Contents

Psychological Testing
Principles and Applications

Sixth Edition

Kevin R. Murphy
Pennsylvania State University

Charles O. Davidshofer
Colorado State University

Pearson Education International

Acquisitions Editor: Jessica Mosher
Editorial Director: Leah Jewell
Editorial Assistant: Kerri Scott
Media Project Manager: David Nusspickel
Assistant Managing Editor: Maureen Richardson
Production Liaison: Fran Russello
Production Editor: Linda Duarte/Pine Tree Composition, Inc.

Manufacturing Buyer: Tricia Kenny
Cover Design: Bruce Kenselaar
Composition/Full-Service Project Management: Pine Tree Composition, Inc.
Printer/Binder: Phoenix Book Tech Park

Pearson Education LTD.
Pearson Education Singapore, Pte. Ltd
Pearson Education, Canada, Ltd
Pearson Education–Japan
Pearson Education Australia PTY, Limited

Pearson Education North Asia Ltd
Pearson Educación de Mexico, S.A. de C.V.
Pearson Education Malaysia, Pte. Ltd
Pearson Education, Upper Saddle River, New Jersey

10 9 8 7 6 5 4 3 2 1

ISBN 0-13-129383-4

Preface

Tests are used to make decisions. This simple sentence describes both the theme and the rationale of this book. Too often, psychological testing is presented as a dry, technical, abstract subject. It is not. Psychological tests have a substantial impact on a variety of important decisions. In some settings, such as the Armed Services, tests represent the only feasible method of making selection and classification decisions. The point is that tests affect people's lives, for good or for ill, and a firm understanding of psychological testing is necessary in many of the settings where important decisions (e.g., college admissions, job placement, clinical assessments) must be made about individuals.

Most students in a testing course have taken many tests and will probably take many more in the future. These students have a real, practical interest in testing. They are also likely to be skeptical about the accuracy and the value of psychological tests. A good part of your job when teaching a testing course is to present a full and fair evaluation of the advantages and drawbacks of psychological testing. We believe that this can best be done by focusing on the impact of tests on decisions. Students generally show little interest in learning a "laundry list" of test names, but they are very interested in knowing how tests are used and whether the use of tests leads to better or worse decisions than would be reached without tests.

Our text is divided into four sections. In Part I (Chapters 1 through 3), we introduce the concepts of psychological testing and discuss the impact of testing on society. Part II (Chapters 4 through 10) discusses the principles of psychological measurement and the techniques used to analyze tests. Part III (Chapters 11 through 17) discusses the development of tests, with particular attention to the domains of cognitive ability, interests, and personality. Part IV (Chapters 18 through 21) discusses the use of psychological tests to make important decisions about individuals.

This book does *not* have several features found in other testing books. First, we do not cover dozens of obscure tests. Rather, we have focused on widely used or technically superior exemplars of the major classes of tests. You will not encounter in this book many tests that are never heard of outside a psychological measurement class, and, frankly, we see no good reason why you should. Second, we do not cover several topics that, although important, have little relevance for decision making. Thus, we do not discuss at length topics such as attitude measurement or the assessment of values.

This book includes some features we think are distinctive and useful to both students and instructors. First, each chapter contains one or more brief sections entitled "Critical Discussion." The Critical Discussion sections present a variety of issues that are controversial (e.g., "Should IQ Scores of Black Examinees Be Based on White Norms?" in Chapter 5), or that illustrate applications of concepts discussed in the chapters (e.g., "Using Item Response Theory to Detect Test Bias," in Chapter 10), or that provide a different perspective of familiar material (e.g., "Personnel Selection From the Applicant's Point of View," in Chapter 19). These critical discussions may provide ideas for further classroom discussions, term papers, or projects, and they are designed to help your students integrate material from this course with their other interests and knowledge bases.

Second, Parts II through IV of the book (i.e., Chapters 4 through 21) include "Problems and Solutions." We start each of these chapters with a problem that is relevant to the material covered in that chapter (e.g., "Determining the Potential Benefits of Testing," in Chapter 9; "What If Different Assessments Disagree?" in Chapter 21). At the end of the chapter, we recap the problem and present a potential solution. The problems involve the sort of questions and issues faced by real test users, and the solutions show students how the material in each chapter can be applied to help solve a real and an important problem.

As you'll note when reading through the text, we are, on the whole, optimistic about psychological testing. There are areas where the technology has failed to keep up with the theory, where the basic theories are flawed, or where the applications of testing have done more harm than good. On the whole, however, psychological tests often provide the fairest and most accurate method of making important decisions. In part, this outcome reflects the strength of tests, and, in part, it reflects the weakness of the competition (e.g., interviews, letters of recommendation, clinical intuition). In any case, we think that psychological tests do make a contribution and are likely to be with us for a long time to come. We hope that this text will contribute to your students' understanding of the advantages and drawbacks of psychological testing.

We have made many changes in preparing this revision. First, we discuss recent revisions of several widely used tests, including the Stanford-Binet, the Wechsler Intelligence Scale for Children, the Wechsler Preschool and Primary Scale of Intelligence, and the Cognitive Abilities Test. Finally, we have added numerous references to research published since the last edition of out book.

ACKNOWLEDGMENTS

This book could not have been produced without the help and encouragement of many of our colleagues. We particularly thank Frank Landy, who encouraged us to write the first edition and who suggested the overall structure for the book. We thank Dennis Roberts, who collaborated in the early development of the book and who also contributed substantially to the overall structure and focus of the book. We also thank the reviewers who have given valuable feedback in developing each edition of this book, Dennis Sweeney, California University of Pennsylvania; K. Elaine Royal, MTSU; Jo Ann Lee, University of North Carolina at Charlotte. Finally, we thank colleagues who have helped us in formulating our ideas and presentations or alerted us to errors and omissions in our first four editions. These include Jeanette Cleveland, George Thornton, Kurt Geisinger, and numerous instructors and students who have provided useful suggestions. We also appreciate feedback from several of our colleagues who identified errors, who suggested alternative interpretations of the reserach, or who have suggested ways of improving the book as we prepared this new edition.

Kevin R. Murphy
Charles O. Davidshofer

Tests and Measurements

The term *psychological test* brings to mind a number of conflicting images. On the one hand, the term might make one think of the type of test so often described in television, movies, and the popular literature, wherein a patient answers questions like, "How long have you hated your mother?" and in doing so reveals hidden facets of his or her personality to the clinician. On the other hand, the psychological test might refer to a long series of multiple-choice questions such as those answered by hundreds of high school students taking college entrance examinations. Another type of "psychological test" is the self-scored type published in the *Reader's Digest*, which purports to tell you whether your marriage is on the rocks, whether you are as anxious as the next fellow, or whether you should change your job or your lifestyle.

In general, psychological tests are neither mysterious, as our first example might suggest, nor frivolous, as our last example might suggest. Rather, psychological tests represent systematic applications of a few relatively simple principles in an attempt to measure personal attributes thought to be important in describing or understanding individual behavior. The aim of this book is to describe the basic principles of psychological measurement and to describe the major types of tests and their applications. We will not present test theory in all its technical detail, nor will we describe (or even mention) all the different psychological tests currently available. Rather, our goal is to provide the information needed to make sensible evaluations of psychological tests and their uses within education, industry, and clinical practice.

The first question that should be addressed in a psychological testing text is, "Why is psychological testing important?" There are several possible answers to this question, but we believe that the best answer lies in the simple statement that forms the central theme of this book: Tests are used to make important decisions about individuals. College admissions officers consult test scores before deciding whether to admit or reject applicants. Clinical psychologists use a variety of objective and projective tests in the process of choosing a course of treatment for individual clients. The military uses test scores as aids in deciding which jobs an individual soldier might be qualified to fill. Tests are used in the world of work, both in personnel selection and in professional certification and licensure. Almost everyone reading this book has taken at least one standardized psychological test. Scores on such a test may have had some impact on an important decision that has affected your life. The area of psychological testing is therefore one of considerable practical importance.

Psychological tests are used to measure a wide variety of attributes—intelligence, motivation, mastery of seventh-grade mathematics, vocational preferences, spatial ability, anxiety, form perception, and countless others. Unfortunately, one feature that all psychological tests share in common is their limited precision. They rarely, if ever, provide exact, definitive measures of variables that are believed to have important effects on human behavior. Thus, psychological tests do not provide a basis for making completely accurate decisions about individuals. In reality, no method guarantees complete accuracy. Thus, although psychological tests are known to be imperfect measures, a special panel of the National Academy of Sciences concluded that psychological tests generally represent the best, fairest, and most economical method of obtaining the information necessary to make sensible decisions about individuals (Wigdor & Garner, 1982a, 1982b). The conclusions reached by the National Academy panel form another important theme that runs through this book. Although psychological tests are far from perfect, they represent the best, fairest, and most accurate technology available for making many important decisions about individuals.

Psychological testing is highly controversial. Public debate over the use of tests, particularly standardized tests of intelligence, has raged since at least the 1920s (Cronbach, 1975; Haney, 1981; Scarr, 1989).[1] An extensive literature, both popular and technical, deals with issues such as test bias and test fairness. Federal and state laws have been passed calling for minimum competency testing and for truth in testing, terms that refer to a variety of efforts to regulate testing and to increase public access to information on test development and use. Tests and testing programs have been challenged in the courts, often successfully.

Psychological testing is not only important and controversial, but it is also a highly specialized and somewhat technical enterprise. In many of the natural sciences, measurement is a relatively straightforward process that involves assessing the physical properties of objects, such as height, weight, or velocity.[2] However, for the most part, psychological attributes, such as intelligence and creativity, cannot be measured by the same sorts of methods as those used to measure physical attributes. Psychological attributes are not manifest in any simple, physical way; they are manifest only in

---

[1]Special issues of *American Psychologist* in November 1965 and October 1981 provide excellent summaries of many of the issues in this debate.

[2]Note, however, that physical measurement is neither static nor simple. Proposals to redefine the basic unit of length, the meter, in terms of the time that light takes to travel from point to point (Robinson, 1983) provide an example of continuing progress in redefining the bases of physical measurement.

the behavior of individuals. Furthermore, behavior rarely reflects any one psychological attribute, but rather a variety of physical, psychological, and social forces. Hence, psychological measurement is rarely as simple or direct as physical measurement. To sensibly evaluate psychological tests, therefore, it is necessary to become familiar with the specialized methods of psychological measurement.

This chapter provides a general introduction to psychological measurement. First, we define the term *test* and discuss several of the implications of that definition. We then briefly describe the types of tests available and discuss the ways in which tests are used to make decisions in educational, industrial, and clinical settings. We also discuss sources of information about tests and the standards, ethics, and laws that govern testing.

PSYCHOLOGICAL TESTS—A DEFINITION

The diversity of psychological tests is staggering. Thousands of different psychological tests are available commercially in English-speaking countries, and doubtlessly hundreds of others are published in other parts of the world. These tests range from personality inventories to self-scored IQ tests, from scholastic examinations to perceptual tests. Yet, despite this diversity, several features are common to all psychological tests and, taken together, serve to define the term *test.*

A psychological test is a measurement instrument that has three defining characteristics:

1. A psychological test is a sample of behavior.
2. The sample is obtained under standardized conditions.
3. There are established rules for scoring or for obtaining quantitative (numeric) information from the behavior sample.

Behavior Sampling

Every psychological test requires the respondent to do something. The subject's behavior is used to measure some specific attribute (e.g., introversion) or to predict some specific outcome (e.g., success in a job training program). Therefore, a variety of measures that do not require the respondent to engage in any overt behavior (e.g., an X-ray) or that require behavior on the part of the subject that is clearly incidental to whatever is being measured (e.g., a stress electrocardiogram) fall outside the domain of psychological tests.

The use of behavior samples in psychological measurement has several implications. First, a psychological test is not an exhaustive measurement of all possible behaviors that could be used in measuring or defining a particular attribute. Suppose, for example, that you wished to develop a test to measure a person's writing ability. One strategy would be to collect and evaluate everything that person had ever written, from term papers to laundry lists. Such a procedure would be highly accurate, but impractical. A psychological test attempts to approximate this exhaustive procedure by collecting a systematic sample of behavior. In this case, a writing test might include a series of short essays, sample letters, memos, and the like.

The second implication of using behavior samples to measure psychological variables is that the quality of a test is largely determined by the representativeness of this sample. For example, one could construct a driving test in which each examinee was required to drive the circuit of a race track. This test would certainly sample some aspects of driving but would omit others, such as parking, following signals, or negotiating in traffic. It would therefore not represent a very good driving test. The behavior elicited by the test also must somehow be representative of behaviors that would be observed outside the testing situation. For example, if a scholastic aptitude test were administered in a burning building, it is unlikely that students' responses to that test would tell us much about their scholastic aptitude. Similarly, a test that required highly unusual or novel types of responses might not be as useful as a test that required responses to questions or situations that were similar in some way to those observed in everyday life.

Standardization

A psychological test is a sample of behavior collected under standardized conditions. The Scholastic Assessment Tests (SAT), which are administered to thousands of high school juniors and seniors, provide a good example of standardization. The test supervisor reads detailed instructions to all examinees before starting, and each portion of the test is carefully timed. In addition, the test manual includes exhaustive instructions dealing with the appropriate seating patterns, lighting, provisions for interruptions and emergencies, and answers to common procedural questions. The test manual is written in sufficient detail to ensure that the conditions under which the SAT is given are substantially the same at all test locations.

The conditions under which a test is administered are certain to affect the behavior of the person or persons taking the test. You would probably give different answers to questions on an intelligence test or a personality inventory administered in a quiet, well-lit room than you would if the same test were administered at a baseball stadium during extra innings of a play-off game. A student is likely to do better on a test that is given in a regular classroom environment than he or she would if the same test were given in a hot, noisy auditorium. Standardization of the conditions under which a test is given is therefore an important feature of psychological testing.

It is not possible to achieve the same degree of standardization with all psychological tests. A high degree of standardization might be possible with many written tests, although even within this class of tests the conditions of testing might be difficult to control precisely. For example, tests that are given relatively few times a year in a limited number of locations by a single testing agency (e.g., the Graduate Record Examination Subject Tests) probably are administered under more standard conditions than are written employment tests, which are administered in hundreds of personnel offices by a variety of psychologists, personnel managers, and clerks. The greatest difficulty in standardization, however, probably lies in the broad class of tests that are administered verbally on an individual basis. For example, the Wechsler Adult Intelligence Scale (WAIS-III), which represents one of the best individual tests of intelligence, is administered verbally by a psychologist. It is likely that an examinee will respond differently to a friendly, calm examiner than to one who is threatening or surly.

Individually administered tests are difficult to standardize because the examiner is an integral part of the test. The same test given to the same subject by two different examiners is certain to elicit a somewhat different set of behaviors. Nevertheless, through specialized training, a good deal of standardization in the essential features of testing can be achieved. Strict adherence to standard procedures for administering various psychological tests helps to minimize the effects of extraneous variables, such as the physical conditions of testing, the characteristics of the examiner, or the subject's confusion regarding the demands of the test.

Scoring Rules

The immediate aim of testing is to measure or to describe in a quantitative way some attribute or set of attributes of the person taking the test. The final, defining characteristic of a psychological test is that there must be some set of rules or procedures for describing in quantitative or numeric terms the subject's behavior in response to the test. These rules must be sufficiently comprehensive and well defined that different examiners will assign scores that are at least similar, if not identical, when scoring the same set of responses. For a classroom test, these rules may be simple and well defined; the student earns a certain number of points for each item answered correctly, and the total score is determined by adding up the points. For other types of tests, the scoring rules may not be so simple or definite.

Most mass-produced standardized tests are characterized by objective scoring rules. In this case, the term *objective* should be taken to indicate that two people, each applying the same set of scoring rules to an individual's responses, will always arrive at the same score for that individual. Thus, two teachers who score the same multiple-choice test will always arrive at the same total score. On the other hand, many psychological tests are characterized by subjective scoring rules. Subjective scoring rules typically rely on the judgment of the examiner and thus cannot be described with sufficient precision to allow for their automatic application. The procedures a teacher follows in grading an essay exam provide an example of subjective scoring rules. It is important to note that the term *subjective* does not necessarily imply inaccurate or unreliable methods of scoring responses to tests, but simply that human judgment is an integral part of the scoring of a test.

Tests vary considerably in the precision and detail of their scoring rules. For multiple-choice tests, it is possible to state beforehand the exact score that will be assigned to every possible combination of answers. For an unstructured test, such as the Rorschach inkblot test, in which the subject describes his or her interpretation of an ambiguous abstract figure, general principles for scoring can be described, but it may be impossible to arrive at exact, objective scoring rules. The same is true of essay tests in the classroom; although general scoring guidelines can be established, in most cases, it is difficult to describe the exact rules that are used in scoring each essay. Thus, two similarly trained psychologists reading the same Rorschach protocol or two teachers reading the same essay generally will not score it in identical ways. However, most psychological tests are designed so that two examiners confronted with the same set of responses will give similar scores. A measure that does not meet this criterion cannot be considered a satisfactory example of a psychological test.

The existence of a set of rules and procedures, which may be general or implicit, for scoring responses to a test is of vital importance in psychological testing. Imagine a personality test in which the method of scoring is left totally to the whim of the person who administers the test. If someone were to take this test and ask three different psychologists to score it, he or she would probably receive three totally different scores. It is likely that the test scores would tell you more about the psychologist who scored the test than they would about the person who took it. Since, in this case, test scores would bear no valid relation to the behavior of the person taking the test, it is impossible to regard such a test as an accurate or a useful measure of some stable characteristic or attribute of the person taking the test.

TYPES OF TESTS

Most psychological tests can be sorted into three general categories:

1. Tests in which the subject performs some specific task, such as writing an essay, answering multiple-choice items, or mentally rotating images presented on a computer screen.
2. Tests that involve observations of the subject's behavior within a particular context.
3. Self-report measures, in which the subject describes his or her feelings, attitudes, beliefs, interests, and the like.

Tests of Performance

The first and most familiar category of tests is one in which subjects are given some well-defined task that they try their best to perform successfully and in which the test score is determined by the subject's success in completing each task. Cronbach (1970) refers to this type of test as a "test of maximal performance." The defining feature of a performance test relates to the intent or the state of mind of the person taking the test. It is assumed in performance testing that the examinee knows what he or she should do in response to the questions or tasks that make up the performance test and that the person being tested exerts maximum effort to succeed. Thus, performance tests are designed to assess what a person can do under the conditions represented by the testing situation.

Standardized tests of general mental ability, referred to as intelligence tests, are among the best exemplars of this type of test. Here, subjects may respond to hundreds of multiple-choice items, and the test score is determined by the number of items answered correctly. Tests of specific abilities, such as spatial ability or mechanical comprehension, are also examples of this type of test. Tests of more specific skills or proficiency, such as a biology test or a music test, also fall into this category.

A number of tests ask the respondent to perform some physical or psychomotor activity. In a typical computerized psychomotor ability test, the examinee might have to use the joysticks to keep a cursor in contact with a specific spot that moves randomly on a screen; performance on this type of task can be assessed in terms of total contact time, number of times contact was broken, or some combination of these factors. Other examples of complex physical performance tests include flight simulators and even the road test you had to take before getting your driver's license. Even video games could be thought of as psychomotor performance tests.

Behavior Observations

Many psychological tests involve observing the subject's behavior and responses in a particular context. To assess salespeople's competence in dealing with problem customers, many stores recruit observers to come into their stores at random intervals and observe and record each salesperson's behavior. They may even play the role of a troublesome customer and record the salesperson's technique (or lack of it) for handling different sorts of problems. This type of test differs from a performance test in that the subject does not have a single, well-defined task that he or she is trying to perform. In fact, in this type of test, the subject may not even know that his or her behavior is being measured. Thus, rather than assessing maximal performance on some well-defined and well-understood task, behavioral observation tests assess typical behavior or performance within a specific context (Cronbach, 1970).

Observations of typical performance or behavior are used in measuring a variety of attributes, ranging from social skills and friendship formation to job performance. Interviews, including both clinical interviews and employment interviews, can be thought of as behavior observation methods. Although an applicant may indeed try to "do his best" in an employment interview, the task confronting that applicant is relatively unstructured, and useful data may be obtained by observing the applicant's behavior in this potentially stressful dyadic interaction.

Systematic observations of behavior in naturalistic situations are particularly useful in assessing attributes such as social skills or adjustment. For example, a school psychologist who wishes to assess a child's ability to relate well with his or her peers might observe, perhaps indirectly, that child's interaction with other children in a variety of structured and unstructured situations (e.g., in the classroom, in a playground) and might systematically record the frequency, intensity, or direction of several types of critical behaviors. Similarly, the behavior of a patient of a mental ward might be systematically observed and recorded in an effort to assess his or her responses to specific treatments.

Self-Reports

The final class of test includes a variety of measures that ask the subject to report or describe his or her feelings, attitudes, beliefs, values, opinions, or physical or mental state. Many personality inventories can be regarded as self-report tests. This category also includes a variety of surveys, questionnaires, and polls.

Self-reports are not necessarily taken at face value. A hypothetical personality test might include an item like "Artichokes are out to get me." The fact that a person endorses (or fails to endorse) such an item may have little to do with his or her true feelings regarding artichokes but may provide valuable information about the respondent's state of mind. Likewise, the subject's indication that he or she prefers going to museums to reading magazines may, by itself, provide little information. However, if we knew that all successful opticians preferred magazines, whereas successful stockbrokers always preferred museums, we would be in a position to predict that in certain respects that person's interests more closely matched those of stockbrokers than those of opticians.

A number of measurement techniques contain features of both behavior observations and self-reports. For example, interviews may include questions dealing with the respondent's thoughts, opinions, or feelings; this is particularly true for clinical interviews. The two methods may not always yield comparable conclusions; a person who describes himself or herself as timid and withdrawn may nevertheless exhibit aggressive behaviors in a variety of settings. However, the two techniques will often yield comparable and complementary information about an individual.

TESTS AND DECISIONS—USES OF PSYCHOLOGICAL TESTS

Origins of Testing

The roots of psychological testing can be traced back to ancient times. Over 3,000 years ago, the Chinese used written tests in filling civil service posts, and systematic testing of both physical and mental prowess was employed by the ancient Greeks. However, as Table 1-1 illustrates, the systematic development of psychological tests is a relatively recent phenomenon. The theory and technology that underly modern psychological testing have, for the most part, been developed within the last 100 years.[3]

Table 1-1   SOME MILESTONES IN THE DEVELOPMENT OF TESTS

1000 B.C.	Testing in Chinese civil service
1850–1900	Civil service examinations in the United States
1900–1920	Development of individual and group tests of cognitive ability, development of psychometric theory
1920–1940	Development of factor analysis, development of projective tests and standardized personality inventories
1940–1960	Development of vocational interest measures, standardized measures of psychopathology
1960–1980	Development of item response theory, neuropsychological testing
1980–Present	Large-scale implementation of computerized adaptive tests

[3]The history of testing in three key areas (i.e., ability testing, interest measurement, and personality assessment) will be examined in more detail in Chapter 2.

At the turn of the century, experimental psychologists such as Cattell and biologists such as Galton and Pearson contributed to the development, construction, and evaluation of psychological tests (Hilgard, 1989). Developments in the theory of intelligence, together with refinements of statistical techniques such as factor analysis, also contributed to the growth of testing. The strongest impetus for the development of psychological tests, however, has been practical rather than theoretical. Consistently throughout the history of testing, major test types have been developed to meet specific practical needs.

The history of intelligence testing provides the clearest example of the influence of practical considerations on the development of psychological tests. The first successful systematic tests of general intelligence, developed by Binet and Simon, were designed to assist the French Ministry of Public Instruction in assessing and classifying mentally retarded students. Binet's tests require a highly trained examiner and are administered on a one-to-one basis. Although these tests provided a reliable method of assessing mental ability, they were not suitable for large-scale testing programs. America's sudden entry into World War I, which brought about a large influx of recruits who needed to be classified according to mental ability, pointed to the need for tests that could be administered to large groups of people. The U.S. Army's attempts to classify recruits led directly to the development of group tests of general mental ability, most notably Army Alpha and Army Beta. Today, the Armed Services Vocational Aptitude Battery, a standardized group-administered test of several abilities, represents the most widely administered test of its kind.

A combination of practical and theoretical concerns has led to several developments in intelligence testing. Most notable is the development of computerized adaptive testing, in which the test is tailored to the individual respondent. Computerized tests take advantage of advances in technology to adapt tests to the responses and capabilities of the individuals examined.

The history of personality testing provides a similar example of how the practical need to make decisions about individuals has fostered test development. The major impetus for the development of a structured measure of psychopathology was, again, the need to screen large numbers of recruits during World War I (P. H. Dubois, 1970). Although developed too late to serve this function, the Woodward Personal Data Sheet became a prototype of other self-report measures. The development of objective tests such as the Minnesota Multiphasic Personality Inventory and projective tests such as the Rorschach inkblot test, though not tied to such large-scale decision problems, nevertheless stemmed from the need to make systematic decisions about individuals.

Yet another similar example can be drawn from the field of scholastic testing. Before the advent of standardized tests, college admissions procedures were typically subjective, cumbersome, and highly variable from one school to another. As the number of students applying to college increased, the need for selection procedures that were fair, accurate, and economical became apparent. Programs initiated by the College Entrance Examination Board led to the development of large-scale scholastic tests such as the SAT and the Graduate Record Examinations (GRE). These tests are extensions of the group-testing techniques developed by the U.S. Army and represent the most extensive civilian applications of psychological testing.

Educational Testing. Educational institutions must make admissions and advancement decisions about millions of students every year. Standardized mass-produced tests, such as the SAT, are widely used in admissions, whereas decisions to advance or hold back students, particularly at the elementary and junior high school levels, are likely to be made largely on the basis of locally constructed classroom tests.

Although admissions and advancement are the most obvious applications of tests in educational settings, they are not the only applications. For example, intelligence tests are likely to be included in the assessment of students for placement in a variety of special education programs. School psychologists might use a number of performance tests and behavior observation tests in diagnosing learning difficulties. Guidance counselors might use vocational interest measures in advising students.

Tests are used by schools and localities in needs assessment and in evaluating the effectiveness of different curricula. Test results may be used in allocating funds to different schools for remedial education. Finally, the publication of average test results for each school in a district is often part of a general drive for accountability in education.

At one time, certification of a student as a bona fide high school graduate was largely the responsibility of the individual school. Today, minimum competency tests are used in many states and communities for the purpose of certifying graduates. A student who successfully completes 4 years of high school but who fails such a test may now receive a certificate of attendance rather than a diploma.

Personnel Testing. Ability tests and tests of specific skills are widely used in personnel selection in both the public and the private sectors. A high score on a written test is necessary to qualify for many jobs in the local, state, and federal governments. Ability tests are also used widely in the military, both for screening new volunteers and for the optimal placement of individual soldiers according to their skills or abilities.

A variety of formal and informal training programs is carried out at the workplace. Tests are used to assess training needs, to assess an individual worker's performance in training, and to assess the success of training programs. Tests might also be used as part of a management development and career counseling program. At regular intervals, supervisors are called on to assess the job performance of their subordinates; such supervisory performance appraisals can be thought of as behavior observation measures. Similarly, interviews and managerial assessment tests can be thought of as applications of behavior observation testing to personnel evaluation.

Clinical Testing. Clinical psychologists employ a wide variety of tests in assessing individual clients. The most common stereotype of a clinical psychologist suggests an extensive use of diagnostic tests. Indeed, a number of objective and projective personality tests and diagnostic tests is widely used by clinical psychologists. However, clinical testing is by no means limited to personality tests.

Clinical psychologists also employ neuropsychological test batteries. For example, perceptual tests are quite useful in detecting and diagnosing many types of brain damage.

Many clinical psychologists receive specialized training in administering individual intelligence tests. Not only do these tests provide data regarding the intellectual performance of individuals, but they also represent a valuable opportunity to observe the subject's behavior in response to a challenging situation. Thus, an intelligence test represents a specialized version of the most common type of clinical measurement, the clinical interview. In some respects, clinical testing is unique in that the clinician is often an integral part of the testing experience. Thus, in clinical testing the clinician must be regarded as a measurement instrument.

TESTING ACTIVITIES OF PSYCHOLOGISTS

The consumers of tests represent a large and varied group, ranging from individual counselors to school principals and personnel administrators. Although there is considerable overlap in the ways in which psychologists and other consumers use these tests, in some ways, psychologists' uses of the tests are specialized. The testing activities of psychologists are of considerable interest to psychology students, and it is useful to describe briefly some of the uses of tests by different types of psychologists.

Psychological assessment is common in several of the fields of applied psychology, although the types of assessment devices and techniques vary widely across different fields. Table 1-2 lists typical assessment activities for several fields of applied psychology; detailed descriptions of many of these assessment activities are presented in Wise (1989). It is important to note two things. First, the table is not comprehensive. Practicing psychologists in each field may carry out a variety of assessment activities not listed here. Second, there is considerable overlap among the assessment activities of the different fields. For example, psychologists in any of the five fields listed in

Table 1-2   TYPICAL ASSESSMENT ACTIVITIES FOR SEVERAL FIELDS OF APPLIED PSYCHOLOGY

Field	*Typical assessment activities*
Clinical Psychology	Assessment of intelligence
	Assessment of psychopathology
Counseling Psychology	Assessment of career interests
	Assessment of skills
	Assessment of social adjustment
Industrial/Organizational Psychology	Assessment of managerial potential
	Assessment of training needs
	Assessment of cognitive and psychomotor ability
School Psychology	Assessment of ability and academic progress
	Assessment of maturity and readiness for school
	Assessment of handicapped children
Neuropsychology	Assessment of brain damage
	Evaluation of Alzheimer's syndrome patients

Table 1-2 might use tests of general intelligence in their assessments; the tests themselves may, however, vary across fields.

There are two differences in the ways in which individuals with training and those without training in psychology typically use these tests. First, psychologists who use tests in their work are more likely than other consumers of tests to have some training in measurement theory. Psychologists are, therefore, often more sophisticated consumers who recognize the limitations of the tests they use. They are better able to effectively use the results of test research. Second, many of the tests used by psychologists require a greater degree of professional judgment in their interpretation than is required for tests used by a wider audience.

There is an ongoing debate within the profession of psychology about the competencies needed to administer and use psychological tests. In particular, questions have been raised about the use of psychological tests by individuals who are not licensed psychologists. In our view, there is no compelling argument in favor of restricting the use of psychological tests to licensed psychologists, nor is there a good argument that holding a license automatically qualifies one to use and interpret all psychological tests. In many states, licensure is restricted to psychologists involved in the mental health areas, and individuals are not always required to demonstrate expertise in psychological testing or test theory to obtain a license as a psychologist. Different types of tests require different competencies (Eyde, Robertson & Krug, 1993), and psychologists in the different fields listed in Table 1-2 might develop expertise in the types of tests used in that field, without developing competencies in other areas of testing. The *Ethical Principles of Psychologists and Code of Conduct* (reproduced in Appendix B) clearly states that a psychologist will limit his or her practice to areas in which he or she has relevant training or expertise, and psychologists who abide by that code are likely to limit their use of tests to the specific areas in which they can demonstrate some competency. The range of tests that is available (and the range of skills needed to administer, score, and interpret these tests) is so vast that very few individuals will have the competencies needed to wisely use all types of psychological tests.

INFORMATION ABOUT TESTS

The greater diversity of psychological tests is both a help and a hindrance to the potential test user. On the positive side, tests are available to meet a wide variety of practical needs, from personnel selection to neurological diagnosis. Unfortunately, many tests might be used in any specific setting, and they vary considerably in cost and quality. Furthermore, new tests are always being developed, and research that points to unsuspected flaws or novel applications of established tests is constantly coming out. To make sensible choices regarding specific tests, the user must know what types of tests are available for specific purposes and must have access to current research involving those tests, as well as to critical evaluations of each test. Fortunately, the *Mental Measurements Yearbooks,* originally edited by O. K. Buros, fulfill these functions.

The *Mental Measurements Yearbooks* have been issued at somewhat irregular intervals over a period of more than 50 years. Together, the *Mental Measurements Yearbooks* provide detailed information regarding most of the tests currently available in English. The yearbook entry for each test indicates the publisher, available forms, and price of the test, together with a comprehensive bibliography of published research involving that test. Of most importance, most tests are critically reviewed by a number of experts. These reviews point out the technical strengths and weaknesses of each test, thereby representing an invaluable evaluation of each test. In the event that a test is judged technically deficient, reviewers are encouraged to indicate whether another commercially available test does a better job of measuring the specific attributes targeted by the test under review. A similar multivolume reference work, entitled *Test Critiques,* contains reviews of a large number of tests. The first volume of this series was released in 1984 (Keyser & Sweetland, 1984), and several additional volumes have been released since then.

Since Buros's death, the task of compiling the yearbooks has been taken over by the Buros Institute, which is affiliated with the University of Nebraska. Figure 1-1 shows a typical *Mental Measurements Yearbook* entry, which describes a popular personality inventory. This entry is quite short because no evaluative review is attached. Other entries, especially those for widely used tests, might run several pages and might include the comments of several reviewers. In addition to the *Mental Measurements Yearbooks,* Buros compiled a comprehensive bibliography of all commercially available tests published in English-speaking countries. *Tests in Print V* and the *Thirteenth Mental Measurements Yearbook* are the latest volumes in the series begun by Buros. Buros also compiled *Intelligence Tests and Reviews* (1975a), *Personality Tests and Reviews* (1975b), and *Vocational Tests and Reviews* (1975c), which contain additional material that had not appeared in any *Mental Measurements Yearbook.* Although by no means as comprehensive as the yearbooks, a list of representative tests, grouped according to their major application (e.g., occupational tests, clerical), is presented in Appendix A.

Research on psychological testing is published regularly in several professional journals. Several journals deal primarily with test theory, or psychometrics, whereas other journals deal primarily with testing applications. A list of some of the professional journals that represent primary outlets for research on psychological testing is presented in Table 1-3. It is important to note that the classification of each journal as primarily psychometric or applications-oriented is by no means ironclad; both applied and theoretical articles appear in all these journals.

STANDARDS FOR TESTING

Given the widespread use of tests, there is considerable potential for abuse of psychological testing. A good deal of attention has therefore been devoted to the development and enforcement of professional and legal standards and guidelines for psychological testing.

The American Psychological Association (APA) has taken a leading role in developing professional standards for testing. The most general document dealing with psychological testing is the "Ethical Principles of Psychologists and Code of Conduct,"

Personal Orientation Inventory. Grades 9–16 and adults; 1962–74; POI; 12 scores; time competence, inner directed, self-actualizing value, existentiality, feeling reactivity, spontaneity, self-regard, self-acceptance, nature of man, synergy, acceptance of aggression, capacity for intimate contact; I form ('63, 8 pages); manual with 1980 supplementation ('74, 56 pages); profile ('65, 2 pages); separate answer sheets (Digitek, IBM 1230, NCS, hand scored) must be used; 1983 price data; $10.50 per 25 tests; $5.50 per 50 Digitek, IBM 1230, or NCS answer sheets; $5.75 per 50 hand scored answer sheets; $10 per set of IBM or hand scoring stencils; $4 per 50 profiles; $2.75 per manual; $3.75 per specimen set; Digitek or NCS scoring service, $.95 or less per test; (30–40) minutes; Everett L. Shostrum; EdITS/Educational and Industrial Testing Service.*

See T3:1789 (98 references); for an excerpted review by Donald J. Tosi and Cathy A. Lindamood, see 8:641 (433 references); see also T2:1315 (80 references); for reviews by Bruce Bloxom and Richard W. Coan, see 7:121 (97 references); see also P:193 (26 references).

Test References

1. Abernathy, R. W., Abramowitz, S. I., Roback, H. B., Weitz, L. J., Abramowitz, C. V., & Tittler, B. The impact of an intensive consciousness-raising curriculum on adolescent women. PSYCHOLOGY OF WOMEN QUARTERLY, 1977, 2, 138–148.

2. Reddy, W. B., & Beers, T. Sensitivity training . . . and the healthy become self-actualized. SMALL GROUP BEHAVIOR, 1977, 8, 525–532.

3. Ware, J. R., & Barr, J. E. Effects of a nine-week structured and unstructured group experience on measures of self-concepts and self-actualization. SMALL GROUP BEHAVIOR, 1977, 8, 93–100.

4. MacVanc, J. R., Lange, J. D., Brown, W. A., & Zayat, M. Psychological functioning of bipolar manic-depressives in remission. ARCHIVES OF GENERAL PSYCHIATRY, 1978, 35, 1351–1354.

5. Paxton, A. I., & Turner, E. J. Self-actualization and sexual permissiveness, satisfaction, prudishness, and drive among female undergraduates. THE JOURNAL OF SEX RESEARCH, 1978, 14, 65–80.

6. DeJulio, S., Bentley, J., & Cockayne, T. Pregroup norm setting: Effects on encounter group interaction. SMALL GROUP BEHAVIOR, 1979, 10, 368–388.

7. Fretz, B. R. College students as paraprofessionals with children and the aged. AMERICAN JOURNAL OF COMMUNITY PSYCHOLOGY, 1979, 7, 357–360.

8. Richards, W. A., Rhead, J. C., Grof, S., Goodman, L. E., DiLeo, F., & Rush, L. DPT as an adjunct in brief psychotherapy with cancer patients. OMEGA, 1979, 10, 9–16.

9. Shadish, W. R., Jr., & Zarle, T. The validation of an encounter group outcome measure. SMALL GROUP BEHAVIOR, 1979, 10, 101–112.

10. Waterman, C. K., Chiauzzi, E., & Gruenbaum, M. The relationship between sexual enjoyment and actualization of self and sexual partner. THE JOURNAL OF SEX RESEARCH, 1979, 15, 253–263.

11. Butterfield, G., & Woods, R. Self actualization and improvement in tennis skills at summer camps for adolescents. ADOLESCENCE, 1980, 15, 429–434.

12. Goldman, J. A., & Olczak, P. V. Effect of an innovative educational program upon self-actualization and psychosocial maturity: A replication and follow up. SOCIAL BEHAVIOR AND PERSONALITY, 1980, 8, 41–47.

13. Wise, G. W., & Strong, L. D. Self-actualization and willingness to participate in alternative marital and family forms. ADOLESCENCE, 1980, 15, 543–554.

14. Mozdzierz, G. J., & Semyck, R. W. Further validation of the social interest index with male alcoholics. JOURNAL OF PERSONALITY ASSESSMENT, 1981, 45, 79–84.

15. Sulzbacher, S., Wong, B., McKeen, J., Glock, J., & MacDonald, B. Long term therapeutic effects of a three month intensive growth group. THE JOURNAL OF CLINICAL PSYCHIATRY, 1981, 42, 148–153.

16. Berndt, D. J., Kaiser, C. F., & Van Aalst, F. Depression and self-actualization in gifted adolescents. JOURNAL OF CLINICAL PSYCHOLOGY, 1982, 38, 142–150.

17. Brown, C. E., Franco, J. N., & DeBlassie, R. R. A computer program for scoring the Personal Orientation Inventory. EDUCATIONAL AND PSYCHOLOGICAL MEASUREMENT, 1982, 42, 843–844.

18. Byrd, J. W., Coble, C. R., & Adler, C. G. A study of personality characteristics of science teachers. SCHOOL SCIENCE AND MATHEMATICS, 1982, 82, 321–331.

19. Dodez, O., Zelhart, P. F., & Markley, R. P. Compatibility of self-actualization and anxiety. JOURNAL OF CLINICAL PSYCHOLOGY, 1982, 38, 696–702.

20. Goldberg, D., Steele, J. J., Johnson, A., & Smith, C. Ability of primary care physicians to make accurate ratings of psychiatric symptoms. ARCHIVES OF GENERAL PSYCHIATRY, 1982, 39, 829–833.

21. O'Brien, M. H., Samonds, K. W., Beal, V. A., Hosmer, D. W., & O'Donnell, J. Incorporating transactional analysis into a weight loss program. JOURNAL OF THE AMERICAN DIETETIC ASSOCIATION, 1982, 81, 450–453.

22. Ware, R., Barr, J. E., & Boone, M. Subjective changes in small group processes: An experimental investigation. SMALL GROUP BEHAVIOR, 1982, 13, 395–401.

23. Perkins, R. J., & Kemmerling, R. G. Effect of paraprofessional-led assertiveness training on levels of assertiveness and self-actualization. JOURNAL OF COLLEGE STUDENT PERSONNEL, 1983, 24, 61–66.

24. Malanowski, J. R., & Wood, P. H. Burnout and self-actualization in public school teachers. THE JOURNAL OF PSYCHOLOGY, 1984, 117, 23–26.

FIGURE 1-1   *Ninth Mental Measurements Yearbook* **entry describing personal orientation inventory.** *Source:* Copyright © 1985 by Buros Institute of Mental Measurements. Reprinted by permission.

Table 1-3   JOURNALS REPORTING RESEARCH ON TEST THEORY AND APPLICATIONS

	Journal	*Orientation*
General	*Psychometrika*	Psychometric
	Educational and Psychological Measurement	Psychometric/Applied
	Applied Psychological Measurement	Psychometric/Applied
Educational Testing	*Journal of Educational Measurement*	Psychometric/Applied
	Journal of Educational Psychology	Applied
Personnel Testing	*Journal of Applied Psychology*	Applied/Psychometric
	Personnel Psychology	Applied
Clinical Testing	*Journal of Consulting and Clinical Psychology*	Applied

published in 2002; this document is presented in Appendix B. Another useful document is the "Code of Fair Testing Practices in Education," which can be accessed at the Web site www.ericae.net/code.txt.

The preamble of the principles states that "psychologists respect and protect human and civil rights, and do not knowingly participate in or condone discriminatory practices." The body of this document outlines the psychologist's responsibility with regard to issues such as competence, confidentiality, and the welfare of consumers of psychological services. The American Psychological Association, in cooperation with several other professional associations, has issued a more specific document, the *Standards for Educational and Psychological Testing* (1999), which discusses in detail the appropriate technical and professional standards to be followed in construction, evaluation, interpretation, and application of psychological tests. These standards represent the most recent revisions of testing standards followed by psychologists for over 30 years.

The International Testing Committee published the "International Guidelines for Test Use" (2000). These ITC Guidelines overlap substantially with the *Standards for Educational and Psychological Testing.* The main points of these guidelines are summarized in Table 1-4. There are two themes running through the guidelines shown in Table 1-4, the need for high standards of ethics when administering and using tests and the need to follow good practice in choosing, administering, interpreting, and communicating the results of tests.

The use of tests in personnel selection has been an area of special concern. The Society for Industrial and Organizational Psychology has issued the *Principles for the Validation and Use of Personnel Selection Procedures* (2003) to cover issues in personnel testing that may not be adequately covered by the standards. As a result of the Civil Rights Act of 1964 and the Civil Rights Act of 1991, the area of employment testing has been the focus of legal as well as professional standards and regulations. A number of federal agencies are charged with enforcing laws that forbid discrimination in employment. The "Uniform Guidelines on Employee Selection Procedures" (1978) has been adopted by the Equal Employment Opportunity Commission, the Departments of Justice and Labor, and other federal agencies; these guidelines describe the technical standards used by the government in evaluating personnel testing programs. Although

Table 1-4   SUMMARY OF THE INTERNATIONAL GUIDELINES FOR TEST USE

Take responsibility for ethical test use

1.1   Act in a professional and an ethical manner
1.2   Ensure they have the competence to use tests
1.3   Take responsibility for their use of tests
1.4   Ensure that test materials are kept securely
1.5   Ensure that test results are treated confidentially

Follow good practice in the use of tests

2.1   Evaluate the potential utility of testing in an assessment situation
2.2   Choose technically sound tests appropriate for the situation
2.3   Give due consideration to issues of fairness in testing
2.4   Make necessary preparations for the testing session
2.5   Administer the tests properly
2.6   Score and analyze test results accurately
2.7   Interpret results appropriately
2.8   Communicate the results clearly and accurately to relevant others
2.9   Review the appropriateness of the test and its use

these guidelines do not have the force of law, they generally are given great deference by the courts when tests are challenged on the basis of possible discrimination.

Taken as a group, the different standards and guidelines deal with two interrelated issues: technical standards and standards for professional behavior. The technical standards are used to evaluate the psychometric characteristics of a test. Chapters 4 through 10, which deal with the principles of psychological measurement, outline the issues that form the core of these technical standards. The standards for professional behavior described in these documents make it clear that psychologists are personally and professionally responsible for safeguarding the welfare of all consumers of psychological tests. The Committee on Professional Standards of APA has issued Speciality Guidelines for clinical, counseling, industrial-organization, and school psychologists. These—together with the "Casebook for Providers of Psychological Services," which is regularly published in the *American Psychologist,* and with *Test User Qualifications: A Data-Based Approach to Promoting Good Test Use* (Eyde et al., 1993)—define in a concrete way the ethical and professional standards that regulate the uses of psychological tests in a variety of contexts.

CRITICAL DISCUSSION:

Ethical Principles Relevant to Psychological Testing

Psychologists are bound by the *"Ethical Principles of Psychologists and Code of Conduct"*; these Principles are shown in Appendix B. They contain many statements that deal directly or indirectly with psychological testing. Four of these that are shown here help to capture the ethical principles that are most relevant to understanding how psychologists use tests:

2.01 Boundaries of Competence

(a) Psychologists provide services, teach, and conduct research with populations and in areas only within the boundaries of their competence, based on their education, training, supervised experience, consultation, study, or professional experience.

4.01 Maintaining Confidentiality

Psychologists have a primary obligation and take reasonable precautions to protect confidential information. . . .

9.01 Bases for Assessments

(a) Psychologists base the opinions contained in their recommendations, reports, and diagnostic or evaluative statements, including forensic testimony, on information and techniques sufficient to substantiate their findings. (See also Standard 2.04, Bases for Scientific and Professional Judgments.)

9.02 Use of Assessments

(a) Psychologists administer, adapt, score, interpret, or use assessment techniques, interviews, tests, or instruments in a manner and for purposes that are appropriate in light of the research on or evidence of the usefulness and proper application of the techniques.

Psychologists who use psychological tests are first and foremost bound to limit their work to areas in which they have appropriate training, experience, and expertise. There are many types of psychological tests, and many of these require specialized training and experience (Chapters 20 and 21 cover many tests that require clinical skills and training). Second, psychologists are obligated to protect the confidentiality of the information they obtain from clients, subjects, and examinees. There are circumstances under which it is impossible to keep test scores completely confidential (e.g., when you are taking an employment test, scores must be shared with the employer), but the principles that bind all psychologists in their work protect the privacy of examinees to the greatest extent possible.

Principles 9.01 and 9.02 oblige psychologists to base their use and interpretation of psychological tests on solid research and reliable evidence. In theory, this principle protects the users of tests from "junk science" or from the use of tests that cannot be substantiated on the basis of reliable evidence. As we will see in Chapter 20, applications of this principle can be challenging, especially in clinical testing, where there are sometimes deep controversies about what practices are or are not supported by acceptable scientific evidence. Nevertheless, the commitment of psychologists to base their use of tests on scientific evidence rather than on personal opinion or traditional interpretations is arguably the ultimate safeguard for consumers of tests. In Chapters 13 through 21, we will review the scientific evidence that supports the use of psychological tests and assessments to measure the interests, abilities, personalities, and pathologies of individuals.

The general goal of the ethical standards that guide the development and application of psychological tests is to safeguard the rights and the dignity of the individual who is tested. The actual ethical problems that arise in psychological testing depend in part on the context in which the test is given and used. In Chapters 18 through 22, we discuss the application of psychological testing in educational, industrial, and clinical settings. Each of these chapters includes examples to help illustrate the potential problems encountered in psychological testing and the ethical principles that are applied to safeguard the individuals tested.

CRITICAL DISCUSSION:

Alternatives to Psychological Tests

A critical issue in the debate over psychological tests is whether there are alternatives that would be better, fairer, or more economical. The answer may depend on the testing context; it may be easier to develop alternatives for some clinical tests than for some employment tests. In general, however, the search for alternatives has been disappointing. One reason for this outcome is that many of the alternatives proposed are themselves psychological tests, albeit poorly structured or badly designed ones.

Consider the debate over the use of tests in academic admissions. Critics have suggested that grade point average (GPA), together with interviews and letters of recommendation, would lead to better decisions than those reached using psychological tests such as the SAT. The GPA clearly reflects an assessment device that meets our definition of a test. That is, it is based on somewhat systematic observations (typically, a large number of observations from several different courses) under reasonably standard conditions, employing systematic (if not always objective) scoring rules. Viewed in this light, the fact that the GPA is such a good predictor of success in college is evidence of the utility of testing rather than the uselessness of tests. Both letters of recommendation and interviews fall within the category of behavioral observations. Considered in this light, it should be clear that these methods are unlikely to be better than well-designed tests in predicting future behavior. These methods are not based on systematic samples of behavior; they lack standardization and are characterized by highly subjective scoring rules. As we will show in later chapters, a substantial body of research evidence shows that methods such as the interview are inferior predictors of a wide range of relevant criteria. One reason for this outcome is that they fail to incorporate the very features that make for a good psychological test: the systematic sampling of behavior, the standardization of the conditions of measurement, and the application of well-defined scoring rules.

In our opinion, much of the opposition to testing can be traced to the perception that psychological tests involve seemingly small samples of behavior, as compared with alternatives such as recommendations from knowledgeable others and interviews. The fear that a single short testing session can undo years of hard work is not altogether unreasonable and should be taken into account. One way to defuse fears of this sort is to preserve flexibility in your testing program by allowing people to retake tests or by allowing for specific handicaps and distractions that may impair test performance. The search for alternatives to testing is not always a reflection of problems with testing per se but, rather, may reflect legitimate concerns over inflexible and seemingly arbitrary testing and decision-making procedures.

SUMMARY

A psychological test is not simply a set of questions compiled by a psychologist. Rather, it is—or it should be—a carefully developed procedure for obtaining meaningful samples of behavior and for attaching numerical scores to those samples that reflect characteristics of the individuals being assessed. Standardized conditions of measurement and well-articulated rules for assigning scores to responses are as much a part of the test as the test items themselves.

Tests might involve performance of mental or psychomotor tasks, observations of behavior, or descriptions of one's own attitudes, beliefs, and values (i.e., self-reports). They are used by psychologists in a variety of specialties to make decisions about individuals. In this book, we will concentrate on three areas—educational testing, personnel testing, and clinical testing—where the use of tests is especially widespread and important.

The sheer number of tests makes it difficult, even for professional psychologists, to stay fully informed about all the options in psychological testing. Fortunately, a number of resources are available for obtaining information about and professional reviews of psychological tests. Also available are a number of documents describing the standards and principles that govern the testing activities of psychologists. Taken together, these books and documents provide a valuable introduction to the complex technical and professional issues involved in psychological testing.

KEY TERMS

Ethical Principles of Psychologists   set of principles (reprinted in Appendix B) that governs professional activities of psychologists

Mental Measurements Yearbooks   series of reference volumes containing reviews of mental tests

Psychological test   measurement instrument that consists of a sample of behavior obtained under standardized conditions and evaluated using established scoring rules

Self-report   type of test in which subject describes his or her feelings, attitudes, beliefs, or subjective state

Standards for Educational and Psychological Testing   standards adopted by several professional societies that define how tests should be developed, evaluated, and used

2

Defining and Measuring Psychological Attributes: Ability, Interests, and Personality

This book focuses on the use of tests for making decisions about individuals. In this chapter we introduce the major types of tests that are used to make these decisions. In particular, we focus on the use of cognitive ability measures, interest measures, and measures of personality in making decisions about individuals and in helping individuals to make their own decisions.

The aim of this chapter is to present a general introduction to these three types of tests. We discuss in general terms the nature of ability, interests, and personality, and we note the implications of differences in these three types of attributes for psychological measurement. We also present the historical foundations of modern ability, interest, and personality measurement, in each case highlighting the impact of practical demands on the development of tests and testing strategies. Finally, we describe general strategies for psychological testing in each of the three domains, and we outline characteristics that one might look for in a good measure of ability, interest, or personality. In the chapter that follows, we will discuss the societal consequences of using these tests to make important decisions about people.

PSYCHOLOGICAL ATTRIBUTES AND DECISIONS

Some psychological attributes are more relevant than others to the problem of making decisions about individuals. In part, this tendency depends on the nature of the decision. For example, in choosing a course of psychotherapy for a client, measures of the person's mathematical ability may not be very useful or relevant, although the same measures might be very useful and relevant in general academic admissions and placement decisions. Nevertheless, some types of psychological tests are likely to be more broadly useful in making decisions than others.

20

There are several ways of classifying the broad domain of psychological testing. One useful dimension is the extent to which the attributes being measured are relatively stable or relatively fluid. Adult intelligence is an example of a stable attribute; attitudes and moods are examples of fluid attributes. In general, stable attributes are more likely to be relevant for making decisions about individuals, particularly if those decisions have a long-term impact (e.g., college admissions).

A second useful dimension for classifying psychological attributes is the type of behaviors through which those attributes are manifested. For example, individual differences in general intelligence are manifest in the performance of cognitively demanding tasks. Individual differences in political beliefs are manifested in how someone votes or in his or her choice of reading matter. Individual differences in interests are manifested in each person's satisfaction with, or reaction to, different choices (e.g., choice of an occupation) or activities. Some behaviors are more relevant to decision makers' goals than others.

Several areas in psychological measurement are not broadly relevant to making decisions about individuals, either because of their fluid nature or because of their limited relevance to important criteria. For example, a large body of research on attitude measurement is important but not highly relevant to decision making. The same can be said for research on measurement of mood, beliefs, values, or narrowly focused abilities or skills (e.g., artistic aptitude). The three domains that are most relevant to decision making are the domains of ability, interest, and personality. General mental ability contributes to performance in a variety of domains, particularly scholastic performance and performance of cognitively demanding tasks. Interests have a substantial bearing on a person's satisfaction with, or reactions to, his or her situation. Personality involves consistency in a person's behavior in a wide range of situations. All three domains represent stable attributes, and all three involve behaviors that are broadly relevant to the goals of both decision makers and the individuals who are the focus of those decisions.

INTELLIGENCE—GENERAL MENTAL ABILITY

The Nature of Intelligence

The first question that must be faced in measuring intelligence is whether there is any such thing as intelligence. It should not be difficult to convince a layperson that intelligence exists; there are clear differences in the way in which people who are commonly labeled "intelligent" and "retarded" deal with the problems of everyday life. The importance of intelligence and the influence of intelligence on behavior clearly show up when individuals are confronted with novel or complex situations. Everyday observation, however, is not sufficient to determine whether intelligence is a scientifically valid and useful construct. The primary scientific basis for asserting that general intelligence exists and that individual differences in intelligence have some impact on behavior is the observation that there is a positive correlation between almost every reliable measure that calls for mental processing, retrieval, or manipulation of information and almost any other measure that involves cognitive activity. In other words, a person who performs very well on one cognitive test, such as a reading comprehension test, is likely to perform well on a number of other cognitive tests, including maze tests, analogy tests, and digit-symbol substitution tests (Eysenck, 1979; Guttman & Levy, 1991; Humphreys, 1979; Jensen, 1980). Furthermore, virtually any combination of scores from ordinary paper-and-pencil tests that involve active information processing (in which scores are positively weighted) yields essentially identical estimates of general cognitive ability (Ree & Earles, 1991b). The combined evidence clearly indicates that people differ along some general continuum, which is usually labeled *intelligence.*

It seems reasonable to conclude that people differ in terms of their general levels of intelligence and that these differences have implications for a variety of behaviors. It is more difficult to arrive at a widely acceptable definition of intelligence that is both precise and useful. Historically, psychologists have shown little agreement in their definitions of intelligence. Both Neisser (1979) and Miles (1957) have provided incisive commentaries on the difficulties in defining psychological constructs such as intelligence. We do not claim to offer a definition that resolves all outstanding controversies, but we do offer some principles that should be considered in developing intelligence tests.

First, intelligence is a construct, not a thing (Eysenck, 1979; Humphreys, 1979). Thus, it is impossible to arrive at a definition of the "essence" of intelligence; it can be defined only in terms of the behaviors that indicate various levels of intelligence. It makes much more sense to try to specify what an intelligent person does than to try to decide what intelligence is. Second, intelligence cannot be defined strictly in terms of one type of behavior but, rather, must be defined in terms of a variety of behaviors that pose cognitive demands. Thus, a test that includes only one type of content, such as a vocabulary test, is not likely to represent an adequate measure of intelligence. Finally, intelligence should, by definition, be related to success in a variety of cognitively demanding endeavors (e.g., school, training programs, work). This correlation need not necessarily be perfect, or even high, but a measure that shows no such correlation is not likely to be a good measure of intelligence.

The concept of general mental ability—a term many prefer to the value-laden term *intelligence*—refers to the existence of systematic individual differences in the performance of tasks that involve the manipulation, retrieval, evaluation, or processing of information. Some evidence suggests that general mental ability is related to very basic cognitive and physiological processes (Jensen, 1980; Sternberg, 1977, 1984), but it is not yet clear whether mental ability can be meaningfully described in terms of these underlying processes. At present, then, definitions of general mental ability must be presented in terms of behaviors rather than in terms of hypothetical causes of those behaviors. Since general mental ability is defined as a consistent facet of performance in all cognitively demanding tasks, it follows that if two individuals differ in their general mental ability, this difference will be consistent across several different types of information-processing tasks.

Specific mental abilities differ from general ability in that they refer to performance in a specific type of task. For example, people who show equivalent levels of general mental ability might nevertheless differ in their performance on a wide range of tasks involving, for example, the mental rotation of objects, the identification of objects presented from unusual perspectives, and the solution of three-dimensional mazes. The consistent differences in the performance of this type of task might be interpreted as differences in spatial ability.

Several theories have been developed to help to identify the different types of mental ability and to clarify the relationships among different abilities. The theories developed by Spearman, Thurstone, Vernon, and Carroll help to illustrate the concepts of general and specific abilities. Guilford's theory represents a very different way of organizing the domain of mental ability.

Two-Factor Theory. The starting point for Spearman's theory (1904, 1927), as well as a number of the theories that followed, is the observation that scores on any two cognitively demanding tests almost invariably show a positive correlation (Allinger, 1988; Humphreys, 1979; Jensen, 1980). Spearman accounts for this fact by positing that scores on every cognitive test are influenced by a person's standing on a general intellectual factor, or level of g, and that correlations among test scores can be explained entirely by the fact that different tests provide partial measures of the same general intellectual factor, g. Spearman recognized that scores on each test are also influenced by measurement error (e) and that each test also measured some specific factor (S) that was unique to each test and independent of one's level of general intelligence. For example, scores on a verbal comprehension test are determined largely by one's level of general intelligence, but they are also affected by one's specific ability to perform verbal comprehension tasks, independent of one's general intelligence.

Spearman's theory has several important implications. First, since specific factors (S's) are unique to individual tests, the theory suggests that important or meaningful individual differences in test performance are due solely to individual differences in general intelligence, g. Second, the theory implies that a good intelligence test will be highly g loaded; that is, the influence of a specific factor or of measurement error will be minimized. The third and most important implication is that a good measure of g will successfully predict performance of all cognitively demanding tasks. The theory clearly suggests that the development of a good measure of g will lead to a substantial payoff, since a test with a high g loading should predict an extremely wide range of "intelligent" behaviors.

Thurstone and Group Factors. While admitting the importance of a general intellectual factor, many psychologists object to the notion that the correlations between psychological tests could be completely explained in terms of their relationship to g. Thurstone (1935, 1938) noted that there are factors common to groups of tests, labeled group factors, that are related to g but clearly not identical to g. For example, tests of reading comprehension, verbal analogies, simple addition, and subtraction involving fractions all will be positively correlated as a consequence of their relationship to g. Yet we would expect higher correlations between the two verbal tests and between the two numerical tests than we would between a verbal test and a numerical test. In Thurstone's terms, we would say that the first two tests share a group factor, labeled verbal comprehension, whereas the third and fourth tests share a different group factor, labeled numerical ability. These group factors are somewhat independent of one another, but both are related to *g*.

Thurstone (1938) suggested that intelligence could best be understood in terms of seven group factors, or primary mental abilities, defined as the following:

Verbal comprehension—vocabulary, reading comprehension, verbal analogies, and the like

Word fluency—the ability to quickly generate and manipulate a large number of words with specific characteristics, as in anagrams or rhyming tests

Number—the ability to quickly and accurately carry out mathematical operations

Space—spatial visualizations as well as ability to mentally transform spatial figures

Associative memory—rote memory

Perceptual speed—quickness in perceiving visual details, anomalies, similarities, and the like

Reasoning—skill in a variety of inductive, deductive, and arithmetic reasoning tasks

Since these mental abilities are seen as at least somewhat independent, it might be possible for two people who are identical in their level of *g* to differ dramatically in terms of their strengths and weaknesses in primary mental abilities. Thus, the most practical implication of Thurstone's theory is that intelligence should be measured at the level of primary mental abilities; the measurement of a single general factor would obscure much of the information conveyed by these seven group factors. While Spearman might argue that our attention should be focused on measuring *g*, Thurstone and his followers suggest that intelligence tests should be developed to tap each of a number of factors.[1]

Fluid and Crystallized Intelligence. R. B. Cattell (1963) has suggested two related but conceptually distinct aspects of general intelligence: fluid and crystallized intelligence. Fluid intelligence is defined as the ability to see relationships, as in analogies and letter and number series; fluid intelligence primarily deals with reasoning ability. Crystallized intelligence, on the other hand, refers to an individual's acquired knowledge and skills; in a sense, crystallized intelligence refers to the size of one's store of factual knowledge. As one might expect, fluid and crystallized intelligence measures tend to be highly correlated, reflecting the fact that people high in fluid intelligence find it easier to quickly build up a large store of factual knowledge (Jensen, 1980). Nevertheless, these two types of intelligence are conceptually distinct, and there is evi-

---

[1]In his later years, Spearman accepted the necessity of group factors; however, he never completely abandoned his original assertion that intelligence tests should be designed to measure *g*.

dence that they show different developmental trends (Horn, 1985; Horn & Cattell, 1967).

Hierarchical Models of Intelligence. Vernon (1960, 1965) suggests that in a sense, both Spearman and Thurstone are right. Vernon's model suggests a general factor, *g*, that pervades all tests of intelligence and that can be broken down into two broad categories, called major group factors. There are two major group factors, verbal-educational and spatial-motor, which can be further divided into minor group factors, such as verbal or spatial factors; in some respects, these minor group factors resemble primary mental abilities. Minor group factors, in turn, summarize patterns of association among individual tests.

Carroll's (1993a) three-stratum model of cognitive ability (based on the results of a large number of factor-analytic studies) nicely illustrates the nature of modern hierarchical models of cognitive ability; this model is illustrated in Figure 2-1. At the most general level, there is a *g* factor, which implies stable differences in performance on a wide range of cognitively demanding tasks. At the next level (the broad stratum), there are a number of areas of ability, which imply that the rank ordering of individuals' task performance will not be exactly the same across all cognitive tasks, but rather will show some clustering. The broad abilities in Carroll's (1993a) model include (1) fluid intelligence, (2) crystallized intelligence, (3) general memory ability, (4) broad visual perception, (5) broad auditory perception, (6) broad retrieval ability, and (7) broad cognitive speediness. The implication of distinguishing these broad abilities from *g* is that some people will do well on a broad range of memory tasks, and these will not be exactly the same set of people who do well on a broad range of tasks tapping cognitive speed, visual perception, and so on. Finally, each of these broad ability areas can be characterized in terms of a number of more specific abilities (the narrow stratum) that are more homogeneous still than those at the next highest level. Examples corresponding to each of the broad spectrum abilities just labeled include (1) induction, (2) language development, (3) memory span, (4) spatial relations, (5) sound discrimination, (6) word fluency, and (7) perceptual speed. Once again, the implication of distinguishing specific narrow abilities from their broad parent abilities is that the individuals who do well on inductive reasoning tasks might not be exactly the same as those who do well on other fluid intelligence tasks (although the groups will once again overlap

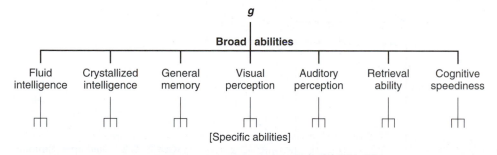

Figure 2-1   Carroll's Hierarchical Model

substantially and also overlap with those classified as high on *g*). This model has received extensive empirical support (McGrew & Flanagan, 1998).

Hierarchical models of intelligence imply that tests designed to measure *g* and tests designed to measure more specific aspects of intelligence both have their place. The choice of a specific level in the hierarchy should be determined by the purpose of testing rather than by personal preference. For example, a psychologist interested in arriving at a very general classification of children might choose a measure of *g*, whereas another psychologist who is interested in selecting people for mechanical abilities might focus on that minor group factor. According to hierarchical theories, there is no reason to argue about the primacy of *g*, or of group factors. Hierarchical theories allow for many levels of organization, depending on the purpose of measurement.

Guilford's Structure of Intellect Model. Guilford's (1967, 1988) model represents a strong departure from the theories discussed so far, in that Guilford does not accept the existence of a general intellectual factor, either in the basic sense, as proposed by Spearman, or in the sense of a higher-order factor, as proposed by Vernon (1965). Rather, Guilford proposes that intelligence is organized according to three dimensions:

1. Operations—what a person does
2. Contents—the material on which operations are performed
3. Products—the form in which information is stored and processed

There are six types of operations, five types of content, and six types of products. Guilford proposes that each combination of a specific operation, a specific type of content, and a specific type of product defines a unique type of intelligence. In other words, there are 180 different types of intelligence, defined by all possible combinations of six operations, five types of content, and six types of product. Later versions of the theory proposed even more types of intelligence. The structure of intellect model is typically as shown in Figure 2-2.

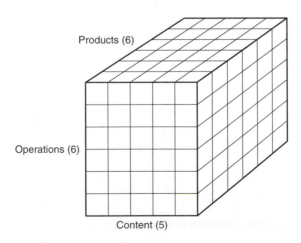

FIGURE 2-2 Guilford's Structure of Intellect Model

Although Guilford and Hoepfner (1971) claim to have identified 98 of the 180 factors suggested by the model (see also Guilford, 1988), the theoretical and practical implications of Guilford's model are unclear (Allinger, 1988; Bachelor, 1989; Ulosevich, Michael, & Bachelor, 1991). In particular, Guilford's model has not greatly affected the practice of intelligence testing.

Gardner's Theory of Multiple Intelligences. Gardner (1983, 1993) suggests that there are seven different types of intelligence: logical-mathematical, linguistic, spatial, bodily-kinesthetic, interpersonal, and intrapersonal. More recent versions of this theory (e.g., Gardner, 1999) have suggested the possibility of a smaller number of intelligences, but this seven-intelligences model is still the most widely cited version. This theory focuses on assessing broad competencies, and many of the proposed applications of this theory have included naturalistic assessment (e.g., assessing intelligences by observing peoples' day-to-day activities). This theory suggests that the concept of general intelligence is not a very useful one, in part because people can be "intelligent" in many different ways.

This theory has potentially profound implications for education. If Gardner's theory is correct, it might be better to tailor education to each individual's patterns of strengths and weaknesses than to focus on global labels such as "gifted" or even "smart." This theory also suggests that global comparisons between people or groups (e.g., describing individuals in terms of IQ) are misleading, because they tend to emphasize only a small portion of the domain of intelligence. For example, if Joe is strong in spatial intelligence and interpersonal intelligence, and Sarah is strong in linguistic and logical-mathematical intelligence, it might be impossible to say which one is "smarter."

As we note later, this theory, like Guilford's, has drawn a good deal of attention but has received relatively little empirical support. The appeal of theories such as Gardner's or Guilford's is based more on ideological positions than on scientific evidence. That is, many people would prefer to believe that everyone is smart in his or her own way, or that a general label such as "intelligent" is just not meaningful, and theories of this sort support the assumption that intelligence is not a unitary phenomenon. The debate over the role of general versus specific facets of intelligence and ability has been hotly contested, and continues to this day.

***The Debate Over* g.** One of the most hotly contested topics in research on cognitive ability is the importance of the general factor g that is central to the theories of Spearman, Vernon, Carroll, and the like (Sternberg & Grigorenko, 2002). On the one hand, abundant evidence suggests that there are broad and general differences in people's performance on a wide range of cognitively demanding tasks and that a general factor emerges from analyses of virtually any set of cognitive tests. People's standing on this general factor is probably the best single predictor of their performance in school, on the job, and in other settings where cognitively demanding tasks must be performed. Finally, once you have taken g into account, considering additional, more specific abilities does not seem to help much in predicting performance in these settings (for extensive recent analyses of these points, see Ree & Carretta, 1994; Ree & Earles, 1991a, 1991b, 1992; Ree, Earles, & Teachout, 1994; see also Hunter & Hunter, 1984; Murphy, 1996). From a pragmatic point of view, it is hard to doubt the utility of the g factor.

On the other hand, critics of "g-ocentric" theories of intelligence (e.g., McClelland, 1993; Sternberg, 1984, 1985; Sternberg & Wagner, 1993) rightly note that if you concentrate too much on the g factor, you are likely to lose sight of key questions such as why a person is intelligent, or what intelligent people do, or how they do it. It is clearly not enough to simply say that people differ on g and leave it at that. Murphy (1996) suggests that models of intelligence that focus on g are most useful for pragmatic purposes (e.g., predicting future performance), whereas models that focus on facets of intelligence other than g may be more useful for structuring research on the nature and origins of intelligent behavior.

Theories of cognitive ability that posit many different types of intelligence are appealing for a number of reasons, not the least of which is the sense that if you don't do well in one type of "intelligence" test, perhaps there is another type that would show just how smart you really are! Unfortunately, theories such as those put forth by Guilford (structure of intellect model), Sternberg (triarchic model), or Gardner (multiple intelligence theory) have not fared well in terms of their empirical support (Cronbach, 1986; Lubinski & Benbow, 1995; McGrew & Flanagan, 1998; Messick, 1992). These theories, all of which downplay the importance of g, fail to explain a wide range of phenomena, especially the tendency for measures of performance on most cognitively demanding tasks to be positively correlated. If g is not an important facet of cognitive ability, it is very hard to explain why people who do well on vocabulary tests also tend to do well on math tests, or why people whose spatial abilities are generally good also tend to do well in remembering long strings of numbers.

Cognitive Processes in Intelligence. Sternberg (1977, 1980, 1981a, 1982, 1985) proposed a very different structure of the domain of intelligence. His theory notes that mental activities can be broken down into components and that different sorts of components are used to acquire information, to carry out specific mental tasks, and to plan, monitor, and evaluate general mental processes. The theory suggests that adaptation to one's environment is a critical measure of intelligence (Sternberg, 1984), a proposition that has been suggested previously by many others (e.g., Mercer, 1979).

Early theories of the cognitive processes involved in intelligence tended to focus on elementary information-processing operations, or the ways in which we perceive, encode, store, and retrieve information (Jensen, 1980). More recent theories have worked from a broader base. For example, Sternberg's (1985) triarchic theory of intelligence features three subtheories. His componential theory, which is concerned with how intelligent behavior is generated, deals with the basic cognitive processes involved in knowledge acquisition and performance. His contextual theory deals with what behaviors are intelligent in what contexts. His experiential theory deals with determining when and why a given behavior is intelligent.

Cognitive theories have had some impact on the design of tests of intelligence (E. B. Hunt & Pellegrin, 1985; Sternberg, 1984). It has been suggested that broad-based theories, such as Sternberg's (1985), could fundamentally alter the way in which we develop, interpret, and use tests of general intelligence; but to date, the links between theories of cognition and mainstream ability testing have not been particularly strong.

Practical Intelligence. Sternberg has made two major contirbutions to research and theory on human cognitive abilities. First, as noted before, he has articulated process theories of cognition that provide an alternative to theories that focus on individual differences in intelligence without giving adequate attention to what intelligent people *do*. Second, he has argued forcefuly that research on cognitive ability should not be limited to academic tasks and domains, and that psychologists should pay more attention to practical intelligence (Sternberg, 1997a, 1997b). He notes that many of our everyday decisions and actions involve solving problems that are not formal or abstract, and that there is a meaningful distinction between the sorts of tasks that are found on typical intelligence tests (e.g., verbal analogies, mathematics problems) and the sorts of problems that people solve each day (e.g., juggling schedules, determining how to pack for a trip, deciding what to include and what to leave out of a letter of recommendation). Sternberg has argued that general factors are less critical in understanding practical intelligence than they are in highly structured academic tasks (Sternberg & Grigorenko, 2002) and that practical intelligence is an important aspect of success in leadership, management, and professional jobs (Sternberg, 1997b; Sternberg & Horvath, 1999). To date, however, there have not been convincing demonstrations that tests of practical intelligence are better predictors of success than more traditional cognitive ability tests (Gottfredson, 2003).

Historical Foundations of Intelligence Testing

Today, intelligence testing represents a multimillion-dollar industry. It may therefore come as a surprise that intelligence testing is a relatively modern phenomenon (see Table 1-1). The term *mental test* did not appear in its modern sense until 1890. The first test that provided a standardized and reasonably valid measure of general intelligence did not appear until 1908. In fact, the term *intelligence* is relatively modern. Before 1900, psychologists (the few who then existed) and philosophers generally did not distinguish intelligence from a number of other human characteristics, such as consciousness, human nature, or soul (Matarazzo, 1972). The concept of intelligence as a general cognitive ability therefore received scant coverage in the writings of early psychologists.

The early development of theories of intelligence and of tests designed to measure general intelligence centered mainly in England and France in the early 1900s. In England, the pioneering work of Galton provided both the impetus and the tools for the systematic study of individual differences. In France, changing attitudes toward the insane and the mentally retarded provided the impetus for developing practical measures of mental ability. These events helped set the stage for the intelligence testing movement.

Measurement of Individual Differences. The contributions of an English biologist, Sir Francis Galton, to scientific psychology are of singular importance. Galton's interest in psychology was secondary to his interest in heredity, and today the theories of intelligence that appeared to pervade his work have been largely repudiated. His contribution is not in terms of what he found but, rather, in terms of his development and synthesis of systematic methods of measuring individual differences. Galton and his students, notably Pearson, developed several of the basic procedures used today in the analysis of individual differences.

James McKeen Cattell helped to bring the study of individual differences to the United States. Although a student of Wundt (an experimentalist who had little patience with the study of individual differences), Cattell was influenced by Galton and developed a set of sensorimotor tests that were used to measure the intellectual level of college students. His tests were similar to Galton's and included measures of strength, reaction time, sensitivity to pain, and weight discrimination. In an article describing these procedures, Cattell (1890) was apparently the first to use the term *mental test*. Although the tests included in his battery would probably no longer be described as "mental," the nomenclature stuck, and the term *mental test* was soon commonplace.

The 1890s saw a flurry of mental tests of the sensorimotor type. A number of early studies, most notably by Wissler (1901), dealt a fatal blow to these mental tests by showing that sensorimotor tests of the type employed by Galton and Cattell were highly unreliable and, worse, showed little or no correlation with other measures of intelligence, such as teachers' estimates of examinees' intellectual level. By this time, however, practical methods of measuring intelligence were being developed successfully in France.

The Classification of the Mentally Retarded. Before the 19th century, treatment of the mentally retarded and the insane frequently was callous and occasionally barbaric; mentally disturbed persons were subject to confinement, neglect, and ridicule. Humanitarian movements in the 19th century helped to change attitudes toward the mentally disturbed and spurred the development of humane and effective methods of treating mental disorders.

One of the first tasks in effectively caring for these patients was the proper classification of mental disorders and deficiencies. At the simplest level, uniform procedures had to be developed for differentiating the insane, who suffered from emotional disorders, from the mentally retarded, who typically suffered from an intellectual deficit. As early as 1838, Esquirol, a French physician, pointed out that there were many degrees of retardation and suggested that an individual's use of language was critical in distinguishing among different degrees of retardation. Esquirol's work anticipated many later developments in measuring intelligence using tests predominantly verbal in content.

The work of another French physician, Seguin, was especially important in providing an impetus for the development of intelligence tests. Seguin rejected the widely held belief that retardation was incurable, and he demonstrated that sensorimotor training could be highly beneficial for retarded children, particularly those with less profound levels of retardation. Seguin's success in training retarded children opened a number of alternatives for children who were not intellectually capable of responding to normal schooling; it also demonstrated the practical need for a standardized measure of general intelligence. Seguin's work was instrumental to a decision by the French Ministry of Public Instruction, nearly 50 years later, to commission the development of a method of quickly and accurately measuring general intelligence.

Individually Administered Tests.   The early mental tests were often nothing more than batteries of psychomotor tests that bore little relation, either theoretically or empirically, to everyday behavior or to success in school. Binet was among the early critics of such tests, insisting that intelligence would be measured better by sampling performance in a variety of more complex tasks that involved functions such as memory, comprehension, and judgment (Binet & Henri, 1895). In 1904, the Ministry of Public Instruction appointed Binet to a commission charged with studying procedures for educating the mentally retarded.[2] One of the primary tasks of this commission was to develop practical measures for identifying schoolchildren who were intellectually unable to profit from education in the public schools and, within this group, to identify children who would be most likely to benefit from special education. In 1905, Binet, in collaboration with Simon, developed the first scale to provide a practical and reasonably valid measure of general intelligence, the 1905 Binet-Simon scale (Binet & Simon, 1905).

The 1905 Binet-Simon scale contained 30 items, or tests, arranged in order of difficulty. Although a few psychomotor tasks were included in this test, most items called for the use of language, reasoning, or comprehension. For example, the first item called for the child to follow a moving object with his or her eyes. Item 11 asked the subject to repeat three spoken digits. Item 20 asked the subject to tell how two common objects were alike, whereas item 30 required the subject to define a set of abstract items (Matarazzo, 1972). The 1905 scale had a number of appealing features: Item difficulties were determined empirically, there was a clear ordering of item difficulties, and there was a broad sampling of the domain of activities requiring intelligence. However, the 1905 scale suffered from a number of drawbacks, the most serious being the lack of any precise method of scoring the test or of interpreting total scores.

The first revision of the Binet-Simon scale appeared in 1908. In the 1908 scale, a few unsatisfactory items from the earlier scale were dropped, and a number of new items were added, bringing the total number of items on the 1908 Binet-Simon scale to 58. The most important revision, however, had to do with the way in which item difficulty was established and the way in which test scores were interpreted. It is well-known that very young children (3 to 4 years old) almost always perform well on tasks similar to those sampled by the easiest items on the Binet-Simon test but that they almost always fail the more difficult items. Similarly, somewhat older children (7 to

---

[2]Binet and his associates in the Society for the Psychological Study of the Child were instrumental in initiating this committee. For an excellent, concise history of Binet's work, see Matarazzo (1972).

8 years old) generally pass all the simplest items and perform well on tests of moderate difficulty, but they almost always fail the most difficult items. In effect, the age at which a typical child first masters a particular task provides an indirect indication of the difficulty of the task. Binet took advantage of this fact to group test items in terms of age levels and to express an overall test score in terms of a mental level, defined as the age of a normal child receiving the same test score as the examinee.

Although Binet preferred the somewhat neutral term *mental level*, the term *mental age* is more common. The method of expressing intelligence test scores in terms of mental age represented a tremendous breakthrough. Whereas previous attempts at measuring intelligence had yielded scores whose interpretations were not immediately obvious (e.g., on the 1905 scale, was a score of 22/30 good, average, or poor?), the score yielded by the 1908 Binet-Simon was concrete and understandable. A score of 7 years meant that the examinee's performance resembled that of a typical 7-year-old. The use of an age scale contributed significantly to the popularity of intelligence tests (Goodenough, 1949; Matarazzo, 1972).

Binet's tests were developed to be used with children. Noting the need for a comparable test for adults, David Wechsler, a psychiatrist at Bellevue Hospital, developed the Wechsler-Bellevue Intelligence Scale. This test was administered on an individual basis to adults and required them to respond to a variety of verbal and performance-oriented items. This test was the forerunner of the highly successful Wechsler Adult Intelligence Scale and of later tests developed by Wechsler for assessing children's intelligence.

The Intelligence Quotient. Since 1908, the Binet-Simon test has undergone many revisions, some of which are discussed in Chapter 13. One of the most influential, carried out by Terman (1916) at Stanford University, resulted in the Stanford-Binet Intelligence Test, in which the intelligence quotient (IQ) first appeared. The IQ was developed to deal with certain difficulties inherent in the 1908 Binet-Simon. For example, if a child received a mental age of 7, this outcome had different implications, depending on the age of the child taking the test. A 5-year-old receiving a mental age of 7 was performing ahead of the level expected for most 5-year-olds, a 7-year-old with a mental age of 7 was showing completely normal performance, and a 12-year-old with a mental age of 7 showed a potentially serious intellectual deficit. To aid in the interpretation of mental age scores, the intelligence quotient was formed by dividing the mental age by the chronological age, as in Equation 2-1.

$$IQ = (MA/CA) \times 100 \hspace{4cm} [2\text{-}1]$$

where

    IQ = intelligence quotient
    MA = mental age
    CA = chronological age

(The ratio of MA/CA is multiplied by 100 in order to remove decimal points.)

When a child is performing at exactly the level reached by other children of the same age, the child's mental age is exactly equal to his or her chronological age, yielding an IQ of 100. Thus, 100 indicates normal, or average performance. When the child's mental age is lower than his or her chronological age, the IQ is less than 100, indicating substandard performance. When a child's mental age is higher than his or her chronological age, the IQ is greater than 100, indicating above-average performance.

Although an IQ score based on mental age has many useful features, this type of IQ measure leads to a number of difficulties. First, there is the technical problem induced by the fact that performance does not show equal levels of variability at all ages. Thus, a 4-year-old with an MA of 5 receives the same IQ score (125) as an 8-year-old with an MA of 10, but it is not clear whether they both show the same degree of superior performance relative to their age group. This problem can be partially dealt with in the test development process, but it does not represent the most serious problem in the use of an IQ score based on mental age. The most serious problem occurs when one tries to measure the intelligence of adults.

Mental age does not increase steadily throughout a person's entire life; an average 85-year-old is not likely to solve many problems that are beyond the grasp of an ordinary 84-year-old. Although there is evidence that many adults continue to add to their score of factual knowledge throughout their entire lives, it seems clear that the rate of development in basic cognitive abilities decreases sharply with age (Eysenck, 1979). In effect, an IQ score based on mental age penalizes the older examinee. Whereas chronological age is progressing at a steady rate, mental age soon levels off. As a consequence, the IQ = MA/CA formulation invariably suggests that as people get older, they steadily become less intelligent. In other words, if you lived long enough, your mental age IQ would invariably approach zero!

Because of the problems previously mentioned, mental age is no longer used in computing IQ scores. On modern tests, a deviation IQ score is computed. The deviation IQ is obtained by computing standard scores on a specific intelligence test and then converting these scores to a scale with a mean of 100 and a standard deviation of 15. For example, a person whose test score is 2 standard deviations above the mean (approximately 98th percentile in a normal distribution) receives a deviation IQ score of 130. Someone whose score is 1 standard deviation below the mean receives an 85, whereas a person whose test score is exactly equal to the mean receives an IQ score of 100. This system preserves many of the desirable features of the mental age IQ without some of the flaws. First, a score of 100 indicates average or normal performance. Second, a score above 100 indicates above-average performance, whereas a score below 100 indicates below-average performance. Third, the size of the difference between the mean score (100) and a person's IQ score indicates, in a very concrete way, the relative standing of the person's score. Intelligence test scores tend to follow a nearly normal distribution; as a consequence, tables of the normal curve can be used to translate deviation IQ scores into percentiles that indicate what percentage of the population would be expected to receive higher or lower test scores.

Standardized Group Testing. The standardized, machine-scored intelligence tests that are used widely today are quite different from Binet's tests. The Stanford-

Binet and similar tests represent complex social interactions in which examinees are faced with challenging tasks. They must be administered on an individual basis by specially trained psychologists, and they require considerable care and professional judgment in their administration and interpretation. Several psychologists, most notably Otis, began in the early 1900s to develop simpler tests that could be administered under standard conditions to groups of examinees.[3]

The real impetus for the development of group tests, however, came with America's entry into World War I. Before the war, the American army had been small and somewhat insular. When our entry into the war led to a sudden influx of high numbers of men, along with an expansion in the complexity of the army and the size of the chain of command, it soon became apparent that the traditional, somewhat haphazard methods of classifying and placing new soldiers—particularly for identifying promising officer candidates—simply would not be sufficient. Hence, some reasonably simple and economical method of classifying recruits was needed. The American Psychological Association (APA) had volunteered its services to the war effort, and an APA committee, headed by Yerkes and including psychologists such as Otis and Terman, was assigned the task of developing a practical method of measuring the intellectual level of a large number of soldiers. Their efforts led to the development of two tests, Army Alpha and Army Beta. Army Alpha was a written test that could be administered to large groups of recruits and that provided a rough measure of general intelligence. Army Beta, a nonverbal test designed for illiterates and for recruits who spoke little or no English, could also be administered in groups and used simple pictorial and nonverbal instructions.[4]

Although there is some debate as to the precise value and validity of Army Alpha and Army Beta (Gould, 1981), the tests were perceived as being useful at the time they were developed. They provided at least a rough classification of men, which was of considerable utility in making the large number of selection decisions necessary at that time.

The apparent success of the army's group tests did not go unnoticed in business circles and educational settings. Soon after the war, the demand arose for similar tests in civilian settings, and many psychologists were happy to fill the bill. By the mid to late 1920s, intelligence testing was widespread, particularly in the schools. Uncritical enthusiasm for group intelligence testing did not fully abate until the 1960s, and even today, standardized group intelligence tests still are used on a routine basis in a number of settings where their validity and utility are questionable. This issue is discussed in later chapters.

[3]See Sokal (1987) for a thorough discussion of the early history of ability testing in the United States.

[4]Gould's (1981) account suggests that the administration of Army Beta was neither simple nor standardized but was a rather harrowing and confusing experience for many people taking the test. The validity of Army Beta scores is doubtful.

Characteristics of a Good Test
of General-Mental Ability

In describing a general strategy for assessing intelligence, we attempt to synthesize some of the theoretical and practical knowledge contained in our survey of the development of intelligence tests and of theories of intelligence to describe a general strategy for measuring intelligence. The purpose of this section is to provide a set of guidelines for evaluating tests that purport to measure intelligence. Some tests embody all the essential characteristics expected in a good intelligence test, whereas others seem to lack them entirely. This is not to say that every test that follows the strategy described here is a good test and that every test that fails to follow this strategy is a bad one. Nevertheless, we think that it is possible to describe the general characteristics of a good measure of intelligence and to use this information in evaluating tests.

The strategy we describe is geared toward measuring general intelligence, although the strategy also might apply when measuring broad abilities (e.g., Vernon's major group factors). Measures of specific intellectual abilities follow the same basic rules of test construction as do measures of nonintellectual abilities or measures of specific personality variables.

Broad Sampling of Tasks. The first principle for measuring general intelligence is that the test should include a broad sampling of cognitively demanding tasks. Every test is a sample of behavior, and since the domain of intelligence is extremely broad, any test of intelligence should feature a similarly broad sample of the domain. One should be very cautious in using a test that claims to measure intelligence but that contains only one type of item (e.g., a vocabulary test, a verbal analogies test, a digit-symbol substitution test). A test that consists exclusively of reading comprehension items is a reading comprehension test, not necessarily a test of general intelligence. Binet was the first to successfully apply the broad sampling principle; the tasks included in his test ranged from simple sensorimotor tasks to questions involving complex abstract concepts.

Broad sampling of cognitive domain may be achieved by including items that tap many different aspects of the domain. For example, a good test of intelligence might include items that measure many (or all) of Thurstone's primary mental abilities. A broad sampling of items and subtests serves to increase the content validity of a test of general intelligence.

Intelligence Tests Are Not Information Tests. There is a long-standing distinction between aptitude tests and achievement tests in psychological testing. Achievement tests are used widely in educational settings. They measure one's mastery of a specific branch of knowledge or of a specific content area. Classroom tests are good examples of achievement tests; professional licensing exams are another. Aptitude tests are more general in nature and are designed to measure cumulative knowledge, skills, and abilities that have developed as a result of the subject's life experience. The distinction between aptitude and achievement is now recognized as being one of emphasis, rather than as the fundamental distinction, as was once assumed (Anastasi, 1982; Angoff, 1988; Jensen, 1980). Indeed, some psychologists maintain that there is no useful distinction between aptitude tests and achievement tests (Humphreys, 1978). In our opinion, the distinction still is useful in terms of describing types of items that should or should not appear on tests of general intelligence.

It seems clear that intelligence tests should not contain a large number of achievement-type items. In other words, intelligence tests should not predominantly measure knowledge of specific facts. Scores on these items typically reflect some combinations of the amount and quality of schooling, together with the level of crystallized intelligence. Although the amount of information at one's disposal is clearly related to the level of general intelligence, knowledge of specific information does not provide a good measure of intelligence. Most intelligence tests are designed to measure something broader and more important than the size of one's store of facts. They are designed to measure and predict performance on a wide variety of tasks in which the knowledge of specific facts may be of little importance.

It is impossible to design a test that does not call for any prior knowledge; all intelligence tests call for some knowledge of specific facts. Critics of intelligence testing have seized on this point to argue that, since the specific facts that are important and relevant to one culture may be less important in another, the tests are inherently culturally unfair. In our opinion, this argument carries much more weight for tests in which knowledge of specific facts is likely to materially affect one's test score. In most good intelligence tests, knowledge of specific facts is likely to have little impact on test scores. Intelligence tests that are in reality achievement tests will tend to be much more prone to cultural bias.

Indifference of the Indicator. One fundamental principle espoused by Spearman (1923) was that of the "indifference of the indicator." Basically, this principle means that on a good test of intelligence, the content of specific items should be irrelevant, since the test is designed to measure the process by which terms are answered. For example, consider a verbal analogies test, in which all the analogies address relationships among parts of the body, as in the following:

Hand is to arm as foot is to _____?

The principle of indifference of the indicator is upheld if the content of each analogy can be changed without changing the essential characteristics of the test. For example:

Uncle is to cousin as father is to _____?

The importance of this principle is that the measurement of intelligence is not restricted to a particular type of item or a particular content area. Rather, any item that poses a cognitively challenging task is a potential candidate for inclusion on an intelligence test. On the other hand, items that presuppose detailed knowledge of some specialized domain are not as likely to provide good measures of intelligence, and an intelligence test that is irrevocably tied to one specific type of item or one specific domain of knowledge is not likely to be a good measure of intelligence.

Sufficient Sample of Items. In psychological testing, there is a built-in conflict between practical and theoretical considerations when determining the length of a test. Test theory shows that the longer the test, the more reliable the test; yet long tests are more time-consuming and more difficult to administer than short tests. It may not be possible to specify the optimal length of an intelligence test, but several factors argue against extremely short tests. First is the concern for the reliability of a short intelligence test. A second and more important concern is the breadth of coverage of a very short test. It may be quite difficult to achieve both reliability and content validity with a small item sample.

It is difficult to draw the line between a short test and a long test. This difficulty is exacerbated by the fact that abbreviated versions of several existing intelligence tests are known to be highly reliable and highly correlated with their longer counterparts. Nevertheless, we suggest that a good test should feature at least a dozen or so of each type of test item. Certainly, a five-item test of general intelligence that features one reading comprehension item, two vocabulary questions, an addition problem, and a subtraction problem should be suspect. A good test should include a sufficient sampling of each of many types of tasks. This requirement is particularly important if subscale scores (e.g., verbal, quantitative) are to be computed.

CRITICAL DISCUSSION:

IQ or EQ?

One of the most potent criticisms of research on cognitive ability is that it implies a very narrow vision of what it means to be "smart." Cognitive ability is clearly relevant to success in school or in performing a wide array of cognitively demanding tasks (everything from completing a crossword puzzle to completing your doctoral dissertation), but there is more to life than cognitively demanding tasks. It is likely that intelligence has many facets, only some of which correspond to the traditional verbal, mathematical, spatial, and other categories studied by most cognitive ability researchers. For example, Gardner (1993) suggests that there are multiple intelligences and that the domain of intelligence should include social-interpersonal skills as well as skills in answering test questions (i.e., cognitive abilities, as traditionally defined).

Empirical research on emotional and social skills has a long history (Salovey & Mayer, 1990; Sternberg, 1985), but it was not until 1995, with Goleman's best-selling book, *Emotional Intelligence: Why It Can Matter More Than IQ,* that the topic received widespread public attention. Emotional intelligence has been the cover story for magazines like *Time* and *Newsweek* and the focus of numerous articles and television reports.

Although some proponents of emotional intelligence, or EQ, suggest that this concept "redefines what it means to be smart" and that it "can matter more than IQ" (both claims are made on the cover of Goleman, 1995), it would be a mistake to throw out cognitive ability tests with the hope of replacing them with measures of social or emotional intelligence. First, we are still far from consensus in defining emotional intelligence. Research in this area suggests that attributes such as impulse control, self-monitoring, and empathy are all part of emotional intelligence, but it is not yet clear how these diverse elements go together or whether social intelligence is a monolithic general ability (e.g., perhaps there is a social or an emotional counterpart to the *g* factor in cognitive ability research) or a set of diverse abilities. Second, and more important, there is no good measure of emotional intelligence that could be used in the ways that cognitive ability tests are currently used.

Consider, for example, the most widely discussed measure of social or emotional intelligence, the marshmallow test. Suppose that you place a marshmallow on a table in front of a 4-year-old and tell him that either he can have this marshmallow now, or if he waits a few minutes until you return from an errand, he can have two marshmallows. If you leave the room, you will find that some children grab the marshmallow right away and eat it, whereas others are able to delay gratification long enough for you to return so that they receive the two-marshmallow reward. Remarkably, children who exhibit the ability to delay gratification in this test turn out to be better students, more well-adjusted, more resilient, confident, and dependable, and these differences are still apparent when they are assessed years later (Goleman, 1995; Shoda, Mischel, & Peake, 1990). In other words, this simple measure of the ability to delay gratification at age 4 predicts a wide range of behaviors and outcomes throughout childhood and adolescence (and perhaps beyond).

The marshmallow test may very well be a good measure of emotional intelligence (although it is still far from clear exactly what this test really measures), but it is still not a good substitute for cognitive ability tests. Similarly, emotional intelligence seems to be a very important attribute, and in some settings it might be more important than IQ, as it is traditionally assessed. Nevertheless, it is unlikely that EQ will someday be a substitute for IQ. Rather, as the concept of emotional intelligence continues to develop and as good measures of this concept start to emerge, it is likely that a combination of IQ and EQ measures will become increasingly common. Rather than being viewed as competitors, it is probably best to view these as complementary aspects of "what it means to be smart" and to look for ways to use information about EQ and IQ in tandem.

INTERESTS

The Nature of Interests

Strong (1943) defined an interest as "a response of liking" (p. 6). It is a learned affective response to an object or activity; things in which we are interested elicit positive feelings, things in which we have little interest elicit little affect, and things in which we are totally disinterested elicit apathy or even feelings of aversion. For example, some people enjoy (are interested in) opera, other people can take it or leave it, and still others hate it.

Interests are different from abilities. The fact that you like opera does not make you an opera singer. However, interests and abilities tend to show some similar patterns. People often learn to like things that they do well and learn to dislike things that they do not do well (Strong, 1943). One practical distinction between abilities and interests is in terms of the variables that they tend to predict. Measures of ability tend to predict measures of performance or efficiency. Interests are typically related to persistence and satisfaction, rather than to performance. Thus, although the fact that a person is extraordinarily interested in opera does not necessarily indicate that he or she will succeed as an opera singer, it does indicate that the person would be happy as an opera singer (the audience, however, might not be so happy).

Interests can be used to predict choices, especially when there are few external constraints. For example, when a person goes to a bookstore, his or her interests (together with the price of the book) have a substantial impact on the choices of which book to buy. Even in decisions that have substantial consequences, such as choosing a career, interests have a substantial effect. A person who hates to work with figures is not likely to choose a career in accounting, even if very lucrative jobs are available.

Interests differ in terms of their specificity. The typical conception of interests is that they are tied to specific objects or activities, such as interest in baseball, ships, or dentistry. However, very broad domains of interest have been identified; examples include scientific interests, masculine interests, and humanitarian interests. Within the occupational domain, interests in specific occupations (e.g., air traffic controller), in broad occupational fields (e.g., medical jobs), and in general types of fields (e.g., business) have been assessed. To date, measures of specific interests have been more useful than measures of general interests in predicting future choices and future satisfaction (Super, 1973).

A distinction is typically made between interests and values; values are regarded as more general and more resistant to change than interests. Super (1973) has suggested that interests and values are best defined in a sort of a means-end relationship. Thus, values are objectives that one seeks to satisfy a need, whereas interests are linked to specific activities through which values can be obtained. Examples of the work values proposed by Super are quality of life, material outcomes, self-expression, and behavior control.

Expressed Versus Inventoried Interests. Early research on interest measurements led to the conclusion that people were unaware of or could not adequately verbalize their interests. The principal support for this conclusion was the finding that scores on interest inventories did a better job in predicting future satisfaction than did claimed interests, which were obtained by simply asking persons to name things in which they were interested. The assumption that people could not identify their interests led to, or at least reinforced, the development of complex, indirect methods of interest measurement.

The assumption that people cannot describe their own interests has long been questioned (Dolliver, 1969; Slaney & Russell, 1981; Zytowski & Borgan, 1983). Studies examining people's ability to describe their core interests suggest that expressed interests show levels of validity in predicting future choices and satisfaction comparable to those achieved by well-constructed interest inventories. It may well be the case that claimed interests are valid interests. Nevertheless, interest inventories continue to serve a useful purpose, especially when used for counseling. Inventories help to clarify interests and to alert clients to specific aspects of their interests that may be unknown to them. For example, even if a person knows exactly the activities in which he or she is interested, inventories provide valid comparisons that could not be carried out by the person being assessed. No matter how much the client knows about his or her interests, the person is probably not sufficiently well informed to validly compare them to those of accountants, physicians, forest rangers, and so on. Interest inventories provide such comparisons.

Historical Foundations of Interest Measurement

The history of interest measurement is concerned largely with the assessment of vocational interests. Although research in interests broader than those linked to occupations can be traced back to Thorndike (1912), applications of interest measures have been linked almost exclusively to vocational counseling.[5] In fact, it is fair to say that measures developed in the years following World War I have provided the foundation for the modern field of vocational guidance and counseling (Zytowski & Borgan, 1983).

The first standardized vocational interest inventories were developed between 1916 and 1923 at the Carnegie Institute of Technology (now Carnegie-Mellon University). E. K. Strong, a member of the Carnegie group, moved on to Stanford, where he supervised a student (K. Cowdery) whose thesis dealt with differentiating lawyers, engineers, and physicians in terms of their interests. The success of Cowdery's study encouraged Strong to undertake a broader line of research, attempting to differentiate many or all occupations in terms of patterns of interests (Strong, 1943). The result of this research was the Strong Vocational Interest Blank. This test, now known as the Strong Interest Inventory (SII), represents one of the most widely used, widely researched tests in existence (Zytowski & Borgan, 1983).

At the same time that Strong was developing and perfecting his test, G. F. Kuder developed a similar test. Although both tests use a person's descriptions of his or her own interests to predict occupational adjustment and satisfaction, the approaches followed by these two researchers differed in important ways. Strong used the responses of people in general as a point of reference and determined how the responses of particular groups (e.g., carpenters, dentists, pilots) differed from this reference group. Kuder's approach was a bit more straightforward. He simply determined the extent to which a person's responses were similar to those of each occupational group. Strong's tests assume that responses that are similar to an occupational group and different from those of people in general tell the most about occupational interests. Kuder's tests assume that any response could provide information about a person's occupational interests, even if that response is not unique to that one occupation. To date, there is little evidence that one method is qualitatively better or worse than the other.

There are two generic approaches to measuring vocational interests, the actuarial approach and the trait-and-factor approach. The tests developed by Strong and Kuder are good examples of the actuarial approach, which searches for consistencies in interest data without necessarily explaining them. Thus, if we knew that most carpenters liked football but that most lawyers like baseball, we could (actuarially) state that interest in football is related to carpentry and that interest in baseball is related to the law. The trait-and-factor approach, on the other hand, represents an attempt to explain or outline the substance of vocational interests. D. P. Campbell and Borgen (1999) review

[5]There are, for example, over 200 vocational interest inventories currently in use.

the impact of Holland's theory on the development and interpretation of vocational interest inventories.

The earliest practitioners of vocational counseling were advocates of the trait-and-factor approach (e.g., Parsons, 1909). This approach gradually lost its popularity, in part because of the very visible success of the actuarial approach. However, later in this century, the trait-and-factor approach reemerged. The dominant theory of vocational choice is the one developed by J. L. Holland (1973), who suggests that vocational interests can be broken down into six basic types: realistic, investigative, artistic, social, enterprising, and conventional. Interests in specific occupations or occupational clusters can be predicted on the basis of these broad factors or themes.

Modern revisions of the SII have successfully combined the actuarial approach with the trait-and-factor approach. The SII has retained the traditional (actuarial) occupational scales but also includes measures of basic interests and of Holland's occupational themes. Thus, it is now possible to give both specific and general feedback in the process of vocational counseling. The addition of general dimensions to the SII greatly increases the usefulness of this measure as a counseling tool.

Characteristics of a Good Interest Measure

As noted, there are two basic approaches to interest measurement, the trait-and-factor approach and the actuarial approach. Because of the two fundamentally different approaches, two very different sets of criteria can be developed for evaluating interest measures.

Actuarial Approach. Actuarial measures compare a person's interests with those of members of specific groups and attempt to predict satisfaction with various activities or occupations. The first requirement for an actuarial measure is criterion-related validity. Thus, if a vocational interest measure indicates that a person's interests are very similar to the interests of carpenters, the most crucial issue in assessing validity is whether the person's interests are similar to those of carpenters.

A number of interest inventories have demonstrated their validity statistically. However, empirical demonstrations, particularly if they are somewhat dated, are not always convincing. An interest inventory that successfully assessed vocational interests 30 years ago might be outdated today. However, the best actuarial instruments are subject to constant research and frequent revision. In general, it is necessary to periodically check and revise the normative bases of interest measures; a measure that has not been revised or renormed for a long time should be used with caution.

Actuarial measures vary considerably in the breadth of the questions asked and of the scores provided. In general, interest inventories are most likely to prove useful when the questions span several different domains and when scores are provided that illustrate several different kinds or levels of interests. For example, the SII asks questions about areas such as work-related interests, preferences for activities, and preferences for types of people; and it provides scores for specific occupational interests (e.g., carpenter, psychologist, policeman), general vocational interests, and broad vocational themes. Such a test is much more useful than a test that samples only a limited domain of interests or provides only a limited range of information.

Trait-and-Factor Approach. With actuarial tests such as the SII, construct validity is not really a relevant concern. In the actuarial approach, no attempt is made to determine which underlying variables or constructs are measured; using this approach, interest measures are judged solely in terms of their ability to predict. When the trait-and-factor approach is followed, however, construct validity is directly relevant.

The principles for evaluating inventories designed to measure a specific interest or group of interests are similar to those that would be followed in evaluating a measure of a specific cognitive ability or personality dimension. First, the interest must be sufficiently well defined to permit an assessment of the relationship between test items and the construct being measured. Second, the relationship between the interest being measured and the other relevant constructs must be spelled out in sufficient detail to allow a detailed assessment of construct validity.

J. L. Holland's (1973) theory of vocational choice can be used to illustrate the application of both of these principles. The theory describes in detail the content of each of six broad vocational themes and, more important, describes in detail the relationships among these themes. This structure allows one to (1) specify item content that is relevant to each theme and (2) compare the empirical relations among measures of the six themes with the theoretical relationships among the constructs themselves.

The most obvious prerequisite for a good trait-and-factor measure is the existence of a reasonably detailed theory or rationale that outlines the set of factors to be measured, the relations among these factors, and the relationships between these factors and behaviors such as occupational choice. As noted in Chapter 8, the better the surrounding theory, the more likely that convincing evidence regarding construct validity will be developed successfully.

PERSONALITY

The Nature of Personality

Frank (1939) noted that "an initial difficulty in the study of personality is the lack of any clear-cut conception of what is to be studied" (p. 389). Subsequent reviews suggested that the situation has not fundamentally changed in the intervening years (Carson, 1989; Pervin, 1985; Rorer & Widigor, 1983). There still is some uncertainty over what personality is, over the usefulness of the term *personality,* and over the contribution of personal factors, as opposed to environmental factors, to the understanding of behavior.

A definition of personality must take into account several facts. First, individuals are unique in the sense that no two people are exactly alike in terms of temperament, behavior, or preferences. Second, individuals do not behave in identical ways in all situations. A person behaves differently at a football game than he or she would in a religious setting. Third, although individuals are unique and are not completely consistent across situations, there is considerable commonality in human behavior. That is, although there are great differences in detail, many people show similar patterns of behavior. The description of broad personality types may allow us to group individuals meaningfully in a way that accurately describes some important behavior patterns.

In theory, two extreme positions could be put forth to explain behavior, the purely trait-oriented position and the purely situational position. The former concentrates solely on the person and ignores the situation in which behavior occurs, whereas the latter ignores the person and concentrates solely on the situation. Neither position represents a fruitful or even an adequate description of personality (Carson, 1989; Pervin, 1985). A more comprehensive definition that considers both the person and the situation has been suggested by Pervin (1980). Personality is defined as the set of characteristics of a person or of people that account for consistent patterns of response to situations.

Consistency in Behavior. During the 1970s and 1980s, the dominant issue in research on personality was the debate over the consistency of behavior across situations (Bem & Funder, 1978; Epstein, 1980; Mischel & Peake, 1982). This controversy can be traced back to the 1930s and probably has roots as old as those of psychology (Maddi, 1984; Pervin, 1985). The core issue in this debate was whether persons do in fact behave in relatively consistent fashions across a wide range of situations.

If we accept (in its most extreme form) the argument that behavior is not at all stable across situations, it would make no sense to measure personality, interests, ability, or any other individual difference variable (Rorer & Widigor, 1983). The data do not support this extreme interpretation, but neither do they support the opposite extreme, that behavior is completely stable across situations.[6] The heart of the person-situation debate is not which factor is completely dominant but, rather, how much emphasis should be placed on consistency versus inconsistency.

Maddi (1984) notes the distinction between absolute and relative consistency. A person may be consistent, relative to others, without being absolutely consistent in his or her behavior. For example, if we observe a person attending a friend's wedding, attending a football game, and attending a scientific conference, that person's behavior might change from setting to setting. This apparent inconsistency does not necessarily mean that behavior is unstable. A person who is more outgoing than another at a wedding will also probably be more outgoing at a football game or at a scientific conference. Thus, when compared with the behavior of others in the same situation, the individual might be highly consistent.

Personality psychologists appear to have reached a consensus that individual behaviors are unstable but that broad patterns of behavior show some consistency (Epstein, 1980) and that persons show more relative than absolute stability in their behavior (Maddi, 1984; Pervin, 1985). This finding suggests that personality measures

---

[6]Pervin (1985) notes that few, if any, of the participants in this debate argued strictly for the person or for the situation and that nearly everyone accepts some consistency and some situational control.

may provide a useful means of predicting individual differences in general patterns of behavior, but that to accomplish this, both the personality dimension(s) measured and the behavior being predicted must not be too narrow or specific.

Traits. Although the study of personality is not the same thing as the study of traits (Pervin, 1985), the trait approach has provided much of the language and framework used in describing personality. For example, if a person always tells the truth, returns a wallet full of money that he or she has found, and files accurate tax returns, we might label that person as honest.

There are three different ways of thinking of traits: (1) Traits are causes of behavior, (2) traits are illusions and exist only in the mind of the beholder, and (3) traits are descriptive summaries. The causal approach uses traits to explain behavior. Thus, if asked why a person returned the wallet full of money, one might answer, "Because he is honest." The difficulty with this approach is its circularity. A person is labeled honest if he or she does honest things; these same honest behaviors are then explained by the fact that the person is honest.

The second approach—that traits exist in the mind of the beholder rather than in external reality—is based on several lines of research in the areas of perception, judgment, and memory (Chapman & Chapman, 1969; Hakel, 1974). This research suggests that we perceive, store, and retrieve information about others' behavior in terms of coherent wholes and units that are very much like traits; hence, some of the coherence we see in others' behavior is imposed by us, rather than being a reflection of external reality.

Although the research just cited does suggest that traits are in part a function of how we process information about behavior, rather than reflections of behavior itself, it does not necessarily suggest that traits are wholly illusory. A more widely accepted conclusion is that there is some consistency or structure to behavior and that traits are merely descriptions of related behavior patterns. Thus, when a person is described as honest, this trait name is a summary term describing an array of related behaviors. The term *honest* is equivalent to saying that the person has done many things in the past that indicate a high regard for the truth and that in the future, similar behaviors are expected in similar sets of circumstances.

The use of traits as descriptive rather than as causal terms has several appealing features. First, the descriptive approach avoids the circularity inherent in the causal approach. Second, the descriptive approach is potentially dynamic. For example, if someone was very aggressive from grade school to college but became comparatively meek as an adult, the causal approach would find it difficult to explain this outcome in terms of underlying traits. However, if traits are regarded as merely descriptive, there is no problem in stating that a person was aggressive in one phase of his or her life and meek in another.

Personality Taxonomies. Although many personality psychologists believe that it is useful to measure traits, there has been a long history of disagreement about what traits to measure. A quick look through the textbook used in any personality course shows that different theories have emphasized very different sets of traits; as you will see in Chapter 17, various personality inventories also seem to tap quite different aspects of personality. Until the 1980s, there was no broad agreement about what traits best summarized the domain of personality.

There is now some consensus that the domain of human personality can be characterized in terms of the five factors listed in Table 2-1; these factors are often referred to as the "big five" (Digman, 1990; McCrae & Costa, 1985, 1986, 1987, 1989; Saucier & Goldberg, 1996; see, however, Block, 1995). These five factors are highly robust and have been replicated in a number of studies using different methods of measurement (e.g., paper-and-pencil inventories, interviews, peer ratings) and in different linguistic and cultural groups. There are personality inventories specifically designed to measure these five factors (e.g., the NEO Personality Inventory; Costa & McCrae, 1992); but perhaps of more importance, several of these five factors seem to be present in many, if not most, well-designed personality inventories (Barrick & Mount, 1991). Thus, this taxonomy provides a basis for organizing and comparing studies involving a wide range of personality inventories.

As you might expect, given the long history of disagreement over the basic structure of personality, this taxonomy is not universally accepted. The meanings and the names of several of the factors, particularly the factor "openness to experience," are still controversial. Several studies show that factors not in this taxonomy are important predictors of a variety of criteria (e.g., performance on the job; Barrick & Mount, 1991; Hough, Eaton, Dunnette, Kamp, & McCloy, 1990; Salgado, 1997; Tett, Jackson, & Rothstein, 1991). Nevertheless, this taxonomy appears to provide a good starting point for describing what personality inventories should measure, and it helps to organize the previously fragmented body of research on personality and its correlates.

Historical Foundations of Personality Measurement

Systematic efforts to describe and categorize human character can be traced back to the ancient Greeks (Eysenck & Eysenck, 1969). From antiquity, differences in temperament were ascribed to the excessive influence of one of the four humors: A

Table 2-1   THE FIVE-FACTOR MODEL OF PERSONALITY

Factor	Definition
Extroversion	People high on this dimension are sociable, gregarious, assertive, talkative, and active.
Emotional stability	People low on this dimension are anxious, depressed, angry, emotional, embarrassed, and insecure.
Agreeableness	People high on this dimension are courteous, flexible, trusting, good natured, cooperative, and tolerant.
Conscientiousness	People high on this dimension are dependable, careful, thorough, responsible, hard-working, and persevering.
Openness to experience	People high on this dimension are imaginative, cultured, curious, original, and artistically sensitive.

sanguine personality reflected strong blood, a melancholic personality reflected the influence of black bile, a phlegmatic personality reflected the influence of phlegm, and a choleric personality reflected an overabundance of yellow bile. This fourfold classification represented both a taxonomy of personality types and a theory regarding the causes of individual differences in personality, and it persisted well into the 19th century.

Early psychological investigations of personality were tied closely to the study of psychopathology; many of the major developments in personality assessment can be traced back to such research. For example, Ketschmer's early taxonomy suggested that personalities could be described on a continuum from schizophrenic to manic depressive (Eysenck & Eysenck, 1969). The link between personality testing and the assessment of psychopathology has remained strong throughout the history of personality measurements. Tests designed solely to predict psychopathology are still often described as personality tests.

As psychology gradually emerged as a discipline separate from both philosophy and medicine, theories of personality became increasingly concerned with understanding and describing the structure of everyday behavior. Thus, by the 1930s, research in personality moved beyond its early focus on abnormal behavior and returned to the general problem of describing and classifying personality types. The 1930s and 1940s were a period of grand theories of personality, which attempted to explain broad consistencies in behavior in relatively universal terms. More recent research is characterized by a middle-level approach (Maddi, 1984), in which more narrow aspects of behavior are the focus of research and theory.

Methods of Personality Assessment. The development of objective measures of personality has many parallels to contemporary developments in intelligence testing. In the latter stages of World War I, it was recognized that psychological assessments might be useful in predicting, and possibly alleviating, cases of shell shock, or "war neurosis." Woodworth developed the Personal Data Sheet, a self-report questionnaire, in an effort to screen out individuals highly susceptible to shell shock. Although his test was developed too late to be widely used for wartime purposes, many of the test development methods developed by Woodworth were applied by later researchers. In particular, Woodworth pioneered the procedure of determining an item's validity by contrasting the responses of normal individuals to those of individuals diagnosed as mentally ill.

The most outstanding application of the method suggested by Woodworth is the Minnesota Multiphasic Personality Inventory (MMPI). The MMPI was developed in the late 1930s and early 1940s in an attempt to provide an objective aid for the diagnosis of psychopathology. It still is one of the most widely used measures in both clinical diagnosis and in research on personality.

The decade following World War I witnessed a development of several projective measures of personality (P. H. Dubois, 1970). Projective methods are ones that give the subject an abstract or unstructured stimulus, such as an inkblot or an incomplete sentence, and require the subject to interpret the stimulus and respond. The assumption of the projective method is that the individual's private world is revealed by the way he or she organizes and interprets unstructured or ambiguous situations (Frank, 1939). Probably the earliest projective method was the method of free verbal association popularized by Carl Jung. Here, subjects were given a list of stimulus words (e.g., *sister*) and asked to give their first response to each one. The most widely known projective technique was developed by Rorschach (1921), who used subjects' responses to inkblots as a diagnostic tool. Other projective methods developed during this decade included the sentence-completion technique and the use of children's drawings in the assessment of personality (P. H. Dubois, 1970). Later decades would see the continuing development of projective methods, such as the Thematic Apperception Test (TAT).

As noted earlier, the 1930s and 1940s were a time of grand theories of personality that attempted to explain an extraordinarily wide range of behaviors within a single theoretical framework (Zucker, Aranoff, & Rabin, 1984). Although these grand theories did not last, they did influence personality psychologists to develop measures that were broader than those concerned exclusively with psychopathology. Examples are provided by the factor-analytic research of Guilford and Guilford (1934, 1939), R. B. Cattell (1957), and Eysenck (1960). Early factor-analytic research on personality provided the conceptual basis for several modern multifactor personality inventories that attempt to describe multiple aspects of personality that are relevant to everyday life, as well as to understanding psychopathology.

Perhaps the best exemplar of a broad, integrated attempt to describe and assess personality is the work of Murray. First at Harvard's Psychological Clinic and later working with the United States Army's Office of Strategic Services (OSS) in assessing candidates during World War II, Murray led teams of psychologists in assessing individuals. Murray's work stressed a holistic view and used multiple measures to study individuals' perceptions, cognitions, emotions, and actions and to form an integrated assessment. The methods employed by the OSS are described in some detail in Chapter 21.

Characteristics of a Good Personality Measure

As noted earlier, there is no clear-cut conception of what personality is, and as a result it is difficult to determine whether a specific test represents an adequate measure of personality. However, it is possible to specify some general principles for evaluating measures of personality. Two issues are especially relevant: their interpretability and their stability.

Interpretability.   Personality inventories differ substantially in what they attempt to measure. Some attempt to measure a single, narrowly focused dimension; others attempt to measure several dimensions that together span a broad domain of behavior; still others attempt to measure a small set of very general or global dimensions. One of the first principles in evaluating a personality inventory is that the results must convey information about the individual that can be interpreted reliably by various users. In other words, personality tests that are reasonably specific in terms of what they are trying to measure are likely to prove more useful than tests that are vague.

In considering the interpretation of personality measures, a trade-off between the precision and breadth of the measure (sometimes referred to as the bandwidth-fidelity trade-off; see Chapter 7) must be kept in mind. Tests that attempt to provide broad statements about the person may provide information that is relevant for understanding a wide range of behaviors, but they also provide information that is vague and potentially unreliable. For example, Eysenck (1976) suggested that the basic dimensions underlying personality were introversion-extroversion and neuroticism-stability. Because of their generality, measures of either of these dimensions would be quite useful, but it also would be difficult to describe precisely what is meant by the terms *introversion* and *stability*. On the other hand, tests that measure one narrowly focused dimension of personality provide precise, interpretable information that is relevant to only a particular subset of behavior.

One of the best compromises between bandwidth and fidelity is found in the multifactor personality inventories that grew out of the work of Guilford, Cattell, and others. These inventories combine breadth and depth by providing scores on multiple well-described dimensions that, taken together, span a fairly broad domain of behaviors. This is not to say that multifactor inventories are the only useful personality tests. Rather, these inventories represent one method of dealing with the inevitable trade-off between the breadth of the domain being measured and the interpretability of test scores.

Stability. Stability can be defined in two different ways, both of which are relevant for evaluating personality measures. First, there is the stability of scoring rules, which affects interjudge agreement. In general, objective measures have simple and significantly more stable scoring rules than are possible with projective measures. As noted earlier, the existence of stable rules connecting the behavior of the examinee to the score he or she obtains is essential to achieve valid measures of personality or of any other attribute.

The second meaning of stability—stability across situations—refers both to the test scores and to the attribute being measured. As the person-situation debate suggests, not all personality measures are consistent across situations. In fact, there are reasons to believe that almost any personality measure would yield inconsistent scores across some situations (Maddi, 1984). It is critical, then, to assess the degree to which a particular personality measure yields consistent scores across the range of situations in which it will be used. The relative stability of two different personality measures can vary, depending on the situations in which they are applied.

All other things being equal, a personality measure that yields consistent scores across the entire range of situations normally encountered would be preferable to another measure that is completely situation bound. However, few measures are likely to be either completely impervious to situations or completely determined by situations.

As a result, careful attention must be given to the range of situations in which a test will be used.

An examination of the dimensions measured might also contribute to the assessment of stability. Some personality dimensions are by definition unstable, in the sense that they can be strongly tempered by a single act or by a small set of behaviors. For example, if a person is happy six days of the week and sad once in a while, we use the trait "happy" as a consistent and generally quite accurate description of that person's behavior. On the other hand, if a person who has been regarded as honest tells one or two lies, one's evaluation of that person's honesty shifts dramatically. Other dimensions might be unstable in a different sense, in that they represent classes of behavior that occur in most but not all situations. For example, a person might be very outgoing at work but quiet at home. Although this behavior is inconsistent in the absolute sense, it is nevertheless predictable.

It is essential that personality measures exhibit levels of stability that are consistent with their intended uses. Thus, there must be a stable, reliable relationship between the behavior of an individual and the score he or she receives. Second, the behavior being measured must show some consistency over a specific (but possibly implicit) range of situations.

CRITICAL DISCUSSION:

The Relationships Among Abilities, Interests, and Personality Characteristics

People differ in their cognitive abilities, their interests, and their personalities, and these individual differences have been the focus of decades of research. A question that is sometimes overlooked in this body of research is the relationship among each of these individual difference domains. Historically, measures of cognitive ability, interests, and personality characteristics have been developed in isolation from one another, and the potential links among domains have not always been made explicit.

In thinking about the relationships among these three domains, two generalizations seem reasonable. First, measures of global personality characteristics (e.g., the "big five" factors) generally show small correlations with measures of general cognitive ability. One exception is the "openness to experience" dimension. Some evidence demonstrates modest positive correlations between cognitive ability and openness to experience. However, on the whole, it appears that cognitive ability is not a major part of what we would typically refer to as personality. Second, both ability and personality are likely to be related to specific aspects of interests.

It seems logical that ability and interests should show some correlation, although the data here are not always clear. However, if you think of interests as a response of liking, it is probable that people will develop interests in things that they are relatively good at and will tend to develop negative responses to things that they do poorly. There are, of course, exceptions. People sometimes have strong interests in things they simply cannot do. However, you could argue that a history of reinforcement in some particular area (i.e., repeated success in certain activities) will probably lead to more and more positive reactions, which in turn should lead to positive relationships between specific interests and specific abilities. It is not clear which should be treated as the chicken and which the egg here. It is possible that interest in an area might lead you to develop abilities or that ability might lead you to become interested. Nevertheless, it is likely that the domains of ability and interest will overlap, at least to some degree.

Interests and personality are also likely to be linked, especially those aspects of personality that are related to peoples' affective reactions (Murphy, 1996). Some people tend to react positively to a broad range of situations and events, whereas others tend to react negatively. Differences in positive and negative affectivity are likely to relate to the breadth and intensity of one's interests. People whose initial tendency is to react negatively to stimuli, people, and events will probably develop a narrow range of interests. Interests are responses of liking, and people whose basic tendencies are to react negatively probably do not like a wide range of things.

It may seem paradoxical that (1) cognitive ability and personality characteristics are largely unrelated, (2) ability is related to interests, and (3) personality is related to interests. One reason that such a pattern of relationships is possible is that ability-interest and personality-interest links tend to be relatively weak and limited in scope. Although these domains are not completely distinct, the relationships between any pair of domains are not so strong or general that they necessarily constrain relationships between other pairs. For example, ability is related to some aspects of interests (e.g., ability in a certain area implies heightened interest in that area), and personality seems to be related to quite different aspects of interests (e.g., the breadth and depth of interests). It is therefore probably useful to think of ability, interests, and personality as relatively distinct sets of individual differences, each of which might be relevant to decisions that are made by or about an individual.

SUMMARY

Tests, scales, and inventories have been developed to measure a wide range of psychological attributes, from attitudes and values to abilities and skills. The domains of cognitive ability, interests, and personality are particularly relevant to the process of making decisions about individuals and helping them make decisions about themselves, and these are reviewed in this chapter.

There are a number of different structural theories of intelligence or mental ability; these theories differ in terms of the importance of general versus specific abilities and in terms of the number of specific types of intelligence proposed. Most ability tests are based on some version of a hierarchical model in which both general cognitive ability and a number of specific types of ability are seen as important.

A survey of the history of intelligence testing shows the strong practical bent of this type of testing. The development of individual and group tests arose in response to the problems encountered in classifying schoolchildren and military recruits. The intelligence quotient was developed to make the interpretation of these tests simpler. Today, ability testing is a multimillion-dollar industry in the United States alone, and it is highly important in many other countries.

We suggested several general principles for evaluating intelligence tests. First, they should include a broad sampling of tasks and should not rely too heavily on items that measure factual knowledge. Second, item content is probably less important than the processes used to answer items. Third, the sample of items should be sufficiently large to provide some basis for making inferences to this broad domain.

Interest measurement has largely revolved around the assessment of vocational interests. Interest measures have been developed using both actuarial and trait-and-factor approaches, and they have included both self-report and more indirect strategies of measurement. A variety of types of measures have been shown to be useful, particularly when based on either current, well-constructed samples (i.e., actuarially developed tests) or well-articulated theories of vocational interest (i.e., trait-and-factor tests).

Personality measurement has been hindered by disagreements over the consistency of behavior and over which factors should be included in an adequate description of normal personality. In recent years, both debates have been to some extent resolved; most researchers believe that behavior is sufficiently stable to allow meaningful measurement and that the five-factor theory provides a reasonable taxonomy of personality. The best measures of personality are likely to provide both consistent and stable measures of some or all of these key traits.

KEY TERMS

Actuarial approach   approach to interest measurement that compares your scores with the scores of members of specific groups

Big Five   personality taxonomy that uses five factors (extroversion, emotional stability, agreeableness, conscientiousness, and openness to experience) to describe normal personality

Crystallized intelligence   acquired store of factual knowledge; sometimes contrasted with fluid intelligence, or the ability to reason and actively process information

EQ   emotional intelligence, or the ability to understand one's own behavior and the behavior of others, and to maintain control over one's own behavior

General mental ability (*g*)   general cognitive ability that appears to underlie performance on a wide array of tests and cognitively demanding tasks

Interest   response of liking to an object or activity

IQ   intelligence quotient, a numerical measure of the overall level of cognitive ability

Projective measures   measures of personality that involve analyzing responses to an abstract or unstructured stimulus

Trait   consistent pattern of behavior in a particular area or domain (e.g., honesty)

Testing and Society

3

As we noted in Chapter 1, the widespread interest in psychological testing is not because of the intrinsic appeal of the tests themselves but, rather, because tests are used to help make decisions that have important consequences for individuals and for society. In this chapter, we will describe how a variety of societal concerns have affected the development, assessment, and use of a variety of psychological tests. The issues raised here will illustrate many of the questions examined in more detail in subsequent chapters. In subsequent chapters, we will describe how test developers and test users have studied, answered, or dealt with specific questions that arise when one considers the societal consequences of psychological testing.

In educational settings, tests are used to select, place, assess, and counsel students. A variety of questions that are of clear interest to society arise in this context, including whether the right individuals are selected, whether the correct placements or treatments are chosen, and whether the progress and achievement of different individuals are fairly and accurately assessed. In work settings, psychological tests and measurement procedures are used to make hiring and placement decisions, to guide and assess training and development, and to evaluate the performance of workers. The societal issues that arise in this context are quite similar to those encountered in education—whether the right individuals are hired for a job, whether they are assessed fairly and accurately, and whether the best methods of training and development are applied to them. In clinical settings, tests are used for a somewhat wider range of purposes, including diagnosis, the selection of treatments, and the assessment of treatment outcomes. Although issues of broad societal concern arise in the context of clinical testing and assessment (e.g., the issue of the invasion of privacy), most of the controversy over the relationship between testing and society has arisen in educational and industrial settings. Therefore, many of the examples we will use in this chapter concentrate more on these two settings, and less on clinical testing.

TYPES OF DECISIONS

The most basic assumption of this book is that the results of psychological tests are relevant to a wide range of decisions that must be made about individuals. It is useful to draw distinctions between several types of decisions that might be made on the basis of, or with the assistance of, psychological tests. Different types of decisions may require different types of tests, or different information from a given test, and may give rise to different types of social concerns. Two distinctions are very useful for classifying decisions: The decision may be (1) individual or institutional and (2) comparative or absolute. These are not the only ways of classifying the types of decisions of concern to society, but these two distinctions are quite useful in understanding the relationship between tests and decisions.

Individual Versus Institutional Decisions

The first distinction that must be made is between the decisions made by the person who takes the test as compared with those made by the institution that administers the test or uses the results of tests. In individual decisions, tests can be used to counsel or advise the examinee; presumably, the results of these tests have some influence on the actions or decisions of the examinee. Two societal concerns are often raised in the context of individual decisions. First, there is concern that psychological tests might have an undue impact on the individual. That is, psychological tests, which appear to be objective and scientific, may be given a great deal of weight, whereas other sources of advice and counsel, such as that of parents or friends, may be ignored. Although we have already noted that psychological tests are often the best single method for making important decisions, this does not mean that other sources of information can be safely ignored or that the results of a brief test are more valuable than the results of all other sources of advice and counsel. Second, tests might change the decisions or actions of individuals, and these changes are not always beneficial. For example, considerable evidence indicates that college admissions tests, such as the Scholastic Assessment Tests (SAT), have an important bearing on the applicant's decisions to apply to or to avoid specific schools (L. S. Gottfredson & Crouse, 1986; Skager, 1982). A student who does not do well on a test such as the SAT may decide not to apply to academically demanding schools, even though he or she might have had a good chance of being accepted and of performing well at these schools. A person who takes a vocational interest test might avoid some careers and gravitate toward others because of test results, and these choices may adversely affect future income, career mobility, satisfaction, and so forth.

The debate over the societal consequences of psychological tests has focused for the most part on institutional decisions. In educational settings, these decisions include those concerning admission, placement in either advanced or remedial programs, and the advancement or retention of students. In industry, these decisions include those concerning personnel selection, identification of fast-track employees who receive special attention and opportunities, placement in training programs, and evaluations of job performance and promotability. Two related issues dominate the controversy over the impact of psychological tests on institutional decisions: (1) the accuracy of the decisions and (2) the fairness of the decisions. For example, the use of tests of general mental ability often results in different decisions for whites than for minorities. Tests of specific abilities and skills, especially spatial abilities, can result in different decisions for males than for females. A substantial research literature is devoted to the question of whether differences of this sort in test scores are real or are the result of bad tests or ineffective test-taking strategies on the part of some examinees. In addition, much literature deals with whether the outcomes of tests of this sort are related to success on the job, in school, or in life in general. We will review some of this literature later in this chapter, and we will return to several of the questions about institutional decisions raised here in several subsequent chapters (especially in Chapters 15, 18, and 19).

Comparative Versus Absolute Decisions

Both individuals and institutions are faced with a variety of decisions and choices, some of which involve comparisons of two or more people, actions, objects, options, and so forth. Other decisions and choices involve assessing a single person, option, action, or object. Personnel selection is a good example of a comparative decision on the part of an organization. If ten people apply for four jobs, the institution must decide the relative merits of different applicants. That is, the organization must try to identify the four best people and hire them.[1] One important feature of comparative decisions is that they often require less information than would be required for an absolute decision.

Absolute decisions do not involve an explicit choice between two well-defined options; rather, they involve a decision about a single person, option, or object. For example, if an employee who is suspected of theft fails a paper-and-pencil honesty test, the employer must decide whether to fire the employee. A student with very low SAT scores must decide whether to apply to college. Note that in both cases, two possibilities are being compared, either to do something (i.e., fire the person; attend the school) or not. However, absolute decisions do not depend so much on a comparison of those two options as they do on an evaluation of whether the information available will lead you to pursue the option being considered.

Absolute decisions often require more precise measurement than is required for comparative decisions. For example, suppose that you were deciding whether a person's visual acuity was sharp enough to qualify as a pilot. This would require (1) fairly exact knowledge of the level of acuity actually needed to fly safely and (2) knowledge of whether the individual's acuity met that standard. In contrast, a comparative decision could be reached by simply devising a task that requires visual acuity and selecting the people who perform best, regardless of their actual acuity levels or the precise visual demands of the job.

---

[1]Comparative decisions might, however, involve some type of absolute assessment. Personnel selection, for example, usually involves some screening to ensure minimal qualifications.

Most of the controversy over the societal impact of psychological testing centers around comparative decisions made by institutions, especially decisions involving educational admissions, personnel selection, and promotions. One troubling issue in this controversy is the frequent failure to distinguish between comparative and absolute decisions. For example, in research on honesty testing in personnel selection, Murphy (1987b) showed that most tests of honesty are not sufficiently accurate to tell with any real assurance who is being honest or dishonest. Some critics suggested that this means that honesty tests should not be used in employment. Sackett, Burris, and Callahan (1989) and Martin and Terris (1991) noted that this conclusion was not warranted, however, and that people who do poorly on honesty tests do indeed often turn out to be poorer employees. Thus, although the tests cannot be used to brand any individual as dishonest, they can be used to make valid and accurate comparisons among individuals.

SOCIETAL CONCERNS

Research, discussion, and debate over the societal effects of psychological tests deal with a wide range of topics and issues. Three issues, however, have dominated this literature: (1) the impact of ability testing on society, (2) the extent to which tests invade privacy, and (3) the fair use of tests. Two of these issues, ability testing and fair use of tests, overlap to some extent in that questions of the fair use of tests are often motivated by the outcomes of ability testing. Nevertheless, we feel that it is useful to present these three issues separately.

Ability Testing

Controversies over tests of general ability, or intelligence, go back to the early years of this century (Cronbach, 1975; Hartigan & Wigdor, 1989; Hilgard, 1989; Sokal, 1987). In fact, it is fair to say that ability tests have been the focus of public debate throughout virtually the entire history of psychological testing. Over the last 50 years, the driving issue in this debate has been the existence and meaning of racial-based, ethnic-based, and gender-based differences in test scores (L. S. Gottfredson, 1988; Lerner, 1989; Scarr, 1989; Shepard, 1982). For example, blacks and Hispanics receive lower average scores on many ability tests used for academic admissions and personnel selection than do whites. The use of these tests as the sole basis for making selection decisions will therefore result in the racial segregation of schools and the workforce (Goldstein & Patterson, 1988). Males and females also differ in the scores that they receive on some tests of academic aptitude. The use of SAT scores, particularly scores from the mathematical section of the test, as the sole criterion for awarding scholarships will result in fewer scholarships for women. Older individuals receive lower scores on tests that require speedy responses. The use of highly speeded tests in personnel selection and placement could therefore result in discrimination against older workers.

As the examples just cited suggest, the debate over ability testing is not purely scientific; rather, it is driven by social and political concerns (Gordon, 1988). Several researchers have noted that the virtual explosion of research on issues such as the nature of ability and test bias can be explained almost entirely in terms of social concerns related to ability testing (Murphy, Cronin, & Tam, 2003; Scarr, 1988; Shepard, 1982). Four specific issues seem especially important: (1) whether score differences reflect real ability differences, (2) whether differences in ability are large enough to matter, (3) whether tests help or hurt minorities, and (4) whether we should emphasize equity or efficiency.

Are the Differences Real? Two plausible explanations exist for group differences in ability test scores. First, these differences may be due to bias in the tests. If this explanation is true, the tests themselves would be the cause of unfair outcomes, such as the loss of jobs, scholarships, and other opportunities (L. S. Gottfredson, 1988). This explanation is intuitively very appealing, especially because test critics can point to items that certainly appear to be biased (e.g., a test item that asks you to define *regatta* seems as if it may be biased against disadvantaged, inner-city respondents). The possibility that test bias explains differences in test scores has been the focus of literally hundreds of studies (L. S. Gottfredson, 1986; Jensen, 1980; C. R. Reynolds & Brown, 1984). The consensus among researchers is that test bias does not by itself explain differences in test scores. Further discussion of research on test bias is included in Chapter 15.

A second possibility is that differences in test scores reflect real differences in ability. Virtually all serious researchers in this area accept the finding that there are some real differences in the cognitive abilities of different groups and that the differences observed in test scores are not solely the result of test bias.[2] The causes of these differences, however, are the subject of acrimonious debate. In particular, arguments rage over the extent to which genetic factors or environmental factors explain differences in ability. Differences in scores might be influenced by the type of test (Chan & Schmit, 1998; Schmitt, Rogers, Chan, Sheppard, & Jennings, 1997), and evaluations of the meaningfulness of these differences might depend on the criteria against which tests are validated (Hattrup, Rock, & Scalia, 1997); but it seems clear that there are differences between many groups in the population in terms of how they are likely to perform on psychological tests, and these differences cannot be ignored.

Further, arguments continue over the implications of high or low levels of genetic influence (Dickens & Flynn, 2001; Jensen, 1969; Lerner, 1989; Scarr, 1989). In later chapters (especially Chapter 15), we will review research on the heritability of cognitive ability and its implications. In our opinion, however, this research shows that differences in cognitive ability are neither fixed nor permanent (there is evidence that differences in ability are shrinking; Williams & Ceci, 1997) and that the most effective means of reducing these differences will be through changes in the learning environment.

---

[2]Snyderman and Rothman's survey (1987) suggested that most testing experts believe that differences in test scores reflect both bias and real differences.

Are the Differences Large? If differences in test scores reflect, at least in part, real differences in ability, the question still remains whether these differences are large enough to be at all important. For example, some researchers suggest that there are gender differences in verbal ability, but that these are so small as to be of little consequence (Hyde & Linn, 1988). A variation on this same theme is the debate over whether cognitive ability is really that important in the real world. It is widely accepted that cognitive ability is important in school, but some critics suggest that it has little relevance in other settings. (L. S. Gottfredson, 1986, and Schmidt, 2002, reviewed evidence suggesting that cognitive ability is important outside school.) If cognitive ability were unimportant outside the classroom, differences in test scores would not be very meaningful.

Another question about the size of the differences in test scores concerns a comparison of the between-group variability (i.e., the differences between groups) to the within-group variability (i.e., the differences in test scores within a single group). A typical finding is that the differences between groups (e.g., the difference in the mean scores for whites as compared with minority examinees) are considerably smaller than the differences within groups and that different groups in the population overlap considerably in test scores.[3] Therefore, although group means may differ, many members of the lower-scoring group will have scores higher than scores of members of the higher-scoring group. Thus, there is controversy over whether findings concerning the means of different groups can be usefully applied to individual members of the group.

Do Tests Help or Hurt? Legitimate questions concern whether cognitive ability tests help or hurt minorities, females, and other specific subgroups. Critics of testing suggest that these tests create artificial barriers to equal employment, equal access to schools, and other opportunities (Goldstein & Patterson, 1988). For example, Gordon (1988) notes that if ability tests were used as the sole criterion for admission to medical school, there would be even fewer black physicians than we presently have. On the other hand, proponents of testing suggest that tests create unique opportunities for individuals who would otherwise not be considered for jobs, college, and other situations (Humphreys, 1989; Jencks, 1972). These researchers argue that tests provide opportunities for talented members of underrepresented groups to demonstrate their abilities and that without tests it would be very difficult for any member of a disadvantaged group to ever get ahead.

It is instructive to consider what would happen if there were no tests. In that case, decisions about college admissions, scholarships, jobs, and other desirable opportunities would be made in the same way as they were before the advent of testing—on the basis of highly subjective criteria such as interviews, references, or personal contacts. Psychological tests may help to control some of the subjectivity in these methods.

---

[3]Scarr (1989) suggests that individual experiences have a greater influence on intelligence than variables such as race, family, or socioeconomic status. See also Plomin and Rende (1991) and Rose (1995).

Efficiency Versus Equity. As we have already noted, research evidence from thousands of studies establishes beyond a doubt that the use of psychological tests to help make decisions about people generally improves the quality of these decisions. For example, the use of ability tests in personnel selection will lead to the selection of more productive workers than would be selected without tests (Hunter & Hunter, 1984; Schmidt & Hunter, 1998). Thus, tests generally contribute to the efficiency of the workforce. On the other hand, the use of ability tests in making decisions may exclude many minority applicants from a particular job. Tests may reduce equity in the assignment of jobs in the sense that they may lead to the hiring of fewer minorities than would be hired without tests.

The trade-off between equity and efficiency has been one of the most difficult and divisive issues in the debate over ability testing (Gordon, 1988; L. S. Gottfredson, 1988; Hunter & Schmidt, 1976; Jensen, 1980). One thing that complicates the debate is that efficiency and equity are measured on very different scales, and so different people might have very different ideas as to how these two concepts should be balanced. Consider a decision about whether to use each of the four tests depicted in Table 3-1 to select job applicants. Many people would agree that test A is probably justified. Even though it has a small negative effect on minority and female hiring, its dramatic effect on profits would, in the minds of many, outweigh its effects on equity in hiring. Most people would agree that test B is probably not justified. It leads to a small increase in profits, but it means a disastrous decline in the hiring of minorities and females. In this case, most reasonable people would agree that the small increase in profits is not worth the human cost of the test. Tests C and D are a much tougher case. If you value efficiency more than equity, you might think that test C would be worthwhile. That is, a person might be willing to live with some decrease in representation for women and minorities in exchange for this increase in profits. On the other hand, perfectly reasonable people whose values were slightly different might conclude that this test was not justified and that test D would be better. It is impossible to choose sensibly between tests C and D without defining the value you place on efficiency versus equity.

Debates over ability testing often boil down to differences in the values that people place on efficiency versus equity (Murphy, 2002). As long as different groups in the population receive systematically different scores on ability tests, the question of efficiency versus equity will be with us. As we will see in Chapter 15, psychological research can help clarify the question, but it cannot provide the ultimate answer to how we should balance concerns of efficiency versus equity in the debate over the use of ability tests in making important decisions about individuals.

Table 3-1   FOUR TESTS THAT ILLUSTRATE THE TRADE-OFF BETWEEN EFFICIENCY AND EQUITY

Effects of test	*Test A*	*Test B*	*Test C*	*Test D*
Number of females and minorities hired	1% decrease	20% decrease	10% decrease	10% increase
Profits	20% increase	1% increase	10% increase	10% decrease

Finally, we should note that the debate over efficiency versus equity has been complicated by the often confusing nature of the data. A very good example comes from analyses of the effects of affirmative action programs in the workplace. *Affirmative action* refers to a wide variety of efforts to attract, recruit, and hire members of underrepresented groups. Some researchers suggest that programs of this kind can result in sizable reductions in productivity, particularly when they involve lowering employment standards (Hunter & Hunter, 1984). Others note that little evidence suggests that existing affirmative action programs have, in fact, had any adverse effect on productivity and that employers strongly support these programs (Goldstein & Patterson, 1988). One reason why different researchers in this area reach such different conclusions is that they typically examine very different types of data and often use the same terms (e.g., the term *productivity*) in very different ways.

Another reason for disagreements in the debate over efficiency versus equity is that the question has become political. Individuals who hold a conservative political philosophy are likely to emphasize efficiency, whereas individuals who hold a liberal political philosophy are likely to emphasize equity. As with all other political questions, valid arguments can be made for either point of view, and the choice of one over the other ultimately boils down to the values that the individual chooses to uphold (Murphy, 2002).

CRITICAL DISCUSSION:

Science and Politics in the Ability-Testing Debate—The Bell Curve

In 1994, Herrnstein and Murray published *The Bell Curve,* a book designed to discuss the relationships among intelligence, class structure, and success (defined in a number of ways) in American society. Their book suggests that differences in cognitive ability are critical determinants of economic success, academic success, and success in living in society (e.g., avoiding crime, keeping families together, etc.), and it makes a number of social policy recommendations based on the authors' interpretation of the data reviewed in this book. It raises questions about the wisdom of affirmative action, the "leveling" of education, and efforts to raise cognitive ability, and it forecasts the coming of a "custodial state," in which those higher in cognitive ability will have the responsibility of taking care of those lower in ability. In one of their less restrained passages, they note that this type of custodial state could degenerate into "a high-tech and more lavish version of the Indian reservation for the substantial minority of the nation's population, while the rest of America tries to go about its business" (p. 526).

As you might imagine, this book has generated a great deal of controversy (see Jacoby & Glauberman, 1995, for critiques of this book; see also *The New Republic,* 1994, special issue entitled "Race"). One particular concern is that the book does not accurately represent current research and theory regarding intelligence (Jacoby & Glauberman, 1995; Sternberg, 1995), which means that the apparently scientific tone of several parts of this work might in fact be misleading to readers. To help set the scientific record straight, the American Psychological Association appointed a task force to summarize what is known and unknown about intelligence; their report (Neisser et al., 1996) notes the following:

1. Scores on intelligence tests are relatively stable and are related to important criteria (e.g., success in school, on the job). However, although scores on these tests have been steadily rising for decades, there has been little apparent rise in the types of performance that is thought to derive from intelligence.

2. Like many personality traits, there is a sizable genetic component to intelligence.
3. Like most personality traits, there are substantial cultural influences on intelligence.
4. There are substantial group differences in scores on intelligence tests, which are likely to reflect a number of cultural, economic, behavioral, and possibly genetic differences.
5. It is possible to raise children's intelligence, but it requires very substantial investments of time and resources.
6. Cognitive ability is one important factor in predicting success in several settings (e.g., school, work), but a substantial portion of the variability in success in these settings cannot be explained in terms of cognitive ability.

Perhaps most importantly, they note that the scientific evidence reviewed by the authors of *The Bell Curve* does not provide a basis for the social policy recommendations provided in that book. Indeed, the book seems to be split into two somewhat unconnected parts: (1) a review of research on intelligence that is generally consistent with the positions laid out above and (2) a set of social policy discussions that appear only tangentially related to the actual scientific evidence reviewed in the book. Thus, while the portrayal of intelligence research in *The Bell Curve* is in many places uncontroversial (see, however, Sternberg, 1995), the use of this research by Herrnstein and Murray to argue for particular political or social recommendations is often questionable.

In our view, the debate over *The Bell Curve* mirrors the more general debate about the role of science and values in ability testing. One regrettable aspect of this book is its tendency to intermix careful scientific reviews with ideological flights of fancy, in which science that seems to support the authors' political convictions is cited and science that seems to refute these strongly held beliefs is ignored. Both science and values play an important part in the debate over psychological testing, and it is best to be clear about the roles of both science and values in shaping conclusions in this contentious area.

Invasion of Privacy

Attitude surveys, personality inventories, integrity tests, and interest inventories all share one thing in common: They often inquire about topics that many people regard as sensitive and private. These topics range from attitudes toward public controversies (e.g., the controversy over abortion) to the most intimate details of one's personal life. Psychological tests and inventories of this kind are widely regarded as unwarranted invasions of privacy.

An outstanding example of a test that might invade one's privacy is the Minnesota Multiphasic Personality Inventory (MMPI and its revision, MMPI-2; see Chapter 20), which contains items dealing with sex, religion, bladder control, family relations, unusual thinking, and other potentially sensitive topics. Responding to the test itself could be embarrassing for many people, and the possibility that test responses might fall into the hands of some unscrupulous person could lead an individual to be very concerned about this seeming invasion of privacy. It is interesting that Gallucci (1986) showed that students objected more to the length and repetitive nature of the MMPI than to the supposedly sensitive items. Nevertheless, it is very reasonable to assume that some people will regard tests like this as an invasion of their privacy.

Psychological tests that explore the respondent's personality, attitudes, beliefs, and so forth pose a greater threat of the invasion of privacy than do ability or achievement tests. In part, this is the case because most people accept the notion that decision makers have some legitimate interest in knowing your abilities, skills, achievements, and such. The same is not necessarily true for personality traits, attitudes, or beliefs. That is, individuals may not see the relevance of tests that measure these things, and they may not wish to reveal the facets of their character that these tests measure.

Invasion of privacy is a growing concern in employment testing. Until a federal law banned the practice, polygraphs (lie detectors) were widely used in preemployment screening. These tests were, to a large extent, replaced by paper-and-pencil tests that purport to measure honesty and integrity (Murphy, 1993; Sackett, Burris, & Callahan, 1989; Sackett & Harris, 1984). Tests of urine and blood samples to determine drug and alcohol use have also become more common. In all these tests, behaviors and experiences away from the workplace may affect test outcomes (e.g., integrity tests may ask whether you have ever stolen anything; weekend drug use may cause you to fail an on-the-job drug test), and many individuals regard these as their personal business, not the business of a potential employer.

Confidentiality. One potential concern is that the results of psychological tests might become available to people who have no legitimate use for these results. The standards that regulate testing professionals (e.g., American Psychological Association, *Standards for Educational and Psychological Testing*, 1999) are very strict with regard to protecting the confidentiality of test results. It is important to realize that virtually all testing professionals accept the idea that the results of a psychological test should never be broadcast indiscriminately; this is especially true of tests whose content or results are sensitive. Nevertheless, the enforcement of these standards can be very difficult. More important, psychological tests and the results of these tests are often available to persons who are in no way regulated by any professional standards and who may be less careful about the confidentiality of test results. The possibility that test results will fall into the hands of individuals who have no business receiving the results is taken very seriously by test publishers and test users, and elaborate methods of maintaining test security are often undertaken. Nevertheless, violations of confidentiality can lead to both serious invasions of privacy and the misuse of test results.

Informed Consent. Some psychological tests and assessment procedures involve deception. For example, some honesty and integrity tests appear to be nothing more than surveys of beliefs or experiences. One widely used test is labeled the "Personal Outlook Inventory"; persons taking this test may never know that they are taking an honesty test. This sort of disguised testing is especially likely to be perceived as an invasion of privacy. To understand why this is so, consider the concept of informed consent.

In psychological research, researchers are usually required to obtain informed consent from subjects before carrying out the research. That is, subjects must be informed of the general purpose and nature of the research, as well as of the possible dangers and threats involved, and they must generally know what they are getting into before participating in a research project. Several testing guidelines also require informed consent for some testing applications (e.g., *Standards for Educational and Psychological Testing, Code of Fair Testing Practices in Education,* and *Guidelines and Ethical Considerations for Assessment Center Operations*). A person who does not know what a test or assessment procedure is designed to measure cannot give fully informed consent to testing. The lack of informed consent in some testing situations probably contributes to feelings that psychological tests invade one's privacy.

Requirements for informed consent can present a real dilemma for test developers and test users. Some kinds of tests simply will not work if test takers are fully informed about the purpose of testing. For example, it is possible to distort responses on many personality tests to either fake mental disturbances or to create specific impressions of your personality (research on test faking is reviewed in Chapter 11). If examinees know the specific purpose of a test, they may distort their responses in such a way that test scores are no longer valid or useful. Sometimes it is necessary to balance the test takers' rights to be informed against the test users' rights to obtain valid information about the individuals who take the test. In general, the balance probably favors test users when the invasions of privacy are minor in nature and when care is taken to preserve the confidentiality of test responses. However, in situations in which tests represent wholesale intrusions on the privacy of test takers, the use of tests will be difficult to justify.

Fair Use of Tests

One of the most significant concerns in the debate over the societal impact of psychological tests is whether tests are used in a fair way. As we have noted in our section on ability testing, the precise definition of fairness is difficult because the concept of fairness involves value decisions; people with different values will disagree over the fairness of some testing practices. Nevertheless, we can clarify the debate over test fairness by making a distinction between the fairness of the testing process and the fairness of the testing outcomes (Greenberg, 1987).

Several factors affect the apparent fairness of the testing process. First, there might be obstacles that prevent some persons from performing well, and unless these are removed or adequately taken into account, the test administration will probably be viewed as unfair. For example, administering a highly speeded test that requires the respondent to fill in small spaces on an answer sheet to a person with a motor impairment is probably unfair. Similarly, having an adult from one culture administer an individual intelligence test to a child from another culture is thought by many to be unfair; the differences between the examiner and the examinee might make it difficult to establish rapport or may cause the examinee to be overly anxious. Second, the tests themselves must not provide unfair advantages to some examinees. One of the most frequent criticisms of intelligence tests is that they ask questions about things that would be familiar to white, middle-class children, but not to others (Jensen, 1980). Other critics cite more subtle biases, such as the use of response formats that are more familiar to some examinees than to others (Berk, 1982).

The outcomes of tests are of even more concern than the process of testing. The most widely cited outcomes that are of societal concern are the differences seen in the ability test scores of whites and minorities, males and females, and other groups. We will discuss research dealing with these differences and its implications for determining the bias and fairness of ability testing in Chapter 15. A variety of other concerns, however, also fall under the heading of the fair use of tests. First, many test experts and critics believe that tests are often used for purposes for which they have little or no validity (Murphy, Cronin & Tam, 2003; Snyderman & Rothman, 1987). In education, ability tests may be used inappropriately for the placement of students in advanced or remedial programs. In industry, tests that have no clear relationship with job performance may be used to select job applicants. Even if the tests do not systematically discriminate against particular groups in the population, the invalid use of a test can cause harm to individuals. Second, tests may be used for purposes that are inherently objectionable. Several reviewers (e.g., Friedman & Williams, 1982; Murphy, 1988) have suggested that occupational and professional licensing examinations often serve no legitimate purpose and are used merely to restrict the number of persons in a job or an occupation (ensuring more profits for those who hold licenses). In the early part of this century, some test researchers used intelligence tests to "prove" theories of racial or ethnic superiority (Gould, 1981; Wigdor & Garner, 1982a); before the Civil Rights Act of 1964, some employers used the same tests as a mere pretext to deny jobs to minorities. Height, weight, and physical ability requirements have also been used to restrict the entry of women into some occupations (J. Hogan & Quigley, 1986). The use of psychological tests to help achieve illegitimate ends is potentially a serious concern of society.

The fair use of test results is a concern of the test developer as well as the test taker and the test user (Messick, 1988). In part, this is a simple matter of survival; tests that appear to cause blatantly unfair outcomes are very likely to be the subject of scrutiny, lawsuits, and legislation, and they are unlikely to be appealing to future test users. There is also an ethical issue involved here. Test developers cannot simply wash their hands after the test is released and ignore the outcomes of testing. Most test developers do indeed consider the likely outcomes of the tests that they release and devote considerable efforts to minimize the potentially unfair outcomes of testing.

CRITICAL DISCUSSION:

High-Stakes Testing

Standardized tests have become increasingly important as a tool for making important decisions in educational settings (e.g., assigning students to programs and schools, determining whether students will be promoted or graduate). As a result of recent changes in federal and state law, it has become fairly common to administer tests in schools and to make decisions about things ranging from graduation criteria to school funding partially or wholly on the basis of test scores. In 2003, half of all high school students attended class in states that required graduation tests, and this figure is likely to grow. The Texas Assessment of Academic Skills (TAAS) is often cited as an exemplar of high-stakes testing in the schools. All public high-school students in Texas take a standardized test

designed to measure statewide curriculum in reading, mathematics, and writing, and they are required to pass this test to graduate.

High-stakes testing in educational settings is nothing new. Tests such as the Scholastic Assessment Tests and the Graduate Record Examination (these are described in Chapter 14) have
long been a part of the admissions process in college and graduate school. Nor is high-stakes testing unique to the American school system. In the United Kingdom and in Ireland, scores that students receive on tests taken at the end of high school have a decisive effect on educational and job
opportunities. In other countries (e.g., Japan, Singapore), high-stakes tests are given in grade
school, and scores on these tests have important consequences throughout the student's academic career.

The increased reliance on high-stakes testing in this country has been controversial. The National Center for Fair and Open Testing claims that high-stakes testing in primary and secondary
school is unfair to students, leads to "teaching to the test," drives out good teachers, and misin-
forms the public. The Association for Childhood Education International has called for a moratorium
on standardized testing.

In reaction to the controversy over high-stakes testing in the schools, the National Academy
of Sciences was asked to examine research on the validity and value of these tests. Their report
(Heubert & Hauser, 1999) suggests that valid tests can be a very useful part of the assessment of
both students and institutions but that testing alone is unlikely to have much impact of learning or
on improving education.

The American Educational Research Association (AERA) suggests that decisions that affect a
student's life chances or educational future should not be made on the basis of test scores alone.
Test scores should be part of high-stakes decisions, but they should not be a substitute for making
careful, well-informed decisions about individuals who take tests. This recommendation is echoed
in the National Academy report, which notes that the ultimate criterion for evaluating the impact of
high-stakes testing is whether it leads to better decisions about individuals and institutions. A high-
stakes test that simply denies diplomas to some high-school students and awards them to others
accomplishes very little. A test that helps educational institutions develop and implement strategies
for improving the achievement of its students can make a tremendous contribution. In the end,
high-stakes testing is neither good nor bad. The critical question for evaluating high-stakes testing
programs is how the information from these tests is used to improve education.

Testing Disabled Examinees. A number of physical or mental disabilities might
affect responses to psychological tests without necessarily affecting the characteristic
that the test was designed to measure. For example, an individual with any of several
types of motor impairment (e.g., as the result of an injury or long-term disability)
might find it very difficult to respond to a speeded, multiple-choice test of scholastic
ability but might nevertheless be extremely bright and capable of high levels of
academic performance. How to test individuals with disabilities fairly (i.e., the
development of testing methods that validly assess their abilities) and how to fairly
use test information in making decisions about disabled individuals are questions that
have received considerable attention in the professional and legal literature.

The Americans with Disabilities Act (ADA) was designed to remove artificial
barriers that have prevented disabled individuals from gaining access to the workplace
and to a variety of public accommodations. Although the precise requirements of ADA
are still not defined, it is likely that this law will profoundly affect the assessment of
disabled individuals. The law requires that otherwise qualified individuals cannot be
discriminated against solely on the basis of their physical or mental disabilities. It does
not require employers or schools to give preference to disabled individuals, but it does

require reasonable accommodation to allow disabled individuals a chance to compete for and to perform in jobs and assignments. Many standardized tests are potential targets for litigation under ADA because the tests may require responses that may not be job related (e.g., filling in small bubbles on an answer sheet, responding to speeded tests, making fine visual discriminations of motor responses). The task of developing assessment procedures that are fair to disabled examinees and that are comparable to those given to nondisabled examinees is a formidable one, and it is likely to occupy test developers for some time to come.

Test Use and Test Fairness. Although the process of testing and the outcomes of testing are separate issues, both of which contribute to perceptions of fairness or unfairness, they are not completely independent. Rather, the process of testing (ranging from test administration practices to decisions about test use) interacts with the outcomes of testing in ways that can substantially affect perceptions of fairness. In general, a test is most likely to be attacked as unfair when (1) it leads to adverse decisions for some groups in the population, (2) it is the sole basis for decisions, and (3) the consequences of doing poorly on the test are harsh (Heubert & Hauser, 1999; Seymour, 1988). For example, if minority group members fail to get jobs because of their test scores, the test is likely to be viewed as unfair and may be the subject of legal action.

The use of multiple assessment procedures is one key to reducing concerns over test fairness. When multiple methods of assessment, which consider many relevant characteristics of the individual, all lead to the same conclusion, the hypothesis that the test itself is the cause of the negative outcome can no longer be supported. When different assessment methods lead to different conclusions, this outcome should lead to a more detailed evaluation of the individual, which should in turn reduce the impact of a single test score. Another key to reducing concerns over test fairness is to employ multiple-stage decision models. Rather than making irreversible decisions about everyone at the point of testing, you might sort individuals into several categories that lead to different outcomes. For example, in educational admissions you might (1) accept the top candidates, who do well on all tests and assessments; (2) reject the lowest-scoring candidates, who do poorly on all tests and assessments; and (3) hold the rest for more detailed examination and consideration (Cronbach & Gleser, 1965).

Another model for reducing the possibility of test unfairness is to use more intensive screening procedures for persons who are most likely to be treated unfairly by a given test. For example, in graduate admissions it is not uncommon for admission committees to closely examine the files of all minority applicants, even those who may have done poorly on one or more tests. This separate examination does not necessarily (or even usually) increase the chances that a given minority applicant with low scores will be admitted, but it does reduce the possibility that unfairly low scores on one test will completely screen out a minority applicant.

Much of the debate concerning test fairness has focused on the outcomes of testing, for example, whether the use of a specific test will affect the likelihood that women or members of minority groups have a fair chance to compete for jobs or for admission to selective universities. A considerable literature also deals with the process of testing.

The key issue here is that many tests are developed, administered, scored, and interpreted by members of the white middle class, and their application to members of other segments of society may not always be optimal or even appropriate.

The debate has to a large extent moved from a question of whether tests and assessment procedures developed by (and perhaps for) one group should be used in other groups to how such tests and assessments should be used. In particular, a good deal of attention has been paid to the ways that cultural and socioeconomic differences can influence the process of testing and the interpretation of test scores. (For a brief sampling of this literature, see Geisinger, 1992, and Ridley, 1995. Books dealing with specific aspects of multicultural assessment and counseling are offered in the Sage *Multicultural Aspects of Counseling* series.) Prediger (1994) has compiled a listing of testing standards from a wide range of documents (e.g., the "Code of Fair Testing Practices in Education") that are relevant to multicultural assessment.

Is There Scientific Consensus About Ability Testing? There is still significant controversy about the use of cognitive ability testing, but in some fields, considerable consensus has been reached. In particular, the debate over the use of cognitive ability tests in employment has led to consensus on several points (Murphy et al., 2003; Schmidt, 2002). Murphy et al. (2003) surveyed Industrial and Organizational psychologists, and reported that they agree that cognitive ability tests are, on the whole, valid predictors of job performance and that their use in personnel selection is generally fair. However, they also agree that cognitive ability tests provide good, but incomplete measures of intelligence, and that different abilities or attributes are likely to be relevant for understanding different aspects of performance or performance in different jobs. Finally, they agree that diversity is valued by organizations and the that adverse impact that would occur if cognitive ability tests were the sole basis for personnel selection should be avoided.

As Murphy et al.'s (2003) survey suggests, scientific opinion is considerably more nuanced than the debates over cognitive ability in the popular press often suggest. There are few scientists who think that ability tests are always good or always bad. Rather, scientists recognize both the strengths and the limitations of cognitive abiliy tests, and most important, they recognize that these tests are often not (and often should not be) the only factor that determines high-stakes decisions about inividuals. There are still settings (e.g., special education placement) where these test scores have a profound effect; but in most places where cognitive tests are used to make important decisions about people, they represent one piece of information that influences but does not determine actual decisions.

CRITICAL DISCUSSION:

The Strange Case of Sir Cyril Burt

Societal concerns about the fairness, accuracy, and meaning of ability tests have led to many heated debates, but perhaps few as strange and bitter as the case of Sir Cyril Burt. Burt was a dominant figure in British psychology, particularly in the areas of mental testing and the heritability of cognitive ability, and is one of three psychologists ever knighted. His research on intelligence had a strong impact on educational practices in Great Britain, and his research was important in establishing the heritability of cognitive ability. In the late 1970s, however, his reputation was virtually destroyed, and opponents of his theories suggested that all the conclusions that were based in part on his work would need to be rejected or at least reexamined.

Dortman (1978), Gillie (1976), and others accused Burt of falsifying important data, of making false claims about coauthors (e.g., it was suggested that some of the coauthors cited in his work did not exist), of making wildy inflated claims about his role in the development and history of factor analysis, and of making inflated claims (perhaps based on falsified data) about the links between intelligence and social mobility (some similar claims are currently made by Herrnstein and Murray, 1994, in *The Bell Curve*). These claims were accepted, even by Burt's biographer, Hearnshaw (1979), and they seemed to cast a great deal of relevant research in doubt.

More recent scholarship (e.g., Fletcher, 1991; Joyson, 1989; Mackintosh, 1995) has rebutted most of these criticisms and suggests that although there may have been some impropriety in Burt's long career as a researcher and an editor, there is not credible evidence of fraud or falsification on his part. Many of the controversies surrounding Burt are a function of the man's complex and often unpleasant character. He was at the same time sloppy and arrogant, paranoid, and supremely sure of his own conclusions. He was incredibly prolific and sometimes published under assumed names (it can be embarrassing when many articles in the same issue of the same journal are published by the same author), a practice that might be interpreted as fraudulent. On top of everything else, critical records from his work were lost for long periods or scattered or destroyed by bombing during World War II; and when records were finally recovered, Burt had the confusing habit of publishing the data without mentioning that they might have spent years or even decades in storage.

The controversy over Burt has cast a long shadow over the legitimacy of a great deal of research on intelligence, and there are still critics who use questions about Burt's work to undermine the work of other scientists. In our view, there is no credible evidence of fraud in Burt's major works, and, more important, there is no important controversy in the area of intelligence whose resolution depends on the work of Sir Cyril Burt. That is, there is a wealth of independent evidence bearing on virtually every important conclusion reached by Burt, and even if his work were removed from the body of relevant research, few well-established conclusions about cognitive ability would change.

ANALYZING THE SOCIETAL CONSEQUENCES OF TESTS

Although test developers and professionals involved in testing agree that the societal impact of testing and the concerns of various groups involved in testing should be taken into account, it is not always easy to identify valid societal concerns. In particular, it is not always clear whose concerns should be given the most weight and whose should be treated as peripheral. This same problem is frequently faced by decision researchers, and the methods that they use to address this problem may be usefully adapted to psychological testing.

W. Edwards and Newman (1983) suggest that the first step in applying decision research to real-world problems is often to identify the stakeholders, or those people who have some real stake in how decisions turn out. (Balzer & Sulsky, 1990, have applied a similar analysis to performance appraisals in organizations.) The *Standards for Educational and Psychological Testing* (American Psychological Association, 1999) identify several participants in the testing process; their roles are described in Table 3-2. Of

Table 3-2   PARTICIPANTS IN THE TESTING PROCESS

Participant	Role
Test developer	Develop, publish, and market the test
Test user	Use test results to make decisions
Test taker	Respond to test items
Test sponsor[a]	Contract with test developer for a specific test or service
Test administrator	Supervise and carry out actual testing
Test reviewer	Conduct scholarly review of technical and practical merits of test

[a]The same organization might serve as test sponsor, test developer, and test administrator, or it may serve any two of these three roles.

these participants, the test developer, the test user, and the test taker are most likely to be identified as stakeholders in decisions concerning test fairness.[4]

The test developer and the test user are likely to consider fairness primarily from the perspective of the institution, whereas the test taker is likely to consider the test's impact on the individual. Furthermore, test users often focus on comparative decisions (e.g., the selection of the best out of a group of applicants), whereas test takers, and possibly test developers, are likely to focus on absolute decisions (e.g., whether a person with a given score is likely to succeed). To help make this more concrete, consider the sometimes competing interests of the three main stakeholders in a debate over the fairness of an aptitude test that is used for academic admissions. Some of the legitimate interests of these three stakeholders are shown in Table 3-3.

Test developers are, in the long run, concerned with the success of the test. Success is defined here in terms of both the extent to which the test is used and the expenses involved in developing and maintaining the test. Thus, a test that is so controversial that users avoid it or so fraught with problems that the test developers devote all their time to defending the test will not be very successful. Test users are, in the long run, concerned with the cost-effectiveness of the test. That is, the user must

Table 3-3   SOME INTERESTS OF VARIOUS STAKEHOLDERS
IN ACADEMIC ADMISSIONS TESTING

Participant	Interests
Test developer	Widespread use of the test
	Avoidance of costly controversies (e.g., lawsuits)
Test user	Selection of best applicants
	Economical, efficient admissions process
Test taker	Fair chance to compete for admission
	Accurate prediction of likelihood of success

[4]When an entire category of tests (e.g., the SAT) is under review, the test sponsor would also have a stake in the assessment.

consider the extent to which the test helps to improve decisions and must balance that assessment against the various costs involved in testing. Costs can range from the dollar cost of test administration to the costs associated with bad publicity that might accompany a controversy over test fairness. Test takers are more concerned with the short-term results of the test than with its long-term success. That is, test takers will naturally be more concerned with how they (and others like them) do on the test and less concerned with the long-term cost-effectiveness of the test. One of the reasons that debates over test fairness are often confusing is that different stakeholders have different perspectives on what is important (e.g., long-term versus short-term perspectives, individual versus institutional outcomes). All these perspectives are legitimate, and a complete examination of test fairness must consider all of them.

The place of advocacy groups, such as the National Association for the Advancement of Colored People (NAACP) or various consumer groups, in the debate over test fairness has not always been well defined. The interests of these groups typically relate more strongly to those of the test takers than to those of test developers and test users (other advocacy groups, however, such as the U.S. Chamber of Commerce, usually take the institutional perspective). Typically, these groups also have political agendas, and these do not always work in favor of individual examinees. Nevertheless, groups concerned with the effects of tests on individuals and society clearly also have a legitimate interest in the debate over test fairness.

The federal guidelines that govern the application of equal employment laws are an example of a system that explicitly considers the perspective of at least two stakeholders, the test taker and the test user. Test takers who believe that they have been discriminated against by a test or an assessment procedure can initiate legal proceedings to reverse the test outcome. It is their responsibility to present evidence that the test does, in fact, have discriminatory impact.[5] The test user must then present evidence that the test serves some legitimate business purpose and that the test contributes to the accuracy of important, job-related decisions. These guidelines, laws, and legal procedures are by no means perfect for balancing the legitimate societal concerns of test takers and test users, but they do give both groups input into the final decision of whether a test that appears to discriminate against some group should be used or abandoned.

In the final analysis, it is in the best interest of all participants in the testing process to develop tests and ways of using tests that satisfy most of the legitimate concerns of all the stakeholders. As we will show in several subsequent chapters, this goal can best be accomplished by developing tests that are highly reliable and valid and in which the influence of variables that are not relevant to the decisions that the test is designed for is reduced or eliminated.

---

[5]A variety of federal and state laws define groups who are specifically protected by antidiscrimination laws. However, anyone who believes that he or she is being discriminated against (including white males) can bring suits under many of these laws.

CRITICAL DISCUSSION:

Are There Technical Solutions to Societal Problems?

Ability testing has a variety of consequences that are of great concern for society. It is important to identify things that psychologists can and should do to help solve societal problems that arise as a result of testing. First, psychologists and other test developers and users have a responsibility to minimize the adverse effects of testing, while at the same time preserving the features of tests that make them useful. This might entail a variety of activities, ranging from efforts to minimize bias in test items to the development of decision-making strategies that reduce the undesirable outcomes of testing. Second, they can help clarify and structure the debate over topics such as test bias and test fairness. For example, by developing precise methods of defining and measuring test-item bias, researchers have been able to focus the debate over bias on precise characteristics of tests and test items, rather than on abstract arguments over terms defined differently by different participants in the debate. By carrying out research on bias and fairness, psychologists can determine whether various testing problems are real or exist primarily in the minds of test critics. One example of this process is in research on the effects of using test items that require knowledge that seems more relevant to upper-class and middle-class persons than to others (e.g., questions about symphonies or polo matches). Most critics of testing have cited this as a serious problem in standardized tests of intelligence (Jensen, 1980), but research has shown that questions of this sort show no more bias than questions about things that are familiar to all classes, races, or sexes.

It is also important to describe the limitations that psychologists face. The most basic limitation is that many societal problems do not have a scientific solution, because they are based on differences in values (e.g., the value of efficiency versus equity). Psychologists can determine what values underlie different positions, and they can describe people's values with some precision, but science cannot dictate what values should or should not be followed.

The word *should* is the key to describing when technological solutions exist for societal problems. As long as the issue is one of fact (i.e., what is happening), scientific and technical solutions are possible. When the issue is one of value (i.e., what should happen), scientists have no special skill or role in solving the problem. Because many of the societal problems that arise from testing do involve values, there will be no technological "quick fix"; in a democratic society, everyone must participate in the solution of these problems.

SUMMARY

Because tests are used to make important decisions about individuals or to help them make decisions for themselves, the potential impact of testing on society is substantial. Proponents of testing believe that psychological tests are preferable to other methods of making these same decisions; but even if they are correct, that condition does not relieve test developers and test users from the responsibility of considering the societal consequences of their actions.

Cognitive ability tests have been the focus of a great deal of discussion and debate. Questions of whether testing helps or hurts different sectors of society, of whether tests lead us to a better understanding of individuals and groups or to an inflated assessment of our differences, still rage. Personality inventories, interest measures, and attitude surveys have not been the focus of as much attention, but issues such as invasions of privacy, confidentiality, and informed consent are of significant concern in our society, and testing of this sort can raise any or all of these issues.

Debates on the fair use of tests involve the process of testing (e.g., how tests might be adapted to validly assess individuals with disabilities) as well as the outcomes of tests. Concerns regarding test fairness seem most pressing when the test is used to screen out individuals or to make irrevocable decisions. Some researchers have suggested that other strategies for using test scores might reduce concerns over unfairness.

Analyses of societal concerns in psychological testing are complicated by the fact that different participants in the process of test development and test use have very different interests. The valid concerns of test developers are likely to be quite different from those of test takers, and a thorough analysis of societal issues in testing must consider the perspectives of multiple stakeholders.

KEY TERMS

Cyril Burt   prominent researcher in the areas of intelligence and heritability who was accused of faking crucial data

Efficiency versus equity   trade-off often encountered in testing between doing what is most beneficial for the institution versus doing what is most beneficial for some or all examinees

High-stakes testing   testing programs in which test scores have substantial implications for participants' educational or career opportunities

Informed consent   the principle that individuals participating in psychological research or assessment should be informed beforehand about the nature of the task and the potential risks and threats inherent in the activity

Institutional decision   decision in which an institution (e.g., school) must make a choice about how to treat an individual (e.g., to offer or refuse admission to graduate school)

Stakeholders   individuals or groups who have valid concerns about the development and use of psychological tests

The Bell Curve   widely discussed book that examines the role of cognitive ability in determining success in several areas and that makes controversial recommendations about the public policy implications of individual and group differences in ability

4

Basic Concepts in Measurement and Statistics

We are all familiar with measurement, or at least with the type of measurement that involves rules, meters, gauges, mileposts, and graduated flasks. Our everyday experience with measurement, which involves assigning numbers to the physical properties of objects, may even suggest that it is impossible to measure most psychological variables. In a sense, it is impossible to measure psychological variables, but this statement is true only if one adopts a highly restrictive definition of the term *measure*. In fact, measurement is an extremely broad term, and the everyday physical measurement with which we are most familiar is a highly specialized case. A psychologist who claims to have successfully measured intelligence, or need for achievement, or knowledge of biology means something different from an engineer's measurement of the span of a bridge. A proper understanding of the term *measurement* is therefore critical for the interpretation and evaluation of psychological tests.

PROBLEMS AND SOLUTIONS—PREDICTING FUTURE PERFORMANCE

The Problem

You and your cousin have applied to Michigan State University. You received a score of 600 on the verbal section of the Scholastic Assessment Test, and he received a score of 500. If you both major in Psychology, what sort of grade point average should you expect to receive? Your SAT-I score suggests that you will have a higher GPA, but how much higher?

PSYCHOLOGICAL MEASUREMENT

Defining Measurement

In the most general sense, measurement is the process of assigning numbers to objects in such a way that specific properties of objects are faithfully represented by properties of numbers (Krantz, Luce, Suppes, & Tversky, 1971). This definition can be refined slightly when applied to psychological measurement, which is concerned with attributes of persons rather than attributes of objects. Psychological measurement is the process of assigning numbers (e.g., test scores) to persons in such a way that some attributes of the persons being measured are faithfully reflected by some properties of the numbers.

It is important to keep in mind that psychological measurement attempts to represent some attributes of persons in terms of some properties of numbers. In other words, psychological tests do not attempt to measure the total person, but only some specific set of attributes of that person. Even more important, many properties of individuals may be represented in terms of specific properties of numbers. Table 4-1 illustrates how several properties of a set of numbers (2, 4, 16) can be used to represent properties of three individuals (A, B, C).

As shown by the table, the term *measurement* might include a wide variety of operations. As long as specific properties of people are faithfully represented by specific properties of numbers, a psychological test provides a valid measure of a person that can be extremely useful, especially when decisions must be made regarding that person.

Table 4-1   PROPERTIES OF NUMBERS THAT COULD BE USED TO REPRESENT PROPERTIES OF PERSONS

Properties of the numbers 2, 4, and 16	*Properties of persons A, B, and C*	*Examples*
1. 2 is different from 4; 4 is different from 16	A is different from B; B is different from C	A is wearing number 2; B is wearing number 4 on his uniform
2. 16 is greater than 4; 4 is greater than 2	C exhibits more of attribute X than B; B exhibits more than A	C came in second, and B came in fourth in a race
3. The difference between 16 and 4 is much greater than the difference between 4 and 2	The difference between the amount of attribute X exhibited by persons C and B is much greater than the difference between the amount exhibited by persons B and A	A, B, and C received scores of 98 (2 wrong), 96 (4 wrong), and 84 (16 wrong) on a vocabulary test
4. 16 is four times as great as 4, and eight times as great as 2	Person C exhibits four times as much of attribute X as does person B, and eight times as much as does person A	C can lift 16 boxes, B can lift 4 boxes, and A can lift only 2 boxes of fruit

Individual Differences

The cornerstone of psychological measurement is the assumption that individuals differ. In particular, there are real, relatively stable differences between individuals in behavior, interests, preferences, perceptions, and beliefs. The task of a psychologist interested in measurement is to devise systematic procedures for translating these differences into quantitative (numeric) terms. In other words, psychological measurement specialists are interested in assigning individuals numbers that will reflect their differences.

It is important to keep in mind what the assumption of stable individual differences means, as well as what it doesn't mean. It means that people differ in discernible and potentially measurable ways in their behavior and that those differences persist over a sufficiently long time to make their measurement useful. If you do not believe that individuals differ at all in their psychological attributes (this belief is unlikely to be true) or that people show no stability in their behavior, there is no sense in trying to attach numerical values to nonexistent or ephemeral differences. We believe that there is enough evidence of stable individual differences in a wide range of psychological characteristics to make the assumption that people really differ a reasonable one. This assumption does not mean that differences are necessarily large or permanent or that differences in psychological attributes indicate differences in people's inherent worth. Rather, it means that there is something out there to measure.

A second point that must be kept in mind is that psychological tests are designed to measure specific attributes of persons, not the whole person. There is not, nor should there be, a test that purports to measure whether one is a good person or a worthy human being. Psychological tests only tell us ways in which individuals are similar or different. Some differences are so small or so specialized that they have little impact on people's lives (e.g., Peter collects stamps from western Africa; Joseph collects stamps from eastern Africa). Other individual differences in psychological attributes affect one's success in school and in business, adjustment, and well-being. Systematic measurement of these differences is a key goal of applied psychology.

Scales of Measurement

As Table 4-1 suggests, a number of different types, or scales, of measurement correspond to the different properties of numbers. Stevens (1946, 1951, 1961) has described four scales of measurement that are of particular importance for psychological testing and research: nominal scales, ordinal scales, interval scales, and ratio scales.[1]

Nominal Scales. A nominal scale of measurement is one in which numbers are used to classify and identify persons. In nominal measurement, numbers are substituted for names or verbal labels. For example, in a football game, each individual is given a specific uniform number, and these numbers are used to identify

---

[1]Coombs, Dawes, and Tversky (1970) note that there are many variations on these four basic scales. See also Narens and Luce (1986).

players throughout the game. Each player receives a different number and retains the same number for the duration of the game. Although the assignment of football numbers may not sound like "measurement," it is, in fact, a very useful level of measurement. Some of the properties of the numbers on those uniforms do indeed reflect some properties of the players; each individual player is a different person, and each receives a different number. Furthermore, the numbers serve the useful function of identifying each player during the game.

Many types of classification result in a nominal level of measurement. For example, a school psychologist may label children as either "normal" or "learning disabled." These labels could easily be replaced by numbers, so that normal children are referred to as "group 1," whereas learning-disabled children are referred to as "group 2." It is important to note that the actual numbers chosen are completely arbitrary. The two groups could just as easily be labeled "group 407" and "group 136"; any set of numbers will do, as long as children who are members of different groups receive unique numbers. The size of the numbers tells nothing about the persons being measured. Thus, a person wearing the football number 82 is not necessarily bigger, faster, or better than someone wearing number 68; he or she merely differs from the person wearing number 68.

Ordinal Scales. People are very often ranked. For example, a class may agree that their psychology professor is more interesting than their accounting professor, but that both of these professors are less interesting than their biology professor. An ordinal scale of measurement is one that assigns numbers to individuals so that the rank order of the numbers corresponds with the rank order of the individuals in terms of the attribute(s) being measured. Consider, for example, the order of finish in a footrace: The person who completes the course in the shortest period of time comes in first, the next person comes in second, and so on. Thus, a runner who finished 17th needed more time to finish the course than the runner who finished 16th, but less time than a runner who finished 18th or 20th. Note that the order of finish does not indicate, in any absolute sense, how close the runners were at the end of the race.

The outcome of a mile race at a recent track meet is shown in Table 4-2. This table illustrates the central difference between ordinal measurement and measurement on an absolute scale. In this race, O'Brien and Taylor finished in what was nearly a dead heat, and both finished well ahead of the pack. Caldwell barely made it around the track, finishing nearly a minute after everyone else. The order of finish reported in the

Table 4-2   ORDER OF FINISH IN A 1-MILE RACE

Runner	Order of finish	Actual time for the mile
O'Brien	1	3:59.35
Taylor	2	3:59.45
Dill	3	4:08
Catton	4	4:16
Caldwell	5	5:10

table, however, merely indicates that O'Brien won, that Taylor came in second, and so on.

Ordinal measurement is extremely common in psychology and education. We can often state with some confidence that a person who receives a high score on an appropriate test is more outgoing or more knowledgeable in the area of mechanics or more likely to exhibit neurotic behavior patterns than someone who received a low score on the same test. However, a comparison of test scores may not tell us how much more outgoing a person with a test score of 40 is than someone with a test score of 22. Nevertheless, a test that yields ordinal information certainly fits our definition of measurement. In addition, ordinal information is often sufficient for decision-making purposes. For example, if ten people apply for six jobs, the decision makers' task is to pick the top six, something that can be done using strictly ordinal information.

Interval Scales. Often we are interested in measuring the differences, or intervals, between objects or people. For example, if you wanted to compare the average temperature in a city in June, July, and December, it would be useful to devise a scale with two essential properties: First, the scale should indicate which month is the warmest and which the coldest (i.e., the rank order); second, the scale should indicate whether the difference between the July and December temperatures is bigger than, smaller than, or the same as the difference between the June and July temperatures. Assuming that the difference between July and December is bigger than the difference between June and July, this scale should indicate the relative sizes of these differences. The Fahrenheit and Celsius scales, which are commonly used in measuring temperature, have these properties.

The scale just described is referred to as an *interval scale.* The defining characteristic of an interval scale is that the size of the difference between the numbers assigned to two persons or objects corresponds to the degree to which these persons or objects differ on the attribute being measured. Assume, for example, that we had an interval scale measure of agility and that Sue, Megan, and Kathleen received scores of 2, 4, and 8, respectively. These scores would tell us (1) that Kathleen is more agile than Megan, who is more agile than Sue and (2) that the difference in agility between Kathleen and Megan is twice as great as the difference between Megan and Sue. Since individual differences are of considerable concern in psychology, interval scales of measurement can be very useful, and many test developers go to great lengths in attempting to construct interval scales. Unfortunately, such scales are somewhat difficult to construct, and, as a result, many psychological tests yield scores with ordinal properties but without the defining characteristics of an interval scale.

Ratio Scales. In many types of measurement, we are concerned with the relative size, weight, speed, or density of two objects. For example, if I measure two boards and find that one is 12 inches long and the other is 36 inches long, I can say that the second board is three times as long as the first. Similarly, a car traveling at 60 miles per hour is going twice as fast as one traveling at 30 miles per hour and 2.4 times as fast as one that is traveling at 25 miles per hour. This type of physical measurement is accomplished using ratio scales. A ratio scale of measurement is one in which ratios between the numbers assigned to persons or objects correspond to ratios between the attributes measured in these persons or objects. For example, if we measure height with a ratio scale and determine that person A is 14 units tall and person B is 7 units tall, this finding indicates that A is twice as tall as B. The difference between interval and ratio scales can be illustrated by returning to our example in which Megan received an (interval level) agility score of 4, and Sue received an agility score of 2. Even though 4 is twice as large as 2, we would not take these scores to indicate that Megan was twice as agile as Sue. Indeed, unless agility could be measured using a ratio scale, the phrase "twice as agile" would be meaningless.

There is a simple but critical difference between interval and ratio scales. In an interval scale, the unit of measurement is arbitrary; interval-level agility ratings of 9, 11, and 15 could be used in place of 2, 4, and 8 without in any way affecting the measurement properties of the scale. In particular, the zero point of an interval scale is completely arbitrary. For example, the Celsius and Fahrenheit scales have different zero points, neither of which would be interpreted in any absolute sense. Hence, an agility rating of zero does not indicate that a person has no agility whatsoever, just as a score of zero on a French test does not indicate that the student knows no French. On a ratio scale, however, the zero point is not arbitrary. Regardless of what is being measured, the zero point on a ratio scale always has the same meaning. An object with a true height of zero inches has no height; an object with a true weight of zero grams is weightless. Thus, although the units of measurement are arbitrary (feet, meters, furlongs), ratio scales are always anchored in terms of a fixed, real zero point. As a result, values on a ratio scale can always be interpreted in terms of their distance from this real zero. Thus, a scale value of 40 (inches, pounds, miles per hour) is twice as far from zero as a scale value of 20. In an interval scale, zero has no intrinsic meaning, so the statement that an interval-level agility rating of 4 is twice as far from a rating of 0 as is a rating of 2 is literally true, but completely uninformative.

There is a clear hierarchy among the four scales of measurement. Nominal scales are the most primitive and least informative scales. Although each person or class of persons receives a unique number that can be used to identify that person, none of the other useful properties of the numbers that make up a nominal scale are reflected in the attributes of the persons being measured.

An ordinal scale has all the useful properties of a nominal scale, plus the ability to portray rank-order information. Thus, when the order of finish in a race is measured, the numbers assigned to each runner (first place, second place, and so on) serve to identify each runner and to indicate the order in which the runners finished. Interval scales, in turn, possess all the useful properties of nominal and ordinal scales, together with the ability to represent the size of the difference between persons or objects. Thus, when individuals receive interval-level agility scores, these scores serve to (1) identify the persons being rated, (2) indicate their rank order in terms of agility, and (3) indicate the relative similarities or differences in the agility of the individuals being rated.

Finally, ratio scales possess all the useful properties of nominal, ordinal, and interval scales, together with the property that ratios between scale values correspond to ratios between the attributes being measured. Thus, if three sections of drainage pipe are measured to be 10, 15, and 30 inches, these numbers (1) identify each pipe, (2) indicate which pipe is longest and which is shortest, (3) indicate which pipes are similar in length and which are relatively dissimilar in length, and (4) indicate that the longest pipe is three times as long as the shortest and twice as long as the second shortest pipe.

Ratio scales, which represent the most useful and informative scales of measurement, are rare in psychology because a meaningful zero point is often difficult to define (in Chapter 10, we describe item-response theory, which sometimes allows one to develop ratio scales). Interval scales can be developed in a wide range of settings, but in practice they are difficult to achieve. Many psychological tests appear to yield ordinal information and may exhibit some interval properties, but they do not always strictly fit the definition of interval scales (Coombs, Dawes, & Tversky, 1970). Finally, many types of classification that appear to be qualitative in nature (e.g., assignment to a particular psychodiagnostic category) can be regarded as a quantitative measurement that employs a nominal scale.

EVALUATING PSYCHOLOGICAL TESTS

The aim of all psychological tests is to assign numbers (i.e., test scores) to individuals so that some attributes of these individuals are faithfully reflected by some properties of the numbers assigned. In Chapter 1 we noted that well-constructed psychological tests do this task better than other available methods that are used in making decisions about people. It is appropriate to ask here just how we know (1) whether tests are any good and (2) whether tests are better than other measurement and decision-making techniques. For example, suppose that you take an intelligence test. How would you really know whether the test measured anything related to your level of intelligence? More important, how would you know whether that test did a better job of measurement than might have been done using another test, an interview, or some other measurement method?

Psychological tests are invariably imperfect, as are all measurement devices; the numbers assigned to individuals do not always correspond exactly to the attributes of those individuals. For example, John may receive a higher score than Mary on a test of spatial ability, yet he may, in fact, possess an equal level, or perhaps even a lower level, of spatial ability than Mary. Furthermore, some tests do a better job of measuring a particular attribute than others. Thus, if Richard receives a higher score than James on a 200-item, professionally developed reading test, we would conclude with more confidence that Richard is a better reader than if the test scores were obtained from a 5-item reading test published in a supermarket tabloid.

One of the central problems in psychological testing is to determine whether a specific test provides an adequate measure of a specific attribute. In other words, to determine how good a job the test does, it is critical to determine whether test scores really reflect the attributes of the persons being measured and whether the test meets some minimal definition of measurement. The evaluation of psychological tests as measurement instruments centers on two related issues: the reliability of the test scores and the validity of inferences that are made about individuals on the basis of the test scores.

Reliability

The consistency of test scores is of considerable importance in evaluating a test as a measurement instrument. A reliable test is one that yields consistent scores when a person takes two alternate forms of the test or when he or she takes the same test on two or more different occasions. The importance of reliability can best be illustrated by examining the outcomes of an unreliable test. Table 4-3 shows the scores of three students on an *unreliable* vocabulary test given first on a Monday morning and then again the following Wednesday.

This test does not appear to measure, in any consistent sense, any attribute of Judy's, Kevin's, and Scott's. It is safe to assume that the verbal ability of the three students did not change dramatically between Monday and Wednesday. Their scores, however, did change dramatically. The test given on Monday suggests that Kevin is best and that Scott is only slightly ahead of Judy. Wednesday's test results suggest that Judy is the best and that Scott and Kevin are tied. In other words, there is no consistent relationship between scores on this test and the attribute being measured. Scores like this might occur if the test included very specialized terms (e.g., vocabulary items involving baseball on Monday's test; items involving history on Wednesday's test). Note that the test may not even provide a nominal scale of measurement, since Scott and Kevin, who may differ dramatically in their verbal ability, received the same score on Wednesday.

Hence, reliability is the first requirement for good measurement. To provide an adequate measure of a particular attribute, a test must at least assign scores in a consistent fashion. Methods of defining, estimating, and increasing test reliability, therefore, are extremely important and have been the focus of a great deal of research. The topic of reliability is examined in Chapters 6 and 7.

Validity

Tests are used to make inferences about people. For example, if John receives a higher score on a spatial ability test than Mary, we may infer that he possesses more spatial ability than she. The validity, or correctness, of these inferences is a major concern in psychological testing.

Table 4-3   SCORES ON AN UNRELIABLE VOCABULARY TEST

Student	Monday	Wednesday
Judy	49%	94%
Kevin	86%	38%
Scott	52%	38%

There are two types of inferences that one might make on the basis of test scores: (1) inferences regarding the attribute being measured and (2) inferences that will affect decisions made about the test taker.

As an example of an inference regarding measured attributes, test scores might be used to infer that one person is more intelligent, more outgoing, or more skilled in French than another. The validity of these inferences is referred to as *validity of measurement.* The central question in assessing the validity of measurement is whether the test adequately measures what it purports to measure. A valid intelligence test, therefore, is one in which more intelligent individuals receive consistently higher scores than do less intelligent individuals.

Not only are tests used to measure specific attributes, but they are also used to make decisions. The decision to admit a college applicant on the basis of his or her test scores represents a second type of inference—the inference that a person with high test scores is more likely to succeed than a person with low test scores. It therefore is important to assess the validity of a test as a basis for making specific decisions. Validity for decisions is the second major facet of test validity; a test that is useful for making accurate decisions about individuals exhibits this type of validity. Chapters 8 and 9 examine validity of measurement and validity for decisions, respectively.

Reliability theory provides a set of procedures for determining whether tests are consistent in assigning scores to individuals. A test that is completely unreliable cannot measure any attribute. A reliable test measures something, but reliability theory does not provide any mechanism for determining what the test measures. To understand fully which attribute or set of attributes is being measured by a test, one must examine the validity of that test. Investigations of the reliability and validity of a test, then, help determine the adequacy with which a test measures a specific attribute of the persons who take the test.

STATISTICAL CONCEPTS

Why Statistics?

One of the authors of this book teaches a statistics course or two every year and often must answer questions such as "What do statistics have to do with psychology?" One way to answer this question is to note that psychological measurement leaves us with lots of numbers and that statistics give us a method for answering questions about the meaning of those numbers. For example, if Susan receives scores of 82, 78, and 75 on math, reading, and history tests, does this outcome mean that she is really better at math than at reading or history? Since tests are imperfect measures, the answer might be yes and might be no. Statistics provide methods for answering questions like this.

Statistics can be used to describe test scores. There are statistics that answer the question "How did people do on the test?" Other statistics answer questions like "Did most people do the same, or were there large individual differences in test scores?"

More important, statistics can be used to make inferences about the meaning of tests scores. Statistical methods can help answer questions like "Is Susan really better at math?" Statistics provide a method for communicating information about test scores and for determining what conclusions can and cannot be drawn from those scores.

Basic Concepts

Three statistical concepts are central to psychological measurement: variability, correlation, and prediction. Of the three, variability is the most basic; it is also the most central. Psychological measurement is concerned with individual differences, and the application of a test is nothing more than a method of expressing individual differences in a quantitative (numeric) form. If there are no individual differences, everyone should, on average, receive the same score on the test. To the extent that individuals really do differ, they will receive scores that differ. Statistical indexes of variability allow us to measure and describe the extent to which test scores differ.

When we ask "Is intelligence related to success in school?" in effect we are asking whether there is any correlation between the two variables. If people who receive high scores on intelligence tests also succeed in school, we can say that the two measures correlate. On the other hand, people who receive high scores on a math test may be no better or worse as golfers than those who receive low scores. In other words, there may be little or no correlation between scores on math tests and scores on the golf course.

Prediction is closely related to correlation but allows us to answer a somewhat more concrete question. Suppose you knew that Scholastic Assessment Tests (SAT) scores were related to college grades (correlation) and also knew that your brother had received scores of 600 and 550 on the verbal and quantitative portions of the test. What grade point average (GPA) would you predict for him? The statistical procedure of linear regression allows us to answer this sort of question.

Variability. If 100 students in an introductory psychology course take a test, you expect that some people will do well, that others will do less well, and that others will do poorly. You could describe the performance of the class as a whole in several ways, the simplest of which would be to report the average test score, or the mean, symbolized by $\overline{X}$. The mean provides a good summary, but it does not describe individual differences. Some people did much better than average (their scores were higher than the mean), whereas others did much worse. It is useful to develop a statistic that measures the extent to which individuals differ. This is most easily done by computing the difference between each person's score and the mean (i.e., subtract the mean from each test score). This deviation score measures the extent to which each individual differs from the mean.

Two basic principles are used in developing most statistics:

1. Statistics are usually based on the average of several scores.
2. Statistics that are based on deviation scores usually work with squared scores rather than raw scores.

Both of these principles are used in defining the basic measure of variability, the variance. The variance is given by

$$\sigma_x^2 = \frac{\sum (X_i - \overline{X})^2}{N}$$ [4-1]

where

σ_x^2 = variance of X

$(X_i - \overline{X})$ = difference between each person's test score and the mean of the test scores (i.e., a deviation score)

N = number of persons

The variance is simply the average of the squared deviation scores.[2] A large variance indicates that individual scores often differ substantially from the mean and therefore from one another. A small variance indicates that most individuals received very similar scores and therefore that most people are very close to the mean.

It may not be obvious why we invoked the second basic rule of statistics ("square everything") in defining the variance. The reason is simple. It can be shown algebraically that the average deviation score is always equal to zero, regardless of the amount of variability in test scores. Since a simple average of the deviation scores will not tell us anything about variability, we do the next best thing and look at the average of the squared deviation scores.

Squaring deviation scores allows us to develop a simple measure of variability. Unfortunately, squaring also changes the unit of measurement. For example, a person who receives a score of 30 on a test in which the mean is 50 has a deviation score of 220. That person's square deviation score is 400. To restore the original unit of measurement, you simply need to take the square root. The square root of the variance is referred to as the *standard deviation* and is symbolized by σ_x. This measure of variability is widely used in psychological measurement and represents one of the most common measures of the variability of a set of scores.

One application of the standard deviation is to form standard scores, or *z scores.* Suppose you knew that your score on a psychology test was 20 points above the mean. This score indicates that you did better than average but does not indicate whether you did *much* better than average or only a little better than average. If most people's scores were within 2 or 3 points of the mean, your score would seem pretty spectacular, and you might expect a grade of A+. However, if the top of the score distribution was 200 points above the mean, your grade would be a C+ rather than an A+. It would be useful in this case to interpret your deviation score in comparison with other people's deviation scores. The *z* score does exactly this.

The *z* score is obtained by dividing a person's deviation score by the standard deviation. That is,

$$z = \frac{X - \overline{X}}{\sigma_x}$$ [4-2]

[2]The sample estimate of the population variance, s_x^2, involves dividing by $N - 1$ rather than N, to correct a slight bias when sample statistics are used to estimate population parameters.

A positive z indicates that you are above the mean, a negative z indicates that you are below the mean, and the size of z indicates, in standard deviation units, how far your score is away from the mean. Together with the normal curve, z scores can be used to provide direct and easily interpretable descriptions of test scores. For example, a z score of 1.0 indicates that you did better on the test than 84% of the people in the class. A z score of 1.65 indicates that you did better than 95% of the class. A z score of 21.25 indicates that you did better than only 10% of the class. The z transformation is discussed in more detail in Chapter 5.

Correlation. The simplest way to describe the relationship between scores is through the use of a scatterplot. A scatterplot is a graph showing the positions of a group of people on each of two variables. The X axis on the graph is used for one variable, the Y axis is used for the second variable, and each person's score is represented by a single dot. For example, consider the data in Table 4-4, which represent general aptitude test scores and grades of 12 undergraduate college students. In tabular form, the relationship between the two variables is not particularly evident. Figure 4-1 presents the same data in the form of a scatterplot. As can be seen in the scatterplot, it appears that grades tend to increase as test scores increase. However, the relationship is far from perfect; that is, it is obvious that each increment in test score is not accompanied by a comparable increment in grade. The data demonstrate a general trend, but also some exceptions.

The relationship shown in Figure 4-1 is called a *positive correlation* because an increase in one variable is associated with an increase in the other variable. That is, the higher the test score is, the higher grades tend to be. Although it is true that the majority of the correlations reported in measurement literature are positive, some variables

Table 4-4   GENERAL APTITUDE TEST SCORES AND GRADES FOR 12 UNDERGRADUATES

Person	Aptitude scores	Grades
A	50	3.1
B	60	3.7
C	20	1.6
D	30	3.4
E	80	4.0
F	50	2.2
G	50	3.7
H	30	1.9
I	30	2.5
J	70	2.2
K	20	2.5
L	70	3.1
$\overline{X}$	46.67	2.83
σ_x	20.59	.78

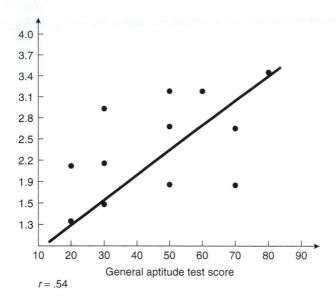

FIGURE 4-1 Relationship Between Aptitude Test Scores and Grades

General aptitude test score

r = .54

tend to show opposite patterns. Such correlations are called *negative correlations* because an increase on one variable is associated with a decrease on the other variable. For example, among adults, age is negatively correlated with running speed; the older you are, the slower you are likely to run.

The simplest and most common measure of correlation is the correlation coefficient, symbolized by r. To compute r, multiply each person's z score on X (e.g., ability test) by his or her z score on Y (e.g., GPA), and take the average of these products.[3] In other words,

$$r = \frac{\sum (z_x \times z_y)}{N} \qquad [4\text{-}3]$$

Once again, this statistic is a simple average. The question is why the average of z_x times z_y provides a measure of the correlation between X and Y.

It may not be immediately obvious why multiplying z scores has anything to do with the correlation between two variables. In fact, the link is simple. Correlation implies that people with high scores on X (large positive z) will also have high scores on Y and that people with low scores on X (large negative z) will also have low scores on Y. The product of two large positive z's is a large positive number; the product of

---

[3]An equivalent formula, which avoids the use of z scores is

$$r_{xy} = \frac{\sum (X - \overline{X})(Y - \overline{Y})}{N \, \sigma_x \sigma_y}$$

two large negative z's is also a large positive number. The r is simply the average of these numbers, so a large r indicates that people with high scores on X also have high scores on Y and that people with low scores on X also have low scores on Y. In other words, the size of r indicates the extent to which two variables are correlated.

When two variables are not correlated, people with high scores on X will sometimes have high scores on Y ($z_x \times z_y$ is large and positive), will sometimes have average scores on Y (zy is near zero, so $z_x \times z_y$ is near zero), and will sometimes have low scores on Y ($z_x \times z_y$ is large and negative). In this case, the average $z_x \times z_y(r)$ will be near zero, and once again, the size of r indicates the strength of the correlation between X and Y.

Correlation coefficients range in absolute value from 0 to 1. A correlation of 0 indicates that two variables are unrelated, and a correlation of 1 indicates that two variables are perfectly related. A positive correlation indicates that high scores on X are associated with high scores on Y (e.g., SAT scores and grades). A negative correlation indicates that high scores on X are associated with low scores on Y. This outcome occurs most frequently when two variables are scored in opposite directions. For example, a high score is good in bowling, whereas a low score is good in golf. Since both variables are influenced by general athletic ability, one might expect a negative correlation between bowling scores and golf scores.

Prediction. One practical use of correlation is in prediction. If scores on one variable, such as performance on the job, are correlated with scores on another, such as a test of mechanical comprehension, one implication is that we can predict job performance from test scores. Many decisions we make about individuals are based (at least implicitly) on predictions. Colleges admit students most likely to succeed. Industries hire people who are predicted to perform well and screen out those predicted to fail. Clinical psychologists often base their treatment decisions on the predicted outcome of different types of therapy. The topic of prediction is therefore of considerable practical importance.

The problem of prediction is complicated by the fact that predictors (X's) and the variables we wish to predict (Y's) are often on different scales of measurement. For example, suppose that scores on a typing test (with scores ranging from 0 to 100, with a mean of 50 and a standard deviation of 15) are used to predict job performance, measured on a 5-point scale (with a mean of 2.0 and a standard deviation of 1.0). The technique used for making predictions must therefore take into account the scale of measurement of both X and Y, as well as the extent to which X and Y are correlated. The technique referred to as *linear regression* accomplishes exactly this task.

The predicted score on Y, based on a person's score on X, is given by the equation

$$\hat{Y} = a + bX \qquad\qquad [4\text{-}4]$$

where

    $\hat{Y}$ = predicted score on Y
    a = intercept
    b = slope or regression coefficient
    X = score on the predictor

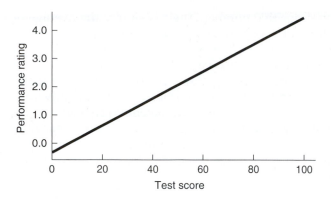

FIGURE 4-2 Predicting Performance Levels From Typing Test Scores

In other words, your predicted score on Y is equal to your score on X multiplied by b, plus a constant, a. The constant (intercept) allows us to adjust for different scales of measurement for X and Y. The regression coefficient, b, indicates the expected change in Y per unit change in X. For example, consider the equation shown next and illustrated in Figure 4-2:

$$\text{Predicted performance} = .35 + .033 \times \text{typing test score} \qquad [4\text{-}5]$$

If the correlation between test scores is .50, an applicant with a test score of 50 would have a predicted performance rating of 2.0.[4] An applicant with a test score of 60 would have a predicted performance rating of 2.33 (i.e., 10 × .033).

The regression equation is a linear equation that predicts that every increase of one unit in X will result in an increase of b units in Y. However, the use of this form of prediction does not imply that the functional relationship between two variables is linear. Psychology abounds with relationships that are nonlinear. The field of psychophysics, which is concerned with the relationship between physical characteristics of stimuli and our perceptions of these stimuli, suggests that a variety of nonlinear functions is needed to describe these relationships. The linear form is used in prediction because it is the most simple and robust form available (Dawes & Corrigan, 1974; Yntema & Torgerson, 1961). In particular, many nonlinear relationships can be described very well using linear equations, simply by transforming the X and Y variables to different forms.

Explaining Correlation: Factor Analysis

Mental tests often show moderate-to-high positive intercorrelations. Factor analysis represents an application of advanced statistical methods to the problem of explaining why two tests are correlated. Suppose, for example, that two tests designed to measure reading comprehension and vocabulary showed a correlation of .53. If

[4]$b = r_{xy} * \dfrac{\sigma y}{\sigma x}; a = \overline{Y} - b\overline{X}$

someone asked you why these tests were correlated, you would probably say that their correlation is explained by the fact that they both measure pretty much the same thing—verbal ability. Your explanation represents an application of inductive reasoning: You identify the more general, abstract, common variable of verbal ability by noting features that the two tests seem to have in common. Factor analysis represents a statistical method of achieving the same result. Factor analysis attempts, through statistical means, to identify the basic underlying variables that account for the correlations between actual test scores. We call these basic variables that account for the correlations among test score *factors;* more than two tests may have the same factor in common, and it is possible that many factors will be needed to explain the intercorrelations among a large group of tests.

Table 4-5 shows the intercorrelations among four tests: a reading comprehension test (RC), a vocabulary test (VOCAB), a figure rotation test (FR), and an exploded figures test (EF). The figure rotation test is one that requires subjects to identify complex geometric figures presented from different vantage points in space. The exploded figures test requires subjects to identify three-dimensional figures in a disassembled state. If you were called on to explain why the correlations between RC and VOCAB and between FR and EF are high, whereas all the other correlations are low, you would probably say that these four tests each measured one or two basic abilities, spatial ability and verbal ability, and that these two abilities were somewhat independent. The fact that RC and VOCAB are highly correlated suggests that they measure the same factor. The fact that RC and VOCAB show very low correlations with FR and EF suggests that the first two variables measure a different factor than is measured by the latter two variables.

When factor analysis is applied to the correlations shown in Table 4-5, the results are very similar to those suggested by our commonsense analysis of these correlations. The analysis suggests that there were two distinct factors; the factor loadings, or the correlations between the original four tests and these two factors, are shown in Table 4-6. In the table, both the reading comprehension and vocabulary show high correlations with the first factor and low correlations with the second; both the FR and EF tests show high correlations with the second factor and low correlations with the first. It seems sensible, therefore, to label the first *verbal ability* and to label the second *spatial ability.*

Table 4-5   CORRELATION AMONG TWO DEPTH-PERCEPTION MEASURES, A READING COMPREHENSION TEST, AND A VOCABULARY TEST

	RC	VOCAB	FR	EF
Reading comprehension (RC)	1.0			
Vocabulary (VOCAB)	.62	1.0		
Figure rotation (FR)	.12	.09	1.0	
Exploded figures (EF)	.04	.11	.76	1.0

**Table 4-6   RESULTS OF A FACTOR ANALYSIS OF THE CORRELATIONS
SHOWN IN TABLE 4-5**

	Factor loadings	
Variables	*Factor I*	*Factor II*
Reading comprehension	.88	.09
Vocabulary	.76	.15
Figure rotation	.04	.72
Exploded figures	.20	.78

You might wonder why psychologists bother with such complex methods when the results are precisely what common sense would suggest. The answer is that in many cases, the pattern of correlations among psychological tests is too complex for seat-of-the-pants methods to produce reliable and valid results. For example, when there are 10 tests, one must examine 45 separate correlation coefficients among the tests. It is generally quite difficult to determine with any precision how many factors are needed to adequately explain the correlations among a number of tests, and it is often even more difficult to identify the factors themselves. To make matters worse, two psychologists looking at the same correlation matrix are likely to disagree in their subjective assessments regarding the number and the identity of the underlying factors. Factor analysis provides an analytic method of determining the number of factors and the statistical characteristics of those factors.

At a more fundamental level, one might ask what is accomplished by carrying out a factor analysis. There are probably two answers: (1) The interpretation of data is simplified by reducing the number of variables, and (2) the focus of research moves from specific tests to more general factors, which have many of the same characteristics of constructs. In the same way that the essential information conveyed by a large number of concrete, observable measures can be summarized and put into some ordered perspective by a small number of constructs, factors serve to summarize and organize the essential information conveyed by a large number of individual tests. One fundamental feature of factor analysis is that the number of important, interpretable factors is always smaller than the number of tests, often considerably smaller. In our verbal-spatial ability tests example, all the important information conveyed by four tests could also be conveyed by the two factors.

There are a number of methods of factor analysis, and they vary considerably in their mathematical sophistication and their usefulness. The most fundamental distinction is between exploratory factor analysis, in which the factors that provide the best statistical fit to the data are derived, and confirmatory factor analysis, in which factors are defined in terms of the specific hypothesis that is being tested by the experimenter. In general, confirmatory analyses are more useful than exploratory ones, but the applicability of these two techniques varies, depending on the specific area of inquiry. For example, psychologists know a great deal about the structure of cognitive abilities, which allows for the application of more powerful confirmatory methods of analysis. On the other hand, we do not yet know enough about some aspects of interpersonal attraction to form specific hypotheses about factors, and we must therefore restrict our efforts to exploratory factor analysis.

CRITICAL DISCUSSION:

Measurement Scales and Statistics

There is an apparent paradox in psychological research: Complex statistical procedures are often employed in analyzing fairly crude (e.g., ordinal-level) measures. If the measures are so crude, is there really any point to the sorts of statistical gymnastics that appear in psychological journals? Some writers say no (e.g., Siegel, 1956), but others say yes (Gaito, 1980; F. M. Lord, 1953). One way to resolve this controversy is to consider the different roles of measurement and statistics in psychological research.

The role of measurement is one of translation. That is, measurement allows us to express very diverse phenomena in a universal language—the language of numbers. The role of statistics is to draw information and inferences from those numbers. Statistics can be thought of as a set of rules for drawing conclusions from numbers. The important point is that statistical conclusions are conclusions about the numbers themselves, not necessarily about the things or people that the numbers represent. An example will help to illustrate this point.

Suppose that there were two day-care centers in town and that one claimed to dramatically improve infants' intellectual ability by exposing them to three hours of flashcards each day. Teachers at this center design a measure, called the Is Your Baby Better? scale, and administer it at both facilities. The means and standard deviations obtained by administering the scale to 100 infants at each site are the following:

	With flashcards	*Without flashcards*
Mean	122	104
Standard deviation	6.1	5.8

The differences between the scores are statistically significant. Does this outcome mean that flashcards work? If not, what does it mean?

It is useful to distinguish between the statistical and the substantive statistical conclusions implied by these results. The statistical conclusion that would be reached is that the mean scores do indeed differ or, more simply, that the numbers differ at the two day-care centers. This finding does not mean that flashcards really do improve intelligence. The substantive conclusion about the meaning of these numbers depends very much on the measure itself. Does this scale really measure infant intelligence? Maybe it measures flashcard knowledge, which may be quite distinct from intelligence. Is the scale at all reliable? Is the scale administered in an unbiased way at both centers? The statistical data presented here do not address these questions. In the chapters that follow, you may find it useful to keep in mind that statistical conclusions, even those drawn from complex analyses, are conclusions only about the numbers themselves. Careful attention to measurement, or to the meaning of those numbers, is required to make sense of psychological research.

SUMMARY

Much of the public controversy over psychological testing is due to a failure to consider what measurement really means. As we noted in this chapter, it is a process of assigning people numbers that faithfully reflect important characteristics of the individuals being assessed. Measurement can range from the simple assertion that two people are consistently different to the assertion that person A has twice as much of an attribute as person B. In this chapter, we noted that there are a variety of scales of measurement and that tests that do no more than indicate who has more or less of a particular attribute nevertheless provide valuable measurement.

Two concepts are basic to evaluating any test. First, the test should yield consistent, or reliable, scores. Second, it should form the basis for correct, or valid, inferences about the persons being measured. Chapters 6 through 10 examine in detail the methods used in evaluating psychological tests. These methods require the application of a variety of statistics, particularly in assessing the variability of test scores and the relationships between test scores and other variables (e.g., the correlation between scores on scholastic ability tests and grades), as well as for predicting scores on other tests and measures on the basis of scores on particular tests. In reading research on psychological tests, you will encounter frequent references to the variance (and standard deviation) of test scores, to the correlations among scores, and to the regression equations used in prediction. Advanced topics such as factor analysis will also be encountered. You do not have to be a statistician to follow this research; as long as you have a firm grasp of the concepts of variability, correlation, and prediction, you will find that even technical studies are relatively easy to follow.

PROBLEMS AND SOLUTIONS—RECAP

The Problem

You received a score of 600 on the verbal section of the Scholastic Assessment Test, and your cousin received a score of 500. If you both major in Psychology at Michigan State University, what sort of a grade point average should you expect to receive?

A Solution

The problem here is predicting the score on one variable (GPA) given the score on another variable (SAT). To answer this question, you would need to know three things: (1) the strength of the relationship between SAT scores and GPA, (2) the mean and the standard deviation of grade point averages in the Psychology department at MSU, and (3) the mean and the standard deviation of the SAT-I Verbal section. Let's say that the correlation between SAT and GPA is .52, the means for SAT and GPA are 500 and 2.95 respectively, and the standard deviations for SAT and GPA are 100 and .80, respectively. Using the formula for linear regression discussed in our section entitled "Prediction," we find:

$$b = .52(.80/100) = .00416$$

$$a = 2.95 - (500^*.00416) = .87$$

So, the predicted GPA for someone who receives a 600 on the SAT-I verbal section is:

$$\text{Predicted GPA} = .87 + (.00416^*600) = 3.37$$

The predicted GPA for someone who receives a 500 on the SAT-I verbal section is:

$$\text{Predicted GPA} = .87 + (.00416^*550) = 3.16$$

These prediction equations suggest that both you and your cousin will be "B" students and that your GPA will be about .20 points higher than his. Of course, these predictions do not always come true, but these figures would represent the best guess, given the information about the SAT, the GPA, and the relationship between the two present in this problem.

KEY TERMS

Correlation coefficient   statistical measure of the association between two sets of scores

Factor analysis   statistical technique used to analyze patterns of correlation among different measures

Interval scale   measurement scale in which the size of the differences between objects is reflected in terms of the size of the differences in the numbers assigned

Linear regression   method for predicting scores on one measure (e.g., success in graduate school) on the basis of scores on some other measure (e.g., scores on a graduate admission test)

Measurement   process of assigning numbers to objects in such a way that specific properties of the objects are faithfully represented by specific properties of the numbers

Nominal scale   measurement scale in which numbers identify objects, but in which the size of the number is meaningless (e.g., numbers on football jerseys)

Ordinal scale   measurement scale in which rank order of the numbers corresponds to rank order of the objects that are measured (e.g., order of finish in a race)

Ratio scale   measurement scale in which ordinal and interval properties are found and in which there is a true and meaningful zero point

Reliability   the consistency of test scores

Validity   the degree to which inferences made on the basis of test scores (e.g., John is more agreeable than Sam) are correct

Variance   measure of the extent to which test scores differ or vary

5

Scales, Transformations, and Norms

Psychological tests involve obtaining samples of behavior to measure attributes such as intelligence, motivation, risk taking, and psychopathology. The score on a scholastic test might reflect the number of questions answered correctly; the score obtained in an observation of mother-child interactions might be the number of times the mother smiles at her baby. This sort of behavior count is simple and concrete, but not necessarily informative. Suppose, for example, that you knew that a student had answered 27 questions correctly on a statistics exam or that a mother had smiled at her baby five times in 30 minutes. It would be impossible, without other information, to determine whether the student had done well or whether the mother was showing unusual warmth in dealing with her baby. In other words, raw scores, which represent simple counts of the behaviors sampled by the test or measuring procedure, do not always provide useful information. It is often necessary to reexpress, or transform, raw scores into some more informative scale.

We use the term *scale* to refer to the set of scores that might be reported for a test. For example, scores on a test of general mental ability might be reported on an IQ scale. Scales are very often transformations of the original raw scores. The goal of this chapter is to discuss the most widely used methods of transforming raw scores into more interpretable, and therefore more useful, scales.

PROBLEMS AND SOLUTIONS—COMPARING SCALES

The Problem

Dan and Alice are collaborating on a research project that involves administering personality inventory designed to measure shyness to high-school children in Wisconsin and Colorado. Participants read 100 statements (e.g., "You would rather work alone than work in a group") and indicate whether they agree or disagree with each. In Wisconsin, Dan uses an older version of the inventory in which students respond to these statements using this scale:

1	3	5
Strongly Disagree	Neither Agree nor Disagree	Strongly Agree

In Colorado, Alice uses the current version of the inventory that uses the same items, but a different response scale, specifically:

1	2	3	4	5	6	7
Strongly Disagree			Neither Agree nor Disagree			Strongly Agree

It is not surprising that they obtain different results. Their hunch is that students in Colorado are more likely to be shy than students in Wisconsin, but they realize that the use of two different scales makes it difficult to directly compare scores. Suppose, for example, that a student in Wisconsin receives a score of 4.0 on a five-point scale. What is the equivalent score on the seven-point scale used in Colorado?

TRANSFORMATIONS

The simplest transformation is one that expresses scores in terms of percentage rather than raw units. Going back to our example in which a student answered 27 test questions correctly, if you knew that there were 40 questions on the test, that student's score could be reexpressed (transformed) as a score of 67.5%. This simple transformation has the three characteristics that many of the most useful transformations exhibit:

1. It does not change the person's score; it simply expresses that score in different units.
2. It takes into account information not contained in the raw score itself—here, the number of items on the test.
3. It presents the person's score in units that are more informative or interpretable than the raw score.

Several of the transformations discussed in this section are more complex than the percentage-correct transformation, but will nevertheless exhibit these three characteristics.

Linear Transformations

A linear transformation is one that takes the form shown in Equation 5-1:

$$\text{Transformed score} = \text{constant} + (\text{weight} \times \text{raw score}) \qquad [5\text{-}1]$$

This equation has the same general form as the regression equation discussed in Chapter 4. As with regression equations, this form of a transformation guarantees a simple, direct relationship between raw scores and transformed scores that can be depicted using a straight line, as in Figure 5-1. As illustrated by the figure; a raw score of 30 would equal a transformed score of 400.

One of the most familiar linear transformations is the z score. As discussed in Chapter 4, the z score that corresponds with a raw score value of X is given by

$$z = \frac{X - \overline{X}}{\sigma_x} \qquad \text{[5-2]}$$

This may look like a linear equation, but a little manipulation allows us to restate the z-score equation in the same form as Equation 5-1. That is,

$$z = -\frac{\overline{X}}{\sigma_x} + \frac{1}{\sigma_x} \times X \qquad \text{[5-3]}$$

The z transformation is extremely useful for a number of reasons. First, the z score indicates each person's standing as compared with the group mean. Those with positive z scores received raw scores that were above the mean, whereas those with negative z scores received raw scores that were below the mean. Second, when the distribution of raw scores is reasonably normal, z scores can be directly converted to percentiles. Figure 5-2 illustrates the relationship between z scores and percentiles for the normal distribution.

For example, 84.1% of the scores in a normal distribution are below a z score of 1.0. Therefore, if you received a z score of 1.0, you could conclude that you received a better score than 84% of the people taking the test. Similarly, a z score of zero indicates that you did better than half of the people taking the test. Most statistics texts include detailed tables for converting z scores to percentiles.

This interpretation of z scores is accurate only when scores are normally distributed. Micceri (1989) and Wilcox (1992) suggest that deviations from strict normality are common. However, the normal distribution is nevertheless a reasonable working approximation in most cases. More important, the deviations from normality that are

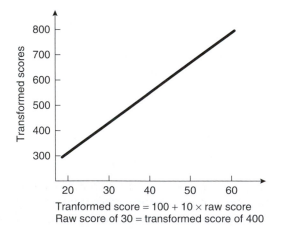

Tranformed score = 100 + 10 × raw score
Raw score of 30 = transformed score of 400

FIGURE 5-1   A Linear Transformation of Raw Scores

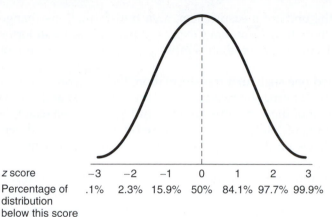

z score	−3	−2	−1	0	1	2	3
Percentage of distribution below this score	.1%	2.3%	15.9%	50%	84.1%	97.7%	99.9%

FIGURE 5-2 Relationship Between z Scores and Percentile for Normally Distributed Variables

most often seen do not greatly affect the relationships between z scores and percentiles. Even when the variable being measured has a distribution that is far from normal, the z score table still provides a working estimate of percentiles; unless the distribution is severely skewed (an abnormally large number of high or low scores), percentiles obtained from a z score table will generally be within 5% to 10% of the true percentile value. Thus, z scores are very useful in interpreting most psychological tests and measurements.

Variations of the z Transformation. There are two features of z scores that many people regard as undesirable. First, half of the z scores in a distribution will be negative. Second, z scores often have fractional values; even when they exceed 11 or 21, they must be carried to at least two decimal places to extract most of the information from each score. Several score transformations can be used to overcome these two disadvantages; T scores illustrate this type of transformation.

The T score is a simple transformation of z that takes the following form:

$$\text{T score} = (\text{z score} \times 10) + 50 \qquad\qquad [5\text{-}4]$$

For example, a z score of 1.30 could be reexpressed as a T score of 63. A z score of 21.97 could be reexpressed as a T score of 31. T scores have a mean of 50 and a standard deviation of 10 and thus have an effective range of 20 to 80. Scores up to 5 standard deviations away from the mean, which represent extraordinary extremes, will have T scores in the range of 0 to 100.

Area Transformations

A second type of transformation, referred to as an *area transformation,* uses the normal curve to create scale score values. Linear transformations simply change the units of measurement; the most familiar example is changing from Fahrenheit to Celsius scales for recording temperature. Area transformations are a bit more complex, because they do more than simply put scores on a new and more convenient scale.

Rather than simply changing the units of measurement, area transformations change the point of reference. That is, these transformations express a person's score in terms of where it falls on a normal curve, rather than simply providing a new unit of measurement.

We have already mentioned one such area transformation, the percentile, or percentile rank. To show how this transformation relates to the concept of area and also to show how it changes the meaning of the test score, we present Figure 5-3, an example of a reasonably normal distribution of 100 test scores expressed in raw scores and percentiles. A test score of 3 represents the 26th percentile; a test score of 6 represents the 76th percentile.

Notice how the percentile transformation changes the relationship between test scores. The difference between a test score of 1 and a score of 2 is the same as the difference between a 5 and a 6. The percentiles, however, differ considerably. Scores near the center of the distribution differ substantially in their percentile ranks (5 = 60%, 6 = 76%), whereas scores at the extremes have more similar percentile ranks (1 = 4%, 2 = 12%). This percentile transformation magnifies differences between individuals at the middle of the distribution and compresses the differences between individuals at the extremes. Area transformations do not change the rank order of scores, but they do change the intervals between scores. As we noted in Chapter 4, scores on many psychological tests are likely to reflect ordinal rather than interval measurement scales (i.e., higher scores indicate higher levels of the attribute being measured, but the size of the difference between two individuals' scores does not necessarily indicate how much

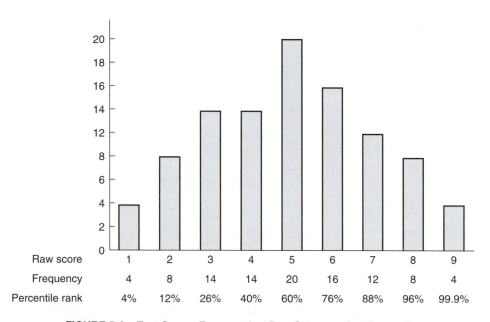

Raw score	1	2	3	4	5	6	7	8	9
Frequency	4	8	14	14	20	16	12	8	4
Percentile rank	4%	12%	26%	40%	60%	76%	88%	96%	99.9%

FIGURE 5-3   **Test Scores Expressed as Raw Scores and as Percentiles**

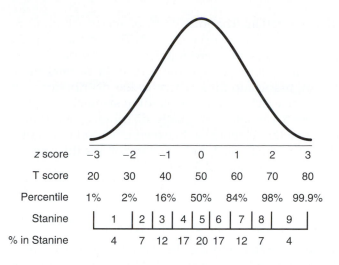

z score	−3	−2	−1	0	1	2	3
T score	20	30	40	50	60	70	80
Percentile	1%	2%	16%	50%	84%	98%	99.9%
Stanine	1	2 3	4 5 6	7 8	9		
% in Stanine	4	7 12	17 20 17	12 7	4		

FIGURE 5-4   Linear and Area Transformation in Relation to the Normal Curve

they differ on that attribute), so the fact that area transformations can change intervals between scores is probably not a major problem.

Figure 5-4 illustrates two area transformations in relation to a normal curve, and it helps to clarify the way in which the concept of area is used to transform raw scores. The data in Table 5-1 are from a test in which scores are normally distributed, with a mean of 100 and a standard deviation of 15. A raw score of 80 has a percentile rank of 9.2, indicating that 9.2% of all scores are 80 or lower. Similarly, the table indicates that over 90% of the scores are 120 or lower. As we noted earlier, most statistics texts include tables that allow you to easily convert z scores (which are themselves transformations of raw scores) into percentile ranks. The transformation to percentile ranks is one of the most common and useful transformations of raw scores.

In addition to the two linear transformations illustrated in Figure 5-4 and the percentile transformation, Table 5-1 and Figure 5-4 include a second area transformation, the *stanine*. The stanine is a contraction of the term *standard nine* and represents one of the simplest transformations available; raw scores are transformed to a single digit, between 1 and 9. The stanine transformation uses the concept of area in a different sense

Table 5-1   TRANSFORMATIONS OF DATA FROM A TEST WITH A MEAN OF 100 AND A STANDARD DEVIATION OF 15

Raw score	z score	T score	Percentile	Stanine
70	−2.0	30	2.3	1
80	−1.33	36	9.2	2
90	− .66	43	25.5	4
100	0	50	50	5
110	.66	56	74.5	6
120	1.33	63	90.8	8
130	2.0	70	97.7	9

than does the percentile rank transformation. The lowest 4% of the distribution receives a stanine of 1. The next lowest 7% receives a stanine of 2. The next lowest 12% receives a stanine of 3, and so on. Whereas the percentile rank transformation expresses raw scores directly in terms of the area in a specific part of the normal curve, the stanine transformation works by first computing where in the distribution each score lies and then transforming the percentile rank into a one-digit stanine.

You may have noted that when a variable is normally distributed, the stanine transformation does not greatly change the relationship between raw scores, except at the extremes. The difference between a stanine of 4 and a stanine of 5 is the same, in raw score terms, as the difference between stanines of 5 and 6.

EQUATING SCALE SCORES

In many instances, it is not possible or desirable to use the same test across different groups of examinees or for the same group of examinees at different times. For example, a topic of recent interest was the decline in performance on tests such as the Scholastic Aptitude Test, precursor to the current Scholastic Assessment Tests (SAT), Graduate Record Examinations (GRE), and other standardized aptitude measures. In these cases, scores of current examinees are compared with those of students who took these tests many years ago. For a variety of practical reasons (e.g., test security), the forms of the tests used today are not exactly the same as those used by the students in the past. The question is, then, how does one compare the performance across different groups of examinees when using different forms of the tests?

Another illustration that is relevant here occurs when comparing the level of performance of the same group of people at two or more times. For example, in many school settings, achievement tests are administered at the beginning and end of the school year as a way of assessing academic growth over that period of time. If the same test is used both times, a variety of factors (e.g., students' ability to remember questions) complicates the interpretation of test scores. Rather than using the same test twice, educators are likely to use alternative forms of the same acheivement test at the beginning and at the end of the year. The question is whether the test publisher can be sure that both forms are equal in terms of their psychometric characteristics (difficulty, etc.). The present discussion illustrates several procedures for equating scale scores across groups of examinees or forms of tests.

Finally, there is growing interest in the problem of equating scores on different versions of the same test that use different testing technologies. For example, it is increasingly common to administer tests via computer (see Chapter 12 for a discussion of computerized testing), but it is not always possible or economical to use computers, and most computerized tests are also given in paper-and-pencil forms. The possibility that test scores will differ as a function of the method of administration has been the focus of a great deal of research, and a good deal of work has gone into equating scores on computerized versus paper-and-pencil forms of the same test.

Equating Alternate Forms Administered
to the Same Examinees

Perhaps the most common type of equating occurs with multiple forms of the same test and the examiners want to make sure that the scores earned on the different forms are interpreted properly. The simplest way to equate two alternate forms of a test is to distribute both forms of the test randomly to a large representative sample of examinees. The random assignment of forms to examinees or examinees to forms is crucial to the accuracy of this procedure. The next step is to generate the descriptive statistics (mean, standard deviation) on both forms of the test. As the final step, a straightforward linear transformation (using z scores) can take place, equating a specific raw score from one test to the scale score that it would equal on the second test.

As an illustration, assume that two different alternative forms of an ability test were developed and then administered to a sample of students. Forms A and B are randomly assigned to a large class of approximately 300 students—150 of each test form. After the tests have been scored, the following results are observed:

	Form A	Form B
Mean	64.72	67.69
Standard deviation	12.66	10.83

Using the z transformation, 64.72 (i.e., $z = 0$) on form A equals 67.69 (i.e., $z = 0$) on form B. Taking various scores from form A, we can convert them to z scores and then transform each z to the appropriate "equivalent" score on form B. For example, a score of 70 on form A has a z value of .42, which is equal to a score of 72.24 on form B. To avoid confusion of interpretation, since the same scores on both forms are interpreted differently, we might find it desirable to further convert the scale scores from both test forms to one of the common linear transformations, such as T scores. As a final step, a table such as Table 5-2 can be prepared and placed in the interpretive and scoring manual of the test. As long as the two test forms do not differ radically in their mean, variability, and shape, the preceding procedure for equating the two forms works quite well.

Equating Alternate Forms Administered
to Different Examinees

Assume that we want to develop a new form of test for a large psychology course but want to make sure that the interpretation of the results will be comparable to a similar test given five years earlier. Obviously, it is not possible to give the previous sample of examinees the new test. However, it is possible to give the new sample of examinees a selection (i.e., minitest) of items from the old test, together with the new

Table 5-2 SCALE SCORE EQUATING FOR FORMS A AND B

Score on form A	z Score for form A	Equivalent score on form B	T Scores for both[a]
75	.81	76.43	58
74	.73	75.60	57
73	.65	74.73	56
72	.58	73.97	56
71	.50	73.11	55
•	•	•	•
•	•	•	•
•	•	•	•
55	−.77	59.35	42
54	−.85	58.48	41
53	−.93	57.62	40
•	•	•	•
•	•	•	•

[a] $\overline{X} = 50$, $\sigma_x = 10$.

test. In this case, we actually have three tests: the old test, the new test, plus the common set of items given to both groups of people. The mechanism for equating the new test form to the old test form is through this common collection of items, referred to as an *anchor test.* Although the technical details of the procedure are beyond the scope of this book, it is informative to describe the rationale behind the technique. The basic idea is that the information obtained from the anchor test provides data that allow one to equate the two test forms.

Consider the situation in Figure 5-5, where both old and new forms of a test (A and B) have 50 items, and the anchor test has 10 items. If people perform differently on

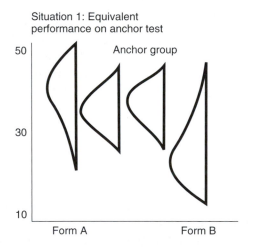
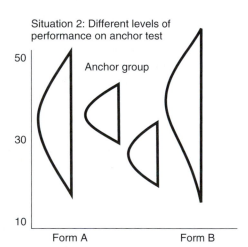

FIGURE 5-5 Using Anchor Tests to Equate Test Forms

test forms A and B, it might be difficult to determine whether this outcome reflects differences in the people taking the test or differences in the tests themselves. The use of a common anchor test, which is taken by both groups of examinees, allows us to separate differences among examinees from differences between the test forms.

Consider the first situation shown in Figure 5-5, in which test scores differ but scores on the anchor test are approximately the same. The anchor test suggests that the groups are similar in terms of their ability, since the two groups receive similar scores, but that form A is easier than form B. In this case, scores on the two tests have to be interpreted differently. In particular, a score of 30 has a higher percentile rank for form B than for form A.

The opposite may occur. Situation 2 in Figure 5-5 illustrates a case in which overall test scores are similar but scores on the anchor test differ. The group of people taking form A scored higher on the anchor test than those taking form B; this outcome suggests that the group taking form A is systematically different from the group taking form B. Since their total test scores are the same, the logical conclusion is that form A must be more difficult than form B. If the tests were equally difficult, we would expect group A to do much better than group B. On the basis of information provided by the anchor test, we can adjust the A and B scale score values so that a raw score of 30 on form A receives a higher scale score than does a raw score of 30 on form B. Scores obtained on the anchor items can be used in developing separate score tables for each form of the test that equates the two forms, meaning that a score of 50 on form A will have the same meaning as a score of 50 on form B.

The procedures described in the previous section and in this one are relatively simple. The technical literature on test development contains a variety of more sophisticated techniques that can be used in equating test scores. We have mentioned some simple methods in order to indicate the general principles involved in equating test scores. Additional information on score-equating procedures can be found in Angoff (1971). Students interested in detailed discussions of advances in score-equating procedures can consult a special issue of *Applied Measurement in Education* (1990, Vol. 3), as well as Kohlen and Brennan (1995).

Although test form equating may seem like a dry, technical topic, one must keep in mind that mistakes in equating can have enormous consequences. Perhaps the most widely discussed equating error was in the scoring of the Armed Services Vocational Aptitude Battery (ASVAB) (see Chapter 14). An equating error in the development of one of the ASVAB forms led to a massive influx of individuals who, had their tests been scored appropriately, would not have been judged qualified to join the armed services. When Congress was informed of the error, questions were immediately raised about how these supposedly unqualified people were performing in their jobs. It was only then that the Congress learned that there were no good measures of the job performance of enlisted personnel, that in fact the armed services did not really know how test scores related to job performance! One result was a massive research program on job performance in the military; the results of this project were summarized in a special issue of *Personnel Psychology* (1990, Vol. 43, No. 2).

NORMS

Scores on psychological tests rarely provide absolute, ratio scale measures of psychological attributes. Thus, it rarely makes sense to ask, in an absolute sense, how much intelligence, motivation, depth perception, and so on, a person has. Scores on psychological tests do, however, provide useful relative measures. It makes perfect sense to ask whether Scott is more intelligent, is more motivated, or has better depth perception than Peter. Psychological tests provide a systematic method of answering such questions.

One of the most useful ways of describing a person's performance on a test is to compare his or her test score with the test scores of some other person or group of people. Many psychological tests base their scores on a comparison between each examinee and some standard population that has already taken the test. The SAT, in which the scores of each individual are compared with the scores of thousands of other high-school students, provides an example of this approach.

When a person's test score is interpreted by comparing that score with the scores of several other people, this comparison is referred to as a *norm-based interpretation.* The scores with which each individual is compared are referred to as *norms,* which provide standards for interpreting test scores. A norm-based score indicates where an individual stands in comparison with the particular normative group that defines the set of standards.

Several different groups might be used in providing normative information for interpreting test scores. For example, the raw score of an entry-level secretary on a typing speed test could be compared with (1) the scores of people in general, such as might be obtained in a random census survey; (2) the scores of experienced typists; or (3) the scores of other entry-level secretaries. The same raw score might be high (i.e., above the mean) when compared with people in general, low when compared with experienced secretaries, and near the mean when compared with other entry-level secretaries. We offer this example to illustrate two essential points: First, no single population can be regarded as the normative group. Second, a wide variety of norm-based interpretations could be made for a given raw score, depending on which normative group is chosen. These two points suggest that careful attention must be given to the definition and development of the particular norms against which a test score will be interpreted.

Types of Norms

In some cases, norms may be developed that are national in scope, as in the case of large achievement test batteries. Results of such tests will be interpreted across the country in many different locations and by many different groups. In these instances, norm groups may involve many thousands of children, and tens of thousands of individuals may take the tests annually.

In the development of local norms to be used in much smaller testing applications, the practical problems are considerably less complex. However, the usefulness of the norms in these local situations is not any less dependent on the care taken during each step in the norming process. For example, a small university may develop a faculty rating scale to be completed by students for purposes of deciding on raises, promotions, and/or tenure. Over several years, only a relatively small number of courses and instructors may be involved in the norming process. Later, during use of the normative data to evaluate the teaching performance of current faculty, the data that are collected may involve 40 to 50 instructors. Although the logistics of compiling local norms are typically less complex than those involved when compiling national norms, the basic process is not really different. When local norms are developed for interpreting test scores, the same care should go into defining and collecting data on the normative sample as is observed in large-scale testing programs.

Regardless of the scope of norms (e.g., national versus local), normative data can be expressed in many ways. Three of the most common forms are percentile ranks, age norms, and grade norms.

Percentile Ranks. The most common form of norms is percentile rank, which represents the simplest method of presenting test data for comparative purposes.[1] For example, one piece of information on the score report form for tests such as the SAT is the percentile rank of the examinee's score. Thus, a person with a score of 500 might be in the 50th percentile. This percentile rank represents the percentage of the norm group that earned a raw score less than or equal to the score of that particular individual. For a test like the SAT, the appropriate norm group is the population of high-school students who are considering applying for college. A score at the 50th percentile indicates that the individual did as well as or better on the test than 50% of the norm group.

It is possible to compare one's score with several different norm groups. For example, scores on the advanced tests on the GRE (i.e., subject matter tests such as chemistry or psychology) sometimes give the examinee several percentile ranks, depending on the specific norm group used. Thus, a particular score may have one percentile rank when compared with the norm group of all graduate school applicants, but a different percentile rank (perhaps lower) when compared with applicants electing to pursue graduate study in a particular academic field.

Table 5-3 illustrates norm data as they are typically presented in a percentile rank format; the table is an adaptation taken from the *Norms Booklet for the Clerical Speed and Accuracy Test of the Differential Aptitude Tests.* The purpose of the test is to see how fast and accurate examinees can be in a 100-item checking task. The score is simply the number of items that are correctly checked in 3 minutes. The norms table is based on both boys and girls who were tested at the beginning of grades 8 through 11.

The data in the body of the table represent the raw scores necessary to achieve various percentile ranks, depending on whether the student was a boy or girl and depending on the examinee's grade. Several interesting conclusions can be drawn from

---

[1]The terms *percentile* and *percentile rank* are used interchangeably by many authors. We find the term *percentile rank* a bit clearer, because it explicitly indicates that this score can be interpreted in terms of where you would rank compared with some norm group.

Table 5-3 CLERICAL SPEED AND ACCURACY TEST PERCENTILE NORMS FOR USE WITH MRC ANSWER SHEETS

| | Raw Scores | | | | | | | | |
| | Grade 8 | | Grade 9 | | Grade 10 | | Grade 11 | | |
Percentile	B Fall	G Fall	B Fall	G Fall	B Fall	G Fall	B Fall	G Fall	Percentile
99	58–100	63–100	62–100	67–100	66–100	73–100	69–100	78–100	99
97	54–57	58–62	56–61	62–66	59–66	65–72	61–68	69–77	97
95	49–53	54–57	52–55	58–61	54–58	61–64	55–60	63–68	95
90	46–48	52–53	49–51	55–57	51–53	58–60	53–54	60–62	90
85	44–45	50–51	47–48	53–54	49–50	56–57	51–52	58–59	85
80	43	48–49	45–46	51–52	48	54–55	49–50	56–57	80
75	42	47	44	49–50	47	52–53	48	54–55	75
70	40–41	46	43	48	46	50–51	47	53	70
65	39	45	42	46–47	45	49	46	52	65
60	38	44	40–41	45	44	48	45	51	60
45	3	41	37	42	41	45	42	47–48	45
40	34	39–40	36	41	39–40	44	41	46	40
35	32–33	38	35	40	38	43	40	45	35
30	31	36–37	33–34	39	37	42	39	44	30
20	28	32–33	30–31	36–37	33–34	38–39	35–36	40–41	20
15	26–27	30–31	28–29	32–35	31–32	36–37	32–34	38–39	15
10	23–25	26–29	25–27	28–31	28–30	32–35	30–31	35–37	10
5	19–22	22–25	21–24	24–27	23–27	26–31	25–29	30–34	5
3	13–18	16–21	14–20	19–23	18–22	22–25	20–24	25–29	3
1	0–12	0–15	0–13	0–18	0–17	0–21	0–19	0–24	1

Source: Taken from the Differential Aptitude Tests, Forms L and M. Copyright 1947, 1948, 1972 by The Psychological Corporation, a Harcourt Assessment Company. Reproduced by permission. All rights reserved. "Differential Aptitude Tests" and "DAT" are trademarks of The Psychological Corporation.

these data. First, the data show a general increase in performance throughout the grades. Second, the very lowest percentile ranks have raw scores that could be classified as in or close to the chance range. Since this test has 100 items, each having 5 options, a chance score would be close to 20. One therefore would have to interpret the lower percentile ranks very carefully. Third, and perhaps most important, notice that often the scores for girls must be several points higher to achieve the same percentile rank as boys. This outcome is true across the entire norm table. Simply stated, girls performed better on this test than the boys.

Age Norms. Many psychological characteristics change over time; vocabulary, mathematical ability, and moral reasoning are examples. Although there may be a general pattern of growth for these types of variables, often there are wide variations among people as to whether they grow at faster or slower rates.

An age norm relates a level of test performance to the age of people who have taken the test. For example, one edition of the Stanford-Binet Intelligence Test has a vocabulary subtest that consists of 46 items, arranged from the easiest to the most difficult. The procedure is to read each word and have the examinee give a definition. This procedure continues until the person is unable to correctly define several words in a row. This yields a score for the examinee that represents the number of words defined correctly. Table 5-4 presents some normative data from this particular vocabulary test. For example, for the typical child at age 6, the average number of correct definitions is about 18; for age 12, the number is about 28. Therefore, if an examinee correctly defined about 25 words, his or her performance is similar to that of the typical child who is 10 years of age.

The principle involved in developing age norms is fairly simple: They can be developed for any characteristic that changes systematically with age—at least up to some age level. In establishing age norms, we need to obtain a representative sample at each of several ages and to measure the particular age-related characteristic in each of these samples. For example, Figure 5-6 presents some hypothetical data showing performance on an intelligence scale at several different age levels. Looking at age 60 months, the 75th percentile rank is approximately 35, the 50th percentile is about 18, and the 25th percentile rank is approximately 8. Of these three values, the median is the most important because it shows what the typical performance level is at each age

Table 5-4   AVERAGE SCORES ON VOCABULARY TEST AT DIFFERENT AGE LEVELS

Age level	Test score
14	31
12	28
10	25
8	22
6	18

Source: Adapted from Thorndike, Hagen, and Sattler (1986).

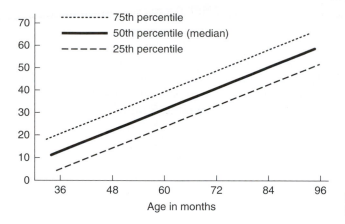

FIGURE 5-6   Age Norms for a Hypothetical Test

level. As can be seen, we can make linear interpolations between any two points if we choose. However, also of importance is the considerable overlap between different age levels. For example, note that the 75th percentile rank for 60 months is about 35 and that it is equal to approximately the median value for age 72 months. Thus, although the typical 60-month-old examinee does not perform as well as the typical 72-month-old examinee, some 60-month-old children do. Although age norms tend to emphasize the average level at a given age, it is important to remember that there is considerable variability within the same age, which means that some children at one age will perform on this test similarly to children at other ages.

    Grade Norms.   Another type of norm commonly used in school settings is called a *grade norm.* Grade norms are very similar to age norms except that the baseline on the graph (see Figure 5-6) is the grade level rather than age. These norms are most popular when reporting the achievement levels of schoolchildren.

    A typical example of normative data in grade-equivalent values is presented in Table 5-5, which shows data from the 1970 edition of the California Achievement Tests, in particular, the vocabulary subtest. The vocabulary subtest has two parts of 20 items each, and scores of these two parts are summed together. Thus, scores on this test could range from zero to 40. This particular version of the test is typically appropriate for students in grades 2 through 4.

    The interpretation of grade norms is similar to that for age norms. For example, on the basis of Table 5-5, the median score for children just beginning the second grade (grade equivalent 2.0) is about 22, whereas the typical score for a beginning fourth grader (grade equivalent 4.0) is approximately 37. What happens if a student who is just beginning grade 2 earns a scale score of 37 on this test? In this case, the child would receive a grade-equivalent score of 4.0. Does this score mean that this child who is beginning second grade is achieving like a typical child who is beginning fourth grade? The answer to this question is both yes and no. It is yes in the sense that this second grader is obtaining a score on this test that we would expect a typical fourth

Table 5-5   GRADE EQUIVALENTS FOR VOCABULARY SCALE SCORES ON THE CALIFORNIA
ACHIEVEMENT TEST

GE	VOCAB	GE	VOCAB	GE	VOCAB
0.6	0–12	2.6	29	5.1	
0.7	13	2.7	30–31	5.2	
0.8		2.8		5.3	39
0.9	14	2.9	32	5.4	
1.0		3.0	33	5.5	
1.1	15	3.1	34	5.6	
1.2		3.2		5.7	
1.3	16	3.3	35	5.8	
1.4	17	3.4		5.9	
1.5		3.5		6.0	
1.6	18	3.6	36	6.1	
1.7	19	3.7		6.2	
1.8	20	3.8		6.3	
1.9	21	3.9		6.4	40
2.0	22	4.0	37	6.5	
2.1	23–24	4.1		6.6	
2.2	25	4.2		6.7	
2.3	26	4.3		6.8	
2.4	27	4.4		6.9	
2.5	28	4.5		7.0	
		4.6	38	7.1	
		4.7			
		4.8			
		4.9			
		5.0			

Source: Adapted from the Examiner's Manual for the California Achievement Tests, Complete Battery, Level 2
Form A, 1970, The McGraw-Hill Companies, Inc. Reproduced by permission.

grader to earn if he or she also took this version of the test. However, the answer is no
in terms of saying that the second grader is at an overall achievement level of a student
entering fourth grade. One needs to be extremely careful when interpreting grade
norms not to fall into the trap of saying that just because a child obtains a certain
grade-equivalent value on a particular test, he or she is like a child of that grade-
equivalent level in all areas. In areas such as emotional and social growth, as well as in
other achievement areas, the child may not perform at that grade equivalent.

Cautions for Interpreting Norms

Normative information can be misinterpreted in many ways. These range from
using normative data that were based on inappropriate target populations to simply
misinterpreting the particular statistics underlying normative data. The most important of these potential sources of misinterpretation occurs when the norms provided in
the test manual or in other types of articles are not based on samples that adequately

represent the type of population to which the examinee's scores are to be compared. A careful reading of the technical manual generally assists in deciding whether the norms are at least close to those desired. However, many times even these statements can be misleading. One way to help to resolve this problem is to develop, over time, local norms on samples for which one has control over selection and testing.

A second difficulty in interpretation that was also mentioned in reference to grade norms should be reemphasized here. Grade norms, and to some extent age norms, can easily be seen as saying that the examinee should be performing at the tested level not only of that specific test but also in other areas and behaviors. It is fairly easy to assume mistakenly that a grade equivalent of 7.5 for a student who is actually in the latter part of the eighth grade means that he or she is capable of acting, in all respects, only like a typical student in the middle of the seventh grade. Since potential for misinterpretation in grade norms is high, one needs to exercise caution when using them and/or listening to interpretive information from others involving grade norms.

Another problem with normative data is that they can become out of date very quickly. Since the process of developing and norming a test is very time-consuming and expensive, most large-scale tests are not renormed very often. This situation is also particularly true for less well-known instruments. Since major events happen at different times and have some important impact on society, then over time, the norms on tests may no longer reflect the current performance levels of the population of interest. This would certainly be the case for achievement batteries that are trying to reflect common content in the schools. Not only should norms be based on samples that represent adequately the target population, but they also should be current.

An additional problem that may be encountered with normative data has to do with the size of the sample taken. Typically, when we look at the norms, there is a tendency to assume that they are fixed and not subject to error. That is, the temptation is to think that, if the same norm group were reexamined with the same test, their scores would produce the same pattern as expressed in the norms manual. However, if norm groups are small, there may be considerable sampling error. That is, if another group similar to the norm were tested to renorm the test, the distributions and data derived from the new group would not necessarily be the same as the first. If the size of the original group is sufficiently large (e.g., for some large tests, the norms groups number into many thousands), changes in norms due to sampling error are generally too small to make a practical difference.

EXPECTANCY TABLES

A method of presenting normative data, referred to as an *expectancy table,* is closely related to the concept of correlation. An expectancy table presents the relationship between test scores and some other variable based on the experience of members of the norm group. For example, an expectancy table might present the likelihood of successful job performance as a function of scores on an employment test, as in Figure 5-7. In

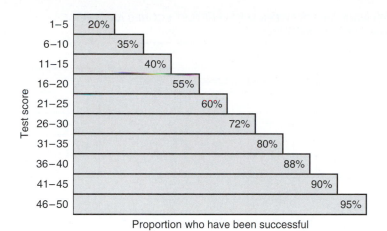

FIGURE 5-7   An Expectancy Table Relating Test Scores to Likelihood of Success on the Job

our example, a job applicant with a test score of 42 would have approximately a 90% chance of success on the job, whereas an applicant with a score of 8 would have a 35% chance.

In principle, there is no limit to the number of expectancy tables that could be developed; test scores could be related to any variable of interest. In general, however, expectancy tables are likely to be developed that relate in some meaningful way to the expected use of the test. For example, a college admissions test is likely to be accompanied by an expectancy table relating test scores to college success. These tables give a rough but concrete illustration of the implication of an individual's score on the test.

Constructing Expectancy Tables

Table 5-6 presents some data collected over several years on 207 students who had taken a math test before enrolling in a statistics course. In general, people who did well on the test also did well in the course; the correlation between pretest scores and course grades was about .70. The table presents a cross-tabulation between test scores with course grades. An expectancy table can be constructed by converting the numbers in Table 5-6 to percentages, or probabilities. The question we seek to answer is the probability of receiving an A, B, C, and so forth, for a person with a specific score on the pretest. To answer this, we take the total from each row in the scatterplot (8, 30, 39, and so on) and change the value within the row to proportions of the total. The resulting expectancy table is shown in Table 5-7. Looking at the lowest row of Table 5-6, note that a total of eight people had pretest scores of 24 or less. Of those eight, six, or .75 of them, earned an F in the course, and two, or .25 of them, earned a D. In Table 5-7, .75 and .25 values are placed in the F and D columns of the lowest row. The upper row, however, has .25 of the eight people earning Bs and .75 of the people earning As. Thus,

Table 5-6   RELATIONSHIP BETWEEN MATH PRETEST SCORES AND GRADES
IN A STATISTICS COURSE

	F	D	C	B	A	Raw total
40				2	6	8
37–39			8	18	9	35
34–36		4	18	17	4	43
31–33		11	19	14		44
28–30	3	14	15	7		39
25–27	8	13	9			30
24	6	2				8
	F	D	C	B	A	207

Grade in Statistics

given a test score on the predictor, one can estimate the probability of earning a specific grade in the course. For example, what was the probability of earning a B if a student got between 28 and 30 on the math test? Since 18% of the students with that type of test score get a B, the probability was .18.

Interpretation and Cautions

An expectancy table is an efficient way of communicating normative information related to predictions that might be based on test scores. For example, think about the situation when a counselor's book could be developed illustrating the relationship between performance on a measure such as the SAT and performance in many different universities. Thus, there might be an expectancy table for the University of Colorado, another for Michigan State, and so on. Not only could there be different tables for different universities, but also separate tables could be developed for males and females, and perhaps for different departments (i.e., English, psychology) within the same university. It all depends on how the specific admission decisions are made.

The real advantage of utilizing expectancy tables is that they give people a simple way of understanding the relationship between test scores and probable levels of success. This book stresses the use of test information in decision making, and providing an individual with one or more relevant expectancy tables may assist that person in making a better decision.

Although expectancy tables have many useful facets, we must be careful when interpreting information from expectancy tables. First, since correlational data can be somewhat unstable from sample to sample, it is important that the sample sizes be fairly large. As with other norms, errors due to sampling could make an important difference in how the data are interpreted. A second factor is the magnitude of correlation

Table 5-7   EXPECTANCY TABLE FOR TABLE 5-6

	F	D	C	B	A	Total
40				.25	.75	1.00
37–39			.23	.51	.26	1.00
34–36		.09	.42	.40	.09	1.00
31–33		.25	.43	.32		1.00
28–30	.08	.36	.38	.18		1.00
25–27	.27	.43	.30			1.00
24	.75	.25				
	F	D	C	B	A	

Grade in Statistics

between the two variables. If the magnitude is high, then we could put more faith in the probabilities in the expectancy table. If the correlation between test scores and success is fairly low, the expectancy table may not be very useful. Finally, one needs to realize that the patterns of relationship between predictors and criteria can change over the years. Also, since there are probably a variety of factors that influence outcomes, it would be wise to not be too discouraged if expectancy tables suggest a low probability of performing well or to be overly confident if the probabilities are high.

Setting Standards and Cutoffs

The use of norms in interpreting test scores usually involves comparing persons. That is, most norm-based scores tell you where you stand with reference to some group of people (i.e., the norm group). Another important basis for interpreting test scores is in relation to standards. That is, rather than finding out how you stand compared with others, it might be useful to compare your performance on a test with some external standard. If most people in a class get F on a test, and you get a D–, your relative performance is good (i.e., a norm-based score that compared you with your classmates would be quite high), but your absolute level of performance is quite poor.

Educational psychologists have devoted a great deal of attention to the development of standards for interpreting test scores (for a sampling of the extensive literature on this topic, see Cizek, 1993; Fischer & King, 1995; Hambleton, 1994). In contrast to norm-referenced tests, which assess your performance relative to other individuals, criterion-referenced tests assess your performance in comparison with some standard or set of standards. For example, if I am teaching a statistics course, I might develop a list of topics and techniques that I expect each student to master and then assess their ability to meet these standards. Although the idea of criterion-referenced test interpretation is both simple and sensible, the technical problems in developing good criterion-referenced tests have turned out to be formidable (Cizek, 1993; Hambleton, 1994). In our view, psychometrically sound criterion-referenced testing is more challenging and more demanding than sound norm-referenced testing. The problem of specifying sensible standards and determining whether people meet or exceed them has not yet been fully resolved, especially in the contexts where this type of testing is more widely applied (i.e., assessments by teachers in the classroom).

A variation on the theme of setting standards is the determination of cutoff scores. In many settings, large numbers of individuals take tests (e.g., civil service examinations), and it is necessary to set cutoffs that determine who passes and who fails the test, for accepting or rejecting applicants or for deciding which individuals should receive further assessment. For example, when jobs such as firefighter or police officer become available, it is common to have many more applicants than jobs. It is also common to start with a written examination and then proceed with a more intensive, and expensive, assessment procedure for those who exceed the cutoff score.

The process of setting cutoff scores on tests involves a complex set of legal, professional, and psychometric issues (Cascio, Alexander, & Barrett, 1988). A variety of methods have been proposed, some of which are quite complex. The most widely accepted, the Angoff method, is, however, quite simple. This method uses expert judges to rate for each test item the probability that a barely qualified or competent person will answer it correctly. For example, an expert examining a test for firefighters might judge that a barely competent firefighter would have a one in four chance of answering a particularly difficult item correctly, thereby giving it a rating of .25. The cutoff score for the test is determined by the average of the item scores. If a barely competent person would be expected to answer about half of the items correctly, the score needed to pass the test will be at least 50%.

CRITICAL DISCUSSION:

Should IQ Scores of Black Examinees Be Based on White Norms?

Scores on tests of general intelligence are often expressed in terms of an intelligence quotient (IQ). The IQ is a norm-based score that compares an individual's score with the scores in a particular normative population. Although there is some variation in the scales employed, most tests that report IQs employ a score distribution with a mean of 100 and a standard deviation of 15. Thus, an IQ of 110 indicates that the individual scored better than average (approximately in the 75th percentile). Scores below 100 indicate below-average performance.

One of the most serious controversies in the field of intelligence testing has to do with differences in the scores obtained by white and black examinees. The average score reported for blacks tends to be lower by about 15 points than the average score reported for whites. The reasons for the differences are the subject of considerable research and debate, but the implication is clear: More blacks will be labeled below average in intelligence than whites. Some critics have suggested that this difference in scores in part reflects the use of inappropriate norm groups (Williams, 1971). In particular, if scores of black examinees are compared with norms based almost exclusively on a white norm sample, the scores will give a biased, unrepresentative indication of blacks' performance.

Table 5.8   POSSIBLE NORMATIVE INTERPRETATIONS
OF A TEST OF BUSINESS KNOWLEDGE

Norm group	Percentile rank
General population	85th
College population	60th
Business majors	48th
Successful businesspersons	35th

Two facts are worth noting in the debate on test norms. If the (largely white) population norms are used to evaluate test scores, more than half of the blacks tested will be labeled below average. On the other hand, if scores of black examinees are compared only with scores of other blacks, one-half of all blacks will be labeled above average and one-half will be labeled below average. Which of these is correct?

In a sense, the debate over norm groups is misleading because both positions cited here are correct. Population norms indicate how well a person does relative to the population as a whole; subgroup norms indicate how well a person does relative to a particular group. Neither of these indicates the "real" level of intelligence; norm-based scores indicate relative, not absolute, performance. The question in evaluating norm-based scores is not which score is correct but, rather, which score is more useful. An example may help to clarify this point.

If a college student took a test of business knowledge, several different normative interpretations might be possible, some of which are illustrated in Table 5-8. The same test score might look quite good when compared with the general population (85th percentile), but it might look bad when compared with successful businesspersons (35th percentile). If this student were applying for admission to an MBA program, comparisons with business majors would be useful. On the other hand, comparisons with the general population would be most useful in answering the question "How much does this person know about business?"

In our opinion, the choice of norm group does not have a pivotal impact on the IQ controversy. The norm group employed does not define the meaning of test scores; rather, each norm group provides another vantage point for interpreting test scores. In deciding whether IQ scores of black examinees should be based on white norms, you first need to determine what it is you want to know. If you want to know how a person did compared with black examinees, use black norms. If you want to know how a person did compared with white examinees, use white norms. Finally, if you want to know how a person did compared with the rest of the people who took the test, you should use norms based on the general population.

SUMMARY

Test scores can be difficult to interpret in their raw score form; knowing that a student answered 62 questions correctly on a multiple-choice test, for example, doesn't necessarily tell you much. To interpret test scores sensibly, one needs to consider other types of information, such as the total number of test items or the performance of other similar individuals who took the same test. Linear transformations, such as the z score or the T score, provide a simple means for comparing an individual's score with the scores obtained by others. Positive z scores (or T scores above 50) indicate above-average performance, and the larger the z (or T) is, the better one's relative performance. Area transformations such as the percentile rank or the stanine provide another simple way of describing a person's relative performance.

Alternate forms are available for many widely used tests, and it is important to guarantee that scores on different forms can be interpreted similarly. A vast and complex body of research examines equating methods, but the basic principles are quite simple. Test-equating studies involve administering parts or all of several different forms to the same set of examinees and comparing their performance. When test forms are well equated, examinees should receive essentially the same scores on any form of the test.

Norms are critical to the interpretation of test scores. A variety of types of norms exists, and more than one set of norms might be used in interpreting test scores. Expectancy tables represent a special type of normative information, which can be used to illustrate the meaning of scores on tests used in admissions, personnel selection, and a variety of other individual and institutional decisions.

PROBLEMS AND SOLUTIONS—RECAP

The Problem

Dan and Alice are collaborating on a research project that involves administering personality inventory designed to measure shyness to high-school children in Wisconsin and Colorado. Participants read 100 statements (e.g., "You would rather work alone than work in a group") and indicate whether they agree or disagree with each. In Wisconsin, Dan uses an older version of the inventory in which students respond to these statements using a five-point scale, where 1 = Strongly Disagree and 5 = Strongly Agree. In Colorado, Alice uses the current version of the inventory that uses the same items, but a different response scale, specifically: where 1 = Strongly Disagree and 7 = Strongly Agree

Suppose a student in Wisconsin receives a score of 4.0 on a five-point scale. What is the equivalent score on the seven-point scale used in Colorado?

A Solution

If the samples in Colorado and Wisconsin are reasonably similar in terms of variables that are relevant to shyness, it is relatively easy to translate scores from one scale to another. There are two things we need to know:

1. Are the samples in fact reasonably equivalent? For example, if the Wisconsin study is carried out in a small-town high school and the Colorado study is carried out in a specialized school for drama and the performing arts, it might be reasonable to believe that students in these two different schools truly differ in their level of shyness and that scores in the two samples are difficult to equate. However, if they are at least reasonably similar samples, it might be relatively easy to equate scores on the two scales.
2. You must know the mean and the standard deviation in each sample. For example, if the mean in Wisconsin is 4.5, a score of 4.0 might indicate relatively low levels of shyness. In order to establish equivalent scores on both scales, you need some concrete frame of reference for interpreting individual scale scores.

Suppose that the mean and standard deviation of the five-point scale are 3.2 and .85, respectively. A score of 4.0 on this scale is equivalent to a standard score (i.e., a z score) of .94.

That is,

$$Z = (4.0 - 3.2)/.85 = .94$$

If the mean and standard deviation on the seven-point scale are 4.5 and .96, respectively, a z score of .94 on this scale is equivalent to a raw score of 5.40.
That is,

$$\text{Raw score equivalent of } z = 4.54 + (.96^* .94) = 5.44$$

Suppose, however, that the two samples were not equivalent (as in our example of a small-town high school versus a school for the performing arts. In that case, it would be better to equate the scale scores on the basis of normative information. So, for example, you might go to the test manual or to published reports to get the best estimate of the mean and standard deviation of each scale. Once you have these figures, you can use the process just laid out. (See also Table 5-2) to transform scores on the five-point scale into equivalent values on the seven-point scale, and vice versa.

KEY TERMS

Age norm   method of describing scores in terms of the average or typical age of the respondents achieving a specific test score

Area transformation   method of transformation based on areas under the normal curve that can change some important characteristics of scores

Criterion-referenced test   test in which you are scored in relation to a specific standard or criterion, rather than having your performance compared with the performance of other examinees

Equating   process of ensuring that identical scores on different versions of a test have the same meaning

Expectancy table   table showing the expected score on some criterion variable (e.g., performance on the job), given your score on a test

Linear transformation   method of transforming test scores to produce a simpler or more useful scale of measurement without changing the essential characteristics of the scores

Norm-referenced test   test in which your score is determined by comparing your own performance with the performance of others

Percentile rank   type of norm that describes a score in terms of the percentage of a norm group who achieves that score or a lower one

Stanine   a simple area transformation that places scores on a nine-point scale (standard nines)

Reliability:
The Consistency
of Test Scores

6

Neither physical measurements nor psychological tests are completely consistent; if some attribute of a person is measured twice, the two scores are likely to differ. For example, if a person's height is measured twice in the same day, a value of 5'10 3/16" may be obtained the first time and a value of 5'9 10/16" the second. A person taking the Graduate Record Examination (GRE) twice might obtain a score of 1060 in the fall and 990 in the spring. A person taking two different forms of a test of general intelligence might obtain an IQ of 110 on one test and 114 on the other. Thus, test scores and other measures generally show some inconsistency. On the other hand, most test scores are not completely random. For example, one is unlikely to obtain a reading of 98.6° using one fever thermometer and a reading of 103° using another. Similarly, a child is unlikely to obtain a score of 95% on a well-constructed reading test and a score of 40% on a second, similar test. Methods of studying, defining, and estimating the consistency or inconsistency of test scores form the central focus of research and theory dealing with the reliability of test scores.

As stated in Chapter 4, measurement is the process of assigning numbers to persons so that some attribute of each person is accurately reflected in some attribute of the numbers. The reliability or consistency of test scores is critically important in determining whether a test can provide good measurement. For example, suppose that you take a test of spatial visualization ability that provides a different score every time you take the test; sometimes your scores are very high, sometimes low, and sometimes moderate. Since spatial visualization ability is a fairly stable characteristic, this test cannot possibly be a reliable measure. The scores vary substantially, even though the attribute that the test is designed to measure does not. In other words, in this case, the numbers do not reflect the attribute they are being used to measure.

The practical importance of consistency in test scores is a direct result of the fact that tests are used to make important decisions about people. For example, many high schools require that students pass a competency test before they are allowed to graduate. Imagine what would happen if test scores were so inconsistent that many students who received low scores on one form of the test received high scores on another form of the same test. The decision to either grant or withhold a diploma might depend more on which form of the test the student took than on his or her mastery of the high school curriculum.

This chapter presents a basic definition of test reliability and describes methods used in estimating the reliability or consistency of test scores. First, we describe sources of consistency and inconsistency in test scores. Next, we present a short outline of the theory of test reliability. Finally, we discuss methods of estimating the reliability of test scores, particularly as they relate to the different sources of consistency or inconsistency described in the first section of this chapter. Questions regarding the use of information about test reliability and factors affecting reliability are discussed in Chapter 7.

PROBLEMS AND SOLUTIONS—EVALUATING A TEST

The Problem

You have applied for a job, and you are asked to take a 20-item test designed to measure your ability to think creatively. The items seem all over the board in terms of what they are designed to measure, and although you think that might be OK for a creativity test, you are still concerned that the test might produce scores that are meaningless. You search the Web for information about this test and find a research report that shows that the items are not highly correlated, with interitem correlations ranging from −.07 to .12, and averaging .08. Should you be concerned about the possibility that this test will produce meaningless scores?

SOURCES OF CONSISTENCY AND INCONSISTENCY IN TEST SCORES

In understanding factors that affect the consistency of test scores, it is useful to ask "Why do test scores vary at all?" For example, if I give a spelling test to a group of fourth graders, what factors are likely to lead to variability in test scores? Thorndike (1949) prepared a list of possible sources of variability in scores on a particular test. This list, presented in Table 6-1, is a useful starting place for understanding factors that may affect the consistency or inconsistency of test scores.

The first category of factors that affects test scores lists some lasting and general characteristics of individuals. For example, we would expect some children to do consistently better than others on a spelling test because they are good spellers or because they are skillful in following instructions and in taking tests. The second category lists lasting but specific characteristics of individuals. For example, some children who are generally poor spellers might nevertheless know how to spell many of the particular words included in the test. If these children were given another test, made up of different words, they might receive very different scores. The third category lists temporary but general characteristics of individuals. For example, a child who is ill or very tired might do poorly this time around but might receive much higher scores if he or she is

Table 6-1 POSSIBLE SOURCES OF VARIABILITY IN SCORES ON A PARTICULAR TEST

I. Lasting and general characteristics of the individual
   A. Level of ability on one or more general traits that operate in a number of tests
   B. General skills and techniques of taking tests (test wiseness or test-naïveté)
   C. General ability to comprehend instructions
II. Lasting but specific characteristics of the individual
   A. Specific to the test as a whole
      1. Individual level of ability on traits required in this test but not in others
      2. Knowledge and skills specific to a particular form of test items
      3. Stable response sets (e.g., to mark A options more frequently than other options of multiple-choice items, to mark true-false items "true" when undecided)
   B. Specific to particular test items
      1. The chance element determining whether the individual knows a particular fact
      2. Item types with which various examinees are unequally familiar (cf. item II.A.2 above)
III. Temporary but general characteristics of the individual (factors affecting performance on many or all tests at a particular time)
   A. Health
   B. Fatigue
   C. Motivation
   D. Emotional strain
   E. Test-wiseness (partly lasting; cf. item I.B. above)
   F. Understanding of mechanics of testing
   G. External conditions of heat, light, ventilation, etc.
IV. Temporary and specific characteristics of the individual
   A. Specific to a test as a whole
      1. Comprehension of the specific test task
      2. Specific tricks or techniques of dealing with the particular test materials
      3. Level of practice on the specific skills involved (especially in psychomotor tests)
      4. Momentary mind-set for a particular test
   B. Specific to particular test items
      1. Fluctuations and idiosyncrasies of human memory
      2. Unpredictable fluctuations in attention or accuracy, superimposed on the general level of performance characteristic of the individual
V. Systematic or change factors affecting the administration of the test or the appraisal of test performance
   A. Conditions of testing: adherence to time limits, freedom from distractions, clarity of instructions, etc.
   B. Interaction of personality, sex, or race of examiner with that of examinee that facilitates or inhibits performance
   C. Unreliability or bias in grading or rating performance
VI. Variance not otherwise accounted for (chance)
   A. Luck in selection of answers by sheer guessing
   B. Momentary distraction

Source: Adapted from Thorndike, R. L. (1949), *Personnel Selection.* Copyright © 1949 by John Wiley & Sons, Inc. Reproduced by permission.

tested when healthy and well rested. The fourth category in the table lists temporary and specific characteristics of individuals. For example, the test may contain the words *Baltimore, Milwaukee,* and *Seattle.* A child who took the test shortly after looking at the sports section of the newspaper might have a temporary advantage on such a test. The fifth category lists some aspects of the testing situation that could lead to inconsistency in test scores. For example, if half the class took the test in a noisy, poorly lit room, we might expect their scores to be lower than they would have obtained under normal conditions. Finally, the sixth category in the table lists some chance factors that may affect test scores. Some of the variability in scores will be due strictly to luck.

In most testing applications, we are interested in lasting and general characteristics of persons, such as spelling ability. Thus, in most cases, the first category in Table 6-1 represents a source of consistency in test scores, and all the remaining categories represent sources of unwanted inconsistency. However, this breakdown is not always quite so simple. For example, we might be interested in measuring a specific characteristic, such as a child's ability to spell *Baltimore* on May 30, 2003. In this case, we might conclude that elements from categories I through IV would all contribute to consistency in measurement and that inconsistency in the child's performance on that particular item at the particular time the child is tested would largely be determined by elements from categories V and VI. The determination of whether each factor listed in the table contributes to consistency or inconsistency in measurement thus depends largely on what one is trying to measure. As will be seen in the sections that follow, the definition of *reliability,* as well as the methods used to estimate the reliability of test scores, ultimately depends on one's definition of precisely what attribute is being measured and of the sources of inconsistency in the measurement of that attribute.

GENERAL MODEL OF RELIABILITY

A perfect measure would consistently assign numbers to the attributes of persons according to some well-specified rule (e.g., if John is more anxious than Teresa, he should receive a higher score on an anxiety test than she does). In practice, our measures are never perfectly consistent. Theories of test reliability have been developed to estimate the effects of inconsistency on the accuracy of psychological measurement. The basic starting point for almost all theories of test reliability is the idea that test scores reflect the influence of two sorts of factors:

1. Factors that contribute to consistency: stable characteristics of the individual or the attribute that one is trying to measure
2. Factors that contribute to inconsistency: features of the individual or the situation that can affect test scores but have nothing to do with the attribute being measured

This conceptual breakdown is typically represented by the simple equation

$$\text{Observed test score} = \text{True score} + \text{Errors of measurement} \qquad [6\text{-}1]$$

Or, more succinctly,

$$X = T + e \qquad\qquad [6\text{-}2]$$

where

X = score on the test
T = true score
e = error of measurement

There is an important distinction between the concept of true score as applied in Equation 6-2 and the notion of ultimate truth or perfect measurement. Thus, true scores on a measure of anxiety are not an indication of a person's "true" or "real" level of anxiety. Rather, the true score represents a combination of all the factors that lead to consistency in the measurement of anxiety (Cronbach, Gleser, Nanda, & Rajaratnam, 1972; Stanley, 1971). As a result, the components that make up the true-score part of a test will vary, depending on what is being measured. Consider, for example, a test of mechanical aptitude given to a U.S. Air Force mechanic in a noisy, poorly lit room. As indicated in Table 6-2, the stressful conditions of measurement could be considered as either part of the true score or part of the error component, depending on whether the test is intended to measure mechanical aptitude in general or mechanical performance under stressful conditions.

Errors in measurement represent discrepancies between scores obtained on tests and the corresponding true scores. Thus,

$$e = X - T \qquad\qquad [6\text{-}3]$$

The goal of reliability theory is to estimate errors in measurement and to suggest ways of improving tests so that errors are minimized.

The central assumption of reliability theory is that measurement errors are essentially random. This does not mean that errors arise from random or mysterious processes. On the contrary, a sizable negative error in a score that a person received on the GRE could easily be accounted for if it were known that the person (1) had stayed up all night, (2) had a hangover, (3) was sitting next to a noisy air conditioner during

Table 6-2   DIFFERENT DEFINITIONS OF TRUE SCORE WHEN AN APTITUDE TEST IS GIVEN UNDER
STRESSFUL CONDITIONS

	Test is used to measure	
	Mechanical performance in general	*Mechanical performance under stressful conditions*
Individual's mechanical aptitude	True score	True score
Stressful conditions of measurement	Error	True score
All other irrelevant sources of variability	Error	Error

the test, and (4) used the wrong part of the form to mark the answers. For any individual, an error in measurement is not a completely random event. However, across a large number of individuals, the causes of measurement error are assumed to be so varied and complex that measurement errors act as random variables. Thus, a theory that assumes that measurement errors are essentially random may provide a pretty good description of their effects.

If errors have the essential characteristics of random variables, then it is reasonable to assume that errors are equally likely to be positive or negative and that they are not correlated with true scores or with errors on other tests. That is, it is assumed that

1. Mean error of measurement $= 0$.
2. True scores and errors are uncorrelated: $r_{te} = 0$.
3. Errors on different measures are uncorrelated: $r_{e_1e_2} = 0$.

On the basis of these three assumptions, an extensive theory of test reliability has been developed (Gulliksen, 1950; F. M. Lord & Novick, 1968). Several results can be derived from this theory that have important implications for measurement. For example, Table 6-1 lists sources of variability in test scores that might contribute to the consistency or inconsistency of measurement. Reliability theory provides a similar breakdown by showing that the variance of obtained scores is simply the sum of the variance of true scores plus the variance of errors of measurement. That is,

$$\sigma_X^2 = \sigma_T^2 + \sigma_e^2$$

[6-4]

In effect, Equation 6-4 suggests that test scores vary as the result of two factors: (1) variability in true scores and (2) variability due to errors of measurement. If errors are responsible for much of the variability observed in test scores, test scores will be inconsistent; if the test is given again, scores may not remain stable. On the other hand, if errors of measurement have little effect on test scores, the test reflects mainly those consistent aspects of performance we have labeled true score.

The reliability coefficient (r_{xx}) provides an index of the relative influence of true and error scores on obtained test scores.[1] In its general form, the reliability coefficient is defined as the ratio of true score variance to the total variance of test scores. That is,

$$r_{xx} = \frac{\sigma_T^2}{\sigma_T^2 + \sigma_e^2}$$

[6-5]

or, equivalently,

$$r_{xx} = \frac{\sigma_T^2}{\sigma_T^2 + \sigma_e^2}$$

[6-6]

[1]Reliability theory deals with population parameters (e.g., ρ_{xy}) rather than sample statistics (e.g., r_{xy}). However, for the sake of simplicity, reliability formulas are presented in terms of r rather than ρ.

There are several interpretations of the reliability coefficient. Perhaps the most straightforward interpretation is that r_{xx} indicates the proportion of variance in test scores that is due to or accounted for by variability in true scores.

SIMPLE METHODS OF ESTIMATING RELIABILITY

The goal of estimating reliability is to determine how much of the variability in test scores is due to errors in measurement and how much is due to variability in true scores. The parallel test model suggests a strategy for accomplishing this goal. According to the parallel test model, it might be possible to develop two forms of a test that are equivalent in the sense that a person's true score on form A would be identical to his or her true score on form B. If both forms of the test were administered to a number of people, differences between scores on form A and form B could be due to errors in measurement only. Thus, if scores on the two forms showed large differences, measurement errors were a major source of variability in test scores. On the other hand, if scores on both tests were highly similar, measurement errors were small and the test was highly reliable.[2]

The parallel test model provides a conceptual solution for estimating reliability but does not necessarily provide a practical solution, because strictly parallel tests are difficult to develop. Four practical strategies have been developed that incorporate many features of the parallel test method and that provide workable methods of estimating test reliability.

1. Test-retest methods
2. Alternate forms methods
3. Split-half methods
4. Internal consistency methods

The methods described here are most likely to be useful in situations when one is interested in measuring lasting, general characteristics of individuals, such as abilities or traits. In these situations, the attributes of the persons being measured represent the sole source of true-score variance, and all other factors that affect measurement combine to represent the error component. As will be discussed in a later section, this sort of testing application is typical but not universal. In many situations, the tester must identify explicitly the purpose and the uses of measurement to determine which factors affect true scores and error. In more complex testing applications, reliability theories that break a measure down into true-score and random-error components may not be sufficient; a more general and complex theory is presented later in this chapter. Nevertheless, for many testing applications, simple methods based on classical reliability theory may be quite useful. Several of these methods are presented in the following sections.

---

[2]The basic equations of reliability theory can also be derived from several models that do not depend on the concept of parallel tests (F. M. Lord & Novick, 1968; Nunnally, 1982).

Test-Retest Method

The test-retest method is one of the oldest and, at least at first glance, one of the most sensible methods of estimating the reliability of test scores. Reliability is concerned with the consistency of test scores; the test-retest method directly assesses the degree to which test scores are consistent from one test administration to the next. The test-retest method involves (1) administering a test to a group of individuals, (2) readministering that same test to the same group at some later time, and (3) correlating the first set of scores with the second. The correlation between scores on the first test and scores on the retest is used to estimate the reliability of the test.

The rationale behind this method of estimating reliability is disarmingly simple. Since the same test is administered twice and every test is parallel with itself, differences between scores on the test and scores on the retest should be due solely to measurement error. This sort of argument is quite probably true for many physical measurements. For example, if a tape measure is used to measure the length of a room and is then used to measure the same room a week later, any difference between the two measurements is likely to be entirely due to measurement error. Unfortunately, this argument is often inappropriate for psychological measurement, since it is often impossible to consider the second administration of a test a parallel measure to the first. Thus, it may be inaccurate to treat a test-retest correlation as a measure of reliability.

The second administration of a psychological test might yield systematically different scores than the first administration for several reasons. First, the characteristic or attribute that is being measured may change between the first test and the retest. Consider, for example, a reading test that is administered in September to a class of third graders and then readministered in June. We would expect some change in children's reading ability over that span of time; a low test-retest correlation might reflect real changes in the attribute measured by the test. Second, the experience of taking the test itself can change a person's true score; this is referred to as *reactivity*. For example, students who take a geography test may look up answers they were unsure of after taking the test, thus changing their true knowledge of geography. Likewise, the process of completing an anxiety inventory could serve to increase a person's level of anxiety. Thus, the first test may serve as a catalyst that causes substantial change in true scores from one administration to the next. Third, one must be concerned with carryover effects, particularly if the interval between test and retest is short. When retested, people may remember their original answers, which could affect their answers the second time around.

In addition to the theoretical problems inherent in the test-retest method, there is a practical limitation to this method of estimating reliability. The test-retest method requires two test administrations. Since testing can be time-consuming and expensive, retesting solely for the purpose of estimating reliability may be impractical.

It is common to distinguish between reliability, which is the ratio of true to observed variance, and temporal stability, which refers to the consistency of test scores over time. If true scores are likely to change over time, this distinction is both theoretically and practically important. Thus, test-retest correlations are often thought of as stability coefficients rather than reliability coefficients. However, even when this distinction is drawn, the test-retest technique has problems. For example, it is not clear whether carryover effects should be regarded as sources of measurement error or as sources of real stability (or instability) in measurement. Nor is it clear whether reactivity effects always contribute to true scores or to error. It could be argued that carryover and reactivity effects are a natural aspect of the attribute being measured and should be taken into account in estimating stability. On the other hand, these effects may inflate (or deflate) one's estimate of the true stability of test scores, thus yielding inaccurate estimates of both reliability and stability.

The test-retest method is most useful when one is interested in the long-term stability of a measure. For example, research on the accuracy of personnel selection tests is concerned with the ability of the test to predict long-term job performance. Several studies in this area have therefore focused on the temporal stability of job performance measures (Schmidt & Hunter, 1977). The argument here is that short-term variations in job performance represent error when the purpose of the research is to predict performance over the long term.

Alternate Forms Method

The alternate forms method of estimating reliability is, on the surface, the closest approximation to the method suggested by the parallel tests model. The key to this method is the development of alternate test forms that are, to the highest degree possible, equivalent in terms of content, response processes, and statistical characteristics. For example, alternate forms exist for several tests of general intelligence; these alternate forms commonly are regarded as equivalent tests. The alternate forms method of estimating test reliability involves (1) administering one form of the test (e.g., form A) to a group of individuals; (2) at some later time, administering an alternate form of the same test (e.g., form B) to the same group of individuals; and (3) correlating scores on form A with scores on form B. The correlation between scores on the two alternate forms is used to estimate the reliability of the test.

The alternate forms method provides a partial solution to many of the problems inherent in test-retest methods. For example, since the two forms of the test are different, carryover effects are less of a problem, although remembering answers previously given to a similar set of questions may affect responses to the present set of questions. Reactivity effects are also partially controlled; although taking the first test may change responses to the second test, it is reasonable to assume that the effect will not be as strong with alternate forms as with two administrations of the same test. The alternate forms method also may allow one to partially control for real changes over time in the attribute being measured. Since carryover effects are less of a problem here than in the test-retest method, it may not be necessary to use a long interval between test administration. It is feasible to administer the second form immediately after the first, which cannot be done in most test-retest studies.

Although the alternate forms method avoids many of the problems inherent in the test-retest method, this technique still has many drawbacks. For example, since two separate test administrations are required, the alternate forms method could be as expensive and impractical as the test-retest method. Second, it may be difficult and expensive to develop several alternate forms of a test. It is questionable that the expense involved in developing alternate forms and in administering two tests rather than one is justified solely for the purpose of assessing the reliability of the test. In addition, it may be difficult, if not impossible, to guarantee that two alternate forms of a test are, in fact, parallel measures. Thus, if alternate forms are poorly constructed, one might obtain low reliability estimates strictly as a function of the lack of equivalence between the two alternative forms.

Split-Half Methods

Split-half methods of estimating reliability provide a simple solution to the two practical problems that plague the alternate forms method: (1) the difficulty in developing alternate forms and (2) the need for two separate test administrations. The reasoning behind split-half methods is quite straightforward. The simplest way to create two alternate forms of a test is to split the existing test in half and use the two halves as alternate forms. The split-half method of estimating reliability thus involves (1) administering a test to a group of individuals, (2) splitting the test in half, and (3) correlating scores on one half of the test with scores on the other half. The correlation between these two split halves is used in estimating the reliability of the test.[3]

The split-half method avoids many of the theoretical and practical problems inherent in test-retest and alternate forms methods. First, this method allows reliability to be estimated without administering two different tests or administering the same test twice. Thus, whenever a multi-item test is administered, the split-half method could be used to estimate reliability. Since there is only one test administration, carryover effects, reactivity effects, and especially the effects of change over time on true scores are minimized. Inconsistencies in scores obtained on two different halves of a test are therefore likely to reflect inconsistencies in responses to the test itself, rather than changes in the individual that may have occurred between administrations of two alternate forms or between a test and retest.

There are several ways of splitting a test to estimate reliability. For example, a 40-item vocabulary test could be split into two subtests, the first one made up of items 1 through 20 and the second made up of items 21 through 40. One might suspect, however, that responses to the first half would be systematically different from responses to the second half, so that this split would not provide a very good estimate of reliability. For example, many vocabulary tests start with the easiest items and then become progressively more difficult. In addition, a person taking the test might be more fatigued during the second half of the test. In splitting a test, the two halves would need

---

[3]As we will note in Chapter 7, this correlation estimates the reliability of each half-test. Scores on the entire test will be more reliable than scores on either half; the Spearman-Brown formula (see Equation 7-5) is used to estimate the reliability of the total test, given the correlation between the split halves.

to be as similar as possible, both in terms of their content and in terms of the probable state of the respondent. The simplest method of approximating this goal is to adopt an odd-even split, in which the odd-numbered items form one half of the test and the even-numbered items form the other. This arrangement guarantees that each half will contain an equal number of items from the beginning, middle, and end of the original test.

The fact that there are many ways a test could potentially be split is the greatest weakness of the split-half method. Consider, for example, the six-item test shown in Table 6-3. There are ten different ways that this test could be split,[4] and each split yields a somewhat different reliability estimate. In other words, the correlation between half A and half B may vary, depending on how the test is split. The question is, Which is the reliability of the test? Although the idea of forming an odd-even split generally makes sense, this particular method of splitting the test is somewhat arbitrary; there is no guarantee that the reliability coefficient obtained from this particular split will be the most reasonable or accurate estimate of the relative contribution of true scores and errors of measurement to the variability of test scores. Since it is difficult to make a strong argument in favor of one particular method of splitting a given test over another, it is difficult to decide which split-half reliability estimate to use.

Internal Consistency Methods

Internal consistency methods of estimating test reliability appear to be quite different from the methods presented so far. Internal consistency methods estimate the reliability of a test based solely on the number of items in the test (k) and the average

Table 6-3   TEN POSSIBLE WAYS OF SPLITTING A SIX-ITEM TEST

Test items, half A	Test items, half B	Reliability estimate
1,2,3	4,5,6	.64
1,2,4	3,5,6	.68
1,2,5	3,4,6	.82
1,2,6	3,4,5	.79
1,3,4	2,5,6	.88
1,4,5	2,3,6	.81
1,5,6	2,3,4	.82
2,3,5	1,4,6	.72
2,4,5	1,3,6	.71
2,4,6	1,3,5	.74

[4]The number of possible splits rises geometrically as the length of the test increases. There are, for example, 126 different ways of splitting a ten-item test into two five-item halves.

intercorrelation among test items ($\bar{r}_{ij}$). These two factors can be combined in the following formula to estimate the reliability of the test:

$$r_{xx} = \frac{k(\bar{r}_{ij})}{1 + (K - 1)\bar{r}_{ij}} \qquad [6\text{-}7]$$

Thus, the internal consistency method involves (1) administering a test to a group of individuals, (2) computing the correlations among all items and computing the average of those intercorrelations, and (3) using Formula 6-7 or an equivalent formula to estimate reliability.[5] This formula gives a standardized estimate; raw score formulas that take into account the variance of different test items may provide slightly different estimates of internal consistency reliability.

There are both mathematical and conceptual ways of demonstrating the links between internal consistency methods and the methods of estimating reliability discussed so far. First, internal consistency methods are mathematically linked to the split-half method. In particular, coefficient alpha, which represents the most widely used and most general form of internal consistency estimate, represents the mean reliability coefficient one would obtain from all possible split halves. In particular, Cortina (1993) notes that alpha is equal to the mean of the split halves defined by formulas from Rulon (1939) and J. C. Flanagan (1937). In other words, if every possible split-half reliability coefficient for a 30-item test were computed, the average of those reliabilities would be equal to coefficient alpha. The difference between the split-half method and the internal consistency method is, for the most part, a difference in unit of analysis. Split-half methods compare one half-test with another; internal consistency estimates compare each item with every other item.

In understanding the link between internal consistency and the general concept of reliability, it is useful to note that internal consistency methods suggest a fairly simple answer to the question, "Why is a test reliable?" Remember that internal consistency estimates are a function of (1) the number of test items and (2) the average intercorrelation among these test items. If we think of each test item as an observation of behavior, internal consistency estimates suggest that reliability is a function of (1) the number of observations that one makes and (2) the extent to which each item represents an observation of the same thing observed by other test items. For example, if you wanted to determine how good a bowler someone was, you would obtain more reliable information by observing the person bowl many frames than you would by watching the person roll the ball once. You would also obtain a more reliable estimate of that person's skill at bowling from ten observations of the person bowling in typical circumstances than if you watched him bowl three times on a normal alley, then watched him bowl five times in a high-pressure tournament, and then watched him bowl twice on a warped alley. If every item on the test measures essentially the same thing as all other items and if the number of items is large, internal consistency methods suggest that the test will be reliable.

[5]Formula 6-7 yields the standardized alpha. Several similar formulas have been developed by Kuder and Richardson (1937), Cronbach (1951), and others.

RELIABILITY ESTIMATES AND ERROR

Each of the four methods of estimating test reliability implies that different sources of variability in test scores might contribute to errors of measurement. Some of these are listed in Table 6-4. As the table shows, both the split-half and the internal consistency methods define measurement error strictly in terms of consistency or inconsistency in the content of a test. Test-retest and alternate forms methods, both of which require two test administrations, define measurement error in terms of three general factors: (1) the consistency or inconsistency of test content (in the test-retest method, content is always consistent); (2) changes in examinees over time; and (3) the effects of the first test on responses to the second test. Thus, although each method is concerned with reliability, each defines true score and error in a somewhat different fashion. Schmidt, Le, and Ilies (2003) note that all of these sources of error can operate simultaneously, and that their combined effects can be substantially larger than reliability estimates that take only one or two effects into account.

The principal advantage of internal consistency methods is their practicality. Since only one test administration is required, it is possible to estimate internal consistency reliability every time the test is given. Although split-half methods can be computationally simpler, the widespread availability of computers makes it easy to compute coefficient alpha, regardless of the test length or the number of examinees. It therefore is possible to compute coefficient alpha whenever a test is used in a new situation or population. A low value for alpha could indicate that scores on the test will not be highly consistent and therefore may form a poor basis for describing the person or for making decisions about the person. However, as noted in the next section, an internal consistency estimate does not necessarily represent the reliability of a test (see also Schmidt, Le, & Ilies, 2003). Indeed, test reliability often depends more on what one is trying to do with test scores than on the scores themselves.

Table 6-4   SOURCES OF VARIABILITY THAT CONTRIBUTE TO ERRORS IN MEASUREMENT

	Method of estimating reliability			
	Test-retest	*Alternate forms*	*Split-half*	*Internal consistency*
Content factors		Inconsistency of test content Nonparallel tests	Inconsistency of test content Nonparallel halves	Inconsistency of test content
Effects of first test on examinee Temporal factors	Reactivity Carryover True change over time	Reactivity Carryover True change over time		

THE GENERALIZABILITY OF TEST SCORES

Reliability theory tends to classify all the factors that may affect test scores into two components, true scores and random errors of measurement. Although this sort of broad classification may be useful for studying physical measurements, it is not necessarily the most useful way of thinking about psychological measurement (Lumsden, 1976). The most serious weakness in applying classical reliability theory is probably the concept of error. As Table 6-4 suggests, the factors that determine the amount of measurement error are different for internal consistency methods than for test-retest or alternate forms methods. We typically think of the reliability coefficient as a ratio of true score to true score plus error, but if the makeup of the true score and error parts of a measure change when we change our estimation procedures, something is seriously wrong.

The theory of generalizability presented by Cronbach and his colleagues (1972) represents an alternate approach to measuring and studying the consistency of test scores. In reliability theory, the central question is how much random error there is in our measures. In generalizability theory, the focus is on our ability to generalize from one set of measures (e.g., a score on an essay test) to a set of other plausible measures (e.g., the same essay graded by other teachers). The central question in generalizability theory concerns the conditions over which one can generalize, or under what sorts of conditions would we expect results that are either similar to or different from those obtained here? Generalizability theory attacks this question by systematically studying the many sources of consistency and inconsistency in test scores.

Suppose that we wish to measure an individual's need for dominance, using a projective test administered by an individual clinician. We are concerned about the possibility that test results would be unreliable, and so we have three different psychologists test the person and, furthermore, repeat the test three times with each psychologist. Scores from such a procedure might look something like those depicted in Table 6-5 and Figure 6-1.

Is this test reliable? It depends on what we mean by reliability. For example, both psychologists B and C give fairly consistent scores over time, but C consistently differs

Table 6-5   TEST RESULTS FOR THREE DIFFERENT PSYCHOLOGISTS, EACH OF WHOM TESTS THE INDIVIDUAL THREE TIMES

Time of testing	Psychologist			Average
	A	*B*	*C*	
January	77[a]	88	70	83
March	85	86	74	81.6
May	92	84	72	82.6
Average	84.6	86	72	

[a]Scores on this hypothetical test range from 1 to 100.

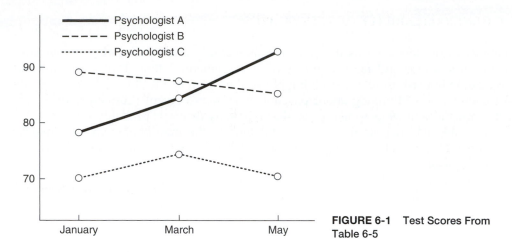

FIGURE 6-1   Test Scores From Table 6-5

from psychologists A and B. The three psychologists agree best in March but agree less well in January or May.

It would be possible to deal with the data in Table 6-5 using classical reliability theory. That is, we could simply treat the inconsistencies in test scores as random error. However, it might be more informative to examine systematic differences between psychologists or between times and to use this information describing circumstances under which one can or cannot generalize test scores. The statistical technique *analysis of variance* (see Cronbach et al., 1972, and Maxwell and Delaney 1990, for detailed descriptions of this method) provides a method for measuring the systematic effects of several variables (psychologists, times, etc.) on the consistency of measurements.

The analysis of variance provides statistical estimates of the variability in test scores associated with systematic differences in the ratings assigned by psychologists and differences in the ratings obtained in January, March, and May. Figure 6-2 illustrates the breakdown of the variability of test scores in Table 6-5 into systematic and unsystematic sources. Average test scores in January, March, and May were quite similar. Therefore, the variability due to the time of testing is small. On the other hand,

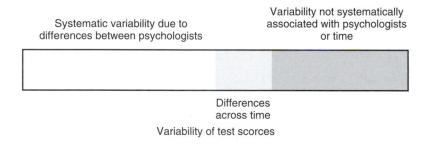

FIGURE 6-2   Systematic and Asystematic Variability in the Test Scores Shown in Table 6-5

there were consistent differences between psychologist C and psychologists A and B. As a result, a larger proportion of the variability in scores is associated with differences between psychologists. Finally, a good deal of the variability is not systematically associated either with the psychologists or the time of measurement.

Analysis of the variance in test scores suggests that scores can be more accurately generalized over time (in the table, average scores obtained at each measurement were quite similar) than other psychologists (psychologists differed in terms of their average scores). Thus, the question of whether this test is reliable would be answered differently if one is concerned with the stability of scores over time, rather than with the stability of scores obtained by different psychologists.

Advantages of Generalizability Theory. Generalizability theory has been the focus of a great deal of research, but, until fairly recently, it was not often used to deal with practical testing problems. Several reviews and texts (e.g., Brennan, 1983; Shavelson & Webb, 1981; Shavelson, Webb, & Rowley, 1989) have brought generalizability theory to the attention of a wider audience, and the techniques of generalizability theory are being applied in a wider variety of research areas. We believe that the primary advantage of generalizability theory over the classical theory is conceptual rather than statistical. That is, generalizability theory forces you to think of reliability as a characteristic of the use of test scores, rather than as a characteristic of the scores themselves. For example, this theory recognizes that you can often make more reliable decisions about people's relative standing (e.g., comparing two people in terms of verbal ability) than about their absolute level on a trait or attribute. Thus, as we have noted earlier, the same set of test scores might have several different levels of reliability, depending on the intended use of the scores. We believe that the uses of test scores are much more important than the scores themselves and that generalizability theory is therefore a considerable improvement over the classical theory of reliability that has dominated the history of psychometrics.

The second major advantage of generalizability theory is that it provides answers to a variety of practical questions that cannot be answered using classical reliability theory. For example, companies that interview job applicants often have the applicant talk to several individuals, each of whom asks several questions. One company might use four people who each ask five questions, whereas another company might use two people who each ask ten questions. Generalizability theory could be used to determine which strategy for combining the number of persons and questions would yield the most reliable assessments.

CRITICAL DISCUSSION:

Generalizability and Reliability Theory

Cronbach and others (1972) note that classical reliability theory, which breaks test scores down into true-score and random-error components, is simply a special case of generalizability theory. The difference between the two theories is that the generalizability approach recognizes that error is not always random and that it often is useful to identify specific, systematic sources of inconsistency in measurement. Generalizability theory identifies both systematic and random sources of inconsistency that may contribute to errors of measurement.[6]

Classical theory is probably most useful in situations in which well-developed tests are given under highly standardized conditions. For example, college entrance examinations, such as the Scholastic Assessment Tests (SAT), are given under nearly identical conditions nationwide. As long as test administration procedures are followed, it is unlikely that the location, the test administrator, or the time of year at which the test is administered will have substantial effects on test scores. Inconsistencies between one administration and the next are likely to be small, and, when they do occur, they are likely to be a function of the test itself and of the individuals responding to the test. Thus, the assumptions that consistency in test scores is due to the true-score component and that inconsistencies reflect essentially random error are probably reasonable.

The more complex methods associated with generalizability theory are likely to be more useful when (1) the conditions of measurement are likely to affect test scores or (2) test scores are to be used for several different purposes. For example, in almost every type of measurement involving human judgment (e.g., interviews, ratings, many clinical tests), there is the possibility of bias. Some interviewers give higher scores to men than to women; attractive people often receive more favorable ratings on a number of dimensions than unattractive people; a clinician whose orientation is Freudian may give a different interpretation of a specific incident than a behaviorally oriented clinician. The point is, human judges could be considered "conditions of measurement," and in a wide variety of circumstances, one might expect systematic differences in human judgment. We might also expect that measures of some attributes and traits will be more strongly affected by the physical conditions of measurement than others. For example, a person might receive different scores on a color discrimination test taken in a room with fluorescent light than in a room with natural light. Finally, we might expect some measures to be more stable over time than others (e.g., measures of basic values as opposed to opinions regarding the outcome of a future sporting event). If scores differ systematically according to when, where, or how the test was taken, these differences will affect the generalizability of test scores. They are not, however, random sources of error, and test theories that treat them as such will lead to erroneous conclusions.

Generalizability theory encourages us to ask questions such as "In what situations is this test reliable?" rather than simply asking whether a test is any good. According to this theory, a test could be reliable for some purposes, but quite unreliable for others. Generalizability theory focuses our attention on what we wish to do with a test, rather than on the test itself.

SUMMARY

Although perfect measures of physical and psychological characteristics would be highly desirable, error-free measurement is impossible; all tests and methods of measurement are subject to some degree of error. Reliability theory provides a method for defining and estimating measurement error in specific testing applications.

In its most basic form, the classic theory of reliability states that all measures are made up of two independent components, true score and error. The reliability coefficient is simply the percentage of the total variance in test scores that is due to the true-score component. A variety of methods have evolved to estimate the reliability of specific tests and measures. These might involve multiple administrations either of the same or of equivalent tests, or they might be based on a single test administration. Internal consistency estimates are the simplest and most practical, and they are the most widely used.

[6]When no systematic differences in test scores are associated with conditions of measurement (e.g., psychologists, time), classical theory and generalizability theory are mathematically identical.

Generalizability theory represents a sophisticated elaboration of the ideas present in the classic theory. Analyses of the generalizability of test scores begin with a description of the intended uses of test scores and the conditions of measurement; they proceed to define the true score and error components in terms of these two factors. The classic theory of reliability, which dominated the field for over 70 years, can be thought of as a special case of the broader theory of generalizability. Although analyses of test reliability are still conducted along the lines laid out in the classic theory, generalizability theory is becoming increasingly popular and is likely to replace the more traditional approach as the method of choice for defining and estimating reliability.

PROBLEMS AND SOLUTIONS—RECAP

The Problem

You took a 20-item test designed to measure creativity and were concerned that the items on the test did not seem to have much in common. You found a research report showing that interitem correlations ranged from $-.07$ to $.12$, and averaging $.08$.

A Solution

Internal consistency formulas can be used to estimate reliability on the basis of the number of items (here, 20), and the average interitem correlation (here, .08). Using formula 6-7, the estimated reliability of the test is the following:

$$r_{xx} = [20^* .08] / [1 + (19^* .08)] = 1.60/2.52 = .63$$

A reliability coefficient of .63 suggests that the test is likely to be almost useless. The theory of reliability suggests that much of the variability in scores will be due to measurement error rather than to differences in creativity. Using this test to make hiring decisions is likely to lead to a number of poor decisions, and if you lose this job solely as a result of a low score on the creativity test, you have every right to be concerned. With a reliability coefficient this small, you can be pretty sure the test does not measure creativity.

KEY TERMS

Alternate forms method   method of estimating reliability that involves administering two parallel forms of a test

Error   difference between obtained score and true score

Generalizability theory   theory of measurement that attempts to determine the sources of consistency and inconsistency in test scores

Internal consistency method   method of estimating reliability that involves assessing consistency in performance across test items

Reliability coefficient   squared correlation between true and observed scores, or the proportion of the variability in observed scores thought to be due to differences in true scores

Split-half method   method of estimating reliability that involves comparing performance on half of the test with performance on the other half

Test-retest method   method of estimating reliability that involves two administrations of the same test

True score   expected value of a test score, or the average you would expect over many measurements

7

Using and Interpreting Information About Test Reliability

In the previous chapter, we discussed different methods of estimating the reliability of test scores. In this chapter, we show how information about reliability can be used in evaluating, interpreting, and improving psychological tests. First we discuss the relationship between reliability and the accuracy of test scores. Although it may be obvious that reliable tests are more accurate than unreliable tests, it is difficult to describe on the basis of reliability information alone how much consistency one can expect in test scores. Next we discuss the relationship between reliability and the validity of inferences that are based on tests. Tests are used both to measure specific attributes of people and to predict their standing on important criterion variables (e.g., success in school, performance on the job), and the reliability of test scores affects the accuracy of both of these uses. We then discuss factors affecting the reliability of test scores. It is difficult to interpret reliability information accurately unless one knows why a test is reliable or unreliable. Finally, we consider several special issues in the interpretation and use of information concerning test reliability.

PROBLEMS AND SOLUTIONS—SHOULD YOU RETAKE THIS TEST?

The Problem

At the beginning of Chapter 6, we described a 20-item test designed to measure your ability to think creatively, and we showed at the end of that chapter that the test was likely to be highly unreliable (using the formula for coefficient alpha, we estimated the reliability of this test to be $r_{xx} = .12$.

You received a score of 12 out of 20 on this test; you need to receive a score of at least 14 to qualify for the job. You have an opportunity to retake the test, but you will have to take the day off without pay from your current job to take this test, and you are not sure whether it is worth the cost. Can you use your knowledge about the reliability of the test to help decide whether it is worthwhile to retake this test?

134

USING THE RELIABILITY COEFFICIENT

The reliability coefficient provides useful information for evaluating tests. In addition to providing a general indication of the effects of true scores and error, the reliability coefficient can be used in two important ways: first, in estimating how much scores might fluctuate as a result of measurement error and, second, in estimating the effects of unreliability on the correlation between tests and criteria of interest (e.g., success in school).

The Standard Error of Measurement

The reliability coefficient provides a relative measure of the accuracy of test scores. Thus, a test with a reliability of .90 is more reliable than a test with a reliability of .80. However, the reliability coefficient does not provide an indication, in absolute terms, of how accurate test scores really are. For example, suppose that a psychologist measured a child's intelligence and obtained a score of 110. Could we be confident that the score obtained was really higher than the average score expected on the test (100), or would we expect test scores to vary more than 10 points simply because of measurement error? Even if we knew that the test was highly reliable (e.g., a reliability coefficient of .93), we would not be able to answer this question. The reliability coefficient simply does not reveal, in concrete terms, how much variability should be expected on the basis of measurement error. To describe the accuracy of test scores concretely, we need to know the size of the standard error of measurement.

The standard error of measurement (SEM) is a function of two factors: (1) the reliability of the test (r_{xx}) and (2) the variability of test scores (σ_x). Thus, the standard error of measurement is given by

$$SEM = \sigma_x \sqrt{1 - r_{xx}} \qquad [7\text{-}1]$$

The standard error of measurement provides a measure of the variability in test scores expected on the basis of measurement errors. For example, imagine that a woman with an IQ of 100 was tested repeatedly with a standard intelligence test. Since tests are not perfectly reliable, she would not receive a score of 100 every time; sometimes she would receive a score higher than 100, and sometimes she would receive a lower score. The total distribution of her test scores might look something like the one shown in Figure 7-1. The standard error of measurement corresponds to the standard deviation of this distribution. In other words, the standard error of measurement indicates how much variability in test scores can be expected as a result of measurement error.

The standard error of measurement can be used to form confidence intervals, which in turn provide a concrete indication of how accurate test scores really are. For example, the scores shown in the figure have a mean of 100 and a standard error of 4.7. In a normal distribution, 95% of all scores fall within 1.96 standard deviations of the mean. Thus, we can form a confidence interval around the mean by multiplying the standard error by 1.96. For this woman, whose true IQ is 100, we would expect 95% of her test scores to fall within 9.2 ($4.7 \times 1.96 = 9.2$) points of the mean. Thus, we would expect 95% of the test scores received by this woman to fall in the 90.8 to 109.2 range.

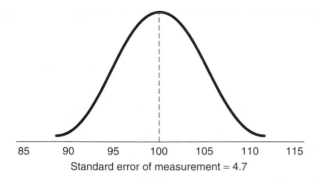

85   90   95   100   105   110   115
Standard error of measurement = 4.7

FIGURE 7-1   Distribution of Scores Obtained by Repeatedly Testing a Woman With an IQ of 100

Many well-developed tests report error bands along with specific scores, and these are usually based on the standard error of measurement. For example, the verbal and quantitative sections of the Scholastic Assessment Tests (SAT) report both a score and a score range (e.g., the report might indicate that you received a score of 550 on the verbal section but that scores could reasonably fall within the range from 520 to 580). The counselor's manual for this test emphasizes that a single score is not an absolute representation of an ability and that the score range gives a more useful indication of the student's performance. The smaller the standard error of measurement is, the narrower the range will be.

The principal drawback of using the standard error to describe the accuracy of the test scores received by an individual is the fact that measurement errors are not always equally large for all test scores. On the contrary, it is generally assumed that measurement errors are small for extreme scores and largest for moderate scores. Ferguson (1981) discusses methods of calculating standard errors for different score levels. These methods, however, rest on debatable assumptions and are not universally accepted (Lumsden, 1976).

Reliability and Validity

Psychological tests are never perfectly consistent or reliable. Our failure to achieve perfect reliability in psychological measurement has implications for the validity of tests, both for the validity of measurement and for the validity of predictions (and decisions) based on test scores. In a nutshell, lack of reliability places a limit on the validity of inferences drawn from test scores. Thus, a test that is not perfectly reliable cannot be perfectly valid, either as a means of measuring attributes of a person or as a means of predicting scores on a criterion. The rationale here is simple. A valid test is one that consistently assigns to persons numbers that reflect their standing on a particular attribute. An unreliable test, which provides inconsistent scores, cannot possibly be valid. A reliable test might or might not provide useful, valid information, but a test that is not reliable cannot possibly be valid

It is important to note that tests that are reliable are not necessarily valid. For example, consider the five-item test of general intelligence shown in Table 7-1. You would expect scores on this test to be almost perfectly consistent. For example, if a per-

Table 7-1   A TEST OF GENERAL INTELLIGENCE THAT WOULD BE HIGHLY RELIABLE BUT NOT AT ALL VALID

1. In what month were you born? _____
2. What is your mother's first name? _____
3. 1 + 1 = _____
4. How many days are there in a week? _____
5. Which of the following is a *triangle*? _____
   (a) □ (b) △ (c) ○

son took this test in January and then again in June, he or she would almost certainly give the same answers. However, we would not accept this test as a valid measure of intelligence, nor would we expect this test to provide accurate predictions of scholastic performance. Thus, consistency in test scores is no guarantee of validity in measurement or prediction.

Less-than-perfect reliability reduces the potential validity of measures. It follows, then, that if the reliability of psychological tests were increased, the validity of those tests would also be expected to increase. The question is how much of an increase in test validity could we expect if measurement errors were somehow reduced or eliminated.

Spearman's (1904) original motivation for developing the true-score theory of reliability stemmed from a question very much like the one previously stated. He reasoned that measurement errors would decrease, or attenuate, the correlation between two tests, X and Y (in other words, the validity of predictions). Thus, the correlation between unreliable measures of X and Y would be lower than the actual correlation between (perfectly reliable measures of) X and Y. He developed the correction for attenuation as a method of estimating the actual relationship between X and Y, given the correlation between two imperfectly reliable measures of X and Y. The correction for attenuation is given by the following equation:

$$r'_{xy} = \frac{r_{xy}}{\sqrt{r_{xx} \times r_{yy}}} \qquad [7\text{-}2]$$

where

r'_{xy} = correlation between x and y (r_{xy}), corrected for attenuation
r_{xx} = reliability of x
r_{yy} = reliability of y

The correction for attenuation provides an estimate of the correlation between perfectly reliable measures of X and Y. As Table 7-2 suggests, the correction can have a substantial effect on r_{xy}, particularly when the reliabilities of X and/or Y are low.

It is now common for researchers in many areas to routinely incorporate the correction for attenuation into their work. For example, research on the validity of tests used in personnel selection usually considers the effects of limited reliability in estimating the usefulness of these tests (Hartigan & Wigdor, 1989; Schmidt & Hunter, 1977; see Chapter 19 for a discussion of validity generalization research). However, although theoretically justified, the correction for attenuation is often criticized on

Table 7-2   CORRECTION FOR ATTENUATION

Observed r_{xy}	r_{xx}	r_{yy}	Corrected r_{xy}
.30	.90	.80	.353
	.70	.60	.462
	.50	.40	.671
	.40	.30	.867
.20	.90	.80	.235
	.70	.60	.308
	.50	.40	.447
	.40	.30	.578
.10	.90	.80	.117
	.70	.60	.154
	.50	.40	.223
	.40	.30	.289

practical grounds. In practice, the correction almost always overestimates the actual correlation between x and y (Lumsden, 1976). In addition, the correction formula assumes the impossible: that one can develop tests with no measurement error. Rather than estimating the correlation that one would obtain using perfectly reliable measures, it is often useful to estimate how much improvement one would expect in r_{xy} if the reliability of either or both tests could be improved by a specific amount. For example, suppose that r_{xy} is equal to .40 for two tests with reliabilities of .70 and .75, respectively. How high would we expect the correlation between x and y to be if we could improve the reliabilities of each test to .90? Equation 7-3 is used to answer this question. The effect of changing the reliability of one or both tests on the correlation between x and y is given by

$$r'_{xy} = \frac{r_{xy}\sqrt{\text{new } r_{xx} \times \text{new } r_{yy}}}{\sqrt{\text{old } r_{xx} \times r_{yy}}} \qquad [7\text{-}3]$$

where

r'_{xy} = correlation between x and y, corrected for change in the reliability of x and/or y

old r_{xx} and old r_{yy} = reliability of x and y at the time the test was given

new r_{xx} and new r_{yy} = new levels of reliability of x and y

Equation 7-3 is the most general form of the correction for attenuation. For example, if both tests could somehow be made perfectly reliable, the new r_{xx} and r_{yy} would be equal to 1.0, and Equation 7-3 would be mathematically identical to Equation 7-2. The most useful aspect of Equation 7-3 is that it allows us to estimate the effects of both raising and lowering the reliability of x and y on the correlation between x and y. Table 7-3 illustrates how a correlation of .40 between x and y was either increased or decreased. As the table shows, the expected correlation between x and y would increase to .52 if highly reliable measures of x and y (e.g., r_{xx} and r_{yy} = .95) could be obtained, but it would decrease to .22 if less reliable measures of x and y (e.g., r_{xx} and r_{yy} = .40) were used.

Table 7-3   CHANGES IN r_{XY} AS A FUNCTION OF THE RELIABILITY OF X AND Y ORIGINAL TEST: $r_{xy} = .40$ $r_{xx} = .70$ $r_{yy} = .75$

Increasing reliability		Corrected	Decreasing reliability		Corrected
r_{xx}	r_{yy}	r_{xy}	r_{xx}	r_{yy}	r_{xy}
.75	.80	.43	.65	.70	.37
.80	.85	.45	.55	.60	.31
.85	.90	.48	.45	.50	.26
.90	.90	.50	.45	.45	.25
.95	.95	.52	.40	.40	.22

Although there is little controversy about the theory that underlies the correction for attenuation, some very real problems are associated with translating that theory into practice (Cronbach, Gleser, Nanda, & Rajaratnam, 1972; Lumsden, 1976; Muchinsky, 1996). In particular, there are many different models of reliability, each specifying different sources of variability as error. In Chapter 6, we noted that a key assumption of generalizability theory was that a particular source of variability in test scores might be interpreted as either true score or error, depending on the particular purpose of testing. As Muchinsky (1996) notes, different researchers in the same area sometimes use fundamentally different definitions of error and therefore apply different corrections to the same data. Furthermore, different types of reliability estimates are sometimes intermixed, especially in meta-analyses of large numbers of studies, making it very difficult to sensibly evaluate the meaning of corrected correlations.

FACTORS AFFECTING RELIABILITY

In Chapter 6 and in the preceding sections of this chapter, we discussed methods of estimating the reliability of a test, along with several ways of using information concerning reliability. In our discussion of internal consistency estimates, we touched briefly on the question of why tests are or are not reliable. In this section, we examine in more detail the factors that affect the reliability of psychological tests. Basically, four factors affect the reliability of a test:

1. Characteristics of the people taking the test
2. Characteristics of the test itself
3. The intended uses of test scores
4. The method used to estimate reliability

Characteristics of the People Taking the Test

The first factor that affects the reliability of psychological measurement is the extent to which people taking the test vary on the characteristic or attribute being measured. As stated earlier, tests are designed to measure individual differences. If individuals do not differ very much on a particular attribute or trait, it is difficult to develop a reliable measure of that attribute. For example, imagine that you are a first-grade teacher trying to estimate individual differences in height of your students as they are seated at their desks. Since children at this age tend to be quite similar in height, this task would be quite difficult. On the other hand, a high-school teacher would find this task much easier, since at that age there is a greater variation in students' heights. Thus, when individual differences are quite large, it is much easier to measure them.

The standard deviation provides a measure of variability, or the extent to which individuals differ. Thus, the larger the standard deviation is, the more likely it is that a test will be reliable. However, a large standard deviation also implies that measures will, in an absolute sense, be inaccurate. Recall that the equation for the standard error of measurement is

$$\text{SEM} = \sigma_x \sqrt{1 - r_{xx}} \qquad [7\text{-}4]$$

Equation 7-4 suggests a paradox. If individual differences are very small, test reliability probably will be low. However, the standard deviation also will be small, and thus the standard error of measurement will be small. Hence, it might be possible to have a test that is unreliable as a measure of individual differences but that, nevertheless, provides an accurate measure of each person's standing on the attribute measured. The clearest example of this phenomenon would occur if everyone received the same score on a test. For example, if a group of physicists took a third-grade mathematics test, each of them would probably receive a score of 100. Since no individual differences in test scores are present, the test would have a reliability coefficient of 0.0; however, the standard error of measurement would also be 0.0. Thus, the test would be perfectly unreliable and perfectly accurate at the same time.

Because the variability of the attribute being measured affects test reliability, it is likely that many tests will show different levels of reliability, depending on the population in which they are used. For example, a test of general intelligence will be more reliable for the population in general than for a population of graduates of highly select colleges. It follows, then, that it will often be difficult to cite any figure as the reliability of a test. Tests will be more reliable in settings where individual differences are extreme and will be less reliable in settings where individual differences are small.

Characteristics of the Test

Internal consistency formulas for estimating reliability suggest that two factors affect the reliability coefficient: (1) the correlations between items and (2) the number of items. This definition suggests that the reliability of a test can be increased in either of two ways: by increasing the correlations between items or by increasing the number of items. Thus, a test made up of 40 mathematics questions is likely to be more reliable than a 40-item test that covers mathematics, spatial visualization, baseball trivia, and knowledge of French grammar; and an 80-item mathematics test is likely to be more reliable than a similar 40-item mathematics test.

The typical strategy for increasing the reliability of a test is to lengthen the test. Psychometric theory provides the Spearman–Brown formula, which can be used to predict the effect of lengthening a test on the reliability of that test. If the length is increased by a factor of n (e.g., double the length, or $n = 2$), the reliability of the new, expanded test is estimated by

$$\text{new } r_{xx} = \frac{n \times \text{old } r_{xx}}{1 + (n - 1) \text{ old } r_{xx}} \qquad [7\text{-}5]$$

where

old r_{xx} = reliability of the original test
new r_{xx} = reliability of the lengthened test

Table 7-4 illustrates the effects of lengthening a 20-item test with a reliability of .60. As shown by the table, it would be possible to substantially increase the reliability of the test by greatly increasing the number of items. Thus, adding 100 more items would raise the reliability from .60 to .90. It may, however, be exceedingly difficult and prohibitively expensive to add 100 extra items.

Equation 7-5 can also be used to predict the effect of decreasing the length of a test. For example, a 200-item test might be highly reliable (e.g., $r_{xx} = .95$), but it also might be too long for many applications. A short form of the same test might show acceptable levels of reliability and be much more practical. For example, a 50-item short form of this test would have an estimated reliability coefficient of .80.

In principle, the reliability of most psychological tests is under the control of the test developer. Internal consistency formulas imply that if a test is sufficiently long, it will be reliable, even if the average interitem correlation is fairly small. For example, a 50-item test in which the average interitem correlation is .20 would have a reliability of .92. A 100-item test in which the average interitem correlation is as small as .05 would still have a reliability of .84. Thus, in theory, there is really no excuse for an unreliable test. On the other hand, a large coefficient alpha is not by itself an indication of a good test if the number of items is large. As Cortina (1993) notes, even a poorly developed test will be reliable if it is sufficiently long. However, though it is theoretically possible to achieve a high level of reliability with any test simply by increasing its length, practical barriers may prevent implementing such a strategy.

Table 7-4   EFFECTS ON RELIABILITY OF LENGTHENING A 20-ITEM TEST WITH A RELIABILITY COEFFICIENT OF .60

Test length	n	Estimated reliability
40 items	2	.75
60	3	.81
80	4	.85
100	5	.88
120	6	.90

First, long tests are more time-consuming and expensive than short tests. The increase in reliability may not be worth the price, especially if tests are not used to make final decisions about people. Second, it often is quite difficult to write good test items. In addition, the new items added to the test must be substantively and statistically similar to the items already on the test; otherwise, the Spearman-Brown formula will not provide an accurate reliability estimate. Thus, in practice it may be quite laborious to lengthen many tests substantially.

Intended Use of Test Scores

In Chapter 6 we noted that tests might have different levels of reliability for different purposes. For example, suppose that schoolchildren take tests of general intelligence at a very early age (e.g., in first grade) and take the same test again many years later (e.g., on entering high school). The test might be highly reliable each time it is given but might show much less temporal stability. Thus, the test would be a more reliable indicator of the children's general mental ability at the time they took each test than it would be as an indicator of their long-term level of intelligence.

In general, the reliability of test scores is related to the breadth (versus narrowness) of the inferences that are made. For example, suppose that a person takes a computer-presented test of spatial visualization that involves mentally rotating three-dimensional geometric shapes. This test would provide a more reliable measure of the person's present level of spatial visualization ability than of his or her ability 10 years down the road. Test scores could probably be better generalized to other computer-presented tests than to similar paper-and-pencil tests. Finally, test scores might generalize better to other tests involving mental rotation than to tests that involve other spatial visualization tasks.

In sum, tests often show different levels of reliability for identifying individual differences at a specific time than for identifying individual differences across time. Tests are more reliable for identifying gross distinctions between individuals than they are for very fine distinctions. For example, one would expect a high degree of reliability for a mastery test (scored either pass or fail) of fifth-grade mathematics given to a sample made up of 50 second graders and 50 college sophomores. Almost everyone in the first group is likely to receive failing scores, and almost everyone in the second group is likely to receive passing scores. On the other hand, it might be difficult to reliably rank-order 100 doctoral candidates in terms of their general intelligence; for although there would be some standouts, this group would tend to be homogeneous. Finally, it is easier to make reliable inferences about stable characteristics of individuals than about characteristics that vary unpredictably. For example, it would be easier to develop a reliable measure of a person's basic values than of a person's mood state.

Methods Used to Estimate Reliability

Test-retest, alternate forms, split-half, and internal consistency methods of estimating test reliability each imply slightly different definitions of true score and error. For example, changes over time in the attribute being measured are considered sources of measurement error in estimating test-retest reliability. When split-half or internal consistency estimates are employed, the temporal stability of the attribute being measured is not a relevant factor.

In general, one might expect internal consistency estimates to be higher than alternate forms correlations, which in turn should probably be higher than test-retest reliability estimates. The reason for this is that more factors contribute to measurement error when test-retest or alternate forms methods are used than when internal consistency methods are used. For example, temporal instability and reactivity affect test-retest estimates but have no effect on internal consistency estimates. There are situations, however, when test-retest reliability can be expected to be higher than internal consistency estimates. For example, if people remembered all their responses to the first test, it would be possible to obtain perfect test-retest reliability, even if the internal consistency estimate was exactly 0.0.

The method used in estimating reliability should correspond with the way in which test scores are used. For example, if test scores obtained on one occasion are used to make inferences across long periods of time, it is important to estimate the temporal stability of test scores. If a clinic employs several different psychologists to score responses to the Rorschach inkblot test, it may be important to determine the extent to which test scores can be generalized across psychologists. No single figure represents the reliability of a test, so the choice of an appropriate method for estimating and defining reliability is potentially very important.

SPECIAL ISSUES IN RELIABILITY

Psychometric theory typically has little to say about the content of a test; a reliability coefficient of .90 is generally interpreted in the same way, regardless of what the test measures or what types of items are included in the test. However, the proper methods of estimating and interpreting test reliability may depend on what the test measures. In particular, some ability and achievement tests measure speed of response, whereas others measure performance irrespective of speed. This distinction has important implications for the estimation and interpretation of test reliability.

A second issue of importance is the reliability of difference scores, or gain scores. In assessing training and educational programs, it is common practice to give a pretest before training and a posttest after training. The difference between pretest and posttest scores is then used to measure the gain associated with training. Difference scores of this sort may present some special problems in terms of their reliability, as is discussed later in this section.

The next issue taken up is the reliability of test batteries, or of composite scores. Very often, scores from a number of tests are combined to form a single composite score. For example, in making graduate admissions decisions, some psychology departments consider the total score on the Graduate Record Examinations (GRE). This total score represents the sum of individual scores on verbal, quantitative, and analytical tests, as well as a psychology test. It is important to determine the reliability of a total score such as this; reliability theory provides methods for doing so. Finally, we will consider the reliability of criterion-referenced tests.

Speed Tests Versus Power Tests

The most widely used type of test is one in which there is a correct answer for each of many individual test items. Tests of this sort are often administered under strict time limits. A person's score on such a test is therefore likely to be affected by two factors: (1) whether the person knew (or guessed) the answer to each item and (2) whether the person had enough time, or worked quickly enough, to respond to each item. Thus, it is not always possible to determine whether a low test score indicates that the person did not know the answers or that he or she worked too slowly (or was given too little time) to respond to all the questions.

In theory, the distinction is often made between speed tests and power tests. A speed test is one in which each item is trivially easy but is administered within such a strict time limit that it is impossible to answer all questions. For example, the examinee might be given 60 seconds for a 100-item test made up of questions such as those shown in Table 7-5. It is assumed that, given enough time, the person could answer every item correctly. However, the strict time limit makes it impossible to complete every item. Individual differences in test scores are thus a function of the speed with which the examinee responds to individual items; the faster the person works, the more items he or she will complete. In contrast, a power test is one in which speed in responding has no effect on the test score. For example, a 20-item introductory psychology exam administered with no time limit would probably be considered a power test. No matter how quickly (or slowly) the examinee works, the final score is determined by the person's knowledge of the material, together with his or her luck in guessing or having studied just the right material.

Split-half and internal consistency methods are inappropriate for estimating the reliability of speed tests. In fact, a pure test of speed should have a split-half reliability of nearly 1.00. For example, suppose that a secretary answered 68 items on a 100-item test of clerical speed. It is safe to assume that practically all items attempted would be answered correctly. An odd-even split of this test therefore should yield two halves with scores of 34 on each half. Another, very slow examinee who attempted only 8 items should receive scores of 4 on each odd-even split. Thus, the halves would almost be perfectly correlated, regardless of how well or poorly the test was constructed.

One alternative is to split the test timewise rather than itemwise (Stanley, 1971). Thus, a 30-minute, 200-item speed test could be split into two 15-minute halves. When

Table 7-5   ITEMS THAT MIGHT APPEAR ON A SPEED TEST

	Are A and B the same or different?		
Item	A	B	
1.	1376493	1376443	_____
2.	John K. Adams	John K. Adams	_____
3.	3749 Parkwood Ct.	3749 Parkwood Dr.	_____
4.	863-4587	863-4587	_____
5.	Sailing Master	Sailing Mister	_____

the number of items completed in the first 15 minutes is compared with the number completed in the last 15 minutes, these numbers should be consistently similar if the test is reliable.

Although the test-retest method is not recommended for most testing applications (Nunnally, 1982), this method is useful for assessing the reliability of speed tests. In a speed test, items are often trivial and fairly meaningless. It is precisely for this reason that the usual barrier to the use of the test-retest method—subjects' tendency to remember their responses—tends not to be a problem with speed tests. When the test content is meaningful, subjects are likely to remember their responses to test items; when test items involve trivial perceptual or motor tasks, over time it becomes more difficult to remember or duplicate one's responses to a large number of test items. Thus, the test-retest method might be quite useful in assessing the reliability of a speed test, particularly in settings where it is difficult to obtain scores on separately timed half-tests.

Reliability of Difference Scores

In evaluating a training program, researchers often look at the difference between scores on a pretest and scores on a posttest. A counselor who wishes to know whether Kathleen is better in mathematics or in English may examine the difference in grades received in these two areas. In both cases, the examiner might be surprised to learn that the change scores or difference scores can show low levels of reliability, even when the two tests being compared are highly reliable.

Suppose that we want to measure how much students have learned in a one-semester statistics course. We might give them a test at the beginning of the semester (X), then give them another, equivalent test at the end of the semester (Y), and compute the difference between the scores on the two tests $(D = X - Y)$. This difference score (D) would have a reliability of

$$r_{DD} = \frac{\dfrac{r_{xx} + r_{yy}}{2} - r_{xy}}{1 - r_{xy}} \qquad [7\text{-}6]$$

where

r_{DD} = reliability of the difference between scores on X and scores on Y
r_{xx} = reliability of X
r_{yy} = reliability of Y
r_{xy} = correlation between X and Y

For example, if the reliability of test X is .85, the reliability of test Y is .80, and the correlation between the two tests is .50, the reliability of the difference between Test X and Test Y is .65.

Examination of Equation 7-6 leads to a somewhat surprising conclusion: All other things being equal, the higher the correlation between X and Y is, the lower the reliability of the difference score.

To understand this apparent paradox, one must remember that both X and Y are made up of true score and error. Thus,

$$X = T_x + e_x \qquad\qquad [7\text{-}7]$$

and

$$Y = T_y + e_y \qquad\qquad [7\text{-}8]$$

The difference between X and Y reflects two factors: (1) differences in true scores and (2) differences due to measurement error. If X and Y are highly correlated, the true-score part of X must overlap considerably with the true-score part of Y. As a result, there will be hardly any difference in the true scores on these variables. Differences between scores on X and scores on Y therefore will be due almost entirely to measurement error. Thus, the more highly correlated X and Y are, the less reliable their difference.

Our discussion of the reliability of difference scores has implications for both research and testing applications. For example, a comparison of pretest and posttest scores might be used to determine who has learned the most in a drivers' education course. If the pretest and posttest are comparable (and it would not make any sense to use completely different types of tests), scores on the two tests are likely to be positively correlated, and difference scores will show low levels of reliability. Thus, in this case, the measure of individual differences in the amount learned (posttest minus pretest) could be quite unreliable. Persons who appear to have learned quite a bit in this drivers' education course (large difference) could show little apparent gain in an equivalent course. This outcome does not reflect instability in their ability to learn; rather, it is a reflection of the potential unreliability of measures of change or gain.

The problems inherent in the use of difference scores have led to a variety of statistical techniques for studying and measuring change (Cohen & Cohen, 1983; Collins & Horn, 1991; J. R. Edwards, 1995, 2001; C. W. Harris, 1963). Although most researchers avoid the use of difference scores for measuring change, you will probably encounter several studies that still use them. In interpreting the results of these studies, it is very important to keep in mind the special problems posed by the typically low reliability of difference scores.

Reliability of Composite Scores

A difference score is obtained by subtracting the score on one test from the score on another. A composite score is obtained by adding the scores on several different tests. Whereas difference scores are often unreliable, composite scores are typically more reliable than the tests that make up the composite. In particular, the more highly correlated the individual tests are, the higher the reliability of the sum of these tests.

The reliability of a composite or summed score is given by

$$r_{ss} = 1 - \frac{k - (k\bar{r}_{ii})}{k + (k^2 - k)\bar{r}_{ij}} \qquad\qquad [7\text{-}9]$$

where

r_{ss} = reliability of the sum
k = number of tests
$\bar{r}_{ij}$ = average test reliability
$\bar{r}_{ij}$ = average correlation between tests

For example, if three tests had reliabilities of .70, .75, and .80 and an average intercorrelation of .39, the reliability of the sum of the scores on these three tests would be .85. If the average intercorrelation among these three tests was .65, the reliability of the sum would be .89.

The basic principles for determining the reliability of a composite score are exactly analogous to those involved in determining the internal consistency of a test. The more tests that are combined and the higher the correlation between them, the higher the reliability of the composite. Adding together scores on several highly correlated tests achieves exactly the same objectives as adding together scores on several positively correlated test items to form a single test score. Each test can be thought of as an observation, or measurement, of a particular attribute, much in the same way that each test item is thought of as a separate observation. Highly correlated tests represent independent observations of similar attributes or of the same attribute. As noted in this chapter and in Chapter 6, the best method to ensure reliability is to obtain as many observations as possible of the attribute that is to be measured.

Reliability of Criterion-Referenced Tests

In Chapter 5, we briefly described criterion-referenced testing. The most common application of this strategy is in classroom assessments, where you might be interested in determining whether a student has mastered a particular skill or topic. In an influential paper, Popham and Husek (1969) suggested that traditional measures of reliability (e.g., internal consistency estimates) were not relevant to this type of testing and that tests with high internal consistency might be inappropriate if the purpose of testing was to evaluate mastery, rather than comparing one student with another. Subsequent studies have shown that this conclusion is not correct and that criterion-referenced tests must show reliability if they are to provide a useful measure of mastery (M. T. Kane, 1986). However, criterion-referenced testing does present challenges not faced when evaluating the reliability of norm-referenced tests.

In criterion-referenced testing, our principal concern is with the reliability of decisions, rather than with the reliability of test scores (Hambleton, 1994; R. G. Taylor & Lee, 1995). That is, if a student takes a criterion-referenced test, we must at some point decide whether that student has mastered the topic or has failed to master the topic. The reliability of these decisions depends on both the quality of the test and the standard used to determine mastery (R. G. Taylor & Lee, 1995).

One method for estimating the reliability of the decisions made on the basis of a criterion-referenced test involves repeated testing. If the test is reliable, students would be consistently classified as mastering or failing to master the material (however, with the passage of time and additional instruction, you expect mastery levels to increase).

R. G. Taylor and Lee (1995) illustrate a simple procedure for computing a coefficient of agreement, often referred to as kappa.

Figure 7-2 illustrates the research design for estimating the agreement between decisions resulting from two administrations of a criterion-referenced test. Here, a refers to the number of persons who pass both the first and the second test, b to the number of persons who fail the first test but pass the second, and so on. Agreement is high when most people receive consistent scores on the two tests (i.e., when they are in cells a or d).

In assessing agreement, it is important to take into account the fact that sometimes two separate tests will yield the same outcome simply as a result of chance, and not as a result of the quality of the test. For example, if 90% of the people pass the first test and 90% also pass the second, the decisions made about people should agree for at least 81% of all those tested, even if the tests are completely unreliable. The closer the passing rate is to 100% (or to 0%), the greater the agreement expected on the basis of chance alone. A good method of assessing the reliability of decisions coming from two separate test administrations must therefore take into account the level of agreement expected on the basis of chance. The kappa coefficient does exactly this.

If we define total and chance agreement levels as

$$\text{Total agreement} = \frac{a + d}{N} \qquad [7\text{-}10]$$

$$\text{Chance agreement} = \left[\left(\frac{\mathrm{a + b}}{N}\right) * \left(\frac{\mathrm{a + c}}{N}\right)\right] + \left[\left(\frac{\mathrm{c + d}}{N}\right) * \left(\frac{\mathrm{b + d}}{N}\right)\right] \qquad [7\text{-}11]$$

then kappa is given by

$$\text{Kappa} = \frac{\text{total} - \text{chance}}{1 - \text{chance}} \qquad [7\text{-}12]$$

Suppose, for example, that you administered a test twice, with the results displayed in Figure 7-3. Here the proportion of total agreement is .80, the proportion expected by chance is .48, and kappa is .61. This outcome indicates a reasonable level of reliability in the decisions that are reached on the basis of this test, but it also indicates that there is still considerable room for improvement.

Second test	First test: Pass	First test: Fail
Pass	*a*	*b*
Fail	*c*	*d*

$N = a + b + c + d$

FIGURE 7-2 Research Design for Evaluating Reliability of Decisions in a Criterion-Referenced Test

HOW RELIABLE SHOULD TESTS BE?

All things being equal, a highly reliable test would always be preferable to a test with little reliability. However, all things are rarely equal; the most reliable test might also be the most expensive or most difficult to administer. Test reliability may be crucial in some settings (e.g., those in which major decisions are made on the basis of tests) but less important in others (e.g., where tests are used only for preliminary screenings). It is impossible to specify any particular figure as the minimum level of reliability needed for all testing applications, but rough guidelines can be established for some of the more common uses of tests.

High levels of reliability are most necessary when (1) tests are used to make final decisions about people and (2) individuals are sorted into many different categories on the basis of relatively small individual differences. For example, tests are used for placement in the armed forces: Individuals can be assigned to any of a number of jobs largely on the basis of their scores on the Armed Services Vocational Aptitude Battery. In this case, measurement error could have a significant effect on decisions (Murphy, 1984a). If the tests used in placement are unreliable, the decisions made regarding thousands of recruits also will be unreliable.

Lower levels of reliability are acceptable when (1) tests are used for preliminary rather than final decisions and (2) tests are used to sort people into a small number of categories on the basis of gross individual differences. For example, if several hundred people apply for a small number of places in a graduate program in clinical psychology, test scores might be used for preliminary screening, in which applicants who essentially have no chance of being admitted (e.g., the bottom 25% of the applicant pool) are screened out. If a test were used in this way, a high level of reliability would be desirable, but not essential.

Table 7-6 illustrates the levels of reliability typically attained by different types of psychological tests and measurement devices. There is, of course, some variability in reported levels of reliability. Thus, some standardized tests of intelligence report levels of reliability in excess of .95, whereas others report reliability estimates closer to .80. Nevertheless, clear differences exist in the levels of reliability achieved by different types of tests. Most standardized tests of general intelligence report reliability

Second test	First test: Pass	First test: Fail
Pass	20	4
Fail	6	22

$N = 52$

Total = .80
Chance = .48
Kappa = .61

FIGURE 7-3 Example of Reliability Assessment

Table 7-6   LEVELS OF RELIABILITY TYPICALLY REPORTED FOR DIFFERENT
TYPES OF TESTS AND MEASUREMENT DEVICES

Typical reliability estimate	Test type	Interpretation
.95		Measurement errors have virtually no effect
.90	Standardized group tests of intelligence	
.85	Standardized achievements tests	High to moderate reliability
.80		
.75	Classroom multiple-choice tests	Moderate to low reliability
.70	Rating scales	
.65		Low reliability
.60	Some projective measures	
.55		
.50		True scores and error have equal effects on test scores

estimates in the neighborhood of .90 (Jensen, 1980). For almost any testing application, this is likely to be regarded as a high level of reliability. Reliability estimates of .80 or more are typically regarded as moderate to high; a reliability coefficient of .80 indicates that 20% of the variability in test scores is due to measurement errors. For most testing applications, reliability estimates around .70 are likely to be regarded as low, although, as noted before, this level of reliability might be sufficient when tests are used for screening or for making preliminary decisions. Finally, reliability estimates lower than .60 usually are thought to indicate unacceptably low levels of reliability.

Generalizability theory encourages us to ask questions that go beyond the simple reliability tests. For example, Buckley, Cote, and Comstock (1990) reviewed research on measures of personality and attitudes, and they then concluded that, on average, 36% of the variance in these measures was due to measurement error, implying a reliability of .64. This does not mean, however, that the constructs measured by these tests account for the other 64%. Buckley and his colleagues (1990) also found that 22% of the variance in scores could be attributed to the method of measurement; they found, in addition, that only 42% of the variance in scores on measures of personality characteristics and attitudes was attributable to the traits that these scales were designed to measure. Thus, in the case of the measures reviewed in this study, a reasonably decent level of reliability may say more about the extent of method bias than about the quality of measurement of personality and attitude scales.

CRITICAL DISCUSSION:

Precise but Narrow—The Bandwidth-Fidelity Dilemma

There are sometimes practical obstacles to maximizing the reliability of tests. For example, a test with a reliability of .90 might be twice as expensive to develop as a test with a reliability of .85. The gain in reliability might not be worth the cost. In addition to the occasional practical problems, there are some theoretical reasons why it may be impossible to achieve high levels of reliability in measuring a particular attribute or trait. In particular, there is an inevitable conflict between the goal of attaining precision (reliability) in measurement and the goal of attaining breadth. This conflict is referred to as the *bandwidth-fidelity dilemma* (Cronbach & Gleser, 1965; Shannon & Weaver, 1949).

The terms *bandwidth* and *fidelity* come from communication theory. *Bandwidth* refers to the amount of information that is contained in a message, whereas *fidelity* refers to the accuracy with which that information is conveyed. The greater the amount of information to be conveyed (bandwidth), the less accurately it can be conveyed (fidelity). The greater the level of accuracy desired, the less information that can be conveyed. The trade-off between bandwidth and fidelity also applies to testing. For any given test, a choice must be made between measuring a very specific attribute with a high degree of accuracy or measuring a broader attribute with less accuracy. Consider, for example, a history test with 20 items. If all 20 items deal with 18th-century American history, one might obtain a highly reliable measure of each student's knowledge of that particular aspect of history. On the other hand, if the 20 items cover all areas of the world, from ancient times to modern, one would be able to measure each student's general knowledge of history, but one would not be able to obtain a very accurate or reliable measure of such a broadly defined area of knowledge.

The time and resources available for testing are typically limited. As a result, we sometimes have to sacrifice reliability and accuracy in measurement in order to measure traits and attributes that are broadly of interest. Thus, it may not be practical, even if it is technically possible, to attain high levels of reliability with every psychological test and measurement device.

SUMMARY

All other things being equal, highly reliable tests are preferable to less reliable ones. However, in most cases, all other things are not equal, and it is important to consider carefully the implications of different levels of reliability. The standard error of measurement, which is determined by both the reliability and the standard deviation of a test, is very useful for describing, in concrete terms, just how much faith can be put into test scores. Tests can be highly reliable, but nevertheless highly imprecise, in the sense that actual test scores can vary considerably from administration to administration.

The correction for attenuation illustrates very concretely the implications of different levels of reliability. When tests are unreliable, the correlation that you obtain between test scores can severely underestimate the strength of the relationship between the characteristics that the tests were designed to measure. The correction formulas presented here allow you to determine the effects of low reliability on the reported validity of tests. They also allow you to determine whether the time and effort needed to increase test reliability is likely to have a concrete payoff in terms of higher validity coefficients.

It is important to correctly estimate and interpret reliability in a number of special testing applications. These include testing applications that involve speeded tests, for which internal consistency methods may be appropriate, and scores that are based either on differences between scores on two different tests or on the sum of scores on two different tests. An important rule of thumb is that difference scores often show very low levels of reliability, whereas composite scores (i.e., those constructed by summing several different tests) may be highly reliable.

PROBLEMS AND SOLUTIONS—RECAP

The Problem

You took a 20-item employment test and received a score of 12 out of 20. You need to receive a score of at least 14 to qualify for the job, and you know that the test is not very reliable ($r_{xx} = .12$). It will be costly to retake the test, and you want to use your knowledge about the reliability of the test to make a decision about whether to retake the test.

A Solution

You might think that the answer is obvious. Since the test is highly unreliable and your score was already near to the cutoff score, it might be reasonable to expect that the next test score could very well fluctuate enough to clear the cutoff. However, as we saw in our discussions of the Standard Error of Measurement, the reliability of the test is not the only thing that matters. In order to estimate the extent to which test scores might vary, you also need to know the variability of test scores, in particular, the standard deviation of the test (σ_x). Suppose, for example, that the mean and standard deviation on this test were 11.8 and 1.75, respectively. Using formula 7.1, the Standard Error of Measurement would be the following:

$$\text{SEM} = \sigma_x{}^*[\text{square root } (1 - .12)] = 1.75{}^*.938 = 1.64$$

If the SEM is 1.64, you should expect scores on a retest to fall roughly within 3.2 points of the original score (i.e., $\text{SEM}^* 1.96$). On the basis of this calculation, it seems feasible that your score on the retest could very well increase by 2 points. Of course, it is also quite possible that you will do worse the second time around, and reliability theory doesn't tell you all that much about your chances of doing better or worse the next time around.[*] It does, however, suggest that it is quite plausible that your score on the retest could exceed the cutoff.

[*] The reason why we can't predict whether your score will go up or down the second time you take the test is that your original test score is very close to the average. If you had received a very high score the first time, the best guess is that your score would go down on a retest, but if you had received a very low score the first time, the best guess would be for an improved score.

KEY TERMS

Bandwidth fidelity dilemma   trade-off between breadth and precision in measurement

Composite score   score obtained by combining scores from multiple tests or measures

Correction for attenuation   estimate of the correlation you would expect between two imperfect measures if the effects of measurement error could be removed

Difference score   score obtained by subtracting one test score from another

Kappa   measure of the agreement between decisions obtained in two separate tests; used in assessing the reliability of criterion-referenced tests

Power test   test in which speed of response has little or no effect on the final score obtained

Spearman-Brown formula   formula for estimating reliability if the test is shortened or lengthened

Speed test   test score in which speed of response is the only factor that influences the final score

Standard error of measurement   measure of the variability in scores that you expect to find as a result of measurement error

Validity of Measurement: Content and Construct-Oriented Validation Strategies

8

Two of the principal problems in psychological measurement are determining whether a test measures what it is supposed to measure and determining whether that test can be used in making accurate decisions. Suppose that a psychologist devises a test and claims that it measures reading comprehension and can be used to predict success in graduate school. These claims would not carry much weight unless they were supported by evidence. Hence, the psychologist must present data to show that the claims are accurate, or valid. For example, if test scores are correlated with grades or with professors' evaluations of graduate students, it is reasonable to conclude that the test is a valid predictor of success in graduate school. If test scores are related to other measures of reading comprehension, or if the test provides a representative sample of tasks that measures reading comprehension, then the test probably does indeed measure what it purports to measure.

This chapter opens our discussion of validity. Tests can be used in many ways; as a consequence, there are many ways of defining validity. We begin this chapter by discussing in more detail the two major aspects of validity: (1) the validity of measurement and (2) the validity for decisions. The validity of measurement is the main focus of this chapter. Ways of defining and estimating the validity of decisions are discussed in the chapter that follows.

PROBLEMS AND SOLUTIONS—WHAT DOES THIS TEST MEASURE?

The Problem

You are employed as a psychometrician at the Allervant Consulting Group. Allervant is in the business of selling and scoring psychological tests that are used to select high-level executives. They have just acquired a new test designed to measure examinees' social skills, and you have been given the task of determining whether the test really measures what it claims to measure.

Test-retest reliabilities are reasonably high (.80-.86 in various samples), but it is not clear whether the test really tells you much about social skills. The test involves giving examinees a list of 20 characters from current television shows (10 male and 10 female, all from different shows), and asking respondents to identify the 10 most compatible couples. Expert ratings of the compatibility of each possible pair have been obtained, and your score is based on the match between your list of compatible pairs and the set of 10 couples judged most compatible by experts. How would you determine whether this is a valid test?

VALIDATION STRATEGIES

In the 1940s and the early 1950s, research on psychological measurement was characterized by a bewildering array of methods of defining and assessing validity. One of the many contributions of the American Psychological Association's *Technical Recommendations for Psychological Tests and Diagnostic Techniques* (1954) was the development of a fairly simple system for classifying procedures for assessing validity. The *Technical Recommendations* recognized four essentially different ways of defining validity:

1. Content validity
2. Construct validity
3. Predictive validity
4. Concurrent validity

These four categories are sometimes referred to as the *four faces of validity.*

For many years it was thought that different types of validity were appropriate for different purposes. For example, for educational testing, content validity might be called for, whereas for personnel testing, predictive validity might be needed. Landy (1987) referred to this approach to matching "types" of validity to specific testing applications as "stamp collecting." Today, it is recognized that these four "faces" represent four different strategies for validating the inferences that are made on the basis of test scores rather than four different types of validity (American Psychological Association, *Standards for Educational and Psychological Testing,* 1999). Rather than describing fundamentally different types of validity, researchers now agree that all validation strategies are designed to pursue the same basic goal: understanding the meaning and implication of test scores. Messick (1989) provides a succinct definition of validation as the "scientific inquiry into test score meaning."

Historically, there has been some confusion about exactly what is "validated" in a validity study. It is not the test itself that is validated, but rather, it is the inferences and conclusions that you reach on the basis of test scores. That is, validity is not a property of the test, but rather a function of what the scores on that test mean. For example, if a college student receives a high score on the Miller Analogies Test, a graduate admissions committee might use that score to predict or infer that he or she will do well in graduate school and make an offer of admission. If that student (and other students with similar scores) subsequently does well in graduate school and if students with lower scores on this test do less well, we can conclude that the admissions committee drew valid conclusions from scores on this test.

In the 1980s, the various strategies for investigating validity were treated as fundamentally different and sometimes incompatible approaches. Today, researchers recognize that all the strategies for investigating validity can be grouped under the broad heading of construct validation. That is, virtually any effort to understand the meaning of test scores is likely to shed light on the attributes or constructs that the test measures, and it is therefore misleading to speak of fundamentally different types of validity. Nevertheless, there is some value in considering separately two different uses of the term *validity*, for measuring particular characteristics or attributes of a person or for predicting future outcomes and making decisions about people. Both content and construct validation strategies represent approaches for determining whether a test provides a valid measure of a specific attribute.[1] In other words, these approaches define validity in terms of measurement: A test is valid if it measures what it is supposed to measure. Predictive and concurrent approaches examine the validity of predictions or decisions that are based on tests: A test is valid if it can be used to make correct or accurate decisions.

To illustrate the differences between validity of measurement and validity for decisions, consider the case of an organization that decides to use an inventory labeled Leadership Skills Profile to help select managers. First, you might ask whether this inventory really tells you anything about a person's leadership skills (validity of measurement). Second, you might ask whether people who receive high scores on this test turn out to be good managers (validity for decisions). The difference between these two aspects of validity is that, in the first case, you are concerned with what the test measures, whereas in the second, you are interested in using the test to make predictions about a variable that is not directly measured by the test (i.e., success as a manager) but that you think is related to what the test measures.

Guion (1991) notes that validity of measurement is not always necessary or sufficient to guarantee validity for decisions. A very good measure of leadership skills may be a poor predictor of performance as a manager, for leadership and day-to-day management are very different things. A poor measure of leadership might nevertheless allow you to identify good managers. It is therefore important to consider the two major aspects of the term *validity* separately.

ASSESSING THE VALIDITY OF MEASUREMENT

It is a simple matter to determine whether a homemade ruler provides a valid measure of length. Simply take the ruler to the Bureau of Weights and Measures and compare it with a standard. This strategy won't work for evaluating the validity of a psychological test. The reason for this inability is simple but fundamental to an understanding of methods of psychological measurement: For many of the characteristics that psychologists wish to measure (e.g., introversion, intelligence, reading comprehension), there

---

[1]It is possible to include all validity research under the heading of construct validity. The rationale here is that all research on the validity of tests and measures is ultimately concerned with constructs and that any validation strategy may ultimately help to establish the relationship between the test and the construct. See Chapter 9 for further discussion of this point.

are no universal standards against which test scores can be compared. In other words, if I measure Paula's general intelligence and come up with an IQ of 112, I cannot go to the Bureau of Weights and Measures to find out whether I was right. Unfortunately, there is no external standard I can use to check this figure or to check scores from most other psychological tests. Rather than validating test scores against some external standard, psychologists must employ more indirect methods in determining the validity of tests. That is, psychologists must collect evidence from a variety of sources to demonstrate that tests measure what they are designed to measure.

In a sense, one's work is never done when attempting to establish the validity of measurement. There is no definitive way of proving that a given test is a measure of general intelligence, of reading comprehension, or of any other trait. Establishing the validity of a specific test is always partially subjective and depends on a researcher's judgment regarding the weight of the available evidence. Nevertheless, although the methods discussed in this chapter are both indirect and partially subjective, judgments regarding the validity of measurement can and should be based solidly on empirical evidence.

Both content- and construct-oriented validation strategies involve the accumulation of evidence that suggests that the test actually measures what it purports to measure. Content validity is established by examining the test itself, whereas construct validity is established by examining the relationship between test scores and a variety of other measures.

CONTENT-ORIENTED VALIDATION STRATEGIES

One way to gather evidence for the validity of measurement is to examine the content of the test. A test that contains 25 addition and subtraction problems is probably a better measure of simple mathematical ability than a test that contains 10 questions about sports and no addition and subtraction problems. Content validity is established by showing that the behaviors sampled by the test are a representative sample of the attribute being measured. Thus, content validity depends both on the test itself and on the processes involved in responding to the test (Guion, 1977). For example, a paper-and-pencil test of job knowledge might not provide a valid measure of a worker's ability to do the job, even if it provides a valid measure of his or her knowledge of what to do on the job.

One can get a rough idea of a test's content validity simply by looking at test items. If all test items appear to measure what the test is supposed to measure, there is some evidence of content validity. The evidence is weak, but it is a start. To develop more detailed evidence of content validity, it is necessary to introduce the concept of content domain.

Content Domains

Every psychological test is a systematic sample from a particular domain of behaviors. A detailed description of the content domain provides the foundation for assessing content validity.

When you say, "I want to measure X," you have specified a particular content domain. A content domain represents the total set of behaviors that could be used to measure a specific attribute or characteristic of the individuals that are to be tested (Guion, 1977). For example, a test designed to measure performance as a baseball player could be constructed by sampling from the total domain of behaviors (running, fielding, hitting) involved in the game of baseball. The domain covered by a test might be very broad (e.g., reading comprehension), or it might be very narrow (e.g., addition problems involving decimals to two places, with sums less than 10). Regardless of its size, every content domain has a number of properties that are useful in assessing content validity.

First, as the name implies, a content domain has boundaries. A great many possible test items within these boundaries could validly be used to measure a person's standing on the content domain; a detailed description of the content domain to be measured allows one to determine whether each test item lies within the boundaries of the domain. There is clearly a problem if a large number of behaviors sampled by the test are outside the boundaries of the domain that one wishes to measure. Returning to an earlier example, a test that is made up of questions about sports will not provide a valid measure of simple mathematical ability. The test might provide an accurate measure of sports knowledge, but questions about sports fall outside the boundaries of the domain of mathematical ability.

Second, content domains are structured. That is, the contents of a content domain can often be classified into several categories. The description of such a content domain presented in Table 8-1 helps to clarify the concepts of boundaries and the structure of content domains. The domain described in the table has well-defined boundaries and

Table 8-1   DETAILED DESCRIPTION OF A CONTENT DOMAIN

1. Domain to be measured: Knowledge of world history as covered in a standard seventh-grade course
2. Areas included in this domain:

A. Issues	B. Areas	C. Time span
1. Social	1. Europe	1. 18th Century
2. Political	2. Americas	2. 19th Century
3. Cultural	3. Africa and Asia	

3. Relative importance of the areas covered.[a]

		Social	Political	Cultural
Europe	18th Century	5%	10%	3%
	19th Century	5%	8%	2%
Americas	18th Century	6%	17%	2%
	19th Century	9%	13%	5%
Africa and Asia	18th Century	2%	0%	0%
	19th Century	6%	5%	2%
				100%

[a]These percentages reflect the relative amount of reading and lecture time dedicated to each area.

structure. Because this domain is very concrete, it is possible to make some precise statements about the areas included in the domain and about the relative importance of each of these areas. This detailed description of the boundaries and structure of the content domain is essential in evaluating content validity.

It should be relatively easy to decide whether specific test items are within or outside the boundaries of the domain described in Table 8-1. It should also be easy to decide whether a test forms a representative sample of this content domain. As discussed in the section that follows, detailed comparisons between the boundaries and structure of the content domain and the structure of the test are at the heart of content validity.

Unfortunately, many content domains cannot be described in the level of detail shown in the table. It is very difficult to provide detailed descriptions of content domains such as mathematical concepts or performance on mechanical tasks. These domains include a broad range of behaviors whose boundaries might be difficult to specify. It may therefore be very difficult to decide whether specific test items are within or outside the boundaries of the domain. If the different areas or classes of behaviors included in the domain cannot be categorized or if the relative importance of those areas cannot be decided on, it may be impossible to determine whether the test provides a representative sample of the content domain.

Assessing Content Validity

There is no exact, statistical measure of content validity. Rather, content validity represents a judgment regarding the degree to which a test provides an adequate sample of a particular content domain (Guion, 1977). Judgments about content validity are neither final nor absolute; tests show various levels of content validity, and experts do not always agree in their judgments. Nevertheless, judgments about content validity are not arbitrary. A detailed description of the content domain provides a framework for the careful evaluation of tests and provides a method for systematic evaluation of the validity of measurement.

The basic procedure for assessing content validity consists of three steps:

1. Describe the content domain.
2. Determine the areas of the content domain that are measured by each test item.
3. Compare the structure of the test with the structure of the content domain.

Although this procedure appears to be simple, in practice it is difficult to implement. The principal difficulty is encountered at the first step, the description of the content domain. Outside the area of classroom testing, it is often difficult to describe content domains in the level of detail shown in Table 8-1. For example, consider applying this strategy in assessing a test of verbal ability. Although it might be possible to decide what sort of tasks were or were not included in this content domain (boundaries of the domain), it would be exceedingly difficult to define in any detail the structure of this domain. In other words, it would be difficult to specify the relative importance or frequency of the different tasks that involve verbal ability. In this case, a test developer might have a general definition of the domain that he or she wishes to measure but might have little detailed knowledge of the structure of that domain. It would be difficult to determine whether a specific test provided a representative sample of this domain; therefore, it would be difficult to argue on the basis of content alone that the test provides a valid measure of verbal ability.

A detailed description of the content domain yields a set of categories that can be used to classify test items. First, each test item can be classified as being within the boundaries of the domain or outside the boundaries of the domain. This type of classification is simple, but important; a test is not likely to show much content validity if the majority of the test items are clearly outside the boundaries of the domain that it is supposed to measure. Those test items that are within the boundaries of the domain can be further classified according to the areas of the domain that they measure. For example, items on a history test designed to measure the domain described in Table 8-1 could be classified as dealing with social, political, or cultural issues and further classified as dealing with European, American, or African and Asian history. In other words, the categories used to describe the content domain can also be used to classify each item on the test.

The final step in assessing content validity is to compare the content and structure of the test with that of the content domain. If none of the test items falls within the boundaries of the domain, then it seems clear that the test will show no content validity. Furthermore, if test items deal with only a specific portion of the domain, the test will not show substantial evidence of content validity.

Consider, for example, the tests described in Table 8-2. The domain we wish to measure is performance as a shortstop, which presumably includes hitting, base running, and fielding a variety of balls. Each of the two tests described in Table 8-2 includes behaviors that are clearly within this content domain, yet neither of them provides a valid sample of the domain. In this example, some combinations of test A and test B might provide a better sample of this particular content domain and thus a better, more valid test. In general, a test that appears to provide a representative sample of the major parts of a content domain will be judged to show high levels of content validity. The closer the match is between the structure of the test and the structure of the domain, the stronger the evidence of content validity. To demonstrate content validity, tests should sample all parts of the content domain and should devote the largest number of items to the larger, more important areas included in the domain, with comparatively fewer items devoted to less important aspects of the domain.

Response Processes and Content Validity. Several researchers, notably Guion (1977) and Sackett (1987), have noted that assessments of content validity focus almost

Table 8-2   EXAMPLES OF TESTS THAT FAIL TO ADEQUATELY SAMPLE A DOMAIN

The Domain: Performance as a shortstop in intermural softball
Test A: Hitting 40 pitches thrown in batting practice
Test B: Fielding 70 ground balls that are hit toward second base

exclusively on the content of test items or assessment exercises. Questions of how stimuli are presented to subjects, how responses are recorded and evaluated, and what is going through the respondent's mind are rarely considered in studies that use content-oriented validity strategies. Failure to consider these issues adequately could be a serious mistake, as can be illustrated through an examination of the underlying logic of content-oriented validation.

The logic of content-oriented strategies of validation is that the test should provide a representative sample of the domain that one wishes to measure. By this logic, validation efforts should be concerned more with the extent to which responses to items provide a representative sample of the domain of responses than with the extent to which stimuli are representative. After all, psychological tests are samples of behavior that are used to draw inferences about the domain of behaviors sampled. Therefore, a test that used unrepresentative stimuli but that sampled the domain of responses well, would be preferable to one that included representative stimuli but unrepresentative responses. An example of the latter is the work sample test, which is often used as a predictor and sometimes as a measure of job performance (see Chapter 19). Work sample tests ask respondents to carry out, under optimal conditions, a standard set of tasks that are part of the job; their performance on each task is carefully observed and scored. In terms of the stimuli employed, these tests are often highly representative and realistic. However, it is clear that these tests typically measure maximal rather than typical performance. That is, people typically perform their best on these tests and probably do not perform as well on the job, where they are not so closely monitored and not so free of distractions. It has long been argued that tests of maximal performance measure different things than tests of typical performance (i.e., how well a person can do a task versus how well he or she does it; see Cronbach, 1970, for an excellent discussion of the typical-maximal distinction). Research has shown that tests of typical versus maximal performance are not highly correlated (Sackett, Zedeck, & Fogli, 1988). A content-oriented analysis of work sample tests would not account for this finding unless it considered the effects of a wide range of variables, such as the respondent's motivation to perform on responses to test items.

Outcome of a Content Validity Study

The principal outcome of a content validity study is a judgment about the adequacy with which the test samples a particular content domain. Lawshe (1975) has proposed a content validity ratio as a measure of the extent to which expert judges agree on content validity, but this statistic measures agreement rather than validity itself. To our knowledge, no single statistic can be used to measure content validity.

Although there is no exact measure of content validity, it is clear that some studies provide more and better evidence for content validity than others. The key to deciding whether it is possible to make systematic and reliable judgments about content validity lies in the description of the content domain. The more detail provided about the boundaries and structure of the content domain, the more confidence that can be placed in judgments about content validity. If a test developer cannot clearly describe the boundaries and the contents of a particular domain, it is difficult to see how he or

she could ever convincingly demonstrate content validity. However, even if we assume that the domain is well understood and that we can, with some confidence, establish that the test is a representative sample from the domain, we are still not out of
the woods. Even if the right types of items are sampled, the way that they are written
may be confusing, or the response formats used may be inappropriate. Thus, two tests
that both show strong evidence of content validity will not necessarily produce identical scores. Although a test that is known to provide a representative sample of a particular domain is very likely to provide a valid and accurate measure of that domain, it is
important to remember that a content validity study cannot, by itself, guarantee the validity of measurement.

Content Validity, Reliability, and the Validity of Decisions

You may have noted the strong similarity between our discussion of reliability
and our discussion of content validity. Although reliability studies and content validity studies address somewhat different questions, reliability and content validity are
conceptually similar (Cronbach, Gleser, Nanda, & Rajaratnam, 1972). The difference is
mainly one of emphasis. Reliability theory assumes that the test represents a sample
from a domain of possible test items; this same assumption provides the basis for studies of content validity. The principal difference between a reliability study and a content validity study lies in the emphasis placed on providing a precise description of the
domain. Reliability theory simply assumes that there is a domain and that the test
could be lengthened by sampling more items from that domain. In a content validity
study, the researcher must describe in detail which domain he or she wishes to measure. Thus, if a test provides a reliable measure of some domain but fails to measure
the particular domain that is of interest, one might achieve a high level of reliability
with little or no content validity.

It seems clear that content validity is important to understanding test scores.
However, there is some controversy over whether content validity can be used to establish the validity of decisions based on test scores. A number of researchers have
suggested that a content validity approach might be useful in determining whether
specific tests could be used in applications such as personnel selection. The basic argument is as follows: (1) Tests are used to predict performance on the job; (2) job performance requires certain abilities and skills; (3) if the tests require the same abilities and
skills as those required on the job, then tests could be used to predict job performance;
and (4) therefore, the validity of a test for selection decisions can be established by
comparing the content of the test with the content of the job. This type of definition of
content validity has been widely accepted both by industry and by the federal government. However, most experts agree that content validity is relevant only in determining the validity of measurement (does the test measure what it claims to measure?), not
in determining the validity of decisions that are made on the basis of test scores.

Carrier, Delessio, and Brown (1990) investigated the hypothesis that judgments
about the content validity of tests would allow one to assess the validity of those tests
as predictors of important criteria. Their results are sufficiently ambiguous to give

comfort to the supporters and the detractors of content-oriented strategies of assessing validity for decisions. They found that expert judgments of content validity were significantly correlated with levels of criterion-related validity but that these correlations were small. Their results suggest that content-related evidence is useful but not sufficient for assessing the criterion-related validity of psychological tests.

CRITICAL DISCUSSION:

Face Validity

Scientific assessments of validity depend heavily on objective data (e.g., test score distributions, correlations between different measures). Another aspect of validity depends much more strongly on subjective reactions to tests, face validity. The term *face validity* refers to assessments of the extent to which a test appears reasonable to those who take it. The topic of face validity received considerable research attention in the 1940s and 1950s (Nevo, 1985), and subjects' reactions to testing procedures continue to be a topic of considerable importance in current research (Thornton, 1993).

Although assessments of face validity are not typically part of modern validation studies, there are good reasons to be concerned about subjects' perceptions of tests. Many tests and inventories ask examinees to perform to the best of their ability (e.g., academic admissions tests) or to provide candid answers to potentially ambiguous or embarrassing questions (e.g., clinical tests). If subjects perceive the test as trivial or irrelevant, they may not provide responses that reflect the attributes that the test is designed to measure.

Face validity is not necessarily a characteristic of the test itself but, rather, represents an interaction between what the test asks the examinee to do and the examinee's understanding of what the test is designed to measure. A test is most likely to be judged to be face valid if the tasks that the examinees are required to perform are in some way related to their understanding of what the test is designed to measure. For example, paragraph-comprehension items (where you are required to read a paragraph and then answer questions that are based on what you read) seem reasonable and appropriate on an academic admissions test, but they might not seem reasonable if the test is designed to measure vocational interests.

Suppose that your test uses an unusual-looking item or procedure. You might be concerned that examinees will not take the test seriously, which might severely limit the validity and usefulness of the test. There are two options for dealing with this problem. First, you might change the items. Sometimes this task might be easy, but the process of test development is usually an arduous one, and changing items is not always possible. Second, you might change the examinees' evaluation of the offending items or tasks. Simply forewarning examinees that they might encounter items that do not look like they should work but that are well-supported in empirical research, can often diminish concerns about face validity.

CONSTRUCT-ORIENTED VALIDATION STRATEGIES

Psychologists are keenly interested in measuring abstract attributes—happiness, intelligence, motivation, sociability. These things do not exist in the literal, physical sense; it is impossible to gather up a pound of happiness or a handful of intelligence. Nevertheless, they must be measured in order to apply, test, and extend psychological theories and principles.

The problem of measuring abstract attributes is by no means restricted to psychology. Physicists routinely measure unobservable properties of matter. Mass provides a good example of this type of property; mass itself cannot be seen or heard, yet this hypothetical property of objects is clearly important and clearly measurable. Attributes such as mass, happiness, or intelligence are referred to as *constructs*. They represent ideas constructed by scientists to help summarize a group of related phenomena or objects. For example, if a person tells the truth in a wide variety of situations, we might label that person as honest. Honesty is a construct; it cannot be directly observed, yet it is a useful concept for understanding, describing, and predicting human behavior.

Tests are often designed to measure psychological constructs. Some tests provide valid measures of important constructs, whereas others show little or no construct validity. Because constructs are abstract in nature, the process of determining whether a test provides an adequate measure of a specific construct is complex.[2] To describe the process of construct validation, we must first discuss the nature of psychological constructs.

Constructs

All constructs have two essential properties: They are abstract summaries of some regularity in nature, and they are related to or connected with concrete, observable entities or events. Gravity provides a good example of a construct: When apples fall to earth, the construct gravity is used to explain and predict their behavior. It is impossible to see gravity itself; all one sees is the falling apple. Nevertheless, it makes perfect sense to measure gravity and to develop theories that employ the construct gravity. It certainly seems more sensible to deal with this abstract force we call gravity than to develop theories and methods that apply only to falling apples.

Constructs are essential to science. They represent departures from our immediate sensory experience that are necessary to form scientific laws (Margenau, 1950). They allow us to generalize from an experiment involving falling apples to situations involving a variety of falling objects. A construct such as gravity is related to a number of concrete objects and events. Thus, once I learn about gravity, I will be able to predict a wide variety of phenomena.

Constructs are not restricted to unseen forces, such as gravity, or to processes, such as learning. Rather, any group of similar things or events may serve to define a construct. Thus, most categories that we use to classify and discuss everyday objects or events are in fact constructs. For example, the color red is a construct. There are plenty of red things, some of which plainly vary in color, but the basic idea of red is an abstraction. Poverty, reading ability, and cognitive style are thus all labels for constructs (Cronbach, 1971).

Although constructs are themselves hypothetical abstractions, all constructs are related to real, observable things or events. The distinguishing feature of psychological constructs is that they are always related, directly or indirectly, to behavior or to experience. Some constructs, such as aggressiveness or achievement motivation, are thought of as causes of particular behaviors. Other constructs, such as pleasure or

---

[2]Angoff (1988) reviewed the history of different definitions of validity and their relations to construct validation.

verbal ability or musical talent, refer to the ability to perform a number of related behaviors. As discussed in the section that follows, still other psychological constructs
show no direct connection with observable behaviors; rather, they are connected with
other constructs that are, in turn, connected with behavior or experience.

Psychological Constructs

Psychological measurement is a process based on concrete, observable behaviors.
Hence, a psychological test is nothing more than a sample of behaviors. To determine
whether a test provides a good measure of a specific construct, we must translate the
abstract construct into concrete, behavioral terms. The process of providing a detailed
description of the relationship between specific behaviors and abstract constructs, referred to as *construct explication,* is the key to determining the construct validity of a test.

The process of construct explication consists of three steps:

1. Identify the behaviors that relate to the construct to be measured.
2. Identify other constructs, and decide whether they are related or unrelated to the construct
   to be measured.
3. Identify behaviors that are related to each of these additional constructs, and on the basis
   of the relations among constructs, determine whether each behavior is related to the construct to be measured.

An example describing the three steps of construct explication is presented in
Table 8-3. In the table, the construct validity of a test designed to measure aggressiveness in schoolchildren is being examined. The first step in the process of construct explication is to describe behaviors that are related to aggressiveness. A child who
assaults other students, who pushes to the head of the line, or who dominates most
games might be labeled aggressive. Many other behaviors might be considered as examples or manifestations of aggressiveness, and at this stage we should try to provide
as many as possible. The more behaviors we are able to list, the clearer the picture will
be of what we mean when we say "aggressiveness."

The second step in providing a detailed description of the construct aggressiveness is to identify other constructs that could sensibly be measured in the subject
population and to determine whether each of these is related or not related to aggressiveness. For example, it is useful to identify other constructs, such as need for power,
that are related to aggressiveness. It is also useful to identify constructs that are clearly
not related to the specific construct to be measured. For example, the statement that the
construct aggressiveness is unrelated to the construct honesty helps to define the
boundaries of both aggressiveness and honesty.

The third step is to identify behaviors that are related to each of these additional
constructs. For example, a child who always makes decisions for groups or who dominates games might exhibit a high need for power. A child who refrains from cheating
and who tells the truth to his or her teacher might be labeled as honest. Because we
have made some statements about the relationships between the constructs of honesty,
need for power, and aggressiveness, it should be possible to state whether each of

Table 8-3   STEPS IN DESCRIBING THE CONSTRUCT "AGGRESSIVENESS IN SCHOOLCHILDREN"

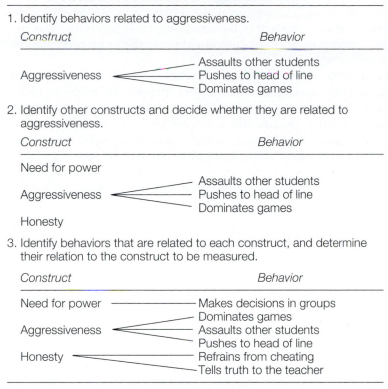

1. Identify behaviors related to aggressiveness.

Construct	Behavior
Aggressiveness	Assaults other students
	Pushes to head of line
	Dominates games

2. Identify other constructs and decide whether they are related to aggressiveness.

Construct	Behavior
Need for power	
Aggressiveness	Assaults other students
	Pushes to head of line
	Dominates games
Honesty	

3. Identify behaviors that are related to each construct, and determine their relation to the construct to be measured.

Construct	Behavior
Need for power	Makes decisions in groups
	Dominates games
Aggressiveness	Assaults other students
	Pushes to head of line
Honesty	Refrains from cheating
	Tells truth to the teacher

Note: Constructs and behaviors that are related to one another are connected with a solid line. Unrelated constructs or behaviors are not connected.

these behaviors is related or unrelated to aggressiveness. For example, if aggressiveness and need for power are related, it is plausible that some behaviors that indicate high levels of need for power (e.g., dominates games) will also indicate high levels of aggressiveness. Similarly, if aggressiveness and honesty are unrelated, then knowing that a student refrains from cheating or tells the truth to the teacher reveals nothing about his or her level of aggressiveness.

The end result of the process of construct explication is a detailed description of the relationships among a set of constructs and behaviors. This system of relationships, referred to as a nomological network, provides a definition of what we mean by aggressiveness (Cronbach & Meehl, 1955). Because constructs are abstract in nature, it is impossible to provide a concrete, operational definition of a term such as aggressiveness. The nomological network provides an alternative way of systematically describing constructs. In our example, aggressiveness is defined as a personal characteristic that is related to a large number of behaviors (e.g., assaulting others) but that is not related to other behaviors (e.g., refraining from cheating). Although a construct cannot be directly observed, it can be inferred from observable behaviors. To put this another way, we cannot say precisely what aggressiveness is, but we can describe how an aggressive child might act, and we can make reliable and meaningful statements about children's levels of aggressiveness by observing their behavior. The more detail included in descriptions of the nomological network, the more precision there will be in describing constructs.

Cronbach (1988, 1989) noted that applications of the methods described in Cronbach and Meehl (1955) have proved to be very difficult. He noted in 1988, "There is no hope for developing in the short run the 'nomological networks' we once envisioned" (p. 13). Thus, construct validity has a somewhat more limited goal than was once hoped for. Rather than embedding each test in a complex network of associations with many other constructs, most construct validity researchers now pursue the goal of determining what inferences about psychological constructs can and cannot be made on the basis of a test score and under what conditions these inferences are or are not valid (Cronbach, 1988).

Assessing Construct Validity

The goal of construct validation is to determine whether test scores provide a good measure of a specific construct. The process of construct explication provides a definition of the construct in terms of concrete behaviors. Although construct explication does not define precisely what a construct such as aggressiveness is, it does tell how that construct relates to a number of behaviors. A child who shows a high level of aggressiveness is likely to show certain behaviors (e.g., assaulting classmates) and is less likely to show other behaviors than a child who is low on aggressiveness. A well-developed nomological network, therefore, provides detailed information about the relationship between the construct and a large number of behaviors. This information can be used to describe the way in which a good measure of a construct can be expected to relate to each of these behaviors. A test shows a high level of construct validity if the pattern of relationships between test scores and behavior measures is similar to the pattern of relationships that can be expected from a perfect measure of the construct. An example will help to clarify this point.

Our explication of the construct aggressiveness (see Table 8-3) suggests that the following behaviors are directly related to the construct: (1) assaulting other students, (2) pushing to the head of lines, and (3) dominating games. In other words, we would expect measures of these behaviors to be positively correlated with a good measure of aggressiveness. The behavior "makes decisions in groups" was related to a construct (need for power) that was in turn related to aggressiveness; we might therefore expect measures of this behavior to show a positive correlation with measures of aggressiveness. Finally, the behaviors "refrains from cheating" and "tells truth to teacher" are not at all related to aggressiveness. We therefore might expect measures of these behaviors to be uncorrelated with a measure of aggressiveness. The correlations we would expect between measures of each of the behaviors and measures of aggressiveness are summarized in Table 8-4.

Table 8-4   EXPECTED CORRELATIONS BETWEEN A GOOD MEASURE OF AGGRESSIVENESS AND MEASURES OF SPECIFIC BEHAVIORS

Behaviors	Relationship with aggressiveness	Expected correlation
Assaulting others	Direct	Strong Positive
Pushing in line	Direct	Strong Positive
Dominating games	Direct	Strong Positive
Making decisions	Indirect — related to need for power	Weak Positive
Refraining from cheating	None	None
Telling truth to teacher	None	None

A detailed description of the construct provides a basis for describing the relationships to be expected between a good measure of that construct and a variety of behaviors. Actual test scores can be correlated with behavior measures, and the results can be compared with the pattern of results expected on the basis of our explication of the construct. The stronger the match between the expected correlations and the actual correlations between test scores and behavior measures, the stronger the evidence of construct validity.

Table 8-5 shows comparisons between expected and actual correlations for two tests designed to measure aggressiveness in schoolchildren. Test A appears to be a valid measure of the construct aggressiveness; the correlations between test scores and behavior measures are very similar to the correlations one would expect on the basis of our theory of aggressiveness. In contrast, the data suggest that test B is a poor measure

Table 8-5   CORRELATIONS BETWEEN TEST SCORES AND BEHAVIOR MEASURES FOR TWO TESTS

Behaviors	Expected correlations	Actual correlations	
		Test A	Test B
Assaulting others	Strong Positive	.59	−.22
Pushing in line	Strong Positive	.70	.14
Dominating games	Strong Positive	.65	.02
Making decisions in groups	Weak Positive	.30	−.40
Refraining from cheating	None	.09	.56
Telling truth to teacher	None	−.04	.39
		(Test with *high* level of construct validity)	(Test with *low* level of construct validity)

of aggressiveness. Behaviors we would expect to correlate strongly with aggressiveness show weak and sometimes negative correlations with test scores. Other behaviors that have nothing to do with aggressiveness show fairly sizable correlations with test B. It appears fair to conclude that test B does not measure aggressiveness as we have defined it.

Construct validity depends on a detailed description of the relationship between the construct and a number of different behaviors. The more we know about the construct, the better are our chances for determining whether a test provides an adequate measure of that construct. One implication is that it will be easier to determine construct validity for measures of well-defined constructs than for measures of constructs that are loosely defined. If I define a new construct but have only a fuzzy idea of what that construct means, it follows that I will never be able to tell whether a given test provides a good measure of that construct.

A very sophisticated version of the validation strategy described here was applied by Mumford, Weeks, Harding, and Fleishman (1988) in their analysis of the relationships among student characteristics, course content, and training outcomes. Their study incorporated measures of 6 student characteristics, 16 measures of course content, and 7 measures of training outcomes. They articulated hypotheses about the relationships between each of these 29 measures and criterion variables, and they developed an integrated model that described the hypothesized relationships. This model allowed them to describe the relationships among the three constructs (i.e., characteristics, content, and outcomes) and to draw conclusions about the relative importance of individual versus situational variables in determining training outcomes.

Another example of this approach is in a study by Pulakos, Borman, and Hough (1988) in which experts were first asked to estimate the correlations that they would expect between specific predictors and criteria. This approach allowed the authors to compare the estimated correlations with the correlations that they actually found. Results of one study of army enlisted personnel, in which there were eight predictors and three criteria, are presented in Table 8-6. In this study, 83% of the obtained correlations were in the predicted direction. Although the observed correlations were typically smaller than the estimated correlations, 87% of the correlations were of the relative magnitude predicted by the experts (i.e., those predicted to be largest were, in fact, usually the largest). These results present strong evidence for the construct validity of the measures employed.

Methods of Construct Validation

Which methods are most appropriate for studying construct validity depends to a large extent on the construct that we wish to measure. A combination of laboratory experiments, field experiments, questionnaires, and unobtrusive observations might be necessary to provide the data that underlie construct validation. Statistics that deal with differences between control and experimental groups, with correlations between various measures, with individual variations, or with change over time might be used to test predictions that are based on our description of the construct. Data about the

Table 8-6   ESTIMATED AND OBTAINED CORRELATIONS FOR ARMY ENLISTED PERSONNEL

	Criteria					
	Technical Skill		Personal discipline		Military bearing	
Predictors	Est.	Obs.	Est.	Obs.	Est.	Obs.
Technical	.38	.21	.11	.00	.09	−.18
Quantitative	.27	.17	.10	.06	.07	−.08
Verbal	.29	.16	.08	.04	.08	−.19
Speed	.16	.09	.07	.04	.06	.07
Achievement orientation	.50	.23	.36	.03	.25	.17
Dependability	.36	.15	.54	.22	.31	.14
Adjustment	.34	.12	.44	.05	.19	.11
Physical fitness	.16	−.01	.10	−.11	.54	.27

Est. = expert judge estimates; Obs. = observed correlations, N = 8,642.
Source: From Pulakos, Borman, and Hough (1988). Reproduced with permission.

reliability of a test under different conditions might contribute to our assessment of construct validity. In fact, it would be fair to say that any type of data or statistic might be useful in determining construct validity.

Although any method might be used to assess construct validity, a few methods seem to be most common. The most basic method is to correlate scores on the test in question with scores on a number of other tests. Here, the word *test* is used broadly to indicate any type of behavioral measure. We have already discussed this basic method in some depth and will return to a specialized application of this method in a later section. Another common method of studying construct validity involves the mathematical technique known as factor analysis (see Chapter 4). Factors are very much like constructs, and factor analysis provides an analytical method for estimating the correlation between a specific variable (a test score) and scores on the factor. Factor analysis also provides a compact summary of information about the relationships among a large number of measures. The description of a construct provides information about the expected relationships among variables; factor analysis helps determine whether this pattern of relationships does indeed exist.

A third common method of studying construct validity involves experimental manipulation of the construct that is to be measured. For example, a test designed to measure anxiety should show higher scores for subjects in an experiment who are led to expect shocks than for subjects who fill out an innocuous questionnaire. On the other hand, if a study has nothing to do with anxiety, the control group and the experimental group would *not* be expected to receive different scores on the test of anxiety. A combination of experiments in which the construct of interest is manipulated and experiments in which that construct is *not* manipulated provide a powerful method for assessing construct validity.

A study by Flynn (1987) illustrates the use of archival data and reviews of existing research in construct validation. This study reviewed research from 14 nations documenting substantial rises in IQ scores over the preceding 30 to 40 years. Flynn (1987) noted several correlates of increasing IQ scores, including increases in scientific achievement, superior performance in schools, and an increase in the number of individuals classified as geniuses. He then surveyed selected newspapers, magazines, and educational journals in countries exhibiting substantial increases in IQ scores and looked for evidence of these phenomena (e.g., an increasing number of patents and inventions, news stories describing an increase in the number of geniuses). His survey showed no evidence of increases in scientific achievement, inventions, and so forth, accompanying the massive increases in IQ, leading him to question whether the IQ tests surveyed really measured intelligence.

Multitrait-Multimethod Approach. D. T. Campbell and Fiske (1959) outlined an approach that is very often used in assessing construct validity. They noted that if we use a number of methods to measure more than one trait or construct, the correlations among these measures will take the form of a multitrait-multimethod matrix. For example, the honesty, aggressiveness, and intelligence of a group of schoolchildren might be measured using three methods: teacher ratings, paper-and-pencil tests, and ratings from outside observers. The correlations among these three traits, measured by each of these three methods, are shown in Table 8-7.

A multitrait-multimethod study provides a great deal of data that are useful in assessing construct validity. First, since each construct is measured using a number of different methods, it is possible to determine whether different methods of measurement produce comparable sources. The correlations between a test measuring honesty, teacher ratings of honesty, and observers' ratings of honesty indicate whether these three methods all measure the same construct. Correlations between different measures of the same construct are underlined in Table 8-7. The data suggest that different methods of measuring honesty, aggressiveness, and intelligence are in pretty close agreement; correlations between different measures of each of the three traits range from .52 to .82. Thus, there is evidence for convergent validity: Multiple measures of each of the three constructs converge to yield similar results. The convergence of different methods serves to increase our confidence that we are, in fact, measuring the constructs that we wish to measure. Therefore, convergent validity is the first link in establishing construct validity.

The correlations between different traits or constructs are enclosed within solid and broken triangles in Table 8-7. In designing a multitrait-multimethod study, the researcher will usually select a group of constructs that are not, in theory, strongly related. Therefore, correlations between measures of different traits should be small— certainly smaller than correlations between different measures of the same trait. The correlations between measures of different constructs or traits serve to indicate the discriminant validity. Constructs are chosen to be clearly different, and measures of those constructs should therefore not correlate highly. Since the correlations between measures of different constructs shown in the table are clearly smaller than the correlations between different measures of the same construct, there appears to be evidence for discriminant validity. That is, the three constructs being measured in this study seem to

Table 8-7   A MULTITRAIT-MULTIMETHOD MATRIX

Method	Trait	Teacher ratings			Tests			Observers' ratings		
		Honesty	Aggressiveness	Intelligence	Honesty	Aggressiveness	Intelligence	Honesty	Aggressiveness	Intelligence
Teacher ratings	Honesty									
	Aggressiveness	.43								
	Intelligence	.36	.32							
Tests	Honesty	.62	.03	.20						
	Aggressiveness	.22	.70	.13	.40					
	Intelligence	.10	.13	.64	.22	.30				
Observers' ratings	Honesty	.59	.11	.02	.60	.20	.21			
	Aggressiveness	.14	.82	−.16	.13	.61	.23	.30		
	Intelligence	.21	.10	.72	.06	.19	.52	.49	.36	

Note: Convergent validity coefficients are underlined. Correlations between different constructs using the same method (e.g., teacher ratings) are enclosed in solid triangles. Correlations between measures of different constructs using different methods are enclosed in broken triangles.

be discriminably different. Since the constructs intelligence, honesty, and aggressiveness are, in theory, unrelated, low correlations between measures of these constructs provide further evidence of construct validity.

The correlations enclosed in solid triangles in Table 8-7 represent measures of different constructs using the same method. For example, the table shows the correlations among teacher ratings of honesty, aggressiveness, and intelligence. The correlations among measures of different traits obtained using a single method (e.g., teacher ratings) are somewhat larger than the correlations enclosed in broken triangles, which represent correlations between different traits measured by different methods. This frequently found pattern indicates method bias. For example, the correlation between honesty ratings and intelligence ratings provided by the teacher is higher than any of the honesty-intelligence correlations that involve two different methods of measurement. When two different constructs are measured using the same method, we expect some correlation solely as a result of the common method of measurement. A multitrait-multimethod study allows us to estimate the effects of this bias.

The multitrait-multimethod approach is an efficient and informative method for studying several questions related to construct validity. This method suggests that a good test of a particular construct has these three characteristics:

1. Scores on the test will be consistent with scores obtained using other measures of the same construct.
2. The test will yield scores that are not correlated with measures that are theoretically unrelated to the construct being measured.
3. The method of measurement employed by the test shows little evidence of bias.

The data from a multitrait-multimethod study can often be difficult to interpret; the simple example presented here contained 36 separate correlation coefficients to consider. A number of analytic methods have been proposed to simplify the interpretation of multitrait-multimethod matrices, ranging from the analysis of variance (Kavanaugh, MacKinney, & Wolins, 1971; Stanley, 1961) to confirmatory factor analysis (Schmitt & Stults, 1986). In addition, sophisticated analytic methods have been developed for answering questions implicit in the multitrait-multimethod design, such as whether two tests measure the same construct (Turban, Sanders, Francis, & Osburn, 1989).

Strong Versus Weak Evidence of Construct Validity

Cronbach (1988, 1989) contrasted two different strategies for construct validation research. The weak version of construct validation involves collecting all the relevant evidence about the relationship between scores on a test and other measures. He dismissed this strategy as "Dragnet empiricism," in the sense that it involves collecting "just the facts," with little regard for their usefulness in understanding the test or the construct being measured. He criticizes most applications of the multitrait-multimethod design as mindless and mechanical; the selection of traits and methods is more often based on convenience than on compelling hypotheses.

In contrast, the strong version of construct validation involves testing your interpretation of test scores against other plausible hypotheses. Landy (1987) notes that all validation studies involve hypotheses testing; but clearly, some hypotheses would allow you to gather strong evidence of construct validity, and others would give only weak support for a particular interpretation of test scores. For example, suppose that you were interested in evaluating the construct validity of situational interviews that are used in personnel selection (Latham, Saari, Pursell, & Campion, 1980). This type of interview presents the interviewee with descriptions of several hypothetical situations that he or she might encounter at work and then asks the interviewee what he or she should do in each situation. Research on criterion-related validity shows that these interviews predict subsequent job performance. The question faced when assessing construct validity is what the scores on such an interview are likely to mean.

A weak program of construct validation would involve gathering as much information as possible about variables that could conceivably be related to outcomes of these interviews (e.g., biographical data, performance data, and scores on standard interviews). A strong program of construct validation would start with specific hypotheses about what such an interview actually measures. Several possibilities come to mind. First, the interviews might measure a social desirability factor; people who know the desirable answer to the questions in these interviews might do well in them and also do well in jobs that require social interactions. Second, these interviews might measure general intelligence; people who are intelligent might be better able to diagnose the situations presented to them and arrive at the best response to each situation. Third, these interviews might measure some type of job knowledge; people with experience in similar situations might be best equipped to perform well in such an interview. A strong program of construct validation would incorporate measures of intelligence, social desirability, and prior experience, and it would determine the extent to which each could account for the situational interview's validity in predicting job performance.

A second difference between a strong and weak program of construct validation may be temporal. Weak construct validation research is often done after the fact (i.e., after the test has been developed) to determine just what an existing test or assessment procedure measured. Strong programs of construct validation often begin at the test development stage (Fiske, 1987; Fredericksen, 1986). That is, a strong program of construct validation is easiest to carry out if the initial decision about what types of items, response formats, and so forth, to use are guided by your understanding of the construct that you wish to measure. If the design of the test does not spring from the nature of the construct, it may subsequently be very difficult to demonstrate that it does indeed measure the construct of interest.

CONTENT AND CONSTRUCT VALIDITY

Content validity is typically determined by examining the sampling plan of the test and seeing whether the test provides a representative sample of the content domain. Construct validity is established by showing that the relationship between test scores and other observable measures is similar to the relationships that would be expected between the construct itself and those observable measures. Furthermore, content validity is typically determined for tests of very concrete domains, such as classroom tests, whereas construct validity is generally determined for tests designed to measure abstract attributes, such as aggressiveness or honesty. It would therefore seem that content and construct validity are very different and perhaps mutually exclusive. Although there is some merit to this point of view, it is better to view content and construct validity as highly related. First, both represent approaches for determining the validity of measurement—for determining whether a test measures what it purports to measure. Second, the distinction between a construct and a content domain is not as fundamental as it might appear (Landy, 1987; Messick, 1988). A content domain represents a group of similar test items whose boundaries and structure are fairly well understood. Although in theory it may be possible to sample all the items in a content domain, in practice, test scores are used to estimate the hypothetical score on the domain. In other words, an individual's standing or score on a content domain is an abstraction, very much like a person's level of a construct such as honesty. Many researchers feel that most content categories are constructs (Cronbach, 1971).

The similarity between content domains and constructs suggests that both content- and construct-oriented approaches may be applicable in a variety of cases. Content validity can be determined whenever the boundaries and structure of a domain can be described in some detail. Construct validity can be determined whenever the researcher can provide a detailed statement about the relationship between the construct and a variety of concrete, observable measures. Both strategies provide evidence that the test measures what it is designed to measure; the combination of content and construct validity represents very strong evidence for the validity of measurement. It is never possible to say with complete certainty that test X measures construct Y or domain Z, but methods described here allow the accumulation of clear and compelling evidence that the test measures what it is supposed to measure. Content validity is established if a test *looks* like a valid measure; construct validity is established if a test *acts* like a valid measure.

There are a few cases in which one must choose to follow either a content validity approach or a construct validity approach. For example, a good deal may be known about the boundaries and structure of a domain such as "knowledge of behavioral statistics" but nothing about how knowledge of statistics should relate to other observable traits or behaviors. In this case, there would be little choice; content validity would represent the most feasible approach for assessing the validity of measurement. On the other hand, one might have a very clear idea of how a construct such as "honesty" relates to a number of observable behaviors, yet be unclear as to the boundaries of the construct. Here, content validity would be out of the question; a construct validity approach would be the only one feasible. Both of these examples represent cases in which the theory of what is being measured has not been fully developed. In other words, both of these cases represent situations in which, because of a poorly developed theory of the domain or construct to be measured, it is impossible to say precisely what would represent a good test or a bad test. In these situations, it is difficult to demonstrate convincingly the validity of measurement.

CRITICAL DISCUSSION:

How Do We Know Whether Intelligence Tests Really Measure Intelligence?

There is considerable controversy over the validity of intelligence tests. In later chapters, we review some of the evidence that bears on this controversy. It is useful here to consider the methods that are used to determine whether intelligence tests really measure intelligence. A brief review of these methods will illustrate the process by which the validity of measurement is determined.

A content validity strategy is not very useful in assessing the validity of intelligence tests. Intelligence is a very broad concept; it would be very difficult to draw up an exhaustive list of the types that could be used to represent intelligence. In other words, it would be nearly impossible to specify the boundaries and content of the intelligence domain.

Several research strategies have been used in assessing the construct validity of intelligence tests. All these strategies depend on key assumptions that are made in defining the construct intelligence. In particular,

1. Intelligence is assumed to involve the processing, retrieval, and manipulation of information.
2. Activities that require complex information processing will draw more heavily on intelligence than will activities that represent simple information-processing tasks.
3. Intelligence is a general construct that is related to a wide range of specific cognitive abilities.

The use of digit span tests illustrates an application of the first two assumptions. For example, if I read to you a list of nine digits, more mental manipulation is required to repeat the list backward from memory (you must store, retrieve, and mentally invert the list) than to repeat the list in its original order (here, you only store and retrieve the list). Since general intelligence involves the processing of information, it follows that mental tasks that involve more complex processes should be more highly correlated with intelligence tests than would tasks that involve simpler processes. In this context, a higher correlation can be expected between intelligence test scores and scores of tests that involve repeating digit spans backward than between intelligence and simple digit span tests. Most good intelligence tests show exactly this pattern (Jensen, 1980). A new test that also showed this pattern of results would exhibit evidence of construct validity.

Another method of validating intelligence tests is to consider situations that, to different extents, involve general intelligence. For example, school places heavy demands on information-processing abilities, whereas in many social situations individual differences in intelligence have very little bearing on behavior. We would therefore expect intelligence test scores to be highly correlated with success in school, but to show much smaller correlations with measures of social skills. Once again, this is exactly the pattern of results found when validating most intelligence tests (see, however, Flynn, 1987).

A third method of validating an intelligence test is to correlate scores on that test with scores on other, well-validated tests of specific cognitive abilities, including other intelligence tests. This procedure may sound circular, but it does provide useful evidence. If there is solid evidence that tests *X, Y,* and *Z* are well-validated measures of intelligence, it follows that any new test of intelligence should yield similar scores to those obtained using the existing tests. If the new test has nothing in common with the existing, well-validated tests of intelligence, it would be difficult to conclude that the new test really measures intelligence. Higher correlations would also be expected between scores on intelligence tests and scores on tests of abilities that are, in theory, strongly related to intelligence (e.g., verbal ability) than between intelligence tests and tests of abilities thought to be minimally related to general intelligence (e.g., simple reaction time).

The best validation research employs multiple methods. It would be difficult to conclude on the basis of any single finding that a test really measures intelligence. Several well-researched intelligence tests present evidence from multiple sources and by multiple methods that test scores act the way that the construct itself is assumed to act. In other words, research involving diverse methods, research questions, and subject populations has provided evidence of the construct validity of these tests that is accepted by many psychologists.

SUMMARY

To understand validation, it is important to keep in mind exactly what is validated. It is not the test that is validated but, rather, the inferences that are made on the basis of test scores. For example, if an individual receives a high score on an inventory designed to measure need for achievement, you might infer that he or she shows high levels of achievement motivation. You might also infer that he or she would do well in a management training course. The first type of inference concerns measurement, and this was dealt with in this chapter. The second type of inference involves a prediction about something other than the attribute that was directly measured, and this is dealt with in the chapter that follows.

Both content- and construct-oriented strategies are used to assess the validity of measurement. Content-oriented strategies are based on the simple premise that tests are samples of behavior. Content-oriented validation strategies involve examining the degree to which the sample is representative of the broader domain that you wish to measure. In applying this strategy, you must not only examine the test items but also consider the response processes and the behaviors elicited by the test. The greater the match between the behaviors actually sampled on the test and those that represent the domain that you wish to measure, the greater your confidence in the validity of measurement.

Construct-oriented strategies start with construct explication—that is, the detailed description of exactly what the test is designed to measure. Psychological constructs are by definition linked to observable behaviors, and the process of construct explication involves describing these links in as much detail as possible. A successful construct explication will give you a very clear idea of how a good measure of the construct should relate to a wide variety of other measures, which in turn gives you a yardstick for evaluating your measure. If the test that you are studying acts like a good measure, in the sense that it is related to other constructs and measures in the same way as the construct that you have explicated, you can infer that it provides valid measurement.

Research provides no definite answers regarding the validity of measurement; you can never be 100% certain that your measure is a valid measure. However, the accumulation of evidence over several studies should increase your confidence that you are indeed measuring the content domain or the construct that you intend to measure. As you will see in Chapters 13 to 22, most of the tests that are used to make important decisions about individuals are supported by large bodies of research, often applying many, if not all, of the methods of validation described in this chapter.

PROBLEMS AND SOLUTIONS—RECAP

The Problem

You have been asked to evaluate the validity of a test of social skills that involves picking the most compatible set of 10 couples from 20 characters on different television shows.

A Solution

As this chapter suggests, there are two basic approaches to this problem. First, you can compare the content of the test to the content domain you are trying to measure. Although the task is arguably relevant (i.e., people with poor social skills might find it hard to predict compatibility), this is probably a case in which construct-oriented methods are likely to be more useful than content-oriented ones. Unless you can specify the content and structure of the domain of social skills in some detail, you probably will not be able to tell how well the tasks that this test involves sample that domain. Rather than asking whether this compatibility-matching task represents a good sample of the domain of social skills, you are more likely to want to ask questions about the characteristics of people who receive high or low scores on this task.

Construct validation starts with an articulation of what "social skills" really means and an identification of the correlates and consequences of high or low social skills. Suppose, for example, that the research literature on social skills showed that people with good skills in this area: (1) made lots of friends, (2) were confident in social situations, (3) had a small number of romantic attachments, each of which lasted a long time, and (4) were more likely to be elected to offices in professional or social associations. This information would give you a variety of hypotheses that could be pursued in validating the social skills test. If the test does indeed measure the respondent's social skills, scores on this test should be positively correlated with measures of friendship formation and social confidence, negatively correlated with the number of romantic relationships but positively correlated with their duration, and positively correlated with election to offices, social honors, and so on.

KEY TERMS

Construct   abstraction that summarizes some regularity in nature (psychological constructs describe some regularity in behavior or experience)

Construct explication   process of describing what a construct means and what it is related to

Construct-oriented validation strategy   method of determining what a test measures by examining the correlates of test scores (e.g., are scores on this test correlated with good measures of some conceptually similar construct?)

Content-oriented validation strategy   method of determining what a test measures by examining test content

Face validity   extent to which a test appears to provide a reasonable and an acceptable measure

Multitrait-multimethod matrix   network of correlations that is obtained if several attributes are each measured using multiple methods

Validity for decisions   extent to which test scores contribute to making correct predictions or decisions about individuals

Validity of measurement   extent to which tests measure what they seem to measure

9

Validity for Decisions: Criterion-Related Validity

As noted in Chapter 1, a major reason for our interest in tests is that they are used to make important decisions about individuals. Tests do not always lead to correct decisions; but compared with other methods for making decisions such as college admissions or job hiring, they are thought to represent the most accurate, fair, and economical alternatives available (Wigdor & Garner, 1982a). In fact, in settings where decisions must be made about large numbers of individuals (e.g., in screening military recruits), psychological tests often represent the only practical method of making systematic decisions.

The validity of tests as decision-making aids is a topic of great practical importance. The accuracy of decisions is directly linked to the validity of test scores; an invalid test can lead to decisions that are both ineffective, from the decision maker's point of view, and unfair, from the individual's point of view. The simplest method of determining whether a test can be used validly in making decisions is to correlate test scores with measures of success or of the outcomes of decisions. These measures are referred to as *criteria*—hence the term *criterion-related validity*. The correlation between test scores and criteria provides a quantitative estimate of validity, which in turn can be used to obtain a detailed picture of the effect of testing on decisions. In particular, measures of criterion-related validity provide means to determine whether tests will serve to reduce particular types of decision errors and whether the gains in the accuracy of decisions are worth the cost of testing. This chapter presents a number of methods of estimating and interpreting the criterion-related validity of a test.

PROBLEMS AND SOLUTIONS—DETERMINE THE POTENTIAL BENEFITS OF TESTING

The Problem

The management of Allervant Consulting Group were very pleased with the job you did in evaluating the validity of their newly purchased social skills test (See Problems and Solutions, Chapter 8). They have given you a new, more complicated task.

Allervant Consulting Group sells a test of verbal ability; a set of careful validation studies suggests that scores on this test are consistently correlated with sales performance (the correlation between test scores and total sales is .45). This finding suggests that people who receive high scores will probably be better salespersons, but the question is how much better. Your managers ask you to estimate the financial benefits that an organization might expect if they used this test in selecting salespersons.

DECISIONS AND PREDICTION

Mathematical decision theory makes a formal distinction between a decision, which involves choosing a particular course of action, and a prediction, which involves estimating the value of some variable, such as success in school, on the basis of what is known about another variable, such as Graduate Record Examination (GRE) scores. Criterion-related validity deals with the correlation between tests and criteria or with the degree to which test scores can be used to predict criteria. Although a prediction is formally different from a decision, there are strong conceptual similarities between predictions and decisions. In fact, these are sufficiently strong that we will treat the correlation between test scores and criteria as synonymous with validity for decisions. An example will help to clarify both the similarities and the differences between predictions and decisions.

Assume that you are a personnel manager trying to pick the best three applicants for the job of master mechanic from the five shown in Table 9-1.

Applicants A, B, and C have reasonably high test scores, whereas D and E have low scores. If you had no other information, you would probably predict that A, B, and C would perform well on the job, and you therefore would hire these three and reject

Table 9-1   MECHANICAL COMPREHENSION SCORES OF FIVE APPLICANTS

Applicant	Scores on mechanical comprehension test (100 = perfect score)
A	98
B	82
C	81
D	43
E	29

D and E.[1] Prediction occurs when you try to estimate a person's score on a particular measure, such as a measure of job performance, on the basis of that person's score on some other measure, such as a mechanical comprehension test. Thus, you predict that applicants with high test scores will perform well on the job. You never know how someone will actually perform, but a good test allows you to make reasonably accurate predictions. A decision represents some action that you take on the basis of your predictions. You hire someone because you predict he or she will perform well on the job; you select a particular course of psychotherapy because you predict that it will be most beneficial for a particular client; you place a child in a special remedial class because you predict that the class will provide a suitable learning environment for the child. Predictions are not always accurate, and therefore tests do not always lead you to make the correct decisions; however, the more accurate your predictions are, the better your decisions will be.

The correlation between test scores and a measure of the outcome of a decision (the criterion) provides an overall measure of the accuracy of predictions. Therefore, the correlation between test scores and criterion scores can be thought of as a measure of the validity of decisions. As will be seen in a later section, thorough investigation of the effect of tests on decisions involves a number of factors in addition to the criterion-related validity of the test. Nevertheless, the validity coefficient, or the correlation between test scores and criterion scores, provides the basic measure of the validity of a test for making decisions.

CRITERIA

A *criterion* is a measure that could be used to determine the accuracy of a decision. In psychological testing, criteria typically represent measures of the outcomes that specific treatments or decisions are designed to produce. For example, workers are selected for jobs on the basis of predictions that the personnel department makes regarding their future performance on the job; the job applicants who are actually hired are those who, on the basis of test scores or other measures, are predicted to perform at the highest level. Actual measures of performance on the job serve as criteria for evaluating the personnel department's decisions. If the workers who were hired actually do perform at a higher level than would have those who were not hired, the predictions of the personnel department are confirmed, or validated. In a similar way, measures of grade point average (GPA) or years to complete a degree might serve as criteria for evaluating selection and placement decisions in the schools. A particular strategy for making college admissions decisions may be a good one if the students who are accepted receive better grades or complete their degrees in a shorter time than the applicants who were rejected would have. Again, in a similar way, measures of adjustment or of symptom severity might be used to evaluate decisions regarding the choice of psychotherapy.

---

[1]Note that, although it is predicted that A will be better than C, the same action is taken toward both (both are hired). This is one of the differences between prediction and decision.

An example will help to illustrate the importance of developing appropriate criterion measures. For years, the military has used the Armed Services Vocational Aptitude Battery (ASVAB) in the selection and placement of new recruits. For a long time, the principal evidence for the validity of the ASVAB was the finding that ASVAB scores were consistently correlated with success in military training courses. However, the ASVAB was designed and has been used to predict performance on the job, not performance in training. Thus, until the late 1980s, it was not proved that the ASVAB leads to correct decisions, although research on the validity of similar tests suggests that it would (Schmidt & Hunter, 1981). To correct this problem, the military undertook large-scale research efforts to develop measures of job performance and to assess the criterion-related validity of the ASVAB.

Unfortunately, the choice of criterion measures used in determining the validity of tests is sometimes made in a careless or haphazard manner (Guion, 1965a). The key to choosing criterion measures is to determine the decision maker's goal. The goal of the personnel department is to select productive workers; the appropriate criterion for evaluating its decision will be a measure of productivity. The goal of admissions directors is to select students who can perform well in classes; measures of classroom performance will supply criteria for evaluating their decision.

CRITERION-RELATED VALIDATION STRATEGIES

There are two general methods for assessing criterion-related validity: *predictive* and *concurrent validation strategies*. Predictive validity is recognized as the most accurate method of estimating validity but is also recognized as presenting the most serious practical and ethical problems. Concurrent validity is a generic term that refers to a variety of more practical procedures for assessing validity. Barrett, Phillips, and Alexander (1981); Guion and Cranny (1982); and Schmitt, Gooding, Noe, and Kirsch (1984) note that the conceptual and empirical distinctions between predictive and concurrent validity are not necessarily fundamental. However, the two general approaches do raise different practical, ethical, and statistical issues and are therefore worth discussing separately. Note that these two approaches represent different strategies for estimating the same quantity: the correlation between test scores and criterion scores. These two strategies differ in a number of practical and operational details, but not in their fundamental goals.[2]

The Ideal: Predictive Validation Strategies

The goal of a predictive validity study is to determine the correlation between test scores, which are obtained before making decisions, and criterion scores, which are obtained after making decisions. Personnel selection represents a typical setting in

---

[2]A third strategy, referred to as *synthetic validity*, has been used to infer or estimate the validity of both tests and test batteries (Guion, 1965b). This strategy provides logical estimates of validity based on the tests' ability to predict various components of the criterion.

which a predictive validity study might be carried out; here, a decision must be made to hire or reject each applicant, and a measure of job performance serves as a criterion for evaluating that decision. In this setting, a predictive validity study consists of the following two simple steps:

1. Obtain test scores from a group of applicants, but do not use the test, either directly or indirectly, in making hiring decisions.
2. At some later time, obtain performance measures for those persons hired, and correlate these measures with test scores to obtain the predictive validity coefficient.

The predictive validity approach is thought of as an ideal for two conflicting reasons. From the scientific point of view, it represents the simplest and most accurate strategy for estimating the correlation between test scores and criterion scores in the population of applicants in general. Yet, in another sense, this strategy is impractical, so although it is considered an ideal strategy for estimating validity, it is not a realistic one. The distinguishing feature of the predictive validity approach lies in the fact that decisions are made about applicants without test scores, either directly or indirectly.

The advantage of the predictive validity approach is that it provides a simple and direct measure of the relationship between scores on the test and performance on the criterion for the population of applicants in general. If the test were used to select applicants, the correlation between the test scores of people who did well on the test (and were therefore hired) and performance measures (which are collected at some later time) would indicate the validity of the test in the population of people with high test scores, rather than the validity of the test in the population in general. In most decision situations, the goal is to select those most likely to succeed from the total population of applicants. To estimate the validity of a test for this type of decision, an estimate of the correlation between test scores and performance scores must be obtained for all applicants. Most practical methods for estimating the validity of decisions involve correlating test scores and criterion scores in some preselected population (e.g., present workers) and therefore fall short of the ideal predictive validity approach.

Practical Objections. The key to the predictive validity approach is the requirement that the population in the validity study be similar to the general population of applicants. The only effective way to carry out a predictive validity study is either to make the same decision for everyone (e.g., hire all applicants) or to make decisions on a random basis (e.g., flip a coin). It is understandable that decision makers object to an approach that forces them to abandon, albeit temporarily, any system of selection in order to guarantee that the sample of people selected is representative of the population of applicants. It is impractical to hire people, admit them to school, or assign them to different types of therapy on a random basis. Of course, if the present system has little or no validity, decisions based on a table of random numbers are not likely to be any worse. Still, as a matter of practical politics, it is difficult to envision many people accepting an explicitly random system, such as would be necessary in a true predictive validity approach.

Ethical Objections. An incorrect decision has negative consequences for both the individual and the decision maker. For example, an organization that hires a worker who has little chance of success on the job is likely to incur substantial losses in terms of training costs and lost productivity. The individual also incurs some serious costs; failure on the job is a very negative experience and may contribute to depression or to loss of self-esteem, not to mention the monetary loss incurred when the employee is subsequently dismissed. Likewise, the psychologist who adopts a predictive validity approach would have to tolerate a number of failures that are probably preventable, with sometimes serious consequences to the clients involved. Thus, the predictive validity approach puts the decision maker in the ethically precarious position of selecting some people who he or she believes are very likely to fail (i.e., those with low test scores).

The Practical Alternative:
Concurrent Validation Strategies

The practical alternative to a predictive validity strategy is simply to obtain both test scores and criterion scores in some intact, preselected population and to compute the correlation between the two. Since many research designs of this type call for obtaining test scores and criterion scores at roughly the same time, they are known as *concurrent validation strategies.* As Guion and Cranny (1982) point out, the delay between obtaining test scores and obtaining criterion scores is not really the most fundamental difference between predictive and concurrent validity. The most fundamental difference is that a predictive validity coefficient is obtained in a random sample of the population about whom decisions must be made, whereas a concurrent validity coefficient is generally obtained in a preselected sample (e.g., present employees, students already accepted into college, patients in therapy) that may be systematically different from the population in general.

Guion and Cranny (1982) describe a number of common concurrent strategies for estimating the validity of a test for predicting scores on a specific criterion; three of these are especially common and can be described in simple terms (see also Sussman & Robertson, 1986). First, one can give the test to individuals who have already been selected (e.g., current workers, college freshmen) from the applicant population and obtain the criterion measure at approximately the same time the test is given. The correlation between test scores and criterion measures is a validity estimate. Next, one can select among applicants using the test (X), following up with a criterion measure (Y) at a later time. Finally, it is possible to use data from personnel files as measures X and Y. In all these designs, the correlation between test scores and criterion scores can be used to estimate the validity of the test, yet the population in which both the predictor and the criterion are measured may be systematically different from the population of applicants in general. The population of workers at a plant or students in a college is much more selective than the population who applied for jobs or who applied for school, since typically large numbers of applicants receive low scores on tests and interviews and hence do not pass the selection process. The fact that the population in a concurrent validity study is significantly more selective than the population of applicants in general has a potentially serious effect on the correlation between test scores and criterion scores. The nature and the extent of this effect are discussed later in this section.

Although in applied settings concurrent validity is much more common than predictive validity, the predictive approach is generally preferred over the concurrent validity approach. The correlation between test scores and criterion scores in some preselected, intact population is in theory not likely to be the same as the correlation between test scores and criterion scores in the population in general. Yet it is the latter correlation that is most important in assessing the validity of decisions. In most cases, tests are used to make decisions about very general populations; the validity of a test in a highly select population will not necessarily reveal much about the validity of the test for making selection decisions in a broader population of applicants.

Advantages. Three factors favor a concurrent validity approach. First, concurrent studies are practical. It is not necessary to select randomly or to allow a significant time lag between testing and criterion measurement in order to obtain concurrent validity coefficients. Second, concurrent validity studies are easier to conduct than predictive studies. In a concurrent study, it might be possible to obtain test scores and performance measures and to correlate them in a single day; a predictive study might last for months or even years. Third, although test theory suggests that concurrent validity coefficients seriously underestimate the population validity, concurrent validities are in fact often similar in size to predictive validities (Barrett et al., 1981; Schmitt et al., 1984). Although there may be considerable theoretical differences between a predictive study and a concurrent study, the outcomes of these two types of studies are often sufficiently similar to justify the more practical concurrent validity approach.

Statistical Problems. Research designs that use the correlation between test scores and criterion measures in a highly selective sample to estimate the validity of a test for making decisions in the population in general give rise to a number of statistical problems. By far the most serious problem in concurrent designs is the range restriction that occurs when people are selected according to their test scores (i.e., only those with high test scores are selected). Range restriction could have a substantial effect on the correlation between test scores and the criterion.

Range restriction also occurs in criterion measures. In work settings, people who perform very poorly are likely to be fired, whereas those who perform well are likely to be promoted. In school, students with consistently low grades are likely to fail or drop out. In clinical settings, clients are not likely to continue treatments that clearly are not working. As a result, the range of criterion scores is likely to be much smaller in an intact, preselected group (workers at a plant, students already admitted to college) than in the population in general.

Range restriction serves to reduce the correlation between test scores and criterion measures. Consider the scattergrams shown in Figure 9-1. In the population of applicants (a), a substantial correlation is shown between the test and the criterion. If

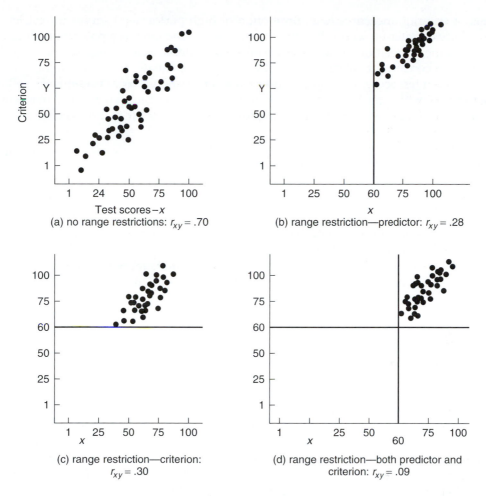

FIGURE 9-1   Effects of Range Restriction on the Correlation Between Test Scores and Criterion Measures

people are selected on the basis of their test scores, the range of the predictor is directly restricted. Scattergram (b) shows the effect of selecting those with test scores above 60. It suggests that the correlation between test scores and criterion measures is much smaller in the group whose test scores are above 60 than in the population in general. Range restriction in the criterion has a similar effect. Scattergram (c) shows the relationship between test scores and criteria for those with criterion scores above 60; the correlation between test scores and criteria also is obviously smaller than the population correlation. Finally, scattergram (d) depicts the correlation between test scores and criteria with range restriction in both the predictor and the criterion; here the concurrent validity coefficient drops to nearly zero. Direct selection of applicants on the basis of test scores serves to restrict the variability of test scores. Indirect selection on the basis of criterion measures (e.g., promotion of high performers) serves to restrict the variability of criterion scores. In either case, range restriction has a potentially dramatic effect on the correlation between test scores and criteria. Since range restriction often occurs in a concurrent validity study, it is critical to estimate its effects on the correlation between test scores (X) and criterion scores (Y). Guion (1965a) presents the following formula, which can be used to estimate the correlation between X and Y that would be obtained if there were no range restriction in the predictor (e.g., no selection):[3]

$$r_c = \frac{r(\sigma u / \sigma res)}{\sqrt{1 - r^2 + r^2(\sigma^2 u / \sigma^2 res)}} \qquad\qquad [9\text{-}1]$$

where

$\qquad r_c$ = estimate of the population r, correcting for range restriction
$\qquad r$ = sample correlation coefficient
$\qquad \sigma u$ = standard deviation of the sample on the predictor before range restriction
$\qquad \sigma res$ = standard deviation of sample after range restriction

The effects of range restriction can be illustrated by computing estimates of the true correlation between a test and a criterion under varying degrees of range restriction. Table 9-2 shows the best estimate of the population correlation coefficient if the r obtained in a range-restricted sample is equal to .30. As the table shows, when range restriction is minimal (e.g., when σ_x is reduced from .8 to .7), its effects are minimal. However, when range restriction is extensive, the correlation in the restricted sample may seriously underestimate the true r. One implication of Equation 9-1 is that the correlation between test scores and a criterion measure is not likely to be large if a concurrent study is carried out in a setting that is very selective, that is, when only those with extremely high test scores are represented. Equation 9-1 implies that concurrent validity coefficients will generally underestimate the validity of the test and that the underestimation may be severe when range restriction is extensive.

Table 9-2   EFFECTS OF RANGE RESTRICTIONS IN THE PREDICTOR X

Standard deviation of X before range restriction	*Standard deviation of X after range restriction*	*Estimated population correlation if the sample r = .30*
.8	.7	.33
.8	.6	.38
.8	.5	.45
.8	.4	.53
.8	.3	.64
.8	.2	.78

[3]A variety of more complicated formulas exist to correct for direct or indirect range restriction on X, Y, or both.

Conceptual Problems. Tests are most often used in an attempt to discriminate superior applicants from marginally acceptable or unacceptable applicants. Specifically, the goal of tests in most selection decisions is to screen out probable failures (see Landy, 1978). A predictive validity study provides a measure of how well a test can accomplish this goal; a concurrent validity study may not. A concurrent study typically contains very few, if any, marginal or poor performers. Because a concurrent study is carried out in a preselected population made up of people who are probably performing at acceptable levels (or better), the correlation between test scores and criterion scores measures the validity of the test in discriminating acceptable performers from superior performers. Therefore, a concurrent validity coefficient does not necessarily reveal much about the validity of decisions. If the population in a concurrent validity study differs significantly from the population of applicants in general, it is possible that a concurrent study will not provide a useful estimate of validity for decisions.

There is a second problem with most concurrent studies. The population in a concurrent study often differs from the population of applicants in a number of ways, and some of these differences could have important implications for the correlation between test scores and criteria. For example, a concurrent validity study conducted in a work setting generally includes a number of workers who have extensive experience on the job. The abilities that contribute to a new worker's performance may be completely different from the abilities that determine an experienced worker's performance (Murphy, 1989). Therefore, a test that predicts the performance of experienced workers may not be as useful in predicting the performance of a new worker.

CONSTRUCT VALIDITY AND CRITERION-RELATED VALIDITY

Virtually any validation strategy can provide information about the concurrent validity of a test or an assessment device. Researchers have moved from thinking that there were fundamentally different types of validity toward a unitary definition of validity, in which all validation is construct validation (Angoff, 1988; Cronbach, 1988; Landy, 1987; Messick, 1988; see also American Psychological Association, *Standards for Educational and Psychological Testing,* 1999). Although this unitary definition of validity is useful for organizing and thinking about validation research, the statement that all validity research is concerned (at least implicitly) with construct validity can be confusing. Consider the example of a personnel selection research project in which the researchers want to determine whether a particular test (e.g., the Wonderlic Personnel Test) predicts supervisory judgments about job performance. This appears to be a very practical question, without any of the abstract subtleties of a construct validity study. In fact, however, construct validity is at the heart of a study of this type.

Binning and Barrett (1989) suggest a framework for describing and analyzing validity studies, which can be used to show how the study described previously involves construct validity. The essential features of this framework are illustrated in Figure 9-2.

In Figure 9-2, actual measures are enclosed in rectangular boxes at the bottom of the figure, and constructs are set above in ellipses. In a typical validation study, the finding of interest is thought to be the relationship between the actual test and the

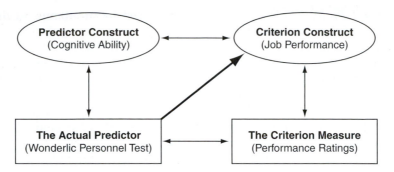

FIGURE 9-2   Inferences in the Validation Process

actual criterion measure (i.e., the arrow between the two boxes). It should be clear, however, that the real concern of the study is the relationship between the predictor and the criterion construct, represented in Figure 9-2 by the heavy arrow. That is, your concern as an applied psychologist is not to predict ratings of job performance but, rather, to predict actual job performance. Ratings are used as an operational criterion because you believe or have evidence to suggest that they are related to the construct of job performance.

What about the predictor construct (i.e., cognitive ability)? The predictor construct enters into a validation study of this type through the selection of actual tests or predictors. Several links are involved here. First, the predictor construct of ability is believed to be linked to the criterion construct of performance (construct-to-construct link). Second, the actual predictor (the Wonderlic) is thought to be linked to the predictor construct of ability (measure-to-construct link). The combination of these two links suggests that the Wonderlic will be related to performance ratings, which, in turn, will provide evidence for the link between that test and the construct of job performance.

The framework presented here suggests that any scientific validation effort will involve constructs on both the predictor side and the criterion side. That is, operational measures of both the predictor and the criterion should be selected on the basis of the constructs that they are thought to measure. Although it would be possible to select predictor tests and/or criteria without considering the criteria that they represent (e.g., you might try out a test that happens to be handy or use the same criteria that some other person has used in the past), a study of this sort would be little more than an exercise in data analysis. A well-designed validity study will always involve inferences about psychological constructs, regardless of the particular validation strategy employed.

Validity Evidence From Meta-Analyses

Novice researchers are often disappointed to find that, no matter how original their ideas seem, it usually turns out that someone else has already done a study similar to the one they are designing. There are tens of thousands of studies in the published literature in psychology, and it is not unusual to find hundreds on a given topic (e.g., Ones, Viswesvaran, & Schmidt's 1993 review of the validity of paper-and-pencil integrity tests included over 180 studies, yielding 665 validity coefficients across over 575,000 observations; this review is discussed in Chapter 19). For any specific test, several studies may be available; and for general classes of tests (e.g., cognitive ability tests), there may be several hundred.

The term *meta-analysis* refers to methods for combining research results from a large number of studies (Hedges & Olkin, 1985; Hunter & Schmidt, 1990). For example, if 50 studies have already been done on the validity of the Wonderlic Personnel Test (see Chapter 19 for a discussion of this test and of meta-analyses of validity studies for similar tests) as a predictor of job performance, the results of those studies can be averaged to give an overall estimate of the validity coefficient. The technical procedures involved in meta-analysis are more complex than computing the mean across all studies; corrections for attenuation and range restriction might be applied, and the results of each study might be weighted by its sample size. Nevertheless, the basic idea of meta-analysis—that the results of previous research should be considered in evaluating the criterion-related validity of any test or group of tests—is a simple one that has gained broad professional acceptance.

One reason for placing our discussion of meta-analysis in a section dealing with construct validity is that a clear specification of the construct is often critical for performing and interpreting a meta-analysis. Rarely do large numbers of studies use precisely the same tests and criterion measures, and it is necessary to make judgments about which studies should be grouped together. Returning to the preceding example, the studies examining correlations between scores on the Wonderlic Personnel Test and measures of job performance might include a variety of specific performance measures ranging from sales figures to supervisory ratings. The decision to group all those studies into the same analysis should be based on a careful assessment that they all represent operational measures of the same basic construct—job performance.

Meta-analyses are increasingly common in virtually all areas of psychology; they are also encountered in fields such as medicine (Olkin, 1992). One of the first steps in evaluating the criterion-related validity of virtually any test (especially commercially available tests or scales that have been in use for some period of time) should be a visit to the library. For many types of tests and criteria, the odds are good that a meta-analysis has already been conducted or that the literature exists that will enable you to conduct one yourself. The results of previous studies will not always address the particular research question you have in mind, but they should prove useful in giving you some guidance in interpreting the results of your own validity study. For example, if your study shows that a test is uncorrelated with an important criterion, but 30 other studies of the same test have shown correlations in the .40 to .60 range, you might expect there to be a flaw in your study that makes your particular findings difficult to interpret or generalize.

We do not believe that meta-analyses of existing research should replace carefully conducted validity studies. If they did, there would soon be nothing left to meta-analyze! However, it is silly to ignore the results of previous validity research, especially if other researchers have already examined the validity of your particular test for predicting the same type of criterion. Meta-analyses provide a means of systematically examining existing research; this examination should be useful in evaluating the criterion-related validity of virtually any measure.

INTERPRETING VALIDITY COEFFICIENTS

A criterion-related validity study provides an estimate of the correlation between test scores and criterion measures. Theoretically, this correlation could range in absolute value from 0.0 to 1.0. In practice, most validity coefficients tend to be fairly small. A good, carefully chosen test is not likely to show a correlation greater than .5 with an important criterion, and, in fact, validity coefficients greater than .3 are not all that common in applied settings. The correlations would almost certainly be higher if more reliable tests and criterion measures were used. Nevertheless, the levels of criterion-related validity achieved by most tests rarely exceed .6 to .7.

The figures shown in Table 9-3 provide a representative picture of the size of the validity coefficients often observed in personnel selection research. These correlations represent average validity coefficients computed across a number of studies, with a total N of over 140,000 (Schmidt, Hunter, & Pearlman, 1981). At first glance, these average validities look quite discouraging; the average of the correlations is .269. The squared correlation coefficient (r^2) indicates the percentage of the variance in the criterion that can be accounted for by the predictor. An average criterion-related validity of .269 indicates that approximately 7% of the variability in job proficiency measures and measures of performance in training can be accounted for (on the average) by test scores. Stated another way, 93% of the variability in performance *cannot* be accounted for by tests.

It is important to keep in mind that the values presented in Table 9-3 represent uncorrected coefficients. If corrected for attenuation *and* range restriction, they could

**Table 9-3   AVERAGE CRITERION-RELATED VALIDITIES
ACROSS A NUMBER OF CLERICAL JOBS**

Test	Job proficiency criteria[a]	Training criteria[b]
General mental ability	.24	.43
Verbal ability	.19	.39
Quantitative ability	.24	.43
Reasoning ability	.21	.22
Perceptual speed	.22	.22
Spatial-mechanical	.14	.21
Clerical aptitude	.25	.38

[a]For example, performance ratings.
[b]For example, training course grades.
Source: Schmidt, Hunter, and Pearlman (1981).

be substantially larger; corrected values in the .50s are often reported for tests of this sort (Hunter & Hunter, 1984). Nevertheless, even a validity of .50 would indicate that tests accounted for only 25% of the variance in the criterion (i.e., if $r = .50$, $r^2 = .25$). In most settings where tests are used to make important decisions, they account for relatively small percentages of the variability in criteria. Critics of testing (e.g., Nairn et al., 1980) have used this point to support their argument that tests are worthless. In fact, things are not as bad as the typically low values of r and r^2 might suggest. The validity of a test as an aid in making decisions should be judged by evaluating the effects of tests on the accuracy of decisions. The validity coefficient does not in itself provide a complete measure of the effects of tests on decisions. In some situations, tests that are extremely accurate predictors lead to only marginal increases in the quality of decisions. In other situations, a test that shows a comparatively low level of criterion-related validity may nevertheless contribute greatly to improving the quality of decisions. The effect of a test on the quality of decisions is affected by a number of factors that may be unrelated to the criterion-related validity of that test.

Tests and Decisions

The validity coefficient is only one of many factors that determine the degree to which a test may improve or detract from the quality of decisions. To fully evaluate the effect of a test on decisions, one must also consider the base rate and the selection ratio of a decision.

The *base rate* refers to the level of performance on the criterion in the population at large. For example, if 95% of all applicants perform successfully in a college course, the base rate is .95. If only 12% of the applicants to a psychology program successfully complete their degrees, the base rate is .12. Thus, the base rate indicates the percentage of the population who can be thought of as potential successes.

The *selection ratio* represents the ratio of positions to applicants. If 30 people apply for 3 jobs, there is a 10% selection ratio; if 10 prospective students apply for an incoming class of 9, there is a 90% selection ratio. Thus, the selection ratio indicates the degree to which the decision maker (e.g., personnel manager, admissions director) can be selective in his or her decisions.

Outcomes of Decisions. A decision represents some action taken with regard to a specific individual. A decision may involve accepting or rejecting a college applicant, or it may involve assigning or not assigning a client to a specific course of psychotherapy. Because predictions are never perfect, each decision may have many possible outcomes. In college admissions, some applicants who are accepted might turn out to be poor students, and others who were rejected might have been excellent students. A clinician might assign some clients to a course of therapy that is less than optimal. Nevertheless, the goal is to make the largest possible number of correct decisions—to accept potential successes and reject potential failures. A valid test should aid in accurately predicting both success and failures and should therefore

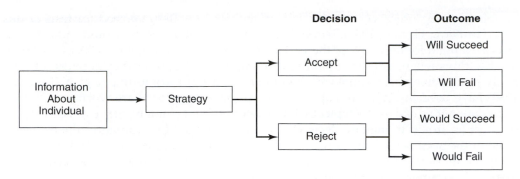

FIGURE 9-3   **The Decision Process**   *Source:* Adapted from Wiggins, 1973, p. 227.

contribute to the quality of decisions. Figure 9-3 presents a schematic representation of the decision process.

Tests, interviews, application blanks, and the like present information about each individual. The formal or informal rules used in making decisions comprise a strategy. For example, a college admissions office might decide to accept all applicants with a B+ average and with Scholastic Assessment Tests (SAT-I) scores over 550. This strategy leads to a decision—accept or reject—for each applicant. Furthermore, there are a number of possible outcomes of this decision. Some students who are accepted will succeed; others will fail. Some students who were rejected would have succeeded, and others would have failed.

The decision to accept an applicant is usually based on the prediction that the applicant will succeed; the decision to reject an applicant implies a prediction of failure, or at least of a lower level of success. One way to evaluate the accuracy of decisions is to compare predictions with the outcomes of decisions. Figure 9-4 presents a cross-tabulation of predicted criterion scores with actual criterion scores. This type of table described all the possible outcomes of a decision. One possible outcome is a true

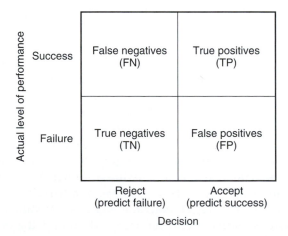

FIGURE 9-4   **Possible Outcomes of a Decision**

positive (TP): a person who is predicted to succeed and who actually does succeed. Another possible outcome is a true negative (TN): a person who is predicted to fail (rejected) and who actually would have failed had he or she been accepted. True positives and true negatives represent accurate, correct decisions; they represent cases in which people who will succeed are accepted and those who will fail are not accepted. One principal goal of psychological testing is to increase the frequency of these correct decisions.

Another possible outcome of a decision is the false positive (FP): Some of the people who are accepted turn out to be failures. Since the decision to accept a person who later turns out to be a failure implies the prediction that that person would succeed, the decision represents an error that is produced as the result of a false prediction. Finally, there are false negative (FN) decisions, in which an applicant who would have succeeded, given the chance, is rejected. False negatives are also decision errors in that they also lead to the wrong course of action for a specific applicant.

Base Rates and Decisions. One factor that strongly affects the outcomes of a decision is the base rate (BR), or the number of potential successes in the population of applicants. If 90% of those who apply are likely to succeed, it should not be too difficult to select a highly successful group. With a base rate of 90%, random selection will on the average lead to successful applicants being chosen 9 times out of 10. Indeed, when the base rate is very high, it may be difficult to devise a test that leads to significantly better decisions than would be reached by flipping a coin. If the base rate is 90%, there may not be very much room for improvement.

A very high base rate practically guarantees a large number of true positive decisions. Unfortunately, it may also lead to a number of false negative decisions. Consider a group of 200 people who apply for 100 positions. A base rate of 90% means that this group has 180 potential successes. Since only 100 positions are available, even the best strategy will result in rejecting 80 potential successes (false negative decisions). Although an extremely high base rate may help to maximize the number of true positives, it may also lead to a number of decision errors, particularly false negative decisions.

Tests are often used to predict criteria that have very low base rates (K. R. Murphy, 1987b). For example, J. Wiggins (1973) discusses applications of personality tests to screen out draftees because of psychiatric disability. The base rate for severe psychiatric problems is undoubtedly low; it is likely that fewer than 5% of the population would be screened out of military service because of psychiatric disorders. Since the base rate is very low, most of the population are, in fact, negatives (no presence of psychiatric disorder). Because positives (those with psychiatric disorders) are very rare, any decision procedure that attempts to isolate this rare group is likely to classify falsely a number of negatives (no disorder) as positives (disorder present). In other words, with a very low base rate, false positive decision errors become much more likely. On the other hand, a low base rate practically guarantees a large number of true negatives. If there are very few psychiatric cases in the population, few people will be screened out by the test, and most of those not screened out will belong to the large group that does not exhibit psychiatric disorders.

In general, tests are more likely to contribute to the overall quality of decisions when the base rate is around .50. When the base rate is extremely high, there is not much room for improvement in terms of locating true positives, and there is little chance of avoiding a substantial number of false negatives. When the base rate is extremely low, a number of false positives is likely. When the base rate is around .50, there is a greater possibility of minimizing decision errors, and it may be possible to make very accurate decisions if a test with sufficient validity can be found.

Selection Ratio and Decisions. The second factor that affects the quality of decisions is the selection ratio (SR), or the ratio of applicants to openings. If 100 people apply for 99 openings at a college, the college cannot be very selective. As a consequence, it doesn't really matter what strategy the college follows; the result will always be pretty much the same. Contrast this with the situation in which 100 people apply for one opening. Here, the validity of the decision strategy has a marked influence on the quality of the decision. A perfectly valid strategy will lead to selection of the best applicant; an invalid strategy could lead to selection of the worst. When the number of openings is large relative to the number of applicants, the selection ratio is high. For example, when ten people apply for eight positions, the selection ratio is equal to .8. In the extreme case when the number of applicants is equal to the number of openings, the selection ratio is equal to 1.0. In this case, there is no choice but to accept everyone.

When the number of openings is small relative to the number of applicants, the selection ratio is small. A small selection ratio indicates that there are few constraints on the decision. For example, if ten people apply for two openings, the selection ratio is .20, which means that eight out of every ten people who apply can be turned down. Of course, if there is no system for selecting among applicants, the freedom to turn down eight out of ten may not represent any real advantage. However, if there is a valid system for making decisions, a low selection ratio allows selection of the "cream of the crop." In fact, when the selection ratio is sufficiently low, a test with very modest validity still can contribute significantly to the accuracy of decisions.

H. C. Taylor and Russell (1939) published a series of tables that dramatically illustrate the effect of the selection ratio on the accuracy of decisions. Taylor-Russell tables indicate the proportion of successes that can be expected, given the validity of the test, the base rate, and the selection ratio. One Taylor-Russell table is shown in Table 9-4; validity coefficients are shown at the side of the table, the selection ratio is shown at the top, and the expected proportion of successes is shown in the body of the table. Several points should be noted in examining the table. First, if the test has a validity of .00 (the first row of Table 9-4), the expected level of success is exactly equal to the base rate (here, .50), regardless of the selection ratio. In other words, a test with no validity yields essentially random decisions. Next, at very high selection ratios (e.g., SR = .90), the expected level of success using an extremely accurate test is not much higher than the level of success one would expect with a validity of .00. Finally, at very low selection ratios (e.g., SR = .10), a test with a reasonably low level of validity still could lead to substantial proportion of "successes"; when a highly valid test is used in a situation

Table 9-4   TAYLOR-RUSSELL TABLE SHOWING THE EXPECTED PROPORTION
OF SUCCESSES WITH A BASE RATE OF .50

Validity	Selection ratio									
	.05	.10	.20	.30	.40	.50	.60	.70	.80	.90
.00	.50	.50	.50	.50	.50	.50	.50	.50	.50	.50
.10	.54	.54	.53	.52	.52	.51	.51	.51	.51	.50
.20	.67	.64	.61	.59	.58	.56	.55	.53	.53	.52
.30	.74	.71	.67	.64	.62	.60	.58	.56	.54	.52
.40	.82	.78	.73	.69	.66	.63	.61	.58	.56	.53
.50	.88	.84	.78	.74	.70	.67	.63	.60	.57	.54
.60	.94	.90	.84	.79	.75	.70	.66	.62	.59	.45
.70	.98	.95	.90	.85	.80	.75	.70	.65	.60	.55
.80	1.00	.99	.95	.90	.85	.80	.73	.67	.61	.55
.90	1.00	1.00	.99	.97	.92	.86	.78	.70	.62	.56
1.00	1.00	1.00	1.00	1.00	1.00	1.00	.83	.71	.63	.56

characterized by a low selection ratio, one can select successful candidates essentially 100% of the time.

It is important to select successes, but the overall quality of a decision strategy is affected not by the number of successes only but by the combination of all the possible outcomes of the decision. For example, with a low selection ratio, a number of potential successes might also be turned down (false negatives). Taylor-Russell tables do not provide a complete picture of the effects of the base rate or the selection ratio on all the outcomes of a decision; the selection ratio, the base rate, and the validity of the test interact in a complex way to affect all the outcomes of decisions. Nevertheless, Taylor-Russell tables do provide important information for interpreting validity coefficients.

Effect of Base Rates, Selection Ratios, and Test Validity on Outcomes. The outcomes of decisions are determined by the base rate, the selection ratio, and the validity of the test. To explain the interaction of these three factors, we first show how the base rate and the selection ratio determine the number of true positives, true negatives, false positives, and false negatives that would occur if one were making decisions on a random basis. Random decisions represent a baseline against which decisions that involve tests can be compared. A test is not useful unless it leads to significantly better, more accurate decisions than would be made at random, without using tests.

When decisions are made on a random basis, the number of true positives, true negatives, false positives, and false negatives can be computed directly from the base rate (BR) and the selection ratio (SR). The probability of a true positive [P(TP)] is given by

$$P \text{ (TP) decision when decisions are made at random} = BR \times SR \qquad [9\text{-}2]$$

With a base rate of .60 and a selection ratio of .50, 30% of the decisions made at random will be true positives. The probability of each other outcome can be solved by subtraction, as shown in Figure 9-5.

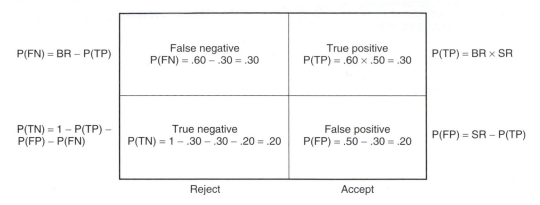

FIGURE 9-5   The Outcomes of Random Decisions With a Base Rate of .60 and a Selection Ratio of .50

Thus, the probability of a false negative is equal to the base rate minus the probability of a true positive [P(TN) = .60 − .30 = .30]; the probability of a false positive is given by the selection ratio minus the probability of a true positive [P(FP) = .50 − .30 = .20]. Finally, the probability of a true negative is given by 1 minus the sum of the other three probabilities [P(TN) = 1 − .30 − .30 − .20 = .20]. In other words, when the base rate is .60 and the selection ratio is .50, 50% of all random decisions will be correct (TP and TN), and 50% of the random decisions will be incorrect (FP and FN). These figures represent a baseline against which decisions involving tests can be evaluated.

When a valid test is used to make decisions, the probability of a true positive increases from $P(TP) = BR \times SR$ to

$$P(TP) = BR \times SR + r_{xy}\sqrt{BR(1 - BR)SR(1 - SR)} \qquad [9\text{-}3]$$

This formula shows that the use of a test increases the probability of making true positive decisions and that the increase in the likelihood of true positive decisionsis a function of the validity of the test (r_{xy}), adjusted by a scaling factor $\left[\sqrt{BR(1 - BR)SR(1 - SR)}\right]$. Thus, when the validity of the test is equal to .00, the probability of a true positive is exactly the same as when decisions are made at random. Whenever the test has a validity greater than .00, true positives are more likely when the test is used to make decisions than when decisions are made at random. As a consequence, both false positives and false negatives are less likely when decisions are based on a valid test than when decisions are made at random.

Figure 9-6 shows how decision errors decrease as test validity increases. With a base rate of .50 and a selection ratio of .40, 50% of all random decisions will be either false positives or false negatives, both of which represent decision errors. When a test with a validity of .40 is used to make decisions, the proportion of correct decisions rises from 50% to 68%; when a test with a validity of .70 is used, the proportion of correct decisions rises to 72%. As shown by the figure, a valid test increases both the number of true positives and the number of true negatives, while decreasing both false positives and false negatives.

Random decisions		Using a test with a validity of .40		Using a test with a validity of .70	
FN .30	TP .20	FN .21	TP .29	FN .19	TP .31
TN .30	FP .20	TN .39	FP .11	TN .41	FP .09

FIGURE 9-6   Outcomes of Random Decisions and Decisions Based on Tests With a Base Rate of .50 and a Selection Ratio of .40

As stated at the beginning of this section, the interpretation of validity coefficients is surprisingly complex. The meaning of a validity coefficient cannot be fully understood unless one understands the context in which a test will be used. A test with a validity of .70 may not be very useful if the base rate or the selection ratio is very high. On the other hand, a test with a validity of .10 might lead to a considerable increase in the accuracy of decisions if the selection ratio is low. Therefore, it makes little sense to say that a validity coefficient of .20 is bad or that a validity of .50 is good. It depends largely on the contexts in which tests will be used.

Tests and the Bottom Line: Applications of Utility Theory

Throughout this book, we focus on the impact of psychological tests on decisions that must be made about individuals. The principal justification for the use of psychological tests is that they allow better decisions to be made than would be made without tests. The question is how much better. Utility theory provides one method of answering this question.

According to utility theory, correct decisions (true positives, true negatives) are valued, whereas incorrect decisions (false positives, false negatives) are to be avoided or have a negative value. Utility theory suggests that two things must be known before the impact of psychological tests can be assessed: (1) how many additional correct decisions will result if tests are used and (2) how much value is placed on good decisions. Methods described earlier in this chapter can be applied to the first question: If the base rate, selection ratio, and validity coefficient are known, the effect of tests on decisions can be determined easily. The trick, then, is to determine the value of outcomes.

One way to determine value is to make a judgment as to what will be gained by making a good decision instead of a bad one. This approach has been widely used in personnel selection and has provided estimates of the financial impact of tests on selection decisions. For example, it is possible to estimate, in dollar terms, the value of the products, goods, and services provided by a superior worker, an average worker, and a poor worker. These estimates can be used to determine the standard deviation of job performance, measured in dollar terms (Judiesch, Schmidt, & Mount, 1992). Since a valid selection test will lead to an increase in the number of superior workers and a decrease in the number of poor workers hired, it is possible to use judgments of the value of performance to provide estimates of the financial impact of valid selection decisions.

Utility theory provides a method for estimating, in dollar terms, the gain (per year) in productivity that will result if valid tests are used in personnel selection. This gain is estimated by

$$\text{Productivity gain} = Kr_{xy}SD_y\overline{Z}_s \qquad\qquad [9\text{-}4]$$

where

$$K = \text{number of persons selected}$$
$$r_{xy} = \text{validity coefficient}$$
$$SD_y = \text{standard deviation of the criterion}$$
$$\overline{Z}_s = \text{average (standard) test score among those selected}$$

Utility estimates have suggested that the use of psychological tests in areas such as personnel selection could lead to substantial gains in performance. For example, Hunter and Hunter (1984) estimate that the use of cognitive ability tests in selection for entry-level federal jobs could lead to a productivity gain of over $15 billion per year. Hunter and Schmidt (1982) estimate that the nationwide gain associated with the use of psychological tests in personnel selection could exceed $80 billion per year.

There are two problems with utility equations such as Equation 9-4. First, they typically overestimate increases in utility (Croons & Alexander, 1985; Murphy, 1986). Second, they ignore the costs associated with incorrect rejection decisions (false negatives; Boudreau, 1991). However, application of this branch of utility theory has greatly increased our understanding of the impact of psychological tests on the quality of decisions made daily by organizations and institutions.

Equation 9-4 suggests that several factors affect the overall quality of decisions. First, of course, is the validity of the test (r_{xy}). Second is the standard deviation of the criterion (SD_y); the larger this standard deviation, the larger the potential gain associated with the use of tests. The rationale here is straightforward. A large standard deviation indicates substantial differences in criterion scores; a small standard deviation indicates that everyone performs at pretty much the same level. If individual differences in performance are large, the quality of selection decisions makes a great deal of difference, but if everyone performs at about the same level, decisions will not affect criterion scores greatly. Finally, the average test score among those selected ($\overline{Z}_s$) affects utility; this average is a function of the selection ratio. The organization that can attract the "cream of the crop" among applicants by being highly selective gains more than another organization that can attract only mediocre applicants (Murphy, 1986). The utility score given by Equation 9-4 represents a complex combination of the characteristics of the applicant pool, the selection ratio, and the decisions of individual applicants.

CRITICAL DISCUSSION:

Values and Validation

We have presented validity and utility as related but distinct topics. Messick (1988, 1989) suggests a different framework, in which values are taken explicitly into account in the process of validation.[4] The central idea in this framework is that we need to consider both the inferences made on the basis of test scores (these are the focus of traditional validity models) and the actions taken as the result of test scores. Thus, in this framework, the validation process might take into account (1) the construct validity of the test, (2) the relevance or utility of the test, (3) the value implications of test scores, and (4) the potential and actual social consequences of test use. The unique aspect of this framework for understanding validity is that both the values that underlie testing (e.g., whether it is valuable to predict college GPA for applicants) and the social consequences of testing (e.g., a selection test that includes many geometric items will lead to the selection of more males than females) are an integral part of validation, rather than concerns that should be addressed by someone other than the scientist investigating validity.

The appropriateness of including social consequences in the definition of validity is somewhat controversial. For example, the fact that, on average, females receive lower scores than males on the mathematical portion of the SAT is taken by some critics as evidence of the invalidity of the test. Virtually any test that produces socially undesirable outcomes is likely to be attacked in this manner (Jensen, 1980; Seymour, 1988; Sharf, 1988).

Messick's (1988) framework is somewhat more sophisticated than the simplistic one suggested by these critics—that tests whose consequences are socially undesirable are necessarily invalid. Messick suggests that we must consider whether the social consequences of a test are a reflection of the test or a reflection of the actual phenomenon being measured. For example, there is clear agreement among testing specialists that there are real differences in the average intelligence levels of different subgroups in the population (see special issues of the *Journal of Vocational Behavior,* 1986, December, and 1988, December, for reviews of this evidence). A test of intelligence that failed to reflect this real difference would probably be judged invalid in Messick's framework. On the other hand, if undesirable social consequences are the result of the test rather than of the phenomenon being measured or predicted, this outcome should be considered in evaluating the validity of a test.

One advantage of Messick's framework is that it encourages us to consider values in the selection of criteria. That is, a researcher applying this framework might not be satisfied with a test if its use not only led to increases in one criterion (e.g., average GPA) but also led to substantial decreases in other relevant criteria (e.g., the representativeness of students admitted). As we noted at the beginning of this chapter, the selection of appropriate criteria is the first and most important step in criterion-related validity studies. Messick's framework may be a very useful tool for accomplishing this end.

SUMMARY

The success of psychological tests in predicting a wide range of important criteria (e.g., academic achievement, performance on the job, outcomes of therapy) helps to explain both their importance and their acceptance. In later chapters, we will review evidence

---

[4]Cronbach (1988) identifies several perspectives on validation, three of which incorporate value or societal concerns: (1) functional, the worth of the test; (2) political, the acceptability of test outcomes; and (3) economic, the contribution of the test to productivity.

of the validity of several types of tests; the aim of this chapter has been to describe the process of collecting and interpreting criterion-related validity evidence.

Both predictive and concurrent validation strategies have been described. Although there are important theoretical differences between these methods, it is not unusual to obtain similar validity estimates from each, especially if factors such as range restriction can be adequately accounted for.

Although it is possible to obtain valid predictors without considering the constructs that tests are designed to measure (strategies for developing such tests are described in Chapter 11), a clear assessment of the constructs involved is usually the first step in a criterion-related validity study. In particular, careful attention must be given to the constructs that your criteria are chosen to represent. In too many studies, criteria are chosen on the basis of convenience (e.g., GPA is an easily obtained metric of academic success, even though it fails to capture many critical aspects of the construct), rather than substantive theory. An examination of the criterion construct is especially important in conducting and interpreting meta-analyses, for a poorly defined meta-analysis might include many irrelevant studies and may not adequately answer your particular research question.

Validity coefficients cannot be sensibly interpreted without considering the context in which tests are likely to be used. Two features of the testing context, the base rate (BR) and the selection ratio (SR), are critically important, and depending on the base rate and selection ratio, a test with high validity may make either a great or a very small contribution to the quality of decisions. In certain situations (e.g., a low SR), tests with modest validity coefficients can nevertheless make a substantial contribution.

Utility theory provides a way of combining information about the validity of the test, the context in which tests will be used, and the value of the good or poor decisions that might result from use of the test. This approach allows you to estimate in very concrete terms what will happen if you decide either to use or to discard tests in making particular decisions.

PROBLEMS AND SOLUTIONS—RECAP

The Problem

You have been asked to estimate the financial benefit of using a valid test (the correlation between test scores and total sales is .45) to select salespeople. This correlation suggests that people with high scores will typically sell more than people with low scores.

A Solution

Equation 9-4 suggests that there are two things that you would need to know before you can determine the actual contribution of this selection test. First, how much variability is there in the performance of salespeople (i.e., what is the value of SD_y). If it turns out that the very best salesperson sells only a few more units than the very worst, there may not be much to gain by increasing the validity of selection. However, if there is a lot of difference in what good versus average versus poor salespeople sell each year, valid selection could make a big difference in the success of the organization.

Second, we need to know how selective the organization is. If 100 people apply and there are 99 sales jobs to fill, it does not make much difference whether your test is a good one or a bad one; you will have to select almost everyone. If 100 people apply and there are 10 jobs to fill, valid selection might make a great deal of difference.

Assume that in this case SD_y = $10,000. That is, in this example, salespeople who are at about the 85th percentile (i.e., those who sell more than do 85% of their peers) will sell about $10,000 more than an average salesperson. Assume also that there are 10 applicants for every job to be filled (i.e., SR = .10, which means that the average standard score of those in the top 10% of the applicant pool will be 1.75; Thornton, Murphy, Everett, & Hoffman, 2000, show how to estimate the mean standard score given the SR). Under these assumptions, the gain in productivity, per person hired, can be estimated by the following:

Estimated gain per person hired = .45 * $10,000 * 1.75 = $7875.00

That is, you would expect that for every salesperson hired using this test, his or her average level of sales performance will be $7,875 higher than you would have expected if you did not have the test. Thus, an organization that uses the test to help fill 500 sales jobs might expect to see their sales increase by over $3.9 million per year!

KEY TERMS

Base rate   proportion of the population who meet a specific criterion (e.g., proportion of an applicant pool who would succeed on the job)

Concurrent validation strategy   strategy that uses scores of a screened sample (e.g., people who received relatively high scores on the test) to evaluate the relationship between a test and a criterion

Criterion   measure that can be used to evaluate the accuracy of a decision

Criterion-related validation strategy   strategy for assessing the validity of decisions by examining the correlation between scores on a test and scores on a criterion measure

False positive   condition in which a positive decision about an individual turns out to be an incorrect decision

Meta-analysis   method for combining the results from multiple studies

Predictive validation strategy   strategy that uses scores of a representative or unscreened sample to evaluate the relationship between a test and a criterion

Range restriction effects   effects of limiting the range of scores on the test or criterion (e.g., by removing people who fail a test from a validity study) on the correlation between tests and criteria; range restriction reduces this correlation

Selection ratio   ratio between the number of applicants for some position or decision and the number of positions available

True positive   condition in which a positive decision about an individual (e.g., decision to admit a person to graduate school) turns out to be the correct decision

Utility theory   theory for combining information about criterion-related validity and the decision context (e.g., base rate, selection ratio) to estimate the gains or losses associated with using a test

Item Analysis

10

Many of the most widely used tests contain a number of multiple-choice items, each of which is designed to measure the same attribute or the same content. The best example is the familiar test of scholastic aptitude. There is usually a correct or preferred answer to each item, and each item is scored as correct, 1; incorrect, 0. The total test score is simply the sum of the scores on all the items. In the preceding four chapters, we discussed properties of test scores, such as reliability and validity. In this chapter, we will deal with the relationship between characteristics of individual test items and the quality of the test as a whole. Some test items contribute to reliability and validity; trick questions or ambiguous items may detract from the overall quality of a test.

The term *item analysis* refers to a loosely structured group of statistics that can be computed for each item in a test. Although many item analyses incorporate common methods of analysis, there are as many "recipes" for item analysis as there are for chili. The exact choice and interpretation of the statistics that make up an item analysis are determined partly by the purpose of testing and partly by the person designing the analysis. Nevertheless, some very general issues are addressed in almost every item analysis. This chapter suggests a set of general questions that should be asked when examining individual test items and shows how information from an item analysis can be used to improve tests.

PROBLEMS AND SOLUTIONS—WHICH ITEMS SHOULD YOU DROP?

The Problem

Your class is up in arms over the Psychology 101 test you just took. There were fifty multiple-choice items, and there were 10 items in which *nobody* chose the correct answer, and you have petitioned to have these items dropped from the exam. Your instructor has pointed out that there were also 12 items in which *everybody* chose the correct answer, and she suggests that there are just as many reasons to drop these items as there are to drop the 10 items you complained about. How should you respond to this argument?

PURPOSE OF ITEM ANALYSIS

Item analysis can help increase our understanding of tests. Close examination of individual tests is essential to understanding why a test shows specific levels of reliability and validity. The reliability coefficient reveals something about the effects of measurement error on test scores. Validity coefficients reveal something about the accuracy of predictions that are based on test scores. A good item analysis can often be very informative when tests are unreliable or when they fail to show expected levels of validity. An item analysis can show why a test is reliable (or unreliable) and may help in understanding why test scores can be used to predict some criteria but not others. Item analysis may also suggest ways of improving the measurement characteristics of a test.

Tests are sometimes limited in their reliability or validity because they contain items that are poorly worded or that are trick questions requiring complex mental gymnastics. Other items may look fine but don't actually measure the construct of the content domain that the test is designed to assess. The reliability and validity of a test can generally be improved by removing such items. At first glance, this solution seems to run counter to one of the basic propositions of reliability theory: the longer the test, the better. Actually, there is no conflict between the policy of removing poor items and the goal of maximizing reliability. Reliability theory assumes that all test items measure the same thing. Item analysis helps locate items that don't meet this assumption, and removing them can improve the reliability of tests.

Critical Features of Test Items

The question that should be asked when examining each test item is whether an item does a good job of measuring the same thing that is measured by the rest of the test. Different computer programs contain a variety of statistics that bear on this general question. Attempts to answer this question usually draw on information provided by three types of measures: distractor measures, difficulty measures, and item discrimination measures.

In examining each item of a test, the first and most natural question to ask is "How many people chose each response?" There is only one correct answer; the rest are referred to as *distractors.* Therefore, examining the total pattern of responses to each item of a test is referred to as *distractor analysis.*

Another natural question is "How many people answered the item correctly?" To answer this question, an analysis is made of item difficulty. A third question is "Are responses to this item related to responses to other items on the test?" Answering this question entails an analysis of item discrimination. In the sections that follow, we present several common procedures for analyzing the total pattern of responses to an item, the difficulty of an item, and the interrelationships among responses to different test items.

DISTRACTOR ANALYSIS

Typically, there is one correct or preferred answer for each multiple-choice item on a test. A lot can be learned about test items by examining the frequency with which each incorrect response is chosen by a group of examinees.

Table 10-1   ITEM FROM INTRODUCTORY PSYCHOLOGY TEST

Item 42. Paranoid schizophrenia often involves delusions of persecution or grandeur. Which
 secondary symptom would be most likely for a paranoid schizophrenic:
 (a) auditory hallucinations
 (b) motor paralysis
 (c) loss of memory
 (d) aversion to food

	Number choosing each answer		*Percent choosing each answer*	
Correct Response	a	47	a	55
	b	13	b	15
	c	25	c	29
	d	1	d	1

Table 10-1 shows data on a single item that was part of an introductory psychology test. The table shows that most of the students answered the item correctly. A fair number of students chose either b or c; very few chose d. Although the calculation of the percentage of examinees choosing each response may not appear to have accomplished anything profound, it constitutes a fairly complete and potentially informative distractor analysis. The percentages convey a great deal of information about the skill with which the item was written.

A perfect test item would have two characteristics. First, people who knew the answer to that question would always choose the correct response. Second, people who did not know the answer would choose randomly among the possible responses. This outcome means that some people would guess correctly. It also means that each possible incorrect response should be equally popular.

For the test item shown in the table, responses b, c, and d served as distractors. Fifty-five percent of the students answered this item correctly. If this were a perfect test item, we might expect the responses of the other 45% of the students to be equally divided among the three distractors. In other words, we might expect about 15% of the students to choose each of the three incorrect responses.

What to Look for in a Distractor Analysis

We can compute the number of people expected to choose each of the distractors using the simple formula

$$\text{Number of persons expected to choose each distractor} = \frac{\text{number of persons answering item incorrectly}}{\text{number of distractors}} \qquad [10\text{-}1]$$

Table 10-1 shows that 39 people answered the item incorrectly. We therefore would expect 13 people to choose each distractor. In fact, 13 people chose response b. More people chose response c than would be expected, and fewer chose d.

When the number of persons choosing a distractor significantly exceeds the number expected, there are two possibilities. First, it is possible that the choice reflects partial knowledge. For this example, someone who knows a bit about psychosis might know that both auditory hallucinations and memory loss are plausible symptoms for a variety of disorders. Therefore, for someone with such partial knowledge, the answer to this question might be a toss-up between a and c. A second, more worrisome possibility is that the item is a poorly constructed trick question. If one more of the distractors is extremely popular among students who have a good knowledge of the domain covered by the item and if the identification of the correct response hinges on some obscure or subtle point, the item is not likely to be a valid measure of the content domain. In some situations, extremely difficult or subtle items are desirable, such as when the intent is to measure individual differences among people at the high end of a score distribution (e.g., competitors for a scholarship). However, in most situations, these types of items do not contribute to the overall quality of a test. For most tests, the presence of items with extremely popular distractors is likely to lower the reliability and validity of the test.

Some distractors are extremely unpopular. Response d for the test item shown in the table is an example. The number of people who actually chose this response is considerably smaller than the number one would expect by chance. The presence of an extremely unpopular or implausible distractor affects a number of important item characteristics. The most obvious effect of an unpopular distractor is that it lowers the difficulty of the item. If a person knows nothing whatsoever about the domain being tested, the probability of choosing the right answer on an item with four possible choices is one in four. If one of those choices is obviously incorrect, it can be eliminated. Thus, if I don't know anything about paranoid schizophrenia but am able to eliminate response d as utterly implausible, the probability of guessing correctly has been raised from one in four to one in three.

ITEM DIFFICULTY

Difficulty is a surprisingly slippery concept. Consider the following two items:

1. $(6 \times 3) + 4 =$
2. $9\pi[1n(-3.68) \times (1 - 1n(+3.68)] =$

Most people would agree that item 2 is more difficult than item 1. If asked why item 2 is more difficult, they might say that it involves more complex advanced procedures than the first. Consider next another set of items:

1. Who was Savonarola?
2. Who was Babe Ruth?

Most people will agree that item 1 is more difficult than item 2. If asked why item 1 is more difficult, they might say that answering it requires more specialized knowledge than item 2.

As these examples might suggest, there is a strong temptation to define difficulty in terms of the complexity or obscurity of the test item. Yet if you were to look at any test that you have recently taken, you would likely find yourself hard pressed to explain precisely why some items were more difficult than others. The only common thread running through the "difficult" items may be the fact that when you took the test, you did not know the answers to these questions.

The psychologist doing an item analysis is faced with a similar problem. Some test items are harder than others, but it is difficult to explain or define difficulty in terms of some intrinsic characteristics of the items. The strategy adopted by psychometricians is to define difficulty in terms of the number of people who answer each test item correctly.[1] If everyone chooses the correct answer, the item is defined as easy. If only one person in 100 answers an item correctly, the item is defined as difficult.

Measuring Item Difficulty

The most common measure of item difficulty is the percentage of examinees who answer the item correctly, or the p value. An item's p value is obtained using the following formula:

$$p \text{ value for item } i = \frac{\text{number of persons answering item } i \text{ correctly}}{\text{number of persons taking the test}} \tag{10-2}$$

The use of p values as a measure of item difficulty has several interesting implications. First, the p value is basically a behavioral measure. Rather than defining difficulty in terms of some intrinsic characteristic of the item, with this method, difficulty is defined in terms of the relative frequency with which those taking the test choose the correct response. Second, difficulty is a characteristic of both the item and the population taking the test. A math problem that is very difficult when given in a high-school course will be very easy when given in a graduate physics course.

Perhaps the most useful implication of the p value is that it provides a common measure of the difficulty of test items that measure completely different domains. It is very difficult to determine whether answering a particular question about history involves knowledge that is more obscure, complex, or specialized than that needed to answer a math problem. When p values are used to define difficulty, it is very simple to determine whether an item on a history test is more difficult than a specific item on a math test taken by the same group of students.

Effects of Item Difficulty on Test Scores

When everyone in a class chooses the wrong answers to a particular test item, there is usually an uproar, and, with luck, the offending item will be dropped from the test. This is exactly the situation considered in this chapter's Problems and Solutions

---

[1]As we will note later, item response theory provides a more sophisticated definition and measure of difficulty.

section. Although infuriated students may not see the problem in technical terms, there is sometimes a sound psychometric basis for dropping such an item.

As stated in Chapter 1, one of the basic assumptions of measurement is that there are systematic individual differences in the construct or the content domain being measured. Tests represent a method of quantifying these differences. When nobody chooses the correct answer (a p value of .0), there are no individual differences in the "score" on that item. Note that the same is true when everyone chooses the correct response (a p value of 1.0). This outcome suggests one of the most important principles of item analysis. An item with a p value of .0 or a p value of 1.0 does not contribute to measuring individual differences and thus is almost certain to be useless.

When we compare the test scores of two people, we are typically interested in knowing who had the higher score or how far apart the two scores were. A test item with a p value of .0 or 1.0 has no effect on the differences between scores received by two subjects; dropping all the test items with p values of .0 or 1.0 from a test will not affect the rank order or the size of the differences between different people's scores. Test items with p values of .0 or 1.0 may affect the test mean, but they have no effect whatsoever on the test's reliability or validity or on the decisions based on the test scores.

Item difficulty has a profound effect on both the variability of test scores and the precision with which test scores discriminate among different groups of examinees. The effects of difficulty on the variance of test scores are fairly obvious when p values are extreme. When all the test items are extremely difficult, the great majority of the test scores will be very low. When all items are extremely easy, most test scores will be extremely high. In either case, test scores will show very little variability. Thus, extreme p values directly restrict the variability of test scores.

The variability of test scores is maximized when p values average around .5. In fact, test scores are more variable when all the p values cluster around .5 than when there is some range of p values. Since most tests are designed to measure some construct or attribute over a range of possible scores, some variability in test scores is to be expected. When tests are designed for the general measurement of some continuous variable (e.g., intelligence, need for achievement), there is little doubt that items with p values near .5 are preferred over extremely easy or extremely difficult items. In most analyses of item difficulty, items with p values near .5 should be considered optimum.

Some tests are not designed to provide equally good measurement at all points on a continuum. For example, a simple reading comprehension test may be used to screen out people whose reading ability is below some minimal level required on a job. If the job demands that the workers be above the 20th percentile in a general reading ability, it makes little difference whether the worker reads at a high-school, college, or postgraduate level. A test will be maximally effective in making this type of screening decision if the item difficulties correspond roughly with the cutting point. To decide whether each applicant is above or below the 80th percentile (i.e., in the top 20% of all applicants), a test that consists of items with p values near .2 would be best (F. M. Lord, 1952). If the objective is to screen the very top group of applicants (e.g., medical admissions), the test should be composed of very difficult items.

ITEM DISCRIMINATION

Every item can be thought of as a separate test. Some items do a pretty good job of measuring the same thing that is measured by the test as a whole. Some items tell nothing at all about individual differences (i.e., items with p values of .0 or 1.0 do not provide information about individual differences); others measure the wrong thing altogether. One principal aim of item analysis is to discover which items best measure the construct or attribute that the test was designed to measure.

If the test and a single item both measure the same thing, one would expect people who do well on the test to answer that item correctly and those who do poorly to answer that item incorrectly. In other words, a good item discriminates between those who do well on the test and those who do poorly. In this section, we discuss three statistics that can be used to measure the discriminating power of an item: the discrimination index, the item-total correlation, and interitem correlations.

Discrimination Index

The method of *extreme groups* can be applied to compute a very simple measure of the discriminating power of a test item. If a test is given to a large group of people, the discriminating power of an item can be measured by comparing the number of people with high test scores (e.g., those in the top 25% of the class) who answered that item correctly with the number of people with low scores (e.g., the bottom 25%) who answered the same item correctly. If a particular item is doing a good job of discriminating between those who score high and those who score low, more people in the top-scoring group will have answered the item correctly.

The item discrimination index, D, is based on the simple rationale just described. The first step in computing this index is to select an upper group and a lower group. Customarily, these extreme groups are made up of either those with scores in the upper and lower 27% or those with scores in the upper and lower 33% of the group taking the test (Cureton, 1957). For all practical purposes, these extreme groups can include anywhere from 25% to 35% of the examinees; any breakdown within this range yields similar discrimination measures. Once extreme groups are formed, the next step is to calculate the percentage of examinees passing each item in both the upper group and the lower group. The item discrimination index is simply the difference between these two percentages.

An example will help to clarify the item discrimination index. A 40-item test was given to 100 students. The 27 students with the highest test scores formed the upper group, and the 27 with the lowest scores formed the lower group. The percentage of those in the upper group and the percentage of those in the lower group passing each item on the test were then computed. Data from four of these items are presented in Table 10-2.

Recall that the p value is a measure of item difficulty. The data in the table suggest that both items 1 and 2 were substantially more difficult for the lower group than

Table 10-2   PERCENT PASSING

Item	Upper group	Lower group	D
1	71	42	29
2	60	24	36
3	47	42	5
4	38	61	−23

for the upper group. The logic of the D statistic is simple. The test itself was, by definition, substantially more difficult for the lower group than for the upper group. If an
item and a test both measure the same thing, the item should also be more difficult for
the lower group than for the upper. The D statistic provides a simple but efficient measure of the discriminating power of each test item (Engelhart, 1965).

Item 3 does not show much discriminating power. The D value for this item is
very small, reflecting the fact that the item was about equally difficult in the upper and
the lower groups. The statistics for item 4 are even more discouraging. This item shows
plenty of discriminating power, but in the wrong direction. A negative D index indicates that an item is easier for people who do poorly on the test than for those who do
well on the test. This outcome is the exact opposite of what would be expected if the
item and the test were measuring the same thing. The D values suggest that both item
3 and item 4 are poor test items. The small D value for item 3 suggests that it does not
make any discriminations between those who do well on tests and those who do
poorly. The negative D value for item 4 suggests that the item discriminates, but in the
wrong direction. One goal of test construction is to generate items that, like items 1 and
2, allow for valid discrimination between high and low scorers.

Shortcuts in Computing D. The procedure for computing D described in the
previous section is fairly simple, but even simpler methods are available. The general
formula for the D statistic is

$$D = \frac{U}{n_u} - \frac{L}{n_l} \tag{10-3}$$

where

U = number of people in the upper group who passed the item
n_u = number of people in the upper group
L = number of people in the lower group who passed the item
n_l = number of people in the lower group

In many cases, the upper group and the lower group are equal in size. In this case,
where $n_u = n_l$, Equation 10-3 reduces to

$$D = \frac{U - L}{n} \tag{10-4}$$

where
$$n = n_l = n_u$$

Thus, in many cases, D can be obtained by computing the difference between the number of people in the upper group who pass an item and the number in the lower group who pass the same item and dividing by n.

Item-Total Correlation

The discrimination index is a simple statistic that provides a good deal of information on the degree to which a particular item and the total test measure the same thing. There is a more familiar statistic, the item-total correlation, that provides the same sort of information. As the name implies, this statistic represents the simple correlation between the score on an item (a correct response usually receives a score of 1; an incorrect response receives a score of 0) and the total test score. This correlation is often referred to as a *point-biserial correlation*. Years ago, when computers were not available, there was some real utility in developing simple computational formulas for different types of correlations. Since computers are now readily available, there is no good reason to treat an item-total correlation differently from any other correlation. Thus, we will avoid the term *point-biserial* and emphasize that the item-total correlation is a simple correlation coefficient.

The item-total correlation is interpreted in much the same way as the item discrimination index, D. A positive item-total correlation indicates that the item successfully discriminates between those who do well on the test and those who do poorly. More important, a positive item-total correlation indicates that the item measures the same thing that is being measured by the test. An item-total correlation near zero indicates that the item does not discriminate between high and low scores. A negative item-total correlation indicates that the scores on the item and scores on the test disagree. Those who do well on an item with a negative item-total r do poorly on the test.

The principal advantage of the item-total correlation is its familiarity. It is the simple correlation between item scores and test scores. Therefore, it is easy to test the statistical significance of an item-total correlation. It also is easy to make judgments about practical significance. If the item-total r is .40, we know that the item can account for 16% of the variability in test scores. An item discrimination index of .40 cannot be reexpressed in such concrete terms. Finally, item-total correlations are directly related to the reliability of a test (Nunnally, 1982).

Interitem Correlations

When conducting an item analysis, it makes sense to compute the correlations among all test items. The resulting interitem correlation matrix is packed with information. First, it is possible to compute the reliability of a test given the average interitem correlation and the number of items on the test. This is a useful fact, but this property of interitem correlations is not the most important. The most important use of interitem correlations is in understanding measures of item discrimination. Up to this point, we have not said why a particular item might show high or low levels of discriminating power. It might be obvious that items that show large positive item-total correlations also will show positive correlations with the most test items. It is not always obvious why other test items show low item-total correlations. Examination of the interitem correlations can help us to understand why some items fail to discriminate between those who do well on the test and those who do poorly.

If the item-total correlation is low, there are two possible explanations. First, it is possible that the item in question is not correlated with any of the other items on the test. In this case, the item should be either substantially rewritten or discarded altogether. The second possibility is that the item shows positive correlations with some test items but shows correlations near zero, or perhaps even negative correlations, with other items on the test. This outcome would occur, for example, if the test measured two distinct attributes. Thus, a mathematics test that contained several complexly worded problems might measure reading comprehension as well as mathematical ability. Reliability theory suggests that such a test, in which different items measure different things (and thus are uncorrelated), would not provide consistent measurement.

INTERACTIONS AMONG ITEM CHARACTERISTICS

An item analysis yields three types of information: (1) information about distractors, (2) information about item difficulty, and (3) information about item discrimination power. These three types of information are conceptually distinct but empirically related. Thus, examining distractors reveals something about difficulty; item difficulty directly affects item discriminating power. In this section, we briefly describe ways in which item characteristics interact.

Distractors and Difficulty

A multiple-choice item that asks the year in which B. F. Skinner published *The Behavior of Organisms* could be very difficult or very easy depending on the distractors. Consider these two versions of the same item:

A. In what year did Skinner publish *The Behavior of Organisms?*
   a. 1457
   b. 1722
   c. 1938
   d. 1996

B. In what year did Skinner publish *The Behavior of Organisms?*
   a. 1936
   b. 1931
   c. 1938
   d. 1942

Even a person who knows very little about the history of psychology is likely to find version A to be an easy item. On the other hand, version B is likely to be extremely difficult. The difficulty of an item is greatly affected by the plausibility of the distractors. If the examinee knows nothing about the domain being tested, any distractor might be equally plausible. In general, however, people taking tests have some knowledge of the domain and are not fooled by ridiculous distractors. On the other hand, examinees usually have an imperfect knowledge of the domain and therefore may be fooled by extremely plausible distractors. Some items are extremely difficult because of one or two extremely popular distractors. In either case, it may be possible to substantially change the item's difficulty by rewriting some distractors.

Difficulty and Discrimination

The level of difficulty places a direct limit on the discriminating power of an item. If everyone chooses the correct response ($p = 1.0$) or if everyone chooses an incorrect response ($p = .0$), item responses cannot possibly be used to discriminate between those who do well on the test and those who do poorly. When the p value is near .0 or near 1.0, the ability to discriminate between individuals is restricted.

Table 10-3 shows the maximum possible value of the item discrimination index (D) for test items at various levels of difficulty. The table shows that items with p values near .50 have the maximum potential to be good discriminators. It is important to keep in mind that a p value near .50 does not guarantee that an item will be a good discriminator. Extreme p values place a direct statistical limit on the discriminating power of an item. When the p values are near .50, there are no statistical limits on discriminating power. Nevertheless, a poor item with a p value of .50 is still a poor item.

Table 10-3   MAXIMUM VALUE OF THE ITEM
DISCRIMINATION INDEX (D) AS A
FUNCTION OF ITEM DIFFICULTY

Item p value	Maximum D
1.00	.00
.90	.20
.80	.40
.70	.60
.60	.80
.50	1.00
.40	.80
.30	.60
.20	.40
.10	.20
.00	.00

Distractors and Discrimination

It is difficult to write a good test item. There usually is no problem in writing the stem of the question or framing the correct response; the trick is to write good distractors. The lack of discriminating power shown by test items often can be attributed to poor distractors. The presence of one or more completely implausible distractors serves to lower the difficulty of an item. As discussed in the previous section, items that are extremely easy have little or no potential for making valid discriminations. The same is true of extremely difficult items.

Distractors should be carefully examined when items show negative D values or negative item-total correlations. When one or more of the distractors looks extremely plausible to the informed reader and when recognition of the correct response depends on some extremely subtle point, it is possible that examinees will be penalized for partial knowledge. Consider, for example, the following item:

Reviews of research on the effectiveness of psychotherapy have concluded that

a. psychotherapy is never effective.
b. psychotherapy is effective, but only in treating somatoform disorders.
c. psychotherapy is effective; there are no major differences in the effectiveness of different types of therapy.
d. psychotherapy is effective; behavioral approaches are consistently more effective than all others.

Choice c is correct. A student who is familiar with research on psychotherapy, but whose professor is strongly committed to praising the virtues of behavior therapy, might mistakenly choose d. Those examinees who have no inkling of the correct answer may choose randomly and do better than those who have some command of the domain being tested but who do not recognize the correct response. This sort of item will not contribute to the overall quality of the test. Rather, it is a source of measurement error and should be either revised or removed. The revision of one or more distractors may dramatically increase the discriminating power of poor items.

ITEM RESPONSE THEORY

Test developers and psychometric researchers have long known that item analyses of the sort just described provide information that can be difficult to interpret. For example, the statement that "Item A is difficult" is both a normative description, in the sense that most people who respond to this item will fail, and a description of the processes involved in responding, in the sense that a person probably needs to have high levels of specific knowledge or abilities to have a good chance of success. Traditional item analyses tell you a good deal about the test items, but they are also heavily influenced by the types of people who take a test. The same test that appears to have difficult, highly discriminating items (measured in terms of p and d values) when administered to a general sample of students may look too easy and insufficiently informative when administered to a sample of gifted students.

Modern approaches to test development and to the analysis of tests do not put a great deal of emphasis on the simple methods of item analysis described so far in this chapter. Rather, they are likely to take advantage of statistics and analytic methods associated with item response theory. This theory allows you to develop informative and interpretable measures of item characteristics, of ability levels needed to pass test items (Carroll, 1993b), and of test scores (Raju, van der Linden, & Fleer, 1995). Many of these measures are obtained from analyses of item characteristic curves.

Item Characteristic Curves

Tests are usually designed to measure some specific attribute, such as verbal ability. The more of this attribute that a person has, the more likely that the person will answer each test item correctly. The item characteristic curve (ICC) is a graphic presentation of the probability of choosing the correct answer to an item as a function of the level of the attribute being measured by the test. The ICC serves as the foundation of one of the most powerful theories in modern psychometrics, item response theory (or latent trait theory). The ICC also summarizes much of the information conveyed by item analysis and suggests how this information might be used to understand the relationships between the attribute being measured and test responses (F. M. Lord, 1977; F. M. Lord & Novick, 1968; Rasch, 1960).

Figure 10-1 shows an ICC for a good item on a test of verbal ability. This theoretical ICC plots the probability of answering the item correctly against a person's level of verbal ability. As verbal ability increases, the probability of choosing the correct answer increases dramatically. This outcome suggests that the item is a fairly good measure of verbal ability.

The ICC is a graphic summary of the key features of a test item: its difficulty, its discriminating power, and the probability of answering correctly by guessing. The

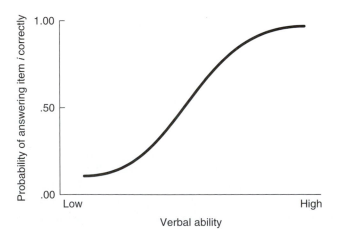

FIGURE 10-1   ICC for Item *i* on a Verbal Ability Test

mathematics involved in estimating the mathematical parameters of this curve are complex, requiring both large samples and sophisticated computer algorithms (Drasgow & Hulin, 1991). However, you can gain an appreciation of the basic ideas behind the ICC by simply graphing the probability of a correct response as a function of the total test score. Figures 10-2 to 10-4 illustrate such graphs.

Suppose that an item was not a very good discriminator. What would a graph of the relationship between item responses and total test scores look like? Figure 10-2 shows such a graph for a very difficult item that shows little discriminating power. Notice that the difficulty of the item (i.e., as indicated by the probability of a correct response) increases, though only slightly, as the total test score increases. That is, people who did well on the test have a slightly higher chance of doing well on this item than those who did poorly on the test. If you compare this graph with the one shown in Figure 10-1, which represents an ICC for an item with high discriminating power, it should be clear how the steepness or slope of the graph indicates discriminating power. A steep upward slope indicates that people who did well on the test (or who possess a large amount of the ability measured by the test) are much more likely to respond correctly to the item than people who did poorly on the test. A flatter slope, as in Figure 10-2, indicates a weaker relationship between test scores and responses to the particular item illustrated in the graph. Figure 10-3 shows an item with negative discriminating power (the item-total r for this item is 2.24). In this graph, the curve slopes downward, indicating that people who did well on the test are less likely to do well on this particular item.

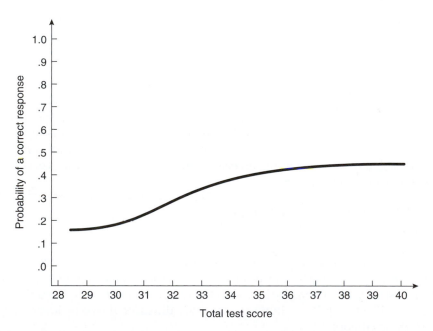

FIGURE 10-2 Graph of Item Versus Test Score for an Item With Little Discriminating Power (p = .24 item-total r = .03)

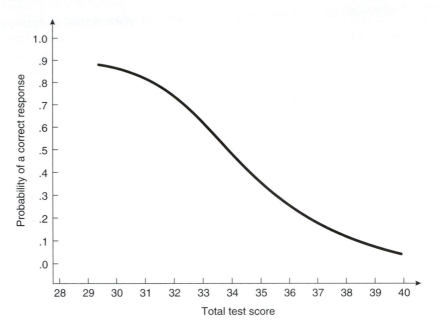

FIGURE 10-3   Graph of Item Versus Test Score for an Item With Negative Discriminating Power (p = .52; item-total r = 2.24)

Graphs of this type can also be used to illustrate item difficulty. Figure 10-4 shows graphs relating item scores to total test scores for three items that show similar discriminating power but that differ in difficulty. Item C is the most difficult, item B is moderately difficult, and item A is the least difficult. The position of the curve gives a good indication of the difficulty of each item. For the most difficult items, the curve starts to rise on the right side of the plot (high total test scores). This feature is simply a graphic illustration of the fact that the probability of answering a difficult item correctly is low for most examinees and rises only in the top group of those taking the test. For the easier items, the curve starts to rise on the left side of the plot (low total test scores); the probability of answering an easy item correctly is high for everyone but the very bottom group of examinees.

Item Characteristic Curves and Item Response Theory

Traditional item analysis procedures supply us with good measures of discrimination and difficulty. If ICCs simply provided alternate measures of these vital item characteristics, they would hardly be worth the trouble. However, some unique advantages are associated with ICCs. In particular, they illustrate the basic ideas that underlie item response theory.

Item response theory was constructed to explain and analyze the relationship between characteristics of the individual (e.g., ability) and responses to individual items

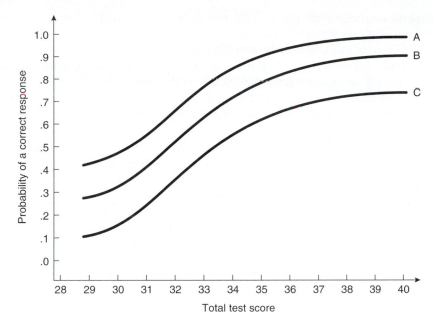

FIGURE 10-4   Graph of Item Versus Test Score for Three Items That Vary in Difficulty

(Hulin, Drasgow, & Parsons, 1983; F. M. Lord, 1980; Thissen & Steinberg, 1988; Weiss, 1983). Reliability and validity theories typically concentrate on test scores and only peripherally deal with individual items. Thus, item analysis represents a sort of ad hoc follow-up analysis when used in the context of explaining reliability or validity. Item response theories, on the other hand, are developed precisely for the purpose of understanding how individual differences in traits or attributes affect the behavior of an individual when confronted with a specific item.

Item response theory starts with a set of assumptions about the mathematical relationship between a person's ability and the likelihood that he or she will answer an item correctly. First, there should be a relationship between the attribute the test is designed to measure and examinees' responses to test items. For example, in a well-constructed test of spatial visualization ability, people who have very good spatial visualization abilities should do well on the test items. Second, the relationship between the attribute that the test measures and responses to a test item should take a form similar to that shown in Figure 10-1; that is, there should be a simple mathematical relationship between the person's ability level and the likelihood that he or she will answer test items correctly. These assumptions form a basis for ICCs, which represent a combination of assumptions regarding underlying relationships and the empirical outcomes of testing. To the extent that these assumptions are true, item response theory allows precise inferences to be made about underlying traits (e.g., ability) on the basis of observed behavior (e.g., item responses).

A principal advantage of item response theory is that it provides measures that are generally sample invariant. That is, the measures that are used to describe an ICC do not depend on the sample from which test data are drawn. The same is not true for standard item analysis statistics. The same reading test that is difficult (low *p* values) for a group of fourth graders may be less difficult and more discriminating for a group of sixth graders, and extremely easy for a group of eighth graders. The invariance of measures obtained using item response theory is thought to be important, since it allows characteristics of items to be analyzed without confounding them, as traditional item analyses do, with the characteristics of the people taking the test.

   Item Response Theory and Test-Taking Behavior. Most proponents of item response theory focus on the technical advantages of this approach, such as sample invariance, or on the fact that this approach allows you to tackle issues that are very difficult to handle in traditional item analysis (applications of this theory to three such issues are described in the section that follows). In our opinion, the real advantage of item response theory may be conceptual rather than mathematical. Unlike the traditional approach to item analysis, this theory encourages you to think about why people answer items correctly.

   The most widely cited model for responses to typical test items suggests that two things explain a correct response: luck and ability. The mathematical methods used in constructing ICCs under this model include a parameter that represents the susceptibility of the item to guessing, another that represents the role of ability in item responses, and a third that represents item discriminating power. Item response theory defines difficulty in terms of the level of ability needed to answer the item correctly, with a given level of probability. In contrast, the traditional definition of difficulty says nothing about what makes an item difficult or easy. Thus, traditionally, an item is difficult if most people answer incorrectly and easy if most people answer correctly. Item response theory states that a difficult item is one that requires a high level of ability to achieve a correct answer, whereas an easy item is one that can be answered by people with lower ability levels.

   In addition to providing a better definition of item difficulty than the traditional approach, this theory provides a better definition of discriminating power. In item response theory, discriminating power is defined in terms of the relationship between item responses and the construct that the test is designed to measure. Thus, if individuals who are very high on spatial ability are more likely to answer an item on a spatial ability test than individuals who are low on that ability, the item shows high discriminating power. The traditional approach links item responses to total test scores rather than to the construct that the test is designed to measure. One implication is that traditional item discrimination statistics are only as good as the test itself. If the test is a poor measure of the construct, the relationship between item scores and total test scores may tell you little about the worth of the item.

   Item response theory has become the dominant theme in modern psychometric research. In several of the chapters that follow (e.g., Chapters 12, 15, and 19), we will discuss contemporary applications of item response theory to practical testing problems. Some of the more specialized applications of the theory are described in the following sections.

Practical Applications of Item Response Theory

Although the mathematical complexity of item response theory has to some extent stood in the way of its widespread use, several advantages unique to item response theory explain why this approach has become increasingly popular among measurement specialists. First, as mentioned earlier, the theory produces measures of item difficulty, discrimination, and so on, that are invariant across different samples of people who take the test. Second, item response theory can be applied to solving several problems that are difficult to solve using traditional approaches. Three examples are noted here: (1) an approach that uses distractors in estimating ability, (2) an approach that tailors the test to the individual examinee, and (3) approaches for analyzing and constructing specialized tests.

Getting Information About Ability From Distractors. In traditional item analysis, an answer is either right or wrong. It makes no difference which distractor is chosen; a right answer receives a score of one, and a wrong answer receives a score of zero. In fact, some distractors are probably better answers than others in that some reflect partial knowledge, whereas others will be chosen only if the person has little or no knowledge.

Item response theory suggests that any response made to an item could provide information about one's knowledge or ability. Rather than concentrate solely on the correct response, the theory encourages construction of a separate ICC for each possible response to a multiple-choice item, distractors as well as the correct response. Figure 10-5 shows a set of ICCs for the possible responses to a single test item. Choice

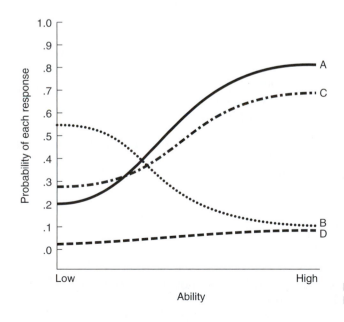

FIGURE 10-5   ICC for Each
Response to a Multiple-Choice Item

A (the correct response) shows positive discriminating power; one of the distractors (choice C) also shows some positive discriminating power. Choice D is extremely unpopular and therefore shows no discriminating power, whereas choice B shows negative discriminating power.

Figure 10-5 suggests that alternative C is nearly as good an answer as alternative A, although it shows less discriminating power. On the other hand, both B and D are bad choices. In particular, the lower a person's ability, the higher the probability that the person will choose B. Rather than scoring the item either right or wrong, an examiner might give nearly full credit for choice C and might give the lowest score for choice B.

Adaptive Testing. Tests are usually constructed for a fairly diverse audience. For example, a test of general mathematical ability might contain several easy items, several items of moderate difficulty, and several very difficult items. For any individual taking the test, many of the items may be inappropriate and uninformative. For example, someone who is gifted in mathematics will find most of the items very easy and will be challenged only by the most difficult items. Someone who has great difficulty with mathematics will find most of the items too difficult and will do better than chance only on the easiest items. Rather than constructing a long test that contains some items appropriate for each ability level, it would be better to construct tests tailored to the ability level of the person taking the test. Developments in computer technology and in psychometric theory have made this technique possible (Urry, 1977).

One of the useful interesting applications of item response theory is in computerized adaptive testing. For any individual, a test is most precise if the difficulty of each item corresponds with his or her level of ability. Item response theory can be used to help tailor tests to individual examinees. When an individual takes a test at a computer terminal, it is possible to estimate his or her ability at each step of testing and then to select the next item to correspond with the person's estimated level of ability. For example, the first item on a tailored test might be moderately difficult. If an examinee passes that item, the computer may select a more difficult question for the second item on the test. If a person fails that item, the next item selected for the test might be less difficult. Tailored testing allows a great deal of precision within a fairly short test. This type of testing is discussed in more detail in Chapter 12.

Item Analysis for Specialized Tests. For the most part, this chapter has dealt with tests designed to measure some attribute or construct over a reasonably wide range (e.g., scholastic aptitude tests). In this type of measurement, three general principles can be applied in evaluating item analyses:

1. Incorrect responses should be evenly distributed among distractors.
2. Item difficulty p values should cluster around .50.
3. Item-total correlations should be positive.

In a number of situations, however, these guidelines do not apply. Screening tests and criterion-keyed tests are outstanding examples.

Screening tests are those that are used to make preliminary decisions or to make decisions as to whether persons exceed some minimum level of knowledge or proficiency needed to qualify for a position. For example, a bus driver must achieve a minimum level of visual acuity and depth perception to qualify for a license. However, visual acuity beyond this minimum does not make the person a better bus driver; rather, subliminal vision disqualifies applicants. Screening tests also are useful when the number of applicants greatly exceeds the number of positions, as is often the case in graduate admissions. A medical school that receives large numbers of applications and that never accepts applicants from the bottom half of the pool would benefit greatly if test scores could be used reliably to screen out this lower group.

A criterion-keyed test is one in which there are no right or wrong answers; it is a test in which a person's score is determined by the similarity of his or her responses to the responses of some known group. For example, the Minnesota Multiphasic Personality Inventory (discussed in Chapter 17) was constructed in such a way that examinees' responses could be compared with those of people diagnosed as schizophrenic, paranoid, and so forth. To the extent that a person's responses are similar to those previously diagnosed as schizophrenic, a diagnosis of schizophrenia would be indicated.

Item response theory is particularly useful in analyzing both screening tests and criterion-keyed tests. For example, consider a test designed to screen out the lower half of the applicant pool for medical school. An ideal item for this test would have an ICC similar to that shown in Figure 10-6. The curve would be very steep at the point about which the school wished to discriminate (the middle of the ability distribution), with a low probability of answering correctly among the low group and a high probability of

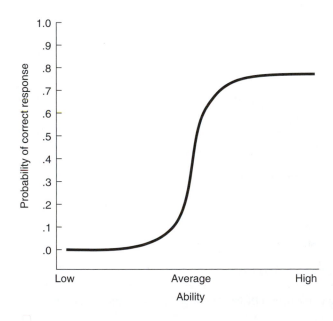

FIGURE 10-6   An Item Ideally Suited for Screening the Upper From the Lower Half of the Ability Distribution

answering correctly among the high group. A short test made up of items such as this would be effective for this type of preliminary screening.

In designing a criterion-keyed test, several ICCs could be developed relating item responses to different criteria. For example, Figure 10-7 illustrates how a particular item response might be related to the likelihood of being diagnosed as depressed, schizophrenic, or paranoid. This figure suggests that the item discriminates well for diagnoses of depression and schizophrenia but is unrelated to diagnoses of paranoia. Further, the ICCs indicate that individuals who answered yes to the item "I disliked school" are likely to be diagnosed as depressed but are unlikely to be diagnosed as schizophrenic.

CRITICAL DISCUSSION:

Using Item Response Theory to Detect Test Bias

As we noted in Chapter 3, the question of whether tests or test items are biased against minorities, females, and others is a very important one, and it is the focus of a great deal of controversy. One reason for this controversy is that there are many ways of defining and detecting test item bias (Berk, 1982; P. W. Holland & Thayer, 1988). These methods range from the very simple, in which a test item is regarded as biased if different groups receive different scores or have different passing rates, to the very complex, in which bias is defined in terms of the relationship between the item and some external criterion. There is a growing consensus among testing experts that measures based on the item response theory are among the best measures of test item bias (Drasgow & Hulin, 1991; Thissen, Steinberg, & Gerrard, 1986).

Although the mathematics of item response theory are quite complex, the application of this approach to the analysis of test item bias is based on a fairly simple idea: The relationship between item scores and the construct being measured by the test is an important consideration, especially when bias in measurement (as opposed to bias in prediction) is at issue. Examination of ICCs and the statistics that describe these curves provides a set of methods for detecting item bias. Figure 10-8 illustrates an item that has different measurement characteristics; that is, it is biased against

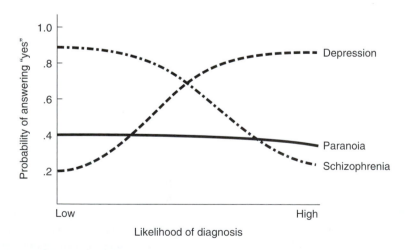

FIGURE 10-7   ICCs Relating Responses to the Item "I Disliked School" to Psychiatric Diagnosis

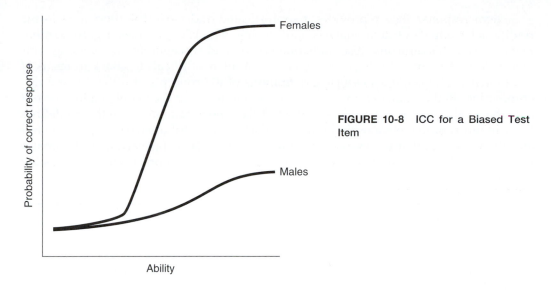

FIGURE 10-8   ICC for a Biased Test Item

males, while favoring females. As you can see, the item is more difficult for males, but it does not discriminate those males with low levels of ability from those with high levels of ability. In contrast, the item is less difficult and is a better discriminator for females.

One of the many advantages of using ICCs and item response theory in the analysis of test item bias is that they illustrate very clearly how items are biased; such an analysis can predict the probable consequences of using particular items on a test. For example, items like the one illustrated in Figure 10-8 would have two effects. First, males would get lower test scores (i.e., the items are more difficult for males). Second, the test would not measure the construct in question as well for males as for females (i.e., it has lower discrimination for males).

SUMMARY

Scores on psychological tests usually represent the sum, average, or some other function of responses to individual items. This chapter has focused on multiple-choice items, for which one of several choices is correct, but the concepts discussed here apply equally to other types of testing (e.g., personality items that have no correct response). In understanding responses to these items and the contribution of information from each item to the total test score, it is important to consider the responses to distractors, the difficulty of the item, and its discriminating power. Distractors that attract an unusually small or large number of responses may need to be rewritten; doing so is likely to improve the item substantially. Items that are too difficult or too easy (i.e., answered incorrectly or correctly by almost all examinees) contribute little to the overall value of the test. Finally, items that show high discriminating power, defined in terms of a *D* value or an item-total correlation, are likely to provide useful measures of the same thing measured by the test as a whole.

Item response theory provides a sophisticated and powerful alternative to the traditional methods of item analysis and scoring. The ICC provides a graphic summary of an item's difficulty, discriminating power, and susceptibility to guessing. This theory provides not only elegant solutions to problems difficult to attack in terms of traditional methods but also sensible definitions of the concepts of difficulty and discrimination. Rather than defining these concepts in terms of the people taking the test (i.e., the p value) or the other items on the test (i.e., the item-total r), the theory defines them in terms of the relationship between the ability or attribute measured by the test and the responses that individuals make to test items. This approach now dominates modern psychometric research, and it opens the way for sophisticated new testing strategies.

PROBLEMS AND SOLUTIONS—RECAP

The Problem

Your Psychology 101 exam (50 multiple-choice items) included 10 items in which *nobody* chose the right answer. You complain to your instructor, who notes that there are also 12 items that everyone answered correctly, and that if you want to drop the 10 difficult items, it is only fair to also drop the 12 easy ones.

A Solution

Your instructor's suggestion might be a reasonable one if the purpose of the test is to measure individual differences in performance. Items that have *p* values of .00 or 1.00 have no effect whatsoever on the ranking of test takers, so you would rank the examinees in exactly the same way if the 10 hard items were dropped, if the 12 easy items were dropped, or if all 22 were dropped. Because there are no individual differences in the "scores" on these 22 items, these items won't tell you anything about who did relatively well or who did relatively poorly on the test. Because of the extreme *p* values, these items also add nothing to the reliability of the test.

However, if the purpose of the test is to determine how much you know about the content area, it might not make any sense to drop *any* of the items. If the students have learned a lot in the course, they *should* choose the right answer pretty frequently, and one interpretation of the 12 perfect items is that the students really knew this content. Unfortunately, it is hard to rule out the alternative explanation, that people did well because the items were too easy. For example, suppose that item 6 (one of the twelve that was answered correctly by everyone) reads as follows:

The science that is most directly concerned with understanding human behavior is:

a. inorganic chemistry
b. paleontology
c. psychology
d. quantum physics

You might conclude that the perfect score was a reflection of a poorly written item rather than a reflection of the knowledge and sophistication of the students.

When everyone chooses the correct answer, item analysis is not very useful for diagnosing the cause of the good performance, and your decision to interpret perfect performance as a reflection of what the students have actually learned versus the simplicity of the items must be based on your knowledge of the content domain and your judgment. Item analysis is potentially more useful in evaluating items on which everyone, or nearly everyone, does poorly. Consider two items for which the correct response alternative is c.

% Choosing	Item 16	Item 24
a	24	2
b	39	92
c	0	0
d	37	6

Both items are equally difficult (p = .00 for both), but it looks as though item 24 is a trick question, in which almost everyone chooses the same incorrect response option, whereas incorrect responses are pretty evenly spread for item 16. We would argue that the pattern or responses to item 24 presents a good case for dropping this item. People seem to get this item wrong because there is something about response b that leads almost everyone to believe (incorrectly) that it is the right answer. The pattern of responses to item 16 suggests another possibility, that there might be something about the way the correct answer is written that makes everyone believe that it is wrong. It is debatable whether or not this item should be removed, but the analysis of distractor choices does help in the diagnosis of why everyone chose the wrong answer to items 16 and 24.

KEY TERMS

Difficulty   defined either in terms of the proportion of examinees who answer an item correctly (classical item analysis) or in terms of the level of ability needed to answer the item correctly (item response theory)

Distractor analysis   analysis of the pattern of responses to incorrect options on multiple-choice tests

Item analysis   set of procedures for analyzing responses to test items and the relationships between item characteristics and test characteristics

Item characteristic curve (ICC)   mathematical function describing the relationship between the construct measured by a test and responses to a specific test item

Item discrimination   extent to which responses to an item discriminate those who receive high versus low scores on the test

Item response theory   modern theory of psychometrics, in which the mathematical relationship summarized by an item characteristic curve is used to analyze test items and tests

Item-total correlation   correlation between scores on an item and scores on the test from which this item is taken

p value   proportion of examinees who answer an item correctly

Tailored or adaptive testing   method of testing in which test items are selected that are most appropriate and informative for the individual being assessed

The Process of Test Development

11

This chapter opens our discussion of the application of the principles of psychological measurement outlined in previous chapters. Up to this point, we have discussed the basic concepts of psychological testing without reference to their application in specific testing situations. In this chapter, we examine the process of test development and highlight some of the problems test developers face as they attempt to measure various psychological traits, attitudes, and behaviors.

Test development can be broken down into three distinct stages. The first stage involves test construction. Issues such as item writing, scale construction, response sets, and selection of test format are of primary interest here. Next, new tests are standardized for use on particular target populations, norms are developed, and considerable research is undertaken to establish estimates of the tests' reliability and validity. Finally, with the passage of time, tests need to be revised to keep them contemporary and current, both with respect to the norms available and item content. This chapter is therefore divided into three sections that deal with these aspects of test development.

PROBLEMS AND SOLUTIONS—SHOULD YOU TRUST YOUR JUDGMENT OR THE TEST?

The Problem

For a number of years after it was first published, the Strong Vocational Interest Blank (now known as the Strong Interest Inventory) included an occupational scale that measured the interests of real estate agents. However, many counselors found that a number of clients whom they tested, who reportedly liked sales-related work and indicated that they thought that they would like to work in real estate sales, did not score well on the real estate sales scale. If scores on that scale were meaningful and interpretable, the best conclusion from the data would have been that these people were not probably well suited for that work and would be unlikely to be satisfied working in real estate sales.

Since the counselors who worked with these clients expected to see testing results that were more consistent with their clients' self-reported interests, they were frequently at a loss to explain why the testing results did not support their clinical impressions. Were their clients not as interested in real estate sales as they thought? Was their clinical judgment suspect? Or was there some problem in the development of that particular scale that produced such surprising results?

CONSTRUCTING THE TEST

Selecting Item Types

The first, and in some ways most fundamental, decision faced by test developers is what type of item(s) they should use. Most of the tests described in this book rely on multiple-choice items, but these are not necessarily the best for all testing applications. In recent years, a great deal of attention has been devoted to the use of items that require a "constructed response," such as essay questions, short-answer questions, or questions that require a concrete demonstration of skill (R. E. Bennett & Ward, 1993; *Goals 2000,* 1994). Guion (1998) notes that item types can be thought of as a continuum rather than as a multiple-choice versus essay dichotomy. For example, items might require examinees to recognize correct responses (traditional multiple choice), to identify or correct problems in material they are presented with, to produce something (essay, drawing), to describe how something can or should be produced (low-fidelity simulations), and so on. Although a range of item types are available to test developers, it is nevertheless true that the choice that they must often face is between a format that requires test takers to produce or construct a response, perhaps with a minimum of structure (e.g., "In 100 words, describe the significance of *Last of the Mohicans* in American literature") and one that requires them to choose or recognize a correct response in a highly structured format.

Advocates of constructed response methods argue that these tests measure a wider and richer array of human abilities and skills than those measured by multiple-choice tests. Multiple-choice tests are often assumed to measure narrow facets of performance (e.g., knowledge of specific facts), and it is often assumed that by allowing examinees to respond in a less structured way (e.g., answering an essay), you can get a much better picture of the individual's true capabilities. However, research comparing these two types of items has not supported the idea that they measure different things, or that essay tests provide more information about the examinee than do traditional multiple-choice tests (R. E. Bennet, Rock, & Wang, 1991; Bridgeman, 1992; Guion, 1998). On the contrary, research on the characteristics of these two types of items typically suggests that multiple-choice items are a better choice than essay or other types of constructed response items. First, it is very difficult to develop reliable methods of scoring constructed-response items. Second, any method of scoring these items is likely to be labor-intensive, expensive, and slow. Multiple-choice tests are relatively easy to develop and score, and these tests can easily be made long and detailed, thereby providing a better chance of broadly sampling the domain to be measured.

Multiple-choice tests with hundreds of items are commonplace, but an essay test including even a few dozen questions would be virtually impossible to administer and score. The assumption in the rest of this chapter and in most of the chapters that follow is that most psychological tests will employ items that involve highly structured responses; tests that follow different measurement strategies (e.g., projective measures of personality and psychopathology) are often severely limited by their low reliability and questionable validity.

Item Writing

The first step in the test construction process is to generate an item pool. Although there have been a few attempts to study item writing (Cantor, 1987; Comrey, 1988; Holden & Fekken, 1990), little attention has been given to item writing in comparison with other aspects of the test development process (e.g., scale construction and response sets) despite the fact that test items form the basic building blocks of tests. Why this is the case is not completely clear. Perhaps it is because item writing has often been seen as much more of an art than a science. Given this view, test developers often rely on statistical item analysis procedures to help them identify and eliminate poor items, rather than focusing on how to improve the item-writing process itself. They appear to be laboring under the assumption that, through much trial and error in writing, eventually subsets of items can be identified that will measure the trait in question.

Some common issues that arise in item writing, however, merit discussion. For example, item length can sometimes be a problem. Examinees may get confused if an item is so long that the major point is missed as it is read. Another critical variable in the item-writing process involves the vocabulary used in the test items. Test developers need to be aware of the reading level of the target group for whom the test is intended. Likewise, the wording of items needs careful consideration to avoid the use of double negatives and possible ambiguity in responding. Items such as "I do not read every editorial in the newspaper every day," from the California Psychological Inventory, often create uncertainty on the part of examinees. Should they respond "true" to this statement if they agree? What would a false response imply? Table 11-1 presents additional hypothetical examples of poorly written, as well as well-written, items.

Table 11-1 EXAMPLES OF POORLY WRITTEN AND WELL-WRITTEN ITEMS

Poorly written items	Well-written items
It is not acceptable to say no when asked to give to charity.	It is considered bad manners to turn down a request to a charitable donation.
I do not believe that all our laws are good for the citizens of this country.	I think that some laws are harmful to particular citizens.
If you ask, people will not tell you what they are thinking most of the time.	I believe that people tend to keep their real thoughts private.

One additional factor that test developers have increasingly taken into account in item writing concerns the presence of sexist, racist, or other offensive language. Although blatantly offensive language is relatively easy to detect and eliminate, subtle linguistic nuances are often overlooked and not perceived as offensive by the developer. A case in point involves interest tests that use occupational titles containing reference to only one sex, for example, using the term "mailman" instead of "mail carrier" or "fireman" rather than "firefighter." Although G. S. Gottfedson (1976) has presented data suggesting that such gender-specific language probably does not appreciably affect most interest test scores, nevertheless, if it promotes sexist attitudes or causes some people to react negatively to testing, then it needs to be eliminated. The best method for eliminating problems inherent in written items is to try them out on sample populations. Test developers generally begin with a large item pool and then weed out unacceptable items until a satisfactory subset is identified.

Item Content

Some test developers use a particular theoretical system to guide them in writing items for their tests. Generally, test constructors draw on one particular theory of personality, career interests, or intellectual ability, and then translate the ideas of that theory into test items.

Allen Edwards adopted this item-writing strategy in developing his personality test, the Edwards Personal Preference Schedule (EPPS). Working from a theory of personality outlined by Murray (1938), Edwards directly translated many of the manifest needs postulated in the theory into behaviorally worded test items. For example, Murray theorized that the need for autonomy often influences people to do things on their own or seek a lifestyle characterized by independence and unconventionality. Edwards took this concept of autonomy and translated it into such test items as "I like to avoid situations where I am expected to do things in a conventional way" and "I like to avoid responsibilities and obligations." You can easily see how these items directly reflect the theorized need.

One particular drawback of items that are generated from theory is that they are often quite transparent. By transparent, we mean that the items are worded in such a way that what the items are trying to measure is usually quite apparent. Thus, examinees often respond to such obvious items as they would like to appear, rather than as they actually perceive themselves.

The other approach used in item writing is much more atheoretical and does not rely on theory to guide the selection of item content. In this method, test developers generate a large item pool with very diverse item content. Often, no common theme binds the items together. The trick is to create items that will differentiate the responses of one group from that of another. The Minnesota Multiphasic Personality Inventory (MMPI) was developed using primarily this approach. Because such items often bear little theoretical significance, they are generally much less transparent than theory-based items and consequently much less subject to examinee distortion.

Item Response Alternatives

The types of item response alternatives used in psychological testing vary widely. Some self-report measures, such as the Personality Research Form, employ a simple true-false response format. Others, such as the Tennessee Self-Concept Scale, employ a multiple-choice answer format in which examinees respond on a 5-point Likert scale, indicating how truthful statements are about them. Projective tests, such as the Rorschach and the Rotter Incomplete Sentences Blank, require examinees to give unstructured, free responses to various test stimuli. Finally, in the case of achievement and aptitude testing, examinees may be required to produce certain kinds of products as part of the testing process.

Sometimes the purpose of the test dictates the type of answer format. Consider the Wide Range Achievement Test, which assesses spelling ability by having the examinee print the correct spelling of a word spoken orally by the examiner. In contrast, the spelling subtest of the Differential Aptitude Test asks test takers to indicate whether stimulus words are spelled correctly. Although both are tests of spelling ability, the former relies on auditory spelling, whereas the latter stresses visual recall skills. Consequently, an examinee may score quite differently on these two measures because a variation in the response format changes the nature of the task.

By far the most popular format in object testing has involved the use of multiple-choice items. Use of this item format provides several advantages over other formats. First, test item scoring is easy and rapid. Second, the error in the measurement process associated with guessing is reduced as the number of alternatives in the item is increased (e.g., a four-alternative item produces a 25% probability of a correct response because of guessing; a five-alternative item reduces the chances of guessing a correct answer to 20%). Finally, no examiner judgment is involved in the scoring of multiple-choice items.

The multiple-choice item format has its shortcomings, however. It is often difficult to write alternative statements for items that will function as good distractors. Another problem with multiple-choice items is that they may contain transparent cues that signal the correct response. This problem occurs when articles such as "a" or "an" are used in the wording of multiple-choice items in a manner that gives the examinee a definite clue as to the correct choice. Similarly, sometimes the tense of verbs used in the stem and in an alternative may aid the test taker in identifying the keyed response. An example of a multiple-choice item that signals the correct response alternative is shown in Table 11-2.

**Table 11-2 CUEING THE CORRECT RESPONSE
IN A MULTIPLE-CHOICE ITEM**

The car featured in the movie *Rain Man* was a
(a) Allante (Cadillac)
(b) Roadmaster (Buick)
(c) Escort (Ford)
(d) Aries (Dodge)

The free-response format also has its advantages and disadvantages. When examinees are permitted to freely respond to test items, the results often convey a richness and depth of thought or reflection that would not otherwise be detectable from the use of a more structured response format. This same strength, however, is also a major contributor to the weakness in this response format. The variability among examinees' responses, as well as their unique characteristics, poses significant scoring problems for examiners.

Recently, researchers have begun to examine whether free-response and multiple-choice items can be combined to measure the same trait or attribute. Some tests, such as the College Board's Advanced Placement Computer Science Test and Advanced Placement Chemistry Test, combine both multiple-choice and free-response formats in the same instrument. Thissen, Wainer, and Wang (1994) used a factor-analytic approach to study student performance on these two tests and concluded that both types of item formats were measuring the same attribute and could be successfully combined in one test. However, although both item formats produced similar scores for these ability tests, there is no assurance that measures of other psychological traits would operate in the same way.

Scale Construction

Each item on a psychological test represents an observation of some particular behavior or trait. By grouping similar items together, test developers can generate multiple observations of the same behavior or trait. As we have seen in Chapters 6 and 7, increasing the number of behavioral observations increases the reliability of our estimates of that variable. However, item grouping can be done in various ways, resulting in psychological scales that have different characteristics and that require different interpretations. Traditionally, three scaling methods have been used in developing psychological tests.

Rational Scales. The oldest method of scaling, the rational method of scale construction, implies that some underlying thought, belief, or rationale is used as the basis for selecting items and grouping them together into a scale. This is precisely what test developers do when they draw on a particular theoretical system to guide them in selecting a set of items to measure a specific theoretical idea. As we have seen before, when A. L. Edwards (1957) wanted to measure various manifest needs within people and to study how they affected behavior, he followed Murray's theoretical ideas about needs and created scales consisting of items reflecting Murray's concepts. The advantage of rationally derived scales is that test developers can then draw on theory to make predictions about behavior, because the scales have been designed to measure the theory's concepts.

Rationally derived scales can also have some severe shortcomings. It is obvious that the usefulness of such scales is tied to the validity of the theory on which they are based. If the theory is sound and leads to accurate predictions about how people will behave, then scales based on the theory should also lead to valid and meaningful predictions. Likewise, if the theory is not substantiated, then scales based on that theory are likely to have questionable validity. Another potential problem arises from the transparent nature of scales constructed using the rational approach. For example, it is not difficult to understand what the item "I have often felt like taking things that do not belong to me" measures. Consequently, examinees can often distort their responses, either consciously or unconsciously, so as to appear in a particular light.

Empirical Scales. Empirically derived scales rely on criterion keying for their validity. With this method, well-defined criterion groups are administered as a set of possible test items. Items that statistically differentiate the groups are included on the test. For example, a group of male adult schizophrenics diagnosed by clinical interview might be contrasted to a group of normal, emotionally well-adjusted male adults. Both groups would be given the same set of items, but only those that clearly separated the schizophrenics from the normal group would be retained. Although this procedure produces reasonably valid tests, it does not permit any analysis of why the groups differ on such items. The major testing purpose served, then, is to discriminate one group from another, rather than to understand the underlying theoretical reasons for their response differences.

In contrast to rational tests, empirical tests are generally difficult to dissimulate because the content of the items that may actually differentiate groups may not be readily apparent. An example is an item from the MMPI-2 such as "I enjoy detective or mystery stories," which if answered false suggests a tendency toward denial. Notice that it is very difficult to determine the psychological significance of such an item and therefore how to respond to it in order to consciously distort your test results.

A variant of the empirical method of scale construction involves the use of factor analysis in the item selection process. In this method, the correlations among items are examined to determine which factors account for most of the variability in responding on the test. Once the items constituting each factor have been identified, they are grouped together and given a label. The labels given to such scales can be somewhat arbitrary, such as letters in the alphabet, as in the case of the 16 Personality Factors test. Generally, however, they are determined by an examination of the item content within the group. Because these groupings were determined by statistical analysis rather than theoretical determination, it is often very difficult to capture the essence of the scales formed by such item groupings or their relationship to clinically useful concepts. Another problem with factor analytically derived tests stems from the variability in item groupings obtained when different methods of factor analysis are used to construct the scales. The strength of this method, however, is that it yields instruments with psychometric properties generally superior to those constructed with the use of the rational method.

Rational-Empirical Scales. Test constructors have begun to combine aspects of both the rational and the empirical approaches to scale construction in the test development process. As is often the case, the combined process allows test developers to utilize the advantages of each method. Tests such as the Personality Research Form (D. N. Jackson, 1967) have been built using elaborate scale development techniques that draw on aspects of the rational approach to ensure that the resultant scales are theoretically meaningful as well as on elements of the empirical approach to ensure that they relate to the desired criteria and are relatively free of unwanted error variance.

Response Sets

To measure various psychological traits, test developers often employ self-report inventories that ask examinees to share information about themselves. However, some examinees believe that the information being requested is too personal or embarrassing to report. Sometimes they may even feel coerced into completing an inventory and then decide not to complete it accurately. On other occasions, they find the questions stated in such vague terms that they are unsure about how to respond in order to present an accurate reflection of their thoughts, feelings, attitudes, or behaviors. In such instances as these, test takers may consciously distort their responses, guess at items when they are stated in vague terms, answer items carelessly, or even unintentionally mismark their answer sheets. Factors such as these add unwanted error variance to test scores and confound the interpretation process. Whenever individuals respond to something other than the actual item content when being tested, the validity of the information obtained is of questionable value. Therefore, better psychological tests have built-in methods for detecting these sources of extraneous variance so that they can be potentially minimized or even eliminated in the interpretation process.

Social Desirability. One of the most pervasive and problematic response sets is social desirability. The effects of this response tendency on measures of personality have been stated most cogently by Allen L. Edwards (1957, 1970). His research demonstrated that people from various backgrounds, educational levels, and cultures generally agree as to which behaviors are socially desirable and which are undesirable. Other researchers (S. T. Smith, Smith, & Seymour, 1993) have also demonstrated the remarkable stability of desirability ratings across diverse cultures. From Edwards's analysis of various personality tests, he concluded that many of the tests did not accurately measure the traits that they were designed to assess but, rather, provided indexes of individuals' propensities for giving socially approved responses. He stated that the rate of endorsement of personality test items was a linearly increasing function of the items' social desirability values. Thus, Edwards was arguing that, when examinees respond to personality test items, they do not attend as much to the trait being measured as to the social acceptability of the statement. Consequently, Edwards proposed that this tendency to give desirable answers is itself a personality trait that is probably more manifest than other traits.

Much research has been done on the issue of social desirability in personality measurement since Edwards first brought the topic to light. Although experts agree that the tendency to give socially desirable responses on personality tests is quite operative, there is sharp disagreement among them as to how much impact this has on test validity and therefore what to do about it. Some researchers (A. L. Edwards, 1970; Walsh, 1990) believe that social desirability represents potentially unwanted variance that needs to be controlled to increase test validity. Others (Nicholson & Hogan, 1990) have argued that social desirability overlaps substantially with personality, and if its effects are statistically removed, then meaningful content is lost. Research evidence reported by McCrae (1986) and by McCrae and Costa (1984) support this latter proposition.

Those who have wanted to control or eliminate the effects of social desirability responding on personality tests have generally attempted to do so by one of the following strategies. The most common methods have been to pair items of equal desirability ratings in an ipsative format, to select neutral items that are neither strongly positive nor strongly negative on the social desirability dimension, or to statistically adjust test scores to eliminate any such effects. This latter method is accomplished by devising a special scale to assess the tendency for examinees to give socially desirable responses and then statistically correcting their other test scores for this distorting factor. However, none of these methods has proved particularly successful in controlling or eliminating the effects of this response set.

Random Responding. The random response set usually results when examinees fail to attend to the content of test items and respond randomly, either because they are unmotivated or incapable of completing the task accurately. Examinees often give random responses on an inventory when they do not want to be evaluated or when they are incapable of validly taking the test (e.g., unable to read the questions or too disturbed to attend to the task). For example, students referred to counseling because of disciplinary infractions might be unwilling to cooperate with any testing efforts, perhaps viewing them as an infringement of their rights. In such cases, their testing results would be of limited clinical value.

To help prevent the clinician from attempting to interpret such results and arriving at faulty conclusions, test constructors often include scales on their tests designed to identify this response pattern. The typical form of these scales includes items that tend to be universally true or false for everyone. If respondents attend to the content of these items, they will answer them in the expected direction. If they respond in a random fashion, however, then by chance they will endorse a significant number of these items in a direction counter to that of the general population and produce a score that is highly suggestive of random responding. Sample items from a scale on the Personality Research Form designed to detect random responding are shown in Table 11-3.

Wise test users generally familiarize themselves with the overall picture generated by random test protocols by experimentally completing a number of answer sheets with random responses. Once the general pattern of scores resulting from a random response set is known, similar score patterns when encountered can be interpreted with caution, and follow-up information on the motivational level of the examinee can be obtained.

Dissimulation. The dissimulation response set generally refers to completing an inventory in such a manner so as to appear overly healthy (faking good) or overly

Table 11-3   SAMPLE ITEMS FROM THE INFREQUENCY SCALE OF THE PERSONALITY RESEARCH FORM

Item	Response
I try to get at least some sleep every night.	False
I make all my own clothes and shoes.	True
I rarely use food or drink of any kind.	True
I have never ridden in an automobile.	True

Source: From Douglas Jackson, *Personality Research Form,* Copyright © 1967, 1974, 1984 by Douglas N. Jackson. Reprinted by permission of Sigma Assessment Systems, Inc., 511 Fort Street, Suite 435, P.O. Box 610984, Port Huron, MI 48061-0984, (800) 265–1285.

disturbed (faking bad). It is produced by the conscious efforts of the respondent to present a picture that is distorted or dissimulated from reality. This response set is most operative in situations in which testing is being done as part of a selection process for jobs, promotions, awards, and the like, or for decision-making purposes relative to the establishment of diminished capacity as part of a defense against culpability in a criminal matter. In such cases, invalid conclusions could be easily drawn if this conscious distortion effort were unknown to the clinician.

Personality tests differ greatly with respect to how successfully they address this problem. Some tests, like the MMPI, contain several sophisticated scales to detect dissimulation, whereas others, like the EPPS, have only a rudimentary check for this response set. However, the absence of scales to check for faking in some personality inventories may not be a serious problem. First, corrections for response distortion rarely help (R. T. Hogan, 1991; Nicholson & Hogan, 1990); if faking is suspected, there may be no good way of estimating what the score would have been without faking. Second, recent research suggests that although personality tests are often fakable, this drawback may not greatly affect their correlations with other tests and measures, and therefore faking may not diminish their validity as predictors of future behavior (Hough, Eaton, Dunnette, Kamp, & McCloy, 1990). Finally, research on the Personality Research Form reported by Jackson and St. John (D. N. Jackson, 1999) has suggested that intentional instructional sets to present a favorable impression may not appreciably affect scores on the Personality Research Form.

CRITICAL DISCUSSION:

How Accurately Can Response Sets Be Detected?

Test constructors have developed several different methods to detect the presence of unwanted response set variance on their tests. One method involves the inclusion of specially developed scales to measure the extent to which examinees utilize various response sets in responding to item content. Typically, scales like the good impression scale from the California Psychological Inventory (CPI) or the F scale from the MMPI are useful in detecting response sets such as attempting to provide an overly favorable picture of oneself or responding in a random fashion. Often, greater precision in detecting response sets can be achieved by combining several validity scales together.

Adding other personality information to the validity scale data in a predictive regression equation can occasionally attain still greater precision. An important question that arises, however, is how well do these scales work? Can they accurately detect such response distortions as faking or random responding?

Several rather sophisticated empirically determined algorithms have been developed for the current edition of the CPI to detect such response sets. For example, the following three equations appear in the CPI Manual (Gough & Bradley, 1996) along with empirically determined cut scores.

Fake good = 41.225 + .273 Dominance + .198 Empathy + .538 Good Impression
  − .255 Well Being − .168 Flexibility

Fake bad = 86.613 − 1.0 Communality − .191 Well Being + .203 Achievement via
  Conformance − .110 Flexibility

Random = 34.096 + .279 Good Impression + .201 Well Being
  + .225 Psychological Mindedness + .157 Flexibility

To test the efficacy of these algorithms in detecting these response sets, sample groups of both men and women were asked to take the CPI under the instructional set to deliberately give false information about themselves so as to appear either very good or very bad. Their CPI protocols were then scored and checked to determine how many of these faked protocols could be accurately identified when these prediction equations were applied to their test scores. Similarly, protocols that were randomly generated either by hand or computer were also examined. Table 11-4 summarizes the results of these investigations.

An inspection of Table 11-4 shows that even though the detection rates varied among groups, the data suggest that those attempting to "fake good" were identified approximately two thirds of the time, those trying to present a negative impression of themselves were spotted over 80% of the time, and protocols that were randomly marked were correctly identified nearly two thirds of the time. However, a sizable number of the randomly generated protocols (22.5%) were identified as "fake bad" rather than random and so were properly identified as invalid, but were misdiagnosed as "fake bad." Consequently, it can be stated that when the random equation was utilized to detect random protocols, approximately 87% of the invalid profiles were correctly identified as invalid, although not all were correctly identified as random (i.e., 64.7% correctly identified as random + 22.5% incorrectly identified as random but correctly identified as invalid). Therefore, we can see that at least in some cases, scoring algorithms designed to detect invalid test scores appear to work reasonably well.

Table 11-4 EFFECTIVENESS OF FAKE GOOD, FAKE BAD, AND RANDOM INDICES ON THE CPI

		Percentage correctly identified		
Instructional Set		Fake good	Fake bad	Random
Fake Good	Males	68.0		
	Females	57.7		
Fake Bad	Males		84.0	
	Females		78.0	
Random Response	Computer Generated			64.6

Response Style

Response style refers to a general tendency to either agree or disagree with statements without attending to their actual content. The tendency to generally agree has been labeled acquiescence; the tendency to disagree is often referred to as criticalness. Both are considered to be problematic when operative in psychological assessment instruments, because client responses are then quite likely to be based on these response tendencies rather than on the specific content of test items. For example, if John gives an agree response to the items "I prefer to not eat meat" and "I believe that eating meat is morally wrong," the clinician cannot unambiguously determine whether John really holds philosophical beliefs in common with vegetarians or if he merely tends to agree with whatever is stated regardless of the content. The potential effects of this problem increase as the imbalance in the number of true and false keyed responses on the test increases. If equal numbers of positive and negative responses are keyed on the test, then any tendency to acquiesce or be critical will not influence the test score markedly. When this balance is not maintained, then profile scores may be affected by these responding styles.

The seriousness of this problem in personality testing has long been debated by experts in the field (A. L. Edwards, 1970; D. N. Jackson, 1967; Rorer, 1965). Some believe that the effects of acquiescence or criticalness are seen only on those items that are ambiguous for the examinee. When the item content is perceived as unclear or confusing, then the response given will likely depend on the examinee's internal preference for agreeing or disagreeing. An example of an ambiguous item would be the statement "I think Lincoln was greater than Washington." There are few clues as to what this item is measuring or what the interpretation of a true or false response might be. On the other hand, clear, unambiguous items such as "I hated my mother" are not likely to induce an acquiescent or critical response but, rather, a response directed at the content of the item.

Unfortunately, some experts in testing state that the most useful items are those that are less obvious and transparent. Use of these subtle items does invite the operation of response styles, however. An example in which this problem has occurred is the F scale measuring authoritarianism developed by Adorno, Frenkel-Brunswik, Levinson, and Sanford (1950).

CRITICAL DISCUSSION:

Do Different Test Formats Give Unique Interpretive Information?

There are two major schools of thought concerning how psychological tests should be developed. One school maintains that a test score should reflect how an examinee has performed in relation to other people who have taken the same test. This testing philosophy has given rise to the normative test format in which norm or comparison groups are used. The intent of this testing format is to answer such questions as "Does Melanie like artistic activities more than other women?" "Is José more outgoing than his peers?" and "Did Melinda respond on the test like other severely depressed adult women?"

Proponents of the other school of test construction have focused their attention more on the individual test taker and the interrelation of his or her various psychological traits. They have been more interested in examining how strong the preferences are for specific attributes within individuals. This testing strategy led to the development of the ipsative format that centered on the individual as the focal point for score comparisons. Some of the types of questions that are addressed using this test format are "Is Trudy more interested in science or business?" "Is Ted more likely to be angry or depressed when frustrated?" and "Will Heidi prefer security or advancement when seeking employment?" In each of these cases, the point of comparison is within the individual and not between the individual and other people.

The interpretive difference between these two test construction strategies lies in the type of information that each provides. Normative tests give an indication of the absolute strength of attributes, since an external reference point (the norm group) is used for comparison purposes. Ipsative tests, on the other hand, give an indication of the relative strength of attributes within the individual, since the central comparison here is how the examinee ranks the strength of his or her attributes.

The standard item format for ipsative tests is to present the examinee with a choice between two or more attributes in each test item. The subject's task is to choose which of the alternatives is preferred. Usually, the attributes being measured by the test are paired, requiring the examinee to choose one trait over another in each item. A rank ordering of all traits results, but it is impossible to determine the absolute strength of each attribute. It can be concluded that trait A is stronger than trait B, since it was chosen more often, but not how strong traits A and B are—both could be very strong, neutral, or very weak. For example, a food preference test might give a choice between spinach and liver. The subject might choose spinach over liver, although he or she may strongly dislike both.

In contrast, normative tests usually permit the examinee to indicate a preference for each item independently. This item format produces test scores that more nearly reflect the absolute level of an attribute within an individual. Following the preceding example, if the examinee can indicate the degree of preference of spinach and liver, he or she will probably respond with strong disliking for both.

Each of these item formats has its advantages and disadvantages. Ipsative tests permit the user to clearly specify which traits are strongest and which are weakest for an individual. Their disadvantage lies in the fact that there is no way to determine how strong or weak the traits are. Another major weakness of ipsative tests is that their scales are not independent of one another, thereby making their use in research very limited. Normative tests, on the other hand, give more precise information about the actual level of trait strength, but they do not always permit the user to know the examinees' preferences among traits of nearly equal strength. An attractive feature of normative tests is that they do allow for independence among scales and therefore are used widely in research.

Which format is the best? This question has never been answered satisfactorily. Each format provides its own unique information about the examinee. The choice between them should depend on the appraisal question being addressed. If intraindividual information is desired, then ipsative measures would be most desirable. If interindividual information is desired, then normative measures should be selected.

NORMING AND STANDARDIZING TESTS

In Chapter 5 we covered some of the general concepts related to both test standardization and norming. We mentioned that because of the problems inherent in the measurement of psychological traits (i.e., the difficulty in establishing a zero point for most traits), researchers use the differential performance of various comparison groups to give test scores meaning. We also discussed the importance of standardizing testing procedures to eliminate additional sources of error from the measurement process. In this chapter we expand our discussion of these two essential features of psychological tests to see how they are actually employed in the construction of psychological tests.

Norming Psychological Tests

Selecting and testing appropriate norm groups for psychological tests are difficult and very expensive tasks. As we discussed in Chapter 5, selecting samples that represent the target population for which the test is intended can be quite complicated. Ideally, good comparison groups provide a representative sample of the population in question, being neither too specific and limited nor too broad and nonapplicable for meaningful score interpretation. Although tests having norm groups consisting of only students living on the East Coast might be very useful for interpretation locally on the East Coast, their value in other parts of the country would be somewhat suspect. On the other hand, tests that employ very general norm groups representative of the United States at large might not be very useful for providing meaningful score interpretation on a more regional basis. Consequently, several different norm groups are usually established for tests so that users can choose the most appropriate comparison group for their particular purposes.

Steps in Developing Norms

Defining the Target Population. As we have seen, a primary concern in the development of norms is the composition of the normative group. A general principle in developing norms is that the composition of the normative group is determined by the intended use of the test. For example, most tests of mental ability are designed to assess an individual's ability relative to that of others in the general population. Here, the appropriate normative group would consist of a random sample of people representing all educational levels. If a more restricted norm group were used (e.g., people with college degrees), it would significantly change the interpretability of test results.

Let us take a look at two more examples, the Law School Admission Test (LSAT) and the Test of English as a Foreign Language (TOEFL). In the case of the LSAT, the target population of interest consists of those college students who plan to attend law school. In the case of the TOEFL, the target group consists of those students whose native tongue is not English but who anticipate studying for a degree for which the language of instruction is English. In both of these situations, the appropriate comparison groups are those that permitted users to determine how successful potential students might be in their academic programs. To compare the performance of a test taker on the LSAT (e.g., prospective law school students) with data based on an inappropriate norm group (e.g., high school dropouts) makes little sense. Generally, incorrect decisions will likely be made if an inappropriate comparison norm group is used. A critical first step in the development and interpretation of norms is to ensure that the target group on which they are based is relevant and appropriate.

Selecting the Sample. Once the test developer has determined the appropriate target group from which to obtain norms, a second important step is to obtain a representative sample from each of these groups. In theory, selecting the sample should be relatively simple, but in practice there are numerous pitfalls. The key in the process is to obtain samples that are a representative cross section of the target population. For example, assume that the target population for norm development for an achievement testing program consists of beginning and end-of-year students in the seventh, eighth, and ninth grades. To construct norms, we need a method of obtaining samples from each of these grades taken at both the beginning and the end of the year that are representative of all students (in the United States, for example) in these grades at these times of the year.

A variety of sampling techniques could be used to obtain a representative sample. However, some techniques could be nearly impossible to implement. For example, a random sample of seventh, eighth, and ninth graders would be completely impractical. Even if one could identify a certain number of schools at random, it is not certain whether the officials at each school would cooperate. Participating in a norming effort takes a lot of time on the part of the school and also disrupts the normal activities; a substantial percentage of the schools may decide against allowing outsiders to use valuable instructional time.

The method most likely to be used when developing large-scale norms is a variation of cluster sampling. The first step is to identify regions of the country that should be represented (Northeast, Southwest, etc.). After identifying regions, further subdivisions may be made into rural and urban areas. Then, on the basis of the overall plan for how many students are needed, a decision is made as to how many school systems within the various regions and rural-urban areas would be needed to obtain the desired number of participants. The last step would be to select the systems at random and convince as many as possible that it would be to their benefit to participate in the norming project. Within each system, one then tries to sample as many of the total number of seventh-, eighth-, and ninth-grade students as possible.

Standardization

After item selection, scale development, and norming have been completed, test developers need to standardize as much of the testing procedure as possible. The goal is to eliminate as many extraneous variables as possible from affecting test performance. Some of the factors that play a role in the determination of an examinee's test performance come immediately to mind. These include such things as test-taking instructions, time limits, scoring procedures, and guidelines for score interpretation.

There are other factors that are not so intuitively obvious, however. Factors such as the physical surroundings in which the testing is done, the health of examinees, the time of the test administration, and many other tangentially related variables may also play a significant role in affecting test scores. For example, what effect would attending a late-night party have on test performance? Would depression significantly affect the scores that an individual might get on an interest test? Is performance affected by the temperature, lighting, or interior design of the testing room? Does testing performance vary as a function of the time of day, day of the week, or month of the year when the test is given? And what effect might a noisy air-conditioner have? Although all these conditions could conceivably affect scores on a test, it would be impossible to try to account for all of them.

The practical solution is to standardize the test administration process. Standardization involves keeping testing conditions as invariant as possible from one administration to another. Adhering to strict rules of test administration and scoring can eliminate many of these extraneous sources of variance, thus permitting more meaningful interpretation of testing results. This process is particularly important when norms are used in the interpretation process. Unless testing conditions remain essentially invariant, valid comparisons of individual test scores with test norms are virtually impossible.

Although standardizing testing procedures would not appear to be difficult, many practical problems arise. Items that are selected for inclusion on tests become outdated or obsolete. When this problem occurs, it is important to remove them to keep the test current. The fact that the test was normed and standardized using the original items raises serious questions about using these original norms for score interpretation. Test developers have circumvented this problem by substituting new items that have similar item characteristics for the out-of-date ones. This solution ensures that the new items discriminate at approximately the same level as their predecessors and, therefore, help to keep the testing task as standardized as possible.

A similar problem is encountered in the standardization of ability tests, such as the Scholastic Assessment Tests or the Graduate Record Examinations. It would be useful to compare the performance of students not only with their peers but also with other students from earlier years. Unfortunately, however, the actual test content is not invariant from one test administration to another. Changes occur because dated items are eliminated, and many items are dropped because they were on forms of the test that have been released to the public for inspection. To permit valid score comparisons with older norm group performances, statistical item replacement is again utilized to maintain a standardized testing procedure.

TEST PUBLICATION AND REVISION

Writing the Manual

The next step in the test development process is the preparation of a manual. It is here that the test developer outlines the purpose of the test, specifies directions for test administration and scoring, and describes in detail each step in its development. Pertinent information concerning the reliability and validity of the test needs to be included so that users can evaluate the test both with respect to its psychometric characteristics and to its applicability to various assessment situations.

Manuals also need to contain detailed information about the norming process. Test developers need to inform the user how the norm groups were selected and how the testing was done. They must provide a thorough description of the samples employed (e.g., the number tested, the age, the race, the sex, and the geographical location). The inclusion of only partial data in this section of the manual makes score interpretation difficult and open to serious error.

When a test manual is initially written, it usually contains only minimal data containing the psychometric characteristics of the test. Much of the research work done up to that time has been conducted solely by the test's author. After the test has been published, other researchers begin to experiment with its use and report their findings. These data frequently lead to modifications of score interpretations as the meaning of certain scales becomes more refined. Similarly, new data are reported on the test's reliability and validity. These data must then be assimilated into new editions of the manual. Keeping the manual up to date is a critical step in the test development process, but, unfortunately, it is often not done in a timely manner.

Revising the Test

When should a test be revised? There is no clear answer to this question. In part, it depends on the timelessness of the content. For example, the Revised Minnesota Paper Form Board Test (MPFB) employs geometric designs to measure an aspect of mechanical aptitude. Items consisting of only two-dimensional geometric figures, such as those on the MPFB, are virtually always contemporary and do not become dated.

Many tests, however, contain items that need updating to keep them current. The Strong Interest Inventory illustrates this point. An early revision of the Strong contained an item that referred to the *Literary Digest*. This item remained on the inventory until it underwent a revision over 30 years later. The problem with this item was that the *Literary Digest* went out of business during the Great Depression of the 1930s. Consequently, individuals responding to this item 10 or 15 years later probably had little or no awareness of what the item meant. What effect this situation may have had on the usefulness of this item in identifying interests is unknown, but it is much more likely that it was negative rather than positive. It is obvious that more frequent revisions are necessary when item content is so definitively dated.

Another factor that influences the timing of test revisions is their popularity. Tests that have generated a great deal of user interest are usually subjected to considerable research activity, thereby leading to the establishment of a substantial database that adds valuable information about the meaning of test scores and their generalizability. These new data often suggest item content modifications, changes in test administration procedures, or alterations in test scoring. The dilemma that test developers face, however, is that to make the indicated revisions entails renorming the test. Scores on the newly revised test cannot legitimately be compared with the older test norms. Since renorming is both expensive and time-consuming, a decision must be made between retaining the less perfect older test or revising it. Often, the revision process is put off until the number of significant modifications required warrants the added costs associated with renorming.

Interpretation and Cautions. Although tests that have been recently revised to take into account current research findings and to eliminate dated item content are often superior to older, less up-to-date tests, some very old, infrequently revised tests still work as well as more contemporary tests. The variables that these tests measure are stable, enduring, and apparently sufficiently robust to overcome any technical shortcomings in the tests. Sometimes even dated item content continues to produce the desired assessment outcomes despite significant developments and changes in our society. As we noted before, the Strong Interest Inventory underwent few revisions during the first 40 years of its existence. Although some of the items containing dated content negatively affected test scores, others had no appreciable effect. Consider the item "Pursuing bandits in a sheriff's posse." Even though this item may have been apropos in the 1920s or 1930s, it certainly is dated today. However, Hansen and Campbell (1985) found that for nearly 60 years this item continued to discriminate well among groups and contributed to the overall validity of the Strong Interest Inventory, although it was dropped for the 1994 revision. The point to be made here is that not all tests can be judged by their age. Newer is not always better.

CRITICAL DISCUSSION:

Should Tests Be Normed Nationally, Regionally, or Locally?

There is no definitive answer to this question. It depends on the purpose for which the testing is being done. Consider the following example. Maria is in the tenth grade in one of the city's four high schools. Maria's counselor is concerned that her grades are not as good as they should be. Is Maria not studying? Are her below-average grades due to a reading deficit or to some other learning problem, or are they really reflective of her ability? To try to answer this question, Maria is given a general intelligence test to determine how she compares with other students. The question arises as to what would be the most meaningful comparison group. Should she be compared with other members of her class? Would it be more beneficial to see how she performs relative to other tenth graders in the city? Perhaps she should be compared with the other tenth graders in the state or even nationally. The choice of which norm group to use is dictated by the specific question to be addressed.

If Maria's counselor wanted to evaluate her performance relative to that of her classmates, then the most appropriate choice would be a locally developed norm group consisting of other tenth graders at her high school. Even using a citywide norm group might not give the most useful information if there were substantial differences among the schools in the city. This possibility might be especially of concern if one school drew heavily from a section of the city where English was a second language. Certainly, regional or national norms would be less useful because Maria's counselor would not know how the average tenth grader in her school scored compared with the national norms. Knowing that Maria is above or below the national mean would not permit an analysis of Maria's score in relation to that of her class.

Ideally, Maria's counselor would have locally developed norms on the intelligence test so that a direct, meaningful comparison could be made between how she scored on the test and how her classmates scored. Unfortunately, local norms frequently do not exist, and so test users must select norm groups that match the characteristics of the local situation as closely as possible. Interpretive errors can arise, however, when this substitution is made.

How specific must local norms be? Sometimes even norms based on the general local population are not adequate for the assessment task. For example, if College X wishes to use a scholastic assessment test to select students for admission into the engineering program, local norms based on all entering freshmen at College X may not provide sufficient information. A student may perform above the mean for all entering freshmen at College X, yet still be considerably below the mean for those who enter the engineering program. Even within the same college, subgroups of students may be quite different. Use of a more general norm group tends to mask these differences, which may be of central importance. Consequently, in this situation, the most appropriate norm group would consist of only enrolled engineering students at College X, rather than the more broadly constructed university-wide freshmen population.

Some testing applications call for more general comparison groups. School administrators are often called on to show that the educational experience being provided for students is effective. One way to demonstrate this is to compare the performance of local students with regional or national norms. Using large, general norm groups for score interpretation reduces the regional and local variability among students and often yields less biased and more meaningful conclusions to be drawn from the data. Frequently, national norm groups become a constant standard against which to assess progress. Using regional or national norms in this manner, school districts look more closely at the change in group performance from one year to another in comparison with the norm, rather than looking at the absolute level of performance attained. In either case, the assessment goals of the user are better served with broad rather than specific norm groups.

Despite this discussion, most test manuals advise users to develop their own local norms whenever possible. We support this position as long as the purpose of testing is consistent with the use of locally generated norms. As we have seen, however, this is not always the case. The selection of which norm group to use should always be based on the testing decision to be made. Whether locally developed norms serve this function best depends on the application.

SUMMARY

The process of test development begins with the basic element of all tests, that is, the items themselves. (A diagram summarizing the essential steps in the test development process is shown in Figure 11-1.) Test constructors first generate a large item pool from which they refine, modify, and reject items generally through statistical analysis of examinees' responses until they arrive at a final set of items that appears to satisfy their requirements. Although this crucial step in the developmental process has not been researched as thoroughly as other aspects of the test construction process (i.e., scale building and norming), attention has been given to several aspects of item writing, such as item length, reading difficulty, and cultural bias, that appear to affect how people respond to test items.

Many different strategies are used in developing tests. The choice of a particular method often depends on the test development philosophies of test authors, whereas the item response format is often a matter of author preference or is determined by the nature of the trait being measured. The two most popular methods of determining item content are (1) to base all test items on a particular theoretical basis and (2) to construct items that are not theory related but reflect extremely diverse activities, behaviors, values, symptoms, and attitudes. Each method has its strengths and weaknesses. The multiple-choice item format is by far the most frequently used, but it is not necessarily superior to other formats and can have serious shortcomings.

Once test items have been chosen, they are usually grouped into scales that intend to provide the user with multiple observations of specific attributes or traits. The

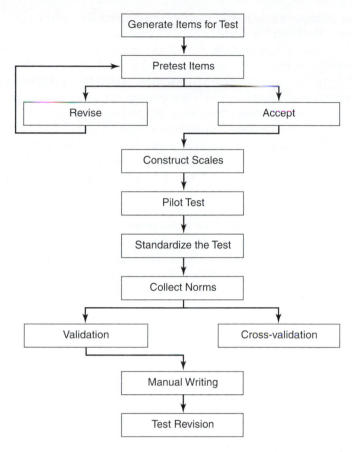

FIGURE 11-1   Diagram of the Test Construction Process

three principal scaling methods in use produce either rational scales, empirical scales, or a combination of the two. Rationally derived scales are theory based; they allow the generation of specific, testable hypotheses, but they permit examinees to easily distort their scores. Empirical derivation produces scales with enhanced validity characteristics that are robust and less subject to examinee distortion than rational scales. Empirical scales have little or no link to theory, however, and therefore make causal interpretation of score differences very difficult or even impossible.

Scaling done through the use of factor analysis is a variant of the empirical method. Scales derived through the use of factor analysis have superior psychometric characteristics, are preferable for research use, but rarely lead to practical, clinically useful information. The rational-empirical method of scale construction combines the best of both strategies to produce theoretically meaningful scales that have sound psychometric characteristics.

A number of factors other than item content affect the responses that examinees give to test items. Examples include the social desirability of items, carelessness, conscious attempts at distortion, and the test taker's response style. Test constructors attempt with varying degrees of success to control for the effects of these response sets either by creating testing formats that reduce their action or by devising statistical correction formulae that can be applied to test scores to account for their presence.

To give test scores meaning, norms are employed to provide points of reference to aid in the interpretation process. Care must go into the selection of samples used in the norming of tests. Factors such as gender, age, geographical location, race, ethnicity, and socioeconomic status need to be considered in choosing appropriate normative groups. The usefulness of a test is often a function of the representativeness of the norm groups provided in the test manual.

The problem of standardizing test procedures and materials to eliminate the effects of extraneous factors on examinee performance has always been a challenge to test developers. Probably countless factors influence test performance, and it is not feasible to attempt to account for all of them. Through explicit standardization of the process and procedures of testing, test developers hope to control or eliminate as many of these factors as possible. The chapter ends with a discussion of the process of test publication and revision.

PROBLEMS AND SOLUTIONS—RECAP

The Problem

The original real estate sales scale on the Strong Vocational Interest Blank (now called the Strong Interest Inventory), even though it remained on the test for years, seemed to give results that were discrepant from what psychologists thought they would see. Users of the test frequently reported that people whom they tested, who reportedly liked sales-related work and indicated that they thought they would like to work in real estate sales, did not score well on the real estate sales scale. If scores on that scale were meaningful and interpretable, the best conclusion from the data would have been that these people were not probably well suited for that work and would be unlikely to be satisfied working in that field. Were their clients not as interested in real estate sales as they thought? Was their clinical judgment suspect? Or, was there some problem in the development of that particular scale that produced the surprising and questionable results?

A Solution

In this chapter, we saw that in developing norms for a test, it is important to define the appropriate target population and to select a representative sample from that target population. In the case of the Strong Vocational Interest Blank, the initial group of workers that E. K. Strong used as his representative sample of real estate sales agents was problematic and not very representative of those in the career as a whole. Strong allegedly had seen an advertisement for a meeting of people selling real estate and decided to test all in attendance at that meeting and to use that group as his normative sample. Unfortunately, what he later discovered was that the group in question was involved primarily in selling cemetery plots and therefore was a poor choice to serve as a norm group for all involved in real estate sales.

Eventually, an appropriate target group was identified that more clearly represented those involved in real estate sales. When a new real estate sales scale was developed, it began to yield results much more in line with expectations. In this instance, the interpretive problems with this scale were the result of choosing an inappropriate norm group. As you can see, the importance of carefully selecting an appropriate norm group cannot be stressed too much.

KEY TERMS

Dissimulation   response set in which an examinee attempts to distort responses in a particular direction (e.g., faking psychopathology in an effort to avoid responsibility for one's actions)

Empirical scales   scales developed to take advantage of empirical regularities in test scores, without necessarily defining any particular construct or concept that one is trying to measure

Ipsative test format   type of test in which score comparisons are made within rather than between individuals (e.g., determining whether one's level of verbal ability exceeds one's level of mathematical ability, rather than comparing one's verbal ability with others' ability levels)

Norms   detailed record of test performance in a norm group, used to assess relative performance levels

Random responding   response set in which there is no apparent relationship between the content of items and examinees' responses

Rational scales   scales developed to measure a specific construct that is defined before developing the test

Rational-empirical scales   scales developed using a combination of these two methods

Response sets   ways of responding to scales or items that reflect particular and identifiable sources of unwanted error variance

Response style   general tendency to agree or disagree with statements, independent of the content of those statements

Social desirability   tendency to respond to items in a fashion that seems most socially acceptable

12

Computerized Test Administration and Interpretation

This chapter discusses the increasingly important role of computers in the administration and interpretation of psychological tests. Computers have long been used in test scoring (Moreland, 1992), but until the 1980s, their role was largely restricted to recording answers and computing test scores. Computers are now used for a much wider variety of purposes in psychological testing, and evidence clearly demonstrates that computer-based testing is beginning to replace traditional paper-and-pencil methods of test administration in many contexts. Furthermore, computers are an increasingly important tool for interpreting test scores, to the extent that some systems of computerized test interpretation seem designed to replace psychologists and other testing professionals in interpreting scores on a variety of tests and inventories.

This chapter explores a number of issues that arise out of the use of computers in administering and interpreting psychological tests. First, the use of a computer keyboard rather than a pencil and paper as a method of responding to test items can change the test taker's strategy for taking the test; it can also change the psychometric characteristics of test scores in unexpected ways. It is not always clear whether responses to a particular set of test items have the same meaning when administering via computer versus paper and pencil. Second, the use of computers in testing provides an opportunity to apply highly sophisticated strategies for adaptive testing, in which tests are tailored to individual respondents. In particular, computerized testing systems allow you to apply the powerful tools of item response theory (described in Chapter 10) to the development and scoring of adaptive tests. This chapter will examine the advantages of this method of testing.

Computerized test interpretation systems make it possible to obtain detailed narrative descriptions of the possible meaning of test scores. For example, individuals responding to inventories designed to assess psychopathology might receive narrative reports that seem highly similar to psychological diagnoses. The possibility that these computer-generated reports might replace or overrule the clinical assessments of psychologists, psychiatrists, and other mental health professionals has generated a great deal of debate. This chapter examines the technical, practical, and ethical issues in the debate over computerized test interpretation.

PROBLEMS AND SOLUTIONS—WHICH TYPE OF TEST IS BEST FOR YOU?

The Problem

Andy has consulted with a career counselor, and he has the opportunity to take an employment test in paper-and-pencil form, or to take a computerized form of the same test. The computerized test costs $10 more, but Andy will receive his score immediately if he takes this form. It will take a week to get a score on the paper-and-pencil test. Andy had done poorly on similar tests in the past, and he is anxious about the result. Would you advise him to go ahead and spend the $10 to take the computerized test?

Finally, this chapter examines the use of computerized testing programs to detect unusual or invalid patterns of responses to test items. For example, ability test scores can be inflated if examinees have opportunities to guess when answering items. Responses to personality and interest inventories may be affected by faking on the part of examinees, that is, by examinees' distorting scores to purposely look good or bad on a particular test. Methods of dealing with guessing, faking, and other response sets exist (some of these were reviewed in Chapter 11), but none of the most widely used methods is completely satisfactory. Computer-based testing provides an opportunity to apply a variety of more sophisticated approaches to the problems created by guessing, faking, and other invalid response patterns.

USE OF COMPUTERS IN TESTING: A TAXONOMY

As the introduction of this chapter suggests, the phrase *computerized testing* can refer to a wide variety of ways in which computers might be used in psychological testing. Hartman (1986) suggested that the involvement of computers in testing and assessment can be classified on a continuum similar to that shown in Figure 12-1. At the simplest level, computers might be used as a simple data-storage device. In cases in which it is important to retain responses to individual items or scores of many individuals, the use of computers to store data is a practical necessity; large-scale testing programs can generate mountains of paper, and the storage and retrieval of hard copies of test responses or testing files can be surprisingly difficult. Although computers are clearly important in this type of testing, we will not use the phrase *computerized testing* to refer to testing programs in which computers are used merely to read answer sheets or to store item responses and test scores. The use of computers solely as data-storage devices does not change the test or its use in any essential way, whereas the use of computers for administering or interpreting tests, or for selecting treatment options, represents a potentially fundamental change from traditional testing practices.

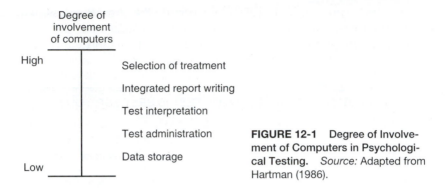

FIGURE 12-1   Degree of Involvement of Computers in Psychological Testing.   *Source:* Adapted from Hartman (1986).

As we noted earlier, computers can be used either to administer the same test that is given via paper and pencil or to administer similar but shorter tests that are specifically tailored to each individual examinee. Computer administration may affect the scores obtained from the test, although evidence we will review later in this chapter suggests that computerized versions of specific tests are often essentially equivalent to their paper-and-pencil counterparts. In fact, many computer-administered tests are interpreted in exactly the same way, often using the same norms, as the paper-and-pencil version.

The military is one of the pioneers and largest users of computerized adaptive testing (Moreno, Segall, & Hetter, 1997). Segall and Moreno (1999) trace the history of a research program extending over 20 years that led to the development and implementation of a computerized adaptive version of the Armed Services Vocational Aptitude Battery (CAT-ASVAB; Waters, 1997, traces the even longer history of the development of ASVAB). CAT-ASVAB is currently administered to over 400,000 individuals each year. This program of research is exemplary for its careful attention to both scientific and practical questions in computerized adaptive testing.

Whereas computerized test administration might represent nothing more than an evolution in testing technology, computerized test interpretation represents a sharp break with the past. Traditionally, the interpretation of test scores has been thought to require specialized training and has represented one of the more important activities of professional psychologists (Wade & Baker, 1977). The use of computerized interpretation systems as an adjunct to or a replacement for clinical judgment is therefore a controversial proposal. Computerized reports are especially controversial when issued in the form of narrative statements. It is common for test interpretation services to offer narrative reports that appear to explain the meaning and implications of scores on tests and inventories such as the Minnesota Multiphasic Personality Inventory (MMPI); these reports are sometimes constructed so that it would be difficult to tell whether they were generated by a person or a machine. The fact that computers can generate narrative reports or diagnoses that are, on the surface, indistinguishable from clinical diagnoses raises a number of troubling questions that will be examined later in this chapter.

The highest level of computer involvement in testing occurs when the computer not only interprets test scores but also decides on the appropriate treatment, therapy, training program, and so on. In principle, a person seeking counseling, advice, or treatment might bypass psychologists, physicians, or other professionals altogether by simply taking a battery of tests and being directed to appropriate types of medication, therapy, training, and so on, by computer algorithms (Web-based counseling, in which testing is done via the Internet and interpretation is delivered via e-mail is occurring, but test interpretation is generally done by a trained psychologist; Bartram, 1997, see also Buchanan, 2002; Sampson, Purgar & Shy, 2003). At the moment, this possibility is more theoretical than real; we do not know of any existing programs in which assessments are done and important treatment decisions are made solely by computer. Nevertheless, the possibility exists that such systems could be designed and implemented.

CRITICAL DISCUSSION:

Test Information on the Internet

Not only are computers useful for administering and scoring tests; they also provide access to a great deal of information about tests, testing programs, and the like. Every day, new sources become available through the Internet, both sources that can be accessed through the World Wide Web and sources that can be accessed through a wide variety of search engines. A sampling of Web sites that provide information about widely used tests follows.

Career Exploration. There are a number of places on the Internet to search for career information. Three sites that are of particular relevance to career exploration and career-related testing are as follows:

www.myfuture.com   Web site with information about careers and career interest assessment

www.careers.org   Web address for Career Resource Center, which contains extensive directories of career information

www.acinet.org/acinet   Web site covering employment trends, careers, tools for career exploration, and certification

Test Information. Information about specific tests or testing programs can often be obtained through the Internet. You might want to try the following sites:

ericae.net/testcol.htm   the Eric/AE Test Locator is a service provided by the ERIC Clearinghouse on Assessment and Evaluation that allows you to locate information on over 10,000 tests and research information, as well as reviews of tests and measurement instruments

www.unl.edu/buros   Web site for Buros Institute of Mental Measurements; contains information about hundreds of tests, as well as directories of test reviews

www.gre.org/cbttest.html   Web site offered in conjunction with the Graduate Record Examination that provides a tutorial on how to take computer-based tests, including opportunities to practice this type of test and tips on testing strategy

www.kaplan.com   Web site prepared by a test-coaching and test-preparation firm (Kaplan), which explains how computerized adaptive tests like the Graduate Record Examination work, gives you practice tests, and gives you tips on how to do well on computerized adaptive tests

www.collegeboard.org   Web site for College Board Online, which contains information and online registration for the Scholastic Assessment Tests (SAT)

COMPUTERIZED TEST ADMINISTRATION

The growing use of computers in psychological testing represents only one aspect of the increasing use of computers in measurement of all kinds. For example, Allran (1989) described computerized systems for measuring physical strength and endurance. Computerized sensors are rapidly replacing mechanical measurement devices in automobile engines and motors of all sorts. However, psychological measurement represents a special case in which the use of computers might change the meaning of test scores. That is, it is possible that people taking psychological tests might respond differently to a computerized test than to a traditional paper-and-pencil test. This concern is especially acute in computerized adaptive testing (which is reviewed in the following section of this chapter), where the test might be considerably shorter and more tightly focused (i.e., containing only those items appropriate for the examinee's ability level) than traditional tests.

The first issue in automated testing is whether the computer format itself affects responses to the test. In other words, do people receive similar scores on a paper-and-pencil version and on a computer-presented version of the same test? Mead and Drasgow's (1993) review suggests that test scores obtained using computer-presented tests are highly correlated with scores on paper-and-pencil tests. Evidence indicates that people view computerized tests more positively than equivalent paper-and-pencil tests and that cultural differences might be smaller on computerized tests than on paper-and-pencil tests (Johnson & Mihal, 1973; see, however, Gallagher, Bridgemen, & Cahalan, 2000). It appears possible, then, that computers could be used to present many ability tests with little loss in the accuracy or acceptability of testing.

Although the evidence suggests that presentation of ability test items on a computer screen, as opposed to a sheet of paper, does not substantially affect the characteristics of the test, the same may not be true of other types of tests and inventories. Davis and Cowles (1989) found that subjects responding to computerized measures of anxiety and locus of control seemed to "fake good"; that is, they seemed to give responses indicating lower levels of test anxiety than they gave to paper-and-pencil versions of the same basic inventory. They speculated that the novelty and apparent scientific rigor of computerized tests might prompt people to answer differently than they would to a more familiar paper-and-pencil test.

Although computerized tests are often equivalent to paper-and-pencil tests, research on the effects of test format suggests that several factors could lead to differences. Mazzeo and Harvey's (1988) review suggested that differences between the two test types might depend on factors such as whether the test was speeded, whether it contained graphics, whether items were based on long reading passages that were difficult to display along with the item on the screen, and whether the computerized tests allowed respondents to omit or return to items. Mead and Drasgow's (1993) meta-analysis confirms that methods of test administration matter substantially when the speed of response is an important factor in scoring the test. Green (1988) outlined a number of ways in which computerized administration could affect the strategies used to respond to items. Finally, computerized tests are often assumed to be equivalent to paper-and-pencil tests, despite the absence of any research on their actual equivalence, and that the standards for developing computerized tests are often considerably less well defined than the standards for paper-and-pencil tests. These studies suggest that test publishers should conduct separate norming and equating studies whenever they introduce computer-administered versions of standardized tests.

Computerized testing is a worldwide phenomenon that is growing rapidly (international research on this topic is presented in *Applied Psychology: An International Review,* Vol. 36, Nos. 3–4). For example, the armed services of each member of the North Atlantic Treaty Organization (NATO) have developed computerized tests, although the United States is the only NATO member that has developed operational computerized adaptive tests to date. For test developers, the question is not whether they should develop computerized tests but, rather, how they should use the capabilities of the computer to improve their tests. As we will note later in this chapter, in many instances, paper-and-pencil tests are still the test of choice. Nevertheless, you can expect to see more and more use of computers in administering and interpreting tests in the near future.

Unique Advantages of Computerized Tests

Although in many areas, practicality constraints may lead you to choose paper-and-pencil tests over computer-administered tests, computerization presents some potentially unique advantages. Computerization has changed not only how you give tests but also what you measure with tests. For example, it is relatively easy to measure response latency, or the time needed to respond to each item. The increasing graphic capabilities of computers make it possible to measure spatial and perceptual abilities that were virtually impossible to measure with paper-and-pencil tests. Perhaps the most promising direction for computerized testing, however, will arise out of interactions between cognitive psychologists, test developers, and computer programmers (Embertson, 1985; Hofner & Green, 1985; Jones & Applebaum, 1989; Ronning, Glover, Conoley, & Witt, 1987).

Hofner and Green (1985) note that computational models are becoming increasingly popular in many areas of psychology, including perception, memory, language acquisition, and reasoning. In the area of intelligence, Sternberg's (1985) triarchic theory includes computational components as part of the definition of intelligence. Psychological tests in all these areas are likely to be presented via computer; in most cases, the processes that these theories describe cannot be adequately measured with conventional tests.

Computerization is most likely to be necessary when the tasks presented in the test require precise timing, stimulus control, dynamic graphic presentation, or limited exposure to the material in each test item. These variables are critical to many theories of cognition, and they can also be relevant to theories of personality and psychopathology (Hofner & Green, 1985). As the influence of cognitive psychology on psychometrics increases, we are more and more likely to see computerized psychological tests that have sophisticated features such as the measurement of response latency or the dynamic presentation of test items.

COMPUTERIZED ADAPTIVE TESTING

An adaptive test is one in which the questions are tailored specifically to the individual being examined. For example, an adaptive test of general mental ability will include items that are neither too easy nor too difficult for the respondent. As a result, when two individuals of different ability take the same version of the same test, they might respond to completely different sets of questions. The idea of adaptive, or tailored, testing has a long history in the area of ability testing. In principle, all the various methods of adaptive testing are similar to the method employed when the Stanford-Binet Intelligence Scale is administered by an individual examiner. First, the examiner (or the computer) must use some data to estimate the subject's ability. On the basis of this estimate, test questions must be chosen that seem appropriate for that ability level, omitting questions that are too easy or too difficult for the subject in question. Using the Stanford-Binet, the clinician first estimates the entry level on the basis of vocabulary test scores and then establishes a subject's ceiling level on the basis of test responses. Computerized adaptive testing provides an alternative strategy that includes continually estimating a subject's level of ability, choosing specific items that are appropriate for that level, and using responses to these items to revise and sharpen the estimate of a subject's ability (Weiss & Davinson, 1981).

A variety of adaptive testing strategies exist. The simplest method is to start testing with a moderately difficult item. If a person fails this first item, it is followed by an easier item. Testing proceeds in this manner, always following a correct answer with a more difficult item and an incorrect answer with an easier item. This strategy is adaptive at every stage of testing but presents some difficulties in scoring.[1] A similar strategy is to divide the test into two or three sections, as in Figure 12-2. Examinees who do well in the first section of the test are routed to the more difficult items in Section 2;

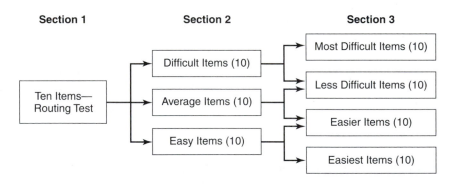

FIGURE 12-2   Adaptive Test With Three Sections

[1]These difficulties are resolved if indexes based on item response theory are employed.

examinees who show average or poor performance are routed to the less difficult items in Section 2. Similarly, a person's performance on the second section of the test determines which items he or she will encounter in the third section of the test. A person who correctly answers most of the difficult items in Section 2 might go on to the most difficult items in Section 3. Examinees who either do poorly on the difficult items or do well on the easy items in Section 2 might go on to the less difficult items in Section 3.

The most sophisticated strategy for computerized adaptive testing involves applying latent trait theory or item response theory to testing (Urry, 1977; Urry & Dorans, 1981: See Chapter 10). The theory provides methods of estimating the difficulty of the item, the discriminating power of the item, and the probability of guessing the correct answer to that item, independent of the sample being tested. Once these item parameters are known, the theory provides procedures for (1) estimating the subject's ability on the basis of his or her response to each item, (2) choosing the optimal test items on the basis of that estimate, and (3) revising that estimate on the basis of responses to each new item. Because the computer continually reevaluates its estimate of the subject's ability and selects optimal items, it is possible to achieve high levels of accuracy in providing estimates of a person's ability using an extremely small set of test questions.

Comparability of Adaptive and Traditional Tests

Much of the recent research comparing computerized and paper-and-pencil tests has examined computerized adaptive tests (CAT). Two reasons explain why these tests might yield scores different from those obtained from more traditional tests. First, they are presented via computer, meaning that examinees do not have opportunities to scan ahead, go back and change answers, and so on. Second, they are adaptive, typically requiring fewer items and less variability in item difficulties than traditional tests. However, research suggests that CAT tests are often highly comparable to their paper-and-pencil counterparts. For example, Henly, Klebe, McBride, and Cudeck (1989) showed that scores from the CAT versions of several subtests from the Differential Aptitude Tests were highly correlated with scores from the traditional test. Cudeck (1985) demonstrated similar results for the CAT and traditional versions of the ASVAB. Mead and Drasgow (1993) analyzed scores from 115 tests in 356 different content areas. Their study showed high levels of equivalence (i.e., correlations between CAT and paper-and-pencil versions in the .90 range) for power tests, but lower equivalence (i.e., correlations in the .60 range) for highly speeded tests. When speed of response is a critical variable, details as trivial as the layout of the answer sheet (e.g., fill in bubbles versus shade the area between two lines) can markedly affect scores. It is no surprise that computerized administration of highly speeded tests, in which you must respond using a keyboard or a mouse, presents special problems.

Advantages of Computerized Adaptive Testing

There are several reasons why CATs might be preferred over traditional tests. First, CATs are highly efficient in the sense that they yield highly reliable and precise scores with a small number of items (Drasgow & Hulin, 1991; Schoonman, 1989; Weiss,

1983). Because they require a smaller number of items than traditional tests, they can also be administered in less time. As we will note later, this time savings can often have a substantial impact on the overall cost of testing.

Second, it is easier to maintain test security with CAT than with traditional testing. There are, unfortunately, many individuals and groups who make their living by helping people cheat on admission tests, personnel selection, and licensing tests. We are not talking about the various schools that offer coaching on tests such as the Graduate Record Examination. Although their tactics are occasionally questionable, these schools are not in the business of pirating the test. Rather, we are referring to individuals or groups who help people obtain unauthorized copies of tests, who sell answers to tests, or who help individuals cheat on tests. In traditional testing, the same test is given to thousands of individuals, and once one copy has been obtained or once someone has memorized the items on that test, test security has been breached. In CAT there often is no hard copy of the test to steal, and an individual who takes the test in order to memorize the items will be exposed only to a small number of potential test items. In contexts where there is a strong incentive to cheat, the added security of CAT is a very important advantage.

When only a small number of tests are given (e.g., when the tests are given by an individual clinician), computerized testing can be an expensive proposition, in part because of the necessary investment in computer hardware and maintenance (Schoonman, 1989). However, in some large-scale testing programs, CAT can be highly cost-effective. Even though a large-scale CAT program requires the purchase of many computers, the savings in testing time can easily offset the expenses of computerization. The armed services' project to develop and implement a computerized adaptive form of the ASVAB (CAT-ASVAB) provides a vivid illustration.

The ASVAB is currently administered in schools and in a number of military testing sites. Because the test takes several hours, it is impractical to bring examinees from a long distance to take the test; the combined travel time and testing time would require an expensive overnight stay. Therefore, there is a need for a large number of testing sites throughout the nation. If the testing time could be cut—which can be accomplished with CAT—the number of testing sites could also be cut, and the savings mount up quickly. The saving of applicants' time also deserves consideration. Anyone who has taken an all-day multiple-choice exam can appreciate the advantage of measuring the same thing with a much shorter test.

The growth of computerized testing has provided an impetus for developing the Guidelines for Computerized-Adaptive Test (CAT) Development and Use in Education (American Council on Education, 1995). One of the most complex set of issues faced in these and other guidelines dealing with computerized testing (e.g., Eyde, Robertson, & Krug, 1993) is determining the proper role of computers in interpreting test scores.

COMPUTER-BASED TEST INTERPRETATION

The use of computers to aid in the interpretation of test scores can take many forms. In its simplest form, a computer program might merely retrieve and display information about the reliability and accuracy of test scores (e.g., when error bands are reported around scores) or about the various norms that might be used to interpret tests. In its most extreme form, it might involve a completely automated testing, diagnosis, and treatment system. Most programs for computer-based test interpretation (CBTI) represent some compromise between the use of the computer solely as an information retrieval system and the use of the computer as a replacement for the psychologist, physician, and so on, whose responsibility it is to give and interpret tests.

Applications of CBTI

The first widely used CBTI systems were developed in the 1960s to aid clinicians in interpreting scores on the MMPI (Moreland, 1990).[2] Although most CBTI systems are still used in interpreting scores on measures of personality and psychopathology, several systems have also been developed for interpreting scores on tests of intelligence and ability (Kramer, 1988), for interpreting structured clinical interviews (Spitzer, Williams, Gibbon, & Furst, 1990), and for diagnosing neuropsychological problems (Adams & Brown, 1986). More than 400 CBTI services and systems are now commercially available, and this number is likely to continue to grow (Butcher, 1987; Butcher & Rouse, 1996; C. W. Conoley, Plake, & Kemmerer, 1991).

CBTI Development. Kramer (1988) describes two basic strategies for developing CBTI systems, the clinical approach and the actuarial approach. Systems that follow the clinical approach attempt to codify clinical experience and judgment into a set of decision rules. For example, if clinical experience suggests that elevated scores on a particular scale (e.g., the hysteria scale on the MMPI) are associated with a particular psychological disorder, the computer program might include commands to notify the test user of this possible diagnosis whenever an individual's test score is above a specific cutoff value. Actuarial strategies are similar in nature, but they use information about the statistical associations between test scores and diagnoses, as opposed to clinical experience or judgments, to create decision rules. A program that follows the actuarial approach might examine the known correlates of test scores and notify the test user whenever specific diagnoses are statistically predicted on the basis of test scores. Most CBTI systems seem to follow the clinical strategy, in which the computer is programmed to mimic the judgment of the clinician, rather than the actuarial approach, in which the computer functions more like a statistician (Moreland, 1990, 1992).

Vale, Keller, and Bentz (1986) provide a clear description of the process of developing a CBTI system for personnel testing in industry. Their study is somewhat of a rarity; the processes used to develop most CBTI systems and the decision rules that characterize the computer programs are often treated as closely guarded secrets. From a business standpoint, this approach makes perfect sense; once the basic workings of a computer program become common knowledge, that program can easily be duplicated, so the test interpretation service loses much of its commercial value. From a

---

[2]The MMPI, as well as computerized systems for interpreting its scores, is described in Chapter 20.

scientific and professional standpoint, however, this secrecy presents a number of problems, some of which will be noted in the sections that follow.

Guidelines for the Use of CBTI

In 1986, the American Psychological Association (APA) developed *Guidelines for Computer-Based Tests and Interpretations;* an updated version of these guidelines was published in 1993. This set of guidelines, which grew out of the more general *Standards for Educational and Psychological Testing* (the CBTI guidelines were based on the 1985 edition of the *Standards*), is designed to encourage responsible use of computerized test interpretation services. However, there are good reasons to believe that many users and CBTI developers are either not aware of or not in compliance with the APA guidelines (Farrell, 1989). Because of the secrecy that surrounds commercial CBTI development, it is often difficult to determine whether the interpretations offered by various services conform to the technical requirements of the guidelines. The potential for abuse by individual test users is an even more worrisome problem. For example, we know of a case in which a licensed psychologist performed a "diagnosis" on an individual by simply reading him the narrative report provided by a commercial test interpretation service, informing him that he was suffering from organic brain damage and probably from depression and schizophrenia, among other things. The only basis for his statements was that the computer printout said that this was the appropriate interpretation of scores from the one test that the individual had taken.

C. W. Conoley et al. (1991) suggest that users of CBTI systems should at a minimum be competent in the use and interpretation of the test in question without the aid of a computer program. That is, users should be sufficiently knowledgeable about the test to recognize when the computer-generated report is either correct or in error. Thus, the role of CBTI should be to act as an aid to the clinician, not as a substitute. A well-developed CBTI system might alert clinicians to aspects or implications of test scores that they had not fully considered, or the scores might provide some independent collaboration of clinicians' interpretations.

The CBTI Controversy

The controversy of CBTI involves several separate issues. First, the validity of computerized interpretations is often in doubt. Second, it is possible that both test users and the individuals who take tests may place undue weight on computer-generated reports. Third, the use of computerized interpretations as a substitute for professional judgment raises a number of ethical questions.

CBTI Validity. Several reviewers note that CBTI systems are extremely difficult to validate (C. W. Conoley, et al., 1991; Moreland, 1990; Snyder, Widiger, & Hoover, 1990). Because the computer algorithms are often proprietary (i.e., the company that develops the CBTI system is unwilling to reveal how interpretative reports are generated), there may be no way to know when or whether the interpretations generated by a particular program are valid. Also, the lack of good criteria makes validity research difficult. If you are going to try to validate computer-generated reports, you need some well-defined standard that defines the "correct" interpretation of each person's test scores. This process is sometimes done using the method of extreme groups, in which computer-generated test interpretations for groups of people with relatively severe and clearly defined psychological problems (e.g., diagnosed schizophrenics) are compared with those of people in general. However, this method provides only a limited view of the validity of CBTI systems, since it is often difficult to assemble identifiable groups that correspond to all the diagnostic interpretations that might be included in a computerized report.

Conoley and his colleagues (1991) suggest that the trend toward easy-to-read narrative reports probably compromises the validity of computer-based interpretations. To generate a natural-sounding report in simple English, it is sometimes necessary to make a large number of statements or predictions, each of which may be based on relatively little evidence. One broad rule of thumb that might be used in estimating the validity of a computerized interpretation is that the more it says about you, the less likely it is to be true.

Vale, Keller, and Bentz (1986) reported an interesting strategy for validating computerized interpretations. Their CBTI system involved generating a library of interpretative statements judged by experts to be appropriate for different test-score levels. In particular, they generated verbal descriptions of the meaning of test scores at the 10th, 25th, 50th, 75th, and 90th percentile on each of the several scales included in their test battery. Their validation strategy represented a variation on the retranslation methods sometimes used in developing rating scales (see Chapter 19 for descriptions of these methods). They gave the tests to a group of individuals and then asked an independent group of experts, individuals who had not been involved in constructing the CBTI system, to read the computer-generated reports and to estimate the test scores received by the individuals described in each report. The relatively high level of accuracy in reconstructing test scores from narrative reports suggests that the two methods of conveying information about performance on the test (i.e., numerical score versus narrative interpretation) were highly equivalent.

Do CBTI Reports Receive Undue Weight? Several authors have expressed concern that computer-generated test interpretations might be given undue weight by both test users, such as clinicians who may defer to the computer's interpretation, and test takers (Matarazzo, 1983, 1986; Skinner & Pakula, 1986). Computer-generated reports might have an aura of objectivity and scientific credibility that cannot be matched by the best professional. That the validity of these reports is often uncertain makes the possibility that they will receive undue weight very worrisome.

Although the idea that computer-generated reports might be seen as more accurate and credible than similar interpretations obtained from human judges seems very reasonable, research suggests that these reports are not seen as more credible or accurate (Andrews & Gutkin, 1991; Honacker, Hector, & Harel, 1986). One possibility is that computers have become so commonplace in modern society that reports of this type have lost their novelty and aura of scientific certainty. Anyone who has worked with computers quickly learns the limitations of this technology—the phrase "garbage in, garbage out" is still the best description of many computer analyses—and the idea that computers can be trusted to arrive at the right answer in psychological assessment may be an anachronism.

   Professional Ethics and CBTI. The standards of professional practice in psychology clearly prohibit using a computerized test interpretation service as a replacement for the informed judgment of a qualified psychologist. Although this restriction may sound a bit self-serving (i.e., psychologists have decided that machines cannot replace psychologists), it is an essential safeguard against potential abuse of computerized test interpretation. First, computerized interpretations often fail to convey information about the limitations of any specific test. Whereas a computer-generated report might be based on scores on one test taken at a single point in time, clinical judgment is supposedly based on many forms of assessment and on data not easily included in a CBTI system (e.g., the client's behavior and demeanor in a clinical interview). Second, complete reliance on CBTI provides no protection against completely and obviously faulty interpretations of test scores.

   Matarazzo (1986) raised an interesting ethical issue in his critique of computerized test interpretations. An individual clinician who interprets a test is ethically responsible for the professional interpretation of that test, and he or she is bound by a strict set of ethical guidelines (American Psychological Association, 1993). No individual has comparable responsibility when a test is sent to a computerized scoring service. The use of computerized test interpretations often fails to include the sorts of safeguards that are implicit in the set of ethical standards that bind licensed psychologists. Probably the best solution is to incorporate both the professional judgment and standards and the power of computerized scoring by using computerized test interpretations in conjunction with clinical interpretations by qualified professionals, rather than relying on computerized test interpretations alone.

DETECTING INVALID OR UNUSUAL RESPONSE PATTERNS

In theory, responses to test items should be determined by two factors: (1) the individual's standing on the construct being measured and (2) random measurement error. This is the central assumption of the classical theory of reliability reviewed in Chapter 6. However, test responses can be influenced by specific response patterns that have nothing to do with what the test is designed to measure and that do not fit the usual definition of measurement error. For example, an individual taking a multiple-choice examination might make a series of lucky guesses and as a result receive an unrealistically high grade. A person taking an interest inventory or a personality inventory might engage in faking, that is, distorting his or her responses to present a specific impression (e.g., giving socially desirable responses). A person might simply be careless in filling out an answer sheet (e.g., filling in the wrong column of bubbles).

It is important to develop methods of detecting and correcting for such invalid or unusual response patterns.

In paper-and-pencil testing, the methods that could be used to deal with invalid response patterns are necessarily somewhat simple and crude. For example, many ability and achievement tests include corrections for guessing in their scoring formulas; the correction is determined from a simple equation that takes into account the number of response options on each question and the total test score. The use of computers in testing makes it possible to apply a wide range of sophisticated detection methods and correction procedures that are either impossible or impractical to apply to paper-and-pencil testing.

Waller (1989) notes that traditional corrections for guessing do not adequately distinguish between random and partial-knowledge guessing. Random guessing occurs when the item is very difficult for the examinee—when he or she has virtually no idea of the true answer. Partial-knowledge guessing occurs when the examinee knows enough about the topic or about the type of question to eliminate some but not all of the response alternatives.[3] The application of item response theory, a strategy used in most computerized adaptive tests, makes it possible to reliably discriminate between these two types of guessing and to apply different correction factors, depending on the degree of partial knowledge used in responding to questions.

Both signal detection theory (Lanning, 1989) and item response theory (Drasgow & Guertler, 1987) have been successfully applied to the problem of detecting inappropriate responses (e.g., random or inconsistent responding). Although these methods are difficult to apply to tests with small numbers of items (Reise & Due, 1991), they are applicable to a wide range of computerized adaptive tests.

Finally, computerized testing may be useful in detecting faking on personality and interest inventories. Research by Holden and his associates (R. R. Holden & Fekken, 1988; R. R. Holden, Fekken, & Cotton, 1991; R. R. Holden & Kroner, 1992) and by George and Skinner (1990) suggests that response latencies, or the time it takes to respond to individual items, might be useful in detecting faking. It is interesting that responses may be faster when people are faking. The rationale here is that people can immediately recognize the socially desirable response, and if they are trying to present a favorable front rather than answering honestly, they do not have to spend as much time thinking about the items.

Although it seems easier to detect and deal with invalid or unusual response patterns to computerized tests than to paper-and-pencil tests, computerization is not the final solution to invalid responses. The best approach to invalid response patterns may be to use multiple methods of measurement and assessment. Consistency in results across several methods of assessment might be a better indicator of careful and honest responding than any of the existing statistical or empirical indexes.

---

[3]Some of the strategies taught at test-coaching academies are, in effect, ways to move from random to partial-knowledge guessing. For example, if you know that on a particular test "None of the above" is virtually never the correct answer, you can eliminate that response option regardless of your knowledge or lack of knowledge of the topic covered by a question.

CRITICAL DISCUSSION:

The Barnum Effect and Computerized Test Interpretation

Suppose that you complete a personality inventory and receive a computerized report that says: YOU ARE A WARM PERSON, BUT OCCASIONALLY INTROSPECTIVE. YOU WORK HARD AND SOMETIMES ARE DISAPPOINTED WHEN OTHERS DO NOT PUT IN AS MUCH EFFORT AS YOU. YOU ARE KIND AND GENTLE, BUT FIRM IN YOUR DEALINGS WITH PEOPLE WHO TRY TO TAKE ADVANTAGE OF YOU.

　　　Does this feedback sound accurate? Many individuals will say yes and rate this description as a highly accurate description of their personality, even if the description has nothing to do with their own personalities or their test scores. Psychologists have labeled the tendency to agree with bogus personality feedback that is vague and generally positive as the Barnum effect. Several researchers have expressed concern about the Barnum effect in computerized test interpretation, that is, the possibility that people will accept virtually any statement on a computerized report as accurate, regardless of its validity or relevance (Guastello, Guastello, & Craft, 1989; Guastello & Rieke, 1990; Prince & Guastello, 1990).

　　　Not only may the Barnum effect be a problem in computerized test interpretation, but it can also be a problem in dealing with the test interpretations provided by a psychologist. There is evidence that the Barnum effect is just as potent when a clinician provides vague and global feedback as when a computer provides exactly the same feedback (Dickson & Kelly, 1985; Furnham & Schofield, 1987). Indeed, some of the concerns that have been raised about the validity of computerized test interpretations apply equally to the test interpretations done by licensed professionals (Murphy, 1987a). Therefore, although you should be wary of accepting a computerized test interpretation at face value, the same advice might apply to accepting the interpretations of clinicians who do not use computers.

SUMMARY

As we noted earlier, the question is not whether to use computers in psychological testing but, rather, when and how. The use of computers in psychological testing ranges from the mundane (e.g., using computers to present the same test that is now done on paper) to the highly controversial (e.g., using computers to make diagnoses). In general, computerized tests and CATs seem closely parallel to their paper-and-pencil counterparts. Computerization can affect highly speeded tests and perhaps some personality inventories, but for ability and achievement tests, the computer is probably the best medium for presenting the test. There are still cases in which the practical advantages of paper-and-pencil testing outweigh the efficiency and security of computerized tests. For example, the full computerization of some large-scale scholastic tests would be very costly. However, it is likely that many testing programs will steadily move from paper-and-pencil formats to computerized adaptive testing.

　　　Computer-based test interpretation is likely to remain controversial. The professional publications that many psychologists read are crammed with ads for test interpretation services, and the claims that some of these ads make are difficult to believe. On the other hand, we are quickly approaching a time when the interpretation of psychological tests without the aid of computers may be a thing of the past (Murphy,

1987a). The challenge ahead of us is to develop optimal strategies for using computerized test interpretational systems.

Finally, computerization opens the possibility that the many technical advances that have dominated the psychometric literature in the past decade, especially developments in item response theory, will make their way into the mainstream of psychological testing in education, industry, and clinical settings.

PROBLEMS AND SOLUTIONS—RECAP

The Problem

Andy is trying to decide whether it is a good idea to spend an extra $10 to take a computerized form of an employment test. He has done poorly on similar tests in the past, and he thinks that the immediate feedback he will receive from the computerized version is worth the $10.

A Solution

In fact, Andy's decision is not a simple issue of weighing the $10 extra cost against the week-long delay that will occur if he takes the paper-and-pencil form of the test. Computerized tests are often more reliable than their paper-and-pencil forms (especially if it as a computerized adaptive test rather than a test that is simply administered via computer), and in this case, reliability might *not* pay off.

If Andy expects that his score is likely to fall in the lower half of the scoring distribution, the use of an *unreliable* test might be to his advantage. If an unreliable test is used, you expect that his score will be upwardly biased, because of regression to the mean, and the more error there is, the stronger the likelihood that his score on this test will be closer to the mean than would be expected with a reliable test. People who expect low scores will typically benefit if the least reliable test is used, whereas people who expect high scores will benefit if the most reliable test is used.

So, Andy has to balance the extra cost *and* the likelihood that he will receive a lower score on a computerized version against the one-week wait that a paper-and-pencil test will require. In Andy's case, it might be worth the wait.

KEY TERMS

Barnum effect tendency to accept as accurate feedback that is vague but positive

CAT-ASVAB computerized adaptive version of the Armed Services Vocational Aptitude Battery

Computer-based test interpretation (CBTI) automated system for interpreting the meaning of test scores

Computerized adaptive testing (CAT) testing method in which the selection of items is done via computer to provide the most efficient and appropriate test to each subject

Computerized test administration using a computer rather than paper and pencil to administer a test

13

Ability Testing: Individual Tests

The measurement of ability represents one of the most widespread applications of psychology in everyday life (Wigdor & Garner, 1982a). Ability tests range from those that tap the general mental ability we refer to as intelligence, to those that tap specific abilities, such as spatial visualization. Measures of general intelligence have broadest application in that they are used in educational, clinical, and work settings as aids in making a wide variety of decisions. Hence this chapter and the two that follow concentrate most heavily on measures of general intelligence and less on tests of more specific abilities.

Jensen (1969) has noted that "intelligence, like electricity, is easier to measure than to define" (p. 5). Although it may at first seem paradoxical, psychologists have developed a number of reliable and valid measures of general intelligence in the absence of a totally satisfactory definition of the construct that these tests are designed to measure. The *Ninth Mental Measurements Yearbook* provided descriptions and reviews of 77 separate intelligence tests. Sixty-one of these were designed to measure general intellectual level, whereas the other 16 measured specific mental abilities. Thirty-two of the general intelligence tests could be administered in groups and could be scored by clerks or by machine; the remaining 29 required individual administration by a specially trained examiner.[1] A thorough review of all these tests would be counterproductive, since many of them are either highly specialized or poorly constructed and thus rarely used. We therefore describe outstanding exemplars of the major types of intelligence tests.

In this chapter we discuss tests that are administered to a single individual by a trained psychologist. Although this type of test dominated the early history of intelli-

[1]The more recent *Mental Measurements Yearbooks* review smaller numbers of intelligence tests.

gence testing, today, standardized tests that can be administered in groups are much more common. In the chapter that follows, we discuss several widely used group intelligence tests.

PROBLEMS AND SOLUTIONS—USING TESTS TO DIAGNOSE READING DEFICITS

The Problem

Your daughter is in the first grade, and she is having a hard time learning to read. She seems to enjoy reading but is making very slow progress relative to her peers. Friends recommend everything from switching to phonics-based instruction to having her vision checked. Can standardized tests provide you with useful information for diagnosing her reading difficulties?

THE ROLE OF THE EXAMINER

As discussed in Chapter 1, a psychological test is nothing more than a standardized sample of behavior. It is relatively easy to ensure standardization in objective tests given to large groups of examinees, such as scholastic tests, since they generally feature simple instructions, multiple-choice questions, and machine-scoreable answer sheets. In an individual test of intelligence, however, a good deal of professional training and skill is required to achieve an acceptable degree of standardization. First, whereas most group tests require the subject to work alone on a well-structured task, an individual mental test requires social interaction between the examiner and the subject. This arrangement has several implications. At the simplest level, both a written test and a psychologist administering an individual test can be thought of as stimuli that prompt responses on the part of the subject. A written test provides a standard set of stimuli to all subjects, whereas a psychologist presents a somewhat unique stimulus in each case. Even if the examiner's overt behavior can be partially standardized, evidence suggests that characteristics of the examiner—including age, sex, race, physical attractiveness, social skills, and nonverbal communication skills—affect a subject's responses during the test (Tagiuri & Petrillo, 1958). Even more important, an individual test represents a social interaction. The behavior of the examiner may change in response to the subject's behavior. For example, if a child refuses to answer a relatively easy question, the examiner may have to depart from his or her usual testing format in an attempt to elicit the child's cooperation. From the subject's point of view, the social nature of the individual test affects his or her perception of the task in several important ways. In an individual test, the subject must respond to a person rather than to a question. A shy examinee may respond in a hesitant manner and might be less willing to employ partial knowledge in making informed guesses while being closely observed by a psychologist. Furthermore, the reactions of the examiner to responses to earlier questions could provide subtle cues that affect responses to later questions.

For the reasons just cited, individual mental testing is typically undertaken only by psychologists who have received extensive professional training. The psychologist's first job is to establish and maintain rapport with the person being tested. The examiner must elicit the subject's interest and motivation to perform well on challenging and demanding tasks; he or she must also ease any anxiety that the subject might have about performing the tasks in the presence of a psychologist. With young children, tests can be presented as a game, but children tend to become easily bored or frustrated when confronted with problems they cannot solve or tasks they cannot comprehend. Adults are likely to be apprehensive and possibly resentful in testing situations in that an intelligence test represents a possible blow to one's self-esteem. In addition, many adults view a visit to a psychologist in a fairly negative light and may initially be defensive and suspicious.

To obtain a valid measure of intelligence, the person taking the test must come to believe that the examiner is trustworthy and nonjudgmental and must view the test as an interesting but nonthreatening task. It takes special skills and training to build and maintain this type of rapport without destroying the standardized nature of the test. A certain amount of training also is necessary to develop a smooth and confident manner in handling the test materials. Many individual tests require subjects to manipulate objects, complete picture series, solve puzzles, or respond to verbal queries, and the psychologist must be careful to observe standard procedures in handling the different sections of the test. An examiner who appears to be nervous, who fumbles in presenting test materials, or who fails to present materials in a standard fashion is not likely to obtain an accurate measure of the subject's intelligence.

The most important objective of the specialized training that psychologists undergo before administering intelligence tests is the development of sound professional judgment in scoring responses to test questions. Individual intelligence tests often employ open-ended questions, such as "What would you do if you found someone's wallet in the street?" Although test manuals provide extensive guidelines for evaluating responses to this type of question, the evaluation of responses to open-ended questions is necessarily subjective, and a thorough understanding of the purpose and nature of each section of an intelligence test is required to ensure standardization in scoring.

Judgments about the quality of responses to open-ended questions are doubly critical, since they can affect the testing process as well as the test scores. A number of individual mental tests are constructed so that the choice of questions and the sequencing of subtests partially depend on the subjects' responses to previous questions. The successors to Binet's early tests provide a good example: The examiner must score the test as he or she goes along to decide when to stop testing. A mistake in scoring could result in an incomplete or improperly sequenced test.

The final aspect of the psychologist's role in individual mental testing lies in the interpretation and communication of test results. Whereas group tests of mental ability are sometimes given as part of a routine testing procedure (e.g., the Scholastic Assessment Test), individual tests generally are given with some particular purpose in mind. Individual testing is both expensive and time-consuming, and a person is not likely to be referred for individual testing unless his or her behavior seems to indicate an unusually high or low level of intelligence. Parents who bring a child to a psychologist for testing are apt to have certain expectations about the results of the test and are likely to interpret results that are ambiguously presented in light of those expectations. Similarly, an agency that refers a child or an adult for testing does so on the basis of hypotheses about the subject's level of intelligence, and these hypotheses tend to color their interpretations of testing reports. It is the psychologist's responsibility to clearly describe the results of the test, the significance and the limitations of these results, and the courses of action that the results suggest.

INDIVIDUAL TESTS OF GENERAL MENTAL ABILITY

The Stanford-Binet

As mentioned in Chapters 1 and 3, the major impetus for the development of intelligence tests was the need to classify (potentially) mentally retarded schoolchildren. The scales developed for this purpose by Binet and Simon in the early 1900s were the forerunners of one of the most successful and most widely researched measures of general intelligence, the Stanford-Binet Intelligence Scale. The Stanford-Binet is used widely in assessing the intelligence of children and young adults, and it is one of the outstanding examples of the application of the principles of psychological testing to practical testing situations.

The scale developed by Binet and Simon in 1905 consisted of a set of 30 problems, varying from extremely simple sensorimotor tasks to problems involving judgment and reasoning. The basic strategy followed in this test and in its many revisions was to observe the subject's reactions to a variety of somewhat familiar, yet challenging tasks. Terman and Merrill (1937) neatly summarize Binet's procedures, noting that this type of test is "not merely an intelligence test; it is a method of standardized interview which is highly interesting to the subject and calls forth his natural responses to an extraordinary variety of situations" (p. 4).

Binet's original scales have undergone several major revisions (Becker, 2003). The fifth edition of the Stanford-Binet (Roid, 2003) represents the cumulative outcome of a continuing process of refining and improving the tests. Following a model adopted with the release of the fourth edition of this test in 1986, the selection and design of the tests included in the Stanford-Binet is based on an increasingly well-articulated theory of intelligence. The fifth edition of the Stanford-Binet leans less heavily on verbal tests than in the past; the current version of the test includes equal representation of verbal and nonverbal subtests. In this edition, both verbal and nonverbal routing tests are used to quickly and accurately adapt test content and testing procedures to the capabilities of the individual examinee.

Each subtest of the Stanford-Binet is made up of open-ended questions or tasks that become progressively more difficult. The examples of items similar to those found in the vocabulary, comprehension, and copying subtests presented in Table 13-1 help to convey the basic nature of the test.

Characteristics of the Stanford-Binet. Like many other tests of general mental ability, the Stanford-Binet samples a wide variety of tasks that involve the processing

Table 13-1 ITEMS SIMILAR TO THOSE USED IN STANFORD-BINET

Vocabulary Test
Define the following terms.
Level

A	ball
E	coin
J	debate
P	prevaricate

Comprehension Test
Answer the following questions.
Level

A	Why do houses have doors?
D	Why are there police?
I	Why do people pay taxes?
O	Why do people belong to political parties?

Copying Test
Copy the following figures.
Level

A	O
C	⌐
F	△
I	□

of information and measures an individual's intelligence by comparing his or her performance on these tests; the Stanford-Binet has employed a well-developed theory of intelligence to guide the selection and development of subtests. Drawing on the work of Vernon (1965), R. B. Cattell (1963), Sternberg (1977, 1981b), and others, the authors of the Stanford-Binet have formulated a hierarchical model of cognitive abilities and have used this model in selecting subtests and in scoring the Stanford-Binet.

The theoretical model used in developing and interpreting the Stanford-Binet is shown in Figure 13-1. The current version of the Stanford-Binet measures five general factors (Fluid Reasoning, Knowledge, Quantitative Reasoning, Visual-Spatial Processing, and Working Memory), using both verbal and nonverbal tasks. In Figure 13-1, the factors measured and the subtest names are shown in boldface, whereas the specific tasks that are used to measure each of these factors are shown in plain text. In several cases, there are different sets of tasks that are appropriate at varying developmental levels. So, for example, in evaluating the Verbal Fluid Reasoning of a young examinee (or an examinee who finds age-appropriate questions too difficult), you might use simple reasoning tasks, whereas verbal absurdities tasks might be used for more advanced examinees and verbal anologies tasks might be appropriate for the oldest and most advanced examinees.

	Verbal	**Nonverbal**
Fluid Reasoning	**Verbal Fluid Reasoning** Early Reasoning (2–3) Verbal Absurdities (4) Verbal Analogies (5–6)	**Nonverbal Fluid Reasoning** Object Series/Matrices
Knowledge	**Verbal Knowledge** Vocabulary	**Nonverbal Knowledge** Procedural Knowledge (2–3) Picture Absurdities (4–6)
Quantitative Reasoning	**Verbal** **Quantitative Reasoning** Quantitative Reasoning (2–6)	**Nonverbal** **Quantitative Reasoning** Quantitative Reasoning (2–6)
Visual-Spatial Processing	**Verbal** **Visual-Spatial Processing** Position and Direction (2–6)	**Nonverbal** **Visual-Spatial Processing** Form Board (1–2) Form Patterns (3–6)
Working Memory	**Verbal Working Memory** Memory for Sentences (2–3) Last Word (4–6)	**Nonverbal Working Memory** Delayed Response (1) Block Span (2–6)

FIGURE 13-1   Theoretical Model for the Stanford-Binet: Fifth Edition

Examinees receive scores on each of the ten subtests (scales with a mean of 10 and a standard deviation of 3), as well as composite scores for Full Scale, Verbal and Nonverbal IQ, reported on a score scale with a mean of 100 and a standard deviation of 15. Historically, the IQ scale based on a mean of 100 and a standard deviation of 15 had been the norm for almost every other major test, but the Stanford-Binet had used a score scale with a standard deviation of 16. This might strike you as a small difference, but what it meant was that scores on the Stanford-Binet were hard to compare with scores on all other tests; a score of 130 on previous versions of the Stanford-Binet was not quite as high a score as a 130 on any other major test (if the standard deviation is 16, 130 is 1.87 standard deviations above the mean, whereas on tests with a standard deviation of 15, it is 2 standard deviations above the mean). The current edition of the Stanford-Binet yields IQ scores that are comparable to those on other major tests.

Administration and Scoring of the Stanford-Binet. Throughout its history, the Stanford-Binet has been an adaptive test (see Chapter 12 for a discussion of computerized adaptive testing) in which an individual responds to only that part of the test that is appropriate for his or her developmental level. Thus, a young child is not given difficult problems that would lead only to frustration (e.g., asking a 5-year-old why we have a Constitution). Similarly, an older examinee is not bored with questions that are well beneath his or her age level (e.g., asking a 10-year-old to add 4 + 5). Subtests in the Stanford-Binet are made up of groups of items that are progressively more difficult. A child taking the test may respond to only a few sets of items on each subtest.

Historically, one of the examiner's major tasks has been to estimate each examinee's mental age to determine the level at which he or she should be tested. The recent revisions of the Stanford-Binet include objective methods of determining each appropriate level for each examinee through the use of routing tests; the current edition uses both verbal (Vocabulary) and nonverbal (Matrices) routing tests.

Evaluation of the Stanford-Binet. One of the principal strengths of this test lies in the continuity between the present Stanford-Binet and the original scales developed by Binet and Simon. The tasks used to tap intelligence have not changed fundamentally over the last 75 years. More important, both the fundamental definition of intelligence as an ability that involves reasoning, comprehension, and judgment and the age-referenced measurement of intelligence have remained constant features of the Stanford-Binet throughout its many revisions. It seems likely that each successive revision has done a better job of measuring the same set of constructs as was measured by preceding versions of the test (Becker, 2003). This trend stands in sharp contrast to many other tests, in which a revision seems to change the character of the test entirely. The continuity of the Stanford-Binet has two implications. First, longitudinal research that measures a person's intelligence at different revisions of the Stanford-Binet is both possible and informative. Since each revision measures the same constructs, changes in test scores tend to indicate real developmental changes in intelligence, rather than changes in the test itself (however, since the change in scoring scales was introduced with the current edition, direct comparisons of test scores have become slightly more complex). Second, the considerable body of research on the reliability, validity, and interpretation of earlier versions of the Stanford-Binet is clearly relevant to the present version of the test.

Considerable evidence supports the reliability of the Stanford-Binet. The correlations between Forms L and M of the 1937 revision (alternative-form reliability coefficients) are greater than .90 for nearly all age levels. The fourth edition of the Stanford-Binet shows even more impressive levels of reliability. Internal consistency reliabilities for the 15 subtests average .88; the composite IQ shows a reliability of .95 or greater at all age levels (Thorndike, Hagen, & Sattler, 1986), and similar levels of reliability are found in the fifth edition (Becker, 2003). Although evidence indicates that the test is somewhat less reliable for very young children (i.e., ages 2 1/2 to 5 1/2) and for children with very high IQs (i.e., above 140), it seems clear that the test very rarely shows low levels of reliability, regardless of the age or IQ of the subjects being measured (McNemar, 1942). Thus, there appears to be a relatively small amount of error variance in Stanford-Binet scores.

Considerable evidence also supports the content, construct, and criterion-related validity of the Stanford-Binet. First, the test is particularly valid as a predictor of academic success. The correlations between the Stanford-Binet and grades, teacher ratings, and achievement test scores typically fall between .40 and .75 (Jensen, 1980). Second, the test is highly correlated with a number of other well-validated ability tests (Becker, 2003; Carvajal, Gerber, Hewes, & Weaver, 1987; Carvajal, Hardy, Smith, & Weaver, 1988; Carvajal & Weyand, 1986; Laurent, Swerdlik, & Ryburn, 1992; Thorndike, Hagen, & Sattler, 1986). Third, inspection of the test suggests considerable content validity. At all age levels, the test samples a broad array of items related to judgment and reasoning. All these factors offer strong evidence that the Stanford-Binet provides a valid measure of the construct of general intelligence.

Historically, the Stanford-Binet has been regarded as one of the best individual tests of a child's intelligence available. The recent revisions of the Stanford-Binet may increase its relevance in adult testing. This test draws on a long history of development and use, and it has successfully integrated theoretical work on the nature of intelligence. It is likely that the Stanford-Binet will remain a standard against which many other tests of general mental ability are judged.

The Wechsler Adult Intelligence Scale

In its earlier versions, the Stanford-Binet provided an age-linked scale of intelligence. A series of tests developed by David Wechsler represent examples of an alternative strategy for measuring intelligence, a point scale (A. J. Edwards, 1972). Rather than developing separate tests that are maximally appropriate for highly specific age ranges, Wechsler designed tests made up of items that are appropriate for a wide range of ages. In Wechsler's tests, a subject receives a certain number of points for each item answered correctly. In this respect, Wechsler's tests are similar to the more familiar group tests of intelligence; a subject often takes the entire test, and the IQ is determined primarily by the number of items answered correctly.

The first in a series of tests developed by Wechsler was the Wechsler-Bellevue Intelligence Scale (Wechsler, 1939). The primary impetus for the development of this test was the growing awareness that the Stanford-Binet, which was designed primarily for children, did not at that time provide an adequate measure of adult intelligence. Not only was the use of mental age inappropriate in measuring adult intelligence, but also, as Wechsler pointed out, the content of Stanford-Binet items was typically oriented toward the interests and concerns of schoolchildren rather than those of adults. In addition, Wechsler noted that adults often were penalized by the emphasis on speed of response characteristic of many Stanford-Binet items. Older persons often work more slowly than young children, and adults do not always take instructions to work quickly at face value. To overcome these faults, the Wechsler-Bellevue was designed as an adult-oriented point scale of intelligence that placed little emphasis on speed.

The Wechsler-Bellevue was replaced in 1955 by the Wechsler Adult Intelligence Scale (WAIS) (Wechsler, 1955, 1958). The WAIS and its successors, which are similar in content but technically superior to the Wechsler-Bellevue, represent the most widely used individual test of adult intelligence (Gregory, 1999; Matarazzo, 1972). The current version of this test, the WAIS-III, carries on a long-standing tradition of improvements in the technical quality and scientific basis of the test without fundamentally changing the concepts that the test measures.

Characteristics of the WAIS-III. The WAIS-III includes 14 separate subtests, 11 of which are used in computing a full-scale IQ score, a Verbal IQ score, and a Performance IQ score. This test also provides scores on a number of more specific indices, including Verbal Comprehension, Perceptual Organization, Working Memory and Perceptual Speed (earlier editions of the WAIS provided Verbal Performance and Full-Scale scores; these indices are new to the WAIS-III). The subtests that make up the WAIS-III are described briefly here.

Verbal Tests

1. *Information.* Included are items covering knowledge of general information that is neither specialized, esoteric, nor academic in nature. The information covered in this test is the type an adult could reasonably be expected to acquire in our culture.

2. *Digit Span.* The examiner reads aloud a list of two to nine digits, which the subject must repeat. This test, which represents one of the most common measures of intelligence, requires the subject to reproduce lists of digits both in the order in which they were presented and in reverse order.

3. *Vocabulary.* A list of up to 33 words is presented, both orally and in writing. The subject must define or explain each word.

4. *Arithmetic.* A set of simple problems that can typically be solved without paper and pencil (e.g., how many inches are there in 4 feet?) are presented orally. This is thought of as a reasoning test rather than a quantitative performance test.

5. *Comprehension.* The subject responds to open-ended questions by explaining why certain things should be done (e.g., why are votes often taken via secret ballot) or by describing what he or she would do in certain situations. This subtest, which is quite similar to a number of the Stanford-Binet tests, reveals the subject's level of understanding or insight.

6. *Similarities.* The subject responds to open-ended questions by telling how two things are alike (e.g., in what way are shoes and socks alike?). This test seems to correspond best to Spearman's suggestion that the ability to see relations is a critical indicator of *g*.

7. *Letter-Number Sequencing.* This is a new subtest in which the examiner presents a series of letters and numbers in mixed-up order (e.g., "X-4-B-2-H-1-C"). The subject must repeat the list by first saying the numbers in ascending order and then saying the letters in alphabetical order (i.e., the correct response is "1-2-4-B-C-H-X"). This test is included as part of the Working Memory index.

Performance Tests

8. *Picture Completion.* Several cards are provided that contain pictures in which some critical detail is missing or out of place. The subject must tell what is wrong with the picture.

9. *Picture Arrangement.* There are several sets of three to six cards, which when arranged in their proper order, tell a story. Each set of cards is presented out of sequence, and the subject must deduce the underlying story in order to put the cards in their correct sequence.

10. *Block Design.* A set of nine cards with geometric designs in red and white corresponds to a set of wooden blocks whose sides are painted red, white, or red and white. The subject must arrange from four to ten blocks to duplicate the figure on the card. This test appears to measure nonverbal intelligence.

11. *Object Assembly.* This test consists of flat cardboard representations of common objects that have been cut up to form a jigsaw puzzle, which the subject must assemble. Since the objects are extremely familiar (e.g., a hand) and the number of pieces is small, this is an

extremely easy test that shows low correlation with other subtests, but that may provide clinically useful data relative to the subject's comprehension of simple tasks if the test score is low. This is an optional test that can be substituted for other Performance tests.

12. *Digit Symbol Coding.* This is basically a code-substitution test, and it represents one of the oldest, best-established psychological tests. A subject is given a code sheet that pairs nine symbols (e.g., #) with digits. The subject is given a list of 133 digits and, using the code sheet, is required to substitute the appropriate symbol for each digit. This is a strictly timed test; the total number of symbols that is provided within 10 minutes determines the subject's subtest score.

13. *Symbol Search.* This is a new subtest in which subjects scan a series of paired groups of symbols, with each pair consisting of a target group and a search group. The subject's task is to indicate, as quickly as possible, whether the target symbol also appears in the search group. This timed test contributes to the Processing Speed index.

14. *Matrix Reasoning.* This is another new subtest, in which subjects identify recurring patterns or relationships between figural stimuli drawn on each of 26 cards.

Examples of several WAIS items are shown in Figure 13-2.

Administration and Scoring of the WAIS-III. Like the Stanford-Binet, the WAIS-III must be administered on an individual basis by a specially trained psychologist. Although the administration and scoring of some subtests (e.g., arithmetic) is a relatively simple matter, many of the subtests, especially those comprising open-ended questions, call for informed professional judgment in scoring responses. As with the Stanford-Binet, a large part of the examiner's job is to establish and maintain rapport with the person taking the test.

The subtests of the WAIS-III are given separately, alternating the verbal and per-formance subtests. The examinee first completes the picture completion subtest, which is simple and nonthreatening (this helps to capture the examinee's interest), then the vocabulary subtest, then the digit-symbol coding subtest, and so on. In each subtest, items are arranged in order of difficulty, with the easier items at the beginning of each subtest and the more difficult items given later. For most subtests, it is neither neces-sary nor useful to administer all test items to every subject. Instead, a fairly easy item is given first, and a subject who answers that item correctly receives credit for that item and for all the easier items of the subtest. If the subject fails the first item, the examiner administers all the easier items to determine what types of problems the subject can or cannot solve. Similarly, if a subject consecutively fails a number of the moderately dif-ficult items, the examiner concludes the subtest, rather than administering the most difficult items. The rationale for this procedure is that subjects tend to lose interest in testing if they are forced to respond to a number of items that are either insultingly easy or impossibly difficult for them.

The WAIS-III manual includes tables that are used to transform raw scores on each of the subtests to standard scores with a mean of 10 and a standard deviation of 3 (the same scale as used by the Stanford-Binet Fifth Edition). These standardized subtest scores provide a uniform frame of reference for comparing scores on the different sec-tions of the WAIS-III. For example, if a person receives a score of 16 on the digit span test and 9 on the block design test, one might reasonably infer that this person is rela-tively better at the functions measured by the digit span test than at those measured by

Picture completion

Picture arrangement

FIGURE 13-2   Sample Items From the WAIS-R.   *Source:* Simulated items similar to those in the Wechsler Adult Intelligence Scale-Revised. Copyright © 1981, 1955 by The Psychological Corporation, a Harcourt Assessment Company. Reproduced by permission. All rights reserved. "WAIS-R" is a trademark of The Psychological Corporation. "Wechsler Adult Intelligence Scale" is a registered trademark of The Psychological Corporation.

the block design test. The question of interpreting differences in subtest scores is a complex one, and it is discussed later in Chapter 21.

Traditionally, interpretation of the WAIS focused on Verbal, Performance, and Full-Scale IQ. These scores are still reported in WAIS-III, but there is growing consensus that the Verbal-Performance dichotomy is not sufficient for understanding individuals' intelligence (McGrew & Flanaghan, 1998). The WAIS-III provides scores for four empirically supported indices: Verbal Comprehension (Vocabulary, Similarities, Information), Perceptual Organization (Picture Completion, Block Design, Matrix Reasoning), Working Memory (Arithmetic, Digit Span, Letter-Number Sequencing), and Processing Speed (Digit-Symbol Coding, Symbol Search). The Picture Arrangement, Comprehension, and Object Assembly subtests do not contribute to these index scores. The WAIS-III manual provides tables for converting verbal, performance, and full-scale scores into deviation IQs based on a mean of 100 and a standard deviation of 15.

Evaluation of the WAIS-III. Like the Stanford-Binet, the WAIS-III is a carefully developed test with many appealing features (Gregory, 1999; McGrew & Flanaghan, 1998). Adequate norms exist for stable and sensible interpretations of most of the scores produced by the WAIS-III. In addition, consistent evidence supports the reliability of three editions of the WAIS. Full-scale IQs typically show split-half reliabilities exceeding .95, whereas the reliabilities of the verbal IQ and the performance IQ are typically in the .90 and .95 range. Individual subtests typically exhibit lower levels of reliability, but subtest reliabilities lower than .70 are fairly rare.

The content, rationale, and procedures of the WAIS-III are basically the same as those of the WAIS and its successor, the WAIS-R. For this reason, research on the validity of the WAIS and WAIS-R provides a good basis for estimating the validity of the WAIS-III. Matarazzo (1972) has summarized research on the criterion-related validity of the WAIS that suggests that WAIS scores are correlated significantly with a number of criteria of academic and life success, including grades and measures of work performance and of occupational level. There are also significant correlations with measures of institutional progress among the retarded. More recent studies of WAIS-R and WAIS-III have reached similar conclusions (McGrew & Flanaghan, 1998). The criterion-related validities of the WAIS are typically smaller than Stanford-Binet validities. In part, this tendency may reflect the fact that intelligence is a more important source of individual differences in children's performance in school than in adults' performance in college or on the job. This is the case because motivation and experience tend to be more important determinants of adult performance. An examination of the WAIS-III itself suggests at least some degree of content validity. The test samples a variety of cognitively demanding tasks, and although some tasks are more clearly related to the construct of general intelligence than others, all the subtests seem to fit the domain of intelligence. There are two lines of evidence for construct validity, internal and external. The consistently high correlations between WAIS scores and scores on other tests of general intelligence (D. Cooper & Fraboni, 1988), such as the Stanford-Binet, provide external evidence of construct validity, and a number of factor-analytic studies provide internal validity evidence. The classification of subtests into verbal and performance categories was done on theoretical rather than empirical grounds (A. J. Edwards, 1972). Factor analysis of the WAIS and of similar tests designed by Wechsler to measure children's intelligence at preschool and school-age levels support the performance-verbal distinction (Cohen, 1957a, 1957b, 1959; Geary & Whitworth, 1988; Kaufman, 1975; Wallbrown, Blaha, & Wherry, 1973). The WAIS-III goes beyond the simple Verbal-Performance classification and provides a more sophisticated model for understanding performance on this test that is consistent with current research on intelligence (McGrew & Flanaghan, 1998).

Because the WAIS-III is a point scale in which most of the items on all the subtests are administered to all examinees, the total testing time tends to be longer for the WAIS than for the Stanford-Binet. One strategy for decreasing the amount of time needed to administer the WAIS-III is to develop short forms of the test. Silverstein (1968, 1970) discusses the characteristics of various short forms of the test, constructed by either dropping specific subtests or by reducing the number of items on each subtest. Ring, Saine, Lacritz, Hynana, and Cullum (2002) summarize evidence on the validity of WAIS-III short forms.

An alternative is to use the Wechsler Abbreviated Scale of Intelligence. This is an individually administered test that yields scores in the three traditional areas: Verbal, Performance, and Full-Scale IQ. The four subtests of Wechsler Abbreviated—Vocabulary, Block Design, Similarities, and Matrix Reasoning—contain new items that are similar in format to the traditional Wechsler counterparts. The two-subtest form (Vocabulary and Matrix Reasoning) provides an estimate of general intellectual ability and can be administered in about 15 minutes (Axelrod, 2002). Kaufman and Kaufman (2001) suggest that tests such as the Wechsler Abbreviated Scale of Intelligence are preferable to WAIS short forms.

The Wechsler Intelligence Scale for Children

The Wechsler-Bellevue and the WAIS represent the most successful application of individual point scales as measures of adult intelligence. In the years following the widespread adoption of his adult intelligence test, Wechsler applied a similar strategy to developing individual point scales for measuring the intelligence of children.

The Wechsler Intelligence Scale for Children (WISC) was developed in 1949 to measure the intelligence of children between 5 and 15 years of age; the scale was basically a downward extension of the Wechsler-Bellevue. Many of the WISC items were taken directly or adapted from Form II of the Wechsler-Bellevue, although all these items were independently restandardized on a large sample of children. This test has been revised several times; the current edition of the test (WISC-IV) was released in 2003. Like the previous revision of WISC, WISC-IV represents an increasingly sophisticated variation on the same theme as the original WISC. It includes updated items, modernized artwork, better norms, new subtests, and more extensive validation research, but it is nevertheless highly similar to the original version of WISC.

Characteristics of WISC-IV

Historically, the WISC was interpreted in terms of a taxonomy that grouped sub-tests into Verbal and Performance factors, but the utility of this distinction has always been in doubt, and the WISC-IV no longer distinguishes between the two areas. The subtests of the WISC-IV include the following:

1. Information
2. Similarities
3. Arithmetic
4. Vocabulary
5. Comprehension
6. Digit Span (an alternative test that may be substituted for one of the verbal tests)
7. Picture Concepts
8. Picture Arrangement
9. Symbol Search
10. Object Assembly
11. Coding
12. Word Reasoning
13. Matrix Reasoning
14. Letter-Number Sequencing
15. Cancellation

The WISC-IV includes better normative data and better assessments of fluid reasoning, working memory, and processing speed than earlier versions of the test.

Administration and Scoring of the WISC-IV. Like the WAIS-III, raw scores on each of the WISC subtests are transformed into standard scores, with a mean of 10 and a standard deviation of 3. The WISC-II yields a full-scale IQ based on a mean of 100 and a standard deviation of 15, as well as composite scores (using the same IQ scoring scale) reflecting Verbal Comprehension, Perceptual Organization, Freedom from Distractibility, and Processing Speed (the same four composite scores are calculated when administering the WAIS-III). As with previous versions of the WISC, psychologists administering the WISC-IV tend to alternate subtests that emphasize verbal tasks with those that emphasize nonverbal tasks, although given the decreasing emphasis on Verbal-Performance distinctions, this practice is less fundamental to the interpretation of the WISC-IV than was the case for earlier versions.

Evaluation of the WISC-IV. Like the WAIS, various versions of the WISC are highly reliable tests. Because the WISC-IV is such a recent test, few studies of the psychometric characteristics of this test exist. However, given the outcomes of previous revisions of the WISC (WISC, WISC-R, and WISC-III scores are highly related, and each test has comparable characteristics), it seems likely that research with earlier WISC versions can be used to draw inferences about the characteristics of the current edition of this test.

Verbal, performance and full-scale IQ scores typically show split-half and test-retest reliabilities exceeding .90, and most individual subtests show reliabilities of .70 and higher. In addition, evidence supports the construct validity of the WISC. Analyses of the WISC scores supported the classification of subtests as measures of verbal and performance IQ (Bannatyne, 1974; Kaufman, 1975), but as noted earlier, this V-P distinction no longer seems useful.

Considerable evidence supports the criterion-related validity of various editions of the WISC. Kaufman (1979) notes that the correlations between WISC-R full-scale IQs and measures of academic achievement (e.g., grades, teacher ratings) are typically in the .50 to .60 range and that validities in the neighborhood of .70 are often attained when the WISC-R is used to predict performance in elementary school. WISC-III short forms provide estimates of full-scale IQ that show validities comparable to those obtained from the full test, and it is likely that the same will be true for WISC-IV. On the whole, the WISC-IV appears to be a well-standardized, carefully developed test that provides accurate estimates of the cognitive ability of children between 5 and 15 years of age.

The Wechsler Preschool and Primary Scale of Intelligence

The Wechsler Preschool and Primary Scale of Intelligence (WPPSI) was developed in 1968 to measure the intelligence of children between the ages of 4 and 6 1/2. The WPPSI was originally conceived as a downward extension of the WISC; its most recent version (WPPSI-III, released in 2003) is appropriate for children ages 3 to 7.

Characteristics of the WPPSI-III. Like the WISC and the WAIS, the WPPSI is composed of a number of subtests; WPPSI tests are still grouped into verbal and performance scales. The content of the WPPSI-III is generally quite similar to that of the WISC-IV, although considerably simpler. Several features of the WPPSI-III were designed to make it easier to test young children; these include more reliance on verbal instructions and responses, as well as the use of very colorful and attractive testing materials.

The WPPSI-III is divided into two age bands. Children 2.5 to 4 years old take four core subtests (Receptive Vocabulary, Information, Block Design, Object Assembly), each of which uses age-appropriate tasks. Older children (ages 4 to 7) take additional subtests, including tests designed to measure Perceptual Speed. The WPPSI-III provides estimates of Verbal, Performance, and Full-Scale IQ for all age levels, and it also provides Perceptual Speed scores for older examinees.

As with the WAIS and WISC, the revision of the WPPSI did not involve fundamental changes in the test but, rather, technical refinements, especially expanded content, and more extensive standardization.

Administration and Scoring of the WPPSI-III. The administration and scoring of the WPPSI-R are highly similar to that of the WAIS and the WISC in that a child alternately completes verbal and performance subtests. Recognizing the complexity of intellectual assessment in younger children, the developers of the WPPSI-III have provided a number of supplemental tests (e.g., very young children who become confused or frustrated with a Receptive Vocabulary test can substitute a Picture Naming test). Raw scores on each subtest are transformed to standard scores (M = 10; SD = 3); and verbal, performance, and full-scale IQs (and perceptual speed scores for older children) are expressed on a scale with a mean of 100 and a standard deviation of 15.

The WPPSI differs from the WAIS and the WISC primarily in the nature and demands of the examiner's role. Using the WPPSI, the examiner must actively maintain a very young child's interest in a series of challenging and potentially frustrating tasks. Children at this age are more likely to become bored and less likely to be motivated to expend significant effort than are older children who are tested with the WISC.

Evaluation of the WPPSI-III. Like the WAIS and the WISC, the WPPSI is highly reliable. Because the WPPSI-III revision is so recent, little data exist that can be used to evaluate this form of the test, but data from previous revisions of the WPPSI suggest that (like the WQAIS and WISC), the most current version of the WPPSI will improve on the already impressive psychometric characteristics of the previous editions of this test.

WPPSI verbal, performance, and full-scale IQs typically show reliabilities near .90, whereas subtest reliabilities typically approach .80. Both factor analyses and correlations with other intelligence tests provide evidence for the construct validity of the WPPSI (Wallbrown et al., 1973). Although some evidence supports the criterion-related validity of the WPPSI, data regarding the predictive power of the WPPSI are relatively sparse. There are a number of potential explanations for the relative lack of criterion-related validity data; perhaps the simplest is that it is difficult to locate appropriate criterion measures for preschool children.

All three of Wechsler's current tests (the WAIS-III, the WISC-IV, and the WPPSI-III) are viewed by many as among the best individual measures of intelligence. It is not entirely clear whether all the subtests of each test are equally necessary, particularly if the intent is to measure a person's general intelligence. However, each subtest has been chosen carefully to provide potentially unique data on a subject's intellectual functioning.

One caution is worth keeping in mind when evaluating tests like the WPPSI. Assessments of intelligence and of specific facets of intelligence are difficult for very young children. Evidence indicates that the psychometric quality of a number of tests declines when used with the youngest examinees (D. P. Flanagan & Alfonso, 1995), and assessments of preschool children should be interpreted with considerable caution.

The Kaufman Assessment Battery for Children

The Kaufman Assessment Battery for Children (K-ABC) is a relatively recent addition to the domain of individual tests of mental ability (Kaufman & Kaufman, 1983a, 1983b). Nevertheless, it has been the focus of extensive research[2] and was used with

---

[2]The fall 1984 issue of *Journal of Special Education* (Vol. 18, No. 3) was devoted to the K-ABC.

over 1 million children in its first 4 years of distribution. This test is noteworthy for several reasons. First, like the fifth edition of the Stanford-Binet, the K-ABC is based on a well-articulated theory of intelligence that is grounded strongly in research in neuropsychology and cognitive psychology. Second, the test is designed to minimize the cultural bias that is thought to exist in many intelligence tests. Third, the test attempts to separate fluid and crystallized intelligence (see Chapter 2) and to provide diagnostic information that helps determine why children perform well on some tasks and poorly on others.

Characteristics of the K-ABC. The K-ABC is designed for assessing children ages 2 1/2 to 12 1/2. The test consists mostly of nonverbal items (e.g., pictorial diagrams) that require children to perform a variety of information-processing tasks. The battery is divided into a mental processing section designed to measure fluid intelligence and an achievement section designed to measure crystallized intelligence, or acquired knowledge (Kaufman, Kamphaus, & Kaufman, 1985). The mental processing scales are divided into tests of two fundamentally different types of information processing: sequential processing and simultaneous processing. Sequential processing occurs when problems are solved in a step-by-step fashion; examples are the digit span test of the WISC-III and everyday mathematics problems. Simultaneous processing occurs when multiple pieces of information must be organized and integrated to solve a problem; problems such as Ravens' Progressive Matrices and comprehending the meaning of a paragraph are examples. The achievement scales measure vocabulary, reading comprehension, general knowledge, and knowledge of arithmetic.

The claim that the K-ABC is less prone to cultural bias than other intelligence tests rests partly on the content of the test and partly on its organization. As noted earlier, K-ABC items are predominantly nonverbal. In fact, it is possible to administer several sections of the test in such a way that neither verbal instructions nor verbal responses are necessary. These nonverbal tests are particularly useful for assessing language-impaired children. The mental processing scales, which are regarded by the test authors as the best measure of intelligence (Cahan & Noyman, 2001; Kaufman et al., 1985), minimize dependence on knowledge of facts or school-related skills and attempt to tap basic information-processing abilities.

Administration and Scoring of the K-ABC. The K-ABC incorporates flexible procedures for administration that are designed to guarantee fair and accurate assessments for all children. In particular, the first three items on the mental processing subtests can be used to "teach the task." The examiner is encouraged to use alternative wording, guidance, or even a foreign language to communicate task expectations to an examinee who fails any of the first three items (Kaufman & Kaufman, 1983a). This flexibility may be particularly important in testing children from minority cultures, who do not always understand the tasks presented to them by examiners.

Like the Stanford-Binet, the K-ABC is partially adaptive to the developmental level of the child taking the test. For example, 12 subtests are administered to children

7 or older, but only 7 subtests would be administered to a 2 1/2-year-old. Some subtests featuring simple recognition tasks are reserved for preschool children (age 2 1/2 to 4), whereas tests that involve reading are administered only after age 5. Total test administration time ranges from 40 to 45 minutes for younger subjects to 75 to 85 minutes for older subjects.

In addition to scores on individual subtests, five global-scale scores are reported, each using a scale with a mean of 100 and a standard deviation of 15 (i.e., a deviation IQ scale). First, an achievement score that represents the child's level of crystallized intelligence is reported. Four different scores that relate to the level of fluid intelligence are reported. A nonverbal score is reported for those subtests that do not involve the use of language by either the examiner or the subject. Separate scores are reported for sequential processing and simultaneous processing tasks. Finally, a mental processing composite score, which represents a weighted composite of sequential and simultaneous scores, is reported. This mental processing composite is most closely identified with the child's level of fluid intelligence.

Evaluation of the K-ABC. Extraordinary care has been taken in the development of the K-ABC, both in selection of information-processing tasks that reflect our current understanding of several aspects of cognition and intelligence and in the administration of the test items themselves (Coffman, 1985; Kaufman et al., 1985). The result has been a test that is technically excellent in many respects. First, test scores show high levels of reliability; internal consistency reliabilities average near .80 for individual subtests and above .90 for the five global-test scores (Kaufman & Kaufman, 1983b). Second, the mental processing composite is positively correlated with several measures of school achievement and shows an average correlation of .70 with the WISC-R full-scale IQ (Cahan & Noyman, 2001; Kaufman et al., 1985). Finally, factor analyses of the K-ABC suggest that the fundamental organization of the mental processing tests (sequential versus simultaneous) is empirically justified, offering some evidence of construct validity (Kaufman & Kamphaus, 1984). However, other researchers have questioned the extent to which the hypothesized factors are in fact measured by the K-ABC (e.g., Strommer, 1988).

The principal attraction of the K-ABC is its claim to measure separately fluid and crystallized intelligence and to further separate fluid intelligence into sequential and simultaneous processes. There is some doubt about these claims (Merz, 1984; Page, 1985); it is not clear whether the mental processing composite really measures fluid intelligence or, indeed, whether there is any such thing as fluid intelligence (Guilford, 1980). Nevertheless, the fact that this test is anchored in cognitive and neuropsychological theory is of definite merit. Until recently, the psychology of intelligence and the technology of intelligence testing seemed to exist independently. The recent revisions of the Stanford-Binet and the emergence of the K-ABC are clear signs of a fundamental and long-awaited change in the nature of intelligence testing. Partly as a result of its strong theoretical base, the K-ABC has proved especially useful in special populations, such as the gifted or the neurologically impaired.

The Individual Intelligence Test
as a Clinical Interview

Individual tests of intelligence are expensive and time-consuming, and they admit at least some subjectivity into the evaluation of a subject's intelligence. Although tests like the Stanford-Binet, the WAIS, the WISC, and the WPPSI appear to be both reliable and valid, several group tests of intelligence, which are relatively simple to administer and score, show comparable levels of reliability and validity. The continuing popularity of individual tests of intelligence can be explained partly by the conviction held by many psychologists that these tests not only measure intelligence but also provide important data on the way in which individuals deal with a variety of demanding tasks (Rapaport, Gill, & Schafer, 1968). It is possible that a skilled clinician can learn a great deal about the person being tested by observing his or her responses to the different tasks that make up each particular test.

At least two sorts of behavioral data might emerge from an individual test of intelligence. First, there is the subject's general reaction or approach to testing. The person may be excited or bored; he or she may respond hesitantly or guess impulsively. The observation of this general orientation to testing may be critical in interpreting test scores. Two people of equal intelligence may receive very different scores if one person approaches the test in a relaxed, confident manner, whereas the other is anxious or hesitant in responding to questions.

The second type of behavioral data that can be gathered in individual tests is the type of data produced by incorrect responses. On a multiple-choice test, errors are not terribly informative, except in their impact on the total test score. The open-ended nature of many individual tests allows for a qualitative analysis of erroneous responses (Rapaport et al., 1968; Robb, Bernardoni, & Johnson, 1972). For example, both "Scott" and "Santa Claus" are incorrect responses to the question "Who was the first man to fly over the North Pole?" but the two answers indicate very different things. The first response probably indicates partial knowledge, since Scott was a polar explorer, whereas the second answer could indicate a flippant attitude or a bizzare view of the world, especially if given by an adult. Errors on performance tests may shed considerable light on problem-solving strategies; a child who completes a large number of digit-symbol substitutions but makes many errors is approaching the task differently from another child who completes fewer substitutions but makes no errors.

In addition to observing test behavior, a clinician obtains important information from test scores. Very childlike behaviors from a 10-year-old with an IQ of 76 have different implications from identical behaviors from a 10-year-old with an IQ of 114. The IQ score helps to determine which types of behaviors one would expect in response to cognitively challenging situations. Tests that provide scores for a number of subtests, such as the WAIS, may be especially useful. Both Rapaport et al. (1968) and Robb et al. (1972) provide extended discussion of scatter analyses of WAIS scores, in which clinical interpretations are assigned to sizable differences in WAIS subtest scores. For example, Rapaport et al. suggest that the picture completion score's being markedly lower than the vocabulary score is a possible indicator of preschizophrenia or of a paranoid condition. Since the early 1980s, a good deal of research has been conducted on scatter analysis, much of which suggests complex statistical limitations on the information that could be obtained from comparisons among intelligence subtest scores. Because this literature is more relevant to the clinical interpretation of intelligence tests than to the tests per se, we defer discussion of scatter analysis to Chapter 20.

INDIVIDUAL TESTS OF SPECIFIC ABILITIES

Although individual tests of general intelligence have been both extensively researched and widely used, the techniques of individual testing have been used only sparingly in measuring more specific abilities. In part, this trend may be a concrete indication of the trade-offs involved in individual assessment. Individual testing is time-consuming and expensive. Although the expense may be justified when assessing broad constructs such as intelligence, it is not likely to be justified in assessing specific aptitudes that are relevant in a narrower range of situations.

One area for which individual tests have been developed is in the assessment of aptitudes relevant to Piaget's developmental theories. A particular concern of Piaget's theory is the development of children's ability to comprehend basic features of their world, such as the conservation of matter. Because many Piagetian concepts are relevant in assessing the level of comprehension exhibited by young (e.g., preschool-age) children, standardized group tests are not feasible. An example of an individual test of one Piagetian concept is presented next.

Concept Assessment Kit—Conservation

The Concept Assessment Kit is a test designed to measure young children's (ages 4 through 7) comprehension of the concept of conservation. Different forms of the test present the child with pairs of objects that are the same with respect to the amount of matter that they contain, their length, or their area. One of these is then changed spatially, and the child is asked whether the amount of matter (area or length) is still the same in the two objects. The child receives one point for each set of objects if he or she answers yes and another point for correctly explaining, in response to a prompt from the examiner, why the objects are still the same.

Each of the three forms of the test yields two scores (correct answer and correct explanation) in each of six areas that correspond to the dimensions varied on the form (e.g., length, area, number). Each form can be administered and scored in 20 minutes or less.

Although the test has demonstrated an acceptable level of reliability, reviews of this test have not been positive (De Vries & Kohlberg, 1969; Hall & Mery, 1969; Lehnert, Rosemier, & Kise, 1986; Smock, 1970). First, the test has been criticized on the basis of the limited information provided by a numerical score. Piaget's methods usually have included in-depth observations that take into account the difficulty of the task and the potential subtleties of responses. Attempts to standardize Piagetian tasks and to provide simple scoring guidelines may sacrifice the essential nature of these tasks (De Vries & Kohlberg, 1969). In a related point, the test has been criticized for insufficient sampling of the domain covered by conservation tasks. Although some evidence supports both content validity and criterion-related validity (Ayers, 1972), the test has not been accepted widely as a valuable measure of Piaget's concept of conservation.

CRITICAL DISCUSSION:

Testing Examinees From Different Racial and Ethnic Groups

The question of whether intelligence tests are equally fair, valid, and useful for white and minority examinees has been the focus of considerable research and debate (McShane & Cook, 1985; Oakland & Parmelee, 1985). Part of the controversy has to do with the administration of individual tests of ability. If children who are members of racial or ethnic minorities are assessed by white examiners (very little research exists on the assessment of white children by nonwhite examiners), will the resulting test scores validly reflect the children's intelligence? Will the same children receive different (probably higher) scores when tested by someone of their own race? If so, which scores are more credible?

In general, the question of whether white examiners can fairly assess minority subjects has revolved around three issues: language, expectations, and orientation to testing. First, it is assumed that whites and minorities may speak subtly different dialects, so a variety of communication problems may result. Second, it is assumed that white examiners have low expectations for the minority individuals that they test and that these expectations might directly affect the performance of the individuals being tested (Steele & Aronson, 1995). Finally, it is assumed that minority examinees might approach the testing situation very differently when interacting with a white examiner than when interacting with a minority examiner. It may be easier to establish rapport and to maintain a high level of interest and motivation if the examiner is of the same race and social class as the person being tested.

Of the three issues just described, the last—the subject's orientation to the testing situation—is probably the most serious. Little evidence indicates that language differences between whites and minorities pose a serious problem in individual assessment, nor is there clear evidence as to the effects of examiners' expectations (Oakland & Parmelee, 1985). There are, however, reasons to believe that white and minority examiners may evoke different reactions from minority subjects.

Rather than focusing exclusively on the examiner's race or social class, it might be more profitable to focus on his or her training and professionalism. Well-trained psychologists generally do a good job in establishing rapport, but they should also be able to recognize situations in which they are not establishing rapport, since psychologists have an ethical obligation to discontinue testing if they cannot establish adequate testing conditions. Unfortunately, the testing field is not made up solely of well-trained professionals; many persons who administer psychological tests are woefully unqualified. A great many of the difficulties in fairly and accurately testing minorities could be minimized by ensuring that competent professionals carry out the assessments.

There is no guarantee that any examiner, white or minority, will do a professional job of assessment. There are, however, practical steps that the consumers of test information can take to maximize the likelihood that minorities will be tested fairly. The most obvious is to see that the assessment is carried out by a licensed psychologist. What is the examiner's background and experience? Is the examiner a diplomate of the American Board of Professional Psychology? A second step is to inquire about the assessment methods themselves. Are important decisions based on a single test score or on multiple, independent assessments? What steps are taken to guarantee rapport? The use of qualified examiners employing multiple assessment methods may provide a remedy to many of the problems that currently exist in testing minorities.

SUMMARY

Individually administered tests of general mental ability are important in both histori-cal and practical terms. This type of test made it possible to reliably and validly mea-sure intelligence, and it addressed a number of practical needs, especially in the field of education. All the various versions of the Stanford-Binet are built on Binet's original insights that (1) the type of problem a child of normal intelligence can reliably solve varies with age and (2) highly intelligent children can solve problems that are usually appropriate for older children, whereas less intelligent children's performance seems like that of a younger child. The current version of the Stanford-Binet represents one of the well-validated measures of intelligence available and serves as a benchmark against which many other tests are evaluated.

Binet's original tests were developed expressly for children. David Wechsler de-veloped comparable tests for adults (i.e., the WAIS, WAIS-R, and WAIS-III). The con-cepts involved in the WAIS were subsequently applied to testing school-age children (i.e., the WISC series of tests) and even preschoolers (i.e., the WPPSI series). All the tests in this series have shown consistent evidence of reliability and validity; because this group of tests provide scores on several separate subtests as well as on the verbal and performance sections, they are widely used by psychologists in diagnosing spe-cific types of learning problems (see Chapter 20).

The K-ABC is a psychometrically sophisticated battery that was designed to re-flect current thinking in cognition and neuropsychology; it was also designed to mini-mize cultural bias. Although there is clear agreement that this battery provides good measurement of intelligence, it is less clear whether the other goals of the K-ABC have been fully met. Nevertheless, it is a useful assessment instrument.

The most critical question in evaluating the tests described in this chapter may be not about the tests themselves but, rather, about the examiner. All these tests require a highly trained examiner, and scores on all of them can be affected by the behavior, de-meanor, and possibly the appearance of the examiner. The chapter that follows re-views tests in which the role of the examiner is less central.

PROBLEMS AND SOLUTIONS—RECAP

The Problem

Your daughter is in the first grade, and she seems to be having trouble learning to read. You think that an ability test might aid in diagnosing her difficulties.

A Solution

Several of the tests described in this chapter might provide useful information for evaluating alterna-tive explanations of her reading difficulties.

A psychologist administers the WPPSI-III to your daughter and reports back the following scale scores:

VIQ—94
PIQ—98

PSQ—92
FSIQ—95

Recall that the WPPSI-III is scored on a scale on which the mean is 100 and the standard deviation is 15. The scale scores that were reported suggest that her Verbal IQ, Performance IQ, Perceptual Speed, and Overall IQ (i.e., her Full-Scale scores are all very near average, and even through all of the scores are slightly below 100, her performance is well within the range of normal or average cognitive ability).

These scores would suggest that her reading problem is probably not a sign of a broader intellectual deficit and that it is likely to be both more specific (perhaps she will do better with a different approach, different teacher, different material) and less worrisome (i.e., it does not indicate that she will have unusual trouble learning or performing well in school) than you might have thought.

There are two caveats that are important to keep in mind. First, the psychologist's report would probably also include information about each subtest, and some practitioners pay a lot of attention to differences in scores across subtests (we take up the issue of interpreting subtest score differences in Chapters 20 and 21). We believe that subtest scores rarely contain much additional information and that users of test like the WPPSI-III tend to overinterpret variation in subtest scores. The pattern of the scores reported here is pretty clear—this child shows normal levels of cognitive ability across several broad domains.

The second important caveat is that assessments of very young children may have less value than assessments done a few years down the line. We would recommend that assessments of six- and seven-year-olds be followed up after a year or two. Cognitive abilities tend to stabilize later in childhood, and we would be more comfortable interpreting test results of a 15-year-old than a 6-year-old. Certainly if a follow-up two years later (e.g., using the WISC-IV) gave similar results, we would be more confident that the reading difficulties your daughter faces were not an indication of broad-based cognitive deficits.

KEY TERMS

Basal level   lowest age level at which the examinee can consistently answer Stanford-Binet items correctly

Ceiling level   highest level at which the examinee can answer at least some Stanford-Binet items correctly

Individual test   test administered on a one-on-one basis by a trained examiner

Performance IQ   norm-based summary score for the Performance scale of the Wechsler series of tests

Point scale   ability test evaluated in terms of how many items are answered correctly, rather than in terms of age grouping of items

Standard age score   score on Stanford-Binet that compares an examinee's performance with the performance of others of the same age in the norm group; similar to IQ

Verbal IQ   norm-based summary score for the Verbal scale of the Wechsler series of tests

14

Ability Testing: Group Tests

Although most people take one or more tests that measure general intelligence or cognitive ability at some time in their lives, the individual tests described in the previous chapter are not the most common type of ability test. Most of us are tested in school, using one or more of the widely distributed group tests of general cognitive ability or scholastic ability, such as the Scholastic Assessment Tests (SAT). This sort of test typically includes a large number of multiple-choice questions that are answered on a machine-scorable answer sheet and is often given to large groups of people. In principle, however, there is no reason why this sort of test could not be given to a single individual.

Group tests have many important features that set them apart from individual tests of mental ability. Most of these features are a direct result of the fact that these tests are designed so that they can be administered to groups of individuals, rather than being administered on a one-to-one basis. First, in individual testing, the examiner's role is both complex and central to the proper administration and scoring of the test. In a sense, the examiner is an integral part of the individual test. The examiner's role in a group test is more distant and routine. His or her primary responsibilities typically include carrying out routine paperwork, issuing standard instructions, maintaining strict adherence to the time limits of each section of the test, and supervising the distribution and collection of test materials. In group testing, the examiner must be as unobtrusive as possible, limiting his or her activities to proctoring and answering an occasional procedural question. It is this simplification of the examiner's role that makes large-scale intelligence testing possible.

Second, the differing roles of the examiners in individual versus group tests may have a significant effect on the responses of those being tested. In an individual test, the examinee is responding to a person, whereas in a group test, the examinee is responding to a question. The individual examiner may give off cues that either inhibit the response of a shy subject or allow another subject to infer the correct answers to specific questions. A paper-and-pencil test provides a standard, identical stimulus to each person being tested. Even more to the point, a paper-and-pencil test provides a relatively anonymous format for responding to questions in which one is not entirely sure of the answer. In face-to-face testing, a person may be reluctant to guess or may feel that a specific answer will not meet with the examiner's approval. The multiple-choice format employed by most group tests encourages guessing whenever one's partial knowledge can be used to eliminate one or more implausible choices.

Third, the use of a multiple-choice format may alter the cognitive process used in answering questions. An open-ended question poses a relatively unstructured task, in which the respondent must discover the optimal response. A multiple-choice question may involve psychological processes ranging from recognition memory to inductive and deductive reasoning, depending on the content of the question and of the choice of possible answers. In addition to differences in the cognitive processes involved, individual and group tests may differ in the problem-solving strategies needed to respond effectively to each type of test. In a group test, the optimal strategy may be to eliminate incorrect alternatives; this strategy does not apply to most individual tests.

PROBLEMS AND SOLUTIONS—IS THIS TEST RIGHT FOR YOU?

The Problem

You have taken a new job as Chief Psychologist for Plangen Industries, the largest aluminum recycling business in Canada. The CEO is a big fan of psychological testing, in particular the WAIS. He took the WAIS in college and received high scores on the Performance section of the test, which convinced him to go into industry rather than becoming a lawyer. Privately, you have your doubts about the utility of the WAIS as a tool for making career choices, but you have read enough of the literature to agree that tests like this could be very useful.

Plangen is starting a new factory in a depressed area of Saskatchewan, and your CEO suggests that you are just the person to administer the WAIS-III to applicants. There are two problems that come to mind immediately. First, you have never been trained to administer the WAIS-III. Second, and perhaps more important, you are expecting hundreds of applicants, and administering the WAIS-III to each one will take a lot of time. What should you do?

ADVANTAGES AND DISADVANTAGES OF GROUP TESTS

Group testing presents two principal advantages: standardization and efficiency. A group test provides the same stimulus to each person. Test examiners' manuals include extensive, detailed instructions for creating and maintaining standard test conditions so that the test is essentially identical, both in its content and administration, regardless of where and when it is given. Objective (often computerized) scoring systems guarantee that a specific test will receive the same score, regardless of who scores the test. As discussed in Chapter 1, one thing that separates a psychological test from other types of behavioral samples is its standardized nature. In many respects, a group test presents a closer approach to the ideal, completely standardized behavior sample than is possible with an individual test.

Group tests are qualitatively more efficient than individual tests. For individual intelligence tests, an examiner might need hundreds of hours to administer and score 100 tests. For group intelligence tests, the number of people being tested has very little impact on the total time and expense involved in administration and scoring. It is clear that without group tests, intelligence testing would never have developed into the large-scale industry that it is today. Whether widespread use of intelligence tests is a good thing or a bad thing is debatable; this issue is examined at the end of this chapter. What is beyond debate is the impact of group tests on the evolution and application of intelligence testing.

Group tests present several disadvantages. First, the impersonal nature of group testing makes it difficult, if not impossible, to collect data on test behavior. An individual test allows one to observe how a person responds to specific challenges and also provides a wide range of cues that may be useful in interpreting test scores (e.g., some subjects may be anxious or impulsive in their response). A group test simply provides data on the number of questions answered correctly. Although it is also possible to gather information about a subject's ability by examining incorrect responses (see Chapter 10), this is rarely done. Generally, it is impossible to determine with any precision why a person chose a particular (correct or incorrect) response to any given question on a multiple-choice group test. The inability to collect qualitative data on a person's test performance may limit the value of the information provided by a group test.

The second major disadvantage of group tests is a function of the test format. As noted earlier, multiple-choice questions probably call for different psychological processes than the open-ended questions typically used in individual testing, and many critics suggest that the functions measured by multiple-choice questions have little to do with intelligence. B. Hoffman (1962) and C. Ryan (1979) argued strongly that multiple-choice questions foster rote learning and penalize original, creative thinkers. However, empirical research provides little, if any, support for the notion that group tests measure knowledge of specific facts and that they fail to measure important intellectual functions that presumably could be measured using other procedures (D. N. Jackson, 1984a; Jensen, 1980; see Chapter 11 for a discussion of the benefits and drawbacks of using various types of items in cognitive ability tests). The more important question of whether comparable psychological processes are involved in responding to different types of problems has not yet been resolved. Some of the evidence that bears on this question is presented in Chapter 15.

MEASURES OF GENERAL COGNITIVE ABILITY

Several group tests designed to measure general cognitive ability also provide information about more specific aptitudes, in much the same way as the Wechsler Adult Intelligence Scale (WAIS-III) provides verbal, performance, and full-scale IQs. Some of these tests are short forms designed for only rough classification, but several techni-cally excellent tests give highly accurate measures with minimal effort on the part of the examiner. Two tests, the Multidimensional Aptitude Battery and the Cognitive Abilities Tests, are good examples.

Multidimensional Aptitude Battery

D. N. Jackson (1984a) noted that although the WAIS and its successors are ex-tremely well developed and useful tests, several factors restrict their more widespread application. First, they must be administered on an individual basis by a highly trained examiner. Second, there is some subjectivity in the scoring of the tests, in that numer-ous judgments must be made regarding the appropriateness of specific answers. Third, these tests do not have sufficient "floor" or "ceiling"; that is, they do not differentiate well at either the high or the low ends of the score distribution. Over a period of more than 10 years, Jackson and his coworkers developed and refined the Multidimensional Aptitude Battery (MAB), a test that retains many of the best features of the WAIS and has substantially overcome all the disadvantages cited by Jackson. The MAB was re-vised in 1998; the current version of this test (MAB-II) uses the same items as MAB but includes better normative information and improved scoring tables.

The MAB can best be described as a machine-scoreable counterpart of the WAIS-R (WAIS-R was the predecessor to WAIS-III; the two tests are similar in their overall structure and in the constructs they measure). In essence, Jackson and his coworkers translated the WAIS-R into a form that is suitable for group testing. Like the WAIS-R, the MAB is divided into a verbal section and a performance section; the sub-tests on the MAB duplicate 10 of the 12 WAIS-R subtests. Thus, the verbal section of the MAB is made up of information, comprehension, arithmetic, similarities, and vo-cabulary subtests. The performance section includes digit symbol, picture completion, spatial visualization, picture arrangement, and object assembly subtests.

Unlike the WAIS-R, which features a free-response format, the MAB is made up of multiple-choice questions. Examples of the types of questions employed are shown in Figure 14-1. In the development of the MAB, careful attention was given to compa-rability with the WAIS-R. Evidence regarding the technical adequacy and the construct validity of the MAB, as well as its comparability with the WAIS-R, is reviewed later.

The MAB has shown levels of reliability comparable to that of the WAIS-R. Sub-test reliabilities, estimated by test-retest, split-half, and internal consistency methods, typically exceed .70 and often exceed .80. Reliabilities for the verbal, performance, and full-scale scores are uniformly high, typically in the neighborhood of .95 (P. A. Vernon, 1985). Factor analysis has been used in assessing the construct validity of the MAB. In general, factor-analytic studies have provided strong evidence of the usefulness of pro-viding separate scores in the verbal and performance sections (see, however, Kranzler, 1991) and evidence of the comparability of the MAB verbal and performance factors to the same factors derived from the WAIS-R (Careless, 2000; Vernon, 1985, 2000), al-though some studies have questioned this distinction (Kranzler, 1991).

Picture Completion—Choose the letter that begins the word describing the missing part of the picture.

A. L
B. E
C. B
D. W
E. F

The answer is **Light** so **A** should be marked.

Arithmetic—Solve the following problem.
1. If it costs $8 for two students to go to the theater, how much will it cost for three students?
A. $10 B. $16 C. $12 D. $4 E. $6

The answer is **C,** $12; therefore, one should mark C.

FIGURE 14-1   Sample Items From the Multidimensional Aptitude Battery
Source: Copyright © 1983 by Douglas N. Jackson. Published by Sigma Assessment Systems, Inc., 511 Fort Street, Suite 435, P.O. Box 610984, Port Huron, MI 48061–0984 (800) 265-1285. Reproduced by permission.

Jackson (D. N. Jackson, 1984a; see also Vernon, 2000) noted the consistently high correlation between the MAB and the WAIS-R. In fact, the correlation between the WAIS-R and the MAB $(r = .91)$ is generally higher than the correlation between the WAIS and other well-constructed tests of general intelligence and even higher than the correlation between the WAIS and the Wechsler-Bellevue (D. N. Jackson, 1984a). The consistency, in terms of both content and test scores, between the MAB and the WAIS is sufficiently high to allow for a meaningful comparison between test scores. In fact, MAB scores can be reported in terms of WAIS-R IQ units. Scores on the MAB are also highly correlated with scores on military testing batteries (Carretta, Retzlaff, Callister, & King, 1998).

Administration of the MAB. The MAB consists of two batteries, verbal and performance, each of which includes five separately timed tests. The number of multiple-choice questions on each test ranges from 20 to 50. There is a 7-minute time limit for each of the 10 tests. Including instructions and practice items, each battery can be administered in 45 to 50 minutes. Computerized administration is possible, and empirical evidence supports the equivalence of computer and paper-and-pencil versions (Harrell, Honaker, Hetu, & Oberwager, 1987).

In the paper-and-pencil version of the MAB, items are arranged in increasing order of difficulty on each of the 10 tests. There is no guessing penalty, and individuals are encouraged to attempt as many items as possible. Nevertheless, the short time limit guarantees that scores on most of the tests will reflect speed as well as power factors.

Tests can be easily hand scored or, alternatively, they can be sent to the publisher for machine scoring. The profile of scores obtained from this test includes T scores for each of the 10 subtests, as well as verbal, performance, and full-scale IQs.

Evaluation of the MAB. There is every indication that the MAB is comparable to the WAIS-R in all major aspects (S. B. Reynolds, 1988). It appears that Jackson and his associates have retained the appealing features of the WAIS-R, such as its broad coverage and its usefulness in assessing adult populations, while achieving the practical advantages of a group-administered test. Jackson (D. N. Jackson, 1984a) cautions that the transition from individual to group testing could affect some examinees' responses and may entail the loss of valuable observational data (see also Silverstein, 1988). Nevertheless, it is clear that the MAB presents an appealing and highly practical alternative to the WAIS.

The Cognitive Abilities Tests

The Cognitive Abilities Tests are widely used in assessing the general mental ability of schoolchildren; the most recent revision of this test, CogAT Form 6 was released in 2001.[1] The CogAT tests can be used, in various combinations, to assess children from kindergarten to grade 12. Students in kindergarten take six subtests; a description of these gives a good flavor of the CogAT:

1. Oral Vocabulary, in which the child must identify pictures of specific objects or animals.
2. Verbal Reasoning, in which children solve simple reasoning problems.
3. Relational Concepts, in which the child must correctly identify specific relations (e.g., indicate which of four pictures depicts a ball under a chair).
4. Quantitative Concepts, in which the child must indicate which picture exemplifies a specific quantitative concept (e.g., find the box with two sets of sticks in it).
5. Figure Classification, in which the child must pick out the picture that does not belong in a specific set or series.
6. Matrices, in which children compare and complete matrices.

Students in grades 3 through 12 complete levels A through H of the Cognitive Abilities Tests. Levels A through H include nine subtests (each made up of questions appropriate to the grade level), which provide verbal, quantitative, and nonverbal scores.[2]

Verbal Battery	Quantitative Battery	Nonverbal Battery
1. Verbal Classification	4. Quantitative Relations	7. Figure Classification
2. Sentence Completion	5. Number Series	8. Figure Analogies
3. Verbal Analogies	6. Equation Building	9. Figure Analysis

[1]The Cognitive Abilities Tests represent revisions of the Lorge–Thorndike Intelligence Tests.

[2]Tests in the Nonverbal Battery employ neither words nor numbers.

Each subtest in the Multilevel Edition is made up of multiple-choice items (15 to 25 per subtest) and the levels are arranged in order of difficulty. Students in the third grade normally take Level A, but it is possible to adjust the choice of levels to the expected performance level of the students. The total testing time for the Multilevel Edition is 45 to 50 minutes per battery.

The Cognitive Abilities Tests are similar in many respects to both the WISC and the Stanford-Binet. First, the Multilevel Edition yields verbal, quantitative, and nonverbal scores, which in turn represent weighted sums of subtest scores. Although the term IQ is avoided, the standard age scores that are reported for the three batteries look very much like deviation IQ scores (Lou, Thompson, & Detterman, 2003). Standard age scores are reported on a normalized standard scale with a mean of 100 and a standard deviation of 16. Second, the Multilevel batteries allow the examiner to adapt the test to the level at which the examinee is most likely to be functioning. As with the Stanford-Binet, the examiner selects items that are neither too easy nor too difficult for the subject being tested. Thus, a child being tested does not respond to all items, but only to those that are appropriately difficult.

Evaluation of the Cognitive Abilities Tests. The Cognitive Abilities Tests have a long history of development and successful application. All three batteries have shown high levels of reliability; alternative form reliabilities of .85 to .95 are typical. In addition, the test manual provides estimates of the standard error of measurement for each test battery as a function of both the score level and the examinee's age. Although it is widely known that the precision of scores on many tests varies as a function of both of these variables, information regarding variation in standard error levels is rarely provided. The availability of this information for the Cognitive Abilities Tests is a definite asset.

The Cognitive Abilities Tests have shown consistently high correlations with other aptitude and achievement tests (Lou et al, 2003; Sax, 1984); these correlations provide some evidence of construct validity. Another piece of relevant information can be obtained from factor analyses of the tests. In general, this research does not support the idea that scores on three separate batteries are useful (K. Hopkins, 1978; Sax, 1984). Some evidence indicates that the Verbal battery measures something that is distinct from the Nonverbal and Quantitative batteries, but it is not clear whether any further meaningful distinctions can be made.

In summation, because the Cognitive Abilities Tests are adaptive to subjects' developmental level, are relatively simple to administer, and show evidence of technical adequacy, they are an appealing alternative to many more complicated or expensive tests of general mental ability.

SCHOLASTIC TESTS

The most widely used group tests of general intellectual level are those used in college and graduate school admissions. Most common are the SAT and the Graduate Record Examinations (GRE), which are administered to many thousands of high-school and college students each year. These tests have a number of characteristics in common: Both are composed of large numbers of multiple-choice questions, both provide measures of a number of different aspects of general scholastic aptitude (i.e., both provide verbal and quantitative scores), and both are typically administered to very large groups. Although similar in content, the two tests are designed for different purposes and hence are described separately.

Scholastic Assessment Tests

The Scholastic Assessment Tests (SAT) include a technically outstanding test designed to measure verbal and mathematical reasoning (SAT I), together with tests assessing knowledge and mastery of particular subject areas (e.g., biology, world history). The SAT is administered nationally by the College Entrance Examination Board and is one of the most familiar and influential tests of its sort. The current SAT represents a revision of the Scholastic Achievement Test, which was also known as the SAT and which was used successfully for several decades before 1994. Although the Scholastic Assessment Tests were specifically designed to be used as an aid in making college admissions and placement, SAT I can validly be classified as a measure of cognitive ability, since it relies primarily on comprehension and reasoning ability rather than on knowledge of specific facts. The two sections of the SAT are described in the next sections.

SAT I: Reasoning Test. SAT I is designed to measure verbal and mathematical reasoning abilities. The test lasts 3 hours and contains seven sections: three verbal, three mathematical (calculators can be used in mathematics section), and an equating section. Questions in this equating section do not count toward final scores and are used to maintain the comparability of test forms and in developing new forms.

The verbal section includes three types of items: analogies, sentence completion items, and critical reading questions; there are 78 items in the verbal section of this test. The mathematics section includes standard multiple-choice questions, quantitative comparison questions, and questions calling for student-produced responses; the mathematics section includes 60 items. Examples of SAT I items are shown in Table 14-1.

SAT I provides separate verbal and mathematical scores. Test scores are reported on a standard score scale, with a mean of 500 and a standard deviation of approximately 100. Thus, a score of 600 on the verbal section and 550 on the mathematics section would indicate that the examinee performed better than 80% of the norm group and 65% of the norm group on the verbal and mathematics sections, respectively.

Earlier versions of the SAT showed impressive levels of reliability (e.g., reliability coefficients in the .90s are routine) and criterion-related validity (e.g., correlations in the .50 to .60 range with performance in college), and the same is true of SAT I. SAT I scores appear to be good predictors of college grades across a wide range of majors and areas of concentration, and they provide meaningful increases in validity over the predictions that can be made on the basis of high school grades alone. Furthermore, SAT validities seem similar for males and females and across racial and ethnic groups.

Table 14-1   SAMPLE ITEMS FROM SAT-I

Medieval kingdoms did not become constitutional republics overnight; on the contrary, the change was _____.
(A) unpopular
(B) unexpected
(C) advantageous
(D) sufficient
(E) gradual

Al, Sonja, and Carol are to divide n coins among themselves. If Sonja receives twice as many coins as Carol and if Al receives twice as many coins as Sonja, then how many coins does Carol receive, in terms of n?
(A) $n/2$
(B) $n/3$
(C) $n/4$
(D) $n/6$
(E) $n/7$

The sum of the digits of a positive two-digit number, x, is 7. The tens digit is greater than the units digit. What is one possible value of x?

Source: SAT items selected from SAT Prep Center: Practice Items (www.collegeboard.com/student/testing/sat/prep_one/practice.html). Reprinted by permission of Educational Testing Service and the College Entrance Examination Board, the copyright owners of the test questions. Permission to reprint SAT materials does not constitute review or endorsement by Educational Testing Service or the College Board of this publication as a whole or of any questions or testing information it may contain.

SAT II: Subject Tests. SAT I assesses basic reasoning abilities that are likely to be relevant to performance in college. The SAT II subject tests measure knowledge of particular subjects and the ability to apply that knowledge. The SAT II tests are 1-hour tests, primarily multiple choice; areas covered by current tests are shown in Table 14-2. Calculators are either allowed or required for some mathematical tests, and some tests require examinees to write essays or to respond to foreign language material presented on tape.

Like the SAT I, the SAT II subject tests are scored on a scale with a mean of 500 and a standard deviation of approximately 100. Although the scales are not identical across areas, scores are roughly comparable. For example, an individual who receives a score of 400 in World History and a 550 in Physics can be said to perform relatively better in physics than in World History. Notice that we used the phrase "relatively better." Scores on the SAT are normative, not ipsative, meaning that we cannot say that this person is better at physics than at world history. What we can say is that this person did better than most people in the reference group in the Physics examination and worse than most people in the reference group in the World History examination.

The SAT Score Scale. For over 40 years, the previous version of the SAT had been interpreted with reference to norms obtained in 1941 from approximately 10,000 examinees, mostly from highly selective schools. Each year, SAT forms were equated back to this sample, so a score of 500 would be equivalent to the average score obtained in this group. By the 1990s, the actual mean score of those taking the test had

Table 14-2   SAT II SUBJECT TESTS

American History
Biology
Chemistry
Chinese, French, German, Japanese, Korean, Latin, or Spanish—
    Reading and Listening
English Language Proficiency test
Literature
Math IC (with calculator)
Math IIC
Modern Hebrew, Italian—Reading only
Physics
World History
Writing (with an essay)

drifted to a level far below 500. For example, the mean SAT-Verbal score of examinees in the early 1990s was approximately 425. That is, examinees in the 1990s did considerably worse, on average, than did the 1941 reference group.

In 1995, a new score scale was adopted, based on a sample of over 1 million examinees from the 1988 to 1989 and 1989 to 1990 school years. This sample was designed to be representative of the current population of SAT examinees (Young, 1995). A score of 500 on this new scale is equivalent to the average score obtained in this reference group; the standard deviation of the recentered scale is approximately 110.

An average performer who took the SAT in 1994 would obtain a verbal score of about 425. An average performer taking the test in 1995 would obtain a score of about 500. It might seem, therefore, that the new score scale is "easier" than the old one. Of course, nothing of the sort is true. Rather, the new score scale simply uses a different and probably more relevant reference group. The old SAT score scale compared each individual with a sample of people attending relatively selective schools in the early 1940s. In the last 50 to 60 years, there have been substantial changes in the populations that complete high school and go on to college, so the average performance in this group might very well be lower than the average performance in the small and selective group that the 1941 norming sample represented. Over the years, there has been a great deal of concern about the apparent downward drift in SAT scores (e.g., the mean Verbal score had drifted from 500 to approximately 425 between the 1940s and the 1990s). Much of this apparent drift (which is often taken as evidence that schools are worse today than they were 50 years ago) is in fact due to the democratization of educational opportunity. Fifty years ago, only a select group ever completed high school and went on to college. Today, a much larger and more diverse portion of the population receives this level of education.

The New SAT

Starting in the spring of 2005, the next major revision of the SAT will be rolled out. The new SAT verbal section will be renamed "Critical Reading." The SAT will no longer use analogies but rather will give examinees many more passages (both long and short) to read and interpret. A new writing section that includes both multiple-choice grammar questions and a written essay will be added. The math section will cover concepts from the three years of high-school math that are most commonly taught across the nation (Algebra I, Algebra II, and Geometry).

These changes are coming in response to decades of criticism of SAT and similar tests as artificial and deficient. Several universities, notably the University of California system, either discontinued the use of SAT in admissions or threatened to do so; it is thought that these changes will make the tests more acceptable to users and possibly more useful as predictors of academic performance. It is less clear, however, whether these changes will make SAT a better test. For example, critics of standardized tests have long clamored for the use of writing samples. It will be very difficult to achieve the level of reliability in scoring these that is easily achieved with multiple-choice items, and therefore it might be very challenging to develop writing assessments that approach the levels of reliability and validity found in standardized tests. Even the problem of replacing analogies with reading passages presents more challenges than one might expect. Reading comprehension items often measure a mix of actual comprehension and prior knowledge. For example, if you give the same passage describing a Civil War battle to a normal student and to a history buff, the history buff probably has a substantial advantage. It is too soon to tell whether these changes will lead to a better SAT, but the principles of measurement articulared in Chapters 1 through 10 of this book suggest that it will be a challenge to produce a new SAT, with fewer items and more subjective scoring, that is nearly as good as the current one. The odds that these changes will lead to meaningful improvements in the SAT or in the decisions made on the basis of SAT scores strike us as slim.

Is the SAT Worthwhile? The SAT and similar testing programs have long been the subject of criticism and debate (e.g., Nairn et al., 1980). Criticisms range from complaints about the narrow coverage of the tests to the way that such tests can destroy an individual's chances for admission to college. In our view, the most serious criticism may be that tests of this sort are not really worth the time, effort, and cost involved.

Evidence suggests that SAT scores can help in making valid and fair decisions about academic admissions and placement, but these same decisions might often be made on the basis of information such as high-school grades (Crouse & Trusheim, 1988; Gottfredson & Crouse, 1986). Combining SAT scores with information from one's high-school transcript does seem to boost the validity of admissions decisions, but the increment is modest.

The main advantage of a test like the SAT is that it makes it easier to compare people coming from very different schools, backgrounds, and so on. High school grades vary as a function of the courses taken and the academic standards of the school, and comparing the transcript of one student who took demanding courses at a school with high standards with another whose curriculum seems less demanding can be very difficult. A second advantage is that SAT measures basic abilities that are broadly relevant. College and high school are different in a number of ways, and an individual who can perform well at one level might not perform as well at the next level. Knowing something about both basic reasoning abilities and a person's past performance probably helps you to make better decisions than would be made on the basis of past performance alone.

The ACT Assessment Program—An Alternative to the SAT

The ACT Assessment Program represents an alternative to the strategy exemplified by the SAT. The ACT Assessment consists of four content-oriented tests of educational development (English, mathematics, reading, and science reasoning), along with an interest inventory measuring vocationally relevant interests similar to those that characterize the J. L. Holland (1973) model discussed in Chapter 2. The ACT educational development tests are characterized by careful attention to content sampling, including the systematic study of high-school curricula and the development of detailed content specifications for every section of the test. For example, the Mathematics test contains 60 items, broken down into four content subcategories: (1) prealgebra and elementary algebra (24 items), (2) intermediate algebra and coordinate geometry (18 items), (3) plane geometry (14 items), and (4) trigonometry (4 items). The goal of this set of tests is to provide information about the student's mastery of four fundamental areas, some or all of which are likely relevant to success regardless of the student's major or area of study.

Two features distinguish the ACT Assessment system from the SAT. First, the ACT represents an integrated assessment system that includes tests of basic competencies that are critical for success in college, as well as including measures of basic interests. ACT assessments may, therefore, be more useful for counseling students (see Chapter 18) than the aptitude or subject scores that result from the SAT. Second, the ACT is more closely tied to secondary school curricula than the SAT. Proponents of achievement tests as alternatives to ability tests find this feature attractive. However, as we note in a later section, the ability-achievement distinction may not be as useful as it appears. Even if the distinction is useful in an academic sense, it may not have much bearing on comparisons between the SAT and the ACT. The most recent revision of the SAT (i.e., 2005 revision) places more emphasis on curriculum-related knowledge and less emphasis on abstract reasoning than the previous versions of SAT.

One of the more interesting applications of ACT assessments has been to use them to scale the difficulty of high-school courses (Bassiri & Schulz, 2003). Because of its ties to the content of high-school curricula, it is thought that scaling courses in terms of their relationships with ACT provides a reasonable metric for comparing courses across schools or across academic programs. Using the methods of Item Responses Theory (Chapter 10), Bassiri and Schulz (2003) were able to develop a universal scale of high-school course difficulty that allows one to adjust for differences in grading standards across courses or schools.

CRITICAL DISCUSSION:
How Did Large-Scale College Admissions Testing Begin?

The history of the SAT is not well-known. How it became the leading test for college admissions being taken by over 2 million college-bound seniors annually is a rather interesting story. Although a partial review of its background is presented here, a more detailed treatment can be found in Lemann (1999). The rise in the popularity of the SAT relies in large part on some of the ideas of James Bryant Conant, who became president of Harvard University in 1933. He observed that most of the students were from upper-class, East Coast backgrounds. He wanted to select some outstanding students from more modest backgrounds from around the country because of his philosophical belief that the best way to keep America strong was by increasing opportunity and social mobility for people. The task of identifying talented students from around the country was somewhat daunting in the 1930s, but the idea eventually emerged of using scores on a scholastic aptitude test for this purpose. The test that was selected, the Scholastic Aptitude Test, was being developed by Carl Brigham, a Princeton psychology professor, who had worked on the massive Army Alpha and Beta Intelligence testing program during World War I. Although originally constructed as an essay exam, it soon was redesigned as a multiple-choice test so that it could be administered to large numbers of students and scored quickly.

It did not take long, however, before Conant's original idea of using the SAT to select a few bright scholarship students began to change to testing large numbers of college applicants to determine which students should be admitted. This change has meant that students now see their test scores as a prime determiner of whether they will be admitted to one of the selective schools of their choice. More and more high schools have developed special courses for their curriculums that are intended to help students prepare to take "the test" and score well. In addition, entrepreneurs have started several flourishing private companies that provide test preparation programs either in face-to-face instructional workshops or online through the Internet. It is highly unlikely that Conant ever could have envisioned the major role that admission testing would eventually play in contemporary society.

Graduate Record Examinations

The SAT is designed to assist in undergraduate admissions and placement decisions. The GREs, which are administered by the Educational Testing Service, serve a similar function in graduate admissions and placement decisions, and they are also used in assigning scholarships, fellowships, and traineeships. Unlike the SAT, which is generally a paper-and-pencil–based testing program, the GRE has become an increasingly computer-based program. The GREs consist of three different tests. (1) The General test, offered only on computer, can be taken year-round at a number of testing sites throughout the country. (2) The GRE Subject tests are offered only in paper-and-pencil format and can be taken only on three testing dates throughout the year. (3) Finally, the newest GRE test, the Writing Assessment, can be taken either on computer throughout the year or in a hand-written format on the three national dates reserved for subject testing.

The GREs include both an aptitude test (GRE General) and advanced achievement tests (GRE Subject tests) in several disciplines. The GRE General test provides verbal ability, quantitative ability, and analytic ability scores; these three scores are thought to reflect verbal comprehension and quantitative skills, as well as ability in logical reasoning. Verbal items include analogies, sentence completions, and reading comprehension. Quantitative items include questions dealing with simple algebra and geometry, as well as quantitative comparisons and data interpretation. Analytic items include syllogisms, interpretations of logical diagrams, and groups of related statements

Table 14-3   SAMPLE GRE® ITEMS

COLOR : SPECTRUM
(A) tone : scale
(B) sound : waves
(C) verse : poem
(D) dimension : space
(E) cell : organism

Early _____ of hearing loss is _____ by the fact that other senses are able to compensate for moderate amounts of hearing loss, so people frequently do not know that their hearing is imperfect.
(A) discovery..indicated
(B) development..prevented
(C) detection..complicated
(D) treatment..facilitated
(E) incidence..corrected

When walking, a certain person takes 16 complete steps in 10 seconds. At this rate, how many complete steps does the person take in 72 seonds?
(A) 45
(B) 78
(C) 86
(D) 90
(E) 115

Source: GRE test questions selected from sample items published in the *GRE Practice General Test*, 2003–2004, Educational Testing Service. Reprinted by permission of Educational Testing Service, the copyright owner. Permission to reprint the above material does not constitute review or endorsement by Educational Testing Service of this publication as a whole or of any other testing information it may contain.

from which one must abstract specific rules. Examples of verbal, quantitative, and analytic items are presented in Table 14-3.

Employing computer-adaptive testing technology (see Chapter 12), the General test assesses an examinee's ability in these areas by starting with a series of test items that are of average difficulty and then progressing with easier or more difficult items, depending on the examinee's responses. Since the computer scores each item when it is answered in order to determine the difficulty level of the next item presented, examinees cannot skip items or return to previous items to change their answers. This feature of computer-adaptive testing may present some problems for those who are unfamiliar with it. For these individuals, acquiring additional familiarity with it can improve their overall test performance. Although those taking the General test do not all receive the same set of test questions, their scores are comparable because of the statistical equating done by the computer. Research done by the Educational Testing Service has also shown that computer-based testing scores are comparable to those generated by the older paper-and-pencil format.

GRE Subject (Advanced) tests are given in 14 different fields, including biology, music, and psychology. Like the SAT, scores on the GRE are reported on a standard scale, with a mean of 500 and a standard deviation of 100. These scores are anchored to a specific reference group who took the test in 1952. Thus, a verbal score of 500 is equal to the average raw score that would have been expected in the reference group. A score of 500 on the music test is the score expected from a person taking this test who has an average aptitude (General) score of 500. Since some disciplines are more selective than others, direct comparisons of scores on different subject tests may be misleading. A score of 600 in sociology could indicate a higher level of (relative) performance than a score of 620 in physics. Similarly, direct comparisons among the verbal, quantitative, analytic, and subject scores of a single applicant are difficult to interpret. Verbal and quantitative scores of 480 and 550, respectively, do not necessarily indicate that a person performs better, in an absolute sense, on quantitative than on verbal tasks. Rather, GRE scores indicate levels of intellectual ability relative to a fixed reference group.

In addition to the standard score, percentile ranks are reported for each test. These percentiles indicate an examinee's performance in comparison with those who have taken the test in a recent 3-year period. The current policy of the Educational Testing Service is to make GRE scores available for 5 years, which means that although an examinee's standard score will remain the same over this entire period, percentile ranks may differ over time (i.e., because scores are compared with different testing populations at different times).

Starting in 1999, the GRE included an essay-based test, the GRE Writing Assessment, which is designed to expand the range of skills evaluated by the General and Subject tests. In particular, this test gives the examinee an opportunity to demonstrate skills in critical reasoning and analytic writing. Student essays are scored by pairs of college and university faculty with experience in teaching writing-intensive courses and additional raters are brought in if the first two raters disagree. Writing samples are evaluated in terms of the extent to which they present clear, well-reasoned analyses.

The GRE has probably made a quicker transition to computer-based testing than any other civilian high-stakes testing program. Starting in the middle of 1999, the GRE General test was available only in its computerized adaptive form (Mills, 1999, traces the extensive program of research and development that led to the development of a computerized adaptive form of the GRE General test); and the GRE Writing Assessment is also administered by computer, although it is still scored by expert judges. GRE subject tests are still given in paper-and-pencil form, but most admissions decisions focus on scores on the General test, and many students are likely to take the computerized General test and bypass the Subject tests altogether.

Evaluation of the GRE and the SAT

Although the GRE and SAT are prepared by different agencies for different purposes, both tests are similar in many fundamentals. First, both represent outstanding examples of careful, professional test development. Test items are extensively screened, edited, and pretested before being included in either test. As a result, both tests are highly reliable (internal consistency reliabilities are consistently above .90), and both are consistently accurate predictors of a variety of measures of academic success. Manuals for both the SAT and the GRE provide detailed information on the interpretation and use of test scores; it is particularly noteworthy that both manuals discuss the limitations of test scores and clearly indicate that these scores should not be the sole basis for academic decisions.

The most fundamental similarity between the SAT and the GRE is in terms of the processes presumably involved in answering questions correctly. The great majority of the questions, whether verbal, quantitative, or analytical, require reasoning and comprehension, rather than knowledge of specific and possibly obscure facts. In some cases, items rely on verbal comprehension; in others, on deducing quantitative relationships; and in others, on symbolic logic. In almost every case, however, the subject is required to actively process, manipulate, and evaluate a good deal of information to arrive at the correct answer to a specific question.

Although critics suggest that the multiple-choice format limits a test to a simple exercise of rote memory, there is little reason to believe that a student can do well on the SAT or the GRE without superior reasoning and comprehension abilities. On the other hand, there is the possibility that intelligent students who are unfamiliar with the demands of multiple-choice group tests may do poorly on either test. It is possible that revisions to the format of the both tests will diminish the importance of this factor. Nevertheless, it is difficult to see how the SAT and GRE could attain such consistent records of validity if they were little more than rote memory tests. For example, Kuncel, Hezlett, and Ones (2001) showed that GRE scores were valid predictors of grade point average, faculty ratings, comprehensive examination scores, and publication citation counts. Similarly, the SAT has repeatedly been shown to predict success in college and beyond. This outcome is not what you would expect if critics of these tests were right in their descriptions of SAT and GRE as limited tests of factual knowledge.

Both the SAT and the GRE have been criticized as potentially biased measures; most of this criticism has been directed at the SAT, which is much more widely used. The root of this criticism is the problem noted in Chapter 3, that different groups systematically receive different scores on most tests of general cognitive ability. For example, both gender differences (C. Holden, 1989) and race differences (Crouse & Trusheim, 1988) in SAT scores have been the focus of controversy, including several lawsuits. Most test researchers agree that the differences in scores are not solely a result of test bias and that the tests are reasonably good measures of ability and scholastic aptitude for males, females, whites, and minorities. The issue of whether the tests should be used in contexts where differences in scores exist is taken up later in this chapter.

Ability Versus Achievement Tests

Psychologists and educators have traditionally distinguished between ability (or aptitude) tests and achievement tests. It is not clear that the ability-achievement distinction is a useful one. (There is a similar debate over fluid versus crystallized intelligence, as can be seen in Guilford, 1980.) For example, research on achievement tests often demonstrates the influence of broad ability factors on achievement scores (Jones & Applebaum, 1989). Nevertheless, it may be useful to distinguish between these two types of tests, at least with regard to the different goals that they serve.

The traditional distinction between ability and achievement tests is that the latter is geared toward specific knowledge or skills that are acquired over a restricted span of time. For example, a person taking a course in auto mechanics may be tested at the end of the semester on the specific knowledge and skills that the course was designed to impart. Ability tests, on the other hand, refer to broad and general abilities that are acquired over long spans of time. Verbal ability and spatial ability are examples. If we think about ability versus achievement tests in terms of the goals of the two types of tests, a somewhat different picture emerges. Achievement tests are retrospective in their purpose. That is, they are designed to assess changes in knowledge and skills acquired in the relatively recent past. In academic settings, achievements are used primarily to determine what a person has learned or mastered, although they may also be useful for determining whether that person is ready to go on to more advanced levels in a particular discipline. In work settings, achievement tests are used to determine whether specific training objectives have been met. Ability tests are prospective in their purpose. That is, they give an indication of how well a person is likely to perform now and in the future on a variety of tasks. They are not tied to specific educational or training experiences but, rather, to broader, more general, and more long-lasting developmental experiences. It is important to note that achievement tests can be used to make predictions of the future (e.g., advanced placement tests) and that ability tests can be used to help diagnose previous deficiencies in performance. Nevertheless, the distinction between the two types of tests that is outlined here is, in our opinion, useful in understanding the research literature on ability versus achievement testing (see also Corno, Cronbach, Kupermintz, Lohman, Mandinach, Porteus, & Talbert, 2002).

Jones and Applebaum (1989) review a number of reports by the National Research Council and other groups that examine achievement tests. A common thread running through virtually every report is that standardized tests that employ multiple-choice response formats are not sufficient to tap critical areas of achievement. The most common criticism of this format is that it puts a premium on the recognition of details and puts too little emphasis on critical thinking skills. There is an increasing call for more open-ended and free-response questions like those incorporated in the new SAT, together with proposals to develop computerized tests that incorporate information such as response latency in diagnosing students' problem-solving skills.

We do not believe that changing response formats is the answer to the current deficiencies of achievement tests. Although the multiple-choice format is undoubtedly restrictive, it is clearly possible to measure things other than recognition of trivial details with multiple-choice items. For example, multiple-choice items in the MAB or in sections of the GRE clearly call for reasoning and problem solving and cannot be adequately answered through rote memorization of facts. Alternatives to multiple-choice questions will contribute to the expense and difficulty of testing and will almost certainly lead to decreased levels of reliability.

The use of achievement tests to certify student progress and teacher competency is a somewhat mixed blessing. On the one hand, there is the perennial complaint that when these tests are required, the emphasis in instruction will shift in such a way that teachers teach to the test (Jones & Applebaum, 1989). In fact, there is little evidence that teachers actually change their instructional methods or the content of their classes to "teach to the test" (Heubert & Hauser, 1999). On the other hand, without some systematic assessment of competency and achievement, we may find that neither teachers nor students know the material. The most critical determinant of the contribution of these tests is their validity. If the tests used to certify competency are themselves poor measures of the domain of knowledge or skill being tested, it is hard to see how achievement testing will contribute to the quality of education. Valid tests of achievement, on the other hand, may allow examiners to accurately assess the progress of individuals as well as the success of various teaching and training strategies.

To date, research on the validity of achievement tests has usually relied on content-oriented validation strategies. That is, the validity of achievement tests has usually been assessed by comparing the test with the educational or training curriculum. The current emphasis on testing understanding and problem-solving abilities suggests that content-oriented strategies will no longer be adequate.[3] As with other tests, the appropriate validation strategy for achievement tests will have to take into account the types of constructs measured by different response modes, as well as the relationships of these constructs to achievement in specific subject areas or domains. Research on the construct validity of tests of educational achievement is still somewhat rare, but it is likely to become more common in the near future.

On the whole, we are not positively impressed by the validity of many achievement tests, some of which are used to make important decisions about people and institutions (e.g., tests that are required to receive a high-school diploma; Heubert & Hauser, 1999). As we have noted earlier in this book, it is considerably easier to make valid comparisons between persons than it is to make comparisons between what a person knows or what that person can do and some standard (Conbach et al., 1972). It is difficult to set good standards, and even more difficult to determine whether or not they have been met. Unfortunately, achievement tests require *more* psychometric sophistication than measures of individual differences, and this characteristic poses a real problem. Few achievement tests show the sort of reliability, validity, and standardization that is common in well-developed ability tests, but there is one important exception—i.e., the National Assessment of Educational Progress (NAEP).

National Assessment of Educational Progress

The National Assessment of Educational Progress (NAEP) is sometimes referred to as "The Nation's Report Card". NAEP is a nationally representative continuing assessment of what students know and can do in the areas of Reading, Mathematics, and Science (Campbell, Humbo & Mazzeo, 2000). It has involved administering achievement tests to large, representative samples of 9, 13, and 17 year old students that assess their performance in these three domains. The tests reflect the state of the art in terms of measurement theory and technology, and they are developed with considerable care and sophistication.

One of the notable accomplishments of the NAEP assessments has been the ability to equate test scores across years, age groups and across content areas. NAEP scores are reported on a 0–500 scale, and concrete descriptions of various performance levels of each scale have been developed. For example, in the Math Assessment, a score of

---

[3]Many researchers would argue that a purely content-oriented strategy never was adequate and that construct validation has always been required for tests of this type.

200 indicates that examinees understand addition and subtraction with two-digit numbers, whereas a score of 250 indicates that examinees have mastered the four basic mathematical operations (addition, subtraction, multiplication, division).

The NAEP provides detailed analyses of patterns of performance over the last three decades, and some of their key findings will come as a real surprise. It is widely believed that our educational systems have failed and that schools (especially public schools) are getting worse all the time. The highly influential report *A Nation at Risk* (U.S. Department of Education, National Commission on Excellence in Education, 1983) included the memorable quote: "If an unfriendly foreign power had attempted to impose on America the mediocre educational performance that exists today, we might well have viewed it as an act of war." The belief that our schools are failing may be widespread, but it is not true. Data from NAEP show that performance levels in Reading, Mathematics, and Science have been remarkably steady over the last 30 years. There were some small drops in performance in the late 1970s but achievement soon recovered and have, if anything, improved slightly over time. There are small variations across age groups and also across ethnic groups (differences in achievement between white examinees and both black and Hispanic examinees have narrowed slightly over time), but on the whole, NAEP data make it clear that achievement has not declined over recent decades.

NAEP does not provide scores to individuals or to schools, but rather it provides summary data for the student population as a whole, for age groups, for males and females, and the like. Participating states can receive statewide data. In part, this decision to report results in terms of average scores in large samples is a recognition of the limited validity and accuracy of individual-level assessments. Even when using the best methods of test development, score equating, sampling, and so on, it is difficult to do a good enough job of assessment to provide valid individual-level achievement. When you consider that most achievement tests are created by teachers and school boards (who do not have access to the resources or expertise to develop state-of-the-art tests), you might appreciate our skepticism about the value of individual-level achievement tests.

MULTIPLE-APTITUDE BATTERIES

The major advantage of group tests is their efficiency. They allow the collection of a large amount of information, under carefully standardized conditions, in a short period of time. This approach makes it possible to achieve several different goals. First, it is possible to measure a single dimension, such as general intelligence, with a wide variety (and a large number) of questions, thus ensuring some degree of reliability as well as construct validity. Alternatively, it might be possible to obtain measures of several distinct abilities, each with a reasonable degree of reliability and within a time frame that is not substantially greater than that often needed to assess general intelligence. This is exactly the strategy followed by several multiple-aptitude test batteries. Rather than measuring several aspects of a more general ability, these batteries attempt to measure several distinct abilities in their own right. Whereas the measurement of several distinct abilities could be both cumbersome and unreliable if individual testing methods were employed, the measurement of several distinct abilities in a single test battery is, in principle, no more difficult than the measurement of a single ability.

The Armed Services Vocational Aptitude Battery

The Armed Services Vocational Aptitude Battery (ASVAB), which is probably the most widely used test in existence, illustrates both the strengths and the weaknesses of multiple-aptitude test batteries. This test, which is administered annually to over a million individuals, is used by the armed services to screen potential recruits and to assign recruits to different jobs, training programs, and career areas. The use of a multiple-aptitude battery, rather than a single test of general intelligence, provides the best chance for successfully meeting the complex set of demands placed on the ASVAB.

The ASVAB consists of a battery of 10 separate subtests, which are listed in Table 14-4. In the paper-and-pencil version of the ASVAB, these subtests range from 15 to 84 items and feature a mix of speed and power tests administered with time limits ranging from 3 to 36 minutes. The entire test can be administered in 3 hours. The computerized adaptive form of the ASVAB (CAT-ASVAB) includes the same subtests but with fewer items and substantially shorter testing times.

Scores on the individual subtests are combined to produce seven separate composite scores:

Academic Composites

1. Academic Ability: word knowledge, paragraph comprehension, and arithmetic reasoning
2. Verbal: word knowledge, paragraph comprehension, and general science
3. Math: mathematics knowledge and arithmetic reasoning

Table 14-4 SUBTESTS OF THE ARMED SERVICES VOCATIONAL APTITUDE BATTERY: PAPER-AND-PENCIL VERSION

1. General Science—25 items measuring general knowledge of the physical and biological sciences.
2. Arithmetic Reasoning—30 items that involve simple calculation but call for the ability to determine the appropriate analysis.
3. Word Knowledge—35 vocabulary items.
4. Paragraph Comprehension—15 items assessing subjects' understanding of several short paragraphs.
5. Numeric Operations—speed test made up of 50 problems involving simple calculation.
6. Coding Speed—speed test made up of 84 items asking the subject to substitute numeric codes for verbal material.
7. Auto and Shop Information—25 items measuring knowledge of automobiles, tools, shop terminology, and shop practices.
8. Mathematics Knowledge—25 items measuring knowledge of high school–level mathematics.
9. Mechanical Comprehension—25 items measuring understanding of basic mechanical principles.
10. Electronics Information—25 items measuring knowledge of electric principles and electronic terminology.

Occupational Composites

4. Mechanical and Crafts: arithmetic reasoning, mechanical comprehension, auto and shop information, and electronics information
5. Business and Clerical: word knowledge, paragraph comprehension, mathematics knowledge, and coding speed
6. Electronics and Electrical: arithmetic reasoning, mathematics knowledge, electronics information, and general science
7. Health, Social, and Technology: word knowledge, paragraph comprehension, arithmetic reasoning, and mechanical comprehension

Several other composites are computed by the individual services. Thus, there is a potential for obtaining a large amount of information about both specific aptitude and major groups of aptitudes that are thought to be relevant to successful performance in training and in a wide variety of jobs within the armed services.

Administration and Use of the ASVAB. The ASVAB program has several noteworthy features. First, the ASVAB is administered in a way that guarantees a level of standardization and precision that is difficult to achieve with many other tests. A large percentage of ASVAB administrations are now done using the CAT-ASVAB. The use of computerization achieves high reliability with a shorter test and also allows much greater levels of test security (Segall & Moreno, 1999). Second, considerable care has gone into the procedures used for disseminating and interpreting ASVAB scores. The ASVAB is given most often in schools, and extensive efforts are made to provide counselors with relevant information about each student's scores, as well as detailed normative information that can be used to interpret those scores. A student who has taken the ASVAB receives reports listing his or her percentile score on each composite. The counseling department of the school receives a more extensive report on each student and also receives a Military Career Guide, which provides expectancy charts for each of approximately 130 clusters of occupations in the various services. This guide indicates the probability that a student with a particular set of scores will qualify for at least one job within each of the clusters. Since many military jobs have clear parallels in the civilian sector, this guide provides a counseling tool that is broadly useful.

In contrast to many other tests, the ASVAB is part of a well-integrated program that includes continual research in all the branches of the armed services on the technical adequacy and practical usefulness of the test, specific procedures for using the test in both selection (i.e., screening recruits) and job placement, and extensive provisions for using the test as a counseling tool (Katz, 1987; for more detail on the ASVAB program, go to the website http://asvabprogram.com). For example, students who take the ASVAB also complete the Interest Finder, a measure of vocational interests developed by the Department of Defense. This inventory helps them to assess their career interests and to determine which civilian and military careers best match their abilities and interests. The ASVAB Career Exploration Program (Defense Manpower Data Center, 1996; J. E. L. Wall & Baker, 1997; J. L. Wall, Wise, & Baker, 1996) is one of the largest integrated assessment programs in the world.

Evaluation of the ASVAB. Evaluations of the technical adequacy of the ASVAB have not been completely favorable (Cronbach, 1979; Murphy, 1984a; Weiss, 1978). Although several specific issues have been raised by different reviewers, most of them revolve around the way that test scores are calculated and reported rather than around features of the test itself. Recall that the ASVAB is a multiple-aptitude battery designed to assess several different aptitudes. This feature is reflected, in part, by the fact that there is no overall ASVAB score. Unfortunately, scores on the individual subtests are not reported to individuals or to counselors. Only the seven composites described earlier are reported. The critical question, then, is whether these composites represent discriminably different pieces of information. Examination of the composites themselves and of the technical manual of the test suggests that they do not (Prediger, 1987).

As can be seen from examining the composites, the same tests appear in many different composites. For example, the arithmetic-reasoning subtest appears in five of the seven composites. Furthermore, the composites are so highly correlated with one another that their scores essentially are redundant. The average intercorrelation among the seven composite scores is .86; corrected for attenuation, the average intercorrelation is an astounding .92. The only reasonable conclusion is that the composites do not provide information about different sets of aptitudes and that, in fact, any one of the composites could be substituted for another with little loss of information. Murphy (1984a) suggested that the composites, particularly the academic ability composite, provide information about the individual's general aptitude but do not provide information about multiple aptitudes.

Although the ASVAB has shown evidence of reliability and criterion-related validity, it nevertheless fails the acid test of a multiple-aptitude battery. The ASVAB (as it is currently used) does not provide the information about multiple abilities needed for successful job placement. For most of its major goals, the military would do just as well with a short test of general intelligence (Murphy, 1984a). Recent research (e.g., Zeidner & Johnson, 1994) suggests that it might be possible to obtain more useful information for classification from the ASVAB if different scoring methods are used. Although the ASVAB is highly "*g*-loaded" (Hunter, Crosson, & Friedman, 1985; Thorndike, 1985), evidence suggests that it can provide information about several separate abilities (Welsh, Kucinkas, & Curran, 1990). However, the process of making even minor changes in a program such as the ASVAB is a daunting one, and it is not clear whether the sort of technical solution suggested by Zeidner and Johnson (1994) will be applicable in a testing program as complex as the ASVAB.

The General Aptitude Test Battery

The General Aptitude Test Battery (GATB) was developed in 1947 by the Department of Labor and is presently used by the U.S. Employment Service for making job referrals in literally hundreds of jobs. The GATB, which is available in at least 12 different languages and is used in over 35 countries (Droege, 1984), rivals the ASVAB in terms of the frequency with which it is used to make decisions about individuals.

Table 14-5   APTITUDES MEASURED BY THE GENERAL APTITUDE TEST BATTERY

Aptitude	Tests
G—General Learning Ability	Vocabulary
	Arithmetic Reasoning
	Three-Dimensional Space
V—Verbal Ability	Vocabulary[a]
N—Numerical Ability	Computation
	Arithmetic Reasoning
S—Spatial Aptitude	Three-Dimensional Space
P—Form Perception	Tool Matching
	Form Matching
Q—Clerical Perception	Name Comparison
K—Motor Coordination	Mark Making
F—Finger Dexterity	Assemble
	Disassemble
M—Manual Dexterity	Place
	Time

[a]As with ASVAB, the same GATB test might be used in measuring several different aptitudes.

The GATB measures 9 aptitudes using 12 separate tests; the tests and the aptitudes measured are listed in Table 14-5. The test is also available in a nonreading form, in which tests are administered orally or by using nonverbal materials (e.g., a number comparison test is used in place of the name comparison test); separate versions of the test are available for deaf examinees and wheelchair-bound examinees.

Like the Stanford-Binet and the WAIS, the GATB includes both verbal and performance tests (e.g., assembly and disassembly tasks). As a result, the administration of the GATB is somewhat laborious and complex; the test typically takes over 2 hours to administer. Factor analyses of the GATB suggest that the test measures three general factors: (1) a cognitive factor representing general learning ability, verbal ability, and numerical ability; (2) a perceptual factor representing spatial aptitude, form perception, and clerical perception; and (3) a psychomotor factor representing motor coordination, finger dexterity, and manual dexterity (Hunter, 1983a). The perceptual factor is almost perfectly correlated with a combination of the other two factors, suggesting that the test measures two basic abilities, cognitive and psychomotor.

Use of the GATB. The GATB has long been a central part of the U.S. Employment Service's job referral program (Delahunty, 1988; Hartigan & Wigdor, 1989). This referral program (which, as we note later, is being updated and revised) includes many elements besides the GATB, such as counseling and workshops, but scores on the GATB can have a pivotal impact on an applicant's chance to be considered for jobs.

The GATB referral system consists of four steps: (1) intake (registration and orientation); (2) assessment (testing and evaluation of credentials); (3) file search (location of appropriate job opportunities); and (4) referral. Employers make the final decisions about individuals referred by the Job Service, but because the referral process is designed to locate qualified candidates, individuals who are referred very often receive job offers.

The U.S. Employment Service has the complex task of referring the most qualified individuals for the job and attempting to ensure that individuals who have been traditionally disadvantaged by standardized testing (e.g., minority group members, individuals with disabilities) have an opportunity to compete for these jobs. During the 1980s, various schemes for computing and reporting scores separately for members of different ethnic and racial groups were proposed and implemented (Hartigan & Wigdor, 1989). This type of race norming led to significant controversies, lawsuits, and a moratorium on the use of the GATB by several agencies. As a result of the Civil Rights Act of 1991, the practice of race norming (i.e., reporting scores in terms of percentiles within one's own racial or ethnic group) has been discontinued.

Evaluation of the GATB. GATB reliabilities are comparable to those of other similar tests, such as the ASVAB (Hartigan & Wigdor, 1989). The validity of the GATB has been researched in hundreds of separate studies. Validity generalization procedures led Hunter (1983c) to conclude that the GATB is valid in all jobs for which it is used and that GATB validities are higher in more complex or demanding jobs than in simpler jobs. Hunter (1983b) also concluded that the GATB was fair to minorities and that the inclusion of a psychomotor composite helps to reduce the adverse impact of this test (i.e., it reduces differences between the average scores of different groups).

The most controversial issue in the evaluation of the GATB has been its utility (see Chapter 20). The GATB referral process was developed and adapted, in part, because of research suggesting that the use of the GATB in job referral could lead to extraordinarily large gains in productivity. The most frequently cited figure is in the neighborhood of $80 billion. It is now clear that a figure such as this is wildly inflated (Hartigan & Wigdor, 1989) and that the use of GATB will not by itself generate this level of productivity. Nevertheless, the use of GATB may help employers locate the most qualified applicants and, in the long run, could result in productivity gains that far exceed the cost of testing and referral.

The GATB Revision. New paper-and-pencil forms of the GATB have been developed, and the test has been renamed (the new test is called the Ability Profiler; you can access this test through http://www.onetcenter.org/AP.html). A computerized adaptive version of the test is also being developed. The process of developing, equating, validating, and implementing a high-stakes test like the GATB (we use the term *high-stakes* in recognition of the extensive use of the test and the important consequences of test scores) is long and complicated, and it is not clear when the new tests will be fully implemented.

In part, the impetus for improving the GATB program is a result of the political and social controversies that surrounded the program in the 1990s, but it is also in part driven by a recognition that the GATB, like many other multiple-aptitude batteries, does not provide as much information as it should to decision makers. As we will note later, a better linkage between test development and research on human cognition might provide a basis for developing more useful and more valid test batteries. The ongoing revision of the GATB (i.e., Ability Profiler) coincided with a large-scale program to develop a comprehensive, modern system for collecting and analyzing occupational information. This system, entitled *O*NET*, includes information on 1,100 occupations, each described in terms of skill requirements, worker characteristics, experience requirements, and so on. One of the most useful features of the Ability Profiler is that scores on this test are linked to the O*NET database, providing examinees with information about how their scores compare with the average scores of incumbents in over 1,000 jobs.

Ability Testing and Cognitive Research

Since the early 1970s, a cognitive revolution swept through most areas of psychology. Research on cognitive processes has come to dominate fields as diverse as motivation (see a special section on motives and goals in human performance, *Psychological Science,* 1992, Vol. 3, No. 3) and psychotherapy (where cognitively oriented therapies emerged). The field of cognitive science provides an exciting integration of psychological, neurological, and computational models of human thought and brain function. However, the explosion of knowledge regarding cognitive processes has had relatively little influence to date on ability testing (Fredericksen, Mislevy, & Bajar, 1993, review the relationships between evolving theories of cognition, test theory, and testing applications). Despite all the advances in cognitive research, the best tests of cognitive ability still follow the basic philosophy and measurement strategies developed by Binet at the turn of the century and by the research team that developed Army Alpha during World War I.

Cognitive research has had a substantial impact on ability testing in at least three areas. First, cognitive researchers have reached some consensus that many higher-level cognitive processes, which presumably include those involving mental abilities, can be best understood through a mental architecture that includes three components: (1) working memory, (2) declarative memory, and (3) procedural memory (R. G. Lord & Maher, 1991). Working memory is that part of memory that is currently activated, whereas declarative and procedural memories store factual information and information about how to do things, respectively (this is a substantial simplification, but it gives a flavor of these three key concepts). Some existing tests (e.g., the K-ABC) and many tests currently being developed (e.g., computerized tests being developed by the armed services) include measures of working memory; other tests (e.g., the fourth and fifth editions of the Stanford-Binet) have been revised to partially accommodate this description of cognitive function. However, few existing tests provide meaningful assessments of all three components.

Second, a number of theories of intelligence attempt to identify multiple types (e.g., Gardner, 1983) or components (e.g., Sternberg, 1984, 1985) of intelligence. Although some tests have been proposed or developed, none of these has proved completely satisfactory, and there is no indication that they will replace current tests of ability (Sternberg, 1981a, 1991).

Third, applied researchers (e.g., Ackerman, 1987; Murphy, 1989) have become increasingly interested in how ability translates into performance on a variety of tasks. Several theories suggest that general mental ability, which is critical to the acquisition of task knowledge, is more critical when the task is new or novel than when an individual has had a chance to practice the task. Although this research does not suggest different ways in which ability should be measured, it does suggest that ability tests should be used in different ways—in particular, to identify those most likely to acquire knowledge and understanding of the task quickly.

Lohman (1992) suggests three reasons why cognitive research has had relatively little impact on ability testing. First, the decomposition of complex, real-world tasks into their basic cognitive components has proved much more difficult than anyone anticipated. Thus, it is often difficult to determine exactly which aspects of the theory apply to which tasks. Second, it is difficult to replace existing psychometric tests with experimental tasks that are designed to measure the same abilities or processes. This problem is related to the first (the difficulty of matching the theory to the task); even when psychometric researchers and cognitive researchers use the same terms, they are not always referring to the same phenomena. Third, measures of speed of response (or latency), which are so central to many cognitive theories, are easier to obtain than to interpret. This is the case because of the well-known speed-accuracy trade-off (Ackerman & Humphreys, 1990). That is, increasing the speed of responses usually results in a decrease in accuracy. If examinees believe that accuracy is important, they tend to respond more slowly; if they believe that speed is important, they tend to be less accurate. Speed of response often has more to do with subjects' orientation to the test than with their basic cognitive processes.

Finally, Sternberg (1991) suggests that practical constraints may prove the most difficult barrier to translating advances in cognitive research into new methods of testing. Test publishing is a big business, and it is difficult to convince publishers of the need to make radical changes in their tests, especially when the familiar testing methods "work" so well. As you saw in Chapter 12, however, developments in computerized testing may open the door for translating advances in cognitive research into new methods of measuring cognitive ability.

CRITICAL DISCUSSION:

The Case Against Large-Scale Testing

The SAT provides an illustration of a large-scale testing program. Here, several thousand students answer hundreds of multiple-choice items that tap areas ranging from vocabulary and reading comprehension to inductive and deductive reasoning. This type of testing has been the focus of extensive criticism (M. Gross, 1963; B. Hoffman, 1962; Nairn et al., 1980; C. Ryan, 1979). Although many specific arguments have been raised in this debate, the case against large-scale testing boils down to two essentials: (1) This type of testing does not measure the right variables, and (2) this type of testing does not provide truly useful information.

In arguments over what group tests measure or fail to measure, the multiple-choice response format is frequently cited as the culprit. Some critics argue that multiple-choice items penalize creative thinkers (B. Hoffman, 1962), whereas others argue that they measure knowledge of specific facts, but not of general abilities (C. Ryan, 1979). In general, research does not support either of these criticisms (Jensen, 1980; Wigdor & Garner, 1982a). It is possible, however, that the psychological processes involved in answering multiple-choice items might be different from those involved in answering the types of open-ended questions that are used in many individual ability tests. Even here, however, the evidence does not suggest that multiple-choice items yield scores that are very different from those that might be obtained with other test formats; scores from tests made up exclusively of multiple-choice items are generally highly correlated with scores from similar tests that include no multiple-choice items (D. N. Jackson, 1984a; Wigdor & Garner, 1982b). Thus, it is difficult to argue that the use of multiple-choice items seriously distorts the measurement of ability.

The best argument *against* large-scale testing is that there may not be good arguments *for* large-scale testing. Tests such as the ASVAB are probably not as useful as they are expensive (Murphy, 1984a). Even the SAT, a test with an impressive level of validity, may not be all that useful. Evidence indicates that SAT scores have only a minor impact on college admission decisions (L. S. Gottfredson & Crouse, 1986) and that the use of these tests might have a very negative effect on minority applicants that, for them, outweighs the potential benefits of the test. Even Jensen (1980), a staunch advocate of testing, recommends against the routine practice of giving tests by the thousands and then deciding what to do with test information. We suspect that if consumers gave more thought to how test information was to be used, fewer tests would be given.

SUMMARY

The development of standardized tests of mental ability that could be administered to groups of examinees has fundamentally changed the face of the testing industry. As we saw in Chapter 13, this type of test was developed to meet a very specific need, the screening of large numbers of military recruits in World War I. The apparent success of this type of testing encouraged psychologists to bring this technology into civilian settings.

The primary difference between individual and group tests is that, with the former, examinees respond to an examiner, who must interpret and score their responses, whereas with the latter, they respond directly to test items. This technique makes it relatively easy to provide highly standardized conditions of measurement, which tends to increase reliability and validity. On the other hand, a heavy reliance on simple response formats (usually multiple choice) may limit the value of a test.

The MAB represents an ingenious adaptation of the WAIS for group administration. The MAB has retained most of the positive features of the WAIS and is substantially easier to administer. The Cognitive Abilities Tests are widely used in testing schoolchildren. The three scholastic tests, described in this chapter—the SAT, the Enhanced ACT Assessment System, and the GRE—should be familiar to many readers. These tests, which are used in making academic admissions decisions, measure both general abilities and more specific competencies or areas of content expertise.

The ASVAB and the GATB represent two of the most widely used cognitive test batteries in existence. Both tests are designed to provide information about general as well as specific abilities, but it is not clear that either has been fully successful in both roles. Nevertheless, evidence indicates clearly that these tests are useful for making important decisions.

The influence of cognitive psychology on psychological testing has been disappointingly small. Current theories of cognition differ in a number of ways from the theories of intelligence that have driven the development of several widely used tests, but to date little progress has been made in translating cognitive principles into useful tests. We reviewed several reasons for the currently limited impact of cognitive research on psychological testing.

PROBLEMS AND SOLUTIONS—RECAP

The Problem

Plangen Industries is opening a new aluminum recycling plant, and the CEO wants you to administer WAIS-III to job applicants. You have not been trained to administer WAIS-III, and since you expect hundreds of applicants, using this individually administered test will be very time-consuming.

A Solution

The Multidimensional Aptitude Battery (MAB–II) is an excellent alternative to the WAIS in this situation. As we note in this chapter, it can be administered in less than an hour to groups of applicants, either via computer or using paper and pencil, and can be scored in a matter of minutes. The MAB-II does not even require administration by a psychologist, although your training and skills should come in handy when interpreting the scores. We suspect that if you come back to the CEO with a proposal to save hundreds of hours and thousands of dollars while obtaining the same information that would have been obtained by administering the WAIS-III to each job applicant, you will look like a genius. It sure beats flying to Saskatchewan to administer several hundred WAIS exams!

KEY TERMS

Achievement tests   tests designed to measure acquired knowledge or skill in a particular area or domain

Group test   test administered to several examinees at the same time, often requiring written responses or responses to multiple-choice items

Multiple-aptitude batteries   groups of tests administered together and designed to measure several distinct abilities

Scholastic tests   tests used in academic admissions and assessment, which often include sections measuring general cognitive abilities

15

Issues in Ability Testing

As discussed in Chapter 1, the apparent success of early tests in classifying recruits during World War I led to a boom in civilian intelligence testing in the 1920s and 1930s, and laid the foundation for the large-scale intelligence testing industry that exists today. Since its inception, however, large-scale intelligence testing has been the focus of sustained public controversy (Cronbach, 1975). Although conflicts between test specialists sometimes revolve around technical or esoteric issues, the primary issue that has fueled the bitter public debate over IQ testing has been the fact that the average test scores for members of minority groups tend to be lower-than-average test scores for white examinees. Furthermore, this difference between the means of white and minority test scores on an intelligence test is generally about the same size as the standard deviation of the test, or approximately 15 points, although this gap appears to be shrinking.

The difference in average test scores means that relatively few minorities will receive high test scores and that minorities will be overrepresented among those receiving low scores on the test. As a result, if tests are used as the sole method of making decisions, fewer minorities will be selected into schools, jobs, and training programs than if decisions are made at random or if quotas are imposed. In very selective contexts (e.g., prestigious schools), the use of tests as the sole means for making decisions effectively rules out most minority applicants.

A number of possibilities have been suggested to account for the difference between white and nonwhite test scores. Hereditarians suggest that genetic factors are partially responsible for individual differences in intelligence test scores. The extreme hereditarian position goes further, suggesting that differences between white and nonwhite test score means are attributable primarily or solely to genetic differences between whites and nonwhites (Schockley, 1972).

Environmentalists suggest that test score differences can best be understood in terms of differences in the environments, particularly in the cultures of white and minority examinees. Extreme environmentalists go further, suggesting that standard intelligence tests are valid only for middle-class whites and that these tests cannot provide valid or useful measures for minorities, who presumably are brought up in a culture that is significantly different from that of middle-class whites. In 1968, the Black Psychological Association called for a moratorium on the use of psychological tests in classifying disadvantaged students on the grounds that these tests showed substantial cultural bias; Jackson (1975) labeled psychological testing as a "quasi-scientific tool for perpetuating racism" (p. 88).

Most psychologists view both extreme hereditarianism and extreme environmentalism as fundamentally incorrect. A good deal of evidence suggests that intelligence is affected by both heredity and environment and that both factors must be taken into account in understanding individual or group differences in scores on intelligence tests. Nevertheless, the debate between the environmentalists and the hereditarians has helped call our attention to three issues that are explored in depth in this chapter: (1) bias and fairness in mental testing; (2) culture-fair or culture-reduced testing; and (3) the heritability and the modifiability of IQ.

PROBLEMS AND SOLUTIONS—DO TESTS UNFAIRLY DISCRIMINATE?

The Problem

Gary has applied for a very attractive job, and he finds out that there are four other applicants, all of them women. All five applicants are asked to take a 12-minute test, and a day later, three of the women are hired. Gary was not all that impressed with the test; it looks as if it has little to do with the job, and he thinks that he is the victim of reverse sex discrimination. What should he do?

BIAS AND FAIRNESS IN MENTAL TESTING

There is a widespread belief that cognitive ability tests are biased and that the use of these tests in educational placement, academic admissions, and personnel selection results in decisions that are fundamentally unfair. One line of evidence that suggests that tests are biased is the existence of systematic differences in test scores as a function of socioeconomic status, sex, and race (Jensen, 1980; Linn, 1982). Researchers on test bias have reported that, in general,

1. Test scores from children and adults in the middle and upper classes tend to be higher than those of children and adults in the lower socioeconomic classes.
2. Whites tend to receive higher scores than minorities.
3. Males receive systematically higher scores on some tests and systematically lower scores on other tests than females.[1]

[1]For a variety of perspectives on the debate over IQ, race, gender, and social class, see Eckberg (1979), Flynn (1980), Herrnstein (1971), Herrnstein and Murray (1994), Jensen (1980), Joseph (1977), Kamin (1974), and Scarr (1981).

These differences have been attributed by some authors to test bias and have been cited as an example of the unfair nature of tests (G. D. Jackson, 1975; Williams, 1974).

The debate about bias and fairness in mental tests has been hampered by a lack of agreement over basic terms. For example, if whites receive higher scores on a given test than minorities, is this outcome an indication of bias, lack of fairness, both bias and unfairness, or neither of these? It is useful at the outset to define bias and fairness in terms that are accepted by most psychologists.

Defining Bias and Fairness

In our everyday language, bias and fairness seem to be closely related, if not identical, concepts. It seems obvious to most people that a biased test is unfair and that an unbiased test is fair. In the context of testing and decision making, however, bias and fairness represent fundamentally different concepts. In some instances, a biased test may lead to decisions that are regarded widely as fair, whereas an unbiased test may lead to decisions that are condemned universally as unfair. It is important, therefore, to distinguish between the two concepts.

Simply put, *bias* is a statistical characteristic of the test scores or of the predictions based on those scores.[2] Thus, bias is said to exist when a test makes systematic errors in measurement or prediction. For example, if test scores indicate that males perform better in verbal reasoning tasks than do females, when in fact they both perform equally well, the test provides a biased measure of verbal reasoning. If a test used in college admissions systematically overpredicts the performance of males and underpredicts the performance of females, that test functions as a biased predictor.

Fairness refers to a value judgment regarding decisions or actions taken as a result of test scores. For example, in selecting firefighters, most cities use some combination of cognitive ability tests, interviews, and tests of physical strength. Quite frequently, the group of applicants selected is predominantly male, even though many females may have applied for the job. Some people regard this situation as fundamentally unfair, since females are largely excluded from this job. Others regard the same situation as completely fair, reasoning that the tests select the best-qualified applicants, regardless of sex. The question of whether the situation is fair depends entirely on one's assessment of what should be done. People who believe that firefighters should be representative of the population in general will regard this situation as unfair; those who believe that persons with the highest scores should be hired will perceive it as fair.

Table 15-1 lists some major differences between bias and fairness. First, bias is a characteristic of the numbers (test scores or predicted criterion scores), whereas fairness is a characteristic of people's actions or decisions. The principle implied here is that numbers are morally and philosophically neutral. People's actions or decisions can be fair or unfair; numbers may be accurate or inaccurate, but they cannot be fair or unfair.

---

[2]Shepard (1982) defines bias as a property of the test or the way the test is used.

Table 15-1   DEFINING CHARACTERISTICS OF BIAS AND FAIRNESS

Bias	*Fairness*
• Refers to *test scores* or to *predictions* based on test scores.	• Refers to *actions* taken or decisions made.
• Is based on *statistical* characteristics of scores or predictions.	• Is a value *judgment* regarding outcomes.
• Is defined *empirically*.	• Is defined in *philosophical* or *political* terms.
• *Can* be scientifically determined.	• *Cannot* be scientifically determined.

Second, bias is a statistical concept, whereas fairness is a judgment based on individual values. The third and fourth defining characteristics of bias and fairness flow directly from this second characteristic. Because bias is a statistical issue, it can be defined empirically, and its existence can be determined scientifically. By examining test data, one can determine the extent to which a test provides biased measures or biased predictions. Fairness, on the other hand, involves a comparison between the decisions that were made and the decisions that "should have" been made. The question of which decisions should have been made depends on the decision maker's values, as well as features of the situation in which decisions were made. Values, in turn, reflect philosophical and political considerations rather than empirical ones. As a result, fairness cannot be determined by scientific methods. Scientific methods can be used to reflect precisely what was done, but they cannot determine what should have been done.

Because bias and fairness are defined in different terms, it follows that a biased test will not necessarily lead to unfair decisions and that decisions based on unbiased tests are not necessarily fair. For example, an unbiased test of upper-body strength could be used to select firefighters. Since such a test would systematically screen out women applicants, many people would regard this outcome as unfair. The same test could be used to select among applicants to dental school, since dentists must occasionally exert physical force. However, in this case, the use of a test that effectively screened out women would be regarded as unfair by almost everyone. On the other hand, it may be regarded as fair to increase the number of minorities hired in a job that they have traditionally been denied. In this case, a biased test might achieve this end more readily than an unbiased one.

Types of Test Bias

As noted in Chapters 8 and 9, tests can be used for two general purposes: to measure a particular characteristic or attribute and to predict scores on some criterion or outcome measure. The major types of test bias parallel these two major uses. Thus, it is useful to distinguish between bias in measurement and bias in prediction.

Bias in measurement occurs when the test makes systematic errors in measuring a specific characteristic or attribute. For example, several psychologists claim that IQ tests may be valid for middle-class whites but that they are not reliable or valid for blacks or other minorities (Joseph, 1977; Williams, 1974). Evidence indicates that employment interviews provide biased measures of the applicants' characteristics; they are, for example, typically biased in favor of attractive applicants (Arvey, 1979).

Bias in prediction, on the other hand, occurs when the test makes systematic errors in predicting some criterion or outcome. It is often argued that tests that are used in academic admissions and in personnel selection underpredict the performance of minority applicants and that the tests therefore have an adverse impact on minority admissions and hiring. In other cases, tests might be useful predictors with one group (e.g., males) but might be markedly less accurate when used to predict the performance of some other group.

Detecting Bias in Measurement

At one time, it appeared that test bias could be assessed by obtaining expert judgments (see our Critical Discussion entitled "Are Judgments of Item Bias Useful?" later in this chapter). There is now consensus that it is virtually impossible to assess the degree to which an item is biased simply by examining its content. Judgmental methods seem to work only when test items contain highly specialized knowledge that is available to some examinees but not to others. For example, an intelligence test that contained nothing but items dealing with terms used in musical notation would probably be biased in favor of music students. For all practical purposes, though, psychological tests are virtually never so transparent in their biases that experts can accurately judge or predict test bias or test item bias. Therefore, methods more sophisticated than those based on armchair judgments are necessary to detect bias.[3]

The methods used in investigating construct validity may be adapted to determine whether a test measures the same thing or whether it measures substantially different things for different groups in the population. For example, suppose that you believed that a scale labeled a test of general intelligence provided a good measure of cognitive ability for whites, but when it was used with minorities, simply measured familiarity with white middle-class culture. To test this hypothesis, you might identify several variables known to be related to general intelligence. Examples include grades in school and performance on problem-solving tasks. You might also identify several variables that reflect familiarity with white middle-class culture. Examples include the number of years in suburban versus inner-city schools and the ability to correctly identify terms and figures uniquely identified with white middle-class culture. If the test measures substantially different things for whites and minorities, you would expect systematic differences in the relationships between test scores and known correlates of intelligence and cultural familiarity. That is, if the test really did measure different things for whites and minorities, you might find correlations similar to those shown in Table 15-2.

---

[3]A variety of methods of detecting bias is discussed in a handbook edited by Berk (1982). See also our Critical Discussion in Chapter 10, "Using Item Response Theory to Detect Test Bias."

Table 15-2   HYPOTHETICAL RESULTS SUPPORTING THE EXISTENCE OF BIAS IN MEASUREMENT

	Correlations with test scores	
Known correlates of intelligence	*White sample*	*Minority sample*
School grades	.48	.03
Problem-solving scores	.39	.10
Known correlates of familiarity with white, middle-class culture		
Number of years in suburban schools	.04	.44
Accuracy in identifying terms and figures unique to this culture	.20	.59

This method of assessing bias in measurement involves examining external correlates of test performance. It would also be possible to test the hypothesis that the test measures substantially different things in different groups by examining internal evidence: the scores on the test itself. One indicator of bias in measurement would be the presence of a group $\times$ item interaction in the difficulty of test items. A group $\times$ item interaction occurs when the relative difficulty of test items varies across groups. Table 15-3 illustrates a short test for which a group $\times$ item interaction might be expected. The interaction described in the table can be more clearly described by graphing the results from the white and minority samples. Figure 15-1 shows, in graphic terms, the group $\times$ item interactions. As can be seen from the figure, the item that is easiest for white examinees (Jane Austen) is most difficult for minorities, whereas the item that is easiest for minorities (Amiri Baraka) is most difficult for whites. It appears here that the test measures exposure to classic literature for whites but measures exposure to modern black literature for minorities. If the test measured the same thing for both groups, items that were relatively difficult for whites would also be relatively difficult for minorities.

In Chapter 10, we noted that item response theory provides a powerful set of tools for examining the hypothesis that test items have different meanings or different implications for particular groups in the population. The group $\times$ item interaction method depicted in Figure 15-1 examines differential patterns of performance across

Table 15-3   AN EXAMPLE OF GROUP $\times$ ITEM INTERACTION

Question	Percent correct	
Identify one work by each of the following authors:	*White sample*	*Minority sample*
Jane Austen	.50	.20
Peter Straub	.42	.43
Amiri Baraka	.15	.47

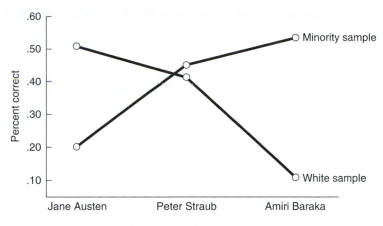

FIGURE 15-1   A Group $\times$ Item Interaction

items. Item response theory-based methods examine differences in the relationships between item responses and the construct being measured within items. These two methods should be thought of as complementary rather than as competing approaches for examining bias in psychological tests.

Evidence Regarding Bias in Measurement

Research on differential validity most clearly addresses the question of whether tests measure different things for different groups, in that it deals with the relationship between test scores and other variables of interest. At one time, the hypothesis that ability tests were differentially valid for predicting criteria such as grades in school, performance on the job, or success in training was widely accepted (Arvey, 1979; Guion, 1965a). The basis for this belief was the fact that many ability tests showed significant correlations with relevant criteria when used with whites but showed nonsignificant validity coefficients when used with minorities. Although some researchers have maintained that differential validity occurs in specific settings (Katzell & Dyer, 1977; Schmitt, Mellon, & Bylenga, 1978), the consensus of most testing specialists is that differential validity is not a widespread phenomenon (Cleary, Humphreys, Kendrick, & Wesman, 1975; Hartigan & Wigdor, 1989; Linn, 1982).

It appears that many instances of differential validity are in fact the result of inappropriate comparisons. Tests of the significance of a correlation coefficient depend largely on the sample size. Because samples of minority examinees are, by definition, likely to be much smaller than samples of white examinees, the same correlation coefficient will often be deemed significant in the large white sample but not significant in the smaller minority sample (V. Boehm, 1977; Hunter, Schmidt, & Hunter, 1979; Schmidt, Berner, & Hunter, 1973). When differences in sample size are taken into account, one rarely finds convincing evidence that ability tests provide substantially better predictions of relevant criteria for some racial or ethnic groups than for others.

Examination of research evidence dealing with group differences in the reliability or the validity of cognitive ability tests provides little support for the hypothesis that bias in measurement is widespread (Cleary et al., 1975; Jensen, 1980). Research using more sophisticated methods of analysis, including analytic methods of comparing factor structures and applications of the item response theory, also suggests that bias in measurement is somewhat rare (Dragow & Kanfer, 1985; Hulin, Dragow, & Parsons, 1983; see Wainer & Braun, 1988, for discussions of methods of detecting bias), although it is sometimes reported (Thissen, Steinberg, & Gerrard, 1986). It is possible, however, that these tests are biased in the predictions that they make.

Detecting Bias in Prediction

Regardless of whether a test provides a biased or an unbiased measure of examinees' cognitive ability, there is a good possibility that the test will provide biased predictions. For example, an academic ability test might routinely overestimate the future academic performance of males and underestimate that of females. In this case, females will be at a disadvantage if the test is used to make academic selection or placement decisions. It is also possible that a test will be highly accurate in predicting the performance of whites, but at the same time it will show relatively little accuracy in predicting the performance of minorities, even though the test does not systematically overpredict or underpredict performance levels for either group. In this case, a high-scoring member of a minority group will be at a considerable disadvantage, since his or her performance on the test will not necessarily lead to a prediction of high performance on the criterion, whereas the high-scoring white applicant will be predicted to perform at a high level.

The typical method of predicting a person's score on the criterion on the basis of his or her score on a test is to use a regression equation (see Chapter 5). That is, the predicted criterion score $(\hat{Y})$ is given by the equation:

$$\hat{Y} = a + bx \qquad\qquad [15\text{-}1]$$

where

$\hat{Y}$ = predicated performance
x = test score
a = the intercept
b = the slope of the regression line[4]

Bias in prediction exists when the regression equations used to predict a relevant criterion in two or more separate groups differ in terms of their intercepts, their slopes, or their standard errors of estimate.

---

[4]The formulas for the regression equation are $\hat{Y} = a + bx$, where $a = \overline{Y} - b\overline{X}$ and $b = r_{xy} \times (\sigma_y/\sigma_x)$.

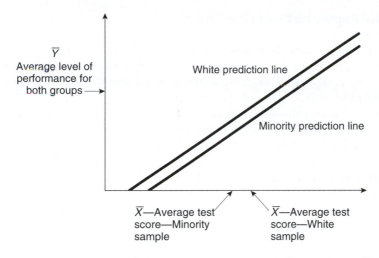

FIGURE 15-2   A Biased Prediction: Groups Show Equal $\overline{Y}$, but Different $\overline{X}$

Regression equations are affected by a number of parameters, most notably the test mean $(\overline{X})$, the mean on the criterion $(\overline{Y})$, the standard deviations of X and Y, and the correlation between X and Y. Bartlett and O'Leary (1969) have illustrated the effects of differences in each of these parameters or predictions. For example, consider the situation depicted in Figure 15-2, where whites and minorities show equal levels of criterion performance $(\overline{Y})$, equal levels of variability in test scores and in performance $(\sigma_x$ and $\sigma_y)$, and equal levels of test validity (r_{xy}). However, the mean test score among whites is higher than the mean test score for minorities. In this situation, the intercepts of the white and minority regression equations differ, and the test will yield biased predictions. Whites and minorities who earn the same test score will receive different predictions regarding their performance on the criterion.

The situation depicted in the figure is of broad concern, since many groups in the population are known to differ in terms of their average test scores. In particular, average scores on most cognitive ability tests are higher for middle-class whites than for minorities or for members of lower socioeconomic classes. Unless these differences in test scores reflect systematic (and comparable) differences in criterion performance, ability tests will yield biased predictions. Bias in prediction could arise as a result of a number of factors: differences in test scores, differences in criterion performance, differences in the variability of test scores or performance, or differences in test validity. In any case, bias in prediction could affect the decisions made about individuals. Since systematic differences are known to exist in the average scores received by whites and minorities on most cognitive ability tests, the possibility of bias in prediction must be seriously examined.

Evidence Regarding Bias in Prediction

The methods for detecting bias in prediction are fairly straightforward: Simply compute a separate regression equation for predicting criterion scores in each group, and compare the equations.[5] We can therefore move directly to an examination of the empirical evidence regarding bias in prediction.

First, it is clear that the question of whether differential validity exists is relevant to understanding both bias in measurement and bias in prediction. If the correlation between test scores and criterion measures differs across groups, it is almost certain that the slope of the regression line will also differ. Evidence reviewed earlier in this book suggests that differential validity is not a widespread phenomenon. It appears, likely, therefore, that differences in slopes and intercepts, when they occur at all, will reflect differences in the means and standard deviations of both tests and criterion measures, rather than reflecting differences in test validity. Evidence indicates that these parameters vary across groups and that some degree of bias in prediction therefore may be present (Jensen, 1980).

In general, the slopes of regression equations computed separately for males and females or for whites and minorities appear to be similar (Arvey, 1979; Jensen, 1980). In other words, within each group, individuals with high test scores are likely to receive high scores on a number of relevant criteria, and the difference in performance between persons with high test scores and persons with low test scores is roughly equivalent across groups. Bias in standard errors also is relatively infrequent, although in some cases, groups who tend to perform most poorly also will have the smallest standard errors. However, there is evidence of a fairly consistent difference in the intercepts of regression equations computed separately for whites and minorities (Cleary, Humphreys, Kendrick, & Wesman, 1975; Hartigan & Wigdor, 1989; Gael, Grant, & Richie, 1975; Linn, 1982). In particular, regression equations computed separately for whites and minorities tend to have similar slopes, but different intercepts, with the white intercept typically higher than the minority intercept. This pattern of results is illustrated in Figure 15-3.

As illustrated by the figure, if separate regression equations are used for whites and minorities, a lower criterion score will always be predicted for a minority group member than for a member of the white sample who has received the same test score. On the other hand, if the regression equation computed for the total sample is used for everybody, whites and minorities who receive the same test score will receive the same predicted criterion score.

Throughout the 1960s and 1970s, it was believed widely that ability tests underpredicted the performance of minorities. This view is no longer accepted. Linn (1982) notes that

> whether the criterion to be predicted is freshman GPA in college, first-year grades in law school, outcomes of job training, or job performance measures,

---

[5]There are statistical tests for determining whether differences between regression equations are significant.

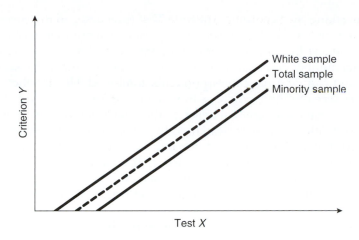

Criterion Y

White sample
Total sample
Minority sample

Test X

FIGURE 15-3 Prediction Equations That Differ in Intercept but Not in Slope

carefully chosen ability tests have not been found to underpredict the actual performance of minority group persons. (p. 384)

In fact, the reverse may be true. If the minority group intercept is lower than the intercept for whites, as is often the case, the use of the total sample's regression equation to predict criterion performance will tend to overpredict the performance of minority group members. This overprediction bias is likely to be small (Cleary et al., 1975). Nevertheless, attempts to reduce intercept bias may actually be unfavorable to minorities. The use of separate regression equations is likely to result in the selection of fewer rather than more minorities if similar selection standards are enforced in each group (Jensen, 1980; Linn, 1982).

Difficulties in Research on Bias and Fairness

Research on bias and fairness in testing is difficult for a number of reasons. First, there is no clear consensus about the precise meaning of terms such as *unbiased* or *fair*, particularly when the debate over bias and fairness goes outside the scientific community. One recurring problem in psychological research is that it deals with concepts and terms that are somewhat familiar to the general public. Thus, terms like *bias, fairness, intelligence,* and so forth, have excess meaning; they convey things to the general public that are not part of their scientific definition. As a result, widespread agreement about many of the topics addressed in this section is virtually impossible because the critical terms in the debate over bias and fairness in ability testing mean different things to different people.

Research on bias and fairness is not only difficult to communicate to the general public but is also quite difficult to do. One surprising difficulty in doing research on the effects of race and gender on test scores arises because the demographic characteristics of test takers are frequently unknown. For example, Wainer (1988) noted that many students taking the Scholastic Aptitude Test (precursor to the current Scholastic Assessment Tests, or SAT) did not respond to questions about their race or ethnic identity. The data suggest that the number of students who did not respond is nearly as large as the total number of responses from black, Asian American, Mexican American, Puerto Rican, and Native American respondents combined. He also shows that failure to identify one's race or ethnic origins is more common in some groups than in others and that this could have a substantial effect on the interpretation of test results.

Another difficulty in doing research on bias and fairness is the sensitivity of the questions raised. Research on race and gender, particularly as they may affect scores on cognitive ability tests, is so sensitive a topic that many researchers seem to have concluded that we should not continue to do research in this area. There are many reasons for this conclusion. First is the possibility that research will be misinterpreted or that research findings will somehow exacerbate the already disadvantaged status of women and minorities. Second, researchers who examine race or gender differences and publicly discuss their results are often subject to harassment and abuse (Gordon, 1988). For example, Scarr (1988) describes the experiences of Arthur Jensen, a psychologist who suggested that intelligence tests were not biased and that racial differences in test scores might be partially genetic in origin, noting that Jensen "was harassed, threatened, and driven into virtual protective custody by colleagues, students, and other radicals who resented his hypothesis" (p. 57).

Scarr (1988) has noted that we probably do more harm than good by trying to avoid sensitive issues, such as race and gender, in psychological research. It is patronizing for investigators (almost always white and usually male) to decide a priori that some research questions about minorities or females are best left unexplored; among other things, this decision makes it difficult to investigate the strengths of underrepresented groups and their ways of functioning well. Scarr does, however, suggest that the way in which research questions are phrased and conceptualized must take into account the sensitive nature of the questions. For example, she suggests that research questions framed in terms of what is wrong with, what is deficient in, or what is in need of change for women and minorities are at best offensive and, at worst, inflammatory.

The bottom line in considering research on race- and gender-related variables may be its value orientation. If the middle-class mainstream is held up as an ideal and a point of comparison, research on race and gender can easily fall into the "what is wrong with these people" frame of mind. On the other hand, research on how and why members of different groups in the population perform important tasks and roles in society is both valuable and important, especially if this research avoids the trap of labeling group differences in terms of the failure of one group to meet another group's standards.

Possible Sources of Bias. There are many possible explanations for why groups might receive systematically different scores on tests or assessments. The first possibility is that there are real mean differences (or real differences in variability) in the attribute being measured. The other general explanation is that differences are a function of the test, not of the attribute being measured.

One obvious possibility is that the content of the test is relevant or familiar to some groups and novel or irrelevant to others; that is, the test might be culturally biased in favor of some groups. In a section that follows, we will examine in some detail the research on cultural bias and on attempts to remove this factor from test scores. As we will show, research does not support this explanation for group differences in test scores. However, blatant cultural bias is not the only possible explanation for group differences in test scores. For example, it is sometimes argued that test bias results if minority groups are not appropriately represented in test development and standardization samples. For example, test items might be selected that tend to favor those in the test development sample, and if this sample does not contain an adequate number of minority group members, test items that favor whites and work against minorities might tend to be selected. However, careful empirical tests of this hypothesis (e.g., Fan, Willson, & Kapes, 1996; Hickman & Reynolds, 1986–1987) have provided little support. Similar tests seem to be developed when the proportion of minorities is large or small in the development sample.

As we will note later in this chapter, the method of presenting a test may be another potential source of bias. It is possible that written tests might show patterns of performance that are different from those of similar tests presented by an individual examiner or via videotape. It is also possible that test bias might result from an interaction between the test administrator and the examinee (e.g., when the individual administering the test comes from a cultural or ethnic group different from that of the individual taking the test). We touched on some of these issues in Chapter 3 and will examine others in more depth in the remaining sections of this chapter.

Are There Remedies for Test Bias? As we noted in Chapter 3, whenever two groups receive systematically different scores on a test that is used to make important decisions, important societal consequences can follow. For example, blacks receive lower scores than whites on some tests used for admission to medical schools (Gordon, 1988). If the test results dictate decisions, the result will be proportionately fewer black doctors. Females receive lower scores on tests of mathematical ability than males. If test scores are used to determine who receives scholarships, fewer females will receive them. Thus, there is considerable interest in methods of reducing test bias.

One possible solution is to change the content of the test to reduce the influence of potentially irrelevant cultural factors on test scores. The next section of this chapter reviews research in this area and shows that this strategy is not effective in reducing group differences in test scores. A more direct route to reducing group differences is in the test development stage. That is, you might develop tests with the specific objective of reducing group differences in test scores. This is the strategy implicit in the Golden Rule agreement.

The Golden Rule refers to a court settlement between the Golden Rule Insurance Company and the Educational Testing Service (ETS) regarding tests developed for insurance licensing exams. According to this settlement, ETS agrees to take steps in test development to reduce the differences in the mean scores received by black and white examinees. Specifically, ETS agrees to give priority in item selection to those test items for which the passing rates of blacks and whites are similar (Type 1 items) and to use items in which the white passing rates are substantially higher only if the available pool of Type 1 items is exhausted. Proponents of this type of solution note that the same thing is sometimes done to reduce sex bias in ability tests.

Although it may look appealing, the strategy implied by the Golden Rule agreement has been criticized (Committee on Psychological Tests and Assessments, 1988). First, this strategy is not necessarily effective. As the report just cited notes, a test developed according to this procedure may have exactly the same impact as a test developed in a standard fashion. Although this method of test development will reduce the size of the difference between scores received by whites and blacks, it does not necessarily change the rank ordering of individuals taking the test. Second, and more important, this procedure is likely to reduce the reliability and validity of the test. Using this procedure, the contribution of items to the technical adequacy of the test is no longer the primary criterion for selecting items. Rather, items will be selected primarily on the similarity of scores received by different groups. The Golden Rule procedure may reduce the reliability, validity, and utility of the test without increasing minority examinees' chances to compete effectively for jobs, academic admissions, and so forth.

There is clear agreement in the scientific community that it is possible to at least partially separate the effects of real differences in the attributes measured by tests from the effects of irrelevant biases in the analysis of test items (a variety of methods for detecting bias are reviewed in Berk, 1982; Hulin et al., 1983; Ironson & Subkoviak, 1979). There is also clear agreement that differences in test scores are not due solely to irrelevant test bias (L. S. Gottfredson, 1986, 1988; Jensen, 1980; C. R. Reynolds & Brown, 1984). Rather, group differences in scores on cognitive ability tests reflect real differences in cognitive ability. There is considerable controversy over the meaning, causes, and modifiability of these differences, but there is little doubt that some of the differences in test scores reflect real differences in ability. One implication of this view is that changing tests will not make the problem of test bias go away.

Cascio, Outtz, Zedeck, and Goldstein (1991) suggest that rather than ranking individuals strictly in terms of their test scores, people with similar scores might be grouped together in a test score band. The idea here is that if two people apply for a job or for admission to college and they have very similar test scores, you should not automatically favor the individual who did the best on the test. If test scores are so similar that the differences between two examinees might represent nothing more than measurement error (see Chapter 7 for a discussion of the standard error of measurement), it probably makes sense to consider things other than their test scores when deciding between them. For example, if one job applicant receives a score of 88 on a test and another has a score of 87 but also has a variety of characteristics that are valuable to the organization (e.g., additional skills or experience, contributions to workforce diversity), it might make sense to prefer the person with a score of 87. Banding procedures have come under heavy criticism (Schmidt, 1991), but as Murphy and Myors (1995) note, it is common in a number of settings to group similar scores together and to treat everyone whose score falls within a specific range as equivalent (e.g., everyone who gets an average of 90 to 100 receives an A in the course).

A second strategy for reducing the effects of test bias is to employ multiple methods of assessment. Test bias is most likely to be a societal problem when a single test score determines each person's fate. The use of a broad array of assessment devices that measures many important attributes may provide the ultimate safeguard against the possibility that irrelevant biases in test scores will unfairly handicap individuals taking the test. Although the use of multiple tests or assessment devices can help to reduce the impact of ability tests on workforce diversity, it is clear that this strategy will rarely eliminate group differences (Hattrup, Rock, & Scalia, 1997; Schmitt, Rogers, Chan, Sheppard, & Jennings, 1997). If group differences are large on one test (e.g., a cognitive ability test), they must be at least as large and in the opposite direction on a second test in order to completely eliminate the effects of test bias. This situation rarely occurs.

Yet another suggestion for reducing test bias has been to change the testing method (e.g., change from written tests to individually administered oral tests). However, as Schmitt, Clause, and Pulakos (1996) note, most studies of this hypothesis tend to confound testing methods with test content. That is, comparison of two different methods of assessment (e.g., paper-and-pencil tests versus work samples) might yield different results because of differences in the way the test is administered and scored, differences in the content of the assessment devices in question, or some combination of the two. In one of the first studies that directly compares differences in methods of test administration, holding test content constant, Chan and Schmitt (1998) obtain some interesting and encouraging results. They developed video-based versus paper-and-pencil versions of a situational judgment test, in which the content of the test was held constant. They showed that group differences were substantially smaller on the video-based version and explained this difference in terms of a number of factors, including differences in reading comprehension and examinees' reactions to the different modes of testing.

CRITICAL DISCUSSION:

Are Judgments of Item Bias Useful?

One method that has been used to determine whether a test or a test item is biased is to assemble a panel of expert judges. If the concern is that items might be biased against a particular group (e.g., females, blacks), the panel will often contain members of that group. Research on these judgments of test or item bias clearly shows that this method is not effective for detecting bias; judgments about the extent to which an item is biased rarely correspond to any of the widely accepted measures of bias (Jensen, 1980; Shepard, 1982). Although panels of judges may not be useful in detecting bias, they may nevertheless serve an important function: They may be critical in ensuring the acceptance of psychological tests by both test users and examinees.

We are not suggesting here that the use of panels of experts to assess test and test item bias is nothing more than window dressing. On the contrary, these panels serve two very real functions. First, they are helpful in screening for items or tests that might be offensive to different segments of the population (Shepard, 1982). Second, they provide some ensurance of due process. That is, the use of panels of experts, particularly panels that include members of minorities or other underrepresented groups, increases the likelihood that the concerns of these groups will be heard and taken into account. Considerable evidence in research on perceptions of justice shows that the use of procedures that are apparently fair and reasonable increases the acceptability of the outcomes of those procedures (Folger & Greenberg, 1985). As Cronbach (1988) points out, a test that is technically excellent but unacceptable to users is worthless as an aid in making practical decisions. Practices such as the review of tests and test items by members of underrepresented groups may increase the acceptability of tests to those groups and to society in general.

CULTURE-REDUCED TESTING

The most common definition of cultural bias refers to "differences in the extent to which the child being tested has had the opportunity to know and become familiar with the specific subject matter or specific processes required by the test item" (Eells et al., 1951, p. 58). For example, it is often assumed that white middle-class children have greater exposure to the cultural activities, such as symphony concerts or reading of classic literature, than do minority children, and that questions such as "What is an oboe?" or "Who wrote *Crime and Punishment*?" will therefore be culturally biased against minorities. Even clearer examples of apparent cultural bias are provided by items in which the "correct" answer may vary from culture to culture. The Wechsler Intelligence Scale for Children–Revised (WISC-R) and the Stanford-Binet include questions such as "What should you do if a younger child hits you?"; in some cultures, the "correct" answer may be different from the answer one would expect from an intelligent, white middle-class child.

Test items that are highly academic in nature are often judged to be culturally biased. The underlying assumption in this assessment is that the school environment is an integral part of the white, middle-class culture. The curriculum planners, teachers, textbook authors, and administrators of school systems are generally white, and the academic environment is assumed to be more foreign to the culture of many minorities—particularly to those living in the inner city—than it is to whites. As a result, items that deal primarily with academic knowledge are likely to be judged culturally biased against minorities. Finally, verbal items are more likely to be regarded as biased than nonverbal items. The rationale here is that verbal items are likely to be presented in standard English, which more closely resembles the everyday language of middle-class whites than that of many minorities, particularly those in lower socioeconomic levels of society.

A composite picture emerges of a test that is likely to show (apparent) cultural bias. A test made up of items that deal with objects or events peculiar to the white, middle-class experience, that are interpreted differently by people from different subcultures, that tap academic as opposed to practical knowledge, or that are primarily verbal in nature may be regarded as culturally biased against minorities. By implication, a test that deals with universal symbols or objects and that is primarily nonverbal rather than verbal is less likely to be judged as culturally biased.

Before describing several tests designed or used to reduce apparent cultural bias, we must first discuss terminology. R. B. Cattell (1940) was among the first to develop what was referred to as a *culture-free* intelligence test. His choice of terms was in many ways unfortunate, since it is difficult to imagine any test in which culture has no effect whatsoever. Learned behavior is, by definition, a function of culture, and it therefore seems pointless to refer to any test as completely culture free. It is somewhat more accurate to describe many tests aimed at eliminating apparent cultural bias as *culture fair*, a term used by Cattell himself in the Culture Fair Intelligence Test. The problem with the term *culture fair* is that there is often disagreement regarding the fairness of specific items for members of different cultures and subcultures, and the test developer may not be the best judge of what is fair. The same argument can be made, of course, in reference to judgments about the degree of cultural bias shown in test items, since these judgments are often subjective rather than data based (Jensen, 1980).

Rather than labeling a test culture free or culture fair, it is more productive to locate the test on a continuum that ranges from heavily *culture loaded* to highly *culture reduced*. A culture-loaded test is one that deals with objects, situations, beliefs, or lore peculiar to one particular culture or subculture. A culture-reduced test is one that deals with objects, information, or symbols that are universal, in the sense that members of any of the cultures or subcultures being tested would have equal familiarity and experience with the content and the demands of the test items. Some characteristics of tests that appear to be culture loaded and culture reduced are presented in Table 15-4.

Intelligence tests vary considerably in their apparent cultural loading. Perhaps the most highly culture-loaded test that purports to measure intelligence is the Black Intelligence Test of Cultural Homogeneity, or the BITCH (Williams, 1972). This test was developed in part to demonstrate the insidious effects of culture loading. The BITCH is basically a vocabulary test that measures knowledge of black inner-city slang and is made up of items similar to the following (the correct answers are starred):[6]

1. Running a game
   a. writing a bad check
   b. looking at something
   c. directing a contest
   d. getting what one wants[*]

Table 15-4   SOME CHARACTERISTICS OF CULTURE-LOADED AND CULTURE-REDUCED TESTS

Culture-loaded	*Culture-reduced*
Paper-and-pencil tests	Performance test
Reading required	Purely pictorial
Written response	Oral response
Speed tests	Power tests
Verbal content	Nonverbal content
Recall of past-learned information	Solving novel problems

Source: Adapted from Jensen, 1980, p. 637.

[6]Reprinted from *Psychology Today*, May 1974, p. 101.

2. Cop an attitude
   a. leave
   b. become angry[*]
   c. sit down
   d. protect the neighborhood

The BITCH, by design, represents an extreme example of culture loading. An examination of this test therefore helps to clarify several of the issues in the debate on culture-loaded tests. First, this test convincingly demonstrates that it is possible to produce sizable differences in test scores by culturally loading the test. Blacks tend to receive considerably higher scores on the BITCH than do whites (Matarazzo & Weins, 1977), and test reviewers have suggested that middle-class whites might gain considerable insight into the debate on culture loading by taking a test such as the BITCH, which is biased in favor of a subculture. Second, it is clear that the type of intentional culture loading employed in the construction of the BITCH is not representative of intelligence tests in general. There are a number of clear differences between standard intelligence tests and this particular culturally loaded test. Taken together, these differences suggest that the BITCH is not merely a mirror image of tests like the Wechsler Adult Intelligence Scale (WAIS) or the SAT and that whatever cultural bias operates in the latter tests does so in a much more subtle manner than in an obviously culture-loaded test such as the BITCH.

The clearest difference between the BITCH and standard intelligence tests lies in the type of items included in the different tests. The BITCH is made up exclusively of items measuring knowledge of a vocabulary employed in a specific subculture, and it does not contain any items that call for the active processing of information (e.g., problem-solving tasks). Most tests of general mental ability are made up of items that tap a variety of cognitive functions, both those involving information retrieval (e.g., vocabulary tests) and those involving active information processing. Apparently, little or no evidence shows that the BITCH provides a valid measure of the intelligence of blacks or whites (Cronbach, 1978; Jensen, 1980; Matarazzo & Weins, 1977).

The conclusion we reach when examining the BITCH is that the blatant cultural bias built into this particular test probably does not exist in standard intelligence tests. It is possible, however, that subtler forms of culture loading exist in many of the widely used intelligence tests, and it is this possibility that has contributed to widespread interest in developing culture-reduced tests of intelligence.

Performance Tests and Quantitative Tests

Although rarely developed for the specific purpose of culture-reduced testing, performance scales and quantitative subtests are standard features of many intelligence tests. For example, the Stanford-Binet includes a variety of nonverbal and performance subtests. Various editions of the WAIS, the WISC, and the Wechsler Preschool and Primary Scale of Intelligence (WPPSI) all contain performance scales as well as verbal scales. Both the Graduate Record Examinations (GRE) and the SAT contain quantitative (mathematical) as well as verbal sections, and the Graduate Record Examinations (GRE) also includes an analytic section. Although none of these performance or quantitative tests necessarily meets all the requirements suggested by various authors for achieving a truly culture-reduced test, these tests all seem to be closer to the culturally reduced than to the culturally loaded end of the continuum.

Many proponents of culture-reduced tests suggest that differences in the test scores obtained by minority and white examinees are due largely to the fact that IQ tests are culturally loaded in favor of whites. This position implies that differences between minority and white test score means should be smaller on performance and quantitative tests, which appear to be culture reduced, than on verbal tests, which appear to be culture loaded. This hypothesis has been extensively researched but to date has received little empirical support.

Several large-scale studies clearly indicate that the difference between white and minority test score means is at least as large for nonverbal tests of intelligence (performance tests as well as quantitative tests) as it is for verbal tests of intelligence. For example, the Coleman report, *Equality of Educational Opportunity* (Coleman et al., 1966), provides test data from over 600,000 schoolchildren in over 4,000 schools. This report shows that the differences between white and black mean IQs are comparable for verbal and nonverbal IQ tests and that these differences are in fact generally a bit larger for nonverbal than for verbal tests. McGurk's (1975) review of 25 studies that compare verbal and performance test scores (mostly WISC, WAIS, or Wechsler-Bellevue scores) of whites and blacks reached a similar conclusion: Black-white differences in performance IQs are generally equal to or larger than differences in verbal IQs.

In response to the Association of Black Psychologists' call for a moratorium on intelligence testing, the Scientific Affairs Board of the American Psychological Association appointed a group of experts to investigate the issue of test bias. Their report included the conclusion that minority-white score differences on nonverbal tests were comparable to differences in scores on verbal intelligence tests and that these differences were "quite general and not narrowly restricted to specific skills involving standard English" (Cleary et al., 1975, p. 16). The fact that minority-white test score differences are equally large for verbal and nonverbal intelligence tests suggests that the cultural-bias hypothesis in its simplest form is incorrect. There can be little doubt that cultural and subcultural differences affect all behavior, including test behavior, and it seems plausible that some tests may be unfairly easier for some people than for others. However, it appears that test score differences are not the result of the predominantly verbal nature of IQ tests, nor are they a reflection of knowledge or understanding of a small set of culturally specific facts. Hence, although cultural bias probably does exist, it is not a simple phenomenon that lends itself to a simple solution.

Raven's Progressive Matrices

Raven's Progressive Matrices, probably the most widely cited culture-reduced tests, have had a long and distinguished history. Factor analyses carried out in Spearman's laboratory in the 1930s suggested that tests made up of simple pictorial analogies showed high correlations with a number of other intelligence tests and, more important, showed high loadings on Spearman's *g*.

Raven's Progressive Matrices (available in both paper and computer-administered forms) are made up of a series of multiple-choice items, all of which follow the same basic principle. Each item represents a perceptual analogy in the form of a matrix. Some valid relationship connects items in each row in the matrix, and some valid relationship connects items in each column of the matrix. Each matrix is presented in such a way that a piece of the matrix, located in the lower-right corner, is missing. The subject must choose from among six or eight alternatives the piece that best completes each matrix. An example of a Progressive Matrix item is presented in Figure 15-4.

There are three forms of Raven's Progressive Matrices. The most widely used form, the Standard Progressive Matrices, consists of 60 matrices grouped into 5 sets. Each of the 5 sets involves 12 matrices whose solutions involve similar principles but vary in difficulty. The principles involved in solving the 5 sets of matrices include perceptual discrimination, rotation, and permutations of patterns. The first few items in each set are comparatively easy, but the latter matrices may involve very subtle and complex relationships.

The Standard Progressive Matrices are appropriate both for children above 5 years of age and adults; because of the low floor and fairly high ceiling of this test, the Standard Matrices are also appropriate for most ability levels. For younger children (ages 4 to 10), and for somewhat older children and adults who show signs of retardation, the Coloured Progressive Matrices seem to be more appropriate. This test consists of three sets of 12 matrices that employ color and are considerably less difficult than those that make up the Standard Progressive Matrices.

Finally, the Advanced Progressive Matrices are appropriate for intellectually advanced subjects who find the Standard Matrices too easy. The Advanced Matrices are made up of 3 sets of 12 matrices, many of which involve extremely subtle principles in

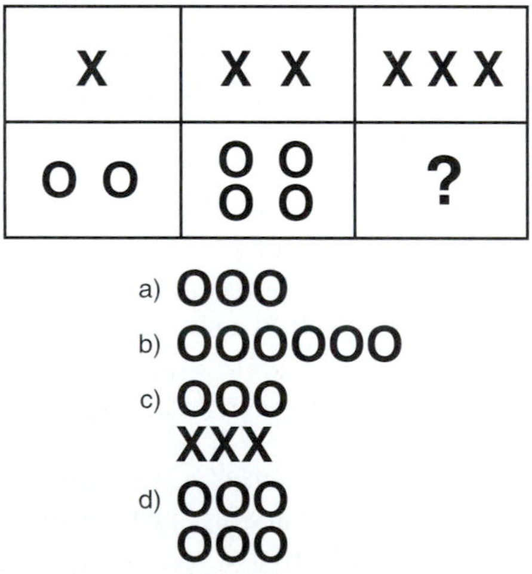

FIGURE 15-4 Type of Item Included in Raven's Progressive Matrices

their solutions. The test effectively discriminates among those who receive extremely high scores on the Standard Progressive Matrices.

Evaluation of Raven's Progressive Matrices. One of the principal attractions of this series of tests is its combination of factorial purity, together with its minimal culture loading. A number of factor analyses of Raven's Progressive Matrices suggest that the only variable that is reliably measured by the test is Spearman's g (Winfred & Woehr, 1993); little evidence suggests that spatial visualization or perceptual abilities significantly affect test scores. The test appears to measure abstract reasoning ability independently of one's factual knowledge or prior experience. Thus, the test appears to be unique in following Spearman's principles for measuring g (induction of relations, indifference of indicators), while at the same time meeting many of the desired characteristics of a culture-reduced test (simple instructions, abstract non-verbal item content, independence from previously learned material).

Scores on the Progressive Matrices are typically reliable (reliabilities generally range from .70 to .90) and show evidence of both construct- and criterion-related validity. Progressive Matrices scores generally show correlations of between .50 and .75 with other intelligence tests, and correlations closer to .80 are sometimes reported (Burke, 1972). Progressive Matrices scores are also correlated with a variety of measures of academic success, although the validities tend to be lower than those typically found with more standard intelligence tests. Finally, the Progressive Matrices show some evidence of content validity.

At first examination, the Progressive Matrices appear to violate our suggestion in Chapter 2 that an intelligence test should comprise a variety of item types. Although all the items on each of these tests are in matrix format, it seems clear that the test in fact samples a wide variety of problem types by varying the principles that govern each matrix. Thus, a person must successfully solve a considerable variety of logical inference problems in order to obtain a high score on the test. The Progressive Matrices provide an excellent demonstration of the plausibility of measuring Spearman's g with a culture-reduced test.

Comparisons of the scores of whites and minorities on Raven's Progressive Matrices provide further evidence that the cultural bias hypothesis, in its simplest form, is incorrect. The Progressive Matrices are clearly culture-reduced tests, yet comparisons between test scores of whites and minorities show that the average score of white examinees is consistently higher than the mean score obtained by minorities. Furthermore, the difference between white and minority test score means is typically as large for the Progressive Matrices as for standard (culture-loaded) intelligence tests (Jensen, 1974; Veroff, McClelland, & Marquis, 1971).

Because of their culturally-reduced content, Raven's Progressive Matrices tests are very useful in cross-cultural studies. For example, Daley, Whaley, Sigman, Espinso, and Neumann (2003) used the Progressive Matrices to study the Flynn effect (discussed later in this chapter) in rural Kenya. The Flynn effect refers to widely observed increases in intelligence test scores over time, and the documentation of this same effect over a 14-year period in rural Africa provides a test of some of the most widely cited explanations for this rise (e.g., that test scores are rising because of increased exposure to news and information or because of increasing computer use). This test is also useful in neuropsychological diagnosis (Hiscock, Inch, & Gleason, 2002), in large part because of the fact that it measures abstract reasoning and fluid intelligence without the confounding influence of content knowledge.

Adaptive Behavior Inventories

Although most general intelligence tests sample a broad array of intellectually challenging problems, considerable justification supports the complaint that the domain sampled by these tests is nevertheless too narrow to provide an adequate measure of how well a person can function in society. In most day-to-day situations, it might be very difficult to detect any difference between the behavior of someone with an IQ of 93 and that of another person with an IQ of 108. A low IQ score may suggest poor performance in a variety of scholastic or intellectual endeavors, but it does not necessarily indicate an inability to cope with the normal demands of day-to-day life. Some people with high IQs function poorly in society, and many people with low IQs function well.

Adaptive behavior inventories represent an attempt to develop broad measures of a person's effectiveness in coping with the normal demands of day-to-day life. These inventories typically represent standardized interviews with persons having frequent contact with the subject (e.g., parents, teachers, siblings) and are aimed at assessing the effectiveness of the subject's reactions to the natural or social demands of his or her environment. These inventories are particularly useful in the diagnosis of mental retardation (Kaufman, 1979). The use of IQ scores as the sole criterion for classifying children as mentally retarded is clearly inappropriate, particularly in the case of minority children. Some children with low IQ scores have difficulties with every phase of their lives, whereas others might show deficits in school settings only. Inventories such as the American Association for Mental Deficiency's Adaptive Behavior Scale (Lambert, Windmiller, Cole, & Figueroa, 1975) help to provide a broader base for diagnosis by including a great deal of information about the subject's social competence. The Adaptive Behavior Assessment System (ABAS–2nd Edition) is also popular for evaluating difficulties in adapting to day-to-day life.

Mercer (1973, 1979) has been concerned with the inappropriate labeling of the mentally retarded, particularly among minorities, on the basis of IQ tests and has developed several adaptive behavior inventories to provide more complete assessments of competence in dealing with one's environment. For example, the inventory described in Mercer (1973) consisted mainly of a household interview, usually with a parent, covering a variety of items from the Vineland Social Maturity Scale (Doll, 1965) and the Gesell Developmental Scales (Gesell, 1948a, 1948b, 1956), together with several original items. Examples of items included in the Mercer inventory are presented in Table 15-5.

As Table 15-5 illustrates, the domain sampled in this test is much broader and less academic than the domain sampled by the Stanford-Binet or the WISC. This type of adaptive behavior inventory is not a substitute for a standard intelligence test, but it

Table 15-5   SAMPLE ITEMS FROM MERCER (1973) INVENTORY

Age in months

7–9	Does _____	recognize a stranger?
13–15	Does _____	walk when only one hand is held?
22–24	Does _____	usually unwrap or peel candy, gum, bananas before eating them?
36–47	Does _____	button clothing without help?
49–59	Can _____	turn pages one at a time?

Age in years

7	Does _____	tie shoelaces?
8–9	Does _____	count by two to twenty?
10–11	Does _____	look up telephone numbers and make telephone calls?
14–15	Does _____	usually give vent to rage by words rather than physical violence or crying?
16–49	Does _____	ever travel to nearby towns alone?

represents an invaluable supplement to an intelligence-testing program. Standard intelligence tests provide psychometrically refined measures of behavior in response to a particular class of problems that involve reasoning, comprehension, or a broad base of factual knowledge. Adaptive behavior inventories provide a less-refined but broader sample of behavior in response to the types of problems encountered in everyday life.

The System of Multicultural Pluralistic Assessment. The culmination of Mercer's research on the assessment of children from a variety of subcultures (i.e., black, Hispanic, Anglo) was the System of Multicultural Pluralistic Assessment (SOMPA) (Mercer & Lewis, 1978). The SOMPA represents an assessment package appropriate for children between the ages of 5 and 11 that includes (1) the WISC-R, (2) interviews with parents, (3) individual interviews with the subject, (4) a medical history, (5) sensorimotor and perceptual testing, and (6) the Adaptive Behavior Inventory for Children, which measures adaptive behavior in family and community settings. Socioeconomic background information may be entered into regression equations to transform WISC-R IQ scores into a standard score referred to as an *estimated learning potential (ELP)*. The ELP indicates the level of test performance in comparison with children of similar racial and socioeconomic background; it is not designed to predict performance in regular public school but to estimate the extent to which a child might benefit from programs that are appropriate for or tailored to the child's cultural background.

Although some questions remain about the value of ELP scores (Brooks & Hosic, 1984; Kaufman, 1979; R. L. Taylor & Richards, 1990), the SOMPA provides a wealth of data that may be useful for corroborating or modifying the interpretation of scores on standard intelligence tests (Matthew, Golin, Moore, & Baker, 1992). These data may be particularly critical for classifying children whose academic deficit is noticeable but not debilitating. Inappropriately labeling a child retarded could have serious social and emotional consequences (Mercer, 1973). Scores on intelligence tests provide hypotheses regarding the effectiveness with which a child deals with both the academic and the nonacademic demands of daily life. A broad-based assessment package such as the

SOMPA provides a means to test these hypotheses more thoroughly before diagnosing and labeling the child. Perhaps because of its breadth and complexity, SOMPA has never reached a wide audience, but the concepts behind SOMPA have captured the attention of researchers in the area of multicultural assessment.

CRITICAL DISCUSSION:

Intelligence and Adaptive Behavior

The problem of what is or is not intelligent behavior has been the focus of a great deal of debate and disagreement in psychology. One way of defining intelligent behavior is to say that it is the set of behaviors that allows one to adapt to one's environment. This definition has been adopted by many psychologists, ranging from those critical of standard intelligence tests (Mercer, 1973; Mercer & Lewis, 1978) to information-processing theorists (Sternberg, 1985). Similar definitions are implicit in several models of skill acquisition (Ackerman, 1987) and performance (Murphy, 1989).

Although defining intelligence in terms of adaptation to one's environment is intuitively appealing, this definition has serious problems. In particular, the phrase "adapting to one's environment" can be hopelessly ambiguous. The reason for the ambiguity is that environment can be defined at several different levels, and different levels of the environment might imply different types of intelligence (Gardner, 1983). For example, a child's environment might be defined in terms of his or her family, neighborhood, playmates, classes, and so forth. At any given time, a person may occupy several different environments, and behavior that is adaptive in one environment may not be adaptive in another.

One potential solution to the problem of defining intelligent behavior in terms of multiple environments is to recognize that environments differ greatly in their salience or importance. Thus, intelligent behavior might be defined as behavior that helps a person adapt to his or her most important environment. Unfortunately, it is seldom clear which environment is most important. Proponents of standard intelligence tests would probably argue that school represents the single most important environment, at least for children, and that existing tests provide very good measures of adaptation to that environment. Proponents of multicultural assessment (e.g., Mercer & Lewis, 1978) would probably argue for a broader definition. Nevertheless, we see some value in shifting the question from "what is intelligence" to "what environments define as intelligent behavior." The latter question helps to focus the debate on why intelligence is being measured, rather than on whether one definition or the other is correct.

HERITABILITY, CONSISTENCY, AND MODIFIABILITY OF IQ

Individual differences in many physical characteristics, such as height or hair color, are substantially affected by genetic factors. Tall parents tend to have tall sons and daughters, although the offspring may not be quite as tall as the parents.[7] The question of whether genetic factors are in any way responsible for individual differences in general intelligence, and if so to what degree, is central to the current controversy over intelligence and intelligence testing.

Interest in the possible genetic basis of intelligence can be traced back to the earliest days of intelligence testing. Galton's (1869) pioneering work on individual differences was largely motivated by his interest in heredity. One hundred years later, the

---

[7]This is because of regression to the mean.

possible influence of genetic factors on intelligence became an issue of heated public debate when Jensen (1969) suggested that scientists must consider the hypothesis that differences between white and minority IQ scores are the result of genetic factors. The outcry was immediate, and the debate over possible genetic factors in intelligence has been intense and bitter ever since.

This section deals with three interlocking issues: heritability, the consistency of IQ, and the modifiability of IQ. Heritability studies attempt to estimate the degree to which both genetic factors and environmental factors contribute to individual differences in intelligence. The mix of genetic and environmental influences will, in turn, affect the degree of consistency and modifiability of IQ. The heritability debate suggests that it is important to both estimate the precise degree of consistency and to understand the way in which IQ may change over one's lifetime. A related issue is the question of whether and under what conditions IQ can be systematically modified.

Heritability of IQ

The available evidence makes it clear that both genetic factors (DeFries & Plomin, 1978; Rose, 1995) and environmental factors (Carroll & Maxwell, 1979) have some impact on individual differences in intelligence. However, neither genetic nor environmental factors by themselves can account for 100% of the variation in scores on intelligence tests. The issue, therefore, is not whether genetic and environmental factors account for some of the variability in test scores, but how much influence each of these factors exerts.

In theory, the total variance in test scores in a single population can be broken down into two components: (1) the variability that is due to all combinations of genetic factors and (2) the variability that is due to all the various combinations of nongenetic or environmental factors (Li, 1975). Symbolically,

$$\sigma^2_T = \sigma^2_G + \sigma^2_E \qquad [15\text{-}2]$$

where

σ^2_T = total test score variance
σ^2_G = varience due to, or explained by, genetic factors
σ^2_E = variance due to nongenetic or environmental factors

Heritability is defined as the proportion or the percentage of the variability in test scores that can be accounted for by genetic factors.[8] Symbolically,

$$h^2 = \frac{\sigma^2_G}{\sigma^2_T} \qquad [15\text{-}3]$$

---

[8]The reader may note the similarity between the heritability equations and the basic equations defining reliability, in which observed score variance is broken down into true score and error components.

where

h^2 = heritability of the trait being measured by the test

Geneticists make a distinction between broad and narrow heritability. *Broad heritability* includes the effects of all genetic factors, including gene dominance and assortive mating (the fact that people do not marry at random but tend to marry others with some similar genetic characteristics). *Narrow heritability* refers to the proportion of additive (nondominant) genetic variance under conditions of random mating (Jensen, 1975). Broad heritability estimates, which are debated by psychologists, can be interpreted as the squared correlation between genotypes (sum total of all genetic factors) and test scores in a specific population.

The basic data used in estimating heritability come from comparisons of intelligence test scores obtained by related and unrelated persons. Members of the same family tend to have more similar IQs than members of different families who are raised in similar environments. Furthermore, the similarity between test scores increases as genetic similarity increases; brothers have more similar scores on intelligence tests than do cousins. The most illuminating data come from studies of twins. Identical (monozygotic) twins have an identical genetic inheritance, whereas fraternal (dizygotic) twins are no more similar genetically than siblings who were born at different times. The intelligence scores of identical twins are highly correlated—and this correlation remains high even when the twins are raised apart—whereas the correlation between the IQs of fraternal twins is lower than that of identical twins.

Several complexities enter into the estimation of heritability. First, siblings or twins are not merely genetically similar; they share very similar environments. At least some of the correlation between the IQs of family members must be due to their similar upbringing and experience. Second, in studies where twins or siblings are raised apart, it still is likely that related persons will experience more similar environments than unrelated persons picked at random. It is unlikely that one monozygotic twin will be adopted by a white, middle-class family and that the other will be adopted by a family of poor, inner-city blacks. At an even subtler level, it has been shown that a person's appearance affects the reactions of others. As a result, identical twins may experience similar social environments solely as a result of their nearly identical appearance.

Finally, the determination of genetic similarity is not always simple. In particular, it is inappropriate to assume that all apparently unrelated persons are equally dissimilar in terms of genetic makeup. Unrelated persons are similar with respect to some genetic factors and dissimilar with respect to others. To complicate matters further, some genes or combinations of genes may be relevant to intelligence, whereas others may be completely irrelevant.

Stoolmiller (1999) notes that adoption studies, which are often cited in support of high heritability estimates for IQ, can be very difficult to interpret because of range restriction. That is, adoptive families are different from families in general. In particular, families that adopt "tend to be White, older, more affluent, higher SES, higher IQ, maritaly [sic] stable, and better functioning" (Stoolmiller, 1999, p. 398). As a result, the family environments for adopted children are systematically different from those experienced by other children, and in general, these environments are favorable to things like educational achievement, high interest in learning, cultural interests, and so on. On the whole, monozygotic twins who are adopted by different families will nevertheless tend to experience similar environments, and those environments will be favorable to developing intelligence. It should come as no surprise, therefore, that monozygotic twins raised apart tend to have IQs that are both relatively high and relatively similar. This tendency is certainly due in part to their shared genetic makeup but is also likely to be a reflection of the similar family environments that they are likely to encounter. Stoolmiller (1999) suggests that IQ heritability estimates based on adoption studies are likely to be artificially high because of this similarity of environments.

Several methods have been proposed for estimating the heritability of intelligence (Li, 1975; Loehlin, Lindzey, & Spuhler, 1975; Rose, 1995). Many of these methods are statistically complex and involve a variety of assumptions about the correlation between genetic effects and environmental effects. There is considerable variability in the size of heritability estimates, but the body of available evidence suggests that the broad heritability of intelligence is at least .4 to .6 and probably higher as examinees age (Cronbach, 1975; Jensen, 1975, 1980; Plomin & Rende, 1991; Rose, 1995; Vandenberg & Vogler, 1985). Heritability estimates are even higher for tests that measure general, as opposed to specific, abilities (Jensen, 1986). In other words, heritability studies suggest that in the population, at least 40% to 60% of the variability in adult intelligence test scores might be explained by genetic factors. This finding does not mean that 50% of an individual's intelligence is genetic. In fact, heritability studies do not attempt to estimate the causes of an individual's intelligence; and even when heritability is very high in the population, genetic factors provide only a rough prediction of an individual's IQ.

A table in Jensen (1980, p. 245), which presents confidence intervals for estimating individual genotypic values, is particularly illuminating. If heritability is equal to 50%, individuals with identical genetic backgrounds might differ by as much as 29 IQ points without exceeding the bounds of chance (95% confidence interval). Even with a heritability of 75%, genetically identical individuals might be expected to differ by as much as 25 IQ points.

The most widespread error in interpreting heritability studies is the assumption that high heritability means that IQ is fixed at birth and is not modifiable. Heritability indicates the degree to which, under present conditions, genetic factors and environmental factors contribute to individual differences in intelligence; it says nothing about the relative importance of genetic factors if the environment were changed in some important way. Therefore, a heritability of 100% does not indicate that the trait being measured is fixed and immutable, but that under present conditions, environmental factors do not contribute to individual differences. For example, height has a heritability coefficient of nearly 1.00, yet there is considerable evidence of massive changes in height over the years (Angoff, 1988; Crow, 1969). This outcome is attributable to several changes in the environment, including improved diet and better medical care. Similarly, changes in environment could have a substantial effect on intelligence regardless of the size of the heritability coefficient for intelligence. Viewed in this light, the heritability index is not a measure of the genetic nature of intelligence but, rather, is an index to which sociocultural conditions, as they presently exist, contribute to individual differences in intelligence (Cronbach, 1975; Li, 1975).

To understand the true nature of heritability ratios, one need only consider what would happen if everyone were raised in identical environments. If the environment were strictly controlled, then the only remaining source of variability would be genetic, and eventually 100% of the variability in test scores would be explained by genetic factors. Similarly, it might be possible to put individuals in environments that are so dissimilar that genetic differences would have a comparatively small effect on their behavior. Therefore, heritability studies reflect the influence of both genetic and environmental variations.

The idea that genetic factors contribute to intelligence is no longer controversial (Plomin & Rende, 1991), although controversies still rage over the extent of the genetic contribution and its implications. There is also evidence that genetic factors are also important determinants of personality, psychopathology (e.g., schizophrenia, affective disorders, autism), alcoholism, temperament, and even attitudes (e.g., job satisfaction) (Bouchard, Lykken, McGue, Segal, et al., 1990; Livesley, Jang, & Vernon, 2003; Plomin & Rende, 1991; Tellegen, Lykken, Bouchard, Wilcox, et al., 1988). Advances in behavioral genetics research hold significant promise for increasing our understanding of how both genetic and environmental factors affect intelligence, personality, and behavior.

Petrill and coworkers (1998) note that the heritability of specific abilities can be explained largely in terms of the heritability of *g*. That is, people who are related are often similar in terms of specific abilities, such as verbal comprehension. This tendency is probably due to the fact that they are also similar in terms of general cognitive ability (*g*). Rather than looking for specific genetic mechanisms that help to transmit specific abilities across generations, it is probably more useful to search for the specific mechanisms by which *g* is inherited. As Lykken (1998) notes, the question is no longer whether genetic factors influence intelligence but, rather, how genes influence behavior (see also Turkheimer, 1999). Tremendous progress has been made in the study of the links between genes and behavior (Plomin, 1997; Rowe, 1999), and it is clear that the processes linking genetic factors and intelligence are complex and multidimensional.

CRITICAL DISCUSSION:

Intelligence and Social Class

Scores on psychometrically sound measures of general cognitive ability differ as a function of socioeconomic status; mean scores for affluent examinees tend to be higher than mean scores for disadvantaged examinees. This pattern has been observed throughout the history of ability testing, but the meaning of these class differences in test scores is still the subject of fierce debate.

As we noted earlier in this chapter, many critics of ability tests have argued that class differences are the cause of differences in test scores. That is, this line of argument suggests that the tests are culturally biased in favor of members of the middle and upper classes and that the difference in test scores does not reflect any real differences in ability. The evidence presented in this chapter suggests that this cultural bias argument is not correct, or at least that it does not provide a complete explanation for test score differences. A more sophisticated version of the argument that class differences cause test score differences is that children in affluent families have greater access to good schools, books, computers, cultural events, and the like, and that they therefore have a better opportunity to develop their abilities. The data are more consistent with this hypothesis.

The authors of *The Bell Curve* argue that the class differences are the effect of differences in intelligence (Hernstein & Murray, 1994). According to this hypothesis, people with higher levels of cognitive ability are more likely to succeed in school and in the workplace and are more likely to go into professions that have higher levels of responsibility and higher pay. This theory suggests that people rise or fall in the social stratum because of their levels of ability.

The argument over whether class differences are the cause or effect of differences in cognitive ability is in many ways the most recent version of an age-old argument about class structures themselves. The argument in favor of hierarchical class structures in society has always included the assumption that members of the upper classes deserve or are better prepared to exercise their privileges because they possess some valued attribute (e.g., ability, character). Viewed in this light, *The Bell Curve* could be thought of as the most recent and "scientific" version of the "divine rights" theory of society. The argument put forth by opponents of class divisions in society holds that privileges are unfairly hoarded by members of the upper classes, who put arbitrary obstacles (e.g., culturally biased tests) in the way of those who seek access to those privileges. Viewed in this light, debates about culturally biased testing could be thought of as the most recent version of the Marxist position on class and privilege (Conway, 1987).

Arguments between such different views of society are unlikely to be settled by data, in part because of the many contradictions that exist in the relationship between class and ability test scores. For example, Sternberg (1995) notes that access to higher education, professional training, and the like, is directly linked to scores on ability tests such as the GRE. It should therefore come as no surprise that people higher on ability also achieve higher salaries and all the other benefits that come with a degree from Harvard, an M.D., or a Ph.D. We cannot necessarily use the correlation between ability and social class to argue that there is any causal link between the two, much less to argue about the direction of the causal flow.

In our view, the data suggest that higher levels of ability do indeed provide more opportunities to advance in life and that starting life with advantages such as educated parents, access to good schools, books, and so on, does indeed provide an optimal environment for developing abilities. In other words, to the extent that causal links exist between ability and socioeconomic status, they probably flow in both directions. High levels of cognitive ability can open doors to opportunity, and low levels of ability can restrict opportunities. Similarly, being raised in an enriched environment can help individuals to develop their abilities, and being raised in an impoverished environment can make it more difficult to develop those same abilities.

Consistency of IQ

As noted in the previous section, the fact that intelligence shows a fairly high degree of heritability does not indicate that an individual's intelligence is a fixed, immutable quantity. If we accept the conclusion that intelligence may be modifiable, several questions emerge. First, under normal conditions, are intelligence test scores stable, or do test scores change dramatically over the course of a person's life? Second, under what conditions might we expect systematic changes in intelligence? This section deals with the first of these questions.

Longitudinal and cross-sectional studies suggest a substantial period of stability in IQs, ranging from early childhood to fairly late adulthood. For example, Rees and Palmer (1970) assessed children at ages 6, 12, and 17, and showed correlations ranging from .75 to .83 between intelligence test scores at these three ages. Furthermore, fewer than 23% of the children tested showed a maximum change of greater than 20 points when their lowest recorded IQ was compared with their highest recorded IQ obtained in three testings; over 58% showed maximum changes of 15 points or less. Large-scale longitudinal studies by Harnqvist (1968), D. K. Hopkins and Bracht (1975), and Magnusson and Backteman (1978) showed IQ correlations ranging from .73 to .78 over age intervals of 13 to 18 years, 10 to 16 years, and 10 to 15 years, respectively. A number of longitudinal and cross-sectional studies combine to show that intelligence scores are comparably stable between age 18 and middle adulthood (Matarazzo, 1972; Wechsler, 1958).

Intelligence scores show less stability in very early childhood and in late adulthood. M. Lewis (1973) has shown that there is little or no consistency in test performance in the first 2 years of life and concludes that infant intelligence is neither stable nor measurable. The stability in test scores in later life has been researched much more widely, and some evidence suggests a systematic change in IQ with age. Normative data from the WAIS show that full-scale IQ scores are at their highest around ages 20 to 35, then decline steadily until age 60, and finally decline precipitously past age 60. This pattern is shown in Figure 15-5.

At first examination, the figure suggests that past age 35 or so, a person's intelligence declines steadily. There are, however, several problems with this interpretation. First, longitudinal studies, in which the same individuals are measured at a number of different ages, yield consistently different results than do cross-sectional studies, in which individuals of different ages are all tested at the same time (Nesselroade & Reese, 1973; Schaie, 1994; Schaie & LaBouvie-Vief, 1974; Schaie & Strother, 1968). Whereas cross-sectional studies typically show steady and sizable declines in IQ scores from middle to late adulthood, longitudinal studies typically show very modest declines that begin much later in life. This pattern is illustrated in Figure 15-6.

The interpretation suggested by Schaie and LaBouvie-Vief (1974) is that the apparent decline in IQ shown in cross-sectional studies reflects generational or cohort differences rather than declines in individual intelligence over time (see also, Schaie, 1994). IQs provide relative rather than absolute measures of intelligence, and in com-

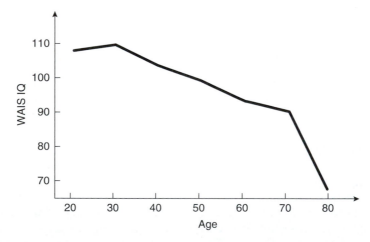

FIGURE 15-5   Average WAIS IQ by Age   *Source:* Adapted from Doppelt & Wallace, 1955, p. 323.

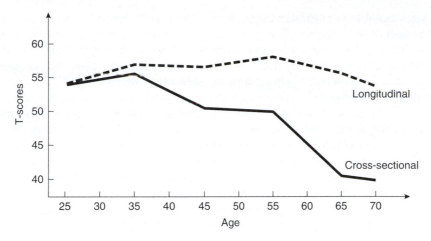

FIGURE 15-6   Trends in Test Scores From Cross-Sectional and Longitudinal Studies   *Source*: Adapted from Schaie & Strother, 1968, p. 675.

parison with an increasingly younger population that is tested during periods of rapid technological and cultural change, the relative performance of older examinees may decline in the absence of any absolute change in performance. In other words, if the normative group becomes increasingly smarter and better educated, the relative performance of any particular individual is likely to decline.

Although there are methodological problems in interpreting apparent cross-sectional declines in intelligence, there are also difficulties in longitudinal studies (Flynn, 1984; Nesselroade & Reese, 1973). One very real problem is that of (literal) subject mortality. The individuals who remain in a study beyond age 70 may differ systematically from those who drop out at the early stages. Thus, it is not clear whether longitudinal results are representative of the population in general. Second, it is not always possible to use identical or even comparable tests at different times (Flynn, 1984).

Taking methodological problems into account, however, the literature on age-related declines in intelligence suggests that the real decline in general intelligence with age is gradual in nature and starts later in life than was previously assumed (Birren & Schaie, 1977; Schaie, 1974, 1994). Intelligence appears to be relatively stable well past age 60, and it may not show noticeable declines until several years later. Thus, although scores on intelligence tests do not describe a fixed aspect of an individual's makeup, considerable evidence supports the consistency of IQ over a large portion of the life span of typical individuals.

Modifiability of IQ

The disparity between the IQs of white, middle-class children and those of minorities has been a source of deep concern since the mid-1960s. In the 1960s, several large-scale remedial programs to increase the IQ scores of minority children were suggested. Most notable was Project Head Start, which is featured in the Critical Discussion at the end of this chapter. The question we consider here is whether it is possible to change (increase) a person's IQ. We think that there is evidence that general cognitive abilities can be significantly increased, although it appears clear that changes cannot be expected as the result of short, simple, or faddish interventions.

Programs that appear to have met with success in increasing participants' cognitive abilities or basic academic skills share several features in common. First and foremost is the careful attention paid to the psychology of learning. Early programs, including many of the pilot programs included in the early years of Project Head Start, often featured untested strategies for improving basic skills that had little scientific or experiential basis. The successful programs described in Bloom (1976) and J. M. Hunt (1975) feature close attention to the processes involved in solving various problems, along with careful consideration of principles of learning and principles of reinforcement. A closely allied feature of successful programs is the careful analysis of the tasks that must be performed in the process of analyzing and solving problems (Whimbey, 1980). These programs are also likely to feature multiple, realistic criteria, rather than vague and perhaps unattainable goals. The lack of realistic goals was a principal problem with some intervention programs. It was overly optimistic to assume that a few weeks of preschool instruction, which varied considerably from location to location, would result in dramatic increases in a wide range of ability and achievement measures. Finally, successful programs are likely to consider both the cognitive and the affective prerequisites to successful compensatory learning (Bloom, 1976). Changes in basic cognitive skills do not come about strictly as a result of learning particular facts, but rather may involve changing attitudes and habits as well as adapting individuals to standard learning environments.

In principle, IQ appears to be modifiable. It is clearly not a simple matter to dramatically raise IQ scores on any large-scale, long-term basis. However, a score on an intelligence test is not a fixed indicator of inborn capacity but, rather, a sample of present behavior. Problem-solving skills can be learned, and other aspects of intelligent behavior can be acquired and reinforced, given the appropriate social environment. There probably are some genetic limitations on the degree to which IQ could be changed through changes in the environment; it is unlikely that everyone could be a genius, no matter how favorable the environment. Nevertheless, most IQ differences that are of concern are those that are well within the normal range (in the statistical sense), and these might be systematically modified by optimal structuring of the learning environment.

The most convincing evidence of the modifiability of IQ comes from studies of long-term changes in average scores on intelligence tests. For example, Flynn (1984) documented massive IQ gains in the United States over the period 1932 to 1978; some of these changes had been obscured in previous research by inconsistencies in the norming of different tests. Similarly, Humphreys (1989) reported evidence of substantial increases in IQ for the periods 1917 to 1942 and 1942 to 1960. Lynn and Hampson (1989) present similar findings from British samples. In an extensive review of studies from 14 nations, Flynn (1987) documented increases of 5 to 25 points in IQ (on an IQ scale with a mean of 100 and a standard deviation of 15) in a single generation.

Changes have been especially notable at the lower ends of the score scale, and differences between groups that receive higher versus lower scores (e.g., white versus black examinees) appear to be diminishing. The data reviewed by Flynn (1987) and others clearly show that IQ can be changed substantially (although the precise sources and mechanisms for this change are still poorly understood; Sternberg, 1995) and that the existence of group differences in IQ does not necessarily imply that these differences will persist over long periods. The important point is that it is possible to observe very large changes in IQ for a group or nation over a relatively short period. Therefore, you cannot assume that current differences in the ability levels of different groups in the population are fixed and permanent.

Flynn (1999) summarized multinational research showing dramatic increases in mean IQ over the years. Gains are largest for heavily g-loaded tests (e.g., Raven's Progressive Matrices), and the rate of growth is relatively uniform across both nations and time. Flynn points out that these data raise at least two important questions: (1) Why has IQ gone up over time? (2) Why haven't real-world achievements shown similar trends? Explanations for IQ gains over time include changes in nutrition, increasing access to education, increasing urbanization, more exposure to tests, and the increasing complexity of daily life (Azar, 1996; Flynn, 1999; Horgan, 1995). Dickens & Flynn (2001) present a compelling analysis of the way that heredity and environment can interact to lead to substantial changes in general mental ability.

The more important question is the implication of these gains for real-world achievement. Flynn (1999) points out that 90% of those born 100 years ago would fall within the bottom 5% of current national norms. A very large proportion of those tested 50 years ago would be classified as "mentally retarded" using current test norms. If we equate IQ with real-world intelligence, it would be hard to escape the conclusion that most people were just plain stupid a few generations ago and that most people today are just plain smarter than their forebearers. If this analysis is correct, we should see massive increases in real-world achievements when we compare each generation with the one before it, but little evidence clearly suggests that people in general are that much "smarter" than they used to be (Flynn, 1999).

CRITICAL DISCUSSION:

Project Head Start

In the 1960s, the federal government embarked on a wide-ranging War on Poverty. One of the goals of this set of programs was to reduce the gap between educational opportunities afforded affluent and poor (mainly minority) Americans (Ziegler & Valentine, 1980). Project Head Start represented one part of this effort.

Project Head Start refers to a number of different educational interventions designed to prepare poor and minority children to compete more effectively in school; in 1995, this program served over 500,000 low-income children. Although the specifics of the different programs initially varied from location to location and have changed significantly over the years, the general theme tying them together was an effort to reach preschool children and to equip them with the knowledge, skills, abilities, and orientation necessary to perform well in school. It was thought that this program would allow educators to catch and remedy problems early and that, as a result, the children who participated would perform at a level more similar to that attained by their more affluent peers.

Tests of general intelligence served as the main criterion in early evaluations of Head Start programs (A. E. Boehm, 1985). Many of these programs did result in gains in IQ of 3 to 4 points that persisted up to 4 years after participation in the program, but there was little evidence of long-term gains sufficiently large to make any difference in the children's school performance (Bouchard & Segal, 1985; Payne, Mercer, Payne, & Davinson, 1973). The apparent failure of Project Head Start in its early years, together with other data, led to Jensen's (1969) controversial conclusion that "compensatory education has failed" (p. 2).

The initial disappointment with Project Head Start does not, in fact, imply that IQ cannot be changed. First, IQ data collected over different time spans and from different tests can be very difficult to interpret (Flynn, 1984); hence, it is not clear whether all Head Start programs really failed. Second, the actual content of Head Start programs varied considerably from site to site, making an evaluation of the project as a whole suspect. Third, the project was, in its early years, chronically underfunded, and it was subject to meddling by well-intentioned but uninformed legislators and administrators.

Over the years, evaluations of the potential contributions of Project Head Start have changed dramatically, to the point that it is one of the few remnants from the War on Poverty that is still evaluated positively by both conservatives and liberals. In part this outcome is due to improvements in the program and to the adoption of more realistic goals; the programs under Head Start are now more likely to be evaluated in terms of how well they prepare children for future success in school than in terms of their impact on overall IQ.

SUMMARY

Differences persist in the average scores received by several racial and ethnic groups on standardized tests of mental ability; the reasons for these differences, their meaning, and the strategies for reducing these differences have been the focus of substantial research and discussion. To understand this research, it is first necessary to distinguish between bias and fairness. Bias is a statistical characteristic of test scores. Systematic differences in test scores, particularly in the regressions between test scores and important criteria, indicate that a test is biased. The assessment of fairness requires a value judgment in which the outcomes of tests are compared with the outcomes that most closely reflect a person's values and preferences. There is no necessary connection between bias and fairness; a biased test can be used fairly, and an unbiased test can be the source of obvious unfairness.

A variety of techniques can be used to evaluate bias in measurement and bias in prediction. On the whole, well-developed tests rarely show bias in measurement. The bias in prediction that these tests show tends to be small, and often the bias is in the opposite direction than that suggested by critics of tests. Although standardized tests might not be seriously biased, the differences in test scores obtained by different groups are often large enough to motivate the search for alternative test types. Attempts to use nonverbal tests to reduce differences in test scores have not been successful, and increasing attention has been devoted to measures of adaptive behaviors.

Research on the heritability and consistency of IQ leads to several general conclusions. First, intelligence (and probably several facets of personality) appears to have a substantial genetic component. Second, IQ shows a high degree of consistency, such that scores obtained relatively early in life might provide a reasonable approximation of intelligence levels throughout one's lifetime. However, this possibility does not mean that it is impossible to modify intelligence. Statements about heritability and stability tell us as much about the environment as about genetics, and large changes in the environment can lead to large changes in such highly heritable and stable traits as height and body type. The same outcome is probably true for intelligence.

PROBLEMS AND SOLUTIONS—RECAP

The Problem

Gary is one of five applicants for a job; the other four applicants were women. It looks as if hiring decisions were based on a 12-minute paper-and-pencil test, and all three of the people hired were women. Gary is not sure whether he should complain that the test was unfair to men.

A Solution

Gary's first step should be to find out more about the test. For example, one widely used test that would fit this description is the Wonderlic Personnel Test (this test is discussed in Chapter 19). It would take only a few minutes to locate research on the Wonderlic on the Web, and what Gary is almost certain to find is that this particular test is not biased in favor of females; male and female average test scores are virtually identical. Furthermore, there is abundant evidence for the construct validity and for the criterion-related validity of the test. If the test is a well-validated instrument like the Wonderlic (particularly if it shows no general pattern of favoring one group over another), Gary might have to conclude that he was less qualified for the job.

Suppose, however, that the test is not as high in psychometric quality as the Wonderlic. In that case, Gary would want to look for evidence relevant to any of the following points:

1. Do women typically do better on this test than men?
2. Do the scores on this test allow you to predict job performance or success?
3. Is the test equally reliable and valid for men and women?
4. If a man and a woman receive the same score on the test, are they likely to perform similarly on the job?

You might conclude that there was real evidence of bias if it turned out that women did better on the test without doing better on the job or if you found that the test was reliable for women but not reliable for men. The most compelling evidence of bias is a demonstration that men and women with identical test scores turn out to perform at substantially different levels on the job.

In our experience, biased tests are a rarity. The process of developing a test is an expensive and a time-consuming one, and test developers have strong incentives to investigate and minimize bias. The end users of tests (here, the employer) have an even stronger interest in avoiding bias, because they can be held liable for discrimination, especially if it can be shown that they made discriminatory decisions on the basis of invalid tests. Test bias will probably never go away entirely, but the likelihood that a modern, professionally developed, commercially distributed test will be substantially biased against particular groups in the population is fairly low.

KEY TERMS

Adaptive behavior inventories inventories that assess the ability to function in day-to-day life situations

Banding grouping together individuals whose test scores are too similar to permit reliable differentiations

Bias tendency of a test to make systematic errors in measurement or prediction for particular groups

Bias in prediction group differences in intercepts, slopes, or standard errors when tests are used to predict specific criteria

Cultural bias hypothesis hypothesis that the content of ability tests unfairly favors some groups over others

Culture-reduced testing strategy for ability testing that minimizes the use of verbal or culturally specific items

Differential validity hypothesis hypothesis that tests might show different levels of criterion-related validity across groups

Fairness value judgment that the outcomes of testing match some desired criterion or end state

Flynn effect steady, long-term increase in levels of intelligence that has been observed in several countries

Group $\times$ item interaction group differences in the relative difficulty of test items

Heritability extent to which an individual difference variable (e.g., cognitive ability) can be explained in terms of genetic factors

Project Head Start series of government initiatives to provide disadvantaged children with better preparation to succeed in school

Interest Testing

16

In the preceding three chapters, we reviewed some of the more frequently used ability tests and examined some of the issues surrounding the measurement of ability. In this chapter, we turn our attention to the measurement of vocational interests. We analyze four widely used interest tests to examine how they are constructed, investigate their psychometric properties, and explore how psychologists use them. The four interest tests chosen for review are the Strong Interest Inventory (SII), the Kuder Occupational Interest Survey (KOIS), the Career Assessment Inventory (CAI), and the Jackson Vocational Interest Survey (JVIS). Each test was selected for a particular reason. To help illustrate their use, a sample test profile and interpretive discussion are presented for each test.

The SII enjoys the heritage of being one of the oldest psychological tests currently in use and has been a dominant force in the field of interest measurement. No survey of interest tests would be complete without an in-depth look at the SII. The KOIS was included because it represents a divergent test construction philosophy and because it also has a rather long and rich history of research and use in the field. The CAI bears many similarities to the SII, but its unique contribution is its ability to measure the interests of people at the lower socioeconomic levels in our society. Finally, the JVIS was included because it is a relatively newly developed test that incorporates several contemporary test development techniques and offers the attractive feature of being hand-scoreable, unlike any of its predecessors. Although other tests could have been selected for review, we believe these four provide a good overview of the entire field of interest measurement.

This chapter is arranged so that the four tests can be compared and contrasted quite easily. Each test is discussed from the same basic four perspectives: purpose, manner of construction, psychometric characteristics, and applications in both counseling and industrial settings.

PROBLEMS AND SOLUTIONS—TESTS AND CAREER COUNSELING

The Problem

Brad is a college freshman who has not yet declared a major. As part of his freshman seminar course, he is required to visit the career center on campus, take an interest test, and begin to formulate a career plan. When he saw his Strong Interest Inventory results, he noticed that he had a few identifiable interests and that one of them was in the agricultural area. His score on the farmer scale was moderately high and actually one of his highest occupational scores on the test. Growing up in an urban area, he had no previous experience with farming or ranching and was quite surprised by his results. Since he has never considered going into agriculture and has little interest in outdoor work, he now wonders whether he should begin exploring this area further or consider the test results as invalid and meaningless for him.

THE STRONG INTEREST INVENTORY

The idea of measuring vocational interests and using this information to help place people in appropriate positions began in earnest during World War I. Following the war, psychologists began to see the potential of using interest test information to help civilians make better educational and career plans. The field of interest measurement as we know it today owes much to the pioneering work of Edward K. Strong, Jr. The development of the instrument that bears his name began while Strong was teaching at Carnegie Institute of Technology in Pittsburgh from 1919 to 1923. At that time, work was well under way in the study of vocational interests. One result of that early effort was the development of a large, 1,000-item pool of interest questions. Using this item pool as a base, Karl Cowdery, a young graduate student advised by Strong, studied whether people in different occupations could be differentiated according to the responses that they made to interest items. He found that the choices people made on a paper-and-pencil interest test could be used to accurately discriminate which occupations they entered. Although Cowdery never pursued this line of research further, Strong was fascinated with the results and set out on a lifetime devoted to the study of interest measurement.

Strong soon moved to Stanford University, where he spent the majority of his academic career. The first published version of his test, the Strong Vocational Interest Blank, appeared in 1927. Strong was an incredibly compulsive, organized, motivated, and dedicated person. He spent many years gathering samples of occupational groups to be tested with his instrument. However, at the beginning he believed that only men should be considered, because women produced responses to the items that were demonstrably different from those of men and chose different career paths. Eventually, Strong decided to devise a separate form for women with the same basic format but with certain unique items. In 1933, he published the first women's form of the test. Strong later revised both the men's and the women's forms of the test in 1938 and 1946, respectively.

About midway through the decade of the 1950s, Strong wanted to revise his test once again. He was getting on in age, however, and enlisted a young graduate student at the University of Minnesota at that time, David Campbell, to help him with the project. Strong eventually died, and Campbell later completed the next set of revisions. The men's form was completed in 1966, followed by the women's form in 1969. Neither of these revisions remained in use for long, however. With the advent of the women's movement, earlier assumptions about the career paths of women being uniquely different from those of men were challenged and eventually abandoned. With the increasing number of women entering the labor market and the change in thinking about the role of women, having two separate, gender-specific forms seemed inappropriate. Consequently, Campbell combined the men's and women's forms into one test, publishing it as the Strong-Campbell Interest Inventory in 1974. Since then, the inventory was revised in 1981, 1985, and finally again in 1994. The current version of the test, the Strong Interest Inventory (SII), still traces its lineage back to the original instrument first published by Strong back in 1927.

Construction of the SII

Strong originally believed that the way to build an interest inventory was to contrast the responses of a specific occupational criterion group to those of a nonspecific, people-in-general group to identify a unique set of items that differentiated the two groups. Strong's method of developing occupational scales involved administering his inventory to workers in various occupations and comparing their responses with those of a general reference group. The workers he chose for his criterion groups had to be satisfied with their jobs and had to have been employed in the occupation for a minimum of at least three years. When he found items that were significantly preferred more or less often by a group of occupational workers than by the general reference sample, he combined them into an interest scale for that occupation. For example, if artists significantly endorsed an item such as "I like to attend symphony concerts" more often than did members of the general reference sample, then Strong included that item on the artist scale. Similarly, if artists marked the item "I like mathematics" significantly less often than the general reference group, then that item was also included on the artist scale, since it still distinguished artists from the reference group.

It should be noted that the essential characteristic of occupational scale items is that they were designed to differentiate the interests of occupational groups from those of a general reference group. Items strongly preferred or rarely liked by both an occupational group and the general reference group did not qualify for inclusion on an occupational scale. This is graphically shown in Figure 16-1. Not only did approximately 95% of the people in occupation X indicate a preference for hunting, so also did the vast majority of the general reference group (90%). In contrast, only about 35% of occupation X members said that they liked gardening. However, even a significantly smaller percentage of the general reference group (10%) indicated a preference for gardening. Consequently, because gardening discriminated between the two groups and hunting did not, only the former would appear on the scale for occupation X, despite the fact that workers in occupation X clearly like to hunt.

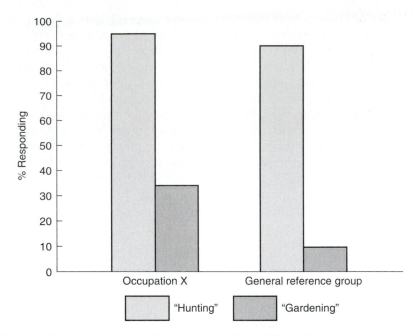

FIGURE 16-1   Comparison Between Two Items and Their Ability to Discriminate Between Groups

The composition of the general reference group posed a very difficult problem for Strong. He initially experimented with several groups that were chosen to represent cross-sections of various socioeconomic strata and vocational interest areas. His studies revealed that the composition of the group was crucial in discriminating between the interests of various occupational groups. For example, he found that if he chose a general comparison group composed mostly of skilled workers (e.g., carpenters, plumbers, printers, etc.), he was able to locate numerous items that differentiated the interests of professional people from those of the skilled workers reference group, but unfortunately he could not then differentiate among the professions. Doctors, lawyers, and business executives all appeared to have similar interests with one another, but they had clearly distinguishable interests from those of the comparison group. His major concern, however, was that he could not separate the interests of one professional group from those of another group of professionals.

In contrast, Strong found that using the skilled worker reference group did allow him to rather easily differentiate one skilled group from another. Carpenters appeared to have quite different interests from plumbers or printers and other skilled workers. He concluded that, as the similarity between the members of occupational groups and the general reference group increased, the discriminating power of the test increased. His conclusions are summarized in Table 16-1. With this discovery in mind, Strong, who was primarily interested in gaining maximum separation among business and professional occupations, decided to select a general comparison group that was biased toward this occupational level. Therefore, the SII provides better separation

Table 16-1   ADVANTAGES AND DISADVANTAGES OF STRONG'S USE OF DIFFERENT GENERAL REFERENCE GROUPS

Composition of general reference sample used	*Advantages and disadvantages*
Sample of workers at the unskilled level	Able to distinguish clearly among workers in unskilled jobs (i.e., construction laborers differed from assembly line workers, window washers differed from farm laborers, etc.). Could only distinguish all professionals from unskilled workers, but could not separate among professionals (i.e., groups such as doctors, lawyers, and engineers could not be clearly distinguished from one another, but as a group could be discriminated from unskilled workers).
Sample of workers at the skilled level	Able to distinguish clearly among workers in skilled jobs (i.e., electricians differed from sheet metal workers, plumbers differed from carpenters, etc.). Could only distinguish all professionals from skilled workers, but could not separate among professionals.
Sample of workers at the business and professional level	Able to distinguish clearly among workers employed in different professional or business occupations (i.e., ministers differed from bankers, professional artists differed from psychologists, etc.). Whereas workers in different areas at the business and professional level could be differentiated from one another, workers at the skilled and unskilled levels all tended to show similar interests and could not be differentiated from one another.

among business and professional occupations than it does among occupations at lower socioeconomic levels; this problem has been partially addressed in the most recent editions of the test. However, recent attempts to extend it to include more nonprofessional and technical occupations have been undertaken (Hansen, 1992).

The current version of the SII consists of 317 items measuring respondents' preferences for various occupations, school subjects, work-related activities, leisure activities, types of people, personal characteristics, and personal preferences. Table 16-2 presents several items similar to those included on the SII. Responses on the inventory are scored by computer and are analyzed in reference to five types of scales: administrative indexes, personal style scales, general occupational theme scales, basic interest scales, and occupational scales.

Administrative Indexes

The administrative indexes reveal information about the type and pattern of choices made by the examinee. They are designed to alert the counselor to possible interpretive problems that might moderate the validity of the results or greatly reduce their usefulness. Several scales are included in this group. One scale, the total response indicator, signals the number of items accurately read by the scoring machine. If the number of items omitted is very large, the validity of the results is doubtful. The most

Table 16-2   SAMPLE SII ITEMS

Mark Like, Indifferent, *or* Dislike *for the following items:*

	Like	Ind.	Dislike		Like	Ind.	Dislike
1. Accountant	L	I	D	7. Buying merchandise for a store	L	I	D
2. Forest ranger	L	I	D	8. Doing research work	L	I	D
3. Word processor	L	I	D	9. Contributing to charities	L	I	D
4. Chemistry	L	I	D	10. Operating machinery	L	I	D
5. Journalism	L	I	D	11. People who assume leadership	L	I	D
6. Sociology	L	I	D	12. Magazines about art and music	L	I	D

common reasons for omitting items seem to be that examinees either are unfamiliar with the terminology used in an item or mark the answer sheet so lightly that the optical reader scanning the sheet fails to pick up some of their responses.

A second validity indicator, the number of infrequent responses marked on the test, provides a check for proper completion of the inventory. Questionable response patterns are suggested when examinees give unusually large numbers of infrequent responses on the test. Invalid profiles due to questionable response patterns often result from poor motivation on the part of examinees, deficiencies in reading ability, confusion about test directions, or language difficulties. In all cases, the detection of such problems is essential in preventing erroneous interpretations from being communicated to the individual.

Finally, a response distribution matrix indicating the percentages of "like," "indifferent," and "dislike" responses enables the counselor to detect other interpretive problems. For example, individuals giving many "indifferent" responses may have trouble making decisions in general and consequently have not clearly differentiated their interests. The usefulness of the SII in such cases may be more to point out their indecision than to measure specific occupational interests. Likewise, unusually large response percentages in either of the other two categories can cause significant modifications in the interpretability of the test results.

Personal Style Scales

Various special scales have appeared on earlier versions of the SII to measure other, more general aspects of people's preferences, but these have been replaced on the current revision by four personal style scales. These scales were designed to assess the types of work and learning environments, as well as the kinds of daily activities that people find rewarding and personally satisfying. Although only one of these scales, the risk-taking–adventure scale, appeared on earlier versions of the SII, the other three show some definite similarities to the older academic comfort and introversion—extroversion special scales on past inventories.

The work style scale was developed to differentiate those who like to have substantial interpersonal contact in their work from those who prefer to work more with data, ideas, and things. The assumption underlying this scale is that those who prefer environments with high levels of people contact will likely be most satisfied in occupations that feature more people contact, such as sales, child care, or counseling. Likewise, people preferring less people contact will find more satisfaction in careers requiring less direct involvement with people (e.g., chemists, biologists, computer programmers).

The learning environment scale provides information about whether examinees' interests are similar to those of people who persist in formal academic settings and pursue advanced educational and professional degrees. It was developed by identifying those items that differentiated the responses of people who had earned postgraduate degrees from those who had not pursued formal education beyond trade school. High scorers on this scale generally like cultural and verbal activities, enjoy school, and frequently pursue advanced degrees. On the other hand, low scorers generally prefer more practical, on-the-job training and pursue more formal advanced education only if required to do so for occupational entry.

The third personal style scale, leadership style, represents an attempt to assess the type of leadership role that people would like to have in their work setting. People who prefer more outgoing, energetic styles of leading and persuading others, such as broadcasters, public officials, realtors, and school administrators, tend to score more highly on this scale. They would most likely find work environments that draw on their strong social and assertive characteristics to be most rewarding and satisfying. In contrast, some people prefer to lead more by example and tend to prefer to do tasks themselves, rather than directing others. They tend to score on the lower side of this scale, often majoring in areas such as physical science, math, or agriculture, and shying away from environments that demand persuasive oratory.

Finally, the risk-taking–adventure scale was included in earlier versions of the inventory but was formerly included as part of the basic interest scales, which we will consider later. Basically, this scale was designed to assess examinees' preferences for physical risk and adventure. In addition to identifying those who enjoy taking risks or who like to act somewhat impulsively, it also appears to have some utility for identifying those who feel quite uncomfortable attempting new activities without more careful planning or experience. This latter aspect of the scale reflects a more general tendency to play it safe and act in more conservative ways.

General Occupational Theme Scales

As more and more occupational groups were added to the inventory, it became desirable to categorize the occupations into some system. Strong experimented with several different classification systems, but he eventually chose one based on the intercorrelations among the occupational scales. This system continued in existence from the mid-1920s until the 1974 revision. Although this classification system worked fairly well, there were always a few occupations that could be classified in more than one group because they shared a number of similarities with various diverse groups (e.g., the veterinarian scale correlated about as well with the scientific group as it did with the outdoor and technical group). In 1974, when the male and female forms of the SVIB were combined into one form, a new classification scheme was needed, since both older forms had some different occupational groupings. The theoretical system of John Holland (J. L. Holland, 1973) was chosen to provide the new organizational schema.

Holland's system postulated that six major interest areas were identifiable that described both work environments and types of people. Holland believed that the optimal vocation choice involved the matching of people with their appropriate environmental type. Holland further postulated that a hexagon best represented the relationship among these six interest areas. A description of each of his six types is presented in Table 16-3. The actual empirical relationships among the types are shown in Figure 16-2.

Inspection of the intercorrelations among the six types suggests that those nearest one another along the hexagon are most similar. As the distance along the hexagon increases, the relationship diminishes. Consequently, the least similar areas are those that lie diagonally across from one another. For example, people with conventional interests do not share much in common with artistic individuals, nor do scientists have many interests in common with people in business.

To adopt Holland's system for use on the SII, it was necessary to select a group of items that reflected each of the six personality types. Twenty or more items were subsequently selected for each type and organized into six theme scales. A general reference sample of 9,484 men and 9,467 women was tested on these six scales to establish a norm group for comparison purposes. This norming of the six theme scales permits the user to formulate a picture of the examinee's interests and personality style in reference to that of a general male and female comparison group.

Basic Interest Scales

The basic interest scales were designed to provide specific information about the likes and dislikes of the respondent. These scales consist of small numbers of items that are reasonably homogeneous with respect to their content. Each scale focuses on a narrow, concentrated interest area.

For example, if examinees gave "like" responses to the sample items listed in the left column of Table 16-4, they would generate high scores on the public speaking scale. Similarly, if they responded "like" to the sample items listed in the right column, they would show a preference for social service–related activities. For all the basic interest scales, norms are reported both on the combined male and female sample as well as on each individually. This arrangement allows the test user to assess the strength of an individual's interests on each of the 25 basic interest scales, both with respect to a combined sex sample as well as in relation to samples of men and women representing a cross-section of the occupations represented on the inventory.

Table 16-3   DESCRIPTION OF THE SIX HOLLAND TYPES

R-Theme: People scoring high here usually are rugged, robust, practical, physically strong; they usually have good physical skills, but sometimes have trouble expressing themselves or in communicating their feelings to others. They like to work outdoors and to work with tools, especially large, powerful machines. They prefer to deal with things rather than with ideas or people. They enjoy creating things with their hands.

I-Theme: This Theme centers around science and scientific activities. Extremes of this type are task-oriented; they are not particularly interested in working around other people. They enjoy solving abstract problems, and they have a great need to understand the physical world. They prefer to think through problems rather than act them out. Such people enjoy ambiguous challenges and do not like highly structured situations with many rules. They frequently are original and creative, especially in scientific areas.

A-Theme: The extreme type here is artistically oriented, and likes to work in artistic settings that offer many opportunities for self-expression. Such people have little interest in problems that are highly structured or require gross physical strength, preferring those that can be solved through self-expression in artistic media. They resemble I-Theme types in preferring to work alone, but have a greater need for individualistic expression, and usually are less assertive about their own opinions and capabilities. They describe themselves as independent, original, unconventional, expressive, and intense.

S-Theme: The pure type here is sociable, responsible, humanistic, and concerned with the welfare of others. These people usually express themselves well and get along well with others; they like attention and seek situations that allow them to be near the center of the group. They prefer to solve problems by discussions with others, or by arranging or rearranging relationships between others; they have little interest in situations requiring physical exertion or working with machinery. Such people describe themselves as cheerful, popular, and achieving, and as good leaders.

E-Theme: The extreme type of this Theme has a great facility with words, especially in selling, dominating, and leading; frequently these people are in sales work. They see themselves as energetic, enthusiastic, adventurous, self-confident, and dominant, and they prefer social tasks where they can assume leadership. They enjoy persuading others to their viewpoints. They are impatient with precise work or work involving long periods of intellectual effort. They like power, status, and material wealth, and enjoy working in expensive settings.

C-Theme: Extremes of this type prefer the highly ordered activities, both verbal and numerical, that characterize office work. People scoring high fit well into large organizations but do not seek leadership; they respond to power and are comfortable working in a well-established chain of command. They dislike ambiguous situations, preferring to know precisely what is expected of them. Such people describe themselves as conventional, stable, well-controlled, and dependable. They have little interest in problems requiring physical skills or intense relationships with others, and are most effective at well-defined tasks. Like the E-Theme type, they value material possessions and status.

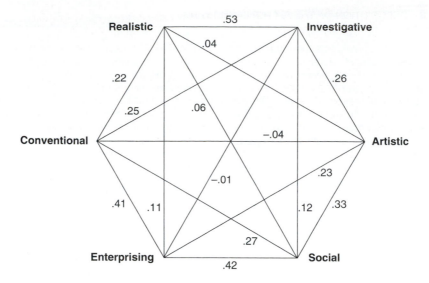

FIGURE 16-2 Intercorrelations Between General Occupational Themes   *Source:* Modified and reproduced by special permission of the Publisher, Consulting Psychologists Press, Inc., Palo Alto, CA 94303 from the *Strong Interest Inventory*™ of the *Strong Vocational Interest Blanks*® Form T317. Copyright 1933, 1938, 1945, 1946, 1966, 1968, 1974, 1981, 1985, 1994 by the Board of Trustees of the Leland Stanford Junior University. All rights reserved. Printed under license from the Stanford University Press, Stanford, CA 94305. Further reproduction is prohibited without the Publisher's written consent. *Strong Interest Inventory* is a trademark and *Strong Vocational Interest Blanks* is a registered trademark of the Stanford University Press.

Occupational Scales The occupational scales are the oldest and most researched scales on the inventory. They were designed to provide information about the degree of similarity between the examinee's interests and those of selected occupational criterion groups. Each occupational scale was empirically derived by comparing the responses given by a sample of workers in an occupation with those given by a

Table 16-4   SAMPLE BASIC SCALE ITEMS FROM THE STRONG INTEREST INVENTORY

Public speaking items	*Social service items*
Public relations director	Social worker
TV announcer	Helping others overcome their difficulties
Making a speech	Contributing to charities
Expressing judgments publicly, regardless of what others say	Youth organization staff member (e.g., YMCA, YWCA, YMHA, YWHA)

Source: Modified and reproduced by special permission of the Publisher, Consulting Psychologists Press, Inc., Palo Alto, CA 94303 from the *Strong Interest Inventory*™ of the *Strong Vocational Interest Blanks*® Form T317. Copyright 1933, 1938, 1945, 1946, 1966, 1968, 1974, 1981, 1985, 1994 by the Board of Trustees of the Leland Stanford Junior University. All rights reserved. Printed under license from the Stanford University Press, Stanford, CA 94305. Further reproduction is prohibited without the Publisher's written consent. *Strong Interest Inventory* is a trademark and *Strong Vocational Interest Blanks* is a registered trademark of the Stanford University Press.

general, nonspecific sample of people and selecting only those items that significantly differentiated the two groups. The resulting items composing each scale are heterogeneous with respect to item content. For example, physicians indicated a definite preference for playing golf, which differentiated them from the general reference group. Although this item does not reflect an occupationally relevant preference, it did significantly differentiate physicians from men in the general population and was therefore included on the physician's occupational scale. On the other hand, the item pertaining to math was highly preferred by both psychologists and the general male reference group. Because this item failed to differentiate the two groups, it was not included on the psychologist scale.

After a group of items was identified that significantly differentiated the occupational criterion groups from the general reference group, the criterion groups were scored on their own scales to determine precisely how many items the members of each group would endorse. Means and standard deviations were then computed for each scale, and these raw scores were transformed into T-score distributions. Thus, a score of 50 represents the average number of items endorsed by each criterion group.

Over the history of the SII, more and more occupational groups have been tested, normed, and added to the profile. Currently, 109 occupational scales have been developed. Finding adequate samples of both men and women for every occupation has often been very difficult, however. Some occupations, such as dental assistant and home economics teacher, have traditionally been so dominated by women that it has been extremely difficult to develop parallel scales for men. Likewise, other occupations have proved to be as problematic for women (e.g., agribusiness manager, plumber).

This difficulty raises the issue of why separately normed groups for the two sexes are needed. It would certainly be more efficient to report only one combined male-female group for each occupation. Although researchers (D. P. Campbell & Hansen, 1981; Hansen, 1976; Johansson & Harmon, 1972; Webber & Harmon, 1978) have attempted to create unisex norms for the occupational scales, they have concluded that because of the empirical differences in the interests of men and women even in the same occupation, separate sex norms are still warranted.

Sex Bias

The issue of sex bias in the measurement of interests historically was addressed only on a superficial level until the women's movement brought widespread attention to it. Before the 1970s, evidence indicated that men and women differed in their interests even if employed in the same job. Consequently, some researchers in the field of interest measurement felt that the way to deal with this discrepancy was to have separate but equal inventories for the sexes. Unfortunately, this solution created additional problems because the inventories for men and women were rarely equal.

Generally, there were far more occupational criterion groups available on the male form of the test than on the female form of the test. The rationale for this discrepancy was that there were so few opportunities for women in historically male-dominated occupations that there was no need to include these occupations on the female form of the SII.

Solving this problem has become a very complex issue. To simply compare both sexes with a combined group of men and women seems unacceptable, given that research has shown gender differences exist for between one quarter and one third of the items on the SII (Harmon, Hansen, Borgen, & Hammer, 1994). To develop both male and female criterion groups for each occupation has been by far the most popular solution. The difficulty with this strategy, as we have seen, is that in certain instances, there are so few workers of one sex in an occupation that finding a representative sample from which to construct a reliable and valid scale has been nearly impossible. Another solution that has some merit is simply to provide score information on all scales (i.e., reporting scores for both male and female criterion groups). This option helps prevent examinees from narrowing their focus based solely on gender issues. Finally, although it may be interesting to speculate about the possibility that gender differences on the SII might decrease in the future—thus eliminating the need for separately gender-normed scales—at the present time, there is no compelling evidence that this is occurring, and therefore the data appear to us to clearly demand their continued use.

Interpretation of the SII

Figure 16-3 presents a modified printout of the SII profile generated by Rebecca, who is a 20-year-old junior majoring in social work. The first step in the interpretation process is to determine whether there are any indications of significant problems in responding that might invalidate her test results. The total number of responses and the number of infrequently given responses both suggest that her results are valid. Similarly, the distribution of her choices across the three response options (i.e., like, indifferent, and dislike) also appears to be well within normal limits.

Her personal style scale scores show that she strongly prefers work that involves people contact. She prefers to learn by experience rather than engaging in a formal educational program. Being in positions of leadership is comfortable for her, but she probably does not mind taking directions from others if needed. Rebecca is not likely to be a risk taker. She prefers activities that are more under her control and predictable.

Rebecca's scores on the basic and occupational scales indicate that she enjoys helping people. She shares many interests in common with child-care workers, elementary teachers, special education teachers, and social workers. She has considerably less interest in allied health, mechanical, and technical activities than most women and has few of the interests generally found among women in science, engineering, and agricultural careers. Overall, her interests as assessed by the SII appear to be focused, stable, and quite consistent with her current major of social work.

Evaluation of the SII

Over the 75-year-span since it was first published, the SII has been subjected to extensive research. Numerous studies have been conducted to determine its reliability and validity. Much of this research has been summarized elsewhere (D. P. Campbell, 1971; Harmon et al., 1994), so only selected findings are reviewed here.

Reliability. The most frequently employed methodology for measuring the reliability of the SII has been to administer the inventory on two occasions separated by an interval of time (i.e., test-retest reliability). The test-retest studies that have been conducted have produced results unparalleled in other areas of psychological testing. Interests as measured by the various forms of the SII have remained exceptionally stable over considerable intervals of time.

Two of the variables that appear to affect the stability of inventoried interest the most are (1) the length of time between testings and (2) the age of individuals when initially tested. With test-retest intervals as short as one week, the stability of SII scores has been reported to exceed .90 (D. P. Campbell, 1971). Recent research on the current revision of the SII (Harmon et al., 1994) reported very stable scores (median test-retest correlations in the mid to high .80s) for four samples tested one to three months apart. As the interval increases, the reliability of the inventory decreases. Conversely, as the age of examinees when first tested increases, the stability of test scores generally increases. D. P. Campbell (1971) has shown how these two variables affect the reliability of the inventory. This information is summarized in Table 16-5.

Validity. The validity of the SII has generally been assessed by two methods. One method involves checking whether different occupational groups can be differentiated clearly from one another on the basis of their interest profiles. As discussed earlier, this type of study is designed to establish the concurrent validity of a test. A second method concerns whether interest scores are predictive of eventual occupational choice and career satisfaction (i.e., predictive validity).

The success of the SII in discriminating between people in different occupations has been assessed using two different methods. In one method, researchers examine how criterion groups score on occupational scales other than their own. For example, attention might be focused on whether chemists actually score as high or higher on their own scale than on other occupational scales. D. P. Campbell (1971) has reported data on a number of SII occupational groups and shown that, in general, criterion groups tended to score highest on their own scales. When exceptions did occur, they were usually in understandable directions. As in the preceding example, when the chemist occupational scale was studied, it was found that physicists actually scored higher on the chemist scale than did the average chemist (the mean score for physicists was 54 as opposed to 50 for chemists). This finding is not too surprising, however, given the similarity in interests among members of these occupational groups.

In the other, more frequently used method of establishing concurrent validity, comparisons are made between the response distributions of the general reference group and each criterion group to determine the percentage of overlap between the distributions. If occupational scales discriminate well, then a small amount of score overlap with the general reference group should occur. That is, members of the general reference sample should not score very high on any occupational scale. If the general reference group does generate high scores on an occupational scale, then the items on that scale are not differentiating the interests of criterion group members from those of a general sample of workers, and therefore it has little concurrent validity. Data

STRONG INTEREST INVENTORY™

Profile report for **REBECCA**
ID: 0000000

OCCUPATIONAL SCALES

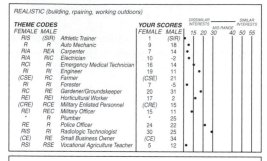

REALISTIC (building, rpairing, working outdoors)

THEME CODES FEMALE	MALE		YOUR SCORES FEMALE	MALE
RIS	(SIR)	Athletic Trainer	1	(SIR)
R	R	Auto Mechanic	9	18
RIA	REA	Carpenter	7	14
RIA	RIC	Electrician	10	-2
RCI	RI	Emergency Medical Technician	16	14
RI	RI	Engineer	19	11
(CSE)	RC	Farmer	(CSE)	21
RI	RI	Forester	7	-5
RC	RE	Gardener/Groundskeeper	20	31
REI	REI	Horticultural Worker	17	2
(CRE)	RCE	Military Enlisted Personnel	(CRE)	15
REI	REC	Military Officer	15	11
*	R	Plumber	*	25
RE	R	Police Officer	24	22
RIS	RI	Radiologic Technologist	30	25
(CE)	RE	Small Business Owner	(CE)	34
RSI	RSE	Vocational Agriculture Teacher	5	12

INVESTIGATIVE (researching, analyzing, inquiring)

THEME CODES FEMALE	MALE		YOUR SCORES FEMALE	MALE
IS	IA	Audiologist	36	28
IRA	IA	Biologist	3	13
IR	IR	Chemist	14	7
IR	IRA	Chiropractor	20	23
IAR	IAS	College Professor	13	12
IR	IAR	Computer Progr./Systems Analyst	20	15
IRA	IR	Dentist	24	17
IES	(SEC)	Dietitian	14	(SEC)
IRA	IA	Geographer	15	0
IRA	IRA	Geologist	7	-2
IRC	ICA	Mathematiciam	-2	-1
IRC	IRE	Medical Technician	14	9
IRC	IRC	Medical Technologist	11	12
IR	IR	Optometrist	23	11
ICR	ICE	Pharmacist	20	20
IAR	IAR	Physician	9	6
IRA	IRA	Physicist	-2	2
IA	IA	Psychologist	13	18
IR	IRC	Research & Development Manager	5	2
IRA	IRS	Respiratory Therapist	17	15
IRS	IRS	Science Teacher	5	5
IAR	(AI)	Sociologist	9	(AI)
IRA	IR	Veterinarian	1	-1

REALISTIC (building, rpairing, working outdoors)

THEME CODES FEMALE	MALE		YOUR SCORES FEMALE	MALE
CE	CE	Accountant	41	31
CI	CI	Actuary	16	15
CE	CE	Banker	47	38
C	C	Bookkeeper	34	37
CES	CES	Business Education Teacher	30	41
CE	CE	Credit Manager	42	31
CSE	*	Dental Assistant	25	*
CSE	(RC)	Farmer	38	(RC)
CES	CES	Food Service Manager	38	35
CIR	CIS	Mathmatics Teacher	13	-1
C	C	Medical Records Technician	31	35
CRE	(RCE)	Military Enlisted Personnel	25	(RCE)
CES	CES	Nursing Home Administrator	41	42
CE	CA	Paralegal	46	40
CES	*	Secretary	36	*
CE	(RE)	Small Business Owner	41	(RE)

ARTISTIC (creating or enjoying art, drama, music, writing)

THEME CODES FEMALE	MALE		YOUR SCORES FEMALE	MALE
AE	AE	Advertising Executive	46	47
ARI	ARI	Architect	16	16
ARI	A	Artist, Commercial	26	41
AR	A	Artist, Fine	20	28
ASE	AS	Art Teacher	18	35
AE	AE	Broadcaster	36	42
AES	AES	Corporate Trainer	42	49
ASE	ASE	English Teacher	21	28
(EA)	AE	Interior Decorator	(EA)	45
A	A	Lawyer	31	39
A	A	Librarian	25	35
AIR	AIR	Medical Illustrator	-4	19
A	A	Musician	28	41
ARE	ARE	Photographer	24	22
AER	ASE	Public Administrator	18	24
AE	AE	Public Relations Director	32	41
A	A	Reporter	27	31
(IAR)	AI	Sociologist	(IAR)	20
AIR	AI	Technical Writer	26	32
A	AI	Translator	16	31

SOCIAL (helping, instructing, caregiving)

THEME CODES FEMALE	MALE		YOUR SCORES FEMALE	MALE
(RIS)	SIR	Athletic Trainer	(RIS)	6
S	*	Child Care Provider	51	*
SE	SE	Community Serv. Organization Dir.	45	41
(IES)	SEC	Dietitian	(IES)	38
S	S	Elementary School Teacher	59	38
SAE	SA	Foreign Language Teacher	21	27
SE	SE	High School Counselor	38	38
SE	*	Home Economics Teacher	36	*
SAR	SA	Minister	15	29
SCE	SCE	Nurse, LPN	22	31
SI	SAI	Nurse, RN	31	25
SAR	SA	Occupational Therapist	36	37
SE	SE	Parks and Recreation Coordinator	37	39
SRC	SR	Physical Education Teacher	11	10
SIR	SIR	Physical Therapist	29	21
SEA	SEC	School Administrator	34	34
SEA	SEA	Social Science Teacher	21	33
SA	SA	Social Worker	55	48
SE	SEA	Special Education Teacher	54	51
SA	SA	Speech Pathologist	49	47

ENTERPRISING (selling, managing, persuading)

THEME CODES FEMALE	MALE		YOUR SCORES FEMALE	MALE
*	ECR	Agribusiness Manager	*	14
EC	EC	Buyer	36	29
ERA	ER	Chef	21	33
EIS	*	Dental Hygienist	28	*
EAS	ESA	Elected Public Official	21	25
EAS	EAS	Flight Attendant	42	55
EAC	EAC	Florist	36	38
EC	EA	Hair Stylist	41	47
ECS	ECS	Housekeeping & Maintenance Supr.	43	32
EAS	ES	Human Resources Director	45	46
EA	(AE)	Interior Decorator	27	(AE)
EIR	ECI	Investments Manager	17	20
E	E	Life Insurance Agent	42	40
EA	EA	Marketing Executive	45	43
ECR	ER	Optician	35	17
ECR	ECR	Purchasing Agent	24	25
E	E	Realtor	25	32
ECR	ECR	Restaurant Manager	32	32
ECA	ECS	Store Manger	38	33
ECA	ECA	Travel Agent	34	44

FIGURE 16-3   SII Report   *Source:* Modified and reproduced by special permission of the Publisher, Consulting Psychologists Press, Inc., Palo Alto, CA 94303 from the *Strong Interest Inventory*™ of the *Strong Vocational Interest Blanks*® Form T317. Copyright 1933, 1938, 1945, 1946, 1966, 1968, 1974, 1981, 1985, 1994 by the Board of Trustees of the Leland Stanford Junior University. All rights reserved. Printed under license from the Stanford University Press, Stanford, CA 94305. Further reproduction is prohibited without the Publisher's written consent. *Strong Interest Inventory* is a trademark and *Strong Vocational Interest Blanks* is a registered trademark of the Stanford University Press.

STRONG INTEREST INVENTORY™

Profile report for **REBECCA**
ID: **0000000**

— — — Female
━━━ Male

GENERAL OCCUPATIONAL THEMES
BASIC INTEREST SCALES

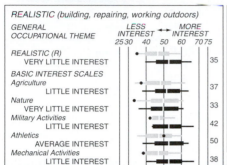

REALISTIC (building, repairing, working outdoors)

GENERAL OCCUPATIONAL THEME	LESS INTEREST ↔ MORE INTEREST	
REALISTIC (R) VERY LITTLE INTEREST		35
BASIC INTEREST SCALES		
Agriculture LITTLE INTEREST		37
Nature VERY LITTLE INTEREST		33
Military Activities LITTLE INTEREST		42
Athletics AVERAGE INTEREST		50
Mechanical Activities LITTLE INTEREST		38

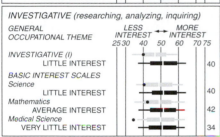

INVESTIGATIVE (researching, analyzing, inquiring)

GENERAL OCCUPATIONAL THEME	LESS INTEREST ↔ MORE INTEREST	
INVESTIGATIVE (I) LITTLE INTEREST		40
BASIC INTEREST SCALES		
Science LITTLE INTEREST		40
Mathematics AVERAGE INTEREST		42
Medical Science VERY LITTLE INTEREST		34

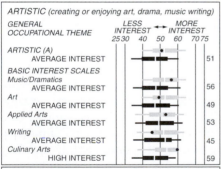

ARTISTIC (creating or enjoying art, drama, music writing)

GENERAL OCCUPATIONAL THEME	LESS INTEREST ↔ MORE INTEREST	
ARTISTIC (A) AVERAGE INTEREST		51
BASIC INTEREST SCALES		
Music/Dramatics AVERAGE INTEREST		56
Art AVERAGE INTEREST		49
Applied Arts AVERAGE INTEREST		53
Writing AVERAGE INTEREST		45
Culinary Arts HIGH INTEREST		59

SUMMARY OF ITEM RESPONSES

ADMINISTRATIVE INDEXES (response percentages)

OCCUPATIONS	27	%L	14	%I	59	%D
SCHOOL SUBJECTS	41	L	5	I	54	D
ACTIVITIES	37	L	22	I	41	D
LEISURE ACTIVITIES	28	L	13	I	59	D
TYPES OF PEOPLE	35	L	35	I	30	D
CHARACTERISTICS	67	Y	33	?	0	N
SUBTOTAL	33	%	16	%	51	%
PREFERENCES: ACTIVITIES	23	L	20	=	57	R
PREFERENCES: WORK	33	L	0	=	67	R

Total responses out of 317: **317**   Infrequent responses: **5**

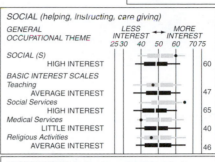

SOCIAL (helping, instructing, care giving)

GENERAL OCCUPATIONAL THEME	LESS INTEREST ↔ MORE INTEREST	
SOCIAL (S) HIGH INTEREST		60
BASIC INTEREST SCALES		
Teaching AVERAGE INTEREST		47
Social Services HIGH INTEREST		65
Medical Services LITTLE INTEREST		40
Religious Activities AVERAGE INTEREST		46

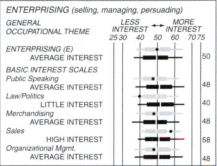

ENTERPRISING (selling, managing, persuading)

GENERAL OCCUPATIONAL THEME	LESS INTEREST ↔ MORE INTEREST	
ENTERPRISING (E) AVERAGE INTEREST		50
BASIC INTEREST SCALES		
Public Speaking AVERAGE INTEREST		48
Law/Politics LITTLE INTEREST		40
Merchandising AVERAGE INTEREST		48
Sales HIGH INTEREST		58
Organizational Mgmt. AVERAGE INTEREST		48

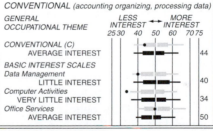

CONVENTIONAL (accounting organizing, processing data)

GENERAL OCCUPATIONAL THEME	LESS INTEREST ↔ MORE INTEREST	
CONVENTIONAL (C) AVERAGE INTEREST		44
BASIC INTEREST SCALES		
Data Management LITTLE INTEREST		40
Computer Activities VERY LITTLE INTEREST		34
Office Services AVERAGE INTEREST		50

PERSONAL STYLE SCALES

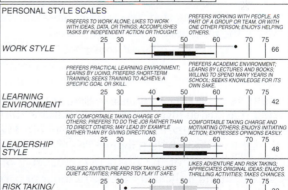

WORK STYLE — PREFERS TO WORK ALONE; LIKES TO WORK WITH IDEAS, DATA, OR THINGS; ACCOMPLISHES TASKS BY INDEPENDENT ACTION OR THOUGHT. / PREFERS WORKING WITH PEOPLE, AS PART OF A GROUP OR TEAM, OR WITH ONE OTHER PERSON; ENJOYS HELPING OTHERS. — 66

LEARNING ENVIRONMENT — PREFERS PRACTICAL LEARNING ENVIRONMENT; LEARNS BY DOING; PREFERS SHORT-TERM TRAINING; SEEKS TRAINING TO ACHIEVE A SPECIFIC GOAL OR SKILL. / PREFERS ACADEMIC ENVIRONMENT; LEARNS BY LECTURES AND BOOKS; WILLING TO SPEND MANY YEARS IN SCHOOL; SEEKS KNOWLEDGE FOR ITS OWN SAKE. — 42

LEADERSHIP STYLE — NOT COMFORTABLE TAKING CHARGE OF OTHERS; PREFERS TO DO THE JOB RATHER THAN TO DIRECT OTHERS; MAY LEAD BY EXAMPLE RATHER THAN BY GIVING DIRECTIONS. / COMFORTABLE TAKING CHARGE AND MOTIVATING OTHERS; ENJOYS INITIATING ACTION; EXPRESSES OPINIONS EASILY. — 48

RISK TAKING/ ADVENTURE — DISLIKES ADVENTURE AND RISK TAKING; LIKES QUIET ACTIVITIES; PREFERS TO PLAY IT SAFE. / LIKES ADVENTURE AND RISK TAKING; APPRECIATES ORIGINAL IDEAS; ENJOYS THRILLING ACTIVITIES; TAKES CHANCES. — 32

Table 16-5   MEDIAN TEST-RETEST CORRELATIONS FOR THE MEN'S OCCUPATIONAL SCALES FOR VARYING AGES AND TEST-RETEST INTERVALS

Age at first testing	Test-retest interval					
	2 Weeks	−1 Year	2–5 Years	6–10 Years	11–20 Years	20+ Years
17–18	—	.80	.70	.65	.64	—
19–20	.91	.80	.73	.67	.67	.64
22–25	—	—	.78	.69	.75	.72
26+	—	—	.77	.81	.80	—

Source: From D. P. Campbell, *Handbook for the Strong Vocational Interest Blank*, p. 82. Copyright © 1971 by Stanford University Press. Reproduced by permission.

presented by Hansen and Campbell (1985) on the amount of score overlap indicate that, on average, approximately one third of the scores from the criterion group distributions overlap with those of the general reference group. The amount of overlap appears to vary as a function of how clearly defined the occupational groups are with respect to interests and specific worker tasks. For example, farmers, artists, and chemists show less overlap and are more clearly defined occupational groups than are college professors and elementary teachers, which show much larger score overlap.

Administering the inventory to different samples of people before occupational entry and following them up later to determine in which careers they eventually became employed generally has been the method used to assess the predictive validity of the SII. Several problems have plagued this line of research. First, it is often difficult to determine whether the occupations entered were predictable from earlier inventory results because current job titles may not have appeared on the original test profiles. Some researchers have dealt with this problem by simply comparing the individual's current occupation with a scale score from the original testing that most closely resembles the current occupation. Others, however, have held that this arbitrary decision process on the part of researchers tends to artificially inflate the predictive validity estimates for the inventory. They believe that only direct-scale comparisons should be done and all other data discarded when predictive studies are conducted. Depending on the strategy selected, researchers have differed somewhat in their conclusions concerning the inventory's predictive validity.

Strong (1955) reported that people tested with his inventory eventually entered occupations for which they had shown an interest when previously tested. Specifically, he stated that the chances were about two in three that people would be in occupations predicted earlier by high test scores on corresponding occupational scales. He also stated that the chances were only about one in five that individuals would be in occupations in which they had shown little interest when tested.

Other researchers (Dolliver, Irvin, & Bigley, 1972) have suggested that the two-in-three estimate of the predictive efficiency of the SII is probably an overestimate, since their data indicated that the number of correct predictions was more in the vicinity of one in two. On the other hand, they reported that the one-in-five estimate for low scores was probably an underestimate. They reported that only one person in eight people was later in an occupation on which he or she had received low scores when tested. Regardless of which is the most accurate estimate of the predictive validity of the test, both indicate that it is quite useful in predicting future occupational entry.

Other factors have also been studied that appear to moderate the predictive efficiency of the SII. For example, McArthur (1954) found that socioeconomic status had an effect on the test's predictive power. He suggested that people from very wealthy families often chose careers less on the basis of interest and more on the basis of opportunities generated by the family's position. Consequently, the SII was found to be more predictive for middle-income people than for those of extremely high socioeconomic status. Brandt and Hood (1968) found that psychological adjustment also played a role. They reported that the test was more predictive for well-adjusted people than for those with emotional problems. Finally, D. P. Campbell (1966) demonstrated that the predictive validity of the SII was higher for those who had well-defined interests when initially tested. Thus, it is apparent that a number of factors affect the overall validity of this test.

A few other studies on the validity of the SII are worthy of note here. Spokane (1979) examined the predictive validity of the 1974 revision of the test for both college men and women over a 3 1/2-year span. Spokane reported good predictive validities for the inventory but also found that students who had expressed interests consistent with their measured interests were also more likely to report satisfaction with their jobs. Donnay and Borgen (1996) have shown that even the nonoccupational scales on the SII such as the personal style scales also accurately predict occupational membership. Other researchers (Hansen & Swanson, 1983; Hansen & Tan, 1992) have reported data suggesting that the inventory can also be used to predict choice of college major. Similarly, Randahl, Hansen, and Haverkamp (1993) suggested that exposing people to the results of the SII can have a positive impact on their career exploration.

Applications of the SII

The SII has long been used as a major tool in helping people to plan their educational and vocational futures. It was designed specifically for this purpose. The SII allows people to compare their interests with those of individuals already in the world of work, providing them with important information necessary to make more informed career choices. This application of the test has been by far the most common, and many experts in the field agree that the SII appears to accomplish this goal quite well (Borgen, 1988).

The SII has also been used rather extensively in selection situations in which employment decisions need to be made; the rationale underlying its use in such cases is that job satisfaction is important for productivity. As we have noted, the SII does predict actual job entry and eventual satisfaction. Therefore, it has been used in selection situations to predict which potential employees are most likely to be satisfied with their work. Selection decisions have thus been based in part on these interest test scores. The use of the inventory for this purpose is somewhat controversial, however.

Counselors have used the SII for other purposes as well. It has been administered in counseling situations to help people to identify their preferences for activities and situations that are unrelated to their work. Using the test in this fashion is intended to assist people to increase their overall life satisfaction by helping them find appropriate outlets for some of their interests not satisfied in their career. The SII is also employed as a tool in counseling to help people to understand why they might be experiencing job dissatisfaction and how to maximize their efforts to meet their needs. For example, a physical therapist with strong interests in the performing arts might find greater satisfaction working as a therapist for a touring dance company than in a setting where there was little chance to interact with other artistically oriented people. Finally, others have used the SII to help to improve counseling outcomes (Kivlighan, Hageseth, Tipton, & McGovern, 1981). The idea here has been to administer the test to clients and then to plan appropriate counseling interventions to more closely match their personal interests (e.g., structured interventions for people preferring structure, active interventions for people who like to be physically active).

To assist counselors in using the SII, a number of administrative and interpretive aids have been developed. Although the SII must be machine scored, options are now available to purchase the necessary software to score the test on an office computer. This method has significantly reduced the amount of time needed to administer and score the test. To extend its use to non-English-speaking people, the SII has been translated into Spanish, French, and Hebrew. Interpretation of the results has been enhanced through the development of a number of score-reporting options. Counselors can choose to use the standard profile report with clients. As the profile report has evolved, efforts have been made to provide test takers with as much interpretive information as possible about their individual scores. Currently, the profile report consists of six pages, each of which has information on the back explaining the score information on the reverse side. In addition to the profile report, expanded descriptions of scores are also available. These narrative reports are computer-generated descriptions that personalize the information and go into greater depth to interpret the examinee's scores. In addition, some of the narrative material provided as a special scoring option contains additional educational and career exploration information that is keyed to the SII results.

THE KUDER INTEREST INVENTORIES

The field of interest measurement has also been significantly affected by the work of Frederick Kuder. His interest inventories date back to 1939, when the University of Chicago Bookstore published the first version of his instrument. This original version utilized a paired-comparison item format to assess preferences for seven interest areas. In 1944, he published the Kuder Preference Record, Vocational (Form B), introducing the now-familiar item triad format that has continued to be a feature of present-day Kuder inventories. The Kuder Preference Record, Vocational (Form C), was added in 1946 and is still available today. This version employed an interesting system for administering and scoring the inventory. Examinees indicated their most and least preferred choices from among three alternatives in each item by punching holes in their multipage answer sheets with a metal stylus. Scoring consisted of counting the number of holes made in the answer sheet in specific places indicated on the reverse side of the answer sheet.

In 1956, Kuder adopted a different vocational interest assessment philosophy. With the publishing of the Kuder Preference Record—Occupational (Form D), his focus shifted from simply assessing the activity preferences of examinees to examining the similarity that existed between examinees' preferences and the preferences of specific occupational groups. Although the methodology he used to accomplish this differed from that employed by Strong on the SII, both instruments basically relied on comparisons with a general reference sample to assess occupational interests. Ten years later in 1966, the Kuder Occupational Interest Survey (Form DD) was published. This version continued the focus on measuring the degree of similarity between respondents' interests and those of people employed in various occupations. It deviated from the strategy used in Form D, however, by eliminating comparisons with a general reference group and using direct comparisons with members of various occupational groups.

In 1988, the Kuder General Interest Survey (Form E) was published. This version represented an adaptation of the older Form C. It could be used with a wider age range and also included additional scoring options. The most recent in the long line of Kuder interest inventories is the Kuder Career Search with Person Match, published in 1999. This version provides person-to-person matching rather than the person-to-group matching used on earlier versions of the Kuder. Since it is quite new and has generated very little research, its effectiveness as an interest measure cannot be adequately evaluated; however, we have previewed it in a critical discussion because it does represent a new and somewhat novel approach to interest assessment.

The Kuder Occupational Interest Survey

In contrast to the SII, the Kuder Occupational Interest Survey (KOIS) employs several different approaches to interest assessment. Specifically, the KOIS differs in two major ways. First, Kuder believed that the best way to assess interests was to use a forced-choice, ipsative item format (e.g., two or more alternatives in each item from which examinees must choose their response). Consequently, he employed a paired-comparison item format on his surveys. As discussed before, this strategy for scale construction produces test results that reveal relative strengths and weaknesses within an individual, rather than the absolute level of a trait or factor within the individual.

Second, Kuder did not share Strong's conviction that the best way to measure interests involved comparing criterion groups with a common comparison group consisting of men or women in general. In place of this method, Kuder chose to use the actual average responses of each criterion group to determine the items for each of the scales on his survey. Thus, he was not interested in identifying only those items that differentiated a criterion group from a general comparison group, such as is the case with the SII, but in selecting all the items actually endorsed by members of a criterion group. His contention was that this method of scale construction provided superior separation among criterion groups and therefore improved the overall validity of the inventory.

Construction of the KOIS

The KOIS maintains the use of the ipsative item format that earlier versions of the test also used. It presents items in a trichotomous format, with instructions to select from each set of three alternatives the one that is most preferred and the one that is least preferred. In effect, a ranking of the three alternatives is thus obtained for each item. A sample of items similar to those on the survey is reproduced in Table 16-6. Descriptions of each of the scales on the KOIS follow.

Verification Scale. This scale was designed to assess whether examinees properly filled out their surveys. Each item on this scale is composed of three alternatives, only one of which is commonly selected by most people. For example, an item contributing to an examinee's score on the verification or V scale may include the following three choices: "be introduced to everyone at a big party made up of strangers," "be introduced to a few people at the party," or "not be introduced to people at the party." Examinees giving a "most like" response to either the first or third choices have responded in a rather unique and statistically infrequent direction.

If a substantial number of infrequently endorsed responses is given throughout the test, the validity of the resulting scores becomes suspect. That is, the probability would be greatly increased that the test scores may have resulted from other factors than item content alone. Such factors as careless marking of the answer sheet, failure to follow the test directions, intentional dissimulation, or random responding are often the cause of suspicious verification scores. However, all questionable verification scores need to be followed up to determine their cause, since examinees with rather

---

Table 16-6   SAMPLE KOIS ITEMS

The directions state that in each group of three activities, examinees are to choose one that they would "most" like to do and one that they would "least" like to do by filling in the appropriate circle. One item in each group of three should be left blank, indicating that it is between the "most" and "least" preferred activity.

1. Visit an art gallery	M	L
Browse in a library	M	L
Visit a museum	M	L
2. Collect autographs	M	L
Collect coins	M	L
Collect stones	M	L

Source: From the Kuder Form DD Occupational Interest Survey, Revised. Copyright © 1985 by Science Research Associates, Inc. Reproduced by permission.

unique interest patterns that are quite different from those of most people may generate verification scores that resemble those of an invalid profile.

Vocational Interest Estimates. A recent addition to the KOIS is the vocational interest estimate (VIE) scales. These broadly defined interest areas provide an overview of the examinee's interests, broken down into 10 major interest fields. In many ways, the VIE scales rather closely resemble the general theme scales on the SII. In fact, Zytowski (1985) has shown how these 10 interest fields can be reclassified into Holland's system of 6 by grouping several of the related areas together (e.g., the outdoor and mechanical areas can be combined to form Holland's realistic theme; the artistic, musical, and literary areas together compose Holland's artistic theme).

Occupational Scales. The occupational scales on the KOIS are similar to those on the SII, in that they are designed to reflect the similarity between the respondent's interests and those of employed workers. The people chosen to represent the various occupational groups had demographic characteristics similar to those used in the construction of the SII; their average age was 45 years, they had been employed in their current occupation for at least 3 years, and they were reportedly very satisfied with their work.

The occupational scales differ from those on the SII, in that they were constructed to reflect all the interests and noninterests of occupational groups, rather than just those that differentiated them from a general comparison group. The significance of this difference is that the occupational scales on the Kuder contain larger numbers of high-base-rate items (i.e., those given very frequently by most people) than do the comparable scales on the SII. You will recall that in the case of the SII, high-base-rate items were essentially eliminated from the occupational scales by the use of a general comparison group in the development of the scales. This difference often means that examinees produce higher interest scores on the Kuder than on the SII because of the presence of these high-base-rate items.

Kuder has maintained that his method of scale construction gives a more accurate picture of the similarity between examinees' interests and those of workers in various occupations than does the method employed on the SII because it permits a direct comparison of all interests and not just a unique subsample. Little evidence at present, however, substantiates that one method is clearly superior to the other.

On the Kuder, the occupational scale scores are reported as correlation coefficients measuring the relationship between the individual's interests and those of workers in various criterion groups. The scores are arranged on the profile in descending order of magnitude, rather than grouped according to any particular theoretical system, such as that proposed by Holland and used on the SII. Kuder believed that the most meaningful arrangement of scores would show a listing of people's interests from strongest to weakest, without regard to the type of interests indicated. This view is in keeping with the overall ipsative nature of the inventory that stresses the relative position of inventory scores.

Although the ranking of the occupational scale scores is of greatest importance on the Kuder, their magnitude is also important. Keeping in mind that correlation coefficients range from .00 to 1.00 in magnitude and increase exponentially, it is rare for occupational scales to exceed values in the mid .70s. In fact, most criterion group members obtain scores ranging between .45 and .75. Therefore, users of the Kuder have found that scores below .45 on the occupational scales are indicative of minimal interest in those areas.

One additional feature of the occupational scales on the KOIS is that they span a much wider spectrum of the world of work than does the SII. This feature permits the user to assess interests not only at the business and professional level but also at the skilled level. This has persuaded some users to select the Kuder over the SII when time is a consideration and additional testing at lower socioeconomic levels is desirable.

College Major Scales. The development of a special set of scales to measure academic interests represented an innovation on the KOIS that was not available on earlier Kuder inventories. These scales were designed to measure the similarity between the respondents' interests and those of college seniors majoring in various academic disciplines. They are of particular value in working with adolescents and young adults because the college major scales were developed with individuals from a similar age group. This feature is in contrast to the occupational scales, which are composed of workers who average 45 years of age. Because of the developmental nature of interests, the availability of peer-criterion groups for score interpretation with younger examinees has been welcomed.

As can be seen from the profile reproduced in Figure 16-4, there are 22 male and 17 female college major scales on the KOIS. Because of the differences in the number and type of college major scales reported for males and females, their usefulness in cases of students with nontraditional interests has been questioned. Nevertheless, their addition to the profile has represented a useful innovation in interest measurement.

Experimental Scales. Eight additional scales have been included on the Kuder to provide supplemental administrative information useful in determining the overall validity of the profile. These scales can be found in the lower-right corner of the example in Figure 16-4. The M and W scales were designed to be used to help determine whether examinees completed the inventory with an open and a truthful attitude. This task is accomplished by comparing an examinee's responses with those of men and women who took the inventory under two separate sets of instructions. On one occasion, the instructions were to respond in a truthful and genuine manner (M and W scales), whereas on a second testing, the instructions were to respond so as to create the best possible impression of themselves (MBI and WBI scales). Consequently, examinees giving overly flattering pictures of their interests are likely to score higher on the "best impression" scales rather than on the other set of scales representing more genuine responses.

Kuder Occupational Interest Survey Report Form

Name

Sex   MALE

Date

Numeric Grid No.   SRA No. 00102

1 Dependability: How much confidence can you place in your results? In scoring your responses several checks were made on your answer patterns to be sure that you understood the directions and that your results were complete and dependable. According to these:

YOUR RESULTS APPEAR
TO BE DEPENDABLE.

2 Vocational Interest Estimates: Vocational interests can be divided into different types and the level of your attraction to each type can be measured. You may feel that you know what interests you have already — what you may not know is how strong they are compared with other people's interests. This section shows the relative rank of your preferences for ten different kinds of vocational activities. Each is explained on the back of this report form. Your preferences in these activities, as compared with other people's interests, are as follows:

Compared with men		Compared with women	
HIGH		HIGH	
MECHANICAL	83	MECHANICAL	99
AVERAGE		MUSICAL	80
MUSICAL	75	AVERAGE	
CLERICAL	67	SCIENTIFIC	58
SCIENTIFIC	49	CLERICAL	55
LOW		LOW	
ARTISTC	23	COMPUTATIONAL	18
SOCIAL SERVICE	19	OUTDOOR	18
OUTDOOR	17	ARTISITC	11
COMPUTATIONAL	11	SOCIAL SERVICE	11
LITERARY	06	LITERARY	06
PERSUASIVE	01	PERSUASIVE	01

3 Occupations: The KOIS has been given to groups of persons who are experienced and satisfied in many different occupations. Their patterns of interests have been compared with yours and placed in order of their similarity with you. The following occupational groups have interest patterns most similar to yours:

Compared with men		Compared with women	
NURSE	.59	ENGINEER	.56
ELEM SCH TEACHER	.58	DENTIST	.54
OPTOMETRIST	.56	COMPUTER PRGRMR	.53
PHOTOGRAPHER	.55	OCCUPA THERAPIST	.53
PHYS THERAPIST	.55	BANKER	.52
DENTIST	.54	ARCHITECT	.50
BUYER	.53	ACCT, CERT PUB	.50
SCIENCE TCHR, HS	.53		
X-RAY TECHNICIAN	.53		
THESE ARE NEXT MOST SIMILAR:			
AUDIOL/SP PATHOL	.49		

Compared with men
THESE ARE NEXT MOST SIMILAR:

POSTAL CLERK	.52
AUDIOL/SP PATHOL	.52
TRAVEL AGENT	.52
TV REPAIRER	.52
MATH TCHR, HS	.52
COMPUTER PRGRMR	.51
ENGINEER	.51
COUNSELOR, HS	.51
BRICKLAYER	.51
SUPERVISOR, INDUST	.50
PODIATRIST	.50
LIBRARARIAN	.49
MATHEMATICIAN	.49
AUTO SALESPERSON	.49
BOOKSTORE MGR	.49
ARCHITECT	.49
FILM/TV PROD/DIR	.49
FLORIST	.49
METEOROLOGIST	.48
PLUMBING CONTRAC	.48
PHARMACIST	.48
POLICE OFFICER	.48
WELDER	.48
BANKER	.48
PLANT NURSRY WKR	.47
PAINTER, HOUSE	.47
MACHINIST	.47
LAWYER	.47
AUTO MECHANIC	.47
PRINTER	.47

THE REST ARE LISTED IN ORDER OF SIMILARITY:

SOCIAL WORKER	.46
FORESTER	.46
INTERIOR DECOR	.46
PHYSICIAN	.46
CHEMIST	.46
ELECTRICIAN	.46
ACCT, CERT PUB	.45
INSURANCE AGENT	.45
REAL ESTATE AGENT	.45
CLOTHER, RETAIL	.45
PERSONNEL, MGR	.45
BLDG CONTRACTOR	.44
PHARMACEUT SALES	.44
BOOKKEEPER	.44
PSYCHOLOGIST	.44
CARPENTER	.44
PLUMBER	.43
VERERINARIAN	.43
STATISTICIAN	.42
RADIO STATION MGR	.42
MINISTER	.41

Compared with women
MOST SIMILAR, CONT.

PHYS THERAPIST	.52
X-RAY TECHNICIAN	.52
VETERINARIAN	.52
PHYSICIAN	.52
ELEM SCH TEACHER	.52
DENTAL ASSISTANT	.51
SECRETARY	.51
MATH TEACHER, HS	.51
FLORIST	.51
EXTENSION AGENT	.50
INSURANCE AGENT	.50
SCIENCE TCHR, HS	.49
FILM/TV PROD/DIR	.49
NURSE	.49
BOOKKEEPER	.49
BANK CLERK	.49
BEAUTICIAN	.49
DIETICIAN	.49

THE REST ARE LISTED IN ORDER OF SIMILARITY:

LIBRARIAN	.48
COUNSELOR, HS	.48
OFFICE CLERK	.47
COL STU PERS WKR	.47
SOCIAL WORKER	.47
BOOKSTORE MGR	.47
PSYCHOLOGIST	.47
INTERIOR DECOR	.47
NUTRITIONIST	.46
PREMED/PHARM/DENT	.46
RELIGIOUS ED DIR	.45
DEPT STORE-SALES	.44
JOURNALIST	.44
LAWYER	.44

Compared with men
REST, CONT.

TRUCK DRIVER	.41
SCHOOL SUPT	.41
EXTENSION AGENT	.40
FARMER	.37
JOURNALIST	.35

4 College Majors: Just as for occupations, the KOIS has been given to many persons in different college majors. The following college major groups have interest patterns most similar to yours:

Compared with men		Compared with women	
ELEMENTARY EDUC	.56	PHYSICAL EDUC	.58
MUSIC & MUSIC ED	.55	MATHEMATICS	.52
ENGINEERING	.54	THESE ARE NEXT MOST SIMILAR:	
PHYSICAL EDUC	.54		
MATHEMATICS	.51	MUSIC & MUSIC ED	.51
PHYSICAL SCIENCE	.50	HEALTH PROFESS	.50
THESE ARE NEXT MOST SIMILAR:		HOME ECON EDUC	.48
		BUSINESS EDUC	.48
ARCHITECT	.49	ELEMENTARY EDUC	.48
FOREIGN LANGUAGE	.49	BIOLOGICAL SCI	.48
FORESTRY	.48	THE REST ARE LISTED IN ORDER OF SIMILARITY:	
BUSINESS ADMIN	.46		
AGRICULTURE	.46	FOREIGN LANGUAGE	.45
BIOLOGICAL SCI	.46	NURSING	.44
PREMED/PHARM/DENT	.46	HISTORY	.41
SOCIOLOGY	.45	DRAMA	.41
ANIMAL SCIENCE	.44	ART & ART EDUC	.41
ART & ART EDUC	.44	PSYCHOLOGY	.41
SERV ACAD CADET	.44	SOCIOLOGY	.38
THE REST ARE LISTED IN ORDER OF SIMILARITY:		POLITICAL SCI	.36
		ENGLISH	.35
ECONOMICS	.43		
PSYCHOLOGY	.43		
HISTORY	.40		
POLITICAL SCI	.36		
ENGLISH	.33		

Experimental Scales.

				V-SCORE	56
M	.52	MBI	.13	W	.47	WBI	.13
S	.53	F	.52	D	.44	MD	.45

7-3881

FIGURE 16-4 KOIS Profile   *Source:* From the Kuder Form DD Occupational Interest Survey, Revised. Copyright © 1985 by Science Research Associates, Inc. Reproduced by permission.

One additional use of the M and W scales is to assess how similar the respondent's interests are to those of adult males and females. Women and men who have atypical interests for their sex often score higher on the opposite-sex scale. This information often alerts the user to expand the exploration process with those examinees to include many nontraditional interest areas that may not have shown up on the profile. It is interesting to note that the M and W scales are really quite similar to the male and female general comparison scales encountered on the SII.

The remaining four scales were designed to give the user information about the developmental stage of a person's interests. The F and M scales were constructed by having a group of fathers and mothers respond to the inventory under the normal instructional set. The S and D scales were constructed by having the sons and daughters of these fathers and mothers also complete the inventory in the usual manner. By comparing the respondent's scores on these scales, users can determine whether the person's interests are more like those of a younger age group or more like those of older adults. The assumption underlying these scales is that if the examinees' interest patterns resemble those of adolescents and young adults, their inventoried interests are probably somewhat unstable and will undergo additional change. In contrast, examinees showing interests more like those of older adults are seen as having more well-defined career interests less subject to change.

Interpretation of the KOIS

The sample profile reproduced in Figure 16-4 can be used to illustrate the interpretation process. Tom, a 34-year-old man seeking vocational counseling, generated this profile. We begin the interpretation by checking the verification score to see whether the results are likely to represent a valid picture of Tom's interests. Since there is a high probability that scores above .45 represent valid interest profiles, we assume that Tom's profile gives an accurate picture of his interests.

Next we can look at the vocational interest estimates to get an overall summary of the results. Tom's scores indicate that he has above-average interests in mechanical activities and below-average interests in artistic, social service, outdoor, computational, literary, and persuasive areas.

The occupational scales reveal that Tom has ranked his interest in social service and allied-health occupations highest, and he has completed the survey in a manner consistent with employed workers in those areas. His interests in technical and mechanical fields are also strong but probably secondary to those in the social and health-related fields. It is interesting to note that Tom rejected few occupational possibilities, as evidenced by the lack of many low occupational scores.

The college major scales show a pattern of ranking most similar to college seniors pursuing various programs in education. The similarity to seniors in some of the sciences and engineering probably reflects Tom's mechanical and technical interests. The academic areas of least interest to Tom appear to be in the social and behavioral sciences.

The experimental scales reveal that Tom has fairly traditional male interests. He also apparently responded to the test in an open and honest manner, without a conscious attempt to dissimulate his results in a particularly favorable way. We can also see that his interests resemble those of older adults and therefore are likely to be rather stable. There are no indications that his results should not be taken as an accurate reflection of his overall vocational interests.

Evaluation of the KOIS

Since the publication of the KOIS in 1966, a number of studies have been conducted in an attempt to establish its psychometric characteristics. Much of this research is reported either in the Manual (Kuder, 1970; Kuder & Diamond, 1979) or in Kuder's book on interest measurement (Kuder, 1977).

Reliability. Two primary types of studies have been done to assess the stability of Kuder scores. As stated earlier, since the Kuder has an ipsative format, the order of the occupational scales is extremely important. Consequently, the ordering of the scales should remain stable over time if the inventory is to be of use in vocational counseling.

One hundred independent determinations of the stability of Kuder scores for both high-school seniors and college students of both sexes were computed to check whether the ordering of scores would remain the same over time (Kuder, 1970). The results indicated that over a 2-week interval, the median correlation coefficient was .90 for all comparisons. Other groups have been similarly tested, with the majority of test-retest coefficients being above .90. Longer intervals up to 3 years have been used with engineering students. The resulting reliability estimates ranged from .35 to .98, clustering just under .90 for most groups.

The second group of studies conducted to assess the reliability of the Kuder involved the consistency of differences among scores on pairs of scales when tested over time. Of concern here is whether the differences between occupational scores remain constant or change as time passes. Data reported in the Manual (Kuder, 1970) indicate that the separation between occupations remains quite constant, as indicated by test-retest correlation estimates ranging from .84 to .92.

Validity. The validity of the KOIS generally has been assessed in two different ways. First, attention has been given to the frequency with which members of one occupational group actually score higher on a scale other than their own (i.e., concurrent validity). On the basis of large samples, the general finding has been that such errors of classification occur approximately 6% of the time.

Similar concurrent validity research also has been designed to determine how well the occupational scales differentiate between groups. Much of this research has focused on the 30 core occupational groups selected to represent the domain of occupations covered on the KOIS. For each of these 30 groups, 100 employees were selected. All 30 groups were scored on all 30 scales. The resulting matrix revealed that many groups did not score highest on their own scale. However, the scales on which they did score highest tended to reflect similar interest dimensions (e.g., school superintendents often scored higher on the personnel manager scale; social workers often scored higher on the clinical psychologist scale). These data seem to suggest that some occupational groups can readily be separated on the basis of interest with a high degree of accuracy, whereas others are more alike and therefore more difficult to separate.

A third demonstration of concurrent validity involves studies comparing criterion group members' highest scores with the scores that they generated on their own occupational scales. As with the reliability studies, the 30 core groups composed of 100 workers each were used. The results showed that 64% of the time, workers' scores on their own occupational scales were within .009 points of their highest scores. Thus, although the KOIS appears to do a reasonable job of differentiating the interests of various occupational groups, this separation is not perfect.

Research on the predictive validity of the KOIS is more sparse. As has been shown, demonstrations of predictive validity are of utmost importance to users of interest inventories. Unfortunately, much of the research on predicting job satisfaction and occupational entry from inventory scores has been done on earlier forms of the test (Lipsett & Wilson, 1954; McRae, 1959). These earlier results have suggested that the likelihood of being dissatisfied in a career is about three times greater if the career chosen was not consistent with previously measured interests. Since these findings were obtained for other forms of the Kuder, however, they cannot be unequivocably extended to the KOIS.

Two more recent predictive studies (Zytowski, 1976; Zytowski & Laing, 1978) have shed some additional light on the validity of the KOIS. Using data gathered on the Kuder Preference Record—Occupational, an earlier version of the KOIS with identical items, these researchers reported that, on average, the accuracy of predicting eventual career selection was comparable to that of other instruments. Specifically, about 50% of the persons in the longitudinal sample were in careers consistent with their top five occupational scores when tested earlier.

Applications of the KOIS

The addition of college major scales on the inventory has been an important attraction for users who desire a direct measure of academic interests. These scales have been used widely to assist students in making important educational decisions, such as course selection and choice of major.

Because of the extended socioeconomic level of occupations provided by the KOIS, it also has found extensive use in those applied settings where the career objectives of people are likely to encompass a rather large span of the world of work. This situation is most often encountered in such settings as vocational-training schools, junior colleges, mental health centers, employment agencies, and employee development offices in business and industry. Here, the primary decisions to be made involve placement of people into specific areas of training, educational programming, or employment based on their inventoried interests.

CRITICAL DISCUSSION:

A Novel Approach to Interest Measurement: The Kuder Career Search With Person Match

As we have discussed, one of the major objectives of the KOIS is to match people with jobs by comparing the interests of examinees with the interests of people in various careers. However, Kuder (1980) has long believed that a potentially more meaningful and useful measure of interest would match a person's interests with another person's interests rather than with a group of people's interests. The KCS (Zytowski, 1999) represents an attempt to implement this interest assessment strategy. The assumption underlying the KCS is that a person is not as much like people in a somewhat heterogeneous occupational group as he or she is like another individual in a specific job. Consequently, more precise and meaningful information about a person can be obtained by matching the interests of a person with those of another person.

The KCS consists of 60 items, each of which is composed of three different activities to which the respondent indicates his or her first, second, and third choices according to his or her preferences for each activitiy. Table 16-7 presents a sample item from the inventory. On the basis of the examinee's ranked preferences, a score is computed for each of the traditional 10 activity preference scales (e.g., nature, mechanical, science/technical, art, music, communications, human service, sales/management, computations, and office detail) included on Kuder inventories. In addition, scores are also included for six cluster scales representing the six Holland interest areas. These scales reflect the examinee's mean score when compared with an aggregate of people constituting all the occupational groups composing each area.

Table 16-7   SAMPLE KCS ITEMS

The directions indicate that examinees should decide which of the three activities they would prefer to do most and blacken the circle with the number 1 inside it. Then they should blacken the number 2 circle for the activity they next prefer and blacken the circle with the number 3 inside for the activity they least prefer from among the three choices.

Write advertising	1	2	3	Work in a candy factory	1	2	3
Be in charge of a public library	1	2	3	Raise chickens	1	2	3
Publish a newspaper	1	2	3	Give eye examinations	1	2	3

The unique feature of the KCS involves the Person Match scoring procedure. Person matching compares the respondent's activity preference profiles with those of all the criterion persons in the database using Spearman's rank order correlation. Respondents are provided with a list of the top 25 matches revealing which people they are most similar to with respect to their preferences and therefore what jobs they may find satisfying given their similar interests with a person doing that kind of work. Finally, biographical information on the people in the database who are the closest interest matches for the inventory taker are given in the summary report to aid in the career exploration process. Figure 16-5 presents a sample of the information provided in the KCS computer-generated summary report.

CAREER ASSESSMENT INVENTORY

The Career Assessment Inventory (CAI) was developed by Charles Johansson and first published in 1976 by National Computer Systems, Inc. It was originally designed to measure the interests of those people considering careers not requiring a

I. Your Activity Preference Profile

Your personal activity preference profile is shown below. It should help you develop a clear picture of yourself, what activities you most and least prefer. Try to keep your top two or three in mind as you think about your future plans.

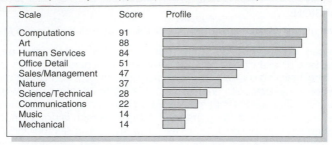

Scale	Score	Profile
Computations	91	
Art	88	
Human Services	84	
Office Detail	51	
Sales/Management	47	
Nature	37	
Science/Technical	28	
Communications	22	
Music	14	
Mechanical	14	

II. Your Preferred Kuder Career Clusters™

Occupations have similarities and differences that enable them to be grouped together into Kuder Career Clusters™. Each cluster has similarities in job duties and outcomes (such as pay level and satisfaction), educational requirements, and career pathways, that make them different from the other clusters. One popular classification system gives six career clusters.

Your activity preferences have been compared with the composite profiles of occupations in six career clusters. They are shown here in order of your similarity. Mark the circle located beside each definition below with a 1 through 6 as it corresponds to your similarity.

① Social & Personal Service
② Business Detail
③ Sales & Management
④ Arts & Communication
⑤ Science & Technical
⑥ Outdoor & Mechanical

Person Match™ ! . . . .

You are a person, not a job title. Yet, when it comes to choosing careers, people tend to only think in terms of job titles or job descriptions, not the individuals behind them. That's why the Kuder Career Search developed Person Match™.

Person Match™ compares your interests with over 1500 real people in satisfying careers. On the following pages are the job sketches of the 5 individuals from the Kuder Career Search reference group whose activity preferences most resemble your own. They have all been fortunate to get into occupations they like – that are satisfying to them in significant ways. By reading about their jobs, you may explore possibilities for your own career.

Read the job sketches. Note from the sketches how the persons describe their work and the way they got into their present occupations; note whether they are working at a job they truly love, at two jobs, or at a job that supports their interest in some activity that is really satisfying to them but doesn't pay, like community theater or volunteer work.

Can you find a theme or several themes common among them? Perhaps it will be a career field, like financial services. Or, it may be a characteristic common to most of them, like being your own boss or working at any level to be a part of an industry that excites you.

Carefully reading and acting on this information is a vital step in your journey toward a satisfying career. Use it well.

. . . .

ACCOUNTING CLERK (330)

Although my educational background, which includes a Bachelor of Arts in psychology degree, does not correspond with my employment, I am fairly satisfied with my job in general accounting and am now planning to continue my education in business. I plan to earn a bachelor's degree in accounting and possibly to become a certified public accountant.

As the general accounting clerk in a small office, I handle the various accounting functions for the company. My regular duties include: handling accounts payable, receivables, payroll once a week, journal entries, and phone calls with vendors and/or customers to discuss account problems.

I like the kind of work I do, and the people I work with. I find job satisfaction in the challenge of my work, in problem-solving and in the socialization within the workplace.

FIGURE 16-5 KCS Computer-Generated Report *Source:* Reproduced with permission by National Career Assessment Services, Inc.™ from the Kuder Career Search with Person Match™ © 1999. All rights reserved.

4-year college degree. Rather than being targeted at the business and professional level, as is the SII, the CAI was intended to assess the interests of workers at the skilled, semiskilled, and unskilled levels of the occupational hierarchy. This is still true today for the vocational version of the test. However, an expanded form of the CAI, the enhanced version (Johansson, 1986), adds a number of professional-level occupations to the test and so extends its applicability to occupations requiring 4-year degrees as well.

Although the item content on the CAI rendered it quite susceptible to sex bias, much careful consideration was given to this issue throughout its development. To eliminate sex bias as much as possible, several notable strategies were employed in the development of the CAI. First, gender-specific occupational titles were avoided in favor of more gender-neutral titles. Second, broad career exploration by both sexes was encouraged by choosing a representative cross section of those careers at the nonprofessional end of the occupational spectrum. Finally, a rather novel procedure has been used in the development of the occupational scales on the current revision of the test. Rather than relying on the established method of developing gender-specific occupational scales (i.e., creating separate male and female scales for each occupation), Johansson (1984) initiated the use of combined-gender occupational scales, thus eliminating the need for separate male and female scores for each occupational group. These three test development procedures have significantly reduced the effect of sex bias on the inventory.

The overall format of the CAI as well as its construction closely resembles that of the SII. The development of the CAI included two substantial modifications, however, which improved its psychometric properties. First, the item response format was expanded to include a 5-point continuum ranging from "very much like" to "very much dislike." Sample items are shown in Table 16-8. This response format enables examinees to make finer discriminations among their preferences than was possible with the 3-point scale provided on the SII. Second, the CAI does not contain as many different type of items as does the SII. Of particular interest here is the fact that the CAI has dropped the ipsative-formatted section on the dyadic preferences (e.g., respondents decide between two statements that they would prefer, "produce an item" or "sell an item"), which always has created complex statistical problems for those desiring to establish reliability and validity estimates.

Table 16-8   SAMPLE CAI ITEMS

201. Be a Bank Cashier	L l l d D	226. Be a Driving Instructor	L l l d D
202. Be a Bartender	L l l d D	227. Be an Electrician	L l l d D
203. Be a Barber	L l l d D	228. Be an Elementary School Teacher	L l l d D
204. Be a Bill Collector	L l l d D	229. Be a Farmer	L l l d D
205. Be a Biologist	L l l d D	230. Be a Fashion Designer	L l l d D

Source: From Johansson, *Career Assessment Inventory.* Copyright © 1973, 1982 by National Computer Systems. Reprinted by permission.

Construction of the CAI

As with the SII, scores on the CAI are organized into four classes of scales for purposes of interpretation. The theme, basic interest, and occupational scales provide a hierarchical analysis of interests into general areas of interests, more specific interests, and very specific interests, respectively. The fourth class of scales—the administrative indexes and special scales—principally provide a check on the validity of the inventory results.

Administrative Indexes and Special Scales. One scale contained in this group— the number of infrequently given responses—involves a measure of whether the examinee correctly followed the directions for filling out the answer sheet and was able to comprehend the written material on the instrument. A second scale—the number of total responses—simply alerts the user if too few responses were given or scored to produce a valid picture of the examinee's interests. Finally, the CAI also contains a response-patterning section analogous to that on the SII that reveals the percentages of all response types given on the inventory. Once again, this array is intended to give information about potential choice problems faced by examinees, such as approach-approach problems (e.g., many interests present, all of which are very desirable), undifferentiated interests (e.g., no clearly defined likes or dislikes), or avoidance-avoidance problems (e.g., strong dislike shown for a major portion of activities surveyed by the CAI).

Several special scales are also included on the CAI that are somewhat similar to the learning environment and leadership style scales on the SII. They provide data on whether examinees like to have close contact with others on their jobs and whether they enjoy formal educational settings, as is characteristic of those who obtain advanced training and academic degrees. In addition to these two scales, a third scale has been added to assess the variety among a respondent's interests and a fourth scale to measure the degree to which examinees prefer artistic and social activities in comparison to mechanical and outdoor work.

Theme Scales. As has been previously described, Holland's theoretical system for classifying occupations provides the basis for grouping the remaining scales on the inventory. The theme scales give the user an overview of the examinee's interest in each of the six Holland areas. They are composed of 20 items chosen to represent each of the Holland types.

Basic Interest Scales. The basic interest scales were constructed to measure the domains of interest assessed by the CAI. Their development was based on the intercorrelations among items on the inventory. Items that were related highly to one another and judged to fit logically into psychologically meaningful categories were grouped into basic interest scales. They differ from those on the SII in that they are generally much more homogeneous and show substantially higher intercorrelations. Their purpose, however, is the same—to indicate areas of specific interest.

Occupational Scales. The occupational scales on the CAI were constructed in much the same manner as those on the SII. Workers representing various occupational groups at the skilled, semiskilled, and unskilled levels of the workforce were tested, and their responses were compared with those of either a general male or female reference sample. These reference groups were designed to represent a cross section of all the occupations on the CAI. Those items differentiating the criterion group's responses from those of the general male or female reference sample were then selected for inclusion on that criterion group's occupational scale. The major difference between the SII and the CAI involves how the item-selection process was done. Whereas the SII forms separate occupational scales for each sex, on the CAI, only those items common to both male and female scales were retained to form a combined-sex scale for each occupation. Following item selection, the scales were then normed for each criterion group and the raw scores transformed to T scores to facilitate the interpretation process.

Just as with the SII, scores on the occupational scales indicate the degree of similarity between the examinee's responses to the CAI and the responses of each occupational criterion group. The assumption on which these scales are based is that, as the degree of similarity in interest increases, the likelihood of career satisfaction also increases. This follows from the fact that the members of each criterion group were selected primarily because they had indicated that they were satisfied with their jobs, and therefore examinees showing similar interest patterns should experience satisfaction if they made the same occupational choices.

Interpretation of the CAI

The sample profile for the CAI appears in Figure 16-6. It reflects the interests of Bill, age 21, who is currently considering taking some vocational courses at the local vocational technical school but is uncertain as to which career path to pursue. Since graduating from high school, he has spent the last 3 years working on a factory assembly line.

The validity indicators in Bill's case all appear to be within normal limits and do not suggest the presence of any unusual test-taking attitudes on his part. His distribution of "like," "indifferent," and "dislike" responses appears to be sufficiently well differentiated to preclude any special decision-making difficulties on his part. Furthermore, he seemed quite clear about his preferences, given the small number of "indifferent" responses he indicated.

The special scales reveal that Bill does not like to work closely with people but, rather, prefers working in environments with minimal interpersonal contact. His level of interest in academic activities resembles that of people who pursue limited formal education beyond high school or vocational school. Bill indicated some diversity among his interests, although they are focused mainly in the outdoor and technical area.

The theme and basic interest scales reveal that Bill has indicated a rather clear preference for agricultural, electronics, carpentry, and mechanical activities. With the exception of some interest in science, Bill showed little interest in any of the other areas on the CAI. His scores on the occupational scales also reflect this same pattern. His

ADMINISTRATIVE INDICES

Career Assessment Inventory™ - Vocational Version
ID 1 BiLL

RESPONSE PERCENTAGES

	LL	L	I	D	DD
Activities	9	21	17	20	34
School Subjects	19	40	9	16	16
Occupations	14	29	4	29	24

Special Scales	Score
Total Responses	305
Fine Arts-Mechanical	76
Occupational Extroversion/Introversion	87
Educational Orientation	16
Variability of Interests	35

GENERAL THEME SCALES

	Scale	Std. Score	Very Low (35)	Low (43)	Average (57)	High (65)	Very High	Average Opp. Sex
R	Realistic	68						40-52
I	Investigative	55			★			42-56
A	Artistic	30	★					46-59
S	Social	29	★					46-59
E	Enterprising	37		★				43-56
C	Conventional	39		★				46-60

Your scores indicate that you should also investigate the additional occupations listed at the end of this report.

OCCUPATIONAL SCALES

Occupational Scales	Std. Score	Very Diss. (15)	Dissimilar (25)	Mid-Range (44)	Similar (54)	Very Sim.	Average Opp. Sex
Realistic Theme							
Aircraft Mechanic (RI)	62					★	12-24
Auto Mechanic (R)	64					★	12-22
Bus Driver (R)	51				★		18-28
Camera Repair Tech (RI)	51				★		10-22
Carpenter (R)	59					★	16-27
Conservation Officer (R)	59					★	9-24
Dental Lab Technician (RI)	50				★		25-35
Drafter (RI)	51				★		14-26
Electrician (R)	63					★	12-22
Emergency Med Tech (RS)	36			★			21-33
Farmer/Rancher (R)	62					★	23-31
Firefighter (R)	56					★	16-29
Forest Ranger (RI)	56	★					0-17
Hardware Store Mgr (RC)	53					★	8-19
Janitor (R)	59					★	22-31
Machinist (R)	67					★	6-18
Mail Carrier (RC)	47			★			17-28
Musical Instrmnt Repair (RIA)	50				★		20-30
Navy Enlisted (RI)	57				★		18-29
Orthotist/Prosthetist (RI)	47				★		20-33
Painter (R)	52				★		20-32
Park Ranger (RI)	42			★			14-28
Pipefitter/Plumber (R)	67					★	14-26
Police Officer (RS)	51				★		23-33
Printer (R)	64					★	16-27
Radio/TV Repair (RI)	55					★	10-20
Security Guard (RC)	46			★			23-30
Sheet-Metal Worker (R)	65					★	5-17
Telephone Repair (RI)	63					★	19-29
Tool/Die Maker (RI)	67					★	1-16
Truck Driver (R)	60					★	17-25
Veterinary Tech (RII)	32			★			14-30
Investigative Theme							
Chiroprctor (IS)	15	★					23-35
Computer Programmer (I)	38			★			18-29
Dental Hygienist (ISA)	12	★					21-34
Electronic Technician (IR)	42			★			13-23
Math/Science Teacher (I)	34			★			20-32
Medical Lab Technician (IR)	43			★			24-34
Radiologic Technician (IRS)	36			★			27-40
Respiratory Ther Tech (IRS)	32			★			26-40
Surveyor (IR)	60					★	11-23
Artistic Theme							
Advertising Artist/Writer (A)	13	★					16-29
Advertising Executive (AE)	8	★					25-37
Author/Writer (A)	4	★					17-29
Counselor-Chem Dep (ASE)	4	★					29-41
Interior Designer (A)	2	★					19-31
Legal Assistant (AE)	11	★					27-38
Librarian (AI)	12	★					26-38
Musician (A)	4	★					17-31
Newspaper Reporter (AE)	0	★					12-26
Photographer (A)	11	★					17-32
Piano Technician (ARI)	35			★			18-30

BASIC INTEREST AREA SCALES

Basic Interest Area	Std. Score	Very Low (35)	Low (45)	Average	High (57)	Very High (65)	Average Opp. Sex
Realistic Theme							
Mechanical/Fixing	71					★	39-51
Electronics	68					★	40-50
Carpentry	64				★		40-53
Manual/Skilled Trades	77					★	40-51
Agriculture	63				★		40-53
Nature/Outdoors	56			★			44-57
Animal Service	58			★			43-57
Investigative Theme							
Science	57				★		42-56
Numbers	49			★			43-57
Aritistic Theme							
Writing	32	★					46-59
Performing/Entertaining	33	★					45-58
Arts/Crafts	34	★					48-60
Social Theme							
Social Service	28	★					46-58
Teaching	36		★				45-58
Child Care	32	★					47-60
Medical Service	41		★				45-59
Religious Activities	34	★					44-58
Enterprising Theme							
Business	35		★				44-57
Sales	45			★			43-56
Conventional Theme							
Office Practices	43			★			47-61
Clerical/Clerking	48			★			46-60
Food Service	36		★				48-60

Occupational Scales	Std. Score	Very Diss. (15)	Dissimilar (25)	Mid-Range (44)	Similar (54)	Very Sim.	Average Opp. Sex
Social Theme							
Athletic Trainer (SR)	26			★			21-34
Child Care Assistant (SA)	7	★					28-38
Cosmetologist (SA)	0	★					17-29
Elem School Teacher (SA)	3	★					30-41
Licensed Practical Nurse (SC)	18		★				30-40
Nurse Aide (SC)	0	★					17-30
Occupational Ther Asst (SR)	9	★					25-37
Operating Room Tech (SR)	27			★			27-38
Physical Ther Asst (S)	16		★				23-37
Registered Nurse (SI)	24		★				24-37
Enterprising Theme							
Barber/Hairstylist (ER)	13		★				11-23
Buyer/Merchandiser (EAS)	3	★					27-38
Card/Gift Shop Mgr (E)	19		★				28-39
Caterer (ES)	6	★					27-36
Florist (E)	22			★			26-36
Food Service Manager (ECS)	13		★				26-36
Hotel/Motel Manager (ECS)	5	★					26-38
Insurance Agent (ESC)	9	★					22-33
Manufacturing Rep (E)	23			★			16-27
Personnel Manager (EAS)	6	★					25-37
Private Investigator (EA)	22			★			25-36
Purchasing Agent (EC)	22			★			23-33
Real Estate Agent (E)	0	★					17-30
Reservation Agent (EAS)	8	★					28-40
Restaurant Manager (ECS)	14		★				28-37
Travel Agent (EC)	2	★					26-37
Conventional Theme							
Accountant (CE)	26			★			20-32
Bank Teller (CE)	3	★					25-38
Bookkeeper (C)	21		★				26-38
Cafeteria Worker (C)	15		★				19-30
Court Reporter (CE)	22			★			26-37
Data Entry Operator (CE)	23			★			29-40
Dental Assistant (CS)	18		★				28-39
Exec Housekeeper (CSE)	20			★			26-35
Medical Assistant (CS)	0	★					22-35
Pharmacy Technician (CS)	16		★				31-41
Secretary (C)	12		★				27-37
Teacher Aide (CS)	0	★					23-36
Waiter/Waitress (CSE)	25			★			30-39

FIGURE 16-6 CAI Pofile *Source:* From Johansson, *Career Assessment Inventory.*
Copyright © 1973, 1982 by national Computer Systems. Reprinted by permission.

FIGURE 16-6   CAI Profile   *Source:* From Johansson, *Career Assessment Inventory.* Copyright © 1973, 1982 by National Computer Systems. Reprinted by permission.

interests resemble those of workers in various outdoor and technical occupations, with little similarity to those of persons in business or social service fields.

Evaluation of the CAI

Much of the research on the psychometric properties of the CAI has come from the efforts of its developer, Johansson. Estimates of the test-retest reliability of the instrument have compared favorably with those reported for the SII and the Kuder. Median test-retest correlations reported in the Manual (Johansson, 1984) on the theme, basic interest, and occupational scales have all ranged from the high .70s to the mid .90s, dropping in magnitude as the amount of time between testings increased from a week to several years.

Studies on the validity of the CAI have been limited to examining its separation among occupations (demonstrations of concurrent validity) and its relationship to other interest inventories (demonstrations of construct validity). In assessing its concurrent validity, the percentage of overlap between various criterion groups and the reference sample of tradespeople in general has been computed. With the switch to the use of combined-gender occupational groups on the 1982 revision of the CAI, the occupational scales lost some power in separating the interests of the criterion groups from those of the general reference sample. Although this outcome has increased the percentage of score overlap, the amount of overlap remains comparable with that reported for other interest inventories, such as the SII. Thus, the evidence tends to support reasonable concurrent validity for the CAI.

Studies examining the intercorrelations of like-named scales on the CAI and other interest inventories have generally produced median coefficients in the .60s. Some important anomalies exist, however (e.g., the female beautician SII scale and the female cosmetologist CAI scale), that produce much lower correlation coefficients, suggesting that they are apparently tapping different aspects of the workers in that occupation. Although this is weak evidence for the construct validity of the CAI, it does offer some encouraging data supporting its current use. Unfortunately, no predictive validity research has been reported on the inventory to substantiate its use in predicting eventual occupational entry. Demonstrations of its predictive validity will be needed before the CAI can claim a permanent place among the established measures of career interests.

Applications of the CAI

Because it was designed to measure the interests of lower-socioeconomic workers, the CAI is not utilized as much in college settings as the SII and the KOIS. It is employed much more often as an aid in educational planning at the junior college and especially vocational-technical school level. Many high-school counselors find it extremely useful in career counseling with students considering entering the world of work immediately after graduation.

The CAI is also utilized in making personnel decisions in business and industry. The information provided by the inventory has proved to be of value in screening new employees for job openings and in facilitating the transfer of currently employed workers to other areas within the organization. Additionally, it has been used to assist in the outplacement of workers displaced by changes in company policy or by a slow economy. In this latter case, the adult workers involved are often older and therefore not likely to return to school to complete an advanced degree or seek postgraduate professional training. The CAI is quite well suited to help them to consider a midlife career change within their financial and educational limitations.

JACKSON VOCATIONAL INTEREST SURVEY

The Jackson Vocational Interest Survey (JVIS) represents a more recent attempt to measure career interests. The JVIS has changed little since it was first introduced in 1977. The main difference between the original and the current version of the instrument is that 16 items have been modified to improve their readability, eliminate dated material, or reduce cultural bias. One of its unique features is that it allows for both hand and machine scoring, which is a very attractive feature when time and financial constraints are present. An advantage of machine scoring is that it allows for the scoring of certain scales not available with the hand-scored version. Thus, some interpretive information is lost when the JVIS is not machine scored.

Because of its relative newness, many of the test construction methods employed in the development of the JVIS were quite sophisticated and advanced. Consequently, Jackson was able to create an instrument with superior psychometric properties. Additionally, great care was taken during its development to suppress the effect of the acquiescence response set that pervades many interest inventories that require examinees to indicate an attraction or aversion for a set of stimulus items.

Construction of the JVIS

The JVIS consists of 289 vocationally relevant activities arranged in an ipsative format. The items are grouped into 34 basic interest scales on the basis of their interrelationships. Each scale was designed to reflect the interest dimension designated by its scale name. In addition, interscale correlation was minimized in an effort to maximize the amount of discrimination possible among interest patterns.

For each of the 289 items, examinees select either an A or B statement, indicating their preferred choice. The items are arranged such that an item from one of each of seventeen basic scales in the A group is paired with an item from each of the seventeen basic scales in the B group. Table 16-9 shows several sample items from the test. Thus, scales within a group are never directly compared with each other. Rather, they can be compared with one another only in reference to how frequently each was chosen when compared with a different common set of scales. Consequently, the JVIS can be thought of as an instrument composed of two separate sets of scales, virtually forming two independent ipsative measures.

All the basic interest scales on the JVIS were developed by employing the rational method of scale construction, by which items are developed according to the theoretical ideas of the author, unlike the three inventories reviewed previously, which utilized an empirical method of scale construction. Jackson chose a rational approach

Table 16-9   SAMPLE JVIS ITEMS

A. Artistically painting sets for a play.
B. Playing records and having young students sing along.

A. Acting in a television comedy.
B. Teaching youngsters how to write.

A. Spending spare time "playing" with difficult algebra problems.
B. Correcting spelling errors on a pupil's lesson.

A. Weaving rugs with unusual designs.
B. Buying and selling stocks for a client.

A. Memorizing lines for a play.
B. Investigating the possibility of buying foreign bonds.

A. Developing unusual mathematical problems for use in a textbook.
B. Studying a company's history of financial growth.

A. Crafting unusual picture frames.
B. Ordering new supplies for a store.

A. Starring in a low-budget movie.
B. Serving as administrative assistant to the head of a large firm.

A. Studying the proof of a complex mathematics problem.
B. Corresponding with customers by mail.

Source: From Jackson Vocational Interest Survey. Copyright © 1977, 1995 by Douglas N. Jackson. Reproduced by permission of Sigma Assessment Systems, Inc., Suite 435, P.O. Box 610984, Port Huron, MI 48061-0984 (800) 265-1285.

based on research showing that scales derived rationally, purified by internal consistency checks, were more stable and valid than those derived empirically (Ashton & Goldberg, 1973; L. R. Goldberg & Slovic, 1967). Of more importance, however, rationally derived scales permit a direct and meaningful interpretation of their content, and Jackson believes that such scales therefore are more useful in counseling.

Work Role Scales. The 34 basic interest scales on the JVIS are composed of two different types. The first group, called the work role scales, bears some resemblance to both the basic interest and the occupational scales encountered on other interest inventories. These scales resemble the basic interest scales in that they are intended to measure specific interests, rather than the degree of similarity between an examinee's interests and those of various occupational groups. Thus, the mathematics work role scale indicates whether individuals like math per se, rather than whether they share interests in common with mathematicians. On the other hand, they function somewhat like the occupational scales in that research has shown that various occupational groups do score highest on the work role scale associated with their area of activity. For example, lawyers score highest on law, and engineers score highest on engineering.

Work Style Scales. The other group of basic interest scales bears some resemblance to the personal style scales on the SII in that they were designed to measure preference for working in environments demanding particular modes of behavior, such as stamina, dominant leadership, security, and the like. The interests measured by this group of scales cut across a number of careers and so are broader in their scope. The additional information they provide helps form a more complete picture of the examinee's personal characteristics. Table 16-10 presents a listing of the 34 basic interest scales on the JVIS and indicates which are work role and work style scales.

Additional Scales. If the JVIS is machine scored, several additional groups of scales are provided. First are the general occupational theme scales. The JVIS provides scores on 10 basic themes, which are very analogous to the theme scales on other instruments. Although the scale names are not always comparable, they can be grouped together to produce a list very similar to Holland's six themes.

Another group of scales provides data on the similarity between the examinee's interests and those of college students majoring in various academic disciplines. Finally, a third cluster of scales indicates the degree of similarity between an individual's interests and those of workers in a variety of careers. These latter scales are comparable to the occupational scales characteristic of other interest inventories.

Interpretation of the JVIS

Figure 16-7 presents the JVIS profile of Linda, a 35-year-old mother of two, returning to the workforce after an absence due to childrearing. The following description of her results demonstrates what type of information can be gained from the survey.

Linda's results suggest that she does not enjoy artistic activities as much as the majority of women. Instead, her interests appear to be much more in the sciences. She appears to like medical and allied-health work, but she may not seek out positions involving considerable social service activity. She will probably choose jobs requiring more technical skill and less direct interpersonal contact if she elects a medical career.

Linda has indicated generally that business is a lower priority for her than it is for most people. She has less interest in sales, clerical work, finance, and managerial activities than in most other areas on the JVIS. Should she enter a business field, the

Table 16-10 JACKSON VOCATIONAL INTEREST SURVEY SCALES

Creative Arts	Medical Service	Supervision
Performing Arts	Dominant Leadership[a]	Human Relations Mgt.
Mathematics	Job Security[a]	Law
Physical Science	Stamina[a]	Professional Advising
Engineering	Accountability[a]	Author-Journalism
Life Science	Teaching	Academic Achievement[a]
Social Science	Social Service	Technical Writing
Adventure	Elementary Education	Independence[a]
Nature-Agriculture	Finance	Planfulness[a]
Skilled Trades	Business	Interpersonal Confidence[a]
Personal Service	Office Work	
Family Activity	Sales	

[a]Denotes work style scales.

Source: From Jackson Vocational Interest Survey. Copyright © 1977, 1995 by Douglas N. Jackson. Reproduced by permission of Sigma Assessment Systems, Inc., 511 Fort Street, P.O. Box 610984, Port Huron, MI 48061-0984 (800) 265-1285.

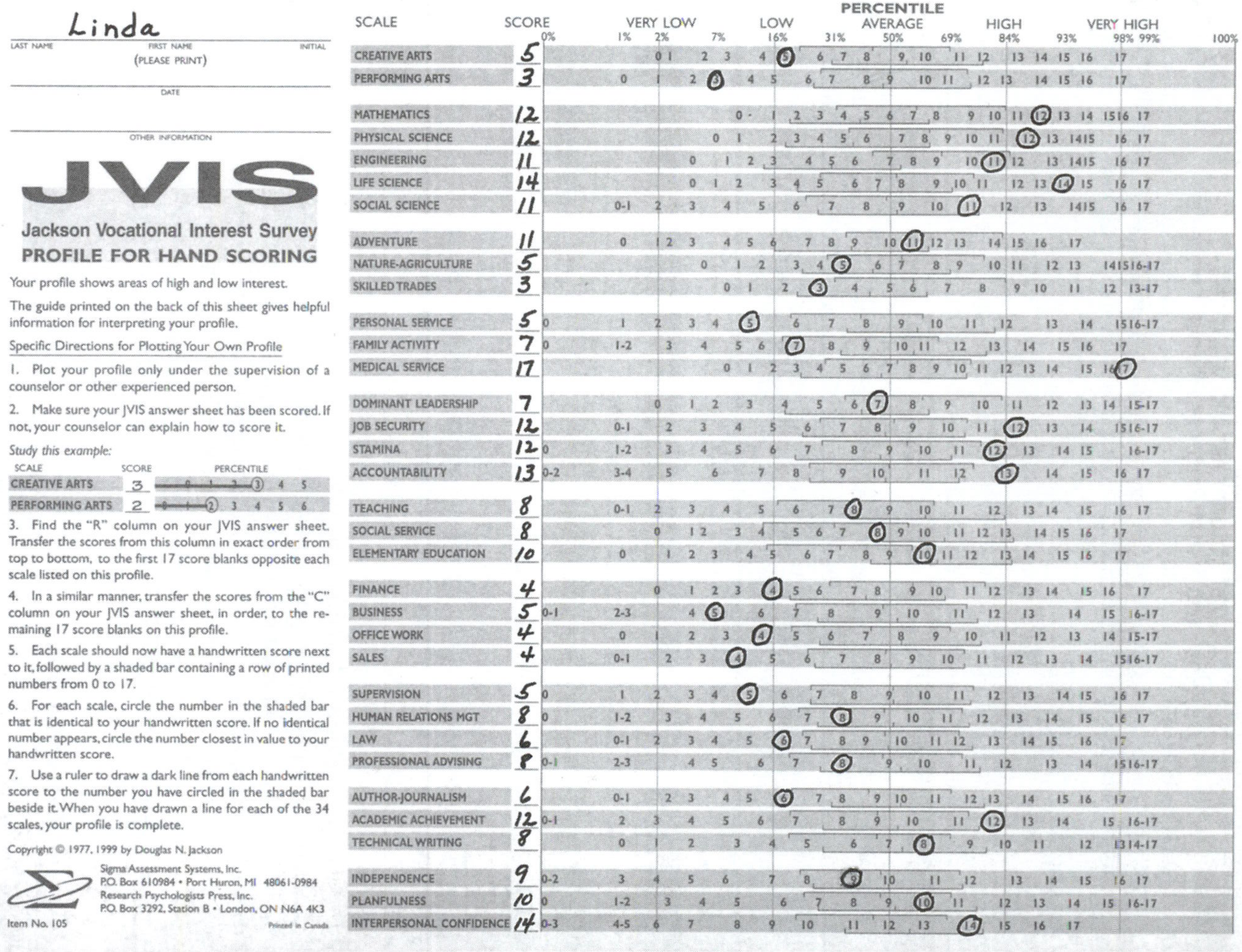

Linda

LAST NAME FIRST NAME INITIAL

(PLEASE PRINT)

DATE

OTHER INFORMATION

JVIS

Jackson Vocational Interest Survey
PROFILE FOR HAND SCORING

Your profile shows areas of high and low interest.

The guide printed on the back of this sheet gives helpful information for interpreting your profile.

Specific Directions for Plotting Your Own Profile

1. Plot your profile only under the supervision of a counselor or other experienced person.

2. Make sure your JVIS answer sheet has been scored. If not, your counselor can explain how to score it.

Study this example:

SCALE	SCORE	PERCENTILE
CREATIVE ARTS	3	0 1 2 (3) 4 5
PERFORMING ARTS	2	0 1 (2) 3 4 5 6

3. Find the "R" column on your JVIS answer sheet. Transfer the scores from this column in exact order from top to bottom, to the first 17 score blanks opposite each scale listed on this profile.

4. In a similar manner, transfer the scores from the "C" column on your JVIS answer sheet, in order, to the remaining 17 score blanks on this profile.

5. Each scale should now have a handwritten score next to it, followed by a shaded bar containing a row of printed numbers from 0 to 17.

6. For each scale, circle the number in the shaded bar that is identical to your handwritten score. If no identical number appears, circle the number closest in value to your handwritten score.

7. Use a ruler to draw a dark line from each handwritten score to the number you have circled in the shaded bar beside it. When you have drawn a line for each of the 34 scales, your profile is complete.

Sigma Assessment Systems, Inc.
P.O. Box 610984 • Port Huron, MI 48061-0984
Research Psychologists Press, Inc.
P.O. Box 3292, Station B • London, ON N6A 4K3

Item No. 105 Printed in Canada

PERCENTILE: VERY LOW (1%, 2%), 7%, LOW (16%), 31%, AVERAGE (50%), 69%, HIGH (84%), 93%, VERY HIGH (98%, 99%), 100%

SCALE	SCORE
CREATIVE ARTS	5
PERFORMING ARTS	3
MATHEMATICS	12
PHYSICAL SCIENCE	12
ENGINEERING	11
LIFE SCIENCE	14
SOCIAL SCIENCE	11
ADVENTURE	11
NATURE-AGRICULTURE	5
SKILLED TRADES	3
PERSONAL SERVICE	5
FAMILY ACTIVITY	7
MEDICAL SERVICE	17
DOMINANT LEADERSHIP	7
JOB SECURITY	12
STAMINA	12
ACCOUNTABILITY	13
TEACHING	8
SOCIAL SERVICE	8
ELEMENTARY EDUCATION	10
FINANCE	4
BUSINESS	5
OFFICE WORK	4
SALES	4
SUPERVISION	5
HUMAN RELATIONS MGT	8
LAW	6
PROFESSIONAL ADVISING	8
AUTHOR-JOURNALISM	6
ACADEMIC ACHIEVEMENT	12
TECHNICAL WRITING	8
INDEPENDENCE	9
PLANFULNESS	10
INTERPERSONAL CONFIDENCE	14

FIGURE 16-7 JVIS Profile *Source:* From Jackson Vocational Interest Survey. Copyright © 1977, 1995 by Douglas N. Jackson. Reproduced by permission of Sigma Assessment Systems, Inc., Suite 435, P.O. Box 610984, Port Huron, MI 48061-0984 (800) 265-1285.

probability is low that Linda will find the work rewarding or satisfying, and it is highly likely that she will leave the field within a few years after entry.

When compared with various occupational patterns established for the JVIS, Linda's results resemble those of radiological and medical technologists, physicians, and other health professionals. Given her preference for high levels of job security, Linda would probably find a career in the medical area quite consistent with her work style.

Evaluation of the JVIS

One of the outstanding features of the JVIS involves its strong psychometric characteristics. Extensive research was undertaken as part of its development, but only highlights are presented here.

Reliability. Several different series of studies have been conducted to establish the reliability of the JVIS. First, data reported by D. N. Jackson (1999) on its test-retest reliability when used with college students revealed that the coefficients ranged from a low of .72 to a high of .91 over a one-week time period. Studies have not been done with time intervals longer than a few months, so its long-term stability remains unknown.

A second research strategy for establishing the reliability of the JVIS has been to check the stability of individual profiles over time. Obviously, if the highest scale score suddenly became the lowest on retesting, the stability of the survey would be suspect. D. N. Jackson (1999) has reported data from two separate studies that indicate that the rank ordering of the profile remains quite stable even over intervals up to 6 months.

Validity. Research activity designed to establish the validity of the JVIS generally has taken two main directions. One avenue has been to employ rather sophisticated factor analytic techniques to confirm that the content of the scales does measure the psychological variables that they were designed to assess. Much of the data reported by D. N. Jackson (1999) appears to substantiate the construct validity of the scales. This result is particularly important for the JVIS, where direct interpretability of the scales is relied on so heavily.

The second important avenue of research concerns demonstrating validity for the occupational clusters. Once again, most of the research in this area has attempted to show that the occupational clusters have concurrent validity (i.e., workers in various occupations score highest on those scales that would be expected on an a priori basis). Few predictive validity studies have been reported to date to substantiate that the JVIS is useful in predicting occupational entry; however, most of the available research suggests that future studies will probably establish that relationship.

Applications of the JVIS

The JVIS has been used mostly with college students as an aid in curriculum selection and career planning. Additional sources of career information are given on the computer-generated profile to facilitate the career exploration process of examinees. The JVIS has not been used very extensively outside educational settings. This trend may be due to the fact that it is such a new interest inventory, but it may also reflect that much of its scale derivation work utilized college students as subjects rather than employed adults. It remains to be seen whether the JVIS will begin to be used in other career counseling situations outside academia, such as for personnel selection or for placement in industry.

CRITICAL DISCUSSION:

Should Interest Tests Be Used in Personnel Selection?

Much controversy has arisen over the issue of whether interest tests should be used in personnel selection. Proponents of their use cite the vast literature indicating that interest tests predict eventual vocational choice and level of career satisfaction. They argue that since satisfied workers are most likely to remain in their chosen field of work, reduced employee turnover would save companies money that would otherwise be diverted to the selection and training of new employees.

On the other side of the controversy, critics argue that although interest tests have proven validity to predict which career fields an individual is likely to pursue, their validity rests on the assumption that examinees give genuine, unbiased responses to the test. They further state that it is inconceivable that potential job applicants are unbiased in responding to interest tests, since they are seeking the position for which they are being tested. Consequently, they are likely to respond to the test items as they believe a "good" employee of the company would. Critics cite several research studies (Steinmetz, 1932; Steward, 1947; Strong, 1943; Wallace, 1950) that have shown that interest tests results can be biased and distorted when test takers make conscious efforts to do so.

However, the issue is by no means resolved. Other studies (Abrahams, Neumann, & Githens, 1968; D. P. Campbell, 1971; Stephenson, 1965) have suggested that real-life intentional distortions may not be as serious as those induced experimentally. Nevertheless, both Kirchener (1961) and Gray (1959) have argued that applicants for jobs can significantly alter their interest test scores.

Although critics have raised many questions about the use of interest testing in personnel selection, few have suggested other selection devices as reasonable alternatives. Perhaps one way to deal with the problem of biased or faked scores on these tests is to create scales to detect this type of response set. If the extent of the tendency to bias the rest results could be determined, then a statistical correction factor could be applied to the results to obtain a more realistic appraisal of the applicant's career interests.

The controversy is likely to continue, however, until future research demonstrates that interest tests can be used validly in the selection process or until other valid, cost-effective alternatives to interest testing are developed.

SUMMARY

Four major interest measures in common use today are the Strong Interest Inventory (SII), the Kuder Occupational Interest Survey (KOIS), the Career Assessment Inventory (CAI), and the Jackson Vocational Interest Survey (JVIS). We examined in some detail how they were constructed and what information they provided to users. Sample cases and their associated profiles illustrated how these tests are used in clinical decision-making situations. Finally, each test was evaluated to determine how closely it reflects the characteristics of a good test outlined in the first section of this book. Table 16-11 provides a summary of this information as an aid in reviewing the tests covered in this chapter.

Table 16-11 COMPARISON OF CHARACTERISTICS OF VARIOUS INTEREST INVENTORIES

Test	Item format	Item content	Types of scales	Benefits and limitations
Strong Interest Inventory	Normative format with three choices: like, indifferent, and dislike	Items range from occupational titles to personal characteristics	Theme scales, basic scales, occupational scales, personal style scales, and administrative indexes	*Advantages* Oldest and most researched, good with business and professional-level occupations *Limitations* Poor discrimination among skilled and lower-level occupations, uses some unfamiliar job titles
Kuder Occupational Interest Survey	Ipsative format with examinees ranking their most- and least-preferred activity from a group of three	Items consist only of work-related activities	Vocational interest estimates, occupational scales, college major scales, and research scales	*Advantages* College major scales, gives ranking of interests for the examinee *Limitations* Reports scores in hard-to-compare correlation coefficients, ipsative format forces client rankings

Career Assessment Inventory	Normative format using 5-point Likert scale from most to least preferred	Items range from occupational titles to school subjects	Theme scales, basic scales, occupational scales, special scales, and administrative indexes	*Advantages* Provides measure of skilled, semiskilled, and unskilled level of interests, uses combined-gender reference groups *Limitations* Has limited representation of occupations in several of Holland's group
Jackson Vocational Interest Survey	Ipsative format pairing two activities in each item	Items consist only of specific activities	Work role scales, work style scales, and additional scales	*Advantages* Permits hand scoring, newest and most technically advanced in item selection and scaling *Limitations* Little research yet to assess its validity

PROBLEMS AND SOLUTIONS—RECAP

The Problem

Brad is a college freshman who has not yet declared a major. As part of his freshman seminar course, he is required to visit the career center on campus, take an interest test, and begin to formulate a career plan. When he saw his Strong Interest Inventory results, he noticed that he had a few identifiable interests and that one of them was in the agricultural area. His score on the farmer scale was moderately high and actually one of his highest occupational scores on the test. Growing up in an urban area, he had no previous experience with farming or ranching and was quite surprised by his results. Since he has never considered going into agriculture and has little interest in outdoor work, he now wonders whether he should begin exploring this area further or consider the test results as invalid and meaningless for him.

A Solution

Despite the fact that Brad's interest test results were quite unexpected, they still are useful and can provide some important information. The tricky part about understanding his results is that there is much more here than is readily apparent. Although at first look it may appear that Brad's interest test results indicate that he has similar interests to those of farmers and therefore should explore that career field, a more thorough analysis of his results is necessary to avoid arriving at this erroneous conclusion. Simply put, Brad's test results look similar to those of farmers primarily because of an anomaly imbedded in some of the occupational scales on the Strong and not because he actually enjoys activities related to farming.

Like all occupational scales on the SII, the item content of the farmer scale is very heterogeneous. The items constituting the scale were selected simply because they discriminated between how workers in the criterion group (i.e., farmers) responded in comparison with workers representing a general reference group (i.e., men or women in general). Although the items on the farmer scale do discriminate farmers from the general reference sample, this result does not mean that these items were necessarily more prefered by farmers than by the general reference sample. Actually, in the case of the farmer occupational scale, a rather high percentage of the items reflect rather strong dislikes on the part of farmers. That is, famers dislike a variety of activities more than do members of the general reference group. Consequently, because of the nature of the farmer scale's being composed of a rather large number of "dislikes," Brad's test responses might resemble those of farmers primarily because he dislikes many of the same activities that farmers dislike (e.g., art, counseling, cooking, etc.) and yet does not necessarily like the agriculturally related activities that farmers like (e.g., working outdoors, operating machinery, growing crops, etc.).

In order to determine whether Brad's score on the farming occupational scale really reflects a clear interest in that field or results from the scale anomaly just discussed, we need to look at some of his other test results. If we examine his basic interest scores in the Realistic area, we gain some critical information needed to solve our problem. If he does not show much interest in those areas highly relevant to farming (e.g., his basic interest scale scores on agriculture, nature, and mechanical are low), then we can conclude that his high score on the farmer occupational scale most likely resulted because he dislikes many of the same things that farmers dislike rather than sharing a common interest with them in specific agricultural activies. We could check this out further by looking at Brad's distribution of responses. We would expect to find that Brad's percentage of dislike responses on the SII was substantially above the normal level (e.g., approximately 40%). In Brad's case, both of these conditions existed. Therefore, his SII results should not be interpreted as supportive of agriculture.

KEY TERMS

Administrative indexes used in conjunction with measures such as the Strong Interest Inventory that provide information about the type and pattern of responses (e.g., how many "like" versus "dislike" responses are made)

Occupational scales scales scored in terms of the similarity of the examinee's responses to those of members of specific occupational groups

Occupational themes broad patterns of occupational interests identified in J. L. Holland (1973); examples include realistic, investigative, and enterprising themes

Verification scale used to assess consistency in responding to essentially identical items (e.g., the Kuder Occupational Interest Survey includes such a scale)

17

Personality Testing

In the preceding chapters of Part III, we discussed a number of important issues related to the measurement of ability and vocational interest, and we reviewed representative tests of these traits, examining their construction, characteristics, and uses. In this closing chapter to Part III, we conclude with a discussion of the remaining domain of psychological interest, personality. We review some of the most widely used measures of personality along with several of the recurring issues in personality assessment. Although the tests described here vary considerably in content and in methods of administration and scoring, they all are designed to provide a general description of the person being tested along one dimension or several dimensions that are thought to be relevant for understanding that person's behavior in everyday situations.

PROBLEMS AND SOLUTIONS—CAN PERSONALITY TESTS HELP IN MAKING SELECTION DECISIONS?

The Problem

Gary, the Director of Housing, is interested in seeing whether he can get some help in selecting resident assistants for the residence halls. In the past, Gary has relied on individual interviews with job applicants to decide who will be hired. This year, the number of resident assistants will be increased and their job duties expanded. They will be expected to conduct interviews with the residents during the middle of each semester to identify students who are struggling academically and then refer them to appropriate services on campus.

Gary consulted a psychologist in the Counseling Center about whether administering a personality test to his applicants would help him in the selection process. He wants to hire students who feel comfortable taking on a leadership role, have good interpersonal skills, and are empathic. Because students who are hired receive free room and board and a small monthly stipend for their work, he is concerned that some students might try to consciously distort their responses to put themselves in a favorable light and yet not have the qualities that he is looking for in a resident assistant.

Can personality testing be of help to Gary? Can traits such as interpersonal warmth, social dominance, and empathy be adequately assessed? Can a personality test successfully detect students who consciously attempt to look overly well suited for the position?

DEVELOPMENT OF PERSONALITY TESTING

Although Chapter 2 briefly introduced us to the history of personality testing, it is useful once again to review the major trends in the field because the diverse tests today still reflect the variety of approaches to personality measurement developed in the early part of this century.

Historically, the first attempt to measure personality or character traits through the use of a test is usually accorded to Fernald. His work involved writing items reflecting his theories about personality and then organizing them into a test of personality. Whereas much of this early work was done at the turn of the century, the next milestone in personality measurement occurred during World War I. The need to select personnel for the military led to the development of instruments designed to predict whether a new recruit would make a satisfactory adjustment to the military. Basically, these early tests were collections of items based on clinical literature describing normal patterns of behavior. They generally attempted to assess only one facet of personality, such as submission to authority, adjustment to the military, or degree of comfort when associating with others.

The most notable improvement in personality measurement during the next two decades was the appearance of multiscaled tests. Typically, personality tests that were introduced in this era measured such things as anxiety, assertiveness, home adjustment, general health, impulsiveness, and interest in masculine or feminine activities. Some attempt at assessing defensiveness or conscious concealment on the test was also included, although these early scales were often quite unsophisticated and obtrusive. For example, a typical item designed to measure defensiveness might ask the examinee to indicate the number of friends that he or she had. The multiple-choice responses available would be "none," "few," or "hundreds." The first choice was judged to measure maladjustment, whereas the third choice was thought to indicate defensiveness.

During the 1930s and 1940s, two new developments in the measurement of personality appeared: empirically derived methods of testing and projective tests. Empirically derived tests represented a change from theoretically based item selection to mathematically based selection. Instead of basing personality instruments on various theories of personality, the basis for decision making shifted to the inherent mathematical relationships that existed among test items. Empirically based personality tests essentially branched out into two major groups, factor-analytically derived tests and criterion-referenced tests.

Projective testing also began to blossom during this period. The work of Murray and his associates on the Thematic Apperception Test and of Rorschach on his inkblot test became the pioneering efforts in projective testing. The development of this approach to personality measurement represented a shift from the use of clear, unambiguous tasks to unstructured, less-defined activities. Proponents of projective testing were interested in developing measures of personality that were more global, less subject to distortion and defensiveness, and more directed at the hidden or unconscious facets of personality.

The decades since the 1940s have seen few significant new trends in personality testing. The emphasis has been much more on researching the established tests and modifying them in an attempt to alleviate their shortcomings. Although new instruments continue to emerge, they all have tended to be variants of earlier themes and have employed similar methods of construction. Later in this chapter, we survey several tests that reflect these major strategies of construction.

OBJECTIVE MEASURES OF PERSONALITY

Tests of personality are often classified as either objective or projective, depending on the structure and clarity of the task required of examinees. According to this classification scheme, objective tests are seen as containing highly structured, clear, unambiguous test items that are objectively scored. Projective tests, on the other hand, are seen as having unstructured, ambiguous items that encourage examinees to project their personality into the tasks utilizing hidden wishes, attitudes, and needs in responding to the stimuli presented. Although this has proved to be a useful distinction for classification purposes, there has been some controversy about the value of this classification system (Lichtenburg, 1985). Nevertheless, we believe that although this historical distinction may be somewhat arbitrary, it is useful in referring to and categorizing the many personality tests in use today.

In surveying the field of objective personality measurement, we examine four instruments that illustrate key developments in personality testing. The California Psychological Inventory provides an example of one of the better, frequently used personality tests, measuring common elements of interpersonal functioning. The Personality Research Form represents one of the newer and more promising instruments. The Sixteen Personality Factor Questionnaire demonstrates the application of factor analysis in the development of a personality inventory, and the Edwards Personal Preference Schedule shows the application of a forced-choice, ipsative format to the problem of personality measurement.

California Psychological Inventory

The California Psychological Inventory (CPI) was initially developed and first published by Harrison Gough in 1957; this inventory was designed to measure normal personality variables in adolescents and adults. Thirty years later, Gough (1987) revised his inventory by adding several new scales and revamping or eliminating a number of dated, sexist, or difficult to read items, and reduced its length to 462 items. It has recently undergone a third revision (Gough & Bradley, 1996), resulting in the elimination of another 28 items that test takers had found objectionable, were considered to violate privacy considerations, or were in conflict with recent legislation dealing with the rights of the disabled. Despite these revisions, the purpose of the test, however, has remained the same, namely, to allow the test user to classify people into specific groups on the basis of their interpersonal behavior and to predict how they will function in specified situations.

The items on the CPI are grouped into 20 scales designed to measure attributes of personality involved in interpersonal behavior and social interaction. Gough chose these scaled variables because he believed that they were important and meaningful personality attributes in all cultures and societies, were readily understandable and interpretable to the test user, and were valid predictors of future behavior in similar social contexts. In addition, three of the scales also provide measures of test-taking attitudes and response sets that, if operable, could reduce the usefulness of the test results. Although not a part of the basic personality scales reported for the CPI, an additional set of 13 special-purpose or research scales (e.g., leadership, managerial potential, anxiety, etc.) have also been developed for use with the inventory. A list of the 20 basic scales and a brief operational description of each scale are presented in Table 17-1.

The CPI was constructed primarily of empirically built scales. The general scheme followed was to select two groups of people who differed with respect to a particular psychological trait (e.g., people rated as high or low in social dominance) and have them complete the inventory. Next, from the examinees' responses, items were identified that significantly differentiated the two groups and were then combined into a scale reflecting that personality attribute. Thirteen of the scales were built using this technique. Four of the scales were constructed to be internally consistent by selecting items that appeared to measure the desired trait and then intercorrelating them to refine the measure. A mixture of the two preceding scale-construction approaches formed the remaining three scales.

Administration and scoring of the CPI is rather quick and easy. It can be administered individually or in a group setting, usually in less than an hour. Scoring consists of counting the number of items endorsed on each scale and plotting the raw scores on a profile. This can be done either by hand or by machine. In either case, the scored profile readily converts raw scores to T scores for ease of interpretation. The current edition of the CPI provides both gender-specific norms for use in most clinical situations and combined-sex norms for use in employment applications. The CPI includes a number of features that enhance its validity and interpretability, including a normative sample three times the size of the original norm sample (current norms are based on 6,000 responses), more detailed reporting (including combined-gender and gender-specific normative profiles), and updated computer-based scoring systems.

Gough maintains that the CPI is most appropriate for evaluating an individual's behavior in and attitude toward interpersonal situations. He states that although the original intent of the scales is relatively clear, the diagnostic implications of certain combinations of scales is less self-evident and requires a trained person to interpret all the nuances inherent in various profile configurations.

Table 17-1   CALIFORNIA PSYCHOLOGICAL INVENTORY SCALES AND DESCRIPTIONS

	Low scorers	*High scorers*
Do (Dominance)	cautious; quiet; hesitant to take the initiative	confident; assertive; dominant; task-oriented
Cs (Capacity for Status)	unsure of self; dislikes direct competition; uncomfortable with uncertainty or complexity	ambitious; wants to be a success; has many interests
Sy (Sociability)	shy; often inhibited; prefers to stay in the background in social situations	sociable; likes to be with people; outgoing
Sp (Social Presence)	reserved; hesitant to express own views or opinions; self-denying	self-assured; spontaneous; versatile; verbally fluent; pleasure seeking
Sa (Self-acceptance)	self-doubting; readily assumes blame when things go wrong; often thinks others are better	has good opinion of self; sees self as talented and personally attractive; talkative
In (Independence)	lacks self-confidence; seeks support from others; tries to avoid conflict; has difficulty in making decisions	self-sufficient; resourceful; detached; persistent in seeking goals whether others agree or not
Em (Empathy)	unempathic; skeptical about the intentions of others; defensive about own feelings and desires; has limited range of interests	comfortable with self and well accepted by others; understands how others feel; optimistic
Re (Responsibility)	self-indulgent; undisciplined; careless; indifferent to personal obligations	responsible; reliable; ethically perceptive; serious about duties and obligations
So (Socialization)	resists rules; does not like to conform; often rebellious; gets into trouble easily; has unconventional views	conscientious; well-organized; finds it easy to accept and conform to normative rules; seldom gets into trouble
Sc (Self-control)	has strong feelings and emotions, and makes little attempt to hide them; likes adventure and new experience	tries to control emotions and temper; takes pride in being self-disciplined; suppresses hostile and erotic feelings
Gi (Good Impression)	insists on being himself or herself, even if this causes friction or problems; dissatisfied in many situations; often complains	wants to make a good impression; tries to do what will please others
Cm (Communality)	sees self as different from others; not conventional or conforming; often change-able and moody	fits in easily; sees self as a quite average person; makes little effort to change things; reasonable

(continued)

Table 17-1   (*Continued*)

	Low scorers	High scorers
Wb (Well-being)	concerned about health and personal problems; pessimistic; tends to complain about being treated unfairly or inconsiderately	feels in good physical and emotional health; optimistic about the future; cheerful
To (Tolerance)	distrustful; fault-finding; often has hostile and vindictive feelings	is tolerant of others' beliefs and values, even when different from or counter to own beliefs; reasonable
Ac (Achievement via Conformance)	has difficulty in doing best work in situations with strict rules and regulations; easily distracted	has strong drive to do well; likes to work in setting where tasks and expectations are clearly defined
Ai (Achievement via Independence)	has difficulty in doing best work in situations that are vague, poorly defined, and lacking in precise specifications	has strong drive to work well; likes to work in settings that encourage freedom and individual initiative
Ie (Intellectual Efficiency)	has a hard time getting started on cognitive tasks and seeing them through to completion	efficient in use of intellectual abilities; can keep on at a task when others might get discouraged
Py (Psychological-mindedness)	more interested in the practical and concrete than the abstract; looks more at what people do than how they feel or think	insightful and perceptive; understands the feelings of others, but is not necessarily supportive or nurturant
Fx (Flexibility)	not changeable; likes a steady pace and well-organized life; conventional and conservative	flexible; likes change and variety; easily bored by routine and everyday experience; may be impatient and even erratic
F/M (Femininity/Masculinity)	decisive, action-oriented; shows initiative; not easily subdued; rather unsentimental; tough minded	among males, high-scorers tend to be seen as sensitive; females with high scores tend to be seen as sympathetic, warm, and modest but also dependent

As an example of a CPI and its interpretation, consider the case of Marianne. At one point in her early academic career, she was undecided about her future career plans. She was uncertain whether she possessed sufficient social skills to succeed in an occupation requiring considerable people contact. As part of career counseling at that time, she completed a CPI. Figure 17-1 presents her score profile.

The interpretation process begins with a check on the three validity scales (Wb, Gi, Cm). Marianne is not particularly concerned about trying to make a good impression. She tends to admit her personal faults and failings as well as her personal successes. She generally is optimistic about her future and feels confident about her ability to cope with the stresses of everyday life. Her test responses are similar to those given by others who conscientiously complete the inventory, suggesting that her profile is likely to render an accurate reflection of her opinions, beliefs, and behavior patterns.

Marianne's profile further reveals that she has good leadership potential. She feels comfortable being in authoritative positions and is perceived by others as strong and self-confident. She interacts readily with others and is generally well received. Although Marianne frequently initiates social contact, she feels comfortable letting others take the lead and will defer to them on occasion. She appreciates humor and wit in others, is very imaginative, and enjoys engaging in playful activities. Since her attitudes and behavior tend to be somewhat conservative, she is not likely to act out radically or impulsively. It is more characteristic for her to inhibit expressing any antagonistic ideas. She accepts responsibility readily and is dependable in carrying out assigned tasks. She prefers structure in her life and performs best when the expectations of others are clear and unambiguous. Being tolerant toward those holding beliefs and values different from her own, she appreciates diversity and is generally nonjudgmental of others. Overall, Marianne appears to be a well-adjusted, interpersonally adept, and socialized woman. Her CPI results suggest that she should have no difficulty succeeding in a career that demands extensive social interaction and interpersonal skill.

Research on the CPI (Megargee, 1972) has established that it is extremely useful in predicting underachievement in academic settings and potential delinquency. The personality dynamics underlying these two behavioral patterns are apparently well assessed by this test. Evidence also indicates that the CPI predicts job performance in a number of careers, as well as performance in school. Factor analyses of the CPI have suggested that its scales are not independent but, rather, show considerable overlap. Such scale overlap should be expected, however, since the CPI was designed to measure common areas of personality hypothesized to be related in the real world. Two studies on the original version of the CPI (Crites, Bechtoldt, Goodstein, & Heilbrun, 1961; Mitchell & Pierce-Jones, 1960) reported that five or six basic factors accounted for most of the variance on the test. Gough (1987) reported that the 20 CPI scales could be reduced to four primary factors (i.e., extroversion, control, flexibility, and consensuality). Wallbrown and Jones (1992) found that two primary factors, interpersonal effectiveness and internal control, accounted for the major portion of the variance on the CPI. Deniston and Ramanaiah (1993) reported that the CPI had factor loadings on four of the five factors comprising the five-factor model of personality (extroversion, openness, neuroticism, and conscientiousness) but did not show significant loadings on

MARIANNE CPISAMPLE
ALPHA 5 FEMALE

PROFILE BASED ON NORMS FOR FEMALES

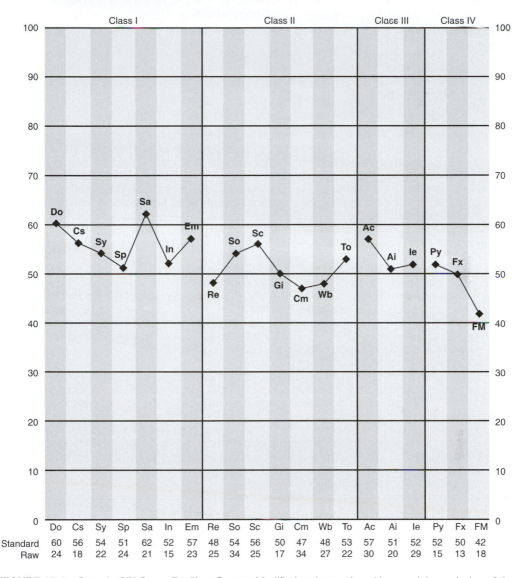

	Do	Cs	Sy	Sp	Sa	In	Em	Re	So	Sc	Gi	Cm	Wb	To	Ac	Ai	Ie	Py	Fx	FM
Standard	60	56	54	51	62	52	57	48	54	56	50	47	48	53	57	51	52	52	50	42
Raw	24	18	22	24	21	15	23	25	34	25	17	34	27	22	30	20	29	15	13	18

FIGURE 17-1   Sample CPI Score Profile   *Source:* Modified and reproduced by special permission of the Publisher, Consulting Psychologists Press, Inc., Palo Alto, CA 93303 from California Psychological Inventory by Harrison G. Gough. Copyright © 1996 by Consulting Psychologists Press, Inc. All rights reserved. Further reproduction is prohibited without the Publisher's written consent.

agreeableness. Recently, however, Fleenor and Eastman (1997) reported data showing that the principal factors underlying the CPI included all five factors.

Although the CPI has been severely criticized for its psychometric shortcomings, its proponents point out that clinicians with sufficient interpretive experience can predict behavior accurately in many social contexts. It remains one of the better researched and more frequently used measures of normal personality (Piotrowski & Keller, 1984).

CRITICAL DISCUSSION:

Can the CPI Be Used to Type People?

Factor analyses of the CPI have offered rather strong evidence that two specific themes, interpersonal poise and confidence and adherence to traditional values, underlie the scales of the inventory and account for much of the variance on the instrument. With this in mind, Nichols and Schnell (1963) initially developed two special scales (Person Orientation and Value Orientation) in an attempt to measure these two main themes or axes of personality. Eventually, Gough developed a model of personality that combined these two concepts into four different personality types labeled alpha, beta, gamma, and delta, based on whether people scored above or below established cut scores on two vector scales designed to measure these personality attributes. He also utilized a third scale to measure the extent to which these personality attributes were actualized and developed in the individual. A diagram of his model is shown in Figure 17-2.

Each of these four personality types is associated with a particular lifestyle, or way of living. For example, alphas tend to be outgoing, socially participative people who respect societal norms and favor having set guidelines for living. Betas also like norms and values but are much more private people who avoid publicly disclosing their thoughts and feelings. Gammas, like alphas, enjoy and seek social participation, but unlike alphas, they are skeptical of rules and social mores, preferring their own values to those of society. Finally, deltas prefer to keep to themselves rather than actively engaging in interactions with others and choose value systems that are more personal and individual rather than communal and public.

This model of personality can be used to type people and see what relationships exist between personality type and other important educational and vocational criteria. For example, Gough and Bradley (1996) reported some interesting relationships between personality type and choice of college major. Alphas tend to major in business, engineering, and preprofessional programs. Deltas tend to pursue majors in the humanities such as art, music, and literature. Students who choose social sciences such as psychology and sociology tend to be gammas, whereas students seeking careers in social service occupations like teaching and nursing tend to be betas. Although there is little published research on the usefulness of this typing system for predicting other criteria, it does present some interesting possibilities for future studies.

Personality Research Form

The Personality Research Form (PRF) was developed and published by Douglas Jackson in 1967. It represents a relatively sophisticated attempt to measure dimensions of the normal personality. It is based on the variables of personality originally defined by Henry Murray and his colleagues at the Harvard Psychological Clinic (Murray, 1938). From Murray's work, Jackson selected 20 personality variables to be assessed by

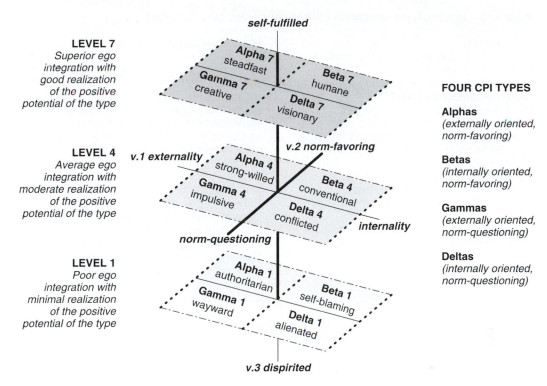

FIGURE 17-2　CPI Model for Type　*Source:* Modified and reproduced by special permission of the Publisher, Consulting Psychologists Press, Inc. All rights reserved. Further reproduction is prohibited without the Publisher's written consent.

his test. However, he believed that a smaller number of variables, 14 personality characteristics, were the most important or most relevant for assessing a wide area of personal living and functioning, so he created a shorter version of the PRF specifically to assess these personality attributes.

Initially, the PRF was available in two sets of parallel forms, differing in item length and number of scales. The shorter forms (A and B) contained 300 items that were scored for these 14 personality variables. In addition, a validity indicator was included to detect possible scoring errors and careless test-taking attitudes (e.g., random responding). The longer forms (AA and BB) contained 440 items comprising 20 personality dimensions and two validity scales. The second validity scale, added to the longer forms, was intended to measure the tendency to give socially desirable responses. Both sets of these parallel forms have been used primarily with college students. Later Jackson developed a shorter 352-item version of the PRF (Form-E) similar to the longer forms AA and BB that also provided measures of all 20 personality variables and both validity indicators.

A list of all 22 scales appearing on the PRF is given in Table 17-2, along with a brief description of each personality dimension being assessed. Jackson designed his

Table 17-2   PERSONALITY RESEARCH FORM SCALES AND DESCRIPTIONS

Abasement—Shows a high degree of humility; accepts blame and criticism, even when not deserved, self-effacing.

Achievement—Aspires to accomplish difficult tasks; maintains high standards and works toward distant goals; enjoys competition.

Affiliation—Enjoys being with friends and people in general, very accepting of others; establishes and keeps relationships with friends.

Aggression—Enjoys combat and argument; easily annoyed; may seek to retaliate with people perceived as causing harm; willing to offend to get own way.

Autonomy—Tries to break away from restraints, confinement, or restrictions of any kind; enjoys being free and unattached.

Change—Likes new and different experiences; dislikes routine and avoids it; adapts readily to changes in environment.

Cognitive Structure—Dislikes ambiguity in information; desires to make decisions based upon definite knowledge rather than probabilities.

Defendence—Ready to defend self against real or imagined harm from others; takes offense easily; does not accept criticism readily.

Dominance—Attempts to control environment and to influence or direct others; enjoys the role of leader.

Endurance—Willing to work long hours; doesn't give up quickly; persevering even in the face of problems.

Exhibition—Enjoys being the center of attention; may enjoy being dramatic or witty; likes an audience.

Harm Avoidance—Dislikes exciting activities, especially if danger is involved; avoids risk of bodily harm.

Impulsivity—Tends to act on the "spur of the moment" without deliberation; gives vent readily to feelings and wishes; speaks freely.

Nurturance—Gives sympathy and comfort, assists others whenever possible; readily performs favors for others; likes caring for others.

Order—Concerned with keeping personal effects and surroundings neat and organized; dislikes clutter, confusion, and disorganization.

Play—Does many things "just for fun"; enjoys jokes and funny stories; maintains an easygoing, light-hearted attitude toward life.

Sentience—Notices smells, sounds, sights, tastes, and the way things feel; remembers the sensations and believes that they are important.

Social Recognition—Desires to be held in high esteem by acquaintances; concerned about reputation and what others think; works for approval.

Succorance—Frequently seeks the sympathy, protection, love, advice, and reassurance of others; may feel insecure or helpless without support.

Understanding—Values synthesis of ideas, logical thought, and verifiable generalizations.

Desirability—Describes self in terms judged as desirable; presents favorable picture of self.

Infrequency—Responds in implausible or pseudo-random manner due to carelessness, confusion, etc.

Source: From *Manual for the Personality Research Form.* Copyright © 1967, 1974, 1984 by Douglas N. Jackson. Reprinted by permission of Sigma Assessment Systems, Inc., 511 Fort Street, Suite 435, P.O. Box 610984, Port Huron, MI 48061-0984 (800) 265–1285.

scales to be bipolar in nature, meaning that a low score on any scale signifies not just the absence of the trait but also the presence of its opposite. For example, if many items were endorsed on the exhibition scale, this pattern would mean that the respondent has a positive need to be conspicuous, dramatic, and colorful in social situations. A low score on the exhibition scale would be interpreted as indicating a fear of group activities and the active avoidance of them.

The PRF scales were constructed by first carefully studying each of the personality constructs outlined by Murray. Then, over 100 items for each scale were written to measure the hypothesized trait or personality dimension in question. Next, these items were reviewed by editors to eliminate redundancy and unclearly worded items. The provisional scales were then administered to large numbers of college subjects. Their responses were used to reduce the scales to a smaller number of internally consistent items, that is, items showing greater correlations with other items in their own scale than with other scales. All items showing extreme endorsement frequencies—above 95% and less than 5% of the samples tested—were eliminated from consideration, since such items generally add little new information that differentiates one respondent from another. The end result was the production of a set of scales that is highly reliable, reasonably free of response set bias, and capable of discriminating examinees along a continuum of personality characteristics.

Jackson had two goals in mind for the PRF. He wanted to design a useful tool for personality research and to develop a measure of the personality dimensions assumed to be of importance in such environments as schools, guidance clinics, and industry. Although the PRF has enjoyed fairly widespread use in a number of different research applications, ranging from the study of group differences and sociometric studies to investigations of academic achievement and creativity, it has also been increasingly applied in clinical settings. With the publishing of the more versatile Form-E, the PRF has been used with junior and senior high school students, in vocational counseling for noncollege populations, in mental health centers, with older populations, and in personnel selection and placement.

Reliability estimates for the original PRF have been reported to be quite positive. Kuder-Richardson formula 20 values for the 20 personality content scales have been shown to range between .87 and .94 with a median of .91 (Jackson, 1999). Test-retest reliability data over a one-week period collected by Bentler (1964) revealed that PRF personality scale scores were quite stable over time, ranging from a low of .69 to a high of .90. As might be expected, reliability estimates for the shorter Form-E have consistently been lower than for the longer versions of the test but are still psychometrically acceptable. Several studies (Jackson & Guthrie, 1968; Kusyszyn, 1968; Ostendorf, Angleitner, & Ruch, 1983) have provided validation data on the PRF. The general strategy of these studies has been to have close acquaintances of the subjects rate them on a number of personality traits and then correlate these criterion ratings with the appropriate PRF scores. The results of these studies have generally substantiated the validity of the PRF scales. Similarly, the PRF has been correlated with other personality and interest tests (Jackson, 1999) and has generally shown positive relationships with conceptually similar variables and low-to-zero-order relationships with conceptually unrelated variables. Consequently, although the PRF is a relatively new test, it appears to be well constructed, has good psychometric characteristics, and offers the promise of becoming one of the more useful measures of important dimensions of the normal personality.

Sixteen Personality Factor Questionnaire

Better known as the 16PF, the Sixteen Personality Factor Questionnaire was developed by Raymond Cattell and first published commercially in 1949 by the Institute for Personality and Ability Testing, Inc. Cattell and his associates believed that a personality test should measure the most fundamental dimensions of personality and comprise all the characteristics and attributes found in adults.

To develop so comprehensive an instrument, Cattell and his associates decided to survey all the words in the English language that described personal characteristics. Other researchers (Allport & Odbert, 1936) had searched through dictionaries and found approximately 4,000 English adjectives that described personality characteristics. Cattell and his coworkers began with this large group of adjectives, intending to factor analyze them to extract a smaller number of more basic adjectives. Because of the limitations of factor analysis at that time, they were forced to categorize the words into 45 groups, based primarily on an inspection of their linguistic similarities. Once they had obtained the 45 categories, they were able to factor analyze this more manageable group into approximately 15 factors, which were simply labeled A through O. The most important factor, accounting for the greatest amount of variance among the 45 characteristics, was assigned the letter A. Each subsequent letter appeared to be less important and was sequentially assigned a lower alphabetic label. However, early work with this set of 15 personality dimensions proved that some of these factors were not consistently found in adults but were more systematically found in children or adolescents. Therefore, they were dropped from consideration (note: the letters D, J, and K are missing from the list of factors presented in Figure 17-3, shown later). Several additional personality variables were identified from factor analyses of other personality questionnaires and were found to be quite important in describing behavior, so these were included on the test. The latter factors were given the designations Q1, Q2, Q3, and Q4 to identify their questionnaire origin. The end result was a personality test built by factor-analytic methods containing 16 factors generally independent of one another that was potentially capable of describing all aspects of normal personality functioning.

Since its initial development, the 16PF has undergone four revisions (1956, 1962, 1968, and 1993). Although the basic nature of the test has remained unchanged, a number of modifications have been made to the original test to both update and improve it. The 1993 revision, the 16PF Fifth Edition, contains 185 items responded to along a 3-point Likert scale. These items are grouped into 16 primary factor scales representing the dimensions of personality initially identified by Cattell. Although the current names attached to these primary factor scales are not particularly difficult to understand and interpret to clients, earlier versions used much more technical and obscure factor labels. These older scale names made interpretation difficult and likely contributed to the lower usage of the 16PF among clinicians. Although there is no item overlap among the 16PF scales, there are interrelationships among them. Further factor analyses of these basic scales revealed five second-order factors that represent broader aspects of personality. These latter global factors are scored along with the basic primary factor scales. In addition, the 16PF also contains scales to measure social desirability, acquiescence, and a check for random responding. Figure 17-3 shows the 16 primary and 5 global factors measured by the test.

Administering and scoring the 16PF requires little special training. Each item response is assigned a unit weight of 0, 1, or 2 points, except for the items on scale B,

16PF® Fifth Edition Individual Record Form
Profile Sheet

Instructions: Write the sten score for each factor in the second column. Starting with Factor A, place a mark over the spot representing the appropriate sten score. Repeat for each factor. Connect the marks with straight lines.

IPAT

Name _____

Date _____

PRIMARY FACTORS

Factor	Sten	Left Meaning	Standard Ten Score (STEN) ← Average →	Right Meaning
			1 2 3 4 5	6 7 8 9 10	
A: Warmth		Reserved, Impersonal, Distant		Warm, Outgoing, Attentive to Others
B: Reasoning		Concrete		Abstract
C: Emotional Stability		Reactive, Emotionally Changeable		Emotionally Stable, Adaptive, Mature
E: Dominance		Deferential, Cooperative, Avoids Conflict		Dominant, Forceful, Assertive
F: Liveliness		Serious, Restrained, Careful		Lively, Animated, Spontaneous
G: Rule-Consciousness		Expedient, Nonconforming		Rule-Conscious, Dutiful
H: Social Boldness		Shy, Threat-Sensitive, Timid		Socially Bold, Venturesome, Thick-Skinned
I: Sensitivity		Utilitarian, Objective, Unsentimental		Sensitive, Aesthetic, Sentimental
L: Vigilance		Trusting, Unsuspecting, Accepting		Vigilant, Suspicious, Skeptical, Wary
M: Abstractedness		Grounded, Practical, Solution-Oriented		Abstracted, Imaginative, Idea-Oriented
N: Privateness		Forthright, Genuine, Artless		Private, Discreet, Non-Disclosing
O: Apprehension		Self-Assured, Unworried, Complacent		Apprehensive, Self-Doubting, Worried
Q_1: Openness to Change		Traditional, Attached to Familiar		Open to Change, Experimenting
Q_2: Self-Reliance		Group-Oriented, Affiliative		Self-Reliant, Solitary, Individualistic
Q_3: Perfectionism		Tolerates Disorder, Unexacting, Flexible		Perfectionisitc, Organized, Self-Disciplined
Q_4: Tension		Relaxed, Placid, Patient		Tense, High Energy, Impatient, Driven

GLOBAL FACTORS

		← Average → 1 2 3 4 5 6 7 8 9 10	
EX: Extraversion	Introverted, Socially Inhibited		Extraverted, Socially Participating
AX: Anxiety	Low Anxiety, Unperturbed		High Anxiety, Perturbable
TM: Tough-Mindedness	Receptive, Open-Minded, Intuitive		Tough-Minded, Resolute, Unempathetic
IN: Independence	Accommodating, Agreeable, Selfless		Independent, Persuasive, Willful
SC: Self-Control	Unrestrained, Follows Urges		Self-Controlled, Inhibits Urges

FIGURE 17-3   **16PF Profile**   *Source:* Copyright © 1993 by the Institute for Personality and Ability Testing, Champaign, IL. Reprinted by permission.

Reasoning, which are either 0 or 1, depending on whether the response is correct or incorrect. Summations of the item weights produce 16 raw scores that, when compared with one of the norm tables provided in the manual, translate these raw scores into standard scores known as *stens* (area transformation scores on a standard ten base). Each sten is then profiled on a graph that shows where the individual stands in reference to the norm group used for comparison. Scoring of the five global factors is a bit more complicated, but specific part scores from the 16 primary scales are combined to form these second-order factor scores. It is worthy of note that 13 of the 16PF scales do not show significant gender differences, and so combined-sex norms are used for profiling them. Three scales (Factor A, Warmth; Factor E, Dominance; and Factor I, Sensitivity) do show gender differences and can be scored either in reference to same-sex norms or to the combined-sex norms at the discretion of the clinician.

The profile used with the 16PF (see Figure 17-3) clearly outlines the normal range of scores for the norm group. Note that the scales on the test are bipolar in that both high and low scores have meaning. The descriptions on the left and right sides of the profile indicate the interpretations to be given to scores deviating in each direction from the middle. Finally, at the bottom of the profile, the global factors are presented with their respective scores. Whereas some find the sten system very easy to use when interpreting test results, others find it somewhat cumbersome to explain and much prefer other score reporting methods (e.g., percentiles, T scores).

Psychometrically, the 16PF continues to be a leader among published personality tests. Its reliability and validity have been amply demonstrated in numerous studies that are documented elsewhere (Conn & Rieke, 1994; Russell & Karol, 1994). In addition, evidence presented by R. B. Cattell and Cattell (1995) has strongly supported its proposed factor structure. Having well-developed norms for high school, college, and adult populations, the 16PF has been used in a wide variety of both research and clinical settings. For example, it has been employed by vocational psychologists to determine the personality profiles of various occupational groups. It has also been used in personnel selection and placement to provide data about employees' management styles and future career development. It has been shown to have some utility to measure workers' leadership potential, decision-making ability, and personal initiative. It has also found use in counseling and mental health centers as a diagnostic, screening, and treatment evaluation tool. It is interesting that despite its superior psychometric properties, however, it has not been the preferred personality test of practicing clinicians.

Edwards Personal Preference Schedule

Developed by Allen Edwards and first published in 1954, the Edwards Personal Preference Schedule (EPPS) represented a novel attempt to reduce the effects of social desirability in personality assessment. Edwards began by operationally defining 15 latent personality needs outlined earlier by Murray and his associates at the Harvard Psychological Clinic (Murray, 1938). After generating a pool of items to reflect these needs, he administered them to various groups of college students with instructions to rate each item according to its social desirability. Once these ratings were determined, Edwards was able to pair items measuring different needs that had equal social desirability ratings. This procedure yielded an ipsative test designed to eliminate the effects of social desirability, while providing a measure of the relative strengths of competing latent personality characteristics.

The 15 latent needs assessed by the EPPS are outlined in Table 17-3. Each need is paired with the other 14 needs twice on the test. Scoring consists of a summation of the number of times a need is chosen out of 28 possible pairs. Raw scores are converted to percentile equivalents, with the use of various norm tables representing both college and general adult populations. One additional scale, a measure of response consistency, provides a check on random responding. It is composed of 15 repeated items. Respondents who carefully complete the EPPS generally answer at least 9 or more of the 15 items consistently. Lower scores are indicative of potential interpretive problems.

The strength of the EPPS in clinical use is that it measures dimensions of personality that are nonthreatening to the client. Open discussion of test results often

Table 17-3   EDWARDS PERSONAL PREFERENCE SCHEDULE SCALES AND DESCRIPTIONS

Achievement—To be successful, to solve difficult puzzles and problems, to be able to do things better than others.

Deference—To get suggestions from others, to find out what others think, to follow instructions.

Order—To have written work neat and organized, to make plans before starting on a difficult job or task.

Exibition—To say witty and clever things, to tell amusing jokes and stories, to have others notice you.

Autonomy—To be able to come and go as desired, to say what you want; to do things that are unconventional.

Affiliation—To be loyal to friends, to participate in friendly groups, to do things for friends.

Intraception—To analyze your motives and feelings, to observe others, to analyze the behavior of others.

Succorance—To have others provide help when in trouble, to seek encouragement from others, to gain sympathy.

Dominance—To argue for your point of view, to be a leader, to persuade and influence others.

Abasement—To feel guilty when you do something wrong, to accept blame when things do not go right.

Nurturance—To help friends when they are in trouble, to assist others less fortunate, to treat others kindly.

Change—To do new and different things, to travel, to experience novelty, to experiment with new jobs.

Endurance—To keep at a job until it is finished, to complete any job undertaken, to work hard at a task.

Heterosexuality—To go out with members of the opposite sex, to engage in social activities with the opposite sex.

Aggression—To attack contrary points of view, to tell others what you think about them, to criticize others.

Consistency—To determine if the responses given on matching pairs are identical and show consistency.

provides an important stimulus for further self-exploration. Sharing the definitional statements that give meaning to the manifest need variables measured with counselees also tends to demystify testing and hence reduce client defensiveness.

Unfortunately, the weaknesses of the EPPS outweigh its advantages. Research (Corah et al., 1958; M. J. Feldman & Corah, 1960) has shown that the effects of social desirability on the test have not been eliminated or even satisfactorily controlled, as Edwards had contended. The additional psychometric problems and limitations that accompany the use of an ipsative, forced-choice item format seems to be a poor trade-off if no benefit of social desirability control is obtained.

It is also quite doubtful that the EPPS measures any latent needs; rather, it provides a picture of how clients see themselves when tested. Since its publication, there has not been much research supporting its validity other than that initially reported in the manual. D. Cooper (1990) used the EPPS with vocational rehabilitation clients and found that they differ significantly from the college norms initially published for the test. He concluded that newer, gender-specific norms are needed. Similarly, Thorson and Powell (1992) have also argued for updated norms but have also raised questions about the stability of test scores. Finally, Piedmont, McCrae, and Costa (1992) presented data suggesting that the use of a forced-choice, ipsative test format on the EPPS may well reduce the overall validity of the test.

Despite the paucity of research data supporting its validity and the apparent problems of its ipsative format, the EPPS still is employed rather widely in guidance centers, vocational counseling, school settings, and employment situations. In a study assessing how frequently various psychological tests were used by clinicians in counseling agencies (Zytowski & Warman, 1982), the results showed that the EPPS was ranked third in overall usage behind the SII and the Kuder OIS. Although it represents an ingenious attempt to improve the art of personality test construction and is rather frequently used, it does not fulfill the requirements of a well-validated and psychometrically sound instrument.

PROJECTIVE MEASURES OF PERSONALITY

All projective tests share in common the utilization of ambiguous stimuli or tasks designed to provide a wide range of responses from examinees. Projective tests are intended to be depth oriented and focused on the unconscious, covert characteristics of personality. They are based on the assumption that the use of ambiguous stimuli eliminates or greatly reduces defensiveness and other conscious attempts to distort test results. Proponents believe that examinees project themselves into the task and respond both to the meaning that they impart to the stimuli and to the feelings that they experience while responding. Interpretation of projective tests depends on the total analysis of examinees' responses, without regard to any preconceived notions about the correctness of any response given on the test.

The history of projective testing dates back to the late 19th century. Early attempts with inkblots were aimed at measuring imagination and intelligence. With the publishing of his inkblot test in 1921, Hermann Rorschach really began the modern era of projective assessment. His use of inkblots to measure personality characteristics was largely an empirical effort at test construction. Henry Murray, however, was more interested in developing a comprehensive theory of personality and needed an instrument for its measurement. The result was the Thematic Apperception Test, published in 1943. These two tests have provided a major impetus in the area of projective testing. They have profoundly affected the practice of psychology, have led to an enormous amount of published research, and have been the models for several later-generation projective instruments.

Rorschach Inkblot Test

The Rorschach, the most widely used projective measure, is not a test in the ordinary sense of the word but a relatively unstructured technique for assessing personality structure, diagnosing psychopathology, and planning psychotherapeutic treatment. The Rorschach consists of a series of 10 bilaterally symmetrical inkblots placed on individual 5-by-9–inch cards. Five of the cards are in black and white only, two cards are basically red and gray, and three are multicolored. Figure 17-4 depicts a typical blot from the test. The cards are presented to the examinee in a predetermined sequential order. Respondents are asked to view each card, relate everything they see, and hand the card back when they are finished, describing as much as they can. Examinees are allowed to turn the cards any way that they wish. Examiners attempt to divulge as little as possible about the task and permit examinees to give as many responses as they wish.

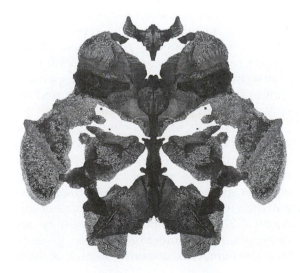

FIGURE 17-4 Typical Blot From **Rorschach** *Source:* From Simon & Schuster, PH College. Reproduced by permission.

After all 10 cards have been responded to, the examiner goes back over all the cards with the examinee during the inquiry phase of testing. The examiner records on a special miniature reproduction of each blot the areas or portion of each blot used as the basis of the examinee's responses. Considerable skill is required to conduct the inquiry so as to extract clarification about their responses and permit examinees the opportunity to give additional information about each card while not influencing their experiences of the inkblots.

Some Rorschach users add a third phase to the testing, during which they test the limits of responding by probing for more examinee responses. This technique is especially useful if earlier responses of the examinee are noticeably lacking in some form of responding commonly found in Rorschach protocols. There is some debate among examiners about the wisdom of this technique, however, because it may have a detrimental effect on any future testing using the Rorschach.

Scoring the Rorschach is a complex and time-consuming process, although computer software has been developed to facilitate the process. To score the Rorschach, clinicians classify examinees' responses on the test as to location, determinants, and content. Location has reference to the area of the blot used by the examinee in determining his or her responses. Some of the possibilities included in scoring are the whole blot, various parts of the blot, and the white space on which the blot is printed. The category of determinants has reference to what qualitative characteristics were perceived on the card that determined the responses. The scored characteristics in this group are the form or shape of the blot, movement inferred to be going on, and the use of color. Content refers to what is reported as actually seen in the blot and is treated as the least important variable scored on the Rorschach. A subcategory here looks at the frequency with which the responses given by the examinee are similar to those frequently given by others.

Unfortunately, in the past, Rorschach users and experts have not been in universal agreement as to which type of responses should be scored or how much emphasis should be placed on them. Various scoring systems have been developed to try to remedy this problem. At least five different popular scoring systems have been developed for the Rorschach over the years, but because of the differences among them, they have often led to disparate interpretations of the same test data (Hunsley & Bailey, 1999). Part of the problem stems from the fact that some of the subcategories of responses that have been identified for scoring were not recognized by Rorschach himself, and consequently they are not accepted universally as necessary or meaningful.

Interpreting the results of a Rorschach consists of examining the relationships that exist among the responses given by examinees. The numbers of responses given in each category and various ratios among them are used to develop an interpretive picture of the individual. One obviously important source of variance on the test, therefore, involves the total number of responses given by the subject. As the number of responses given increases, the amount of data from which to draw interpretive conclusions also increases. Hersen and Greaves (1971) have reported that simply saying "good" after each response often increased the total number of responses given by as much as 50%. However, the variability in the number of responses to each of the blots can cause significant interpretive problems. Although some researchers have suggested that the number of responses be controlled, the majority of Rorschach users have consistently resisted attempts to place any restrictions on the responding patterns of examinees. They view the Rorschach's strength as providing a richer and more individualized measure of personality than other instruments and therefore want to enhance this idiographic aspect of the test. An attempt to control for this weakness in the Rorschach has been offered by Holtzman, who developed an analogous set of inkblots but expanded the number of cards to 45 and limited the number of responses to one per card.

In analyzing the relationships that exist among responses given by an examinee, certain diagnostic patterns have been formulated. These include such things as the use of color, indicating the presence of emotionality; movement, indicating imagination; the ratio of total responses to movement responses, suggesting over- or underachievement; and time required to respond, being an indicator of anxiety. Certain combinations of categories are also used to diagnose emotional disorders such as neuroses, psychoses, and brain damage.

Psychometrically, the Rorschach has continually been shown to be woefully inadequate (Dawes, 1994; Gleser, 1963; McCann, 1998; Zubin, Eron, & Schumer, 1965). The reliability and validity data on the test do not meet the accepted values established for objective measures of personality (see, however, Hiller, Rosenthal, Bornstein, Berry, & Brunell-Neulieb, 1999). Despite decades of research on the Rorschach, there is still little evidence that an unstructured administration of this test (i.e., use of the Rorschach without a standardized scoring scheme, as discussed later) tells the examiner much about the person being assessed (Dawes, 1994; Schontz & Green, 1992). Nevertheless, this test is widely used by clinicians (Dawes, 1994; Wade & Baker, 1977) and enjoys a position of prominence among the diagnostic tools utilized in daily clinical practice.

A special section of the journal *Psychological Assessment* (1999, Vol. 11, No. 3) discusses research on the utility of the Rorschach in clinical assessment. A series of papers by distinguished scholars (both advocates and opponents of the Rorschach) suggest that the Rorschach is widely used as a tool for clinical diagnosis, that it can contribute to clinical assessments, that it is rarely used to its full advantage, and that it might not offer much additional information over and above that provided by standardized scales, such as the Minnesota Multiphasic Personality Inventory (MMPI) scales. Empirical reviews of the literature have supported the notion that the Rorschach shows lower validity than other comparable tests. For example, Garb, Florio, and Grove's (1999) review suggests that the MMPI explains 23% to 30% of the variance in a variety of clinically relevant criteria, whereas the Rorschach explains only 8% to 13% of the variance.

Many of the tests and assessments used in personality assessment, particularly in clinical settings, are relatively unstructured and often depend heavily on the clinician's interpretation. The Exner (1974, 1978) and Holtzman (1968) modifications help to reduce subjectivity and error in the interpretation of the Rorschach, but nevertheless, the psychometric properties of Rorschach scores are far from encouraging. As Exner (1999) notes, it is probably not possible to assess the validity of the Rorschach inkblot test.

There are so many ways that a Rorschach might be scored or interpreted that it is difficult to pin down what is being validated. The best we can do is ask questions about the usefulness of the data that come from administrations of the Rorschach, and here, the answers are rarely comforting (Dawes, 1994).

Modifications of the Rorschach Technique. The Rorschach is not a test, in the ordinary sense of the word, but represents a relatively unstructured technique for personality measurement and assessment. Recently, Aronow, Reznikoff, and Moreland (1995) have argued that the value of the Rorschach lies in its use as a tool to delve into the unique qualities of the individual. They believe that attempts to quantify and standardize the Rorschach actually run counter to the original purpose for which it was intended. They contend that it is inappropriate to view the Rorschach as a psychological test and therefore hold that psychometric standards for tests should not apply to it. It is not clear whether the psychometric deficiencies of the Rorschach represent problems with the inkblots themselves, the various scoring systems in use, or the clinicians who use the test. Several attempts have been made to improve the Rorschach technique, and some of these have increased the psychometric adequacy of the Rorschach substantially. Two of the most notable efforts in this direction have been undertaken by Exner (1974, 1978) and Holtzman (1968).

The Holtzman Inkblot Technique represents a psychometrically sophisticated adaptation of Rorschach's basic approach. The Holtzman consists of a set of 45 inkblots empirically selected to maximize scorer reliability and clinical diagnostic validity. Unlike the Rorschach, however, Holtzman's technique allows only one response per card. There are standardized procedures for scoring the 45 responses on many of the major Rorschach dimensions.

One of the most serious problems with the Rorschach technique has been the lack of standardization in its administration, scoring, and interpretation. Exner (1993) has attempted to integrate the empirically supported aspects of five major Rorschach scoring systems into a single comprehesive system to establish greater standardization to the test. Exner's efforts to systematize the Rorschach and bring it closer into compliance with the standards required of a psychological test have been both positive and laudable. Although Exner's Comprehensive System has not been adopted uniformly, it is in sufficient widespread use to provide a reasonable normative base and to provide useful data about the reliability and validity of Rorschach scores derived from its use.

In general, even though some of the research on the reliability of the Exner scoring system has been somewhat encouraging, its validity as a personality measure continues to be questioned. Proponents of the Rorschach such as Viglione (1999) and Stricker and Gold (1999) maintain that the research evidence supports the use of the Rorschach for individual case conceptualization, assessing the structure of personality, and predicting therapeutic outcomes. Opponents such as Dawes (1994) and Hunsley and Bailey (1999) argue that much of the research data offered in support of the Rorschach's validity are seriously flawed and therefore uninterpretable. They contend that even though certain Exner scales and ratios can be reliably scored, their integration into a complete clinical picture requries substantial judgment on the part of clinicians and therefore introduces the potential for significant variability and error in the interpretive process. Ben-Shakhar, Bar-Hillel, Bilu, and Shefler (1998) have similarly shown that the interpretations of tests like the Rorschach given by expert clinicians can be appreciably affected by their initial clinical hypotheses of patients. Finally, Lilienfeld, Wood, and Garb (2000) noted that there is little convincing evidence that Rorschach scores are systematically related to psychopathology or personality traits. Therefore, the most parsimonious conclusion that we feel can be drawn about the Rorschach is that its psychometric characteristics still do not meet the accepted values established for objective measures of personality and that despite decades of research, there is little convincing evidence demonstating its usefulness in making clinical decisions. Nevertheless, the Rorschach enjoys widespread use by clinicians (Camara, Nathan, & Puente, 1998; Dawes, 1994; Wade & Baker, 1977), although some evidence suggests that its popularity may be waning somewhat (Norcross, Karg, & Prochaska, 1997).

Thematic Apperception Test

Henry Murray (1938) developed another major projective instrument using pictures rather than inkblots. The Thematic Apperception Test (TAT) consists of 31 picture cards that provide stimuli for examinees to create stories concerning relationships or social situations suggested by the pictures (Morgan, 1995, presents the history of each of the images appearing in the TAT). One of the cards in the set is actually blank to provide a maximally ambiguous stimulus. Although Murray recommended that approximately 20 cards be used during an assessment, normally the clinicians administer about 10 cards, selecting ones appropriate to the referral question.

Murray postulated that respondents would project into their stories information concerning their needs, emotions, conflicts, attitudes, and emotional difficulties. Particular attention is paid to the protagonist of each story and the environmental stresses that impinge on him or her. The hero is presumed to represent the examinee. Scoring involves subjectively analyzing all story content and evaluating it for various themes. Particular themes that emerge are seen as indicative of various personality dynamics.

Figure 17-5 illustrates a typical card from the TAT. Interpretations of the narratives that are provided for each card are combined to establish themes suggestive of hypotheses about the personality dynamics of the individual. Some themes occur sufficiently frequently in disturbed examinees to be indicative of pathology. Examples of some commonly occurring themes include extreme attention to detail, suggesting an obsessive-compulsive personality; violent stories, suggesting impulse-control difficulties; and delays in responding, reflecting possible depression.

As with the Rorschach, the psychometric characteristics of the TAT have not been shown to be very impressive (Zubin, Eron, & Schumer, 1965). Various coding systems have been developed to improve the scoring reliability of the TAT, and some have shown promise (Cramer, 1997, 1999; Westen, Lohr, Silk, Gold, & Kerber, 1990). However, the validity of the TAT as yet remains unsubstantiated. Although the TAT is still popular in some settings, its use has clearly declined over the last 10 to 15 years

FIGURE 17-5   Typical Card From TAT   *Source:* Reprinted by permission of the publishers from Henry A. Murray, *Thematic Apperception Test*, Cambridge, Mass.: Harvard University Press. Copyright © 1943 by the President and Fellows of Harvard College, © 1971 by Henry A. Murray.

(Dana, 1996; Rossini & Moretti, 1997, have suggested ways that the use of TAT might be reinforced in clinical settings). It is possible that the lack of validity evidence or of any well-accepted scoring method has finally caught up with this venerable assessment instrument. However, as Dana (1996) notes, it is likely that variations on the basic story-telling technique will continue to be an important component of clinical assessment.

Rotter Incomplete Sentences Blank

The incomplete-sentence method of assessing personality has its roots in the work of Ebbinghaus around the beginning of the 20th century. Many different sentence-completion instruments have been developed, but the work of Julian Rotter and his associates has led to the development of the best standardized, most objectively scored, and most rigorous of all such instruments. His original work began with the Army (Rotter & Willerman, 1947) but later led to the construction of the Rotter Incomplete Sentences Blank (RISB) for college students (Rotter & Rafferty, 1950). It was later expanded for use with noncollege adults and adolescents of high-school age. As a result, this test has enjoyed greater usage than other sentence-completion methods that have emerged in the field of personality assessment. The Second Edition of this test, published in 1992, built on the success of its 1950 edition.

The RISB is generally considered to be a semistructured, projective test, because the items consist of sentence stems that must be woven into a complete thought by the examinee. As is the case with other projective methods of personality assessment, the underlying assumption is that examinees project their wishes, desires, fears, and attitudes into the sentences that they create. It differs from other projective tests, however, in several respects.

Whereas examinees responding to tests like the Rorschach and TAT are rarely aware of what they are revealing about themselves, partly because of the ambiguous nature of the test items, examinees responding to the RISB are generally more aware of the feelings, attitudes, and fears that they are disclosing because the task is more structured. A second difference concerns the purpose of testing. Other projective instruments have been designed to reveal information about the inner, deeper dimensions of personality, whereas the RISB and other sentence-completion methods have been designed principally to screen for emotional maladjustment.

The RISB consists of 40 items, each containing a sentence stem that the examinee uses to create a complete sentence dealing with the content of the item. A couple of examples from the test are shown in Table 17-4. An interesting feature of the RISB is its ease of administration. It can be given either individually or in a group setting, and it requires no special training to administer. Unlike many of its projective counterparts, the RISB has a rigorous and systematic scoring system that research has shown yields extremely high interscorer reliability (Rotter, Rafferty, & Lotsof, 1954; Rotter, Rafferty, & Schachtitz, 1949).

Scoring consists of assigning a weight to each item ranging from 0 to 6, depending on the content of the sentence formed. Responses are scored as to the degree of conflict expressed, the amount of optimism shown, the presence of qualifying statements, the length of responses, and omissions. The manual provides a number of sample responses and indicates the appropriate item weights to be assigned to each. Since it is impossible to include an example for all possible responses, guidelines are given to aid in scoring responses not found in the manual. A total score is summed over all items, which provides a measure of general emotional adjustment. Rasulis, Schuldberg, and Murtagh's (1996) study suggests that a computer-administered version of the RISB yields similar scores to those obtained from the paper-and-pencil version, at least when dealing with nonclinical levels of maladjustment. Many clinicians go beyond this score, however, and examine the content of the responses for particular insights into major areas of difficulty for the individual.

The positive psychometric properties of the RISB as reported in the manual have generally been sustained by later research (L. R. Goldberg, 1965; Lah, 1989). Research has shown it to be a rather sensitive measure of emotional maladjustment among college students and adults. Its psychometric advantage over other projective tests, however, has not significantly impacted its use. Clinicians continue to use it less often than other projective instruments, in large part because they are critical of its failure to

Table 17-4   SAMPLE RISB ITEMS

---

1. The happiest time _____
2. I want to know _____

Source: From the Rotter Incomplete Sentences Blank. Copyright © 1950, renewed 1977 by The Psychological Corporation, a Harcourt Assessment Company. Reprinted by permission. All rights reserved.

examine more dynamic, deeper levels of personality functioning. Some of its proponents do attempt such analyses through examining the content of the sentences generated on the RISB, but little research supports this method of interpretation (L. R. Goldberg, 1965). Nevertheless, the RISB continues to offer the clinician the advantages of group administration, quick administration and scoring capability, acceptable reliability and validity estimates, and an objective scoring system, all of which are absent in the more popular projective tests.

Draw-a-Person Test

The Draw-a-Person Test (DAP) grew out of the work of Karen Machover (1949). Although originally developed to assess children's intelligence, its use was extended to assess personality and diagnose psychopathology. The basic hypothesis underlying the development of the DAP was that examinees project themselves into the human figures that they are asked to draw. These reproductions are believed to reveal their impulses, anxieties, and other internal emotional states.

The DAP consists of having examinees draw two human figures. First they are instructed to simply draw a person and, following completion of that task, are told to draw a person of the opposite sex from that of the first drawing. While the examinee goes about these tasks, the clinician observes such things as the sequence of body parts drawn, verbalizations made by the examinee, and other factors associated with the actual drawing process. Occasionally, a period of questioning occurs after both drawings have been completed. During this inquiry, information is elicited about the figures, such as age, occupation, and family relationship.

Scoring and interpreting the DAP are complex, subjective tasks. Machover outlined a number of structural and formal aspects of the drawings that are important in the interpretation process. These include such aspects as the size and placement of the figures on the paper, the amount of action depicted in the drawings, the systematization followed in doing the task, erasures, shading, and differential treatment of male and female figures. Attention is also given to specific body parts. A partial list of these structures along with their hypothesized significance is summarized in Table 17-5.

Table 17-5   SIGNIFICANCE OF BODY PARTS EMPHASIZED ON THE DRAW-A-PERSON TEST

Body part	Psychological significance
Head size	Perceived intellectual ability, impulse control, narcissism
Facial expression	Fear, hate, aggression, meekness
Emphasis on mouth	Eating problems, alcoholism, gastric distress
Eyes	Self-concept, social problems, paranoia
Hair	Sign of virility, potential sexual dysfunction
Arms and hands	Degree of contact with the environment, openness to others
Fingers	Ability to manipulate and experience others
Legs and feet	Amount of support, sexual concerns, aggression
Emphasis on breasts	Sexual immaturity, preoccupation, and neurosis

Despite the intuitive appeal of tests like the DAP, research has generally failed to demonstrate that human drawings can be successfully utilized to assess personality, behavior, or psychopathology (Kahill, 1984; Motta, Little, & Tobin, 1993; D. Smith & Dumont, 1995). The research evidence summarized by Swensen (1957, 1968) and Roback (1968) on the DAP has not supported many of the theoretical relationships hypothesized by Machover concerning particular diagnostic signs and emotional disturbance. Some evidence suggests that interpreting the significance of overall patterns of signs, rather than the individual signs themselves, may have some validity as indications of general adjustment level. The relationships that have been shown are not sufficiently impressive, however, to warrant the use of the DAP over most other personality measures. Quantitative scoring systems have been developed for the DAP, which may help to reduce unreliability due to subjectivity in scoring (Naglieri, 1988). However, the validity of the scores obtained from the DAP, even with objective scoring, remains in doubt. Nevertheless, the DAP ranks among the 10 most frequently used assessment devices by clinicians (Lubin, Larsen, & Matarazzo, 1984).

CRITICAL DISCUSSION:

Are Scales on Personality Tests Interpreted Independently?

In studying several personality test profiles and examining what they reveal about the people who complete them, the interpretation process would probably appear to be fairly straightforward and uncomplicated. Interpretation might seem to be nothing more than a collection of statements made about each scale individually, with no provision for interactions between or among the scales. Things are not so simple.

In interpreting a personality test, three major characteristics of the test profile need to be taken into consideration. First, the average score of all scales on the test needs to be noted. A second characteristic of personality test profiles involves the degree of scatter among the scales. The focus here is on the amount of variability among the scores: Are all scores relatively at the same level, or is there great variation among the scales? Finally, the shape of the profile must be taken into consideration: Which scales are elevated? Which are depressed? It is particularly this last feature of test profiles that has led to the study of scale interactions.

The pattern of scores on a personality test must be taken into account when interpreting the test profile. Scales often interact with each other, such that the resulting combination of two scales yields a different interpretation of the individual than either scale would indicate if considered alone. To illustrate this point, we will focus on the CPI.

Heilbrun, Daniel, Goodstein, Stephenson, and Crites (1962) have studied several scale interactions on the original CPI and have presented clear evidence of scale blending. It is as if the characteristic measured by one scale is moderated or slightly changed by the influence of another personality characteristic. For example, these researchers found that, when scores on the Responsibility (Re) and the Capacity for Status (Cs) scales were both significantly above average on a profile, the individual was described as efficient, forceful, persevering, poised, and resourceful. When the Re score was above average but the Cs score was below average, however, the individual was described as sincere, conscientious, mild, patient, and unassuming. A different clinical picture was generated when the Re score was below average and the Cs score was above average. In this case, the individual was usually described as aggressive, manipulative, self-centered, skeptical, and opportunistic. Finally, when both Re and Cs were below average on a profile, the adjectives used to describe such an individual were apathetic, awkward, distrustful, indifferent, and undependable.

In their work with the CPI, Heilbrun and his colleagues studied several additional pairs of scales and found similar patterns of scale interactions between them. This type of research clearly illustrates the complexity of profile analysis and suggests that scores on any one personality scale cannot be interpreted in isolation.

CRITICAL DISCUSSION:
Reliability and Validity of Projective Tests, Personality Inventories, and Intelligence Tests

The sheer volume of research on popular psychological tests makes it difficult to establish with any precision the psychometric characteristics of these tests. For example, the number of studies before 1980 on the MMPI and the Rorschach alone exceeded 10,000 and probably far exceeds this figure by now. The recent growth of meta-analysis (see Hedges & Olkin, 1985; Hunter, Schmidt, & Jackson, 1982), which represents a group of statistical techniques for summarizing the results of large numbers of studies, provides one way of potentially keeping up with the voluminous literature on specific psychological tests.

Parker, Hanson, and Hunsley (1988) applied meta-analysis to research on the MMPI, the Rorschach, and the Wechsler Adult Intelligence Scale (WAIS); this study provides a unique opportunity to compare the psychometric qualities of widely different types of tests. Their study summarized findings from 411 studies published between 1970 and 1981 in two leading journals. They found that all three tests were highly reliable and that all three were correlated with criteria of interest. Their most interesting findings, however, involved comparisons of the three tests. The WAIS was selected as a point of comparison because it is widely acknowledged as a psychometrically superior test. However, measures of reliability and temporal stability of the three tests were comparable; this result runs counter to the widely held belief that personality inventories and projective tests are necessarily less reliable than tests of intelligence. The WAIS showed higher levels of validity for predicting theoretically relevant criteria (e.g., academic success), but the other two tests also showed respectable levels of validity.

The Parker, Hanson, and Hunsley (1988) study illustrates both the strengths and the weaknesses of meta-analysis. On the one hand, this technique provides a means for dealing with long-standing controversies, such as the reliability and validity of different types of tests. On the other hand, a meta-analysis is only as good as the data that are incorporated into the analysis. For example, Parker and his colleagues (1988) note that all their data on the Rorschach were obtained from a single journal with a long history of association with the Rorschach, and so there might be editorial bias in favor of that test. Because of the potential problems in interpreting meta-analyses, it is not yet clear whether Parker and his associates' results are accurate. However, they do suggest that a variety of types of tests can show high levels of reliability and validity.

SUMMARY

The history of personality measurement has progressed through several relatively distinct stages. Initially, testing was deeply rooted in personality theory. Test developers drew heavily on personality theory to direct the writing of items and the determination of what constituted the dimensions of personality. These early instruments were subject to much distortion but provided easily interpretable data. Next came the emergence of empirically derived tests. The basis for item selection shifted from the author's theory about personality to empirically observed relationships between item endorsement and criterion-group differences. Although this method yielded tests with high criterion-related validity, it did not produce theoretically meaningful scores that could easily be related to established personality theory. During this same period, projective testing also became prominent. The content of projective test items was designed to provide less structured, more ambiguous stimuli to assess the deeper aspects of personality.

With the development of advanced statistical procedures and computer technology, test constructors turned to factor analysis as the basis for item selection. A more recent development in the field of testing is to combine both rational and empirical approaches in order to select theoretically meaningful items that clearly distinguish various criterion groups.

The field of projective testing has seen the development of strongly theoretically based, yet poorly validated, instruments. The two most widely used tests, the Rorschach inkblot test and the Thematic Apperception Test (TAT), were developed initially during the 1920s. Little attention was paid to established practices of test development; consequently, issues such as reliability and validity were not addressed adequately. The years since their initial appearance have been marked by countless attempts to modify or standardize the administration and scoring of these tests to attain desirable psychometric characteristics. Despite these efforts, there has been little success.

The Rotter Incomplete Sentences Blank (RISB) provides an example of a projective test designed to have acceptable psychometric properties, but it unfortunately does not enjoy the extensive use of its less well-constructed counterparts. The Draw-a-Person Test (DAP), while fascinating in its speculation about the relationships between certain features of human drawings and personality dynamics, has not generated much solid evidence to substantiate its claims. Nevertheless, it ranks among the top 10 tests in total overall use among clinicians.

The appeal of projective tests would appear to be their rich source of exploratory hypotheses about the inner dynamics of the individual. However, their importance and widespread use in personality measurement cannot be justified on the basis of current research data.

PROBLEMS AND SOLUTIONS—RECAP

The Problem

Gary, the Director of Housing, consulted a psychologist in the Counseling Center about whether using a personality test would help him select resident assistants for the coming year. He wants to hire students who feel comfortable taking on a leadership role, have good interpersonal skills, and are empathic. Because students who are hired receive free room and board and a small monthly stipend for their work, he is concerned that some students might try to consciously distort their responses to put themselves in a favorable light and yet not have the qualities that he is looking for in a resident assistant.

Can personality testing be of help to Gary? Can traits such as interpersonal warmth, social dominance, and empathy be adequately assessed? Can a personality test successfully detect students who consciously attempt to look overly well-suited for the position?

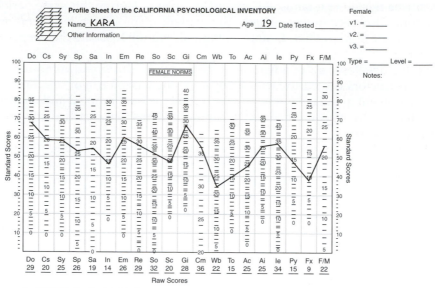

Kara: 7.917 + 5.148 + 15.064 − 5.61 − 1.52 = 62.77

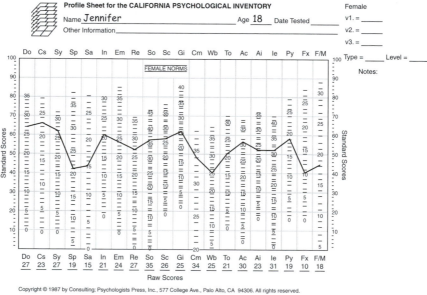

Jennifer: 7.371 + 4.752 + 13.45 − 6.375 − 1.68 = 58.743

FIGURE 17-6   Detecting Faking on the CPI   *Source:* Modified and reproduced by special permission of the Publisher, Consulting Psychologists Press, Inc., Palo Alto, CA 93303 from *California Psychological Inventory* by Harrison G. Gough. Copyright © 1996 by Consulting Psychologists Press, Inc. All rights reserved. Further reproduction is prohibited without the Publisher's written consent.

A Solution

Tests like the California Psychological Inventory (CPI) have been frequently used to successfully screen applicants for a variety of jobs. The CPI contains scales that are designed to measure a number of dimensions related to interpersonal functioning. The Dominance scale, for example, was specifically developed to differentiate students who took leadership roles and were persuasive with their friends from those who tended to shy away from assuming positions of authority and who were less socially confident. Similarly, the CPI also contains scales that give information about empathy and interpersonal warmth. Consequently, having all the applicants complete the CPI as part of the screening process could be of significant help in ranking applicants along several of important selection criteria for the Resident Assistant positions.

Finally, although Gary is concerned about some students trying to create an overly favorable impression on the test, research has shown that by combining several of the scores on the CPI in a special algorithm, it is possible to identify attempts to give untruthful responses. Consider the following two CPI profiles for Kara and Jennifer (these profiles are shown in Figure 17-6). If the algorithm developed to detect conscious efforts to appear overly well-adjusted is applied to both sets of scores (i.e., $41.225 + .273$ Dominance $+ .198$ Empathy $+ .538$ Good Impression $- .255$ Well Being $- .168$ Flexibility > 60.59), the profile generated by Kara ($7.917 + 5.148 + 15.064 - 5.61 - 1.512 = 62.77$) exceeds the established validity limit, whereas Jennifer's profile ($7.371 + 4.752 + 13.45 - 6.375 - 1.68 = 58.743$) does not. Thus, students trying to present themselves as overly qualified for the position should be detected.

KEY TERMS

Drawing tests   personality tests that use drawings of human figures or other stimuli to make inferences about personality

Empirically derived test   test in which items are selected or scored on the basis of their ability to distinguish between specific groups

Holtzman scoring technique   standardized scoring method for the Rorschach Inkblot Test

Incomplete sentence tests   tests that ask examinees to complete partial sentences

Objective measures   measures that imply clear items and/or standardized scoring systems

Validity scales   administrative scales that can be used to assess the consistency or appropriateness of scores on specific clinical or personality scales

18

Tests and Educational Decisions

In Part I of this book (Chapters 1 through 3), we introduced you to the field of testing with discussions about the behavioral domains that are measured and the potential consequences of such measurement activities. In Part II (Chapters 4 through 10), we examined various aspects of test theory and reviewed the basic psychometric properties that are essential in the development of sound psychological tests. Part III (Chapters 11 through 17) dealt with the transformation of these basic principles into functional tests and continued with an examination of several frequently used measures of ability, interest, and personality. Now, in the fourth and final section of the book, we will focus on how tests are actually used to make decisions in people's lives. Specifically, we will examine some of the questions that arise in applied situations and will explore how tests are used to make clinical decisions.

PROBLEMS AND SOLUTIONS—HOW SHOULD YOU INTERPRET A LOWER THAN AVERAGE SCORE?

The Problem

Samantha is a high-school senior who will be going to college in the fall. She took the ACT and obtained a composite score of 24 on the test. She has been thinking about what to study in college and talking with her counselor about career possibilities. Lately, she has been thinking about going into civil engineering because she really liked her job last summer working for a bridge construction company. She wonders whether she will be able to handle the academic work, however. Her counselor suggested that she do some research on the college she wants to attend in order to determine whether she will have a difficult time competing with the other students enrolled there. Samantha checked the academic ability of the college's student body in several national guidebooks and also on the college's Web site. She found that her ACT composite score was slightly higher than the average score of entering freshmen there.

Should Samantha be excited and optimistic about her chances of success in engineering, given what she learned about how she compares with the average student enrolling at the college she plans to attend?

This section is divided into three units corresponding to the specific types of settings that rely most heavily on psychological testing. Chapter 18 begins this final section with a discussion on the use of psychological measurement in educational settings. Here we focus on a few of the major decision-making questions faced by institutions and on some of the major testing instruments available to try and answer those questions. Chapter 19 deals with the role that psychological tests play in business and industrial settings. In this chapter, the discussion focuses on how specific job performance and selection questions are addressed through the use of psychological testing. Finally, Chapters 20 and 21 focus on clinical assessment and diagnosis as we investigate how psychological tests are used in clinical decision making.

We now turn our attention to how ability and interest tests are used in making educational decisions at both the institutional and the individual levels. The types of decisions made at each of these levels often demand different kinds of information, however. At the college and university level, administrators need information about the academic abilities of prospective students to make appropriate admissions decisions. They are interested in selecting those students who have the ability to succeed and in eliminating those who are likely to fail. At the primary and secondary school levels, educators are usually more interested in identifying those students who have special educational needs. At this level, standardized tests are used to identify both those who are especially intellectually gifted and those who may need specific remedial help. Tests are also used in making decisions about how to best group students within a school system so that the instructional level chosen will be appropriate for their developmental level.

Whereas institutions are usually concerned with admissions and selection decisions, individuals want information about their interests, strengths, and weaknesses to help them plan for their educational and vocational futures. Counselors are interested in knowing what kinds of skills individuals possess, what they are capable of learning, and what course of study and type of work they should pursue.

In this chapter we discuss how tests are used in making the decisions that confront both individuals and institutions. We begin by examining the central role that testing plays in making institutional decisions. Next, we focus on how tests are used by individuals in making decisions about their own educational goals. Finally, we discuss the impact of psychological testing on both the individual and society as it relates to career planning and the effective use of human resources.

APPLICATIONS IN INSTITUTIONAL DECISION MAKING

Admissions Decisions

Since the turn of the century, colleges and universities have been interested in finding cost-effective, efficient ways of selecting students. This institutional need has given rise to the development and, eventually, large-scale implementation of aptitude testing programs designed to provide postsecondary schools with information about the potential success of students if admitted to various programs of study. These programs rely on the premise that scholastic aptitude tests can effectively measure the abilities that are required to successfully learn course material.

These testing programs have not been without their critics, however (e.g., Crouse & Trusheim, 1988; Lemann, 1999; Miller, 2001; Sheehan & Gray, 1992). They have raised issues about their possible bias in favor of middle-class, white students, their inability to predict academic performance accurately, their gender bias, the overreliance placed on such tests in making academic decisions, and the alleged ease with which test scores can be inflated through coaching. Nevertheless, many admissions decisions are based, at least in part, on such standardized aptitude tests. Consequently, few prospective students entering postsecondary educational programs escape coming into contact with these assessment instruments. Therefore, we will examine how such tests are used in making institutional decisions and how efficient they are in the process.

How are aptitude tests like the American College Test (ACT), Scholastic Assessment Tests (SAT), and Graduate Record Examination (GRE) actually used by institutions? The answer varies with the school in question. Some institutions rely more heavily on test scores than others. Typically, however, test scores are combined with data on past academic performance in a regression equation statistically designed to yield the highest possible predictive equation for potential academic success. The rationale for this approach is that past academic history alone does not always accurately reflect the actual potential of the individual, since extraneous factors such as family difficulties, social problems, health concerns, or motivational deficits may be operative in lowering performance levels.

Should institutions use scholastic aptitude tests as aids in the admissions process? Do they really provide any critical data? How well do they work? These are the issues that we will now discuss by examining some of the criticisms leveled against admissions tests and their use, and by evaluating the impact of these tests on higher education.

Retaking Scholastic Aptitude Tests. Because of the perceived importance of aptitude tests in the selection process, students often retest in an effort to improve their scores. Whether they are likely to show significant score gains has been a matter of some controversy (American College Test Program, 1995; College Entrance Examination Board, 1998). Data reported by the College Entrance Examination Board on SAT retesting indicated that on the revised SAT I, which debuted in the spring of 1994, only about 55% of the 408,000 juniors taking the test improved their scores when they retested as seniors. Approximately 10% of these juniors obtained the same score, and about 35% generated lower scores when they retested as seniors. It is interesting to note that the average improvements in verbal and math scores were approximately 13 and 12 points, respectively. Given the standard error of measurement on the SAT, such gains are of questionable interpretable value. Less than 4% of the retest cases had score gains approaching a magnitude of 100 points or more, and slightly more than 1% saw their scores decline 100 or more points.

Similarly, research conducted by Wilson (1989) on the long-term stability of GRE scores tends to support the notion that students show only modest increases in their test scores as a result of retest. He studied 3,614 test takers who took the GRE on two occasions more than 5 years apart. His results revealed gains of approximately 40 points on the verbal section and 17 points on the math portion of the test.

There are instances when substantial score gains are more likely to occur, however. Information provided by ACT (1995) suggests that students who experienced difficulty with test directions on the day of the test were highly anxious and unable to concentrate, were under considerable emotional stress, or were physically ill when they initially tested will probably achieve a somewhat lower score than they deserve. Likewise, students who have had limited or no experience taking standardized multiple-choice tests may perform substantially below their capacity because of their inability to employ successful test-taking strategies. Under such circumstances, retesting may substantially improve scores.

Admission of the Educationally Disadvantaged. Scholastic aptitude tests have been severely criticized for being biased toward white, middle-class students. Critics point to the substantial body of research that shows that educationally disadvantaged students, often from minority groups, typically do not perform as well on aptitude tests as their white peers (Freedle, 2003; Jencks & Phillips, 1998; Lawlor, Richman, & Richman, 1997). They argue that it is this differential in performance that leads to underrepresentation of minorities in colleges, graduate programs, and professional schools.

On the other hand, proponents of scholastic aptitude testing have countered with research showing that although educationally disadvantaged students do score lower on such tests than their peers, they also achieve lower grades in school. They contend that scholastic aptitude tests substantially predict actual school performance just as they were designed to do. The educational deficits reflected in lower test scores are assumed to be the same ones that are related to poorer performance in the actual school setting. Fleming (2002) found that in even predominately white colleges, the average black-white differences in predictive validity using SAT scores was quite small (less than 2%). Data reported by the College Entrance Examination Board (1993) showed that regardless of ethnicity, the students performing best on the SAT were those with four or more years of study in challenging high school course work. Similarly, Pennock-Roman (1990) found that the overall accuracy of grade prediction using the SAT was as good for Hispanic students as for non-Hispanic, white students. Some researchers (e.g., Manning, 1976) have even presented data suggesting that in some cases, tests like the Law School Admissions Test may, in fact, overpredict rather than underpredict actual school performance for some minority groups. Thus, the controversy rages on concerning to what extent aptitude tests are biased against minority students. The data would appear to indicate that bias is present, but whether it is the result of poor test construction or merely reflective of educational inequities in society has yet to be clearly resolved.

Should scholastic aptitude tests be used in making admissions decisions? There are strong arguments for both points of view. It appears to us, however, that such tests are probably likely to enjoy widespread use by institutions until some other selection tool becomes available. Although the data reported by Crouse and Trusheim (1988) support the earlier findings of the National Academy of Sciences (Wigdor & Garner,

1982b), suggesting that the role aptitude testing plays in making admission decisions has been greatly overrated, there are still no reasonable alternatives to their use.

We believe that the problem with using them does not really reside within the tests themselves. The research data seem to suggest that tests of scholastic aptitude actually accomplish what they were designed to do, that is, to pick out those who are most likely to perform well in school. The difficulty appears to be much more a societal concern involving how these tests are used. It is precisely at this level that institutions need to abandon rigid admission policies based on aptitude scores and select a more diverse student body, knowing that some students will need additional supportive services to achieve their educational goals. Thus, selection tools such as scholastic aptitude tests can be used either to maintain the status quo or move beyond it to create more opportunities for all segments of our society.

Prediction Efficiency. How well do scholastic aptitude tests work? A great many studies have been undertaken to determine the validity of scholastic aptitude tests for predicting future academic performance. Typically, researchers have compared grades in high school against admission test scores to see which would predict future college performance most accurately. The evidence has shown consistently that past academic history is superior to aptitude testing in predicting future school achievement. In general, the correlation between former grades in school and future grades is usually between .40 and .50, whereas test scores manage correlations only with future grades in the .30 to .35 range.

Should institutions continue to use test scores for making admissions decisions? Certainly, the amount of variance in academic grades that is accounted for by scholastic test scores is not very impressive (approximately 10% to 15%). Nevertheless, a small portion of the variance that is accounted for is unique to these tests and not assessed by past academic history alone. Because both sets of data do contribute some unique information, most institutions now combine them into a regression equation to maximize their ability to predict future grades. Utilizing such statistical procedures, the correlations obtained between predictor and criterion are often increased substantially (e.g., $r = .55$ to .60).

Tests produce their most impressive predictive successes when used with individuals who have performed poorly in school for reasons other than lack of ability. Similarly, testing provides a way of more equitably assessing students who come from very localized educational systems; in these cases, identical grade records tend to vary in meaning from one school system to another. In both instances, institutions can make more informed admission decisions based on the tested ability levels of those students.

Effects of Coaching. Because of the presumed importance of test scores in institutional decision making, many people have sought help from various test preparation organizations, hoping to learn how to take the tests so as to get the best score. These commercial ventures report gains in test scores ranging from 1.0 to 2.5 standard deviations (e.g., 100 to 250 points on the SAT or GRE). In addition to formal instructional programs, many students purchase one or more of the many self-help books to better prepare for taking the exam. Computer software and online materials are also available that allow students to diagnose their academic deficiencies and strengthen their skills with the expectation of improving their performance. Some reviewers have suggested that coaching can have a significant impact on test scores (Owen, 1985), although the validity of these claims has been questioned (Wigdor & Garner, 1982b).

Two corporations, Educational Testing Service and American College Testing Program, are actively involved in the testing controversy. They have conducted much research on the efforts of coaching and exam preparation on actual test performance. Most of their research has reported much more modest gains than suggested by their critics. Data from research on the SAT suggest that average score improvement after coaching is more in the range of a one-fourth to a one-third standard deviation, or 25 to 35 points. The most conservative evaluation to be made, given the data reported from all sources, is that the probability of some improvement in scores is quite high; how much improvement is another matter. Undoubtedly, there is considerable interindividual variation in score improvement. Those who claim very large gains in test performance have probably seen outstanding increases for some individual students. However, when aggregate data from a large population of students are considered, the gains are generally much less exciting (Powers, 1993; Powers & Rock, 1999).

It is our belief that those individuals who are most apt to benefit from coaching or tutoring are those whose academic skills are rusty or nonexistent. Therefore, people who have been out of school for a period of time or who are particularly deficient in one or more essential academic skill area, such as written communication or mathematics, will probably benefit most. In addition, it is possible that the practice and basic skill building involved in coaching will improve their ability to handle additional course work.

Selection Decisions

Identification of Exceptionality. Institutions have long had a need to identify those individuals who are at either end of the ability continuum. One group of students needing rather early detection and remedial work consists of those who experience developmental delays in their maturation. The earlier these people can be identified and provided with learning environments designed to stimulate their intellectual and emotional development, the more likely it is that they will be able to maximize their talents. Aptitude tests are employed to make these decisions, while recognizing that some decisional errors will inevitably occur. Typically, the inaccurate decisions that are usually made are more likely to be false negative errors (i.e., individuals being classified as less able than they are), rather than false positive errors (i.e., students being classified as more talented than they really are). Consequently, even when errors are made, it is likely that those students who have been misclassified will be given special remedial treatment until the errors are detected. Thus, all who need special educational intervention will not be overlooked. However, testing errors can lead to the potential loss of educational opportunities and possible stigma for the students involved.

A second area of exceptionality that is receiving considerable attention today involves the identification of intellectually gifted students. Institutions need to identify those talented individuals who will benefit most from an enriched educational curriculum. To properly challenge these students, more demanding and complex learning environments need to be made available. Failure to provide adequate stimulation often leads to poor motivation and performance on the part of gifted students. They often become discouraged and fail to channel their talents in productive directions. Again, ability tests play a major role in the identification of these especially talented people.

Classroom Selection. Perhaps one of the more inventive uses for aptitude tests in educational settings has been their application to the problem of tracking in the classroom. In this case, students are grouped according to ability in order to provide instruction that is consistent with their ability level. This application of aptitude testing seeks to maximize the motivation of students and minimize their frustration by placing them in classes where the material presented is neither too easy (and therefore boring) nor too difficult (which often leads to frustration). Although tests are far from perfect tools in accomplishing this purpose, they are helpful aids in the decision-making process. The biggest danger in their use is that administrators may rely on them too heavily, without taking into account other important data that are essential to sound decision making. Certainly, this is the case when talented students with a history of performing very well academically are not placed in more challenging class sections because of low test scores resulting from some extraneous factor, such as test anxiety or emotional upset.

Evaluation Decisions

Standardized ability tests have long played a major role in evaluating the effectiveness of educational programs. Achievement tests such as the Iowa Tests of Basic Skills, the Iowa Tests of Educational Development, and the California Achievement Test are typically administered to students within an institution to determine how they are performing in relation to their peers across the country. Strengths and weaknesses among students are noted, but from an institutional perspective, administrators are more interested in evaluating whether the curriculum has the breadth and depth characteristic of other programs. Administrators who give these tests are, therefore, very concerned about the overall effectiveness of their instructional program.

This institutional application of achievement testing has recently raised some troubling issues. Several years ago, a West Virginia physician, Dr. John Cannell, noted in a report that schoolchildren in West Virginia were reported to be above the national norm in their performance on a standardized ability measure. Because West Virginia has a very high illiteracy rate, he decided to investigate the issue further. He subsequently found that not only West Virginia but also every one of the 50 states had reported that the achievement scores of their schoolchildren were above the national average on standardized test batteries. This rather startling finding has been coined the

"Lake Wobegon Phenomenon" after author Garrison Keillor's mythical town where all the children are above average.

How can everyone be above the national average? From our earlier study of the meaning of test scores, we know that theoretically this situation is impossible (i.e., 50% must be above the mean and 50% below). The findings reported by Cannell have since been confirmed by an independent study conducted by the U.S. Department of Education. The answer to this paradox lies in the characteristics of the national norm group against which student performance is compared. Because of the great expense involved in renorming standardized tests on a yearly basis, test companies usually rely on well-developed norm groups that are often five or more years old. Consequently, when student performance is compared with the "national norm," it is really being compared with the performance of students who took the test several years earlier. It is therefore quite possible for everyone to be above the average because the comparison group is not composed of students taking the current test.

Why would we necessarily see an improvement in scores when a new test group is compared with the older norm group? One factor is that teachers often "teach to the test." That is, they note what content is covered on the various standardized tests in use at their school and then modify their teaching to cover that material in their classes. Curricula are often modified by administrators to better reflect the test content so that students will have exposure to the material and consequently perform well when tested. This "curriculum alignment" (McNeil, 2000; Shanker, 1988) process probably accounts for much of the "Lake Wobegon Phenomenon."

The unresolved issue that testing and curriculum experts are now debating is whether teaching to the test and curriculum alignment are reasonable methods of attaining educational goals. Proponents claim that modifying curricula to reflect test content ensures that our educational programs are up to date and responsive to the needs of society. Critics, on the other hand, claim that as long as we use test content to guide our teaching, we jeopardize our ability to effectively evaluate how well we are really teaching. With all the external pressures from people outside the school system to show positive educational progress, it appears as though teaching to the test will probably continue.

CRITICAL DISCUSSION:
The National Assessment of Educational Progress

American schools are frequently criticized on the grounds that students no longer attain basic skills (e.g., literacy, a working knowledge of mathematics) and that we are falling behind other nations in terms of educational attainment. Although some of these criticisms are probably justified, it is in fact quite difficult to sensibly evaluate the quality of our schools or the attainments of our students.

The National Assessment of Educational Progress (NAEP), which started in 1969, represents a systematic effort to assess what American students know and can do. A special issue of the 1992 *Journal of Educational Statistics* provides a detailed discussion of the NAEP program, which involves a complex sampling plan for both students and test items. In 1990, for example, over 145,000 students in more than 20 distinct samples provided data for NAEP. NAEP employs highly sophisticated applications of item response theory to provide consistent scaling of proficiency across a wide range of grades and content areas.

NAEP provides assessments of proficiency in science, mathematics, and reading. This assessment does not report scores for individual students, schools, or school districts; rather, it estimates proficiency at a national level. It also provides proficiency levels in individual participating states. On the whole, the results of NAEP do not support the idea that students are declining in their proficiency. Math proficiency was higher in 1990 than in the late 1970s. Performance in science declined in the 1970s but improved in the 1980s. For 9- and 13-year-olds, science proficiency levels in the 1990s were similar to those in the 1970s, although for older students, proficiency levels have dropped somewhat. Reading proficiency was at least as high, and for some age groups, higher in the 1990s than in the 1970s.

The technical descriptions of the NAEP methods make it clear just how difficult it is to determine whether students are really improving or declining in their skills. Most comparisons of different nations, different school districts, different states, or trends over time confound real differences in proficiency with differences in curriculum, differences in the student population, and differences in the tests used to estimate performance. Although most people seem to believe that our educational system is failing, the data from careful assessments, such as that provided by NAEP, suggest that the picture is not so simple, and perhaps not so grim.

APPLICATIONS IN INDIVIDUAL DECISION MAKING

Although it is difficult to completely separate institutional from individual applications of testing in decision making, we have chosen the target or purpose for which the testing is done as our point of reference in making this distinction. Up to this point, we have focused on how tests are used by institutions to help make administrative decisions. Now we shift our focus to how tests are employed in the educational and career decisions made by the individual.

As students progress through the educational system, they encounter many decision points. Questions arise such as whether to prepare for college or to take vocationally relevant course work. Likewise, they face decisions about how much formal education to pursue, what academic major to select, which electives to take, and what career path to follow. How are psychological tests applied to these individual decision-making tasks? How useful are they? These are some of the issues that are examined here.

Educational Planning

Selecting an appropriate educational program is an extremely important goal in our society, yet many people are reluctant to seek help. They try to avoid a lengthy trial-and-error process, opting instead to narrow their alternatives to a small, manageable number of possibilities that seem to have potential for success and personal satisfaction. Testing can play an important role in the decision-making process as can be seen in the following four case studies that illustrate how psychological tests can affect educational and vocational decisions.

Case example—Bob. Take the case of Bob, who is a college sophomore currently taking a liberal arts curriculum. Although he came to college somewhat undecided about what he wanted to pursue, he felt little pressure to make a commitment until now. In the past, it seemed that most decisions had been made for him. He had few choices open to him as he progressed through elementary and junior high school. In high school he simply followed a college preparatory program, since he knew that he was going on to college. Bob's hope was that as he got involved in college, the decision-making process would get easier. Unfortunately, he became more rather than less confused.

Bob sought help from the counseling center on campus and was administered two interest tests as part of the counseling process. What he learned from the test results was that he shared a similar interest pattern with people engaged in certain business occupations. Specifically, Bob's tests indicated a rather strong interest in the aspect of business that was people oriented. He immediately began to think about selling, but his counselor pointed out to him that his strong secondary pattern of interest in art and design, combined with his business interests, would suggest a career in advertising. Although Bob was aware that he liked to draw at times, he had not pursued art with much interest because he was certain that he lacked sufficient ability to be successful as an artist. The thought of combining art with business and taking an introductory advertising course to check out his ability level was intriguing. Encouraged by the data supplied by these tests, Bob decided to explore advertising further.

How useful were these test data for Bob? Why had he not gravitated toward business or advertising on his own? Bob, like many of us, had some stereotypic ideas about business that kept him from taking any course work in that field. He had just assumed that he would not like business. What the testing did for Bob was to give him some important information about how his interests compared with the interests of people in various jobs who were quite satisfied with their work. Although the tests did not reveal any major surprises about what he liked or disliked, they did help him reconsider his thinking about business and rekindle his interest in art.

Case example—Dawn. Sometimes the issue in question is not so much interest as ability. For an example, consider the case of Dawn, who always had an interest in mechanical activities. She grew up with three brothers and learned to repair just about anything that was mechanical, including her bicycle and her car. As she approached college, however, she questioned whether she could successfully major in mechanical engineering. To assist Dawn in deciding about her future college plans, she was given a mechanical aptitude test. Coupled with other data, such as her excellent grades in math and science during high school and her scholastic aptitude test scores, the results of the mechanical aptitude test suggested that she had a better than average chance of completing that major.

Case example—Bill. Sometimes testing results do not coincide with an individual's current plans or past experience. Bill, for instance, was a second-semester sophomore with a C average who recently had begun to experience severe problems in his math course. As his course work was becoming more difficult, Bill was studying more and more, yet finding it harder to keep up. Because he had always been an A and a B student in high school, Bill attributed his failing marks in math to the quality of the instruction he was getting and his lack of background in math (i.e., his high school had required only one year of math). Bill's math professor suggested that he take some tests to see whether he had a learning disability.

The results of a battery of both aptitude and achievement tests administered to Bill revealed that his current academic difficulty was probably due to his being less intellectually able than his peers. Interest testing was then done to help him formulate some alternatives to his current plans. He eventually decided to cut back to a part-time basis, monitor his progress for another semester, and reevaluate his educational plans at that time.

Case example—Bonnie. Sometimes too much reliance can be placed on tests, causing costly delays in the educational development and career planning of the individual. Bonnie was not a very motivated student. She did enough to get by, but rarely applied herself beyond the bare minimum. She had other priorities in her life besides school. She worked at various part-time jobs throughout high school and spent considerable time with her steady boyfriend.

When Bonnie was a sophomore in high school, she was given an ability test and an interest inventory to help her set some educational and career goals. Her interest scores indicated that she liked working with people and doing artwork and mechanical-technical activities. The results of the ability test, however, indicated that she did not have the aptitude for college work. Since this finding was consistent with her mediocre grades in school, her counselor advised her to take the vocationally oriented track and to not consider attending college.

Now at age 24, Bonnie is a divorced, single parent of a 3-year-old son. She is finding it difficult to live on her minimum wage as a hospital ward clerk, and so she has decided to reconsider attending college. During career counseling, she discovered that she was much brighter and more academically able than prior testing and school grades had shown. Both she and her counselor decided that lack of motivation and a poor self-concept were probably responsible for her marginal performance in the past. She was therefore encouraged to pursue her career ambition of becoming an occupational therapist. Had less weight been given to the earlier ability testing data, she might have gone to college much sooner.

In all four of the preceding cases, testing played a key role in helping individuals make important decisions about their educational plans. Testing provided either unique, new information or confirmation of past or present plans.

Career Planning

Perhaps one of the most frequent applications of individual testing in educational settings involves career decision making. Throughout their life spans, people are faced with decisions about what type of work to pursue. At an early developmental age, there is a need for general areas to be identified so that further exploration can be undertaken. During young adulthood, the need is often for more specific information concerning the probabilities of both success and satisfaction in various careers. Persons undergoing midlife career changes present another problem. They are searching for support and encouragement in the change process and are seeking data that either reinforce or contraindicate their plans. At all stages of development, then, testing can play a significant role in the vocational decision-making process. Three case studies illustrate this role.

Case example—Megan. Megan, a high-school sophomore, has been wondering what she should do after she finishes school. She has recently been thinking about taking some secretarial classes and going to work after graduation. As part of the career counseling process in her high school, Megan was given an interest test revealing that she had a rather definite preference for science. What had happened, however, was that Megan had never considered herself college material and therefore had not pursued science in school. When further ability testing was done, she learned that college was within her reach if she wanted to try. This information opened a whole new set of alternatives for her that she would not have explored without the use of tests.

Case example—Juan. Juan, on the other hand, was facing a midlife crisis. He was a 32-year-old high school history teacher, but he was becoming increasingly disenchanted with teaching. He had entered the field partly by accident. As a student in college, Juan had not known exactly what he wanted to do. After taking a variety of courses for 2½ years, he decided to major in history because he had more hours in that area than in any other and he had always liked to study it. As he approached graduation, he realized that there were not too many jobs for history majors, so he completed the necessary hours in education to become a teacher. Now, 10 years later, he thought he wanted a change.

Testing revealed that Juan's choice of teaching was quite consistent with his interests. Test data indicated that he had a rather clearly defined interest in social science and education. Further discussion with Juan indicated that the major source of his dissatisfaction was not his choice of work but was job-related factors, such as the new principal recently hired at his school. Using this information, Juan decided to remain in teaching because he had enjoyed it in the past, but he considered changing to a new school system.

Case example—David. Our final case is David, a college junior majoring in biological science with plans to go on to veterinary school. David began thinking that he might need a backup plan in case he was unsuccessful in gaining admission to the veterinary program. Even though he had always received excellent grades, he knew that admission to that field was very competitive. David found that his test results were very supportive of his veterinary goal but that they were also consistent with a number of other medically related fields as well as with computer-oriented work. The test results helped David to take several additional computer courses as electives while completing his major in biological science. In this way, he would leave college with an employable skill to fall back on if he were not able to gain acceptance into veterinary school. This course of action gave him an alternative to his current vocational plans should he need it in the future.

This chapter has illustrated a number of ways in which psychological tests are used in making educational and career decisions, both on an institutional level and on an individual level. In both cases, tests often have significant impact on the decisions made. Although tests do not provide infallible data, they can be useful tools enabling decision makers to gather systematic information relatively quickly and accurately. Finally, as several clinical case studies illustrated, tests of ability and interest often form the basis for much decision making in the educational and career area.

CRITICAL DISCUSSION:

What Is Portfolio Assessment? Should It Be Used for Educational Assessment?

Portfolio assessment refers to an evaluation technique by which expert judges rate the performance of workers on a series of work-sample tasks. The work that is evaluated is contained in a portfolio. Typically, this is a collection of an individual's work that exhibits his or her effort, progress, and achievement in a particular area. Recently, there has been much interest in applying this assessment technique to educational issues. LeMahieu, Gitomer, and Eresh (1995) noted that portfolio assessment has its strong proponents who argue its superiority over standardized testing for educational assessment. They report that portfolio assessment provides more information about how students think and solve problems, enables students to take a more active role in their own assessment, provides assessment tasks that are more comprehensive, and permits students to be evaluated on more meaningful and educationally relevant material than is the case when typical standardized tests are used. They further state that portfolio assessment also benefits institutions in that they can more effectively evaluate their programs and develop common performance-based criteria across various disciplines. Advocates of portfolio assessment also maintain that this technique is more equitable to minority students, in that it eliminates the differential performance between majority and minority students that is often shown on standardized tests. However, Dunbar, Koretz, and Hoover (1991) have presented evidence that this gap in performance probably still exists and therefore question this contention.

Detractors of portfolio assessment have raised a number of issues about the use of this technique in educational settings. They question whether there is an acceptable level of agreement among judges in the scoring of the portfolio. They have also questioned whether there is sufficient agreement about the standards to be used when portfolios are judged. Similarly, there is concern that the judgments made about the performance of students might vary as a function of the work samples chosen. Finally, they seriously question whether large-scale performance-based assessment is practical or feasible.

Given that performance-based assessment has been successfully utilized in industry for some time, however, it might seem that this technique could effectively be applied to educational assessment as well. However, researchers have generally reported rather disappointing results (Baker, O'Neil, & Linn, 1993; Koretz, 1993; Linn, Baker, & Dunbar, 1991), indicating that the standards for reliability and validity that are expected of psychological assessment have not been shown when portfolio assessment was used in evaluating educational achievement. Why has this technique produced better results when used in industry? Camara and Brown (1995) have suggested that a part of the problem may lie in the fact that educational objectives are often vague and open to various interpretations, whereas in industrial settings, the criteria to be judged are much clearer and more sharply defined. Ambiguity leads to less interjudge reliability. Consequently, the promise of portfolio assessment has just not been realized. Unless the variables involved in educational evaluation are much more clearly explicated and quantified, there is little hope of establishing reliable and valid performance-based measures of educational outcomes.

CRITICAL DISCUSSION:

What Is Criterion-Referenced Testing?

Criterion-referenced testing is not a new idea. It closely resembles the concept mastery approach to testing that has been used in educational settings for years. The essence of criterion-referenced testing lies in comparing the test performance of examinees with some objectively stated goal or standard of achievement to determine how much examinees have learned or at what level they are able to perform the tasks in question.

Our focus throughout this book has been primarily on norm-referenced tests. How do they differ from criterion-referenced tests? The answer lies in the frame of reference that each uses to give meaning to test scores. In the case of norm-referenced tests, the scores that examinees receive are compared with the scores of other people taking the same tests. The focus is not on how many items were answered correctly but, rather, on whether the number answered correctly was greater or less than that of a comparison group. Criterion-referenced tests, on the other hand, use a specified content area as the basis for comparison. These tests are designed to measure how much of the content area has been learned, mastered, or performed. Consequently, the focus is on the absolute number of items correctly answered in relation to the total number of correct responses on the test, rather than on the number responded to correctly relative to a comparison group.

Criterion-referenced tests have been used most extensively in educational settings where the instructional goal consists of clearly defined, objective content. For example, they are particularly well suited as aids in making decisions about the level of math or spelling proficiency attained by examinees or the English reading fluency found among a class of foreign students. In addition, they have been used rather extensively in conjunction with computer-aided instruction. For example, criterion-referenced tests are frequently used to determine how much students have learned in a particular subject so that a structured program of instruction can be given. Then, following a specified learning period, testing is done again to measure the amount of gain achieved by the students as a result of the instruction. The ease with which students' progress can be monitored through the use of computers enables educators to employ criterion-referenced tests to tailor instructional programs to each student's individual needs.

While criterion-referenced tests have been increasingly utilized in educational decision-making situations, they are not likely to supplant the premier role played by norm-referenced tests in psychological assessment. Several significant problems still plague developers of criterion-referenced tests and prevent their wide-scale application. For instance, there is the rather thorny issue of what constitutes an acceptable level of mastery for the attribute in question. Should mastery be defined as achieving a score of 100% on the test? Should answering 80% of the items correctly be considered adequate mastery of the material? Should the required level of mastery change as a function of other student characteristics, such as intelligence, sex, or grade level? Answers to these difficult questions are not yet readily available.

Finally, another problem involving criterion-referenced tests concerns how to evaluate them adequately. The methods reviewed earlier in this book for estimating the reliability of psychological tests do not work with criterion-referenced tests. For example, reducing the variability among test scores influences the size of the correlation coefficient that is employed in estimating the reliability of tests. However, in the case of criterion-referenced tests, which have an established level of mastery that everyone eventually attains through additional instruction, the amount of intersubject variability becomes zero. With such a restricted range of scores, our correlational techniques for estimating reliability do not work. In Chapter 7, we showed how to assess reliability when multiple tests were used (i.e., with coefficient kappa). For additional discussions of methods of assessing the reliability of criterion-referenced tests, see Cizek (1993) and Hambleton (1994).

SUMMARY

Colleges, universities, and professional schools have long had a need to find methods of identifying academically able students to be admitted to their institutions. Historically, they have turned to academic aptitude testing programs to provide them with predictive information about the academic potential of student applicants. Although institutions differ on how much emphasis should be placed on academic aptitude test scores, there has been solid support for including them along with past academic record in some type of regression equation as an aid in making admissions decisions.

Students often retake academic aptitude tests in an effort to raise their scores. Although significant score improvement occurs in a few isolated cases, the majority of research indicates that only modest gains are usually achieved.

Critics have raised substantive issues about the use of academic aptitude tests in making admission decisions for educationally disadvantaged students. Claiming clear evidence that such tests are biased toward the majority group, they contend that such tests discriminate against certain subgroups and prohibit their entry into postsecondary education. Although the bulk of the research suggests that academic aptitude tests predict academic success for disadvantaged students about as well as for others, it was suggested that institutions might want to modify their use of test scores in working with certain subgroups in an effort to create greater equality among all groups within our society.

Others question the continued use of scholastic aptitude tests in admissions decisions because they account for so little of the variance in students' grades. Typically, scholastic aptitude scores correlate in the .30 to .35 range with first-year grades. Proponents counter that, although it is small, the contribution that scholastic aptitude tests make in predicting grades is unique and should not be disregarded.

Because scholastic aptitude tests can have such a profound effect on people's lives, many individuals attend special coaching clinics, tutoring sessions, or preparation classes to help them maximize their score. Although some students do improve their test scores dramatically, most people do not substantially improve their scores.

In addition to admissions decisions, scholastic aptitude tests are also utilized to identify individuals with specialized educational needs, to group students according to ability levels for program-planning purposes, and to evaluate the overall effectiveness of educational programs. Because our society places such a heavy premium on academic excellence, there has been the temptation to misuse the data generated from scholastic testing to support various political or personal aims.

Finally, academic testing is frequently used in clinical counseling situations to help people make realistic decisions about their futures. Several examples were discussed, showing how testing can be employed to confirm people's plans, alert them to possible future problems or difficulties, and suggest new, unexplored career avenues for possible consideration.

PROBLEMS AND SOLUTIONS—RECAP

The Problem

Samantha is a high-school senior who will be going to college in the fall. She took the ACT and obtained a composite score of 24 on the test. She has been thinking about what to study in college and talking with her counselor about career possibilities. Lately, she has been thinking about going into civil engineering because she really liked her job last summer working for a bridge construction company. She wonders whether she will be able to handle the academic work, however. Her counselor suggested that she do some research on the college she wants to attend in order to determine whether she will have a difficult time competing with the other students enrolled there. Samantha checked on the academic ability of the college's student body in several national guidebooks and also on the college's Web site. She found that her ACT composite score was slightly higher than the average score of entering freshmen there.

Should Samantha be excited and optimistic about her chances of success in engineering, given what she learned about how she compared with the average student at the college she wants to attend?

A Solution

Using test data such as scores on a college admissions test like the ACT to predict academic performance can be useful in academic planning. Certainly knowing that one compares generally with other students at a given school can be very reassuring. The problem with the data presented in this scenario is that Samantha's test scores are being compared with those of the average student at the college and not with those of other students majoring in engineering. The picture might look considerably different if the more relevant norm group was used.

When Samantha met with her engineering advisor to register for fall courses, she found that although her composite score of 24 compared favorably with that of the average entering freshman at the college, it was slightly below average when compared with the scores of students who were declaring engineering as their major. What was potentially more problematic, however, was that her math score of 23 was substantially below that of entering engineering students who averaged 28 on the ACT math test. Given that the standard deviation on the ACT is approximately five points, her advisor pointed out that she might encounter some difficulty with math since nearly nine out of ten engineering students with whom she would be competing appeared to be stronger in math than she is. With this new information, Samantha now has a better understanding of how she stands in relation to her potential engineering classmates and is more aware of the challenges before her. As we can see, test data can be very helpful in educational and career planning, but selecting the most meaningful comparison group is essential for making good decisions.

KEY TERMS

Admissions tests   tests used by colleges and universities to assist in determining which applicants to admit or to reject

Coaching   using courses, workbooks, or other methods to improve performance on admissions tests

Identification of exceptionality   using tests to identify individuals who would be most likely to benefit from special placement (either for gifted students or for students with special developmental needs)

Mastery testing   criterion-referenced testing strategy in which examinees are asked to demonstrate mastery of a specific skill or body of knowledge

National Assessment of Educational Progress   systematic, nationwide effort to assess the knowledge, skills, and performance of American schoolchildren

Portfolio assessment   evaluation of student performance on the basis of a sample of completed tests

19

Psychological Measurement in Industry

In work settings ranging from small businesses to large corporations, from local, state, and federal agencies to the various arms of the military, decisions must be made regarding hiring, placement, training, promotion, raises, and the like. For the most part, personnel decisions involve either predictions or evaluations of job performance. Workers are hired, promoted, or placed in new jobs to achieve maximal levels of productivity; accuracy in prediction of job performance is therefore the cornerstone of successful personnel administration. Similarly, organizational rewards are in part based on evaluations of past performance. The allocation of promotions, raises, bonuses, and awards depends on evaluations of past and present performance. The accurate measurement of present and past performance is therefore central to many decisions regarding the allocation of organizational rewards. This chapter addresses both the tests and the assessments that are used to predict future performance and the methods used to measure current and past performance.

We start with a discussion of the types of tests that are used in industry to predict job performance. Before discussing specific tests, it is useful to consider the context of testing, or the extent to which psychological tests are used for making work-related decisions.

PROBLEMS AND SOLUTIONS—SCREENING A LARGE APPLICANT POOL

The Problem

Following the lead of Honda, Toyota, and other major automobile manufacturers, a German company is thinking about building a manufacturing facility in the United States, preferably in the Midwest. There is a huge turnout for their first job fair, and they realize that they are likely to attract thousands of applicants (many of whom have experience working in factories and manufacturing) to fill 135 semiskilled jobs. Your task as a consultant is to design a system for selecting the best workers from this pool.

EXTENT AND IMPACT OF PERSONNEL TESTING

If one adopts a broad definition of the term *test*, a definition that includes interviews and work samples as well as traditional paper-and-pencil tests, then it is safe to conclude that personnel testing is almost universal. An interview of some sort precedes nearly every job offer, and those candidates who are not interviewed are almost certain to have filled out a standard job application, which in some cases could be used as a form of test. Even if the definition of test is narrowed to include only paper-and-pencil measures, testing is still widespread. Ability tests have long been used in the United States (Friedman & Williams, 1982) and are used in other countries, although perhaps to a lesser extent than in the United States. Personality measures and standardized assessments of background and experience are increasingly common. Tests designed to measure dependability or integrity are now widespread (Murphy, 1993).

The use of written tests is much more common for office positions than for production and sales jobs. In particular, candidates for clerical jobs represent the most heavily tested group of applicants in the private sector. Between 60% and 80% of the companies that use written tests use clerical tests. Testing is also common for positions involving highly specific skills or abilities (e.g., master electrician).

The fact that a test is given and that test scores may be entered into an applicant's file does not necessarily mean that the tests will be used in making personnel decisions. Tenopyr (1981) notes that although a number of tests may be given to each applicant, scores on written tests actually often have a minor impact on personnel decisions. Private employers tend to rely heavily on interviews, credentials, and recommendations in making selection decisions, and they may pay little attention to scores on standardized tests.

Testing in Government and the Military

Written tests are very widely used for selection and placement in the federal government; they are used somewhat less, although still extensively, by state, county, and local governments. For the most part, civil service hiring is done using a merit system in which applicants must receive high scores on competitive examinations in order to be considered for the job. Nearly 90% of all federal employees work in jobs that are filled using the merit system; for state, county, and local employees, the figure is nearer to 80% (Friedman & Williams, 1982).

The military represents the largest consumer of employment tests. Although the military workforce is considerably smaller than the workforce in the private sector or in civilian government, tests are used so widely and so frequently in the military that the total number of tests used per year far exceeds the total figure for either the private sector or civilian government. For example, over a million people per year take the

Armed Forces Vocational Aptitude Battery (ASVAB). In addition to this basic test, the military uses over 900 separate skill classification tests. Finally, a large amount of basic and applied research on the validity of tests is carried out by the military.[1]

The military faces very different testing problems from those encountered in the private sector. Testing in the private sector is often designed to select from a pool of applicants the persons most qualified for a specific job. Although the military does set minimum selection standards, much of its testing is used in making placement rather than selection decisions. In other words, the military must plan carefully to use the talents, skills, and abilities of its recruits effectively. As a result, tests used in the military are likely to stress a combination of aptitudes and skills that are useful across a broad range of military jobs. Military testing very often includes the use of wide-ranging test batteries, such as the ASVAB, together with tests of skills that are necessary for specific military assignments.

Occupational and Professional Licensing

More than 2,000 occupations may require licensing or certification, ranging from accountants to physical therapists; in some states up to 25% of the workforce consists of licensed practitioners. Both oral and written tests are frequently used as part of the certification process. Testing for a license or a professional certificate therefore represents a fairly large-scale activity.

A sizable array of state, local, and nongovernmental licensing boards exist. For the most part, examinations are prepared by board members, although national examinations prepared by professional testing agencies have become increasingly common (Friedman & Williams, 1982). Tests prepared by licensing boards vary extremely in quality; locally prepared exams almost always are technically inferior to nationally prepared ones (Wigdor & Garner, 1982a). Finally, licensing boards do not always demonstrate or even investigate the content, construct, or criterion-related validity of their exams. It is likely that many of the tests currently used in professional and occupational licensure are of limited validity.

Viewed as a whole, testing for professional licensure and occupation certification is in a state of near chaos (Murphy, 1988). National tests are used widely in some occupations but do not exist for many others. Licensing requirements typically vary from state to state, and the licensing exams used in different states and localities for the same occupation may show little overlap. Although testing for professional and occupational certification represents a potentially important application of psychological testing, as yet, the available measurement technology is not being used to its fullest potential.

---

[1]Unfortunately, little of this research is published in widely accessible journals; most validity studies are described in technical reports whose circulation is sporadic (e.g., see Vinberg & Joyner, 1982).

PREDICTING PERFORMANCE

Psychological tests provide information about those skills, abilities, experiences, and characteristics of individuals that can be used to predict job performance. One striking feature of personnel testing is the diversity of techniques used to obtain predictor data. In part, this range is a reflection of the diversity of the world of work; "performance" as a middle manager is a very different thing from "performance" as a bus driver, and the abilities, skills, and experiences that contribute to performance in one job may be less relevant in another. The diversity of measurement techniques is also a reflection of the apparent diversity of factors that affect job performance. Depending on the job in question, performance may be a function of basic cognitive or noncognitive abilities (e.g., verbal comprehension, manual dexterity), previous experience, social skills, specific task-oriented skills (e.g., the ability to type 40 words per minute), levels of motivation, or some combination of all these factors.

Some testing techniques (e.g., paper-and-pencil tests, interviews) appear to be more appropriate than others for assessing specific attributes of the individual that might help predict job performance. For example, it is often assumed that basic cognitive abilities are best measured by paper-and-pencil tests, whereas the interview might be best for evaluating social skill. Other examples are shown in Table 19-1. The question of whether specific measurement techniques (e.g., interviews) are in fact most effective for assessing specific skills, abilities, knowledge, or personal characteristics is an empirical issue; we return to this question at the end of this section.

Standardized Tests

There is considerable overlap between the paper-and-pencil tests used in industry and those used in other settings, such as educational or clinical testing programs. In particular, the tests of general intelligence that are used widely in personnel selection and placement are essentially similar to those used in many other contexts. General intelligence tests used in industry are most typically group-type tests and are likely to be relatively short, but otherwise they do not differ in essential ways from other group tests of intelligence. The Wonderlic Personnel Test, a 50-item multiple-choice test that includes verbal, mathematical, pictorial, and analytic items, is a good example of the kind of intelligence test likely to be used in personnel testing and selection. This test

Table 19-1 METHODS OF OBTAINING JOB-RELEVANT INFORMATION

Information desired	Method most likely to be used
Basic abilities, aptitudes	Paper-and-pencil or computerized test
Social skills, motivation	Interview
Background experience	Application blank, references, background checks
Current performance	Work-sample test
Holistic evaluation	Assessment centers

has demonstrated high levels of reliability (alternative-form reliabilities typically exceed .90) and is significantly correlated with measures of performance in a wide variety of jobs (Murphy, 1984b). Considerable evidence also shows that scores on this brief test are very highly correlated with scores on more complex tests, such as the Wechsler Adult Intelligence Scale (WAIS) (Dodrill & Warner, 1988). The Wonderlic is also available in a computerized version designed to assess both ability and personality factors.

Several test batteries are widely used in personnel selection and placement; examples include the General Aptitude Test Battery (GATB) Ability Profiler and the ASVAB. These test batteries provide measures of specific aptitudes that are relevant to work. More important, these tests are dominated by the same general factor that dominates other ability tests. That is, scores on these tests are strongly influenced by the respondent's level of general mental ability. This characteristic is critical for the simple reason that general mental ability is recognized as the single most important predictor of performance in a wide variety of jobs. That is, no other predictor shows comparable levels of validity in an equally wide range of settings (Ree & Earles, 1992; Schmidt & Hunter, 1998.) Schmidt and Hunter's (1998) review does suggest that structured interviews and integrity tests both show validity that is nearly as high as that shown by cognitive ability tests, but it is not clear whether these methods work across such a wide range of jobs and settings as cognitive tests.

Employers are showing increasing interest in computerized tests and assessments. While these tests are often psychometrically equivalent to their paper-and-pencil counterparts (see Chapter 12), moving to computerized testing can pose a challenge when testing older applicants or applicants with little prior computer experience (Sinar, Reynolds, & Paquet, 2003)

Although intelligence tests used in industry are not fundamentally different from the tests used in other contexts, several tests of specific skills and aptitudes are used almost exclusively in personnel selection and placement. Outstanding exemplars include several clerical tests and tests of mechanical comprehension.

Clerical Tests.   Outside the military, clerical workers represent the most widely tested category of workers. Approximately two thirds of all companies use written tests as aids in making hiring and promotion decisions, and between 60% and 80% of these companies use clerical tests.[2] These tests vary considerably in their emphasis, ranging from tests that sample one highly specific facet of clerical work to tests that tap several broadly defined abilities thought to be necessary to perform clerical jobs.

The Minnesota Clerical Test is an example of a test that measures a highly specific clerical function. The Minnesota Clerical Test is composed of two subtests, Number Comparison and Name Comparison. Both subtests are made up of long lists of pairs of numbers or pairs of names in which each pair is either identical or differs in some minor detail. Examples of items similar to those used on the Minnesota Clerical Test are shown in Table 19-2.

---

[2]Many of these companies also test nonclerical workers.

Table 19-2   ITEMS SIMILAR TO THOSE ON THE MINNESOTA CLERICAL TEST

Number comparison

1. 34796	34796
2. 246738	246638
3. 594327	594321
4. 6674532	6674532
5. 47948672	47948672

Name comparison

1. Mitchell Tools	Mitchell Tools
2. Anderson, J. A.	Andersen, J.A.
3. Biloxi, Miss.	Biloxi, Miss.
4. Gleason's Motors	Gleson's Motors
5. McNally, John	McNally, John

A person taking this test must read each pair of names or numbers, compare them, and mark each pair that is identical. There is a very strict time limit, and the total score is determined by the number of pairs checked. Although there is some deduction for errors (checking a nonidentical pair, failure to check an identical pair), scores on the Minnesota Clerical Test are determined almost entirely by speed. In fact, this test is a perfect example of a speed test; if there were no time limit, almost anyone who understood the test instructions would answer all the test items correctly.

The Minnesota Clerical Test is a reliable measure of perceptual speed and accuracy; test-retest reliabilities typically exceed .70. Evidence also shows consistent positive correlations between scores on this test and supervisory performance ratings. However, questions may be raised about the importance of perceptual speed and accuracy in most clerical jobs. Although filing and data-retrieval tasks are frequently performed by clerical workers, little evidence shows that individual differences in perceptual speed contribute greatly to the variability in job performance. Thus, although the Minnesota Clerical Test possesses a certain amount of face validity (i.e., it looks like tasks often performed by clerical workers), it is not clear whether the criterion-related validity of this test is due to the importance of perceptual speed in job performance or to the overlap between perceptual speed and general intelligence.

The Minnesota Clerical Test was first developed at a time when clerical tasks were virtually all done manually and in paper-and-pencil media. The nature of clerical work has changed dramatically since then, and many organizations are working toward developing the "paperless office" in which all clerical tasks are done via computer. Computerized versions of the Minnesota Clerical Test have been developed (Silver & Bennett, 1987; Vale, 1990), but it is not clear whether they will be better predictors than the venerable paper-and-pencil version. One reason for the apparent usefulness of this paper-and-pencil task for predicting performance in an increasingly paperless setting may be that the test measures more than it appears to measure. This test shows a number of similarities to the tasks used by many cognitive psychologists to assess intelligence (E. B. Hunt & Pellegrin, 1985). It is possible that the performance-related abilities measured by this type of test are more cognitive (e.g., speed of mental operations, speed in comparing messages) than perceptual (Jensen, 1980).

Tests of Mechanical Comprehension.   A variety of skilled and semiskilled blue-collar jobs call for an understanding of basic mechanical principles, as well as the ability to predict the outcome of mechanical activities or to reason backward from effects to probable mechanical causes. For example, people holding repair jobs of all types, machinists, many types of construction workers and laborers, and, of course, mechanics use mechanical abilities in their work. Although mechanical knowledge and mechanical reasoning ability are not completely distinct from general intelligence, there is some utility in employing measures of mechanical comprehension rather than measures of academic intelligence in many blue-collar jobs. Measures of mechanical comprehension have face validity as well as a solid record of criterion-related validity (Ghiselli, 1966).

The Bennett Mechanical Comprehension Test (2nd Ed.) is an outstanding example of an occupational test of basic mechanical knowledge and mechanical reasoning (Bennett, 1980). The Bennett is available in two forms (Forms S and T); each is a 68-item test designed to be administered using a 30-minute time limit. The pictorial multiple-choice items on this test vary widely in difficulty but share a common theme. The respondent is required to apply simple principles of physics and mechanics in responding to questions concerning the operations of common machines, tools, and vehicles. Examples of items from the Bennett are presented in Figure 19-1.

The Bennett Mechanical Comprehension Test has been shown to be highly reliable (internal consistency of reliabilities range from .81 to .93) and has shown respectable levels of criterion-related validity. Scores on the Bennett typically have shown correlations of approximately .30 with measures of performance in training courses and with measures of job proficiency in studies involving machinists, mechanics, and machine operators (Ghiselli, 1966). Because of its well-documented reliability, validity, and simplicity, the Bennett is one of the most popular tests of mechanical comprehension (Muchinsky, 1996). However, as Wing (1992) noted, one criticism of the Bennett is that it "just looks old"; if you look at the sample items in Figure 19-1, you will probably agree. It is not clear whether the appearance of the test influences the way in which individuals respond, but you can make the case that the individuals will not take the test as seriously if most or all of the items represent items no longer found in a modern workplace.

Personality Inventories.   The use of personality inventories as predictors of job performance has been a subject of controversy since the mid-1960s. An influential review by Guion and Gottier (1965) concluded that the research available at that time did not support the validity of personality measures as selection instruments. Although the intentions of Guion and Gottier (1965) were to encourage better research on the relationship between personality and job performance, almost the opposite

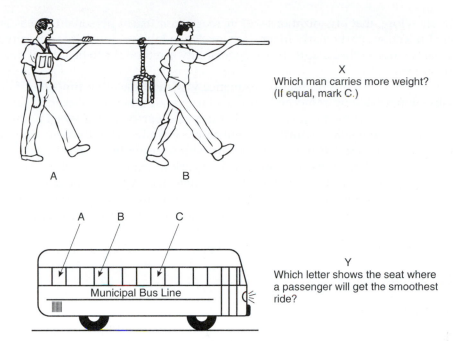

X
Which man carries more weight?
(If equal, mark C.)

Y
Which letter shows the seat where
a passenger will get the smoothest
ride?

FIGURE 19-1 Sample Items From Bennett Mechanical Comprehension Test
Source: From the Bennett Mechanical Comprehension Test. Copyright 1942, 1967–
1970, 1980 by The Psychological Corporation, a Harcourt Assessment Company.
Reproduced by permission. All rights reserved. "Bennett Mechanical Comprehension
Test" and "BMCT" are registered trademarks of The Psychological Corporation.

happened. For the two decades that followed the Guion and Gottier review (1965), the accepted wisdom in personnel psychology implied that personality was not really relevant to job performance and that personality scales should not be used in selecting among job applicants. As a result of several recent reviews (Barrick & Mount, 1991; Hough et al., 1990; Salgado, 1997; Tett, Jackson, & Rothstein, 1991), this view has changed.

Evidence indicates that a variety of personality characteristics are consistently related to job performance, including three of the "big five": agreeableness, conscientiousness, and openness to experience. Average validities for measures of these traits typically fall in the .15 to .25 range, which, though not as high as validities demonstrated by cognitive ability tests, is clearly large enough to suggest that personality inventories can make a worthwhile contribution. The validity of specific personality scales, chosen in terms of their relevance to specific jobs or organizations, can be substantially higher (Tett et al, 1991; Tett, Steele, & Beauregard, 2003). Although measures of these and other personality characteristics are susceptible to faking (e.g., job applicants may distort their responses to appear more dependable or agreeable than they really are; see Chapter 11), response distortion does not appear to substantially affect the validity of personality inventories as predictors of performance (Hough et al., 1990). It is likely, therefore, that organizations will increase their use of personality measures in personnel selection, particularly in jobs where dependability, integrity (integrity tests are discussed later in this chapter), or responsibility are thought to be critical determinants of success.

The general proposition that performance is a multiplicative function of ability and motivation has a long-standing history. A large-scale study by Sackett, Gruys, and Ellingson (1998) tested the proposition that ability and personality interact in this way. They examined personality characteristics most closely aligned with motivation (most theories assume that aspects of personality that show strong ties to motivation should also show strong interactions with ability). Contrary to expectations, the results indicate that ability-personality interactions are not detected at above-chance levels. This study suggests that personality is an important determinant of performance but that traditional theories about how personality influences job performance may need to be revised.

Application Blanks

Standardized application blanks, which include questions dealing with the applicant's personal and work history, as well as questions about his or her present status (e.g., age, address, marital status), have been used in industry since at least 1894 (Owens, 1976). Although application blanks are used routinely in almost every organization, these are not always recognized as tests. This omission is unfortunate, since it is well-known that information from standard application blanks (background data, or biodata) can be used to successfully predict job performance. In fact, biodata have consistently been shown to be one of the best, if not the best, predictors of job performance (Mumford, Uhlman, & Kilcullen, 1992; Owens, 1976; Reilly & Chao, 1982).

There are two different strategies for using background data to predict job performance: (1) the development of empirical keys, or systems for scoring application blanks, and (2) the assignment of persons to groups that are homogeneous with respect to biographical information but differ in terms of expected job performance. The empirical keying strategy is the older of the two; to date, many of the papers reporting substantial correlations between background data and job performance have followed this strategy. However, more recent research on the use of background data in predicting job performance has moved in the direction of theories that classify persons on the basis of their patterns of past behavior and that predict future performance on the basis of those classifications (Mael, 1991; Mumford et al., 1992; Owens & Schoenfeldt, 1979; Stokes, Mumford, & Owens, 1994).

The empirical method of scoring biographical information blanks rests on the assumption that successful workers (defined in terms of performance, tenure on the job, salary, etc.) systematically differ from unsuccessful workers in a number of ways and that at least some of the variables on which they differ are measured by standard application blanks. If an applicant's responses to a biographical information blank are highly similar to those of successful workers and dissimilar to those of unsuccessful workers, success would be predicted for that applicant. On the other hand, a person whose responses are highly similar to those of the unsuccessful group would be predicted to fail. Thus, it is possible to assign to each person's total set of responses to a standard application blank a score that measures the degree to which the responses are similar to those given by successful workers, as opposed to those given by unsuccessful workers. Considerable evidence indicates that biodata scores of this type can be used to predict both job performance and turnover (Cascio, 1976; Reilly & Chao, 1982).

The simplest method of scoring application blanks is the horizontal percentage method described by Stead and Shartle (1940), which is similar to the method used in scoring the Strong Interest Inventory. The first step in applying the horizontal percentage method is to divide a pool of current or past workers into "success" and "failure" categories. Next, the number of successes and failures who endorse each possible response on an application blank is compared. A weight is computed for each possible response to each item on the application blank; this weight corresponds to the proportion of successes in the group of workers who endorsed that particular response.

Table 19-3 illustrates the process. In the group of workers described in the table, 60 had previous employment experience. Fifteen of these were failures, yielding a success rate of 25%. The item weight for the response "Yes" to the question "Have you ever been employed?" is therefore 25. The item weight for the response "No" is 50 (25 successes of 50 workers with no previous experience, or 50%). Using this same method, weights are developed for each of the possible responses to the item "Education" and to any other items contained in the application blank. The applicant's total score for the application blank is then computed by summing the weights assigned to each response chosen by the applicant. As a further illustration, an applicant who indicated "Yes" and "Grade School" in response to the two questions shown in the table would receive

Table 19-3   ILLUSTRATION OF THE HORIZONTAL PERCENTAGE METHOD

Item	Responses	Number of successes	Number of failures	Total	Success rate	Weight
Have you previously been employed?	Yes	45	15	60	15/60 = 25%	25
	No	25	25	50	25/50 = 50%	50
Education	Grade school	5	20	25	5/25 = 20%	20
	High school	25	20	45	25/45 = 55%	55
	College	20	5	25	20/25 = 80%	80
	Postgraduate	13	2	15	13/15 = 93%	93

Illustrative total scores

Responses to biographical information blank	Weights	Total score
Experience, grade school	25 + 20 =	45
No experience, high school	50 + 55 =	105
Experience, college	25 + 80 =	105
Experience, postgraduate	25 + 93 =	118

a total score of 45, whereas an applicant who indicated "Yes" and "College" would receive a score of 105. Another applicant who indicated "No" and "High School" would also receive a score of 105.

The item weight reflects the proportion of successes among those who endorsed a particular response. If many successes and few failures occur among those who give the same responses to a demographic item (e.g., "Postgraduate"), the item discriminates successes from failures and receives a large weight. If many failures and few successes occur (e.g., "Grad School"), the item discriminates failures from successes and receives a small weight. The total score therefore reflects the degree to which an applicant's responses are similar to those of the successful group. The total score is large if the applicant endorses many items with large weights—those chosen frequently by successes but infrequently by failures. The total score is low if the applicant endorses many items with low weights—those endorsed most frequently by failures.

Many problems occur with the purely empirical approach to scoring biographical information blanks. First, the theoretical base of this method of scoring is sorely lacking. There is generally no attempt to determine why some items should receive large weights and others small weights. The determination of weights is done on a strictly empirical basis, and if the success rate in one group (e.g., males) is lower than in another, new applicants from that group will be penalized. This procedure creates some potentially explosive problems, since it presents the clear appearance of discrimination. Furthermore, the lack of any theoretical base makes it very difficult to explain why someone is penalized for membership in certain groups. Although equal employment opportunity laws make it unlikely that someone will be denied a job solely on the basis of membership in the "wrong" demographic group, the logical implication of the purely empirical strategy is to do precisely that—to select some groups and reject others, without necessarily being able to explain how group membership affects job performance.

Statistical difficulties also occur with the purely empirical approach. Empirically derived scoring systems take advantage of any relationships between group membership and success, even those that are due to chance or to insufficient sampling. It is therefore necessary to cross-validate empirically derived scoring keys by demonstrating the validity of those keys in several independent samples (Darlington, 1968; Murphy, 1983; for a critical review of cross-validation methods, see Mitchell & Klimoski, 1986). A surprising number of studies fail to cross-validate empirical scoring keys (Schwab & Oliver, 1974). Many scoring keys are developed on a completely empirical basis, with little theory either to guide the researcher's initial hypothesis or to alert researchers to possibly spurious results. Results from a single sample will seriously overestimate the validity of an empirical scoring key, and it is unlikely that a useful validity estimate can be obtained unless the key is cross-validated in another, independent sample.

Another concern is the stability of empirical scoring keys. There is evidence that the validity of empirically scored biographical information blanks systematically deteriorates over time and that a key that is highly valid in one year may show little or no validity in ensuing years (Wernimont, 1962).

Owens and his associates developed an alternative strategy for predicting behavior on the basis of background data (Owens & Schoenfeldt, 1979). This approach, referred to as the Developmental-Integrative Model, involves sorting people into a small number of groups that are relatively homogeneous with respect to a wide variety of background data. The data used in classifying individuals include standard demographic measures as well as measures pertaining to facets of one's life experience, such as academic achievement, group participation, financial responsibility, family adjustment, and situational stability (Baehr & Williams, 1967). The underlying assumption of this approach is that people whose background and experience are fundamentally similar will show similar patterns of behavior in the future, whereas people whose backgrounds are different will behave differently. Considerable evidence supports this assumption; people who differ in basic patterns of background data are also likely to differ in social attitudes, goals, personality orientation, and levels of achievement (Owens, 1971). Even more to the point, persons who differ in basic patterns of background data are likely to differ in job performance and in the rapidity of job turnover (Brush & Owens, 1979).

Considerable progress has been made in identifying the constructs that underlie responses to biodata items (Mael, 1991; Mumford et al., 1992); this research is likely to help explain why biodata items are so successful in predicting future performance. The emergence of construct-oriented models represents a definite advance in the use of biodata in predicting job performance. Rather than examining individual responses to an application blank in an attempt to differentiate good from poor performers, this approach encourages researchers to classify persons into groups with similar life histories and to search for differences in performance among these groups. The classification of persons rather than items allows one to take into account considerable amounts of data from different sources, rather than relying on an arbitrary classification of present or past workers into successes or failures. At a more fundamental level, these models provide a scientific rationale for the use of background information in predicting job performance. The model encourages one to view biodata as an indicator of what a person has done, which in turn provides a solid basis for predicting what the person will do. However, the same problems that are present in empirically based uses of biodata may also be present here. Any use of biodata in making decisions about individuals ultimately rewards some people and penalizes others for their demographic characteristics (race, sex, income, etc.). This practice is regarded by many, including the authors of this book, as fundamentally unfair and, as will be noted later, may violate the civil rights of applicants.

The Employment Interview

Although considerable diversity exists in the types of tests used in making personnel selection decisions, one component of all systematic personnel selection strategies is nearly universal—the interview. Surveys suggest that well over 95% of all employers use interviews as part of the selection process and that the number of interviews conducted yearly may run as high as 20 per person hired (Landy & Trumbo,

1980). Not only is the interview widespread; it also appears to have a substantial effect on selection decisions (Ahlburg, 1992). It is therefore no surprise that the employment interview has been the focus of a tremendous amount of research.

From the 1940s to the 1980s, research on the reliability and validity of the employment interview portrayed a consistently negative picture (Arvey & Campion, 1982). Validity coefficients rarely exceeded the teens and were often embarrassingly close to zero (Hunter & Hunter, 1984; Reilly & Chao, 1982). Indeed, one of the most interesting research questions in the early 1980s was why organizations continued to rely so heavily on such an invalid method of making selection decisions (Arvey & Campion, 1982).

More recent research suggests that interviews can indeed be a useful and valid method of selecting employees, as long as structure is imposed (Campion, Pursell, & Brown, 1988; Wiesner & Cronshaw, 1988). Most of the interview research cited in earlier reviews focused on unstructured interviews, in which different interviewers might ask different sets of questions or in which the same interviewer might ask different questions of different applicants. Interviews of this sort are widely regarded as poor predictors of future performance (although, as McDaniel, Whetzel, Schmidt, and Maurer, 1994, note, they can show higher levels of validity than was suggested in earlier reviews). However, when care is taken to develop a consistent set of job-related questions and a consistent method for scoring or evaluating responses, interviews can show very respectable levels of validity.

Latham, Saari, Pursell, and Campion (1980) recommended an extremely structured interview format, referred to as a *situational interview,* in which examinees are asked to describe how they would behave in several hypothetical but critical situations. For example, an applicant for a baker's job might be asked what he or she would do if two oven thermometers gave readings that varied widely. Responses are independently rated by multiple interviewers, and composite ratings are used to make decisions about examinees. Although this structure may not be optimal in all settings, it represents a clear advance over the unconnected series of spontaneous questions that an untrained interviewer tends to ask (Wiesner & Cronshaw, 1988).

An alternative is to structure interviews around discussions of past behavior on the job (Janz, 1982). Rather than asking what a person might do in a hypothetical situation, interviewers might ask what he or she did do in specific situations encountered previously on the job. A review by McDaniel et al. (1994) suggests that such job-related interviews show higher levels of validity than unstructured interviews but lower validity than the situational interview method described before. Salgado and Moscoso (2002) conclude that interviews that focus on past behavior probably measure different constructs than interviews that deal with responses to hypothetical situations; a combination of behavioral and situational interviews might represent the best format for interviewing applicants.

Campion, Palmer, and Campion (1997) note that although adding structure to an interview generally improves its reliability and validity, one might add structure in many ways. Campion et al. review the effects of 15 components of structure (e.g., standardizing the set of questions, tying questions to a job analysis, rating each answer on a fixed scale, using multiple interviewers, and so on). Just about all methods of adding structure seem to help, and there is no professional consensus about which methods of structuring interviews are best or worst. Unfortunately, managers appear reluctant to impose structure when interviewing job applicants, probably because a structured interview reduces their discretion in making selection decisions (VanderZee, Bakker, & Bakker, 2002).

Interviews are probably most useful when they cover areas that are not already covered by paper-and-pencil tests or other assessment devices. A number of researchers have suggested that interviews should focus on behaviors, rather than on attitudes or skills (Janz, 1982; Motowidlo et al., 1992; Orpen, 1985). Evidence indicates that a clear focus on behavioral information increases the reliability and criterion-related validity of measures obtained on the basis of interviews.

It is reasonably clear that the interview is better for measuring some attributes of applicants than others. For example, interviews may not be appropriate for measuring basic cognitive abilities. In addition, since an interview represents a relatively short sample of behavior, this technique may not be appropriate for measuring traits or personality characteristics that are manifest only over a long period of time, such as honesty or dependability (McCormick & Ilgen, 1980). Rather, the interview is probably optimal for measuring characteristics such as social skills, which are manifest during the period of the interview itself and which are exceedingly difficult to measure using other testing techniques.

Work-Sample Tests

Wernimont and Campbell (1968) distinguish between two strategies for predicting future job performance: the use of signs and the use of samples. An example of the former is when a paper-and-pencil test of mechanical comprehension is used to predict performance as a machinist. The applicant's level of mechanical comprehension is viewed as a sign, or probably a causal agent, in determining future job performance. Thus, people who receive high scores are predicted to perform better than those who receive low scores, on the basis of the assumption that ability is one of the signs of performance. The latter strategy, which involves using a sample of present performance to predict future performance, is considerably simpler and more direct. The use of signs assumes the existence of some theory regarding the relationship between the characteristics that are measured and job performance; the use of samples of present performance to predict future performance involves the simpler assumption that performance shows some consistency across time and tasks. Wernimont and Campbell (1968) argue that predictions of future behavior that are based on samples of the characteristic behavior of individuals are likely to be more accurate than predictions that are based on measures of specific skills, ability, or knowledge (signs). Reviews by Asher and Sciarrino (1974) and Reilly and Chao (1982) provide at least partial support for this argument.

Work-sample tests range from those that involve relative simple tasks, such as a 5-minute typing sample, to those involving complex samples of performance, such as those obtained using flight simulators. Two features common to all work-sample tests should be examined in evaluating these tests. First, every work-sample test puts the applicant in a situation that in some way is essentially similar to a work situation and measures performance on tasks reasonably similar to those that make up the job itself. Second, every work sample differs in important ways from the job in which it will be used. Even when the tasks are identical to those required on the job, it is reasonable to expect that examinees, who are trying to impress their prospective employers, will show higher levels of motivation in work-sample tests than they will on the job. Thus, it is most reasonable to regard a work sample as a measure of maximal performance rather than a measure of typical performance. This is an important distinction, because measures of maximal performance are not necessarily correlated with measures of typical performance (C. Dubois, Sackett, Zedeck, & Fogli, 1993; Sackett, Zedeck, & Fogli, 1988).

When tests are used as signs of future performance, criterion-related validity is a function of the content or construct validity of both the test and the criterion, as well as the validity of the theory linking a particular ability or set of abilities to performance. When a sample of present behavior is used to predict future performance, validity is primarily a function of the representativeness of the work sample. Thus, Asher (1972) hypothesized that the criterion-related validity of a work-sample test would be highest when the point-to-point similarity between the test and the job itself was maximized. A later review by Asher and Sciarrino (1974) provided strong support for this hypothesis—the greater the similarity between the content of the work-sample test and the content of the job, the more accurate the test in predicting job performance.

The principle that validity is maximized when the test most closely resembles the job itself provides useful guidance for designing work-sample tests for many blue-collar and clerical jobs. It is often possible to have candidates perform the actual tasks that comprise the job (e.g., operating specific machines, typing, filing, retrieval); and if an adequate job analysis has been performed, it should be a reasonably simple matter to determine the match between the test and the job. However, as we noted in Chapter 8, assessing the content similarity between the test and the job can sometimes involve complex questions about the examinees' motivation and state of mind when responding to the test versus performing their jobs.

Managerial Work-Sample Tests. Although it is more difficult to develop a comprehensive and valid work-sample test in managerial jobs than in many nonmanagerial jobs, the potential payoff of a valid managerial work-sample test is considerable. Managerial effectiveness is not the simple result of possessing one or two key traits or abilities; it is the result of a complex interaction between characteristics of the individual and characteristics of the situation. Samples of behavior in situations that seem to capture many of the salient characteristics of day-to-day management are thus particularly valuable in predicting performance as a manager (Cascio, 1982).

Probably the most widely used type of managerial work-sample test is the in-basket (Fredericksen, 1962). As its name implies, an in-basket test is a simulation that presents the applicant with the types of memos, letters, notes, and other materials found in a typical manager's in-basket. The applicant is given background information on the job and is instructed to play the role of a new manager in the job. In response to the materials in the in-basket, the applicant is required to write letters, memos, agendas, and so forth, indicating how he or she would respond to the information in the in-basket. The applicant's responses can be scored in terms of their overall appropriateness, the order in which the applicant responds to items, the responses to specific critical pieces of information, or some combination of these factors.

Although in-basket tests vary considerably in content, generally being tailored to individual jobs and organizations, considerable consistency is found in the results achieved using this type of test. Brass and Oldham (1976) and Wollowick and McNamara (1969) report correlations ranging from .24 to .34 between ratings obtained from in-basket tests and a number of measures of managerial performance and effectiveness. Furthermore, there are clear differences between the in-basket responses of management trainees and those of experienced managers. Trainees tend to choose strategies for solving the problems posed in the in-basket that are less flexible, less feasible, and less effective than those chosen by experienced managers (Lopez, 1966). Research also suggests that the in-basket test effectively discriminates promising managerial candidates from applicants who are less likely to succeed. However, more recent research (e.g., Schippman, Prien, & Katz, 1990) has questioned the reliability and validity of scores obtained from in-basket tests. On the whole, we believe that carefully constructed in-basket tests can yield useful information but that the construction of these tests is more difficult than it at first appears. Like other types of tests, it is probably easier to produce a bad in-basket test than a good one.

Another popular managerial work-sample test is the leaderless group discussion (Bass, 1954). This is an exceedingly simple simulation, yet one that has considerable potential for measuring characteristics of potential managers that are important for successful job performance but are not readily measured using other types of tests. In a leaderless group discussion, a group of participants is asked to carry on a discussion of a specific, usually job-related topic for a period of time. For example, a group of applicants might be told to conduct a 45-minute discussion of career planning. By design, there is no formal discussion leader. Several raters may observe the discussion, but these raters do not participate in any way. Group members are therefore responsible for initiating, maintaining, and directing the group discussion.

It should be obvious that this procedure provides some information about aggressiveness, ability to provide structure, and leadership: Inevitably, some group members take active or controlling roles, whereas others have little to say (Bass, 1954). This technique has also been used to assess characteristics such as persuasiveness, self-confidence, resistance to stress, oral communication ability, and interpersonal skills (Wollowick & McNamara, 1969).

Both Bass (1954) and Wollowick and McNamara (1969) suggest that the leaderless group discussion technique shows levels of reliability and validity comparable to those shown by other personnel tests. To some extent, reliability and validity depend on the characteristics that the leaderless group discussion is used to measure. This technique seems particularly appropriate for measuring the tendency or ability to impose structure on a relatively ambiguous and unstructured situation but may be less suitable for measuring specific skills or knowledge. The combination of the leaderless group discussion with other types of managerial work sample might be particularly useful (Lopez, 1966).

Thornton and Cleveland (1990) reviewed the use of simulation methods in management development. All work samples involve simulating some aspects of the job, but such simulations differ considerably in their complexity and their fidelity. For example, complex business games, in which individuals assume various roles and make numerous decisions over periods of hours or even days with regard to a simulated business problem are popular for both assessing and developing managerial competencies. Although, at an operational level, such games are a far cry from the leaderless group discussion, at a conceptual level, they represent the same strategy for measurement, that is, observing behavior in a setting that reflects some aspect of the job itself.

Assessment Centers

The assessment center is not, as its name might imply, a place, nor is it a single, unified method of predicting job performance. Rather, an assessment center is a structured combination of assessment techniques that is used to provide a wide-ranging, holistic assessment of each participant. This technique is most likely to be used in making managerial selection and promotion decisions, although assessment centers are also employed for many other jobs. Assessment centers also can play a critical role in employee development (Spychalski, Quiñones, Gaugler, & Pohley, 1997).

The assessment center as it exists today is a lineal descendant of the multiple assessment procedures used by German and British psychologists in World War II and adopted by the American Office of Strategic Services (OSS) as aids in selecting agents and operatives (OSS, 1948). By the early 1970s, over 1,000 companies had experimented with this method, prompting Hinrichs (1978) to refer to the assessment center as "one of the more phenomenal success stories of applied psychology" (p. 596).

Although the assessment centers used in different organizations differ widely in terms of content and organization, nearly all assessment centers share several features in common and that are distinctive to this approach (Bray, Campbell, & Grant, 1974; Bray & Grant, 1966; Finkle, 1976). They include the following:

Assessment in groups.   In an assessment center, small groups of participants are assessed simultaneously. Since group activities and peer evaluations are an integral part of most assessment centers, it would be impossible to use this technique to its fullest advantage in assessing a single individual.

Assessment by groups.   The assessment team may be made up of managers, psychologists, consultants, or some mix of these three groups. Each participant's behavior is observed and evaluated by a number of different assessors, and the final ratings represent the assessment team's consensus regarding the individual being evaluated.

The use of multiple methods.   Assessment center activities might include ability tests, personality tests, situational tests, interviews, peer evaluations, and performance tests. The central assumption of this method is that each test has its strengths and weaknesses and that a combination of diverse tests is necessary to capitalize on the strengths of each individual test.

The use of situational tests.   Although the specific tests used vary from organization to organization, nearly every assessment center uses some type of work-sample or situational test. Both the in-basket and the leaderless group discussion tests are popular, as are other role-playing exercises.

Assessment along multiple dimensions.   The end result of an assessment center is a consensus rating along each of several dimensions. For example, candidates going through an assessment center at AT&T are rated on 25 dimensions, including organizational planning, resistance to stress, energy, and self-objectivity (Thornton & Byham, 1982). Each exercise in the assessment center typically provides information relevant to one or more dimensions, and ratings of a specific dimension (e.g., energy) might reflect data obtained from several different exercises.

The appeal of assessment centers is a function of the face validity, practicality, and, to a lesser extent, the empirical evidence documenting the criterion-related validity of this technique. In contrast to several paper-and-pencil tests that might be used in selection, the assessment center appears valid. The exercises included in many assessment centers resemble essential features of the manager's job, and the assessment team typically includes a number of actual managers. As a result, managers are much more likely to react favorably to an assessment center than to other, more objective selection tests (Finkle, 1976). In addition, an assessment center is likely to be surprisingly practical, since it does not generally require the extended service of psychologists or other testing specialists. Although early assessment centers relied on psychologists to form their assessment teams, it is now clear that trained managers are every bit as good as psychologists for most assessment tasks and that participation in assessment centers is often highly beneficial for the managers who serve as assessors (Finkle, 1976; Greenwood & McNamara, 1967). Thus, although assessment centers involve a complex set of activities, a major portion of the assessment tasks may be carried out by members of the organization, rather than by outside consultants.

Psychometric evaluations of the assessment center generally have been favorable. Interrater reliabilities of assessment center ratings show considerable variability but are generally in the .60 to .95 range (Schmitt, 1977). Sackett and Hakel (1979) report comparable levels of temporal stability in assessment ratings. Evidence for the validity of the assessment center has also been consistently positive (Borman, 1982; Finkle, 1976; Gaugler, Rosenthal, Thornton, & Bentson, 1987; Hinrichs, 1978; Howard, 1974; Huck, 1973; Thornton, 1992). For example, Borman (1982) reported a correlation of .50 between composite assessment ratings obtained at the beginning of an army recruiter training course and later performance in training. Data presented by Hinrichs (1978) suggest comparable levels of validity in predicting advancement within organizations. What is more important is that the validity of assessment center ratings for predicting promotion appears to increase as one moves into higher levels of management.

Finally, assessment centers appear to be fair and relatively unbiased methods of making selection and promotion decisions. In a carefully balanced study, Huck and Bray (1976) showed that assessment centers showed nearly identical levels of validity for white and black employees in predicting job performance and potential for advancement; furthermore, it showed that the regression equations for whites and blacks did not differ significantly.

Although an impressive body of evidence supports the validity of the assessment center method, Klimoski and Strickland (1977) have raised important questions about interpretations of the validity evidence. They note that assessment centers, which consist largely of managers (acting as assessors) making evaluations of participants, are validated against performance ratings and promotions, both of which are managers' on-the-job evaluations of these same participants. Thus, studies documenting the validity of the assessment center method do little more than demonstrate that one set of managerial ratings of a particular person (assessment ratings) are positively correlated with another set of managerial ratings (performance ratings and promotability ratings) of the same person. It is possible that assessment center ratings are "valid" because they share the same biases that affect performance ratings and promotion judgments. Thus, one hypothesis that would account for the validity of the assessment center method is that the same "fair-haired boys" who receive high ratings in a managerial assessment center will receive high performance ratings and quick promotions on the job, irrespective of their actual effectiveness. Although it is unlikely that the validity of assessment centers is totally illusory (a product of shared biases), it is likely that biases inherent in all ratings tasks inflate the validity of the assessment center method (Cascio, 1982).

COMPARATIVE ASSESSMENT OF PERSONNEL TESTS

The availability of paper-and-pencil tests, interviews, biographical information blanks, work samples, and assessment centers as alternative methods of predicting job performance leads to the question of which method is best. Reilly and Chao's (1982) review provides an excellent starting point for this comparative assessment. They examined research on alternatives to standard ability tests and focused on eight alternative methods of predicting future job performance: biodata, interviews, peer evaluations, self-assessments, reference checks, academic performance, expert judgments, and objective tests. They evaluated each technique in terms of its criterion-related validity, practicality, and likelihood of providing unbiased predictions of future performance. Their review suggests that only biodata and peer evaluations show levels of validity that are in any way comparable to the validity of paper-and-pencil tests. They also suggest that none of the alternatives shows comparable levels of validity with less adverse impact against minority applicants and that when the issue of practicality is considered, paper-and-pencil tests are by far the best single selection device. A report by the National Academy of Sciences (Wigdor & Garner, 1982a) reached a similar conclusion: that in employment testing, there are no known alternatives to standard ability tests that are equally informative, equally fair, and of equal technical merit (see also Hartigan & Wigdor, 1989; Hunter, 1986; Hunter & Hunter, 1984).

Schmidt and Hunter (1998) summarize the practical and theoretical implications of 85 years of research on the validity and utility of selection tests. Their meta-analysis examines the validity of 19 selection procedures for predicting job performance and training. Table 19-4 summarizes some of their key findings.

Table 19-4   ESTIMATES OF THE VALIDITY OF WIDELY USED TESTS AND ASSESSMENTS

	Job performance	*Performance in training*
General mental ability tests	.51	.56
Work samples	.54	
Integrity tests	.41	.38
Conscientiousness measures	.31	.30
Structured interviews	.51	.35 (combined structured/unstructured)
Unstructured interviews	.38	
Assessment centers	.37	
Graphology	.02	

Source: Data from Schmidt and Hunter (1999).

Organizations rarely use a single test as a basis for making decisions, and Schmidt and Hunter's (1998) review suggests that using combinations of tests can lead to high degrees of accuracy in predicting job performance. For example, combining general mental ability tests with a work-sample test could yield a validity as high as .63; the same validity might be attained by combining a structured interview and an ability test. Ability tests combined with integrity tests might do even better (an estimated validity of .65).

Although standard ability tests appear to be the best aids available for making selection decisions, it is unrealistic to expect that ability tests will be used as the sole method of making selection decisions. Managers' distrust of paper-and-pencil tests and their attachment to alternative selection devices (e.g., the interview) are not likely to be significantly affected by reviews of the research literature. Alternatives to paper-and-pencil tests are here to stay; the question is not whether they should be used but, rather, how they might best be combined with standard ability tests to maximize accuracy in predicting performance.

Surveys of personnel managers (Ahlburg, 1992; Dankin & Armstrong, 1989) reveal two depressing findings. First, personnel and human resource professionals are often unaware of the most basic findings of research on the validity of various personnel assessment and selection methods. For example, personnel managers in several countries, including the United States, consistently rank cognitive ability tests as among the least valid and useful tools for selection, and they rank interviews as among the most valid and useful tools for selection. The available body of research, which includes literally thousands of studies conducted in a wide variety of settings, shows that the opposite is true. Second, even those individuals who know which techniques have been shown to have the most or the least validity (e.g., individuals holding recent graduate degrees, who would have had extensive exposure to this research) do not seem to translate their knowledge into concrete action. That is, even when they are aware of the relevant evidence, well-trained personnel managers are more likely to use techniques such as the interview or assessments of experience, which they know to show less validity in most settings than ability tests or other relatively objective assessment methods. It appears that personnel managers' habit of using less valid methods is a difficult one to break.

The most general suggestion that we can make is to optimize each type of selection test for obtaining specific sorts of information about the applicant (see Table 19-1). In designing a selection program, it would be best to decide, first, what information is needed and then select the tests, interviews, or other methods that are most appropriate for obtaining it.

Our second suggestion is that each type of selection should be used only for a specific purpose. The interview provides a good example of a test that can be used for a broad variety of purposes, including gathering background information, making inferences about specific cognitive abilities, or arriving at a holistic evaluation of the applicant; yet it should be used almost exclusively for assessing characteristics such as social skills and motivation.

Our third and final suggestion is that conflicts between different tests (e.g., high test scores but poor interview ratings) should be used to guide further inquiries about the applicant. If different methods are used to assess truly different aspects of each individual's qualifications, conflicts should be expected rather than avoided, and these conflicts should be used to provide the basis for more in-depth evaluations.

CRITICAL DISCUSSION:
Can Graphology Predict Occupational Success?

Graphology, or the analysis of handwriting, is surprisingly common in personnel selection. It is routinely used in Europe and in Israel, and it has been used by over 3,000 American firms (Ben-Shakar, Bar-Hillel, Blum, Ben-Abba, & Flug, 1986). Despite its widespread use, virtually no research supports the validity of graphology for predicting job performance or occupational success; the few methodologically strong studies that have been done suggest that graphology does not work and that the predictions of graphologists may be no better than predictions made by chance (Ben-Shakar et al., 1986). There is no shortage of companies offering handwriting analysis services (e.g., www.handwriting.com is a Web site for Handwriting Research Corporation), and there seems to be no shortage of consumers. Given the lack of scientific support for this technique, it is important to understand why graphology is so widespread.

One reason for the popularity of graphology is face validity. Graphology is used primarily to make inferences about the writer's personality, and handwriting seems to the lay audience a very reasonable indicator of personality, especially when it is analyzed according to a complex and arcane set of rules (Murphy, 1993). The idea that personality is revealed in one's face, mannerisms, and so forth, is a recurring theme in Western literature, and the use of handwriting to analyze personality is a simple extension of this theme.

Another reason for the apparent validity of graphology, in the eyes of consumers, is that it makes predictions that are both vague and difficult to verify, a characteristic that this alleged science shares with astrology. Graphologists typically make holistic assessments and describe candidates with terms such as "honest" or "insightful," and it is very difficult to prove or disprove these assessments. It is notable that graphologists refuse to predict some easily verifiable characteristics of writers, such as their gender (Ben-Shakar et al., 1986). Untrained individuals can predict a writer's gender approximately 70% of the time, and if graphology has any validity whatsoever, graphologists should be able to do even better in predicting gender.

   A third reason for the acceptance of graphologists is that some of their predictions are valid. For example, graphologists involved in personnel selection will often ask a candidate to write a brief biographical essay and will base their recommendations on a graphological analysis of this document. Research has demonstrated that the validity of these readings is due to the content of the biographical essay and not to graphological analysis of the handwriting. That is, untrained individuals given the same information contained in those essays can make predictions that are as valid as those of the graphologists. All in all, the available evidence does not support the use of graphology in personnel selection or placement (Schmidt & Hunter, 1998).

THE VALIDITY OF PERSONNEL TESTS

Although the level of validity achieved by some personnel tests is lower than desired, a far more serious problem is the apparent variability in validity coefficients from job to job and from organization to organization. Ghiselli's (1955) review suggested that tests that showed significant validity coefficients in one job often showed little evidence of validity for predicting performance in other, similar jobs. Furthermore, tests that were shown to be valid predictors of performance in one organization were not necessarily valid predictors of performance in apparently identical jobs in other organizations. The extensive variability in validity coefficients has been confirmed by Ghiselli's later reviews (1966, 1970) and also by Albright, Glennon, and Smith (1963) and Guion (1965a). The extensive variability in test validities suggest that it is difficult, if not impossible, to predict whether a test that is known to be a valid predictor of performance in one job or organization will show comparable levels of validity in another setting.

Validity Generalization

   In a series of papers, Schmidt, Hunter, and their colleagues challenged the assumption that validities of personnel tests are typically low and that they are highly variable from job to job and from organization to organization. They note that the size of the validity coefficient obtained in any particular study is affected by statistical artifacts, such as sampling error, range restriction, and unreliability, and that failure to take these statistical artifacts into account has led to an overestimation of the true variability of test validities.

   Schmidt and Hunter (1977) note that the variability in validity coefficients from job to job or from organization to organization can be broken down into two components:

1. True differences in validity: The validity of a test of mechanical comprehension may be truly higher for predicting the performance of mechanics than for predicting the performance of typists.
2. Variability due to statistical artifacts: Sampling error, range restriction, and unreliability all affect the size of the validity coefficient. Variability in validity coefficients that is due to these statistical artifacts represents not true score, but error variance. That is, differences in

validity coefficients that are caused by these artifacts do not reflect true differences in the validities of tests.

Schmidt and Hunter have developed a validity generalization model that estimates the effects of statistical artifacts on the variability of test validities. By subtracting the variability due to artifacts (error variance) from the total variability in validity coefficients, it is possible to estimate the true variability in the validity of a test in predicting performance in different jobs, organizations, and so forth.

The Schmidt-Hunter validity generalization model has been applied to estimate the validity of predictor tests in clerical occupations (Pearlman, Schmidt, & Hunter, 1980); in the petroleum industry (Schmidt, Hunter, & Caplan, 1981); for computer programming (Schmidt, Gast-Rosenberg, & Hunter, 1980); and in the life insurance industry (Brown, 1981); and it has been the focus for considerable research and debate (Callender & Osburn, 1980, 1981, 1982; Hunter, Schmidt, & Pearlman, 1982; Osburn, Callender, Greener, & Ashworth, 1983; Schmidt, Hunter, & Pearlman, 1982; Schmidt, Hunter, Pearlman, & Shane, 1979). Although some inconsistency is exhibited in the results obtained when different sets of validity generalization equations are applied, the general trend suggested by the model is unmistakably clear. The Schmidt-Hunter validity generalization model suggests that in almost every case, true validities are (1) substantially larger and (2) much less variable than psychologists have traditionally believed.

Results presented in Pearlman et al. (1980) help to illustrate the validity generalization process. In their research, data were collected from hundreds of validity studies to test the hypothesis that variability in validity coefficients could be explained primarily by the existence of statistical artifacts. Data bearing on the validity of quantitative ability tests, reasoning tests, and spatial and mechanical ability tests for predicting performance in production and stock clerk jobs are illustrated in Figure 19-2.

As can be seen, the observed validity coefficients were not particularly large (none larger than .30). However, the validity generalization model assumes that range restriction and low levels of reliability for both the test and the criterion serve to artificially depress test validities.[3] On correcting for these statistical artifacts, the average validities increase dramatically, ranging from .31 to .60.

Statistical artifacts serve as sources of error variance; the validity generalization model allows an estimation of the true variability in validities by removing the probable effects of error. Figure 19-2 also illustrates the effects of statistical artifacts on the mean of validity coefficients: The cumulative effect of correcting for these statistical artifacts is apparent. When statistical artifacts are taken into account, it appears likely that the validity of employment tests is fairly substantial and, further, is fairly constant from job to job or organization to organization.

The debate over validity generalization and its meaning has been extensively documented. (See Hartigan & Wigdor, 1989; James, Demaree, & Mulaik, 1986; Kemery,

---

[3]Corrections for range restriction and attenuation due to less-than-perfect reliability are discussed in Chapter 9.

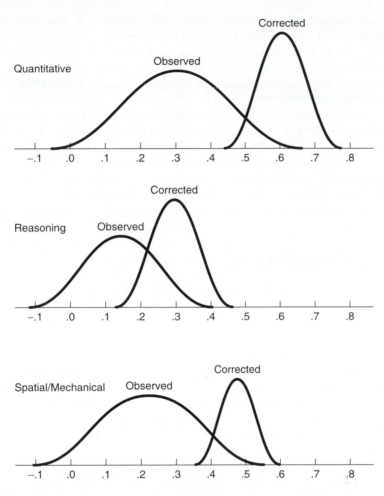

FIGURE 19-2   Distributions of Validity Coefficients Before and After Correcting for Statistical Artifacts

Mossholder, & Roth, 1987; Murphy, 2003; Schmidt, Hunter, & Pearlman, 1982; Schmidt et al., 1985; Thomas, 1988, for a sample of this literature.) Although controversies over specific technical features of validity generalization remain, the general findings of validity generalization research are now well accepted (Hartigan & Wigdor, 1989). See Hunter and Schmidt (1990) for an overview of validity generalization methods.

THE SOCIAL AND LEGAL CONTEXT OF EMPLOYMENT TESTING

Before 1964, employment testing was of concern to a relatively small number of testing specialists and business people who used tests in personnel selection and placement. The Civil Rights movement, together with the Civil Rights Act of 1964, served to focus

the attention of society and the legal system on the political and economic consequences of widespread discrimination against minorities. Discriminatory employment
practices were seen as both an immediate cause of economic deprivation suffered by
minorities and as a symptom of the broader problem, the denial of civil rights to minorities in America. Attempts by Congress, the courts, and society at large to define,
detect, and remove discriminatory employment practices, as well as to partially undo
the effects of past discrimination, have changed greatly both the nature and the practice of employment testing. For example, many companies, worried about the possibility of lawsuits, have stopped employment testing altogether (Arvey, 1979; Hale, 1982).
Other companies have struggled to develop nondiscriminatory hiring practices or to
demonstrate that their current practices do not discriminate. Still other organizations
have attempted to repair the damage done by past discrimination, sometimes to the
disadvantage of applicants from groups who had traditionally benefited from prejudice against minorities.

The Law and Personnel Testing

The Civil Rights Act of 1964 is the major piece of federal legislation dealing with
fair employment practices. (The more recent Civil Rights Act of 1991 reinforces many
of the key provisions of the 1964 law and reverses a series of Supreme Court decisions
in the 1980s that appeared to weaken the 1964 act.) The Civil Rights Act of 1964 was divided into several sections, or titles, forbidding discrimination in voting, housing, public education, and the like; Title VII of the Civil Rights Act deals with employment
practices. Basically, the act as amended states that it shall be an unlawful employment
practice . . . to hire or to refuse to hire or to discharge an individual or to discriminate
against any individual with respect to his compensation, terms, conditions, or privileges of employment, because of such individual's race, color, religion, sex, or national
origin.

The interpretation and enforcement of the Civil Rights Act is a complex en-
deavor. At the heart of the problem is the fact that the act does not forbid employers
from using a selection procedure that validly identifies good and poor performers,
even if that procedure has the unintended consequence of discriminating against
women, minorities, or members of specific ethnic groups. In other words, if an employer can demonstrate the "business necessity" of using a specific selection procedure, that procedure is deemed lawful.

The Equal Employment Opportunity Commission (EEOC), which is charged with
enforcing the Civil Rights Act, has a substantial responsibility for determining the
standards to be used in evaluating the validity and the business necessity of a specific
employment procedure. The EEOC Guidelines provide an indication of the principles
and procedures used by the EEOC to determine whether a specific procedure meets
with requirements implicit in the commission's interpretation of the act and of relevant
case law. Since the EEOC is empowered to bring suits in federal court to enforce antidiscrimination laws, the guidelines issued by the EEOC are viewed by many as defining the legally acceptable standards for most tests (Arvey, 1979).

In evaluating the EEOC Guidelines, it is important to consider the conflict between the rights of the employer and the rights of applicants. The use of tests in selection (or promotion, transfer, etc.) often results in different selection rates for whites and minorities or for men and women. If these differences in selection rate are the result of real differences in ability to perform the job, the employer has the right to use the test. For example, in a job that requires frequent use of substantial upper-body strength, such as a center in professional football, the use of a physical strength test that discriminated against women might nevertheless be entirely legal. On the other hand, if differences in test scores have nothing to do with ability to perform the job, the employer who uses the test arbitrarily violates the civil rights of applicants with low test scores. If the same physical strength test just described were used in selecting computer programmers, the test would unfairly discriminate against women and would be illegal. The EEOC Guidelines are used in an effort to determine whether a test that has adverse impact is in fact related to ability to perform the job.

The Search for Equal Employment Opportunity

In the early debates on the Civil Rights Act of 1964, many people assumed that the removal of explicitly discriminatory employment practices would bring about an end to the economic and occupational stratification of our society. It soon became clear that a policy that simply banned overt discrimination would not achieve significant results within the foreseeable future. Attempts to increase the representativeness of the workforce have taken a number of directions, ranging from attempts to recruit and train qualified minorities to the use of selection systems that impose different selection criteria on whites and minorities or on men and women.

Affirmative action represents one of the most straightforward and misunderstood efforts to achieve equal employment opportunity. The basic premise of affirmative action is that a person's right to be considered for a job should be limited only by his or her ability to perform that job. Affirmative action involves a voluntary effort on the part of the employer to ensure that all qualified applicants are considered for the job. Affirmative action programs represent a series of activities including recruitment, workforce analyses, efforts to redesign jobs to provide more opportunities for entry-level workers, and efforts to retrain workers in dead-end jobs. Since the mid-1980s, the scope of affirmative action programs has been significantly narrowed, and the use of quotas or even targets for defining the makeup of a workforce has been restricted substantially. However, organizations doing business with the federal government are still required to file affirmative action plans outlining the steps that they will take to attract qualified applicants from protected groups.

Many analysts have suggested that the policies of the EEOC represent an alternative—some would say covert—strategy for achieving a representative workforce (Wigdor & Garner, 1982a). Wigdor (1982) notes that although the EEOC Guidelines go into great detail regarding the technical standards for validating tests, the EEOC appears to have no intrinsic interest in test validity; rather, its mission is to increase the representativeness of the workforce. By choosing a very broad definition for the term *test* and by setting stringent standards for labeling a test valid, the EEOC has nearly outlawed tests, or at least has outlawed those for which minorities, women, or other protected groups receive lower scores. Although this strategy of covertly banning tests may increase the representativeness of the workforce, it may do so at considerable cost, especially since it is not necessary to abandon tests altogether to increase the proportion of minorities or women who are hired.

Hough, Oswald, and Ployhart (2001) caution against assuming that valid selection devices will necessarily have adverse impact on the employment opportunities of members of traditionally underrepresented groups. Tests that measure general cognitive abilities have the highest validity but also have the most negative impact on workforce diversity. Other valid alternatives will sometimes be preferable to cognitive ability tests, even if they do not yield the optimal prediction of job performance (Murphy, 2002).

CRITICAL DISCUSSION:

Personnel Selection From the Applicant's Point of View

We usually think of personnel selection from the organization's point of view, and we focus on the validity and cost-effectiveness of various tests and assessment methods. It is useful to consider personnel selection from the applicant's point of view, since applicants are likely to be concerned with issues different from those that concern organizations. We comment briefly on three of these issues: local accuracy, deception, and the impact of selection procedures on applicant decisions.

Local accuracy.   From the organization's point of view, the validity coefficient provides a measure of the test's worth. The applicant is more likely to be concerned with the accuracy of the test at or around the cutting score (i.e., the lowest score needed to get the job). We refer to this type of accuracy as *local accuracy.* Assume, for example, that an applicant needs a score of 50 to be hired. Applicants whose scores are near 50 will be concerned most with their placement relative to the cutting score but less with the overall accuracy of the test. A test might be highly valid if those with very high scores (e.g., over 80) perform better than those with very low scores (e.g., below 10), yet it might yield essentially random decisions for the majority of the applicants if the cutting score is near the test mean.

Deception.   Some tests are straightforward (e.g., mechanical ability tests), but others disguise their purpose. The Personal Outlook Inventory is an example of such a test. This inventory asks a series of innocuous questions such as "What are your goals in life?" and "How often are you sick?" and purports to yield scores that predict employee theft. Deceptive tests are regarded by some as an invasion of privacy (B. Hoffman, 1962). Even if job applicants waive their right to privacy, the use of deceptive tests effectively destroys the principle of informed consent (Adair, 1973), for if the applicant is not informed about the purpose of testing, he or she will have no meaningful protection against unreasonable invasions of privacy. Concerns over deception in testing are particularly serious in the area of honesty testing.

Applicant decisions.   Once an organization has made its selection decisions, applicants who receive job offers must make decisions about organizations. It is at this point that many organizations lose their top prospects, which can be very costly (Murphy, 1986). Evidence indicates that the selection process itself can affect applicants' decisions (Rynes, Heneman, & Schwab, 1980; Schmitt & Coyle, 1976). Organizations that employ tedious or arduous selection procedures may alienate applicants and may eventually do themselves more harm than good.

Some selection procedures look offensive; routine drug tests in jobs where the likelihood of drug-related problems is low and polygraph examinations are examples.[4] Other procedures are inoffensive in themselves but convey such a negative image of the organization that they may repel qualified applicants; a long, rambling interview with a prospective boss might convince an applicant to take a job elsewhere. Applicants use selection procedures as one means of gaining information about the organization. Failure to consider this fact and to take steps to ensure that the organization is viewed by the applicant in the most favorable light possible can cost organizations dearly.

ASSESSING INTEGRITY

Dishonesty in the workplace, ranging from employee theft and white-collar crime to the unauthorized use of equipment, materials, and supplies (e.g., making personal long-distance calls from the office, taking home tools and materials), is extremely costly; estimates of the costs of employee theft alone often exceed $40 billion per year. Employers are therefore very interested in evaluating the honesty or integrity of job applicants and incumbents.

The whole question of assessing honesty or integrity is highly controversial. First, it is not clear whether honesty is a stable trait or whether it is primarily determined by situational factors (Murphy, 1993; Salgado, 2002). Second, the methods used in the past to assess or infer honesty were often seen as coercive and inaccurate. For example, before the Employee Polygraph Protection Act of 1988 banning the practice, the polygraph (often called the lie detector) was widely used to screen job applicants. Research on this method of assessing honesty suggested that it was both inaccurate and highly offensive. Third, honesty is a uniquely valued characteristic, and assessment methods that brand some people as dishonest may provoke extreme reactions. Suppose, for example, that you apply for the job of master machinist. You will probably react differently to the news that you did not get the job because you did not possess a sufficient degree of fine visual discrimination ability than to the news that you were turned down because you are dishonest!

As a result of the controversy over integrity testing, these tests have been the focus of a great deal of recent research. The tests, as well as the research on the validity of these tests, are described next.

Integrity Tests

Although paper-and-pencil integrity tests have been in existence since at least the 1950s (Ash, 1976), their widespread use is relatively recent. O'Bannon, Goldinger, and Appleby (1989) report that these tests are used by 10% to 15% of all employers, that they are concentrated in the retail sales, banking, and food service industries, and that over 2.5 million tests are given by over 5,000 employers each year.

---

[4]The routine use of the polygraph in employment testing is now illegal, although it may still be used in some jobs (e.g., security-related jobs) and in some circumstances (e.g., where there is specific evidence of wrongdoing).

Although the individual tests differed in a number of specifics, a number of features were common to virtually all integrity tests. In particular, integrity tests usually include items that refer to one or more of the following areas: (1) direct admissions of illegal or questionable activities, (2) opinions regarding illegal or questionable behavior, (3) general personality traits and thought patterns believed to be related to dishonesty (e.g., the tendency to think constantly about illegal activities), and (4) reactions to hypothetical situations that may or may not feature dishonest behavior.

A distinction is usually drawn between tests that enquire directly about integrity, asking for admissions of past theft or asking about the degree to which the examinee approves of dishonest behaviors, and tests that indirectly infer integrity on the basis of responses to questions that are not obviously integrity related (Sackett, Burris, & Callahan, 1989). Examples of tests usually classified as either clear-purpose or veiled-purpose integrity tests, together with descriptions of dimensions measured by the tests (in some cases, these refer merely to the labels attached to scale scores reported), are presented in Table 19-5; detailed descriptions of the dimensions measured by 43 integrity tests are presented in O'Bannon, Goldinger, and Appleby (1989).

Validity of Integrity Tests

Sackett and his colleagues have conducted several reviews of research on the reliability, validity, and usefulness of integrity tests (Sackett & Decker, 1979; Sackett & Harris, 1984, 1985; Sackett, Burris, & Callahan, 1989); Ones, Viswesvaran, and Schmidt (1993) and McDaniel and Jones (1988) have subjected some of the same studies to meta-analyses that are designed to quantitatively summarize the outcomes of multiple validity studies. O'Bannon and his colleagues (1989) have also reviewed this research and have given attention to a variety of practical issues that surround the administration and use of integrity tests. Although each review raises different concerns and most reviews lament the shortcomings of research on the validity of integrity tests, the general conclusion of the more recent reviews is positive. Earlier reviews of research on integrity tests were sharply critical, but now both the research and the tests themselves

Table 19-5   EXAMPLES OF CLEAR-PURPOSE AND VEILED-PURPOSE INTEGRITY TESTS

Clear purpose	*Dimensions measured or scores reported*
Reid Report	Honesty, attitude, social behavior, substance abuse, personal achievements, service orientation, clerical/math skills
Stanton Survey	Honesty, attitude, admissions of previous dishonesty
Personnel Selection Inventory (Version 7)	Honesty, drug avoidance, customer relations, work values, supervision, employability index, validity scales

Veiled purpose	*Dimensions measured or scores reported*
Personnel Reaction Blank	Dependability/conscientiousness
Hogan Reliability Scale	Hostility to rules, thrill seeking, impulsiveness, social insensitivity, alienation
PDI Employment Inventory	Productive behavior, tenure

appear to have improved, partly as a result of the earlier criticism. A reasonable body of evidence now shows that integrity tests have some validity for predicting a variety of criteria that are relevant to organizations. This research does not say that tests of this sort will eliminate theft or dishonesty at work, but it does suggest that individuals who receive poor scores on these tests tend to be less desirable employees.

There are several challenges in evaluating the validity of integrity tests. First, it is exceedingly difficult to define honesty, integrity, or whatever attribute these tests are designed to measure. Different tests seem to focus on very different attitudes, beliefs, or behaviors. For example, there are a number of definitions of employee theft. Researchers often distinguish between trivial and nontrivial theft; conclusions about the extent of theft depended largely on whether taking articles of little value (e.g., pencils, paper, supplies) was included in one's definition of theft. Goldbricking, taking long lunch breaks, using company time to carry out personal business, and similar activities are sometimes labeled time theft.

A related issue has been a source of controversy since the time of Hartshorne and May (1928)—the question of whether honesty is a distinct trait. Most researchers believe that situational factors have a very strong impact on the tendency to engage in honest versus dishonest behaviors (Saxe, 1990) and that labeling a person as honest or dishonest is a serious oversimplification. It is not completely clear what integrity tests measure, but whatever it is, it is not quite the same thing as "honesty."

Second, informed consent is a potentially serious issue in integrity testing. The Office of Technology Assessment (1990) review of integrity testing notes that integrity test publishers advise against informing examinees of their test scores. This practice implies that if an individual is denied employment on the basis of a score on an integrity test, he or she should not be so informed. The "Standards for Educational and Psychological Testing" and the "Ethical Principles of Psychologists" make it clear that psychologists involved in integrity testing are obliged to inform examinees of the risks and consequences of taking the test versus refusing to take the test, the purpose and nature of the test, and the way in which test scores will be used (Lowman, 1989). The ethical standards described in these documents do not imply that examinees need to know their final test scores, but they do seem to imply that examinees receive a good deal more information about the tests and their use than is typical in actual testing situations.

Third, there are serious concerns over the way in which integrity tests are scored and in which scores are reported. Despite the claims of some test publishers, it is common to use some sort of dichotomous scoring (e.g., pass-fail) in integrity testing. More sophisticated tests sometimes report test scores in terms of a small number of "zones": high danger, moderate danger, average danger, or low danger of theft, substance abuse, and so on. An extensive literature deals with the highly complex psychometric and legal issues involved in setting cutting scores (see Cascio, Alexander, & Barrett, 1988, for a review), but it is not clear whether any of this literature is taken into account by some test publishers. Test scores that are reported on a pass-fail basis are inherently suspect because they blur potentially meaningful differences between individuals in each of the two categories (e.g., it is unlikely that all individuals who fail present the same risks).

The marketing of integrity tests is, in some cases, a disgrace, and tests are sometimes used inappropriately (Kay, 1991). The American Psychological Association's review of integrity testing (APA Task Force, 1991) notes that the claims made for some of these tests are so excessive and overblown as to be fraudulent. Indeed, if you want to see examples of dishonesty in the workplace, you do not need to look much farther than the marketing brochures for some integrity tests.

MEASURES OF JOB PERFORMANCE AND EFFECTIVENESS

Three general classes of data might be used, singly or in combination, to measure the performance of an individual worker. First, and most obvious, are data arising from some sort of production count. It might be possible to count the number of bricks laid by a mason, the number of calls answered by an operator, the number of parts produced by a machinist, or the number of arrests carried out by a policeman and to use this production count to measure job performance. A second type of data that might be used in measuring performance is personnel data. It can be argued that workers who are frequently late or absent or who frequently lose time because of accidents produce at a significantly lower level than workers who put in eight hours every day. Finally, it is possible to use judgmental methods, such as supervisory performance ratings or rankings, or peer nominations, which depend on the judgment of a specific person or set of persons, to measure an individual worker's performance.

Of the three, judgmental methods are by far the most widely used; over 80% of studies published since the mid-1960s have used judgmental ratings or rankings as the primary, if not the sole, method of measuring job performance (see Austin & Villanova, 1992, for a review of the history of criterion research). When you consider that both production counts and personnel data are objective, whereas judgmental methods are necessarily subjective, the overwhelming predominance of judgmental methods may come as a surprise.[5] However, close examination of production counts and personnel data suggest that there are serious limitations to these types of measures and that judgmental methods are often the only practical methods of measuring job performance.

Difficulties in the Objective Measurement of Job Performance

At first glance, production counts appear to be ideal objective measures of job performance. In fact, these measures pose several problems that greatly limit their applicability (Borman, 1991; Guion, 1965a).

First, production counts are not applicable in many jobs, particularly professional and managerial ones. It is not clear what types of units one should count to obtain an

---

[5]We use the term *objective* here in the same sense as do Landy and Farr (1983). Objective data are perceptible to persons other than the evaluator, whereas subjective data are unique to the single evaluator.

objective measure of the performance of a night-shift manager, a judge, or a dentist. Although almost every job involves producing some concrete, quantifiable objects (e.g., widgets, memos, records), a simple count of these objects often fails to capture the essence of the job; a dentist who drills hundreds of cavities is not necessarily a good dentist.

Advances in technology have led to an increasing reliance on computerized monitoring of work performance; over 6 million workers were being monitored by computers and that computerized performance monitoring was growing; federal laws have been proposed to limit computerized monitoring in some circumstances. A number of "spying software" programs exist that allow employers to monitor and record every keystroke that employees make at their computers and to track the Web sites that they browse and the e-mail that they send and receive; systems for remotely observing worksite behaviors are also available. Although computerized monitoring may help solve some of the problems found in using typical objective measures of performance, this method is not without its own problems. Most notably, the presence of a computerized monitoring system probably changes the behaviors of workers and not necessarily in a positive way (Safayeni, Irving, Purdy, & Higgins, 1992). For example, a salesperson whose calls are counted by computer is likely to make many short calls, even though longer discussions with promising customers might, in fact, be more effective. In addition, computerized monitoring may lead to stress, dissatisfaction, and, eventually, to lower performance (Aiello & Kolb, 1995a). Computerized performance-monitoring systems have attracted a good deal of attention. Research on these systems is reviewed in special issues of the *Journal of Applied Social Psychology* (1993, Vol. 23, No. 7) and *Applied Ergonomics* (1992, Vol. 23, No. 1).

Second, many jobs do result in concrete, countable products, but in which the rate of production is not under the control of the worker whose performance is to be evaluated. For example, it might be possible to measure the performance of an assembly line worker in terms of the number of parts he or she successfully bolted on to passing cars. The problem with this approach is that performance is determined almost entirely by the speed of the assembly line. Since the number of cars that comes by each hour tends to be constant, there are very strict limits on the potential variability of this performance measure. If there is no variability in the performance measure, it cannot be a valid measure of individual differences in performance.

Data obtained from personnel files are often used as objective measures of performance. Absenteeism, which represents one of the most widely studied criterion measures in organizational research, illustrates many of the problems encountered in using personnel data to measure job performance. Foremost is the difficulty in arriving at an operational definition of absenteeism. Absenteeism can be defined in any number of ways—as frequency of absences, duration of absences, total time lost due to absences, voluntary absences (e.g., taking a day off to go to a ball game), or involuntary absences (e.g., sick days) (Chadwick-Jones, Brown, Nicholson, & Sheppard, 1971; Landy & Farr, 1983; Steers & Rhodes, 1978). Landy and Farr (1983) and Gaudet (1963) describe over 40 separate indexes that have been used to measure absenteeism in organizations. The choice of a particular index is by no means unimportant; a worker who is out for

2 weeks with a medical excuse might receive a high score on some absenteeism indexes (e.g., duration of involuntary absence) and a very low score on other indexes (e.g., frequency measures). Since different measures of absenteeism are frequently unrelated (Landy & Farr, 1983), the choice of one index over another could have a profound impact on the evaluation of a particular worker's performance.

A second major problem with absenteeism as a measure of job performance has to do with the distribution of absenteeism in the workplace. No matter how it is measured, most people have very low levels of absenteeism, whereas a few people are absent quite a lot (Hammer & Landau, 1981). The distribution of absenteeism raises some serious statistical problems, but it also suggests a serious conceptual problem. The great majority of workers typically have zero, one, or two absences per year and thus receive nearly identical scores on this measure of performance, yet it is unlikely that all these workers are performing at the same level.

Similar problems emerge when accidents are used to measure performance. Very few people have any accidents over the course of a normal year; yet it is unlikely that everyone who did not have an accident performs at the same level or that everyone who did have an accident performs at a lower level than everyone who did not.

The final problem with using personnel data to measure job performance lies in the low levels of reliability of personnel data. For example, Latham and Pursell (1975), Chadwick-Jones and others (1971), Ilgen and Hollenback (1977), and Hammer and Landau (1981) report reliability coefficients of approximately .30 for a variety of absence measures over time spans ranging from 12 weeks to 30 months. Similarly low levels of test-retest reliability have been noted for many other indexes that are based on personnel data. The lack of reliability places some rather obvious limits on the value of personnel measures as indicators of job performance.

One interesting finding in research on objective versus subjective measures of job performance is that the validity of tests and other selection measures is typically higher when objective criteria are used than when subjective ratings are used to measure performance (Schmitt, Gooding, Noe, & Kirsch, 1984). This finding is important because it suggests that validation research that relies on subjective criteria (this would include the great majority of studies) will probably produce a conservative estimate of the validity of selection tests. Thus, methods that are valid for predicting well-developed, subjective measures of performance may be even more valid for predicting objective indexes of performance.

JUDGMENTAL MEASURES

Two general types of judgments might be used in measuring performance: rankings, which involve comparing workers with one another, and ratings, which involve comparing each worker with some standard. There is reason to believe that rating and ranking involve different psychological processes and that ratings and rankings may not always be comparable (Landy & Farr, 1980). Of the two methods, ratings are used more widely, although both methods have advantages and disadvantages.

Ranking Techniques

Suppose that a manager supervises the work of eight construction electricians. The simplest method of evaluating their performance might be to rank order the employees in terms of their overall effectiveness. There is no doubt that some employees are more effective than others; a ranking is merely a systematic recognition of this fact.

Several different ranking methods exist, ranging from those that provide a crude, partial rank order to those that provide very exact data on the relative (perceived) effectiveness of each employee. One of the simplest of the partial ranking methods is the forced distribution. This ranking method is designed to deal with a very common problem in judgmental performance evaluations: the tendency of most supervisors to rate almost all their employees in the top 5% to 10% and to describe the worst employees as merely "above average."[6] A forced-distribution scale requires the supervisor to designate a fixed number of workers as belonging to the lowest category, a fixed number as belonging to the highest category, and the rest as belonging to a middle category. It is, of course, possible to employ more than three categories if necessary.

An example of a forced-distribution scale is shown in Table 19-6. In the table, eight workers have been sorted into three ordered categories, top, middle, and bottom. It might be more informative to obtain a full ranking, which involves determining the rank order of each of the eight workers and, in effect, sorts the workers into eight ordered categories. Thus, the principal difference between a forced distribution and a full ranking is that in the latter, the number of categories is equal to the number of workers,

Table 19-6   A TYPICAL FORCED DISTRIBUTION SCALE

Top 25%	Middle 50%	Bottom 25%
A	B	C

Total Number of Subordinates: 8
Your top 2 subordinates belong in category "A"
Your bottom 2 subordinates belong in category "C"
Your remaining subordinates belong in category "B"

Subordinates	Category
1. Small, M.	_____
2. O'Reilly, J.	_____
3. Stetson, K.	_____
4. Witherspoon, R.	_____
5. Dobson, T.	_____
6. Murchinson, A.	_____
7. Archer, S.	_____
8. Houston, J.	_____

[6]This tendency is referred to as *leniency*.

whereas in a forced distribution, the number of categories may be considerably smaller than the number of workers.

A third method of ranking is the pair-comparison method. An example of a pair comparison involving four workers is shown in Table 19-7. As is evident from the table, a pair-comparison task involves an extremely simple judgment: For each pair of subordinates, the supervisor must judge which worker is more effective. Although the judgment required is very simple and seemingly crude, the pair-comparison method allows for very exact scaling of the relative effectiveness of each worker. Application of scaling techniques allows one to transform the ordinal data that arise out of pair comparisons to interval-level measures of effectiveness (Thurstone, 1927; Torgerson, 1958). This precision in measuring the effectiveness of each employee is made possible by the fact that a relatively large number of comparisons must be obtained in the course of a pair-comparison task. A total of $[n(n-1)/2]$ comparisons is necessary when comparing n employees. Thus, with four employees, six comparisons are necessary $[(4 \times 3)/2 = 6]$; in comparing 10 employees, 45 separate pair comparisons must be made.

Chiu and Allinger (1990) proposed a method that combines aspects of ranking and rating. Using this method, raters must place each individual that they evaluate in different ordered categories, but the spread between people can be used to indicate relatively large or relatively small differences between individuals. Suppose, for example, that you thought that Joe and Mary were both poor workers (although Mary was slightly better) and that Sue and Kathleen were both quite good (and that Kathleen was slightly better). You might assign scores of 1, 2, 6, and 7 (on a 7-point scale) to Joe, Mary, Sue, and Kathleen, respectively.

In practice, the method suggested by Chiu and Allinger (1990) is likely to be more similar to a rating scale than to a ranking method. It does, however, force raters to make distinctions between individuals, and it might be useful in settings where it is necessary to rank everyone.

Comparison of Ranking Methods. In choosing among ranking techniques, a trade-off must be made between the effort involved in ranking and the precision of the

---

Table 19-7   A TYPICAL PAIR-COMPARISON TASK

Workers to be compared:	Wallsten, A.
	Block, S.
	Barrow, K.
	Carr, M.
Which worker is performing better? Circle one.	
Wallsten or Block?	
Wallsten or Barrow?	
Wallsten or Carr?	
Block or Barrow?	
Block or Carr?	
Barrow or Carr?	

information that will result. A forced distribution provides a relatively crude measure: Workers in the top category are judged to be more effective than those in the bottom category. A full ranking provides a more exact comparison of individual workers, but at the price of considerable effort. A pair-comparison procedure provides an interval-level measure of relative effectiveness, but it does so at the price of requiring a large number of comparisons.

In part, the choice of a technique depends on the way in which rankings will be used. For certain promotion decisions or for allocating cutbacks, a forced-distribution ranking may be appropriate. On the other hand, for evaluating the extent to which employees differ in their levels of performance, a pair-comparison ranking might be necessary.

Rating Scales

Rating scales represent the single most common measure of job performance (Landy & Farr, 1980, 1983). As opposed to ranking techniques, which call for comparisons between persons, rating scales require the supervisor to evaluate each worker with regard to a particular standard that may be vaguely described (e.g., good, average, poor) or that may be described in concrete behavioral terms (e.g., "This teacher could be expected to miss class frequently"). Whereas ranking methods require supervisors to decide on a relative basis which of two workers is a better performer, rating scales require supervisors to evaluate and describe the level of each individual worker's performance.

A variety of rating scale formats are available, ranging from scales that are quite simple and straightforward to those that involve complex scoring rules or extremely concrete behavioral anchors. Two types of rating scales that are widely used and that have been the object of considerable research are graphic rating scales and behavior-based scales.

Graphic Rating Scales. The most common and the simplest form of rating instrument is the graphic rating scale. This format asks the rater to make a direct judgment about the quality of each worker's performance and to indicate this judgment on a specific response scale. Examples of several different types of graphic rating scales are presented in Table 19-8. Response scale (a) requires the rater to mark, on a 21-centimeter line, the point that corresponds to his or her evaluation of a particular employee. A numeric rating can be obtained by measuring the distance between the lower end of the scale and the supervisor's check mark. In this case, worker A received a rating of 18, whereas worker B received a rating of 1.

Rating scales (b) and (c) are verbally anchored scales that are divided into a small number of discrete categories. The supervisor's check mark can be translated into a numeric rating by assigning values to each category. For example, scale (c) can be numbered from 1 to 5, where 1 indicates "Consistently Unsatisfactory" and 5 indicates "Consistently Superior." A worker who was rated "Below Average" would receive a score of 2.

Table 19-8 EXAMPLES OF GRAPHIC RATING SCALES MEASURING THE QUALITY OF WORK

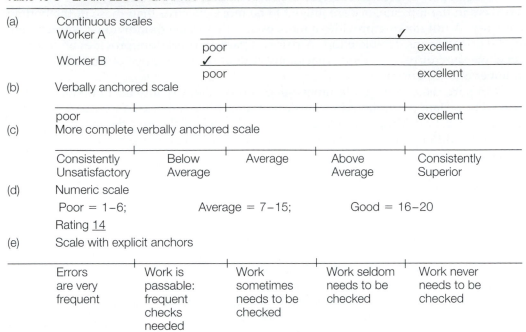

Rating scale (d) is an example of a numeric scale. A rater using this scale could indicate with some apparent precision his or her evaluation of each applicant. Thus, if a worker received a rating of 14, as in the table, this rating would indicate performance that was somewhat better than average but was lower than the level typically described as "good."

The obvious advantage of a graphic scale is its simplicity. Once it is decided what is to be measured, the construction of a graphic scale is quite simple. Three general principles should be followed in constructing a graphic rating scale, but within the confines of these principles it probably does not matter what type of scale one decides to construct. First, the number of responses probably should be somewhere between 5 and 9. Second, to whatever degree possible, scale anchors should be fairly explicit. Scale (e) in the table is an example of a scale that meets these two requirements. The third requirement is that the behaviors or traits being measured be defined explicitly.

Unfortunately, the simplicity of a graphic rating scale is also the source of considerable ambiguity. First, there is a good deal of ambiguity with regard to the precise meaning of the performance dimensions being rated. Graphic scales are typically used to measure somewhat broad dimensions of performance, such as "Quality of Work," "Oral Communication," or "Planning." It is never clear precisely what behaviors are included in a dimension such as "Quality," and it is therefore likely that different raters will have different ideas regarding the aspects of employee performance that they should consider when rating the "Quality" of each employee's work.

Second, there is often a good deal of ambiguity in the interpretation of the scale anchors. Supervisors almost certainly have different interpretations of what is meant by good or average performance, and in most cases, scale anchors do not really provide a concrete, detailed description of the behavior that best represents good, average, or poor performance. Behavior-based scales—a category that includes mixed standard scales, behaviorally anchored rating scales, and behavioral observation scales—were developed in an attempt to remove several sources of ambiguity in rating.

Behavior-Based Scales. One of the most heavily researched rating scale formats, behaviorally anchored rating scales (BARSs),[7] were developed to deal with the two principal sources of ambiguity that plague graphic rating scales: (1) ambiguity in the dimensions being rated and (2) ambiguity in the scale anchors. BARSs provide concrete behavioral statements that are used to identify particular levels of performance and that, taken together, provide a series of clear behavioral exemplars of the performance dimension under consideration (P. Smith & Kendall, 1963). An example of a BARS used to measure the job knowledge of police patrol officers is presented in Table 19-9.

The development of BARSs typically involves extensive input from the supervisors and workers who use the scale (Landy, 1985). The goal of this input is to develop behavioral anchors that have three properties. First, they should be relevant to the work setting. Second, they should provide good illustrations of the dimension being measured. Thus, a police officer who was not sure exactly what is meant by "job knowledge" could consult the scale shown in the table for behavioral examples. Third, the behavioral anchors should provide a good illustration of a particular level of performance. Thus, an officer who consults the scale shown in the table should have a good idea of what is meant by good, average, and poor performance.

Various aspects of the voluminous literature on BARSs have been reviewed by Bernardin and Smith (1981), Jacobs, Kafry, and Zedeck (1980), Landy and Farr (1980), Kingstrom and Bass (1981), and Schwab, Heneman, and DeCotiis (1975). Researchers generally agree that BARSs have not lived up to their promise; ratings obtained using BARSs do not appear to be substantially more accurate or less prone to bias than ratings obtained using simpler graphic scales (Borman, 1991). However, the process of developing a BARS may itself be highly beneficial to an organization, and it may very well justify the investment of the organization's time and resources.

First, as the result of developing a BARS, the organization arrives at fairly precise, agreed-upon behavioral definitions of performance in specific aspects of the job (Landy & Farr, 1980). This outcome contrasts sharply with that achieved by organizations that employ graphic rating scales, in which every supervisor might have a unique definition of average performance. Second, the process of scale-development involves many members of the organization (Borman & Vallon, 1974). A good deal of evidence shows that participation in the scale-development process itself contributes to the acceptance of performance appraisal systems and to the perception that these systems are fair and accurate (Dipboye & de Pontbriand, 1981; Landy & Farr, 1980).

---

[7]These scales are sometimes referred to as behavior expectation scales (BES).

Table 19-9   BEHAVIORALLY ANCHORED RATING SCALE FOR POLICE PATROL OFFICERS' JOB
KNOWLEDGE: AWARENESS OF PROCEDURES, LAWS, AND COURT RULINGS AND
CHANGES IN THEM

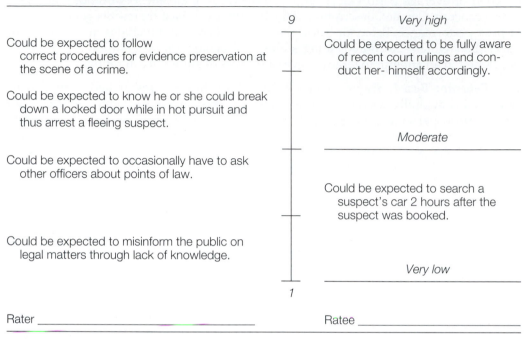

	9	*Very high*
Could be expected to follow correct procedures for evidence preservation at the scene of a crime.		Could be expected to be fully aware of recent court rulings and conduct her- himself accordingly.
Could be expected to know he or she could break down a locked door while in hot pursuit and thus arrest a fleeing suspect.		
		Moderate
Could be expected to occasionally have to ask other officers about points of law.		
		Could be expected to search a suspect's car 2 hours after the suspect was booked.
Could be expected to misinform the public on legal matters through lack of knowledge.		
		Very low
	1	

Rater _____   Ratee _____

  Latham and Wexley (1977) have criticized both graphic rating scales and BARSs;
they note that the former require raters to make vague, unanchored judgments,
whereas the latter require raters to indicate what sort of behaviors they would expect,
even though in many cases none of the behavioral anchors included in the scale have
been observed. They suggest a simpler alternative, the behavioral observation scale
(BOS). A BOS is made up of a list of behaviors believed to be critical for effective job
performance. An example of a BOS used in measuring the performance of teachers is
presented in Table 19-10.
  The rater who uses a BOS is asked to indicate how frequently each of the critical
incidents on the scale has occurred over a specific period of time (Latham, Fay, & Saari,
1979). Items that depict ineffective performance, such as items 3, 4, 8, 9, or 12 in the
table, are rescaled so that large-scale values indicate low frequency of occurrence, and
scores are obtained by summing the frequency ratings assigned to each item. Thus, a
worker who frequently performs effective critical behaviors and who very rarely performs ineffective behaviors receives a high rating, whereas a worker who frequently
performs ineffective behaviors receives a low rating.
  One of the principal advantages of the BOS technique is its apparent simplicity.
Rather than asking supervisors to make complex, unreliable judgments about workers,
this type of rating scale merely asks raters to report how frequently different behaviors

Table 19-10 A BEHAVIORAL OBSERVATION SCALE FOR TEACHERS

Rate the frequency with which each of the following behaviors has occurred this month. Use the following scale to rate frequency.

1	2	3	4	5	6	7
Never	Almost never	A few times	About half of the time	Often	Most of the time	All of the time

1. Examples were presented that were clearly related to the central topic. _____
2. Lecturer used purposeful nonverbal behaviors (smiles, points) to emphasize points. _____
3. Lecturer stops in midsentence. _____
4. Lecturer is hesitant, says "uh" or "um." _____
5. Lecturer establishes eye contact with audience. _____
6. Lecturer provides facts or evidence to support broad generalizations. _____
7. Lecturer speaks clearly. _____
8. Lecturer acts nervous. _____
9. Lecturer speaks in a monotone for a sustained period. _____
10. Lecturer gives clear answers to questions. _____
11. Lecturer varies his or her facial expression. _____
12. Lecturer appears unsure of what he or she is saying. _____

have occurred; the psychological process involved in completing a BOS therefore seems considerably simpler and more straightforward (less prone to error) than with other types of scales (Latham, Saari, & Fay, 1980). However, several investigators have suggested that the processes involved in filling out a BOS are neither simple nor straightforward but, rather, may depend on the same general impressions and vague judgments that affect ratings obtained using other types of scales. Murphy, Martin, and Garcia (1982) suggest that supervisors cannot recall the frequency of critical behaviors over extended periods of time; rather, they infer the frequency with which effective behaviors have occurred on the basis of their general impressions of each worker. Murphy and Balzer (1981, 1986) have gone further, suggesting that behavioral observation scales are, in fact, trait-rating scales in disguise. Supervisors infer that workers whom they perceive as good must have carried out many effective work behaviors, rather than inferring that a worker is good because he or she carried out the specific behaviors included in the BOS.

Comparing Performance-Appraisal Scales

Landy and Farr (1980) suggest that 30 years of research on scale formats have failed to produce an alternative that is demonstrably more efficient or more psychometrically sound than simple graphic rating scales. On this basis, they called for a moratorium on format-related research. Although this recommendation may represent a somewhat extreme reaction, their review does bring into focus the relatively minor impact of rating scale formats on the outcomes of rating. A good graphic scale is probably adequate for measuring the performance of one's workers, and the use of a complex behavioral format is unlikely to improve the quality of rating data.

Although rating scales have little effect on the outcomes of rating, they may dramatically affect the process of rating. As Table 19-11 suggests, the psychological processes implied by graphic rating scales, mixed standard scales, BARSs, and BOSs are quite different. Although research on rating-scale formats has failed in its original mission—to develop the one best scale for rating job performance—future research on rating-scale formats may shed light on the judgment processes involved in performance evaluation (Murphy & Constans, 1987, 1988).

The question of who evaluates your performance may be more important than the question of what type of scale is used. Many organizations use peer ratings (i.e., evaluations obtained from coworkers rather than supervisors) and even self-ratings as supplements to supervisory ratings (Bracken, Timmreck, & Church, 2001). Clear evidence shows that (1) self-ratings are consistently higher than peer or supervisory ratings and (2) peers and supervisors agree more closely with one another than either agrees with self-ratings (M. M. Harris & Schaubroeck, 1988; Murphy, Cleveland, & Mohler, 2001). A number of explanations for these differences have been suggested (Murphy & Cleveland, 1995), but the implications of this research are clear: If you want high ratings, do them yourself!

The Validity of Criterion Measures

In the introduction to this chapter, we noted that most applications of psychological testing in industry are concerned, in one way or another, with the construct of job performance. Selection tests are used to predict future job performance; therefore, the validity of these predictions is of major importance in assessing the overall worth of the test. The second broad class of measures frequently encountered in personnel administration is the set of indexes used to measure job performance. Except in a limited number of cases in which meaningful production counts can be obtained, judgmental methods (i.e., ratings or rankings) are used to measure the performance of workers. The validity of these measures is the central concern of this section.

Table 19-11 PSYCHOLOGICAL PROCESSES PRESUMABLY INVOLVED WHEN USING DIFFERENT RATING SCALES

Scale	Processes involved
Graphic rating scale	Unanchored judgment
Behaviorally anchored rating scale	Continuous comparison that involves matching performance levels with behavioral anchors
Behavioral observation scale	Observation and recall of behavior frequency

There is no simple way to determine or to demonstrate the validity of most measures of job performance. Consider, for example, supervisory performance ratings. Ideally, the validity of ratings might be determined by correlating these ratings with other measures of job performance (Kavanaugh, 1971). The problem with this approach is that ratings are often the only available measure of the worker's performance; there is rarely any other acceptable standard against which ratings can be compared.[8] In short, there are rarely "criteria for criteria"; it is rarely possible to demonstrate convincingly that a particular measure of job performance is, in fact, a valid measure of the performance of individual workers. Because there are typically no standards against which most criterion measures can be compared, it is difficult to use the predictive or concurrent validity strategies in assessing the validity of criteria.

Recognizing that the strategy of determining the validity of a criterion measure directly by comparing that measure with some standard is often impossible, a number of authors have suggested indirect strategies to assess the validity of criterion measures. For example, it is often possible to determine the extent to which raters discriminate among individuals or differentiate among performance dimensions in their ratings of job performance (Kavanaugh, MacKinney, & Wolins, 1971; Saal, Downey, & Lahey, 1980; Stanley, 1961). It is assumed that raters who are sensitive to differences in their subordinates' levels of performance are more accurate than those who give everyone similar ratings. Other authors suggest that interrater agreement be used as an indirect indicator of the validity of ratings (Bernardin, Alveres, & Cranny, 1976; Lawler, 1967). Although it is true that valid ratings also should be reliable, several authors have noted that reliability does not necessarily imply validity and on this basis have questioned the use of interrater agreement as an indicator of valid ratings (Buckner, 1959; Freeberg, 1969; Wherry & Bartlett, 1982).

Finally, James (1973) has proposed the most comprehensive approach to assessing the validity of criterion measures—the construct validity approach. He notes that performance can be thought of as a construct and that the relationships between a measure of performance and a number of other observable behaviors could be compared with the pattern of relationships implied by the theoretical network in which the construct performance is embedded to assess the validity of a criterion measure.

Research on the construct validity of performance ratings has progressed significantly in recent years. For example, the research teams involved in U.S. Armed Forces Project A relied on careful explications of the construct domain of job performance to develop concrete performance measures (see *Personnel Psychology*, Vol. 43, No. 2, for a detailed description of this project). Kraiger and Teachout (1990) illustrated ways in which analyses of the generalizability of ratings (see Chapter 6 for an overview of generalizability theory) could be used to assess construct validity. Other authors (e.g., Lance, Teachout, & Donnelly, 1992; Murphy, 1989; Murphy & Shiarella, 1997) have suggested methods for identifying dimensions that underlie the performance domain.

---

[8]Heneman's (1986) review suggests that subjective and objective measures show only modest correlations.

Rater Errors. Research in organizations suggests that supervisors fall prey to several errors in evaluating the performance of subordinates. Some raters fail to discriminate good performers from bad ones; others fail to identify the strengths and weaknesses of individual workers. A number of indexes have been proposed to measure raters' tendencies to commit these errors; these rater-error measures represent the most common criteria for evaluating performance ratings. Rater-error measures are used by some researchers as indirect measures of rating accuracy, in that ratings that show little or no evidence of specific rater errors are assumed to be more accurate than ratings that show strong evidence of such errors (Jacobs, Kafry, & Zedeck, 1980).

Rater errors fall into three categories:

1. Halo errors, which represent a failure to identify employee strengths and weaknesses
2. Leniency errors, which represent a tendency to assign ratings that are either unduly lenient or unduly harsh
3. Range-restriction errors, which represent a failure to discriminate among workers in terms of their overall level of performance

Halo errors are thought to reflect raters' tendencies to allow their overall evaluation of each worker to affect their evaluation of each specific aspect of that person's performance (W. Cooper, 1981; Thorndike, 1920). Thus, a worker who receives a favorable overall rating might also receive high marks for all specific aspects of performance on which he or she is rated; a worker who receives a poor overall rating might also receive poor ratings on every specific performance dimension. In fact, it is unlikely that many workers are either very good, very bad, or even average in all aspects of their work. It is therefore likely that the supervisor who rates individual workers as uniformly good or uniformly poor is not providing accurate ratings, at least on some dimensions.

Halo error is most clearly manifest in the correlations between ratings of different performance dimensions. When raters commit halo error, ratings of apparently unrelated performance dimensions show substantial positive correlations. The correlation between different performance dimensions is therefore used as a measure of halo error (Saal, Downey, & Lahey, 1980). The higher the correlation between ratings of different performance dimensions, the greater the likelihood that halo error is present.

Leniency errors are thought to reflect an inappropriate judgmental standard held by the rater. When a supervisor indicates that all of his or her workers are top performers or, conversely, that all workers are extremely poor performers, it is likely that the ratings tell us more about the rater than they do about the people being rated. Leniency errors are thought to be most clearly indicated by the mean rating; it is assumed that when the average rating is 9.5 on a 10-point scale, the rater is unduly lenient.[9] Conversely, when the average rating is 2 on a 10-point scale, it is assumed that the rater is unduly severe.

---

[9]A similar assumption underlies the perennial debate over grade inflation.

Range-restriction errors are thought to reflect supervisors' inability or unwilling-
ness to discriminate good from poor workers. For example, some supervisors rate most
or all workers as average, and they seem to be unwilling to go out on a limb in describing specific workers as either good or poor. Range-restriction error is most clearly
manifest in measures of the variability in ratings, such as the standard deviation. If the
range, or the standard deviation, of the ratings assigned by a specific supervisor to a
group of workers is very near zero, it is probably safe to assume that range-restriction
error is present.

Rater-error measures have been used widely in evaluating performance appraisal
scales (Landy & Farr, 1980) and rater-training programs (Spool, 1978). Nevertheless,
these measures have been the focus of considerable criticism. First, there is a great deal
of inconsistency in the operational definitions of these measures (Balzer & Sulsky,
1992; Murphy, 1982; Murphy & Balzer, 1981; Saal, Downey, & Lahey, 1980). Alternate
measures of halo, leniency, or range restriction are rarely equivalent and sometimes
are unrelated. Second, the assumptions underlying rater error measures often are inappropriate. Finally, and most important, there is little empirical or theoretical support
for the position that rater errors are related to rating accuracy (Borman, 1977;
W. Cooper, 1981; Murphy & Balzer, 1989). As a result, the use of rater-error measures
as criteria for evaluating ratings is becoming increasingly rare (Balzer & Sulsky, 1990,
1992).

Rating Accuracy. Borman (1977) has noted that, to evaluate the accuracy of the
rating assigned to a specific worker, ratings must be compared with a true score
measure of the worker's performance. In real work settings, it is generally impossible
to obtain measures against which performance ratings can be directly evaluated, and,
as a result, indirect measures such as rater-error measures must be used. However, in
laboratory experiments in which performance is preserved on videotape, it is possible
to develop direct measures of rating accuracy. Methods of measuring the accuracy of
ratings of videotaped performance have been developed and applied by Borman
(1977, 1978) and others (Murphy, Balzer, Kellam, & Armstrong, 1984; Murphy, Garcia,
Kerkar, Martin, & Balzer, 1982; Penn & Bowser, 1977).

To date, much of the research on rating accuracy has examined aspects of the rating process that contribute to accuracy in evaluating performance. For example, Murphy, Garcia, and their colleagues (1982) showed that accuracy in observing behavior is
related to accuracy in rating performance, although this relationship is not a simple
one, owing to the multiple definitions of rating accuracy (Cronbach, 1955; J. Wiggins,
1973).

Landy and Farr (1980) have suggested that a number of contextual variables,
such as the timing, format, and purpose of rating, affect the accuracy of performance
evaluations. For example, several studies have suggested that ratings collected for the
purpose of making administrative decisions (i.e., salary and promotion decisions) are
systematically more lenient than ratings collected for research purposes. However,
other research casts some doubts on the relationship between the purpose of rating
and the accuracy of ratings (Murphy et al., 1984; Murphy, Philbin, & Adams, 1989).

Research on rating accuracy suggests that under optimal conditions, raters can achieve high levels of accuracy in evaluating the performance of others. Thus, the central issue in current research on rating accuracy is not whether raters are capable of accuracy but, rather, under what conditions they will achieve accuracy. For example, Mohrman and Lawler (1983) suggest that supervisors are rarely motivated to provide accurate ratings and that in several instances they may actually be motivated to provide inaccurate ratings. Since organizations rarely reward supervisors for accuracy in assessing their workers' performance, the supervisor often has nothing to gain—and quite a bit to lose—if he or she gives a poor evaluation to a worker (Murphy & Cleveland, 1995).

Other researchers suggest that the accuracy of ratings is affected by characteristics of the rater, characteristics of the worker, the variability of performance, the use of memory aids, such as behavior diaries, and the broader social context in which rating occurs (Bernardin & Walter, 1977; Landy & Farr, 1980, 1983; Lerner, 1983; Locke, 1983; Murphy & Cleveland, 1995; Wherry & Bartlett, 1982). More research is needed before the circumstances under which ratings provide an accurate measure of an individual worker's performance can be described clearly.

SUMMARY

A variety of methods are used to predict job performance, ranging from interviews and work samples to standardized tests designed to measure ability and personality characteristics. Paper-and-pencil testing is widespread, and consistent evidence shows that both general ability tests and more specialized tests (e.g., measures of clerical speed and accuracy or mechanical comprehension) are valid predictors of performance. Contrary to the beliefs of many personnel managers, standardized tests are probably the best predictors, especially when both psychometric and practicality criteria are considered.

The biographical and demographic data that are typically collected on application blanks can be used to predict performance, absenteeism, job tenure, and so on. In recent years, considerable progress has been made over the blind empirical methods that dominated biodata research in the past. Researchers have attempted to document the constructs that are potentially measurable in terms of biographical data and have constructed detailed theories to link biographical data to job performance.

The employment interview is a source of continuing frustration to industrial psychologists. This technique is probably the most widely used and the worst predictor of performance. Interviews can be valid predictors, especially if they are structured, with a strong emphasis on behavioral information. In most cases, however, organizations seem to rely on unstructured interviews, which are known to show much lower levels of reliability or validity.

Work samples are used in both blue- and white-collar jobs. In blue-collar jobs, work samples often involve carrying out actual job tasks under controlled conditions (e.g., typing tests). Managerial work samples often represent simulations of key aspects of the manager's job. Both types have shown relatively consistent evidence of validity. Managerial work samples are a frequent component of assessment centers, which represent a strategy for collecting and integrating multiple sources of information about an individual's strengths, weaknesses, present performance, and future potential.

Psychological tests are an important component of the process of personnel selection and classification. Because of their potential impact on members of minority groups (see Chapter 15 for a more extended discussion of this issue), tests have become the center of legal and ethical debates. Although significant controversy over the proper use of psychological tests in personnel selection remains, most reviews suggest that well-developed tests are more valid and fair than other methods, such as unstructured interviews, that might be used in their place.

With the demise of the polygraph as a means of inferring honesty at work, paper-and-pencil integrity tests have become increasingly common. Although they are the focus of considerable controversy, there is some consensus that they can be valid in predicting criteria such as workplace theft and perhaps overall job performance.

A variety of measures are available to measure job performance, including both objective methods, in which little or no judgment is required to obtain adequate measures, and subjective methods, which rely on the judgments of one or more evaluators to "measure" job performance. Given all the potential problems associated with subjective methods, their popularity is at first difficult to understand. However, in many jobs, it is essentially impossible to obtain objective measures that adequately represent the performance of the individuals being assessed, meaning that subjective measures are the only practical choice.

Judgmental measures might require ranking (i.e., comparisons of persons with one another) or rating (i.e., comparisons of persons with some standard). On the whole, rating methods are more common, and a great deal of research has been devoted to developing the best possible rating scales. A number of scale formats have been developed that use behavioral examples to define or measure levels of performance, but although behavior-based scales are popular, little evidence indicates that the rating scale format makes much of a difference in the psychometric quality of the ratings.

Two general methods have been used to evaluate the validity of ratings. First, an increasing number of researchers have applied construct validation methods to the analysis of performance ratings, and there is some consensus that supervisors in organizations can provide reasonably valid measures of their subordinates' performance (Milkovich & Wigdor, 1991). Second, researchers have developed a number of rater-error measures, which are designed to reflect specific types of judgment errors (e.g., excessive leniency in rating subordinates). Although these measures are still somewhat popular, an increasing body of research demonstrates their shortcomings. Finally, these measures are limited to laboratory experiments and other artificial settings, and they have had relatively little applicability to field settings.

PROBLEMS AND SOLUTIONS—RECAP

The Problem

A car manufacturer expects to receive thousands of applications to fill 135 semiskilled jobs in a new manufacturing plant; many of these applicants will have prior experience in similar jobs. Your job is to design a system for selecting the best candidates out of this pool.

A Solution

There are three factors that are likely to be relevant in making a recommendation. First, the large number of applicants is both a blessing and a curse. It is a blessing in the sense that the selection ratio will be very small, which means that an employer using valid tests is likely to be very successful in identifying good candidates for the job (See Chapter 9). It is a curse in the sense that you will have to screen thousands of applicants, making it difficult to use assessment methods that are time- or labor-intensive. You are very likely to do well in selection, but you will be limited to relying on short and simple assessments. Second, the job is not a highly skilled one. When selecting candidates for highly complex or advanced jobs, it might be necessary to consider highly specific knowledge or skills, or more advanced abilities, but if the job is simpler, the range of assessment methods that might be appropriate is probably less constrained. Third, many applicants have successfully performed similar jobs in the past; the likelihood of hiring people who are completely unable to do the job is relatively low.

The design of a personnel selection system starts with a careful analysis of the job, assessing the knowledge, skills, and abilities needed to perform the job. In the preceding example, you would probably want to use written or computerized tests rather than in-depth, one-on-one interviews to assess these abilities and skills. If you are expecting to screen large numbers of candidates in a short period of time, paper-and-pencil tests might turn out to be preferable to computerized tests (unless there are large numbers of computers available, it will be logistically difficult to administer computerized tests). It would be feasible here to use assessments of past experience (e.g., in similar jobs) to predict future success; but in jobs where skill levels are lower, applicants with no previous experience would probably be able to acquire the knowledge and skills to perform the job in a reasonably short time, so it might be better to select a promising candidate with no prior experience over an applicant with lower test scores who has performed similar jobs in the past. It is likely that you will end up with a multistage selection model, in which a test or some other assessment that can be used with large numbers of applicants is used to narrow down the applicant pool, with more time- and labor-intensive assessments used for individuals who pass this first screen.

KEY TERMS

Assessment center   assessment method that uses multiple methods and multiple assessors to evaluate examinees on several work-related dimensions

Behavior-based rating scale   scale that includes specific behavioral examples of the dimension to be rated and/or the levels of performance on that dimension

Biodata   data about an individual's background, life accomplishments, or present status that can be used to predict future performance

Computerized performance monitoring   computerized monitoring systems that continuously track rates of output or production in specific jobs or tasks

EEOC—Equal Employment Opportunity Commission   a federal agency responsible for enforcing the provisions of the Civil Rights Acts of 1964 and 1991 related to employment

Graphic rating scale   scale that includes only simple descriptions of the dimension to be rated and the levels of performance on that dimension

Graphology   use of handwriting analysis to draw inferences about an examinee's personality or behavior; this method has not been shown to be valid

Halo error   tendency to base ratings of specific dimensions on one's overall evaluation of the person being rated

Horizontal percentage method   method of empirically scoring biodata by comparing responses of various groups

Integrity test   paper-and-pencil test used to draw inferences about an individual's honesty, dependability, or likelihood of engaging in dishonest or destructive behaviors

Leniency error   tendency to assign ratings that are unrealistically high

Objective measures   measures that require minimal levels of judgment to obtain (e.g., production counts)

Ranking methods   methods that involve comparing individuals with one another

Rating methods   methods that involve comparing individuals with some standard (e.g., "average" or "good" performance)

Structured interview   interview format in which questions and perhaps scoring criteria for responses are defined in advance of the interview

Validity generalization   application of meta-analysis to determine whether validity coefficients are similar across tests, jobs, and settings

Work-sample test   test of maximal performance, which involves carrying out a sample of tasks under optimal conditions

20

Diagnostic Testing: Clinical Applications

In Chapter 17, we considered several personality tests that are used widely in clinical settings. Although these tests may be used in the diagnosis of psychopathology, their primary purpose is somewhat broader—to provide a multifaceted measure of the personality of the individual taking the test. This chapter considers a set of tests and measurement techniques that are geared toward a more limited purpose, the differential diagnosis of psychopathology.

First, we discuss two of the most widely used diagnostic tests, the Minnesota Multiphasic Personality Inventory (MMPI) and the Bender-Gestalt test. Both tests are thought to be useful in diagnosing a wide array of problems that the clinician might encounter. Second, we consider the diagnostic use of intelligence test scores. There is some reason to believe that patterns of subtest scores on tests of general intelligence convey information that is not conveyed by an overall test score (i.e., IQ). Finally, we describe the classification system most commonly used in clinical diagnosis.

The chapter closes with a discussion of the value—or lack of value—of clinical diagnosis. For too long, psychodiagnosis has seemed to be an end in itself, rather than a means for directing therapy and treatment. It is important to determine whether accurate diagnosis does in fact contribute to the progress of treatment or to the determination of the client's prognosis. It if does not, clinical diagnosis may not be worth the considerable time and effort devoted to it.

PROBLEMS AND SOLUTIONS—COMPARING PERFORMANCE ON SUBTESTS

The Problem

Mitch is a 9-year-old who is being assessed by a local psychologist. Mitch has had some difficulty in school, and the psychologist administers a test designed to tap general intelligence. Mitch's scores suggest differences in his level of performance on verbal versus nonverbal tasks, and the psychologist suggests that this pattern of scores might indicate underlying neurological problems.

Mitch scores a bit better than average on the verbal section, and substantially below average (40th percentile) on the nonverbal section of this test. You are not convinced that the psychologist is interpreting the test correctly. What would you need to know to make sense of the psychologist's diagnosis?

THE MINNESOTA MULTIPHASIC PERSONALITY INVENTORY

The MMPI, first published in 1943, represents one of the most widely used and researched psychological tests in existence. It is estimated that there are well over 10,000 published articles and reports dealing with the original MMPI; a major revision of this instrument, MMPI-2, which is discussed later in this section, has also received considerable research attention.[1] Although the MMPI has been the focus of a great deal of debate and criticism (Butcher, 1972; Newmark, 1979), it nevertheless is recognized as one of the most broadly useful diagnostic tests currently available. King (1978) noted, "The MMPI remains matchless as the objective instrument for the assessment of psychopathology" (p. 616), and the same could probably be said today. The MMPI has been adapted for use in Europe (Butcher, Derksen, Sloore, & Sirigatti, 2003), and is used for a variety of purposes, ranging from forensic assessment (Wise, 2002) to assessing faking of physical and mental disorders (Bury & Bagby, 2002).

The test itself is made of 550 affirmative statements, similar to those listed here:

I was often in trouble at school.
Most of the time I feel happy.
Someone is controlling my thoughts.
When I play cards or games, it is important that I win.

A person taking the test responds to each item by indicating "true," "false," or "cannot say." As typically administered, the MMPI yields scores on 10 clinical scales:[2]

1. Hypochondrias (HS)—a neurotic pattern characterized by extreme concern for health and bodily functions
2. Depression (D)—an affective disorder usually characterized by sadness, feelings of lack of worth, loss of energy and interest
3. Hysteria (Hy)—a neurotic condition in which physical symptoms are used to avoid or solve conflicts and to avoid reponsibilities
4. Psychopathic Deviate (Pd)—a personality disorder characterized by an extreme and flagrant disregard for social and moral norms

---

[1]Research on the MMPI before 1975 is reviewed extensively in a two-volume MMPI handbook (Dahlstrom, Welsh, & Dahlstrom, 1972, 1975).

[2]Originally, there were eight clinical scales. Masculine-Feminine and Social Introversion were added later.

5. Masculine-Feminine (Mf)—the extent to which the respondent accepts extreme, stereotypic sex roles
6. Paranoia (Pa)—delusions of reference, influence, grandeur, persecution
7. Psychasthenia (Pt)—obsessive-compulsive behavior or thought patterns
8. Schizophrenia (Sc)—a disorder characterized by a lack of connection between affect and cognition
9. Hypomania (Ma)—a disorder characterized by overactivity, flight of ideas, emotional excitement
10. Social Introversion (Si)—a disorder characterized by withdrawal, avoidance of social contact

Self-report measures can be influenced by a number of conscious and unconscious response tendencies, and measures like MMPI that ask many sensitive questions might be especially prone to conscious faking. To aid in the interpretation of MMPI scores, scores on three administrative scales are typically reported:

1. Lie score (L)—a scale made up of items that are quite unlikely to be true and that put the respondent in a very favorable light (e.g., "I never do anything bad"). A high score may indicate an attempt to distort one's responses.
2. Validity score (F)—a scale made up of a set of extremely infrequent responses. A high score may indicate a careless or random response pattern.
3. Correction score (K)—a measure of psychological defensiveness that can indicate a tendency to "fake good" (high score) or "fake bad" (low score). Scores are used to correct certain clinical scales for artificially low scores that might result from defensiveness in responding to the MMPI.

The total set of clinical scores, together with the administrative indexes, is typically displayed on a score profile such as the one shown in Figure 20-1. Scores on each clinical scale are reported on a T-score scale with a mean of 50 and a standard deviation of 10; norms for T-score conversion were obtained from the group of normal control subjects used in constructing the clinical scales (see the following section). Scores of 70 or higher (2 standard deviations above the mean) are considered to have possible clinical significance; scores within 2 standard deviations of the mean are regarded as within the normal range.

Development of the MMPI

The MMPI is an outstanding example of the empirical or criterion-keying approach to test development. The original clinical scales were developed by contrasting the responses of groups of psychiatric patients diagnosed as exhibiting hypochondriasis, depression, paranoia, and other disorders, with the responses of normal subjects, a group primarily composed of approximately 700 visitors to the University of Minnesota hospital. Statements were included in a particular clinical scale if the responses of psychiatric patients exhibiting that particular condition were reliably different from the responses of normal subjects and of patients exhibiting other psychiatric syndromes. The Masculine-Feminine scale is made up of items that are answered differently by apparently normal males and females. The Social Introversion scale is made

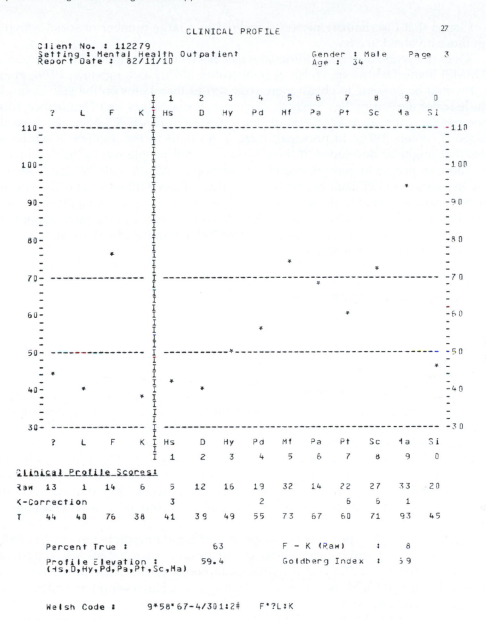

FIGURE 20-1   MMPI Score Profile   *Source:* Minnesota Multiphasic Personality Inventory. Copyright © University of Minnesota, 1942, 1943, (renewed 1970). This form 1948, 1976, 1982. Reprinted by permission of the University of Minnesota Press. "MMPI" and "Minnesota Multiphasic Personality Inventory" are trademarks and owned by the University of Minnesota.

up of items that discriminate persons involved in a large number of social activities
from those involved in a few.

Over the years, over 500 additional scales have been developed from the pool of
550 MMPI items (Dahlstrom, Welsh, & Dahlstrohm, 1975; Faschingbauer, 1979); in theory it would be possible to obtain more scale scores than items on the test. Examples
include scales measuring Ego Strength, Prejudice, Social Status, and Dominance. More
exotic special scales, such as one predicting "Success in Baseball," have also been developed (Clopton, 1979). In principal, there is no limit to the number of additional
scales that might be developed: If the responses of tall people were reliably different
from those of people in general, one could develop an MMPI scale labeled "Height."
Thus, in a sense, it is difficult to describe or evaluate the MMPI itself. The MMPI is not
so much a test as a set of responses from which any number of scales might be devised.
Nevertheless, most applications rely on the ten clinical scales and the three administrative scales; hence, for the most part, our descriptions and evaluations of the MMPI
refer to this standard set of scores.

Interpretation of MMPI Scores

Although as a general rule, scores above 70 on any of the clinical scales are considered potentially significant, scores on individual scales do not yield a simple interpretation. For example, a score of 75 on the depression scale does not lead
automatically to a diagnosis of clinical depression. Rather, patterns or configurations
of test scores are considered in the diagnostic use of the MMPI (Webb & McNamara,
1979). For example, Graham (1977) described a number of 2-point code types based on
profiles grouped according to their two highest clinical scales. Figure 20-2 depicts hypothetical MMPI profiles that illustrate the 2-point code types 12 and 18, together with
a brief description of the modal pattern associated with that code. Although both of
these profiles show elevated scores on the Hypochondriasis scale, the combination of a
high score on this scale with a high score on Depression (code 12) produces a very different diagnosis than a high score on Hypochondriasis coupled with a high score on
Hypomania (code 18).

The 2-point code represents the simplest configural interpretations of the MMPI.
More complex configural interpretations are suggested in several atlases (Dahlstrom,
Welsh, & Dahlstrom, 1972) and actuarial code books (Gilberstadt & Druker, 1965;
Marks & Seeman, 1963; Marks, Seeman, & Haller, 1974). However, little evidence indicates that the complex scoring codes are significantly more valid or more useful than
the simpler 2-point codes (Graham, 1977; Marks et al., 1974). In addition, complex scoring rules are more difficult to apply consistently than the 2-point scoring method. As a
result, although the interpretation of the MMPI is essentially configural, very simple
rules for identifying a small number of possible configurations typically are applied.

A number of computerized MMPI scoring and interpretation services are available in the United States (Fowler, 1979; Graham, 1977; Matarazzo, 1986). These range
from relatively simple machine-scoring systems that provide scores on the clinical

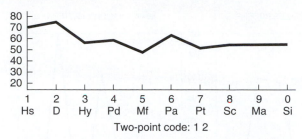

Two-point code: 1 2

Description—characterized by semantic discomfort and pain, with no evidence of organic basis; individuals are anxious, self-conscious, may be prone to excessive use of alcohol.

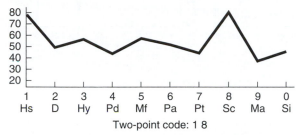

Two-point code: 1 8

Description—individuals harbor feelings of hostility and aggression but cannot express these in an adaptive manner; feel socially inadequate, especially with the opposite sex; may present intense somatic concerns (e.g., severe headaches).

FIGURE 20-2 Hypothetical MMPI Profiles Illustrating Different Two-Point Code Types

scales and several special scales to systems that provide various types of reports, depending on the expertise of the user, and that provide computer-generated narrative reports in addition to scale scores. Figure 20-3 presents an example of a computerized MMPI report.

Computerized interpretation of the MMPI has three obvious advantages. First, computerized systems allow complex scoring rules to be applied in a completely reliable fashion. As long as a set of scoring rules can be translated into a computer program, it is possible to apply these rules consistently to every test processed. Furthermore, it is no more difficult to apply extremely complex scoring rules than it is to apply simple ones. Thus, computerized interpretation services might allow users to obtain the maximum benefit from the configural interpretation of the MMPI.

Second, computerized scoring systems provide a workable means for integrating the vast accumulation of data on the MMPI in interpreting an individual's test scores. For example, Fowler (1979) notes that evidence indicates that the optimal interpretation of test scores may depend on the age, sex, or other demographic characteristics of the respondent. It is unlikely that the individual clinician will be able to take all the relevant demographic variables into account when interpreting each test profile.

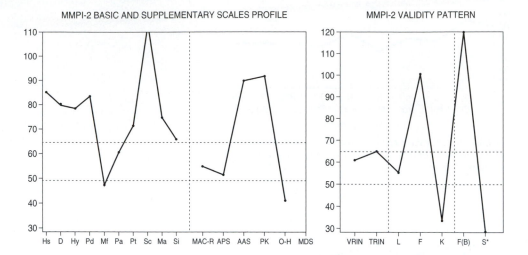

PROFILE VALIDITY

This MMPI-2 profile should be interpreted with caution. There is some possibility that the clinical report is an exaggerated picture of the client's present situation and problems. He is presenting an unusual number of psychological symptoms. This response set could result from poor reading ability, confusion, disorientation, stress, or a need to seek a great deal of attention for his problems.

His test-taking attitudes should be evaluated for the possibility that he has produced an invalid profile. He may be showing a lack of cooperation with the testing or he may be malingering by attempting to present a false claim of mental illness. Determining the sources of his confusion, whether conscious distortion or personality deterioration, is important because immediate attention may be required. Clinical patients with this validity profile are often confused and distractible and have memory problems. Evidence of delusions and thought disorder may be present. He may be exhibiting a high degree of distress and personality deterioration.

The client's responses to items in the latter portion of the MMPI-2 were somewhat exaggerated in comparison to his responses to earlier items. There is some possibility that he become more careless in responding to these later items, thereby raising questions about that portion of the test. Although the standard validity and clinical scales are scored from items in the first two-thirds of the test, caution should be taken in interpreting the MMPI-2 Content Scales and supplementary scales, which include items found throughout the entire item pool.

SYMPTOMATIC PATTERNS

This report was developed using the Hs and Sc scales as the prototype. Individuals with this MMPI-2 clinical profile tend to show a pattern of chronic psychological maladjustment. The client is likely to be a rather ineffective person who is experiencing a great deal of confusion and personality deterioration at this time. He is likely to be chronically disoriented, alienated, and withdrawn. He is reporting vague physical concerns that may have no organic basis and are possibly delusional.

DIAGNOSTIC CONSIDERATIONS

This profile suggests the possibility of a borderline psychotic condition. The existence of somatic delusions and the possibility of Schizophrenia should be considered in developing a diagnosis. Individuals with this profile might be diagnosed as having a severe somatoform disorder in a schizoid or schizotypal personality.

TREATMENT CONSIDERATIONS

Individuals with this MMPI-2 clinical profile are experiencing a severe psychological disorder that requires treatment. They are usually treated with antipsychotic medication.

Patients with this MMPI-2 clinical profile are typically difficult to approach psychotherapeutically. They persistently maintain that the basis of the is problems is physical and are not very willing to accept a psychological interpretation of their difficulties. This individual probably has difficulty verbalizing his feelings and trusting other people; thus, he is not likely to be able to form a working psychotherapeutic relationship. His unusual thinking related to his bodily processes also makes it difficult for him to view his psychological problems in a flexible way.

Behavioral management or psychosocial therapy might be attempted to decrease his somatic complaints and increase his interpersonal adjustment.

FIGURE 20-3 Computerized MMPI Report

Finally, computerized interpretation can be substantially less expensive than individual clinical interpretation. If individual clinical interpretation were the only method available, it is likely that many patients would, for economic reasons, receive no psychological or psychiatric screening (Fowler, 1979).

Most reviews conclude that computerized interpretation of the MMPI is useful, but that it is not an adequate substitute for professional clinical judgment (Graham, 1977; Matarazzo, 1986; see, however, Murphy, 1987a). First, in most clinical applications, the MMPI is not the only test or assessment device employed. Thus, computerized MMPI interpretations do not take into account a good deal of information that is available to the clinician. Second, the validity of the narrative descriptions that form a major part of most computerized MMPI reports is not always well established (Layon, 1984; Meehl, 1972). Since many people overestimate the accuracy of computer-generated reports, it is particularly important to demonstrate the validity of these interpretations. There is a very real possibility that some test users will disregard potentially valid and important information that is at variance with the computer summary. Nevertheless, if proper caution is observed in the use of the reports, computerized MMPI interpretations may be a quite useful addition to the clinician's arsenal.

Evaluation of the MMPI

One of the most striking features of the MMPI is the amount of data available for interpreting and evaluating test scores. The archive of empirical data on the MMPI probably exceeds that available for any other test. For example, Swenson, Pearson, and Osborne (1973) established norms for medical (nonpsychiatric) outpatients on a sample of 50,000 completed MMPIs.

Given the widespread use of the MMPI and the veritable mountain of data available regarding this test, the test itself is a bit disappointing. As we note later, a major revision of the MMPI has helped to overcome some of the shortcomings of the original instrument. However, the transition between the original and the revised MMPI is likely to be long and difficult, and many of the criticisms of the original MMPI raised here will continue to be relevant for a long time to come.

First, the MMPI clinical scales are based on an outmoded set of diagnostic categories; most psychologists refer to the clinical scales by number rather than by name, in part out of recognition of the dubious value of the diagnostic labels attached to each scale (Faschingbauer, 1979; Graham, 1977). Second, the norms that are used to convert raw scores to T scores are widely viewed as unrepresentative. Thus, a T score of 70 indicates a raw score that is 2 standard deviations above the mean. It is not entirely clear, however, whether the mean (or the standard deviation) of the normative sample is in any way representative of the mean that one would expect from the population of people who are now likely to take the test.

There are related concerns regarding the samples of psychiatric patients employed in constructing the original clinical scales, because as few as 50 patients in the psychiatric group were employed in constructing the scales. Updated norms, using larger and more representative groups, have been developed (Colligan, Osborne,

Swenson, & Offord, 1983), but to date, these new norms have not had any major impact on the interpretation of the MMPI.

Evaluations of the measurement properties of the test are not altogether encouraging. As is frequently the case for tests that yield scores on many different scales, the reliability of scores on individual clinical scales is disappointingly low. This problem is offset partially by the use of conservative decision rules in interpreting test scores; for example, scores within 2 standard deviations of the mean, which represent the great majority of test scores, are not considered clinically significant. Nevertheless, the lack of reliability detracts from the potential value of individual scale scores. In addition, scale scores tend to be positively intercorrelated. As a result, persons with high scores on any one scale are likely to show high scores on many, if not most, of the other scales. The fact that the clinical scales tend to be positively correlated severely restricts the usefulness of any configural interpretation of the MMPI.

Meehl (1972) reminds us that it is difficult to evaluate the MMPI itself, independently of the way in which the MMPI is scored or used. Thus, a defect in a particular clinical or research scale is not necessarily a defect in the MMPI itself; the particular scores that are typically obtained using the MMPI are not necessarily the optimal scores for any particular purpose. Thus, deficiencies in interpretation or in the decisions that are made on the basis of the test may reflect an inappropriate choice of scales or scoring strategy, rather than a shortcoming of the test itself.

Meehl notes that the MMPI seldom is used as well as it could be used. For example, a combination of clinical judgment and computerized scoring would probably yield more valid results than are typically obtained using either clinical judgment without the aid of computers or computer judgment. Thus, the question of whether the MMPI is a good or useful test depends as much on the test user's ability to glean relevant information out of the test responses as on the content or form of the test itself.

MMPI-2

In 1990, the first major revision of the MMPI was completed. The University of Minnesota Press discontinued publication and distribution of the original MMPI in 1999; currently the MMPI-2 is the only authorized version of the full MMPI. The test publishers argue that the simultaneous availability of the original and revised forms of the MMPI test has become a source of confusion for test users, and they are probably right.

The MMPI-2 represents the culmination of a long and difficult process of research and test development. (See D. T. Campbell, 1972; Hathaway, 1972; C. Holden, 1986, for discussions of the difficulties in revising a test like the MMPI.) It goes a long way toward solving many of the technical problems noted previously for the MMPI. The MMPI-2 retains the same basic test format as the MMPI, and it reports scores on the same basic scales, together with additional validity scales, new clinical scales, and measures of gender roles; an example of a computerized MMPI-2 report (see Chapter 12) is presented in Figure 20-3.

There are four major features to the revision of the MMPI. First, new items have been written, duplicate items and items with objectionable content have been removed, and the total number of items has been increased to 567. Items have been rearranged so that it is possible to score all the basic scales from the first 370 items, greatly facilitating abbreviated testing sessions. Second, new norms have been developed from larger samples (the total N exceeds 2,500) that are much more representative of the U.S. population than previous normative samples. Third, T scores on the clinical scales have been standardized in a way that makes it easier to validly compare scores across scales. Fourth, content-oriented scales (e.g., scales indicating levels of anxiety, obsessiveness, social discomfort, and family problems) have been added (Butcher, Graham, Williams, & Ben-Porath, 1990). In contrast to the original MMPI, in which scales were developed solely on an empirical basis, these content-oriented scales were developed on a rational basis to provide interpretable measures of constructs judged to be important in assessing personality and clinical disorders.

The MMPI-2 includes three new validity scales. One (Back-F) evaluates responses to infrequently endorsed responses that are near the end of the test. The idea here is that some examinees may begin to respond randomly or carelessly as the test wears on; the Back-F scale can help detect this response pattern. There are two inconsistency scales (Variable Response Inconsistency Scale and True Response Inconsistency Scale) that assess inconsistent or contradictory responses.

To help ease the transition from the MMPI to MMPI-2, efforts were made to ensure that most of the items and many of the special scales developed for the original MMPI survive intact in the MMPI-2 and that score profiles from the two instruments will be comparable (Levitt, 1990; Munley & Zarantonello, 1990). In addition, several handbooks have been developed for applying the MMPI-2, and most of these refer extensively to comparisons between the MMPI and the MMPI-2 (Butcher, 1990; Graham, 1990; Greene, 1991). Empirical assessments suggest high levels of convergence, especially when strict criteria are used to define the MMPI-2 code types (Graham, Timbrook, Ben-Porath, & Butcher, 1991).

The MMPI and MMPI-2 were designed to be administered to adults. The MMPI-A is a version of this inventory that was designed to be used with adolescents (ages 14 to 18). The MMPI-A was developed at about the same time as the MMPI-2 and is very similar in content and in psychometric characteristics to the MMPI-2. The development of the MMPI-A and MMPI-2 has added a degree of breadth and sophistication to the venerable MMPI and has probably extended the life of this instrument for at least a generation. Reviewers (e.g., Nichols, 1992) note that the revised versions of the MMPI retain many of the weaknesses of the original instrument (e.g., the inventory still refers to diagnostic categories that have long been abandoned), but that the new versions of the MMPI are nevertheless useful and are likely to supplant the original MMPI as one of the widely used and widely researched diagnostic inventories.

To assess the status of changing MMPI practice, Downey, Sinnett, and Seeberger (1999) mailed a questionnaire to licensed psychologists, almost all of whom had experience with the MMPI. They found that psychologists are quite likely to use computerized scoring and computerized test administration, but they also found that many practitioners still cling to outmoded systems for interpreting the MMPI, and many incorrectly assumed that the same interpretive standards could be applied to the MMPI-2 as to the MMPI.

THE BENDER-GESTALT

The Bender Visual-Motor Gestalt Test is a deceptively simple measure that is thought to be useful in the differential diagnosis of perceptual disorders and organic brain damage, as well as a diagnosis of many types of psychopathology (e.g., schizophrenia, depression). It is one of the most widely used tests in clinical practice (Raphael, Golden, & Cassidy, 2002; Sellbom & Meunier, 2003); however, evidence for the validity and usefulness of this test is ambiguous, at best. As we note later in this section, there is still some uncertainty about what this test actually measures.

In its simplest form, the Bender-Gestalt is a picture-copying task in which the respondent is required to copy geometric forms similar to those shown in Figure 20-4. In the process of copying the figures, subjects make errors that (it is assumed) are not simply a function of a lack of artistic skill, and these distortions form the basis of the clinical interpretation of the Bender-Gestalt. An example of a Bender-Gestalt protocol produced by a patient suffering from organic brain damage is presented in Figure 20-5.

In developing this test, Bender (1938) applied the principles of Gestalt psychology to the selection of stimulus figures and to the interpretation of distortions made when persons taking the test reproduced the figures. According to Bender, "The final product is a visual motor pattern which reveals modifications in the original pattern by the integrating mechanisms of the individual who has experienced it" (p. 3). More modern interpretations of the Bender-Gestalt have placed less emphasis on the principles of Gestalt psychology and more emphasis on the systematic differences in response as a function of organic brain damage or of psychopathology.[3] Alternative

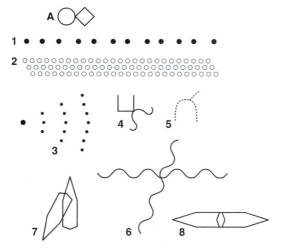

FIGURE 20-4   The Bender-Gestalt Test   *Source:* From Bender Visual-Motor Gestalt Test, published by American Orthopsychiatric Association, 1938.

[3]Several explanations, other than those implied by Gestalt principles, have been offered for the diagnostic power of the Bender-Gestalt. For example, Pascal and Suttell (1951) claim that the test measures, among other things, "attitude toward reality," or the degree to which one is in contact with external reality.

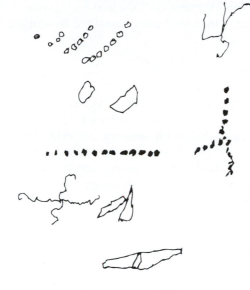

FIGURE 20-5   Bender-Gestalt
Protocols From Patient Suffering
From Organic Brain Damage
Source: From Lacks, 1984, p. 34.
Copyright © 1984 by John Wiley &
Sons. Reprinted by permission.

scoring systems have developed since the test was first introduced (Murray, 2001), and even though there is now better normative data available to interpret Bender-Gestalt scores, there are still serious questions about the construct validity of this test. In particular, there is no agreed-upon theory of what the test measures or what test scores mean.

Interpretation of the Bender-Gestalt

A variety of methods for scoring and interpreting the Bender-Gestalt have been proposed. For example, Spraings (1966) and Labrentz, Linkenhoker, and Aaron (1976) have developed multiple-choice scoring formats. Probably the most widely researched scoring method is referred to as the Hutt adaptation of the Bender-Gestalt (Hutt, 1977). This adaptation treats the Bender-Gestalt as a projective test. It is assumed that, in the process of generating, elaborating, and describing his or her drawings, the respondent projects important needs or conflicts.

The Hutt adaptation consists of three separate phases:

1. Copy phase, in which the respondent is shown the standard set of Bender-Gestalt figures and is asked to copy them freehand
2. Elaboration phase, in which the subject is given both his or her drawings and the original figures and is asked to modify or change the drawings in any way he or she wishes to make them "better" or "more pleasing."

3. Association phase, in which the respondent looks at both the stimulus card and the elaborated drawings and tells the examiner what each figure calls to mind

The interpretation of the respondent's test protocol takes into account the features of the drawings themselves, the types of elaborations done to make the original drawings "better" or "more pleasing," and the associations that they evoke. Table 20-1 lists several of the 26 features of the drawings that are considered in scoring Bender-Gestalt protocols.

Evaluation of the Bender-Gestalt

As was the case with the MMPI, the Bender-Gestalt is regarded as useful in the diagnosis of a wide variety of disorders. For example, Bender's (1938) original manuscript discussed response patterns associated with sensory aphasia, organic brain disease, schizophrenia, manic-depressive psychosis, mental retardation, and psychoneuroses. More recent research suggests that the Bender-Gestalt may be useful in diagnosing depression, anxiety states, and a variety of adjustment problems and learning disorders (Tolor & Brannigan, 1980). As might be expected, given the perceptual-motor emphasis of the test, the Bender-Gestalt is most useful in diagnosing brain damage and other forms of organic dysfunction (Tolor & Brannigan, 1980). Marley (1982) has presented evidence that suggests that the Bender-Gestalt may be used to localize some types of brain pathology and to provide information useful in estimating prognosis under different forms of therapy.

Evidence for the validity of the Bender-Gestalt in the differential diagnosis of nonorganic pathologies is not so well established, although evidence indicates that in psychotic patients, the degree of distortion in Bender-Gestalt drawings is related to the degree of pathology.

As with the MMPI, the Bender-Gestalt is not so much a single, well-defined test as a general technique for diagnosis. The validity of diagnoses based on the Bender-Gestalt depends on a number of factors, such as the particular scoring system chosen and the clinician's skill and reliability in applying that system (Canter, 1996). The reliability and validity of Bender-Gestalt diagnoses also depend on the type of condition being diagnosed and on the level of specificity of the diagnosis. The test is likely to be more successful in diagnosing brain dysfunction than schizophrenia and more useful in making gross diagnoses than in making highly localized diagnoses of lesions or brain damage.

**Table 20-1   SOME OF THE FEATURES CONSIDERED IN SCORING THE
              HUTT ADAPTATION OF THE BENDER-GESTALT TEST**

1. Sequence of drawings	5. Use of margin
2. Position of first drawing	6. Closure difficulty
3. Use of space	7. Simplification
4. Collision	8. Consistency in direction of movement

The essential strategy behind most Bender-Gestalt scoring systems is similar to that employed by the MMPI. With some exceptions, Bender-Gestalt systems are the product not of well-developed theories of psychopathology but, rather, of systematic differences in test responses as a function of type and severity of psychopathology. However, with the exception of multiple-choice versions of the test (e.g., Spraings, 1966), the scoring of the Bender-Gestalt is more subjective than objective. Thus, it is not as easy to apply the empirical criterion-keying strategy to the Bender-Gestalt as is the case with the MMPI. It is therefore even more difficult to determine whether the Bender-Gestalt test is as useful as it could be in diagnosing organic and nonorganic pathologies. Although the Bender-Gestalt is one of the most widely used psychological tests, a Bender-Gestalt database comparable to that which exists for the MMPI is simply not feasible.

SCATTER ANALYSIS

Intelligence tests are widely viewed as useful components of a total diagnostic testing package. Tests such as the Wechsler Intelligence Scale for Children—Third Edition (WISC-III) or the Wechsler Adult Intelligence Scale—Third Edition (WAIS-III), which provide scores on individual scales and subtests, are regarded as especially useful, since they provide information not only about general levels of mental ability but also about patterns of strengths and weaknesses in relatively specific areas of cognitive functioning (Rapaport, Gill, & Schafer, 1968; Robb, Bernardoni, & Johnson, 1972). These patterns of performance, in turn, are believed to have diagnostic significance. For example, both McFie (1960) and Meyer and Jones (1957) claimed that patterns of performance on the WAIS and the WISC, particularly comparisons of verbal and performance scores, could be useful in diagnosing and locating specific types of brain lesions; more recent research supporting these claims is reviewed by Matarazzo and Herman (1985) and Zimmerman and Woo-Sam (1985).

Rapaport, Gill, and Schafer (1968) suggest that comparisons of individual subtest scores can be revealing. For example, a subject who takes the WAIS and receives high scores on the vocabulary and information subtests but a low score on the comprehension subtest is likely to give inappropriate responses to questions as a result of impaired judgment, rather than a lack of knowledge.

The most extensive literature dealing with pattern interpretation of scores on intelligence tests examines the diagnostic significance of differences between verbal and performance IQ scores (Kaufman, 1979; Rapaport, Gill, & Schafer, 1968). The existence of sizable differences in verbal and performance scale scores on tests such as the WISC-III or WAIS-III is believed by many to be significant in the diagnosis of a variety of cognitive, affective, and behavioral disorders. However, reviews of the research on verbal-performance differences suggest considerable inconsistency in the apparent effects of these differences (Dumont & Willis, 1995; Matarazzo, 1972; Zimmerman & Woo-Sam, 1972).

One reason for the inconsistency in the apparent effects of verbal-performance differences is the tendency of some researchers to attempt to interpret relatively trivial differences in scale scores as an indication of clinically significant discrepancies in performance. In fact, examination of the confidence intervals around scores on the WAIS or the WISC suggests that verbal-performance IQ differences of as much as 15 points could be attributed to chance (Kaufman, 1979). A second reason for the inconsistency of the research dealing with verbal-performance difference is the inherent unreliability of difference scores (see Chapter 7). There is some degree of error in the measurement of verbal and performance IQs; a score that represents the difference between these two IQ measures necessarily will be less reliable than either measure.[4]

Limited reliability poses problems when comparing verbal and performance IQ scores, although some investigators question the seriousness of these problems (Matarazzo & Herman, 1985). Such problems probably are most severe when scores on individual subtests are compared. For example, Rapaport et al. (1968) discuss the clinical significance of vocabulary scatter, defined as the difference between the scale score on the WAIS vocabulary subtest and the score on any other subtest. It is quite likely, however, that substantial differences between subtest scores arise through chance alone, since individual subtests show comparatively low levels of reliability (Conger & Conger, 1975). For example, Kaufman (1979) notes that two thirds of all normal children who are tested using the WISC have scale score ranges (difference between highest and lowest subtest score) of 7 ± 2. The maximum possible scale score range is 18, and ranges of 5 points or more often are regarded as significant. Unless we assume that two thirds of all apparently normal children exhibit clinically significant abnormalities in their cognitive functioning, the relatively high frequency of substantial scatter in subtest scores seems to argue against giving such patterns substantial weight in clinical predictions. Charter (2002) reported reliability coefficients as low as .00 (making them no more reliable than a set of random numbers) for some discrepancy scores used in clinical practice.

The most likely explanation for the widespread scatter in subtest scores is the low level of reliability exhibited by many subtests. A good deal of scatter may be attributed to measurement error, rather than to clinically significant differences in specific mental abilities. Although the research evidence clearly indicates that large degrees of scatter are common and that simple measures of scatter are not related in any consistent way to brain damage or to mental dysfunction (Golden, 1990; Kamphaus & Reynolds, 1987; J. J. Ryan, Paolo, & Smith, 1992), many test users still view scatter as useful evidence in forming a diagnosis (Kramer, Henning-Stout, Ullman, & Schellenberg, 1987). In clinical diagnosis, it is not uncommon for personal experience, clinical tradition, and personal beliefs about the effectiveness of specific tests or diagnostic techniques to outweigh beliefs about the effectiveness of specific tests or diagnostic techniques to outweigh negative research results (e.g., tests with doubtful validity, such as the Draw-a-Person Test, are quite popular). However, clinicians are not alone in ignoring evidence that contradicts their preferred methods of practice. As Dawes (1979, 1980) notes, although many

---

[4]Recall from Chapter 7 that the correlation between two tests also affects the reliability of difference scores. Verbal and performance IQ scores are positively correlated, which serves to lower the reliability of their differences.

psychologists are well aware of the doubtful validity of interviews and of subjective methods of judging candidates, they still use them in selecting faculty and students (see Chapter 21 for further discussion of this issue).

The bandwidth-fidelity dilemma described in Chapter 7 has serious implications for the clinical interpretations of patterns of test scores. Basically, there are two choices when the amount of testing time is limited: (1) Measure a few variables with a high degree of accuracy, or (2) measure many variables with very little accuracy. In the context of clinical testing, this dilemma suggests that attempts to measure many different variables (e.g., multiple subtest scores) with a limited number of items, observations, and so on, will often lead to limited reliability in each test score—the more subtests, the lower the reliability of each. Furthermore, the more subtests considered, the more likely that scores on at least two tests will differ substantially. Thus, increasing the number of subtests to be considered in a search for clinically significant patterns (defined by differences between subtest scores) creates a snowball effect: The more tests, the lower the reliability; the lower the reliability, the greater the likelihood that two test scores will differ greatly because of measurement error (chance); and the more unreliable tests compared, the greater the likelihood that an individual will exhibit a substantial range of test scores and the greater the likelihood of a "clinically significant" scatter pattern.

Although reliability considerations limit the usefulness of diagnostic strategies that depend on patterns or configurations of test scores, these strategies are by no means useless. Rather, their application should be limited to specific situations in which several conditions are met.

First, there should be clear evidence that a pattern of test scores has some validity as a predictor of important clinical criteria. Furthermore, consideration of the pattern of test scores must improve the validity of the predictions that could be made on the basis of average test scores alone (Nystedt & Murphy, 1979).

Second, the reliability of individual tests must be considered in determining the significance of apparent patterns obtained in a single test administration. The use of confidence intervals would help discourage the natural tendency to overinterpret patterns that in fact may be due to measurement error, rather than to real differences in the abilities and traits being compared.

Finally, the number of tests being compared and the number of possible patterns under consideration should be as small as possible. If the results of 10 different tests are compared with 45 different diagnostic patterns, the likelihood of a misdiagnosis is considerable. When a smaller number of tests and patterns are considered, the likelihood that test scores will, by chance, match any present pattern is significantly reduced.

DIAGNOSTIC CLASSIFICATION SYSTEMS

Clinical assessment typically results in a classification of the individuals being assessed. For example, a patient at a mental institution may be diagnosed as schizophrenic or as psychotic without signs of schizophrenia. A school psychologist may determine that certain children suffer from specific learning disabilities and on this basis may assign them to special education programs. An industrial psychologist may help in determining which management trainees represent fast-track employees and hence should be given challenging assignments as soon as possible. In each case, the individual being assessed is classified as a member of a specific category of persons who exhibit similar behavior in specific situations and who are demonstrably different from other categories of persons.

In some contexts, classification involves the use of few categories (e.g., learning disabled versus not disabled) that may be poorly defined (e.g., fast-track employees at one company may fail at another). However, in the practice of clinical psychology and psychiatry, a complex, standard set of categories is used to classify or diagnose mental disturbances. The classification system used in the diagnosis of mental illness is described in the American Psychiatric Association's (1994) *Diagnostic and Statistical Manual of Mental Disorders, Fourth Edition,* commonly referred to as DSM-IV. The most recent update of this test (DSM-IV-TR, American Psychiatric Association, 2000) provides additional detail for several diagnostic categories.

DSM-IV

The DSM-IV (American Psychiatric Association, 1994; see also DSM-IV-TR, 2000) is designed to provide clear descriptions of diagnostic categories that enable clinicians to diagnose, treat, study, and communicate about mental disorders. The manual describes nearly 300 diagnostic categories and calls for multiaxial classification, which entails the use of a number of different facets, or axes, in the assessment and diagnosis of an individual patient. The five axes described in the DSM-IV include the following:

Axis I   Clinical disorders and other conditions that may be the focus of clinical attention
Axis II   Personality disorders and mental retardation
Axis III General medical conditions
Axis IV Psychosocial and environmental problems
Axis V   Global assessment of functioning

Axes I and II comprise the primary classification of mental disorders. The possible behavioral effects of physical disorders are recognized in Axis III. Axis IV represents the clinician's assessment of the severity of occupational, financial, legal, familial, and other psychosocial and emotional stressors affecting the individual. Finally, Axis V represents the clinician's assessment of how well the individual has adapted to the demands of everyday life.

Some of the axes of DSM-IV require the clinician to identify specific disorders or conditions (e.g., Axes I, II, and III), whereas others require ratings on a continuum. For example, assessment of Axis V (global assessment of functioning) requires a rating on the 100-point scale illustrated in Table 20-2. In DSM-IV, mental disorders are defined as involving clinically significant impairment or distress, and assessments of global functioning levels can provide critical information for determining whether a disorder is present.

Table 20-2   GLOBAL ASSESSSMENT OF FUNCTIONING SCALE

Consider psychological, social, and occupational functioning on a hypothetical continuum of mental health—illness. Do not include impairment in functioning due to physical (or environmental) limitations.

Code	(**Note:** Use intermediate codes when appropriate, e.g., 45, 68, 72.)
100 | 91	**Superior functioning in a wide range of activities, life's problems never seem to get out of hand, is sought out by others because of his or her many positive qualities. No symptoms.**
90 | 81	**Absent or minimal symptoms** (e.g., mild anxiety before an exam), **good functioning in all areas, interested and involved in a wide range of activities, socially effective, generally satisfied with life, no more than everyday problems or concerns** (e.g., an occasional argument with family members).
80 | 71	**If symptoms are present, they are transient and expectable reactions to psychosocial stressors** (e.g., difficulty concentrating after family argument); **no more than slight impairment in social, occupational, or school functioning** (e.g., temporarily falling behind in schoolwork).
70 | 61	**Some mild symptoms** (e.g., depressed and mood and mild insomnia) **OR some difficulty in social, occupational, or school functioning** (e.g., occasional truancy, or theft within the household), **but generally functioning pretty well, has some meaningful interpersonal relationships.**
60 | 51	**Moderate symptoms** (e.g., flat affect and circumstantial speech, occasional panic attacks) **OR moderate difficulty in social, occupational, or school functioning** (e.g., few friends, conflicts with peers or co-workers).
50 | 41	**Serious symptoms** (e.g., suicidal ideation, severe obsessional rituals, frequent shoplifting) **OR any serious impairment in social, occupational, or school functioning** (e.g., no friends, unable to keep a job).
40 | 31	**Some impairment in reality testing or communication** (e.g., speech is at times illogical, obscure, or irrelevant) **OR major impairment in several areas, such as work or school, family relations, judgment, thinking, or mood** (e.g., depressed man avoids friends, neglects family, and is unable to work; child frequently beats up younger children, is defiant at home, and is failing at school).
30 | 21	**Behavior is considerably influenced by delusions or hallucinations OR serious impairment in communication or judgment** (e.g., sometimes incoherent, acts grossly inappropriately, suicidal preoccupation) **OR inability to function in almost all areas** (e.g., stays in bed all day; no job, home, or friends).
20 | 11	**Some danger of hurting self or others** (e.g., suicide attempts without clear expectation of death; frequently violent; manic excitement) **OR occasionally fails to maintain minimal personal hygiene** (e.g., smears feces) **OR gross impairment in communication** (e.g., largely incoherent or mute).
10 | 1	**Persistent danger of severely hurting self or others** (e.g., recurrent violence) **OR persistent inability to maintain minimal personal hygiene OR serious suicidal act with clear expectation of death.**
0	Inadequate information.

Source: Reprinted with permission from the *Diagnostic and Statistical Manual of Mental Disorders, Fourth Edition.* Copyright © 1994 American Psychiatric Association.

DSM-IV is essentially a medical taxonomy that attempts to classify mental disorders in the same way that medical taxonomies classify diseases. DSM-IV was designed to be compatible with current and future international systems for classifying diseases (e.g., ICD-10; Kendell, 1991). Companion volumes, such as the *DSM-IV Casebook* (Spitzer, Gibbon, Skodol, Williams, & First, 1994) and the *DSM-IV Guidebook* (Frances, First, & Pincus, 1995) are designed to help clinicians learn and apply this diagnostic system.

As mentioned, DSM-IV is the fourth edition of a widely used manual. Changes in this manual often reflect broad changes in the way that clinicians think about and classify mental disorders. For example, early editions of the DSM distinguished neuroses from psychoses, on the basis of the assumption that different symptoms and etiologies were involved. The term *neuroses* is no longer used by scientists, and the term was dropped when the third edition of the manual was prepared. A major change in preparing DSM-IV is that there is no longer any attempt to distinguish organic from nonorganic syndromes. In part, this reflects steady progress over the last several years in understanding the relationship between biological processes and behavior; it now seems naive to assume that investigations of how the brain functions are important for understanding some disorders and irrelevant to understanding others.

Previous revisions of DSM have sometimes been the focus of heated controversy (McReynolds, 1989), particularly with regard to the scientific justification (or lack thereof) of specific diagnostic categories. In preparing DSM-IV, careful attention was given to this issue; the results of extensive literature reviews, field trials, and reanalyses supporting the structure of DSM-IV are reported in a multivolume series entitled *DSM-IV Sourcebook* (for Volume 1, see Widiger et al., 1994). This work seems to have paid off; DSM-IV seems to have made better use of the body of research on mental disorders than its predecessors (Clark, Watson, & Reynolds, 1995). There are, of course, criticisms of DSM-IV (e.g., Caplan, 1995), but so far DSM-IV seems to have received a more cordial welcome than some other versions of this manual (e.g., criticism of DSM-III was so intense that a revision was needed shortly after its release, leading to DSM-III-R).

The most serious criticism of DSM-IV is that it continues to rely on a categorical system of diagnosis. That is, individuals diagnosed under DSM-IV are sorted into one of nearly 300 categories. A number of serious problems occur with a categorical approach, but the two that are most frequently discussed are the sheer number of categories and comorbidity (Clark et al., 1995). As we note later, the number of categories needed to build a reasonably comprehensive system greatly limits the usefulness of this approach. Diagnoses that require choosing among hundreds of categories might be better made by assessing patients on a small number of dimensions.

The term *comorbidity* refers to the fact that individuals rarely come to a psychiatrist or a clinical psychologist with one well-defined problem. Clark et al. (1995) note that comorbidity estimates in the range of 60% to 80% are common (i.e., in some studies only 20% to 40% of those diagnosed appear to fit in a single diagnostic category). In earlier versions of DSM, clinicians were forced to choose among possible categories, and although rigid exclusionary rules are no longer part of DSM, the very fact that diagnoses are categorical, whereas the problems seen by clinicians are not, suggests a serious problem with the structure of DSM-IV.

Is Clinical Diagnosis Useful?   The debate over the relative merits and demerits of DSM-IV is part of a larger debate over the relative merits of psychological diagnosis itself. In medical settings, diagnosis is clearly important, since different medical treatments are necessary for different diseases. For example, a patient suffering from chronic high blood pressure should receive different treatment from that for a patient with leukemia. However, in the case of psychological disturbances, it is not always clear whether accurate diagnosis is necessary, or even helpful, for the choice of appropriate therapies or treatments (in part because of the weak research base of many therapies; Lilienfeld, Lynn, & Lohr, 2002).

Two conditions must be met to demonstrate the usefulness of psychological diagnoses. First, different treatments (e.g., psychotherapy, hospitalization, drug therapy, no treatment) must be indicated for individuals who receive different diagnoses. Second, the treatments must be differentially valid for people with different diagnoses.[5] In other words, if different treatments are chosen for individuals who receive varying diagnoses, it must be demonstrated that it makes a difference which persons are assigned to which treatments. Differential diagnosis of psychopathology would clearly not be useful if everyone received the same therapy, regardless of their diagnosis, or if the success of a particular course of therapy did not depend in any way on the diagnosis.

Some evidence indicates that gross differences in diagnosis have value in choosing treatments. The course of treatment that is most likely to alleviate depressive symptoms differs from the treatment that would be chosen in cases of mental retardation, phobia, or sociopathic personality disorder. In some cases, more detailed diagnoses may have clear treatment implications (Rahman & Eysenck, 1978). However, little evidence indicates that the hundreds of diagnostic categories that make up the DSM-IV all have different implications for treatment (Clark et al., 1995; R. C. Miller & Berman, 1983; M. Smith & Glass, 1977). Thus, the value of distinguishing among hundreds of different types of pathology, as opposed to a very small number of major syndromes, is in doubt; little evidence has been presented to date to suggest that all these different categories of psychopathology would call for different types of treatment. As a result, the usefulness of fine-grained psychological diagnoses such as those suggested by DSM-IV is questionable.

Eysenck, Wakefield, and Friedman (1983) note that psychological problems are generally not analogous to medical diseases in that psychological problems are often extreme examples of behavior that is exhibited by "normal" persons every day, whereas many medical problems represent separate categories that often can be traced to a single pathogen (see also, Frances et al., 1991; Millon, 1991). As long as the diagnostic classification systems in use are drawn up by psychiatrists, the medical tradition of categorical diagnosis is likely to persist. It is likely, though, that the most useful diagnostic systems eventually will adopt a dimensional rather than a categorical approach (Clark et al., 1995; Eysenck et al., 1983; Lang, 1978). That is, rather than assigning each individual being assessed to a discrete diagnostic category (e.g., a typical paranoid disorder), it might be useful to describe each individual along several psychologically meaningful and adequately measured dimensions. Examples include

---

[5]Cronbach and Snow (1977) make a similar argument in evaluating educational programs.

intelligence, extroversion, psychoticism, and neuroticism (Eysenck, 1976, 1981). Thus, rather than saying that a patient is suffering from a borderline conversion disorder, it might be more useful to describe the individual's functioning in terms of a relevant set of cognitive, emotional, and behaviorial dimensions.

The debate over the utility of clinical diagnosis is related to a somewhat more narrow debate over the contribution of psychological tests and assessment devices to the treatment of psychological and behavioral disorders. Hayes, Nelson, and Jarrett (1987) note that despite the long history of the clinical application of psychological assessment, "clinical assessment has not yet proven its value in fostering favorable treatment outcomes" (p. 963). They identified several problems with current research on the utility of psychological assessment for diagnosis and the selection of treatments, and they proposed an integrated framework for designing, conducting, and evaluating research on this critical topic. We agree that there is a substantial need for more and better research on the contribution of psychological assessment to clinical practice, but we are pessimistic about the possibility of this research happening, at least in the short run. Throughout the long history of clinical assessment and treatment, research on validity and utility has been a very low priority, and the research that has been carried out is often ignored by practitioners. It seems likely that clinical lore and subjective judgments will continue to play a dominant role in assessments of the extent to which psychological tests and assessment devices contribute to treatment outcomes.

CRITICAL DISCUSSION:
Professional Ethics and Clinical Testing

Psychological tests are an important part of the process of clinical diagnosis, and some of the tests used by clinicians are so poorly constructed, administered, or scored that they are at best worthless. In the preceding chapter and in this one, we discussed tests such as the Rorschach Inkblot Test, the Thematic Apperception Test, the Draw-a-Person Test, and the Bender-Gestalt. Literally thousands of studies have been conducted of these and similar tests, and the results of this research are absolutely clear. These tests, as typically used in clinical practice, are not valid measures and do not contribute to the accuracy or usefulness of clinical diagnoses. Claims by individual clinicians that they find the tests useful and valid are simply inconsistent with the results of empirical research.

In his book *House of Cards: Psychology and Psychotherapy Built on Myth,* Dawes (1994) forcefully raises the question of whether the use of tests and assessment methods that either have not yet been shown to be valid or whose lack of validity has been convincingly shown is consistent with professional ethics. The "Ethical Principles of Psychologists and Code of Conduct" (American Psychological Association, 2002), reproduced in Appendix B of this text, states that "Psychologists administer, adapt, score, interpret, or use assessment techniques, interviews, tests, or instruments in a manner and for purposes that are appropriate in light of the research on or evidence of the usefulness and proper application of the techniques" (Principle 9.02a). It is difficult to see how the typical administration and use of the Rorschach or the Draw-a-Person Test in clinical settings could be consistent with this principle (Lilienfeld et al., 2002; Wood, Nezworski, Lilienfeld, & Garb, 2003). There have been calls to limit the use of such tests (e.g., Garb, 1999, called for a moratorium on the use of the Rorschach; see also Wood et al., 2003), but to our knowledge, there have not yet been sucessful challenges to these tests on ethical grounds. Perhaps it is time for such a challenge.

To make matters worse, abundant evidence indicates that many of these tests can be improved, simply by developing valid standardized scoring systems. The best example is the Exner system for scoring the Rorschach. Similarly, a great deal of research, some of which will be reviewed in the chapter that follows, demonstrates that clinical assessment and diagnosis can be improved by incorporating base rate information, computerized decision aids, and statistical (as opposed to intuitive) prediction models. Sadly, little evidence shows that clinicians are willing to incorporate these improvements, and a great deal of evidence shows that they continue to rely on tests and assessment methods that are either unproved or known to be faulty. Dawes (1994) offers the following advice: "If a professional psychologist is 'evaluating' you in a situation where you are at risk, and asks you for responses to ink blots or to incomplete sentences, or for a drawing of anything, walk out of that psychologist's office. Going through with such an examination creates a danger of having serious decisions made about you on totally invalid grounds" (pp. 152–153). Although this advice may sound harsh, we believe that the time has passed when professional psychologists can ignore the body of research showing that widely used tests and assessment devices simply do not work. Professional ethics require that credible evidence supports the use of tests to make important decisions about people, and the knowing use of invalid tests by a psychologist appears to constitute a serious breach of professional ethics.

NEUROPSYCHOLOGICAL ASSESSMENT

The relationship between the brain and behavior is one of the most important and active areas of research in psychology and is also one that unites the interests of researchers in a wide range of fields. One of the many applications of this research is in the field of clinical neuropsychology. Clinical neuropsychologists work with assessment of memory disorders, brain injury, cerebral disorders, Alzheimer's disease, attention disorders, learning disabilities, and mental retardation (Horton, 1997a). They often work in conjunction with neurologists (who usually specialize in the peripheral nervous system), psychiatrists (who often need assistance in evaluating neural bases of behavior impairments), practitioners in vocational education and rehabilitation medicine (e.g., examining the impact of brain injuries on ability to return to work) and clinical psychologists, and they provide important information about the possible neural bases of behavioral dysfunctions. Neuropsychological assessments typically include a range of methods, from simple tests to complex neuroimaging techniques (for a thorough review of imaging techniques, see Bigler, Lowry, & Porter, 1997). This chapter discusses tests that are widely used in neuropsychological assessment, as well as special issues encountered when using psychological tests in neuropsychological assessment.

The Halstead-Reitan Neuropsychological Test Battery and the Luria-Nebraska Neuropsychological Battery represent the most widely used neuropsychological tests (Horton, 1997a). However, the range of tests that are used in neuropsychological assessment is extensive. Lezak (1995) provides a compendium of dozens of tests that are used in neuropsychological assessment in the areas of orientation and attention, perception, memory, verbal functioning and language skills, construction and drawing, concept formation and reasoning, and executive functioning and motor performance. One reason for the wide range of tests is that neuropsychological assessments often involve the use of multiple tests. For example, Lezak (1995) describes a testing protocol for a patient with epilepsy that includes four attention measures, six memory tests, three verbal tests, two figure construction tests, two sensory-motor tests, and two inventories designed to measure emotional status. A similar protocol for assessing a patient with multiple sclerosis included 15 different tests.

Testing and Neuropsychological Assessment

Brain damage and other neurological problems often affect a person's cognitive, emotional, and psychomotor functioning (Uomoto, 1991). Furthermore, damage to specific portions of the brain can affect highly specific functions. It should be possible, therefore, to use performance on a variety of psychological tests to assist in the diagnosis of several types of brain damage and dysfunction (R. L. Kane, 1986). This is exactly what is done by clinical neuropsychologists. Tests such as the Bender-Gestalt, discussed in the previous section, are often useful in such assessments. In addition to the Bender-Gestalt, neuropsychologists employ three broad classes of tests, brief screening tests, tests of specific neuropsychological functions, and neuropsychological test batteries. Screening tests are often short and imprecise, but they are used to make tentative rather than final decisions (see Chapter 7); people who perform poorly on screening tests often receive more extensive follow-up testing. Tests that are geared toward assessing specific functions are sometimes part of this follow-up. Finally, broad-based test batteries are an important part of the neuropsychologists' inventory.

Screening Tests. Neuropsychological screening tests typically do not provide a detailed assessment or diagnosis, but they can provide a useful first step in determining what sorts of assessments are needed or justified (Berg, 1997). The 7-Minute Screen is an example of such a screening test that has received considerable attention in recent years.

Solomon et al. (1998) note that this test is a highly sensitive tool for making initial diagnoses of Alzheimer's disease (see also Solomon & Pendlebury, 1998). The 7-Minute Screen—which consists of four brief tests that focus on orientation, memory, visuospatial skills, and expressive language (enhanced cued recall, temporal orientation, verbal fluency, and clock drawing)—has shown high levels of reliability and considerable sensitivity in distinguishing between patients experiencing cognitive changes related to the normal aging process and those experiencing cognitive deficits related to disorders such as Alzheimer's disease.

One test used to evaluate orientation asks subjects to identify the present month, date, year, day of the week, and time of day. The degree of error is graded, so that a 1-day error in date is scored as 1, whereas a 1-month error is scored as 5 errors. In a memory test, subjects are asked to identify 16 items drawn on 4 cards, with the help of a clue or hint from the tester (e.g., "there's a piece of fruit on this page—what is it?"). After successful identification, the card is hidden, and the subject is asked to recall the item after being given the clue again. After all 4 cards have been completed, the subject is distracted by having him or her recite the months of the year backward. The subject is then asked to recall as many of the 16 items as possible, without hints. Visuospatial skills are measured by having the subject draw a clock face, with the hands drawn at 20 minutes before 4 o'clock. Scoring is based on the correctness of the drawing (e.g., the hour hand should be shorter than the minute hand). To test expressive language or verbal fluency, the subject is asked to name as many animals as possible within 1 minute.

Test-retest reliabilities for individual tests ranged from 0.83 to 0.93. Test-retest reliability for the entire battery was 0.91. Interrater reliability for the entire battery was 0.92. Estimates of validity have largely generally been presented in terms of ability to distinguish Alzheimers' patients from other patients, and in virtually all cases, the 7-Minute Screen has been extremely sensitive (Tsolaki, Iakovidou, Papadopoulou, Aminta, Nakopoulou, Pantaxi, & Kazis, A., 2002). These studies have been based on somewhat small samples, but they are highly encouraging.

Table 20-3 presents examples of several other neurological screening tests. Brief assessments can be used to evaluate attention, memory, and verbal performance; although none of these tests is itself an overly impressive measure, they can be highly effective as initial screens.

Tests of Specific Neuropsychological Functions. Spreen and Strauss (1991) describe a wide variety of tests used in neuropsychological assessment. They note that many of the tests used by practicing neuropsychologists to evaluate specific neuropsychological functions are experimental in nature or are developed by in-house research teams, so information about the norms and psychometric characteristics of these tests is often unavailable. The Wechsler Memory Scale is an important exception.

The Wechsler Memory Scale—Revised (Wechsler, 1987) contains a variety of subtests designed to tap different aspects of short-term memory, including (1) Mental Control (ability to correctly say a series of letters or numbers); (2) Figural Memory

Table 20-3   EXAMPLES OF NEUROPSYCHOLOGICAL SCREENING TESTS

Attention tests
Digit Span—similar to tests used in WISC-III, digit span backward is a more sensitive indication of brain dysfunction than a simple forward memorization test
Continuous Performance Tasks—perform simple mental tasks, such as signaling whenever the letter "C" is read from a randomized list
Cancellation tests—cross out a target letter from a randomized list

Memory tests
Logical Memory scale (WAIS-R)—repeat a story, immediately and after delay
Inglis Memory Task—learn word pairs (*cabbage–pen*), respond with paired word when initial word (cabbage) is read out
Rey-Osterrieth Complex Figure Test—immediate and delayed recall of complex drawn figure

Verbal
Boston Naming Test—name 60 line drawings
Controlled Word Association Test—name as many words as possible starting with a particular letter

(recognition memory for abstract designs); (3) Logical Memory (ability to recall ideas in stories presented verbally); (4) Visual Paired Associates (ability to learn simple associations); (5) Visual Reproduction (ability to draw geometric designs after brief exposure); (6) Digit Span (ability to repeat sets of digits either forward or backward); and (7) Visual Memory Span (ability to duplicate the sequence of colors touched by the examiner). The Wechsler Memory Test—Third Edition (WMS-III) has shown evidence of both reliability (test-retest reliabilities in the .70s, interscorer reliabilities in the .90s) and construct validity. The test manual also provides unusually good normative information, making WMS-III one of the most psychometrically sophisticated instruments commonly used for neuropsychological assessment (Butler, Retzlaff, & Vanderploeg, 1991; Reynolds, 2001).

The tasks included on the Wechsler Memory Scale and on other neuropsychological test batteries are usually quite simple in the sense that individuals with no impairment do very well on most of these tasks. Neuropsychological assessment is often reserved for individuals who show some evidence of severe impairment on one or more cognitive or behavioral functions, especially when there are reasons to suspect organic brain damage (e.g., in cases of severe cognitive deficits that emerge after exposure to toxic substances). Despite the proven validity of some neuropsychological tests, the results of neuropsychological assessments are not always viewed as reliable. In particular, several court cases in the last few years have involved the use of neuropsychological assessments as evidence of brain damage in lawsuits over industrial accidents, exposure to toxins, and the like. In most cases, the courts have been reluctant to admit the testimony of psychologists regarding diagnoses of brain damage or dysfunction, largely on the basis of the nonmedical nature of the diagnoses. Whereas the courts are likely to admit the testimony of neurologists, especially if their opinions are based on standard medical tests, they often question psychologists' ability and expertise in diagnosing brain damage. Wide-ranging test batteries might provide more compelling evidence of the validity of neuropsychological assessments.

Neuropsychological Test Batteries. Horton (1997b) noted that the Halstead-Reitan Neuropsychological Test Battery is the most widely used neuropsychological test battery, in part because of the extensive base of research on its validity and the availability of credible norms for the test. The Halstead-Reitan is usually administered together with a test of cognitive ability (e.g., an age-appropriate version of the WAIS), but even without this supplemental test, it can take 5 to 6 hours to administer.

The major subtests of this battery (see Horton, 1997b) include the following:

1. *Category test.* This is a test of visual concept formation, in which the examinee is asked to determine what principle or principles several stimulus items have in common.
2. *Tactual Performance.* This is a test in which the examinee is blindfolded and asked to place shaped blocks into corresponding holes on a formboard and then to draw the board and place the blocks from memory.
3. *Speech Sounds test.* The examinee is asked to match spoken words to alternatives in a multiple-choice test sheet.

4. *Rhythm test.* The examinee is asked to determine whether pairs of rhythmic beats are identical or different.

5. *Trail Making test.* The examinee is asked to draw a line connecting consecutively numbered circles or alternating numbers and letters (e.g., 1-A-2-B-3-C, etc.) printed on a page.

6. *Finger Oscillation test.* This is a test of finger tapping speed.

7. *Reitan-Indiana Aphasia Screening test.* This is a gross measure of language skill used to assess difficulties in reading, writing, spelling, naming, counting, and so on.

8. *Reitan-Klove Lateral Dominance examination.* This test uses a series of simple physical tasks (e.g., kicking an imaginary ball) to assess preferences for hand, foot, and eye use.

9. *Strength of grip.* A dynometer is used to test hand-grip strength.

The Halstead-Reitan yields a number of scores, including several general impairment indices (Horton, 1997b). Many of the tests in this battery are sensitive to the subject's age, education, or gender, and separate age and gender norms are often used in evaluating scores on various tests. The subtests in this battery vary considerably in their reliability and diagnostic sensitivity, but evidence shows that the Halstead-Reitan can contribute to the accuracy of neuropsychological diagnoses. In particular, a number of tests in the battery can be used to help identify the location, type, and status of brain lesions (Reitan & Wolfson, 2004). However, because this battery yields such a variety of scores on individual tests and composites, it can be difficult to determine the overall psychometric quality of the Halstead-Reitan. Probably the most useful score coming out of this test battery is provided by the General Neuropsychological Deficit Scale (a composite of 42 separate scores from the test battery), which has been shown to be a valid indicator of the presence or absence of cerebral damage (Reitan & Wolfson, 2004)

Moses (1997) reviewed research on the Luria-Nebraska Neuropsychological Battery (see also Leark, 2004, who reviews the childrens' version of this battery). The Luria-Nebraska has two forms (with 269 and 279 items, respectively), and it can usually be administered in 2 to 3 hours. Like the Halstead-Reitan, this battery is usually administered together with a measure of general cognitive ability, normally the WAIS.

The Luria-Nebraska is built around the idea that behavior involves sensory input, cognitive processing, and behavioral responses, and that disruptions in any of these three areas can be manifest in behavior. This battery includes 11 clinical scales and 5 summary scales, which are listed in Table 20-4.

All of the clinical and summary scales yield reliable scores. Coefficient alphas are .80 or higher for all scales, test-retest reliabilities are in the .80 to .95 range, and inter-rater reliabilities are similarly high (Moses, 1997). Moses (1984a, 1984b, 1984c) reports the results of several factor-analytic studies that support the factor structure of this test. Purisch (2001) reviews evidence for the predictive validity of Luria-Nebraska scores. However, because many of the tasks included in this test are relatively simple, the Luria-Nebraska may not be useful for screening high-functioning examinees. When used with low-functioning examinees, this battery is a valid predictor of several neurological criteria, but with examinees who are less obviously impaired, it might not provide much useful diagnostic information (Golden, 2004).

Table 20-4   SCALES OF THE LURIA-NEBRASKA NEUROPSYCHOLOGICAL BATTERY

Clinical scales

C1	Motor—involves a graded variety of movements of hands, arm, and face
C2	Rhythm—simple and complex pitch and rhythm discrimination
C3	Tactile—finger sensation and discrimination scale
C4	Visual—visual naming of clear and degraded pictures
C5	Receptive speech—appropriate response to simple verbal directions
C6	Expressive speech—repetition of words and word series of increasing complexity
C7	Writing—sequencing letters, spelling, copying, writing words
C8	Reading—reading material ranging from single words to paragraphs
C9	Arithmetic—number recognition, calculation, analysis of arithmetic symbols
C10	Memory—recall of words, visual stimuli, stories, visual arrays
C11	Intellectual processes—conceptual analysis of pictures and texts, mental calculation

Summary scales

S1	Pathognomic—empirically derived scales that distinguish brain dysfunctional patients from controls
S2	Left hemisphere—motor and tactile items from C1 and C3 scales performed with right hand
S3	Right hemisphere—motor and tactile items from C1 and C3 scales performed with left hand
S4	Profile elevation—experimental empirically derived scale that appears to indicate acuteness of brain dysfunction
S5	Impairment—experimental empirically derived scale that appears to indicate global cognitive deficit

In evaluating the validity of neuropsychological test batteries, it is important to distinguish between the measurement validity of each subtest (e.g., does the Motor scale of the Luria-Nebraska provide a valid measure of Motor performance?) and the validity of diagnoses and decisions that are made on the basis of test scores. The relationship between neuropsychological test batteries and diagnoses is far from simple, and different neuropsychologists looking at the same set of test scores might arrive at different diagnoses. As is the case with many other diagnostic tests, the validity of the Halstead-Reitan or the Luria-Nebraska is not a simple function of the test itself but is also a function of how the test is used.

Special Issues in Neuropsychological Test Administration

Sbordone (1997) notes that the usual practice of testing people in quiet, structured, calm environments can decrease the validity of neuropsychological tests, especially when assessing individuals with specific dysfunctions (e.g., orbital frontal lobe pathologies). Many people can function in calm, structured environments but fall apart in noisy, distracting, or demanding environments. Lezak (1995) also noted that testing environments may need to be tailored to the examinees. Because these tests are used in quite special populations, general evidence of their reliability, validity, and performance under normal testing conditions is not always useful for assessing the tests.

Neuropsychological tests might work best in settings where examinees are asked to function in a natural environment rather than in the sort of controlled environment that is sought for most other types of testing. In Chapter 1, we noted that standardization is an important issue in psychological testing. However, when symptoms of a neurological disorder are more clearly manifest in a noisy, confusing, unstructured environment than in a quiet, calm setting, it might be necessary to sacrifice some level of standardization to obtain accurate diagnoses.

Computerized testing has not made the sorts of inroads in neuropsychological assessment that it has in other contexts (Horton, 1997a), but some computerized tests are widely used. Examples include MicroCog, Cognitive Screen—Aeromedical Edition, and Neurobehavioral Evaluation System 2 (R. L. Kane & Reeves, 1997). Evidence indicates that computerized tests have comparable psychometric characteristics to their paper-and-pencil counterparts (K. A. Campbell et al., 1999), and it is likely that these tests will soon take greater advantage of the technological advances associated with computerized testing (see Chapter 12). However, neuropsychologists' reliance on large numbers of short and simple tests may reduce the attractiveness of computerization. For example, some of the tests in the 7-Minute Screen are very simple (e.g., show the subject a picture of a tiger, and a minute later, ask the subject whether he or she remembers what he or she saw in the picture), and computerized administration or scoring has few meaningful advantages. Some tests likely will move toward computerization, but it is unlikely that paper-and-pencil tests will disappear any time soon in the practice of neuropsychological assessment.

SUMMARY

A wide variety of tests are used for diagnostic purposes in clinical settings; this chapter has discussed only a handful of the available tests. The Minnesota Multiphasic Personality Inventory (MMPI) is one of the most widely researched psychological tests, and it continues to be used in contexts ranging from clinical diagnosis to personnel selection (although the validity of this instrument for that purpose is doubtful; Lowman, 1989). The release of the MMPI-2 represents an advance along several fronts. First, the test now incorporates both empirical and rational test-development strategies (see Chapter 11). The continued use of the empirically developed scales maximized the comparability of MMPI and MMPI-2, while the addition of content-oriented scales addresses one of the most frequent criticisms of this inventory. Second, better norms, scoring procedures, and validity research make the interpretation of MMPI-2 considerably simpler than was true for MMPI.

The Bender Visual-Motor Gestalt Test is used for a variety of purposes, from neuropsychological assessment to psychiatric diagnosis. A variety of other tests are used in neuropsychological assessment, ranging from short screening tests designed to assess specific conditions (e.g., the 7-Minute Screen, which is used in evaluating

Alzheimer's disease) to test batteries that can take over an hour to administer (e.g., Luria-Nebraska Test Battery). One common practice in neuropsychological assessment, the use of scatter (i.e., differences among subtest scores) in diagnosing brain damage and learning disabilities, presents some serious problems. Differences among test scores can arise for a number of reasons, and many instances of "clinically significant" scatter appear to represent nothing more than measurement error.

The diagnostic classification system embodied in DSM-IV has several appealing features, including the use of multiaxial diagnosis and attempts to increase the scientific credibility of the diagnostic categories and rules in DSM-IV. However, the contribution of a well-defined diagnostic classification scheme is not as clear for psychological and psychiatric complaints as for some purely medical ones. Although DSM-IV will probably contribute to the reliability of diagnoses, it is not clear whether it will make a large contribution to the usefulness of these diagnoses.

PROBLEMS AND SOLUTIONS—RECAP

The Problem

Mitch is a 9-year-old who received discrepant scores on the verbal (55th percentile) and nonverbal (40th percentile) sections of a cognitive ability. The psychologist who administers the test suggests that this difference might be clinically significant. You are not sure. What else would you need to know to evaluate the psychologist's diagnosis?

A Solution

First and foremost, you would need to know a good deal about the reliability of the verbal and nonverbal sections of the test. Differences in scale scores or in subtest scores can arise as a result of measurement error, and you would certainly want to rule this explanation out. Second, you would need to know the correlation between the two sections of the test. In general, most measures of intelligence are positively correlated, and as we showed in Chapter 7, differences in scores on positively correlated tests are considerably *less* reliable than scores obtained from two independent measures.

Earlier in this chapter, we noted that "clinically significant" scatter in subtests on the WISC occurs in nearly 2/3 of all children tested, and that much of this scatter is explainable in terms of the limited reliability of WISC discrepancy scores. Unless the evidence for the reliability of both the subtests and the discrepancy scores is compelling, we are deeply suspicious of diagnoses based on differences in performance on various sections of a test of cognitive ability.

KEY TERMS

Clinical scales   scales on the MMPI that identify individuals whose responses are most similar to individuals in specific diagnostic groups

DSM-IV   diagnostic classification system currently used by psychologists and psychiatrists for classifying mental disorders

Global assessment of functioning   assessment of overall ability to function in day-to-day life that is used as part of the diagnostic process with DSM-IV

Hutt adaptation   adaptation of Bender Visual-Motor Gestalt Test that treats it as a projective test

Inconsistency scales   scales embedded in diagnostic instruments that assess consistency in responding to the same question or to equivalent questions

Lie scale   administrative scale on MMPI made up of items that are socially desirable but very unlikely to be true

Neuropsychological assessment   use of psychological tests and performance on motor and cognitive tasks to diagnose neurological disorders

Scatter analysis   use of differences in performance on various sections of intelligence tests to help diagnose learning disorders and neurological disorders

Two-point code   method of interpreting MMPI scores that focuses on the two highest clinical scores in a profile

21

Issues in Multimethod Assessment

Intelligence tests, personality tests, behavioral assessments, and clinical interviews all yield potentially important information about the person being tested, but none of these techniques provides an overall assessment of the examinee's level of functioning. In other words, no individual test provides a complete picture of the individual; it provides only a specific piece of information about that person. One major task of psychologists involved in assessment is to evaluate information provided by many tests, interviews, and observations, and to combine this information to make complex and important judgments about individuals. For example, when an individual shows evidence of difficulty in adjusting to the demands of daily life, a clinician must decide whether therapy would be helpful and, if so, what type of therapy would be most appropriate.

Psychologists also are called on to assess individuals in a variety of nonclinical settings. For example, school psychologists might consider information about a child's intellectual performance, social skills, and home environment in recommending placement in special education programs. Industrial psychologists might be asked to evaluate management trainees who participate in a series of assessment exercises. In each case, it is assumed that the assessment is more than a simple combination of test scores—it is a judgment on the part of a trained professional.

PROBLEMS AND SOLUTIONS—WHAT IF DIFFERENT ASSESSMENTS DISAGREE?

The Problem

Janet has completed a psychological assessment designed to evaluate her fitness for highly stressful defense-related work involving sensitive classified material. She received very good scores on the first two tests, but a poor score on the clinical interview. The interviewer is well-trained and highly experienced. Should the organization take the risk and hire her (on the basis of her test scores) or turn her down (on the basis of the interview)?

Although expert judgment plays a part in each form of psychological measurement, the practice of clinical assessment and the implementation of structured assessment programs—both broadly defined as the integration of multiple pieces of information into an overall evaluation of the present state of the individual being assessed—is somewhat unique in that human judgment is an integral component of the process. This chapter deals principally with the individual assessor's contribution to the reliability and validity of psychological measurement in a variety of clinical and nonclinical settings in which decisions must be made on the basis of multiple tests or assessments. In particular, this chapter examines the impact of the assessor's judgment on the quality of psychological measurement and clinical decisions.

First we discuss the general nature of multimethod assessment, together with a brief consideration of the tests that are used most often in assessment. Next we describe several methods of studying expert judgment in assessment contexts. In particular, we note that a number of influential reviews have suggested that individual assessor judgments (usually referred to as clinical judgments in this research literature) often can be duplicated and perhaps even improved through the use of mechanical or statistical methods of prediction. Finally, we describe several structured programs of psychological assessment. Many of the functions carried out by individual clinicians in a relatively unstructured way are also carried out by groups of psychologists in large-scale assessment programs.

THE NATURE OF CLINICAL ASSESSMENT

Korchin and Schuldberg (1981) define psychodiagnosis as a process that

> (a) uses a number of procedures, (b) intended to tap various areas of psychological functions, (c) both at a conscious and unconscious level, (d) using projective techniques as well as more objective and standardized tests, (e) in both cases, interpretation may rest on symbolic signs as well as scorable responses, (f) with the goal of describing individuals in personological rather than normative terms. (p. 1147)

Korchin and Schuldberg's definition of psychodiagnosis might be applied more aptly to the neutral term *clinical assessment.* The central difference between clinical assessment and other testing applications is that the clinician, rather than the test, is at the center of the assessment process. Indeed, as J. Wiggins (1973) notes, the clinician has two distinct functions, both of which are essential to the assessment process. First, the clinician must gather data. Although standardized tests are used in clinical assessment, projective tests, interviews, and behavioral observations represent the clinician's most important measurement tools (Korchin & Schuldberg, 1981; McReynolds, 1968; Wade & Baker, 1977). Second, the clinician must integrate data from various tests, interviews, and observations to form an overall assessment of the individual.

The data-gathering function has clear implications for the quality of psychological measurement. A clinician who makes inaccurate observations, conducts poorly structured interviews, or misinterprets or misrecords responses to open-ended questions or ambiguous stimuli (e.g., responses to Rorschach cards) is not likely to produce valid assessments. The clinician often functions as a measurement instrument, and it is important to assess the reliability and validity of the clinical data he or she gathers.

Although it may not be immediately obvious, the clinician's second function—the integration of clinical data—also affects the quality of psychological measurement in clinical settings. Assessment represents an attempt to arrive at a valid classification of each individual patient or client. In some cases, clinicians may be called on to diagnose or assist in the diagnosis of mental or behavioral disorders. In others, the clinician must make recommendations regarding the placement of children or adults in remedial education or in therapeutic programs. In any case, the classification of individuals represents a fundamental type of measurement (see Chapter 1), and the clinician's skill in integrating diverse sources of data may be a critical factor in determining the validity of his or her classifications and assessments of individuals.

Testing, Assessment, and Clinical Practice

At one time, psychological testing represented one of the most important activities of clinical psychologists (Korchin & Schuldberg, 1981; McReynolds, 1968; Rabin, 1981). Since the early 1980s, the practice of clinical psychologists has shifted steadily from an emphasis on assessment and diagnosis to an emphasis on psychotherapy and adjustment (Matarazzo, 1992; Rabin, 1981). Several reviews of research and practice (e.g., Matarazzo, 1992), however, suggest that testing will remain an important activity and that many of the tests now widely used (e.g., standardized measures of intelligence, the MMPI-2) will remain popular even if they are partially supplemented by new testing technologies.

Although clinicians do not appear to devote as much of their time to testing as in the past, psychological testing still represents an important activity for practicing clinicians. Wade and Baker's (1977) survey suggested that over 85% of practicing clinical psychologists used tests and that over one third of their therapy time was devoted to test administration and evaluation. Patterns of test use have been quite stable since the 1970s (Lubin, Larsen, & Matarazzo, 1984; Piotrowski & Keller, 1989a, 1989b) and probably will remain so for the foreseeable future. Psychological testing appears to be a common activity, regardless of the psychologist's therapeutic orientation (e.g., behavioral, cognitive).

The most widely used clinical tests can be divided into three types: (1) individual tests of general mental ability, (2) personality tests, and (3) neurological tests. The Wechsler Intelligence Scales (WISC-III and WAIS-III) and the Stanford-Binet represent the most popular tests of general mental ability (Korchin & Schuldberg, 1981). These tests serve a dual function in forming assessments of individuals. First, an evaluation of general mental ability often is crucial for understanding an individual's behavior, since many behavioral problems are linked to intellectual deficits. Second, individual intelligence tests present an opportunity to observe the examinee's behavior in response to several intellectually demanding tasks, and thus they provide data regarding the subject's persistence, maturity, problem-solving styles, and other characteristics.

The Rorschach, the Thematic Apperception Test (TAT), and the Minnesota Multiphasic Personality Inventory (MMPI) represent three of the most popular personality tests. Of the three, the MMPI is most closely associated with the diagnosis of psychopathology, whereas the TAT is most closely associated with the assessment of motives and drives. The Rorschach may be used for a variety of purposes, ranging from the assessment of specific personality traits to the diagnosis of perceptual disorders, depending on the scoring system used.

The Bender-Gestalt and the Luria-Nebraska Neuropsychological Test Battery are widely used in the diagnosis of neurological disorders. The Bender-Gestalt is used in the assessment of perceptual disorders and organic dysfunctions, although, as noted in Chapter 20, it may be used for a wide range of diagnostic purposes, whereas the Luria-Nebraska Battery provides a wide-ranging assessment of perceptual, motor, and intellectual functions that might be affected by damage to specific portions of the brain.

Piotrowski, Belter, and Keller (1998) examined the relationship between the constraints imposed by managed care and psychological assessment practices. The majority of respondents reported that their use of tests has changed in the recent years as a result of managed care directives and that they have tended to restrict their pool of assessment instruments. The Rorschach inkblot technique and the TAT were cited as particular examples of tests that are less common under managed care than under systems in which psychologists are free to choose any test they want.

Normally, psychologists are, and should be, skeptical of efforts to limit their professional practice, especially when decisions about the type of care to give or the type of test to use are driven by cost concerns rather than by the best interests of the client. In this case, managed care directors may be doing everyone a favor. There are very good reasons to question the validity and usefulness of tests such as the Rorschach and the TAT, and the fact that their use might be declining as a result of managed care is not necessarily a bad thing.

The Clinical Interview.   Most clinical tests (e.g., the WAIS, the Rorschach) represent structured interactions between the clinician and the individual being examined. In other words, most clinical tests require the examinee to respond to specific, standardized stimuli (e.g., an inkblot) presented by the examiner, and the clinician must record and interpret the individual's responses. These structured interactions between the examiner and the examinee represent one of the major sources of information to be used in assessing the examinee.

The clinical interview, which represents a less-structured interaction between the examiner and the examinee, is the second major source of information used in assessing individuals (Sundberg, 1977). In many ways, the clinical interview is similar to the employment interview (see Chapter 19). In both cases, the interview represents an opportunity to obtain information about an individual that is not obtained readily from written tests. In addition, the interviewer is likely in both cases to pay attention to the content of the examinee's responses and to the examinee's behavior in responding to (or avoiding) questions.

Despite the similarity between employment interviews and clinical interviews, a critical difference between the two has important implications for the quality of the clinical interview as a measurement tool: The goal of an employment interview is known beforehand; the interviewer's task is to select applicants who best fill the demands of a particular job or set of jobs. As a result, employment interviews often are fairly structured and may be directed toward obtaining a few relatively concrete types of information. In contrast, clinical interviews are almost certain to be unstructured. Although most clinical interviews strive to fulfill the same general goal (e.g., obtain important information about examinees), the specific goal of a particular clinical interview depends almost entirely on the needs and the conditions of the particular individual being interviewed. As a result, the specific goals of a clinical interview may be quite difficult to determine in advance. For example, in theory there is a clear distinction between a therapeutic interview, which entails both an attempt to obtain information and an attempt to alleviate the client's problem, and a research interview, which is aimed strictly at obtaining specific information.

Research interviews can be broken down further into types, the case history and the intake or "pinpointing" interview (Nay, 1979). In practice, the distinction between information gathering and therapeutic intervention is not always so sharp. For example, in gathering information, it may not be clear what questions the clinician should ask or which topics should be pursued until the interview gets under way. Nor will it be clear whether all the relevant information has been obtained until well after the conclusion of the initial interview. Furthermore, the process of gathering information may itself have therapeutic value, and the clinician may intersperse attempts to elicit factual information with attempts to resolve problems that are uncovered during the interview.

Because the clinical interview is a relatively unstructured search for relevant information, it is important to consider factors that may affect the accuracy and comprehensiveness of this search. Research on hypothesis confirmation bias (Darley & Fazio, 1980) suggests that it may be difficult to conduct a search for unbiased and comprehensive information in an unstructured setting such as the clinical interview. This research suggests that decision makers form hypotheses to explain the behavior of others and then actively search for information that confirms their hypotheses. More important, decision makers typically ignore or actively discount information that runs counter to their hypotheses. In the context of the clinical interview, this research suggests that clinicians are likely to conduct biased searches for information that confirms their early impressions of each examinee. Information that is ambiguous tends to be interpreted to support first impressions; information that contradicts the initial hypotheses may receive little weight.

Research on self-fulfilling prophecies (Dipboye, 1982) suggests a second factor that may limit the validity of interviews in general and may be especially problematic in unstructured clinical interviews. This research suggests that the interviewer's expectations affect the behavior of the person being interviewed and that interviewees may change their behavior to match the interviewer's expectations. For example, a clinician may develop the hypothesis that family problems are the root cause of the client's problems and therefore may focus on familial issues during the interview. The interviewer's persistence in examining this topic may, in turn, lead the client to believe that family problems are responsible for his or her troubles, and as a result, that client may present or emphasize information that tends to confirm the clinician's hypothesis.

Research on confirmatory biases and self-fulfilling prophecies suggests that early impressions could have a decisive impact on the scope and conduct of the interview. If the clinician's early hypotheses are largely correct, the interview may serve as a valuable source of valid information. However, if early hypotheses are incorrect, it may be difficult for the clinician (or the client) to recognize the problem and to redirect the search for relevant information.

Clinicians typically regard the interview as a highly useful source of information and often place more weight on the interview than on written tests in their assessments of individuals (Korchin & Schuldberg, 1981; J. Wiggins, 1973). Unfortunately, empirical evidence regarding the validity of the clinical interview is spotty at best (J. Wiggins, 1973). As was the case with the employment interview, research suggesting that clinical interviews are limited in their validity has not had a major impact on their popularity or perceived worth. Possible reasons for the continuing popularity of the clinical interview parallel those cited by Arvey and Campion (1982). First, there is a widespread belief that clinical interviews should work; clinicians are highly trained in observing and interpreting behavior, and if anyone is able to gather valid information using highly unstructured techniques, clinical psychologists and psychiatrists certainly are the most likely candidates. Second, there is a pervasive tendency to overestimate the accuracy of one's judgments. Thus, individual clinicians are likely to believe that they are accurate interviewers, even if the research evidence suggests that most of their colleagues are not. Finally, clinicians rely heavily on the interview because it may provide important information about individuals that tests alone cannot provide. The validity of this information is open to doubt; but practicing clinicians argue that if they are confined to the role of passively interpreting test scores, they will be severely handicapped in their efforts to understand the individuals whom they are asked to assess (Holt, 1969).

Several efforts have been made to provide more structure for clinical interviews, thereby (hopefully) increasing their reliability and validity (McReynolds, 1989; Robins & Helzer, 1986). A variety of interview schedules, including the Structured Clinical Interview for the *Diagnostic and Statistical Manual, Third Edition—Revised* (SCID), Schedule of Affective Disorders and Schizophrenia (SADS), and Personality Disorder Examination (PDE), have been developed to provide structure for either wide-ranging clinical interviews (e.g., the SCID) or interviews that are more narrowly focused (e.g., the SADS). These interview schedules typically include a mix of objective and open-ended questions and often call for clinical judgments at various branching points in the interview (i.e., at points where the next line of inquiry depends on your interpretation of what has been said so far). These structured interview schedules are likely to increase the reliability of clinical interviews; it is still not clear whether they lead to increased validity (McReynolds, 1989).

STUDYING CLINICAL JUDGMENT

A variety of methods might be used to study clinical judgment. For example, Klein-muntz (1968, 1970) described several applications of the think-aloud technique, in which the clinician attempts to describe the different steps he or she follows while evaluating individual examinees or case reports. These methods are useful in that they shed light on the processes involved in clinical judgment. The implications of this type of research for the accuracy of clinical judgments, however, are not entirely clear.

Other methods focus on the outcomes of clinical judgments; research of this type seems more directly relevant for determining the factors that affect the accuracy of clinical inference. In particular, applications of Brunswick's lens model seem especially useful in understanding features of the clinician's judgment that may contribute to or detract from the accuracy of assessments (Brunswick, 1956; Hammond, 1955, 1966; P. Hoffman, 1960).

The lens model describes the relationship between the individual being assessed, the information used in assessing that individual, and the judgment of the clinician, as portrayed in Figure 21-1. The model suggests that to understand the factors affecting the accuracy of clinical judgments, we must examine two factors: (1) the validity of the information provided by tests, observations, interviews, and the like and (2) the way in which the clinician uses this information. For example, the model suggests that the ac-curacy of clinical judgments is limited by the validity of the information available to the clinician. If the tests that are chosen provide little information about the status of the individual being assessed, it is unreasonable to expect the clinician to make accu-rate judgments. On the other hand, if the information provided by tests is highly valid, there is still no guarantee that the clinician's judgments will be accurate. The accuracy

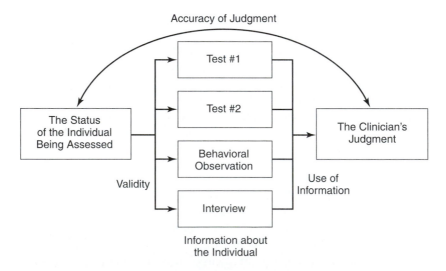

FIGURE 21-1 The Lens Model Applied to Clinical Judgment

of these judgments also depends on the way in which the clinician uses the available information.

Correlational methods have typically been used to study the accuracy of judgments, the validity of information, and the use of that information. In this setting, accuracy can be defined by the correlation between the clinician's judgments regarding an individual and the actual status of that individual. Validity can be defined in terms of the relationship between the available information (e.g., test scores) and the status of the individual. The clinician's use of the available information in part can be described in terms of the relationships between different pieces of information and the clinician's final judgment (Beach, 1967; Castellan, 1992; Christal, 1968; L. R. Goldberg, 1968; Slovic & Lichtenstein, 1971).

Clinical Versus Statistical Prediction

The lens model suggests two different ways that information might be used to predict or assess the status of a particular individual. First, the information could be used indirectly. That is, test scores and measures obtained from interviews and observations could be given to a clinician, who would then make judgments about the individual being assessed. This method is referred to as *clinical prediction.* A second, simpler alternative would be to use the information directly in making predictions about the individual. Statistical techniques such as multiple regression analysis are designed to predict scores on one variable (e.g., the status of the individual) on the basis of information provided by other variables (e.g., test scores). Using these techniques, it would be possible to bypass the clinician altogether and make predictions solely on the basis of test scores. This method is referred to as *statistical prediction.*

As stated at the beginning of this chapter, of central concern in clinical assessment is the effect of human judgment on the accuracy of clinical assessments and decisions. Comparisons between the accuracy of clinical prediction and the accuracy of statistical predictions would seem to shed considerable light on this issue. A statistical system of prediction represents a simple, mechanical method of combining information to arrive at an overall assessment of an individual.[1] It is useful to determine whether a clinician, given the same information, arrives at judgments that are more accurate or less accurate than the predictions obtained using statistical techniques. On the one hand, one might expect a trained, experienced professional to make better decisions than can be made on the basis of some statistical combination of test scores. On the other hand, human judgment is not perfectly valid or reliable, and errors in human judgment can lead to predictions or assessments that are less accurate than those obtained using statistical techniques.

---

[1]The simplest statistical method is to take the average of all test scores and to predict one outcome for people who receive high averages and another outcome for people who receive low averages. Regression equations produce a weighted average rather than a simple unweighted average.

The accuracy of clinical and statistical predictions has been extensively studied. A typical method is to obtain information from the files of a number of patients whose diagnoses are known and to present that information to clinicians in a form such as that shown in Table 21-1. The clinician's task is to read each case description and to make a diagnosis. Since the actual diagnosis for each case is known in advance, it is possible to directly assess the clinician's accuracy. Similarly, the scores on the different tests can be combined using a statistical technique such as multiple regression, and the predicted diagnosis can be compared with the actual diagnosis to assess the accuracy of the statistical prediction.

In a highly influential review, Meehl (1954) examined 20 studies comparing the accuracy of clinical and statistical predictions. He concluded that in almost every case, statistical methods produced predictions that were at least as accurate as clinical predictions, and they were often more accurate than the judgments of trained professionals. Later reviews by Meehl (1957, 1965) reached essentially similar conclusions. These reviews seemed to suggest that clinicians did not make more accurate assessments than could be achieved using simple statistical procedures for combining the available information and that clinicians might, in fact, do worse than statistical methods in predicting the status of individuals.

Some years after Meehl's reviews, research in judgment and decision making dealt a second blow to the proponents of clinical prediction. Several researchers used statistical techniques to predict, or model, the clinicians' decisions, rather than predicting the actual diagnoses. This process is referred to as *bootstrapping*. It was found that,

Table 21-1   A HYPOTHETICAL CASE REPORT USED TO STUDY CLINICAL VERSUS STATISTICAL PREDICTION

Case #122		
Edwards Personal Preference Schedule— Percentiles		*WAIS-R Scores*
Achievement	55	Full 118
Deference	42	Verbal 123
Order	78	Performance 113
Exhibition	35	
Autonomy	40	*Health and adjustment:* Client complains of
Affiliation	55	stomach disorders, with no diagnosed
Intraception	62	causes. Shows no clear signs of maladjust-
Succorance	35	ment, but is occasionally undependable.
Dominance	44	
Abasement	67	
Nurturance	32	
Change	25	
Endurance	50	
Heterosexuality	38	
Aggression	60	

in general, the statistical models were highly accurate in predicting the clinician's behavior (Dawes & Corrigan, 1974). More important, these statistical models were often
more accurate in predicting the actual diagnoses than were the clinicians whose decision behavior was being modeled (Dawes, 1971; Dawes & Corrigan, 1974; L. R. Goldberg, 1970).

Meehl's reviews, together with research on bootstrapping, seem to suggest that
(1) clinicians very rarely make better predictions than can be made using simple statistical methods, (2) statistical methods are in many cases more accurate in predicting relevant criteria than are highly trained clinicians, and (3) clinical judgment should
therefore be replaced, wherever possible, by simple statistical methods of integrating
the information used in forming assessments. As one might imagine, these sorts of
conclusions do not always sit well with clinical psychologists.

Arguments Against Statistical Prediction.   Meehl's reviews (1954, 1957, 1965)
and the research on statistical prediction that followed stimulated several papers
questioning the relevance of studies comparing clinical and statistical prediction and
disputing the supremacy of statistical techniques. For example, both Holt (1958) and
McArthur (1968) suggested that the comparison between clinical and statistical
prediction in most studies was essentially unfair and that most studies were biased
strongly in favor of statistical models.

First, they noted that the clinician's task in these studies was quite different from
the clinician's task in his or her day-to-day practice. Clinicians do not merely read a set
of test scores or brief descriptions of clients and then make snap diagnoses; rather, they
interact with clients for a substantial period of time before making their diagnoses.
Thus, the task that clinicians typically performed in studies of clinical prediction was
not really a clinical judgment task but rather was a simulation for which clinicians did
not have access to the type of direct observational data that they would normally use
in forming their assessments.

Second, the criterion used to evaluate both clinical and statistical predictions is
the correlation between predicted and actual judgments. Statistical models are designed to produce the highest possible correlation between the information used to
make decisions and the decisions themselves, which means that the clinician cannot
beat the statistical model unless he or she has access to information that is not readily
integrated into statistical models (e.g., observations of the client) or can validly recognize cases in which statistical methods will err. Neither of these conditions is likely to
occur in the typical study of clinical versus statistical prediction (Nystedt & Murphy,
1979).

Sawyer (1966) noted a second shortcoming in studies on clinical versus statistical
prediction—the failure to separate the clinician's role in data collection from his or her
role in integrating the available information to form an overall assessment. In most
studies, the clinician was put in a relatively passive role and asked to make a decision
solely on the basis of numerical information presented in a case report. Sawyer noted
that in actual clinical settings, both clinical and mechanical (e.g., objective tests) methods are used to collect data that may contain important information about the person

being assessed. Similarly, both clinical (judgmental) and statistical methods often are used to integrate the data obtained from tests and judgments. Most of the studies cited by Meehl and others concentrated exclusively on the relative accuracy of clinical and statistical methods of data integration and paid no attention to clinical methods of data collection or to the interaction between data collection and data integration methods.

Sawyer suggested that the debate over clinical versus statistical is somewhat artificial. The critical issue is the accuracy of clinical predictions, not the method by which those predictions are made. Hence, rather than trying to decide which method is best, we should try to determine how best to use each method to improve the accuracy of clinical predictions and decisions. Clinicians may be uniquely qualified to collect certain types of data via interviews and behavioral observation, whereas objective tests may be optimal for predicting specific psychopathologies or other diagnostic or treatment criteria. Clinical judgment is important in deciding which tests or pieces of information are relevant, whereas statistical methods, such as computing a weighted average of a person's test scores, may be optimal for summarizing trends in the data collected from that individual. Indeed, Sawyer's review suggested that clinical predictions were most accurate when (1) both clinical and mechanical (i.e., objective) methods of data collection were used and (2) mechanical or statistical methods were used to combine the data collected.

What Have We Learned From the Clinical Versus Statistical Debate?   For many years, the debate over the supremacy of clinical or statistical methods obscured the more important (and more illuminating) question of why simple statistical methods performed so well. To put it another way, why is it that a clerk with an adding machine could often make better predictions than those made by highly trained, experienced clinicians? The answer to this question sheds light on several of the most pressing measurement issues in the context of clinical assessment.

One secret to the success of statistical models is their reliability (Dawes & Corrigan, 1974). If the same numbers are fed into a particular regression equation today, tomorrow, and next week, the prediction will always be the same. This outcome is not true of clinical prediction. Clinicians, being human, are not perfectly reliable; if confronted with identical or essentially identical information about a case on two different occasions, they may make different predictions. This lack of perfect reliability puts the clinician at a considerable disadvantage when competing with statistical techniques. When a clinician makes two different predictions based on the same set of test scores, at least one of those predictions must be in error. If the clinician used the same strategy as is implied by the statistical approach (i.e., "take the average of all test scores and predict from that"), the unreliable clinician, in the long run, always would perform worse than the perfectly reliable statistical model. Thus, for a clinician to produce more accurate predictions than those produced using statistical models, he or she must devise a strategy for combining information that is more valid than the simple strategy implied by the statistical model.

The second secret to the success of statistical predictions lies in the robust nature of the statistical models employed (Dawes, 1979; Dawes & Corrigan, 1974). Simple statistical methods, such as using the average of many test scores to predict a specific outcome, are often highly accurate and may be nearly as accurate as the best possible strategy. Furthermore, the decision to employ statistical techniques that either give all tests equal weight or give some tests more weight than others has little effect on the accuracy of the model's predictions (Einhorn & Hogarth, 1975; Wainer, 1976). Thus, in many clinical judgment situations, a wide variety of simple statistical strategies could be applied that would be equally (and highly) accurate in predicting relevant clinical criteria. Although complex clinical strategies may exist that, in theory, are more accurate than statistical strategies, the robust nature of the type of statistical models typically employed in studying clinical judgment guarantees that the difference between the accuracy of a statistical prediction and the accuracy attained by the best clinical strategy will generally be small.

A third secret is that statistical models avoid the all-too-human tendency to "see" relationships that do not, in fact, exist and to "identify" individual exceptions to general actuarial trends that do not, in fact, apply (Dawes, Faust, & Meehl, 1989). Well-trained clinicians are no more immune than anyone else to the tendency to ignore relevant background information (e.g., base rates) and to treat each case as a unique individual, to whom general trends that exist in the population do not apply. This issue surfaced in the debate over computerized versus clinical interpretations of psychological tests. Matarazzo (1986) complained that computerized interpretations were "all mean and no sigma," meaning that they reflected actuarial trends in the data but did not consider the individual characteristics of the respondent in the same way that a clinician would. Murphy (1987a) retorted that clinical judgments often incorporate too much irrelevant information; clinical judgments might be characterized as too much sigma and not enough mean (i.e., they incorporate information about irrelevant differences but ignore information about general trends in the population).

The most valuable outcome of the clinical-versus-statistical debate is the recognition that the clinical judgment process can be broken down into several subtasks (e.g., data collection, integration of information) and that some of these tasks are done most efficiently using statistical techniques. Rather than regarding statistical techniques as a replacement for clinical judgments, these methods should be regarded as tools that clinicians can use to enhance the accuracy of their predictions. Statistical methods are superior to human judgment when it comes to very specific tasks, such as determining the average or the trend in responses to several tasks. However, in the long run, the automation of clinical prediction would limit the accuracy of clinical decisions, since it would preclude the use of behavioral observation data or the selection of appropriate tests to optimally assess the status of each individual client. The combination of clinical and statistical prediction in most cases is preferable to the use of purely clinical or purely statistical methods of prediction.

Practicing clinicians still appear to prefer using their own judgment rather than using statistical models or rules when combining data from multiple assessments. This preference may change as more clinicians develop the capability of at least determining what a statistical combination rule would say. Garb (2000) noted that clinicians have increasing access to statistical software that can instantly tell them what the outcome of a statistically valid model for combining test scores would look like. Clinicians are not likely to allow these statistical models to make decisions for them (indeed, the ethical guidelines for psychologists shown in Appendix B do not allow this practice), but there are few excuses for not at least considering what a statistical model would say. As clinicians learn to treat statistical models as a decision aid rather than as a replacement for their own decisions, they are likely to be both more able and more willing to take advantage of the strengths of the statistical method for combining information from different tests or assessments.

Patterns, Configurations, and Clinical Judgment

Experiments designed to obtain statistical representations of clinical judgment have shown consistently that a simple model, in which the average of all test scores for an individual are used to predict his or her status, is highly accurate in predicting the assessments reached by clinicians (J. Wiggins, 1973). This finding led several investigators to conclude that this simple model provided a fairly good representation of the clinician's decision-making strategy (Christal, 1968; Hursch, Hammond, & Hursch, 1964). Clinicians, however, insist that they do more than simply add test scores together when they assess individuals; they also try to pay attention to patterns or configurations of test scores.

Table 21-2 presents a simple example that illustrates the distinction between the average test score and the pattern of test scores. Although the average scores for the three individuals depicted in the table are identical, the patterns are very different. Individual A received average scores on all three tests; individual B is highly immature and very concerned with health; and individual C shows evidence of paranoia, together with little concern for his health. Clinicians maintain that patterns of scores on tests, interviews, and the like reveal important information that is not revealed by average test scores. Experimental studies of clinical judgments frequently demonstrate that clinicians consider patterns or configurations of test scores in their assessment of individuals (Dana, Cocking, & Dana, 1970; L. R. Goldberg, 1965; P. Hoffman, 1960; N. Wiggins & Kohen, 1971). The question of whether efforts to consider patterns of test

Table 21-2   TEST SCORES THAT DIFFER IN PATTERN, BUT NOT IN AVERAGE

Individual	Maturity[a] scale	Paranoid thought scale	Health concern scale	Average score
A	5	5	5	5
B	2	4	9	5
C	6	8	1	5

[a]All three indexes employ a 10-point scale, where 1 = low, 5 = average, 10 = high.

scores as well as average test scores contribute to the accuracy of clinical predictions is exceedingly complex. For example, one aspect of this question concerns the validity of clinicians' interpretations of specific patterns. Granted, a high score on a paranoia scale coupled with a low score on a depression scale may mean something different than a medium score on both. It is not always clear, however, precisely what that specific pattern may indicate. A second aspect of this question involves the way in which patterns are defined. Consider, for example, a diagnostic system that includes the following as indicators of the hypothetical mental disorder called Brunswick's egonia:

1. Lower-than-average full-scale IQ (less than 100)
2. Performance IQ higher than verbal IQ
3. Verbal IQ not less than 70

In Table 21-3, each of the cases appears to fit the pattern for Brunswick's egonia, but in some cases, the data more clearly fit the pattern than in others. For example, individual A clearly appears to meet all three diagnostic criteria. Individuals B and C also meet the criteria, but there is reason to doubt that they really exhibit the pattern that the diagnostic manual describes. For example, one might question whether individual A's performance IQ really exceeds his or her verbal IQ and whether the verbal score really exceeds the cutoff suggested by the third diagnostic criterion. Similarly, one might question whether individual C, who has a reported IQ of 99, should really be regarded as "below average" in intelligence. In both cases, the limited reliability of psychological tests leaves room for doubt regarding the degree of fit between the characteristics of the individual and the characteristics of the specific pattern of scores used to predict Brunswick's egonia. For example, if individual B were to be retested, it is not at all unlikely that she would receive an IQ of 100 or more. Of course, it is possible that each individual would receive the same scores on his or her second testing. It is more likely, however, that scores would vary somewhat and that all trivial differences between test scores observed in the first testing (e.g., the difference between the performance and the verbal scores of individual B) would not recur in the second.

Table 21-3   CASES THAT APPEAR TO FIT THE DIAGNOSTIC PATTERN FOR BRUNSWICK'S EGONIA

	Criteria		
(a) Full IQ is less than 100			
(b) Performance IQ is higher than verbal IQ			
(c) Verbal IQ is not less than 70			

Case	*Full IQ*	*Verbal IQ*	*Performance IQ*
A	86	80	95
B	70	70	71
C	99	85	113

The limited reliability of psychological tests has important implications for clinical assessment strategies that involve examining patterns or configurations of test scores. The reliability of psychological tests is not, however, the only issue in assessing the clinician's ability to react to patterns or configurations of test scores. Rather, in examining the clinician's use of score configurations, it may also be important to consider the clinician's reliability in applying complex diagnostic rules. As has been discussed, one major advantage of statistical as opposed to clinical methods of prediction is that the former are highly reliable, whereas the latter are not. There are good reasons to believe that judges will be less reliable in applying complex diagnostic strategies than they will be in applying a relatively straightforward, simple one (Murphy, 1979). Thus, attempts to develop complex clinical prediction strategies designed to outperform simple statistical prediction methods may actually reduce rather than increase the accuracy of clinical predictions.

Can We Improve Clinical Judgment?

If your goal is to improve the reliability and validity of clinical judgment, two strategies seem reasonable. First, you might try to improve the judges, perhaps through better training. Second, you might try to improve the judgment process, perhaps through the use of statistical methods for the integration of data. We have already reviewed evidence suggesting that the second strategy can be effective. Less is known about whether the first strategy (improving the judges) will work.

One way to determine whether new and better methods of training clinicians will improve clinical judgment is to look at the impact of the training (both formal and on the job) that clinicians currently receive on the validity of their judgments. Garb (1989) reviewed the results of 55 studies on the effects of clinical training and professional experience on the validity of clinical judgments. These studies compared the clinical judgments of experienced and less-experienced clinicians, of clinicians and graduate students, of advanced and beginning graduate students, and of clinicians (including graduate students) and laypersons. The results of these studies were fairly clear: On-the-job experience is not related to the validity of clinical judgments, and training is only weakly related to validity. In other words, an experienced Ph.D. makes clinical judgments that are not substantially better than those made by someone with essentially no training or experience. Garb notes that similar findings have been reported in medicine. High-school graduates, given a few weeks of training and explicit protocols for diagnosis and treatment, are as effective as fully trained physicians in treating a limited range of problems (Shortliffe, Buchanan, & Feigenbaum, 1979).

Clinicians typically receive several years of postgraduate experience and deal with large numbers of clients each month. Since this level of training and experience has so little effect on the validity of clinical judgment, it seems unlikely that a little more training or experience will really make a difference. Unfortunately, research on the effects of training and experience on clinical judgment has had little to offer in the way of concrete suggestions for improving the ability of clinicians to make these critical judgments. Garb (1989) suggests that clinicians must rely more heavily on relevant research in making judgments (and less on intuition and experience) and that automated decision-making aids might help.

Rapid developments in technology make it likely that the strategy of improving the judgment process (rather than improving the judge) will dominate efforts to increase the validity of clinical judgments. In the early years of the clinical-versus-statistical-prediction debate (i.e., the 1950s and 1960s), the issue was somewhat academic because individual clinicians rarely had access to computers capable of carrying out complex statistical integration tasks. Now, the most complex clinical integration tasks are easily handled by computers that, in terms of cost and ease of use, are accessible to virtually any clinician. In addition, software for performing statistical integration or for assessing normative databases is widely available and easy to use. Finally, computerized test interpretation services are available; several issues in computerized assessment were discussed in Chapter 12. Although these will not and should not replace the individual clinician (Matarazzo, 1986), they can provide a valuable tool for increasing the reliability and validity of clinical judgments.

Garb and Schramke's (1996) review of the role of judgment in neuropsychological assessment illustrates the potential impact of decision aids in increasing the reliability and validity of these judgments. For example, it seems possible to increase the validity of diagnostic assessments by simply providing base rate information to the psychologists (i.e., information about the relative frequency of different conditions). This review suggests that the use of automated assessment programs and statistical prediction methods as an adjunct to clinical judgment might further increase reliability and validity.

STRUCTURED ASSESSMENT PROGRAMS

Up to this point, we have concentrated on applications of clinical assessment in which an individual clinician gathers and integrates various types of information in forming an integrated diagnosis of an individual client's current status and future prognosis. The same sorts of activities that are carried out by individual clinicians on a case-by-case basis are also carried out on a larger scale as part of a number of structured assessment programs. One of the most notable examples of a structured assessment program was the one carried out by the Office of Strategic Services (OSS) in selecting intelligence agents during World War II. This program, which is described in the section that follows, was the forerunner of a number of large-scale assessment programs carried out today by both the government and private industry.

The most obvious difference between individual clinician assessment and structured programs of assessment is that of scale. For example, the OSS program assessed over 5,000 recruits over a period of approximately three years. Other differences, which may not be so obvious, are even more important for understanding the similarities and differences between individual assessment and structured programs of assessment.

First, in structured assessment, the goal of the program is likely to be fairly well defined. The OSS program was designed to select effective intelligence agents; similar assessment programs are used widely in business to identify and develop promising candidates for higher levels of management. Although it may be difficult to specify exactly what one is looking for in a secret agent or in a manager, structured programs nevertheless typically have clearer goals than the individual clinician whose goals are in part shaped by the clients' problems.

Second, structured programs often, though not always, are standardized in such a way that the assessment activities do not vary as a function of the behavior of the person or persons being assessed. Individual assessment, by contrast, is typically adaptive rather than fixed (Cronbach & Gleser, 1965). Rather than using the same set of tests, interviews, and observations with every client, individual clinicians must tailor their assessment activities to fit the client's apparent status.

Third, structured assessment programs very frequently involve multiple assessors (e.g., psychologists, psychiatrists, physicians, and managers). Research on group decision making is therefore relevant to understanding the outcomes of structured assessment programs.

Finally, large-scale assessment programs are typically concerned with individual differences within the wide range of behavior that we typically label as normal, and they are likely to be less concerned with psychopathology. Thus, the goal of structured assessment is rarely to understand and alleviate psychological or behavioral problems experienced by the individuals being assessed. There are, however, exceptions; later in this chapter, we discuss a structured assessment program used in assessing and designing treatment for children with learning disabilities.

The OSS Assessment Program

The OSS, forerunner of the CIA, was created shortly after the United States entered World War II. Among the functions of the OSS was the selection and training of agents to work, often behind enemy lines, in gathering intelligence, conducting sabotage and propaganda campaigns, and assisting resistance movements. In many respects, the task facing the OSS during World War II was reminiscent of that facing the U.S. Army in World War I. That is, they were charged with developing a large and effective force of agents in a short period of time, starting pretty much from scratch. In World War I, group-administered tests of general intelligence (i.e., Army Alpha and Army Beta) had provided a partial solution to the army's problem of identifying officer candidates. The task facing the OSS in World War II was much more complex, however. The OSS had to select agents from a very heterogeneous group of recruits, under conditions that precluded testing for specific, assignment-related skills, for a wide variety of ill-defined jobs and missions (Office of Strategic Services Assessment Staff, 1948). Psychologists and staff members affiliated with the OSS developed a complex "multiform organismic system of assessment" to cope with this task.

The system of assessment employed by the OSS had its roots in the methods employed by both British and German military psychologists, as well as those employed by Murray at the Harvard Psychological Clinic (J. Wiggins, 1973). The cornerstone of the assessment technique employed by the OSS was the use of several different types of procedures and several procedures of each type to assess each recruit's standing in several different dimensions. These dimensions are listed in Table 21-4. For example, each candidate received a rating on the dimension Social Relations, based on information obtained from (1) interviews, (2) informal observation, (3) individual situational tests, (4) group situational tests, (5) projective tests, and (6) sociometric questionnaires. The situational tests were an especially important part of the assessment procedures developed by the OSS. Each of these tests put the recruit in a lifelike situation that was designed to illustrate specific aspects of the recruit's behavior in difficult or demanding situations. For example, three individual situational tests were used in assessing the recruits' skill in Social Relations:

1. *Construction test.* The recruit was asked to build a simple structure with the help of two assistants. The assistants were, in fact, confederates of the assessment staff and were consistently uncooperative, argumentative, and ineffective; their "assistance" made it nearly impossible to complete the structure.
2. *Recruitment test.* The person being assessed played the role of a recruiter interviewing an applicant. The applicant was, once again, a confederate of the assessment staff.
3. *Improvisation.* A role-playing test in which the recruits were given a description of a situation and were required to interact in the roles of the characters in that situation.

Typical OSS assessments involved a group of 18 recruits who were studied extensively over a 3-day period. Over these 3 days, each recruit completed a number of tests, interviews, and exercises; was observed and rated by his peers and by a number of psychologists on the assessment staff; and participated in the evaluation of other recruits. At the end of this period, the assessment staff compiled all the available information to form an overall assessment of each recruit's suitability for assignment in the OSS. This information was combined in assessment staff conferences to reach a consensus on a coherent, comprehensive description of each recruit's strengths and weaknesses. One of the most important products of the assessments was a written personality sketch of each assessee that attempted to "predictively describe him as a functioning member of the organization" (Office of Strategic Services Assessment Staff, 1948, p. 53).

Several features of the OSS assessment program distinguish it from other methods that might have been used in evaluating recruits. First, the program represented an attempt to carry out assessment in a natural social setting. Recruits spent three days living, eating, and drinking with the assessment staff in a remote location; observation of the recruits' behavior in nontest situations was thought to provide especially useful

Table 21-4   AREAS RATED IN OSS ASSESSMENTS

1. Motivation for assignment	6. Leadership
2. Energy and initiative	7. Security
3. Effective intelligence	8. Physical ability
4. Emotional stability	9. Observing and reporting
5. Social relations	10. Propaganda skills

information. Second, assessment included a number of lifelike tasks. Rather than relying on tests of specific skills, abilities, or traits, the assessment staff used behavior in natural settings to predict future behavior in similar settings. Third, the assessment included multiple, overlapping procedures. Thus, each important variable was measured using a number of distinct methods. Finally, there was an attempt to arrive at agreement regarding each recruit's personality. Rather than attempting to assess several specific abilities, aptitudes, and skills, the OSS assessment procedure was designed to reach a coherent impression of each recruit as a person.

The OSS assessment program has set the pattern for many large-scale assessment exercises. Several of its features have been carried over to the assessment centers that have become increasingly popular for assessing managers and executives (see Chapter 19). In the early 1960s, an assessment program was developed by the Peace Corps that drew on, and in many ways improved, the assessment techniques developed and applied by the OSS.

Assessment in the Peace Corps

The Peace Corps was established in 1961 to provide a wide range of medical, educational, and technical assistance to developing countries. Volunteers typically spend two years in the host country, often living under conditions of considerable hardship. The assessment problem initially facing the Peace Corps was strikingly similar to that facing the OSS some years earlier. A large number of volunteers were available for difficult, ill-defined missions that varied tremendously from country to country and also varied over time (Henry, 1965). In addition, many Peace Corps volunteers were young and inexperienced (Hobbs, 1963). Thus, there often was little in the volunteers' background that could give firm indications of success or failure overseas.

The assessment procedure developed by the Peace Corps in the 1960s consisted of two separate stages: suitability screening and field selection.

Suitability Screening.   Peace Corps training was both expensive and arduous. Rather than admitting all applicants to training, the Peace Corps developed a method of screening out applicants who were unlikely to succeed in their assignments before they entered training. Each applicant filled out a questionnaire assessing his or her training, experience, and technical qualifications; took written placement tests, which included measures of language aptitude; and provided academic transcripts and references.[2] On the basis of this information, a number of applicants were invited to training. Those applicants who accepted training were then subject to a civil service background examination and a strict medical exam. Those applicants who cleared these final hurdles were admitted to the training program. The Peace Corps's suitability screening process is diagrammed in Figure 21-2.

Several features of the suitability screening process are noteworthy. First, the process was quite intensive: Approximately one applicant out of six passed this initial screening and reached the training site. However, as the figure shows, the majority of

---

[2]As many as 22 letters of reference were solicited for any given candidate.

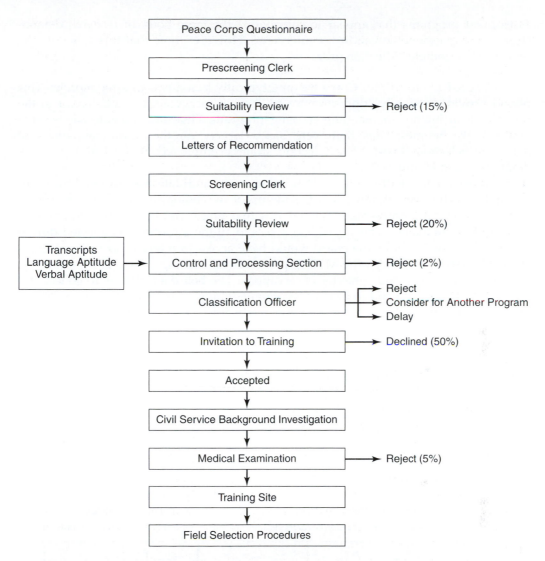

FIGURE 21-2   Peace Corps's Suitability Screening Process   *Source:* Adapted from Wiggins, 1973, p. 587. Copyright © 1972 by Newbery Award Records, Inc., and Random House, Inc. Reproduced by permission.

the screening decisions were made by individual applicants, rather than by the Peace Corps itself; approximately half of the applicants invited to training decided not to accept. Second, despite intensive pressure to conduct personal interviews with each applicant, the entire suitability screening process was accomplished without any personal contact with the applicants (Hobbs, 1963; J. Wiggins, 1973). Thus, the screening procedure developed by the Peace Corps represents one of the few large-scale assessment programs that appear to corroborate the large body of research demonstrating the questionable validity of interviews. However, note that this was only the first step in a complex selection program.

Field Selection. Peace Corps training typically lasted two to three months. This period provided extensive opportunities to observe each volunteer's behavior in the context of an intense, demanding training program. Final selection decisions were made at the training sites that were based largely on the recommendations of Advisory Selection Boards. The selection strategy employed at the training site is diagrammed in Figure 21-3.

Approximately halfway through training, each candidate was assessed by an Intermediate Advisory Selection Board made up of psychologists, psychiatrists, physicians, training staff, representatives familiar with overseas conditions, and experienced Peace Corps volunteers. This board had access to all the information collected during the training. For example, the board would have access to interviewer ratings, scores on psychological tests (e.g., the MMPI), peer ratings, training course grades, medical records, staff ratings, and behavior observations. The board's task was to collect and integrate relevant data and to present recommendations to the Field Selection Officer, who was responsible for making decisions regarding each candidate. At this stage, candidates could be rejected, transferred to another program or site, or retained for

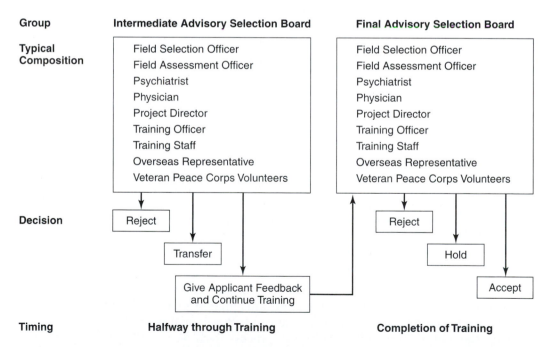

FIGURE 21-3 Peace Corps's Field Selection Strategy *Source:* From Wiggins, 1973, p. 587. Copyright © 1972 by Newbery Award Records, Inc., and Random House, Inc. Reproduced by permission.

further training. Those candidates who were retrained received extensive feedback re-garding their strengths and weaknesses, with special attention given to shortcomings that could be corrected during the remainder of the training period.

At the end of training, the Final Advisory Selection Board met to consider the total information available for each remaining candidate. At this point, the Field Selection Officer made a decision, on the basis of information provided by the board, to accept, reject, or hold the candidate for another project or assignment. Approximately 70% of the candidates who began training were eventually accepted for assignment overseas.

Comparison of OSS and Peace Corps Programs

The assessment programs developed by the OSS and the Peace Corps were simi-lar in many ways. Both employed multiple methods of measurement, and both relied on the diagnostic council, a meeting of assessors that attempted to forge a coherent pic-ture of each volunteer as a potential member of the organization. Yet several important differences suggest that the Peace Corps program had a greater potential for produc-ing valid, useful assessments. First, the Peace Corps employed a largely objective screening system that eliminated a large number of unsuitable candidates. Admittedly, much of the screening involved self-selection, and some of those who were eliminated at the screening stage might have performed successfully overseas. Nevertheless, the use of a multistage assessment procedure was definitely an advance, particularly in light of the fact that the selection ratio (number of assignments per number of appli-cants) was known to be low. Second, the Peace Corps program formally separated the roles of data collection (e.g., by physicians, training staff), data integration (e.g., by field assessment officer), and decision making (e.g., by field selection officer) (J. Wig-gins, 1973). In contrast, members of the OSS assessment staff carried out all three activ-ities on an ongoing basis. Third, each decision made in the Peace Corps program was made on the basis of the cumulative weight of evidence. Although there is a good pos-sibility that previous evaluations of a candidate can bias later evaluations of that same candidate (Murphy, Balzer, Lockhart, & Eisenman, 1985), nevertheless, this procedure made it possible to test and reevaluate early impressions of the candidate.

Because of difficulties in obtaining useful criterion measures (especially in the case of the OSS program), it is difficult to determine which program was, in fact, more successful. The OSS staff concluded that there was little definitive evidence for the pre-dictive validity of their assessments (Office of Strategic Services Staff, 1948). However, later analyses of data presented by the OSS (J. Wiggins, 1973) suggest that the use of psychological assessment resulted in at least a modest increase in the number of cor-rect decisions made by the OSS.

Several sorts of data are available for evaluating the accuracy of the Peace Corps's selection decisions. Of particular interest are statistics regarding the number of volun-teers who were unable to complete their two-year tour of duty because of emotional or physical illness, adjustment problems, or situations at home necessitating their return. In the early years of the Peace Corps, it was assumed that between 20% and 50% of all volunteers would be unable to complete their tours (Hobbs, 1963). It is worth noting that between 10% and 15% of the age cohort from which most volunteers were drawn, under normal circumstances, will suffer clinical impairment due to emotional illness at some point in their lives. However, through 1964 only approximately 8% of the volunteers sent overseas had returned prematurely, and fewer than 1% returned for psychiatric reasons (Menninger & English, 1965). It has been estimated that 95% of those selected for overseas assignment represented true positive decisions (i.e., were correctly sent overseas) (J. Wiggins, 1973).[3]

Behavioral Assessment in Mental Retardation. The final structured assessment program to be discussed is not a program per se, at least not in the sense of the large-scale programs of the OSS and the Peace Corps. Rather, it is a structured set of measurement activities used to assess severe learning disabilities in children and to design training programs tailored to the individual child's weaknesses and capabilities. The core of this assessment program is the Learning Potential Assessment Device (LPAD), developed by Feuerstein (1970) and his colleagues (cf. Haywood, Filler, Shifman, & Chatelant, 1975; Luther & Wyatt, 1997, who describe recent applications of LPAD in assessing the performance of disadvantaged children).

In a sense, the LPAD integrates the functions of training and assessment. Using the LPAD, a psychologist asks a child to perform a number of tasks, some of which are quite novel and complex. The amount and type of training necessary to achieve successful performance on each task are critical aspects of the clinician's assessment. Thus, LPAD assesses a child's level of functioning in part by examining the extent and the means necessary to modify his or her performance. It is assumed that functions that are easily modifiable show less impairment than those that require extensive training to modify.

The LPAD is made up of four distinct tests:

1. *Organization of Dots.* The child is required to detect geometric patterns in a cloud of dots and to construct them by connecting the dots. Successful performance is a function of ability to plan and delay responses, analytic ability, and ability to learn new performance strategies as the patterns become more complex.
2. *Plateau Test.* The test materials consist of four plates, each with nine buttons on its surface. One or more of the buttons is fixed in place. The child's task is to locate a fixed button and remember its location as the plates are stacked, rotated, or represented in a drawing. This task taps associative learning, memory, and spatial transformation ability.
3. *LPAD Matrices Test.* Essentially similar to Raven's Progressive Matrices, this test taps reasoning ability and ability to discriminate relevant from irrelevant dimensions.
4. *Representational Stencil Design Test.* The test consists of 20 stencils, each of which has a unique design. The child is shown models, which are constructed by overlaying two or more stencils, and must pick out the stencils needed to reproduce the design and indicate their order of placement. This test taps color, form, and size discrimination; mental manipulation; and ability to integrate feedback from earlier solutions.

Each of the tests that make up the LPAD can be varied independently on three different dimensions: (1) the novelty or complexity of the task, (2) the modality of

---

[3]However, because over 85% of those who applied were not accepted for overseas assignment, a larger number of false negative errors were almost certainly made.

presentation, and (3) the cognitive operations required for successful task perfor-mance. The clinician can systematically manipulate these dimensions in any or all of the LPAD tests to probe the child's capabilities and limits. Thus, the LPAD is at the same time a structured, multitest program and an assessment method that can be tai-lored to the performance levels exhibited by the child being assessed.

The LPAD is clearly different in its structure and its goals from the large-scale structured programs described earlier. Nevertheless, this assessment technique shares several essential features with the methods employed by the OSS and the Peace Corps. First, the LPAD employs multiple tests that assess, in part, overlapping functions. Sec-ond, the LPAD incorporates performance tests. Although these are not as naturalistic or complex as some of the situational tests employed by the OSS, they nevertheless re-quire the child to actively solve problems, rather than simply to answer the clinician's question. Finally, this technique requires the clinician to integrate information from a variety of different sources (e.g., test, effects of manipulating novelty of the material presented, mode presentation, cognitive demands) to form an overall assessment of the child's level of functioning.

The LPAD is one of several methods of dynamic assessment that rely heavily on the observation of performance in novel or complex tasks for evaluating cognitive abil-ities and skills. Although these assessment methods in general, and the LPAD in par-ticular, have attracted favorable reviews (e.g., Hamilton, 1983), other researchers have expressed concerns (Buchel & Scharnhorst, 1993). Research on both the reliability and the construct and criterion-related validity of the LPAD suggests that this method does not meet the same psychometric standards as more traditional paper-and-pencil de-vices (Glutting & McDermott, 1990; Hamilton, 1983). Nevertheless, LPAD has been used in assessing a variety of clinical and learning interventions (Hada, Katz, Tyano, & Weizman, 2001; Skuy, 2002).

Evaluating Structured Assessment Programs

Structured assessment programs typically incorporate many features that are consistent with the general principles of measurement discussed in Chapters 4 through 10. For example, they employ multiple observations and often multiple assessors. This feature should help to increase the reliability and possibly the validity of assessments and reduce their susceptibility to bias. On the other hand, the frequent reliance on clin-ical (judgmental) methods of integrating data seems justified more on the basis of tra-dition than on the basis of empirical evidence. Despite a significant body of research showing that mechanical methods are generally preferable to judgmental methods of combining information from multiple sources (e.g., Dawes, 1979, 1980; J. Wiggins, 1973), assessment programs stubbornly cling to some version of the "diagnostic coun-cil," in which an individual clinician or a group of clinicians attempts to form a unified, coherent impression of the mass of data collected in assessment.

Sawyer (1966) noted that predictions seemed to be most accurate when objective and judgmental methods were used to collect data, whereas mechanical methods were used to integrate data. Even departments of psychology are reluctant to rely solely on statistical methods to make final decisions (Dawes, 1979). It may be unrealistic, therefore, to expect assessment programs to adopt the statistical method. As currently conducted, structured assessment programs often lead to better decisions than simpler methods of prediction (e.g., written tests), although the increase in accuracy may not always offset the high cost of assessment. However, considering their potential level of accuracy (if optimal measurement and prediction strategies were adopted), structured assessment programs, as currently designed, are not all that impressive. In other words, structured assessment may be better than simpler testing methods, but the structured assessment approach is probably not as useful as it could be if better use were made of statistical prediction models and other automated data-integration aids.

There is an extensive body of research on the use of assessment centers for predicting and developing managerial performance (cf. Thornton, 1992; Thornton & Byham, 1982). This literature illustrates several of the issues that are relevant for evaluating assessment programs in general. As was discussed in Chapter 19, assessment centers involve the use of multiple methods and multiple evaluators to assess managerial candidates on dimensions such as verbal ability, leadership, delegation of authority, and planning ability. Data from several distinct exercises and testing techniques are combined, and a consensus is then reached as to each candidate's overall assessment.

Research on assessment centers suggests several conclusions that may apply quite broadly to other assessment programs. First, it is not easy to evaluate the validity of assessment centers, largely as the result of problems in developing adequate criteria. To evaluate the validity of any assessment program, assessment outcomes must be compared against some external criterion, and many of the criterion measures employed are of questionable reliability and validity or, worse yet, are directly biased by assessment outcomes (Klimoski & Strickland, 1977). Structured assessment programs are likely to be used to make complex predictions (e.g., predicting managerial success, success of remedial training programs), and these predictions are difficult to validate.

Second, there is little support for the continued use of judgmental rather than statistical methods of aggregating assessment data (Borman, 1982; Borman, Eaton, Bryan, & Rosse, 1983; Sackett & Wilson, 1982). Each assessment exercise typically yields a set of scores for each assessee; the research cited before consistently showed that a simple sum of all these ratings was as good as and often better than assessment reached by consensus in terms of its ability to predict relevant criteria. Sackett and Wilson (1982) suggest that "diagnostic councils" rarely need to meet and that statistical methods of combining assessment data would be more practical and more valid than the judgmental methods currently employed.

Assessment programs typically are designed to measure several attributes, in much the same way that multiple-aptitude test batteries are designed to measure several distinct abilities and skills. For example, the managerial assessment centers of American Telephone and Telegraph (AT&T) at one time included ratings on 25 or more separate characteristics, ranging from passivity to work motivation. As noted in Chapter 14, the measurement of several distinct attributes is difficult and not always successful. Research on assessment centers suggests that similar difficulties may be encountered when several distinct methods are used to measure multiple attributes of the persons being assessed. Sackett and Dreher (1982) suggest that various assessment exercises provide valid measures of a person's overall performance but do not provide valid measures of several distinct attributes. In part, this outcome is a result of the strong reliance on individual and group assessment techniques that depend on assessors' judgments (e.g., interviews, behavior observations). Human judges are notorious for exhibiting general evaluative bias and have difficulty assessing individual attributes in a way that is not affected by their overall evaluation of the assessee (Murphy, 1982).

In general, structured assessment programs have shown consistent evidence of reliability and criterion-related validity (Thornton, 1992; Thornton & Byham, 1982), although there is still some uncertainty about why assessment center predictions are valid (Klimoski & Brickner, 1987). Evidence regarding their content and construct validity is somewhat less consistent. In part, this tendency is a reflection of too much optimism in the design of assessment programs. Returning to an earlier example, managerial assessment centers used by AT&T attempted to evaluate 25 separate dimensions. There are reasons to doubt that there are that many discriminably different dimensions or if that many dimensions really do exist, that any assessment technique could yield valid information about all of them. Thus, the failure of assessors to discriminate among this large set of dimensions may tell us more about the domain being measured than about the shortcomings of the assessment technique.

Structured assessment programs present many appealing features, especially their reliance on multiple testing techniques. Clearly, there is room for improvement in most assessment programs, but these programs could potentially represent the most comprehensive and valid method of measuring the attributes of individuals. In evaluating these programs, it may be necessary to move away from the traditional criteria used to evaluate individual tests (e.g., reliability, validity) and focus attention on the one criterion that has been emphasized throughout this book: A method is useful only if it results in better decisions. On the whole, multiple assessment techniques do seem to help in making fair and accurate decisions. The full potential of this approach has probably not been exploited, but it seems clear that the use of a single test score in making important decisions has become a thing of the past. It is therefore likely that research on the best (i.e., most accurate and most practical) methods of combining information from multiple assessment devices will become an increasingly important aspect of the application of the principles of psychological measurement to decision making.

CRITICAL DISCUSSION:

Psychological Assessment in the Courtroom

There is a strange link between the nation's first and its most recent presidential assassination attempts: the successful use of insanity as a legal defense. The first known assassination attempt was made against President Andrew Jackson, by Richard Lawrence. Lawrence's defense was one of the first in this nation to be based successfully on a plea of insanity (Zonana, 1984). When John Hinkley attempted to assassinate President Reagan, his successful insanity defense touched off a legal and psychiatric controversy that continues today.

Psychological assessment in criminal trials must often deal with two separate issues: the defendant's competence to stand trial and the defendant's sanity at the time the crime was committed. Although questions of sanity have received considerable attention in the press, the issue of competence has greater impact on the conduct and dispensation of legal proceedings. It is much more likely that a disturbed defendant will be found incompetent to stand trial than not guilty by reason of insanity.

Competence refers to the defendant's present state of mind. A defendant is ruled not competent to stand trial if, because of some mental disorder, he or she is unable to understand the charges and/or is unable to participate in his or her own defense. *Insanity* refers to the defendant's state of mind at the time the crime was committed. The American Law Institute's definition of insanity states that "A person is not responsible for criminal conduct if at the time of such conduct, as a result of mental disease or defect, he lacks substantial capacity either to appreciate the wrongfulness of his conduct or to conform his conduct to the requirements of the law" (Zonana, 1984, p. 311).

There is no standard procedure for assessing competency or sanity. It is common, however, to use psychological tests such as the MMPI as evidence. More specific diagnostic tools, such as the Schedule of Affective Disorders and Schizophrenia or the Competency Screening Test (Nicholson & Kugler, 1991; Nicholson, Robertson, Johnson, & Jensen, 1988; Rogers, Thatcher, & Cavanaugh, 1984) exist but are not always used. The use of interviews and self-report measures in assessment has probably contributed to juries' skepticism when evaluating insanity pleas. As a result, successful insanity pleas are much less frequent than one might think. For example, in 1980 there were 259 successful insanity pleas out of over 50,000 defendants tried in California. More recent surveys suggest that the insanity plea frees defendants in about 3 of every 1,000 criminal cases tried and that the plea is even less successful in serious cases (e.g., murder trials). The insanity plea is not an easy way out.

In general, assessments of sanity are more difficult and more controversial than assessments of competence. First, it is difficult to obtain reliable information about a defendant's past behavior (i.e., at the time of the crime); in assessing competence, past behavior is irrelevant. Second, there is not as much incentive to fake incompetence as there might be to fake insanity. If a defendant is found incompetent to stand trial, the judge may simply defer the charges and commit the defendant to a mental institution until he or she is ready to stand trial. (Note, however, that indefinite commitment may be unconstitutional, since it infringes on the defendant's right to a speedy trial.) A defendant who is found not guilty by reason of insanity might also be committed to a mental institution, but he or she must be freed and cannot be retried if "cured."

Significant scientific and professional criticisms have come to surround the practice of forensic psychology. Several studies and reviews of the literature seem to show that psychologists do a poor job of predicting the future behavior of violent individuals or of evaluating the sanity of defendants (Dawes, 1989, 1994; Faust, 1989; Faust & Ziskin, 1988). On the whole, this research suggests that mental health professionals do not have any special skill, in the sense that their judgments are not demonstrably better than those of laypersons, in evaluating sanity or competency to stand trial. Like laypersons, psychologists and other professionals in related fields make a substantial number of errors in these judgments. Although detailed ethical guidelines have been drawn up to regulate the practice of psychology as it relates to the legal system (Committee on Ethical Guidelines for Forensic Psychologists, 1991), strong doubts have been expressed about the usefulness of the testimony of forensic psychologists. Like Nicholson and Kugler (1991), we believe that part of the answer to improving the quality of practice in forensic psychology is the development of well-validated, objective screening instruments that can replace the often bewildering array of techniques now used in the assessment of competency and sanity.

SUMMARY

Clinical assessment is one of several methods of psychological measurement in which subjective judgment is an integral part of the process of measurement and evaluation (other examples include employment interviews and performance appraisals). Clinical assessments usually involve psychological tests, and thus they can be thought of as a second level of psychological measurement. That is, psychological tests provide many sorts of information about individuals, information that is integrated, together with clinical interviews, observations, life history data, and other information, to form an overall assessment or diagnosis. The use of tests with consistent evidence of reliability and validity contributes to, but does not guarantee, the validity of these assessments.

Research on clinical judgment suggests that it is very difficult to reliably apply complex judgment strategies in assessing individuals. The task of integrating information from multiple tests can often be done with a calculator; the average of several test scores often provides a more valid assessment than does the unaided judgment of a well-trained clinician. Clinical skills and experience are probably useful for collecting and interpreting data on individuals, but the task of integrating scores on several tests is not one that should be done via subjective judgment.

Three structured assessment programs or systems were discussed. The OSS assessment program established the ground rules for several types of behavioral assessment, including the assessment centers that are widely used to evaluate managers and job applicants in industry. The assessment program developed by the Peace Corps is a clear success, and it suggests that clinical assessment can be done with a high level of reliability and validity. On the other hand, assessment systems such as LPAD illustrate some of the difficulties in clinical assessment.

Chapters 4 through 10 of this book were largely devoted to evaluating psychological tests. As we note here, it can be more difficult to evaluate assessment programs. The best programs incorporate many of the suggestions that come out of psychometric theory (e.g., they use multiple tests and multiple methods of measurement), but they also often incorporate features, such as clinical rather than statistical integration, that have been widely criticized in the technical literature. Nevertheless, the research on assessment suggests that the use of subjective judgment as part of the measurement process does not mean that the resulting assessments will be unreliable or invalid. If they are carefully carried out, clinical assessments can show high levels of reliability and validity.

PROBLEMS AND SOLUTIONS—RECAP

The Problem:

Janet is being screened for a highly sensitive job. She received good scores on two tests and a poor score from a clinical interview (the interviewer is highly experienced). What should the organization do?

A Solution

There are at least three issues that are relevant here. First, the fact that the interviewer is well-trained and highly experienced might turn out to be irrelevant. There is compelling evidence that training and experience do not do much to improve the validity of interviews. Second, interviews are often suspect, and given the good indications from the two tests she took, they should be regarded with extra caution here. Third and most important, the organization cannot simply consider the risks if it hires Janet (despite the bad interview). It must also consider the risk of not hiring Janet. That is, the decision to go with the results of the interview increases the risks of a false positive error (see Chapter 9); the decision to pass her up as a candidate increases the risk of a false negative error. The organization might decide that a false negative is not so bad if there are other viable candidates, but if Janet is the best on all other criteria, going with the results of a clinical interview might lead to a truly costly error in hiring.

KEY TERMS

Brunswick's lens model   model widely used in research on judgment that examines links between the information available to the judge (clinician) and his or her judgments

Clinical assessment   integration of information from multiple procedures by a clinician to arrive at assessment or diagnosis of an individual

Clinical interview   relatively unstructured interview used to obtain case histories or to start the process of clinical assessment

Configural interpretation   use of patterns or configurations of test scores to arrive at predictions or diagnoses

Forensic assessment   use of psychological tests and clinical assessment in legal proceedings (e.g., evaluating claims of insanity)

Hypothesis confirmation bias   tendency to search for and pay attention to information that confirms one's initial impressions

OSS assessment program   method of assessment developed for Office of Strategic Services (forerunner of the current CIA) that served as the model for assessment centers currently used in work settings

Statistical prediction   use of a mathematical formula, rather than clinical judgment, to combine information from multiple tests or assessments

Forty Representative Tests

INTELLIGENCE AND SCHOLASTIC APTITUDE

Group Tests

Scholastic Assessment Tests (SAT)
ACT Assessments
Graduate Record Examinations (GRE)
Cognitive Abilities Tests
Multidimensional Aptitude Battery (MAB-II)

Individual Tests

Kaufman Assessment Battery for Children (K-ABC)
Stanford-Binet Intelligence Scale—Fifth Edition
Wechsler Adult Intelligence Scale—III (WAIS-III)
Wechsler Intelligence Scale for Children—IV (WISC-IV)

MULTIPLE APTITUDE BATTERIES

Armed Services Vocational Aptitude Battery (ASVAB)
Ability Profiler—General Aptitude Test Battery
Differential Aptitude Tests

NEUROPSYCHOLOGICAL

Halstead—Reitan Neuropsychological Test Battery
Luria—Nebraska Neuropsychological Test Battery
Wechsler Memory Test

PERSONALITY/PSYCHOPATHOLOGY

California Psychological Inventory
Edwards Personal Preference Schedule (EPPS)
The Holtzman Inkblot Technique

Jackson Personality Inventory
Millon Adolescent Personality Inventory
Minnesota Multiphasic Personality Inventory (MMPI-2)
Myers-Briggs Type Indicator
NEO Personality Inventory—Revised
Rorschach Inkblot Technique
Sixteen Personality Factor Questionnaire (16PF)
State-Trait Anxiety Inventory
Tennessee Self-Concept Scale
Thematic Apperception Test (TAT)

SENSORY-MOTOR

Bender-Gestalt Test
Fine Dexterity Test
Peabody Developmental Motor Scales

VOCATIONAL

Interest

Jackson Vocational Interest Survey
Self-Directed Search
Strong Interest Inventory (SII)
Vocational Preference Inventory

Aptitude and Skills

Minnesota Clerical Tests
NOCTI Student Occupational Competency Tests
The Short Employment Tests
Wonderlic Personnel Test
Bennett Test of Mechanical Comprehension

Ethical Principles of Psychologists and Code of Conduct

The American Psychological Association's (APA's) Ethical Principles of Psychologists and Code of Conduct (hereinafter referred to as the Ethics Code) consists of an Introduction, a Preamble, five General Principles (A–E), and specific Ethical Standards. The Introduction discusses the intent, organization, procedural considerations, and scope of application of the Ethics Code. The Preamble and General Principles are aspirational goals to guide psychologists toward the highest ideals of psychology. Although the Preamble and General Principles are not themselves enforceable rules, they should be considered by psychologists in arriving at an ethical course of action. The Ethical Standards set forth enforceable rules for conduct as psychologists. Most of the Ethical Standards are written broadly, in order to apply to psychologists in varied roles, although the application of an Ethical Standard may vary depending on the context. The Ethical Standards are not exhaustive. The fact that a given conduct is not specifically addressed by an Ethical Standard does not mean that it is necessarily either ethical or unethical. This Ethics Code applies only to psychologists' activities that are part of their scientific, educational, or professional roles as psychologists. Areas covered include but are not limited to the clinical, counseling, and school practice of

psychology; research; teaching; supervision of trainees; public service; policy development; social intervention; development of assessment instruments; conducting assessments; educational counseling; organizational consulting; forensic activities; program design and evaluation; and administration. This Ethics Code applies to these activities across a variety of contexts, such as in person, postal, telephone, internet, and other electronic transmissions. These activities shall be distinguished from the purely private conduct of psychologists, which is not within the purview of the Ethics Code.

Membership in the APA commits members and student affiliates to comply with the standards of the APA Ethics Code and to the rules and procedures used to enforce them. Lack of awareness or misunderstanding of an Ethical Standard is not itself a defense to a charge of unethical conduct.

The procedures for filing, investigating, and resolving complaints of unethical conduct are described in the current Rules and Procedures of the APA Ethics Committee. APA may impose sanctions on its members for violations of the standards of the Ethics Code, including termination of APA membership, and may notify other bodies and individuals of its actions. Actions that violate the standards of the Ethics Code may also lead to the imposition of sanctions on psychologists or students whether or not they are APA members by bodies other than APA, including state psychological associations, other professional groups, psychology boards, other state or federal agencies, and payors for health services. In addition, APA may take action against a member after his or her conviction of a felony, expulsion or suspension from an affiliated state psychological association, or suspension or loss of licensure. When the sanction to be imposed by APA is less than expulsion, the 2001 Rules and Procedures do not guarantee an opportunity for an in-person hearing, but generally provide that complaints will be resolved only on the basis of a submitted record.

The Ethics Code is intended to provide guidance for psychologists and standards of professional conduct that can be applied by the APA and by other bodies that choose to adopt them. The Ethics Code is not intended to be a basis of civil liability. Whether a psychologist has violated the Ethics Code standards does not by itself determine whether the psychologist is legally liable in a court action, whether a contract is enforceable, or whether other legal consequences occur.

The modifiers used in some of the standards of this Ethics Code (e.g., *reasonably, appropriate, potentially*) are included in the standards when they would (1) allow professional judgment on the part of psychologists, (2) eliminate injustice or inequality that would occur without the modifier, (3) ensure applicability across the broad range of activities conducted by psychologists, or (4) guard against a set of rigid rules that might be quickly outdated. As used in this Ethics Code, the term *reasonable* means the prevailing professional judgment of psychologists engaged in similar activities in similar circumstances, given the knowledge the psychologist had or should have had at the time.

In the process of making decisions regarding their professional behavior, psychologists must consider this Ethics Code in addition to applicable laws and psychology board regulations. In applying the Ethics Code to their professional work, psychologists may consider other materials and guidelines that have been adopted or endorsed by scientific and professional psychological organizations and the dictates of their own conscience, as well as consult with others within the field. If this Ethics Code establishes a higher standard of conduct than is required by law, psychologists must meet the higher ethical standard. If psychologists' ethical responsibilities conflict with law, regulations, or other governing legal authority, psychologists make known their commitment to this Ethics Code and take steps to resolve the conflict in a responsible manner. If the conflict is unresolvable via such means, psychologists may adhere to the requirements of the law, regulations, or other governing authority in keeping with basic principles of human rights.

PREAMBLE

Psychologists are committed to increasing scientific and professional knowledge of behavior and people's understanding of themselves and others and to the use of such knowledge to improve the condition of individuals, organizations, and society. Psychologists respect and protect civil and human rights and the central importance of freedom of inquiry and expression in research, teaching, and publication. They strive to help the public in developing informed judgments and choices concerning human behavior. In doing so, they perform many roles, such as researcher, educator, diagnostician, therapist, supervisor, consultant, administrator, social interventionist, and expert witness. This Ethics Code provides a common set of principles and standards upon which psychologists build their professional and scientific work.

This Ethics Code is intended to provide specific standards to cover most situations encountered by psychologists. It has as its goals the welfare and protection of the individuals and groups with whom psychologists work and the education of members, students, and the public regarding ethical standards of the discipline.

The development of a dynamic set of ethical standards for psychologists' work-related conduct requires a personal commitment and lifelong effort to act ethically; to encourage ethical behavior by students, supervisees, employees, and colleagues; and to consult with others concerning ethical problems.

GENERAL PRINCIPLES

This section consists of General Principles. General Principles, as opposed to Ethical Standards, are aspirational in nature. Their intent is to guide and inspire psychologists toward the very highest ethical ideals of the profession. General Principles, in contrast to Ethical Standards, do not represent obligations and should not form the basis for imposing sanctions. Relying upon General Principles for either of these reasons distorts both their meaning and purpose.

Principle A: Beneficence and Nonmaleficence

Psychologists strive to benefit those with whom they work and take care to do no harm. In their professional actions, psychologists seek to safeguard the welfare and rights of those with whom they interact professionally and other affected persons, and the welfare of animal subjects of research. When conflicts occur among psychologists' obligations or concerns, they attempt to resolve these conflicts in a responsible fashion that avoids or minimizes harm. Because psychologists' scientific and professional judgments and actions may affect the lives of others, they are alert to and guard against personal, financial, social, organizational, or political factors that might lead to misuse of their influence. Psychologists strive to be aware of the possible effect of their own physical and mental health on their ability to help those with whom they work.

Principle B: Fidelity and Responsibility

Psychologists establish relationships of trust with those with whom they work. They are aware of their professional and scientific responsibilities to society and to the specific communities in which they work. Psychologists uphold professional standards of conduct, clarify their professional roles and obligations, accept appropriate responsibility for their behavior, and seek to manage conflicts of interest that could lead to exploitation or harm. Psychologists consult with, refer to, or cooperate with other professionals and institutions to the extent needed to serve the best interests of those with whom they work. They are concerned about the ethical compliance of their colleagues' scientific and professional conduct. Psychologists strive to contribute a portion of their professional time for little or no compensation or personal advantage.

Principle C: Integrity

Psychologists seek to promote accuracy, honesty, and truthfulness in the science, teaching, and practice of psychology. In these activities psychologists do not steal, cheat, or engage in fraud, subterfuge, or intentional misrepresentation of fact. Psychologists strive to keep their promises and to avoid unwise or unclear commitments. In situations in which deception may be ethically justifiable to maximize benefits and minimize harm, psychologists have a serious obligation to consider the need for, the possible consequences of, and their responsibility to correct any resulting mistrust or other harmful effects that arise from the use of such techniques.

Principle D: Justice

Psychologists recognize that fairness and justice entitle all persons to access to and benefit from the contributions of psychology and to equal quality in the processes, procedures, and services being conducted by psychologists. Psychologists exercise reasonable judgment and take precautions to ensure that their potential biases, the boundaries of their competence, and the limitations of their expertise do not lead to or condone unjust practices.

Principle E: Respect for People's Rights and Dignity

Psychologists respect the dignity and worth of all people, and the rights of individuals to privacy, confidentiality, and self-determination. Psychologists are aware that special safeguards may be necessary to protect the rights and welfare of persons or communities whose vulnerabilities impair autonomous decision making. Psychologists are aware of and respect cultural, individual, and role differences, including those based on age, gender, gender identity, race, ethnicity, culture, national origin, religion, sexual orientation, disability, language, and socioeconomic status and consider these factors when working with members of such groups. Psychologists try to eliminate the effect on their work of biases based on those factors, and they do not knowingly participate in or condone activities of others based upon such prejudices.

ETHICAL STANDARDS

1. Resolving Ethical Issues

1.01 Misuse of Psychologists' Work

If psychologists learn of misuse or misrepresentation of their work, they take reasonable steps to correct or minimize the misuse or misrepresentation.

1.02 Conflicts Between Ethics and Law, Regulations, or Other Governing Legal Authority

If psychologists' ethical responsibilities conflict with law, regulations, or other governing legal authority, psychologists make known their commitment to the Ethics Code and take steps to resolve the conflict. If the conflict is unresolvable via such means, psychologists may adhere to the requirements of the law, regulations, or other governing legal authority.

1.03 Conflicts Between Ethics and Organizational Demands

If the demands of an organization with which psychologists are affiliated or for whom they are working conflict with this Ethics Code, psychologists clarify the nature of the conflict, make known their commitment to the Ethics Code, and to the extent feasible, resolve the conflict in a way that permits adherence to the Ethics Code.

1.04 Informal Resolution of Ethical Violations

When psychologists believe that there may have been an ethical violation by another psychologist, they attempt to resolve the issue by bringing it to the attention of that individual, if an informal resolution appears appropriate and the intervention does not violate any confidentiality rights that may be involved. (See also Standards 1.02, Conflicts Between Ethics and Law, Regulations, or Other Governing Legal Authority, and 1.03, Conflicts Between Ethics and Organizational Demands.)

1.05 Reporting Ethical Violations

If an apparent ethical violation has substantially harmed or is likely to substantially harm a person or organization and is not appropri-ate for informal resolution under Standard 1.04, Informal Resolution of Ethical Violations, or is not resolved properly in that fashion, psychologists take further action appropriate to the situation. Such action might include referral to state or national committees on professional ethics, to state licensing boards, or to the appropriate institutional authorities. This standard does not apply when an intervention would violate confidentiality rights or when psychologists have been retained to review the work of another psychologist whose professional conduct is in question. (See also Standard 1.02, Conflicts Between Ethics and Law, Regulations, or Other Governing Legal Authority.)

1.06 Cooperating with Ethics Committees

Psychologists cooperate in ethics investigations, proceedings, and resulting requirements of the APA or any affiliated state psychological association to which they belong. In doing so, they address any confidentiality issues. Failure to cooperate is itself an ethics violation. However, making a request for deferment of adjudication of an ethics complaint pending the outcome of litigation does not alone constitute noncooperation.

1.07 Improper Complaints

Psychologists do not file or encourage the filing of ethics complaints that are made with reckless disregard for or willful ignorance of facts that would disprove the allegation.

1.08 Unfair Discrimination Against Complainants and Respondents

Psychologists do not deny persons employment, advancement, admissions to academic or other programs, tenure, or promotion, based solely upon their having made or their being the subject of an ethics complaint. This does not preclude taking action based upon the outcome of such proceedings or considering other appropriate information.

2. Competence

2.01 Boundaries of Competence

(a) Psychologists provide services, teach, and conduct research with populations and in areas only within the boundaries of their competence, based on their education, training, supervised experience, consultation, study, or professional experience.

(b) Where scientific or professional knowledge in the discipline of psychology establishes that an understanding of factors associated with age, gender, gender identity, race, ethnicity, culture, national origin, religion, sexual orientation, disability, language, or socioeconomic status is essential for effective implementation of their services or research, psychologists have or obtain the training, experience, consultation, or supervision necessary to ensure the competence of their services, or they make appropriate referrals, except as provided in Standard 2.02, Providing Services in Emergencies.

(c) Psychologists planning to provide services, teach, or conduct research involving populations, areas, techniques, or technologies new to them undertake relevant education, training, supervised experience, consultation, or study.

(d) When psychologists are asked to provide services to individuals for whom appropriate mental health services are not available and for which psychologists have not obtained the competence necessary, psychologists with closely related prior training or experience may provide such services in order to ensure that services are not denied if they make a reasonable effort to obtain the competence required by using relevant research, training, consultation, or study.

(e) In those emerging areas in which generally recognized standards for preparatory training do not yet exist, psychologists nevertheless take reasonable steps to ensure the competence of their work and to protect clients/patients, students, supervisees, research participants, organizational clients, and others from harm.

(f) When assuming forensic roles, psychologists are or become reasonably familiar with the judicial or administrative rules governing their roles.

2.02 Providing Services in Emergencies

In emergencies, when psychologists provide services to individuals for whom other mental health services are not available and for which psychologists have not obtained the necessary training, psychologists may provide such services in order to ensure that services are not denied. The services are discontinued as soon as the emergency has ended or appropriate services are available.

2.03 Maintaining Competence

Psychologists undertake ongoing efforts to develop and maintain their competence.

2.04 Bases for Scientific and Professional Judgments

Psychologists' work is based upon established scientific and professional knowledge of the discipline. (See also Standards 2.01e, Boundaries of Competence, and 10.01b, Informed Consent to Therapy.)

2.05 Delegation of Work to Others

Psychologists who delegate work to employees, supervisees, or research or teaching assistants or who use the services of others, such as interpreters, take reasonable steps to (1) avoid delegating such work to persons who have a multiple relationship with those being served that would likely lead to exploitation or loss of objectivity; (2) authorize only those responsibilities that such persons can be expected to perform competently on the basis of their education, training, or experience, either independently or with the level of supervision being provided; and (3) see that such persons perform these services competently. (See also Standards 2.02, Providing Services in Emergencies; 3.05, Multiple Relationships; 4.01, Maintaining Confidentiality; 9.01, Bases for Assessments; 9.02, Use of Assessments; 9.03, Informed Consent in Assessments; and 9.07, Assessment by Unqualified Persons.)

2.06 Personal Problems and Conflicts

(a) Psychologists refrain from initiating an activity when they know or should know that there is a substantial likelihood that their personal problems will prevent them from performing their work-related activities in a competent manner.

(b) When psychologists become aware of personal problems that may interfere with their performing work-related duties adequately, they take appropriate measures, such as obtaining professional consultation or assistance, and determine whether they should limit, suspend, or terminate their work-related duties. (See also Standard 10.10, Terminating Therapy.)

3. Human Relations

3.01 Unfair Discrimination

In their work-related activities, psychologists do not engage in unfair discrimination based on age, gender, gender identity, race, ethnicity, culture, national origin, religion, sexual orientation, disability, socioeconomic status, or any basis proscribed by law.

3.02 Sexual Harassment

Psychologists do not engage in sexual harassment. Sexual harassment is sexual solicitation, physical advances, or verbal or nonverbal conduct that is sexual in nature, that occurs in connection with the psychologist's activities or roles as a psychologist, and that either (1) is unwelcome, is offensive, or creates a hostile workplace or educational environment, and the psychologist knows or is told this or (2) is sufficiently severe or intense to be abusive to a reasonable person in the context. Sexual harassment can consist of a single intense or severe act or of multiple persistent or pervasive acts. (See also Standard 1.08, Unfair Discrimination Against Complainants and Respondents.)

3.03 Other Harassment

Psychologists do not knowingly engage in behavior that is harassing or demeaning to persons with whom they interact in their work based on factors such as those persons' age, gender, gender identity, race, ethnicity, culture, national origin, religion, sexual orientation, disability, language, or socioeconomic status.

3.04 Avoiding Harm

Psychologists take reasonable steps to avoid harming their clients/patients, students, supervisees, research participants, organizational clients, and others with whom they work, and to minimize harm where it is foreseeable and unavoidable.

3.05 Multiple Relationships

(a) A multiple relationship occurs when a psychologist is in a professional role with a person and (1) at the same time is in another role with the same person, (2) at the same time is in a relationship with a person closely associated with or related to the person with whom the psychologist has the professional relationship, or (3) promises to enter into another relationship in the future with the person or a person closely associated with or related to the person.

A psychologist refrains from entering into a multiple relationship if the multiple relationship could reasonably be expected to impair the psychologist's objectivity, competence, or effectiveness in performing his or her functions as a psychologist, or otherwise risks exploitation or harm to the person with whom the professional relationship exists.

Multiple relationships that would not reasonably be expected to cause impairment or risk exploitation or harm are not unethical.

(b) If a psychologist finds that, due to unforeseen factors, a potentially harmful multiple relationship has arisen, the psychologist takes reasonable steps to resolve it with due regard for the best interests of the affected person and maximal compliance with the Ethics Code.

(c) When psychologists are required by law, institutional policy, or extraordinary circumstances to serve in more than one role in judicial or administrative proceedings, at the outset they clarify role expectations and the extent of confidentiality and thereafter as changes occur. (See also Standards 3.04, Avoiding Harm, and 3.07, Third-Party Requests for Services.)

3.06 Conflict of Interest

Psychologists refrain from taking on a professional role when personal, scientific, professional, legal, financial, or other interests or relationships could reasonably be expected to (1) impair their objectivity, competence, or effectiveness in performing their functions as psychologists or (2) expose the person or organization with whom the professional relationship exists to harm or exploitation.

3.07 Third-Party Requests for Services

When psychologists agree to provide services to a person or entity at the request of a third party, psychologists attempt to clarify at the outset of the service the nature of the relationship with all individuals or organizations involved. This clarification includes the role of the psychologist (e.g., therapist, consultant, diagnostician, or expert witness), an identification of who is the client, the probable uses of the services provided or the information obtained, and the fact that there may be limits to confidentiality. (See also Standards 3.05, Multiple Relationships, and 4.02, Discussing the Limits of Confidentiality.)

3.08 Exploitative Relationships

Psychologists do not exploit persons over whom they have supervisory, evaluative, or other authority such as clients/patients, students, supervisees, research participants, and employees. (See also Standards 3.05, Multiple Relationships; 6.04, Fees and Financial Arrangements; 6.05, Barter With Clients/Patients; 7.07, Sexual Relationships With Students and Supervisees; 10.05, Sexual Intimacies With Current Therapy Clients/Patients; 10.06, Sexual Intimacies With Relatives or Significant Others of Current Therapy Clients/Patients; 10.07, Therapy With Former Sexual Partners; and 10.08, Sexual Intimacies With Former Therapy Clients/Patients.)

3.09 Cooperation With Other Professionals

When indicated and professionally appropriate, psychologists cooperate with other professionals in order to serve their clients/patients effectively and appropriately. (See also Standard 4.05, Disclosures.)

3.10 Informed Consent

(a) When psychologists conduct research or provide assessment, therapy, counseling, or consulting services in person or via electronic transmission or other forms of communication, they obtain the informed consent of the individual or individuals using language that is reasonably understandable to that person or persons except when conducting such activities without consent is mandated by law or governmental regulation or as otherwise provided in this Ethics Code. (See also Standards 8.02, Informed Consent to Research; 9.03, Informed Consent in Assessments; and 10.01, Informed Consent to Therapy.)

(b) For persons who are legally incapable of giving informed consent, psychologists nevertheless (1) provide an appropriate explanation,

(2) seek the individual's assent, (3) consider such persons' preferences and best interests, and (4) obtain appropriate permission from a legally authorized person, if such substitute consent is permitted or required by law. When consent by a legally authorized person is not permitted or required by law, psychologists take reasonable steps to protect the individual's rights and welfare.

(c) When psychological services are court ordered or otherwise mandated, psychologists inform the individual of the nature of the anticipated services, including whether the services are court ordered or mandated and any limits of confidentiality, before proceeding.

(d) Psychologists appropriately document written or oral consent, permission, and assent. (See also Standards 8.02, Informed Consent to Research; 9.03, Informed Consent in Assessments; and 10.01, Informed Consent to Therapy.)

3.11 Psychological Services Delivered To or Through Organizations

(a) Psychologists delivering services to or through organizations provide information beforehand to clients and when appropriate those directly affected by the services about (1) the nature and objectives of the services, (2) the intended recipients, (3) which of the individuals are clients, (4) the relationship the psychologist will have with each person and the organization, (5) the probable uses of services provided and information obtained, (6) who will have access to the information, and (7) limits of confidentiality. As soon as feasible, they provide information about the results and conclusions of such services to appropriate persons.

(b) If psychologists will be precluded by law or by organizational roles from providing such information to particular individuals or groups, they so inform those individuals or groups at the outset of the service.

3.12 Interruption of Psychological Services

Unless otherwise covered by contract, psychologists make reasonable efforts to plan for facilitating services in the event that psychological services are interrupted by factors such as the psychologist's illness, death, unavailability, relocation, or retirement or by the client's/patient's relocation or financial limitations. (See also Standard 6.02c, Maintenance,

Dissemination, and Disposal of Confidential Records of Professional and Scientific Work.)

4. Privacy And Confidentiality

4.01 Maintaining Confidentiality

Psychologists have a primary obligation and take reasonable precautions to protect confidential information obtained through or stored in any medium, recognizing that the extent and limits of confidentiality may be regulated by law or established by institutional rules or professional or scientific relationship. (See also Standard 2.05, Delegation of Work to Others.)

4.02 Discussing the Limits of Confidentiality

(a) Psychologists discuss with persons (including, to the extent feasible, persons who are legally incapable of giving informed consent and their legal representatives) and organizations with whom they establish a scientific or professional relationship (1) the relevant limits of confidentiality and (2) the foreseeable uses of the information generated through their psychological activities. (See also Standard 3.10, Informed Consent.)

(b) Unless it is not feasible or is contraindicated, the discussion of confidentiality occurs at the outset of the relationship and thereafter as new circumstances may warrant.

(c) Psychologists who offer services, products, or information via electronic transmission inform clients/patients of the risks to privacy and limits of confidentiality.

4.03 Recording

Before recording the voices or images of individuals to whom they provide services, psychologists obtain permission from all such persons or their legal representatives. (See also Standards 8.03, Informed Consent for Recording Voices and Images in Research; 8.05, Dispensing With Informed Consent for Research; and 8.07, Deception in Research.)

4.04 Minimizing Intrusions on Privacy

(a) Psychologists include in written and oral reports and consultations, only information germane to the purpose for which the communication is made.

(b) Psychologists discuss confidential information obtained in their work only for appropriate scientific or professional purposes and only with persons clearly concerned with such matters.

4.05 Disclosures

(a) Psychologists may disclose confidential information with the appropriate consent of the organizational client, the individual client/patient, or another legally authorized person on behalf of the client/patient unless prohibited by law.

(b) Psychologists disclose confidential information without the consent of the individual only as mandated by law, or where permitted by law for a valid purpose such as to (1) provide needed professional services; (2) obtain appropriate professional consultations; (3) protect the client/patient, psychologist, or others from harm; or (4) obtain payment for services from a client/patient, in which instance disclosure is limited to the minimum that is necessary to achieve the purpose. (See also Standard 6.04e, Fees and Financial Arrangements.)

4.06 Consultations

When consulting with colleagues, (1) psychologists do not disclose confidential information that reasonably could lead to the identification of a client/patient, research participant, or other person or organization with whom they have a confidential relationship unless they have obtained the prior consent of the person or organization or the disclosure cannot be avoided, and (2) they disclose information only to the extent necessary to achieve the purposes of the consultation. (See also Standard 4.01, Maintaining Confidentiality.)

4.07 Use of Confidential Information for Didactic or Other Purposes

Psychologists do not disclose in their writings, lectures, or other public media, confidential, personally identifiable information concerning their clients/patients, students, research participants, organizational clients, or other recipients of their services that they obtained during the course of their work, unless (1) they take reasonable steps to disguise the person or organization, (2) the person or organization has consented in writing, or (3) there is legal authorization for doing so.

5. Advertising and Other Public Statements

5.01 Avoidance of False or Deceptive Statements

(a) Public statements include but are not limited to paid or unpaid advertising, product endorsements, grant applications, licensing applications, other credentialing applications, brochures, printed matter, directory listings, personal resumes or curricula vitae, or comments for use in media such as print or electronic transmission, statements in legal proceedings, lectures and public oral presentations, and published materials. Psychologists do not knowingly make public statements that are false, deceptive, or fraudulent concerning their research, practice, or other work activities or those of persons or organizations with which they are affiliated.

(b) Psychologists do not make false, deceptive, or fraudulent statements concerning (1) their training, experience, or competence; (2) their academic degrees; (3) their credentials; (4) their institutional or association affiliations; (5) their services; (6) the scientific or clinical basis for, or results or degree of success of, their services; (7) their fees; or (8) their publications or research findings.

(c) Psychologists claim degrees as credentials for their health services only if those degrees (1) were earned from a regionally accredited educational institution or (2) were the basis for psychology licensure by the state in which they practice.

5.02 Statements by Others

(a) Psychologists who engage others to create or place public statements that promote their professional practice, products, or activities retain professional responsibility for such statements.

(b) Psychologists do not compensate employees of press, radio, television, or other communication media in return for publicity in a news item. (See also Standard 1.01, Misuse of Psychologists' Work.)

(c) A paid advertisement relating to psychologists' activities must be identified or clearly recognizable as such.

5.03 Descriptions of Workshops and Non-Degree-Granting Educational Programs

To the degree to which they exercise control, psychologists responsible for announcements, catalogs, brochures, or advertisements describing workshops, seminars, or other non-degree-granting educational programs ensure that they accurately describe the audience for which the program is intended, the educational objectives, the presenters, and the fees involved.

5.04 Media Presentations

When psychologists provide public advice or comment via print, internet, or other electronic transmission, they take precautions to ensure that statements (1) are based on their professional knowledge, training, or experience in accord with appropriate psychological literature and practice; (2) are otherwise consistent with this Ethics Code; and (3) do not indicate that a professional relationship has been established with the recipient. (See also Standard 2.04, Bases for Scientific and Professional Judgments.)

5.05 Testimonials

Psychologists do not solicit testimonials from current therapy clients/patients or other persons who because of their particular circumstances are vulnerable to undue influence.

5.06 In-Person Solicitation

Psychologists do not engage, directly or through agents, in uninvited in-person solicitation of business from actual or potential therapy clients/patients or other persons who because of their particular circumstances are vulnerable to undue influence. However, this prohibition does not preclude (1) attempting to implement appropriate collateral contacts for the purpose of benefiting an already engaged therapy client/patient or (2) providing disaster or community outreach services.

6. Record Keeping and Fees

6.01 Documentation of Professional and Scientific Work and Maintenance of Records

Psychologists create, and to the extent the records are under their control, maintain, disseminate, store, retain, and dispose of records and data relating to their professional and scientific work in order to (1) facilitate provision of services later by them or by other professionals, (2) allow for replication of research design and analyses, (3) meet institutional requirements, (4) ensure accuracy of billing and payments, and (5) ensure compliance with law. (See also Standard 4.01, Maintaining Confidentiality.)

6.02 Maintenance, Dissemination, and Disposal of Confidential Records of Professional and Scientific Work

(a) Psychologists maintain confidentiality in creating, storing, accessing, transferring, and disposing of records under their control, whether these are written, automated, or in any other medium. (See also Standards 4.01, Maintaining Confidentiality, and 6.01, Documentation of Professional and Scientific Work and Maintenance of Records.)

(b) If confidential information concerning recipients of psychological services is entered into databases or systems of records available to persons whose access has not been consented to by the recipient, psychologists use coding or other techniques to avoid the inclusion of personal identifiers.

(c) Psychologists make plans in advance to facilitate the appropriate transfer and to protect the confidentiality of records and data in the event of psychologists' withdrawal from positions or practice. (See also Standards 3.12, Interruption of Psychological Services, and 10.09, Interruption of Therapy.)

6.03 Withholding Records for Nonpayment

Psychologists may not withhold records under their control that are requested and needed for a client's/patient's emergency treatment solely because payment has not been received.

6.04 Fees and Financial Arrangements

(a) As early as is feasible in a professional or scientific relationship, psychologists and recipients of psychological services reach an agreement specifying compensation and billing arrangements.

(b) Psychologists' fee practices are consistent with law.

(c) Psychologists do not misrepresent their fees.

(d) If limitations to services can be anticipated because of limitations in financing, this is discussed with the recipient of services as early as is feasible. (See also Standards 10.09, Interruption of Therapy, and 10.10, Terminating Therapy.)

(e) If the recipient of services does not pay for services as agreed, and if psychologists intend to use collection agencies or legal measures to collect the fees, psychologists first inform the person that such measures will be taken and provide that person an opportunity to make prompt payment. (See also Standards 4.05, Disclosures; 6.03, Withholding Records for Nonpayment; and 10.01, Informed Consent to Therapy.)

6.05 Barter With Clients/Patients

Barter is the acceptance of goods, services, or other nonmonetary remuneration from clients/patients in return for psychological services. Psychologists may barter only if (1) it is not clinically contraindicated, and (2) the resulting arrangement is not exploitative. (See also Standards 3.05, Multiple Relationships, and 6.04, Fees and Financial Arrangements.)

6.06 Accuracy in Reports to Payors and Funding Sources

In their reports to payors for services or sources of research funding, psychologists take reasonable steps to ensure the accurate reporting of the nature of the service provided or research conducted, the fees, charges, or payments, and where applicable, the identity of the provider, the findings, and the diagnosis. (See also Standards 4.01, Maintaining Confidentiality; 4.04, Minimizing Intrusions on Privacy; and 4.05, Disclosures.)

6.07 Referrals and Fees

When psychologists pay, receive payment from, or divide fees with another professional, other than in an employer-employee relationship, the payment to each is based on the services provided (clinical, consultative, administrative, or other) and is not based on the referral itself. (See also Standard 3.09, Cooperation With Other Professionals.)

7. Education and Training

7.01 Design of Education and Training Programs

Psychologists responsible for education and training programs take reasonable steps to ensure that the programs are designed to provide the appropriate knowledge and proper experiences, and to meet the requirements for licensure, certification, or other goals for which claims are made by the program. (See also Standard 5.03, Descriptions of Workshops and Non-Degree-Granting Educational Programs.)

7.02 Descriptions of Education and Training Programs

Psychologists responsible for education and training programs take reasonable steps to ensure that there is a current and accurate description of the program content (including participation in required course- or program-related counseling, psychotherapy, experiential groups, consulting projects, or community service), training goals and objectives, stipends and benefits, and requirements that must be met for satisfactory completion of the program. This information must be made readily available to all interested parties.

7.03 Accuracy in Teaching

(a) Psychologists take reasonable steps to ensure that course syllabi are accurate regarding the subject matter to be covered, bases for evaluating progress, and the nature of course experiences. This standard does not preclude an instructor from modifying course content or requirements when the instructor considers it pedagogically necessary or desirable, so long as students are made aware of these modifications in a manner that enables them to fulfill course requirements. (See also Standard 5.01, Avoidance of False or Deceptive Statements.)

(b) When engaged in teaching or training, psychologists present psychological information accurately. (See also Standard 2.03, Maintaining Competence.)

7.04 Student Disclosure of Personal Information

Psychologists do not require students or supervisees to disclose personal information in course- or program-related activities, either orally or in writing, regarding sexual history, history of abuse and neglect, psychological treatment, and relationships with parents, peers, and spouses or significant others except if (1) the program or training facility has clearly identified this requirement in its admissions and program materials or (2) the information is necessary to evaluate or obtain assistance for students whose personal problems could reasonably be judged to be preventing them from performing their training- or professionally related activities in a competent manner or posing a threat to the students or others.

7.05 Mandatory Individual or Group Therapy

(a) When individual or group therapy is a program or course requirement, psychologists responsible for that program allow students in undergraduate and graduate programs the option of selecting such therapy from practitioners unaffiliated with the program. (See also Standard 7.02, Descriptions of Education and Training Programs.)

(b) Faculty who are or are likely to be responsible for evaluating students' academic performance do not themselves provide that therapy. (See also Standard 3.05, Multiple Relationships.)

7.06 Assessing Student and Supervisee Performance

(a) In academic and supervisory relationships, psychologists establish a timely and specific process for providing feedback to students and supervisees. Information regarding the process is provided to the student at the beginning of supervision.

(b) Psychologists evaluate students and supervisees on the basis of their actual performance on relevant and established program requirements.

7.07 Sexual Relationships With Students and Supervisees

Psychologists do not engage in sexual relationships with students or supervisees who are in their department, agency, or training center or over whom psychologists have or are likely to have evaluative authority. (See also Standard 3.05, Multiple Relationships.)

8. Research and Publication

8.01 Institutional Approval

When institutional approval is required, psychologists provide accurate information about their research proposals and obtain approval prior to conducting the research. They conduct the research in accordance with the approved research protocol.

8.02 Informed Consent to Research

(a) When obtaining informed consent as required in Standard 3.10, Informed Consent, psychologists inform participants about (1) the purpose of the research, expected duration, and procedures; (2) their right to decline to participate and to withdraw from the research once participation has begun; (3) the foreseeable consequences of declining or withdrawing; (4) reasonably foreseeable factors that may be expected to influence their willingness to participate such as potential risks, discomfort, or adverse effects; (5) any prospective research benefits; (6) limits of confidentiality; (7) incentives for participation; and (8) whom to contact for questions about the research and research participants' rights. They provide opportunity for the prospective participants to ask questions and receive answers. (See also Standards 8.03, Informed Consent for Recording Voices and Images in Research; 8.05, Dispensing With Informed Consent for Research; and 8.07, Deception in Research.)

(b) Psychologists conducting intervention research involving the use of experimental treatments clarify to participants at the outset of the research (1) the experimental nature of the treatment; (2) the services that will or will not be available to the control group(s) if appropriate; (3) the means by which assignment to treatment and control groups will be made; (4) available treatment alternatives if an individual does not wish to participate in the research or wishes to withdraw once a study has begun; and (5) compensation for or monetary costs of participating including, if appropriate, whether reimbursement from the participant or a third-party payor will be sought. (See also Standard 8.02a, Informed Consent to Research.)

8.03 Informed Consent for Recording Voices and Images in Research

Psychologists obtain informed consent from research participants prior to recording their voices or images for data collection unless (1) the research consists solely of naturalistic observations in public places, and it is not anticipated that the recording will be used in a manner that could cause personal identification or harm, or (2) the research design includes deception, and consent for the use of the recording is obtained during debriefing. (See also Standard 8.07, Deception in Research.)

8.04 Client/Patient, Student, and Subordinate Research Participants

(a) When psychologists conduct research with clients/patients, students, or subordinates as participants, psychologists take steps to protect the prospective participants from adverse consequences of declining or withdrawing from participation.

(b) When research participation is a course requirement or an opportunity for extra credit, the prospective participant is given the choice of equitable alternative activities.

8.05 Dispensing With Informed Consent for Research

Psychologists may dispense with informed consent only (1) where research would not reasonably be assumed to create distress or harm and involves (a) the study of normal educational practices, curricula, or classroom management methods conducted in educational settings; (b) only anonymous questionnaires, naturalistic observations, or archival research for which disclosure of responses would not place participants at risk of criminal or civil liability or damage their financial standing, employability, or reputation, and confidentiality is protected; or (c) the study of factors related to job or organization effectiveness conducted in organizational settings for which there is no risk to participants' employability, and confidentiality is protected or (2) where otherwise permitted by law or federal or institutional regulations.

8.06 Offering Inducements for Research Participation

(a) Psychologists make reasonable efforts to avoid offering excessive or inappropriate financial or other inducements for research participation when such inducements are likely to coerce participation.

(b) When offering professional services as an inducement for research participation, psychologists clarify the nature of the services, as well as the risks, obligations, and limitations. (See also Standard 6.05, Barter With Clients/Patients.)

8.07 Deception in Research

(a) Psychologists do not conduct a study involving deception unless they have determined that the use of deceptive techniques is justified by the study's significant prospective scientific, educational, or applied value and that effective nondeceptive alternative procedures are not feasible.

(b) Psychologists do not deceive prospective participants about research that is reasonably expected to cause physical pain or severe emotional distress.

(c) Psychologists explain any deception that is an integral feature of the design and conduct of an experiment to participants as early as is feasible, preferably at the conclusion of their participation, but no later than at the conclusion of the data collection, and permit participants to withdraw their data. (See also Standard 8.08, Debriefing.)

8.08 Debriefing

(a) Psychologists provide a prompt opportunity for participants to obtain appropriate information about the nature, results, and conclusions of the research, and they take reasonable steps to correct any misconceptions that participants may have of which the psychologists are aware.

(b) If scientific or humane values justify delaying or withholding this information, psychologists take reasonable measures to reduce the risk of harm.

(c) When psychologists become aware that research procedures have harmed a participant, they take reasonable steps to minimize the harm.

8.09 Humane Care and Use of Animals in Research

(a) Psychologists acquire, care for, use, and dispose of animals in compliance with current federal, state, and local laws and regulations, and with professional standards.

(b) Psychologists trained in research methods and experienced in the care of laboratory animals supervise all procedures involving animals and are responsible for ensuring appropriate consideration of their comfort, health, and humane treatment.

(c) Psychologists ensure that all individuals under their supervision who are using animals have received instruction in research methods and in the care, maintenance, and handling of the species being used, to the extent appropriate to their role. (See also Standard 2.05, Delegation of Work to Others.)

(d) Psychologists make reasonable efforts to minimize the discomfort, infection, illness, and pain of animal subjects.

(e) Psychologists use a procedure subjecting animals to pain, stress, or privation only when an alternative procedure is unavailable and the goal is justified by its prospective scientific, educational, or applied value.

(f) Psychologists perform surgical procedures under appropriate anesthesia and follow techniques to avoid infection and minimize pain during and after surgery.

(g) When it is appropriate that an animal's life be terminated, psychologists proceed rapidly, with an effort to minimize pain and in accordance with accepted procedures.

8.10 Reporting Research Results

(a) Psychologists do not fabricate data. (See also Standard 5.01a, Avoidance of False or Deceptive Statements.)

(b) If psychologists discover significant errors in their published data, they take reasonable steps to correct such errors in a correction, retraction, erratum, or other appropriate publication means.

8.11 Plagiarism

Psychologists do not present portions of another's work or data as their own, even if the other work or data source is cited occasionally.

8.12 Publication Credit

(a) Psychologists take responsibility and credit, including authorship credit, only for work they have actually performed or to which they have substantially contributed. (See also Standard 8.12b, Publication Credit.)

(b) Principal authorship and other publication credits accurately reflect the relative scientific or professional contributions of the individuals involved, regardless of their relative status. Mere possession of an institutional position, such as department chair, does not justify authorship credit. Minor contributions to the research or to the writing for publications are acknowledged appropriately, such as in footnotes or in an introductory statement.

(c) Except under exceptional circumstances, a student is listed as principal author on any multiple-authored article that is substantially based on the student's doctoral dissertation. Faculty advisors discuss publication credit with students as early as feasible and throughout the research and publication process as appropriate. (See also Standard 8.12b, Publication Credit.)

8.13 Duplicate Publication of Data

Psychologists do not publish, as original data, data that have been previously published. This does not preclude republishing data when they are accompanied by proper acknowledgment.

8.14 Sharing Research Data for Verification

(a) After research results are published, psychologists do not withhold the data on which their conclusions are based from other competent professionals who seek to verify the substantive claims through reanalysis and who intend to use such data only for that purpose, provided that the confidentiality of the participants can be protected and unless legal rights concerning proprietary data preclude their release. This does not preclude psychologists from requiring that such individuals or groups be responsible for costs associated with the provision of such information.

(b) Psychologists who request data from other psychologists to verify the substantive claims through reanalysis may use shared data only for the declared purpose. Requesting psychologists obtain prior written agreement for all other uses of the data.

8.15 Reviewers

Psychologists who review material submitted for presentation, publication, grant, or research proposal review respect the confidentiality of and the proprietary rights in such information of those who submitted it.

9. Assessment

9.01 Bases for Assessments

(a) Psychologists base the opinions contained in their recommendations, reports, and diagnostic or evaluative statements, including forensic testimony, on information and techniques sufficient to substantiate their findings. (See also Standard 2.04, Bases for Scientific and Professional Judgments.)

(b) Except as noted in 9.01c, psychologists provide opinions of the psychological characteristics of individuals only after they have conducted an examination of the individuals adequate to support their statements or conclusions. When, despite reasonable efforts, such an examination is not practical, psychologists document the efforts they made and the result of those efforts, clarify the probable impact of their limited information on the reliability and validity of their opinions, and appropriately limit the nature and extent of their conclusions or recommendations. (See also Standards 2.01, Boundaries of Competence, and 9.06, Interpreting Assessment Results.)

(c) When psychologists conduct a record review or provide consultation or supervision and an individual examination is not warranted or necessary for the opinion, psychologists explain this and the sources of information on which they based their conclusions and recommendations.

9.02 Use of Assessments

(a) Psychologists administer, adapt, score, interpret, or use assessment techniques, interviews, tests, or instruments in a manner and for purposes that are appropriate in light of the research on or evidence of the usefulness and proper application of the techniques.

(b) Psychologists use assessment instruments whose validity and reliability have been established for use with members of the population tested. When such validity or reliability has not been established, psychologists describe the strengths and limitations of test results and interpretation.

(c) Psychologists use assessment methods that are appropriate to an individual's language preference and competence, unless the use of an alternative language is relevant to the assessment issues.

9.03 Informed Consent in Assessments

(a) Psychologists obtain informed consent for assessments, evaluations, or diagnostic services, as described in Standard 3.10, Informed Consent, except when (1) testing is mandated by law or governmental regulations; (2) informed consent is implied because testing is conducted as a routine educational, institutional, or organizational activity (e.g., when participants voluntarily agree to assessment when applying for a job); or (3) one purpose of the testing is to evaluate decisional capacity. Informed consent includes an explanation of the nature and purpose of the assessment, fees, involvement of third parties, and limits of confidentiality and sufficient opportunity for the client/patient to ask questions and receive answers.

(b) Psychologists inform persons with questionable capacity to consent or for whom testing is mandated by law or governmental regulations about the nature and purpose of the proposed assessment services, using language that is reasonably understandable to the person being assessed.

(c) Psychologists using the services of an interpreter obtain informed consent from the client/patient to use that interpreter, ensure that confidentiality of test results and test security are maintained, and include in their recommendations, reports, and diagnostic or evaluative statements, including forensic testimony, discussion of any limitations on the data obtained. (See also Standards 2.05, Delegation of Work to Others; 4.01, Maintaining Confidentiality; 9.01, Bases for Assessments; 9.06, Interpreting Assessment Results; and 9.07, Assessment by Unqualified Persons.)

9.04 Release of Test Data

(a) The term *test data* refers to raw and scaled scores, client/patient responses to test questions or stimuli, and psychologists' notes and recordings concerning client/patient statements and behavior during an examination.

Those portions of test materials that include client/patient responses are included in the definition of *test data*. Pursuant to a client/patient release, psychologists provide test data to the client/patient or other persons identified in the release. Psychologists may refrain from releasing test data to protect a client/patient or others from substantial harm or misuse or misrepresentation of the data or the test, recognizing that in many instances release of confidential information under these circumstances is regulated by law. (See also Standard 9.11, Maintaining Test Security.)

(b) In the absence of a client/patient release, psychologists provide test data only as required by law or court order.

9.05 Test Construction

Psychologists who develop tests and other assessment techniques use appropriate psychometric procedures and current scientific or professional knowledge for test design, standardization, validation, reduction or elimination of bias, and recommendations for use.

9.06 Interpreting Assessment Results

When interpreting assessment results, including automated interpretations, psychologists take into account the purpose of the assessment as well as the various test factors, test-taking abilities, and other characteristics of the person being assessed, such as situational, personal, linguistic, and cultural differences, that might affect psychologists' judgments or reduce the accuracy of their interpretations. They indicate any significant limitations of their interpretations. (See also Standards 2.01b and c, Boundaries of Competence, and 3.01, Unfair Discrimination.)

9.07 Assessment by Unqualified Persons

Psychologists do not promote the use of psychological assessment techniques by unqualified persons, except when such use is conducted for training purposes with appropriate supervision. (See also Standard 2.05, Delegation of Work to Others.)

9.08 Obsolete Tests and Outdated Test Results

(a) Psychologists do not base their assessment or intervention decisions or recommendations on data or test results that are outdated for the current purpose.

(b) Psychologists do not base such decisions or recommendations on tests and measures that are obsolete and not useful for the current purpose.

9.09 Test Scoring and Interpretation Services

(a) Psychologists who offer assessment or scoring services to other professionals accurately describe the purpose, norms, validity, reliability, and applications of the procedures and any special qualifications applicable to their use.

(b) Psychologists select scoring and interpretation services (including automated services) on the basis of evidence of the validity of the program and procedures as well as on other appropriate considerations. (See also Standard 2.01b and c, Boundaries of Competence.)

(c) Psychologists retain responsibility for the appropriate application, interpretation, and use of assessment instruments, whether they score and interpret such tests themselves or use automated or other services.

9.10 Explaining Assessment Results

Regardless of whether the scoring and interpretation are done by psychologists, by employees or assistants, or by automated or other outside services, psychologists take reasonable steps to ensure that explanations of results are given to the individual or designated representative unless the nature of the relationship precludes provision of an explanation of results (such as in some organizational consulting, preemployment or security screenings, and forensic evaluations), and this fact has been clearly explained to the person being assessed in advance.

9.11 Maintaining Test Security

The term *test materials* refers to manuals, instruments, protocols, and test questions or stimuli and does not include *test data* as defined in Standard 9.04, Release of Test Data. Psychologists make reasonable efforts to maintain the integrity and security of test materials and other assessment techniques consistent with law and contractual obligations, and in a manner that permits adherence to this Ethics Code.

10. Therapy

10.01 Informed Consent to Therapy

(a) When obtaining informed consent to therapy as required in Standard 3.10, Informed Consent, psychologists inform clients/patients as early as is feasible in the therapeutic relationship about the nature and anticipated course of therapy, fees, involvement of third parties, and limits of confidentiality and provide sufficient opportunity for the client/patient to ask questions and receive answers. (See also Standards 4.02, Discussing the Limits of Confidentiality, and 6.04, Fees and Financial Arrangements.)

(b) When obtaining informed consent for treatment for which generally recognized techniques and procedures have not been established, psychologists inform their clients/patients of the developing nature of the treatment, the potential risks involved, alternative treatments that may be available, and the voluntary nature of their participation. (See also Standards 2.01e, Boundaries of Competence, and 3.10, Informed Consent.)

(c) When the therapist is a trainee and the legal responsibility for the treatment provided resides with the supervisor, the client/patient, as part of the informed consent procedure, is informed that the therapist is in training and is being supervised and is given the name of the supervisor.

10.02 Therapy Involving Couples or Families

(a) When psychologists agree to provide services to several persons who have a relationship (such as spouses, significant others, or parents and children), they take reasonable steps to clarify at the outset (1) which of the individuals are clients/patients and (2) the relationship the psychologist will have with each person. This clarification includes the psychologist's role and the probable uses of the services provided or the information obtained. (See also Standard 4.02, Discussing the Limits of Confidentiality.)

(b) If it becomes apparent that psychologists may be called on to perform potentially conflicting roles (such as family therapist and then witness for one party in divorce proceedings), psychologists take reasonable steps to clarify and modify, or withdraw from, roles appropriately. (See also Standard 3.05c, Multiple Relationships.)

10.03 Group Therapy

When psychologists provide services to several persons in a group setting, they describe at the outset the roles and responsibilities of all parties and the limits of confidentiality.

10.04 Providing Therapy to Those Served by Others

In deciding whether to offer or provide services to those already receiving mental health services elsewhere, psychologists carefully consider the treatment issues and the potential client's/patient's welfare. Psychologists discuss these issues with the client/patient or another legally authorized person on behalf of the client/patient in order to minimize the risk of confusion and conflict, consult with the other service providers when appropriate, and proceed with caution and sensitivity to the therapeutic issues.

10.05 Sexual Intimacies With Current Therapy Clients/Patients

Psychologists do not engage in sexual intimacies with current therapy clients/patients.

10.06 Sexual Intimacies With Relatives or Significant Others of Current Therapy Clients/Patients

Psychologists do not engage in sexual intimacies with individuals they know to be close relatives, guardians, or significant others of current clients/patients. Psychologists do not terminate therapy to circumvent this standard.

10.07 Therapy With Former Sexual Partners

Psychologists do not accept as therapy clients/patients persons with whom they have engaged in sexual intimacies.

10.08 Sexual Intimacies With Former Therapy Clients/Patients

(a) Psychologists do not engage in sexual intimacies with former clients/patients for at least two years after cessation or termination of therapy.

(b) Psychologists do not engage in sexual intimacies with former clients/patients even after a two-year interval except in the most unusual circumstances. Psychologists who engage in such activity after the two years following cessation or termination of therapy and of having no sexual contact with the former client/patient bear the burden of demonstrating that there has been no exploitation, in light of all relevant factors, including (1) the amount of time that has passed since therapy terminated; (2) the nature, duration, and intensity of the therapy; (3) the circumstances of termination; (4) the client's/patient's personal history; (5) the client's/patient's current mental status; (6) the likelihood of adverse impact on the client/patient; and (7) any statements or actions made by the therapist during the course of therapy suggesting or inviting the possibility of a posttermination sexual or romantic relationship with the client/patient. (See also Standard 3.05, Multiple Relationships.)

10.09 Interruption of Therapy

When entering into employment or contractual relationships, psychologists make reasonable efforts to provide for orderly and appropriate resolution of responsibility for client/patient care in the event that the employment or contractual relationship ends, with paramount consideration given to the welfare of the client/patient. (See also Standard 3.12, Interruption of Psychological Services.)

10.10 Terminating Therapy

(a) Psychologists terminate therapy when it becomes reasonably clear that the client/patient no longer needs the service, is not likely to benefit, or is being harmed by continued service.

(b) Psychologists may terminate therapy when threatened or otherwise endangered by the client/patient or another person with whom the client/patient has a relationship.

(c) Except where precluded by the actions of clients/patients or third-party payors, prior to termination psychologists provide pretermination counseling and suggest alternative service providers as appropriate.

Reprinted with permission from "Ethical Principles of Psychologists and Code of Conduct," 2002, *American Psychologist, 57*, 1060–1073.

References

Abrahams, N. M., Neumann, I., & Githens, W. H. (1968, February). *The Strong Vocational Interest Blank in predicting NROTC officer retention. Part II, Fakability.* U.S. Naval Personnel Research Activity, *Technical Bulletin STB*, 68–69.

Ackerman, P. L. (1987). Individual differences in skill learning: An integration of psychometric and information processing perspectives. *Psychological Bulletin, 102,* 3–27.

Ackerman, P. L., & Humphreys, L. G. (1990). Individual differences theory in industrial and organizational psychology. In M. Dunnette & L. Hough (Eds.), *Handbook of industrial and organizational psychology* (2nd ed., Vol. 1, pp. 223–282). Palo Alto, CA: Consulting Psychologists Press.

Adair, J. G. (1973). *The human subject: The social psychology of the psychological experiment.* Boston: Little, Brown.

Adams, K. M., & Brown, G. C. (1986). The role of the computer in neuropsychological assessment. In I. Grant and K. Adams (Eds.), *Neuropsychological assessment of neuropsychiatric disorders.* New York: Oxford University Press.

Adorno, T. W., Frenkel-Brunswik, E., Levinson, D. J., & Sanford, R. N. (1950). *The authoritarian personality.* New York: Harper Bros.

Ahlburg, D. A. (1992). Predicting the job performance of managers: What do the experts know? *International Journal of Forecasting, 7,* 467–472.

Aiello, J. R., & Kolb, K. J. (1995a). Electronic performance monitoring: A risk factor for workplace stress. In I. S. Sauter and L. Peters (Eds.), *Organizational risk factors for job stress* (pp. 163–179). Washington, DC: American Psychological Association.

Aiello, J. R., & Kolb, K. J. (1995b). Electronic performance monitoring and social context: Impact on productivity and stress. *Journal of Applied Psychology, 80,* 339–353.

Albright, L. E., Glennon, J. R., & Smith, W. J. (1963). *The uses of psychological tests in industry.* Cleveland, OH: Allen.

Allinger, G. M. (1988). Do zero correlations really exist among measures of different intellectual abilities? *Educational and Psychological Measurement, 48,* 275–280.

Allport, G. W., & Odbert, H. S. (1936). Trait names: A psycholexical study. *Psychological Monographs, 47* (1, Whole No. 211).

Allran, K. D. (1989). *The reliability of a computerized method for assessment of anaerobic power and work capacity using maximal cycle ergometry.* Eugene, OR: Microform Publication, College of Human Development and Performance, University of Oregon.

American College Test Program. (1995). *Using the ACT assessment on campus.* Iowa City, IA: American College Test Program.

American Council on Education. (1995). *Guidelines for computerized-adaptive test (CAT) development and use in education.* Washington DC: Author.

American Psychiatric Association. (1980). *Diagnostic and statistical manual of mental disorders* (3rd ed.). Washington, DC: American Psychiatric Association.

American Psychiatric Association. (1994). *Diagnostic and statistical manual of mental disorders* (4th ed.). Washington, DC: American Psychiatric Association.

American Psychiatric Association. (2000). *Diagnostic and statistical manual of mental disorders: 4th Edition—Text Revision.* Washington, DC: American Psychiatric Association.

American Psychological Association. (1954). *Technical recommendations for psychological tests and diagnostic techniques.* Washington, DC: Author.

American Psychological Association. (1985). *Standards for educational and psychological testing.* Washington, DC: Author.

American Psychological Association. (1986). *Guidelines for computer-based tests and interpretation.* Washington, DC: Author.

American Psychological Association. (1992). Ethical principles of psychologists and code of conduct. *American Psychologist, 47,* 1597–1611.

American Psychological Association. (1993). Guidelines for computer-based tests and interpretations. Washington, DC: Author.

American Psychological Association. (1999). *Standards for educational and psychological testing.* Washington, DC: Author.

American Psychological Association. (2002). Ethical principles of psychologists and code of conduct. *American Psychologist, 57,* 1060–1073.

Anastasi, A. (1982). *Psychological testing* (5th ed.). New York: Macmillan.

Andrews, L. W., & Gutkin, T. B. (1991). The effects of human versus computer authorship on consumers' perceptions of psychological reports. *Computers in Human Behavior, 7,* 311–317.

Angoff, W. H. (1971). Scales, norms and equivalent scores. In R. L. Thorndike (Ed.), *Educational measurement* (2nd ed.). Washington, DC: American Council on Education.

Angoff, W. H. (1988). The nature-nurture debate, aptitudes, and group differences. *American Psychologist, 43,* 713–720.

APA Task Force. (1991). *Questionnaires used in the prediction of trustworthiness in pre-employment selection decisions: An A.P.A. Task Force Report.* Washington, DC: American Psychological Association.

Aronow, E., Reznikoff, M., & Moreland, K. L. (1995). The Rorschach: Projective technique or psychometric test? *Journal of Personality Assessment, 64,* 213–228.

Arvey, R. D. (1979). *Fairness in selecting employees.* Reading, MA: Addison-Wesley.

Arvey, R. D., & Campion, J. E. (1982). The employment interview: A summary and review of recent research. *Personnel Psychology, 35,* 281–322.

Arvey, R. D., & Faley, R. H. (1988). *Fairness in selecting employees* (2nd ed.). Reading, MA: Addison-Wesley.

Ash, P. (1976). The assessment of honesty in employment. *South African Journal of Psychology, 6,* 68–79.

Asher, J. J. (1972). The biographical item: Can it be improved? *Personnel Psychology, 25,* 251–269.

Asher, J. J., & Sciarrino, J. A. (1974). Realistic work sample tests: A review. *Personnel Psychology, 27,* 519–553.

Ashton, S. G., & Goldberg, L. R. (1973). In response to Jackson's challenge: The comparative validity of personality scales constructed by the external (empirical) strategy and scales developed intuitively by the experts, novices, and laymen. *Journal of Research in Personality, 7,* 1–20.

Association of Test Publishers. (1996). *Model guidelines for preemployment integrity testing.* Washington, DC: Author.

Austin, J. T., & Villanova, P. (1992). The criterion problem 1917–1992. *Journal of Applied Psychology, 77,* 836–874.

Axelrod, B. N. (2002). Validity of the Wechsler Abbreviated Scale of Intelligence and other very short forms of estimating intellectual functioning. *Assessment, 9*(1), 17–23.

Ayers, J. D. (1972). Review of the Concept Assessment Kit—Conservation. In O. K. Buros (Ed.), *The eighth mental measurements yearbook.* Highland, NJ: Gryphon Press.

Azar, B. (1996). People are becoming smarter—why? *American Psychological Association Monitor, 27*(6), 20.

Bachelor, P. A. (1989). Maximum likelihood confirmatory factor-analytic investigation of factors within Guilford's structure of intellect model. *Journal of Applied Psychology, 74,* 797–804.

Baehr, M., & Williams, G. B. (1967). Underlying dimensions of personal background data and their relationship to occupational classification. *Journal of Applied Psychology, 51,* 481–490.

Baker, E. L., O'Neil, H. F., Jr., & Linn, R. L. (1993). Policy and validity prospects for performance-based assessment. *American Psychologist, 48,* 1210–1218.

Balzer, W. K., & Sulsky, L. M. (1990). Performance appraisal effectiveness. In K. Murphy & F. Saal (Eds.), *Psychology in organizations: Integrating science and practice* (pp. 133–156). Hillsdale, NJ: Erlbaum.

Balzer, W. K., & Sulsky, L. M. (1992). Halo and performance appraisal research: A critical examination. *Journal of Applied Psychology, 77,* 975–985.

Banks, C. G., & Murphy, K. R. (1985). Toward narrowing the research-practice gap in performance appraisal. *Personnel Psychology, 38,* 335–345.

Bannatyne, A. (1974). Diagnosis: A note on the recategorization of the WISC scaled scores. *Journal of Learning Disorders, 7,* 272–273.

Barrett, G. V., Alexander, R. A., Doverspike, D., Cellar, D., & Thomas, J. C. (1982). The development and application of a computerized information-processing test. *Applied Psychological Measurement, 6,* 13–29.

Barrett, G. V., Phillips, J. S., & Alexander, R. A. (1981). Concurrent and predictive validity designs: A critical reanalysis. *Journal of Applied Psychology, 66,* 1–6.

Barrick, M. R., & Mount, M. K. (1991). The Big Five personality dimensions and job performance: A meta analysis. *Personnel Psychology, 44,* 1–26.

Bartlett, C., & O'Leary, B. (1969). A differential prediction model to moderate the effects of heterogeneous groups in personnel selection and classification. *Personnel Psychology, 22,* 1–17.

Bartram, D. (1997). Distance assessment: Psychological assessment through the Internet. *Selection and Development Review, 13,* 15–19.

Bass, B. M. (1954). The leaderless group discussion. *Psychological Bulletin, 51,* 465–492.

Bassiri, D., & Shulz, E. M. (2003). Constructing a universal scale of high school course difficulty. *Journal of Educational Measurement, 40,* 147–161.

Beach, L. (1967). Multiple regression as a model of human information utilization. *Organizational Behavior and Human Performance, 2,* 276–289.

Becker. K. A. (2003*). History of the Stanford-Binet intelligence scales: Content and psychometrics. Stanford-Binet Intelligence Scales, Fifth Edition.* Assessment Service Bulletin No. 1. Itasca, IL: Riverside.

Bem, D. J., & Funder, D. C. (1978). Predicting more of the people more of the time: Assessing the personality of situations. *Psychological Review, 85,* 485–501.

Bender, L. (1938). A visual motor gestalt test and its clinical use. *Research monograph, No. 3, American Orthopsychiatric Association.*

Bennett, G. (1980). *Tests of Mechanical Comprehension.* New York: Psychological Corporation.

Bennett, G., Seashore, H., & Wesman, A. (1974). *Fifth edition manual for the Differential Aptitude Tests.* New York: The Psychological Corporation.

Bennett, R. E., Rock, D. A., & Wang, M. (1991). Equivalence of free-response and multiple-choice items. *Journal of Educational Measurement, 28,* 77–92.

Bennett, R. E., & Ward, W. C. (1993). *Construction versus choice in cognitive measurement: Issues in constructed response, performance testing, and portfolio assessment.* Hillsdale, NJ: Erlbaum.

Ben-Shakar, G., Bar-Hillel, M., Bilu, Y., & Shefler, G. (1998). Seek and ye shall find: Test results are what you hypthesize they are. *Journal of Behavioral Decision Making, 11,* 235–249.

Ben-Shakar, G., Bar-Hillel, M., Blum, Y., Ben-Abba, E., & Flug, A. (1986). Can graphology predict occupational success: Two empirical studies and some methodological ruminations. *Journal of Applied Psychology, 71,* 645–653.

Ben-Shakar, G., Lieblich, I., & Bar-Hillel, M. (1982). An evaluation of polygraphers' judgments: A review from a decision theoretic perspective. *Journal of Applied Psychology, 67,* 701–713.

Bentler, P. M. (1964). *Response variability: Fact or artifact?* Unpublished doctoral dissertation, Stanford University.

Berg, R. A. (1997). Screening tests in clinical neuropsychology. In A. Horton, D. Wedding, & J. Webster (Eds.), *The neuropsychology handbook* (2nd ed., Vol. 1, pp. 331–364). New York: Springer.

Berk, R. A. (1982). *Handbook for detecting test bias.* Baltimore, MD: Johns Hopkins University Press.

Bernardin, H. J., Alveres, K. M., & Cranny, C. J. (1976). A recomparison of behavioral expectation scales to summated scales. *Journal of Applied Psychology, 61,* 564–570.

Bernardin, H. J., & Smith, P. C. (1981). A clarification of some issues regarding the development and use of behaviorally anchored rating scales (BARS). *Journal of Applied Psychology, 66,* 458–463.

Bernardin, H. J., & Walter, C. S. (1977). Effects of rater training and diary-keeping on psychometric error in ratings. *Journal of Applied Psychology, 62,* 64–69.

Biglcr, E. D., Lowry, C. M., & Porter, S. S. (1997). Neuroimaging in clinical neuropsychology. In A. Horton, D. Wedding, & J. Webster (Eds.), *The neuropsychology handbook* (2nd ed., Vol. 1, pp. 171–220). New York: Springer.

Binet, A., & Henri, V. (1895). La psychologie individuelle. *Annee Psychologique, 2,* 411–463.

Binet, A., & Simon, T. (1905). Methodes nouvelles pour le diagnostic du nivau intellectuel des anormaux. *Annee Psychologique, 11,* 191–244.

Binning, J. F., & Barrett, G. V. (1989). Validity of personnel decisions: A conceptual analysis of the inferential and evidential bases. *Journal of Applied Psychology, 74,* 478–494.

Birren, J. E., & Schaie, K. W. (1977). *Handbook of the psychology of aging.* New York: Van Nostrand Reinhold.

Block, J. (1995). A contrarian view of the five-factor approach to personality description. *Psychological Bulletin, 117,* 187–215.

Bloom, B. S. (1976). *Human characteristics and school learning.* New York: McGraw-Hill.

Boehm, A. E. (1985). Educational applications of intelligence testing. In B. Wolman (Ed.), *Handbook of intelligence: Theories, measurements and applications.* New York: Wiley.

Boehm, V. (1977). Differential prediction: A statistical artifact. *Journal of Applied Psychology, 62,* 146–154.

Borgen, F. H. (1988). Strong-Campbell Interest Inventory. In J. T. Kapes & M. M. Mastic (Eds.), *A counselor's guide to career assessment instruments* (2nd ed.). Alexandria, VA: National Career Development Association.

Borman, W. C. (1977). Consistency of rating accuracy and rating errors in the judgment of human performance. *Organizational Behavior and Human Performance, 20,* 238–252.

Borman, W. C. (1978). Exploring the upper limits of reliability and validity in job performance ratings. *Journal of Applied Psychology, 63,* 135–144.

Borman, W. C. (1982). Validity of behavioral assessment for predicting military recruiter performance. *Journal of Applied Psychology, 67,* 3–9.

Borman, W. C. (1991). Job behavior, performance, and effectiveness. In M. Dunnette & L. Hough (Eds.), *Handbook of industrial and organizational psychology* (2nd ed., Vol. 2, pp. 271–326). Palo Alto, CA: Consulting Psychologists Press.

Borman, W. C., Eaton, N. K., Bryan, J. D., & Rosse, R. L. (1983). Between-assessor differences in assessment validity. *Journal of Applied Psychology, 68,* 415–419.

Borman, W. C., & Vallon, W. R. (1974). A view of what can happen when behavioral expectation scales are developed in one setting and used in another. *Journal of Applied Psychology, 59,* 197–201.

Bouchard, T. J., Lykken, D. T., McGue, M., Segal, N. L., et al. (1990, October). Sources of human psychological differences: The Minnesota Study of Twins Reared Apart. *Science, 250,* 223–228.

Bouchard, T. J., & Segal, N. L. (1985). Environment and IQ. In B. Wolman (Ed.), *Handbook of intelligence: Theories, measurements and applications.* New York: Wiley.

Boudreau, J. W. (1991). Utility analysis for decisions in Human Resource Management. In M. Dunnette & L. Hough (Eds.), *Handbook of industrial and organizational psychology* (2nd ed., Vol. 2, pp. 621–745). Palo Alto, CA: Consulting Psychologists Press.

Bracken, D., Timmreck, C., & Church, A. (2001). *Handbook of multisource feedback.* San Francisco: Jossey-Bass.

Brandt, J. E., & Hood, A. B. (1968). Effect of personality adjustment on the predictive validity of the Strong Vocational Interest Blank. *Journal of Counseling Psychology, 15,* 547–551.

Brass, D. J., & Oldham, G. R. (1976). Validating an in-basket test using an alternative set of leadership scoring dimensions. *Journal of Applied Psychology, 61,* 652–657.

Bray, D. W., Campbell, R. J., & Grant, D. L. (1974). *Formative years in business: A long-term AT&T study of managerial lives.* New York: Wiley.

Bray, D. W., & Grant, D. L. (1966). The assessment center in the measurement of potential for business management of potential for business management. *Psychological Monographs, 80* (Whole Number 17).

Brennan, R. L. (1983). *Elements of generalizability theory.* Iowa City, IA: American College Test Program.

Brewer, N., & Ridgway, T. (1998). Effects of supervisory monitoring on productivity and quality of performance. *Journal of Experimental Psychology: Applied, 4,* 211–227.

Bridgeman, B. (1992). A comparison of quantitative questions in open-ended and multiple-choice formats. *Journal of Educational Measurement, 29,* 253–271.

Brief, A. P., & Motowidlo, S. J. (1986). Prosocial organizational behaviors. *Academy of Management Review, 11,* 710–725.

Brooks, B. L., & Hosie, T. W. (1984). Assumptions and interpretations of the SOMPA in estimating learning potential. *Counselor Education and Supervision, 23,* 290–299.

Brown, S. H. (1981). Validity generalization and situational moderation in the life insurance industry. *Journal of Applied Psychology, 66,* 664–670.

Brunswick, E. (1956). *Perception and the representative design of psychological experiments.* Berkeley: University of California Press.

Brush, D. H., & Owens, W. A. (1979). Implementation and evaluation of an assessment classification model for manpower utilization. *Personnel Psychology, 32,* 369–383.

Buchanan, T. (2002). Online assessment: Desirable or dangerous? *Professional Psychology: Research and Practice, 33,* 148–154.

Buchel, F. P., & Scharnhorst, U. (1993). The Learning Potential Assessment Device (LPAD): Discussion of theoretical and methodological problems. In J. Hamers, K. Sijtsma, & A. Ruijssenaars (Eds.), *Learning potential assessment: Theoretical, methodological and practical issues* (pp. 83–111). Amsterdam: Swets & Zeitlinger.

Buckley, M. R., Cote, J. A., & Comstock, S. M. (1990). Measurement errors in the behavioral science: The case of personality/attitude research. *Educational and Psychological Measurement, 50,* 447–474.

Buckner, D. N. (1959). The predictability of ratings as a function of interrater agreement. *Journal of Applied Psychology, 43,* 60–64.

Burke, H. R. (1972). Raven's progressive matrices: Validity, reliability, and norms. *The Journal of Psychology, 82,* 253–257.

Buros, O. K. (1974). *Tests in print II.* Highland Park, NJ: Gryphon Press.

Buros, O. K. (1975a). *Intelligence tests and reviews.* Highland Park, NJ: Gryphon Press.

Buros, O. K. (1975b). *Personality tests and reviews II.* Highland Park, NJ: Gryphon Press.

Buros, O. K. (1975c). *Vocational tests and reviews.* Highland Park, NJ: Gryphon Press.

Buros, O. K. (1978). *The eighth mental measurements yearbook.* Highland Park, NJ: Gryphon Press.

Bury, A. S., & Bagby, R. M. (2002). The detection of feigned uncoached and coached posttraumatic stress disorder with the MMPI-2 in a sample of workplace accident victims. *Psychological Assessment, 14,* 472–484.

Butcher, J. N. (1972). *Objective personality assessment: Changing perspectives.* New York: Academic Press.

Butcher, J. N. (1987). *Computerized psychological assessment: A practitioner's guide.* New York: Basic Books.

Butcher, J. N. (1990). *MMPI-2 in psychological treatment.* New York: Oxford University Press.

Butcher, J., Derksen, J., Sloore, H., & Sirigatti, S. (2003). Objective personality assessment of people in diverse cultures: European adaptations of the MMPI-2. *Behaviour Research and Theory, 41,* 819–840.

Butcher, J. N., & Rouse, S. V. (1996). Personality: Individual differences and clinical assessment. *Annual Review of Psychology, 47,* 87–111.

Butcher, J. N., Graham, J. R., Williams, C. L., & Ben-Porath, Y. S. (1990). *Development and use of the MMPI-2 content scales.* Minneapolis: University of Minnesota Press.

Butler, M., Retzlaff, P., & Vanderploeg, R. (1991). Neuropsychological test usage. *Professional Psychology: Research and Practice, 22,* 510–512.

Cahan, S., & Noyman, A. (2001). The Kaufman Ability Battery for Children Mental Processing scale: A valid measure of "pure" intelligence? *Educational and Psychological Measurements, 61*, 827–840.

Callender, J. C., & Osburn, H. G. (1980). Development and test of a new model for validity generalization. *Journal of Applied Psychology, 65*, 543–558.

Callender, J. C., & Osburn, H. G. (1981). Testing the constancy of validity with computer-generated sampling distributions of the multiplicative model variance estimate: Results for petroleum industry validation research. *Journal of Applied Psychology, 66*, 274–281.

Callender, J. C., & Osburn, H. G. (1982). Another view of progress in validity generalization. *Journal of Applied Psychology, 67*, 846–852.

Camara, W. J., & Brown, D. C. (1995). Educational and employment testing: Changing concepts in measurement and policy. *Educational Measurement: Issues and Practice, 14*, 5–11.

Camara, W., Nathan, J., & Puente, A. (1998). *Psychological test usage in professional psychology: Report to the APA Practice and Science Directorates.* Washington, DC: American Psychological Association.

Campbell, D. P. (1966). Occupations ten years later of high school seniors with high scores on the SVIB life insurance salesman scale. *Journal of Applied Psychology, 50*, 369–372.

Campbell, D. P. (1971). *Handbook for the Strong Vocational Interest Blank.* Stanford, CA: Stanford University Press.

Campbell, D. P., & Borgen, F. H. (1999). Holland's theory and the development of interest inventories. *Journal of Vocational Behavior, 55*, 86–101.

Campbell, D. P., & Hansen, J. C. (1981). *Manual for the SVIB-SCII* (3rd ed.). Stanford, CA: Stanford University Press.

Campbell, D. T. (1972). The practical problems of revising an established psychological test. In J. Butcher (Ed.), *Objective personality assessment: Changing perspectives.* New York: Academic Press.

Campbell, D. T., & Fiske, D. W. (1959). Convergent and discriminant validation by the multitrait-multimethod matrix. *Psychological Bulletin, 56*, 81–105.

Campbell, J. R, Humbo, C. M., & Mazzeo, J. (2000). *Trends in Academic Performance: Three decades of student performance.* Washington, DC: U.S. Department of Education.

Campbell, K. A., Rohlman, D. S., Storzbach, D., Binder, L. M., Anger, W. K., Kovera, C. A., Davis, K. L., & Grossmann, S. J. (1999). Test-retest reliability of psychological and neurobehavioral tests self-administered by computer. *Assessment, 6*, 21–32.

Campion, M. A., Palmer, D. K., & Campion, J. E. (1997). A review of structure in the selection interview. *Personnel Psychology, 50*, 655–702.

Campion, M. A., Pursell, E. D., & Brown, B. K. (1988). Structured interviewing: Raising the psychometric properties of the employment interview. *Personnel Psychology, 41*, 25–42.

Canter, A. (1996). The Bender-Gestalt Test (BGT). In C. Newmark (Ed.), *Major psychological assessment instruments* (2nd ed., pp. 400–430). Boston: Allyn & Bacon.

Cantor, J. A. (1987). Developing multiple-choice items. *Training & Development Journal, 41* 85–88.

Caplan, P. J. (1995). *They say you're crazy: How the world's most powerful psychiatrists decide who's normal.* Reading, MA: Addison-Wesley.

Careless, S. A. (2000). The validity of scores on the Multidimensional Aptitude Battery. *Educational and Psychological Measurement, 60*, 592–603.

Carretta, T. R., Retzlaff, P. D., Callister, J. D., & King, R. E., (1998). A comparison of two U.S. Air Force pilot aptitude tests. *Aviation Space and Environmental Medicine, 69*, 931–935.

Carrier, M. R., Delessio, A. T., & Brown, S. H. (1990). Correspondence between estimates of content and criterion-related validity values. *Personnel Psychology, 43*, 85–100.

Carroll, J. B. (1993a). *Human cognitive abilities: A survey of factor-analytic studies.* Cambridge, UK: Cambridge University Press.

Carroll, J. B. (1993b). Test theory and behavioral scaling of test performance. In N. Frederiksen, R. Mislevy, and I. Bejar (Eds.), *Test theory for a new generation of tests* (pp. 297–322). Hillsdale, NJ: Erlbaum.

Carroll, J. B., & Maxwell, S. E. (1979). Individual differences in cognitive abilities. *Annual Review of Psychology, 30*, 603–640.

Carson, R. C. (1989). Personality. *Annual Review of Psychology, 40*, 227–248.

Carson, R. C. (1990). Assessment: What role the assessor? *Journal of Personality Assessment, 54*, 435–445.

Carvajal, H., Gerber, J., Hewes, P., & Weaver, K. (1987). Correlations between scores on Stanford-Binet IV and Wechsler Adult Intelligence Scale—Revised. *Psychological Reports, 61*, 83–86.

Carvajal, H., Hardy, K., Smith, K., & Weaver, K. (1988). Relationships between scores on Stanford-Binet IV and Wechsler Preschool and Primary Scale of Intelligence. *Psychology in the Schools, 25*, 129–131.

Carvajal, H., & Weyand, K. (1986). Relationships between scores on Stanford-Binet IV and Wechsler Intelligence Scale for Children—Revised. *Psychological Reports, 59*, 963–966.

Cascio, W. F. (1976). Turnover, biographical data, and fair employment practice. *Journal of Applied Psychology, 61*, 576–580.

Cascio, W. F. (1982). *Applied psychology in personnel management* (2nd ed.). Reston, VA: Reston.

Cascio, W. F., Alexander, R. A., & Barrett, G. V. (1988). Setting cutoff scores: Legal, psychometric, and professional issues and guidelines. *Personnel Psychology, 41*, 1–24.

Cascio, W. F., Outtz, J., Zedeck, S., & Goldstein, I. L. (1991). Statistical implications of six methods of test score use in personnel selection. *Human Performance, 4,* 233–264.

Castellan, N. J. (1992). Relations between linear models: Implications for the lens model. *Organizational Behavior and Human Decision Processes, 51,* 364–384.

Cattell, J. (1890). Mental tests and measurements. *Mind, 15,* 373–381.

Cattell, R. B. (1940). A culture-free intelligence test: Part I. *Journal of Educational Psychology, 31,* 161–179.

Cattell, R. B. (1957). *Personality and motivation structure and measurement.* Yonkers, NY: World Book.

Cattell, R. B. (1963). Theory of fluid and crystallized intelligence: A critical experiment. *Journal of Educational Psychology, 54,* 1–22.

Cattell, R. B., & Cattell, H. E. (1995). Personality structure and the new fifth edition of the 16PF. *Educational and Psychological Measurement, 55,* 926–937.

Chadwick-Jones, J. K., Brown, C. A., Nicholson, N., & Sheppard, C. (1971). Absence measures: Their reliability and stability in an industrial setting. *Personnel Psychology, 24,* 463–470.

Chan, D., & Schmitt, N. (1998). Video-based versus paper-and-pencil method of assessment in situational judgment tests: Subgroup differences in test performance and face validity perceptions. *Journal of Applied Psychology, 82,* 143–159.

Chapman, L. J., & Chapman, J. P. (1969). Illusory correlation as an obstacle to the use of valid psychodiagnostic signs. *Journal of Abnormal Psychology, 74,* 271–280.

Charter, R. A. (2002). Reliability of the WMS-III discrepancy comparisons. *Perceptual and Motor Skills, 94,* 387–390.

Chiu, K., & Allinger, G. M. (1990). A proposed method to combine ranking and graphic rating in performance appraisal: The quantitative ranking scale. *Educational and Psychological Measurement, 50,* 493–503.

Christal, R. (1968). Selecting a harem—and other applications of the policy capturing model. *Journal of Experimental Education, 36,* 35–41.

Cizek, G. J. (1993). Reconsidering standards and criteria. *Journal of Educational Measurement, 13,* 21–26.

Clark, L. A., Watson, D., & Reynolds, S. (1995). Diagnosis and classification in psychopathology: Challenges to the current system and future directions. *Annual Review of Psychology, 46,* 121–153.

Cleary, T., Humphreys, L., Kendrick, S., & Wesman, A. (1975). Educational use of tests with disadvantaged students. *American Psychologist, 30,* 15–41.

Clopton, J. (1979). Development of special MMPI scales. In C. Newmark (Ed.), *MMPI: Clinical and research trends.* New York: Praeger.

Coffman, W. E. (1985). Review of Kaufman Assessment Battery for Children. In *The ninth mental measurements yearbook.* Lincoln, NB: Buros Institute of Mental Measurement.

Cohen, J. A. (1957a). A factor-analytic based rationale for the Wechsler Adult Intelligence Scale. *Journal of Consulting Psychology, 21,* 451–457.

Cohen, J. A. (1957b). The factorial structure of the WAIS between early childhood and old age. *Journal of Consulting Psychology, 21,* 283–290.

Cohen, J. A. (1959). The factorial structure of the WISC at ages 7–6, 10–6, and 13–6. *Journal of Consulting Psychology, 23,* 285–299.

Cohen, J. A., & Cohen, P. (1983). *Applied multiple regression/correlation analysis for the behavioral sciences* (2nd ed.). Hillsdale, NJ: Erlbaum.

Cole, N. S. (1973). Bias in selection. *Journal of Educational Measurement, 10,* 237–255.

Coleman, J. S., et al. (1966). *Equality of educational opportunity.* Washington, DC: U.S. Office of Education.

College Entrance Examination Board. (1987). *ATP guide for high schools and colleges.* Princeton, NJ: Educational Testing Service.

College Entrance Examination Board. (1993). *The College Board News, 22,* 1. New York: College Entrance Examination Board.

Colligan, R. C., Osborne, D., Swenson, W. M., & Offord, K. P. (1983). *The MMPI: A contemporary normative study.* New York: Praeger.

Collins, L. M., & Horn, J. L. (1991). *Best methods for the analysis of change.* Washington, DC: American Psychological Association.

Comrey, A. L. (1988). Factor-analytic methods of scale development in personality and clinical psychology. *Journal of Consulting & Clinical Psychology, 56,* 754–761.

Committee on Ethical Guidelines for Forensic Psychologists. (1991). Specialty guidelines for forensic psychologists. *Law and Human Behavior, 15,* 655–665.

Committee on Psychological Tests and Assessment. (1988). *Implications for test fairness of the "Golden Rule" company settlement.* Washington, DC: American Psychological Association.

Conger, A. C., & Conger, J. C. (1975). Reliable dimensions from WISC profiles. *Educational and Psychological Measurement, 35,* 847–863.

Conn, S. R., & Rieke, M. L. (1994). *The 16PF Fifth Edition technical manual.* Champaign, IL: Institute for Personality and Ability Testing, Inc.

Conoley, C. W., Plake, B. S., & Kemmerer, B. E. (1991). Issues in computer-based test interpretative systems. *Computers in Human Behavior, 7,* 97–102.

Conoley, J. C., & Kramer, J. J. (1989). *Tenth mental measurements yearbook.* Lincoln, NB: University of Nebraska Press.

Conway, D. (1987). *A farewell to Marx: An outline and appraisal of his theories.* New York: Penguin Books.

Coombs, C. H., Dawes, R. M., & Tversky, A. (1970). *Mathematical psychology: An elementary introduction.* Englewood Cliffs, NJ: Prentice Hall.

Cooper, D. (1990). Factor structure of the Edwards Personal Preference Schedule in a vocational rehabilitation sample. *Journal of Clinical Psychology, 46,* 421–425.

Cooper, D., & Fraboni, M. (1988). Relationship between the Wechsler Adult Intelligence Test—Revised and the Wide Range Achievement Test—Revised in a sample of normal adults. *Educational and Psychological Measurement, 48,* 799–803.

Cooper, W. (1981). Ubiquitous halo. *Psychological Bulletin, 90,* 218–244.

Corah, N. L., Feldman, M. J., Cohen, I. S., Gruen, W., Meadow, A., & Ringwall, E. A. (1958). Social desirability as a variable in the Edwards Personal Preference Schedule. *Journal of Consulting Psychology, 22,* 70–72.

Corno, L., Cronbach, L. J., Kupermintz, H., Lohman, D. F., Mandinach, E. B., Porteus, A. W. & Talbert, J. E. (2002) *Remaking the concept of aptitude: Extending the legacy of Richard E. Snow.* Mahwah, NJ: Erlbaum.

Cortina, J. M. (1993). What is coefficient alpha?: An examination of theory and applications. *Journal of Applied Psychology, 78,* 98–104.

Costa, P. T., & McCrae, R. R. (1992). Normal personality assessment in clinical practice: The NEO Personality Inventory. *Psychological Assessment, 4,* 5–13.

Cramer, P. (1997). Identity, personality and defense mechanisms: An observer-based study. *Journal of Research in Personality, 31,* 58–77.

Cramer, P. (1999). Future directions for the Thematic Apperception Test. *Journal of Personality Assessment, 72,* 74–92.

Crites, J. O., Bechtoldt, H. P., Goodstein, L. D., & Heilbrun, A. B., Jr. (1961). A factor analysis of the California Psychological Inventory. *Journal of Applied Psychology, 45,* 408–414.

Cronbach, L. J. (1951). Coefficient alpha and the internal structure of tests. *Psychometrika, 16,* 297–334.

Cronbach, L. J. (1955). Processes affecting scores on "understanding of others" and "assumed similarity." *Psychological Bulletin, 52,* 177–193.

Cronbach, L. J. (1970). *Essentials of psychological testing* (3rd ed.). New York: Harper & Row.

Cronbach, L. J. (1971). Test validation. In R. L. Thorndike (Ed.), *Educational measurement* (2nd ed.). Washington, DC: American Council of Education.

Cronbach, L. J. (1975). Five decades of public controversy over psychological testing. *American Psychologist, 30,* 1–14.

Cronbach, L. J. (1978). Review of the BITCH Test. In O. K. Buros (Ed.), *The eighth mental measurements yearbook.* Highland Park, NJ: Gryphon Press.

Cronbach, L. J. (1979). The Armed Services Vocational Aptitude Battery—A test battery in transition. *Personnel and Guidance Journal, 57,* 232–237.

Cronbach, L. J. (1986). Signs of optimism for intelligence testing. *Educational Measurement: Issues and Practice, 5,* 23–24.

Cronbach, L. J. (1988). Five perspectives on the validity argument. In H. Wainer & H. Brown (Eds.), *Test validity.* Hillsdale, NJ: Erlbaum.

Cronbach, L. J. (1989). Construct validation after thirty years. In R. Linn (Ed.), *Intelligence: Measurement, theory, and public policy.* Urbana, IL: University of Illinois Press.

Cronbach, L. J., & Gleser, G. (1965). *Psychological tests and personnel decisions* (2nd ed.). Urbana, IL: University of Illinois Press.

Cronbach, L. J., Gleser, G. C., Nanda, H., & Rajaratnam, N. (1972). *The dependability of behavioral measurements: Theory of generalizability for scores and profiles.* New York: Wiley.

Cronbach, L. J., & Meehl, P. E. (1955). Construct validity in psychological tests. *Psychological Bulletin, 52,* 281–302.

Cronbach, L. J., & Snow, R. E. (1977). *Aptitudes and instructional methods: A handbook for research on interactions.* New York: Halstead Press.

Cronshaw, S. F., & Alexander, R. A. (1985). One answer to the demand for accountability: Selection utility as an investment decision. *Organizational Behavior and Human Decision Processes, 35,* 102–118.

Crouse, J., & Trusheim, D. (1988). *The case against the SAT.* Chicago: University of Chicago Press.

Crow, J. F. (1969). Genetic theories and influences: Comments on the value of diversity. *Harvard Educational Review, 39,* 301–309.

Cudeck, R. (1985). A structural comparison of conventional and adaptive versions of the ASVAB. *Multivariate Behavioral Research, 20,* 305–322.

Cureton, E. E. (1957). The upper and lower twenty-seven percent rule. *Psychometrika, 22,* 293–296.

Dahlstrom, W., Welsh, G., & Dahlstrom, L. (1972). *An MMPI handbook: Vol. I. Clinical interpretation.* Minneapolis, MN: University of Minnesota Press.

Dahlstrom, W., Welsh, G., & Dahlstrom, L. (1975). *An MMPI handbook: Vol. II. Research developments and applications.* Minneapolis, MN: University of Minnesota Press.

Daley, T. C., Whaley, S. E., Sigman, M. D., Espinosa, M. P., & Neumann, C. (2003). IQ on the rise: The Flynn effect in rural Kenyan children. *Psychological Science, 14,* 215–219.

Dana, R. H. (1996). The Thematic Apperception Test (TAT). In C. Newmark (Ed.), *Major psychological assessment instruments* (2nd ed., pp. 166–205). Boston: Allyn & Bacon.

Dana, R. H., Cocking, R., & Dana, J. (1970). The effects of experience and training on accuracy and configural analysis. *Journal of Clinical Psychology, 26,* 28–32.

Dankin, S., & Armstrong, J. S. (1989). Predicting job performance: A comparison of expert opinion and research findings. *International Journal of Forecasting, 5,* 187–194.

Darley, J., & Fazio, R. (1980). Expectancy confirmation processes arising in the social interaction sequence. *American Psychologist, 35,* 867–881.

Darlington, R. B. (1968). Multiple regression in psychological research and practice. *Psychological Bulletin, 69,* 161–182.

Davis, C., & Cowles, M. (1989). Automated psychological testing: Method of administration, need for approval, and measures of anxiety. *Educational and Psychological Measurement, 49,* 311–337.

Dawes, R. (1971). A case study of graduate admissions: Application of three principles of human decision making. *American Psychologist, 26,* 180–188.

Dawes, R. (1979). The robust beauty of improper linear models in decision making. *American Psychologist, 34,* 571–582.

Dawes, R. (1980). Apologia for what works. *American Psychologist, 35,* 678.

Dawes, R. M. (1989). Experience and the validity of clinical judgment: The illusory correlation. *Behavioral Sciences and the Law, 7,* 457–467.

Dawes, R. (1994). *House of cards: Psychology and psychotherapy built on myth.* New York: Free Press.

Dawes, R., & Corrigan, B. (1974). Linear models in decision making. *Psychological Bulletin, 81,* 95–106.

Dawes, R. M., Faust, D., & Meehl, P. E. (1989). Clinical versus acturial judgment. *Science, 243,* 1668–1674.

Defense Manpower Data Center (1996). *Counselor manual for the Armed Services Vocational Aptitude Battery Career Exploration Program.* Seaside, CA: Author.

DeFries, J. C., & Plomin, R. (1978). Behavioral genetics. *Annual Review of Psychology, 29,* 473–515.

Delahunty, R. J. (1988). Perspectives on within-group scoring. *Journal of Vocational Behavior, 33,* 463–477.

Deniston, W. M., & Ramanaiah, N. V. (1993). California Psychological inventory and the five-factor model of personality. *Psychological Reports, 73,* 491–496.

De Vries, R., & Kohlberg, L. (1969). The Concept Assessment Kit—Conservation. *Journal of Educational Measurement, 6,* 263–266.

Dickens, W. T., & Flynn, J. R. (2001). Heritability estimates versus large environmental effects: The IQ paradox resolved. *Psychological Review, 108,* 346–369.

Dickson, D. H., & Kelly, I. W. (1985). The Barnum effect in personality assessment: A review of the literature. *Psychological Reports, 57,* 367–382.

Digman, J. M. (1990). Personality structure: Emergence of the five-factor model. *Annual Review of Psychology, 41,* 417–440.

Dipboye, R. (1982). Self-fulfilling prophecies in the selection-recruitment interview. *Academy of Management Review, 7,* 579–586.

Dipboye, R. L., & de Pontbriand, R. (1981). Correlates of employee reactions to performance appraisals and appraisal systems. *Journal of Applied Psychology, 66,* 248–251.

Dodrill, C. B., & Warner, M. H. (1988). Further studies on the Wonderlic Personnel Test as a brief measure of intelligence. *Journal of Consulting and Clinical Psychology, 56,* 145–147.

Doll, E. E. (1965). *Vineland social maturity scale, condensed. Revised edition. Manual of direction.* Minneapolis, MN: American Guidance Service.

Dolliver, R. H. (1969). Strong Vocational Interest Blank versus expressed occupational interests: A review. *Psychological Bulletin, 72,* 94–107.

Dolliver, R. H., Irvin, J. A., & Bigley, S. E. (1972). Twelve-year follow-up of the Strong Vocational Interest Blank. *Journal of Counseling Psychology, 19,* 212–217.

Donnay, D. A., & Borgen, F. H. (1996). Validity, structure, and content of the 1994 Strong Interest Inventory. *Journal of Counseling Psychology, 43,* 275–291.

Doppelt, J. E., & Wallace, W. L. (1955). Standardization of the Wechsler Adult Intelligence Scale for older persons. *Journal of Abnormal and Social Psychology, 51,* 312–330.

Dorfman, D. (1978). The Cyril Burt question: New findings. *Science, 201,* 1177–1186.

Downey, R. G., Sinnett, E. R., & Seeberger, W. (1999). The changing face of MMPI practice. *Psychological Reports, 83,* 1267–1272.

Drasgow, F., & Guertler, E. (1987). A decision-theoretic approach to the use of appropriateness measurement for detecting invalid test and scale scores. *Journal of Applied Psychology, 72,* 10–18.

Drasgow, F., & Hulin, C. L. (1991). Item response theory. In M. Dunnette & L. Hough (Eds.), *Handbook of industrial and organizational psychology* (2nd ed., Vol. 1, pp. 577–636). Palo Alto, CA: Consulting Psychologists Press.

Drasgow, F., & Kanfer, R. (1985). Equivalence of psychological measurement in heterogeneous populations. *Journal of Applied Psychology, 70,* 662–680.

Droege, R. C. (1984). The General Aptitude Test Battery and its international use. *International Review of Applied Psychology, 33,* 413–416.

DuBois, C., Sackett, P. R., Zedeck, S., & Fogli, L. (1993). Further exploration of typical and maximum performance criteria: Definitional issues, prediction, and white-black differences. *Journal of Applied Psychology, 78,* 205–211.

Dubois, P. H. (1970). *A history of psychological testing.* Boston: Allyn & Bacon.

Dumont, R., & Willis, J. O. (1995). Intrasubtest scatter on the WISC-III for various clinical samples vs. the standardization sample: An examination of WISC folklore. *Journal of Psychoeducational Assessment, 13,* 271–285.

Dunbar, S. B., Koretz, D. M., & Hoover, H. D. (1991). Quality control in the development and use of performance assessments. *Applied Measurement in Education, 4,* 289–303.

Eckberg, D. L. (1979). *Intelligence and race: The origins and dimensions of the IQ controversy.* New York: Praeger.

Educational Testing Service. (1995). *Admission officer's handbook for the SAT program.* New York: College Board.

Edwards, A. J. (1964). Social desirability and performance on the MMPI. *Psychometrika, 29,* 295–308.

Edwards, A. J. (1972). *Individual mental testing. Part II, measurement.* San Francisco: Intext Educational Publishers.

Edwards, A. L. (1957). *Techniques of attitude scale construction.* New York: Appleton-Century-Crofts.

Edwards, A. L. (1970). *The measurement of personality traits by scales and inventories.* New York: Holt, Rinehart & Winston.

Edwards, J. R. (1995). Alternatives to difference scores as dependent variables in the study of congruence in organizational research. *Organizational Behavior and Human Decision Processes, 64,* 307–324.

Edwards, J. R. (2001). Ten difference score myths. *Organizational Research Methods, 4,* 265–287.

Edwards, W., & Newman, J. R. (1983). *Multiattribute evaluation.* Beverly Hills, CA: Sage.

Eells, K., et al. (1951). *Intelligence and cultural differences.* Chicago: University of Chicago Press.

Einhorn, H., & Hogarth, R. M. (1975). Unit weighting schemes for decision making. *Organizational Behavior and Human Performance, 13,* 171–192.

Embertson, S. E. (1985). *Test design: Developments in psychology and psychometrics.* New York: Academic Press.

Engelhart, M. D. (1965). A comparison of several item discrimination indices. *Journal of Educational Measurement, 2,* 69–76.

Epstein, S. (1980). The stability of behavior II. Implications for psychological research. *American Psychologist, 35,* 790–806.

Exner, J. E. (1974). *The Rorschach: A comprehensive system.* New York: Wiley.

Exner, J. E. (1978). *The Rorschach: A comprehensive system, Vol. 2: Current research and advanced interpretations.* New York: Wiley-Interscience.

Exner, J. E. (1986). *The Rorschach: A comprehensive system* (2nd ed.). New York: Wiley.

Exner, J. E. (1993). *The Rorschach: A comprehensive system* (3rd ed.). New York: Wiley.

Exner, J. E. (1999). The Rorschach: Measurement concepts and issues of validity. In S. Embretson, S. Hershberger, et al. (Eds.), *The new rules of measurement: What every psychologist and educator should know* (pp. 159–183). Mahwah, NJ: Erlbaum.

Eyde, L. D., Robertson, G. J., & Krug, S. E. (1993). *Responsible test use : Case studies for assessing human behavior.* Washington, DC: American Psychological Association.

Eysenck, H. J. (1960). *Experiments in personality.* London: Routledge & Kegan Paul.

Eysenck, H. J. (1976). *The measurement of personality.* Baltimore, MD: University Park Press.

Eysenck, H. J. (1979). *The structure and measurement of intelligence.* New York: Springer-Verlag.

Eysenck, H. J. (1981). *A model for personality.* Berlin: Springer.

Eysenck, H. J. (1987). A critique of contemporary classification and diagnosis. In T. Millon & G. L. Klerman (Eds.), *Contemporary directions in psychopathology: Toward DSM-IV.* New York: Guilford Press.

Eysenck, H. J., & Eysenck, S. B. (1969). *Personality structure and measurement.* San Diego, CA: Knapp.

Eysenck, H. J., Wakefield, J., & Friedman, A. (1983). Diagnosis and clinical assessment: The DSM-III. *Annual Review of Psychology, 34,* 167–193.

Fan, X., Willson, V. L., & Kapes, J. T. (1996). Ethnic group representation in test construction samples and test bias: The standardization fallacy revisited. *Educational and Psychological Measurement, 56,* 365–381.

Farrell, A. D. (1989). Impact of standards for computer-based tests on practice: Consequences of the information gap. *Computers in Human Behavior, 5,* 1–11.

Faschingbauer, T. (1979). The future of the MMPI. In C. Newmark (Ed.), *MMPI: Clinical and research trends.* New York: Praeger.

Faust, D. (1989). Data integration in legal evaluations: Can clinicians deliver on their promises? *Behavioral Sciences and the Law, 7,* 469–483.

Faust, D., & Ziskin, J. (1988, July 1). The expert witness in forensic psychology and psychiatry. *Science, 241,* 31–35.

Feldman, M. J., & Corah, N. L. (1960). Social desirability and the forced choice method. *Journal of Consulting Psychology, 24,* 480–482.

Ferguson, G. (1981). *Statistical analysis in psychology and education.* New York: McGraw-Hill.

Feuerstein, R. (1970). A dynamic approach to the causation, prevention, and alleviation of retarded performance. In H. Haywood (Ed.), *Social-cultural aspects of mental retardation.* New York: Appleton-Century-Crofts.

Finkle, R. B. (1976). Managerial assessment centers. In M. Dunnette (Ed.), *Handbook of industrial and organizational psychology.* Chicago: Rand McNally.

Fischer, C. F., & King, R. M. (1995). *Authentic assessment: A guide to implementation.* Thousand Oaks, CA: Corwin Press.

Fisher, K. (1986, July). DSM-III-R protest. *APA Monitor, 177(7),* 4.

Fiske, D. W. (1987). Construct invalidity comes from method effects. *Educational and Psychological Measurement, 47,* 285–307.

Flanagan, D. P., & Alfonso, V. C. (1995). A critical review of the technical characteristics of new and recently revised intelligence tests for preschool children. *Journal of Psychoeducational Assessment, 13,* 66–90.

Flanagan, J. C. (1937). A proposed procedure for increasing the efficiency of objective tests. *Journal of Educational Psychology, 26,* 17–21.

Flanagan, J. C. (1954). The critical incidents technique. *Psychological Bulletin, 51,* 327–358.

Fleenor, J. W., and Eastman, L. (1997). The relationship between the five-factor model of personality and the California Psychological Inventory. *Educational and Psychological Measurement, 57,* 698–703.

Fleming, J. (2002). Who will succeed in college? When the SAT predicts Black students' performance. *Review of Higher Education, 25,* 281–296.

Fletcher, R. (1991). *Science, ideology and the media: The Cyril Burt scandal.* New Brunswick, NJ: Transaction Publishers.

Flynn, J. R. (1980). *Race, IQ and Jensen.* London: Routledge & Kegan Paul.

Flynn, J. R. (1984). The mean IQ of Americans: Massive gains 1932 to 1978. *Psychological Bulletin, 95,* 29–51.

Flynn, J. R. (1987). Massive IQ gains in 14 nations: What IQ tests really measure. *Psychological Bulletin, 101,* 171–191.

Flynn, J. R. (1999). Searching for justice: The discovery of IQ gains over time. *American Psychologist, 54,* 5–20.

Folger, R., & Greenberg, J. (1985). Procedural justice: An interpretive analysis of personnel systems. In K. Rowland & J. Ferris (Eds.), *Research in personnel and human resources management* (Vol. 3). Greenwich, CT: JAI Press.

Fowler, R. (1979). The automated MMPI. In C. Newmark (Ed.), *MMPI: Clinical and research trends.* New York: Praeger.

Frances, A. J., First, M. B., & Pincus, H. A. (1995). *DSM-IV guidebook.* Washington, DC: American Psychiatric Association.

Frances, A. J., First, M. B., Widiger, T. A., Miele, G. M., Tilly, S. M., Davis, W. W., & Pincus, H. A. (1991). An A to Z guide to DSM-IV conundrums. *Journal of Abnormal Psychology, 100,* 407–412.

Frank, L. K. (1939). Projective methods for the study of personality. *Journal of Psychology, 8,* 389–409.

Fredericksen, N. (1962). Factors in in-basket performance. *Psychological Monographs, 76* (22, Whole No. 541).

Fredericksen, N. (1986). Construct validity and construct similarity: Methods for use in test development and test validation. *Multivariate Behavioral Research, 21,* 3–28.

Frederiksen, N., Mislevy, R., & Bejar, I. (1993). *Test theory for a new generation of tests.* Hillsdale, NJ: Erlbaum.

Freeberg, N. E. (1969). Relevance of rater-ratee acquaintance in the validity and reliability of rating. *Journal of Applied Psychology, 53,* 518–524.

Freedle, R. O. (2003). Correcting the SAT's ethnic and social-class bias: A method for reestimating SAT scores. *Harvard Educational Review, 73,* 1–43.

Friedman, T., & Williams, E. B. (1982). Current use of tests for employment. In A. Wigdor & W. Garner (Eds.), *Ability testing: Uses, consequences and controversies, Part II: Documentation section.* Washington, DC: National Academy Press.

Furnham, A., & Schofield, S. (1987). Accepting personality test feedback: A review of the Barnum effect. *Current Psychological Research and Reviews, 6,* 162–178.

Gael, S., Grant, D., & Richie, R. (1975). Employment test validation for minority and nonminority clerks and work sample criteria. *Journal of Applied Psychology, 60,* 420–426.

Gaito, J. (1980). Measurement scales and statistics: Resurgence of an old misconception. *Psychological Bulletin, 87,* 564–567.

Gallagher, A., Bridgeman, B., & Cahalan, C. (2000). The effect of computer-based tests on racial/ethnic, gender and language groups. *GRE Research Bulletin No. 96–21P,* Princeton, NJ: Educational Testing Service.

Gallucci, N. T. (1986). General and specific objections to the MMPI. *Educational and Psychological Measurement, 46,* 985–988.

Galton, F. (1869). *Hereditary genius: An inquiry into its laws and consequences.* London: Macmillan.

Garb, H. N. (1989). Clinical judgment, clinical training, and professional experience. *Psychological Bulletin, 105,* 387–396.

Garb, H. N. (1999). Call for a moratorium on the use of the Rorschach Inkblot Test in clinical and forensic settings. *Assessment, 6,* 313–317.

Garb, H. N. (2000). Computers will become increasingly important for psychological assessment: Not that there's anything wrong with that. *Psychological Assessment, 12,* 31–39.

Garb, H. N. (2003). Clinical judgment and mechanical prediction. In J. R. Graham and J. A. Naglieri (Eds.) *Handbook of psychology: Assessment psychology, Vol. 10.* (pp. 27–42). New York: Wiley.

Garb, H. N., Florio, C. M., & Grove, W. M. (1999). The validity of the Rorschach and the Minnesota Multiphasic Personality Inventory: Results from meta-analyses. *Psychological Science, 9,* 402–404.

Garb, H. N., & Schramke, C. J. (1996). Judgment research and neurological assessment: A narrative review and meta-analysis. *Psychological Bulletin, 120,* 140–153.

Gardner, H. (1983). *Frames of mind: The theory of multiple intelligences.* New York: Basic Books.

Gardner, H. (1993). *Multiple intelligences: The theory in practice.* New York: Basic Books.

Gardner, H. (1999). *Intelligence reframed: Multiple intelligences for the 21st century.* New York: Basic Books.

Gaudet, F. J. (1963). *Solving the problems of employee absence.* New York: American Management Association.

Gaugler, B. B., Rosenthal, D. B., Thornton, G. C., III, & Bentson, C. (1987). Meta-analysis of assessment center validity. *Journal of Applied Psychology, 72,* 493–511.

Geary, D. C., & Whitworth, R. H. (1988). Dimensional structure of the WAIS-R in a simultaneous multi-sample analysis. *Educational and Psychological Measurement, 48,* 945–959.

Geisinger, K. (1992). *Psychological testing of Hispanics.* Washington, DC: American Psychological Association.

George, M. S., & Skinner, H. A. (1990). Using response latency to detect inaccurate responses in a computerized lifestyle assessment. *Computers in Human Behavior, 6,* 167–175.

Gesell, A. L. (1948a). *The first five years of life.* New York: Harper & Bros.

Gesell, A. L. (1948b). *Studies in child development.* New York: Harper & Bros.

Gesell, A. L. (1956). *Youth: The years from ten to sixteen.* New York: Harper & Bros.

Ghiselli, E. E. (1955). *The measurement of occupational aptitude.* Berkeley, CA: University of California Press.

Ghiselli, E. E. (1966). *The validity of occupational aptitude tests.* New York: Wiley.

Ghiselli, E. E. (1970). The validity of aptitude tests in personnel selection. *Personnel Psychology, 26,* 461–477.

Gilberstadt, H., & Druker, J. (1965). *A handbook for clinical and actuarial MMPI interpretation.* Philadelphia: Saunders.

Gillie, O. (1976, October 24). Crucial data faked by eminent psychologist. *Sunday Times,* London.

Ginton, A., Dail, N., Elaad, E., & Ben-Shakar, G. (1982). A method for evaluating the use of the polygraph in a real-life situation. *Journal of Applied Psychology, 67,* 131–137.

Gleser, G. C. (1963). Projective methodologies. *Annual Review of Psychology, 14,* 391–422.

Glutting, J. J., & McDermott, P. A. (1990). Childhood learning potential as an alternative to traditional ability measures. *Psychological Assessment, 2,* 398–403.

Goals 2000: Educate America Act. (1994, March 31). Public Law, 103–226. 108 STAT. 125/.

Goldberg, L. R. (1965). Diagnosticians versus diagnostic signs: The diagnosis of psychosis versus neurosis from the MMPI. *Psychological Monographs, 79*(9, Whole No. 602).

Goldberg, L. R. (1968). Simple models or simple processes? Some research on clinical judgments. *American Psychologist, 23,* 483–496.

Goldberg, L. R. (1970). Man versus model of man: A rationale plus evidence for a method of improving clinical inference. *Psychological Bulletin, 73,* 422–432.

Goldberg, L. R., & Slovic, P. (1967). The importance of test item content. An analysis of a corollary of the deviation hypothesis. *Journal of Counseling Psychology, 14,* 462–472.

Goldberg, P. A. (1965). A review of sentence completion methods in personality assessment. *Journal of Projective Techniques and Personality Assessment, 29,* 12–45.

Golden, C. J. (1990). *Clinical interpretation of objective psychological tests* (2nd ed.). Boston: Allyn & Bacon.

Golden, C. J. (2004). The adult Luria-Nebraska Neuropsychological Test Battery. In G. Goldstein and S. Beers (Eds.), *Comprehensive Handbook of Psychological Assessment, Vol. 1* (pp. 133–146). New York: Wiley.

Goldstein, B. L., & Patterson, P. O. (1988). Turning back the Title VII clock: The resegregation of the American work force through validity generalization. *Journal of Vocational Behavior, 33,* 452–462.

Goleman, D. (1995). *Emotional intelligence: Why it can matter more than IQ.* New York: Bantam.

Goodenough, F. L. (1949). *Mental testing: Its history, principles, and applications.* New York: Rinehart.

Gordon, R. A. (1988). Thunder from the left. Review of "Storm over biology: Essays on science, sentiment, and public policy." *Academic Questions, 1,* 74–92.

Gottfredson, G. S., (1976). A note on sexist wording in interest measurement. *Measurement and Evaluation in Guidance, 8,* 221–223.

Gottfredson, L. S. (1986). Societal consequences of the g factor in employment. *Journal of Vocational Behavior, 29,* 379–410.

Gottfredson, L. S. (1988). Reconsidering fairness: A matter of social and ethical priorities. *Journal of Vocational Behavior, 33,* 293–319.

Gottfredson, L. S. (2003). Dissecting practical intelligence theory: Its claims and evidence. *Intelligence, 31,* 343–397.

Gottfredson, L. S., & Crouse, J. (1986). Validity versus utility of mental tests: Example of the SAT. *Journal of Vocational Behavior, 29,* 363–378.

Gough, H. G. (1987). *California Psychological Inventory administrator's guide.* Palo Alto, CA: Consulting Psychologists Press.

Gough, H. G., & Bradley, P. (1996). *California Psychological Inventory, manual* (3rd ed.). Palo Alto: Consulting Psychologists Press.

Gould, S. J. (1981). *The mismeasure of man.* New York: Norton.

Graham, J. R. (1977). *The MMPI: A practical guide.* New York: Oxford University Press.

Graham, J. R. (1990). *MMPI-2: Assessing personality and psychopathology.* New York: Oxford University Press.

Graham, J. R., Timbrook, R. E., Ben-Porath, Y. S., & Butcher, J. N. (1991). Code-type congruence between MMPI and MMPI-2: Separating fact from artifact. *Journal of Personality Assessment, 57,* 205–215.

Gray, C. W. (1959). *Detection of faking in vocational interest measurement.* Unpublished doctoral dissertation, Minneapolis, University of Minnesota.

Green, B. F. (1988). Construct validity of computer-based tests. In H. Wainer & H. Brown (Eds.), *Test validity.* Hillsdale, NJ: Erlbaum.

Greenberg, J. (1987). A taxonomy of organizational justice theories. *Academy of Management Review, 12,* 9–22.

Greene, R. L. (1991). *The MMPI-2/MMPI: An interpretative manual.* Boston: Allyn & Bacon.

Greenwood, J. M., & McNamara, W. J. (1967). Interrater reliability of situational tests. *Journal of Applied Psychology, 31,* 101–106.

Gregory, R. J. (1999). *Foundations of intellectual assessment: The WAIS-III and other tests in clinical practice.* Boston: Allyn & Bacon.

Gross, A. L., & Su, W. (1975). Defining a "fair" or "unbiased" selection model: A question of utility. *Journal of Applied Psychology, 60,* 345–351.

Gross, M. (1963). *The brain watchers.* New York: New American Library.

Guastello, S. J., Guastello, D. D., & Craft, L. L. (1989). Assessment of the Barnum effect in computer-based test interpretations. *Journal of Psychology, 123,* 477–484.

Guastello, S. J., & Rieke, M. L. (1990). The Barnum effect and the validity of computer-based test interpretations. The Human Resource Development Report. *Psychological Assessment, 2,* 186–190.

Guilford, J. P. (1967). *The nature of human intelligence.* New York: McGraw-Hill.

Guilford, J. P. (1980). Fluid and crystallized intelligences: Two fanciful concepts. *Psychological Bulletin, 88,* 406–412.

Guilford, J. P. (1988). Some changes in the Structure-of-Intellect model. *Educational and Psychological Measurement, 48,* 1–4.

Guilford, J. P., & Guilford, R. B. (1934). An analysis of the factors in a typical test of introversion-extraversion. *Journal of Abnormal and Social Psychology, 28,* 377–399.

Guilford, J. P., & Guilford, R. B. (1939). Personality factors D, R, T and A. *Journal of Abnormal and Social Psychology, 34,* 21–26.

Guilford, J. P., & Hoepfner, R. (1971). *The analysis of intelligence.* New York: McGraw-Hill.

Guion, R. M. (1965a). *Personnel testing.* New York: McGraw-Hill.

Guion, R. M. (1965b). Synthetic validity in a small company: A demonstration. *Personnel Psychology, 18,* 49–63.

Guion, R. M. (1977). Content validity—The source of my discontent. *Applied Psychological Measurement, 1,* 1–10.

Guion, R. M. (1991). Personnel assessment, selection, and placement. In M. Dunnette & L. Hough (Eds.), *Handbook of industrial and organizational psychology* (2nd ed., Vol. 2), pp. 327–398. Palo Alto, CA: Consulting Psychologists Press.

Guion, R. M. (1998). *Assessment, measurement and prediction for personnel decisions.* Mahwah, NJ: Erlbaum.

Guion, R. M., & Cranny, C. J. (1982). A note on concurrent and predictive validity designs. *Journal of Applied Psychology, 67,* 239–244.

Guion, R. M., & Gottier, R. F. (1965). Validity of personality measures in personnel selection. *Personnel Psychology, 18,* 135–164.

Gulliksen, H. (1950). *Theory of mental tests.* New York: Wiley.

Guttman, L., & Levy, S. (1991). Two structural laws for intelligence tests. *Intelligence, 15,* 79–103.

Hada, L. N., Katz, N., Tyano, S., & Weizman, A. (2001). Effectiveness of dynamic cognitive intervention in rehabilitation of clients with schizophrenia. *Clinical Rehabilitation, 15,* 349–359.

Hakel, M. (1974). Normative personality factors uncovered from readings or personality descriptions: The beholder's eye. *Personnel Psychology, 27,* 409–421.

Hale, M. (1982). History of employment testing. In A. Wigdor & W. Garner (Eds.), *Ability testing: Uses, consequences, and controversies, Part II: Documentation section.* Washington, DC: National Academy Press.

Hall, V. C., & Mery, M. (1969). The Concept Assessment Kit—Conservation. *Journal of Educational Statistics, 6,* 263–266.

Hambleton, R. K. (1994). The rise and fall of criterion-referenced measurement. *Educational Measurement: Issues and Practice, 13,* 21–26.

Hamilton, J. L. (1983). Measuring response to instruction as an assessment paradigm. *Advances in Learning and Behavioral Disabilities, 2,* 111–133.

Hammer, T. H., & Landau, J. (1981). Methodological issues in the use of absence data. *Journal of Applied Psychology, 66,* 574–581.

Hammond, K. R. (1955). Probabilistic functioning in the clinical method. *Psychological Review, 62,* 255–262.

Hammond, K. R. (1966). *The psychology of Egon Brunswick.* New York: Holt, Rinehart & Winston.

Haney, W. (1981). Validity, vaudeville, and values: A short history of social concerns over standardized testing. *American Psychologist, 36,* 1021–1034.

Hansen, J. C. (1976). Exploring new directions for SCII occupational scale construction. *Journal of Vocational Behavior, 9,* 147–160.

Hansen, J. C. (1992). A note of thanks to the women's movement. *Journal of Counseling and Development, 70,* 520–521.

Hansen, J. C., & Campbell, D. P. (1985). *Manual for the SVIB-SCII Fourth Edition.* Stanford, CA: Stanford University Press.

Hansen, J. C., & Swanson, J. L. (1983). Stability of interests and the predictive and concurrent validity of the 1981 Strong-Campbell Interest Inventory for college majors. *Journal of Counseling Psychology, 30,* 194–201.

Hansen, J. C., & Tan, R. N. (1992). Concurrent validity of the 1985 Strong Interest Inventory for college major selection. *Measurement and Evaluation in Counseling and Development, 25,* 53–57.

Harmon, L. W., & Borgen, F. H. (1995). Advances in career assessment and the 1994 Strong Interest Inventory. *Journal of Career Assessment, 3,* 347–372.

Harmon, L. W., Hansen, J. E., Borgen, F. H., & Hammer, A. L. (1994). *Strong Interest Inventory Applications and technical guide.* Palo Alto, CA: Consulting Psychologists Press.

Harnqvist, K. (1968). Relative changes in intelligence from 13 to 18, II. *Scandinavian Journal of Psychology, 9,* 65–82.

Harrell, T. H., Honaker, L. M., Hetu, M., & Oberwager, J. (1987). Computerized versus traditional administration of the Multidimensional Aptitude

Battery—Verbal scale: An examination of reliability and validity. *Computers in Human Behavior, 3,* 129–137.

Harris, C. W. (1963). *Problems in measuring change.* Madison, WI: University of Wisconsin Press.

Harris, M. M., & Schaubroeck, J. (1988). A meta-analysis of self-supervisory, self-peer, and peer-supervisory ratings. *Personnel Psychology, 41,* 43–62.

Hartigan, J. A., & Wigdor, A. K. (1989). *Fairness in employment testing: Validity generalization, minority issues, and the General Aptitude Test Battery.* Washington, DC: National Academy Press.

Hartman, D. E. (1986). Artificial intelligence or artificial psychologist? Conceptual issues in clinical microcomputer use. *Professional Psychology: Research and Practice, 17,* 528–534.

Hartshorne, H., & May, M. A. (1928). *Studies in deceit.* New York: Macmillan.

Hathaway, S. (1972). Where have we gone wrong? The mystery of the missing progress. In J. Butcher (Ed.), *Objective personality assessment: Changing perspectives.* New York: Academic Press.

Hattrup, K., Rock, J., & Scalia, C. (1997). The effects of varying conceptualizations of job performance on adverse impact, minority hiring, and predicted performance. *Journal of Applied Psychology, 82,* 656–664.

Hayes, S. C., Nelson, R. O., & Jarrett, R. B. (1987). The treatment utility of assessment: A functional approach to evaluating assessment quality. *American Psychologist, 42,* 963–974.

Haywood, H., Filler, J., Shifman, M., & Chatelant, G. (1975). Behavioral assessment in mental retardation. In P. McReynolds (Ed.), *Advances in psychological assessment* (Vol. 3). San Francisco: Jossey-Bass.

Hearnshaw, L. S. (1979). *Cyril Burt: Psychologist.* London: Hodder & Soughton.

Hedges, L. V., & Olkin, I. (1985). *Statistical methods for meta-analysis.* New York: Academic Press.

Heilbrun, A. B., Jr., Daniel, J. L., Goodstein, L. D., Stephenson, R. R., & Crites, J. O. (1962). The validity of two-scale pattern interpretation on the California Psychological Inventory. *Journal of Applied Psychology, 46,* 409–416.

Heilman, M. E., & Saruwatari, L. R. (1979). When beauty is beastly: The effects of appearance and sex on evaluations of job applicants for managerial and non-managerial jobs. *Organizational Behavioral and Human Performance, 23,* 360–372.

Heneman, R. L. (1986). The relationship between supervisory ratings and results-oriented measures of performance: A meta-analysis. *Personnel Psychology, 39,* 811–826.

Henly, S. J., Klebe, K. J., McBride, J. R., & Cudeck, R. (1989). Adaptive and conventional versions of the DAT: The first complete battery comparison. *Applied Psychological Measurement, 13,* 363–372.

Henry, E. (1965). What business can learn from Peace Corps selection and training. *Personnel, 42,* 17–25.

Herrnstein, R. (1971). IQ. *The Atlantic Monthly, 228*(3), 43–64.

Herrnstein, R. J., & Murray, C. (1994). *The bell curve: Intelligence and class structure in American life.* New York: Free Press.

Hersen, M., & Greaves, S. T. (1971). Rorschach productivity as related to verbal performance. *Journal of Personality Assessment, 35,* 436–441.

Heubert, J. P. & Hauser, R. M. (1999). *High stakes: Testing for tracking, promotion, and graduation,* Washington, DC: National Academy Press.

Hickman, J. A., & Reynolds, C. R. (1986–1987). Are race differences in mental test scores an artifact? A test of Harrington's experimental model. *Journal of Special Education, 20,* 409–430.

Hilgard, E. R. (1989). The early years of intelligence measurement. In R. Linn (Ed.), *Intelligence: Measurement, theory, and public policy.* Urbana, IL: University of Illinois Press.

Hiller, J. B., Rosenthal, R., Bornstein, R. F., Berry, D. T. R., & Brunell-Neulib, S. (1999). A Comprehensive meta-analysis of the Rorschach and MMPI validity. *Psychological Assessment, 11,* 278–297.

Hinrichs, J. R. (1978). An eight-year follow-up of a management assessment center. *Journal of Applied Psychology, 63,* 596–601.

Hiscock, M., Inch, R., & Gleason, A. (2002). Raven's Progressive Matrices performance in adults with traumatic brain injury. *Applied Neuropsychology, 9,* 129–138.

Hobbs, N. (1963). A psychologist in the Peace Corps. *American Psychologist, 18,* 47–55.

Hoffman, B. (1962). *The tyranny of testing.* New York: Crowell-Collier.

Hoffman, P. (1960). The paramorphic representation of clinical judgment. *Psychological Bulletin, 57,* 116–131.

Hofner, P. J., & Green, B. F. (1985). The challenge of competence and creativity in computerized psychological testing. *Journal of Consulting and Clinical Psychology, 53,* 826–838.

Hogan, J., & Quigley, A. M. (1986). Physical standards for employment and the courts. *American Psychologist, 41,* 1193–1217.

Hogan, R. T. (1991). Personality and personality measurement. In M. Dunnette & L. Hough (Eds.), *Handbook of industrial and organizational psychology* (2nd ed., Vol. 2, pp. 874–919). Palo Alto, CA: Consulting Psychologists Press.

Holden, C. (1986). Researchers grapple with problems of updating classic psychological test. *Science, 233,* 1249–1251.

Holden, C. (1989). Court ruling rekindles controversy over SATs. *Science, 243,* 885–886.

Holden, R. R., & Fekken, G. C. (1988). *Using reaction time to detect faking on a computerized inventory of psychopathology.* Presented at Annual Convention of Canadian Psychological Association: Montreal.

Holden, R. R., & Fekken, G. C. (1989). Three common social desirability scales: Friends, acquaintances, or strangers? *Journal of Research in Personality, 23,* 180–191.

Holden, R. R., and Fekken, G. C. (1990). Structured psycholpathological test item characteristics and validity. *Psychological Assessment, 2,* 35–40.

Holden, R. R., Fekken, G. C., & Cotton, D. H. G. (1991). Assessing psychopathology using structured test-item response latencies. *Psychological Assessment, 3,* 111–118.

Holden, R. R., & Kroner, D. G. (1992). Relative efficacy of differential response latencies for detecting faking on a self-report measure of psychopathology. *Psychological Assessment, 4,* 170–173.

Holland, J. L. (1973). *Making vocational choices: A theory of careers.* Upper Saddle River, NJ: Prentice Hall.

Holland, P. W., & Thayer, D. T. (1988). Differential item performance and the Mantel-Haenszel procedure. In H. Wainer & H. Brown (Eds.), *Test validity.* Hillsdale, NJ: Erlbaum.

Holt, R. R. (1958). Clinical and statistical prediction: Reformulation and some new data. *Journal of Abnormal and Social Psychology, 56,* 1–12.

Holt, R. R. (1969). The evaluation of personality assessment. In I. L. Janis (Ed.), *Personality: Dynamics, development and assessment.* New York: Harcourt, Brace & World.

Holtzman, W. H. (1968). Holtzman inkblot Technique. In A. Rabin (Ed.), *Projective techniques in personality assessment.* New York: Springer.

Holtzman, W. H., Thorpe, J. S., Swartz, J. D., & Herron, E. W. (1961). *Inkblot perception and personality: Holtzman Inkblot Technique.* Austin, TX: University of Texas Press.

Honacker, L. M., Hector, V. S., & Harel, T. H. (1986). Perceived validity of computer-versus clinician-generated MMPI reports. *Computers in Human Behavior, 2,* 77–83.

Hopkins, D. K., & Bracht, G. (1975). Ten-year stability of verbal and nonverbal IQ scores. *American Educational Research Journal, 12,* 469–477.

Hopkins, K. (1978). Review of the Cognitive Abilities Tests. In O. K. Buros (Ed.), *The eighth mental measurement yearbook.* Highland Park, NJ: Gryphon Press.

Horgan, J. (1995, November). Get smart, take a test: A long-term rise in IQ scores baffles intelligence experts. *Scientific American,* pp. 2–14.

Horn, J. L. (1985). Remodeling old models of intelligence. In B. Wolman (Ed.), *Handbook of intelligence: Theories, measurements and applications.* New York: Wiley.

Horn, J. L., & Cattell, R. B. (1967). Age differences in fluid and crystallized intelligence. *Acta Psychologica, 26,* 107–129.

Horton, A. M. (1997a). Human neuropsychology: Current status. In A. Horton, D. Wedding, & J. Webster (Eds.), *The neuropsychology handbook* (2nd ed., Vol. 1, pp. 3–30). NewYork: Springer.

Horton, A. M. (1997b). The Halstead-Reitan Neuropsychological Test Battery. In A. Horton, D. Wedding, & J. Webster (Eds.), *The neuropsychol-* *ogy handbook* (2nd ed., Vol. 1, pp. 221–254). New York: Springer.

Hough, L. M., Eaton, N. K., Dunnete, M. D., Kamp, J. D., & McCloy, R. A. (1990). Criterion-related validities of personality constructs and the effect of response distortion on those validities. *Journal of Applied Psychology, 75,* 581–595.

Hough , L. M., Oswald, F. L., & Ployhart, R. E. (2001). Determinants, detection and amelioration of adverse impact in personnel selection procedures: Issues, evidence and lessons learned. *International Journal of Selection and Assessment, 9,* 152–194.

Howard, A. (1974). An assessment of assessment centers. *Academy of Management Journal, 17,* 115–134.

Huck, J. R. (1973). Assessment centers: A review of the external and internal validities. *Personnel Psychology, 26,* 191–193.

Huck, J. R., & Bray, D. W. (1976). Management assessment center evaluations and subsequent job performance of white and black females. *Personnel Psychology, 29,* 13–30.

Hulin, C. L., Drasgow, F., & Parsons, C. K. (1983). *Item response theory: Application to psychological measurement.* Homewood, IL: Dow Jones-Irwin.

Humphreys, L. G. (1978). Relevance of genotype and its environmental counterpart to the theory, interpretation, and nomenclature of ability measures. *Intelligence, 2,* 181–193.

Humphreys, L. G. (1979). The construct of general intelligence. *Intelligence, 3,* 105–120.

Humphreys, L. G. (1989). Intelligence: Three kinds of instability and their consequences for policy. In R. Linn (Ed.), *Intelligence: Measurement, theory, and public policy.* Urbana, IL: University of Illinois Press.

Hunsley, J., & Bailey, J. M. (1999). The clinical utility of the Rorschach: Unfulfilled promises and an uncertian future. *Psychological Assessment, 11,* 266–277.

Hunt, E. B., & Pellegrin, J. W. (1985). Using interactive computing to expand intelligence testing. *Intelligence, 9,* 209–236.

Hunt, J. M. (1975). Reflections on a decade of early education. *Journal of Abnormal Child Psychology, 3,* 275–330.

Hunter, J. E. (1983a). *The dimensionality of the General Aptitude Test Battery (GATB) and the dominance of general factors over specific factors in the prediction of job performance.* USES Test Research Report No. 44. Washington, DC: U.S. Department of Labor.

Hunter, J. E. (1983b). *Fairness of the General Aptitude Test Battery: Ability differences and their impact on minority hiring rates.* USES Test Research Report No. 45. Washington, DC: U.S. Department of Labor.

Hunter, J. E. (1983c). *Overview of validity generalization for the U.S. Employment Service.* USES Test Research Report No. 43. Washington, DC: U.S. Department of Labor.

Hunter, J. E. (1986). Cognitive ability, cognitive aptitudes, job knowledge, and job performance. *Journal of Vocational Behavior, 29,* 340–362.

Hunter, J. E., Crosson, J. J., & Friedman, D. H. (1985). *The validity of the Armed Services Vocational Aptitude Battery (ASVAB) for civilian and military job performance.* HQUSAF/ MPXOA (Contract No. F41689-83-C-0025). Washington, DC: Department of Defense.

Hunter, J. E., & Hunter, R. F. (1984). Validity and utility of alternate predictors of job performance. *Psychological Bulletin, 96,* 72–98.

Hunter, J. E., & Schmidt, F. (1976). A critical analysis of the statistical and ethical implications of various definitions of "test bias." *Psychological Bulletin, 83,* 1053–1071.

Hunter, J. E., & Schmidt, F. L. (1982). Fitting people to jobs: The impact of personnel selection on national productivity. In M. Dunnette & E. Fleishman (Eds.), *Human performance and productivity: Human capability assessment.* Hillsdale, NJ: Erlbaum.

Hunter, J. E., & Schmidt, F. L. (1990). *Methods of meta-analysis.* Newbury Park, CA: Sage.

Hunter, J., Schmidt, F., & Hunter, R. (1979). Differential validity of employment tests by race: A comprehensive review and analysis. *Psychological Bulletin, 86,* 721–735.

Hunter, J. E., Schmidt, F. L., & Jackson, G. B. (1982). *Meta-analysis: Cumulating research findings across studies.* Beverly Hills, CA: Sage.

Hunter, J. E., Schmidt, F. L., & Pearlman, K. (1982). History and accuracy of validity generalization equations: A response to the Callender and Osburn reply. *Journal of Applied Psychology, 67,* 853–856.

Hursch, C., Hammond, K., & Hursch, J. (1964). Some methodological considerations in multiple-cue probability studies. *Psychological Review, 71,* 42–60.

Hutt, M. (1977). *The Hutt adaptation of the Bender-Gestalt test* (3rd ed.). New York: Grune & Stratton.

Hyde, J. S., & Linn, M. C. (1988). Gender differences in verbal ability: A meta-analysis. *Psychological Bulletin, 104,* 53–69.

Ilgen, D. R., & Hollenback, J. (1977). The role of job satisfaction in absence behavior. *Organizational Behavior and Human Performance, 19,* 148–161.

International Guidelines for Test Use. (2000). New York: International Testing Commission.

Ironson, G. H., & Subkoviak, M. J. (1979). A comparison of several methods of assessing bias. *Journal of Educational Measurement, 16,* 209–225.

Jackson, D. N. (1967). Acquiescence response styles: Problems of identification and control. In I. A. Barg (Ed.), *Response set in personality assessment.* Chicago: Aldine.

Jackson, D. N. (1977). *Jackson Vocational Interest Survey manual.* London, Ontario: Research Psychologists Press.

Jackson, D. N. (1984a). *Multidimensional Aptitude Battery manual.* Port Huron, MI: Research Psychologists Press.

Jackson, D. N. (1984b). *Personality Research Form manual.* Port Huron, MI: Research Psychologists Press.

Jackson, D. N. (1999). *Personality Research Form manual* (3rd ed.). Port Huron, MI: Sigma Assessment Systems, Inc.

Jackson, D. N. (2000). *Jackson Vocational Interest Survey manual* (2nd ed.). Port Huron, MI: Sigma Assessment Systems, Inc.

Jackson, D. N., & Guthrie, G. M. (1968). Multitrait-multimethod evaluation of the Personality Research Form. In *Proceedings of the 76th Annual Convention of the American Psychological Association* (Vol. 3, pp. 177–178). Washington, DC: American Psychological Association.

Jackson, G. D. (1975). On the report of the ad hoc committee on educational uses of tests with disadvantaged students. *American Psychologist, 30,* 88–93.

Jacobs, R., Kafry, D., & Zedeck, S. (1980). Expectations of behaviorally anchored rating scales. *Personnel Psychology, 33,* 595–640.

Jacoby, J., & Glauberman, N. (1995). *The bell curve debate.* New York: Random House.

James, L. R. (1973). Criterion models and construct validity for criteria. *Psychological Bulletin, 80,* 75–83.

James, L. R., Demaree, R. G., & Mulaik, S. A. (1986). A note on validity generalization procedures. *Journal of Applied Psychology, 71,* 440–450.

Janz, T. (1982). Initial comparisons of patterned behavior description interviews versus unstructured interviews. *Journal of Applied Psychology, 67,* 577–582.

Jencks, C. (1972). *Inequality: The reassessment of the effect of family and schooling in America.* New York: Basic Books.

Jencks, C., and Phillips, M. (Eds.) (1998). *The Black-White test score gap.* Washington, DC: Brookings Institution Press.

Jensen, A. R. (1969). How much can we boost IQ and scholastic achievement? *Harvard Educational Review, 39,* 1–123.

Jensen, A. R. (1972). *Genetics and education.* London: Methuen.

Jensen, A. R. (1974). How biased are culture-loaded tests? *Genetic Psychology Monographs, 90,* 185–244.

Jensen, A. R. (1975). The meaning of heritability in the behavioral and social sciences. *Educational Psychologist, 11,* 171–183.

Jensen, A. R. (1980). *Bias in mental testing.* New York: Free Press.

Jensen, A. R. (1982). The chronometry of intelligence. In R. J. Sternberg (Ed.), *A componential approach to intellectual development* (Vol. 1). Hillsdale, NJ: Erlbaum.

Jensen, A. R. (1986). *g:* Artifact or reality? *Journal of Vocational Behavior, 29,* 301–331.

Johansson, C. B. (1976). *Manual for the Career Assessment Inventory.* Minneapolis, MN: National Computer Systems.

Johansson, C. B. (1984). *Manual for Career Assessment Inventory.* Minneapolis, MN: National Computer Systems.

Johansson, C. B. (1986). *Career Assessment Inventory, the enhanced version.* Minneapolis, MN: National Computer Systems.

Johansson, C. B., & Harmon, L. W. (1972). Strong Vocational Interest Blank: One form or two? *Journal of Counseling Psychology, 19,* 404–410.

Johnson, D. F., & Mihal, W. L. (1973). The performance of blacks and whites in manual vs. computerized testing environments. *American Psychologist, 28,* 694–699.

Joint Committee for Educational Evaluation. (1985). *Personnel evaluation standards.* Newbury Park, CA: Sage.

Joint Committee on Testing Practices. (1988). *Code of fair testing practices in education.* Washington, DC: Author.

Jones, L. V., & Applebaum, M. I. (1989). Psychometric methods. *Annual Review of Psychology, 40,* 23–43.

Joseph, A. (1977). *Intelligence, IQ, and race—When, how, and why they became associated.* San Francisco: R & E Research Associates.

Joyson, R. B. (1989). *The Burt affair.* London: Routledge.

Judiesch, M. K., Schmidt, F. L., & Mount, M. K. (1992). Estimates of the dollar value of employee output in utility analyses: An empirical test of two theories. *Journal of Applied Psychology, 77,* 234–250.

Kahill, S. (1984). Human figure drawing in adults: An update of the empirical evidence, 1967–1982. *Canadian Psychology, 25,* 269–292.

Kamin, L. (1974). *The science and politics of IQ.* Hillsdale, NJ: Erlbaum.

Kamphaus, R. W., & Reynolds, C. R. (1987). *Clinical and research applications of the K-ABC.* Circle Pines, MN: American Guidance Service.

Kane, M. T. (1986). The role of reliability in criterion-referenced tests. *Journal of Educational Measurement, 23,* 221–224.

Kane, R. L. (1986). Comparison of Halstead-Reitan and Luria-Nebraska Neuropsychological Batteries. In T. Incagnoli, C. Goldstein, & C. Golden (Eds.), *Clinical application of neuropsychological test batteries.* New York: Plenum.

Kane, R. L., & Reeves, D. L. (1997). Computerized test batteries. In A. Horton, D. Wedding, & J. Webster (Eds.), *The neuropsychology handbook* (2nd ed., Vol. 1, pp. 423–468). New York: Springer.

Katz, M. R. (1987). Theory and practice: The rationale for a career guidance workbook. *Career Development Quarterly, 36,* 31–44.

Katzell, R., & Dyer, F. (1977). Differential validity revived. *Journal of Applied Psychology, 62,* 137–145.

Kaufman, A. S. (1975). Factor analysis of the WISC-R at eleven age levels between 6Z\x and 16Z\x

years. *Journal of Consulting and Clinical Psychology, 43,* 135–147.

Kaufman, A. S. (1979). *Intelligence testing with the WISC-R.* New York: Wiley.

Kaufman, A. S., & Kamphaus, R. W. (1984). Factor analysis of the Kaufman Assessment Battery for Children (K-ABC) for ages 2 1/2 through 12 1/2 years. *Journal of Educational Psychology, 76,* 623–637.

Kaufman, A. S., Kamphaus, R. W., & Kaufman, N. L. (1985). New directions in intelligence testing: The Kaufman Assessment Battery for Children (K-ABC). In B. Wolman (Ed.), *Handbook of Intelligence: Theories, measurements, and applications.* New York: Wiley.

Kaufman, A. S., & Kaufman, N. L. (1983a). *K-ABC administration and scoring manual.* Circle Pines, MN: American Guidance Service.

Kaufman, A. S., & Kaufman, N. L. (1983b). *K-ABC interpretive manual.* Circle Pines, MN: American Guidance Service.

Kaufman, J. C., & Kaufman, A. S. (2001). Time for the changing of the guard: A farewell to short forms of intelligence tests. *Journal of Pscyhoeducational Assessments, 19,* 245–267.

Kavanaugh, M. J. (1971). The content issue in performance appraisal: A review. *Personnel Psychology, 24,* 653–668.

Kavanaugh, M. J., MacKinney, A., & Wolins, L. (1971). Issues in managerial performance: Multi-trait-multimethod analysis of ratings. *Psychological Bulletin, 75,* 34–49.

Kay, G. G. (1991). Casting stones at integrity testing, not at integrity tests. *Forensic Reports, 4,* 163–169.

Kemery, E. R., Mossholder, K. W., & Roth, L. (1987). The power of the Schmidt-Hunter additive model of validity generalization. *Journal of Applied Psychology, 72,* 30–37.

Kendell, R. E. (1991). Relationship between DSM-IV and ICD-10. *Journal of Abnormal Psychology, 100,* 297–301.

Keyser, D. J., & Sweetland, R. C. (1984). *Test critiques* (Vol. 1). Kansas City, MO: Test Corporation of America.

King, G. (1978). Review of the MMPI. In O. Buros (Ed.), *The eighth mental measurement yearbook.* Highland Park, NJ: Gryphon Press.

Kingstrom, P. O., & Bass, A. R. (1981). A critical analysis of studies comparing behaviorally anchored rating scales (BARS) and other rating formats. *Personnel Psychology, 34,* 263–289.

Kirchener, W. K. (1961). "Real-life" faking on the Strong Vocational Interest Blank by sales applicants. *Journal of Applied Psychology, 45,* 273–276.

Kivlighan, D. M., Jr., Hageseth, J. A., Tipton, R. M., & McGovern, T. V. (1981). Effects of matching treatment approaches and personality types in group vocational counseling. *Journal of Counseling Psychology, 28,* 315–320.

Kleinmuntz, B. (1968). *Formal representation of human judgment.* New York: Wiley.

Kleinmuntz, B. (1970). Clinical information processing by computer. In *New Directions in Psychology* (Vol. 4). New York: Holt, Rinehart & Winston.

Klimoski, R., & Brickner, M. (1987). Why do assessment centers work? The puzzle of assessment center validity. *Personnel Psychology, 40,* 243–260.

Klimoski, R. J., & Strickland, W. J. (1977). Assessment centers—Valid or merely prescient? *Personnel Psychology, 30,* 353–361.

Kohlen, M. J., & Brennan, R. L. (1995). *Test equating: Methods and practices.* New York: Springer-Verlag.

Korchin, S. J., & Schuldberg, D. (1981). The future of clinical assessment. *American Psychologist, 36,* 1147–1158.

Koretz, D. (1993). New report of the Vermont Portfolio Project documents challenges. *National Council on Measurement in Education Quarterly Newsletter, 1,* 1–2.

Kraiger, K., & Teachout, M. S. (1990). Generalizability theory as construct-related evidence of the validity of job performance ratings. *Human Performance, 3,* 19–36.

Kramer, J. J. (1988). Computer-based test interpretation in psychoeducational assessment: An initial appraisal. *Journal of School Psychology, 26,* 143–154.

Kramer, J. J., Henning-Stout, M., Ullman, D. P., & Schellenberg, R. P. (1987). The viability of scatter analysis on the WISC-R and the SBIS: Examining a vestige. *Journal of Psychoeducational Assessment, 5,* 37–47.

Krantz, D. H., Luce, R. D., Suppes, P., & Tversky, A. (1971). *Foundations of measurement, Vol. 1: Additive and polynomial representations.* New York: Academic Press.

Kranzler, J. H. (1991). The construct validity of the Multidimensional Aptitude Battery: A word of caution. *Journal of Clinical Psychology, 47,* 691–697.

Kuder, G. F. (1970). *Kuder DD Occupational Interest Survey general manual.* Chicago: Science Research Associates.

Kuder, G. F. (1977). *Activity interests and occupational choice.* Chicago: Science Research Associates.

Kuder, G. F. (1980). Person matching. *Educational and Psychological Measurement, 40,* 1–8.

Kuder, G. F., & Diamond, E. E. (1979). *Kuder DD Occupational Interest Survey general manual* (2nd ed.). Chicago: Science Research Associates.

Kuder, G., & Richardson, M. (1937). The theory of the estimation of test reliability. *Psychometrika, 2,* 151–160.

Kuncel, N. R., Hezlett, S. A., Ones, D. S. (2001). A comprehensive meta-analysis of the predictive validity of the Graduate Record Examinations: Implications for graduate student selection and performance. *Psychological Bulletin, 127,* 162–181.

Kusyszyn, I. (1968). Comparison of judgmental methods with endorsements in the assessment of personality traits. *Journal of Applied Psychology, 52,* 227–233.

Labrentz, E., Linkenhoker, F., & Aaron, P. (1976). Recognition and reproduction of Bender-Gestalt figures: A developmental study of the lag between perception and performance. *Psychology in the Schools, 13,* 128–133.

Lacks, P. (1984). *Bender-Gestalt screening for brain dysfunction.* New York: Wiley.

Lacks, P. (1999). *Bender-Gestalt screening for brain dysfunction* (2nd ed.). New York: Wiley.

Lah, M. I. (1989). New validity, normative, and scoring data for the Rotter Incomplete Sentences Blank. *Journal of Personality Assessment, 53,* 607–620.

Lambert, N., Windmiller, M., Cole, L., & Figueroa, R. (1975). *Manual for the AAMD Adaptive Behavior Scale, public school version, 1974.* Washington, DC: American Association on Mental Deficiency.

Lance, C. E., Teachout, M. S., & Donnelly, T. M. (1992). Specification of the criterion construct space: An application of hierarchical confirmatory factor analysis. *Journal of Applied Psychology, 77,* 437–452.

Landy, F. J. (1978). Adventures in implied psychology: On the value of true negatives. *American Psychologist, 33,* 756–760.

Landy, F. J. (1985). *The psychology of work behavior* (3rd ed.). Homewood, IL: Dorsey Press.

Landy, F. J. (1987). Stamp collecting versus science: Validation as hypothesis testing. *American Psychologist, 41,* 1183–1192.

Landy, F. J., & Farr, J. L. (1980). Performance rating. *Psychological Bulletin, 87,* 72–107.

Landy, F. J., & Farr, J. L. (1983). *The measurement of work performance: Methods, theory, and applications.* New York: Academic Press.

Landy, F. J., & Trumbo, D. A. (1980). *Psychology of work behavior* (Rev. ed.). Homewood, IL: Dorsey Press.

Lang, R. J. (1978). Multivariate classification of daycare patients: Personality as a dimensional continuum. *Journal of Consulting and Clinical Psychology, 46,* 1212–1226.

Lanning, K. (1989). Detection of invalid response patterns on the California Psychological Inventory. *Applied Psychological Measurement, 13,* 45–56.

Larry, P. v. Wilson Riles. (1972). U.S. District Court for the Northern District of California. No. C-71-227ORFP.

Latham, G. P., Fay, C. H., & Saari, L. M. (1979). The development of behavioral observation scales for appraising the performance of foremen. *Personnel Psychology, 32,* 299–316.

Latham, G. P., & Pursell, E. D. (1975). Measuring absenteeism from the opposite side of the coin. *Journal of Applied Psychology, 60,* 369–371.

Latham, G., Saari, L., & Fay, C. (1980). BOS, BES, and baloney: Raising Kane with Bernardin. *Personnel Psychology, 33,* 815–821.

Latham, G. P., Saari, L. M., Pursell, E. D., & Campion, M. A. (1980). The situational interview. *Journal of Applied Psychology, 65,* 422–427.

Latham, G., & Wexley, K. (1977). Behavioral observation scales. *Journal of Applied Psychology, 30,* 255–268.

Laughon, P. (1990). The dynamic assessment of intelligence: A review of three approaches. *School Psychology Review, 19,* 459–470.

Laurent, J., Swerdlik, M., & Ryburn, M. (1992). Review of validity research on the Stanford-Binet Intelligence Scale: Fourth Edition. *Psychological Assessment, 4,* 102–112.

Lawler, E. E. (1967). The multitrait-multimethod approach to measuring managerial job performance. *Journal of Applied Psychology, 51,* 369–381.

Lawlor, S., Richman, S., and Richman, C. L. (1997). The validity of using the SAT as a criterion for black and white students' admission to college. *College Student Journal, 31,* 507–515.

Lawshe, C. H. (1975). A quantitative approach to content validity. *Personnel Psychology, 28,* 563–575.

Layon, R. (1984). Personality assessment. *Annual Review of Psychology, 35,* 667–701.

Leark, R.A. (2004). The Luria-Nebraska Neuropsychological Test Battery—Children's Revision. In G. Goldstein and S. Beers (Eds.), *Comprehensive Handbook of Psycholgical Assessment*, Vol. 1 (pp. 147–156). New York: Wiley.

Lehmann, N. (1999). *The big test: The secret history of the American meritocracy.* New York: Farrar, Straus & Giroux.

Lehnert, L., Rosemier, R., & Kise, L. (1986). Psychometric properties of the concept assessment kit-conservation. *Journal of Research and Development in Education, 19,* 77–83.

LeMahieu, P. G., Gitomer, D. H., & Eresh, J. T. (1995). Portfolios in large-scale assessment: Difficult but not impossible. *Educational Measurement: Issues and Practice, 14,* 11–28.

Lemann, N. (1999, September 6). Behind the SAT. *Newsweek, 134,* 52–57.

Lerner, B. (1983). Reality, utopia, and performance appraisal: Another view. In F. Landy, S. Zedeck, & J. Cleveland (Eds.), *Performance measurement and theory.* Hillsdale, NJ: Erlbaum.

Lerner, B. (1989). Intelligence and the laws. In R. Linn (Ed.), *Intelligence: Measurement, theory, and public policy.* Urbana, IL: University of Illinois Press.

Levitt, E. E. (1990). A structural analysis of the impact of MMPI-2 on MMPI-1. *Journal of Personality Assessment, 55,* 562–567.

Lewis, L., & Sinnett, E. R. (1987). An introduction to neuropsychological assessment. *Journal of Counseling and Development, 66,* 126–130.

Lewis, M. (1973). Infant intelligence tests: Their use and misuse. *Human Development, 16,* 108–118.

Lezak, M. D. (1995). *Neurological assessment.* New York: Oxford.

Li, C. C. (1975). *Path analysis—A primer.* Pacific Grove, CA: Boxwood Press.

Lichtenberg, J. W. (1985). On the distinction between projective and nonprojective assessment. *Journal of Counseling and Development, 64,* 3–4.

Lieblich, I., Ben-Shakar, G., Kugelmass, S., & Cohen, Y. (1978). Decision theory approach to the problem of polygraph interrogation. *Journal of Applied Psychology, 63,* 489–498.

Lilienfeld, S. O., Lynn, S. J. & Lohr, J. M. (2002). *Science and pseudoscience in clinical psychology.* New York: Guilford.

Lilienfeld, S. O., Wood, J. M., and Garb, H. N. (2000). The scientific status of projective techniques. *Psychological Science in the Public Interest, 1,* 27–66.

Linn, R. (1982). Ability testing: Individual differences, prediction, and differential prediction. In A. Wigdor & W. Garner (Eds.), *Ability testing: Uses, consequences, and controversies* (Part II). Washington, DC: National Academy Press.

Linn, R. L., Baker, E. L., & Dunbar, S. B. (1991). Complex, performance-based assessment: Expectations and validation criteria. *Educational Researcher, 20,* 15–21.

Lipsett, L., & Wilson, J. W. (1954). Do suitable interests and mental ability lead to job satisfaction? *Educational and Psychological Measurement, 11,* 373–380.

Livesley, W. J., Jang, K. L. & Vernon, P. A. (2003). Genetic basis of personality structure. In T. Millon & M. J. Lerner (Eds), *Handbook of psychology: Personality and social psychology,* (Vol 5, pp. 59–83). New York: Wiley.

Locke, E. A. (1983). Performance appraisal under capitalism, socialism, and the mixed economy. In F. Landy, S. Zedeck, & J. Cleveland (Eds.), *Performance measurement and theory.* Hillsdale, NJ: Erlbaum.

Loehlin, J. C., Lindzey, G., & Spuhler, J. N. (1975). *Race differences in intelligence.* San Francisco: Freeman.

Lohman, D. F. (1992). *Implications of cognitive psychology for selection and classification: Three critical assumptions.* Presented at ARI Conference on Selection and Classification in the Military, Alexandria, VA.

Lohman, D. F. (1994). Implications of cognitive psychology for ability testing: Three critical assumptions. In M. G. Rumsey & C. B. Walker (Eds), *Personnel selection and classification* (pp. 145–172). Hillsdale, NJ: Erlbaum.

London, M., & Bray, D. W. (1980). Ethical issues in testing and evaluation for personnel decisions. *American Psychologist, 35,* 890–901.

Lopez, F. M. (1966). *Evaluating executive decision making. Research Study 75.* New York: American Management Association.

Lord, F. M. (1952). The relation of the reliability of multiple-choice tests to the distribution of item difficulties. *Psychometrika, 17,* 181–194.

Lord, F. M. (1953). On the statistical treatment of football numbers. *American Psychologist, 8,* 750–751.

Lord, F. M. (1977). Practical applications of item characteristic curve theory. *Journal of Educational Measurement, 14,* 117–138.

Lord, F. M. (1980). *Applications of item response theory to practical testing problems.* Hillsdale, NJ: Erlbaum.

Lord, F. M., & Novick, M. (1968). *Statistical theories of mental test scores.* Reading, MA: Addison-Wesley.

Lord, R. G., & Maher, K. J. (1991). Cognitive theory in industrial and organizational psychology. In M. Dunnette & L. Hough (Eds.), *Handbook of industrial and organizational psychology* (2nd ed., Vol. 2, pp. 1–62). Palo Alto, CA: Consulting Psychologists Press.

Lou, D., Thompson, L. A., & Dettermen, D. K. (2003). The causal factor underlying the correlation between psychometric g and scholastic performance. *Intelligence, 31,* 67–83.

Lowman, R. (1989). *Pre-employment screening for psychopathology: A guide to professional practice.* Sarasota, FL: Professional Resource Exchange.

Lubin, B., Larsen, R., & Matarazzo, J. (1984). Patterns of psychological test usage in the United States. *American Psychologist, 39,* 451–454.

Lubinski, D., & Benbow, C. P. (1995). An opportunity for empiricism. *Contemporary Psychology, 40,* 935–940.

Lumsden, J. (1976). Test theory. *Annual Review of Psychology, 27,* 251–280.

Luther, M. G., & Wyatt, F. (1997). A comparison of Feuerstein's method of (LPAD) assessment with conventional I.Q. testing on disadvantaged North York high school students. In M. G. Luther & E. Cole (Eds.), *Dynamic assessment for instruction: From theory to application* (pp. 168–181). North York, Ontario: Captus Press.

Lykken, D. T. (1979). The detection of deception. *Psychological Bulletin, 86,* 47–53.

Lykken, D. T. (1998). The genetics of genius. In A. Steptoe (Ed.), *Genius and mind: Studies of creativity and temperament* (pp. 15–37). New York: Oxford University Press.

Lynn, R., & Hampson, S. (1989). Secular increases in reasoning and mathematical abilities in Britain, 1972–84. *School Psychology International, 10,* 301–304.

Lyu, C. F., & Lawrence, I. (1998). Test taking patterns and average score gains for the SAT I. *ETS Statistical Report No. 98-05,* Educational Testing Service, Princeton, NJ.

Machover, K. (1949). *Personality projection in the drawing of the human figure.* Springfield, IL: Thomas.

Mackintosh, N. J. (1995). *Cyril Burt: Fraud or framed?* Oxford: Oxford University Press.

Maddi, J. (1984). Personology for the 1980's. In R. Zucker, J. Aranoff, & A. Rabin (Eds.), *Personality and the prediction of behavior.* New York: Academic Press.

Mael, F. A. (1991). A conceptual rationale for the domain of attributes of biodata items. *Personnel Psychology, 44,* 763–792.

Magnusson, D., & Backteman, G. (1978). Longitudinal stability of person characteristics: Intelligence and creativity. *Applied Psychological Measurement, 2,* 481–490.

Manning, W. H. (1976). Some current controversies in educational measurement. *Educational Testing Service Reports,* 25–43.

Margenau, H. (1950). *The nature of physical reality.* New York: McGraw-Hill.

Marks, R., & Seeman, W. (1963). *Actuarial description of abnormal personality.* Baltimore, MD: Williams & Wilkins.

Marks, R., Seeman, W., & Haller, P. (1974). *The actuarial use of the MMPI with adolescents and adults.* Baltimore, MD: Williams & Wilkins.

Marley, M. (1982). *Organic brain pathology and the Bender-Gestalt test: A differential diagnostic scoring system.* New York: Grune & Stratton.

Martin, S. L., & Terris, W. (1991). Predicting infrequent behavior: Clarifying the impact on false-positive rates. *Journal of Applied Psychology, 76,* 484–487.

Maser, J. D., Kaebler, C., & Weise, R. E. (1991). International use and attitudes toward DSM-III and DSM-III-R: Growing consensus in psychiatric classification. *Journal of Abnormal Psychology, 100,* 271–279.

Matarazzo, J. D. (1972). *Wechsler's measurement and appraisal of adult intelligence.* Baltimore, MD: Williams & Wilkins.

Matarazzo, J. D. (1983). Computerized psychological testing. *Science, 221,* 323.

Matarazzo, J. D. (1986). Computerized clinical psychological test interpretations: Unvalidated plus all mean and no sigma. *American Psychologist, 41,* 14–24.

Matarazzo, J. D. (1992). Psychological testing and assessment in the 21st century. *American Psychologist, 47,* 1007–1018.

Matarazzo, J. D., & Herman, D. O. (1985). Clinical uses of the WAIS-R: Base rates of differences between VIQ and PIQ in the WAIS-R standardization sample. In B. Wolman (Ed.), *Handbook of intelligence: Theories, measurements, and applications.* New York: Wiley.

Matarazzo, J. D., & Weins, A. N. (1977). Black Intelligence Test of Cultural Homogeneity and Wechsler Adult Intelligence Scale scores of black and white police applicants. *Journal of Applied Psychology, 62,* 57–63.

Matthew, J. L., Golin, A. K., Moore, M. W., & Baker, C. (1992). Use of SOMPA in identification of gifted African-American children. *Journal for the Education of the Gifted, 15,* 344–356.

Maxwell, S. E., & Delaney, H. D. (1990). *Designing experiments and analysing data.* Belmont, CA: Wadsworth.

Mayfield, E. C., Brown, S., & Hamstra, B. W. (1980). Selection interviews in the life insurance industry: An update of research and practice. *Personnel Psychology, 33,* 225–239.

Mazzeo, J., & Harvey, A. L. (1988). The equivalence of scores from automated and conventional educational tests: A review of the literature. *College*

Board Report, No. 88-8. New York: College Entrance Examination Board.

McArthur, C. (1954). Long term validity of the Strong Interest Test in two subcultures. *Journal of Applied Psychology, 38,* 346–354.

McArthur, C. (1968). Comment on studies of clinical versus statistical prediction. *Journal of Counseling Psychology, 15,* 172–173.

McArthur, C. (1992). Rumblings of a distant drum. *Journal of Counseling and Development, 70,* 517–519.

McCann, J. T. (1998). Defending the Rorschach in court: An analysis of admissibility using legal and professional standards. *Journal of Personality Assessment, 70,* 125–144.

McClelland, D. C. (1993). Intelligence is not the best predictor of job performance. *Current Directions in Psychological Science, 2,* 5–6.

McCormick, E. J. (1979). *Job analysis: Methods and applications.* New York: Amacom.

McCormick, E. J., & Ilgen, D. (1980). *Industrial and organizational psychology* (7th ed.). Upper Saddle River, NJ: Prentice Hall.

McCrae, R. R. (1986). Well-being scales do not measure social desirability. *Journal of Gerontology, 41,* 390–392.

McCrae, R. R., & Costa, P. T., Jr. (1984). *Emerging lives, enduring dispositions: Personality in adulthood.* Boston: Little, Brown.

McCrae, R. R., & Costa, P. T., Jr. (1985). Updating Norman's "adequate taxonomy": Intelligence and personality dimensions in natural language and questionnaires. *Journal of Personality and Social Psychology, 49,* 710–721.

McCrae, R. R., & Costa, P. T., Jr. (1986). Clinical assessment can benefit from recent advances in personality psychology. *American Psychologist, 51,* 1001–1002.

McCrae, R. R., & Costa, P. T., Jr. (1987). Validation of the five-factor model of personality across instruments and observers. *Journal of Personality and Social Psychology, 52,* 81–90.

McCrae, R. R., & Costa, P. T., Jr. (1989). The structure of interpersonal traits: Wiggin's circumplex and the five-factor model. *Journal of Personality and Social Psychology, 56,* 586–595.

McDaniel, M. A., & Jones, J. W. (1988). Predicting employee theft: A quantitative review of the validity of a standardized measure of dishonesty. *Journal of Business and Psychology, 2,* 327–345.

McDaniel, M. A., Whetzel, D. L., Schmidt, F. L., & Maurer, S. D. (1994). The validity of employment interviews: A comprehensive review and meta-analysis. *Journal of Applied Psychology, 79,* 599–616.

McFie, J. (1960). Psychological testing in clinical neurology. *Journal of Nervous and Mental Disease, 131,* 383–393.

McGrew, K. S., & Flanaghan, D. P. (1998). *The intelligence test desk reference (ITDR): Gf-Gc cross-battery assessment.* Boston: Allyn & Bacon.

McGurk, F. C. (1975). Race differences—Twenty years later. *Homo, 26,* 219–239.

McNeil, L. M. (2000). *Contradictions of school reform: Educational costs of standardized testing.* New York: Routledge.

McNemar, Q. (1942). *The revision of the Stanford-Binet Scale: An analysis of the standardization data.* Boston: Houghton-Mifflin.

McRae, G. G. (1959). *The relationships of job satisfaction and earlier measured interests.* Unpublished doctoral dissertation, Gainesville, University of Florida.

McReynolds, P. (1968). An introduction to psychological assessment. In P. McReynolds (Ed.), *Advances in psychological assessment* (Vol. 1). Palo Alto, CA: Science and Behavior Books.

McReynolds, P. (1989). Diagnosis and clinical assessment: Current status and major issues. *Annual Review of Psychology, 40,* 83–108.

McShane, D., & Cook, U. (1985). Transcultural intellectual assessment: Performance by Hispanics on the Wechsler Scales. In B. Wolman (Ed.), *Handbook of intelligence: Theories, measurements, and applications.* New York: Wiley.

Mead, A. D., & Drasgow, F. (1993). Equivalence of computerized and paper-and-pencil cognitive ability tests: A meta-analysis. *Psychological Bulletin, 114,* 449–458.

Meehl, P. E. (1954). *Clinical versus statistical prediction: A theoretical analysis and a review of the evidence.* Minneapolis: University of Minnesota Press.

Meehl, P. E. (1957). When shall we use our heads instead of formula? *Journal of Counseling Psychology, 4,* 268–273.

Meehl, P. E. (1965). Seer over sign: The first good example. *Journal of Experimental Research in Personality, 1,* 27–32.

Meehl, P. E. (1972). Reactions, reflections, projections. In J. Butcher (Ed.), *Objective personality assessment: Changing perspectives.* New York: Academic Press.

Megargee, E. I. (1972). *The California Psychological Inventory handbook.* San Francisco: Jossey-Bass.

Meier, M. J. (1985). Review of Halstead-Reitan Neuropsychological Test Battery. In *The ninth mental measurements yearbook.* Lincoln, NE: Buros Institute of Mental Measurements.

Menninger, W., & English, J. (1965). Psychiatric casualties from overseas Peace Corps service. *Bulletin of the Menninger Clinic, 29,* 148–158.

Mercer, J. R. (1973). *Labelling the mentally retarded.* Los Angeles: University of California Press.

Mercer, J. R. (1979). Theoretical constructs of adaptive behavior: Movement from a medical to a socioeconomic perspective. In W. A. Coulter & H. W. Morrow (Eds.), *Adaptive behavior: Concepts and measurement.* New York: Grune & Stratton.

Mercer, J. R., & Lewis, J. F. (1978). *System of multicultural pluralistic assessment (SOMPA).* New York: Psychological Corporation.

Merz, W. R. (1984). *Kaufman Assessment Battery for Children. Test critiques* (Vol. 1). Kansas City: Test Corporation of America.

Messick, S. (1988). The once and future issues of validity: Assessing the meaning and consequences of measurement. In H. Wainer & H. Brown (Eds.), *Test validity.* Hillsdale, NJ: Erlbaum.

Messick, S. (1989). Meaning and values in test validation: The science and ethics of assessment. *Educational Researcher, 18* (2), 5–11.

Messick, S. (1992). Multiple intelligences or multilevel intelligence? Selective emphasis on distinctive properties of hierarchy: On Gardner's Frames of Mind and Sternberg's Beyond IQ in the context of theory and research on the structure of human abilities. *Psychological Inquiry, 3,* 365–384.

Meyer, G. J., Finn, S. E., Eyde, L. D., Kay, G. G., Moreland, K. L., Dies, R. R., Eisman, E. J., Kubiszyn, T. W., & Reed, G. M. (2001). Psychological testing and psychological assessment: A review of evidence and issues. *American Psychologist, 56,* 128–165.

Meyer, V., & Jones, H. G. (1957). Patterns of cognitive test performance as functions of lateral localization of cerebral abnormalities in the temporal lobe. *Journal of Mental Science, 103,* 758–772.

Micceri, T. (1989). The unicorn, the normal curve, and other improbable creatures. *Psychological Bulletin, 105,* 156–166.

Miles, T. R. (1957). Contributions to intelligence testing and the theory of intelligence. I. On defining intelligence. *British Journal of Educational Psychology, 27,* 153–165.

Milkovich, G. T., & Wigdor, A. K. (1991). *Pay for performance: Evaluating performance appraisal and merit pay.* Washington, DC: National Academy Press.

Miller, D. W. (2001). Scholars say high-stakes tests deserve a failing grade. The Chronicle of Higher Education, March 2, 2001.

Miller, R. C., & Berman, J. S. (1983). The efficacy of cognitive behavior therapies: A quantitative review of the research evidence. *Psychological Bulletin, 94,* 39–53.

Millon, T. (1991). Classification in psychopathology: Rationale, alternatives and standards. *Journal of Abnormal Psychology, 100,* 245–261.

Mills, C. N. (1999). Development and introduction of a computer adaptive Graduate Record Examinations General Test. In F. Drasgow & J. Olson-Buchanan (Eds.), *Innovations in computerized assessment* (pp. 117–136). Mahwah, NJ: Erlbaum.

Mischel, W., & Peake, P. K. (1982). Beyond déjà vu in the search for cross-situational consistency. *Psychological Review, 89,* 730–755.

Mitchell, J. V. (1985). *The ninth mental measurements yearbook.* Lincoln, NB: Buros Institute of Mental Measurements.

Mitchell, J. V., & Pierce-Jones, J. (1960). A factor analysis of Gough's California Psychological Inventory. *Journal of Consulting Psychology, 24,* 453–456.

Mitchell, T. R., & Klimoski, R. J. (1986). Estimating the validity of cross-validity estimation. *Journal of Applied Psychology, 71,* 311–317.

Mohrman, A. M., & Lawler, E. E. (1983). Motivation and performance-appraisal behavior. In F. Landy, S. Zedeck, & J. Cleveland (Eds.), *Performance measurement and theory.* Hillsdale, NJ: Erlbaum.

Moreland, K. L. (1990). Some observations on computer-assisted psychological testing. *Journal of Personality Assessment, 55,* 820–823.

Moreland, K. (1992). Computer-assisted psychological assessment. In M. Zeidner & R. Most (Eds.), *Psychological testing: An insider's view.* Palo Alto, CA: Consulting Psychologists Press.

Moreno, K. E., Segall, D. O., & Hetter, R. D. (1997). The use of computerized adaptive testing in the military. In R. Dillon (Ed.), *Handbook on testing* (pp. 204–219). Westport, CT: Greenwood Press.

Moreno, K. E., Wetzel, C. D., McBride, J. R., & Weiss, D. J. (1984). Relationship between corresponding Armed Services Vocational Aptitude Battery and computerized adaptive testing-subtesting. *Applied Psychological Measurement, 8,* 155–163.

Morgan, W. G. (1995). Origin and history of the Thematic Apperception Test images. *Journal of Personality Assessment, 65,* 237–254.

Morrison, T., & Morrison, M. (1995). A meta-analytic assessment of the predictive validity of the quantitative and verbal components of the Graduate Record Examination with graduate grade point average representing the criterion of graduate success. *Educational and Psychological Measurement, 55,* 309–316.

Moses, J. A. (1984a). An orthogonal factor solution of the Luria-Nebraska Neuropsychological Battery items: 1. Motor, Rhythm, Tactile, and Visual Scales. *International Journal of Clinical Neurology, 5,* 181–185.

Moses, J. A. (1984b). An orthogonal factor solution of the Luria-Nebraska Neuropsychological Battery items: 2. Receptive Speech, Expressive Speech, Writing and Reading Scales. *International Journal of Clinical Neurology, 6,* 24–38.

Moses, J. A. (1984c). An orthogonal factor solution of the Luria-Nebraska Neuropsychological Battery items: 3. Arithmetic, Memory, and Intelligence Scales. *International Journal of Clinical Neurology, 6,* 103–106.

Moses, J. A. (1997). The Luria-Nebraska Neuropsychological Battery: Advances in interpretation. In A. Horton, D. Wedding, & J. Webster (Eds.), *The neuropsychology handbook* (2nd ed., Vol. 1, pp. 255–290). New York: Springer.

Motowidlo, S. J., Dunnette, M. D., Carter, G. W., Tippins, N., Werner, S., Griffiths, J. R., & Vaughan, M. J. (1992). Studies of the behavioral interview. *Journal of Applied Psychology, 77,* 571–587.

Motta, R., Little, S., & Tobin, M. (1993). The use and abuse of human drawings. *School Psychology Quarterly, 8,* 162–169.

Muchinsky, P. M. (1996). The correction for attenuation. *Educational and Psychological Measurement, 56,* 63–75.

Mumford, M. D., Uhlman, C. E., & Kilcullen, R. N. (1992). The structure of life history: Implications for the construct validity of background data scales. *Human Performance, 5,* 109–137.

Mumford, M. D., Weeks, J. L., Harding, F. D., & Fleishman, E. A. (1988). Relations between student characteristics, course content, and training outcomes: An integrated modeling effort. *Journal of Applied Psychology, 73,* 443–456.

Munley, P. H., & Zarantonello, M. M. (1990). A comparison of MMPI profile types with corresponding estimated MMPI-2 profiles. *Journal of Clinical Psychology, 46,* 803–811.

Murphy, K. R. (1979). *Convergent and discriminant validity of regression models and subjectivity weighted models of decision-making processes.* Unpublished doctoral dissertation, Pennsylvania State University.

Murphy, K. R. (1982). Difficulties in the statistical control of halo. *Journal of Applied Psychology, 67,* 161–164.

Murphy, K. R. (1983). Fooling yourself with cross-validation. Single-sample designs. *Personnel Psychology, 36,* 111–118.

Murphy, K. R. (1984a). Review of Armed Services Vocational Aptitude Battery. In D. Keyser & R. Sweetland (Eds.), *Test critiques* (Vol. 1). Kansas City, MO: Test Corporation of America.

Murphy, K. R. (1984b). Review of Wonderlic Personnel Test. In D. Keyser & R. Sweetland (Eds.), *Test critiques* (Vol. 1). Kansas City, MO: Test Corporation of America.

Murphy, K. R. (1986). When your top choice turns you down: Effects of rejected offers on selection test utility. *Psychological Bulletin, 99,* 133–138.

Murphy, K. R. (1987a). Accuracy of clinical vs. computerized test interpretations. *American Psychologist, 42,* 192–193.

Murphy, K. R. (1987b). Detecting infrequent deception. *Journal of Applied Psychology, 72,* 611–614.

Murphy, K. R. (1988). Psychological measurement: Abilities and skills. In C. Cooper & I. Robertson (Eds.), *International review of industrial and organizational psychology* (Vol. 3). New York: Wiley.

Murphy, K. R. (1989). Is the relationship between cognitive ability and job performance stable over time? *Human Performance, 2,* 183–200.

Murphy, K. R. (1993). *Honesty in the workplace.* Pacific Grove, CA: Brooks/Cole.

Murphy, K. R. (1996). Individual differences and behavior in organizations: Much more than *g.* In K. R. Murphy (Ed.), *Individual differences and behavior in organizations* (pp. 3–30). San Francisco: Jossey-Bass.

Murphy, K. R. (2002). Can conflicting perspectives on the role of "g" in personnel selection be resolved? *Human Performance, 15,* 173–186.

Murphy, K. R. (2003). *Validity generalization: A critical review.* Mahwah, NJ: Erlbaum.

Murphy, K. R., & Balzer, W. K. (1981). *Rater errors and rating accuracy.* Paper presented at the annual conference of American Psychological Association, Los Angeles.

Murphy, K. R., & Balzer, W. K. (1986). Systematic distortions in memory-based behavior ratings and performance evaluations: Consequences for rating accuracy. *Journal of Applied Psychology, 71,* 39–44.

Murphy, K. R., & Balzer, W. K. (1989). Rater errors and rating accuracy. *Journal of Applied Psychology, 74,* 619–624.

Murphy, K. R., Balzer, W. K., Kellam, K., & Armstrong, J. (1984). Effects of the purpose of rating on accuracy in observing teacher behavior and evaluating teacher performance. *Journal of Educational Psychology, 76,* 45–54.

Murphy, K. R., Balzer, W. K., Lockhart, M., & Eisenman, E. (1985). Effects of previous performance on evaluations of present performance. *Journal of Applied Psychology, 70,* 72–84.

Murphy, K. R., & Cleveland, J. N. (1995). *Understanding performance appraisal: Social, organizational and goal-oriented perspectives.* Newbury Park, CA: Sage.

Murphy, K. R., Cleveland, J. N., & Mohler, C. (2001). Reliability, validity and meaningfulness of multisource ratings. In D. Bracken, C. Timmreck, and A. Church (Eds), *Handbook of MultiSource Feedback* (pp. 130–148). San Francisco: Jossey-Bass.

Murphy, K. R., & Constans, J. I. (1987). Behavioral anchors as a source of bias in rating. *Journal of Applied Psychology, 72,* 573–579.

Murphy, K. R., & Constans, J. I. (1988). Psychological issues in scale format research: Behavioral anchors as a source of bias in rating. In R. Cardy, S. Puffer, & J. Newman (Eds.), *Advances in information processing in organizations* (Vol. 3). Greenwich, CT: JAI Press.

Murphy, K. R., Cronin, B., & Tam, A. P. (2003). Controversy and consensus regarding the use of cognitive ability testing in organizations. *Journal of Applied Psychology, 88,* 660–671.

Murphy, K. R., Garcia, M., Kerkar, S., Martin, C., & Balzer, W. (1982). Relationship between observational accuracy and accuracy in evaluating performance. *Journal of Applied Psychology, 67,* 320–325.

Murphy, K. R., Martin, C., & Garcia, M. (1982). Do behavioral observation scales measure observation? *Journal of Applied Psychology, 67,* 562–567.

Murphy, K. R., & Myors, B. (1995). Evaluating the logical critique of banding. *Human Performance, 8,* 191–201.

Murphy, K. R., Philbin, T. A., & Adams, S. R. (1989). Effect of purpose of observation on accuracy of immediate and delayed performance ratings. *Organizational Behavior and Human Decision Processes, 43,* 336–354.

Murphy, K. R., & Shiarella, A. (1997). Implications of the multidimensional nature of job performance for the validity of selection tests: Multivariate frameworks for studying test validity. *Personnel Psychology, 50,* 823–854.

Murray, H. A. (1938). *Explorations in personality.* Cambridge, MA: Harvard University Press.

Murray, J. B. (2001). New studies of adults' responses to the Bender-Gestalt. *Psychological Report, 88,* 68–74.

Naglieri, J. A. (1988). *Draw-a-Person: A quantitative scoring system.* New York: Psychological Corporation.

Nairn, A., et al. (1980). *The reign of ETS: The corporation that makes up minds. The Ralph Nader Report on the Educational Testing Service, New York.*

Narens, L., & Luce, R. D. (1986). Measurement: A theory of numerical assignments. *Psychological Bulletin, 99,* 166–180.

Nay, W. (1979). *Multimethod clinical assessment.* New York: Gardner Press.

Neisser, U. (1979). The concept of intelligence. *Intelligence, 3,* 217–227.

Neisser, U., Boodoo, G., Bouchard, T. J., Boykin, A. W., Brody, N., Ceci, S., Halpern, D. F., Loehlin, J. C., Perloff, R., Sternberg, R. J., & Unbina, S. (1996). Intelligence: Knowns and unknowns. *American Psychologist, 51,* 77–101.

Nesselroade, J. R., & Reese, H. W. (1973). *Life-span developmental psychology: Methodological issues.* New York: Academic Press.

Nevo, B. (1985). Face validity revisited. *Journal of Educational Measurement, 22,* 287–293.

Newmark, C. (1979). *MMPI: Clinical and research trends.* New York: Praeger.

Nichols, D. S. (1992). Review of the Minnesota Multiphasic Personality Inventory-2. In J. Kramer & J. Conoley (Eds.), *The eleventh mental measurements yearbook* (pp. 562–565). Lincoln, NB: University of Nebraska Press.

Nichols, R. C., & Schnell, R. R. (1963). Factor scales California Psychological Inventory. *Journal of Consulting Psychology, 27,* 228–235.

Nicholson, R. A., & Hogan, R. (1990). The construct validity of social desirability. *American Psychologist, 45,* 290–292.

Nicholson, R. A., & Kugler, K. E. (1991). Competent and incompetent criminal defendants: A quantitative review. *Psychological Bulletin, 109,* 355–370.

Nicholson, R. A., Robertson, H. C., Johnson, W. G., & Jensen, G. (1988). A comparison of instruments for assessing competency to stand trial. *Law and Human Behavior, 12,* 313–321.

Nisbett, R., & Ross, L. (1980). *Human inference: Strategies and shortcomings in social judgment.* Upper Saddle River, NJ: Prentice Hall.

Nisbett, R., & Wilson, T. D. (1977). Telling more than you can know: Verbal reports on mental processes. *Psychological Review, 84,* 231–259.

Norcross, J. C., Karg, R. S., & Prochaska, J. O. (1997). Clinical psychologists in the 1990s: Part II. *The Clinical Psychologist, 50,* 4–11.

Nunnally, J. C. (1982). *Psychometric theory* (2nd ed.). New York: McGraw-Hill.

Nystedt, L., & Murphy, K. (1979). Some conditions affecting the utility of subjectively weighted models in decision making. *Perceptual and Motor Skills, 49,* 583–590.

Oakland, T., & Parmelee, R. (1985). Mental measurement of minority group children. In B. Wolman (Ed.), *Handbook of intelligence: Theories, measurements, and applications.* New York: Wiley.

O'Bannon, R. M., Goldinger, L. A., & Appleby, J. D. (1989). *Honesty and integrity testing: A practical guide.* Atlanta: Applied Information Resources.

Office of Strategic Services (OSS) Assessment Staff. (1948). *Assessment of men: Selection of personnel for the Office of Strategic Services.* New York: Rinehart.

Office of Technology Assessment. (1990). *The use of integrity tests for preemployment screening.* Washington, DC: U.S. Congress Office of Technology Assessment.

Olkin, I. (1992). Reconcilable differences: Gleaning insight from conflicting scientific studies. *Sciences, 32*(4), 30–36.

Ones, D. S., Viswesvaran, C., & Schmidt, F. L. (1993). Comprehensive meta-analysis of integrity test validities: Findings and implications for personnel selection and theories of job performance. *Journal of Applied Psychology, 78,* 679–703.

Orpen, C. (1985). Patterned behavior description interviews versus unstructured interviews: A comparative validity study. *Journal of Applied Psychology, 70,* 774–776.

Osburn, H. G., Callender, J. C., Greener, J. M., & Ashworth, S. (1983). Statistical power of tests of the situational specificity hypothesis in validity generalization studies: A cautionary note. *Journal of Applied Psychology, 68,* 115–122.

Ostendorf, F., Angleitner, A., & Ruch, W. (1983). *Convergent and discriminant validation of the German Personality Research Form.* West Germany: University of Bielefeld.

Owen, D. (1985). *None of the above: Behind the myth of scholastic aptitude.* Boston: Houghton Mifflin.

Owens, W. A. (1971). A quasi-actuarial basis for individual assessment. *American Psychologist, 26,* 992–999.

Owens, W. A. (1976). Background data. In M. Dunnette (Ed.), *Handbook of industrial and organization psychology.* Chicago: Rand McNally.

Owens, W. A., & Schoenfeldt, L. F. (1979). Toward a classification of persons. *Journal of Applied Psychology, 65,* 569–607.

Page, E. B. (1985). Review of Kaufman Assessment Battery for Children. In *The ninth mental measurements yearbook.* Lincoln, NE: Buros Institute of Mental Measurements.

Parker, K. C. H., Hanson, R. K., & Hunsley, J. (1988). MMPI, Rorschach, and WAIS: A meta-analytic comparison of reliability, stability, and validity. *Psychological Bulletin, 103,* 367–373.

Parkinson, C. N. (1957). The short list of principles of selection. In *Parkinson's law.* New York: Houghton Mifflin.

Parsons, F. (1909). *Choosing a vocation.* Boston: Houghton Mifflin.

Pascal, G. R., & Suttell, B. J. (1951). *The Bender-Gestalt test: Quantification and validity for adults.* New York: Grune & Stratton.

Payne, J. E., Mercer, C. D., Payne, A., & Davinson, R. G. (1973). *Head Start: A tragicomedy with epilogue.* New York: Behavioral Publications.

Pearlman, K., Schmidt, F. L., & Hunter, J. E. (1980). Validity generalization results for tests used to predict job proficiency and training success in clerical occupations. *Journal of Applied Psychology, 65,* 373–406.

Penn, S., & Bowser, S. (1977). *Assessment of rater bias in performance evaluations.* Presented at American Psychological Association Annual Convention, New York.

Pennock-Roman, M. (1990). *Test validity and language background: A study of Hispanic American students at six universities.* New York: College Entrance Examination Board.

Pervin, L. A. (1980). *Personality theory and assessment.* New York: Wiley.

Pervin, L. A. (1985). Personality: Current controversies, issues, and directions. *Annual Review of Psychology, 36,* 83–114.

Petrill, S. A., Plomin, R., Berg, S., Johansson, B., Pedersen, N. L., Ahern, F., & McClearn, G. E. (1998). The genetic and environmental relationship between general and specific cognitive abilities in twins age 80 and older. *Psychological Science, 9,* 183–189.

Piedmont, R. L., McCrae, R. R., & Costa, P. T. (1992). An assessment of the Edwards Personal Preference Schedule from the perspective of the five-factor model. *Journal of Personality Assessment, 58,* 67–78.

Piotrowski, C., Belter, R. W., & Keller, J. W. (1998). The impact of "managed care" on the practice of psychological testing: Preliminary findings. *Journal of Personality Assessment, 70,* 441–447.

Piotrowski, C., & Keller, J. W. (1984). Psychodiagnostic testing in APA-approved clinical psychology programs. *Professional Psychology: Research and Practice, 15,* 450–456.

Piotrowski, C., & Keller, J. W. (1989a). Psychological testing in outpatient mental health facilities: A national study. *Professional Psychology: Research and Practice, 20,* 423–425.

Piotrowski, C., & Keller, J. W. (1989b). Use of assessment in mental health clinics and services. *Psychological Reports, 64,* 1298.

Plomin, R. (1997). Identifying genes for cognitive abilities and disabilities. In R. J. Sternberg & E. Grigorenko (Eds.), *Intelligence, heredity, and environment* (pp. 89–104). New York: Cambridge University Press.

Plomin, R., & Rende, R. (1991). Human behavioral genetics. *Annual Review of Psychology, 42,* 161–190.

Podlesny, J. A., & Raskin, D. C. (1977). Physiological measures and the detection of deception. *Psychological Bulletin, 84,* 782–799.

Popham, W. J., & Husek, T. R. (1969). Implications of criterion-referenced measurement. *Journal of Educational Measurement, 6,* 1–9.

Powers, D. E. (1993). Coaching for the SAT: A summary of the summaries and an update. *Educational Measurement: Issues and Practice, 12,* 24–39.

Powers, D. E., and Rock. D. A. (1999). Effects of coaching on the SAT I: Reasoning Test scores. *Journal of Educational Measurement, 36,* 93–118.

Prediger, D. J. (1987). Validity of the new Armed Services Vocational Aptitude Battery cluster scores in career planning. *Career Development Quarterly, 36,* 113–125.

Prediger, D. J. (1994). Multicultural assessment standards: A compilation for counselors. *Measurement and Evaluation in Counseling and Development, 27,* 68–73.

Prince, R. J., & Guastello, S. J. (1990). The Barnum effect in a computerized Rorschach interpretation system. *Journal of Personality, 124,* 217–222.

Pulakos, E. D., Borman, W. C., & Hough, L. M. (1988). Test validation for scientific understanding: Two demonstrations of an approach to studying predictor-criterion linkages. *Personnel Psychology, 41,* 703–716.

Purisch, A. D. (2001). Misconceptions about the Luria-Nebraska Neuropsychological Test Battery. *NeuroRehabilitation, 16,* 275–280.

Rabin, A. I. (1981). Projective methods: A historical introduction. In A. Rabin (Ed.), *Assessment with projective techniques: A concise introduction.* New York: Springer.

Rahman, M., & Eysenck, S. (1978). Psychoticism and response to treatment in neurotic patients. *Behavioral Research and Therapy, 16,* 183–189.

Raju, N, S., van der Linden, W. J., & Fleer, P. F. (1995). IRT-based internal measures of differential functioning of items and tests. *Applied Psychological Measurement, 19,* 353–368.

Randahl, G. H., Hansen, J. C., & Haverkamp, B. E. (1993). Instrumental behaviors following test administration and interpretation: Exploration validity of the Strong Interest Inventory. *Journal of Counseling and Development, 71,* 435–439.

Rapaport, D., Gill, M. M., & Schafer, R. (1968). In R. Holt (Ed.), *Diagnostic psychological testing* (Rev. ed.). New York: International Universities.

Raphael, A. J., Golden, C., & Cassidy, F. S. (2002). The Bender-Gestalt Test (BGT) in forensic assessment. *Journal of Forensic Psychology Practice, 2,* 93–106.

Rasch, G. (1960). *Probabilistic models for some intelligence and attainment tests.* Copenhagen: Danish Institute for Educational Research.

Rasulis, R., Schuldberg, D., & Murtagh, M. (1996). Computer-administered testing with the Rotter Incomplete Sentences Blank. *Computers in Human Behavior, 12,* 497–513.

Raven, J. C. (1938). *Progressive Matrices: A perceptual test of intelligence, Individual Form.* London: H. K. Lewis.

Raven, J. C. (1947). *Coloured progressive matrices.* London: H. K. Lewis.

Raven, J. C. (1960). *Guide to the Standard Progressive Matrices.* London: H. K. Lewis.

Ree, M. J., & Carretta, T. R. (1994). The correlation of general cognitive ability and psychomotor tracking tests. *International Journal of Selection and Assessment, 2,* 209–216.

Ree, M. J., & Earles, J. A. (1991a). Predicting training success: Not much more than g. *Personnel Psychology, 44,* 321–332.

Ree, M. J., & Earles, J. A. (1991b). The stability of g across different methods of estimation. *Intelligence, 15,* 271–278.

Ree, M. J., & Earles, J. A. (1992). Intelligence is the best predictor of job performance. *Current Directions in Psychological Science, 1,* 86–89.

Ree, M. J., Earles, J. A., & Teachout, M. S. (1994). Predicting job performance: Not much more than g. *Journal of Applied Psychology, 79,* 518–524.

Rees, A. H., & Palmer, F. H. (1970). Factors related to changes in mental test performance. *Developmental Psychology Monograph, 3* (No. 2, Part 2).

Reilly, R. R., & Chao, G. T. (1982). Validity and fairness of some alternate employee selection procedures. *Personnel Psychology, 35,* 1–67.

Reise, S. P., & Due, A. M. (1991). The influences of test characteristics on the detection of aberrant response patterns. *Applied Psychological Measurement, 15,* 217–226.

Reitan, R. M., & Wolfson, D. (2004). Theoretical, methodological and validation bases of the Halstead-Reitan. Neuropsychological Battery. In G. Goldstein and S. Beers (Eds.), *Comprehensive handbook of psychological assessment* (Vol. 1, pp. 105–132). New York: Wiley.

Reynolds, C. R. (2001). Test Review of the Wechsler Memory Scale III. In B. S. Plake & J. C. Impara (Eds.), *The fourteenth mental measurements yearbook.* Lincoln, NB: Buros Institute of Mental Measurement.

Reynolds, C. R., & Brown, R. (1984). *Perspectives on bias in mental testing.* New York: Plenum.

Reynolds, C. R., & Kamphaus, R. W. (1997). The Kaufman Assessment Battery for Children: Development, structure, and applications in neuropsychology. In A. Horton, D. Wedding, & J. Webster (Eds.), *The neuropsychology handbook* (2nd ed., Vol. 1, pp. 221–330). New York: Springer.

Reynolds, S. B. (1988). Review of the Multidimensional Aptitude Battery. In K. Conoley, J. Kramer, & J. Mitchell (Eds.), *Supplement to the ninth mental measurements yearbook.* Lincoln, NB: University of Nebraska Press.

Ridley, C. R. (1995). *Overcoming unintentional racism in counseling and therapy: A practitioner's guide to intentional intervention.* Thousand Oaks, CA: Sage.

Ring, W. K., Saine, K. C., Lacritz, L. H., Hynana, L .S., & Cullum, C. M. (2002). Dyadic short forms of the Wechsler Adult Intelligence Scale-III. *Assessment, 9,* 254–260.

Roback, H. B. (1968). Human figure drawings: Their utility in the clinical psychologist's armentarium for personality assessment. *Psychological Bulletin, 70,* 1–19.

Robb, G. B., Bernardoni, L. C., & Johnson, R. W. (1972). *Assessment of individual mental ability.* Scranton, PA: Intex Educational Publishers.

Robins, L. N., & Helzer, J. E. (1986). Diagnosis and clinical assessment: The current state of psychiatric diagnosis. *Annual Review of Psychology, 47,* 409–432.

Robinson, A. L. (1983). Using time to measure length. *Science, 220,* 1367.

Rogers, R., Thatcher, A., & Cavanaugh, J. L. (1984). Use of the SADS Diagnostic Interview in evaluating legal insanity. *Journal of Clinical Psychology, 40,* 1537–1541.

Roid, G. H. (2003). *Stanford-Binet Intelligence Scale, Fifth Edition.* Itasca, IL: Riverside.

Ronning, R. R., Glover, J. A., Conoley, J. C., & Witt, J. C. (1987). *The influence of cognitive psychology on testing.* Hillsdale, NJ: Erlbaum.

Rorer, L. G. (1965). The great response-style myth. *Psychological Bulletin, 63,* 129–156.

Rorer, L. G., & Widigor, T. A. (1983). Personality structure and assessment. *Annual Review of Psychology, 34,* 431–463.

Rorschach, H. (1921). *Psychodiagnostik.* Berne: Birchen.

Rose, R. J. (1995). Genes and human behavior. *Annual Review of Psychology, 46,* 625–654.

Rossini, E. D., & Moretti, R. J. (1997). Thematic Apperception Test (TAT) interpretation: Practice recommendations from a survey of clinical psychology doctoral programs accredited by the American Psychological Association. *Professional Psychology—Research and Practice, 28,* 393–398.

Rotter, J. B., & Rafferty, J. E. (1950). *Manual: The Rotter Incomplete Sentences Blank.* New York: Psychological Corporation.

Rotter, J. B., Rafferty, J. E., & Lotsof, A. B. (1954). The validity of the Rotter Incomplete Sentences Blank: High school form. *Journal of Consulting Psychology, 18,* 105–111.

Rotter, J. B., Rafferty, J. E., & Schachtitz, E. (1949). Validation of the Rotter Incomplete Sentences Blank for college screening. *Journal of Consulting Psychology, 13,* 348–356.

Rotter, J. B., & Willerman, B. (1947). The incomplete sentence test. *Journal of Consulting Psychology, 11,* 43–48.

Rowe, D. C. (1999). Heredity. In V. J. Derlega & B. A. Winstead (Eds.), *Personality: Contemporary theory and research* (2nd ed.). Chicago: Nelson-Hall.

Rulon, P. J. (1939). A simplified procedure for determining the reliability of a test by split-halves. *Harvard Educational Review, 9,* 99–103.

Russell, M. T., & Karol, D. L. (1994). *The 16PF Fifth Edition administrator's manual.* Champaign, IL: Institute for Personality and Ability Testing, Inc.

Ryan, C. (1979). *The testing maze.* Chicago: National Parent Teachers Association.

Ryan, J. J., Paolo, A. M., & Smith, A. J. (1992). Wechsler Adult Intelligence Scale—Revised scatter in brain-damaged patients: A comparison with the standardization sample. *Psychological Assessment, 4,* 63–66.

Rynes, S. C., Heneman, H. G., III, & Schwab, D. P. (1980). Individual reactions to organizational recruitment: A review. *Personnel Psychology, 33,* 529–542.

Saal, F. E., Downey, R. G., & Lahey, M. A. (1980). Rating the ratings: Assessing the psychometric quality of rating data. *Psychological Bulletin, 88,* 413–428.

Sackett, P. R. (1987). Assessment centers and content validity: Some neglected issues. *Personnel Psychology, 40,* 13–25.

Sackett, P. R., Burris, L. R., & Callahan, C. (1989). Integrity testing for personnel selection: An update. *Personnel Psychology, 42,* 491–529.

Sackett, P. R., & Decker, P. J. (1979). Detection of deception in the employment context: A review and critique. *Personnel Psychology, 32,* 487–506.

Sackett, P. R., & Dreher, G. F. (1982). Constructs and assessment center dimensions: Some troubling empirical findings. *Journal of Applied Psychology, 67,* 401–410.

Sackett, P. R., Gruys, M. L., & Ellingson, J. E. (1998). Ability-personality interactions when predicting job performance. *Journal of Applied Psychology, 83,* 545–556.

Sackett, P. R., & Hakel, M. D. (1979). Temporal stability and individual differences in using assessment information to form overall ratings. *Organizational Behavior and Human Performance, 23,* 120–137.

Sackett, P. R., & Harris, M. M. (1984). Honesty testing for personnel selection: A review and critique. *Personnel Psychology, 37,* 221–245.

Sackett, P. R., & Harris, M. M. (1985). Honesty testing for personnel selection: A review and critique. In H. J. Bernardin & D. A. Bownas (Eds.), *Personality assessment in organizations.* New York: Praeger.

Sackett, P. R., & Wilson, M. A. (1982). Factors affecting the consensus judgment process in managerial assessment centers. *Journal of Applied Psychology, 67,* 10–17.

Sackett, P. R., Zedeck, S., & Fogli, L. (1988). Relationship between measures of typical and maximal job performance. *Journal of Applied Psychology, 73,* 482–486.

Safayeni, F. R., Irving, R. H., Purdy, L., & Higgins, C. A. (1992). Potential impacts of computerized monitoring systems: Eleven propositions. *Journal of Management Systems, 2*(3), 73–84.

Salgado, J. F. (1997). The five-factor model of personality and job performance in the European Community. *Journal of Applied Psychology, 82,* 30–43.

Salgado, J. F. (2002). The big five personality dimensions and counterproductive behaviors. *International Journal of Selection and Assessment, 10,* 117–125.

Salgado, J. F., & Moscoso, S. (2002). Comprehensive meta-analysis of the construct validity of the employment interview. *European Journal of Work and Organizational Psychology, 11,* 299–324.

Salovey, P., & Mayer, J. D. (1990). Emotional intelligence. Imagination. *Cognition and Personality, 9,* 185–211.

Sampson, J. P., Purgar, M. P., & Shy, J. D. (2003). Computer-based test interpretation in career assessment: Ethical and professional issues. *Journal of Career Assessment, 11,* 22–39.

Saucier, G., & Goldberg, L. R. (1996). The language of personality: Lexical perspectives on the five-factor model. In J. S. Wiggins (Ed.), *The five-factor model of personality: Theoretical perspectives* (pp. 21–50). New York: Guilford.

Sawyer, J. (1966). Measurement and prediction, clinical and statistical. *Psychological Bulletin, 66,* 178–200.

Sax, G. (1984). The Lorge-Thorndike Intelligence Tests/Cognitive Abilities Test. In D. Keyser & R. Sweetland (Eds.), *Test critiques* (Vol. 1). Kansas City, MO: Test Corporation of America.

Saxe, L. (1990). *The social significance of lying.* Invited address, Annual Convention of the American Psychological Association, Boston.

Sbordone, R. J. (1997) The ecological validity of neuropsychological testing. In A. Horton, D. Wedding, & J. Webster (Eds.), *The neuropsychology handbook* (2nd ed., Vol. 1, pp. 365–392). New York: Springer.

Scarr, S. (1981). *Race, social class, and individual differences in I.Q.* Hillsdale, NJ: Erlbaum.

Scarr, S. (1988). Race and gender as psychological variables: Social and ethical issues. *American Psychologist, 43,* 56–59.

Scarr, S. (1989). Protecting general intelligence: Constructs and consequences for interventions. In R. Linn (Ed.), *Intelligence: Measurement, theory, and public policy.* Urbana, IL: University of Illinois Press.

Schafer, C. (1989, May). Curriculum alignment behind nation's above-average scores. *Guidepost, 31,* 29.

Schaie, K. W. (1974). Translations in gerontology: From lab to life. Intellectual functioning. *American Psychologist, 29,* 802–807.

Schaie, K. W. (1994). The course of adult intellectual development. *American Psychologist, 49,* 304–313.

Schaie, K. W., & LaBouvie-Vief, G. (1974). Generational versus ontogenetic components of change in adult cognitive behavior. A fourteen-year cross-sequential study. *Developmental Psychology, 10,* 305–320.

Schaie, K. W., & Strother, C. S. (1968). A cross-sequential study of age changes in cognitive behavior. *Psychological Bulletin, 70,* 671–680.

Schippman, J. S., Prien, E., & Katz, J. A. (1990). Reliability and validity of in-basket performance measures. *Personnel Psychology, 43,* 837–859.

Schmidt, F. L. (1991). Why all banding procedures in personnel selection are logically flawed. *Human Performance, 4,* 265–278.

Schmidt, F. L. (2002). The role of general cognitive ability and job performance: Why there cannot be a debate. *Human Performance, 15,* 187–211.

Schmidt, F. L., Berner, J., & Hunter, J. (1973). Racial differences in validity of employment tests: Reality or illusion? *Journal of Applied Psychology, 58,* 5–9.

Schmidt, F. L., Gast-Rosenberg, I., & Hunter, J. E. (1980). Validity generalization results for computer programmers. *Journal of Applied Psychology, 65,* 643–661.

Schmidt, F. L., & Hunter, J. E. (1977). Development and a general solution to the problem of validity generalization. *Journal of Applied Psychology, 62,* 529–540.

Schmidt, F. L., & Hunter, J. E. (1981). Employment testing: Old theories and new research findings. *American Psychologist, 36,* 1128–1137.

Schmidt, F. L., & Hunter, J. E . (1998). The validity and utility of selection methods in personnel psychology: Practical and theoretical implications of 85 years of research findings. *Psychological Bulletin, 124,* 262–274.

Schmidt, F. L., Hunter, J. E., & Caplan, J. R. (1981). Validity generalization results for two jobs in the petroleum industry. *Journal of Applied Psychology, 66,* 261–273.

Schmidt, F. L., Hunter, J. E., & Pearlman, K. (1981). Task differences as moderators of aptitude test validity in selection: A red herring. *Journal of Applied Psychology, 66,* 166–185.

Schmidt, F. L., Hunter, J. E., & Pearlman, K. (1982). Progress in validity generalization: Comments on Callender and Osburn and further developments. *Journal of Applied Psychology, 67,* 835–845.

Schmidt, F. L., Hunter, J. E., Pearlman, K., Hirsch, H. R., Sackett, P. R., Schmitt, N., Tenopyr, M. L., Kehoe, J., & Zedeck, S. (1985). Forty questions about validity generalizations and meta-analysis with commentaries. *Personnel Psychology, 37,* 407–422.

Schmidt, F. L., Hunter, J. E., Pearlman, K., & Shane, G. S. (1979). Further tests of the Schmidt-Hunter Bayesian validity generalization procedure. *Personnel Psychology, 32,* 257–281.

Schmidt, F. L., Le, H., & Ilies, R. (2003). Beyond alpha: An empirical examination of the effects of different sources of measurement error on reliability estimates for measures of individual difference constructs. *Psychological Methods, 8,* 206–224.

Schmitt, N. (1977). Interrater agreement in dimensionality and confirmation of assessment center judgments. *Journal of Applied Psychology, 62,* 171–176.

Schmitt, N., Clause, R. Z., & Pulakos, E. D. (1996). Subgroup differences associated with different measures of some common job relevant constructs. In C. L. Cooper & I. T. Robertson (Eds.), *International review of industrial and organizational psychology.* New York: Wiley.

Schmitt, N., & Coyle, B. W. (1976). Applicant decisions in the employment interview. *Journal of Applied Psychology, 61,* 184–192.

Schmitt, N., Gooding, R. Z., Noe, R. A., & Kirsch, M. (1984). Metaanalysis of validity studies published between 1964 and 1982 and the investigation of study characteristics. *Personnel Psychology, 37,* 407–422.

Schmitt, N., Mellon, P., & Bylenga, C. (1978). Sex differences in validity for academic and employment criteria and different types of predictors. *Journal of Applied Psychology, 63,* 145–150.

Schmitt, N., Rogers, W., Chan, D., Sheppard, L., & Jennings, D. (1997). Adverse impact and predictive efficiency of various predictor combinations. *Journal of Applied Psychology, 82,* 719–730.

Schmitt, N., & Stults, D. M. (1986). Methodology review: Analysis of multitrait-multimethod matrices. *Applied Psychological Measurement, 10,* 1–22.

Schockley, W. (1972). Dysgenics, geneticity, and raceology: A challenge to the intellectual responsibility of educators. *Phi Delta Kappan, 53,* 297–307.

Schontz, F. C., & Green, P. (1992). Trends in research on the Rorschach: Review and recommendations. *Applied and Preventative Psychology, 1,* 149–156.

Schoonman, W. (1989). *An applied study of computerized adaptive testing.* Amsterdam: Swete & Zeitlinger.

Schwab, D. P., & Heneman, H. G. (1969). Relationship between interview structure and inter-interviewer reliability in an employment situation. *Journal of Applied Psychology, 53,* 214–217.

Schwab, D. P., Heneman, H., & DeCotiis, T. (1975). Behaviorally anchored rating scales: A review of the literature. *Personnel Psychology, 28,* 549–562.

Schwab, D. P., & Oliver, R. L. (1974). Predicting tenure with biographical data: Exhuming buried evidence. *Personnel Psychology, 27,* 125–128.

Segall, D. O., & Moreno, K. E. (1999). Development of the Computerized Adaptive Testing version of the Armed Services Vocational Aptitude Battery. In F. Drasgow & J. Olson-Buchanan (Eds.), *Innovations in computerized assessment* (pp. 35–65). Mahwah, NJ: Erlbaum.

Sellbom, M., & Meunier, G. (2003). Assessing antisocial characteristics in females: Can the Bender-Gestalt test provide clinically meaningful information? *Journal of Forensic Psychology Practice, 3*(2), 39–51.

Senna, C. (1973). *The fallacy of IQ.* New York: Third Press.

Seymour, R. T. (1988). Why plaintiff's counsel challenge tests, and how they can successfully challenge the theory of validity generalization. *Journal of Vocational Behavior, 33,* 331–364.

Shanker, A. (1988, April 24). Time for truth in testing. *New York Times,* p. 4.

Shannon, C., & Weaver, W. (1949). *The mathematical theory of communication.* Urbana, IL: University of Illinois Press.

Sharf, J. C. (1988). Litigating personnel measurement policy. *Journal of Vocational Behavior, 33,* 235–271.

Shavelson, R. J., & Webb, N. M. (1981). Generalizability theory—1973–1980. *British Journal of Mathematical and Statistical Psychology, 34,* 133–166.

Shavelson, R. J., Webb, N. M., & Rowley, G. L. (1989). Generalizability theory. *American Psychologist, 44,* 922–932.

Sheehan, K. R., & Gray, M. W. (1992). Sex bias in the SAT and the DTMS. *Journal of General Psychology, 119,* 5–14.

Shepard, L. A. (1982). Definitions of bias. In R. Berk (Ed.), *Handbook for detecting test bias.* Baltimore: Johns Hopkins University Press.

Shoda, Y., Mischel, W., & Peake, P. (1990). Predicting adolescent cognitive and self-regulatory competencies from preschool delay of gratification. *Developmental Psychology, 26,* 978–986.

Shortliffe, E. H., Buchanan, B. G., & Feigenbaum, E. A. (1979). Knowledge engineering for medical decision making: A review of computer-based clinical decision aids. *Proceedings of the IEEE, 67,* 1207–1224.

Siegel, S. (1956). *Nonparametric statistics for the behavioral sciences.* New York: McGraw-Hill.

Silver, E. M., & Bennett, C. (1987). Modification of the Minnesota Clerical Test to predict performance on video display terminals. *Journal of Applied Psychology, 72,* 153–155.

Silverstein, A. B. (1968). Validity of a new approach to the design of WAIS, WISC, and WPPSI short forms. *Journal of Consulting and Clinical Psychology, 32,* 478–479.

Silverstein, A. B. (1970). Reappraisal of the validity of WAIS, WISC and WPPSI short forms. *Journal of Consulting and Clinical Psychology, 34,* 12–14.

Silverstein, A. R. (1988). Review of the Multi-dimensional Aptitude Battery. In K. Conoley, J. Kramre, & J. Mitchell (Eds.), *Supplement to the ninth mental measurements yearbook.* Lincoln, NB: University of Nebraska Press.

Sinar, E. F., Reynolds, D. H. & Paquet, S. (2003). Nothing but Net? Corporate image and web-based testing. *International Journal of Selection and Assessment, 11,* 150–157.

Skager, R. (1982). On the use and importance of tests of ability in admission to post-secondary education. In A. Wigdor & W. Garner (Eds.), *Ability testing: Uses, consequences, and controversies.* Washington, DC: National Academy Press.

Skinner, H. A., & Pakula, A. (1986). Challenge of computers in psychological assessment. *Professional Psychology: Research and Practice, 17,* 44–50.

Skuy, M. (2002). The development of MLE-based intervention programmes in the context of education in South Africa. *School Psychology International, 23,* 85–111.

Slaney, R. B., & Russell, J. E. (1981). An investigation of different levels of agreement between expressed and inventoried interests among college women. *Journal of Counseling Psychology, 28,* 221–228.

Slovic, P., & Lichtenstein, S. (1971). Comparison of Bayesian and regression approaches to the study of information processing in judgment. *Organizational Behavior and Human Performance, 6,* 649–744.

Smith, D., & Dumont, F. (1995). A cautionary study: Unwarranted interpretations of the Draw-A-Person Test. *Professional Psychology: Research and Practice, 26,* 298–303.

Smith, M., & Glass, G. V. (1977). Meta-analysis of psychotherapy outcome studies. *American Psychologist, 32,* 752–760.

Smith, P., & Kendall, L. (1963). Retranslation of expectations: An approach to the construction and unambiguous anchors for rating scales. *Journal of Applied Psychology, 47,* 149–155.

Smith, S. T., Smith, K. D., & Seymour, K. J. (1993). Social desirability of personality items as a predictor of endorsement: A cross-cultural analysis. *Journal of Social Psychology, 133,* 43–52.

Smock, C. D. (1970). Goldschmid-Bentler Concept Assessment Kit—Conservation. *Professional Psychology, 1,* 491–493.

Snyder, D. K., Widiger, T. A., & Hoover, D. W. (1990). Methodological considerations in validating computer-based test interpretations: Controlling for response bias. *Psychological Assessment, 2,* 470–477.

Snyderman, M., & Rothman, S. (1987). Survey of expert opinion on intelligence and aptitude testing. *American Psychologist, 42,* 137–144.

Society for Industrial and Organizational Psychology, Inc. (2003). *Principles for the validation and use of personnel selection procedures* (4th ed.). Bowling Green, OH: Author.

Sokal, M. (1987). *Psychological testing and American society, 1890–1930.* New Brunswick, NJ: Rutgers University Press.

Solomon, P. R., Hirschoff, A., Kelly, B., Relin, M., Brush, M., DeVeaux, R. D., & Pendlebury, W. W. (1998). A 7 minute neurocognitive screening battery highly sensitive to Alzheimer's disease. *Archives of Neurology, 55,* 349–355.

Solomon, P. R., & Pendlebury, W. W. (1998). Recognition of Alzheimer's disease: the 7 minute screen. *Family Medicine, 30,* 265–271.

Spearman, C. (1904). The proof and measurement of association between two things. *American Journal of Psychology, 15,* 72–101.

Spearman, C. (1923). *The nature of "intelligence" and principles of cognition.* London: Macmillan.

Spearman, C. (1927). *The abilities of man.* New York: Macmillan.

Spitzer, R. L. (1985). DSM-III and the politics-science dichotomy syndrome: A response to Thomas E. Schacht's "DSM-III and the politics of truth." *American Psychologist, 40,* 522–526.

Spitzer, R. L., Gibbon, M., Skodol, A. E., Williams, J. B., & First, M. B. (1994). *DSM-IV casebook.* Washington, DC: American Psychiatric Association.

Spitzer, R. L., Williams, J. B., Gibbon, M. G., & Furst, M. B. (1990). *SCID-II.* Washington, DC: American Psychiatric Press.

Spitzer, R. L., Williams, B. W., & Skodol, A. E. (1980). DSM-III: The major achievements and an overview. *American Journal of Psychiatry, 137,* 151–164.

Spokane, A. R. (1979). Occupational preference and the validity of the Strong-Campbell Interest Inventory for college women and men. *Journal of Counseling Psychology, 26,* 312–318.

Spool, M. D. (1978). Training programs for observers of behavior: A review. *Personnel Psychology, 31,* 853–888.

Spraings, V. (1966). *The Spraings multiple choice Bender-Gestalt test.* Olympia, WA: Sherwood Press.

Spreen, O., & Strauss, E. (1991). *A compendium of neuropsychological tests: Administration, norms, and commentary.* New York: Oxford University Press.

Spychalski, A. C., Quiñones, M. A., Gaugler, B. B., & Pohley, K. (1997). A survey of assessment center practices in organizations in the United States. *Personnel Psychology, 50,* 71–90.

Stanley, J. C. (1961). Analysis of an unreplicated three-way classification with applications to rater bias and trait independence. *Psychometrika, 26,* 205–219.

Stanley, J. (1971). Reliability. In R. Thorndike (Ed.), *Educational measurement* (2nd ed.). Washington, DC: American Council on Education.

Stead, W. H., & Shartle, C. L. (1940). *Occupational counseling techniques.* New York: American Book.

Steele, C. M., & Aronson, J. (1995). Stereotype threat and the intellectual test performance of African Americans. *Journal of Personality and Social, 69,* 797–811.

Steers, R. M., & Rhodes, S. R. (1978). Major influences on employee attendance: A process model. *Journal of Applied Psychology, 63,* 391–407.

Steinmetz, H. C. (1932). Measuring ability to fake occupational interest. *Journal of Applied Psychology, 16,* 123–130.

Stephenson, R. R. (1965). *A comparison of responses to a vocational interest test taken under standard conditions at recruiting stations and responses to the same test taken as a self-administered test at home.* Paper presented at the annual convention of the American Personnel and Guidance Association, Minneapolis, MN.

Sternberg, R. J. (1977). *Intelligence, information processing, and analogical reasoning: The componential analysis of human abilities.* Hillsdale, NJ: Erlbaum.

Sternberg, R. J. (1980). Sketch of a componential subtheory of human intelligence. *Behavioral and Brain Sciences, 3,* 573–584.

Sternberg, R. J. (1981a). Testing and cognitive psychology. *American Psychologist, 36,* 1181–1189.

Sternberg, R. J. (1981b). Toward a unified componential theory of human intelligence, I. Fluid abilities. In M. Friedman, J. Das, & N. O'Connor (Eds.), *Intelligence and learning.* New York: Plenum.

Sternberg, R. J. (1982). A componential approach to intellectual development. In R. J. Sternberg (Ed.), *Advances in the psychology of human intelligence* (Vol. 1). Hillsdale, NJ: Erlbaum.

Sternberg, R. J. (1984). What should intelligence tests test? Implications of a triarchic theory of intelligence for intelligence testing. *Educational Research, 13,* 5–15.

Sternberg, R. J. (1985). *Beyond IQ: A triarchic theory of human intelligence.* New York: Cambridge University Press.

Sternberg, R. J. (1991). Death, taxes, and bad intelligence tests. *Intelligence, 15,* 257–269.

Sternberg, R. J. (1995). For whom the bell curve tolls: A review of *The Bell Curve. Psychological Science, 6,* 257–261.

Sternberg, R. J. (1997a). *Successful intelligence.* New York: Plume.

Sternberg, R. J. (1997b). Tacit knowledge and job success. In N. Anderson & P. Herriot (Eds.), *International handbook of selection and assessment* (pp. 201–213). New York: John Wiley & Sons Inc.

Sternberg, R. J. & Horvath, J. A. (1999). *Tacit knowledge in professional practice.* Mahwah, NJ: Erlbaum.

Sternberg, R. J & Grigorenko, E. L. (2002). *The general factor of intelligence: How general is it?* Mahwah, NJ: Erlbaum.

Sternberg, R. J., & Wagner, R. K. (1993). The g-ocentric view of intelligence and performance is wrong. *Current Directions in Psychological Science, 2,* 1–5.

Stevens, S. S. (1946). On the theory of scales of measurement. *Science, 103,* 677–680.

Stevens, S. S. (1951). Mathematics, measurement, and psychophysics. In S. S. Stevens (Ed.), *Handbook of experimental psychology.* New York: Wiley.

Stevens, S. S. (1961). The psychophysics of sensory function. In W. A. Rosenblith (Ed.), *Sensory communication.* New York: Wiley.

Steward, V. (1947, January). The problem of detecting fudging on vocational interest tests. In *Personnel Reports for Sales Executives.* Los Angeles.

Stokes, G., Mumford, M., & Owens, W. (1994). *Biodata handbook: Theory, research, and use of biographical information in selection and performance prediction.* Palo Alto, CA: CPP Books.

Stoolmiller, M. (1999). Implications of the restricted range of family environments for estimates of heritability and nonshared environment in behavior-genetic adoption studies. *Psychological Bulletin, 125,* 392–409.

Stricker, G., & Gold, J. R. (1999). The Rorschach: Toward a nomothetically based, ideographically applicable configurational model. *Psychological Assessment, 11,* 240–250.

Strommer, E. (1988). Confirmatory factor analysis of the Kaufman Assessment Battery for Children: A reevaluation. *Journal of School Psychology, 26,* 13–23.

Strong, E. K. (1927). *Vocational Interest Blank.* Stanford, CA: Stanford University Press.

Strong, E. K. (1943). *Vocational interests of men and women.* Stanford, CA: Stanford University Press.

Strong, E. K. (1955). *Vocational interests 18 years after college.* Minneapolis, MN: University of Minnesota Press.

Sundberg, N. D. (1977). *Assessment of persons.* Upper Saddle River, NJ: Prentice Hall.

Super, D. E. (1973). The Work Values Inventory. In D. Zytowski (Ed.), *Contemporary approaches to interest measurement.* Minneapolis: University of Minnesota Press.

Sussmann, M., & Robertson, D. U. (1986). The validity of validity: An analysis of validation study designs. *Journal of Applied Psychology, 71,* 461–468.

Swensen, C. H. (1957). Empirical evaluations of human figure drawings. *Psychological Bulletin, 54,* 431–466.

Swensen, C. H. (1968). Empirical evaluations of human figure drawings. *Psychological Bulletin, 70,* 20–44.

Swensen, W., Pearson, J., & Osborne, D. (1973). *An MMPI sourcebook: Basic item, scale, and pattern data on 50,000 medical patients.* Minneapolis, MN: University of Minnesota Press.

Tagiuri, R., & Petrillo, L. (1958). *Person perception and interpersonal behavior.* Stanford, CA: Stanford University Press.

Tarvis, C. (1992). *The mismeasure of woman.* New York: Simon & Schuster.

Task Force on Assessment Center Guidelines. (1989). *Guidelines and ethical condsiderations for assessment center operations.* Pittsburgh, PA: Author.

Taylor, H. C., & Russell, J. T. (1939). The relationship of validity coefficients to the practical effectiveness of tests in selection. *Journal of Applied Psychology, 23,* 565–578.

Taylor, R. G., & Lee, E. (1995). A review of methods and problems in measuring reliability for criterion-referenced tests. *Journal of Instructional Psychology, 22,* 88–94.

Taylor, R. L., & Richards, S. B. (1990). Validity of the Estimated Learning Potential and other measures of learning potential. *Perceptual and Motor Skills, 71,* 225–229.

Tellegen, A., Lykken, D. T., Bouchard, T. J., Wilcox, K. J., et al. (1988). Personality similarity in twins reared apart and together. *Journal of Personality and Social Psychology, 54,* 1031–1039.

Tenopyr, M. L. (1981). The realities of employment testing. *American Psychologist, 36,* 1120–1127.

Tenopyr, M. L., & Oeltjen, P. D. (1982). Personnel selection and classification. *Annual Review of Psychology, 33,* 581–618.

Terman, L. M. (1916). *The measurement of intelligence.* Boston: Houghton Mifflin.

Terman, L. M., & Merrill, M. A. (1937). *Measuring intelligence.* Boston: Houghton Mifflin.

Terman, L. M., & Merrill, M. A. (1960). *Stanford-Binet Intelligence Scale: Manual for the third revision, Form L–M.* Boston: Houghton Mifflin.

Terman, L. M., & Merrill, M. A. (1973). *Stanford-Binet Intelligence Scale: 1972 norms edition.* Boston: Houghton Mifflin.

Tett, R. P., Jackson, D. N., & Rothstein, M. (1991). Personality measures as predictors of job performance: A meta-analytic review. *Personnel Psychology, 44,* 703–742.

Tett, R. P., Steele, J. R., & Beauregard, R. S. (2003). Broad and narrow measures on both sides of the personality-job performance relationship. *Journal of Organizational Behavior, 24,* 335–356.

Thissen, D., & Steinberg, L. (1988). Data analysis using item response theory. *Psychological Bulletin, 104,* 385–395.

Thissen, D., Steinberg, L., & Gerrard, M. (1986). Beyond group-mean differences: The concept of item bias. *Psychological Bulletin, 99,* 118–128.

Thissen, D., Wainer, H., & Wang, X. (1994). Are tests comprising both multiple-choice and free-response items necessarily less unidimensional than multiple-choice tests? An analysis of two tests. *Journal of Educational Measurement, 31,* 113–123.

Thomas, H. (1988). What is the interpretation of the validity generalization estimate $S^2_p = S^2_r - S^2_e$? *Journal of Applied Psychology, 73,* 679–682.

Thorndike, E. L. (1912). The permanence of interests and their relation to abilities. *Popular Science Monthly, 81,* 449–456.

Thorndike, E. L. (1920). A constant error in psychological ratings. *Journal of Applied Psychology, 4,* 25–29.

Thorndike, R. L. (1949). *Personnel selection.* New York: Wiley.

Thorndike, R. L. (1951). Reliability. In E. Lindquist (Ed.), *Educational measurement.* Washington, DC: American Council on Education.

Thorndike, R. L. (1985). The central role of general ability in prediction. *Multivariate Behavioral Research, 20,* 241–254.

Thorndike, R. L., Hagen, E. P., & Sattler, J. M. (1986). *The Stanford Binet Intelligence Scale, fourth edition: Technical Manual.* Chicago: Riverside.

Thornton, G. C., III. (1992). *Assessment centers in human resource management.* Reading, MA: Addison-Wesley.

Thornton, G. C., III. (1993). The effect of selection practices on applicants' perceptions of organizational characteristics. In H. Shuler, J. Farr, & M. Smith (Eds.), *Personnel selection and assessment: Individual and organizational perspectives* (pp. 57–69). Hillsdale, NJ: Erlbaum.

Thornton, G. C., III, & Byham, W. C. (1982). *Assessment centers and managerial performance.* New York: Academic Press.

Thornton, G. C., III, & Cleveland, J. N. (1990). Developing managerial talent through simulation. *American Psychologist, 45,* 190–199.

Thornton, G. C., III, Murphy, K. R, Everest, T. M., & Hoffman, C. C. (2000). Higher cost, lower validity and higher utility: Comparing the utilities of two tests that differ in validity, costs, and selectivity. *International Journal of Selection and Assessment, 8,* 61–75.

Thorson, J. A., & Powell, F. C. (1992). Vagaries of college norms for the Edwards Personal Preference Schedule. *Psychological Reports, 70,* 943–946.

Thurstone, L. L. (1927). A law of comparative judgment. *Psychological Review, 34,* 273–286.

Thurstone, L. L. (1935). *Vectors of the mind: Multiple-factor analysis for the isolation of primary traits.* Chicago: University of Chicago Press.

Thurstone, L. L. (1938). Primary mental abilities. *Psychometric Monographs,* No. 1. Chicago: University of Chicago Press.

Tolor, A., & Brannigan, G. (1980). *Research and clinical applications of the Bender-Gestalt test.* Springfield, IL: Thomas.

Torgerson, W. (1958). *Theory and methods of scaling.* New York: Wiley.

Tsolaki, M., Iakovidou, V., Papadopoulou, E., Aminta, M., Nakopoulou, E., Pantaxi, T., & Kazis, A. (2002). Greek validation of the Seven-Minute Screening Battery for Alzheimer's disease in the elderly. *American Journal of Alzheimer's Disease and Other Dementias, 17,* 139–148.

Turban, D. B., Sanders, P. A., Francis, D. J., & Osburn, H. G. (1989). Construct equivalence as an approach to replacing validated cognitive ability selection tests. *Journal of Applied Psychology, 74,* 62–71.

Turkheimer, E. (1999). Heritability and biological explanation. *Psychological Review, 105,* 782–791.

Ulosevich, S. N., Michael, W. B., & Bachelor, P. (1991). Higher-order factors in structure-of-intellect (SOI) aptitude tests hypothesized to portray constructs of military leadership: A re-analysis of an SOI data base. *Educational and Psychological Measurement, 51,* 15–37.

Uniform guidelines on employee selection procedures. (1978). *Federal Register, 43* (166), 38296–38309.

Uomoto, J. (1991). *The neuropsychological evaluation in vocational planning.* Boca Raton, FL: St. Lucie Press.

Urry, V. W. (1977). Tailored testing: Successful application of latent trait theory. *Journal of Educational Measurement, 14,* 181–196.

Urry, V. W., & Dorans, N. J. (1981). *Tailored testing: Its theory or practice, Part I. The basic model, the normal ogive submodel, and the tailoring algorithms.* San Diego, CA: Navy Personnel Research Development Center.

U.S. Congress Office of Technology Assessment. (1987). *The electronic supervisor: New Technology, new tensions (OTA-CIT-333).* Washington, DC: U.S. Government Printing Office.

Vale, C. D. (1990). The Minnesota Clerical Assessment Battery: An application of computerized testing to business. *Measurement and Evaluation in Counseling and Development, 23,* 11–19.

Vale, C. D., Keller, L. S., & Bentz, V. J. (1986). Development and validation of a computerized interpretation system for personnel tests. *Personnel Psychology, 39,* 525–542.

Vandenberg, S. G., & Vogler, G. P. (1985). Genetic determinants of intelligence. In B. Wolman (Ed.), *Handbook of intelligence. Theories, measurements and applications* (pp. 3–57). New York: Wiley.

VanderZee, K. I., Bakker, A. B., & Bakker, P. (2002). Why are structured interviews so rarely used in personnel selection? *Journal of Applied Psychology, 87,* 176–184.

Vernon, P. A. (1985). Review of Multidimensional Aptitude Battery. In D. Keyser & R. Sweetland (Eds.), *Test critiques* (Vol. 2). Kansas City, MO: Test Corporation of America.

Vernon, P. A. (2000). Recent studies of intelligence and personality using Jackson's Multidimensional Aptitude Battery and Personality Research Form. In Goffin, R. D., & Helmes, E. (Eds.), *Problems and Solutions in Human Assessment: Honoring Douglas N. Jackson at Seventy* (pp. 195–212). New York, NY: Kluwer Academic/Plenum Publishers.

Vernon, P. E. (1960). *The structure of human abilities* (Rev. ed.). London: Methuen.

Vernon, P. E. (1965). Ability factors and environmental influences. *American Psychologist, 20,* 723–733.

Veroff, J., McClelland, L., & Marquis, K. (1971). *Measuring intelligence and achievement motivations in surveys.* Ann Arbor, MI: Survey Research Center. Institute for Social Research, University of Michigan.

Viglione, D. J. (1999). A review of recent research addressing the utility of the Rorschach. *Psychological Assessment, 11,* 251–265.

Vinberg, R., & Joyner, J. N. (1982). Performance measurement in the military services. In F. Landy, S. Zedeck, & J. Cleveland (Eds.), *Performance measurement and theory.* Hillsdale, NJ: Erlbaum.

Wade, T. C., & Baker, T. B. (1977). Opinions and use of psychological tests. *American Psychologist, 32,* 874–882.

Wainer, H. (1976). Estimating coefficients in linear models: It don't make no never mind. *Psychological Bulletin, 83,* 213–217.

Wainer, H. (1988). How accurately can we assess changes in minority performance on the SAT? *American Psychologist, 43,* 774–778.

Wainer, H., & Braun, H. I. (1988). *Test validity.* Hillsdale, NJ: Erlbaum.

Wainer, H., Wang, X., & Thissen, D. (1994). How well can we compare scores on test forms that are constructed by examinees' choice? *Journal of Educational Measurement, 31,* 183–199.

Wall, J. L., & Baker, H. E. (1997). The interest-finder: Evidence of validity. *Journal of Career Assessment, 5,* 255–273.

Wall, J. L., Wise, L. L., & Baker, H. E. (1996) Development of the Interest-Finder: A new RIASEC-based interest inventory. *Measurement and Evaluation in Counseling and Development, 29,* 134–152.

Wallace, W. L. (1950). The relationship of certain variables to discrepancy between expressed and inventoried vocational interest. *American Psychologist, 5,* 354.

Wallbrown, F. H., Blaha, J., & Wherry, R. J. (1973). The hierarchical factor structure of the Wechsler Preschool and Primary Scale of Intelligence.

Journal of Consulting and Clinical Psychology, 41, 356–362.

Wallbrown, F. H., and Jones, J. A. (1992). Reevaluating the factor structure of the revised California Psychological Inventory. *Educational and Psychological Measurement, 52,* 379–386.

Waller, M. I. (1989). Modeling guessing behavior: A comparison of two IRT models. *Applied Psychological Measurement, 13,* 233–243.

Walsh, J. A. (1990). Comment on social desirability. *American Psychologist, 45,* 289–290.

Waters, B. K. (1997). Army alpha to CAT-ASVAB: Four-score years of military personnel selection and classification testing. In R. F. Dillon (Ed.), *Handbook on testing* (pp. 187–203). Westport, CT: Greenwood Press.

Watkins, C. E., Jr., Campbell, V. L., Nieberding, R., & Hallmark, R. (1995). Contemporary practice of psychological assessment by clinical psychologists. *Professional Psychology: Research and Practice, 26,* 54–60.

Webb, J., & McNamara, K. (1979). Configural interpretation of the MMPI. In C. Newmark (Ed.), *MMPI: Clinical and research trends.* New York: Praeger.

Webber, P. L., & Harmon, L. W. (1978). The reliability and concurrent validity of three types of occupational scales for two occupational groups: Some evidence bearing on handling sex differences in interest scale construction. In C. K. Tittle & D. B. Zytowski (Eds.), *Sex-fair interest measurement: Research and implications.* Washington, DC: National Institute of Education, Department of Health, Education, and Welfare.

Wechsler, D. (1939). *The measurement of adult intelligence.* Baltimore: Williams & Wilkins.

Wechsler, D. (1955). *Manual for the Wechsler Adult Intelligence Scale.* New York: The Psychological Corporation.

Wechsler, D. (1958). *The measurement and appraisal of adult intelligence* (4th ed.). Baltimore: Williams & Wilkins.

Wechsler, D. (1987). *Wechsler memory scale—revised.* New York: Psychological Corporation.

Weiss, D. J. (1978). Review of Armed Services Vocational Aptitude Battery. In O. K. Buros (Ed.), *The eighth mental measurements yearbook* Highland Park, NJ: Gryphon Press.

Weiss, D. J. (1983). *New horizons in testing: Latent trait testing and computerized adaptive testing.* New York: Academic Press.

Weiss, D. J., & Davinson, N. L. (1981). Test theory and methods. *Annual Review of Psychology, 32,* 629–658.

Welsh, J. R., Kucinkas, S. K., & Curran, L. T. (1990). *Armed Services Vocational Aptitude Battery (ASVAB): Integrative review of validity studies.* Brooks Air Force Base.

Wernimont, P. F. (1962). Re-evaluation of a weighted application blank for office personnel. *Journal of Applied Psychology, 46,* 417–419.

Wernimont, P. F., & Campbell, J. P. (1968). Signs, samples, and criteria. *Journal of Applied Psychology, 52,* 372–376.

Westen, D., Lohr, N. E., Silk, K., Gold, L., & Kerber, K. (1990). Object relations and social cognition in borderlines, major depressives, and normals: A thematic apperception test analysis. *Psychological Assessment: A Journal of Consulting and Clinical Psychology, 2,* 355–364.

Wherry, R. J., & Bartlett, C. J. (1982). The control of bias in ratings: A theory of rating. *Personnel Psychology, 35,* 521–551.

Whimbey, A. (1980). Students can learn to be better problem solvers. *Educational Leadership, 37,* 560–565.

Widiger, T., Frances, A. J., Pincus, H. A., Ross, R., First, M. B., & Davis, W. W. (1994). *DSM-IV sourcebook* (Vol. 1). Washington, DC: American Psychiatric Association.

Widiger, T. A., & Trull, T. J. (1991). Diagnosis and clinical assessment. *Annual Review of Psychology, 42,* 109–133.

Wiesner, W. H., & Cronshaw, S. F. (1988). A meta-analytic investigation of the impact of interview format and degree of structure on the validity of the interview. *Journal of Occupational Psychology, 61,* 275–290.

Wigdor, A. (1982). Psychological testing and the law of employment discrimination. In A. Wigdor & W. Garner (Eds.), *Ability testing: Uses, consequences and controversies, Part II: Documentation section.* Washington, DC: National Academy Press.

Wigdor, A. K., & Garner, W. R. (1982a). *Ability testing: Uses, consequences, and controversies, Part I: Report of the committee.* Washington, DC: National Academy Press.

Wigdor, A. K., & Garner, W. R. (1982b). *Ability testing: Uses, consequences, and controversies, Part II: Documentation section.* Washington, DC: National Academy Press.

Wiggins, J. (1973). *Personality and prediction: Principles of personality assessment.* Reading, MA: Addison-Wesley.

Wiggins, N., & Kohen, E. (1971). Man versus model of man revisited: The forecasting of graduate success. *Journal of Personality and Social Psychology, 19,* 100–106.

Wilcox, R. (1992). Why can methods for comparing means have relatively low power and what can you do to correct the problem? *Current Directions in Psychological Science, 1,* 101–105.

Williams, R. L. (1971). Abuses and misuses in testing black children. *Counseling Psychologist, 2,* 62–77.

Williams, R. L. (1972). *The BITCH-100: A culture-specific test.* Paper presented at the annual convention of the American Psychological Association, Honolulu, HI.

Williams, R. L. (1974). Scientific racism and IQ: The silent mugging of the black community. *Psychology Today, 7*(12), 32–41.

Williams, W. M. & Ceci, S. J. (1997). Are Americans becoming more or less alike?: Trends in race, class, and ability differences in intelligence. *American Psychologist, 55,* 1226–1235.

Wilson, K. M. (1989, Spring). A study of the long-term stability of GRE test scores. Report No. 86-18R. In J. Pfleiderer, *GRE Board Newsletter,* 5. Princeton, NJ: Graduate Record Examinations Board.

Winfred, A., & Woehr, D. J. (1993). A confirmatory factor analytic study examining the dimensionality of the Raven's Advanced Progressive Matrices. *Educational and Psychological Measurement, 53,* 471–478.

Wing, H. (1992). Review of the Bennett Mechanical Comprehension Test. In J. Kramer & J. Conoley (Eds.), *Eleventh mental measurements yearbook.* Lincoln, NB: Buros Institute of Mental Measurements.

Wise, E. A. (2002). Relationships of personality disorders with MMPI-2 malingering, defensiveness, and inconsistent response scales among forensic examinees. *Psychological Reports, 90,* 760–766.

Wise, P. S. (1989). *The use of assessment techniques by applied psychologists.* Belmont, CA: Wadsworth.

Wissler, C. (1901). The correlation of mental and physical traits. *Psychological Monographs, 3*(6, Whole No. 16).

Wolfe, J. (1976). The effects and effectiveness of simulations in business policy teaching applications. *Academy of Management Review, 1,* 47–56.

Wollowick, H. B., & McNamara, W. J. (1969). Relationship of the components of an assessment center to management success. *Journal of Applied Psychology, 53,* 348–352.

Wood, J. M., Nezworski, M. T., Lilienfeld, S. O., & Garb, H. N. (2003). *What's Wrong with the Rorschach? Science Confronts the Controversial Inkblot Test.* San Francisco: Jossey-Bass.

Yntema, D., & Torgerson, W. (1961). Man-computer cooperation in decisions requiring common sense. *IEE Transactions on Human Factors in Electronics, 2,* 20–26.

Young, J. (1995). "Recentering" the SAT score scale. *College and University, 70,* 60–62.

Zeidner, J., & Johnson, C. D. (1994). Is personnel classification a concept whose time has passed? In M. Rumsey, C. Walker, & J. Harris (Eds.), *Personnel selection and classification* (pp. 377–410). Hillsdale, NJ: Erlbaum.

Ziegler, E., & Valentine, J. (1980). *Project Head Start: A legacy of the war on poverty.* New York: Free Press.

Zimmerman, I. L., & Woo-Sam, J. M. (1972). Research with the Wechsler Intelligence Scale for Children, 1960–1970. *Psychology in the Schools, 9,* 232–271.

Zimmerman, I. L., & Woo-Sam, J. M. (1985). Clinical applications. In B. Wolman (Ed.), *Handbook of intelligence: Theories, measurements, and applications.* New York: Wiley.

Zonana, H. V. (1984). The first presidential assassination attempt. *Bulletin of the American Academy of Psychiatry and Law, 12,* 309–322.

Zubin, J., Eron, L. D., & Schumer, F. (1965). *An experimental approach to projective techniques.* New York: Wiley.

Zucker, R. A., Aranoff, J., & Rabin, A. I. (1984). *Personality and the prediction of behavior.* New York: Academic Press.

Zytowski, D. G. (1976). Predictive validity of the Kuder Occupational Interest Survey: A 12- to 19-year follow-up. *Journal of Counseling Psychology, 3,* 221–233.

Zytowski, D. G. (1985). *Kuder DD manual supplement.* Chicago: Science Research Associates.

Zytowski, D. G. (1992). Three generations: The continuing evolution of Frederic Kuder's interest inventories. *Journal of Counseling and Development, 71,* 245–248.

Zytowski, D. G. (1999). How to talk to people about their interest inventory results. In M. Savickas and A. R. Spokane (Eds.), *Vocational interests: Meaning, measurement, and counseling use* (pp. 277–293). Palo Alto, CA: Davies-Black.

Zytowski, D. G., & Borgan, F. H. (1983). Assessment. In W. Walsh & S. Osipaw (Eds.), *Handbook of vocational psychology* (Vol. 2). Hillsdale, NJ: Erlbaum.

Zytowski, D. G., & Laing, J. (1978). Validity of other-gender-normed scales on the Kuder Occupational Interest Survey. *Journal of Counseling Psychology, 3,* 205–209.

Zytowski, D. G., & Warman, R. W. (1982). The changing use of tests in counseling. *Measurement and Evaluation in Guidance, 15,* 147–152.

Subject Index

Author Index

MODERN
MEAT KITCHEN

MODERN
MEAT KITCHEN

How to choose, prepare and cook meat and poultry

Miranda Ballard

photography by Steve Painter

LONDON · NEW YORK

DEDICATION
To my parents, Edward and Jude.

DESIGN, PROP STYLING AND
PHOTOGRAPHY Steve Painter
EDITOR Kate Eddison
PRODUCTION MANAGER Gordana Simakovic
ART DIRECTOR Leslie Harrington
EDITORIAL DIRECTOR Julia Charles
PUBLISHER Cindy Richards

FOOD STYLIST Lucy McKelvie
US CONTRIBUTING EDITOR Toponia Miller
INDEXER Vanessa Bird

First published in 2015 by
Ryland Peters & Small
20–21 Jockey's Fields
London WC1R 4BW
and
341 E 116th St
New York NY 10029

www.rylandpeters.com

10 9 8 7 6 5 4 3 2 1

Text copyright © Miranda Ballard 2015
Design and photographs copyright
© Ryland Peters & Small 2015 with the exception
of the farm animal pictures on pages 8, 9, 13, 16, 20,
23, 38, 41, 42, 44, 46, 47, 58, 60–61, 68, 70, 71, 80,
83, 88, 240, copyright © Steve Painter.

Printed in China

UK ISBN: 978-1-84975-652-5
US ISBN: 978-1-84975-726-3

A CIP record for this book is available from
the British Library.

US Library of Congress CIP data has been
applied for.

NOTES
• All eggs are medium (UK) or large (US), unless
otherwise specified. Uncooked or partially cooked
eggs should not be served to the very old, frail,
young children, pregnant women or those with
compromised immune systems.
• Fruit and vegetables are medium-sized, unless
otherwise stated.
• When a recipe calls for the grated zest of citrus
fruit, buy unwaxed fruit and wash well before
using. If you can only find treated fruit, scrub
well in warm soapy water before using.
• Ovens should be preheated to the specified
temperatures. We recommend using an oven
thermometer. If using a fan-assisted oven, adjust
temperatures according to the manufacturer's
instructions.

FOOD SAFETY
• The information in this book is based on the
author's experience. Guidelines for safety are
included within recipes, and these should be
followed. Neither the author nor the publisher can
be held responsible for any harm or injury that
arises from the application of ideas in this book.
• Use the freshest meats possible for home-curing.
Ensure all tools and working surfaces are clean.
Store all meats in a refrigerator.
• Uncooked or partially cooked meats should not
be served to the very old, frail, young children,
pregnant women or those with compromised
immune systems.

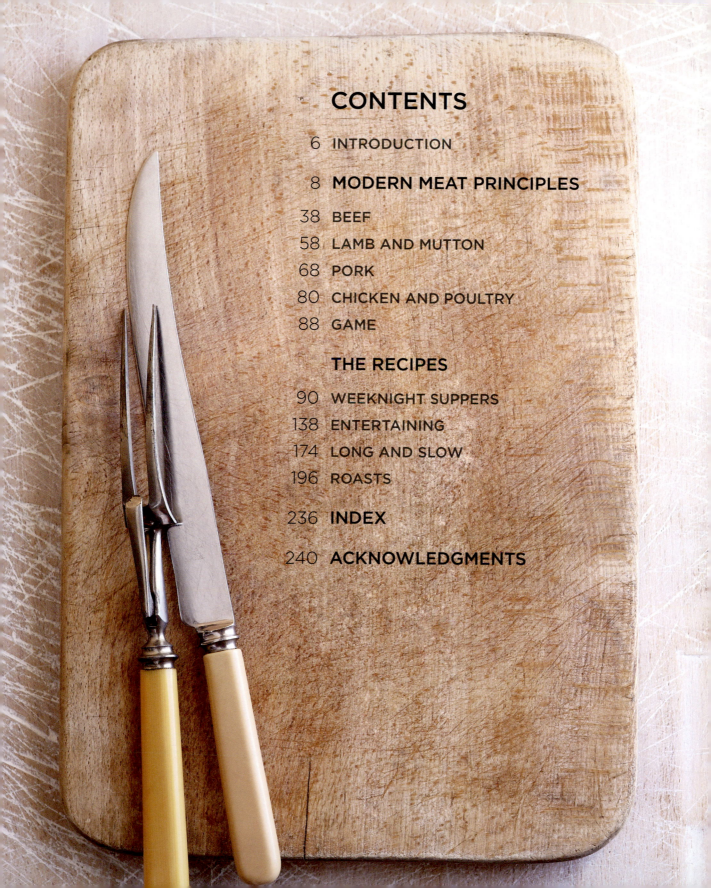

CONTENTS

INTRODUCTION

Writing this book was an absolute treat for me: I'm a meat eater; I'm an enthusiastic cook; I'm a lover of great farming; I own a meat company; I don't have an unlimited budget for food shopping; and I always seem to be really (really) busy, largely because of starting up our meat company! So here was an opportunity to put together a great collection of recipes that work within the demands of a modern lifestyle (mine included) and based on the needs of the shoppers who buy their meat from our shop.

Of course the recipes in my book (and every other meat recipe ever written) actually start with the farming: the life and origin of the meat and our relationship with it. We don't have to spend a lot of time making a recipe, but we do have an obligation to understand the origins of our meat, and you can do this simply by asking questions of the person selling it to you. In this book I exclusively endorse well-farmed meat, both for the ethics of animal husbandry and for the eating experience. I do this confidently due to the work that I have had the pleasure of doing with some of the UK's finest farmers over the past six years.

I also feel confident proposing that a 'modern meat cook' does not need to be detached from the handling of meat. Some recipes here use cuts of meat that I show you how to butcher yourself from larger pieces of meat. I've been delighted to discover a demand for simple home butchery, or 'cooktchery' as we call it at the shop: the simple cutting of meat at home for cooking, rather than for retail presentation or commercial efficiency. This is exciting, really satisfying and surprisingly easy to do.

I also mention my own limited budget, because as a consumer and as the owner of a business, I'm not naive about the difficult balance between ethical ideals and a realistic commercial viability. However I do believe I can prove that there is a balance; there is a point where the contract of animal husbandry works and we can still afford it. You'll see that nearly all my recipes have value in mind, from how to utilize a more affordable cut to how to buy a larger piece of meat, which is cheaper per kg/lb., and portion it yourself by freezing batches and chilling leftovers for other recipes.

The average cooking time for the evening meal in the UK has reduced from 55 minutes in the 1970s to just 18 minutes today. Of 2,000 people asked at 4 pm, 1,500 hadn't yet planned what they were going to have for dinner that night. This isn't necessarily a bad thing – we have to embrace these significant changes in our lifestyles and routines, and meat recipes can be some of the easiest, quickest and most nutritious you can choose. Even the recipes with longer cooking times, such as large roasts and braises, are designed with leftovers for later in the week in mind.

This book is about how to get the absolute best and most out of every cut of meat you buy and every recipe you choose to make in your own 'modern meat kitchen'.

MODERN MEAT PRINCIPLES

Meat has been a fundamental part of our ancestral history and human evolution. Now, in modern society, our relationship with meat has completely evolved too. Though it is still absolutely intrinsic to our lives, we no longer actually need to eat it to survive.

So, here we are, in a new era of meat consumption, a modern collaboration with farming and a modern definition of animal husbandry. Although there are failings, there is also sincerity, commitment and a celebration of good flavour.

The most positive thing that we in the meat industry can do (and the only thing we should be doing) is asking you what you want to know. More than that, we should first ask you if we can help you find the questions you want to ask us. We should never make you feel that, just because you eat meat, you should understand how, for example, we get it to you, why it was priced as it is, how it was farmed, and so on. I'm typing these words on a computer, but I don't understand how the processor is working, nor how it just auto-saved to a 'cloud' thing, and I would be offended if an IT expert made me feel stupid for asking. So, transparency in the meat industry and a true willingness by suppliers like us to have an open conversation about our meat will empower you with enough knowledge to make the right choices.

So I'm going start this book with by asking four questions – the four questions most often asked in our shop. I hope that one or more of them will appeal to your priorities, too.

1 *How do I tell the difference between 'good' meat and 'cheap' meat?*
2 *What price should I be paying?*
3 *Where is the meat from?*
4 *What do I do with it?*

These are the four questions you should ask your butcher and feel confident about asking them. To give you a bit of a head start, I'm going to start with the first one – I think it's the most important question for me to try to answer before we begin a collection of recipes that very confidently advocates the use of good meat. On the following pages, we will take a look at the differences between the production of 'cheap' meat and 'good' meat.

Now this is a rather coarse approach to defining farming practices and I don't mean to ignore the complexities and subjectivity of farming, nor do I suggest there isn't a middle ground between these extremes. However I intend for this to be a general case study to compare a chronology of the two ends of the market. I haven't simplified this because I think you need it this way and I do this because it is how I first came to learn about farming myself. It's how I started to become more confident to ask the questions I needed to ask to be able to find where the balance lay between commercial viability and ethics in our meat business.

I've chosen beef because I come from a beef farming background and I've worked with beef more than any other meat in the last seven years, but the chart is similar for other commercially farmed animals and, indeed, for the breeding of dairy cattle, too. So, let's start right at the beginning, from conception…

'GOOD' MEAT VERSUS 'CHEAP' MEAT

So let's tackle the question – how do we tell the difference between 'good' meat and 'cheap' meat? And why should we care? Well, we should care for two simple reasons: taste and principles.

'GOOD' MEAT	'CHEAP' MEAT
The pedigree and/or registered bull is rotated through the herd to impregnate the cows.	The cows are artificially inseminated with a stock semen developed from a number of breeds for optimum growth and weight.
The pregnant cow is outdoors (except during extreme temperatures) for the 9-month gestation and fed pasture food: grass, silage, barley, peas.	The pregnant cow is kept indoors, with the rest of the herd, and fed a mixture of pasture, grain, soya, genetically modified (GM) feed, cereals and antibiotics.
The cow will come indoors for labour and be monitored. The calf is born with any assistance necessary. Cow and calf stay indoors for a day or two before returning to the field together.	The cows are scheduled for assisted birthing. The calf may stay for colostrum (first milk) but will be removed from the mother's stall soon after birth to begin its own developed feeding regime of formula milk.
The calf weans for six to eight months, as it naturally moves from the teat to eating grass. A bull calf may be castrated to make a 'steer' for beef, or be assigned for bull breeding in the herd. A female will be assigned to beef or breeding.	The calf has been growing away from the mother the whole time and the mother is being prepared for another insemination or for slaughter.
If assigned to beef, the cow continues to feed itself grass and silage. Some beetroot/beets in the winter, too, perhaps.	The cow is fed growth hormones and high-fat cereals and grain for optimum growth, weight and fats (marbling) in the meat.
The cow might be moved (in a minimum of pairs) from a breeding farm to a finishing farm, depending on the size of the farms involved.	The cow may be moved from a breeding lot to a finishing/feed lot (both indoors). A foreign born calf may be moved to the UK for rearing and finishing.
The cow is scheduled for slaughter between the age of 24 and 30 months old, at an average weight of 400 kg/900 lbs.	The cow is scheduled for slaughter from 18 months old, as soon as it reaches target weight. It may be moved to a third farm for fattening/finishing.
The cow is taken (in a pair to avoid stress and the release of adrenalin) to the slaughterhouse, often the day before, to settle in 'layerage' overnight to calm.	The cow is packed into a cattle lorry/truck with the other cows and taken to the slaughterhouse for immediate slaughter.

'GOOD' MEAT	'CHEAP' MEAT
The cow walks between two high, winding walls – cattle and sheep will inquisitively walk around a corner and this means the cow walks to slaughter without being handled.	The cow is packed into the slaughter space along with the other cows. They are then taken one at a time to the crush and bolt gun.
The soundproof wall goes up. The cow takes its place on the slaughter platform. The soundproof wall goes down. The head is raised up by a slow mechanical arm and the bolt gun moves to the precision-programmed location on the front of the head. The bolt completely implodes the brain. There is no consciousness or brain activity. There is minimized stress for the animal, preventing the release of adrenalin, which toughens the meat.	The wall goes up. The cattle is crushed to be held in position. There are humans around, so the animal is aware of danger and may instinctively release the stress hormone, adrenalin, into the blood (this strengthens the muscles in order to run away). The precision-programmed bolt gun is moved into place and the brain is completely imploded. There is no consciousness or brain activity.
The animal is strung by a rear ankle and the neck is sliced to drain all the blood. The stomach and all fecal matter is drawn. The capacity and pace per bolt-gun line per day is approximately 250 cattle.	The animal is strung by a rear ankle and the neck is sliced to drain all the blood. The capacity and pace per bolt gun line per day is a minimum of 400 cattle.
An independent vet adjudicates the process, grades the animal and authorizes the traceability tag to be attached to both halves of the carcass, which has been split and the spinal cord removed – the main risk of bovine spongiform encephalopathy (BSE or 'mad cow disease') and Creutzfeldt-Jakob disease (CJD) contamination to the meat.	
The carcass is skinned, offal removed and the body moved to a fridge to cool	The carcass is skinned, offal and stomachs removed, and the body moved to a refrigerator to cool.
The meat is butchered: each traceability marking kept with each quarter; offal trimmed for pet and human food; fats rendered for oils; bones used for marrow and stock; collagen, bone, hooves, hide, etc., removed for by-products ('fifth quarter' refers to the utilization of the entire animal).	The meat is butchered: all commercial meat and products are removed; anything else is refuse. Often intensive slaughterhouses do not have the budget for long-term investment in low-margin by-products and 'fifth quarter'. Sometimes these parts will be shipped for outsourced handling.
The meat is butchered for wholesale or retail. It is marked with the slaughterhouse's hygiene and traceability code and any accreditations and certifications. Prime cuts may be dry-aged or matured in a humidity-controlled refrigerator.	The meat is (often mechanically) butchered, processed for wholesale or retail and coded with the legal requirements. Prime cuts may be wet-aged in vac-pack bags. Small pieces of meat are mechanically separated from the carcass, minced and processed (often called 'pink slime').
It is sold packaged to the consumer through reputable retailers (including supermarkets).	It is packaged and sold to the consumer through national retailers (in particular supermarkets).

TASTE

The taste of meat is a fascinating study because it is entirely due to our ancestral history that a sequence of sensory reactions occur at the sight, smell and taste of meat. If you flip the idea from 'I eat this because it's tasty' to 'This is tasty because I eat it and because our ancestors ate it', it gets really interesting.

The ultimate fuel

Like all living things, we need fuel. We ingest food and convert it to fuel. About 2 million years ago, at the *Homo erectus* stage in our evolution, our bodies became bipeds. We were moving, we were evolving, we were making tools, we were hunting and we were eating meat. There is even evidence that we were starting to cook, too.

The energy from the calories in meat did wonders for us – we could hunt, gather, fight and flee better than we ever could before, and we had the strength to survive adverse weather, harsh climates, attacks and other threats to our continued evolution. And as we converted this new fuel, we also absorbed the protein in it, which made our muscles stronger and bigger, and our brains grow and advance. We started to develop social skills, very early communication and a sense of self.

Irresistible taste

Meat is fundamental to our history and we are still hardwired, instinctively, to recognize foods with high fats, sugars, proteins and salts as fuel and, significantly, 'fast fuel'. We love vitamins, minerals and the things that make us feel healthy and alert, but our most basic animal instinct is to survive and if there's something that will make the muscles in our bodies stronger, then we're going to crave it. Indeed, this is why cured meat is often described as 'tasty' and 'flavourful' when our body actually senses 'usable' and 'valuable'.

One of the most common confessions of vegetarians is a yearning for bacon when it is being cooked near them. This is no coincidence at all: the smell triggers the alerts in our heads for salts, fats and proteins mixed together, a super-fuel signal to our caveman ancestors and to us now, too. The tricky part is that we're still tuned to follow this thirst for fats and proteins when we no longer live in a world where we need to run from a wild animal or kill with handheld tools. Today, we think we have control over whether a food tastes good to us, but it's still the food that dictates to us whether we want to eat it – our body's response to a food is what manifests as 'tasty' and our instincts haven't caught up with modern life yet.

Meat in modern diets

One could argue that we don't need meat at all these days, as it has done its job of getting us this far. Though we're not fighting and fleeing so much any more, without the nutritional content of 'good' meat our bodies still lack strength and ability. We must have a well-designed, careful diet of substitutes, inspired by the effects of meat on our bodies, to survive. We have the luxury of the kind of global food chain and food technology that our ancestors – even recent ancestors – could have never imagined, so we can easily choose to follow a vegetarian diet. A lot of how we look and behave and a lot of what we're capable of doing is thanks to eating meat, and good meat is vital to our modern meat-eating diet. I can't stress enough that the difference between 'good' meat and 'cheap' meat is everything. It is the whole point of meat; the need to prove this distinction in our modern world is something so important to us that my husband and I have turned down three of the biggest retailers in the world and bet our livelihoods on defining it. I'll try to explain why.

PRINCIPLES

So, to the principles of 'good' meat and their origin. If our history is where I argue taste comes from, where and when was the source of our principles? And what do they look like in a modern world?

I have a dream that we could reclassify the term 'meat'. Like how an Aston Martin is a 'car', and a Fiat is a 'car'... but they are not compared as 'cars', in neither price nor product. In fact, you would laugh if a Fiat was suggested as a direct alternative for less money. So when you look down the comparable chronologies in farming practice on pages 10–11, the end product should not equally be called 'meat' because we can prove that the products have been produced in very different ways. That in the same way that one can measure the engineering, design, metalwork, performance, and so on of an Aston Martin so too can you define and value the end product from the good farming chronology. And, incidentally, the 'cheap' meat column is still the regulated lower end of our market: it does not come near to the criminal activity that occurs in the meat industry.

Maybe the word 'cheap' is too flippant and ambiguous, but could we call the two grades, 'good' meat and 'fast' meat perhaps? That doesn't seem unfair or misleading, as the process to produce cheaper meat is much faster. Then if someone says they are totally happy with 'fast' meat, its flavour and its processes, then that is fine – we accept that they have made an informed decision and are totally aware that they're buying a different product.

I realize, at the same time, that this is the real world and we cannot start a campaign with the scale of meat retail. But just think what a difference it makes, every time a customer asks, 'Excuse me, is this "good" meat?' it sends a ripple through the meat industry, all the way to the farm, and one more animal is reared a little better. That we can individually have such an effect on something as unimaginably immense as our global meat industry is what I love the most – these measurable effects and our fantastically exciting role in supply and demand.

So why are there principles in the first place and what are they? Christien Meindertsma completed an incredible three-year study called 'Pig 05049', in which she tracked the journey of one pig and its by-products to 184 counts of different uses from one pig's body, so unbelievably far beyond pork chops and sausages. She followed the parts to their use in concrete, bread manufacturing, paint, pharmaceuticals, military armament and it is wonderful and fascinating – I recommend the book or 'How Pig Parts Make The World Turn' (2010) introduction on TED online.

And this is where I also have some fun when talking to vegans and vegetarians. To define our principles, one first has to accept the role that meat plays in our modern world, beyond the steak on our plate and the recipes in this book.

The principles of veganism

I would go so far as to say that one can never cut animal products out of one's life completely. I should say that I love debating this point with vegans; I do so with respect and a cheeky smile because I admire anyone making a positive and rational commitment to their beliefs. That said, here are some things to consider before deciding to go vegan:

1 Evolution, as we've already covered, is where meat had a massive impact on what we look like and are capable of doing today.

2 Good vegetables, which are fertilized by livestock waste, would need science and pesticides to grow without it. If we all stopped eating meat, there would be no meat farms. In the short term, the animals would all be killed

and burnt, and in the long term, there would be no organic or natural fertilizer for the farming and production of crops.

3 Arable farming in general, ploughing/plowing a field of crop kills far more living beings than even a mass intensive livestock farm could kill in a year. It's just that they're little insects, ground-feeding birds and rodents… and it's harder to imagine that they have feelings.

4 Soil is made up of carbon from millions and millions of years of the corroded bodies of these small animals and every size animal.

5 Indeed, it is compressed carbon that is fueling our electricity, our houses, our cars…

6 Meat by-products are used in all kinds of manufacturing and production. There is no meat in your can of green beans, but the production of the mould to make the aluminium can they come in will have likely used pig by-product to make the shape.

7 Of course, there's leather, gelatine in cakes, etc. – the consumer items that are easier to avoid as a vegan, which more directly relate to the animal as we can picture them – but there are animal by-products in soap, toothpaste, shampoo and medicine.

I'm not just trying to antagonize; I mean it from a good place and I'm still very early on in my own journey to understand meat and our relationship with animals. But I feel strongly that to study veganism, vegetarianism and our principles, we must stop looking at meat only in the context of eating meat. For example, there are many uses of animal products, such as the commercial bread raising-agent that includes an ingredient from pig hair. We can live without meat products, we can buy bread that isn't mass produced, we can buy sweets that don't contain gelatine… it's just that our relationship with living beings, and indeed their relationship with each other, goes far beyond purely the rearing and slaughter of livestock. We are blessed with the mental capacity to challenge and question this larger context where we're a significantly smaller aspect of the symbiosis of all living things, and we should absolutely do that. This earth, this ecology and this biology existed before we were able to question it and so we shouldn't dismiss the wider picture and its limitless impact on our lives and evolution. Examine, challenge… have the conversations.

Once again, it comes back to the practice of 'good' meat versus 'fast' meat, and on the journey of trying to imagine the bigger picture, I become ever more confident to denounce 'fast' meat as the practices can in no way be described as 'natural'. For example, the process of force-feeding geese to produce foie gras from their liver is not 'natural'. Eating a goose – if we compare our practices to wild carnivores – is 'natural'. Hounds killing a fox is 'natural'; they will do this without human training and assistance; but humans following on a horse and not eating the fox at the end isn't necessarily 'natural'. Maybe the discipline, 'WWWAD?', could be introduced: What Would Wild Animals Do? It's not as simple as this, I do understand that, but to question a few smaller parts of an impossibly large overall question, can surely do no harm. The chronology for 'fast' meat on page 10 is an achievement for modern science but it is so different to our own history and to any other carnivorous animal today. It has gone so far.

If a vegan tells me they would still choose for the animal never to be born, I'm listening. If they say that to die to be eaten is not worth the life they have before slaughter, even if it is the life that the animal would lead if there were no farmers, no human intervention and absolutely no conscious awareness of the lead-up to nor moment of slaughter, I'm listening. I'll obviously ask them how we will redesign not just agriculture but our society, economy and human survival, but I am listening. Vegetarians who are vegetarian for reasons relating to animal welfare, on the other hand, have it all upside down.

I'D RATHER BE A BEEF COW

In the chronology of 'good' meat versus 'cheap' meat on pages 10–11, there was a period of up to 30 months when the animal (either bred outdoors or indoors) is largely left alone to, on a good farm, eat what they want to eat and do what they want to do. If we do a quick chronology for that section for the life for a dairy cow, it offers another view of the role of meat beyond steaks and burgers.

It may surprise you to learn that dairy cows are slaughtered, too. They cannot stay on a farm to die a natural death; it just doesn't happen. To consume dairy without taking responsibility for the end of the life of that dairy-producing animal is irresponsible and infinitely more detached from its life than eating meat.

I would choose not to eat dairy if I were to make a stand against the treatment of animals, and I would certainly choose to be a beef cow over a dairy cow.

Again, I'm not trying to be antagonistic about this, but it's part of the wider argument about animal husbandry, to find a meat and dairy supply that we trust.

Below you'll find a table detailing the differences between what I consider to be 'good' dairies versus 'cheap' dairies.

'GOOD' DAIRY (EXTENSIVE FARMING)	'CHEAP' DAIRY (INTENSIVE FARMING)
The calf is born. If it's a female it will stay with the mother for a few weeks. If the breed, or cross-breed, has a market demand for its beef as well as milk, a bull calf may stay with its mother for milk-fed and/or rosé veal for a few weeks. Usually, though, the bull calf is killed straight away as it will never produce milk for the dairy farm	The calf is born. If it's a pure dairy herd, the bull calf is killed immediately. If there is a market for the beef, it is taken from the mother after the first day, reared on formula, castrated to become a steer and slaughtered for beef. A female calf may stay with the mother for a short time, but the milk from the mother is the product, so the calf is kept indoors and fed formula.
After weaning, the female calf is fed formula until she becomes a dairy cow and twice a day, she will be herded into the milking parlour, have the pumps attached to her udders and be milked. She will then be herded back to the field.	The female cow becomes a dairy cow. She is kept indoors all day, the pumps are attached to her udders twice a day and she is milked.
The cow may be used for breeding. The most common challenge is mastitis, when the teat ducts contract a bacterial infection, either from the pump (cleanliness and hygiene), the water, or another aspect of the milking parlour.	
The udders need to be 'dipped' to fend off infection. Infection needs to be treated with antibiotics.	
The cow is either slaughtered for beef if it's within the legal killing age or slaughtered for by-products once it stops producing milk or can't be used for breeding.	

WHAT ABOUT PRICE?

It's weird that we buy meat from big national chains of supermarkets. We don't have to comprehend how the system works, but we should try to picture it.

Picture the nearest supermarket to your home, and then picture the meat counter: the ground meat, sausages, burgers, steaks, roasting joints, chicken, ham, bacon, ready-to-eat meals, salamis... Then picture the lorry/truck coming to the back of the store every day to restock the aisle. Now picture the next nearest 10 stores all having a delivery of their own. Then imagine the next 100 nearest, then the next 1,000... and, for the UK, about 5,500 stores of the six main national supermarket chains. In America, over 14,500 supermarket outlets for just the national chains. Then there are regional companies, convenience stores, online retailers, wholesalers and so on. Walmart and Tesco, for example, own more than 3,000 stores each – 3,000 of those meat sections running simultaneously, the whole time, all across the country, with fresh meat.

I don't find it as strange to imagine pallets of ketchup or, for example, breakfast cereals or toilet paper or long-life/shelf-stable products. But meat? How many cows, pigs, lambs, chickens? Fish, how many fish? And all the dairy: milk, cheese, yogurt, ice cream, butter...? The scale is unbelievable.

This brings us to the question of price, by far the biggest factor in our modern meat industry and our modern lives. If our meat is considered too expensive, shoppers won't buy it, we will not make any money and our company will go bust. If our meat is priced too cheaply, there may be no money left after we have paid the farm, slaughterhouse, chilled delivery company, butchers, electricity and water bills, and for the ingredients, packaging, regulations, etc. So we have to identify the price point where people will buy it and we can afford to produce it.

And what is 'too expensive'? Factors like income, geography and economy all have to be taken into account but, simply put, if a shopper wants it, they will pay for it. Or maybe the better way to phrase it is: if the customer doesn't want it, they simply won't pay for it. It's up to us to find the people who want to buy our products.

Be confident asking about pricing – why one pack of chicken breasts is so much cheaper than another. Be polite (it's a sensitive subject), but you should feel comfortable asking about price.

Mass production

Going back to the thousands upon thousands of meat aisles, the competitive price 'wars' have brought the average price of meat right down, so much so that a lot of our meat in the UK as well as in the USA costs less than it did in the 1970s, despite inflation and above-inflation increases in costs of production and transport (such as fuel). This is because:

1 The quality of farming, production, slaughter, butchery, processing, packaging, retailing, etc. has had to come down.

2 The scale of production (to supply those 3,000 stores owned by one company) has had to go up to produce efficiencies.

Put simply, and I know I'm telling you what you already know, the cost of making two beef burgers isn't double the cost to make one; you already had to put the meat through the grinder and weigh out the ingredients and pack it – it's not double the work for the second burger since you were already making one. Similarly, the lorry/truck going to the back of one of the stores was going there anyway, another pack of burgers doesn't double the cost of the fuel. Mass production means the cost of every unit comes down, which is fantastic and where I am least anti-supermarket because they can achieve, through taking on huge risks and liabilities, the economies of scale that small companies can't achieve. These savings are passed onto customers who undoubtedly benefit.

Mass production versus premium quality

Is large-scale mass production really a good thing in meat, given that we haven't yet worked out a way to farm 'good' meat any faster than we do? Or have we found a secret formula to find the balance between the quality of farming and the commercial viability and sustainability of the product any cheaper?

My question to my own industry is: if we accept mass, how can we make mass better? If supermarket meat cost 10 per cent more, would it be so bad if we bought and ate 10 per cent less? Especially if 10 per cent more on the price meant it was 10 per cent better tasting and better farmed? I know it's not as simple as this, but I'm not going to stop thinking of pricing and principles in simplified questions like this. I'll also accept just as much that if I find something 'too expensive' then maybe I just don't want or need it right now. 'Too expensive' is often used in the place of 'it's just not something I'm looking for at the moment'. If you don't want something then the price will always be expensive. To you.

The economist Richard Thaler used the term 'mental accounting' to describe the sequence of valuations that happens separately in each of our minds when we process the cost of a transaction within the context of the things on which we spend our money, i.e. our priorities, our interests, our restraints, and so on. Things can be expensive to some people and very good value to others. It's fascinating seeing this with the customers in our shop, witnessing their mental accounting of their values whilst they decide whether to buy our products or not.

The average family's grocery bill has dropped 5 per cent in the last 10 years, which may not seem like much, but the significance is that there are still the same number of items in the average shopping trolley/cart. The same groceries just cost 5 per cent less. For this to be the case, all the suppliers of those groceries need to either reduce their prices or reduce the cost of making their product. The majority of meat companies and retailers I've been in the fortunate position to be able to meet are not crooks, they do not think that the consumer is stupid and they are not making enormous profits by exploiting the unquantifiable, unregulated price of your food products. In chilled food, particularly, with the very high additional costs of something as simple as refrigerated storage and transport, the margins are very small. For the 'good guys', taking 5 per cent off their price just isn't realistic for the survival of the company; it has to come out of the product and, for meat, it always comes back to where and how it was farmed.

Very often with meat, it is what falls in and out of favour. I'm at peace with media coverage of meat, even the sensationalized coverage. It exists, it taints and it can mislead, but it generally only targets or appeals to those who probably wouldn't come and ask me questions anyway, nor would they welcome the chance to have a conversation with me about meat and farming. 'Good' meat just isn't important to everyone. I'm not being a defeatist, I'd just rather do a really, really good job for those to whom it is important. In the long term, the positive movement of these people, who have access to good meat and the ripples they make through a national, even global, meat industry is more powerful than I could ever be by howling at the moon about how we need a revolution. Little changes and little improvements to the system will be what regains the grace and respectability of our meat industry. So to our next question...

WHERE IS THE MEAT FROM?

This is a great question to encapsulate all the major factors of farming and producing meat. Don't ever feel like you need to understand the whole process of producing meat. You are responsible for the meat that you purchase and for finding a source that suits your principles, tastes and budget. There is a short answer and a more in-depth answer, and very often trusting the short answer to this question is enough.

The short answer
We source our meat from a small network of exceptional farms across the country. We know and trust them. And it's our name on the packs.

The more in-depth answer
There are three important points: traceability, practice and accountability.

There are a lot of national certifications and accreditations for meat in different countries. I admire them as they are founded on a base of honest beliefs and integrity. They are brilliant at defining where lines can be drawn in practices and helping to communicate these to a consumer who may have very little time (or interest) to carry out the studies themselves. However, they are also brilliant at allowing a consumer to believe that they are the 'right way' and that foods without these accreditations are inferior. They are, however, just accreditations; they're still an optional subscription for the farm to undertake and a cost for them to absorb.

Let's take the 'Organic' certificate (Soil Association in the UK, AOM in Australia, the NOP in conjunction with the USDA in America, ECOCERT in Europe, and so on...). We are better for these regulating bodies, undeniably so. They filter and define practices and have a symbol that is easily recognisable. They reassure you that meat production follows certain principles without you needing to understand the details.

However, I believe they stifle the questions that I'm so desperate for us to be asked and answer. They go too far to market meat and stop us from just asking one of the four simple questions I'm trying to answer now. I don't think that's as positive as the initial objective started out to be because all farms are not owned by one organisation and certainly I have never been to even two farms that practise farming the same way. Carrots, for example, are more easily defined – organic vegetables and arable farming are far from an easy science and rely on massive amounts of skill and experience (and instinct), but the same acreage that can produce 10 tonnes of carrots will produce perhaps 40 beef cattle a year. That's 40 different animals, with different genetics, health and feeding needs, unknowns and variables. Classifying and certifying the farming of animals (pastoral farming) is harder to centralize than for grains, vegetables, etc (arable farming).

What's the answer? The language and labelling at retail level. All those thousands of meat categories in stores – the labelling on the packaging should go beyond a small symbol on the back. If we in the industry put our names/company names/a picture of the founders (or all three) on the packaging, then that company is accountable for the entire process, from birth to plate, including the farming, slaughter, butchery, recipe, packaging and regulations. Shouldn't it be that we're the ones who should be putting our name on it? Not a governing body for one part of it. And, importantly, shouldn't retail, as the final stage in the meat chain, take responsibility for their customers and their customers' questions by representing their own standards? It's no less responsibility for the farm and the slaughterhouse, as there is a vital trust between them and the retailer, and the retailer will not choose to work with them if they don't trust them (or will cease trading with them immediately if the trust is broken). It is not okay for the retailer to say, 'Not my fault' as happened in the UK with the 2013 horsemeat scandal. Any regulation or certification paperwork that means that the retailer can avoid taking responsibility for their customers themselves is massively detrimental.

What's really strange is that, in supermarkets' defence, they do put their name on it. The dominance of 'own label' branded lines on supermarket shelves is massive now and it suggests they should have the greatest accountability and liability of all, but these supermarket brands have become so completely dominated by the message of 'price' that any attempt to prioritize taste and principles in this branding is lost. These 'own label' products are produced by contract to third parties, who in turn source through third parties (does that make a ninth party?) and we're back to 'Not my fault,' and 'There's no way we could have known'... This is not good enough. Rather than national certificates for the rearing of the animals, let's put the accountability back on the retailers for selling it. It's a lot of pressure on us, but it's a more practical definition of who is the final gatekeeper for this control and the retailer is the only person to whom most consumers have access to be able to ask these questions.

In the short answer, to say, 'We know them and we trust them' sums up this agreement. It's the role that the farm and the supply has in keeping their side of the bargain if the retailer is going to put their name on the pack and take full accountability. We must meet the farmers, shake their hands and ask them the same questions that consumers will ask us. Maybe it's impossible immediately and we can use a blueprint and a contract to get started with a farm, but I think we should meet every farmer from whom we buy our meat. That's why mass-produced meat just isn't good enough – how is it possible to stock 3,000 shelves every single day and still know where the animals are from?

What if marketing was in charge of procurement and sourcing? Too often now, the marketing department is there for damage control, when the pressures of a price-driven modern food market make the brand and the message fall apart. What if the people who are responsible for the message and the brand, plus the sales team on the shop floor who need to answer their questions, what if they were in charge of where the contents of those packs are from? Wouldn't that be a better way around than the financial department delivering annual targets for increasing margin, volume and market share? We could put the responsibility back on the marketing departments, and then we'd see how hard it is to sell something you know isn't good enough.

The traceability question is also important to understand. In the short answer, I say 'farms across the country' (for me, this means the UK, but the same applies wherever the retailer is). With further interest, I can explain (and prove) that the animal was born, reared, slaughtered and processed in the UK. That's what I would call British meat. It's not just patriotism or investing in my own economy; it stands for another set of checks and regulations to help me (the retailer) tell the customer that I trust the sourcing and I know where the meat is from. It's not to say that meat from other countries isn't just as good, or as well farmed, it is simply to demonstrate that I know the farms and I know how they get the meat to me. The same applies for American retailers or Australian or French and so on. If you can trace the meat to a number of farms in the same country, you can show that you know where it came from. Of course there are extreme examples: for example, a pig's carcass can be exported whole, but once a distribution wholesaler in the receiving country removes the trotters, they are then permitted to say that the whole animal is the product of their country. This is an extreme, and there are mass suppliers that run checks and audits and strict sourcing regimes to import meat and who are not crooks, but it is being detached from the actual product that puts traceability at risk. Is it the marketing and sales team who are auditing the supply, ready to answer the questions properly? Almost certainly not.

I'm not entirely naive, just an idealist and an optimist. Let's not move animals around so much while they're alive. Let's not move carcasses around so much when they're dead.

Let's all start using 'I' where we've been using 'our policy'. A national meat supply is brilliant. It's challenging, expensive and (given the ticking clock of shelf life constantly chipping away at your sanity) completely exhausting, but it can be a beautiful, admirable thing when it's done properly. In a small country like Britain, 'local' is a bonus but 'national' isn't usually more than about 300 miles away on average. In larger countries like Australia and America, using a similar geography to the one that humans use for their own sense of identity (regions or states, for example) is a pretty good start for working out how far your chilled/fresh food should travel. Again, I'm an idealist; it's not that I don't accept that the global food chain is out there, I just want to question those little parts of it that I could understand if I just try.

And now on to the last of my four questions, and the one that leads (seamlessly!) into the collection of cuts and recipes for this book...

WHAT DO I DO WITH IT?

This is my favourite question because it really covers all the other questions. When someone asks what to do with a piece of a meat, they're showing an interest in the taste, where it's from, what the price is, and whether it's 'good meat'. People asking this question are looking for more than a microwave lasagne or a pack of deli ham. To come to a meat shop and ask for cooking ideas is the start of a celebration of the taste of meat and nothing makes me happier than seeing that.

First and foremost, I like to eat meat. Which is why so far we've looked at what makes up our 'taste' response and hopefully have some ideas to help find our principles and priorities. However, more than this, I like to cook with meat as well as simply eat it. I like what a plate of different food becomes when one of the components is good meat, and I love the endless ideas and possibilities for cooking with it. That the same pig can be used to make anything from sausages needing 5 minutes to cook to a bone-in pulled pork shoulder (page 180) taking 4 hours to cook is amazing.

So to the question, 'What do I do with it?', we often respond with, "How much time do you have to cook it?", because the possibilities and ideas are endless. And that's the idea with the recipe collection here – a lot of classic recipes and my takes on classic recipes, which are put into an order to hopefully suit how much time you have to cook them.

Our modern meat kitchens are busy places, with ovens, microwaves, food processors, freezers... Not to mention tablets, televisions and mobile/cell phones... We cook and eat in a totally different environment from 40 years ago and, literally, millennia removed from when we started to eat meat in the first place. Though the wonderful thing is that the practice is still essentially the same. We do, fundamentally, follow the same cycle of sleeping and eating to fuel ourselves.

Look how the methods of Western medical science have transformed because of inventions and discoveries in recent history; how feats of engineering and design have revolutionized the way we can travel in cars, planes and trains; how the invention of the phone completely flipped how we communicate, let alone the way we shop and pay for food, with the development of credit cards, the internet, and so on.

But we still, 1.9 million years later, cook and eat meat. There is no reason for any of us, even a cooking novice or someone who has never eaten meat before, not to have the confidence to handle meat as part of this history. When it comes to cooking meat, all this practice has made us really, really good at it, and when it comes to cutting and preparing meat for cooking, we already have all the basic instincts and capabilities that we need to be able to do it (I will show this later).

More than anything I've ever been taught, confidence has been the most valuable. I'm pretty sure that confidence means you can do about 90 per cent of anything in the world and 100 per cent with a lot of training and practice on top. The same goes for cooking, especially for cooking meat. So I'm going to start with a quick list of some general and practical dos and don'ts – the don'ts have been learned from my own valuable mistakes – to start our celebration of cooking and eating good meat and building our confidence to know what to do with it.

DOS	DON'TS

DOS

✻ Do buy a meat thermometer; they're not just for dads and BBQs, they're brilliant for getting the consistency of the meat right.

✻ Do get your hands in – we have nails (claws!) and opposable thumbs. There is nothing better for stripping the cold leftovers of roast chicken than our hands. Buy some disposable latex food gloves – they're so cheap and great for handling meat, and you'll never again think twice about handling garlic, onion or smoked salmon either.

✻ Do seal meat well before freezing. The best way to stop 'freezer burn' (when the moisture crystallizes) is to dry it with paper towels and wrap it tightly in clingfilm/plastic wrap or a sandwich bag.

✻ Do keep some chorizo or other cured meats in your fridge. Curing is the simplest way (as our ancestors learnt) to keep meat for longer and makes a tasty addition to recipes, especially if you haven't had time for a fresh food shop.

✻ Do try offal. I'm not a fan of liver, even after trying it a few times, I just don't love it on its own (though I like it in haggis and faggots), but I think heart and lungs/lights are great when available. And…

✻ …do serve 'fries' (testicles, also known as 'Rocky Mountain oysters', 'prairie oysters' and 'cowboy caviar') at a dinner party, just once!

✻ Do ask for opinions on food, but remember that, as we all eat, we all have a very different set of tastes. If you ask someone for an opinion, they will (out of goodness) give you one, even if they didn't actually have one until you asked.

✻ Do rest meat – it's nothing more complicated than letting the temperature drop a little, the meat relax and the small veins of fat thicken a little so that our taste buds can detect them better. Serve meat warm, not piping hot.

✻ Do sharpen your knives regularly; it makes preparing your meals more of a pleasure.

DON'TS

✻ Don't be embarrassed to order your steak well done if you like it that way. There's a strange culture that rarer meat is more sophisticated. It's just a different cooking time and flavour.

✻ Don't trim the fat. Keep it on for cooking, even if you don't eat it. Try cooking the edge of a sirloin steak or the rind of bacon for longer so that it becomes crispy. It's a totally different product from the lean muscle and can be just as delicious cooked to your taste. If you don't like the taste, don't be shy to leave it on the plate.

✻ Don't watch YouTube videos of abattoirs; there are so few videos of good abattoirs, it will completely skew your view.

✻ Don't worry if you're not fully on board with a media campaign for food. They are not dishonest or misleading, but they are produced by a television company whose audience data might not include you. Better to make lots of tiny ripples with your better meat purchases than wait to find the time to campaign.

✻ Don't only assign the the phrase 'processed meat' to cheap food. Grinding a well farmed rump steak is still classified as 'processed'.

✻ Don't be scared of salt. Too much is bad for you, but a sprinkle on meat you're cooking will largely dissolve and remain in the dish/pan. It's better to use salt for cooking than add salt to cooked food. Find salt with the strongest flavour and then you'll use less as well.

✻ Don't forget to taste with your nose – it's the best translator of flavour. If you're cooking a meat dish like a ragù and you hold dried basil up to your nose, your nose will tell you if you want to put it in more effectively than tasting the dried basil. The smell is the best indicator of the contributing flavour for a recipe.

✻ Don't forget kitchen foil to catch the juices and grease from roasting meat. If you're scouring away at your roasting pan every time, you'll be less excited to start the next recipe.

Most importantly, please remember...

...that there is no perfect taste. There are popular tastes, cuisines and dishes, but there is no single perfect taste. Food awards are helpful promotional tools, but there is such a fallacy that anything is the 'best tasting'... there is no such thing. There is only 'My favourite...' and everyone has a their own. Otherwise, there would be one film at the movies, one song in the charts, one item on a menu, and so on.

So, the reason I say this is because it is very hard to completely fail when making food for yourself or for guests. There will always be things – flavourings, seasoning, cooking time – that you might do differently next time, but it's hard to fail completely, and the worst possible outcome is that you have to serve something else (that's why I like to keep leftovers in the freezer!). Is that so bad? In the pursuit of confidence, will you agree to these four things?

1. You will always start with 'good meat' (following the parameters we have covered), which makes it so much harder to fail.

2. You will treat this collection of recipes as a guide and adapt them in any way you like. They're ideas, some classic and conservative and some a bit different and more adventurous, but they are just ideas to try. Shake them up with anything that you know you like or take out the things you don't.

3. You will remember that I'm a home cook, not professionally trained. I made recipes first as a hobby and then as a business, where all of my product development is down to trial, error and customer feedback. The error is the most helpful part of the process, and though you want to avoid error 5 minutes before dinner guests arrive, don't be afraid to try something different when you aren't under pressure. We are on our seventh evolution of our range of sausages (with at least 10 sub-recipes per evolution) and we're still not 'there'. The sausages are good, we get positive feedback but they're not 'there' yet...

'There' is the closest you come to a real 'taste award'. Once you've found the eating experience of which you're most proud, you will realise that it takes no effort at all to sell it – for me, that's selling it to customers, to you, it's presenting it to dining guests. So with this in mind, lastly...

4. You will, on presenting a recipe to anyone else, accompany it with the words, 'There. Nailed it!' Nothing excites the sensory reaction and anticipation of the taste buds more than confident presentation – it's the foundation of all food packaging and brand design. After years of celebrity chefs, television shows and so many experts in food, we've lost the ability to sit down for a meal without first listing a) whose recipe it is b) what went wrong c) what went wrong last time we tried it d) miscellaneous list of things for which we should apologize. We just don't need to do it. Our grandparents would have never dreamed of discussing whether the food was any good, and not out of stifled courtesy, just because there was no chink in the armour of confidence from the person who made it. Imagine if there was a bottle of wine on the shelf and the label said, 'You can buy this but I have to say that it's not our best year. Last year's was better. I'm not really sure why, but I think it was that we kept the grapes on the vines a little bit longer. So, anyway, drink up but just remember, it's not our best.' Nobody would buy it. If they did, they wouldn't enjoy it because not only has it failed to trigger the taste buds, the salivation, the anticipation, it's completely turned them off.

If I can leave you with one skill, beyond butchering your own pork shoulder or filleting your own chicken, it's to present the plates of your culinary creation with total pride, even a little smugness. The effect this will have on the tastes and eating experience of your dining companions is wonderful. And if they still don't like it... well, it's just their tastebuds. And there's nothing you can do about that!

So, now, to what to do with it...

COOKTCHERY

'Cooktchery' is a term we use in our shop for cutting meat at home. Essentially it is butchery for cooking, rather than retail.

Skilled and trained butchery is a beautiful thing to watch – the effortless flow and controlled pace of an experienced butcher cutting down some meat is utterly mesmerizing. It is, however, a craft for a profession and it has been developed for two main reasons: the commercial value of using the maximum amount of meat on a carcass and achieving the best presentation to appeal to customers.

There is no value to a meat retailer for muscle that is sliced in a way that it can't be sold on its own. Minced/ground and cubed meat makes the best use of all the trim, even the small pieces around the bones. It's worth mentioning the ethical position with this as well: if you're wasting a single piece of meat, you are not honouring the life of the animal.

This is not to say that I endorse the process of mechanically reclaimed meat, which captures every single 'non-bone' part in the manufacture of 'pink slime'. This process uses machines to strip every piece off a carcass and then another machine to pulverise it until it's edible, which is far from butchery. But what I most object to is the result being sold as 'meat'. Commercially skilled butchery will use every part of the muscle, as well as the offal and the 'fifth quarter' for by-products, and it will be sold as such, too.

The other reason for trained butchery is to present meat attractively, which shows care and precision and inspires trust in the product. If it doesn't look good, our brains will not send the signals that we want to eat it, our 'mental accounting' (page 19) will put this at a lower value than its price tag and we won't buy it. We shop with our eyes – it's not just marketing speak. When Muddy Boots started trading at farmers' markets, our sales doubled after 7 months, when we finally got branded packaging, and it wasn't even very good packaging then. We all get a kick out of spending our hard-earned money on something we want to buy.

However, cutting a piece or joint of meat in your own home isn't the same as cutting it for retail. You don't need to worry about the cumulative cost of a few grams/ounces of meat going to waste on 1,000 carcasses in a month, for example, and you don't need to worry that it's looking perfect for retail. You're simply going to cook it.

So let's start doing a bit of cutting ourselves in our own kitchens. We already do this when we trim a bit of rind on bacon or remove the skin on chicken breasts, for example. If it's any interest to you to take it a step further, you'll see that's it really easy, very satisfying and (to suit our modern lives and budgets), much better value than pre-packaged cuts.

And you won't be surprised to hear me say again, if you start with 'good meat' you simply can't go wrong. Butchery for the purpose of cooking is wonderfully easy, I promise.

We're going to do a rib of beef, a leg of lamb, a shoulder of pork and a whole chicken. The chicken is interesting because chicken is the most price-pressured meat in the world. There is so much of a range in its pricing that it is difficult to know what is the 'right' price for chicken. Indeed, people always ask why 'good chicken' is so expensive, when they should be asking why cheap chicken is so cheap, so as well as listing the processes involved in cutting it down into pieces, I'll have a go at explaining the cost savings you'll make here too.

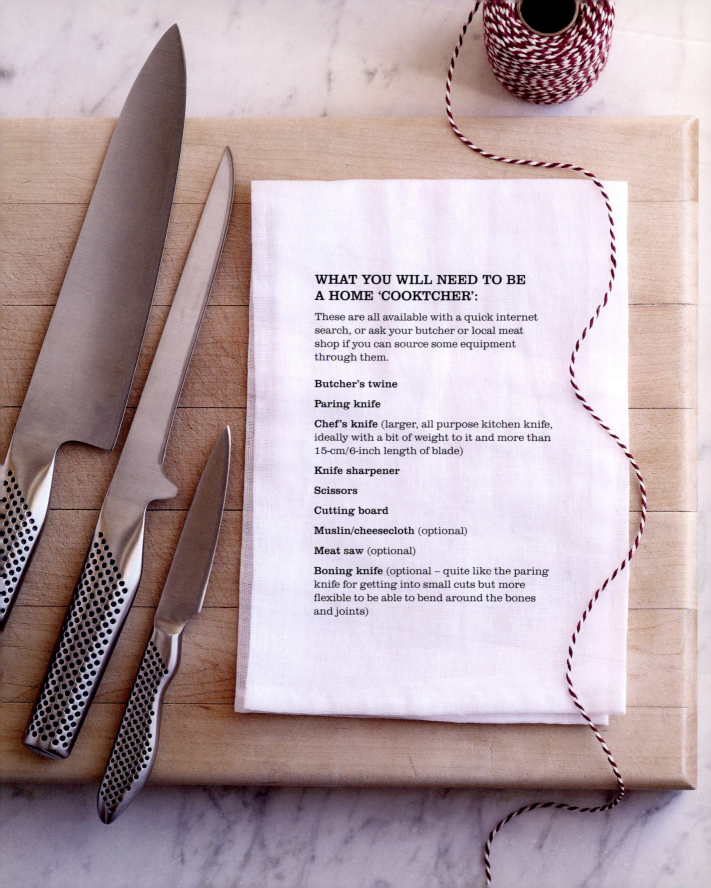

WHAT YOU WILL NEED TO BE A HOME 'COOKTCHER':

These are all available with a quick internet search, or ask your butcher or local meat shop if you can source some equipment through them.

Butcher's twine

Paring knife

Chef's knife (larger, all purpose kitchen knife, ideally with a bit of weight to it and more than 15-cm/6-inch length of blade)

Knife sharpener

Scissors

Cutting board

Muslin/cheesecloth (optional)

Meat saw (optional)

Boning knife (optional – quite like the paring knife for getting into small cuts but more flexible to be able to bend around the bones and joints)

COOKTCHERY TIPS

Here are a few cooking hints and tips that will help you become a successful and confident cooktcher!

Rolling with twine

The stronger the twine or string, the easier and better. Red and white (or blue and white) butcher's twine is best.

Simply explained, you need to tie the meat back together after you've boned it. You can make individual ties: cut a piece of twine, wrap it under the meat, tie it on top tightly with a double knot, then trim the ends. And repeat. If you're doing this, it's easiest to start in the middle of the piece of meat to hold the centre together (the first knot is always the hardest), then do the next one to the right and to the left, and then back to the right, etc. The benefit of this style is that you can string a whole piece of meat and then cut it down into smaller pieces between the strings. Also, as you can imagine for a butcher, this helps them roll a larger piece and then cut it down at the customer's request without having to retie it.

However, the other way to tie, which I find easier, can be used if you don't need to cut the meat down to a smaller size. Tie the first piece of twine at one end (I tend to go left to right), tie it tightly with a double knot. Then run the twine around the outside of the cut of meat 2 cm/1 inch along. Next you need to bring it back over the top, but use your finger to pull back the join of the twine that's attached to the previous knot and thread the end between the twine and the meat – this creates a lever so that you can pull it tighter and with the tension from turning the meat away from you, it'll hold the string long enough for you to repeat the process at intervals along the stretch of the meat. You'll have a 'spine' of string along the base of the meat, so you'll see that you can't cut between the ties or you'll cut through this twine spine and it'll untie the whole lot. However, if you're just tying and 'cooktchering' for your own cooking (and you don't need to resize the piece of meat), it's a very easy way of tying.

Tunnel boning

As the name suggests, this is tunnelling out a bone. It is, for example, how you could get the bone out of a pork leg without having to cut a line down the middle to reach the bone and open out the meat. It's only recommended if you're going to slow cook the piece of meat. This is because, by tunnelling in from either end with a knife until the bone can be twisted out, you get a neat and tidy result but you haven't had access to the sinews and tissue inside, so you won't have trimmed it back to lean muscle. Therefore a fast, dry roast will mean that the 'chewy' bits inside don't have a chance to dissolve and tenderize.

Sharpening your knife

My favourite method of sharpening a knife is by using a 'steel' (a handled, long rod of metal). A sharp knife makes everything easier. A butcher will have their steel by them (or connected to their belt) and will do three quick sharpens every 10–15 slices of meat. It becomes a habit and keeps the knife razor-sharp. I hold the steel with the tip down and the weight of my arm holding the handle in place and then run the blade of the knife either side of the steel, just a few times. The best advice I can give you is to keep playing with it. Wait until it sounds right and feels satisfying. Have a lemon nearby, as that's great for testing for sharpness (and cheaper than slashing up a piece of meat). If you pinch your thumbnail on the blade edge too, you'll hear a click on a ridge one way and feel a rounded curve on the other side. There is a dominant side to your knife – don't worry about this too much, but if you do two strokes on the soft side and one on the ridge side, you'll have a sharp knife in three strokes.

Hand-cutting and cubing

Cubing is very simple. The longer you're going to cook the meat, the less you need to trim it, as the tissue and proteins will break down in the liquid (for example in a cassoulet or stew). However, if you're using diced meat for a shorter or dry cooking process (for example in a stir-fry), trim off all the fats and sinew so that you just have lean meat, as the strips or cubes of meat won't have long enough to tenderize.

Mincing/grinding seems like something that needs a mincer/grinder but it really isn't more complicated than finely dicing an onion, for example. Just keep slicing it until it's in really small pieces. You'll get to experience a wonderfully different texture and flavour with hand-cut mince in dishes like Spaghetti Bolognese or Chilli Con Carne. If you're cutting it for burgers, meatballs or meatloaf, try and go even more fine so that it binds together well.

MEAT AND POULTRY COOKING GUIDES

RED MEAT

As a general guide for all red meat (beef, veal, lamb, mutton, venison and pork), I plan for around 250 g/9 oz. of boneless meat per person (a little more for bigger appetites) and 350–400 g/12–13 oz. to allow for bone-in roasts, so that it yields the same amount of boneless meat.

If you're serving a lot of accompaniments (chips or roasted vegetables with a steak, for example), then reduce the weight of the meat a little to 225 g/8 oz. For beef sirloin though, for example, with the lovely spine of fat down the side, keep in mind that you or your guest might not eat this part and, although it is essential for flavour in the cooking, you might look for a slightly thicker-cut steak to compensate for how much might be left on the plate.

Roasting

Unless stated in a recipe, roasting is always uncovered, in a roasting pan, on the middle shelf of the oven, usually turned halfway or basted with the juices from the pan.

You'll see in some of the roasting recipes in this book, there's a lovely benefit from 'browning'. Do this by either heating a pan with a little oil or butter and turning the meat in it for a few minutes to 'sear' the edges, or preheat your oven to 200°C (400°F) Gas 6 and start cooking the roast, whatever its weight, unwrapped, for 15 minutes at this temperature. Then begin the usual cooking following the temperatures and timings opposite.

The temperatures are recommended for preheated ovens. I didn't appreciate the value of this until I started to adhere to it; it's not just to count the minutes properly, it has a better effect on the meat to put it into a hot oven rather than a cold oven that only heats up slowly with the joint already in there.

Braising and pot-roasting

For braising and pot-roasting, it's similar proportionally, just a lot lower and slower. This method is great for rolled beef brisket, boneless leg of lamb ('butterflied lamb'), boneless leg or 'haunch' of venison, and any cuts that need long, slow, moist cooking to tenderize them.

Pan-frying and griddling

This quick cooking method is for cooking steaks, medallions, tournedos, chops, cutlets, fillets, etc. The guide opposite is based on 2-cm/1-inch thick steaks, but you will need to increase the times for thicker cuts and take note of the visual and 'prod' test to keep an eye on it. Although you can cook beef and lamb steaks rare, you should make sure that pork is cooked through.

Like the importance of pre-heating an oven before roasting, the secret to pan-frying is to get the pan really hot before putting the piece in. This browns or 'sears' the outside straight away, which produces a lovely, soft, burnt, caramelized flavour.

POULTRY AND FEATHER GAME

For whole smaller birds (chicken, duck, guinea fowl, pheasant, partridge, etc.) the United States Department of Agriculture (USDA) Food Safety and Inspection Service (FSIS) recommends cooking whole chicken to a safe minimum internal temperature of 74°C (165°F). Check the temperature using a thermometer in the inner part of the thigh and the thickest part of the breast. You should also check the colour of the meat juices. When you've followed the cooking guide opposite, remove the chicken from the oven, scratch the surface of the thickest bit of the leg and press down with a fork. If the juices are still pink, it needs longer in the oven. Test it again after 10 minutes and repeat if necessary.

RED MEAT ROASTING TIMES

Target	Oven temp	Cooking time per 1 kg/2¼ lbs.	Meat temp
Rare	190°C (375°F)	30 minutes	55°C (130°F)
Medium	180°C (350°F)	45 minutes	65°C (150°F)
Well done	180°C (350°F)	55 minutes	72°C (162°F)

RED MEAT BRAISING AND POT-ROASTING TIMES

Target	Oven temp	Cooking time per 1 kg/2¼ lbs.	Meat temp
Tender	160°C (325°F)	60 minutes	55°C (130°F)
Melt-in-the-mouth	145°C (275°F)	80 minutes	65°C (150°F)
Seriously tender melt-in-the-mouth	130°C (250°F)	90 minutes	65°C (150°F)

RED MEAT PAN-FRYING AND GRIDDLING TIMES

Target	Hob temp	Cooking time	Visual and 'prod' test
Rare	Mark 6	2 minutes either side	Brown coating but still very soft when you prod it. The fats will still be light and soft.
Medium	Mark 6 then turn down to Mark 3	2 minutes either side then a further 2 minutes either side	Brown all over. Any fat will be brown and starting to crisp. It will be a little harder when you prod it, like pressing your eyeball through your eyelid.
Well done	Mark 6 then turn down to Mark 3	2 minutes either side then a further 3 minutes either side	Very dark brown all over. All fats brown and crispy and reduced in size. *Much harder to prod, like pressing the tips of your finger and thumb together.

POULTRY AND FEATHER GAME ROASTING TIMES

Bird	Oven temp	Cooking time per 1 kg/2¼ lbs.	Meat temp
Small whole birds (chicken, duck, guinea fowl, etc.)	190°C (375°F)	40 minutes	74°C (165°F)
Larger birds (turkey, capon, etc.)	190°C (375°F)	45 minutes	74°C (165°F)
Whole turkey up to 6 kg/ 13 lbs. (unstuffed weight)	190°C (375°F)	30 minutes	74°C (165°F)
Whole turkey 6–11 kg/ 13–24 lbs. (stuffed weight)	200°C (400°F) for 25 minutes then 190°C (375°F)	30 minutes	74°C (165°F)

COOKING STYLES

Braising

For 'thicker', more protein-rich cuts, such as beef brisket, this cooking method uses liquid in a sealed pan to cook the meat slowly with maximum moisture. These guidelines should help you braise a piece of meat to perfection:

1 Preheat the oven according to the table on page 33.

2 Heat a little butter in a flameproof casserole with a lid and brown the outside of the piece of meat for 2 minutes.

3 Remove the joint and set aside for a moment. Add a little more butter to the casserole, if needed, and then cook some chopped onions, carrots and celery (known as a '*mirepoix*') in the butter until softened. This will give you the base.

4 Place the browned meat on top of the base and pour in enough stock to submerge the joint, probably around 750 ml–1 litre/3–4 cups.

5 See the braising timings in the table on page 33 and calculate the timing for your weight and desired consistency. Cook in the preheated oven according to these timings and temperatures.

6 This is an optional stage. Work out the half-way stage of cooking. At this time, remove the meat for a moment and strain the liquid. Discard the vegetables and pour a little of the liquid stock (about 2 cm/1 inch deep) back into the pan, put the joint of meat back in and return to the oven. Pour the rest of the liquid stock into another pan and boil hard on the hob until it reduces and thickens. Meanwhile, keep turning and basting the meat every 15 minutes.

7 To serve, remove the joint to carve. Chill the stock for use another time or, if you've thickened the stock following step 6, serve it as a sauce to pour over the top of the carved meat. (Save any leftover sauce and chill in the fridge for jellied stock another time.)

Pot-roasting

This is very similar to braising but it uses less liquid, so it produces a drier, richer-flavoured meat, which might be a little less succulent. Therefore, if it's a lean piece of meat like venison or beef topside/silverside/round then a 'bard' is a great idea for cooking. (To 'bard' a piece of meat basically means to wrap or coat it in extra fat, such as bacon or pork fat.)

1 Preheat the oven according to the table on page 33.

2 Heat a little butter in an flameproof casserole with a lid and brown the outside of the piece of meat or the 'bard', if using, for 2 minutes.

3 Remove the joint and set aside for a moment. Add a little more butter to the casserole, if needed, and then cook some chopped onions, carrots and celery (the *mirepoix*) in the butter until softened. This will give you the base.

4 Place the browned meat on top of the base and pour in 2 cm/1 inch of stock to moisten.

5 See the pot-roasting timings in the table on page 33 and calculate the timing for your weight and desired consistency. Cook in the preheated oven according to these timings and temperatures.

6 Turn the joint halfway and baste with the liquid at the bottom of the casserole. If it's getting dry, add a little more water or stock.

7 To serve, remove the joint to carve. If you've added a bard, then cut that off and either fry it off in a pan to brown or pop it under the grill/broiler with a sprinkle of sea salt to crackle and offer it on the side.

Grilling

One for a barbecue/outdoor grill (or under a grill/broiler when the weather isn't ideal for a cook-out). Here are some general tips for cooking meat outdoors:

1 Preheating is very important. Make sure the barbecue/outdoor grill is really hot ('white hot') before putting meat on to cook. It's the best for searing the edges and helping the binding, particularly holding together things like burgers, and makes the most of that smoky flavour.

2 To make sure the middle of the pieces are cooked well or medium, make good use of a lid or cover. So sear the meat over high heat first, then put the lid down to intensify the temperature and help cook through to the middle. Gas or electric barbecues/outdoor grills can be controlled to reduce the temperature a bit at this stage too or, for charcoal, move the meat to the sides or away from the hottest section of coals.

3 Don't turn meat too quickly, especially for tender pieces and minced/ground products like burgers. Let them sit for 2 minutes first so they cook through on the one side. Constantly turning runs the risk of breaking them up or damaging the surface too much. Have the confidence to let them sit for at least 2 minutes to start with.

4 Don't use forks to turn, try and use soft tongs. There isn't a pan or dish below to catch the meat juices so we want to keep as much in the meat as possible.

5 Avoid using lighter fuel or firestarters, as they'll add a rather toxic taste to the meat.

6 Keep a meat thermometer handy, if you have one. Meat cooked on a barbecue/outdoor grill can be the trickiest to test and you need to make sure that chicken and pork are fully cooked through.

Boiling

This is simply placing a piece of meat into water or stock and lightly simmering (rather than actually boiling). It's a great way to tenderize thicker cuts of meat like a horseshoe gammon/ham (see Honey and Mustard Ham Hocks, page 224) or a rolled breast of lamb.

Poaching

This is very similar to boiling and can be used for the same process, but it is often used specifically for submerging a wrapped piece of meat in water (either covering or sitting in a few cm/inches of liquid) and then lightly simmering until cooked. (See Poached Whole Ballotine Chicken with Basil Pesto, page 155.)

Sautéing

This method of cooking is good if you want to keep meat pieces quite rare. Heat a little oil or butter in a frying pan/skillet and just brown until the outside of the pieces of meat are browned. (Remove the meat if you need to use the pan to sauté vegetables or make a sauce, then pop the meat pieces back in to reheat to serve.)

Stir-frying

This is the same process as above, but the meat is fully cooked through and you can fry the other vegetables with it. Start with garlic and onions before the meat so that the meat absorbs those flavours, then add the other ingredients.

Chargrilling and griddling

These cooking methods are lovely for attractive presentation, particularly for steaks, as the strips/grates of heat singes dark lines across the meat, but this also adds a lovely caramelized flavour. It's a great way to keep the meat rare, while also crisping up the surface.

1 Get the griddle pan smoking hot and use just a little oil (or not at all if the pan is non-stick).

2 Place the meat (steaks or chicken breasts work well) into the griddle pan.

3 Don't turn too quickly, let them sear and acquire the dark markings along the meat.

4 Turn them over to sear the other side.

5 If the first side needs more time, try and turn to match the angle of the lines again (although this is just a presentation thing!).

WHITE CHICKEN STOCK

This is distinct from Brown Chicken Stock – it is a simpler, shorter option that doesn't include roasting the carcass first. If you're cutting your own whole chicken, follow the instructions to debone it on page 86.

1.5 litres/2⅔ pints water
1 white onion, chopped
2 garlic cloves (optional), chopped
1 carrot, chopped
2 celery sticks, chopped
1 bay leaf
a big pinch of black pepper
1 teaspoon whole pink peppercorns
carcass of 1 whole chicken

MAKES ABOUT 150 ML/⅔ CUP

Bring the water to the boil in a pan with a lid. Then add the vegetables, bay leaf, black pepper and peppercorns and return to the boil.

Add the chicken carcass and then reduce the heat to a simmer and leave to cook over low heat, covered, for 3 hours. Occasionally, skim the surface. You can just use a sieve/strainer or some paper towels to run over the top of the water.

After 3 hours, strain the liquid into a bowl and allow to cool. Once it's at room temperature, transfer it to the fridge. Keep chilled for up to 8 days or freeze in portions (a good tip is to use an ice cube tray, which means you can just defrost as much as you need in future).

BROWN CHICKEN STOCK

The 'brown' here refers to roasting the chicken bones before making the stock. I think it adds an oaky flavour and makes it perfect with red meat dishes. If you're cutting your own whole chicken, this will use all the bones (see pages 85–86).

carcass of 1 whole chicken
1 white onion, roughly chopped
1 carrot, roughly chopped
1 celery stick, roughly chopped
2 garlic cloves, roughly chopped
1 bay leaf
a big pinch of black pepper
2 tablespoons olive oil
1.5 litres/2⅔ pints water

MAKES ABOUT 250 ML/1 CUP

Preheat the oven to 180°C (350°F) Gas 4.

Place the chicken bones in a roasting pan, scatter the vegetables around and add the bay leaf and pepper. Drizzle the olive oil on top and roast, uncovered, in the preheated oven for 30 minutes.

Bring the water to the boil in a pan with a lid. Add the contents of your roasting pan. Reduce the heat to a simmer and cook over low heat, covered, for at least 3 hours. Occasionally, skim the surface. You can just use a sieve/strainer or some paper towels to run over the top of the water.

Strain the liquid into a bowl and allow to cool. Once it's at room temperature, transfer it to the fridge to help it turn to a jelly consistency. Cover and keep in the fridge up to 1 week or freeze in portions (use an ice-cube tray, so you can just defrost as much as you need in future).

BEEF BROTH

For a really hearty nutritious broth or to chill and use as stock, this is such an easy throw-in-a-pan-for-another-time recipe or something to make as a large batch and portion for the freezer. As with the Brown Chicken Stock, we're going to roast the bones first to release the goodness in the marrow and enhance the flavours.

1 beef bone (or the ribs from the rib, see pages 54–56)

800 g/3½ cups cubed beef

100 g/⅔ cup chopped streaky/fatty bacon

2 tablespoons olive oil

30 g/2 tablespoons butter

1 white onion, roughly chopped

1 garlic clove, roughly chopped

1 carrot, unpeeled and roughly chopped

1 parsnip, unpeeled and roughly chopped

1 celery stick, roughly chopped

a big pinch of black pepper

1 bay leaf

a pinch of dried thyme or a sprig of fresh

3 litres/12 cups water

1 tablespoon plain/all-purpose flour (optional)

MAKES ABOUT 400 ML/ ¾ PINT OR SERVES 2 AS A SOUP

Preheat the oven to 180°C (350°F) Gas 4.

Put the bone, cubed beef and bacon in a roasting pan, drizzle the olive oil over the top and roast in the preheated oven for 25 minutes.

Meanwhile, heat the butter in a large pan on the hob. Add the onion, garlic, carrot, parsnip and celery and cook for 5 minutes.

Add the pepper, bay leaf and thyme, then pour in the water and bring to the boil.

If you want to serve this as a soup with meaty chunks in it, rather than a liquid broth, keep half the beef and bacon pieces to the side after roasting to add later. Place the rest (or all) of the contents of the roasting pan into the water, reduce the heat to a simmer and cook over low heat, covered, for up to 3 hours.

Occasionally, skim the surface. You can just use a sieve/strainer or some paper towels to run over the top of the water.

Strain the liquid into a clean pan. Either serve it as it is, as a lovely, rich broth or add the reserved beef and bacon back in with the flour and heat through until thickened. Alternatively, allow to cool to room temperature then transfer to the fridge for up to 1 week or freeze in portions (use an ice-cube tray, so you can just defrost as much as you need in future).

BEEF

I don't believe there is a better meat than beef to demonstrate good farming – and of course, by contrast, poor farming. My top meat-eating experiences have all been beef, and if I had to choose just one meat for the rest of my life, it would be beef. I'll cover a lot about general livestock in this beef section, as I did on pages 10–11 because the qualities and practices of beef farming extend to most handling of other livestock. I find beef is the best general case study for red meat, and I hope you'll allow me to use the considerations here as the reference for the subsequent veal, lamb and pork sections too.

'The feeling of friendship is like that of being comfortably filled with roast beef....' SAMUEL JOHNSON

If we're going to track the role of meat in our evolution, we need to go back to our Neolithic ancestors (between 10,000 and 6,500 years ago). This was when the domestication of animals was developed, and cattle, particularly towards the end of this period, were a massively significant part of this 'agricultural revolution'. This is when we became farmers, not hunters, and we tamed the wild auroch into our control. It was their domestication that evolved into what we have as cattle today. Incidentally the word cattle comes from the Anglo-French word 'chattel', meaning 'possession'. By this stage, we are now owning animals, not hunting wild ones.

Not to get too bogged down in anthropology, but this move to farming made us settlers. We no longer had to travel to find our fuel – we could keep our food with us. With settled lives, we developed society and culture, as well as the responsibility of a live food source. This was the start of animal husbandry. Maybe that's why live animals are so impressive to us still today, and why to butcher and handle raw meat always feels, to me, like an honour.

BEEF FOR BEGINNERS

For the cook in our modern meat kitchen, there is no greater head start than a good bit of beef (steak, minced/ground beef, roasting cut or cubed). It's the meat that you can worry about the least in terms of cooking time, succulence and flavour, as it is perfectly structured and balanced to offer the 'whole package' for eating experience. From a practical point of view, it's also got the longest chilled shelf life, it holds up pretty well in the freezer, it has a great range of uses for its by-products, and the structure of it (meat to bone ratio) makes it much more straightforward to butcher. Though it seems like a whole fore-rib/rib section might be a daunting place to begin one's first attempt at butchery, it's an awful lot easier than the tighter design of, for example, lamb shoulder, where sinews, muscle and bones are far more tightly packed together, fiddly and more prone to shards and chips. So, as we'll do in a moment, starting with a hunk of beef is actually the best place to start building up our meat-handling skills.

THE SCIENCE OF COLOUR

Beef is a naturally dense muscle, made up of water, fats and protein (as is all muscle), but it undergoes an exciting process of change from slaughter, through ageing and cooking that makes it a masterclass in biology, food science and the pursuit of great-tasting food. Not to go too much into this (as I'm afraid I would still find myself out of my depth), but visible colour changes are a key indicator of the taste quality of the meat. More so than any other meat, the high myoglobin (the deep-red iron- and oxygen-holding protein) demonstrates the quality and tenderness of the piece of meat. Even a small amount of hanging after slaughter (at minimum to chill the carcass to a safe temperature before cutting), will show this protein start to break down and dull in colour. Hanging/ageing further will see this dull more every day. And finally, when you come to cook the piece of beef, what can start as still 'red' becomes a brown-grey, as the myoglobin breaks down completely.

I mention this example of the life of the piece of meat because, contrary to popular belief and marketing, bright red meat is not always fresher. Indeed, when you take a piece of meat out of packaging, or if you mince/grind it, it will become, for a short period, bright red again due the contact that it has with the oxygen in the air. Oxygen-flushing or 'gas-flushing' was developed to pump pure oxygen into the sealed pack to keep the meat pink, but it doesn't indicate the freshness of the meat. It doesn't do any harm and it's a helpful tool for increasing shelf-life, but I just want to mention it so that you have the knowledge to make informed decisions. The discolouring of the myoglobin is a natural occurrence and not an indicator of 'old meat'.

TENDERNESS

The number-one quality people desire with beef is tenderness. This isn't a recipe requirement or a food trend, it's simply the enjoyment that the majority of us have when we have a piece of beef that doesn't need sawing and chewing. Here are the questions to ask your butcher to have the best chance of tender beef:

1. Do you like the abattoir or slaughterhouse? Meat retailers should have all witnessed the slaughter of our meat supply; it is not a huge ask for us and it's fundamental to the accountability that we must have for your meat supply. What this question asks is: was the animal stressed when it was killed? As I've mentioned, a worried animal will flood adrenalin into its muscle if it's scared. If I came into the room you're in now, slammed my hand down on the table and shouted your name, you would feel a physical surge of adrenalin through your muscles, particularly right to the ends of your arms and legs. This is to enable you to either fight me or run like the wind and, though I'm not scary or actually attacking you, you can't control it. And neither can other mammals; it's a fundamental element in our survival. Then, when you have the next split second to see that it's just me, your brain will send the follow signal to your adrenal glands to say, 'It's okay, false alarm, it's just Miranda trying to prove a point' and the adrenalin leaves the muscles. What happens when the mammal is slaughtered is that the brain can't follow up with this release and the adrenalin never leaves the muscles. Clench your fist now and see the difference in the strength of your forearm, then imagine that that never unclenches. Therefore, what is best for the animal is also best for the product.

2. How old is it? This question covers three things: the age of the animal, the shelf life and the ageing, and I'll quickly cover these three points and their role in our beef cooking and eating experience. Firstly the age of the beef cow or steer when it was slaughtered is relevant to taste and tenderness because of how much the animal has moved around. The older the animal, the more it has used its muscles and the more the connective tissues have grown and strengthened. Without intervention, a piece of 18-month-old animal's beef will be more tender

than that of a 30-month-old animal. However, there is a point in an animal's life where the age and the yield of the animal meet for the most sustainable but viable commercial balance.

By this, I mean that if an animal not fully grown, it is small. Therefore you don't get as much meat from it or, of course, as much money for the animal. The price paid for the whole animal on a per kg/lb. calculation for the weight and grade of its yield would be less than for a fully grown animal. That difference, across a herd of 100 or 1,000 cattle is a massive factor for a farm's income and business.

At the same time, we need to find the balance between what is best for the animal and for the business. It honours the life of the animal far more to slaughter it once it can yield the most it can produce, rather than to slaughter it before maturity. What was the purpose of its life if you didn't produce everything you could? It would be like harvesting a field of wheat when the 'ear' is only half grown. The older age does have some cost to the tenderness and flavour of the meat though, so that's why ageing, butchery and cooking come into play to tenderize and further finish the beef.

Secondly, shelf life is pretty straightforward across all foods as everything is eventually perishable. Simply put, when the level of bacteria has overcome the piece of food, it is bad for us to eat it. We have bacteria around and inside us all the time, and most of it is harmless. However, bacteria develops as fast as it can, which is why humans have invented salt-curing, smoking, fridges, freezers, post-pack-pasteurizing, aluminium cans, heat-sealing, gas-flushing, vac-packing, etc. All of these techniques and products developed to fend off the inevitable triumph of bacteria over our food. So asking, 'How old is it?' is a great way to ask how many more days you will be able to keep it in your fridge until they would recommend you eat it safely. This will be based on

microbiological testing in the labs as well as sensory (sight, taste and smell) experience over the years. You are totally right to ask for the longest possible shelflife, but also please remember that if you're eating it that night, shelf life is, indeed, still 'life' and the cost of all food products in the world will go down if we are more willing to buy products with just enough life for when we plan to eat them, rather than longer. In other words, if you're not planning to eat it until next Thursday, of course ask if there is a newer product with enough life, but if you're planning to eat it that night, there is no need for the longer life. Indeed (as we'll look at next) your beef, if it's 'good meat', will be better towards the end of its commercial shelflife anyway.

Lastly, on to ageing, though to define what is 'better' in the case of ageing beef is a little tricky, because tastebuds, like snowflakes are all different. However, some understanding of ageing can really help you pick the best beef, in terms of tenderness in particular, if you ask the right questions about it.

A popular and somewhat trendy (or perhaps 'marketable') process is dry-ageing. This basically means leaving the meat on the carcass in a fridge for a period of time after slaughter. You have to hang it for a minimum of 2 days to reduce the temperature and see out rigor mortis (another process that causes tension in the muscles, but this one dissipates). But ageing it for longer than a couple of days means that a process naturally occurs in the meat. It accumulates lactic acid, which has the effect of reducing the pH, helping some of the protein present in the muscle to break down. It doesn't break down the connective tissues, but it tenderizes the meat and small protein fibres around them.

There is plenty of debate about the best length of time to dry-age meat, and the benefits of dry-ageing over wet-ageing (which is vacuum-sealing the meat in a plastic bag and keeping it in the fridge). It's a long and complex study of individual preferences and commercial gains but, for what it's worth, my preferred experience is that it is dry-aged on the bone for up to 2 weeks and then it doesn't seem to matter if it's vacuum-sealed for a short amount of time after that and, indeed, I would rather meat is transported in sealed, labelled bags for cleanliness and traceability. I recommend removing a cut joint or steak from a sealed bag for at least 20 minutes before cooking, for the simple reason that the blood and moisture coating the steak will be the first thing to cook and add an iron/metallic taste to the meat.

I will (yet again!) cite the distinction between 'good' meat and 'cheap' meat, as you could add all the trimmings and mod-cons to a Fiat but it still wouldn't be an Aston Martin... Asking if the butcher likes the farm is going to tell you yet more.

3. Do you like the farm? So as I keep mentioning throughout this book, good farming is the key to good meat. Our friends and fantastic suppliers of British cured meats at Trealy Farm in Monmouthshire helped me answer this question further. I asked, 'Given that curing meat is arguably the most handling one can do with a piece of meat...' (for salamis and chorizos, for example, this involves chopping up all the meat, turning it inside out, mixing it with salts and seasonings and then controlling the temperature for 40 days) '...do you believe that the most important part of any meat production, for eating experience, taste and succulence, is what happens to the animal when it's alive?"

They said, 'Yes'. That no matter how much cutting, cooking, curing, handling, processing, etc., is done, a commitment to starting with well-farmed raw meat will always result in a superior end product. In other words, back to

my analogy, you can't make an Aston Martin out of a Fiat.

So the question for your butcher, 'Do you like the farm?' covers the rearing and all the stages in the chronology on pages 10–11. The feeding is incorporated into this question too, unless you would prefer to ask about it separately. In other words, is it slowly or traditionally farmed? Or is it intensively farmed? Even more simply, did the animal eat what it wanted to eat and do what it wanted to do? If this sounds like a version of the question a 7-year-old might ask, it's because it is. It's the very simple introduction I give to the children who come to our 'Little Boots' burger-making classes in our shop. I obviously don't go a lot into the farming and slaughter processes, although, incidentally, children, untarnished so far by sensationalized media, often bring me the most wonderfully inspiring reasoning and rational understanding of the practice of eating animals. Even in cities and suburbs, they are unoffended by a balance of life for the purpose of death. To arm them with an initial understanding, I ask them, 'What's your favourite food?' And they'll say something like, 'Spaghetti.' And I'll ask, 'What's your favourite game?" And they'll say something like, 'Football.' And then I'll say, 'Well, a cow's favourite food is grass, and her favourite thing to do is be in a field with her friends... so imagine if your teachers let you eat spaghetti whenever you wanted and play football whenever you wanted?' ...that usually does it! They're on board with good farming and know the most important question to ask of anyone selling meat – did the animal eat what it wanted to eat and did it do what it wanted to do during its lifetime?

Even better, animals (including humans) like to find their own food and to be in control of it. We don't like to be fed and we certainly wouldn't like to be force-fed. If you're a hunter and/or gatherer, your instinct is to feed yourself.

Cattle that are grass-fed have cleaner bodies alive and on the butcher's block. Feeding only grain and cereal (and worse) is not natural for the cattle's digestion. With many more years of this, they will evolve, but like many of the food-science advances made in producing commercially 'efficient' foods, we just can't process that food easily. So on a simple level at the slaughterhouse, a cereal- and grain-fed carcass has a dirty gut, and when the gut is removed, the e-coli and potentially harmful bacteria is released into the air and onto the floor. Now of course it is totally possible to control this and food standards and regulations ensure (or at least request) that this faecal matter doesn't contaminate the parts that continue on for meat, but it just isn't as simple to handle the carcass from a hygiene perspective.

Incidentally, I'm not a fan of Kobe and Wagyu beef. The marbling and tenderness is impressive, and it sounds like the animals are treated with care as they're regularly massaged, but they're 'encouraged' to eat as much grain and cereal as possible to produce the fats in the meat (the marbling). Also, although technically 'domesticated', the physical human handling of livestock is still unnatural to the animals. In other words, they're not eating what they want to eat and not doing what they want to do... Food should grow the skeleton, not just the muscle. You could feed a child nothing but chocolate bars and it would be huge, but it would be horrifically unhealthy. It's the same with animals. This leads us back to taste and principles. What is best for one, is undeniably better for the other.

CUTS OF BEEF

Beef is butchered into slightly different cuts in different countries, and each cut can have various names. If in doubt, ask your butcher, as he or she will be familiar with the varied names of pieces of meat and which part of the animal they come from.

BRITISH BEEF CUTS

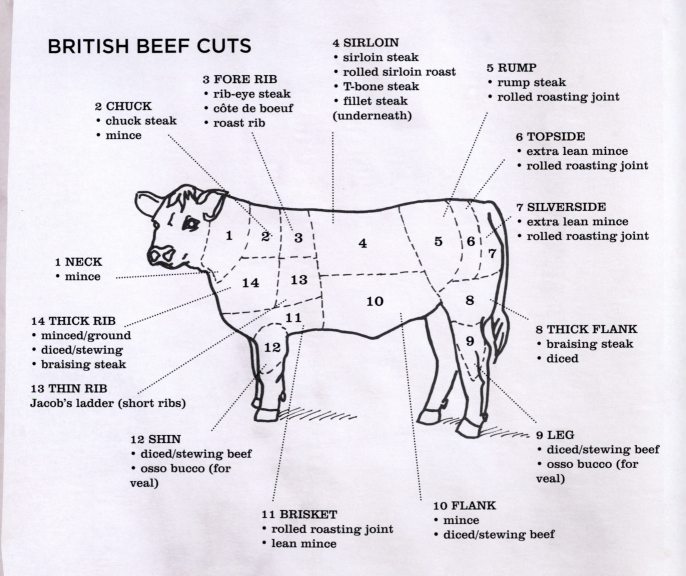

4 SIRLOIN
• sirloin steak
• rolled sirloin roast
• T-bone steak
• fillet steak
(underneath)

5 RUMP
• rump steak
• rolled roasting joint

3 FORE RIB
• rib-eye steak
• côte de boeuf
• roast rib

2 CHUCK
• chuck steak
• mince

6 TOPSIDE
• extra lean mince
• rolled roasting joint

7 SILVERSIDE
• extra lean mince
• rolled roasting joint

1 NECK
• mince

14 THICK RIB
• minced/ground
• diced/stewing
• braising steak

13 THIN RIB
Jacob's ladder (short ribs)

8 THICK FLANK
• braising steak
• diced

12 SHIN
• diced/stewing beef
• osso bucco (for veal)

9 LEG
• diced/stewing beef
• osso bucco (for veal)

11 BRISKET
• rolled roasting joint
• lean mince

10 FLANK
• mince
• diced/stewing beef

AMERICAN BEEF CUTS

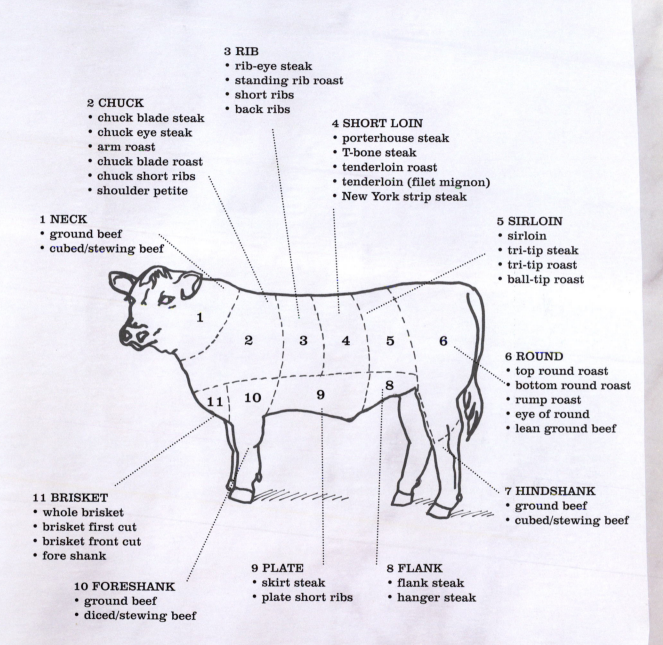

3 RIB
- rib-eye steak
- standing rib roast
- short ribs
- back ribs

2 CHUCK
- chuck blade steak
- chuck eye steak
- arm roast
- chuck blade roast
- chuck short ribs
- shoulder petite

4 SHORT LOIN
- porterhouse steak
- T-bone steak
- tenderloin roast
- tenderloin (filet mignon)
- New York strip steak

1 NECK
- ground beef
- cubed/stewing beef

5 SIRLOIN
- sirloin
- tri-tip steak
- tri-tip roast
- ball-tip roast

6 ROUND
- top round roast
- bottom round roast
- rump roast
- eye of round
- lean ground beef

11 BRISKET
- whole brisket
- brisket first cut
- brisket front cut
- fore shank

7 HINDSHANK
- ground beef
- cubed/stewing beef

10 FORESHANK
- ground beef
- diced/stewing beef

9 PLATE
- skirt steak
- plate short ribs

8 FLANK
- flank steak
- hanger steak

UNDERSTANDING BEEF CUTS

Once you've identified which cut you've got and which part of the cow it's come from, it's time to work out how to get the most out of it.

The names, styles, butchery and cooking methods vary a little bit between countries, but the main approach is the same: if it's lean, cook it good and fast, and if it's fibrous, nice and slow. See the main cuts diagrams (pages 48–49). Each of these is then broken up into sub-cuts and all of those have different varieties of butchery and presentation within them too. However, generally, the main cuts can be put into three cooking categories:

Dry, which means it should be fried on its own, or with just a little bit of oil, and roasted without any need to be covered/steamed/braised. **Wet**, which basically needs us to help maintain or add to the moisture to prolong the cooking time, so that the connective tissue and fibres have enough time to break down (wet cooking keeps the moisture in, stopping the piece of meat from drying out). **Comminuted**, which means minced/ground and cubed beef. Often these are the same cuts as are used for 'wet', but the mincing/grinding and cubing breaks down the tissue and any sinew. (The burger developed as the 'poor man's steak' for the very reason that a cheaper source of beef was far more palatable if it was minced/ground to tenderize it and seasoned to give it more flavour. The same applies to meatloaf and meatballs for beef and sausages for pork.)

DRY-COOKING CUTS
The headline pieces and cuts, accounting for 90% of butchered steaks and joints, are covered here, but there might be other cuts available throughout the world, or other lesser-known and lesser-used pieces of beef. Ask your butcher for advice if you're unsure.

Sirloin (UK)/Short loin (US)
This is the strip of muscle along the top of the back; imagine where a saddle would go on a horse. It has a lovely coating of fat over the top (always look for light, cream fat, as darker fat means either a much older animal or, more commonly, grain- and cereal-fed), which gives it a lovely flavour for frying as steaks.

It makes a good roast, cut top to bottom to the length required and then rolled to thicken the mass of lean muscle underneath and keep it nice and juicy, while capping it with the fat to crisp under the roasting heat and release the juices into the meat. It can also be trimmed and broken down into various steaks and pieces. **Steaks** are best cut 2.5 cm/1 inch thick. In America, the **New York Strip Steak** is a thick-cut steak, often 5 cm/2 inches thick, from the leaner, higher end of the short loin. The **T-bone steak** and **porterhouse steak** are cut straight through the top end of the sirloin/short loin, including the connecting bone (a T-shape) and part of the fillet/tenderloin.

Stir-fry strips are often made from trimmed sirloin/short loin, because it's so lean and stir-frying needs only a short cooking time.

Rump (UK)/Sirloin (US)
The chunk of meat between the sirloin/short loin and the topside/round has various names depending on where you are in the world. In the UK, what is known as the rump is called the sirloin in the US, and then sub-divided into the top sirloin (used for roasting, grilling and stir-frying) and the tri-tip (which is grilled, roasted or slowly cooked). It can be trimmed and broken down into various cuts.

Steaks can vary in size from 250 g/8 oz. all the way up to 500 g/1 lb., as the cut is wide, so you can make a very large steak without having to cut too thick. **Rolled rump** is a roasting joint and it can be cut to your preferred size. It's best to use the top of the rump with the fat covering for the roasting and roll with twine. It's still fine for open roasting, but it's happier on a slightly lower heat for longer. **Cubed pieces** make fantastic stir-fries and pies. They're a little more expensive per kg/lb. so they're not used in mainstream restaurants, but if you want really good meat in, for example, the Cornish Pasties (page 118), a rump/sirloin or round steak, cubed finely, is exceptional.

Fillet (UK)/Tenderloin (US)

This muscle runs along the sirloin and rump (UK) or short loin and sirloin (US) and does very little work. It is therefore the leanest and, because of this lack of fat and fibres through the meat, the most tender of steaks. It's so lean that it can be eaten raw as in Steak Tartare (page 153) or 'blue', which means barely cooked, just seared on the outside as in Beef Carpaccio (page 150). In other words, there is no connective tissue or fat to break down, so it's the quickest part to cook. Just be wary that, for this reason too, it can quite easily become dry, so I'd advise you to serve it cooked any more than medium to keep it succulent.

The whole fillet/tenderloin can be cooked whole as a quick or 'flash' roast (see page 169) or wrapped in pastry to make Beef Wellington (see page 170), or it can be broken down into various cuts. **Beef tournedos/filet mignon** comes from the tail end of the fillet/tenderloin, and can be roasted whole or cut into steaks. **Medallions** are square-cut steaks through the round, middle section. **Chateaubriand** is the 400–500 g/14 oz.–1 lb. of wider, uneven cut at the thick end of the piece, and is often cooked as one piece to share between two people.

Fore rib (UK)/Rib (US)

This is the muscle between the rib cage and spine, before the cavity for the lungs and organs begins. It's a lovely thick, rich cut of beef, with the best foundations for natural marbling (the fibres of fats that run through the meat) and perfect for roasting on the bone to add the extra conduction of heat and to release the juices from the marrow and reduced collagens that connect the to the bone. It's great for making delicious gravy.

The fore rib/rib can be trimmed and cut down into **rib-eye steaks**, which are about 2.5 cm/ 1 inch thick, boneless steaks. They are perfect for frying and griddling, and because there is a lot of fat running through the meat, which makes it almost impossible to overcook a well-farmed rib-eye steak. The longer you cook it, the more flavour will be released from the saturated fats, a short time and these will be chewy and fatty. **Rib on the bone** makes the ultimate roast in my opinion and can be cut to whichever size you require (roughly one rib bone for every 2–3 people). This is my favourite roasting meat and I go into more detail about prepping and roasting it on pages 54–56 and 215. **Côte de boeuf** is a trimmed, bone-in roast or thick rib steak – the rib-eye steak with the rib bone still attached.

WET-COOKING CUTS

These mid-priced cuts make up about 10% of our sales for pieces of meat. They tend to need more preparation or marinating, plus lower temperatures and higher moisture control.

Thin rib (UK)/Short rib (US)

Sometimes called 'Jacob's Ladder' in the UK, this is where the fore-rib is cut (basically to fit in a household oven!) and there is still very flavoursome meat between and over the outside of the bones. See page 187 for a slow-cooked Jacob's Ladder recipe.

Brisket (UK)/Brisket and plate (US)

Great for braising (see page 34), this is a flat piece of muscle on the underside of the animal. The section known as brisket in the UK includes the brisket and some of the plate in the US. This muscle does a lot of work and therefore requires long, slow cooking to tenderize it. It is popular as a rolled joint, so that the thin coating of fats is helpfully running through the middle. It is also often salted/brined to make salt beef/pastrami. **The hanger steak** or **onglet** is the muscle that works the diaphragm. The way it's used during the animal's life makes it very dark and bloody and it's not as tender as the prime cuts, but it's great for anyone who likes a rare piece of beef with a good bit of bite to it.

Topside (UK)/Top round (US) and Silverside (UK)/Bottom round (US)

The UK likes to separate the topside and silverside from the rump, but it's all part of the round in the US. It's very similar meat, but this far end, over the rear and down the back of the animal, is slightly leaner. These make great roasts if you braise or pot-roast them, covered, at a low temperature for a long period of time.

THE TRIM

And then we have the 'trim', which isn't a very flattering word, but it describes the rest of the body, which is still really good-quality, flavoursome meat. It's just that it's best for mincing and cubing. You'll sometimes hear it described by 'vl' (visual lean). This is an estimate of the share of fat in or on the meat so, for example, 95vl is very lean (like the topside/top round above) because that only leaves 5 per cent for fat. This lean grade is minced/ground and mixed with either fattier meat to balance it out or is used in recipes where you'd be cooking with butters or oils so aren't reliant on the natural fats present in the meat. A trim of 85vl is your reliable beef mince/ground beef that we use for burgers and meatballs, as it won't shrivel up and still has lots of flavour.

However, for **mincing/grinding**, I think the best cut is from the neck and shoulder, sometimes called 'chuck' or 'blade'. This tends to be about 85vl or 15% fat.

For **cubed or stewing meat**, shin/fore shank is terrific. If you imagine leg muscles and their role, you can see that there would need to be a lot of connective tissue. Thicker bits of sinew can be removed with a knife, but the collagen within and around the shin melts wonderfully in a slow-cooked casserole and turns to gelatine, naturally thickening your recipe.

OTHER CUTS

Ox cheek (UK)/beef cheek (US)

I'm not sure why the term 'ox' is still used in the UK for the cheek and tail; it's just beef. The ox is a working or 'draft' cattle and we don't use them for much work any more, but we still use the name for these. This is a dark, rich, sinewy cut – perfect for a slow-cooked casserole (see Ox Cheek and Blackberry Casserole, page 188).

Oxtail

This is, as the name suggests, the tail muscle. It is usually sliced widthways through the bone and it's great for a slow casserole/braise to break down all the connective tissue. It's also brilliant for making stock; you'll end up with a lovely, thick jelly stock, as the collagen will turn to gelatine and thicken it up naturally. Oxtail soup is a popular choice for chefs because the consistency basically looks after itself while it's simmering.

COOKTCHERY: RIB OF BEEF

This might just be my beef favouritism showing itself again, but this my favourite type of cooktchery to do and it looks very impressive. The bones are large and not as fiddly as lamb or pork, so you can really get stuck into it with knives to take off as much or as little as you'd like.

1. The 'chine' is the flat side of bone running from the corner where the ends of the ribs meet. We want to take this off whatever we do, as it's great for flavour but a pain when trying to carve. So get a knife underneath it and slice along to detach the bone from the meat. Wiggle a boning knife along the corner **(A)** to remove the piece completely – it's quite tough at the join of the ribs, so just be determined, it will come away. Remember not to worry if you leave a bit of meat on the bone, it doesn't matter.

2. Keep the chine to the side as we're going to use it for a roasting joint.

3. Then turn the rib on its end and, depending on which side of the animal it's from, you'll find a blade bone in the side of the piece. This is the end of the scapula. This might have already been taken out, but you'll see it and be able to feel it if it's there. Just slide a knife around the top and the bottom and twist it out.

4. Next we need to remove the nuchal ligament or 'paddywhack' **(B)**. This is in all quadrupeds and basically, it helps hold the head up. It's almost pure protein, so would be very nutritious, but it's also like a big thick rubber band, and no amount of slow-cooking or tenderizing would make it good in terms of taste or to digest. However, dogs love it and it's the best natural dog chew – as the English nursery rhyme goes, 'Nick nack paddywhack, give a dog a bone, this old man came rolling home.' Just dry it for a couple of days to harden even more – leave it out on the side or in your fridge. It's not good for dogs if they swallow it, so keep it really dry so they're not tempted to swallow it whole (apologies to our friend, his dog and the results of the upset stomach from swallowing one whole...).

To get to the nuchal ligament, look again at the joint side on. Pointing towards where you started to cut the chine will be a thick yellow piece, about 3 cm/1¼ inches wide **(C)**. It runs all the way through, so you can't cut it out like the scapula; just pull back the top, or 'jacket', of the rib (use a knife to help) so that you can cut or pull out the paddywhack.

5. Now, if we're roasting, we might want to cut or saw through to make a smaller piece, or we might roast the whole piece. The smaller piece is called the 'fore rib' because it's at the fore end of the animal, not to be confused with a 'four rib' if it has four ribs on it... that's technically a fore four rib!

6. It's up to you if you want to trim the top of the bones. You don't have to, you can just cook it like this and it will be lovely. For a bit more presentation, cut down around the tops of the bones to expose about 2.5 cm/1 inch at the top. Scrape well so they're nice and clean after roasting. The meat you cut off is delicious and fatty and it's lovely in casseroles, so either keep it in the fridge for up to a week or pop it in the freezer for another time.

7. For roasting, though this isn't vital, you can now tie the 'chine' back onto the bottom **(D)**. Like all cooking with the bone, the chine works as a natural heat conductor and helps the heat run through the main part ('eye') of the joint. It

also helps to keep the moisture in by sealing this side of the beef. And it will help produce more and richer liquids in the bottom of the roasting tray for if making gravy. You just put it back along the bottom and use the butcher's twine to tie it back on. Once the meat is roasted, just snip the strings and discard the chine so that the joint is easier to carve. Put the joint rib-side down and just carve from the top of the muscle.

8. If we're going to break the joint down some more or just use half of it for a roasting joint, we can remove the whole or half 'jacket' **(E)**. There is a natural seam that you'll see with the fat through the meat where you can cut the top off. Essentially, it's the rib-eye joint still on the bone. This is 'côte de boeuf' and it's sometimes sold as trimmed joints, the width of two or more ribs, or it's sliced between the ribs for very large steaks (for two to share), which, as you can imagine, have all the juice and flavour of a rib-eye steak plus the moisture and the cooking benefits of

having the rib still attached. It's a terrific cut and looks impressive for entertaining, too.

9. To use the jacket, either dice or hand-mince (see page 31) for really flavoursome cuts or make a mini roast by folding it into a round bend and using the twine to cut it. It's such a terrific cut of meat that it's great to use it for something like this, and it's so juicy that dry-roasting even a small piece like this can't fail.

10. For the remaining part, we can now also remove the rib bones and slice just the centre meat into rib-eye steaks **(F)**. The cut in the middle is, helpfully, already very even, so you just need to get equal widths for a perfect set of steaks, which will be ready to fry, griddle or cook on the barbecue/outdoor grill as you wish.

E

F

VEAL

Veal is an interesting subject. It's strange that we're comfortable eating lamb (more so than sheep's meat – mutton), but there is strong cultural concern about eating veal. Indeed, pigs, although fully grown because of their fast growth rate, tend to be younger than veal at slaughter. I agree with honouring an animal by eating it as late as you can, so that it has as long a life as possible and yields the most meat. However, there is a strong argument in favour of eating veal when reared well.

The main argument in favour of eating veal is when the breed of beef is for dairy. There are some dairy breeds that yield so little meat, even fully grown, that they can't be used for beef. However dairy cows are often mixed (or cross-bred) with some more muscular breeds. So in a dairy herd, if a bull calf is born to a dairy cow, it is going to be killed instantly, because there is no value in keeping the animal alive on a dairy farm. Is it better to rear the animal for a short time and sell it for veal?

Veal tends to be reared to 18–20 weeks. These are pretty big animals by now, weighing around 200 kg/550 lbs. – they look like small cows. In an ideal situation, the calves would remain with the mother and be milk-fed for this entire time. Unfortunately, the dairy farm is in a difficult position because their income is from the milk. So, not only are they rearing an animal that can't produce milk, they're assigning it the share of the milk they need to be getting from the mother as well. So, often, the calves are reared on formula, which is designed to have the nutrients and steady growth, like human baby milk formula.

In the UK, the RSPCA (the Royal Society of the Prevention of Cruelty to Animals) worked with farms (and dairy farms in particular) on the welfare and rearing of dairy calves. They designed the category, 'rose veal', which refers to the pink colour of the meat, which only occurs after a certain age (around 35 weeks).

Elsewhere in Europe, this meat is called 'young beef', another distinction from the young, white meat of veal.

So there are the principles of veal; the other question is the taste. What veal offers, which beef doesn't, is tenderness and very soluble fats and proteins, as well as very light (coloured and tasting) offal, such as heart and liver. Osso Bucco (page 172) for example, can't be made with the shin of beef, because the sinew around the bottom of the leg has been worked so much that it is very hard to break down, even with the slowest simmer, and the marrow has ossified and calcified. Veal bones and tissue don't add the strong dark 'beefy' taste to a stock either. The lean muscle, under 35 weeks, is a very light grey colour as the myoglobin still hasn't developed – another factor that makes the lean muscle very tender. Even rose veal, after 35 weeks, is only light pink.

The liver, kidney and heart are young and tender, in the same way that lamb's liver is infinitely more palatable than mutton liver, simply because it hasn't been used for as long.

LAMB AND MUTTON

The preference for lamb over mutton is similar in the UK, America and Western Europe and it's a very odd one. Meat is something that is so natural to us from an ancestral and evolutionary point of view, but it is also still something that challenges us, including my husband and me with our meat company.

I embrace the way we challenge our carnivorous practices and try to comprehend the ethics of killing and eating other living beings. On top of these individual questions, we are subjected to meat as an interminably 'hot' topic in the media… Meat is great for headlines, but this doesn't actually help us figure it out. You'd think it would encourage us to ask more questions, but it doesn't have that effect, not long term, because it sensationalizes it, fixates on the extremes and polarizes the argument so that the majority of the industry who fall between the extremes are either mislabelled and stereotyped or overlooked completely. That we eat mainly lamb rather than mutton in the UK and America is simply because mutton stopped being 'cool'.

Lamb and mutton in the UK

Lamb is more popular in the UK and Europe than it is in America. Before we began using synthetic materials, there was a booming wool trade in the UK in the mid-19th century. If a sheep got larger and older, you got more wool, so the bigger the better from the fleece point of view. Mutton was enjoyed as a welcome by-product. Cows at the time were very often 'draft' or working cattle, used for ploughing and harvesting. They were solid and muscular and therefore a bit chewy. Sheep weren't required to do anything but grow nice big fleeces of valuable wool.

In the early twentieth century the wool industry slowly started to diminish due to the development of synthetic materials and moving manufacturing abroad for cheaper production. At the same time, the two world wars had a big effect on rations. The infrastructure and supply set up for the (now greatly reduced) wool trade meant that there were a lot of sheep. There was therefore more mutton available for rations and this devalued it socially.

Following that, the increasing immigrant population from Arab states, the Caribbean and North Africa (and their religious traditions) arrived with mutton recipes, and it was further dissociated with 'traditional' Britain. However, it's a fantastic meat. It's got a little more fat, but the chops and loin are just as tender as lamb and I tend to slow-cook or braise a lot of lamb anyway, so why wouldn't I use mutton? It's cheaper, despite needing to be farmed for longer and not yielding much more meat, given that lamb is still 'lamb' up to 1 year old.

However, lamb is the big seller, so it is lamb we will celebrate in this collection of meat recipes, although I would happily have a go at all the lamb recipes with mutton, with the slightest reduction in temperature and the slightest increase in time.

Lamb and mutton in the US

Lamb was brought to the US by Spanish soldiers in the 16th century. Although lamb is easy to buy in the US, it has never become as popular here as it is in the UK and Europe, and the terms 'mutton' and 'hogget' (a sheep aged 12–18 months, between lamb and mutton) are more rarely used.

CUTS OF LAMB

Although there are not as many variations as with beef, lamb is butchered into slightly different cuts in different countries, and each cut can have slightly different names. If in doubt, ask your butcher.

BRITISH LAMB CUTS

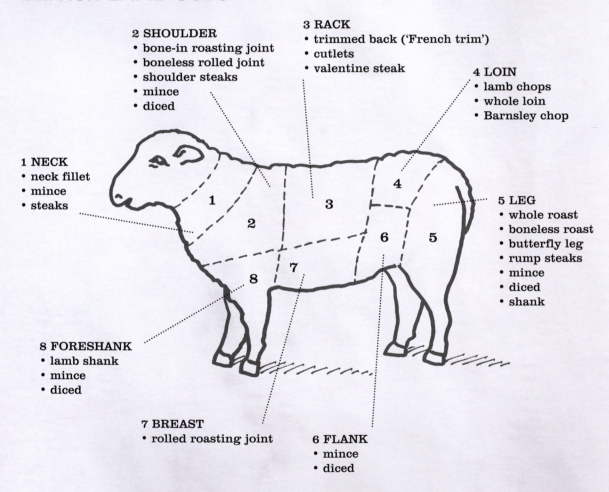

2 SHOULDER
- bone-in roasting joint
- boneless rolled joint
- shoulder steaks
- mince
- diced

3 RACK
- trimmed back ('French trim')
- cutlets
- valentine steak

4 LOIN
- lamb chops
- whole loin
- Barnsley chop

1 NECK
- neck fillet
- mince
- steaks

5 LEG
- whole roast
- boneless roast
- butterfly leg
- rump steaks
- mince
- diced
- shank

8 FORESHANK
- lamb shank
- mince
- diced

7 BREAST
- rolled roasting joint

6 FLANK
- mince
- diced

AMERICAN LAMB CUTS

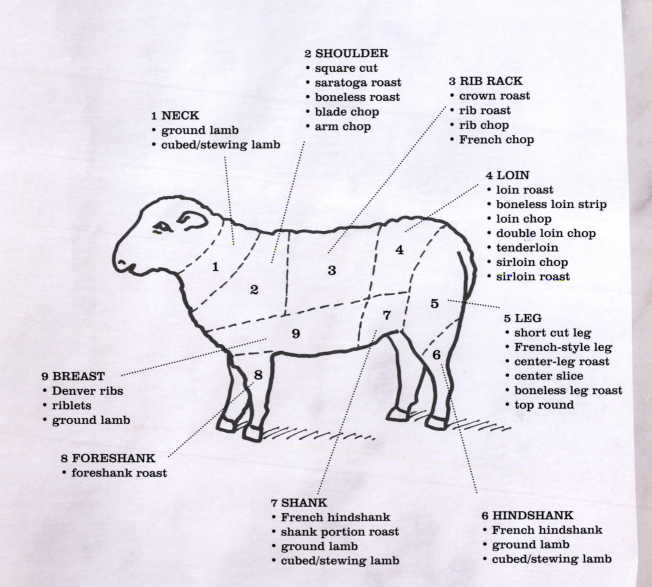

2 SHOULDER
- square cut
- saratoga roast
- boneless roast
- blade chop
- arm chop

3 RIB RACK
- crown roast
- rib roast
- rib chop
- French chop

1 NECK
- ground lamb
- cubed/stewing lamb

4 LOIN
- loin roast
- boneless loin strip
- loin chop
- double loin chop
- tenderloin
- sirloin chop
- sirloin roast

5 LEG
- short cut leg
- French-style leg
- center-leg roast
- center slice
- boneless leg roast
- top round

9 BREAST
- Denver ribs
- riblets
- ground lamb

8 FORESHANK
- foreshank roast

7 SHANK
- French hindshank
- shank portion roast
- ground lamb
- cubed/stewing lamb

6 HINDSHANK
- French hindshank
- ground lamb
- cubed/stewing lamb

UNDERSTANDING LAMB CUTS

A 'spring lamb' is under three months old and the most tender. Again, like veal, they grow faster than you'd imagine and already look quite sheep-like at this stage. Most lamb is slaughtered around 5–6 months old, to yield more meat. Up to 1 year old it is 'lamb'; for its second year, it's called 'hogget', and then, from its second summer, it's called 'mutton'. A lot of the cuts and cooking methods are the same as for beef, it's just smaller and, as I discovered, a bit more fiddly!

DRY-COOKING CUTS
Rump (UK)/Round (US)
On the shape of a lamb, this is the top of the leg. It is also sometimes called the 'chump' in the UK or sirloin in the US. This can be sliced as steaks (see opposite) or rolled into a small roast.

Loin
This is often trimmed of all bone and sinew and sold as fillet or loin, or cleavered between the thin ribs/vertebrae and sold as loin chops. There is a small fillet/tenderloin too.

Rack
This is the rib section. This is often French trimmed/Frenched to clean along the top, which looks impressive, yields very tender and juicy meat, it doesn't take very long to roast. The rack, with smaller bones than the loin chop end, can be cut down the middle, between the bones to create **cutlets or rib/rack chops**, ideal for grilling/broiling or cooking in griddle pans.

Leg
Ideal for a large bone-in roast or butterflied to remove the bone. (See pages 65–66.)

WET-COOKING CUTS
Shank
This is the muscle around the front or hind leg with the hoof removed. It is best slow-cooked, as it has a lot of connective tissue.

Shoulder
Some recipes just remove the top end of the ribs and keep both shoulder bones and the scapula, but often the bones and scapula are removed, the front shank tunnel-boned and the muscle trimmed and rolled for a slow-roasting joint, ideal for braising or pot-roasting. In the US, it is more likely that the shoulder includes the scrag but not any part of the shank.

Breast
This is a thin strip of meat, which is cut off the breast bone, trimmed and rolled. It benefits from even slower and lower time and temperature.

Neck and scrag end (UK)/upper shoulder (US)
Great for mincing/grinding for burgers, meatballs or sausages.

OTHER BITS
Offal (UK)/variety meats (US)
The **'pluck' (kidney, liver, heart** and **lungs/ lights)** are tender and have a lighter taste than grown sheep. Ideal for Homemade Haggis (page 114) if they are available. **Intestines** are used for natural casings for non-pork sausages.

Bones
The marrow and connective tissue from lamb are ideal for making stock, as the viscosity from the collagen naturally thickens to a jellied stock or as the base for a delicious casserole.

COOKTCHERY: LEG OF LAMB

A

Doing your own cooktchery more than halves the cost of buying a lot of the lamb leg pieces pre-cut. It's all surprisingly easy to do when you don't have to do it the 'right' way, in terms of what constitutes butchery. Just ask yourself the simple question, does this bit look like I want to eat it? If not, cut it out. To start with, please begin with a clean surface, give it a really good wash down with very hot water and cleaning liquids – the same for the chopping board, knives and your hands, of course.

1. Ask for a whole leg of lamb with the rump/round still attached to the top to get the most out of this. (If you have bought a meat saw, ask for the shank to be on, even the hoof too, as you can remove that if you like.)

2. Your fingers are your best guide for removing the bits that don't cook well or taste nice. Bone, obviously, is easy to detect, but also connective tissues and ligaments that are hard to break down. It's easiest to push your fingers into the meat and if these bits resist or feel thick and tough, like elastic bands or string, then you'll know to cut them out, particularly if you're not slow-cooking the meat.

3. Lay the leg, inside facing up, so that the fat coating is flat on the chopping board. In line with the top of the hip bone, maybe a little bit before the end of the bone if you can get the knife in, slice clean through to take all of the top muscle off **(A)**.

4. This top muscle can be rolled with twine to make a small roasting joint or sliced into steaks. You'll see a small grey sphere among the meat, which is a gland. Cut it out. Incidentally, if you slice this through the middle, check the colour – it's a good indication of the quality and age of the lamb. It should be a very light grey – if it's dark grey or brown-grey, then it's an older lamb and possibly not in the best health. The meat will likely still be fine, just give it a good sniff to check that it doesn't smell off or 'tainted' and perhaps choose a recipe with a good bit of marinating to balance the flavour, rather than the traditional dry roast. The top muscle can also be sliced into rump/round steaks. Lovely for pan-frying in a frying pan/skillet or popping on the barbecue/outdoor grill.

5. Below that, you have the main leg of lamb, great for a Classic Roast Leg of Lamb (page 204) but there's still more you can do with it too...

6. If you have a saw, you can make a lamb shank. Feel where the bulge in the muscle has a small ridge, approximately 12 cm/5 inches above the start of the muscle on the leg bone. Use your knife to cut through the meat and around the bone, and then use your meat saw to cut through the bone to detach it. Stand the triangular piece of meat on its end and use your paring knife to slice the thin end of meat away from the bone; keep it attached but bring it a little off the bone and scrape the bone clean. This is just a presentation thing so that the bone looks very clean after cooking and the connective tissue at the end there has some help breaking down during cooking too.

7. On the outside of the leg, cut off any thick or very hard bits of fat from the surface or from around the edges of the leg. The white, crumbling fat will dissolve when you cook it but any larger bits will be better to be cut off.

8. For a boneless leg joint, you can happily keep the shank on or off. The whole leg bone can be tunnel-boned (see page 31) but it's easier to slice it out and then either roll the joint or butterfly it. Put the piece with the inside leg facing up again and, with the tip of your knife, slice into the meat tightly next to one side of the hip bone **(B)**. Then bring the knife all the way down the one side of the bone so you make a clean cut through the middle of the meat. Come all the way down to the other end, if you like, as it's easier. Don't be afraid to angle the tip of the knife into the bone to make sure that you're staying nice and close to it; you probably won't take a chip off the bone but, if it's a young ('spring') lamb, or you have a very well-sharpened knife, you might take a bit off. But we're going to trim the inside of the meat anyway, so you'll soon see the small, flat white disc of hard bone attached to the meat and know to cut it out.

Use your fingers to pull back the meat to give some tension, then you can keep using your paring knife to cut close to the top of the bone and then, very simply down the other side and under the bottom, just by pulling the meat **(C)** gently away from the bone to get some tension and putting the sharp, thin tip of the paring knife into the meat to slice it **(D)**.

9. Now you have a boneless leg of lamb, just open out the meat, use your fingers to squeeze the surface and cut out anything hard or stringy. Just leave all the lovely, rich, dark, lean meat where it is.

10. Then to butterfly it, imagine that you're trying to cover as much of the chopping board with a single piece as possible. You basically angle the knife parallel to the board and slice in sideways to halve the depth of the lamb meat and then fold that piece out to increase the surface size of the joint, like a flat butterfly **(E)**. You can then, if it's still thick, do the same to that piece to fold it out in another angle. This is great for chucking on the barbecue/outdoor grill or under the grill/broiler and lovely with a marinade too.

11. You can also butterfly-cut it for the benefit of marinating (so that the flavours and acids reach much further into the meat) and then roll it, following the instructions on page 30.

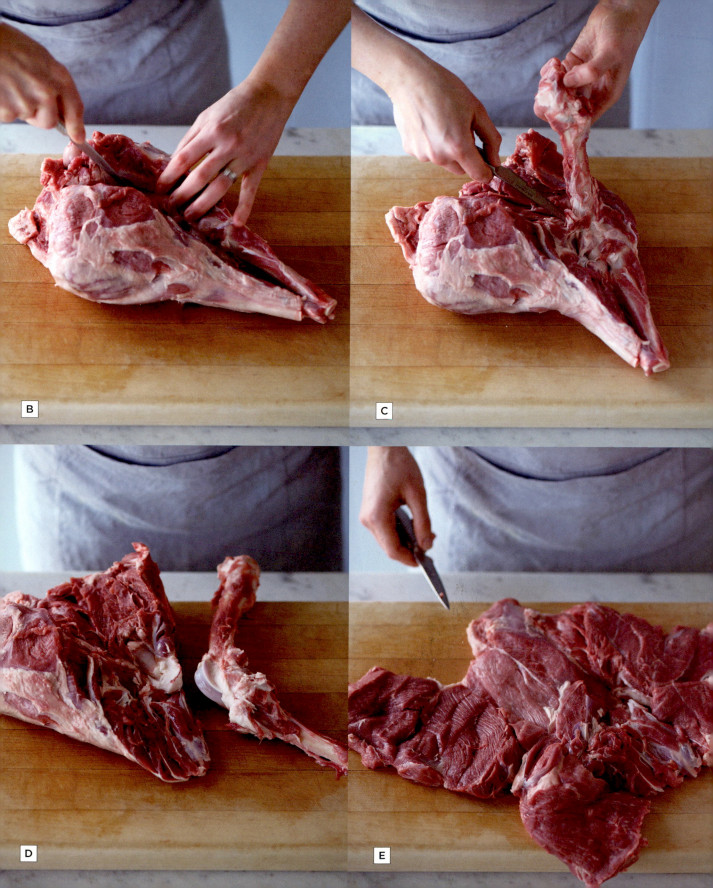

PORK

Pork is a fascinating meat to study, both in terms of taste and principles. Pork gives the widest range of taste and recipes once you take into account not just the raw meat cuts, listed below, but the popularity of minced/ground products (such as sausages), semi-cured or brined products (such as bacon), and fully cured products (known as charcuterie) to which the pig lends far more varieties and traditions than any other meat. For the same reason that pork dominates the popular cured-meat products, it is (along with chicken) the most consumed meat on average around the world. This is because they can be farmed so fast... not necessarily 'fast' as in 'cheap' or unethical, but pigs breed and grow at an astonishing rate.

Even a slow, traditional, 'free-range' pig farm can produce 2.2 rounds (or generations) of pigs in a year. The impregnating and gestation is often described as 'three months, three weeks, three days'. The piglets wean (even unaided) far quicker than other animals and their growth rate to 'full-grown' (i.e., when there is no further commercial value to keep finishing them) is under 5 months. Indeed, a lot of breeds (developed for just this sort of rate) are 'finished' in under 14 weeks.

Incidentally, this provides an interesting angle on the controversy around the age of an animal when it's killed – what constitutes a full life when pigs are technically still within the 'milk-fed veal' age or the 'spring lamb' age. 'Suckling pig' is even younger – around 4–6 weeks old.

On top of this fantastic productivity, they have big litters; 6–12 piglets at a time! Compared to singles, twins and (very occasionally) triplets in sheep and cows.

Cured pork

Because of this availability, our palates and our processes with pork are more advanced, especially with curing meats. We borrow the French word 'charcuterie', which comes from the 'charcutier' or the 'pig butcher'. The range of pig products was so vast that the 'boucher' (butcher) took all other meats, and the 'charcutier' took the pig products. Curing meats was man's battle against bacteria, and our friends in Italy, France and Spain were leagues ahead in developing salami, saucisson and chorizo respectively.

On top of all the fully cured meats, we eat a vast amount bacon and ham.

Pork principles

There are religious considerations for pork, as it is not permitted by the laws of Islam and Judaism. However, pork is extremely popular in China, America, the UK and Europe.

From a principles point of view, I feel that pork challenges the conscience more than any other meat. Having spoken to other people in farming and slaughter, I'm not alone in detecting far more 'thought' in pigs than any other animal. I describe this now only to further examine the accountability and responsibility of a modern meat supply.

If you look a cow or sheep in the eye, it doesn't look back. Humans begin interpreting non-verbal communication and signals from a surprisingly young age, just a few weeks, in fact. We are genetically and instinctively programmed to read faces and communicate with other humans. A cow or sheep will look straight past you. If they happen to make eye contact, it is very little more than coincidence. There is very little searching in their look. A pig however... well, it was really a race to opposable thumbs with these ones, I reckon. They'll look right back at you, they can be trained and be taught their name (like a dog), they are happiest in groups like 'tribes', they have hierarchies within these groups like humans and apes, and they're carnivores like humans too; they'll eat anything... and when they look at you, you know that they're thinking this as well. In fact, I'm sure they'd have as many cuts, curing methods and make crackling out of us too, if we weren't as nimble.

The significance of this is the responsibility to witness slaughter. I had seen a lot of cattle and lambs slaughtered before I first saw a pig being slaughtered. I was surprised at what a different effect it had on me to stand on the live side and help lead the pigs to the stun (or gas and stun). As with all good abattoirs/slaughterhouses, the pigs in the two systems that I have been to (and the two that we still use), the animals are calm, there is no rough handling by the staff and (for the benefit of the meat and the animals) the pigs are led in twos, so that they remain calm and there is less adrenalin released.

However, they all look at you before they go in, properly, I feel, look at you, and there is a searching in the eyes. If you are still happy with and confident in the abilities, practices and ethics of the abattoir/slaughterhouse and the slaughtermen after this, then you have found your supply (with, of course, the farm(s) you trust, too). It was one of the hardest challenges for me and I'm pleased to have done it, to have respected it and, most importantly, to now trust the abattoir/slaughterhouse.

CUTS OF PORK

BRITISH PORK CUTS

2 LOIN
- loin rack
- pork chops
- fillet
- boneless loin joint
- loin steak
- back bacon (cured)

1 SHOULDER
- rolled boneless joint
- bone-in roast
- knuckle shank
- mince
- diced lamb
- neck/collar joint
- hock

3 LEG
- boneless roast joint
- pork bucco
- mince
- diced pork

4 BELLY
- rolled roasting joint
- belly strips
- spare ribs
- streaky bacon (cured)

AMERICAN PORK CUTS

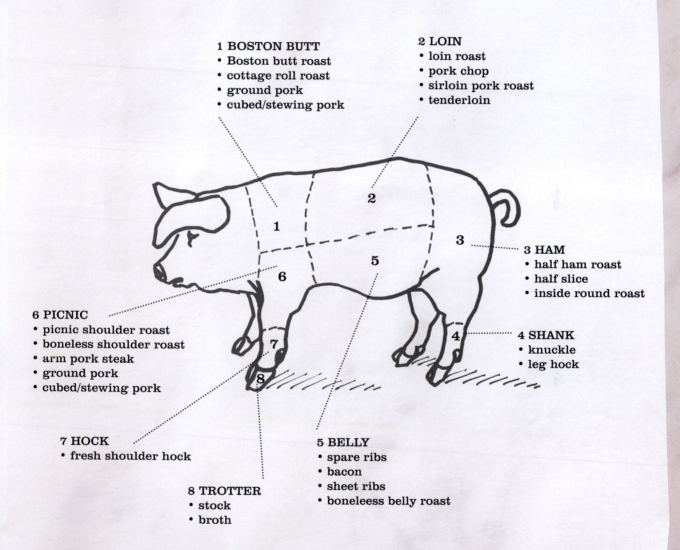

1 BOSTON BUTT
- Boston butt roast
- cottage roll roast
- ground pork
- cubed/stewing pork

2 LOIN
- loin roast
- pork chop
- sirloin pork roast
- tenderloin

3 HAM
- half ham roast
- half slice
- inside round roast

6 PICNIC
- picnic shoulder roast
- boneless shoulder roast
- arm pork steak
- ground pork
- cubed/stewing pork

4 SHANK
- knuckle
- leg hock

7 HOCK
- fresh shoulder hock

5 BELLY
- spare ribs
- bacon
- sheet ribs
- boneleess belly roast

8 TROTTER
- stock
- broth

UNDERSTANDING PORK CUTS

There are some cuts (like the Boston butt), used for pulled pork, which benefit from being covered when roasted but, generally, the high water content in the pork means that it's quite wet to begin with and all the cuts can be cooked using dry-cooking methods, such as roasting or grilling/broiling. For this same natural 'wetness' reason, pork doesn't hang well. It will tenderize, but its wetness is too productive for the growth of bacteria, so it is only chilled in the fridge for 2-4 days before cutting and packing.

DRY-COOKING CUTS
Shoulder
See the cooktchery feature (page 77–78) for cutting the shoulder into boneless and bone-in roasting cuts, neck fillet, collar and shank. In the US, the shank is rarely considered part of the shoulder, which is instead divided into the Boston butt (used for pulled pork) and picnic cuts. For cured products, the shoulder is transformed into coppa.

Loin
Much like the sirloin in beef, this is the 'saddle' along the top of the pig. It can be a loin rack joint or cut into pork chops. It is very popular cured for bacon (known as 'back bacon' in its uncooked form the UK and, when cooked, 'Canadian bacon' in the US).

Spare ribs
These lead down the side/belly, like short ribs in beef. These are sawn left to right (to remove the loin, above) and can be left whole or cut between the ribs so that there is a coating of the intercostal muscle around them.

Belly/Side
This is the long strip along the underside of the body. It is very versatile and can be roasted whole, rolled with butcher's twine (see page 30) and roasted, cut into slices (see Pork and Boston Beans, page 179) or diced for lardons. It's also very popular for bacon (known as 'streaky bacon' in the UK or 'fatty bacon' in the US).

The Leg
It's large, so the leg is usually portioned into boneless rolled roasting joints, rather than being sold whole. Along the top, from inside, is the fillet/tenderloin for roasting whole or cutting into steaks/medallions. Also leg steaks, similar to rump/round. The leg is famous for bone-in curing, such as gammon/bone-in ham, Parma Ham and Jamón Ibérico, and boneless for general prosciutto and ham.

WET-COOKING CUTS
Pig cheek, like ox/beef cheek, is more fibrous, but makes great cubed pork for casseroles and slower cooks.

OFFAL (UK)/VARIETY MEATS (US)
The 'pluck' or **heart**, **lung**, **liver** and **kidneys** can be used for faggots (like the recipe on page 103), if you can get hold of them in your country.

   Trotters can be stripped for mincing/grinding and cubed or boiled for stock.

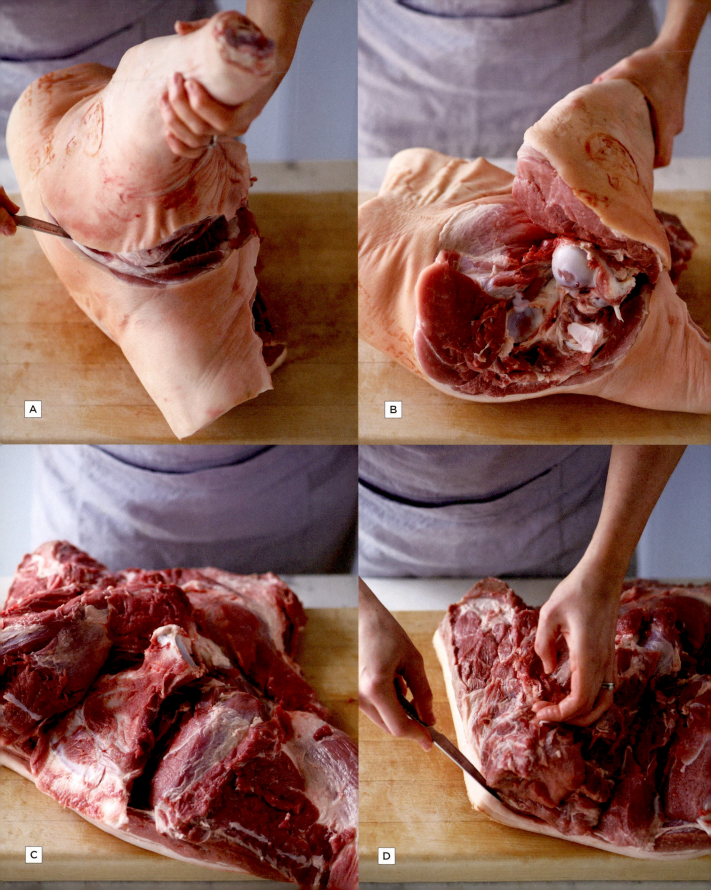

COOKTCHERY: PORK SHOULDER

This follows similar fundamentals to the leg of lamb, basically cutting out the bones and then using the pieces separately. Again, buying the whole piece tends to work out at less than half the price per kg/lb. on average than buying the cut pieces. Remember that a pork shoulder is very big – three times the size of a leg of lamb, for example, so make sure you have a big gathering or enough room in your freezer to make use of all that you cut down.

You can request for the trotter to be removed first or just use a meat saw to take it off.

Pigs have skin (or 'rind'), unlike cows that have a hide, so this is why there is rind on the pork and, with some scoring, salt and high heat, we'll get crackling too. If you'd prefer not to have crackling and would just like the coating of light fat underneath, then just use a sharp knife to take if off in strips from around the whole shoulder. This is easier done at this stage (or order a rindless whole shoulder to make it even easier) and though there are some skills for removing the rind, they are a bit fiddly, so just keep cutting it off in strips with a chef's knife (or a paring knife first to get between the rind and the skin) until it's all off.

If you're keeping the rind on, always score diagonal lines across it. This helps release the juices from the fat below as well as (for crackling) penetrating the surface with salt to dehydrate the fats underneath and make it dissolve and harden.

1. You'll probably still have the top of the rib cage attached – skip to the next point if you don't. For this, as with all cooktchery, it's common sense – you want to get the bones off. I tend to hold it up on its 'end' so that the top of the ribs is towards me. Then I use a paring knife (or boning knife) to wiggle under the flat bones and tightly underneath them (be careful not to take too much off the collar joint beneath them, as this is lovely pork) and then up, under

and around the inside of the ribs. You can score a line down each side of the ribs first to try and keep the intercostal muscles attached as well but, again, you're not a commercial operation and the difference of this tiny bit of meat from in between the bones isn't going to make much difference. So keep wiggling along the bones until that plate of ribs comes off completely. You can use this for broth, although there isn't a lot of marrow in these thin bones, so a stock won't quite have the flavour or the thickness.

2. You have three bones and an elbow to deal with. I'd recommend removing the main leg bone (radius) from the top first. This piece of meat is best for a slow bone-in roast or pulled pork. With the rind facing up, feel and look for a natural curve at the base of the leg. There's usually a ridge, a natural dip in the muscle formation **(A)**. Just use a big knife to cut that end off; you might need to feel for the end of the central bone to be able to cut through the connecting socket **(B)**. Score the rind and use for Pulled Pork Shoulder with BBQ Sauce (see page 180) or a roasting joint.

3. Keeping the rind facing down, feel for the remaining bones. The humerus comes away from the elbow, back through the shoulder. Use your paring (or boning) knife to cut along one side of the bone. Once you've done one side, you'll be able to see the bone the top and prise away the meat with the tip of your knife. Cut underneath it to remove the bone fully. Don't worry that the meat is opening out – you're going to roll it anyway and now we want to get to the connective tissue to cut out any thicker bits of sinew, so just feel for any tough strains or silvery sinews.

4. Once that bone is out (which looks most like a classic dog bone if you have a willing dog waiting patiently!), you'll be able to feel where the top of it was to find the scapula (the shoulder blade bone, which looks like a triangle **(C)**). This has a deceptively knobbly top to it because of the elbow, so you need to wiggle the knife in and around the top with a good bit of confidence. Slice down one side and then use the sharp tip of the knife to cut the lean muscle away from the top of the bone. Cut through the connective tendon that attaches the top to the radius. Then scrape under the scapula a little and you'll see that the top end has come away from the meat. You can either get a good grip and pull this towards you to pull it out, or you can just keep using the sharp tip of your paring knife to cut it out. Discard the bone.

5. You now have a big expanse of meat. Use your eyes and your fingers to cut out as much of the non-pink, non-meaty looking tissue. Remember that you're going to roll it so try not to cut through the rind, but otherwise don't worry about the appearance of the underside of the meat **(D)**.

6. You have a neck joint along the top. Depending on how far back the shoulder was cut will determine how much of this piece you'll get. You'll find the neck joint along the top of the piece, with natural lines to show where to cut it. You can roast this as a piece, 'bard' it with some fat from elsewhere on the shoulder, or you can cut it into steaks. It's also used to make coppa, a delicious cured meat **(E)**.

7. With the remaining shoulder piece, you can either cube or mince/grind it for casseroles, pork burgers, sausages, etc., or roll it into one very large or two small shoulder joints. You can weigh the whole piece to get an idea of what you're dealing with – 250 g/8 oz. per person is a good serving suggestion, so you can cut it to the size you need **(F)**. if your kitchen scales don't go above a very high weight, just put some greaseproof paper or something on your bathroom scales, or weigh yourself holding the joint and subtract your weight without!

8. You can roll the joints with separate ties (see page 30 on rolling) and score the rind to help make crackling **(G and H)**.

9. You can also butterfly the shoulder like we did with the leg of lamb (see page 66) to produce more surface area for a marinade or stuffed joint recipe (see Stuffed Rolled Pork Shoulder on page 203).

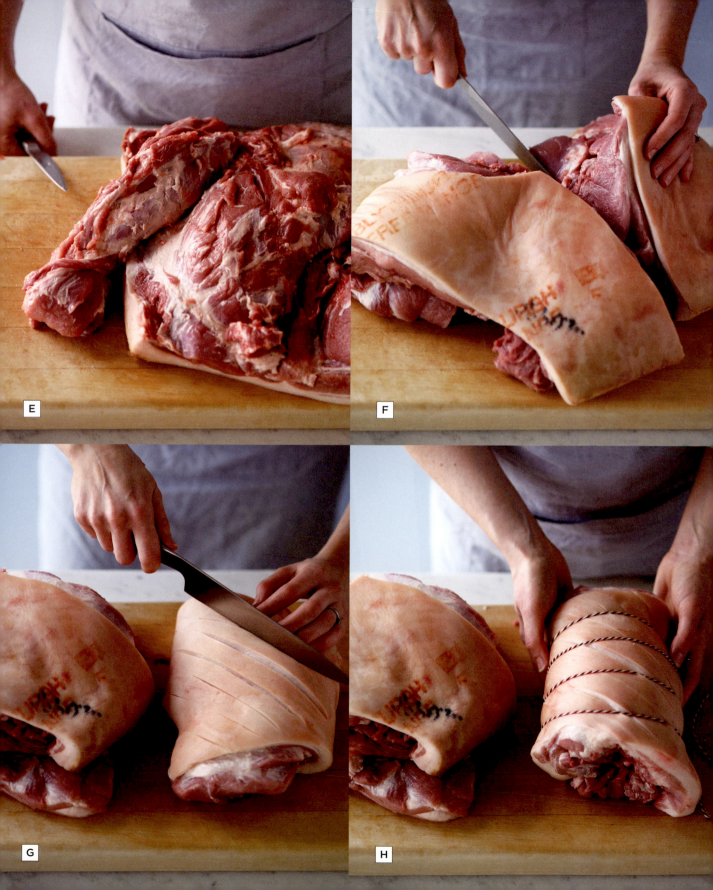

CHICKEN AND POULTRY

Chicken is by far the most popular and common member of the poultry family, and it is consumed more than any other meat. Like the pig, it breeds extremely efficiently and grows to full size in 6 weeks in a fairly intensive system or 18–20 weeks for a slow-farmed free-range chicken.

Chicken's popularity is the bird's downfall. The market for it is huge, so the competition is high and the race to be the cheapest has come entirely at the cost to the bird's quality of life. The popularity of the meat, and possibly because we're more detached from birds than other mammals, with whom we share certain qualities, means that some of the worst cases of ill treatment occur in poor chicken farming. As ever, the cost to principles is undeniably reflected in the taste too. If you roast a well-farmed chicken in the same oven as an intensively farmed chicken for the same amount of time and with the same amount of care, preparation and basting, you will end up with two very different pieces of meat. Though, as I mentioned, it is impossible to define tastes as 'better', one can definitely identify what is superior and a dry, shrivelled, chewy chicken is vastly inferior to a luscious, succulent, flavourful one that hasn't shrunk to a third of its raw size. Fast-farmed chicken will leave you with little meat and even less flavour.

Health and safety
Chicken is a headliner for health and hygiene risks. The meat, in fact, is no more susceptible to bacteria than other animals, but the nature of the mass slaughter and handling makes for a higher-risk product. There is some 'dry-plucking' but it's an expensive, labour-intensive method, so usually the birds are clamped onto a rail after gassing (you couldn't stun a chicken because you wouldn't be able to hold it place and the head is too small) and then flushed with jets of water to help the pluckers remove the feathers. The high levels of water combined with the warm body of the bird make it a perfect place for bacteria, plus the plucking leaves punctures in the skin for these to hide. The 'drawing' (or gutting) has to happen very fast for the volume of birds coming through even a high-level killing floor, so there is a risk of fecal contamination as well.

Types of chicken
In the category of chickens, there are many varietes of bird. **Poussins** are very young chickens (4–6 weeks old, or 'double poussins' are 6–12 weeks old). **Spring chicken** is 10–12 weeks old. **Roasting chicken** (usually just called 'whole chicken') is generally around 3 months. The better farmed, the more plump. Free-range chickens will be 1.4–2.2 kg/3–5 lbs. Capon (a castrated cockerel) can be up to 4 kg/8½ lbs. Not as popular any more, capon is quite tough, so a slower roasting, like a goose, is better.

Free range
Well-farmed chicken will be 'free-range', in other words, free to walk around. They choose to go under cover, even if not ushered, for night, as do pigs. They will peck at the ground and eat clover and pasture and often have troughs of corn undercover to top up their feed as they wish. A good chicken is usually large and plump and can be cut down to be used for lots of meals (see page 85).

Duck
A naturally more fatty bird, with proportionally less edible muscle. A 1.8 kg/4 lbs. chicken will serve 4–5 people, whereas the same weight duck will go around 2–3 people and there isn't much use serving the thighs or legs separately, unless you add multiple accompaniments. The breasts are delicious though, with more flavour and almost as much meat as chicken. Great cubed as well: see Duck, Venison and Halloumi skewers (page 156).

Goose
We had a retired butcher in the shop before Christmas, remembering how goose used to be more popular than turkey at Christmas in the UK. The trend has definitely moved to turkey (we sold about 15:1 turkey:geese last Christmas). Quite like duck, it's a lot of fat and bone to not as much muscle, which is probably why turkey has taken over. See (Roast Goose, page 221). The strained fats from cooking a goose or a duck make a very thick, flavoursome cooking fat, a real treat for perfect roast potatoes.

Turkey
The traditional Thanksgiving meal, turkey is popular in the UK, as well as America now. The meat is very lean, often recommended for low-fat/high-protein diets. For a classic holiday roast, see page 228.

Cooking poultry
The lean meat can benefit from the 'bard' method of wrapping bacon or pork fats over the top for roasting. Similarly, minced/ground chicken and turkey often have minced pork fat in them to prevent shrivelling and drying when cooked. (Check the ingredients on minced/ground poultry products to avoid other meats or added fats.)

Poaching is great for rolled and stuffed chicken or for keeping the tenderness on a lower temperature. Steamed chicken is popular for people following extremely-low fat diets.

POULTRY CUTS
Whole bird
Great for roasting whole (with some basting, particularly for turkey) or boned out (see pages 85–86) and stuffed (see Poached Whole Chicken Ballotine with Basil Pesto, page 155).

Crown/whole breast
This is the name for the breast joints on the bone but with the back bone, legs/thighs (and sometimes wings) removed. It's most popular with turkey because it makes a much smaller joint, but still has the moisture and juices from the bones. It's ideal for making gravy.

Breast fillets/boneless breasts
Birds are totally different from mammals in that they carry their muscles on the front (because of their wings). Breast fillets are cut off the rib cage and are great for roasting or stuffing and coating.

Legs
Legs can subsequently be jointed into thighs and drumsticks. This meat is darker and a bit richer, making it great for casseroles, such as Coq au Vin (page 176) on the bone. You can also use them boneless (see page 86 for how to do this).

Wings
Often marinated and cooked on the barbecue/outdoor grill or in a griddle pan. The meat is very succulent and has lots of flavour, but they're fiddly – best for picking up and nibbling.

OTHER BITS
Liver
Chicken liver is popular as it has a light flavour and fries well. It is most popular for pâtés (see Chicken Liver Pâté, page 143).

Bones
The carcass is great for making delicious stock and nutritious broth (see page 36).

COOKTCHERY: CHICKEN BREAKDOWN

Chicken is the meat that tragically boasts some of the worst examples of criminal animal-rearing. People ask why good chicken is so expensive but they don't ask why cheap chicken is so cheap. A good chicken is usually large and plump and can be used for lots of meals, so here's a way to make the most of it. It's always better value to buy a whole chicken and break it down into portions yourself. If you buy butchered breasts and thighs, you understandably pay for the cost of the cutting, packaging, transportation, space on the shelf and labour.

1. Start with the whole chicken, plucked and drawn. Remove any remaining entrails and giblets inside but nearly all trade in chickens is for fully eviscerated birds.

   2. Take off any holding ties around the legs or wings too. These are just used to hold its shape for presentation as well as ease of getting it into any packaging.

3. With the breast side up, pull one of the legs away from the body to make the skin more taut and, with a sharp knife, cut towards the body through the middle of the skin that attaches it **(A)**.

   4. Then carry on with the knife around the very base of the leg, alongside the bone of the body, as close as you can **(B)**. You want a funnel

A

B

shape at the top of the thigh so that you haven't left too much chicken on the bone on this side because it's not attached to another piece of muscle so you want to keep it attached to the thigh.

5. When you've cut all around, it's just the hip bone attached – bend it back/away from you to crack it and then you'll be able to use the knife to cut through the cartilage in the middle. You can then cut around the joint in the middle to detach the thigh and drumstick in the same way. Set them aside for now

6. Then the breasts. The smaller and sharper the knife, the better (a paring knife), and remember that it's really just the end bit you want to work with. Little 'nicks' are better than deep slices, which might result in you cutting a piece off that you can't see from the surface and you can't reattach. Start along the top, straight down the middle **(C)** and try and cut along the ridge of the bone, either start just to the left or just to the right. Angle the knife as you come around and take your time so that you try not to leave any meat on the carcass. These boneless breasts retail for, on average, three times the price per kg/lb. than a whole chicken.

7. Cut off the wings, just clean through the joint – pull the wing away from the body to create the tension **(D)**. Great in stock or marinated and cooked on the barbecue/outdoor grill. Do the same on the other side.

8. Take the thigh, cut around with the knife, snap the bone **(E)**, snip the attaching tendons and separate. Now you have a bone-in thigh and a drumstick – perfect for cooking on the barbecue/outdoor grill or putting in casseroles.

9. You can lay the thigh skin-side down and cut out the bone to make a boneless thigh too. Just run the knife along the sides of the bone and cut it out, then remove anything that looks 'sinewy' – basically, let your instincts take over. If it looks like it'll be chewy and hard to digest,

cut it out. Lean muscle looks totally simple to us, it's amazing to see people in the shop very unfazed by the distinction between what to cut out and what to leave in. This boneless thigh that you've made in about 5 minutes would retail at double the price you paid for it attached to the whole chicken.

10. Do the same to the other side so that you have two sets of thighs and drumsticks to go with the wings you've already removed **(F)**. (You can take the meat off the drumsticks, but you're working with three different muscles and some fiddly bones and tendons. Better to use the drumstick for the barbecue/outdoor grill or cooking whole in casseroles or roasts, then you can take the meat off the bone once cooked, as it falls off easily.)

11. Use the carcass to make lovely chicken stock (see page 36).

12. Tightly wrap the parts you're not using straight away to keep in your fridge (for up to the use-by date stated on the whole chicken) or pop in the freezer for up to 3 months.

13. To make a boneless whole chicken, start with a pair of scissors to cut just to the left or right of the breast bone. Then switch to a knife to cut out all the bones – don't worry too much about the order, just be careful not to nick the skin because that, particularly around the legs, is what's going to hold it together so you can stuff and roll it. The wings are too small to bone out, and if you cut them off, you make two large holes in the bird, so I just leave them where they are and then cut them off after. It's fiddly, but there's no wrong way if you just take each section at a time and remove all the bone. For the back plate, turn the bird carefully over and slide a knife in, just a little at a time to cut the skin away from the bone. You'll find a knack that works for you.

GAME

The term 'game' refers to wild animals, killed either for sport or breeding control (known as culling) and then eaten. There are mammals and poultry under this category, the most popular of which I will cover here, although there may be other popular or more unusual local game meats in your area. Ask your butcher for seasonal recommendations.

Both types of game will usually be hung for a least a couple of weeks. Feather game will be hung with the feathers still unplucked to extend the life (meaning there is less access for bacteria and less water in the handling to encourage the multiplying of bacteria on the skin).

There's a strong 'gamey' flavour to this meat and it's not for everyone. The recipes to cook with it often include marinating in some degree of acidity (vinegar or citric juices) to help break down that strong flavour as well as tenderize the meat by dissolving some of the proteins.

MAMMALS (AKA FUR GAME)
Deer (venison)
Roebuck
Wild boar
Rabbit
Hare

BIRDS (AKA FEATHER GAME)
Guinea fowl
Partridge
Pigeon
Grouse
Pheasant
Quail
Wild duck
Woodcock

Fur game

These animals are very lean. They are more active than domestic livestock and burn a lot of calories. 'Barding' (coating with fats, see page 34) is popular for these meats, as is mixing them into recipes that contain more oils or fats and flavours (see Rabbit and Seafood Paella, page 160). The cuts and joints are similar to the other quadrupeds/mammals and can be fried, roasted, rolled or braised in much the same way.

Feather game

These birds are plucked and drawn (gutted) just like poultry. They are best roasted whole, as the individual pieces are small and fiddly, or deboned and cubed for casseroles, such as Pheasant and Gammon Pie (see page 159) or stir-frying.

WEEKNIGHT SUPPERS

CHICKEN KIEVS

When buying chicken breasts for this, find the largest and plumpest possible; it will really help with keeping the garlic butter in the middle. If you're cutting your own whole chicken, remove the breast joints from the bone (see pages 84–7). Free-range chicken breasts are noticeably better for this recipe from a practical as well as ethical point of view. They aren't pumped with water or flushed with too much water in the plucking stage, so they won't shrivel, which would make the garlic butter leak or release water into the oil so that it doesn't brown.

2 large, skinless, free-range chicken breasts

1 teaspoon freshly chopped tarragon

40 g/5 tablespoons plain/all-purpose flour

3 eggs, beaten

100 g/2 cups dried breadcrumbs

300 ml/1¼ cups sunflower oil, for frying

Buttery Crushed Potatoes, to serve (see page 233)

GARLIC BUTTER

50 g/3½ tablespoons butter, softened

1 garlic clove, finely chopped

2 big pinches of freshly chopped parsley

a squeeze of lemon juice (approximately ¼ lemon; save the rest to serve)

salt and black pepper, to season

SERVES 2

Start by mixing the garlic butter so you can chill it in the fridge to harden. Mix the butter, garlic, parsley and lemon juice in a bowl, and season with salt and pepper. Portion the butter into two flat, thin pieces, approximately 2 cm/1 inch wide and 4 cm/2 inches long, so that they'll slot into the cut in the chicken breast. Wrap in foil and put in the fridge to harden while you prepare the chicken.

Cut the 'false fillet' (the small piece of muscle on the side, which is attached can be prized apart by pulling it) off the chicken breasts, as you're going to use this to plug the hole in the side.

Lay each breast flat, push down on the top to level it and carefully slice through the middle, front to back, so that there's a cut down one side. Don't cut all the way through; the cut needs to go about three-quarters of the way through.

Take the garlic butter from the fridge and place a piece inside each breast. Take the false fillet and push one end in first, at the edge of the cut, then slot the other end into the other end of the cut to help 'plug' it.

Mix the tarragon with the flour. Roll each stuffed breast in the seasoned flour, dip in the egg and then cover really well with breadcrumbs. You can then fry it straight away, but I like to double-dip! Wrap in foil and place in the fridge for 30 minutes for it to 'set'.

Take out the kievs out of the fridge and repeat the coating process: flour first, then egg and then breadcrumbs.

Heat the sunflower oil in a heavy-bottomed pan or deep-fryer until a cube of bread browns in 20 seconds. Carefully lower the kievs into the hot oil and fry for 20 minutes, or until cooked through, turning carefully once halfway through cooking.

Drain on paper towels, then serve with a lemon quarter to squeeze over the top, salad leaves and buttery crushed potatoes, if you like.

CHICKEN TIKKA MASALA

Many polls have concluded that chicken tikka masala is the most popular dish in the UK and it's also a much-loved Indian dish in the USA, so let's see if I can do its popularity justice. It's a great one to batch-cook and portion, too, and it's delicious cold for lunch. If you're cutting your own chicken, dice the breasts and use the boneless thigh meat (see pages 84–7).

4 teaspoons olive oil

1 red onion, diced

1 garlic clove, finely chopped

4 chicken breasts (or 2 breasts and 2 boneless thighs), diced

1 red chilli/chile, deseeded and finely chopped

a pinch of ground ginger

a pinch of ground turmeric

a pinch of ground cumin

a pinch of paprika

freshly squeezed juice of ½ lime (the rest can be cut for serving)

3 tablespoons tomato purée/paste

a big pinch of freshly chopped coriander/cilantro, plus extra whole leaves to garnish

1 teaspoon soft dark brown sugar

200 g/7 oz. canned chopped tomatoes

5 tablespoons double/heavy cream

salt and black pepper, to season

cooked basmati rice and naan bread, to serve

SERVES 4

Heat the oil in a pan set over a high heat and fry the onion and garlic for about 5 minutes until they start to brown.

Add the diced chicken, the chilli/chile, all the pinches of scrummy seasoning, a pinch of salt and pepper, and the lime juice (if you cut the lime lengthways, you can make longer wedges with the other half to serve – it's easier to squeeze).

Stir in the tomato purée/paste, coriander/cilantro and sugar. Lastly, add the chopped tomatoes and double/heavy cream.

Bring to the boil, then reduce the heat to low and simmer for 15–20 minutes, until the chicken is cooked through.

Taste and check the seasoning. A good trick is to taste the sauce and then smell each of the seasonings – your nose will tell you whether you want to add a pinch more of anything or just a little salt and pepper.

Serve with rice and naan bread, and a sprinkling of extra whole coriander/cilantro leaves.

PERFECTLY TENDER PORK CHOPS

Pork loin chops are a delicious and very quick meat dish – they can be fancy for entertaining or just quick and easy for a weeknight supper. One thing that is often a challenge, though, is keeping them soft. Of course, I'm going to say again (every time!) that if you start with well-farmed pork, more than half the work is done for you, which makes it so much easier to impress with your skills... but there's also a good method for cooking this pork that will really ensure it is soft and succulent, and it's always fun to get a few flames going in the kitchen...

2 tablespoons olive oil

1 white onion, sliced

2 sticks/ribs celery, strings peeled and sliced

a big pinch of freshly chopped parsley

2 pork chops

3½ tablespoons brandy

100 ml/7 tablespoons cider

100 ml/7 tablespoons Brown or White Chicken Stock (see page 36) or 1 tablespoon jellied stock

3 tablespoons crème fraîche (optional)

grated zest and freshly squeezed juice of 1 lemon (optional)

salt and black pepper, to season

SERVES 2

Heat half of the oil in a frying pan/skillet set over a medium heat and fry the onion and celery with some salt and pepper and the parsley for 5 minutes. Transfer to a plate and set aside.

Put the other half of the oil in the pan and, over a high heat, fry the pork chops for 30 seconds on each side to brown the surfaces.

Pour in the brandy and set alight (tilt the pan to ignite if you're using a gas hob/stovetop, or use a match to light the brandy if you're using an electric hob/stovetop). This is called 'flambéing' – the flames burn off the alcohol to soften the flavour of the brandy as well as leave behind the flavour of flash-heated pork that you wouldn't get from just simmering the chops. It also looks cool.

Let the flames die down and then pour in the cider and the stock, and let boil for 5 minutes.

Reduce the heat to medium, half-cover with a lid or piece of foil and leave gently bubbling for 10 minutes (or 15 minutes if they're thick chops).

Make a slice in one of the chops to check that they're cooked through and not pink at all. Cook for a few minutes more if not.

You can make a simple sauce here by spooning in crème fraîche and adding the lemon zest and juice, or just serve the pork chops as they are.

PORK MEDALLIONS AND LINGUINE

If you're cutting the pork shoulder at home, this recipe is great using the neck fillet as well, or buy a fillet/tenderloin or pre-cut medallions, about 2-cm/¾-inch thick.

40 g/3 tablespoons butter

1 garlic clove

4 rashers/strips of bacon (smoked bacon is great for flavour, if you like the smoky taste), chopped

6 spring onions/scallions, trimmed and chopped

4 asparagus spears (optional)

a big pinch of freshly chopped tarragon

4 pork medallions

100 ml/scant ½ cup white wine

340 g/12 oz. linguine

200 ml/¾ cup crème fraîche or sour cream

salt and black pepper, to season

freshly chopped flat-leaf parsley, to garnish

SERVES 4

Heat the butter in a ridged griddle pan (or a frying pan/skillet is fine if you don't have a griddle pan).

Fry the garlic, bacon, spring onions/scallions and asparagus (if using) for a minute to mix with the butter and coat the pan.

Add a pinch of salt and pepper and the tarragon.

Use a wooden spoon or other utensil to clear four spaces in the pan and add the pork medallions to the spaces in the pan. Cook over a high heat for about 2 minutes on each side.

Turn the heat down to medium and add the white wine. Cover with a lid or piece of kitchen foil and cook for a further 12 minutes, turning the pork pieces again halfway through. Meanwhile, start cooking the linguine in a large pan of salted water following the packet instructions.

Once the pork is cooked, put the four pieces on a plate and set aside for a moment.

Drain the linguine and stir in the crème fraîche. Then tip in the mixture from the griddle pan and stir to coat the pasta in the creamy sauce. Spoon the linguine into four pasta bowls and place a piece of pork on the top.

Add a crunch of black pepper and some chopped parsley to garnish, and serve with a cold beer.

PORK AND APPLE SLIDERS

For anyone who doesn't know, a 'slider' is a mini burger and it makes a great canapé for entertaining or a lovely choice for children's plates. They are usually served in mini bread rolls, but this recipe uses fried potato discs instead – happily use either, depending on what you fancy.

10 g/2 teaspoons butter

50 g/½ cup finely diced dessert or cooking apple

180 g/6 oz. really good pork mince/ground pork (see page 31 for hand-mincing/hand-cutting)

10 g/2 teaspoons dried breadcrumbs

10 g/2 teaspoons tomato purée/paste

a pinch of freshly chopped parsley

salt and black pepper, to season

POTATO 'BUNS'

4 new potatoes

10 g/2 teaspoons butter

MAKES 4

Heat the butter in a frying pan/skillet over a medium heat and fry the diced apple pieces for about 6 minutes until they brown and start to go sticky.

Remove the apple from the pan and set on a plate to cool (you can chill a plate in the fridge before you start to help speed this up). Don't worry about washing up the pan – we're going to use it again.

Mix the pork mince/ground pork with a pinch of salt, the breadcrumbs, tomato purée/paste and parsley really well in a bowl. Add the apple pieces once they've cooled a bit and mix.

Divide the mixture in half and then in half again to get four even pieces (weighing approximately 60 g/2 oz. each). Shape and flatten each portion – flatter sliders are easier to cook and serve.

Meanwhile, for the potatoes, bring a pan of water to the boil. Leave the skins on the new potatoes and slice them, not too thin, approximately 1 cm/½ inch thick. You need two slices per slider, but I would make a few spares in case any break... and to nibble whilst the sliders are cooking later... you'll see what I mean! Perhaps make 12 slices to be on the safe side.

Add the potato slices to the boiling water and parboil them for just 2 minutes to soften. Drain and set aside.

Heat the butter in the same frying pan/skillet from earlier over a medium heat and pick out the best-looking potato slices to fry with a good crack of black pepper.

Fry well and then set aside on a wire rack or paper towel, with the slices not touching each other to keep them crispy.

Add the sliders to the same pan and fry for 3–4 minutes on each side, until cooked through. This is when you want to nibble a potato slice, is that right?

To serve, put a slider between two potato slices and use a cocktail stick/toothpick to keep the slider together, then serve.

TOAD IN THE HOLE

An absolute favourite in my house growing up, and a special treat on a Saturday if our grandma came for lunch... Grandma would then explain that she had 'far too much' and we would get to eat the rest of hers. An even better result all round!

140 g/1 cup plain/all-purpose flour

2 eggs, beaten

150 ml/generous ½ cup milk

150 ml/generous ½ cup water

25 g/2 tablespoons butter

8 good-quality, thick pork sausages (to make your own skinless sausages, see below)

salt and black pepper, to season

Red Onion Gravy (opposite), to serve

HOMEMADE SKINLESS SAUSAGES

500 g/1 lb. 2 oz. good-quality pork mince/ground pork (see page 31 for hand-mincing/hand-cutting)

½ teaspoon salt

25 g/1 tablespoon dried breadcrumbs

20 g/4 teaspoons tomato purée/paste

1 egg, beaten

a pinch of freshly chopped parsley

a 25 x 35-cm/10 x 14-inch roasting pan, greased

SERVES 4 (OR 4½ WITH GRANDMA!)

Whizz the flour, a pinch of salt, the eggs, milk and water together in a food processor to make a batter. Put in the fridge to rest for at least 30 minutes.

Preheat the oven to 180°C (350°F) Gas 4.

Heat the butter in a frying pan/skillet over a medium–high heat and fry the sausages so that they're browned all over – don't worry about the middle not being fully cooked here, as they'll be baked later in the batter; this is just to brown them for flavour.

Place the browned sausages evenly in the base of the greased pan and pour the batter over the top.

Bake in the preheated oven for 45 minutes, but check it after 30 minutes; if the batter is crisping already, turn the temperature down and only bake for a further 5 minutes; if it hasn't started to crisp yet, turn up to 200°C (400°F) Gas 6 for the last 15 minutes.

Season with salt and pepper and serve with red onion gravy.

Homemade Skinless Sausages

Mix the pork mince/ground pork and salt first of all until the mince becomes sticky (this is the salt breaking down the proteins in the pork and will help with texture and binding). Mix in the rest of the ingredients and a pinch of pepper and shape into eight sausage shapes. Use as above, frying them gently so that they don't break up in the pan.

FAGGOTS WITH RED ONION GRAVY

Faggots don't have a great reputation. They need a big marketing campaign or maybe we all just need to try making them and learn how delicious, simple and great value they are. If there is ever a recipe for the modern meat budget, this is it.

1 whole pig pluck (the heart, lungs, liver and kidneys of a pig), trimmed

100 g/3½ oz. streaky/fatty bacon, chopped

200 g/7 oz. pork mince/ground pork (see page 31 for hand-mincing/hand-cutting)

120 g/¾ cup porridge oats/oatmeal

30 g/2 tablespoons tomato purée/paste

1 red onion, finely chopped

2 eggs, beaten

a big pinch each of freshly chopped parsley, sage and thyme

a big pinch each of nutmeg, allspice and cayenne pepper

salt and black pepper, to season

Buttery Crushed Potatoes or Fancy Mashed Potatoes (see page 233), to serve

RED ONION GRAVY

20 g/4 teaspoons butter

4 red onions, finely sliced

1 tablespoon brown sugar

2 tablespoons red wine vinegar

250 ml/1 cup Brown or White Chicken Stock (see page 36)

a pinch each of freshly chopped or dried sage and tarragon

a pinch of salt

baking parchment, greased with butter (optional)

SERVES 4

Preheat the oven to 170°C (325°F) Gas 3.

Trim any hard or dark blood parts off the pluck and cut it into pieces. (I like to use only half of the liver, or one-third if it's a very large pluck, as it's the strongest flavour and can overpower the other elements, but it's totally up to you.)

Bring a large pan of water to the boil and boil the pluck for 20 minutes. Drain, chop into small pieces and transfer to a mixing bowl.

Add all the other ingredients with a pinch of salt and pepper, and mix with your hands until it's really soft. Shape into a big, long sausage and then cut into eight pieces. Roll the pieces into balls.

Like with homemade haggis (see page 114), I bake these in baking parchment, so that they're soft inside and slightly crisp on the outside, but you can bake them as they are for a crisp outside. Put a faggot on each sheet of greased baking parchment and twist the ends like a sweet/candy wrapper, if you want to bake them in parchment.

Bake in the preheated oven for 50 minutes, until cooked through. Season with salt and pepper and serve with buttery crushed potatoes or fancy mashed potatoes.

Red Onion Gravy

Heat the butter in a pan over a medium heat and fry the onions until they are very soft and browning. Stir in the sugar until it's dissolved and sticky. Add the red wine vinegar, stir well and then slowly pour in the chicken stock. Add the sage, tarragon and a pinch of salt, and keep stirring over the heat until it thickens.

PORK STROGANOFF

Such an easy pot dish and a great use of pork shoulder. It's great with all the easiest accompaniments like rice, potatoes or pasta, so it's a perfect one to make in a larger batch and freeze in portions for easy lunches and dinners.

15 g/1 tablespoon butter

1 small white onion, diced

1 garlic clove, chopped

110 g/1½ cups mushrooms, sliced

200 g/7 oz. pork shoulder, diced (see pages 31 and 76–9)

1 teaspoon wholegrain mustard

a pinch of freshly chopped parsley

a pinch of freshly chopped tarragon

4 tablespoons double/heavy cream

1 tablespoon brandy

Fancy Mashed Potatoes (see page 233) and some green vegetables, to serve

salt and black pepper, to taste

SERVES 2

Heat the butter in a pan over a medium heat and fry the onion, garlic and mushrooms until they start to brown. Add a pinch of salt and pepper and then the diced pork. Continue to fry for 4–5 minutes to cook the pork through.

Stir in the mustard, parsley, tarragon, cream and brandy. Reduce the heat to low, pop a lid on top and simmer. For this two-portion quantity, it will only need 15–20 minutes; for a larger batch, double the time and just give it a stir occasionally until the sauce thickens.

Serve hot with potatoes (my favourite with this is mashed) and greens seasoned to taste with salt and pepper. Or, cool the mixture right down and portion in sealed containers or sandwich bags and freeze for up to 3 months.

SWEET CHILLI PORK BELLY AND NOODLES

The crispier the better for these pork pieces. I like to make the pieces really dark and crunchy, and adding the lime towards the end of frying is a great way to crisp them up and perfect the balance with the sweetness.

400 g/14 oz. rindless pork belly, diced

1 red chilli/chile, deseeded and finely chopped, plus extra to serve (optional)

2 tablespoons clear honey

2 teaspoons ground paprika

1 garlic clove, finely chopped

1 tablespoon sesame oil

1 tablespoon vegetable oil

8–10 spring onions/scallions, trimmed and finely sliced

1 red (bell) pepper, deseeded and finely chopped

2 pak choi/bok choy, trimmed and chopped

1 tablespoon plain/all-purpose flour

a pinch each of salt and black pepper

freshly squeezed juice of 1 lime, plus 1 lime, cut into wedges, to serve

noodles and soy sauce, to serve

SERVES 2

A few hours in advance, or the day before, marinate the pork belly to really give it flavour. Put the diced, rindless belly pieces in a bag or bowl with the chilli/chile, honey, paprika, garlic and sesame oil. Seal and leave in the fridge for a few hours or overnight.

Heat the vegetable oil in a wok or high-sided frying pan/skillet and fry the spring onions/scallions, red (bell) pepper and pak choi/bok choy over a high heat until they are soft and starting to brown. Transfer them to a plate and set aside.

Spoon the belly pieces out of the marinade (keep the marinade) and coat them in the flour. Add to the wok and fry over a high heat until they become crisp (and smell amazing!), then add the marinade and fry for 4–5 minutes until the pork is cooked through.

Squeeze in the lime juice to help them crisp some more. Return the cooked vegetables to the wok along with a pinch of salt and pepper. Stir well, then serve with noodles and soy sauce. Sprinkle some more chopped red chilli/chile on the top to add an extra fresh kick, if you like.

ROGAN JOSH

This is such a quick and easy weeknight supper... though I think it has the longest and most tantalizing list of herbs and seasonings in the whole book, showing perfectly that speedy or easy recipes don't have to lack a flavour punch.

400 g/14 oz. diced lamb rump (see pages 65–6 to cut the rump from a leg of lamb)

2 tablespoons olive oil

2 garlic cloves

a 2-cm/1-inch piece of peeled fresh ginger, or 1 teaspoon ground ginger

1 teaspoon ground cinnamon

a pinch of fennel seeds

1 teaspoon ground cumin

1 teaspoon ground coriander

½ teaspoon chilli/chili powder

2 bay leaves

200 ml/scant 1 cup Greek-style yogurt

1 teaspoon garam masala

4 handfuls of spinach leaves (optional)

boiled rice, a pinch of saffron, a pinch of salt and some freshly squeezed lime juice, to serve

a big pinch paprika and a little fresh coriander/cilantro, to garnish

SERVES 2

Trim the lamb well so that it's nice and lean, as we won't be cooking this for very long.

Heat the olive oil in a frying pan/skillet and start by browning the garlic, ginger and diced lamb over a medium heat. Add the cinnamon, fennel seeds, cumin, coriander, chilli/chili powder and bay leaves and mix well.

Stir in the yogurt, then add the garam masala. Reduce the heat to low and simmer for 5 minutes.

Mix in the spinach leaves, if using, and cook until soft.

To serve, season some plain rice with a pinch of saffron, salt and a big squeeze of lime juice. Spoon over the rogan josh, sprinkle a little ground paprika on the top and garnish with a little fresh coriander/cilantro. Accompany with a cold lager or perhaps a chilled, fruity rosé wine.

LAMB AND ROSEMARY MEATBALLS

This is a lovely way to flavour and cook lamb mince. If you're cutting your own lamb leg, follow the instructions on page 31 to hand-mince/hand-cut the trim.

400 g/14 oz. lamb mince/ground lamb (see page 31 for hand-mincing/hand-cutting)

30 g/2 tablespoons dried breadcrumbs

30 g/2 tablespoons tomato purée/paste

a pinch of freshly chopped rosemary, or ½ teaspoon dried rosemary

1 garlic clove, very finely chopped

½ teaspoon mustard powder

20 g/4 teaspoons butter, for frying

a pinch of salt and black pepper

cooked pasta, to serve

SAUCE (OPTIONAL)

5 tablespoons white wine

200 ml/scant 1 cup crème fraîche or sour cream

a big pinch of freshly chopped parsley

MAKES 16 MEATBALLS

Mix the lamb, breadcrumbs, tomato purée/paste, rosemary, garlic, mustard powder, salt and pepper together well in a bowl. Divide the mixture into 16 meatballs – the easiest way to make these even is to shape the mixture into a ball, halve it, halve each of those, then again and again, so you have 16 meatballs. It's easier to halve pieces by sight and feel than to take off a meatball piece at a time.

To cook the meatballs, put the butter in a frying pan/skillet and fry on a medium–high heat for 10–12 minutes until browned and cooked through.

For a simple sauce, add the wine to the frying pan/skillet once the meatballs are cooked. Bring to a boil, then add the remaining sauce ingredients and season with salt and pepper. Serve with pasta.

LAMB, OLIVE AND FETA BURGERS

These are a bestseller in our shop. I love them because they're juicy but still quite light and fresh-tasting. Perfect for serving in the summer.

500 g/1 lb. 2 oz. lamb mince/ground lamb (see page 31 for hand-mincing/hand-cutting)

60 g/4 tablespoons dried breadcrumbs

1 egg, beaten

50 g/½ cup pitted black olives, chopped

50 g/2 oz. feta cheese, crumbled

30 g/2 tablespoons tomato purée/paste

a big pinch of freshly chopped parsley

1 garlic clove, finely chopped

2 teaspoons olive oil, plus extra for frying

4 pitta breads, shredded romaine lettuce, sour cream and lemon wedges, to serve

salt and black pepper, to taste

MAKES 4 BURGERS

Mix all the ingredients, apart from those to serve, in a bowl really well, squeezing the mixture together to help it to bind.

Split the mixture in half, and then half each again to make four even burger patties. Flatten them down and try to make the thickness as even as possible.

Heat a little olive oil in a frying pan/skillet over a high heat and lay the burgers in the oil. Fry for 30 seconds each side, then turn the heat down to medium and fry for a further 5 minutes on each side.

These are delicious in pitta breads with shredded romaine lettuce, sour cream and a squeeze of fresh lemon juice. Season with salt and pepper to taste.

SHEPHERD'S PIE

Shepherd's pie uses lamb mince, whereas cottage pie uses beef mince – but in my opinion this comforting pie is lovely wlth either. The porridge oats help to make the mixture soft and squishy but stop it from going slimy, which flour can sometimes do when you use it to thicken the base of a pie.

600 g/1 lb. 5 oz. all-purpose potatoes, such as Maris Piper or Yukon Gold, peeled and chopped into 2-cm/1-inch chunks

1 garlic clove

2 carrots, chopped

1 white onion, chopped

45 g/3 tablespoons butter

500 g/1 lb. 2 oz. lamb mince/ground lamb (see page 31 for hand-mincing/hand-cutting)

20 g/4 teaspoons tomato purée/paste

200 ml/scant 1 cup red wine

150 ml/⅔ cup vegetable stock

a pinch of dried rosemary

a pinch of dried thyme

40 g/generous ⅓ cup old-fashioned rolled oats

50 ml/3½ tablespoons milk

20 g/⅓ cup finely grated Parmesan, plus extra for sprinkling on top (optional)

salt and black pepper, to season

a 20 x 25-cm/8 x 10-inch ovenproof dish, greased

SERVES 4

Preheat the oven to 180°C (360°F) Gas 4.

Bring a large pan of water to the boil and boil the potatoes for about 20 minutes, until soft enough to mash.

Meanwhile, heat 15 g/1 tablespoon of the butter in a frying pan/skillet over a medium heat and add the garlic, carrots and onion. Fry for about 4–5 minutes, until softened and starting to brown.

Add the lamb and fry until cooked, breaking it up as it cooks using a wooden spoon.

Add the tomato purée/paste and stir in. Then add the red wine, vegetable stock, rosemary, thyme and some salt and pepper. Stir well and then add the oats, a little at a time. Mix well and cook, stirring, until the mixture is nice and thick and the oats have absorbed the liquid.

By now the potatoes should be soft, so drain and mash them, mixing in the milk, Parmesan and remaining 30 g/2 tablespoons of the butter.

Spoon the lamb mixture into the greased ovenproof dish and press down to make it level. Then spread the mashed potatoes over the top evenly.

Put the dish in the preheated oven and bake for 20 minutes. To brown the top, add a little more Parmesan (or sprinkle with grated mature Cheddar) and place under a hot grill/broiler for the last 5 minutes.

HOMEMADE HAGGIS

This is such a delicious, good-value and nutritious meal. I love the full tradition with the offal and stomach casing, but they're not always easy to source, so this has an alternative version to achieve an equally delicious flavour and texture.

75 g/2½ oz. lamb's liver

100 g/3½ oz. each of lamb's heart and lamb's lights/lungs or 200 g/7 oz. lamb mince/ground lamb (see page 31 for hand-mincing/hand-cutting)

100 g/3½ oz. beef suet or vegetable shortening

a big pinch of allspice

a pinch of cayenne pepper

1 small red onion, finely chopped

1 garlic clove, finely chopped

a big pinch of freshly chopped parsley, plus extra to garnish

1 tablespoon white wine vinegar

30 g/2 tablespoons tomato purée/paste

120 g/¾ cup old-fashioned rolled oats

salt, to season

1 sheep's stomach (alternatively, use baking parchment)

'NEEPS AND TATTIES'

1 swede/rutabaga

2 baking potatoes

a large knob/pat of butter

black pepper, to taste

butcher's string/twine

SERVES 2

Pre-heat the oven to 160°C (325°F) Gas 3.

Finely chop the liver, heart and lights/lungs, if using, or chop the liver and mix it into the lamb mince/ground lamb. Transfer to a mixing bowl and add the chopped suet/vegetable shortening, allspice, salt, cayenne pepper, onion, garlic, parsley, white wine vinegar, tomato purée/paste and oats.

Then either stuff into the stomach and seal the end with butcher's string/twine or squeeze into a tight ball. Place into the centre of a square of baking parchment and twist or tie the ends to lock it in.

Wrap in a layer of foil and place into 1 cm/⅜ inch of water in the bottom of an ovenproof pan. Set a lid on top and cook in the preheated oven for 2 hours. Remove the haggis from the casing, season with salt and slice it to serve.

'Neeps and Tatties'

While your haggis is cooking, you can make your 'neeps and tatties', the accompaniments for this famous Scottish meal. Peel and chop the swede/rutabaga and potatoes into small dice. Boil separately (or together, if you prefer), drain and mash with the butter and freshly ground black pepper.

MUTTON, PEAR AND ROQUEFORT SALAD

I love mutton and this is a lovely way to lighten the richness of the meat in a dressed salad. The sweetness of pear provides the perfect balance.

2 ripe pears, quartered lengthways and cored

40 g/3 tablespoons butter

1 mutton fillet/ tenderloin, about 500 g/1 lb. 2 oz.

4 large handfuls of romaine or Little Gem/ Bibb lettuce leaves

125 g/4½ oz. Roquefort cheese, or other rich and creamy cheese

7–8 fresh basil leaves

salt and black pepper, to taste

DRESSING

2 tablespoons olive oil

1 tablespoon balsamic vinegar

freshly squeezed juice of ½ lime

SERVES 2

Preheat the grill/broiler to high.

Arrange the quartered and cored pears on a baking sheet. Melt half the butter in a frying pan/skillet and drizzle over the pears. Spread it over the top of the pears. Place under the grill/broiler for 5 minutes.

Meanwhile, heat the rest of the butter in the frying pan/skillet over a high heat. Add the mutton to the pan and roll it in the butter for 5 minutes, until the surface is completely browned. (If you'd prefer your meat more well done, cook it for 10 minutes over a medium heat.) Set aside to rest.

Make the dressing and toss the leaves in it. Divide the leaves between two plates. Tear the cheese into pieces and sprinkle over the top. Layer the grilled/broiled pear on top. Slice the fillet/ tenderloin very thinly using a sharp knife. It should still be pink in the middle. Place on the plates and add a good scrunch of salt and black pepper and a few torn basil leaves.

AFRICAN GOAT AND PLANTAIN CURRY

This African-inspired dish also works well with lamb, mutton or veal.

2 tablespoons olive oil or argan oil

2 garlic cloves, chopped

1 white onion, chopped

a 3-cm/1¼-inch piece of fresh ginger, peeled and grated

1 red chilli/chile, deseeded and chopped

800 g/1 lb. 12 oz. goat loin or shoulder, diced (or use lamb, mutton or veal)

4 green plantains

a big pinch of freshly chopped coriander/ cilantro

6–8 fresh basil leaves

a handful of freshly chopped parsley

2 beef/beefsteak tomatoes, diced

200 ml/scant 1 cup Brown or White Chicken Stock (see page 36)

salt and black pepper, to season

lemon wedges, to serve

a 20-cm/8-inch ovenproof dish, greased

SERVES 4

Preheat the oven to 170°C (350°F) Gas 4.

Heat the oil in a frying pan/skillet over a medium heat and fry the garlic, onion, grated ginger, chilli/chile and a pinch of salt and pepper for a few minutes until soft.

Add the meat and stir to brown all over.

Peel the plantain, halve them lengthways and lay them flat in the base of the prepared ovenproof dish. Put the goat meat and all the mixture from the frying pan/skillet over the top, then cover with the coriander/cilantro, basil, parsley and diced tomatoes. Add the stock. Cover with a lid and cook in the preheated oven for 1 hour.

Remove the lid, stir the mixture away from the sides and just lift the plantain pieces gently off the bottom to make sure they're not catching. Return to the oven, uncovered, for another 30 minutes. Season and serve with wedges of lemon and a cold ginger beer.

CORNISH PASTIES

The manager of our shop kitchen, Bev, makes the best traditional Cornish pasties. We bring them out hot from the oven on a Saturday morning and the smell of these delicious pasties once even lured in a vegetarian! I reckon we can convert him soon, too...!

500 g/1 lb. 2 oz. diced beef (rump/round is lovely for these, see page 50)

160 g/5½ oz. swede/rutabaga, finely diced

160 g/5½ oz. carrot, finely diced

75 g/2½ oz. onion, finely diced

a pinch of fresh thyme leaves

a pinch each of salt and black pepper

FOR THE PASTRY

500 g/1 lb. 2 oz. butter

1 kg/2 lb. 4 oz. plain/all-purpose flour, plus extra for dusting

cold water, to bind

a pinch each of salt and black pepper

1 beaten egg, to glaze

a 25-cm/10-inch pastry/cookie cutter

MAKES 6 LARGE PASTIES

Preheat the oven to 180°C (360°F) Gas 4.

Make the pastry first by crumbling the butter and flour, plus some salt and pepper together with your fingertips. Then add a little cold water, just a splash at a time, until the pastry comes together.

Sprinkle a little more flour over a work surface and use a rolling pin to roll out the pastry to a thickness of about 5 mm/¼ inch. Use the cutter to cut out six 25-cm/10-inch circles.

Either leave the circles out if you've space or layer them with a little baking parchment in between to keep them separate.

Put the steak, swede/rutabaga, carrot, onion, thyme and some salt and pepper in a bowl and mix well. Divide the filling among the pastry circles and spread it out evenly on the right side of each circle, so that you can fold over the other side. Pull the left side over and press it together to seal 1 cm/½ inch away from the edge of the right hand side of the pastry. This allows a little room to fold the edge back over the fold to seal in the filling nice and tightly.

Lay some baking parchment onto a baking sheet (you can grease this a little with some butter, too, to be safe), slide a palette knife/metal spatula under the pasties and lift them carefully onto the paper.

Bake in the preheated oven for 45 minutes and serve straight away or chill in the fridge for up to a week.

Pastry Tip

You can also wrap the uncooked pastries and filling in clingfilm/plastic wrap or foil and freeze them for up to 3 months, as long as the meat hasn't been previously frozen. It's a really handy thing to have ready in the freezer and bakes perfectly well from frozen in a preheated oven at 160°C (325°F) Gas 3 for 90 minutes.

OVEN MEATLOAF

In the UK, we're way behind the Americans in appreciating the ease, taste and versatility of the unassuming meatloaf. I don't know why it isn't more popular; it will be one day. This is a classic recipe combination but, as with burgers, you can have some fun putting more ingredients in and trying out the hard-boiled/hard-cooked egg in the middle thing. Serve it with your choice of vegetables or chips/fries, or put it in a brioche sandwich with Chunky Barbecue Sauce (see page 127).

150 g/5½ oz. really good beef mince/ground beef (see page 31 for hand-mincing/hand-cutting)

120 g/4 oz. really good pork mince/ground pork (see page 31 for hand-mincing/hand-cutting your own)

50 g/3 tablespoons dried breadcrumbs

50 g/2 oz. white onion, diced

1 teaspoon wholegrain mustard

20 g/4 teaspoons tomato purée/paste

½ garlic clove, chopped

a pinch of dried parsley

½ beaten egg

salt and black pepper, to season

SERVES 2

Preheat the oven to 180°C (360°F) Gas 4.

Mix all the ingredients really well together in a mixing bowl. Shape the whole mixture into a large sausage shape, trying to keep the thickness as even as possible.

There are two tricks for cooking it. Either put a stainless-steel skewer through the middle (lengthways) to help the roasting balance, place it in a roasting pan and roast for 35 minutes. Or wrap it in some baking parchment and twist the ends (like for homemade haggis on page 114) and bake it in the oven for 40 minutes.

Leave to stand for 5 minutes so that the juices settle and it is easier to slice. Season with salt and pepper and serve.

THE PERFECT KITCHEN STEAK

How to get the steakhouse taste experience in your own home, whatever your favourite cut.

15 g/1 tablespoon butter

225–340 g/8–12 oz. steak of your choice

salt

a sheet of muslin/cheesecloth (optional)

Colour
The colour of your steak will depend on the packaging. A bright red shade only means that it's been gas-flushed with oxygen to help eliminate as much bacteria as possible in the packaging process and to keep the bright red look. It doesn't do any harm to the meat – it's just a process – but don't be afraid to choose a darker grey-red colour, either unpacked or vacuum-sealed.

Marbling
This is the term given to the intramuscular fat in the meat. It's not a sure sign of quality farming though. Indeed, pumping as much grain and corn into cattle, enough to reach the point just before they get ill and can't digest it, produces the most marbling, so be aware if the marbling is a yellow colour, as this likely suggests the presence of corn and grain. We're looking for bright, white marbling, so it's clean and will dissolve beautifully when you cook it. The marbling is best found in rib-eye and sirloin steaks. You will find some in the fillet/ tenderloin, though this cut is celebrated for its lean tenderness with or without marbling.

Labelling
The label should tell you about the breed, feed and hanging. Certain breeds are naturally more inclined to marble, like Aberdeen Angus, so that will help you know whether the marbling has occurred naturally. The feed should proudly say that the animals have been reared mostly on grass and pasture, the things they can digest, with any grain only in the last 10–12 weeks for the optimum yield of marbling. The meat needs to be marbled for the hanging to really have an effect, as the weight and stretch in the meat helps to tenderize these veins of fat, which means they'll dissolve more easily when being cooked, coating the meat in flavour.

Packaging

If you've started with a vacuum-sealed steak, your steak will be wet. This is what kept your steak fresh and why I support this method for the time between abattoir and your fridge, but you need to dry it out before cooking. Drying it out will get rid of the metallic, 'iron' taste in the steak, which is from the coating of blood that remains on the outside of the steak and which cooks first and sticks to the meat. The simplest thing to do is remove it from the packaging about 30 minutes before, pat it with paper towels and leave it on a plate at room temperature (turn it over halfway through if you remember) before cooking it.

If you have some muslin/ cheesecloth, then it's lovely to wrap it up for up to two days before cooking (and if you want to be really fancy, you could hang it from a shelf in your fridge – see page 150 – so it isn't touching anything). Using quality beef would mean wrapping it isn't vital – it does add to the taste, but just a fraction, so it's mostly just to look fancy. Whatever you do, removing the wet blood from the steak means the first thing you're cooking, and therefore tasting, is meat, not blood.

Cooking

My absolute favourite way to cook a steak is frying or griddling. It celebrates the best of the flavours and is so quick and easy. Get the frying pan/skillet or griddle pan really hot first over a high heat, then put in a scoop of butter and a sprinkle of sea salt and let that just start to brown slightly. The temperature of the butter and pan here is important, so here are a few pointers:

• You're looking for the butter to bubble and just start to brown; too soon and your steak will be greasy.

• If the pan starts to smoke, that's too hot and the steak will scorch and taste burnt, even if the middle is still pink. Just hold the pan off the heat for a minute to let it cool and then return to the heat for 10 seconds and add the steak.

• Don't turn too quickly the first time, do wait for 30 seconds so that the first side tightens and browns and seals in the flavour.

• Don't put a lid on the pan – we don't want any moisture at this stage.

• If you have a nice square griddle pan, then you can do two or three steaks at a time. If you have a round pan, be careful not to do too many steaks at the same time, as they won't cook evenly; you want them evenly placed above the best heat to control the temperature. If you need to fry one at a time, still serve them as they are ready, after resting for 2 minutes, rather than try and keep them warm in the oven – just explain to your guests that staggered presentation means better steaks.

Timings

First cook the steak for 30 seconds on each side on this very high heat, then reduce the heat right down to low–medium and let the steak cook for:

• 30 seconds either side for rare;

• 2 minutes either side for medium;

• 4 minutes either side for well done.

These are for an average 1.5–2-cm/½–¾-inch thick steaks. For thicker medallions, Porterhouse, Chateaubriand and so on, see page 51.

If you're cooking a steak with a spine of fat, such as sirloin or the top cuts of rump/round, then I would recommend using tongs to pick up the steak and hold it on its side for 30 seconds, to crisp up the fat and release even more flavour into the pan for the cooking. Once cooked, remove from the pan and allow to rest for 2 minutes, then sprinkle with a little cracked black pepper.

DIANE SAUCE

A bit of a retro choice for a sauce, as it was a victim of its popularity and was a little overused on menus in the 1950s and '60s. Popular it was, though, and a good freshly made one will remind you why.

1 tablespoon olive oil
1 red onion, finely chopped
1 garlic clove, finely chopped
2 tablespoons Worcestershire sauce
2 tablespoons tomato ketchup
150 ml/⅔ cup double/heavy cream

**MAKES ABOUT 150 ML/⅔ CUP
(2–3 SERVINGS)**

In the same pan in which you have cooked your steak, put the heat back up to high and add the olive oil.

Fry the onion and garlic for 4–5 minutes until they are brown, then add the Worcestershire sauce and ketchup, and stir well for a minute.

Finally mix in the double/heavy cream and bring back to the boil. Serve with the rested steak.

BÉARNAISE SAUCE

This is a lovely light balance for a steak accompaniment. It takes just a little extra time for the cooling and adding the egg, but it's worth it for a really impressive fresh sauce.

85 g/6 tablespoons butter
2 shallots, chopped
4 tablespoons white wine vinegar
a pinch of soft brown sugar
a pinch of dried tarragon
1 egg yolk
75 g/5⅓ cups butter, melted
a pinch of freshly chopped parsley
salt and black pepper

**MAKES ABOUT 150 ML/⅔ CUP
(2–3 SERVINGS)**

In the same pan in which you have cooked your steak, put the heat up to medium, melt 10 g/ 2 teaspoons of the butter and fry the shallots for 4–5 minutes until brown.

Add the white wine vinegar, sugar, tarragon and some pepper, and bring to the boil. Cook for 5 minutes to reduce slightly, then remove from the heat and allow to cool.

Strain the sauce through a fine mesh sieve/ strainer into a food processor.

Add the egg yolk and whizz until it changes colour and starts to go fluffy.

Meanwhile, melt the remaining butter over a medium heat. Turn the speed right down and slowly drizzle in the melted butter.

Season with salt and freshly chopped parsley. Serve with the rested steak.

PINK PEPPERCORN SAUCE

Peppercorn sauce is definitely my favourite steak accompaniment, but this one uses pink peppercorns, which have a lovely flavour and are very pretty.

2 teaspoons pink peppercorns
20 g/1½ tablespoons butter
2–3 shallots, finely chopped
a handful of mushrooms, finely chopped
1 tablespoon red wine vinegar
1 tablespoon brandy
100 ml/⅓ cup Beef broth or Brown Chicken Stock (see pages 36–37)
50 ml/3 tablespoons double/heavy cream

MAKES ABOUT 200 ML/GENEROUS ¾ CUP (4 SERVINGS)

First crush the peppercorns with a pestle and mortar (or just in a mixing bowl with the bottom of a shatterproof tumbler or the end of a large rolling pin).

Heat the butter in a frying pan/skillet and fry the shallots until they're soft and brown.

Add the mushrooms and stir until they soften fully, then add the crushed peppercorns and stir.

Pour in the red wine vinegar, brandy and stock, and cook over a high heat for 3–4 minutes, until the sauce has reduced.

Mix in the double/heavy cream and serve with the rested steak.

CHUNKY BARBECUE SAUCE

A poor-quality barbecue sauce can ruin a great plate of meat for me. It's so easy to make it at home and I hope you taste the difference when enjoying fresh barbecue sauce as quickly as I did.

50 g/3½ tablespoons butter
1 onion, chopped
2 teaspoons tomato purée/paste
2 tablespoons soft/packed brown sugar
1 teaspoon paprika
a pinch of chipotle powder
2 teaspoons Worcestershire sauce
1 teaspoon English/hot mustard powder
2 tablespoons white wine vinegar
a pinch each of salt and black pepper

MAKES ABOUT 125 ML/½ CUP (2 SERVINGS)

Melt the butter in a frying pan/skillet over a medium heat, then add the onion and fry until soft and browned. Add the tomato purée/paste, sugar, paprika and chipotle powder, and stir well. Add the Worcestershire sauce, mustard powder and vinegar, and season with salt and pepper, then as soon as it bubbles, pour in 150 ml/⅔ cup water. Increase the heat to high and bring to the boil, then let it boil hard, uncovered, for about 10 minutes, until the mixture reduces and thickens.

Remove from the heat and let cool, then whizz it in a food processor. I like to keep barbecue sauce nice and chunky, but you can keep whizzing until it's smooth, if you prefer.

CHILLI CON CARNE

A great recipe to make in a large batch and freeze in portions. After a quick bit of prep, you can leave this bubbling on the hob for as long as you like. It's a good one for the budget, too, with minced/ground beef, kidney beans and chopped tomatoes, all very inexpensive ingredients to buy.

2 tablespoons olive oil

1 red onion, finely chopped

1 garlic clove, finely chopped

800 g/1 lb. 12 oz. beef mince/ground beef (see page 31 for hand-mincing/hand-cutting)

1 fresh chilli/chile, deseeded and finely chopped

a pinch of cayenne pepper, plus extra to serve

a pinch of ground cumin

a pinch of ground coriander

2 teaspoons dark muscovado/molasses sugar

1 tablespoon plain/all purpose flour

a pinch each of salt and black pepper

½ beef stock/bouillon cube (or 30 g/1 oz. veal stock)

a 400-g/14-oz. can kidney beans, drained (drained weight 250 g/9 oz.)

1 tablespoon tomato purée/paste

100 ml/⅓ cup red wine

200 g/7 oz. canned chopped tomatoes

rice and sour cream, to serve

SERVES 4

Heat the oil in a saucepan or deep frying pan/skillet over a medium heat and fry the onion and garlic for about 4–5 minutes until they start to brown.

Add the beef mince/ground beef and fry for another minute, using a wooden spoon to break up the meat.

Add the chilli/chile, cayenne pepper, cumin, coriander, sugar, flour and some salt and pepper, and stir until it forms a paste. Then slowly crumble in the beef stock/bouillon cube or add the veal stock.

Then add the kidney beans, tomato purée/paste, red wine and chopped tomatoes and bring to the boil.

Once it bubbles, reduce the heat to low and let it simmer for 45 minutes, or up to an hour if you can, so that it thickens.

Serve straight away with rice, a dollop of sour cream and a pinch of cayenne pepper on the top.

Chilli con carne freezes brilliantly: portion it into freezerproof containers or sandwich bags and freeze for up to 3 months. Once defrosted, just check the flavours and add a little chilli/chili powder, salt or cayenne pepper to liven it up a bit if necessary.

CLASSIC BOLOGNESE

I love bolognese and I love Italian food. Although serving this classic meat ragù with spaghetti is not traditional in Italy, it's a must for me! I think the classic bolognese has also done more for beef mince/ground beef than any other recipe.

10 g/2 teaspoons butter

½ white onion, finely chopped

1 garlic clove, finely chopped

25 g/scant ½ cup chopped mushrooms

2 rashers/strips streaky/fatty bacon, sliced

300 g/10½ oz. beef mince/ground beef (I recommend 20% fat, see page 31 for hand-mincing/hand-cutting)

20 g/4 teaspoons tomato purée/paste

200 g/7 oz. canned chopped tomatoes

50 ml/3½ tablespoons red wine

3–4 leaves fresh basil, torn

a pinch of oregano

1 bay leaf

salt and black pepper, to taste

SERVES 2

Heat the butter in a pan over a high heat and start by browning the onion and garlic for 4–5 minutes. Then add the mushrooms and bacon and cook for 4–5 minutes, until brown.

Add the mince (a lot of people start with this, but it's better not to overcook it, as it can go chewy). As soon as it is cooked (it will turn from pink to grey), stir in the tomato purée/paste and cook for a couple of minutes, then stir in the chopped tomatoes, red wine, basil, oregano, bay leaf and some salt and pepper. Mix well, bring to the boil and then reduce the heat right down to low to simmer. Cook for at least 20 minutes, and up to 45 minutes if you can.

If you've time, I'm a big fan of letting bolognese cool and then reheating it to serve – it helps to bring out the richness in the tomatoes and the flavour of the beef. It's not vital, but if you can, make this the day before, then just reheat it on the stovetop for 10 minutes. You can cool it quickly by lowering the pan into a shallow sink of cold water and stirring well. Reheating is not vital, but the strength of the flavours really comes through even more.

It's a great pot to take to heat for lunch as well, as long as I haven't eaten it cold for breakfast, another favourite meaty meal of mine!

SQUIDGY MEATBALLS

So called because they have a mozzarella pearl centre so they go super squidgy when you cook them! This is one of the first recipes I made for our farmers' markets when we started our meat company and it's still popular in our meals section in the shop today.

800 g/1 lb. 12 oz. beef mince/ground beef (see page 31 for hand-mincing/hand-cutting)

200 g/2½ cups dried breadcrumbs

80 g/1 cup freshly grated Parmesan cheese, plus extra to serve

3 tablespoons tomato purée/paste

1 teaspoon dried oregano

1 teaspoon dried basil

20 mozzarella pearls

a pinch each of salt and black pepper

cooked spaghetti, to serve

TOMATO SAUCE

30 g/2 tablespoons butter

1 garlic clove, chopped

1 white onion, chopped

1 teaspoon ground cinnamon

1 tablespoon tomato purée/paste

800 g/1¾ lbs. canned chopped tomatoes

a pinch of freshly chopped basil

a pinch each of salt and black pepper

SERVES 4

Make the sauce first so it can cook while you're making the meatballs. Melt half the butter in a pan over a high heat and fry the onion and garlic for 4–5 minutes, until brown. Add the cinnamon and stir well. Add the tomato purée/paste and stir for a couple of minutes, then pour in the chopped tomatoes and stir well. Add some salt and pepper, and the basil, reduce the heat to a simmer and cook for 20 minutes to thicken.

Meanwhile, while the sauce is simmering, make the meatballs. Mix the beef mince/ground beef, breadcrumbs, Parmesan, tomato purée/paste, oregano, basil and some salt and pepper in a bowl with your hands, making sure they combine really well.

Divide the mixture into 20 even portions (about 55 g/2 oz. each), then round each one in your hand and flatten on the work surface. Place a mozzarella pearl in the middle of each one and fold the meat around to seal it in.

Preheat the oven to 180°C (360°F) Gas 4.

By now, the sauce should be cooked well. Remove it from the heat and either keep it chunky or use an electric hand mixer to whizz it up and make it really smooth.

Transfer the sauce to an ovenproof dish and set aside. Return the pan to the stovetop (there's no need to clean it) and set it over a high heat. Put the other half of the butter in (don't worry about any of the sauce that remains stuck to the sides of the pan, as it will all mix together!). Fry the meatballs for 8 minutes, being careful to stir them gently so that the mozzarella stays safely in the middle, until the outsides are browning. Transfer the meatballs to the sauce and bake in the preheated oven for 15 minutes.

Serve with spaghetti and top with a sprinkle of Parmesan and a pinch of black pepper. This dish is lovely with a glass of Chianti for a celebration of Italian delights.

SUPERFOOD BURGERS

These are the ultimate superfood beef burgers, with a tasty hit of protein, iron and antioxidants, as well as vitamins A, B6 and C.

300 g/10½ oz. beef mince/ground beef (see page 31 for hand-mincing/hand-cutting)

1 cooked beetroot/beet, grated

½ cooking apple, peeled and diced

20 g/4 teaspoons tomato purée/paste

1 teaspoon powdered spirulina (optional)

20 g/4 teaspoons dried breadcrumbs (optional)

1 garlic clove, finely chopped

a pinch each of salt and black pepper

oil, for frying

wholemeal/whole-wheat rolls, spinach leaves and some hoummus, to serve

MAKES 2

Mix the beef mince/ground beef, grated beetroot/beet, diced cooking apple, tomato purée/paste, spirulina and breadcrumbs (if using), garlic, salt and pepper together with your hands until well mixed.

Divide the mixture in half and shape into two burgers, making sure they're not too fat, so that it's easier to cook them through.

Heat a little oil in a frying pan/skillet over a high heat and put the burgers in. Don't turn them too quickly; let them sear fully on the first side for 4–5 minutes before you move them. Turn and cook on the other side for 5–6 minutes, until they're cooked thoroughly in the middle.

For extra goodness, serve in a lightly toasted wholemeal/whole-wheat roll with a few spinach leaves and a dollop of hoummus on the top.

MICHAELMAS PIE

The filling for this pie is such a simple throw-together recipe, but it tastes terrific with the sweetness of the redcurrant jelly. It's up to you if you'd like to serve mini pies or make one large pie, but I like mini pies the best!

250 g/9 oz. game, such as venison, rabbit and pheasant, diced (alternatively, diced beef is delicious in this pie too)

25 g/2 tablespoons butter

½ garlic clove, chopped

100 g/1½ cups chopped mushrooms

40 g/generous ¼ cup plain/all-purpose flour

20 g/4 teaspoons tomato purée/paste

100 ml/scant ½ cup red wine

80 ml/⅓ cup Beef Broth (see page 37)

40 g/2 tablespoons redcurrant jelly

a sprig of fresh thyme

2 bay leaves

salt and black pepper, to season

1 beaten egg or 20 ml/4 teaspoons milk, for glazing

greens or salad, to serve (optional)

PASTRY

100 g/7 tablespoons salted butter

225 g/1¾ cups plain/all-purpose flour

a pinch of salt

3–4 tablespoons chilled water

8 individual round pie dishes or a 25 x 20-cm/10 x 8-inch pie dish, greased

MAKES 8 MINI PIES OR 1 LARGE PIE TO SERVE 4

Start by making the pastry. Rub the butter, flour and a little salt together with your fingertips until the mixture resembles breadcrumbs. Then keep adding a little chilled water, a tablespoonful at a time, until you can combine the crumbled mixture into a ball of pastry. Don't add too much water. Wrap in clingfilm/plastic wrap and place in the fridge while you make the pie filling.

Preheat the oven to 180°C (350°F) Gas 4.

Put the diced game, butter, garlic, mushrooms, flour, tomato purée/paste, red wine, stock, redcurrant jelly, thyme, bay leaves and some seasoning into a stewing pot (or a pan with a lid) stir, cover with the lid and cook in the preheated oven for 90 minutes. Every 20 minutes or so, take it out and give it a stir; everything will cook really easily and the mixture will start to thicken. Just make sure the flour hasn't stuck to the side or formed an unintentional dumpling – if it has, break it up with a spoon.

On a flour-dusted work surface roll the pastry out to a thickness of 5 mm/¼ inch using a floured rolling pin. Cut out 8 circles or 1 large circle large enough to cover the base and sides of your pie dish(es) and place them into your pie dish(es). Make sure there's enough pastry left over to make the lid(s).

Remove the filling from the oven, but leave the oven on. Remove the sprig of thyme and bay leaves from the mixture and divide the filling between the pastry-lined pie dish(es).

Use the rest of the pastry to make the lid(s) and place these on top of the pie(s), using a little beaten egg or milk to stick the edges to the lid(s), crimping the pastry together with your fingers.

Brush the remaining beaten egg or milk over the top and use a sharp knife or skewer to make one or two little holes in the middle of the lid(s).

Cook the mini pies in the oven for 25 minutes (or 45 minutes for a large pie), until the pastry is cooked and browning.

It's a lovely rich recipe with the meat and red wine, so serve with some greens or salad, or serve the mini pies on their own as luxurious canapés.

ENTERTAINING

PEPPERED VENISON AND PRUNE TERRINE

This terrine is rich and filling. Follow with a light main if serving as an appetizer or serve as a meal in itself with seasonal roast vegetables or a lightly dressed salad as accompaniments. It's perfect for portioning into lunches, too.

a 600-g/1¼-lb. piece of boneless venison (steak or loin)

2 teaspoons olive oil, plus extra for greasing

1–2 bay leaves

2 tablespoons butter, at room temperature

1 garlic clove, crushed

1 egg, beaten

3½ tablespoons double/heavy cream

1 teaspoon wholegrain mustard

1 tablespoon brandy

10 dried, stoned/pitted prunes, roughly chopped

1 teaspoon fresh thyme leaves

1 teaspoon freshly chopped tarragon

6–8 rashers/slices smoked streaky/fatty bacon

salt and black pepper, to season

toasted and buttered ciabatta and dressed mixed salad leaves, to serve

a 20 x 10-cm/9 x 4-in. loaf pan, greased with butter

SERVES 4

Preheat the oven to 180°C (350°F) Gas 4.

Cut 200 g/7 oz. of venison off the piece, ideally widthways so it's as thin a piece as possible, cover and reserve until needed.

Secure a large piece of foil in a roasting pan or on a baking sheet. Set the larger piece of venison on the foil and rub in the olive oil using your hands. Add a few generous pinches of freshly ground black pepper, place the bay leaf/leaves on top, wrap the foil over the top to form a parcel and seal.

Transfer to the preheated oven and roast for 30 minutes.

Remove the venison from the oven, unwrap it, discard the bay leaf/leaves and shred the cooked meat. The easiest way to do this is with two forks. Keep as much of the peppered oil in the shredded meat as you can. Cover and set aside to cool.

When you are ready to bake the terrine, preheat the oven to 180°C (350°F) Gas 4.

Trim any fat off the reserved piece of raw venison and dice the flesh into very small pieces.

Combine the butter, garlic, egg, cream, mustard, brandy, prunes, thyme, tarragon and a pinch of salt in a mixing bowl and lightly beat with a wooden spoon to combine. Add the shredded, peppered venison to the bowl and mix until well combined before adding and mixing in the diced raw venison.

Lay the bacon across the width of the prepared loaf pan, leaving the ends overhanging. Leave a small gap between them so that the terrine is easier to slice when cooked. Spoon the venison mixture into the pan and press down firmly with the back of a spoon. Fold over the overhanging bacon to seal. Cover with a sheet of oiled foil, press down firmly and bake in the middle of the preheated oven for 50 minutes.

Remove the terrine from the oven and cool it as quickly as possible, either by an open window if it's cold outside or partially submerge it in a sink of cold water, making sure the water doesn't seep inside the pan, for the first 30 minutes and then transfer to the fridge. Don't serve the terrine until it has cooled completely and set.

Remove the terrine from the fridge 20 minutes before serving to bring the temperature up a little and bring out the flavours. Slice and serve with toasted ciabatta and a simply dressed salad.

PÂTÉ DE CAMPAGNE

This French classic is easy to make and ideal served as a cold appetizer or a simple yet sophisticated lunch. The recipe makes terrific use of the diced cuts of a pork shoulder if you're cutting your own (see pages 31 and 76–9). It takes a good few hours to set, so is best made the day before you intend to serve it.

2 tablespoons butter

2 tablespoons brandy

4 shallots, finely chopped

1 garlic clove, finely chopped

1 egg, beaten

4 tablespoons double/heavy cream

½ teaspoon Dijon mustard

1 teaspoon finely chopped fresh parsley

1 teaspoon finely chopped fresh tarragon

400 g/14 oz. pork loin (as lean as possible)

6 slices prosciutto

2 hard-boiled/hard-cooked eggs, peeled (optional)

salt and black pepper, to season

oatcakes, crispbread or fried green beans, to serve

a 20 x 10-cm/9 x 4-inch loaf pan, greased with butter

an ovenproof roasting pan, large enough to hold the loaf pan

SERVES 4

Preheat the oven to 180°C (350°F) Gas 4.

Melt the butter in a frying pan/skillet over a medium heat, then add the brandy. Let it come to the boil and then reduce for 1 minute.

Add the shallots and garlic to the pan. Once those have softened, remove the pan from the heat and let cool.

Combine the egg, cream, mustard, parsley and tarragon in a mixing bowl and season with salt and pepper.

Trim any remaining fat from the pork and dice it. (Note: as this recipe isn't cooked for very long in the oven, there isn't time for the fat to break down, so the leaner the meat the better.)

Add the cooled shallot mixture and juices from the pan to the other ingredients in the mixing bowl and stir to combine.

Lay the prosciutto across the width of the prepared loaf pan, leaving the ends overhanging. Leave a small gap between them so that the pâté is easier to slice when cooked. Spoon half of the pork mixture into the prepared pan and, if using the eggs, lay these on top of the mixture now.

Spoon the remainder of the pork mixture on top and fold over the overhanging prosciutto to seal. Cover tightly with oiled kitchen foil.

Put the loaf pan inside the roasting pan and carefully pour about 2.5 cm/1 inch cold water around it. Transfer to the preheated oven and cook for 1 hour, until the meat is firm to the touch. Don't worry if there is liquid around the edge of the pâté or melted butter on the top, as this will set as it cools.

Leave the pâté to cool to the touch before moving to the fridge to cool completely and set – this will take a few hours so, if possible, leave it overnight.

Remove the pâté from the fridge 20 minutes before serving to bring the temperature up a little and bring out the flavours. Slice and serve with oatcakes or crispbread, or try a slice of it on a bed of fried green beans for a warm dish.

CHICKEN LIVER PÂTÉ

I'm in the habit of grabbing lunch on the go. I eventually realized that a chunk of cheese and some bread wasn't keeping me going through the afternoon and it wasn't particularly interesting or memorable to eat. I now find a pâté of any sort is a good option for me, as it's nutritious as well as being utterly delicious. I usually enjoy this recipe spread on some freshly made wholemeal/whole-wheat toast.

45 g/3 tablespoons butter

2 shallots, finely chopped

1 garlic clove, chopped

75 g/3 oz. rindless pork belly, diced

200 g/7 oz. chicken livers, chopped

1 teaspoon freshly chopped thyme, plus a few leaves to garnish

1 tablespoon brandy

1 bay leaf

freshly squeezed lemon juice, to taste

black and pink peppercorns, to garnish (optional)

salt and black pepper, to season

wholemeal/whole-wheat toast, to serve

4 x 150-ml/5-oz. capacity ramekins or similar small ovenproof dishes

SERVES 4

Melt half the butter in a frying pan/skillet set over a medium heat. Add the shallots and garlic and fry for 1 minute.

Add the pork belly, chicken livers, thyme, brandy and a pinch each of salt and pepper, and stir well.

Add the bay leaf to the mixture. Cook for 10 minutes, stirring, until everything is browned and the chicken livers and pork are cooked through.

Remove the pan from the heat and leave to cool until the mixture is warm but not hot.

Remove and discard the bay leaf and then transfer the mixture to a food processor (don't wash the pan just yet, you'll use it again). Add a squeeze of lemon juice to the mixture and whizz until blended. It's up to you how smooth you want it. I like it quite smooth, but you can keep it coarse by stopping just as the mixture starts to stick to the sides of the processor.

Spoon the mixture into the ramekins, leaving about 5 mm/¼ inch at the top.

Melt the rest of the butter in the original frying pan/skillet set over a medium heat, until it starts to bubble. Remove from the heat and carefully pour over the top of each ramekin of pâté. Decorate with a sprinkling of thyme leaves and some black and pink peppercorns, if using.

Transfer the ramekins to the fridge and allow at least 1 hour for the butter to set before serving with wholemeal/whole-wheat toast. The pâté will keep for up to 9 days in the fridge if the seal isunbroken. Eat within 3 days if you break the butter.

You can also freeze the pâté in the ramekins for up to 3 months (before sealing with butter) by wrapping each one in clingfilm/plastic wrap. If you do this, it's best to defrost them in the fridge slowly overnight before serving rather than with any heat or microwaving. You can still pour melted butter on top after defrosting, or just enjoy them without.

GAME RILLETTES

A traditional way of preserving meat in fat, rillettes are a delicious alternative to a heartier terrine and one of my favourite ways to enjoy game. It really celebrates the flavours as well as extending the shelf-life and tenderizing the meat. I've tried this recipe with pheasant, duck, pigeon and rabbit and it works really well for each.

200 g/7 oz. boneless game meat of your choice (see recipe introduction), diced

100 g/3½ oz. pork belly (this is optional but especially recommended for pigeon and rabbit, as they're more lean)

1 tablespoon salt (preferably sea salt flakes or crystals)

25 g/2 tablespoons butter

1 garlic clove, finely chopped

1 bay leaf

1 sprig fresh rosemary

1 teaspoon finely chopped fresh parsley

100 ml/⅓ cup white wine

100 ml/⅓ cup White or Brown Chicken Stock (see page 36), or made from a stock cube

freshly squeezed juice of 1 lemon (if using duck or pigeon, use juice of ½ lemon plus 1 orange instead), plus extra to season

black pepper, to season

crusty baguette and butter, to serve

2 x 150-ml/5-oz. capacity ramekins or similar small ovenproof dishes

SERVES 2

Put the diced game and pork belly in a mixing bowl and add the salt. Massage the salt into the meats really well then cover and leave for a minimum of 2 hours to allow the salt to break down the proteins and start to soften the meat.

Drain away the resulting liquid, rinse the meat and dry with paper towels.

Heat the butter in a frying pan/skillet over a medium heat and brown the meat for 5 minutes.

Add the garlic, herbs, white wine and stock to the pan. Bring to the boil and then reduce the heat to a gentle simmer, cover the pan with a lid and leave for 1½ hours. (Note: for rabbit and pigeon, check the pan after 1 hour. If you can shred the meat at this stage, remove it from the heat – you don't want it to be dry.)

Remove the pan from the heat, add the lemon juice (and orange juice, if using) and stir. Discard the bay leaf and rosemary sprig and leave to cool.

Once it's cold enough to handle, use your fingers to tear up the meats. You can use two forks for this but I find fingers are best.

Taste and adjust the seasoning to taste with black pepper and lemon juice. Spoon the meat into the ramekins and serve warm with slices of crusty baguette and butter, or keep it for another time.

If sealed with butter (see page 143), it will keep in the fridge for up to 9 days. Remove the rillettes from the fridge 30 minutes before serving to bring out the flavours.

You can also freeze the rillettes in the ramekins for up to 3 months (before sealing with butter) by wrapping each one in clingfilm/plastic wrap. If you do this, it's best to defrost them in the fridge slowly overnight before serving rather than with any heat or microwaving. You can still pour melted butter on top after defrosting, or just enjoy them without.

ROAST MARROW BUTTER WITH LEMON, PARSLEY AND CAPER OATCAKES

This is ideal served as a canapé for a drinks party or a hearty appetizer if you're following it with a lighter main dish, as the marrow is lovely and rich, like a pâté. I have paired the recipe with the zesty lemon, parsley and caper oatcakes to balance the buttery richness of the marrow topping, and it works brilliantly.

6 pieces veal or lamb marrow bone, each about 5 cm/2 inches long

20 g/1½ tablespoons butter

1 tablespoon capers, finely chopped, plus a few extra to garnish

1 teaspoon finely chopped fresh parsley

freshly squeezed juice of ½ lemon

LEMON, PARSLEY AND CAPER OATCAKES

50 g/½ cup old-fashioned rolled oats

25 g/3 tablespoons plain/all-purpose flour

20 g/1½ tablespoons butter (at room temperature)

a pinch of baking powder

finely grated zest and freshly squeezed juice of ½ lemon

1 tablespoon freshly chopped parsley

2 teaspoons capers, finely chopped

a pinch each of salt and black pepper

milk, for glazing

a 4-cm/1½-inch round fluted cookie cutter

a large baking sheet, lined with baking parchment

SERVES 4

Preheat the oven to 180°C (350°F) Gas 4.

Cover a roasting pan with kitchen foil (to catch any of the marrow that may melt out of the bones) and arrange the bones on top. Stand them up if the shape will allow you to do so.

Bake in the preheated oven for 15 minutes (no longer, to avoid melting the marrow and making it harder to scoop up – check after 10 minutes). Remove from the oven and set aside until cool enough to handle.

Melt the butter in a frying pan/skillet over a medium heat. Scoop out the roasted marrow from the bones and add it to the pan. Add the capers, parsley and a squeeze of lemon juice, and cook for 2 minutes. Spoon the mixture into a food processor and blend until smooth. Transfer to a dish or other suitable container and chill in the fridge for at least 2 hours, until just set.

While the marrow is setting, make the oatcakes. Preheat the oven to 180°C (350°F) Gas 4.

Put the oats, flour, butter, baking powder, lemon zest and juice, parsley and capers in a bowl and the salt and pepper. Rub in the butter with your fingertips until the mixture is flaky. Add a few drops of water to the mixture just to soften it enough to shape it into a ball. Lightly flour the work surface and use a rolling pin to roll out the oat mixture as you would pastry dough.

Using the cutter, stamp out rounds and arrange them on the prepared baking sheet. Bring the scraps together and re-roll to get as many oatcakes from the mixture as possible. Brush with a little milk. Bake in the preheated oven for 15 minutes, until firm. Transfer the oatcakes to a plate or cooling rack. (Tip: if you want to cool and serve the oatcakes straightaway, chill a plate in the fridge before you start and transfer the oatcakes to it to speed up the cooling time.)

Spread each oatcake with some chilled marrow butter and finish with a sprinkling of chopped capers and a squeeze of lemon juice. I like to pair these with a crisp, cool white wine such as a Pouilly Fuissé to cut through the richness of the marrow.

CHICKEN DRUMSTICK CROQUETTES

These hot and crispy croquettes are a clever way of using up the drumstick and wing meat from a chicken. Serve with a pot of sour cream on the side for dipping.

2 skinless* chicken drumsticks and 2 wings

½ white onion, finely chopped

1 teaspoon smoked paprika

a pinch of chilli/chili powder (or ½ a fresh chilli/chile, finely chopped)

1 tablespoon olive oil

salt and black pepper, to season

100 g/3½ oz. chorizo, diced

50 g/3½ tablespoons butter

190 g/1½ cups plus 1 tablespoon plain/all purpose flour

300 ml/1¼ cups milk

2 eggs, beaten

75 g/1½ cups dried breadcrumbs

300 ml/1¼ cups sunflower oil

tomato ketchup and sour-cream dip of your choice, to serve (optional)

MAKES 8

* If cooking in the US where skinless wings and drumsticks are not available, you can skin the meat after cooking or substitute boneless, skinless thighs, if preferred

Preheat the oven to 180°C (350°F) Gas 4.

Put the drumsticks and the wings in a roasting pan with the onion, paprika, chilli/chili powder and season with salt and pepper. Drizzle the olive oil over the top. Roast in the preheated oven for 30 minutes.

Meanwhile, melt the butter in a frying pan/skillet set over a medium heat. Sprinkle 140 g/1 cup plus 1 tablespoon of the flour into the pan (reserving the rest for cooking) and stir with a wooden spoon to combine and form a paste. Slowly add the milk, stirring until it's mixed in and the mixture is smooth.

Remove the pan from the heat and set aside to cool.

Once the chicken is cooked through and brown, take it out of the oven and leave until cool enough to handle.

Tear the meat off the drumstick and wing bones with your fingers and put it into a mixing bowl. Tip the cooked onions and seasoned oil from the roasting pan into the bowl and pour in the flour and butter mixture (batter). Add the chorizo and stir to combine.

Put the remaining flour (50 g/heaping ⅓ cup flour) and breadcrumbs on 2 separate plates and the eggs into a shallow bowl. Flour your hands and use them to work the chicken mixture into 8 small sausage shapes of equal size. Roll each croquette first in the flour, then in the egg and finally roll gently to coat well with the breadcrumbs.

Warm the sunflower oil into a heavy-based pan set over a medium–high heat. Meanwhile, line a large plate with paper towels.

Using metal tongs, carefully put each of the croquettes into the oil and fry for 5 minutes. Turn the croquettes over and fry for a further 5–8 minutes, until crisp and golden brown.

Serve hot with tomato ketchup and small dish of sour-cream dip on the side if liked.

HOMEMADE SCOTCH EGGS

Who doesn't love a Scotch egg? This British classic has enjoyed a revival in recent years and is surprisingly simple to make at home. They are a fun choice for entertaining too – served warm with a soft yolk middle and accompanied with some well-dressed salad leaves, they make the perfect appetizer or light lunch.

8 eggs

600 g/21 oz. really good pork mince/ground pork (see page 31 for hand-mincing/hand-cutting)

30 g/2 tablespoons tomato purée/paste

1 garlic clove, finely chopped

1 teaspoon freshly chopped parsley

1 tablespoon freshly chopped chives

½ teaspoon mustard powder

20 g/1½ tablespoons plain/all-purpose flour, plus extra for sprinkling

1.5 litres/6 cups vegetable oil

200 g/2½ cups dried breadcrumbs

salt and black pepper, to season

lemon wedges and mixed salad leaves or pickle of your choice, to serve (optional)

MAKES 6

Bring a large pan of water to the boil. Using a slotted spoon, lower 6 of the eggs into the water. Boil for 5 minutes for softer centres, 8 minutes for hard-boiled/hard-cooked eggs.

Meanwhile, put the minced/ground pork in a mixing bowl. Add the tomato purée/paste, garlic, parsley, chives and mustard powder and mix to combine. Season with salt and pepper.

Lightly flour a work surface or board. Flour your hands and use them to break the pork mixture into six pieces of equal size, roll them into balls and then flatten them on the surface with the heel of your hand to make round patties. These need to be big enough to fold around the whole eggs.

Remove the boiled eggs from the water. Drop them into a bowl of cold water. When they are cool enough to handle, peel off the shells.

Pour the vegetable oil into a heavy-based pan and warm over a medium–high heat. Meanwhile, line a large plate with paper towels.

Put each peeled egg in the middle of a pork patty, then fold the patty around the egg, using your fingers to move and squeeze the pork around the egg until it is completely sealed inside.

Put the flour and breadcrumbs on separate plates. Beat the remaining 2 eggs and pour into a shallow bowl. Roll each pork ball first in the flour, then roll in the beaten egg and finally roll gently to coat with the breadcrumbs.

Using metal tongs, carefully put two of the balls into the hot oil and deep-fry for 15 minutes, until crisp and golden brown. Remove each ball from the oil and transfer to the paper-towel-lined plate to drain. Repeat with the remaining Scotch eggs.

Serve warm with a wedge of lemon for squeezing and mixed salad leaves. Alternatively, chill and enjoy as a cold cut with pickles.

The Scotch eggs will keep in the fridge for up to 1 week and should be stored in an airtight container.

BEEF CARPACCIO WITH ROCKET AND PARMESAN SALAD

This recipe celebrates beef fillet/tenderloin as does the Flash Fillet Roast on page 169. Because we're serving it almost raw here you get a very different but equally fantastic eating experience. If you're cutting your own fillet/tenderloin, the middle section is best for Beef Wellington (see page 170) or fillet steaks but here, the tail end works well. It takes up to seven days to prepare, so do plan ahead!

a 800-g/1¾-lb. piece of beef fillet/tenderloin (allow about 200 g/7 oz. per person)

1 tablespoon olive oil

about 100 g/3 cups wild rocket/arugula

80 g/3 oz. Parmesan cheese, shaved

extra virgin olive oil, to drizzle

salt and black pepper, to season

a 20-cm/8-inch square piece of muslin/cheesecloth or cotton

kitchen twine

SERVES 4

The real trick to carpaccio is to get the piece of beef as dry as possible before preparing it. You will be searing the outside of the meat, so don't worry about hanging it for a couple of days beforehand to help it dry (see Note on page 153 about serving rare beef).

Wrap the piece of beef in the muslin/cheesecloth and secure with twine. Suspend it by tying it to a shelf in your fridge. To do this, pull out your fridge shelf so you can tie the twine around the back and tighten to lift the meat into the air underneath. Ideally you should leave it for at least 2–3 days (and up to 4 days) but even a few hours of this will help the result if you don't have more time available.

When you are ready to serve, remove the beef from the fridge, unwrap it and discard the muslin/cheesecloth and twine.

Heat the olive oil over a medium–high heat in a heavy-based frying pan/skillet until it bubbles.

Add a pinch of salt to the pan then lift the beef into the pan and sear it by rolling it in the hot oil, just a few seconds on each side, but ensuring that the heat has made contact with the entire surface of the meat.

Remove from the pan and transfer to a board. Using a very sharp knife, slice it as thinly as possible.

Put a few slices of carpaccio on each serving plate and drop a handful of rocket/arugula on top. Scatter with some Parmesan shavings, add a crack of black pepper and a drizzle of a good fruity olive oil. Serve immediately.

STEAK TARTARE

Use the best-quality meat you can find to get the most out of this classic French dish made with raw beef. And if you are worried about food safety, let me reassure you. This recipe requires 350 g/¾ lb. of beef, but you'll only in fact be eating around 200 g/7 oz. of it and this will be the meat at the centre of the piece. You're going to mix it with the other ingredients and enjoy it straightaway, before any bacteria has a chance to make contact with it, let alone contaminate it. It is only contact with the air that carries the bacteria that will spoil perishable foods. What you trim off won't be wasted either. It will be fresh for a few more days, ideal to use in a stir fry, and once cooked, any bacteria will have been killed. It's a refreshing and sophisticated plate and well worth trying if you've not done so before.

40 g/⅓ cup very finely diced red onion

1 gherkin/pickle or 4 small cornichons, finely diced

2 teaspoons capers, crushed or finely chopped

½ garlic clove, finely chopped (optional)

1 teaspoon tomato purée/paste

5–6 drops Tabasco (or other hot pepper sauce), to taste

2 teaspoons Worcestershire sauce

1 teaspoon finely chopped fresh parsley

350 g/¾ lb. beef, ideally fillet/tenderloin or trimmed sirloin

1 very fresh egg (optional)

salt and black pepper

snipped chives, to garnish

horseradish, to serve

SERVES 1

First wash your hands in hot water with plenty of soap. Also wash a chopping board, mixing bowl, sharp knife and serving plate really thoroughly in piping hot water and washing liquid and dry with a clean kitchen cloth.

Put the onion, gherkin, capers, garlic (if using), tomato purée/paste, Tabasco, Worcestershire sauce and parsley in a mixing bowl and stir to combine. Set aside.

Using the knife, cut thin strips off the beef, from all around the edge of the piece of meat and set aside (see recipe introduction). Then chop the remaining meat from the centre into tiny pieces, aiming to get it as close to mince/ground meat in appearance as you can.

Tip the beef into the mixing bowl with the other ingredients and mix really well, using your hands to rub flavour into the meat so it is seasoned and tender. Check the seasoning and add salt, pepper and more Tabasco to taste.

Spoon the mixture directly onto a serving plate. Press down with your thumb to make an indentation in the middle. Crack and separate the egg and drop the yolk only into the dent. Add a spoonful of horseradish to the side, grind a little black pepper over the top, sprinkle with chives and serve immediately.

POACHED WHOLE BALLOTINE CHICKEN WITH BASIL PESTO

Ballotine is a French term for a boned, stuffed and poached piece of poultry, from the word '*balle*' meaning 'a package of goods'. The description is now sometimes used to refer to other stuffed meat joints like lamb and pork but, staying true to the traditional recipe, we're going to use chicken here. Chilled leftovers (known as '*galantine*', which refers to poached, chilled and sliced meat) can be used to make a delicious sandwich. Split and butter a soft, oaty wholemeal/whole-wheat roll, add slices of the ballotine, some goat's cheese, sun-blush tomatoes and lettuce.

1 boned*, whole, free-range chicken (weighing about 2 kg/4½ lbs.)

braised red cabbage and Fancy Mashed Potatoes (see page 233), to serve (optional)

BASIL PESTO

50 g/scant ½ cup pine nuts

12–15 large fresh basil leaves

2 garlic cloves

50 ml/3½ tablespoons extra virgin olive oil

60 g/1 cup finely grated fresh Parmesan cheese

freshly squeezed lemon juice

salt and black pepper, to season

butchers' string or kitchen twine (optional)

SERVES 6–8

* If you're cutting your own whole chicken, see page 86 for instructions on how to debone

To make the pesto, heat a small frying pan/skillet without oil and dry-fry the pine nuts for 2–3 minutes until brown and lightly toasted. Watch the pan closely, as they can quickly catch and burn. Remove the pan from the heat and let cool.

Tip the cooled pine nuts into a food processor and add the basil and garlic. Season with salt and pepper.

Whizz the ingredients, whilst slowly adding the olive oil so it blends in a little at a time. Add the Parmesan and a little lemon juice and blend until smooth.

Transfer the pesto into a small dish (a rubber spatula is helpful for scraping around the bowl of the food processor to get it all out). Check the seasoning and add more salt and pepper to taste. Use your hands to rub the pesto all around the inside of the boneless chicken. Make sure you coat as much of the surface as you can, getting into all the nooks.

Next, roll the bird up tightly. Use the butchers' string method on page 30 to roll it and then wrap in clingfilm/plastic wrap. Alternatively you can wrap it tightly in clingfilm/plastic wrap without tying it, which will still work okay. Wrap it securely in kitchen foil.

Fill a large lidded pan with water (to match the height of the wrapped bird; it doesn't need to cover it) and bring just to the boil.

Carefully lower the foil-covered parcel into the water and simmer over a low heat for 35 minutes, until poached. Be careful not to let the water boil around it, as the chicken will dry out if it's too hot.

Remove the parcel from the water and leave to rest in the foil for 10 minutes before unwrapping and transferring to a board or plate. Carve into slices straight away and serve hot with red cabbage and fancy mashed potatoes, if liked, or chill to eat cold.

DUCK, VENISON AND HALLOUMI SKEWERS

Duck and venison are often used in recipes that combine sweet and savoury flavours. Here, a delightfully rich, fruity marinade prepares these skewers for grilling or barbecuing.

2 tablespoons olive oil

1 tablespoon Cointreau (or other orange-flavoured liquor)

2 teaspoons soft/light brown sugar

1 red onion, finely chopped

2 teaspoons finely chopped fresh flat-leaf parsley, plus extra to garnish

a 400-g/14-oz. venison loin, trimmed

1 boneless duck breast, skin on

200 g/7 oz. halloumi (a semi-hard, unripened, brined cheese from Cyprus) or similar

6 fresh plums, halved and stoned/pitted

salt and black pepper, to season

lime wedges, to serve

6 stainless steel or wooden skewers (soak wooden skewers in water before use to prevent them from burning)

MAKES 6

To prepare the marinade, combine the olive oil, Cointreau, sugar, red onion and parsley in a small bowl, season with salt and pepper and mix well.

Cut the venison and duck into chunks of equal size. Keep the skin on the duck at this stage. You can remove it later when you come to assemble the skewers, but as the venison and the duck look very similar after marinating, leaving the skin on will help you tell them apart and distribute the meats evenly along the skewers.

Transfer the marinade to a sealable bag or a bowl suitable for marinating. Add the duck and venison to the bag or bowl and shake or toss to coat the meats really well with the marinade. Seal the bag or cover the bowl with clingfilm/plastic wrap. Put in the fridge and chill for at least 1 hour.

Cut the halloumi into pieces the same size as the chunks of meat. Remove the meats from the marinade (reserving the marinade). Thread the marinaded meats, halloumi cubes and plum halves alternately on the skewers (aiming for 2–3 pieces of each on a single skewer).

Brush, spoon or rub the reserved marinade over the skewers.

These can be cooked by a number of methods. You can grill them over a preheated charcoal or gas barbecue, on the stovetop in a very hot ridged griddle pan/skillet, turning every minute. Or lastly, under a preheated grill/broiler for about 15 minutes, turning them a couple of times. (It's advisable to line the grill pan with foil to catch the juices.)

Scatter over some chopped flat-leaf parsley and serve hot with wedges of lime for squeezing (which just sharpens and balances the rich sweetness of the flavours).

PHEASANT AND GAMMON PIE

Like a lot of game, pheasant is delicious when paired with sweet and salty flavours, so the addition of gammon and cranberries here is a winner. This is a brilliant way to make use of any leftover Glazed Roast Gammon (see page 227).

2 tablespoons olive oil

1 red onion, diced

1 leek, split lengthways, rinsed and thinly sliced

1 garlic clove, chopped

600 g/21 oz. boneless pheasant, diced

a handful of fresh or frozen cranberries

1 teaspoon soft brown sugar

a handful of roughly chopped fresh flat-leaf parsley

20 g/2⅓ tablespoons plain/all-purpose flour

100 ml/⅓ cup white wine

150 ml/⅔ cup White or Brown Chicken Stock (see page 36)

150 ml/⅔ cup double/heavy cream

salt and black pepper, to season

200–300 g/7–10½ oz. cooked gammon, bacon or ham, diced

Fancy Mashed Potatoes (see page 233) and steamed vegetables, to serve

PASTRY

200 g/1½ cups plain/all-purpose flour, plus extra for sprinkling

100 g/7 tablespoons butter, at room temperature, plus a little extra for greasing

1–2 teaspoons finely chopped fresh tarragon (optional)

1 egg, beaten

a 25–30-cm/9¾–12-inch deep pie dish

a pie funnel (optional)

SERVES 4

Heat the oil in a large frying pan/skillet and add the onion, leek and garlic. Gently sauté until soft and translucent.

Add the pheasant to the pan and cook for 4–5 minutes over a medium heat, until browned.

Add the cranberries, sugar and parsley, season with salt and pepper and stir well to mix. Sprinkle the flour over the top and wait for it to take on colour, then stir it in.

Pour the white wine and stock into the pan, increase the heat and bring the mixture to the boil. Add the cream, bring back to boil, then reduce the heat to a simmer. Add the gammon and cook for 15 minutes.

Meanwhile preheat the oven to 180°C (350°F) Gas 4.

To make the pastry, put the flour in a mixing bowl and add the butter. Rub the butter into the flour using your fingertips. Add the tarragon, if using, and a pinch of salt and then 3–4 tablespoons of cold water, 1 tablespoon at a time. Use your hands to bring the dough together into a ball.

Lightly dust a work surface with flour. Use a rolling pin to roll out the dough to a size sufficient to generously cover your pie dish. Use your finger to run butter around the top 2 cm/¾ inch outside edge of the pie dish. If you have a pie funnel, put this in the centre of the dish. (This enables the steam to escape and thus keeps the filling thick and the pastry crisp.)

Pour the filling mixture into the pie dish/pan. Lift up the pastry and place it on the top of the filling. Use a sharp knife to cut a small cross in the centre of the pastry lid (directly on top of the pie funnel, if using). Trim the edges or let them overhang, as preferred, and press around the edge to seal it to the sides of the dish.

Using a pastry brush, glaze the top of the pie with the beaten egg. Transfer the dish to a baking sheet to catch any escaping filling and bake in the preheated oven for 30–40 minutes, until the top is golden brown and crisp.

Serve hot with mashed potatoes and a steamed vegetable, such as green beans or broccoli, if liked.

RABBIT AND SEAFOOD PAELLA

What most people know as a Spanish paella (and what is offered in restaurants all over Spain) is a chicken and seafood rice dish. But in some regions of Spain rice dishes featuring rabbit are more commonplace and include hunter's rice (rich with foraged mushrooms) like Valencian paella, which includes rabbit as well as chicken. I have found that the oakier, darker meat of rabbit works well with cured meats, so my recipe pairs it with chorizo and bacon as well as seafood, with delicious results.

1 tablespoon olive oil

10 g/2 teaspoons butter

1 red onion, finely chopped

2–3 spring onions/scallions, chopped

2 garlic cloves, finely chopped

1 fresh red chilli/chile, deseeded and finely chopped

120 g/¼ lb. rabbit meat, diced

100 g/3½ oz streaky/fatty bacon, chopped

100 g/3½ oz. chorizo, diced

1 red (bell) pepper, diced

80 g/¾ cup peeled raw prawns/shrimp

4–6 raw scallops

100 ml/⅓ cup plus 1 tablespoon white wine

2 tablespoons frozen peas

1–2 teaspoons smoked Spanish paprika (pimentón)

3–4 saffron strands, ground or 1 teaspoon ground saffron

80 ml/⅓ cup White or Brown Chicken Stock (see page 36) or made from a stock cube

150 g/¾ cup short-grain rice (such as Arborio or Calasparra)

1 tablespoon chopped fresh flat-leaf parsley

salt and black pepper, to taste

sour cream (optional) and lemon wedges, to serve

SERVES 2

Heat the oil and butter in a large frying pan/skillet set over moderate heat. Add the onion and spring onions/scallions and fry for 2 minutes. Add the garlic and fresh chilli/chile to the pan and fry for a further 1 minute or so, until the onions are soft and browning.

Add the rabbit, bacon and chorizo to the pan and fry over medium heat for 8–9 minutes, until the rabbit is golden brown.

Add the red (bell) pepper, prawns/shrimp and scallops to the pan and cook, stirring for 4–5 minutes.

Add the peas, paprika and saffron to the pan and stir.

Pour the white wine and chicken stock into the pan, stir well, and increase the heat to bring the liquid to the boil.

Once boiling, tip in the rice, reduce the heat and simmer, uncovered and stirring occasionally, for 20 minutes, or until the rice is soft and 'al dente' to the bite. (If the paella starts to dry and catch on the bottom of the pan, just add a little more stock or water and stir).

Taste and add salt and pepper to taste, sprinkle with parsley and serve straight away with sour cream on the side (if using) and lemon wedges for squeezing.

LAMB KLEFTIKO WITH SPICED YOGURT

Kleftiko is one of the most popular Greek dishes. Lamb is seasoned with rosemary, garlic and lemon, and slow-roasted with potatoes in a sealed earthenware pot, but it can be cooked at home in a paper parcel with equally delicious results.

6 garlic cloves

finely grated zest and juice of 1 lemon

2 tablespoons fresh oregano leaves, chopped

½ teaspoon ground cinnamon

¼ teaspoon ground nutmeg

¼ teaspoon mustard powder

3 tablespoons olive oil

a 2-kg/3½-lbs. leg of lamb, bone in

1 kg/2¼ lbs. waxy potatoes, peeled and quartered

2 sprigs fresh rosemary

3 bay leaves

salt and black pepper, to season

SPICED YOGURT

2 fresh red chillies/chiles, deseeded

1 garlic clove, crushed

1 tablespoon each of chopped fresh flat-leaf parsley, chives and coriander/cilantro

2–3 fresh mint leaves

½ teaspoon ground cumin

200 ml/¾ cup natural/plain Greek yogurt

SERVES 6

Preheat the oven to 180°C (350°F) Gas 4.

With their skins still on, flatten the garlic cloves with the side of a knife. Put them on a baking sheet and roast in the preheated oven for 20 minutes.

Put the lemon zest and juice in a small bowl with the oregano, cinnamon, nutmeg, mustard powder and half of the olive oil. Add a pinch each of salt and pepper and whisk with a fork to combine.

Remove the garlic cloves from the oven and, once cool enough to handle, squeeze out the roasted soft centre and discard the skins.

Using a sharp knife, score lines across the outer surface of the lamb and rub the garlic cloves and then the lemon and herb mixture into the lines and coat the outside.

Put a large sheet of baking parchment on a roasting pan that will fit on a shelf in your fridge. Place the lamb leg on top. Wrap the paper tightly and then wrap the whole thing in clingfilm/plastic wrap. Transfer to the fridge for at least 1 hour or ideally overnight.

When you are ready to cook the lamb, preheat the oven to 160°C (325°F) Gas 3.

Toss the peeled potatoes in rest of the olive oil and season with salt and pepper.

Lay a large sheet of foil on a baking sheet, enough to fold right over the potatoes and the lamb leg. Remove the clingfilm/plastic wrap from the lamb and put it (still wrapped in its baking parchment) on top of the foil; open out the baking parchment.

Move the joint to the side and pop the seasoned potatoes in the bottom of the parcel. Add the sprigs of rosemary and the bay leaves and then place the joint of lamb on top. Transfer to the preheated oven. After 20 minutes of cooking time, fold the baking parchment and the foil over the top tightly and return to the oven for 2½–3 hours. Then pull out the oven shelf, carefully open out the foil and baking parchment and baste the joint with the cooking juices. Increase the heat to 200°C (400°F) Gas 6 and return to the oven for about 10 minutes. This will brown the lamb and crisp the potatoes.

To make the spiced yogurt, whizz all the ingredients except the yogurt in a food processor. Scoop out and mix with the yogurt. Serve chilled with slices of the hot lamb and the potatoes.

MARINATED LAMB STEAKS

We sell about 20 beef rump or leg steaks to every lamb rump or leg steak in our Modern Meat Shop – they just don't seem to be an obvious choice for a cut of lamb – but, especially marinated, I think they're terrific and easy to cook and eat.

This recipe is inspired by Moroccan flavourings, but you can substitute a sweet redcurrant marinade, or use the kleftiko marinade (see left) here, adding the rosemary and bay leaves to the marinading liquid. If you're cutting your own lamb leg, this is an especially easy part to extract, see pages 65–66.

2 tablespoons olive oil (or argan oil, if available), plus extra for cooking

1 teaspoon paprika

½ teaspoon cayenne pepper

1 tablespoon ground cumin

½ teaspoon whole pink or black peppercorns

2 trimmed lamb rump/leg steaks (usually 200 g/7 oz. each)

2 tablespoons of chopped fresh flat-leaf parsley, to garnish

a generous pinch of salt

TO SERVE

plain couscous

a pinch of saffron threads or 1 teaspoon ground saffron

salad of peeled and sliced orange segments and pitted/stoned black olives (optional)

SERVES 2

Start this recipe the day before you want to serve it.

Combine the olive oil, paprika, cayenne pepper, cumin and peppercorns in a bowl and add the salt. Whisk the mixture with a fork to combine.

Pour into a sealable bag or suitable container and add the steaks. Shake the bag or spoon the marinade over the meat to cover. Put in the fridge and leave to marinade overnight.

When ready to serve, prepare sufficient couscous for 2 servings according the instructions on the packet, adding the saffron to the liquid you are using, usually water or vegetable stock, as preferred. Cover and set aside until needed.

Warm a ridged griddle/grill pan (or heavy frying pan/skillet) over a high heat and add a drop of olive oil. Remove the steaks from the bag or container and reserve the marinade.

When the pan is very hot, add the steaks and sear for just 20 seconds on each side, using tongs to gently turn the meat over.

Reduce the heat and pour the reserved marinade over the steaks. Cook for a further 2 minutes on either side for medium-rare or 3–4 minutes for medium-well done.

Sprinkle with chopped parsley and serve straight away with spoonfuls of saffron couscous and a simple Moroccan-style orange and olive salad on the side, if liked.

APPLE, PLUM AND CINNAMON LAMB TAGINE

Inspired by a Belvoir fruit cordial we were served on a break during the lamb cutting section of a butchery course... I thought I'd try the combination for a type of tagine! If you're cutting your leg of lamb, this recipe is perfect for the rump/chump top meat. Just trim it and cut into 2 cm/1-inch dice.

20 g/1 tablespoon butter

800 g–1 kg/1¾–2 lbs. lamb, diced

6 small shallots, peeled and halved

4 fresh plums, peeled, stoned/pitted and quartered

1 small cooking apple, peeled, cored and diced

1 teaspoon finely chopped fresh sage

1 teaspoon ground cinnamon

2 teaspoons dark brown sugar

200 ml/⅔ cup Brown Chicken Stock (see page 36) or a chicken stock cube dissolved in 200 ml/⅔ cup boiling water

couscous, to serve

freshly chopped flat-leaf parsley, to garnish

salt and black pepper, to season

SERVES 4

Preheat the oven to 160°C (325°F) Gas 3.

Set a large lidded heatproof casserole dish on the stovetop over a medium heat. Add the butter, lamb and the shallots to the casserole and fry for 6–8 minutes until the lamb is browned, stirring often. Add the plums, apple, sage, cinnamon, sugar and stock.

Bring to the boil then reduce the heat and simmer for 5–10 minutes. Place the lid on the casserole and transfer it to the preheated oven. Cook for 2 hours, until the meat is tender and the sauce rich and sticky.

Meanwhile, prepare enough couscous for 4 servings according to the instructions on the packet.

Remove the tagine from the oven, taste and adjust the seasoning with salt and pepper.

Serve hot, spooned over a bed of couscous and sprinkled with chopped parsley.

KOREAN-STYLE BUTTERFLIED LAMB

This butterflied lamb joint is marinated in Asian flavourings ahead of cooking. It looks really impressive (and smells just as good!), so is perfect for entertaining a larger number of people. It's an easy idea for a barbecue, too, as you produce a big piece of boneless, really flavoursome meat, which is easy to carve up and tuck into. The joint needs to be marinated overnight, so start preparing the recipe the day before you intend to cook it.

1 butterflied lamb joint (see pages 65–6 for cutting your own lamb leg)

MARINADE

3 tablespoons sesame oil

3 garlic cloves, chopped

4 spring onions/scallions, roughly chopped

a 2-cm/1-inch piece of fresh ginger, peeled and chopped or 1 teaspoon ground ginger

2 tablespoons soy sauce

2 tablespoons mirin (Japanese rice wine)

1 tablespoon tomato purée/paste

1 teaspoon miso paste (optional)

½ teaspoon mustard powder

a generous pinch each of salt and black pepper

SERVES 6–8

The day before you plan to cook the joint, prepare the marinade. Put the oil, garlic, spring onions/scallions, ginger, soy sauce, mirin, tomato purée/paste and miso paste (if using) in a food processor and add a generous pinch each of salt and black pepper. Whizz until combined.

Lay the joint out flat on a clean work surface or baking sheet. Remove the marinade from the food processor using a spatula and rub it all over the meat, using your fingers to push it into every join and dip in the meat. Reserve any leftover marinade for later.

Fold the joint back up and put it into a large sealable bag or suitable container. Pour the rest of the marinade into the bag or container and seal. Transfer to the fridge and leave overnight.

The following day, take the joint out of the fridge and remove it from its marinade. You can cook it on a barbecue, on the stovetop or under the grill/broiler.

To cook on the barbecue, put the joint on the hottest part of the barbecue and cook for 3 minutes on either side. Move the meat away from the heat and cover with the lid. Cook for 8–10 minutes on either side then place it back over the hottest part for a few minutes to make it crisp before serving.

Indoors, a large enough griddle/grill pan will do the job. Heat the pan to a medium heat. Cover the main part of the joint with foil so that it doesn't char and cooks through properly, cook for 10 minutes on each side then remove the foil, increase the heat to high and cook for 8–10 minutes on either side to crisp up the surface.

Alternatively, cook it under a preheated grill/broiler. Preheat to medium and cook the joint on the middle shelf for 25 minutes, turning halfway through cooking time until it's starting to crisp on the outside. Turn the grill/broiler up to the highest setting and cook for a further 5–6 minutes on either side.

To serve, either slice from it flat or, for a bit of theatre, fold the meat back to its original shape, roll it with your utensils (it'll be too hot to handle yet), stick a meat fork through the middle to lift it to a board and then slice like a roasting joint so it falls into juicy pieces.

FLASH FILLET ROAST WITH MUSTARD SAUCE

The joy of a fillet/tenderloin is that, as the name suggests, it is so tender it is the perfect choice for serving rare or, indeed, raw as in Steak Tartare (page 153).

If you're cutting your own fillet, this is a great way to use the thinnest end, including the tail. We're only flash-roasting here, so we don't have to worry about balancing the cooking time of the different thicknesses of meat. I would go for about 200 g/7 oz. of meat per person. Start with more than you think, because you can always cut a steak off the thicker end for another time, which is better than starting with a piece that is too small for the number of you eating, and having to cook a lonely steak on the side to make up for it!

a 800-g/1¾-lbs. piece of beef fillet/tenderloin (allow about 200 g/7 oz. per person)

20 g/1½ tablespoons butter

salt and black pepper, to rub

Buttery Crushed Potatoes (see page 233), cooked spinach and greens, to serve

MUSTARD SAUCE

1 garlic clove, finely chopped

½ teaspoon Dijon mustard

1–2 tablespoons crème fraîche

SERVES 4

Preheat the oven to 200°C (400°F) Gas 6.

Take the beef and rub some salt, pepper and half the butter all over it.

Heat a frying pan/skillet with the other half of the butter over a high heat, so that it is completely hot and the butter starts to brown. Put the piece of fillet/tenderloin in the frying pan/skillet and roll it over every 5 seconds, lightly pressing on the top for each side. You need to sear the whole surface, but just the surface rather than cooking it through. Use tongs to hold it upright to sear the ends too.

Transfer the meat to a roasting pan (do not wash the frying pan/skillet yet) and cook in the hot oven for 15 minutes.

Once the meat is cooked, remove it from the oven and set it aside to rest for a few minutes while you make the sauce.

Put the same frying pan/skillet you used to cook the meat over a low heat and throw the garlic in to brown. Add the Dijon mustard and crème fraîche and stir. Keep over the heat while you slice the meat for serving.

Serve the fillet/tenderloin with the sauce. This is great with buttery crushed potatoes, some baby spinach and other greens.

BEEF WELLINGTON

This is a classic dinner party dish that, when executed perfectly, will never fail to impress your guests. Fillet/tenderloin is an expensive cut of beef, so this dish should be reserved for special occasions.

50 g/3½ tablespoons butter

salt, to season

1 kg/2 lbs. trimmed beef fillet/tenderloin (ask for an even cut from the middle)

1 garlic clove, finely chopped

3 shallots, finely chopped

100 g/3½ oz. button/white mushrooms, finely chopped

40 g/1½ oz. lamb's liver, finely diced

1 teaspoon Dijon mustard

4 tablespoons tomato purée/paste

a pinch of freshly chopped thyme

a pinch of freshly chopped parsley

salad and steamed new potatoes, to serve (optional)

PASTRY

150 g/⅔ cup butter

325 g/scant 2½ cups plain/all-purpose flour, plus extra for dusting

1–2 tablespoons cold water

salt and black pepper

1 egg, beaten

SERVES 4

Take the butter out of the fridge for at least 20 minutes in advance to soften a little.

Heat a frying pan/skillet with a little of the butter and a sprinkle of salt. Sear the piece of fillet/tenderloin for just a minute, rolling it constantly to brown the whole surface and use tongs to hold it upright to sear the ends too. Remove and set on a plate to cool.

In the same pan, add the rest of the butter to fry the chopped garlic, shallots, mushrooms, liver, mustard, tomato purée/paste, thyme and parsley. Add some salt and pepper and fry until nice and soft – the more finely the shallots and mushrooms are chopped the better, so that it becomes more like paté. Remove from the heat.

To make the pastry, rub the butter, flour and a pinch of salt together with your fingertips until the mixture resembles breadcrumbs. Add the cold water, a tablespoonful at a time, until you can combine the crumbled mixture into a ball of pastry. Don't add too much water.

Sprinkle some flour on a surface and roll out three-quarters of the pastry into a large square; try to keep it to 5 mm/¼ inch thick and as even as possible. At this stage, lift the pastry square onto a piece of baking parchment so that it's easier to transfer to the baking sheet later. Spread the mushroom mixture over three-quarters of the pastry, leaving the top quarter uncoated.

Roll the remaining pastry out to the same thickness as before and trim lengths 5 mm/¼ inch wide. Cut half of these in half.

Preheat the oven to 170°C (325°F) Gas 3.

Place the seared fillet/tenderloin across the top of the coated area and fold over the pastry so as much of the meat is covered with the mushroom mixture as possible. Brush a little of the beaten egg along the top and fold the uncoated quarter of pastry over so it's wrapped like a parcel. Smudge down the join of the pastry with your fingertips to help it stick across the top. Pinch together the ends to seal as well. Brush the rest of the beaten egg over the top of the pastry then lay the long strips of trimmed pastry over the top. Weave the shorter lengths beneath these and glaze.

Lift the baking parchment onto a baking sheet and place in the oven on the middle shelf. Roast for 45 minutes, until the pastry is browned and cooked. Let stand for 10 minutes before serving.

OSSO BUCCO

Italian for 'bone with a hole', osso bucco is named after the cross-cut veal shin/shank from which it is made. The emphasis is on the flavour the cut has from being attached to the bone and from its delicious marrow. Veal is excellent for this recipe because the bone and marrow are still young and soft; if you did this with a beef shin, you would have lovely soft meat from the slow-cooking but not nearly as much of the rich flavour in the sauce from the bone and marrow.

2 pieces of veal shin/shank, about 4-cm/1¾-inches thick

1 tablespoon plain/all-purpose flour

30 g/2 tablespoons butter

1 white onion, chopped

2 garlic cloves

finely grated zest of ½ lemon

4 teaspoons tomato purée/paste

100 g/3¾ oz. drained canned chopped tomatoes or 1 fresh beef/beefsteak tomato, deseeded and chopped

a pinch of freshly chopped sage

a pinch of freshly chopped basil

80 g/1¼ cups chopped mushrooms, optional

200 ml/scant 1 cup white wine

200 ml/scant 1 cup White or Brown Chicken Stock (see page 36)

salt and pepper, to season

saffron rice, to serve

SERVES 2

Coat the pieces of veal shin/shank in the flour. Heat half the butter in a pan over a medium heat and brown the coated meat for 1 minute on either side. Remove the meat pieces and set aside.

In the same pan, add a the rest of the butter and fry the onion and garlic over a high heat for 5–6 minutes, until softened.

Add the lemon zest, tomato purée/paste, chopped tomatoes, sage, basil, mushrooms, if using, and some salt and pepper. Give it a stir and then pour over the wine and stock.

Bring to the boil, then reduce the heat to a low simmer. Lift the veal pieces back into the sauce and turn them over a couple of times to coat. Put a lid half over the top of the pan and leave to cook over a low heat for 1 hour.

You want the sauce to darken and go sticky. If it's still light after an hour, remove the lid, increase the heat and cook until the sauce thickens a little. Serve on saffron rice.

VEAL INVOLTINI

Whereas the Osso Bucco (opposite) really needs to be made with veal, this recipe works well when made with beef, too; some lean topside/top round, really flattened with a tenderizer/pounded thin is lovely and cooks just as well as veal. It's an impressive-sounding dinner party main course, but it is actually quite simple to make: quick and fresh when you have guests coming for lunch on a warm summer's day.

4–6 pieces of tenderized/thinly pounded veal loin or beef topside/top rump, about 8 cm/ 3½ inches long and 4 cm/ 1¾ inches wide

a small handful of freshly chopped basil

a small handful of freshly chopped parsley

4–6 slices of prosciutto

4–6 anchovy fillets

4–6 slices of Parmesan cheese

3 tablespoons olive oil

crusty bread or Foolproof Roasties (see page 216), to serve (optional)

TOMATO SAUCE

3 tablespoons olive oil

2 beef/beefsteak tomatoes, chopped

1 red onion, diced

1 garlic clove

1 tablespoon red wine vinegar

salt and black pepper, to season

SERVES 2

Start by making the tomato sauce. Heat the olive oil in a pan and fry the tomatoes, onion, garlic, red wine vinegar and some seasoning lightly for a few minutes – you want to keep a little crunch, as this should be more like a hot salsa than a smooth sauce.

Meanwhile, take one piece of the meat at a time. Sprinkle a little of the basil and parsley on the top and season with salt and pepper

Lay a prosciutto slice flat on a surface, and then top with an anchovy fillet, a slice of Parmesan and a piece of veal. Roll up the meat and use a cocktail stick/toothpick to hold the join of the meat together. (Don't let the fold come too far back around the rolled piece or it will take too long to cook through the double layer of meat. Aim for a crossover of about 2.5 cm/1 inch at the join and trim the rest of the meat away.) Repeat with the remaining ingredients to make 4–6 rolls.

Heat the olive oil in another pan over a medium heat and fry the involtini for 8–10 minutes, turning often to ensure even cooking.

Add the tomato sauce and a little more seasoning to taste and then reduce the heat to a simmer. Cook for 10 minutes, until the veal is cooked through.

Serve just as they are with some crusty bread for a light lunch or with some herby foolproof roasties for a fuller meal. A glass of Chianti will complete the Italian spread!

LONG AND SLOW

COQ AU VIN

Some of my favourite meat dishes were once considered to be a 'poor man's' meal and often they used an abundance of seasonings to help to disguise cheaper meats or so-called 'lesser' cuts. In fact, they actually celebrate the flavours and combinations that work amazingly with good meat. They're often not difficult to make, and the meat will collapse off the bone or dissolve in your mouth. This recipe still takes a little time in the oven but it's a simpler approach with fewer stages than are sometimes traditionally involved. Serve with rice for a heartier meal.

1 whole jointed chicken (see pages 85–86), or 2 thighs, 2 drumsticks and 2 breasts

250 ml/1 cup red wine

3 bay leaves

2 garlic cloves

3 tablespoons olive oil

45 g/3 tablespoons butter

salt and black pepper, to season

75 g/generous 1 cup chopped mushrooms

6 shallots, chopped

85 g/3 oz. pancetta, diced

2 tablespoons plain/all-purpose flour

400 ml/1²/₃ White Chicken Stock (see page 36)

freshly squeezed juice of ½ lemon

green beans, to serve

SERVES 4

Keep the thighs and drumsticks on the bone but debone the breast joint and cut it into smaller thirds. I don't use the wings in this recipe as they can be a bit fiddly to debone before serving so cover and refrigerate to cook at another time.

Put the chicken in a bowl or sandwich bag with the red wine, bay leaves, chopped garlic and 1 tablespoon of the olive oil. Seal the bag or cover the bowl and leave in the fridge to marinate for at least 1 hour, or ideally overnight.

Preheat the oven to 160°C (325°F) Gas 3.

Heat half the butter in a large, deep frying pan/skillet and fry the salt, pepper, pancetta, shallots and mushrooms over a high heat for about 5 minutes, until the pancetta browns.

Take the chicken pieces out of the bag or bowl, leaving the marinade in there for the moment, and add the chicken pieces to the mushrooms, shallots and pancetta for a few minutes, until they are sealed all over.

Add the marinade from the bag or bowl and stir well. Sprinkle the flour over the top and undisturbed there for a minute to absorb the flavours, then stir in.

Add the stock and lemon juice. Mix well and then transfer the contents to a casserole dish. Cover with a lid (or with foil) and cook in the preheated oven for 1½ hours.

If you want to remove the bones, remove the thighs and drumsticks and carefully pinch them to remove the bones – make sure you find the fibula bone on both drumsticks (the very thin, needle like bone). Return the meat to the casserole and use a fork to break the tender chicken chunks into shreds. Mix together. Alternatively, leave the meat on the bone and serve in whole pieces.

Serve with green beans or with rice for a fuller meal. A crisp dry white wine or cider is lovely with this.

PORK AND BOSTON BEANS

Inspired by a lovely regular to our shop (an American adopted by London), who came to a bacon-making course, I thought I'd have a crack at some Boston Baked Beans. Hoping just to do it justice, I had not anticipated the joy of making my own baked beans and will never be able to go back to flavourless canned ones again! Whether you use good-quality pork sausages or strips of pork belly, this will become a firm favourite in your home, too. Try serving on some toasted brioche.

400 g/14 oz. soaked haricot/navy beans (use 200 g/7 oz. dried beans and follow the pack instructions to soak them and keep the liquid to make it up to 400 g/14 oz. in weight)

1 teaspoon mustard powder

2 tablespoons tomato purée/paste

1 tablespoon black treacle/molasses or soft dark brown sugar

1 tablespoon runny honey

1 red onion, finely chopped

1 garlic clove, finely chopped

salt and black pepper, to season

6 chunky pork sausages or 2 strips of boneless pork belly, about 4-cm/2-inches wide (250 g/9 oz. total weight), rind still on

30 x 20-cm/12 x 8-inch roasting pan, greased

SERVES 2

Preheat the oven to 140°C (275°F) Gas 1.

Pour the soaked beans into the greased roasting pan. Mix in the mustard powder, tomato purée/paste, black treacle/molasses, honey, onion, garlic, salt and pepper and pour over the beans.

If you're using pork belly strips, use a sharp knife to score lines in the rind and press salt into the scored lines to help the rind to crackle by dehydrating the fat layer beneath.

Clear little beds in the beans and place the sausages or pork belly strips into the dish.

Cover with foil and bake in the preheated oven for 1½ hours.

Uncover, stir the beans, turn the temperature up to 190°C (375°F) Gas 5 and roast for another 15–20 minutes, until the sausages brown or the pork strips have crackled. (If the beans have dried a little before this happens, just pour in a few tablespoons of water to loosen them.

To serve, divide the bean mixture between two plates and place the sausages or pork strip on top.

PULLED PORK SHOULDER

This is my very favourite way to have pork shoulder, as it has such a fantastic result when you take really good-quality piece of pork and slow-cook it to break down the meat. Boneless shoulder pulls really well, but bone-in is even better as you have the bone and the collagen to contribute to the juices and moisture. It's like you're making stock from the inside of your joint to come out through the meat and it produces more juices at the bottom of the pan. If you're cutting your own shoulder, follow the simple way to remove this part (see pages 76–9).

3 kg/6½ lb. free-range, bone-in pork shoulder (rind on, if you would like to make crackling)

1 tablespoon sea salt (flakes or crystals)

3 tablespoons olive oil

1 teaspoon paprika

a big pinch of cayenne pepper

warm brioche rolls, to serve

BARBECUE SAUCE

1 tablespoon olive oil

1 white onion, chopped

1 garlic clove, chopped

2 red (bell) peppers, deseeded and chopped

a pinch of fennel seeds

a pinch of cumin

½ teaspoon mustard powder

½ teaspoon salt

1 tablespoon soft brown sugar

a pinch of black pepper

400 g/14 oz. canned tomatoes, drained

1 cooking apple, cored, peeled and diced

100 ml/generous ⅓ cup cider vinegar

3½ tablespoons maple syrup

100 ml/generous ⅓ cup apple juice

½ teaspoon Dijon mustard

SERVES 10–12

Preheat the oven to 190°C (375°F) Gas 5.

If you want to make crackling, use a sharp knife to score diagonal lines across the rind and push the salt into the cuts in the rind. This draws the moisture out of the rind and fat so that the surface crackles.

Fold a large piece of foil in two to make it double-strength and place it in a roasting pan. You're going to need enough foil either side to cover and seal the pork. Place the pork on top. Drizzle the olive oil over the surface and sprinkle over the paprika and cayenne.

Keeping the foil open at this stage, place the meat in the oven and roast for 25 minutes so that the outside has a chance to brown. Then turn the temperature right down to 150°C (300°F) Gas 2, fold in the sides of the foil so that the meat is totally covered and cook for at least 3 hours, or 4 hours if you can. Every hour, open up the foil and baste the meat by spooning the juices from the bottom of the pan back over the top of the joint. After 3–4 hours, prod it with a fork and see if it is easy to 'pull' (the strips in the muscle should have 'melted' apart). Return for a little longer if it still feels tight.

Open the foil, increase the heat to 200°C (400°F) Gas 6 and continue to cook for 5 minutes to crisp up the top. Remove the crackling and set aside. Use two forks to 'pull' the pork to shreds. Use scissors to cut the crackling into thin strips. Serve the pork in warm brioche rolls with barbecue sauce and crackling on the side.

Barbecue Sauce

Heat the oil in a pan over a medium heat and sauté the onion, garlic and red (bell) pepper for 4–5 minutes, until softened. Stir in the fennel seeds, cumin, mustard powder, salt, sugar and pepper. Add the remaining ingredients and bring to the boil, then turn the heat down to a simmer and cook for 1 hour, stirring occasionally. If it's looking very thick, add a drop more apple juice. Remove from the heat and allow to cool a little, then whizz in a food processor until smooth. Store in a sterilized bottle in the fridge for up to 3 weeks, or freeze in portions to keep for up to 3 months.

SLOW-COOKED LAMB SHANKS

The lamb shank is often thought of as a restaurant cut, but it has become especially popular in recent years. This is partly because it presents really well on the plate and looks very cool. However, it's actually very simple to cook at home. If you're cutting your own leg of lamb, follow the instruction on page 66 to remove the end. I always serve this with Buttery Crushed Potatoes (see page 233).

2 bone-in lamb shanks

20 g/1½ tablespoons butter

2 garlic cloves, roughly chopped

1 lemon, halved

4–6 fresh mint leaves

salt and black pepper, to season

Buttery Crushed Potatoes (see page 233) and Red Onion Gravy (see page 103), to serve

SERVES 2

Pre-heat the oven to 190°C (375°F) Gas 5.

Fold a large piece of foil in two to make it double-strength and place it in a roasting pan. You're going to need enough foil either side to cover and seal the lamb shanks inside.

Rub the butter over all the sides of the meat. Stand the lamb shanks on their flat ends and add the garlic, lemon and mint leaves, and season well.

Keeping the foil open at this stage, place the meat in the oven and roast for 10 minutes, then fold in all the sides of the foil so that the shanks are sealed inside and fully covered. Reduce the oven temperature to 160°C (325°F) Gas 3 and cook for 1 hour.

Remove the foil and prod the meat with a fork. If it feels tender and looks like it's falling off the bone then it's ready. If it still resists the pressure of the fork, you might have a nice chunky-sized shank that will need another 15 minutes or so.

Once it's tender, open up the foil and turn up the temperature again to 190°C (375°F) Gas 5. Pop the lamb shanks back in the oven for 5 minutes to brown and crisp a little.

To serve, spoon the meat juices over the shanks and then put them on serving plates with the Buttery Crush Potatoes and drizzle more of the meat juices over the top, if you like. Accompany with Red Onion Gravy.

LANCASHIRE HOT POT

This is another example of how some of our traditional recipes, designed for a different time, still perfectly suit our modern meat kitchens. The history of this dish was for the heavily industrialized Northern England to have a recipe that was so easy to throw together in the morning, leave on a low heat in the oven all day, to be devoured after a good day's work. Most of us don't work in jobs that require the physical labour of those times, but we've filled our days and lives with so many other things to keep us just as busy, so to return home to a slow-cooked meal is, in my mind, the very best type of 'ready meal' for a weeknight supper.

6 potatoes

40 g/3 tablespoons butter

100 g/3¾ oz. hard cheese, such as mature/sharp Cheddar (optional)

FILLING

500 g/1 lb. 2 oz. diced mutton or lamb shoulder or loin

2 lamb's kidneys (optional), chopped

2 white onions, diced

2 carrots, peeled and chopped

½ swede/rutabaga, peeled and chopped

300 ml/1⅓ cups stock

2 tablespoons plain/all-purpose flour

a pinch of dried thyme or a sprig of fresh

1 bay leaf

4 shelled oysters (optional)

salt and black pepper, to season

SERVES 4

Preheat oven to 120°C (250°F) Gas ½.

Start by slicing the potatoes (skins left on) widthways so that they're in oval discs, about 5-mm/¼-inch thick.

Take a large casserole or ovenproof dish (with a lid) and use half the butter to grease it.

Lay half the potatoes across the bottom (this stops the filling catching, too) and up the sides of the pot, if they'll stick.

Throw all the ingredients for the filling into a mixing bowl and mix well. I'm a fan of oysters, but I don't love them in this dish. They were popular at a point but then became expensive so were phased out. It's up to you if you want to add them.

Pour the filling over the potato base and cover the top with the other half of the potatoes, making sure you cover as many of the gaps as possible.

Melt the other half of the butter in a pan or in the microwave and drizzle it over the top of the potatoes. Add a sprinkle more of salt and pepper on the top, then cover with the lid (or with double layer of foil, sealing it very tightly) and bake in the preheated oven for 8–10 hours. For a faster result, preheat the oven to 160°C (325°F) Gas 3 and cook it for 2–3 hours instead.

Just before serving, remove the lid or foil, turn the heat up to 200°C (400°F) Gas 6. If using, grate the cheese onto the top at this stage. Cook for 10 minutes to brown the topping and serve.

JACOB'S LADDER

The short ribs of beef are known as Jacob's Ladder, and the flavour and tenderness of the meat on the bones is delicious. They're great indoors or on the barbecue, and they make a very snazzy 'Surf & Turf' spread with crayfish tails and corn on the cob alongside, as you can pick everything up with your hands and gnaw!

4 beef short ribs

3 tablespoons olive oil

3 garlic cloves, in their skins

4 tablespoons runny honey

3 tablespoons soft brown sugar

400 ml/1²/₃ cups apple cider vinegar

100 g/7 tablespoons butter

salt and black pepper, to season

SURF 'N' TURF

4 crayfish tails or king prawns/jumbo shrimp

15 g/1 tablespoon butter

a big pinch of chopped fresh parsley

a squeeze of fresh lime juice

4 corn on the cobs, to serve

SERVES 4

Preheat the oven to 180°C (350°F) Gas 4.

Roast the garlic in the oven for 20 minutes with their skins on, then squeeze out the centre. This will give you a sweeter flavour, but if you are short of time, you can just peel and chop the garlic instead.

Cut between the short ribs, through the muscle, and put the separated ribs into a sealable bag or container with a lid. Season with salt and pepper and add the olive oil, honey, 1 tablespoon of the sugar, roasted garlic and apple cider vinegar. Seal the bag or place a lid on the container and set in the fridge for at least 1 hour, but ideally a few hours or overnight.

When you are ready to cook the ribs, preheat the oven to 150°C (300°F) Gas 2.

Take just the ribs out of the marinade and lay them flat in an ovenproof or casserole dish. Cover with a lid or foil and bake in the preheated oven for 2 hours.

Melt the butter in a pan, add the remaining 2 tablespoons of sugar and bring to the boil. Take the ovenproof dish out of the oven and remove the lid. Pour the liquid from around the meat into the pan with the butter and sugar. This has some of the vinegar flavour and a rich stock from cooking the meat on the bone.

Continue cooking the sauce over a high heat until the sauce starts to thicken to a syrupy texture, about 8–9 minutes.

Pour half the sauce back over the ribs, turn the oven up to 200·C (400°F) Gas 6 and return the ribs, uncovered, to the oven for 20 minutes. Turn the ribs over half way through.

Meanwhile, cool the rest of the sauce to thicken it a bit more. Fill a sink with a little very cold water, then lower the bottom of the pan in and stir until it thickens. Pour over the top of the ribs to serve, or serve on the side.

Surf 'n' Turf

To serve this as a classic surf 'n' turf, cook some crayfish tails or king prawns/jumbo shrimp in a pan with some butter until pink and cooked through, then sprinkle with freshly chopped parsley and squeeze with fresh lime. Serve with some corn on the cobs.

OX CHEEK AND BLACKBERRY CASSEROLE

Simply another name for beef cheek, ox cheek is the traditional name in the same way that 'oxtail' is used to describe beef tail. It is too tough to eat if only cooked for a short time. You can imagine how overused the muscle in the cheek is from a lifetime of chewing grass, but also, famously 'chewing the cud', which is the second process of cows' digestion, where the food is chewed all over again! So ox cheek is tough when it's raw and it's a case of the slower the better for cooking it. Like with the Lancashire Hot Pot (see page 184), this could be your 'ready meal' for when you get home from a long day at work.

20 g/1½ tablespoons butter

800 g/1 lb. 12 oz. trimmed, diced ox cheek

2 red onions, chopped

2 tablespoons plain/all-purpose flour

2 carrots, peeled and chopped

2 sticks celery, chopped

400 ml/2⅔ cups Beef Broth (see page 37), or 200 g/7 oz. jellied stock

½ teaspoon all-spice

100 g/3¾ oz. streaky/fatty bacon, diced

1 tablespoon red wine vinegar

2 teaspoons soft dark brown sugar (or 50 g/2 oz. very dark/bittersweet chocolate, minimum 70% cocoa content)

150 g/generous 1 cup blackberries

¾ bottle of red wine

Fancy Mashed Potatoes (see page 233) and green vegetables, to serve

SERVES 4

Preheat the oven to 150°C (300°F) Gas 2.

Melt the butter in a flameproof casserole over a medium heat and brown the diced ox cheek for 1–2 minutes to seal all over.

Add the red onion and fry that for 1 minute. Sprinkle over the flour and don't stir until it changes colour, then add all the other ingredients and give it a good stir.

Put the lid on (or cover with two layers of kitchen foil, sealed tightly) and cook in the preheated oven for 3 hours. If you want to cook it all day, preheat the oven to 120°C (250°F) Gas ½ and cook it for 8 hours instead.

To thicken the sauce a little before serving, move the casserole back to the stovetop and stir it over a very high heat for a few minutes until it thickens – don't worry, the cheek won't toughen again, they are already very tender.

This dish is dark and rich but still lovely and sweet. I like to serve it with mash and some green vegetables.

Want to make it even easier? Don't worry about browning the cheek first. It adds a little extra roasty flavour but there is still so much flavour and richness, you can just chuck all the ingredients in the casserole, mix it around, and pop it in the oven.

BEEF CASSEROLE WITH HERBY DUMPLINGS

This casserole couldn't be easier, as you just throw it all in a pan and leave it to cook in the oven. The herby dumplings are optional, but they make a lovely addition if you like the sound of them. Serve with some fresh green vegetables. This is a perfect winter warmer to divide into portions and freeze. You can freeze the dumplings separately too, if you want to make extra for other dishes.

20 g/1½ tablespoons butter

1 red onion, chopped

60 g/1 cup chopped mushrooms

1 red (bell) pepper, deseeded and chopped

400 g/14 oz. diced beef (cut from the rib joint, see page 54)

75 ml/6 tablespoons red wine

90 ml/7 tablespoons Brown Chicken Stock (see page 36) or ½ chicken stock/bouillon cube

1½ tablespoons plain/all-purpose flour

1 bay leaf

a pinch each of salt and black pepper

green vegetables, to serve

HERBY DUMPLINGS

70 g/¾ cup beef suet or vegetable shortening

150 g/generous 1 cup plain or all-purpose flour

a pinch of dried rosemary

a pinch of dried thyme

SERVES 4

Preheat the oven to 160°C (325°F) Gas 3.

Put all of the casserole ingredients into a pan over a medium heat and bring to the boil with a lid on, stirring a few times to make sure nothing catches on the bottom and the flour breaks up.

Once boiling, keep the lid on and transfer to the preheated oven. Cook for 1 hour, giving it a stir after 30 minutes. (Meanwhile, see below to make the herby dumplings, if you want to add them.) If the casserole isn't quick thick enough after an hour of cooking, return it to the oven for a further 15 minutes.

Serve with some green vegetables and the herby dumplings.

Herby Dumplings

Mix the suet, flour and herbs in a bowl. Add 1–2 tablespoons of water, a little at a time, until you can squeeze the mixture into a solid ball. Pinch off a piece at a time – a sphere to fit in the circle you make when you join your index finger and thumb is a good size. Roll them tightly and place on a baking sheet. After the casserole has been in for 30 minutes, put the baking sheet in the oven and bake the dumplings for 15 minutes. Then throw them into the casserole for the last 15 minutes of the casserole's cooking time.

STEAK AND KIDNEY PIE

This is another age-old meat dish that still works fantastically well in our modern meat kitchens. It's also a good one for entertaining because it can be prepared earlier in the day or the day before and then simply put in the oven when ready.

20 g/1½ tablespoons butter, plus extra if needed

750 g/1 lb. 10 oz. diced beef (cut from the rib joint, see page 54)

250 g/9 oz. beef or lamb's kidneys, diced

2 white onions, chopped

3 carrots, peeled and chopped

60 g/1 cup mushrooms, chopped

1½ tablespoons plain/all-purpose flour

a pinch of freshly chopped thyme leaves

a pinch of freshly chopped sage

4 teaspoons tomato purée/paste

2 teaspoons Worcestershire sauce

800 ml/3⅓ cups Beef Broth (see page 37)

salt and pepper, to season

PASTRY
200 g/1½ cups plain/all-purpose flour, plus extra for dusting

100 g/7 tablespoons butter, at room temperature

a pinch of freshly chopped tarragon (optional)

a pinch of salt

1–2 tablespoons cold water

1 beaten egg, to glaze

20-cm/8-inch round pie dish, greased with butter

SERVES 4

Melt the butter in a frying pan/skillet over a medium heat and set a large pan on another burner over a medium heat.

Brown the diced beef first in the frying/pan, in batches, and add it to the pan as soon as is it sealed. Do the same with the diced kidneys – you don't need to cook these through, it's just browning for flavour at this stage.

Add the onion, carrots and mushrooms to the frying pan/skillet, adding a little more butter if necessary, and soften them for a few minutes, letting them loosen any meaty bits from the bottom of the frying pan/skillet. Pour the vegetables into the pan and give it a stir, then sprinkle the flour over the top don't stir again until the flour starts to change colour. Stir in the thyme, sage, tomato purée/paste and Worcestershire Sauce and season with salt and pepper. Pour in the beef broth and bring to the boil, then reduce the heat to a low simmer and leave for up to 2 hours, with the lid half-on.

It might be thick enough after 90 minutes, so just keep giving it a stir occasionally and making sure none of the flour has caught on the bottom. Add a little more beef broth if it's too thick. If it isn't thickening, remove the lid completely and increase the heat a little.

Preheat the oven to 180°C (350°F) Gas 4.

Make the pastry by rubbing the flour and butter together with your fingertips until it resembles breadcrumbs. Add the salt and the cold water, a tablespoon at a time, until the pastry holds together.

Lightly dust a work surface with flour. Use a rolling pin to roll out the dough to a size sufficient to generously cover your pie dish. Use your finger to run butter around 2 cm/¾ inch of the outside edge of the pie dish. If you have a pie funnel, put this in the centre of the dish. (This enables the steam to escape, keeping the pastry crisp.)

Pour the filling mixture into the pie dish. Lift up the pastry and place it on the top of the filling. Use a sharp knife to cut a small cross in the centre of the pastry lid (directly on top of the pie funnel, if using). Trim the edges or let them overhang, as preferred, and press around the edge to seal it to the sides of the pie.

Using a pastry brush, glaze the top of the pie with the beaten egg. Transfer the dish to a baking sheet to catch any escaping filling and bake in the preheated oven for 30–40 minutes, until the top is golden brown and crisp. Serve with peas and a glass of amber ale.

VENISON AND CHORIZO CASSOULET

A cassoulet is a slow-cooked casserole and it is actually often the easiest and least fiddly approach to a casserole, so it suits our modern meat kitchens perfectly.

a 400-g/14-oz. piece of venison loin, diced

100 g/3¾ oz. chorizo, diced

20 g/1½ tablespoons butter

50 g/scant 1 cup sliced mushrooms

1 red (bell) pepper, deseeded and diced

1 red onion, diced

1 garlic clove, chopped

150 ml/⅔ cup red wine

2 tablespoons plain/all-purpose flour

200 g/1¼ cups dried haricot/navy beans, soaked and drained or 250 g/1¾ cups pre-soaked canned haricot/navy beans, drained

a pinch of fresh or dried tarragon

2 teaspoons redcurrant jelly

300 ml/1¼ cups White Chicken Stock (see page 36)

salt and pepper, to season

SERVES 2

Preheat the oven to 150°C (300°F) Gas

Put all of the ingredients into a casserole with a lid, give it a good stir and put the lid on. Put it in the preheated oven and cook for 2½–3 hours. That's it!

It'll keep chilled for a week in the fridge or it freezes really well if you make a larger batch and freeze it in portions. Just increase the cooking time by 15 minutes per extra serving, if you are increasing the quantities.

ROASTS

CLASSIC ROAST CHICKEN

If you've been good enough to read the introduction to this book, you'll know how much value I place on the life of the animal. There is no better visual aid for demonstrating the difference between good farming and cheap farming than a roast chicken. Start with a well-farmed, free-range chicken and, whatever your ethics, you will be rewarded with a succulent, flavoursome, easy-to-carve roast, which doesn't disappear to half its original size.

20 g/1½ tablespoons butter, softened

1 whole chicken, approx. 2 kg/ 4 lbs., trimmed and prepared (see pages 84–7)

1 lemon

1 garlic clove, sliced lengthways

2 sprigs of fresh thyme

salt and black pepper, to season

Easy Roast Gravy (see page 216) and your choice of accompaniments, to serve

SERVES 6

Preheat the oven to 180°C (350°F) Gas 4.

Rub the butter over the whole chicken, being careful not to break the skin.

Wash and roughly zest half of the lemon, and rub the zest into the skin. Rub the cut sides of the garlic halves over the skin too. Set the garlic aside; do not discard it.

Lay the chicken in a roasting pan, breast down to start with, so you start with the flat side (its back) facing up.

Cut the lemon in half and squeeze the juice of half the lemon over the top of the chicken. Don't throw the squeezed lemon half away – add it to the roasting pan. Sprinkle a big pinch of salt and black pepper over the top.

Put the other half of the lemon inside the chicken, along with the sprigs of thyme and reserved pieces of garlic.

Roast the chicken in the preheated oven for 45 minutes. After this time, turn it over in the dish so it is breast-side up. Sprinkle salt and black pepper on the top and return to the oven for another 45 minutes.

Press a fork into the thickest part of the leg. If the juices are still pink, it needs to be cooked for longer – return to the oven for another 10 minutes and check again.

Serve with gravy and your choice of veg.

Leftovers
Any leftover roast chicken can be whipped into a delicious chicken noodle soup the next evening (see page 201).

LEFTOVER ROAST CHICKEN NOODLE SOUP

A lovely leftover idea for Classic Roast Chicken (page 198) or Roast Turkey (page 228), and so easy to throw together for a light and nutritious weeknight supper.

1 tablespoon olive oil

1 red chilli/chile, deseeded and chopped

1 garlic clove, finely chopped

1 tablespoon Thai fish sauce

1 teaspoon tamarind paste

1 teaspoon soft brown sugar

1 teaspoon turmeric

a pinch of cumin

a pinch of ground ginger
(or 1.5 cm/¾ inch root ginger, finely chopped)

4 spring onions/scallions, chopped (and/or other stir-fry vegetables as you like)

150 ml/⅔ cup coconut milk

about 300 g/10½ oz. leftover roast chicken (or however much you have), shredded

700 ml/scant 3 cups White or Brown Chicken Stock (see page 36)

100–200 g/3¾–7 oz. dried noodles, depending on how hungry you are

salt and black pepper

fresh coriander/cilantro leaves, to serve

a sprinkle of sesame seeds, to serve (optional)

SERVES 2

Heat the oil in a pan with tall sides that is large enough to hold a litre/quart of liquid over a medium heat. Fry the chilli/chile and garlic with the fish sauce, tamarind paste, sugar, turmeric, cumin, ginger and a good pinch each of salt and pepper.

Add the spring onions/scallions and cook until golden. Pour in the coconut milk, add the shredded leftover chicken and cook until the mixture starts to bubble. Pour in the stock and bring back to the boil. Bubble the soup for 4–5 minutes.

Follow the packet instructions to cook your noodles, but most need only a few minutes cooking time, so add them into the soup and cook for the required amount of time.

Serve with a sprinkle of fresh coriander/cilantro on top. To add a bit of toasty crunch, heat a dry frying pan/skillet over a medium heat and toast a handful of sesame seeds for 1–2 minutes until brown. Sprinkle them on the top, too.

STUFFED ROLLED PORK SHOULDER

This is a fantastic Sunday roast and it looks very impressive despite its relatively low cost. The shoulder/butt is an inexpensive cut, but it contains lots of fat under the skin which makes for a moist and flavourful piece of meat.

1.2–1.4 kg/2¾–3 lbs. boneless pork shoulder/butt, ideally unrolled with skin still on

Easy Roast Gravy (see page 216), roast potatoes, honey parsnips and green beans, to serve

STUFFING

30 g/¼ stick butter

a pinch of salt

1 red onion, finely diced

1 garlic clove, finely diced

300 g/10½ oz. chicken livers

1 cooking apple, finely diced

a pinch of freshly chopped parsley

a pinch of freshly chopped or dried sage

100 ml/scant ½ cup red wine

a pinch of black pepper

butcher's twine, about 60 cm/2 feet in length

SERVES 4

Start with the stuffing. Heat a pan with the butter and salt over a high heat and then sauté the onion, garlic, chicken livers and cooking apple for 4–5 minutes until softened.

Reduce the heat a little and add the parsley, sage and pepper, and stir well. Add the red wine and bring to the boil for 2–3 minutes to thicken.

Remove from the heat and allow to cool – to speed up the cooling process, fill a sink with cold water, submerge the base of the pan in the cold water and stir until the mixture has cooled. Alternatively, make the stuffing mix earlier in the day and move to the fridge once it's at room temperature.

Preheat the oven to 180°C (350°F) Gas 4.

Lay the pork flat on a board, skin-side up. Take a very sharp knife and score lines across the skin of the pork. You do not want to cut all the way through to the meat; just score through the surface of the skin.

Turn the pork over. Take the cooled stuffing mixture and rub it into the underside of the shoulder, across the pink pork meat. Really push it into the gaps and corners so it's spread across the whole side.

Roll the shoulder/butt and secure it using butcher's twine (see page 30 for instructions on how to tie). Now push salt into the scored gaps in the skin; this will help draw out the moisture in the rind to produce crackling.

Transfer the rolled meat to a roasting pan, with the skin facing up, and roast in the middle of the oven for 80 minutes. Use a meat thermometer to check the inside of the joint (see charts on page 33) and insert a skewer into the meat to check if the meat juices are running clear. Roast for longer if necessary, until cooked through.

Cut lovely, big, thick slices to serve with easy roast gravy, roast potatoes, honey parsnips and green beans.

CLASSIC ROAST LEG OF LAMB

A rich and juicy roast lamb is often such a popular option, and you can't go too wrong with the cooking of it either, because the shape and ratio of meat to bone makes it the perfect cut for a well-balanced roasting. If you're cutting your own lamb leg, follow the preparation instructions on pages 65–6. I like the classic combination of mint sauce with roast lamb, so I've included an easy recipe here.

bone-in, trimmed leg of lamb (usually around 2 kg/4 lbs.)

2 sprigs of fresh rosemary

2 garlic cloves, chopped (optional)

salt and black pepper, to season

Easy Roast Gravy (see page 216) and your choice of accompaniments, to serve

MINT SAUCE

10–12 fresh mint leaves, chopped finely

2 tablespoons soft brown sugar

2 tablespoons boiling water

2 tablespoons white wine vinegar

SERVES 6–8

Preheat the oven to 180°C (350°F).

Place the leg of lamb in a roasting pan and sprinkle the rosemary, garlic (if using), and some salt and pepper on top.

If you like, put your vegetables to roast around the edge (I recommend parboiling for a couple minutes first, if you're doing potatoes or root vegetables, so that they don't dry out too much).

Cook in the preheated oven for about 90 minutes, but check it a couple of times before the end of that time, as cooking times depend on the shape of the leg – they can be short and plump or long and thin, depending on the breed. For rare/pink meat, it may only need 60 minutes.

I find the easiest way to carve is to start in the middle and slice towards the ankle end first. Then you can hold that and turn it to slice in the opposite direction. There's lots of meat on the hind leg, so don't worry too much about technique; you'll be able to get all the meat off one way or another.

Serve with the mint sauce (see below), easy roast gravy and vegetables of your choice. If you have any leftover, why not use it in the leftover roast lamb moussaka (see page 207).

Mint Sauce

Put the chopped mint leaves and brown sugar in a cold frying pan/ skillet and pour over the boiling water (or just enough to soak up and dissolve the sugar).

Put the pan over a high heat and bring to the boil. Add the white wine vinegar and boil for another couple of minutes.

Leave to cool; ideally cool it to room temperature then let it chill in the fridge overnight. Alternatively, submerge the bottom of the pan in a sink of cold water and stir so that the mint sauce cools and thickens a bit. Serve cold with the roast lamb.

LEFTOVER ROAST LAMB MOUSSAKA

You can use the leftovers from Classic Roast Leg of Lamb (see page 204) or the Lamb Kleftiko with Spiced Yogurt (see page 162) for this simple and delicious Greek-inspired recipe. It is a perfect comforting Monday-night dinner to use up the remnants of your Sunday roast. Serve it simply with some crisp salad.

2 potatoes

olive oil, for drizzling and frying

salt and black pepper, to season

1 aubergine/eggplant

1 white onion, diced

1 garlic clove, finely chopped

a pinch of fresh or dried oregano

a pinch of ground nutmeg

a pinch of cinnamon

2 tablespoons plain/all-purpose flour

150 ml/²⁄₃ cup white wine

120 ml/½ cup full-fat/whole milk

freshly squeezed juice of ½ lemon

300–400 g/10½–14 oz. leftover roast lamb (from the Lamb Kleftiko or Classic Roast Leg of Lamb on pages 162 and 204)

200 g/7 oz. drained canned chopped tomatoes

salad, to serve

SERVES 2

Preheat the oven to 180°C (350°F) Gas 4.

Slice the potatoes widthways, 5-mm/¼-inch thick to make oval discs (leave the skins on). Layer the potato discs flat on a greased baking sheet and drizzle olive oil on the top. Season with a good pinch of salt and black pepper. Bake in the preheated oven for 20 minutes until they start to brown.

Meanwhile, slice the aubergine/eggplant widthways, into similar sized discs. Heat a little olive oil in a frying pan/skillet and fry the aubergine/eggplant discs in batches in one layer, until soft and starting to brown, and then remove and lay on paper towels to absorb some of the excess oil.

In the same pan, fry the onion and garlic over a medium heat until soft and brown. Mix in a pinch of salt and pepper, and the oregano, nutmeg and cinnamon. Add the flour and stir to make a paste, then add the white wine. Stir until smooth and then slowly add the milk, a little at a time, to make a smooth sauce. Stir in the drained chopped tomatoes.

Pour half the mixture from the frying pan/skillet into a greased roasting pan. Tear or cut the leftover lamb pieces into bite-sized strips or pieces and layer half of the lamb on top of the mixture in the roasting pan.

Then layer half the potato discs followed by half the aubergine/eggplant on top.

Repeat with the remaining ingredients, following the same order, finishing with the potatoes on top.

Cover with foil and bake in the preheated oven for 15 minutes. Remove the foil and place under a hot grill/broiler for 5–10 minutes until the potatoes have crisped on top. Serve with a crisp salad.

ROAST RACK OF LAMB

For a modern meat kitchen, this is a great recipe for a really quick roast. The little cutlets have all the flavour and tenderness of a slow-cooked leg roast, but they take just 25 minutes to cook to perfection.

1 top end rack of lamb, French trimmed/Frenched (about 6–7 ribs)

4 garlic cloves, roughly chopped

salt and black pepper, to season

6–7 tablespoons olive oil

2–3 Maris Piper or Yukon Gold potatoes, peeled, quartered and parboiled

2 carrots, peeled and cut into large chunks

1 red onion, chopped into large chunks

a handful of cherry tomatoes

SERVES 2

Preheat the oven to 190°C (375°F) Gas 5.

Lay the rack bone-side down. Score the top and put the garlic pieces in some of the lines. Sprinkle salt and pepper on the top and drizzle over 3 tablespoons of the olive oil.

Place the parboiled potatoes, carrots, red onion and cherry tomatoes in a roasting pan. Drizzle over the remaining olive oil and sprinkle with some salt and black pepper.

Put this in the oven for 20 minutes, then give it all a good shake and place the lamb on top. Return to the oven for 25–30 minutes (25 minutes will keep the lamb a little pink inside).

Remove the lamb from the pan and allow to rest for a few minutes, before slicing between the bones to make cutlets. Serve with the roast vegetables.

WHISKY LAMB SHOULDER

The marinade for this makes the absolute most of the lamb flavours. As the lamb falls apart in your mouth, I hope you'll also have the same experience of the sweetness first, then the lovely lamb and herb combinations, and then a bold finale of the whisky taste.

4 teaspoons vegetable oil

2 tablespoons runny honey

5 tablespoons whisky (I used a single malt Scotch whisky)

a big pinch of fresh rosemary

a splash of apple cider vinegar

bone-in shoulder of lamb (around 1.5 kg/3 lbs.)

salt and black pepper, to season

your choice of vegetables, to serve

SERVES 4

Mix the vegetable oil, honey, whisky, rosemary, cider vinegar and some salt and pepper in a large mixing bowl. Add the lamb and coat it in the marinade.

If you have a large, sealable food bag, move the meat and all the marinade to the bag and seal with as little air inside as possible. Place in the fridge to marinate for at least 2 hours, ideally overnight.

Preheat the oven to 160°C (325°F) Gas 3.

Remove the lamb shoulder from the bag, reserving the marinade. Place it on a large piece of foil. Pour all the marinade over the top and fold up the sides of the foil to scrunch and seal over the top of the meat. Place in a roasting pan.

Place in the preheated oven and roast for at least 2½ hours, but ideally 3 hours for really tender meat.

To serve, lift the meat out of the foil, but make sure you reserve the juices to pour onto the lamb once you have carved it. (If you plan to make the leftover whisky lamb shoulder wrap on page 212 the next day, it's a good idea to set aside some of the juices in a jug/pitcher. Slice only what you will need for now, and keep the rest of the lamb on the bone, as this will keep it nice and moist until the next day.)

Serve with accompanying vegetables of your choice.

LEFTOVER WHISKY LAMB SHOULDER WRAP

This is an easy supper or lunch to enjoy the day after you make the Whisky Lamb Shoulder (see page 211), especially nice on a warm evening in the summer. This will fill 2 large tortilla wraps or 4 smaller ones. Place all the filling ingredients on the table for both diners to fill their own wraps.

1 aubergine/eggplant

2 tablespoons olive oil

2–4 flour tortilla wraps

2–4 tablespoons natural/plain yogurt

2–4 teaspoons redcurrant jelly

2–4 handfuls of baby leaf spinach

100 g/3¾ oz. feta cheese (optional)

300–400 g/10½–14 oz. leftover roast lamb (from Whisky Lamb Shoulder, see page 211), torn into pieces

SERVES 2

Slice the aubergine/eggplant into 5-mm/¼-in. thick slices.

Heat the olive oil in a ridged griddle/grill pan or frying pan/skillet over a high heat, then fry the aubergine/eggplant slices, in batches if necessary. Once cooked, transfer them to paper towels to soak up some of the excess oil. Leave the pan over the heat.

Wet the tortilla wraps slightly on both sides to help them crisp, then add them to the pan you have just cooked the aubergine/eggplant in, heating them one at a time. Cook them on one side (to keep the other side grease-free) until warmed and slightly crispy. Alternatively, heat them according to the packet instructions.

To serve, place a tortilla wrap (greasy-side up) on a plate and spread the yogurt and redcurrant jelly down the middle.

Lay the shredded lamb on top and sprinkle the spinach and feta cheese, if using, on top.

Fold the end and sides over the middle to make a wrap.

ROAST RIB OF BEEF

I think this is the most impressive-looking cut of beef and, with a bit of prep, it can deliver the most incredible beef experience – my favourite. I recommend planning for about 400 g/14 oz. per person of raw beef rib, which will yield about 250 g/ 9 oz. of meat each, or work it out as 1 rib bone per 2–3 people.

For step-by-step techniques and advice on preparing your rib of beef for roasting, see pages 54–6.

three-bone rib of beef (about 3 kg/6 lbs.)

salt and black pepper, to season

Yorkshire Puddings (see page 217), Foolproof Roasties (see page 216), Easy Roast Gravy (see page 216) and your choice of vegetables, to serve

SERVES 6–8

Preheat the oven to 190°C (375°F) Gas 5.

Put your prepared rib of beef in a roasting pan and sprinkle a good pinch of salt over the top cap of fat as well as a little black pepper.

Roast in the preheated oven for 20 minutes and then reduce the heat to 160°C (325°F) Gas 3 and roast for a further 2 hours (or 20 minutes per 500 g/1 lb.) for medium.

Turn off the oven, open the door to let the heat out and then shut the door again, leaving the beef to sit in the warm oven, still uncovered, for 15 minutes. (This is not ideal if you're roasting vegetables at the same time, so you can remove the meat and leave it to stand in as warm a place as possible if you are cooking vegetables in the oven.)

Remove the twine and place the meat on a carving board. Don't throw away any of the juices – you can use them to prepare the gravy. Serve the meat with yorkshire puddings, foolproof roasties, easy roast gravy and your choice of vegetables.

ACCOMPANIMENTS

EASY ROAST GRAVY

One of the many joys of a good roast dinner is that it's really easy to make a gravy at the end, in the few minutes while the meat is resting.

2 tablespoons plain/all-purpose flour

100 g/3¾ oz. Brown Chicken Stock (see page 36) or 200 ml/scant 1 cup chicken stock from a stock/bouillon cube

2 teaspoons redcurrant or cranberry jelly

salt and black pepper, to season

SERVES 6

Once your meat is fully roasted, move it to a board to rest (don't put kitchen foil over the top; you'll only be a few minutes, so just let it breathe).

Drain nearly all of the meat juices from the roasting pan into a jar, but leave the last 3–4 tablespoons in there – this is usually the fattier portion, which is what we want.

Put the roasting pan over a medium heat on the stovetop and let the reserved fatty meat juices start to bubble.

Stir in the flour and then add the stock and stir well until smooth. Add the redcurrant or cranberry jelly and keep cooking until thickened and glossy. Season to taste.

Transfer to a gravy boat or spoon over the carved meat.

FOOLPROOF ROASTIES

We put a lot of pressure on ourselves to make the perfect roasties. Here's a simple recipe for the way that always works best for me.

6 Maris Piper or Yukon Gold potatoes, peeled and quartered

100 g/3¾ oz. goose fat or 100 g/7 tablespoons butter

1 tablespoon plain/all-purpose flour

salt, for the water

SERVES 4

Preheat the oven to 200°C (400°F) Gas 6 and put a roasting pan in the oven to heat up.

Put the potatoes in a pan of water with a pinch of salt. Bring to the boil then reduce the heat to low and simmer for 2 minutes.

Meanwhile, remove the hot roasting pan from the oven and put the goose fat or butter in. Return it to the oven to get really hot.

Drain the potatoes well in a colander. Take the lid from the pan and hold it securely over the top of the colander, then shake, shake, shake for 15 seconds to roughen the edges a little. Sprinkle with the flour.

Carefully put the potatoes into the hot fat (be wary of splashing) and roast in the preheated oven for 15 minutes. Turn all the potatoes over and return to the oven for a further 15 minutes. If they're still not quite crispy, turn them again and replace for a further 10 minutes, until golden brown and crispy.

YORKSHIRE PUDDINGS

Made from a basic batter of eggs, flour and milk, these classic British puddings remain a traditional part of a Sunday roast, however modern our tastebuds become!

3 eggs, beaten

200 g/1½ cups plain/all-purpose flour, sifted

250 ml/1 cup full-fat/whole milk

salt and black pepper, to season

an 8–10-hole muffin pan, greased well with butter or dripping

MAKES 8–10

Preheat the oven to 180°C (350°F) Gas 4.

Beat the eggs into the sifted flour, then use a whisk or electric hand-held whisk to mix while you add the milk. Mix until smooth and season with salt and pepper.

Place the batter in the fridge for 30 minutes to rest.

To help the batter brown well on the underside and ensure a good rise, put the greased muffin pan in the preheated oven for the last 5 minutes of the batter's resting time.

Take the hot pan out of the oven and divide the batter between the holes. Put it back in the oven and cook for 25–30 minutes, but keep checking the puddings after 20 minutes and remove once risen and golden brown.

HONEY PARSNIPS

This is an easy-peasy accompaniment that's scrummy with a roast dinner and heavenly for leftovers. You could also give carrots the same treatment, or try swapping the honey for maple syrup.

2 tablespoons olive oil

4–5 parsnips (depending on how chunky they are), peeled and quartered

4 tablespoons runny honey

1 teaspoon mustard powder (optional)

salt, for the water

SERVES 4

Preheat the oven to 180°C (350°F) Gas 4.

Put the olive oil in a roasting pan and place in the oven to heat up.

Bring a pan of water to the boil over a high heat, add the quartered parsnips and a pinch of salt and boil for 2 minutes. Drain well.

Take the hot roasting pan out of the oven and tip the parboiled parsnips into the hot oil carefully, being wary of spitting oil. Toss the parsnips in the hot oil to coat them all over.

Roast the parsnips for 5 minutes in the preheated oven to dry them out a little. Then drizzle the honey over the top, sprinkle with salt and return to the oven for 15–20 minutes, until sticky and brown. You can also add mustard power along with the honey, if you like.

LEFTOVER ROAST BEEF SANDWICH

This is the ultimate leftovers lunch and one of my favourite sandwiches. It is perfect for using up leftovers from the Roast Rib of Beef (see page 215) or the Flash Fillet Roast (see page 169). Use whatever bread you prefer for your sandwich – sliced, bagel, roll or anything you fancy.

2 slices of bread, or a bagel or roll of your choice

1 garlic clove, skin still on

2 rashers/slices streaky/fatty bacon, optional

20 g/1 oz. Stilton or other blue cheese, thinly sliced

2–3 slices of leftover roast beef

1–2 cherry tomatoes, as ripe as possible, sliced

SERVES 1

Preheat the oven to 200°C (400°F) Gas 6.

Put the garlic clove (skin still on) on a baking sheet and cook in the preheated oven for 10 minutes.

Fry the bacon in a frying pan/skillet over a medium heat until crisp and cooked to your liking. Set aside on paper towels to soak up any excess oil.

Meanwhile, lightly toast the bread, bagel or roll.

Set the roasted garlic aside to cool, then once it's cool enough to handle, squeeze out the inside of the garlic clove by cutting off the hard end and gently squeezing the soft centre.

Butter the bread, bagel or roll and then spread the soft garlic purée on top. Place the Stilton or blue cheese slices on top, then add your leftover roast beef, followed by the tomato slices and finally the crispy bacon.

If you are taking this to work, wrap it in brown paper and secure it with twine, then try to pretend you don't notice the envy of all your work colleagues when you get it out at lunch time.

ROAST GOOSE

Roast goose makes a pleasant alternative to roast turkey at Christmas or for a special Sunday roast. It has a very different flavour to turkey, but a similar approach is taken for roasting it and for keeping it as succulent as possible. A goose is much more about the breasts than turkey or chicken – in fact, you don't get an awful lot off the thighs and drumsticks. There is something really special about the dark, rich taste of roasted goose breast though, a delight. See page 230 for the Roast Turkey Stuffing and Turkey Giblet Gravy. As a guide, I suggest 500 g/1 lb. per person to yield about 200 g/7 oz. boneless meat.

a whole goose, about 4.5 kg/ 9 lbs.

100 g/7 tablespoons butter

1 quantity Roast Turkey Stuffing (see page 230, optional)

salt and black pepper, to season

about 200 ml/scant 1 cup chicken stock or any other type of stock that you have

a handful of fresh sage and parsley

SERVES 8–10

Preheat the oven to 160°C (325°F) Gas 3.

Use tweezers to remove any stubborn feathers left in the skin of the goose. Rub the butter over the skin of the bird. Fill with the stuffing, if using.

Sprinkle salt and black pepper all over the bird and place the goose breast-side down on a rack inside a roasting pan.

Pour in the stock up to a depth of 2 cm/¾ inch, along with the fresh sage and parsley.

Roast in the preheated oven for 20 minutes, then turn the goose over and spoon the juices over the top (the breasts).

Return to the oven for a further 20 minutes per 1 kg/2 lbs. of unstuffed goose weight.

Baste every 20 minutes to keep it succulent.

Increase the heat to 200°C (400°F) Gas 6 for the last 15 minutes to brown the surface and crisp the skin without drying out the meat.

LEFTOVER ROAST GOOSE, MANGO AND AVOCADO SALAD

The richness of goose makes it a terrific meat for salads. It works well in wraps and rolls, but it turns a salad into a hearty, flavoursome meal and there are lovely dressing options to go with it too. This is an excellent recipe idea for using up the leftovers from the Roast Goose (see page 221). However it also works well with duck breasts; you'll need 1 duck breast per person.

about 400 g/14 oz. leftover Roast Goose (see page 221), or 2 duck breasts

2 handfuls of salad leaves

2 spring onions/scallions, trimmed and finely sliced lengthways

1 avocado, stoned/pitted, peeled and sliced

1 mango, ripe as possible, stoned, peeled and sliced

8–10 baby plum tomatoes, halved

DRESSING

2 tablespoons soy sauce

freshly squeezed juice of 1 lime

1 teaspoon ground ginger

2 tablespoons sesame oil

a big pinch of chilli powder

salt and black pepper, to season

SERVES 2

If you are using leftover roast goose, tear the meat into shreds and set it aside. If you are roasting duck breasts for this salad, preheat the oven to 180°C (350°F) Gas 4. Score the skin of the duck breasts and season with salt and pepper. Heat a little olive oil in an ovenproof frying pan/skillet and cook the duck breasts over a high heat, skin-side down, for a few minutes until the fat starts to crisp. Turn the duck breasts over and transfer to the preheated oven. Roast the duck breasts in the preheated oven for 15–20 minutes, or until cooked to your liking.

Mix all the dressing ingredients together and season to taste.

Divide the salad leaves and spring onions/scallions between two serving plates and toss them with half the dressing.

Layer the avocado, mango, tomatoes and goose or duck on top, and drizzle over a little extra dressing.

HONEY AND MUSTARD HAM HOCKS

Lovely served as a roast with accompaniments or cold for picnics or sandwiches, this is a classic flavour combination for ham and works perfectly with the juiciness of meat from a well-used cut like the hock.

1 large or 2 small ham hocks, smoked or unsmoked

1 carrot, trimmed and roughly chopped (unpeeled)

1 white onion, roughly chopped

1 celery stick, roughly chopped

2 garlic cloves, roughly chopped

a sprig of fresh tarragon

3 teaspoons wholegrain mustard

1 teaspoon English mustard powder

4 tablespoons clear honey

2 teaspoons soft brown sugar

salt and black pepper (or pink peppercorns if you have them), to season

SERVES 4

Cut the rind off the ham hock(s) and discard. Put the ham hock(s) in a large pan or pot. Add the carrot, onion, celery, garlic and enough water to cover and bring to the boil over a high heat. Reduce the heat to low and leave to simmer for 1 hour 30 minutes.

Preheat the oven to 180°C (350°F) Gas 4.

In a bowl mix the tarragon, mustards, honey, sugar and a pinch of salt and pepper (or pink peppercorns, if using).

Remove the ham hock(s) from the pan or pot, place in a roasting pan and cover with the honey and mustard glaze. Roast in the middle of the preheated oven for 1 hour, but turn and baste it (or them) every 10–15 minutes by using a spoon to scoop up the liquid from the bottom of the pan and drizzle it back over the top.

GLAZED ROAST GAMMON

I've tried this marinade on a few types of gammon/ham – smoked, unsmoked, sweet-cured – and it seems to work well with all of them. My favourite with these flavours is an unsmoked (sometimes called 'green') shoulder (or 'horseshoe') gammon/ham. Allow about 200 g/7 oz. per person or serving... and plan for lots of cold leftovers! This is best when marinated for a few hours or overnight.

1–1.2 kg/2–2 lbs. 7 oz. gammon joint/boned ham

bread and butter and piccalilli or other pickle, to serve (optional)

CRANBERRY GLAZE

20 g/1½ tablespoons butter

1 red onion, finely chopped

2 handfuls of fresh cranberries (frozen cranberries, defrosted, work well here)

a big pinch of ground cinnamon

2 tablespoons white wine vinegar

1 tablespoon soft dark brown sugar

freshly squeezed juice of ½ lemon

SERVES 4

Start by making the glaze. Heat the butter in a frying pan/skillet over a medium heat and fry the red onion for about 4–5 minutes until soft and brown.

Add the cranberries and cinnamon, fry for 1 minute and then pour in the white wine vinegar. When the vinegar comes to the boil, sprinkle in the sugar and stir well.

Add the lemon juice, stir again and remove from the heat. Leave to cool until it is cool enough to touch (you don't want the heat of the glaze to cook the meat at all).

Lay out a piece of foil that is large enough to fold around the gammon/ham fully. Score lines all over the gammon/ham and spread the glaze all over it. Push the glaze mixture into the scored lines with your fingers to really push the flavour into the meat.

Move the gammon/ham to the foil and wrap it tightly, then put it in the fridge for a minimum of 3 hours or overnight, ideally.

Preheat the oven to 190°C (375°F) Gas 5.

Put the gammon/ham, still in the foil, onto a baking sheet. Open out the top of the foil, then put in the preheated oven. Roast for 10 minutes, then reduce the heat to 170°C (340°F) Gas 4. Baste the meat by spooning the mixture at the bottom of the foil over the top of the meat and return to the oven for 20 minutes.

Baste again and return to the oven for another 40 minutes.

If you want to crisp up the top any more, just turn the heat back up to 190°C (375°F) Gas 5 for the last 5 minutes of cooking.

Allow to rest for 6–8 minutes, then carve and serve warm or leave to cool completely and serve cold with piccalilli or other pickle of your choice.

ROAST TURKEY

This recipe is for Thanksgiving, Christmas or any gathering requiring something bigger than a chicken! I've learned (via plenty of trial and error!) that turkey is the best thing to prove that 'good meat' is easier to cook than cheaper alternatives. On top of that, there are a couple of things you can do to help keep it really juicy.

a whole turkey, about 4.5 kg/ 9 lbs.

100 g/7 tablespoons butter, softened

salt and black pepper, to season

about 1 kg/2 lb. Roast Turkey Stuffing (see page 230, optional)

Turkey Giblet Gravy (see page 230), Foolproof Roasties (see page 216), Honey Parsnips (see page 217) and any other vegetables of your choice, to serve

PIGS IN BLANKETS
16–20 chipolatas
8–10 slices streaky/fatty bacon

SERVES 8–10

Preheat the oven to 190°C (375°F) Gas 5.

Use tweezers to remove any stubborn feathers left in the skin of the turkey. Place the bird on a rack, breast-side down, and then place the rack into a roasting pan.

Take the butter and rub it all over the skin of the bird, making sure you get it into the folds of the legs too. Sprinkle salt and black pepper all over the bird. Fill with the stuffing, if using.

Pour 2 cm/¾ inch of water into the base of the roasting pan, underneath the rack.

Roast on the bottom shelf of the preheated oven for 45 minutes, then turn the bird over and baste by using a spoon to scoop the liquid from the bottom of the pan over the bird. Sprinkle over a little more salt and black pepper.

Return to the oven for 1 hour more, but remove the bird and baste it every 15 minutes. After this time, check to see if it's cooked: at the thickest part of the leg, scratch the surface with a fork and press down. If the juices are still pink, return to the oven for another 10 minutes and check again. If your turkey is bigger or smaller than the one used here, you can work out the total cooking time at 25 minutes per 1 kg/2 lbs. unstuffed weight.

Follow the instructions on page 230 to make turkey giblet gravy while your turkey is roasting, if you like.

Allow the turkey to rest for 8–10 minutes. Serve with the gravy, stuffing, roast potatoes, parsnips, pigs in blankets and any other accompaniments you choose.

Pigs in Blankets

Preheat the oven to 180°C (350°F). Cut each slice of bacon in half and wrap each half-slice around a chipolata. Roast in the preheated oven for 15–20 minutes, until the bacon is crisp and the sausages are cooked through.

ROAST TURKEY STUFFING

Cooking time for your turkey or goose needs to be calculated for the unstuffed bird, so make sure you weigh it before stuffing. This recipe also works really well for stuffed goose too – I just replace the chestnuts with 2 peeled, cored and chopped cooking apples. I have also included a recipe for making delicious gravy using the giblets from your bird. Perfect for Christmas or Thanksgiving.

20 g/1½ tablespoons butter

1 white onion

a big pinch of fresh sage

a big pinch of freshly chopped parsley

a handful of dried apricots

50 g/½ cup beef suet or vegetable shortening

80 g/1 cup dried breadcrumbs

1 beaten egg

150 g/5 oz. cooked chestnuts

1 lemon, halved

200 g/7 oz. minced/ground pork

salt and black pepper, to season

TURKEY GIBLET GRAVY

giblets from the turkey

1 carrot, roughly chopped

1 celery stick, roughly chopped

1 white onion, roughly chopped

60 ml/¼ cup red wine

2 tablespoons plain/all-purpose flour

salt and black pepper, to season

a pinch of freshly chopped tarragon or parsley and a squeeze of lemon juice (optional)

SERVES 8–10

Put the butter, onion, sage, parsley, apricots, suet or shortening, breadcrumbs, beaten egg and chestnuts into a food processor. Squeeze in the lemon juice from both halves, but keep one of the squeezed halves for later. Whizz until finely chopped.

Transfer the stuffing mixture to a mixing bowl and add the ground/minced pork. Mix together and season well. Stuff into the cavity of the bird and used the reserved lemon half to partly seal the entrance.

Turkey Giblet Gravy

While your turkey is roasting, put the giblets in a pan, add the chopped carrot, celery and onion. Cover with water and bring to the boil. I like to remove the liver from the giblets as it's a stronger flavour than I prefer in my gravy, but feel free to use it if you like. Reduce the heat to a low simmer and cook for as long as it takes to roast the turkey.

Once your turkey is cooked, take the bird and the rack out of the roasting pan and place the roasting pan (if it is flameproof) over a low heat on the stove top to keep it bubbling.

Be sure to scrape off any crispy bits from the edge of the dish to get all the flavour into the gravy. Add 150 ml/⅔ cup of the giblet stock and the red wine, and mix well.

Sprinkle in the flour, let it colour and then stir well until the gravy starts to thicken. Taste and add salt and pepper. Tarragon is also lovely in a gravy for turkey or a pinch of parsley and a squeeze of lemon juice, if you want to lighten it.

ROAST DINNER SAUCES

BREAD SAUCE

500 ml/2 cups full-fat/whole milk

50 g/3½ tablespoons butter

2 shallots, chopped

1 teaspoon cloves

1 teaspoon black peppercorns

2 garlic cloves, chopped

1 bay leaf

1 sprig of thyme

a big pinch of ground or freshly grated nutmeg

100 g/scant 2 cups fresh white breadcrumbs

3 tablespoons double/heavy cream

salt, to taste

SERVES 4–6

Put all the ingredients except the breadcrumbs and cream in a pan and bring to the boil.

Reduce the heat to low and simmer for 25 minutes.

Remove from the heat and strain to capture just the liquid.

Return to the heat and add the breadcrumbs, then keep stirring until it starts to thicken. Add the double/heavy cream and stir well. Add salt to taste.

Serve warm straight away or make it up to 3 days before you need it and store it chilled in the fridge.

APPLE SAUCE

10 g/2 teaspoons butter

5–6 cooking apples, peeled, cored and diced

finely grated zest of ½ lemon

freshly squeezed juice of 1 lemon

a pinch of ground cinnamon

1 tablespoon soft light brown sugar

100 ml/scant ½ cup water

salt, to taste

SERVES 4–6

Melt the butter in a pan over a medium heat. Add all the other ingredients and bring to the boil, then reduce the heat to a low simmer and leave for 20–30 minutes until thick and the apples are soft, stirring occasionally to make sure it's not catching on the base of the pan. Add salt to taste.

Either mash it with a potato masher or purée it in a food processor, or just dish it up chunky, depending on your preference.

Store in the fridge for up to 2 weeks in a sealed container.

CRANBERRY SAUCE

20 g/1½ tablespoons butter

1 red onion, finely chopped

2 handfuls of fresh cranberries (frozen cranberries, defrosted, work well here)

a big pinch of cinnamon

2 tablespoons white wine vinegar

1 tablespoon soft dark brown sugar

freshly squeezed juice of ½ lemon

SERVES 4–6

In a frying pan/skillet, heat the butter over a medium heat and fry the onion until soft and golden brown.

Add the cranberries and cinnamon, then fry for 1 minute. Pour in the white wine vinegar and bring to the boil, then sprinkle in the sugar and keep mixing well.

Add the lemon juice, stir and remove from the heat.

Serve immediately while hot or chill and serve as a cold accompaniment.

Store in the fridge for up to 2 weeks in a sealed container.

PERFECT POTATOES

TRIPLE-COOKED CHIPS

3–4 potatoes, depending on size
vegetable oil, for deep-frying

SERVES 2

Wash the potatoes and remove any blemishes. Keep the skins on and slice into chunky chips/fries.

Bring a pan of water to the boil, add the chips/fries and boil for 8 minutes to soften.

Drain in a colander, then use the lid of the pan to cover and shake for a few seconds – not as hard as for roast potatoes, as you don't want the chips/fries to break.

Heat the oil for deep-frying in a large pan until it bubbles – use a tester chip/fry first to make sure it sizzles as you put it in.

Tip the chips/fries in and fry for 8 minutes, then use a slotted spoon to fish them out and drain on paper towels to cool.

Preheat the oven to 200°C (400°F) Gas 6.

Transfer the chips/fries to a baking sheet, making sure they are in one layer and not touching each other.

Cook in the preheated oven for 8 minutes, or until as crispy as you like. Serve immediately.

DAUPHINOISE POTATOES

400 ml/scant 1¾ cups double/heavy cream
400 ml/scant 1¾ cups full-fat/whole milk
4 garlic cloves, roughly chopped
a little freshly grated nutmeg, to taste
a sprig of fresh thyme
salt and black pepper, to season
4–5 potatoes, peeled
150 g/1⅓ cups grated Gruyère cheese (or mature/sharp Cheddar cheese)

a 20-cm/8-inch square baking dish, greased

SERVES 4

Preheat the oven to 180°C (350°F) Gas 4.

Put the cream, milk, garlic, nutmeg and thyme into a pan, add a pinch of salt and pepper, and bring to the boil.

Slice the potatoes widthways into oval discs, about 3-mm/⅛-inch thick.

Add the potato slices to the simmering cream mixture and cook for 10 minutes.

Use a slotted spoon to scoop out the slices of potato and lay them into the prepared dish. Discard the thyme.

Pour the rest of the liquid over the top until it's just about to cover the top layer of potatoes.

Sprinkle the grated cheese on top.

Bake in the preheated oven for 30 minutes until browned on top and the liquid is absorbed. If they're still not browning, you can cook them under a hot grill/broiler for 5 minutes.

FANCY MASHED POTATOES

3–4 potatoes, peeled and quartered
20 g/1½ tablespoons butter
40 g/½ cup finely grated Parmesan cheese (optional)
2 tablespoons double/heavy cream
salt and black pepper, to season

SERVES 4

Bring a pan of salted water to the boil, add the potatoes and cook for 25 minutes until totally soft when you prod them with a fork.

Drain and return to the pan. Add the butter and mash until lovely and soft.

Mix in the Parmesan, if using, and then the double/heavy cream, salt and pepper.

Serve immediately or use within in 2 days (keep sealed in the fridge and make sure you cool it fully before moving it to the fridge so that it doesn't sweat).

BUTTERY CRUSHED POTATOES

8–10 new potatoes
20 g/1½ tablespoons butter
salt and black pepper, to season

SERVES 2

Heat a grill/broiler to medium.

Boil the new potatoes (skins on) in a pan of salted boiling water for 20 minutes, until soft.

Drain and return to the pan.

Add the butter and swirl to melt.

Tip the buttery potatoes onto the greased baking sheet and crush with a fork.

Sprinkle salt and pepper on the top and pop under the preheated grill/broiler for 5 minutes to brown.

BOXING DAY PIE

The ultimate celebration of leftovers! Boxing Day is a bank holiday celebrated on 26 December in the UK. This is my mother's recipe and she realized, even from when my sister and I were very young, that we were asking for tiny portions of the separate meats and vegetables on Christmas Day because we were trying to stockpile as much as possible for her Boxing Day pie! If you're out and about for the few days after Christmas, this is also a brilliant way to trim and freeze all the leftovers for another time. It just takes 15 minutes without cooking, so you can sort out the whole fridge in a single recipe.

about 1.5 kg/3 lbs. Christmas or Thanksgiving leftovers, such as turkey or goose, ham, bacon, sausages, stuffing, sprouts, roast potatoes, carrots, parsnips, bread sauce or peas

WHITE WINE SAUCE

50 g/3½ tablespoons butter

1 teaspoon mustard powder

50 g/6 tablespoons plain/all-purpose flour, sifted

700 ml/scant 3 cups full-fat/whole milk

150 ml/⅔ cup white wine

salt and pepper, to season

TOPPING

100 g/scant 2 cups fresh breadcrumbs

100 g/1⅓ cup finely grated Parmesan cheese or grated Cheddar cheese

SERVES 4

Preheat the oven to 180°C (350°F) Gas 4.

To make the sauce, melt the butter in a pan over a medium heat and sprinkle in the mustard powder and flour.

Add a pinch of salt and pepper and then slowly add the milk, a little at a time, mixing well with the butter and flour base.

Once all the milk is added, keep stirring continuously over the heat until the sauce begins to thicken. Once it is the consistency of double/heavy cream, add the wine and reduce to a low simmer.

Taste and add more seasoning as you like.

Then take all the leftovers and slice everything you can into strips and discs. My mother even slices the roast potatoes and sprouts, and there are always lovely big chunks of the ham shredded in there too. Any leftover sausages are sliced lengthways to make thin strips.

Layer them all in a large roasting pan, however you like. We tend to be a bit particular and have separate layers of each, but you can honestly just throw it all in. Pour the white wine sauce over the top.

Mix the breadcrumbs and Parmesan or Cheddar together in a bowl and sprinkle over the top.

Bake in the preheated oven with foil on top for 20 minutes, then remove the foil for another 20 minutes. If you want to brown the top a little more to serve, just pop it under a preheated grill/broiler for a few minutes until crispy and browned.

I like to serve this with lots of ketchup on the side, but it's also nice with leftover cranberry sauce.

SOURCES

UK
INGREDIENTS

BLYTHBURGH REAL FREE RANGE PORK
St Margaret's Farm
Mells, Halesworth
Suffolk, IP19 9DD
+44 (0)1986 873 298
www.freerangepork.co.uk

FOREST PIG CHARCUTERIE
Bell Farm, Far Forest
Kidderminster
Worcestershire, DY14 9DX
+44 (0)1299 266 771
www.forestpig.com

ISLE OF MAN MEATS
Meat Plant,
Ballafletcher Farm Road
Tromode, Douglas
Isle of Man, IM4 4QE
+44 (0)1624 674 346
www.iommeats.com

J. F. EDWARDS
42 Central Markets
West Market Building
London, EC1A 9PS
www.jfedwards.uk.com

LITTLE GATE FARM
Horseshoe Lane, Beckley
East Sussex, TN31 6RZ
+44 (0)7811 464 202
www.littlegatecarefarm.co.uk

MUDDY BOOTS
29 Broadway Parade
London, N8 9DB
+44 (0)20 8245 4240
www.muddybootsfoods.co.uk

OCADO
Ocado Limited
Freepost 13498
PO BOX 3 62
Hatfield, AL9 7BR
+44 (0)345 656 1234
www.ocado.com

PACKINGTON FREE RANGE
Blakenhall Park
Barton-under-Needwood
Staffordshire, DE13 8AJ
+44 (0)1283 711 547
www.packingtonfreerange.co.uk

TREALY FARM CHARCUTERIE
Park Farm, Plough Rd
Goytre, Abergavenny
Wales, NP4 0AL
+44 (0)1495 785 090
www.trealyfarm.com

WAITROSE
Customer Service
Waitrose Ltd.
Doncastle Road, Bracknell
Berkshire, RG12 8YA
+44 (0)1344 825 232
www.waitrose.co.uk

EQUIPMENT

BUTCHERS' SUNDRIES
TruNet Packaging
Services Ltd., Westminster
Industrial Estate
Measham, Swadlincote
Derbyshire, DE12 7DS
+44 (0)1530 272 396
www.butchers-sundries.com

NISBETS CATERING SUPPLIES
Nisbets Plc., Fourth Way
Avonmouth
Bristol, BS11 8TB
+44 (0)117 307 5606
www.nisbets.co.uk

JOHN LEWIS
www.johnlewis.com

LAKELAND
Alexandra Buildings
Windermere
Cumbria, LA23 1BQ
+44 (0)1539 488 100
www.lakeland.co.uk

PROCOOK®
3 iO Centre, Hurricane Road
Gloucester Business Park
Gloucester, GL3 4AQ
+44 (0)330 100 1010
www.procook.co.uk

DIVERTIMENTI
227–229 Brompton Road
London, SW3 2EP
+44 (0)330 333 0351
www.divertimenti.co.uk

STEAMER TRADING COOKSHOP
The Malthouse
Daveys Lane
Lewes, BN7 2BF
+44(0)1273 483 300
www.steamer.co.uk

US
INGREDIENTS

BROKEN ARROW RANCH
3296 Junction Highway
Ingram, TX 78025
+1 (800) 962-4263
www.brokenarrowranch.com

FATTED CALF
644 C First Street
Napa, CA 94559
+1 (707) 256-3684
and 320 Fell Street
San Francisco, CA
+1 (415) 400-5614
www.fattedcalf.com

HERITAGE FOODS U. S. A.
790 Washington Ave.
PMB 303
Brooklyn, NY 11238
+1 (718) 389 0985
www.heritagefoodsusa.com

MAINE MEAT
7 Wallingford Square #104
Kittery, ME 03904
+1 (207) 703 0219
www.memeat.com

PARADISE LOCKER MEATS
405 W. Birch St.
Trimble, MO 64492
+1 816-370-MEAT
www.paradisemeats.com

REVIVAL MARKET
550 Heights Boulevard
Houston, TX 77007
+1 (713) 880-8463
www.revivalmarket.com

THE BUTCHER & LARDER
Chicago, IL
+1 (773) 687-8280
www.thebutcherandlarder.com

THE SPOTTED TROTTER
Atlanta, GA
www.thespottedtrotter.com
+1 (470) 428-2509

TAILS & TROTTERS
Portland, OR
www.tailsandtrotters.com
+1 (503) 477-8682

EQUIPMENT

BUTCHER PACKER
www.butcher-packer.com
+1 (248) 583-1250

EMILIO MITI
www.emiliomiti.com

NATURAL CASING COMPANY
www.naturalcasingco.com
+1 (877) 515-0270

THE SAUSAGE MAKER
www.sausagemaker.com
+1 (888) 490-8525

INDEX

ACKNOWLEDGMENTS

Julia, Kate, Leslie, Cindy, Maria, Mel and all the team at Ryland, Peters & Small, who put such incredible effort into getting any book commissioned, edited, produced, printed, listed, distributed... It is a total pleasure working for you and I'm immensely grateful for the opportunities.

Steve Painter, the calm, skilled, amazing photographer, prop stylist and designer, I loved working with you in Hastings. Thank you for all your work. And Lucy McKelvie the gorgeous daffodil – thank you for your wonderful food styling. Alex and Hilary McNeill and their chickens, and Claire and Dave Cordell and everyone at Little Gate Farm who let us shoot on location.

Georgina, Sean, Sam, Beth and Bev, our founding shop crew, and all the current Muddy Boots team for freeing up my time to get to have a go at this book and for being on this crazy journey with us.

Francesca, Lauren and the team at Prestbury for letting me camp out in their offices to focus on writing the introduction. Nick, Sandy and Mike for welcomed breaks from the typing. And these three with Jon for making up our ambitious little Muddy Boots family.

The farms, abattoirs, producers and inspiring food companies my husband Roland and I get to work with. Thank you for the incredible supply and all the hard work you do.

My father-in-law, John – the inspiration behind all the respect I have for land and farming. We saw you still be exhilarated by the birth of every calf and your honorable sadness when they left fully grown. Thank you for letting us live at your farm and learn about what you do.

Sarah, Dan, Linda, Dunc, Alex, Amelia, Totty, Harry, Freddie – I completely adore you, Ballards!

My brother-in-law, Paddy, and two incredible girls, Orla and Nuala. And my big sister, Olivia... I still just basically want to be you.

My bonkers parents, Edward and Jude. You crack me up. I have too much to thank you for.

And Ro... I still haven't found the words. I'll find them, I promise.